1870

Deutsche Bank
The Global Hausbank

Werner Plumpe, Alexander Nützenadel & Catherine R. Schenk

2020

BLOOMSBURY
LONDON · OXFORD · NEW YORK · NEW DELHI · SYDNEY

Translated from the German by:
Patricia C. Sutcliffe: *In the Age of the First Globalisation, 1870–1914,*
Sally Hudson Dill: *Between State and Market, 1914–1989* (I.-II.3),
Andrew Evans: *Between State and Market, 1914–1989* (II.4-III.).

BLOOMSBURY BUSINESS
Bloomsbury Publishing Plc
50 Bedford Square, London, WC1B 3DP, UK

BLOOMSBURY, BLOOMSBURY BUSINESS and the Diana logo are
trademarks of Bloomsbury Publishing Plc

First published in Great Britain 2020

A catalogue record for this book is available from the British Library

Library of Congress Cataloguing-in-Publication data has been applied for

ISBN: 978-1-4729-7732-8; eBook: 978-1-4729-7730-4

2 4 6 8 10 9 7 5 3 1

Typeset by seagulls.net

Printed and bound in Italy by L.E.G.O. S.p.A.

To find out more about our authors and books visit www.bloomsbury.com
and sign up for our newsletters

Contents

Between State and Market, 1914–1989

ALEXANDER NÜTZENADEL

Globalisation and Crisis, 1989–2020

CATHERINE R. SCHENK

Preface

As we celebrate 150 years of Deutsche Bank this year, we can look back on a long and eventful history. It began with the founding of the bank on the first floor of a nondescript house in a central Berlin street. It spans two world wars and nearly fifty years in which Deutsche Bank had to focus on the domestic German market. And it includes what is, for now, the bank's last chapter in which it re-established itself on the global stage.

Our corporate history has been analysed at great length; virtually no other company in Germany has had – and continues to have – so much written about it. We, too, have looked into our history on several occasions. For example, on our 125th anniversary 25 years ago we became the first German corporate to comprehensively investigate our responsibility during the Nazi era.

So why bring out another book now?

It has a lot to do with our role and our corporate identity. The respected historians Werner Plumpe (Goethe University Frankfurt am Main), Alexander Nützenadel (Humboldt University Berlin) and Catherine R. Schenk (University of Oxford) have analysed our 150-year development by looking at the different phases of internationalisation and globalisation of the economy. This is an approach that couldn't be any more topical for Deutsche Bank. Today we still consider our calling to be that of a facilitator of investment and trade worldwide for German companies – as their global 'Hausbank'. The very first statute of the bank dated March 1870 underlined the great importance of foreign business: the business purpose is 'in particular the promotion and easing of trade relations between Germany, other European countries and overseas markets'.

Accordingly, Deutsche Bank built out its international business rigorously from the very beginning. Within just a few years of being founded it had already opened branches in Yokohama, Shanghai and London. The international expansion was successful. In spring 1914 the *Frankfurter Zeitung* newspaper called Deutsche Bank the 'biggest bank in the world'. It had benefited from globalisation more than virtually any other financial institution, while also being a driving force behind it. Werner Plumpe provides an impressive description of the first phase from the founding in 1870 until 1914. He highlights particularly well where the roots and the strength of Deutsche Bank lie – namely in business with companies. This is precisely the area that we made the focus of our bank last year with our new strategy.

One can only vaguely imagine which alternative course not only the history of Germany would have taken but also of our bank, if two world wars had not originated in Germany. World War I saw a large share of international client relationships terminated overnight, German industry had to focus much more heavily on the domestic market – as did its biggest bank, too.

The history of Deutsche Bank is thus closely intertwined with that of Germany and Europe. The long phase of focusing on the German market shaped the bank's activities until the end of the 1980s. After the end of World War II Deutsche Bank was able to participate in the 'economic miracle' and shape it. But although European integration advanced, banking remained a largely national affair. It's not by chance that we considerably accelerated our international expansion only once the Iron Curtain had fallen. Even though the geopolitical circumstances restricted opportunities for a long time, Deutsche Bank did not abandon its aim to be a global Hausbank, as Alexander Nützenadel describes in the second section of the book.

It is this aim that triggered a new wave of global expansion by Deutsche Bank following the collapse of the Berlin Wall. The takeover of the British merchant bank Morgan Grenfell ushered in an expansion into the global capital markets business in order to satisfy the growing requirements of German corporates.

This development was by no means linear, as Catherine R. Schenk details in the third section. It yielded a number of successes, but there were also serious setbacks. Insufficient controls and excessive growth targets especially prior to and during the financial crisis resulted in missteps and misdevelopments for which we had to pay large settlements and sometimes even fines. We have learned our lessons from the over-exuberance. One of the things we have done during the past years is to introduce far tighter controls in all areas of business. In addition, we as a bank issued an official apology at the beginning of 2017.

That said, it is safe to say that only by expanding since 1989 are we today one of the few European banks with a global network. We are the world's biggest clearer of euro-denominated transactions and the biggest dollar clearer outside the US. We have a unique global infrastructure that sets us apart from all other German and European banks. This makes us a natural, reliable and versatile partner for virtually all German corporates with international operations.

History shows that the recent past has not been Deutsche Bank's most difficult chapter. This great institution has already dealt with serious crises. And one thing it has repeatedly epitomised is resilience. Our bank is today less complex, safer and more robust. In a nutshell, we have performed a radical clean-up. Now we are once again in a position to grow sustainably and successfully. Our strategy, which we announced in summer 2019, builds on our roots. And on what generations of people who worked for our bank have created: for 150 years we have been connecting worlds to help people and businesses get to where they want to be. We continue to be the global Hausbank. And it is our mission to deliver a positive impact – for our clients, employees, the economy and society as a whole.

Deutsche Bank again threw open the doors of its archives to the authors of this new book. And they have succeeded in casting our bank in a new light – on an academically independent basis. Their analyses therefore do not necessarily reflect the opinion of our bank – all the more reason for readers to reflect on and discuss the book's content.

I hope you find the book interesting and a source of inspiring insights.

Christian Sewing
Frankfurt, January 2020   *Chief Executive Officer, Deutsche Bank AG*

Introduction

The history of Deutsche Bank, which celebrates its 150th anniversary in 2020, reflects both the dramatic international political and economic events through which it operated as well as the volatile path of the German domestic environment. The bank survived and adapted through two eras of globalisation (in the 19th century and the late 20th century), the rise of economic nationalism and dictatorship in the interwar period, two world wars and through many booms and busts in global economic relations. The bank was also deeply affected by the evolution of the German economy and Germany's place in Europe, while also in turn influencing these developments.

The bank originated in Berlin in 1870, during the boom that followed the foundation of the German Empire, and grew quickly in the first phase of globalisation before the First World War. It was in this period that it established its role as an adviser for the innovative and successful German industrial and commercial base and followed its customers into a strategy of internationalisation. In Germany, the model of bank-dependent finance rather than market-led finance created opportunities for Deutsche Bank to be closely embedded in the industrial success of the German economy. In the heyday of globalisation in the late 19th century Deutsche Bank assumed its role as global Hausbank for German industry and commerce. The term 'Hausbank' infers a close and primary, if not exclusive, relationship between a company or enterprise and its bank across a range of services. In Germany's case this closeness was enhanced by banks holding shares in industry and cross-directorships.

Deutsche Bank's original international business model was largely destroyed by the Great War and the thirty years of turmoil and violence that followed. The implications for the bank of Germany's defeat in 1918 quickly became clear: the loss of a large part of its international operations, international branches and investments, but also the erosion in the domestic capital market business. The rise of National Socialism and the renewal of aggression between Germany and its European neighbours ensured that these losses were not merely a brief interruption related to the war and its immediate aftermath. After short-term efforts to regain international business in the interwar period, the bank remained largely restricted to the German territory under Hitler's National Socialist dictatorship and during the Second World War. The global Hausbank of the years before 1914 was transformed into a German universal bank that was primarily reliant on the domestic market. Politics played an ever greater role in the bank's business. During the Nazi period politics became the single determining factor of the bank's strategy. As the most prominent financial institution in Germany, Deutsche Bank was collaborating with the regime, being part of the National Socialist war economy and involved in crimes committed by the Nazis. Even after the end of the Second World War, it was not possible to return to the older traditions from the period before 1914. The political and economic division of Germany by the occupying powers cut the bank off from its origins in Berlin. In the western sphere, the American occupying power sought to break up the corporate structures of the big banks, which were linked to the armaments and war policies of the Third Reich. The Americans also sought to increase competition in the banking sector. A plethora of smaller regional institutions emerged from the three Berlin big banks – Deutsche Bank, Dresdner Bank and Commerzbank. During the period of Germany's post-war economic recovery, these banks quickly gained importance, but at the same time efforts were directed towards the restoration of larger corporate structures, which was completed by the reunification of Deutsche Bank's successor institutions in 1957. Meanwhile, with Berlin isolated, Frankfurt emerged as the new West German banking hub.

In consequence, Deutsche Bank's post-1957 business model was a different one than before 1914. As the bank no longer had an international infrastructure, its employees concentrated their expertise on domestic business and industrial loans. The continued weakness of the German capital market in the 1950s made it impossible to finance industry through capital market products, which had worked excellently in the pre-1914 German Empire. These restrictions did not, however, seem as important when measured against the stabilisation and expansion of good relations with major industrial clients. Close Hausbank relationships linked corporate customers' foreign trade and investment needs. In addition, various factors contributed to the establishment of permanent equity holdings in industrial firms by the financial services sector and cross-shareholdings between banks and insurance companies. Deutsche Bank, alongside Dresdner Bank, Allianz and Munich Re, was undoubtedly among the most important players in what later became known as 'Deutschland AG' (or 'Germany Inc.') and remained as such until the 1990s.

These shifts in the bank's strategy caused by the upheavals of the first half of the century and the specific conditions of Germany's reconstruction were less deliberative decisions or even a strategic repositioning by the bank's top management, even if their actions were of great significance. At the core was entrepreneurial understanding of the market conditions, ultimately created by politics, that gradually narrowed the bank's scope for action after 1914. This was by no means unsuccessful, especially in the reconstruction after the Second World War, and in this respect the bank rightly saw itself at the top of the financial system of one of the economically most important countries in the world on the occasion of its 100th birthday in 1970. But the risks and disadvantages connected with the repeated changes of its profile became apparent with the opening of the world economy in the course of the second globalisation from the 1980s.

In view of the structural changes in global financial markets on the one hand, and the end of the industrial boom in the 1970s on the other, international markets steadily gained in importance. Initially, this was simply due to the sheer volume of money and capital flows (such as Euro- and petrodollars). With stagnating or only moderately growing profit opportunities in the traditional business of trade and industrial finance, and the restructuring of many large companies in the context of intensifying global competition, the importance of capital markets was greatly enhanced. Only gradually did it become clear that this renewed transition towards an open global economy, which bridged national characteristics, would make serious changes in the bank's business model necessary. At first, in Deutsche Bank and more generally in the European financial industry, there was a reluctance to expand actively internationally, partly because the war-related losses from foreign business were still firmly anchored in the minds of many bankers. Only gradually did the bank adapt to global financial markets by taking its own strategic decisions and setting its own course – measures that did not entail a restoration of the situation before 1914, but were intended to build on the original model of being a leading internationally active bank, with a prominent profile developed through an extensive network of correspondent banks, representative offices, branches and subsidiaries.

But this was all easier said than done. Although the bank had great earning power (not least because of its strong position in 'Deutschland AG') and enormous reserves (including substantial industrial holdings), the loss of international competence after 1914 and the specialisations of the organisational structure and personnel profile, which were typical of reconstruction, were not particularly good preconditions for a powerful return to the competitive international arena. A small number of efficient and highly competitive finance companies dominated global financial markets, particularly American investment banks, which had grown after the Glass Steagall Act of 1933 separated out retail banking from investment banking in the US. These banks particularly thrived during the rapid growth of securities and equity trading from the 1980s onward. Barriers to entry were high for a latecomer, especially for a bank that had been doing most of its business in this market from the sidelines. Deutsche Bank now faced establishing its position in international financial centres where its presence was relatively minor. It was soon clear that the existing organisational and personnel resources would not support the bank's international expansion and its return to the world's major financial markets. This was especially true for the necessary growth of its international capital markets business, where the global standard was now modelled on American investment banking. In consequence, from the end of the 1980s the bank stepped up its international expansion through acquisition (partly by using the proceeds from the gradual dissolution of 'Deutschland AG'), first in London and later New York, and finally worldwide. In this way it was able to become a leading European player in investment banking, especially in securities and derivatives business, but also in foreign exchange trading. Despite initial difficulties, this strategy seemed so successful in the boom of the financial markets before the 2007–08 crisis that it dramatically changed the shape and nature of the entire bank.

As before 1914, after the acquisition of Morgan Grenfell in 1989, London was an important hub for the bank and the centre for the new investment banking operations. New York, where the bank had been represented until the Great War through numerous co-operative agreements and friendly relations with other banks, also became – after the acquisition of Bankers Trust in 1999 – a central location for the now truly global financial conglomerate, catapulting Deutsche Bank into the league of the world's leading global banks. The boom in financial markets after the turn of the millennium was both a curse and a blessing: a blessing because it created an extremely favourable environment for global expansion; a curse because it intensified competition among leading institutions to such an extent that increasingly risky strategies were pursued in the search for higher returns and greater scale, which ultimately contributed significantly to bloated balance sheets and opaque risk structures. At the same time, the role of investment bankers, who joined the bank in their thousands from the 1990s, became decisive for the bank's strategy. In a highly competitive environment, the true asset of the bank was its people and their ability to compete, to innovate and to win over customers. In investment banking, this required a change in the norms of incentives and compensation that increased the focus on the short term and contributed to the overheating of the business – a shift in strategy whose consequences could not be controlled from the top of the bank in Frankfurt. As long as the results for the shareholder were positive, this seemed acceptable, indeed desirable. But the rapid expansion in the bank's scale and scope created managerial challenges and operational risks that quickly became apparent when the growth in underlying markets abruptly ended.

The bursting of the real estate bubble in the United States in 2007–08 sent shock waves through the global financial system because of the complex web of securitisation that the global investment banks had spun since the 1990s. At first, Deutsche Bank itself appeared to have got off fairly lightly compared to other major banks. However, the crisis revealed the ways in which the bank had extended itself beyond the competence of its governance and operational systems. In the ten years after the crisis, the bank struggled to reinvent itself and return to consistent profit, eventually retreating from global equity trading and reorienting its strategy to the global Hausbank model, with a renewed emphasis on corporate and transaction banking and wealth management.

History shows, of course, that this was not the first time the bank had faced such challenges. Even in the extensive reports by Berlin financial journalists on the bank's 25th anniversary in 1895, it was clear that by no means all the bank's projects went smoothly. But the bank's management repeatedly found ways to learn from its mistakes and had the resources for quite painful write-downs. The banking crisis at the beginning of the 1930s, for example, hit the bank hard. In contrast to other banks, Deutsche Bank was able to recover from the crisis relatively quickly and had to make only limited use of state aid. During the Nazi Third Reich this proved to be an advantage and gave the bank a higher degree of autonomy than was the case with Dresdner Bank, for example. In May 1945, however, it was on the brink of ruin, a fate shared with the entire German economy. But the bank succeeded in finding its way back to the top of the German financial system by mobilising its remaining resources, and taking advantage of the favourable circumstances of the rapid post-war economic recovery. This gave the bank a reputation for resilience that was to be tested in the next century.

The history of the bank was and is anything but a simple success story, and it has not been portrayed as such in earlier anniversary volumes, even though each time period has left its mark on these depictions. The milestone birthdays in 1920 and 1945 were not times for celebration. The commemorative *festschrift* for the 100th birthday in 1970, written by the financial journalist and archivist of the bank, Fritz Seidenzahl,[1] took a critical but positive look at the bank's early history, the First World War and the

---

1 Fritz Seidenzahl, *100 Jahre Deutsche Bank 1870–1970*, Frankfurt am Main 1970.

early 1920s, which was borne out by the self-confidence of the bank's reconstruction success. On the other hand, the description of the Great Depression and the banking crisis failed to stand up to critical scrutiny, as is also the case for the cursory treatment of the role of the bank during the Nazi dictatorship and the Second World War. This was already of great concern to the general public back then, when attack and defence were in balance for a while.[2] Eventually, however, it became increasingly clear that such deliberate 'silence' could not be justified. Not least to make up for these obvious omissions, a much-acclaimed scholarly account followed for the 125th anniversary of the bank in 1995. This substantial collection of essays not only met the expectations of the German and American public through Harold James' critical reappraisal of its history in the Third Reich, but also set a milestone in German business history.[3] Acting as a role model, the leading company of 'Deutschland AG' no longer dodged a reappraisal of its history during the period of National Socialism nor played it down, but instead gave independent historians the opportunity to examine precisely this problematic period of the bank's history and to present the results of their work to a broad public.

Now, on the occasion of the bank's 150th anniversary, the circumstances have once again changed and other, quite new questions about the history of the bank have become urgent and are taken up with this account. On the initiative of the Historical Institute of Deutsche Bank, the concept underlying this book was developed as early as 2015 together with a team of authors consisting of economic, financial and business historians. What is new is not only that the international dimension of Deutsche Bank's activities is given a prominent role from the very beginning. Another new dimension is the ability to address the bank's history over the past 25 years in the context of its longer term historical evolution. At the same time, it is possible to identify continuities and discontinuities which are discernible right up to the present. This inevitably shifts the overall perspective. The turmoil in the decade after 2008 highlights turning points in the history of the bank that were less obvious at the beginning of the 1990s and even less so at the end of the 1960s. Today it is clear that the period between the beginning of the First World War through the end of the Cold War was a period of politically determined market structures and that politics played a decisive role, in many important respects, in defining the bank's scope for action. This was not only because of the destruction of the international division of labour and open capital markets between the wars, but also due to the creation of the European economic area and its increasingly intensive institutional regulation since the 1950s. On the other hand, in the periods before 1914 and since 1989 the prominence of political factors was different in essential respects. Politics certainly played a role in the period of the German Empire and is by no means insignificant for business development today – even in the present, with the instability of the Eurozone and the emergence of a kind of Neo-Mercantilism in the United States, new political fractures are looming, whose medium-term significance are certainly hard to envisage. For the bank, however, the politically determined turning points between 1914 and 1989 had even more far-reaching implications. In this period, the bank's

---

2 Martin Walser, Ist die Deutsche Bank naiv?, *Der Spiegel* 35/1970; Wilhelm Treue, Eine (deutsche) Bank, zwei Geschichten, *Die Zeit* 33/1970.
3 Lothar Gall *et al.*: *The Deutsche Bank 1870–1995*, London 1995.

business model had to follow political requirements that did not exist before 1914 and are hardly tangible after 1989. The bank was able to adapt to the change in underlying conditions, including the emergence of freer global economic structures after 1945 (at least in the western hemisphere). It also succeeded in continuing its operations successfully in West Germany. However, considering the foundation and the development of the first decades, this era was distinct from the fundamental identity of the company, which always understood itself as a global actor and consequently acted as such.

In some respects, Deutsche Bank returned to its historical roots after 1989, but under completely different conditions. These altered conditions did not necessarily mean greater risks than in the period before 1914. The volume, tempo and technological capabilities were certainly on a greater scale than during the first era of globalisation, but the risk of losses on the American or Asian market was always only too well known to the bank's directors before the First World War. Yet before 1914, while business was global, the bank itself and its milieu, as well as that of British, French and American institutions, continued to be nationally inflected, despite the fact that bankers of the pre-war era were already a kind of cosmopolitan elite. While today the national milieus in global finance have retreated somewhat in favour of a more homogenous global investment business culture, the times before 1914 and after 1989 are nevertheless more similar than the short 20th century in between these dates, in which the political implications of the two world wars and the Cold War that ensued created 'camps' which were only partially capable of cooperation among themselves.

This tripartite division of the period of one and a half centuries is the starting point for the study. Throughout, the bank is understood as a financial actor that was unable to escape fully from the changing external economic and political market conditions. In some cases, the bank attempted to influence market developments, making use of its multiple political and economic relationships. However, the bank's power and influence should not be overestimated. In much of the existing literature, the bank has been characterised almost as a spider at the centre of a web, shaping economic and political conditions. But this clearly misrepresents the character of the institution that had to respond to difficult and changing market conditions. The bank usually followed the markets, not the other way around. As much as there was lobbying on the one hand, as much as politicians were keen to use the bank as an ally and even as an aid to its foreign policy ambitions, the bank was not eager for political significance unless this fit in with its business needs. Individual bank directors may have had political convictions and stood up for them; the bank's day to day operations were rather indifferent to this, and the directors, who were always bound by collective decisions anyway, knew that the bottom line held the last word.

Accordingly, each major chronological section first examines the question of how the bank understood and defined its scope for action and developed its strategy under the prevailing market conditions and competitive context. Moreover, the bank's strategic orientation was closely linked to the evolution of the structure of the organisation and its personnel, which supported and enabled each other. We place particular emphasis on the importance of the bank's early internationalisation, which began in London and East Asia in the 1870s and soon also in Latin America, as well as its very early willingness to be present in Germany in important commercial centres outside Berlin. Strategy and organisation determined the ability to identify and exploit opportunities for action, both in deposit-taking and lending business, in its international presence and in national operations. This global ambition re-emerged in the 1980s partly as a defensive strategy to retain the bank's customers in Germany, but also to follow the huge short-term revenues available in the new global securities trading environment. This in turn transformed the structure, personnel and operations of the bank.

The division of the bank's history into three main phases was also a deciding factor in the choice of authors, as it was less a matter of setting out technical banking details than of tracing historical lines; of examining the processes to handle and manage changes, over which the bank itself often had limited influence. The focus is on aspects of business and economic history in the parts written by Werner Plumpe and Alexander Nützenadel, while Catherine R. Schenk's exploration of the bank's structural change in the context of renewed globalisation reveals more recent perspectives on financial history. The differences between the sections are therefore easy to notice, but there are also continuities as each section addresses questions of organisational and personnel development, the image and public reputation of the bank. Although the authors wrote their contributions on behalf of the bank, they were scientifically independent and were able to explore the themes that they chose without interference. Importantly, the views of the authors do not necessarily reflect the views of the bank's management. To support the project, the bank made great efforts to make all the documents requested available as far as possible, thus resulting, for the first time, in the history of a bank based on extensive archival records almost up until the present. Inevitably, the legal repercussions of more recent episodes have constrained the details that can be disclosed, but this does not affect the overall arc of the narrative. We benefited hugely from the work and advice of Martin L. Müller, director of the Historical Institute of Deutsche Bank. Matthias Kemmerer provided invaluable day-to-day support facilitating the work with the sources, frequently offering constructive criticism and useful suggestions. Moreover, the staff of the bank's Historical Institute were decisively involved in the selection of images, without which the book would have much less lustre and vividness. The archive of the Historical Institute of Deutsche Bank is a crucial resource for understanding the development of the German economic and financial system as well as providing scholars with the records of a key player in the development of the global economic system. Without it, our collective understanding of the course of world history would clearly be weakened in many ways.

In addition to the extensive written sources, leading former and active managers of the bank were available to Catherine R. Schenk as contemporary witnesses for extensive discussions.

At a workshop at the University of Frankfurt am Main in July 2018, the authors were able to present their concept to a larger group of experts and discuss it critically. Their suggestions have been incorporated into the manuscripts. All participants of this meeting deserve our thanks.[4]

---

4   The participants present in addition to the three authors were Ralf Ahrens, Boris Barth, Harold James, Jan Pieter Krahnen, Mary O'Sullivan, Morten Reitmayer, Jörg Rocholl, Friederike Sattler, Reinhard H. Schmidt and Cornelius Torp.

Ian Hallsworth from the Bloomsbury Publishing group was very committed to this project, as was editor Allie Collins and copy-editor Richard Collins, who reviewed the manuscripts and gave important hints on how to improve them. Patricia C. Sutcliffe, Sally Hudson Dill and Andrew Evans did an admirable job in translating the sections by Werner Plumpe and Alexander Nützenadel from the German. It goes without saying, of course, that the authors alone are responsible for any remaining deficiencies.

Werner Plumpe
Alexander Nützenadel
Catherine R. Schenk

IN THE AGE
OF THE FIRST
GLOBALISATION,
1870–1914

WERNER PLUMPE

I. The Founding of Deutsche Bank and the Beginnings of the Business, 1870–1875

1. The Beginnings of the Industrial Boom

'What's breaking into a bank compared with founding a bank?'[1] asks the bandit Mack the Knife in Brecht's *Threepenny Opera* at the end of the 1920s. In saying this, he is trying to suggest – not very subtly – that the banking business is no more honest than robbing a bank, but certainly more profitable. With a bank, one can make money, in some cases lots of it; in the nineteenth century at least this was not controversial and successful bankers like the Rothschilds even managed to acquire wide public recognition. The problem was more how one ought to begin such a business. Brecht does not mention this; rather, he simply implies that if you found a bank you will become rich. But it is not as straightforward as that. The nineteenth century knew this, and the twentieth century knows it, too. There are as many new banks being founded as there are bank crises and bankruptcies. Big names in the world of finance have already evaporated into thin air – and by no means only as a result of major crises. Day-to-day business, too, overtaxed many banks that failed to consolidate their business, made dubious investments, or took risks that ultimately turned out not to be justified.

Even if founding a bank may still be relatively easy, managing one successfully certainly is not. There is no obvious path to success, and, if achieved, nor is it guaranteed to last. The conditions of the banking business are constantly changing. Recipes for success from the past may not help in the future; it can even be a disadvantage if one hangs on too tightly to a successful past and fails to shift in time to take a new course. And even the business of founding a bank can be difficult. In the middle of the nineteenth century, there were considerable barriers to founding a bank. The financial sector was by no means underdeveloped; there were numerous relevant institutions, including private banks in which bankers conducted banking business with their own personal assets, mostly concerned with extending credit, trade finance and financing governments. Those who lacked the necessary assets and, above all, had no relevant expertise had little prospect of opening a profitable banking business. It was very different from what Brecht imagined it to be: without already being wealthy, you could hardly become a successful banker. And even that would not have been enough by itself: without sufficient experience, on the one hand, and without the relevant public reputation, on the other, the banking business was doomed to fail from the outset. Almost all the large private banks followed a tradition – often based on their family – that ranged from beginnings in regional and supra-regional trade and simple loan transactions up to the high art of state financing. Above all, the Rothschilds embodied this combination of affluence, family and experience, with the generations involved in managing the business always striving to maintain it.[2] It was no different with banks like Bethmann in Frankfurt am Main, Mendelssohn, Bleichröder and Warschauer in Berlin or Warburg in Hamburg. Keeping the family together was by no means a trivial matter, either, because the banking business was passed down both in terms of assets and knowledge. It was not possible to get a formal education along these lines outside the private banks. The families' sons or very promising candidates, often related in some way, initially learned in their own bank and continued their 'education' in friendly banks in international locations, preferably significant ones, before they finally returned home to their fathers' banking businesses. At the same time, marital ties among banking families were pursued. It was not uncommon for sons and daughters of bankers to marry into other banking families; indeed, in certain families, there was an unspoken, but also sometimes openly expressed, expectation that their children would find a way to make personal interests and business prospects work together in harmony. All in all, the European and, at least partially, also the American banking world was not necessarily a 'closed shop' in the final analysis, but it was a very homogeneous world of a few families, which were quite often related by marriage. To succeed in this environment was not impossible, but it was certainly quite difficult. Above all, newly founded banks hardly managed to penetrate state financing, the 'Holy Grail' of big banking business, for a long time because you had to have good connections and correspondingly great financial strength in order to do so. Without the comprehensive change in the structure of the economy that was associated with the emergence of industrial capitalism in the middle of the nineteenth century, the rise of new banks would hardly have been conceivable. Only the emergence of major industry generated new conditions for financing; initially with the great railway projects and later in the industrial sector there were financial squeezes that could not be handled by private bankers alone. Private bankers still played a considerable part in the founding of railway corporations, and stock market transactions and bond issues also fitted well with their previous practices, but the mobilisation of capital for the ongoing operations of industry, and, thus, especially of working credits and long-term financing, were not necessarily to the taste of traditional institutions. Consequently, alternative models came into being, of which the founding of Crédit Mobilier by the Péreire brothers in Paris became an archetype because in this case, an incorporated bank – new in and of itself – engaged in 'crowdfunding' for the first time on a large scale; that is, it used wide-ranging deposit banking as the basis for expanding its lending business in the industrial sector. This seemed like a model for success but was also very risky because the share capital of the bank was limited and would hardly have been sufficient, in the face of a crisis, to satisfy all the depositors if there were larger defaults. In the end, the Parisian bank failed for precisely this reason, despite the consistently favourable support of the French government. In 1867, it was liquidated.

But no one could have known this when the bank was founded in 1852. Far from it: Crédit Mobilier was fascinating. The French model attracted a great deal of attention east of the Rhine as well, although it was not yet held in high regard. On the contrary, the Prussian government, above all, considered this sort of banking business to be highly speculative. As it was restrictive in the licensing of joint-stock companies anyway, between 1848 and 1870 the Berlin government consistently rejected all attempts to establish incorporated banks based on the French model in Prussian territory. The first incorporated banks in the 1850s, therefore, were not established in Prussia but, rather, in other German states, such as in Darmstadt, Gotha, Hamburg and Hanover, or in Austria. Some of those interested in such banks in Prussia, among them merchants from the

David Hansemann (1790–1864), the founder of Disconto-Gesellschaft.

Rhineland and members of Berlin's high-finance sector who recognised the growing financial needs of industry, which was expanding considerably in the so-called *Gründerjahre*, or founders' years, tried to avoid this problem by founding limited partnerships, and in this they were quite successful. Disconto-Gesellschaft (1851), founded by David Hansemann, and Berliner Handels-Gesellschaft (1856), whose founders came from the big private banks of Berlin, combined some of the traits of the older private bankers – company owners who were personally liable with their own capital contributions made up their management boards – and the variant of a joint-stock company (*KGaA – Kommanditgesellschaft auf Aktien*, partnership limited by shares). Subsequently, both banks were heavily involved in the field of industrial financing, sometimes even taking on the management of industrial companies or holding larger equity stakes in companies in their own portfolios in order to be able to list them later on the stock market under more favourable conditions.

In light of the economic boom of the era during the tremendous industrial expansion of the 1850s and 1860s, this was not a bad business. Towards the end of the 1860s, however, this boom began to take on highly speculative characteristics. Because of rising share prices, more and more joint-stock companies were being founded, and existing companies were being transformed into joint-stock companies. When stock corporation law was liberalised in June 1870 within the North German Confederation, which meant that the licensing requirement for joint-stock companies was also dropped in Prussia, such company transformations became easier, and incorporated banks could now also be founded that dealt primarily with transforming companies into stock corporations and, thus, engaging in stock price arbitrage in a big way.[3] This form of business, called agiotage, was quite popular. Beginning in 1870, a multitude of new incorporated banks sprang up, often in the form of so-called brokerage banks,[4] whose essential purpose was to profit from the potential founding earnings in the stock market boom. With the business practices of some of these banks, one is reminded of Bertolt Brecht's cunning protagonist Mackie the Knife. Whereas in the entire period before 1870, joint-stock

4

Political cartoon about the Panic of 1873 in the satirical magazine Kladderadatsch.

companies with 9.2 billion marks in capital were founded in Prussia, those founded between 1870 and 1874 alone managed to reach the dizzy heights of 12.87 billion marks.[5] This could not turn out well. The *Gründerkrach*, or the Panic of 1873, put an early end to this boom. The majority of the brokerage banks had to shut down almost as quickly as they had opened. But even many reputable banks that had participated in the speculative investments of the founders' boom, and had bet on a persistent rise of the numerous new industrial joint-stock companies, were now a shambles. The Panic of 1873 and the founders' crisis left considerable dents in their balance sheets and severely depressed their stock prices. The stock value of Disconto-Gesellschaft was almost halved between late 1872 and late 1873; Darmstädter Bank für Handel und Industrie and Berliner Handels-Gesellschaft, too, had to cope with serious drops in their stock prices. Dividends were drastically reduced or had to be discontinued altogether, as in the case of Berliner Handels-Gesellschaft.[6]

2. The Idea of a German Bank for World Trade

When Deutsche Bank was founded as an incorporated bank in March 1870, it is not altogether surprising that the public assumed it was merely another agiotage bank. But the men who had already been planning the founding of Deutsche Bank since the late 1860s were not driven by the wave of speculative investments. In any case, they represented banks and trading companies that either took part in this boom, or could have done so if they had wanted to. The motives behind the founding of Deutsche Bank were altogether different. They were an expression of the economic boom of those years, but they had a different starting point. The rise of German industry, which, as we have seen, grew significantly and extensively in the 1850s and 1860s – commercial production alone doubled between 1850 and 1870[7] – was closely associated with a corresponding expansion in German foreign trade. The demand for imports of raw materials rose dramatically. At the same time, German exports increased as well, with commercial products playing an ever-greater role. Imports rose from 545 million marks to 2.188 billion marks between 1850 and 1870, whereas exports grew from 522 million to 1.967 billion marks in the same period.[8] All in all, therefore, foreign trade increased in this period even more than the gross domestic product. There was clearly a great business opportunity in the financing of foreign trade, but also in the expansion of the large infrastructure associated with trade, which German companies had barely taken notice of up to that point.[9] Moreover, it was obvious that the expansion of the global economy – the growth in foreign trade was by no means limited to Germany – was not a transient phenomenon. It was the beginning of a new age.

Even if it would be wrong to speak of this period as a first wave of globalisation, the character of the global economic division of labour nonetheless changed. New transportation possibilities, be they now railways or steamships, meant that distances were shrinking; travel times dropped dramatically, transport costs declined significantly, worldwide price differences levelled out – a unified global economy at least appeared on the horizon as a future possibility.[10] At the same time, the nations of the world all knew more about each other. Undersea cables connecting Europe and America made it possible to exchange information between the great world trade centres in New York, London and Hamburg within minutes – communications that had previously taken days or weeks. Telegraph cables were not limited to the Atlantic, but were soon connecting all the important locations of the global economy with one another; the Near and Middle East were included just as India, China, and Japan were, not to mention Australia as an important outpost of the British Empire.[11] Although the global economic boom of the 1850s and 1860s had contributed, in any case, to intensified international trade, it was additionally spurred on by more than technological innovations; there were other factors of great significance. The discovery of gold in California and Australia favoured a significant expansion in the money supply, originating in Great Britain, where the

A centre of German foreign trade: the Port of Hamburg around 1870.

gold standard had been implemented. The basic deflationary tenor of the years before the Revolution of 1848 was over. And the end of the American Civil War, which had brought cotton export from the Southern US states to a standstill, normalised Atlantic trade. Thereafter, extensive cotton exports from the same states were resumed, quickly reaching their old level; before the Civil War, cotton imports had been the single greatest item of the German import balance and would soon become that again.[12] It was not lost on close observers that it was foreign banks that provided German exporters and importers with the necessary loans for financing foreign trade in exchange for good interest rates and commissions. After the founding of Deutsche Bank, there was talk of 50 million marks being lost to the German national economy every year on account of there being either no domestic finance infrastructure for foreign trade or only a very rudimentary one. Franz Urbig, who would later become proprietor of Disconto-Gesellschaft and after the merger in 1929 was Chairman of the Supervisory Board of Deutsche Bank and Disconto-Gesellschaft, even estimated the sum of commissions flowing to England alone in the mid-1880s at £5 million, which would have amounted to about 100 million marks. The volume of credit behind this, which German trading firms were perpetually taking advantage of, he even estimated at £300 million.[13] This was a tremendous amount of business that German banks were allowing to slip away. The few institutions, such as traditional private bankers in Bremen and Hamburg, who got involved at all were dependent on assistance from the London banks as long as bills of exchange denominated in German currency could not be discounted internationally. Thus, there were obviously considerable opportunities in this which, if properly exploited, seemed to promise high returns. This was shown in the successes of the large London merchant bankers and Paris's Comptoir d'Escompte, which often also carried out their business with German employees.[14]

The memoirs of Hermann Wallich, who worked for overseas branches of Comptoir d'Escompte from 1863 to 1870 and would become an influential figure at Deutsche Bank in its first decades, provide not only an accurate reflection of these business opportunities, but also of the difficulties that representing a bank on Réunion or in East Asia on a daily basis entailed at that time.[15] Wallich's biography also presents a prime example of how closely connected the European banks between the Rhineland, Paris and London, and above all, their personnel, already were, precisely because of the financing of international trade. This was because in order to be able to take part in international financial transactions of any kind, the respective banks had to depend on partners with whom they could co-operate at key locations of world trade.[16] Such connections were absolutely vital to the private German bankers; the close relationship between Bleichröder, the leading Berlin bank at the time, and the Rothschilds of Paris may serve as proof of this in this context.[17] In the Berlin circles that were pushing the idea of founding a foreign trade bank in the late 1860s, these conditions were known; indeed, they were part of everyday conversation because both of the two leading thinkers in the founding circle of Deutsche Bank, Adelbert Delbrück and Ludwig Bamberger, had relevant experience. Adelbert Delbrück was the head of a private bank and Ludwig Bamberger came from a Jewish banking family from Mainz and was a member of the customs parliament, or the North German Reichstag, and, before that, had been a banker in Rotterdam, London and Paris.[18] That the idea of becoming active in financing foreign trade suggested itself is evident, moreover, in the fact that other simultaneous initiatives pointed in the same direction, above all the plan to found the Internationale Bank in Hamburg. The background was most probably the same as Ludwig Bamberger attributed to the founding of Deutsche Bank in his memoirs:

> Some coincidence or another initially brought about the first connections with Brazil, and these built upon a series of others, namely, with the La Plata states. A large part of these, as well as the East Asian transactions that also flowed in, always had to be directed through London, where the loans were opened and the products were consigned, and these experiences gave the impetus for me, when Adelbert Delbrück […] spoke with me upon my first longer stay in Berlin at the end of the Sixties about the business of founding a Deutsche Bank while asking me to participate in its formation and organisation, to willingly engage with this in respect of the expansion of German banking business in transatlantic areas that would need to be achieved, for which I was confident I had some knowledge.[19]

Thus, it was the private banker Adelbert Delbrück, the head of the bank Delbrück, Leo & Co., and, furthermore, the cousin of the head of the Reich Chancellery, Rudolf von Delbrück, who got the ball rolling. The co-operation with Ludwig Bamberger made sense not only because of his experience in the international banking business. Bamberger was also an influential liberal politician, who had quite a history of revolutionary activity, whose competence, above all in the field of currency and monetary policy, was considerable. Since the late 1860s, Bamberger had sided with Bismarck,

The founders: Adelbert Delbrück (1822–1890) and Ludwig Bamberger (1823–1899).

not only defending Bismarck's policies before the French public but also becoming an influential adviser to him during the war of 1870–1.[20] It would surely be going too far to attribute direct political influence to the founding circle of Deutsche Bank around Delbrück and Bamberger. Yet both men were held in very high regard by both the chancellor of the North German Confederation and the Prussian prime minister Bismarck. Bismarck had set aside his old differences with Bamberger during this time, although he never really warmed to Johannes von Miquel, who was likewise an influential National Liberal politician and banker and, for a time, a member of the Management Board of Disconto-Gesellschaft.[21] Bamberger's position of trust with Bismarck, though, was probably not only favourable to the process of obtaining a concession for Deutsche Bank; his currency and monetary policies in the early 1870s were also decisive for its further development.[22] One roadblock to German banks becoming involved in international banking was the lack of an internationally recognised German currency. Even in the area of the Customs Union, which more or less corresponded to the later Reich territory, no uniform currency had really been achieved. When the German Empire was founded, there were, in fact, still six different currency zones in Germany, which had already seriously impeded national economic exchange, not to mention the difficulty these currencies presented for participation in international trade.[23] Ludwig Bamberger was one of the staunchest advocates for transitioning from the federally fragmented bimetallism with its numerous gold and silver coins and various denominations to a gold standard orientated around the British model. In his book *Reichsgold*,[24] published in 1876, he presented himself as an ardent supporter of gold, which, he claimed, provided a guarantee and was also a prerequisite for smart fiscal policy and for a bank system capable of withstanding resistance.[25] In Bamberger's view, the gold standard had two advantages: it forced governments to have cautious monetary and fiscal policies, and it rendered the German currency capable of competing internationally, even though the mark did not achieve an equal footing in the leading financial and capital markets before, at best, 1900. This was a crucial point for the business policy of the banks, and Deutsche Bank remained entirely loyal to its founder in its defence of the gold standard against its key critics. Karl Helfferich, who was promoted to the Management Board of Deutsche Bank in 1908, owed his career not least to his energetic defence of Ludwig Bamberger's life's work; Helfferich was closely allied both personally and in terms of his programmatic positions to Bamberger.[26] To a certain extent, therefore, the bank inherited a left-liberal legacy. Adelbert Delbrück, too, had after all been a member of the Progress Party and had been involved along these lines in municipal politics in Berlin as well as in the Management Board of Deutscher Handelstag (the German Chamber of Commerce). This inheritance shaped Deutsche Bank's political positioning because its advocacy of a liberal monetary and fiscal policy was oriented towards the gold standard; in addition, its support for international trade that was as free as possible and tied to the liberal tradition put it at odds with the agriculturalists as well as their political representatives, namely the conservative parties. Thus, the liberalism embodied by the bank by no means merely expressed the convictions of its early representatives but, rather, to a certain extent also followed their interests, which stood to profit from a restrictive trade policy just as little as from lax and undisciplined monetary and financial policies.

3. From the Idea to the Initiative

The project Adelbert Delbrück initiated to found a bank for foreign trade began in rather auspicious circumstances. The economic situation was good, the general conditions for an initial public offering (IPO) were promising and the circle of potential supporters and interested parties was anything but small. However, Delbrück was aware that the founding of a new institution would not necessarily be well received by the established banks. Thus, it made sense to signal that this new initiative would not compete with the existing banks. On the contrary – they were prompted to either directly or indirectly participate in the establishment of a bank that was supposed to deal in a business field that, until then, had hardly been addressed, and not at all from Berlin. For banks that were not active in cross-border trade or were not able to become active in this field, participation in this sort of a specialised institution must have been an attractive prospect. The initiators advertised this project '[t]hrough confidential discussions and letters in the circles initially most interested'.[27] The founding circle expanded bit by bit, especially because many of the men who were experienced in the international exchange of goods appeared to be quite open to the idea. Clearly, Delbrück and Bamberger had hit upon an important issue, even though they never managed to establish the co-operative agreement with Berlin's leading bank Mendelssohn & Co. that they had aimed for. Yet private bankers and major merchants from Berlin, Frankfurt, the Hanseatic cities and Elberfeld with the surrounding Bergisches Land and Rhineland all belonged to the founding committee, and they at least also maintained close relationships in the international business world, particularly in the United States.[28] In New York especially, the crucial founders who had already known one another for a decade before the bank was founded had crossed paths.[29] The Bremen merchant Hermann Henrich Meier also had an abundance of experience in the United States.[30] He had been employed there in the 1830s in his father's trading company and had staunchly advocated the importance of trade and the shipping industry between Bremen or Bremerhaven and the United States. In 1857, he was counted among the co-founders of Norddeutscher Lloyd. Meier was also the person who, after an initially positive reception, had recommended an expert for the overseas business, who was commissioned to write a memorandum about the structure and tasks of the envisaged bank. The Dutchman Gustav Dufresne was chosen.[31] In 1863, he had opened an agency in Batavia, at that time Dutch India (and Jakarta today), for the Chartered Bank of India, Australia & China, which had its headquarters in London. In 1867, he had returned to Amsterdam.[32] Thus, after many years of experience, he was familiar with the East Asian market, which would become one of the business fields of the planned bank. The aspiration of the bank that was to be founded was clearly spelled out in the memorandum. It had something to do with utilising the opportunities that the strong growth in German foreign trade seemed to afford such an institution, and, thus, it was explicitly about breaking the dominant position of British banks in the financing of German foreign trade by establishing a German institution that would compete with them. Dufresne listed the financial successes of the British Oriental Bank, the Chartered Mercantile Bank of India, London & China, the Chartered Bank of India, Australia &

China and the Hong Kong & Shanghai Banking Corporation, but, above all, also of the French Comptoir d'Escompte, which, he noted,

> has been opening establishments in East India, China, and Japan for 8 or 9 years and – though dispensing with the support of reputable French banks in various locations in the East, [...] the operations of these branches are achieving such brilliant results that the management in its last annual report wished to point to the establishments in India, China and Japan as an essential support of this tremendous creation of the year 1848. In this time period from 1 July 1867 to 15 June 1868 the branches in Calcutta, Bombay, Hong Kong, Shanghai, Réunion and London earned a total sum of c. frcs. 4 250 000 for Comptoir d'Escompte in interests and profit and the last annual report particularly emphasises the high value of the branches in times when low discount rates in Europe would have significantly reduced the profits, if the branches had not offered this compensation.[33]

Dufresne also projected similar profit prospects to the founding circle in relation to the proposed bank project.

The financial incentives were framed in a national rhetoric that accompanied the founding of the bank from the beginning. In this and all the following narratives, the interest of the institution to be founded, which by the summer of 1869 already bore the name 'Deutsche Bank', was equated with the interest of the country.[34] In this respect, the naming of the bank was already part of the programme,[35] and playing the patriotic card in representing one's own interest quickly became routine, not least because the spirit of the times between the wars of unification and the founding of the Reich was particularly conducive to this sort of talk of the fatherland. However, the founders

A model for the founding of Deutsche Bank: Comptoir d'Escompte, which financed French foreign trade with its branches in India and East Asia. The branch in Shanghai was led from 1867 to 1870 by Hermann Wallich, who transferred after that to Deutsche Bank in Berlin.

were clearly aware that the matter had to do with a private bank asserting itself in a competitive international field of business. The national rhetoric may thus have helped in the German public, but in some circumstances it involved more disadvantages from a business perspective. For example, from the outset the bank was open to international co-operation and also stated this in the memorandum in a way that did not preclude the possibility of international investment in the share capital of the new bank: 'But exclusively German participation is not needed to support the company, which should take a cosmopolitan point of view.'[36] This was not just empty talk. Later, as well, responsible executives of the bank were always clearly aware of the meaning that cross-border co-operation implied. They were entirely self-confident as Germans and also defined themselves clearly in relation to the national market, yet the entanglement of this market in the world market likewise conditioned the bank's international involvement. Thus, even in the 1890s, Georg Siemens, Deutsche Bank's Spokesman, was able to state matter-of-factly that he did not wish to participate in an initiative to support the development of a Kaiser Wilhelm Library, and thus Germanness, in Posen: 'We are not national, but international.'[37]

This openness was simply a condition for international co-operation, which was of necessity closely associated with the financing of foreign trade. The founding committee, which was formed in the summer of 1869, was, consequently, anything but nationally narrow-minded. Victor von Magnus, the head of the Berlin bank F. Mart. Magnus, had assumed the chairmanship. Thus, a renowned individual held the reins and thoroughly concealed the fact that the notable bank Mendelssohn was not willing to enter into a co-operative agreement, particularly since the committee had another Berlin private banker in the shape of Adelbert Delbrück. The other members of the founding committee were mostly active in the international sphere as private bankers or merchants, individuals such as Hermann Zwicker from the Berlin bank Schickler & Co., and Adolph vom Rath, the co-proprietor of the Cologne bank Deichmann & Co. The merchant Gustav Kutter was not necessarily known to the German public. He had gone to New York in around 1850 in order to found the dry goods suppliers Kutter, Luckemeyer & Co. with his business partner Eduard Luckemeyer.[38] Twenty years later, the company had agencies in New York, Zurich, Lyons and Berlin. In addition, Kutter was the discreet representative of the overseas interests of the Frankfurt bank Sulzbach. This private bank would also play a prominent role in the founding of Deutsche Bank as it gathered Frankfurt investors, thus becoming the largest single shareholder of the new bank. Gustav Müller was hardly less important; after two decades as an export merchant in Szczecin, he had settled in Berlin as a private banker in 1865. He had valuable ties with the south-western financial scene and represented 162,000 thalers' worth of shares, including his own shares, comprising about 10 per cent of the capital, which included the voting rights of Köster & Co. in Mannheim, Bamberger & Co. in Mainz, and Königlich Württembergische Hofbank in Stuttgart. Like many in the founding circle, he was also politically active among the National Liberals, and he was a representative for several years respectively in the Prussian state parliament, the Reichstag of the North German Confederation, the Customs Parliament and the first all-German Reichstag.[39]

If one adds Ludwig Bamberger to this group, it completes the picture. A circle of nationally and internationally active private bankers and wholesale merchants who were already closely connected and mostly had liberal backgrounds got down to the business of conquering a field of business – which was obviously lucrative – by founding a new bank as the respective investors alone lacked the capacities and competencies. And because the conditions for founding an incorporated bank, as noted above, could not have been better, they seized the moment and sent out invitations for a sort of founding assembly in Berlin that would take place on 22 January 1870. There, a temporary Administrative Board with 10 members was elected. This was in accordance with the draft of the company statute, which stipulated a division of labour between the Administrative Board as the authoritative body for the owners and the directorate as the body that would manage operations. Later, the Administrative Board came to be known as the Supervisory Board, and the directorate became the Management Board. In addition to the seven members of the founding committee, three other figures with experience in international business were also members. One of these was the Altona merchant Wilhelm von Pustau, the owner of the trading company of the same name and who, in 1845, had simultaneously opened a branch in Canton and the first German trade agency in China.[40] The merchant Hermann Marcuse was even more significant; from his retirement home in Rheingau, he nonetheless held the third largest block of shares of Deutsche Bank. As early as the 1850s, he had worked as a banker in New York. As a shareholder in the 1860s, he formed the New York bank Marcuse & Baltzer, which the *New York Times* called one of the leading foreign banks in the United States.[41] After the American Civil War, he returned to Germany having retired and created, among other things, the Special Administrative Council for Europe of the Germania Life Insurance Company of New York together with Eduard von der Heydt, Heinrich Hardt and Friedrich Kapp; the company had established a branch in February 1868 in Berlin, thus expanding quite successfully to Europe.[42] Like Marcuse, the private banker von der Heydt, the cloth merchant and National Liberal politician Hardt and the journalist Friedrich Kapp had been active in business in New York since the middle of the century and would be members of the circle of founders, or first members of the Administrative Board, of Deutsche Bank.

The founding assembly also approved the draft of the company statute, which listed the purpose of the founding of the bank, alongside 'conducting bank transactions of all kinds', above all as the 'fostering and simplification of trade relations between Germany, the other European countries and overseas markets'.[43] The first of these was rather a severability clause so as not to saddle the bank with any unnecessary restrictions, but the second point was more germane to the matter. This is where the clear focus of the future bank was to lie. The first financial advertisement of Deutsche Bank after it received its licence, which appeared in the *Frankfurter Zeitung* edition of 24–25 March 1870, also made this abundantly clear:

> The purpose of the company, whose statute was approved by His Majesty the King of Prussia on 10 March 1870, is to supply the German capital market with extraordinarily rewarding and secure money transactions, which is required by the

ever more powerfully developing trade in goods between Germany and overseas markets, and to secure the position for German capital in the tremendous world trade that it is entitled to on account of its significance in Europe. For this purpose, the bank is authorised to found agencies, branches, and subsidiaries both at home and abroad. The firms and institutions active in this business field in England and France show glowing results of their activity.[44]

There it was, this patriotic tone that equated the interests of Deutsche Bank unequivocally with the growth of the German capital market. Competitors may well have read these grandiose announcements with rather mixed feelings; the business press's first reactions to these announcements were also quite lukewarm, as we will see below. Naturally, it was not dishonest because it was quite obvious that the new bank, as with the foreign banks that looked on enviously, wanted a big slice of the pie that was international trade financing. By contrast, the indication in the financial advertisement that the new company also intended to 'conduct banking transactions of all kinds, such as those that have proven to be very successful for the other similar banking institutions in Germany'[45] seemed harmless enough, although it would later turn out to be the more explosive statement of intent.

Deutsche Bank's first financial advertisement in Frankfurter Zeitung *of 24–25 March 1870.*

4. Patriotic Fantasies?

The founding assembly proceeded uneventfully, and the statute and temporary Administrative Board were passed and elected without any major conflicts. Shortly thereafter, a petition to have a licence granted for operating an incorporated bank was submitted to the Prussian Trade Ministry. Nevertheless, members of the temporary Administrative Board were obviously of the opinion that an explanatory letter to the federal chancellor of the North German Confederation and the Prussian prime minister, Count Otto von Bismarck, could not hurt. This letter, sent on 8 February 1870,[46] is a prime example of the kind of keen rhetoric that might have put off Bismarck, who was known for his hearty dislike of such camouflaged communications, but apparently it did not. Indeed, the members of the Administrative Board made sure to lay it on thick, initially suggesting that their initiative in founding the bank had come about as a result of Bismarck's policies. The very thought of explaining the basic idea for founding Deutsche Bank to the Reich chancellor, the letter stated, 'had imposed itself on his account, because this same [idea] makes use of the honour of having derived its starting point from the new formation of the national circumstances, [and] having generated its deeper meaning from the founding of a Germany that stands strong and united under the protective power of the North German Confederation and the Customs Union'.[47] Bismarck's policies, the letter continued, thus contributed to the great rise of the German economy, whose successes these policies could only harvest, of course, in a limited way, since Germany's international financial relations were handled, with the exception of those with the United States, by French and British banks. This, the letter argued, disadvantaged the German merchant and also contributed to considerable costs.

> The new bank is supposed to remedy this renunciant position of the world of German foreign trade [...]. And, indeed, in the form of an institution located in the capital of Germany and eventually represented by branches in the harbour locales, which will be in a position to offer credit, information, and encouragement to foster this business sector, which is so significant for the entire culture of a people.

Ludwig Bamberger asserted very confidently on behalf of the temporary Administrative Board that Deutsche Bank had already been acknowledged 'by the trading class of the entire nation' as this sort of institution ever since the plans had first been made known:

> One look at the enclosed list of the businesses of every stature and career, which rushed to partake in the formation of the institution at the first announcement, may suggest to Your Excellency that the thought of this creation has been taken up as a long overdue good deed, and the diplomatic representatives abroad will surely welcome the news of this beginning with the same warmth.

This can already be seen as quite a presumptuous statement about the future meaning of an institution that had not yet even been approved, but there was more to come because the founders of Deutsche Bank put themselves on a par with Bismarck himself:

The feeling of security and the self-confidence to which the German shipmaker and merchant in the Far East and West have become privy since the new German protective power took up its great position in international relations will now experience not inconsiderable growth through the certainty of having the protection and support of their own compatriots by their side in the most important monetary matters.[48]

These testimonies sounded both harmless and selfless and would, indeed, make the 'work just undertaken [and] arising from a truly patriotic thought' appealing to 'Your Excellency'. Nor did the petitioners forget to highlight the use Berlin could make of the new bank, emphasising, in particular, 'that the capital market of Frankfurt addressed the matter with the greatest zeal'.[49] This was true, but highlighting it was also intended to show that Frankfurt seemed to have overcome its rancour about Prussia's annexation of the city, which had occurred a few years earlier. Despite all the patriotic rhetoric, however, it was of course about benefits to business. The initiators of Deutsche Bank, after all, were not the only ones who hoped to make a lot of money in the financing of foreign trade. Other attempts were in the works, and in Hamburg a similar bank, Internationale Bank, was about to be founded. The founding committee in Berlin was simply afraid of losing time in a drawn-out licensing process and having to chase after the competition. The letter writer, Ludwig Bamberger,[50] openly admitted this in the end. Because the Berlin initiative had not remained a secret, the great interest in Frankfurt alone had awakened other circles 'which are contemplating outrunning the present company from other points in Germany, [and] which, unfortunately, in more favourable conditions in terms of legislation, came immediately to life and were able to gain an important advantage as a consequence because they were not required to wait for approval from the top'. Thus, the letter writer asked Bismarck to limit the time the licensing process would take to 'the bare minimum'.[51]

5. The Founding

Thus, the company needed to be presented as a sort of patriotic necessity in order for the founders to receive the necessary incorporated bank licence as quickly as possible. It is highly likely that the circumstances also dictated the reason for the name chosen for the bank; 'Deutsche Bank' was a rather striking name, at least when compared with other names typical of the period, and later on it would also repeatedly lead to misunderstandings, since many observers believed that the institution was a government establishment. The founding circle of the bank achieved success with this strategy. Early on, the trade ministry signalled that it would treat the bank benevolently. On 20 February 1870, the petition was answered, and the submitted statute was returned for revision. The 34 complaints primarily constituted editorial changes. One issue was that the founders intended to grant themselves subscription rights for the beginning and for later capital increases at face value. As such rights could then be sold during a boom when share prices rise rapidly, the ministry only demanded greater assurances. The founding committee immediately provided these assurances. On 25 February 1870, the revised statute was resubmitted, and on 10 March 1870 'the highest level of permission was granted'.[52]

Notarised copy of the permission for 'the establishment of a joint-stock company under the firm "Deutsche Bank, Actien-Gesellschaft" with headquarters in Berlin' granted by Prussian King Wilhelm I on 10 March 1870.

In light of the fact that no incorporated bank licence had previously been granted in Prussia despite numerous applications since A. Schaaffhausen'scher Bankverein was transformed into a joint-stock company in 1848, the speed with which this occurred is surprising, as was the rather large room to manoeuvre granted to the bank. The planned share capital was 5 million thalers, of which 2 million thalers initially needed to be deposited. The precaution taken to prevent agiotage consisted of requiring that initial stock subscribers would only receive further stock options when share capital was increased at face value 'to the extent that they are still in possession of shares from the first issuance'. This was, incidentally, a right that the initial subscribers voluntarily dispensed with later on.[53] Moreover, the statute[54] planned for the usual governing instruments of a joint-stock company, including an Administrative Board (Supervisory Board), directorate (Management Board) and a general meeting, although in this it granted the Administrative Board extensive authorities, also in the operative business, which was still quite possible in 1870 because a clear legal differentiation between the competencies and tasks of the various bodies in a joint-stock company was only created when the amended stock law of 1884 was passed. The stock law of the North German Confederation passed in June 1870 did not undertake to draw a clear distinction between the functions, which contributed significantly to the practical blurring of the boundaries between supervisory and management bodies.[55] Up until 1884, the directorate had to carry out its tasks 'according to the measure of this statute and the instruction given it by the Administrative Board',[56] so that it was, in fact, dependent on orders. The large Administrative Board, ultimately consisting of 24 members, was hardly in a position to intervene in day-to-day business, but those who drafted the statute had anticipated this and had prescribed the formation of a five-person committee of the Administrative Board: 'This committee has all the rights to which the entire Administrative Board is entitled in relation to the directorate. It will convene as often as required by business transactions, or one of the director's requests. Every member of this [same committee] is entitled to convene the committee.'[57] This could lead to tight control of the directorate; indeed, at its core, it meant that it had little room to manoeuvre. Whether there were fears within the founding committee that the bank could slip out of the founders' grasp in the day-to-day business and not conduct itself according to their ideas is not known, but it appears to be obvious. Perhaps the habits of the private bankers prevailed, as such banks did not have a division between supervisory and management boards anyway. In this sense, the statute took the organisational structures of a joint-stock company into account in a purely formal way, whereas the founders possibly assumed that they would be able to conduct business entirely in the traditional manner with the new institution. Although this is largely speculation, the conflicts which soon emerged between the supervisory body and the ideas of the Management Board demonstrate that this passage of the statute by no means corresponded to the reality of dynamically developing joint-stock companies.

Of course, in the beginning this was hardly noticeable. On 21 March 1870, the first general meeting took place; it utilised a 24-man Administrative Board that did have two foreign representatives and appointed Wilhelm Platenius and Georg Siemens (who was ennobled in 1899) as directors, with Wilhelm Platenius himself being a member of the Administrative Board.[58] The expectations of the bank, as well as the fevered speculation of the time, became apparent when the first 2 million thalers of the 5 million in share capital had their initial public offering: in the end, 294 million thalers came in, making them oversubscribed by a factor of 150. As was correctly observed, this had a primarily speculative character, because the stocks were offered at face value, as already noted. Everyone in the world assumed that rates would rapidly increase, so people subscribed to large sums just to be considered.[59] Thus, at the beginning of the company's history, a portion of the share capital was already comprised of free-floating shares. But even among the initial 76 who subscribed to the remaining millions and set the founding assembly, no dominant group of owners emerged with the weight to determine the course of the bank.[60] Consequently, the list of initial subscribers is interesting primarily in its depiction of the reach and significance of Deutsche Bank's network of founders; it extended from Paris (S. H. Goldschmidt) to Moscow (Achenbach & Coller, Jr) and from Zurich (Otto Wesendonck, who, of course, had earned his wealth as a merchant in Elberfeld) to London (Bischoffsheim & Goldschmidt). Two of the biggest subscribers came from the greater Frankfurt area: the Sulzbach brothers and Hermann Marcuse (Walluf) subscribed 850,000 and 334,000 thalers, respectively, and were granted 799,000 and 314,000 worth of shares, respectively. Ahead even of Marcuse, who, like the Sulzbach brothers, represented a number of investors, was the Berlin bank E. J. Meyer (500,000/470,000 thalers). Most of the remaining subscribers invested less than 100,000 thalers each. Mostly only representatives of banks with which Deutsche Bank later co-operated closely, as a rule, had invested above this threshold; examples include

Schlesischer Bankverein in Breslau (133,000/125,000 thalers); the Berlin banks F. Mart. Magnus (175,000/164,600 thalers), the Schickler brothers (150,000/141,000 thalers) and Delbrück, Leo & Co. (112,000/105,200 thalers); in Cologne the Schaaffhausen'scher Bankverein (150,000/141,000 thalers) and Deichmann & Co. (175,000/164,000 thalers); as well as, in Stuttgart, G. H. Kellers Söhne (100,000/94,000 thalers) and Württembergische Vereinsbank (150,000/141,000 thalers). The close relationship with this last bank, which had likewise only been founded a short time before, would become quite significant in the first years of Deutsche Bank's activity, not least because the leading figures of both banks, Georg Siemens and Kilian Steiner, got along well.[61]

There were certainly already influential investors, but there was no controlling group of investors. This would not change before the First World War despite numerous increases in the capital stock. Rather, the bank's shareholders reflected its broad basis of business and – in this context the term can for once be used in a precise sense – its commercial network, which grew wider and wider over the course of the years.[62] Recently, on the basis of an analysis of registrations for general assemblies or shareholder meetings, it was shown that

> Deutsche Bank had many shareholders and probably free-floating shares between 1870 and 1930, thus distinguishing itself from other German companies. At the general meeting, too, no controlling major shareholder was registered who was able to block important decisions or make them single-handedly. The ownership of shares among inside shareholders was not high and declined by 1930, so that a certain separation between share ownership and management control prevailed.[63]

This shareholder structure was very significant because it noticeably weakened the Administrative Board, which had great significance from the statute. Its ability to take action was dependent on the unity of its representatives, and this unity was not easy to achieve in light of the various interests of the investors. Initially, everything depended on Adelbert Delbrück, who became the most notable figure of the Administrative Board in the following years on account of his significance as the *spiritus rector* of the bank's founding, even though Victor von Magnus was the first chairman of the Administrative Board. Hermann Wallich speaks in his memoirs of having been brought to 'President Delbrück' when he entered Deutsche Bank in the autumn of 1870.[64] As early as 1871, Delbrück took over the chairmanship of the Administrative Board, which he would retain until 1889. Of the members of the founding committee, Gustav Kutter and Ludwig Bamberger soon left the Administrative Board, so that it was, above all, the 'major shareholders' or their representatives, Eduard von der Heydt, Rudolf Sulzbach, Hermann Marcuse and Gustav Müller, along with Delbrück, who initially set the tone. Von der Heydt became Delbrück's long-serving deputy. But Müller, too, had already left the Administrative Board in 1877.[65] In the day-to-day work that quickly commenced, a great deal depended on how the two leading boards dealt with each other. It was very unlikely that decrees were simply uttered in this sort of governance structure, even though the powers of the Committee of Five in the Administrative Board were so extensive that it had to approve all transactions that exceeded 1,000 marks. Not without

Front page of the list of initial subscribers to Deutsche Bank of 21 March 1870.

bitterness, Hermann Wallich said that the aim of the Administrative Board had been 'to reduce the directors to mere clerks'.[66] It is known that things were supposed to have been different, and that derived from the fact that the directors would not allow themselves to be continually treated this way.

6. Administrative Councils and 'mere clerks'

Nevertheless, the decisive question for the bank was initially who could be found for the directorate. Experienced individuals who were satisfied with the role intended for them by the Administrative Board were by no means easy to find, particularly since the bank itself was not necessarily positively received by the interested public after its founding. The Frankfurt financial newspaper *Der Aktionär*, for example, mistrusted the newly founded bank on principle and suspected it was driven purely by interest in agiotage, not least on account of the high level of share capital it was aiming for, because one could hardly think of serious foreign business:

It cannot be asserted that the project would have been taken up on the stock market with satisfaction; it is doubtful whether the ostensible purpose of this [bank] alone can guarantee sufficient occupation for a bank institution with such significant means as are supposed to be provided to Deutsche Bank, and one believes that the core of the matter will be less the very nicely conceived support of German trade than agiotage on a grand scale on the model of the Viennese and Parisian institutions [...] In addition, the banks that have placed themselves at the top of this company, as honourable and solid as they all undoubtedly are, are not regarded as capable of managing this sort of institution in accordance with 'modern' requirements.[67]

This problem, along with the more or less open rejection of the project on the part of the Berlin banks that had led the sector up to this point, which in the best case only invested minimally in the founding of the bank, did indeed make the new bank's future prospects seem doubtful. The capital increase from 5 to 10 million thalers already announced for 1871 was, likewise, not suited to eliminating doubts; rather, it strengthened them even more since such an enormous sum was not even needed, should the bank wish 'to establish limited partnerships among pirates, kaffirs and black-footed Indians' along with the planned foreign branches, as *Der Aktionär* sarcastically remarked.[68] None of this was a good advertisement for the bank, and it would not necessarily have attracted suitable candidates for the directorate. And the names of the first two directors who became known after the founding assembly only seemed to reinforce the widespread scepticism.

In any case, up to this point Wilhelm Platenius and Georg Siemens had not yet struck the interested public as financial geniuses. Both of them were considered rather unknown quantities, something that Siemens still liked to play around with years later. On the occasion of the twenty-fifth anniversary of the bank, which had meanwhile become quite successful, the Berlin journalist Friedrich Dernburg reported that he had helped Georg Siemens drink a small keg of Rüdesheimer in the 1870s 'on a long summer night,' and they had come around to the subject of Siemens's career at Deutsche Bank.

Our host bore his dignity with a certain derision, the meaning of which we were not mistaken about at that time. We did not yet know what a profound art of living was coming to light in him presenting himself in this form. Georg Siemens was still a long way off from getting out of the saddle in which he had traversed Persia as a telegraph installer. Now he mockingly told us about his first day as manager of the bank, how someone brought him a bill of exchange and he was absolutely at a loss as to what to do with a piece of paper like that ...[69]

This was also mischievous because early on Siemens had been included on the list of suitable candidates for the Management Board of the bank. During his work in London and Persia, where he had been independently responsible for laying an important telegraph cable for Siemens & Halske, the electronics company run by his uncle Werner, Adelbert Delbrück had taken notice of him and had hired him as a sort of adviser who was to help him in the founding of the bank and also in the selection of directors because of his extensive foreign experience.[70] In the search for suitable candidates on 26 January 1870 Siemens turned to the younger brother of his uncle Werner, Carl Siemens, to whom he disclosed his own ambitions:

> Now the question arises whether you and namely Wilhelm [Wilhelm Siemens, another brother of Werner] in London know a suitable man. My personal interest is also at play in this. I would like to become director, but since I cannot become the first one, I would like to become the second or third. Now since, of course, the first man has a significant vote in the selection of the second and third, it is important to me that I find the first one so that he can propose me as the second or third.[71]

If as a lawyer Siemens lacked the necessary professional requirements for banking, he could nonetheless, despite being only 30 years old, point to his international experience and his obvious skill as a negotiator, which he had proved in difficult circumstances in Persia, where he had more or less had to fend for himself. He probably let Delbrück know this as well, because on 22 March 1870, just a day after the first general meeting of the newly founded Deutsche Bank, Siemens and Delbrück had reached an agreement. Siemens declared himself willing 'to assume a position on the Management Board of Deutsche Bank for the duration of one year for a salary of 1,500 thalers'. He finally left the Prussian judicial service, but retained his right to 'temporarily continue his position as the legal adviser of the local company Siemens & Halske as long as this does not clash with the business affairs of Deutsche Bank'.[72] In other words, Georg Siemens kept a back door open for himself – returning to his uncle's company – if the new bank failed to develop as he hoped.

Initially, there were no other candidates; Ludwig Bamberger helped them out of a jam. Through personal relationships, he knew two potential candidates who were willing to switch to Deutsche Bank. In any case, Bamberger, who had made inquiries about them previously in an entirely noncommittal way, suggested the two men to Adelbert Delbrück. They met with his approval in the founding circle of Deutsche Bank because they could demonstrate relevant experiences and competence. Wilhelm Platenius, a German-American, did not have training as a banker, but he had run a discount business in the United States and had traded in American securities in Stuttgart after his return to Germany. He put himself forward because of the significance of the American market, even though Kilian Steiner, the director of Württembergische Vereinsbank, candidly

Georg Siemens (1839–1901) at the age when he joined Deutsche Bank's Management Board.

expressed certain concerns. On 14 February 1870, he wrote to Ludwig Bamberger. Praising Platenius for his qualities, he did not hold back on criticism, either:

> You see, he is more arrogant than is good for reasonable people. But that is all that I can say against him. He has grown used to comporting himself in a noble manner, and so makes a noble impression in all he does; in his case, this is not an original quality but rather good self-training. You see that I gather only all sorts of material for your judgement; about the whole person I myself have nothing constant. One always feels he is lacking something because everything seems very prepared. One thus always thinks that something else will reveal itself that is his actual nature. In sum, I believe that he would fill such a post with dignity and success when those around him and the conditions support him in that which he seems to be lacking. To put it more precisely, you must tell me which branch should become his.[73]

It was predictable that a personality so described would come into conflict with the Administrative Board's assertion of control in day-to-day matters.

Bamberger recommended Platenius for the Management Board of the bank just as he did his distant relative Hermann Wallich – the latter suggestion was his lucky strike. Hermann Wallich actually had all the experience and qualifications needed in the new bank; it was just that he could not take up his position in Berlin immediately, but only in the autumn of that year, since he was still managing the branch of Comptoir d'Escompte in Shanghai in January 1870. Wallich was unquestionably the right man for this future area of activity at the bank, also because of his experiences in Paris and because he had less need for approval than Platenius and probably also Siemens.[74] In any case, at the founding assembly of the bank there were three people in the directorate, of which two directors began their work for the bank, and thus the work *of* the bank, in April 1870. Georg Siemens wrote numerous letters to his relative in which he described the 'troubles of the plains' that had to be overcome after the mountain of the bank's founding had been scaled. Initially, the way of working was probably rather clueless because neither Platenius nor Siemens was an experienced banker, and they admitted as much: 'Platenius later explained how he and Georg Siemens sat across from each other at the desk on the first day of their new job. One asked the other: "What do we do now? Do you actually have any idea about the banking business?" Both said no and then broke out into redemptive laughter.'[75] But none of this was really very funny. The press had little faith in the two of them. Siemens took this as a challenge and sought to learn the ropes with great zeal:

> Though I understand little of American and Indian banking, I nevertheless try to look very erudite, give the occasional shrug, grin from ear to ear – this is my sneering smile – and secretly refer, when I get home, to my encyclopaedia or dictionary or 'How to become a banker in 24 hours' when I want to find a word I didn't under- stand. I've already just about grasped the difference between ask and bid.[76]

Behind all of this jokiness was a serious problem. Since the bank had been entered into the trade registry, the directorate had considerable sums of money at its disposal, but for what purpose? The Administrative Board was petty in its control over the directors; at the same time, the industrial boom was in full swing, and those who would undertake big projects gathered in droves trying to win the financial support of the new bank. Whereas Siemens first had to learn the ropes of the day-to-day banking business and by no means knew what direction it should go in, Platenius early on already had bigger things in mind with his good US contacts, but he came into conflict again and again with the restrictive stance of the Administrative Board. Strategic decisions about the direction of business were improbable in this situation, particularly since the outbreak of the war against France in the summer, in which Siemens participated as an enlisted officer, forced them to take a break.

7. The Beginnings of Foreign Trade Financing and Overseas Business

When Georg Siemens was called up for military service in the war against France in the summer of 1870, the newly founded Deutsche Bank had only been in business for a few weeks. On 8 April 1870, three days after it was entered into the trade registry, the business – consisting of lending, bills of exchange, acceptances and current accounts business – had been opened in rented rooms at Französische Straße 21 in rather primitive conditions. At Siemens's urging, the new bank also entered into deposit banking. The annual report for 1870 listed a profit of a good 87,000 thalers (261,000 marks) with a turnover of almost 80 million thalers, which corresponded to 240 million marks after the currency conversion of 1873; a small part of this profit resulted from revenues from bills of exchange, and a large part from revenues in the securities, lombard and current accounts business.[77] Deposit banking, already with a volume of more than 1.135 million thalers (3.405 million marks), did not result in any noteworthy gains, but it did contribute significantly to the bank's consolidation, because from the outset

Deutsche Bank took up business operations on the first floor of this building at Französische Straße 21 in Berlin (building on the left) in April 1870.

the bank had made an effort to offer its depositors all its banking transactions, that is, also current accounts and loans. It is probable that business ties and customer contacts were pursued from the founding circle and the first Administrative Board, which made this beginning – which was, all things said, satisfactory – possible in the first place. Gustav Kutter and Hermann Marcuse, for example, may have played a role in brokering American business dealings, which initially were a focal point.

In the summer of 1870, Wilhelm Platenius found himself working alone for some months. He obviously had some precise ideas, especially about American business dealings, yet he failed in this because of the Administrative Board. Exasperated, Platenius threw in the towel at the end of the year, and his quickly appointed successor was not successful either, so that now Hermann Wallich, who had first taken up his position on 1 November 1870, had to run the business. 'My colleague Platenius ...' Hermann Wallich recalled, 'who was not a trained banker, had made valuable connections with New York in accordance with his speciality in the meantime [probably in the autumn of 1870], but he was not able to get used to the dependent relationship on the Administrative Board, grew disgruntled and quit.' 'It gratifies me,' Wallich continued, 'that I was not involved in his resignation, nor in that of his successor, the Privy Financial Councillor Mölle, who realised after working for one year that the qualification of a high-level civil servant did not suffice for taking over the management of a commercial institution.'[78] He had expressed this cautiously. Ludwig Bamberger was much clearer in his memoirs: 'The man was neither stupid nor inexperienced, but I have never come across a greater degree of incompetence in such a position. The civil service and the world of business certainly are poles apart.'[79] Consequently, as Wallich later recalled, the bank was sitting on a tremendous amount of unused capital in the autumn of 1870. When he then suggested 'investing the capital of the bank temporarily in the 5%-North German Confederation Treasury bills just coming out in November 1870, which were being issued at 95%', he suffered a bitter defeat. Although Sedan had been fought, the outcome of the war was not in doubt, and it was indisputable that the bills would certainly be repaid, Wallich's suggestion was rejected, 'and the gentlemen went into a discussion of whether it had been wise to entrust the management of the bank to such a young person, who was, after all, displaying the cravings of a wild speculative investor'.[80]

Even though Wallich was rebuffed in this instance, his plan, which he had worked out before taking up his position in the bank and had presented to the Administrative Board almost immediately upon his arrival, was much more important. It was titled 'On the future business activity of Deutsche Bank with organisational branches of Deutsche Bank (Domestically and Abroad)'.[81] His experience with Comptoir d'Escompte formed the basis of this draft. The core of foreign trade financing, in Wallich's view, consisted in connecting the most important places in the world economy with one another, so Deutsche Bank needed trusted partners in all the places where German merchants purchased products or where they delivered goods. The worldwide exchange of goods worked solely, or at least primarily, by means of credit relations,[82] in which one had to make sure that the exporter received the value of his goods when he shipped them and, in turn, that the importer got the necessary loans to be able to pay for the goods for which he would only earn revenues after further processing them and then selling them.

Hermann Wallich (1833–1928) joined the Management Board in late 1870. He was a proven expert in East Asian markets and foreign trade financing.

The difficulties arising from this were considerable. Nevertheless, the point was that Deutsche Bank's acceptances had to be recognised internationally, which would only be possible if the bank had the requisite financial strength and an unimpeachable reputation. Moreover, Deutsche Bank would be dependent on partners in foreign countries who would be able to accept the bank's own letters of credit and take care of financial affairs abroad. The greatest difficulty, however, lay in the fact that the most convenient and least expensive way to manage foreign trade financing was via London in pounds sterling, not only for British merchants but also for all businesses conducting trade around the world, so that London's central position and the overseas and colonial banks existed there not by coincidence but because of a compelling economic logic. And the banks located in London were regarded as the most professional financiers, particularly since the London money market was able to offer the highest degree of liquidity and thus comparably the lowest international interest rates.

It was thus clear to every expert who understood the technique of foreign trade financing[83] – and Wallich knew this only too well[84] – that the bank could not even consider participating successfully in international business unless it had a foothold of its own in London:

The occasionally, if not on average, cheaper, discount rate of the English bank, combined with the ease of placement of the English foreign currency when compared to other foreign currencies, make it necessary to conduct this business via London for the most part. If we thus really wish to offer our German customers an advantage, we will have to do it by means of an institution to be founded in London. In this context, I do not wish to be more specific about the form of such an institution, but I do wish to recommend the founding of a special agency of our bank as the most appropriate.[85]

In addition, it would be rather naive to assume that London banks concentrated primarily on British foreign trade; they saw themselves as financiers of global trade who aimed to finance world trade in its entirety, regardless of the connections concerned, and were also doing so quite successfully. If Deutsche Bank wished to achieve success, it would have to fit into this context. The point could not be to push London out of the business; rather, the point had to be to utilise the advantages of London as a financial centre, from which the financial centre itself could only profit, as was clear to astute observers, and which did, in fact, occur. The volume of German trade financed via London did not decrease in the years before the First World War but increased significantly; it was just that Deutsche Bank was now directly involved in this.[86]

Securing a foothold in London, therefore, was a matter of survival. Yet in order even to be able to begin with the programme for the bank, it was necessary not only to create bases abroad but also to be represented in the most important German port cities, the centres of German foreign trade. Wallich had also sketched this out in his report. As early as 1871, a branch was opened in Bremen, followed by another in Hamburg in 1872, which were appropriately endowed with funds after the capital stock was raised to 10 million thalers and had been fully paid up.[87] Likewise, the establishment of the Asian branches in Shanghai and Yokohama also took place as early as 1872 on this basis.[88] They were not only supposed to finance foreign trade but also, above all, conduct the arbitrage transactions – that is, exploiting the differences in interest rates between Europe and Asia. The similarly central question of how to find suitable personnel for the newly established

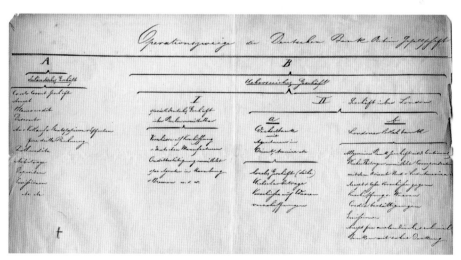

'Operational branches of Deutsche Bank' Hermann Wallich wrote on the first organisational chart in the autumn of 1870. It distinguished domestic from overseas business and gave the 'business through London' a prominent position.

branches was solved by the historical circumstances of the time, as the bank recorded in its annual report for 1871: 'It so happened to us that Comptoir d'Escompte, which was pursuing the same aims with us in France, suddenly laid off its German employees out of national considerations, and that, consequently, a number of competent men, who were entirely familiar with the customs and practices, became available.'[89] Gustav Pietsch, Emil Seligmann and Julius Mammelsdorf, all laid-off managers of Comptoir d'Escompte, took on the management of the agencies in London, Shanghai and Yokohama.[90]

One alternative to founding branches that suggested itself was to invest in other institutions so as not to bear the entire business risk. The Administrative Board opted for this solution with regard to the question of how the bank should be represented in London. Deutsche Bank and its sub-participants alone put £250,000 into the German Bank of London Limited, which was newly founded in March 1871 with share capital of £600,000.[91] The Mitteldeutsche Creditbank and the Frankfurt bank Sulzbach, which were also counted among the first shareholders of Deutsche Bank, made investments of about the same size; the remaining shares were acquired by limited partners from England. Along with limiting the risk, this path, above all, had legal advantages since in the early 1870s British law still did not yet permit the constitution of a branch of Deutsche Bank in London as an independent legal entity. This was not achieved until 1874 with a German–British government agreement that was pushed forward, not least, by Deutsche Bank's interest in maintaining a branch in London as well. Nevertheless, despite Deutsche Bank's large investment in the German Bank of London, the line of credit the latter provided to Deutsche Bank proved, as early as 1872, to be too small for its rapidly expanding business.[92] Additionally, from the outset there were conflicts with the management of the German Bank of London concerning the size of the commissions it was to receive,[93] and there was internal debate about the question of which branch could gain access to the limited London credit line and how much could be borrowed.[94] Wallich's early thoughts about founding a Deutsche Bank branch in London were, thus, never aired. After another capital increase, now to 15 million thalers, had been undertaken in November 1872,[95] the bank had enough room to manoeuvre to endow a functional branch on the Thames. As early as March 1873 – one year before the branch achieved the status of a legal entity – it opened its doors under the name 'Deutsche Bank London Agency'. There was no time for the new branch to grow gradually into the business because, from the outset, it was required to replace the tight line of credit and the high commissions of the German Bank with its own acceptance business. By 15 March 1873 already, Wallich wrote the following to Gustav Pietsch,[96] whom he knew personally from Comptoir d'Escompte in Asia and who had transferred to the management of the London branch from the German Bank, a position he would hold until 1897:

> Our idea was, as you know, to only gradually & only slowly allow your branch to enter into the circulation of acceptances, & to use, as before, the German Bank for 'reimbursement' business. On account of the unexpected position that the German Bank recently took towards us, the situation is totally changed. […] We would, therefore, need to ask ourselves whether we would not find the replacement in ourselves in the near future, & would need to test the capacity of your

branch much earlier than originally intended. [...] It is obvious that we would then have to make use of our circulation of reimbursements and bills of exchange exclusively for our business and that of our branch, & that it would temporarily not be advisable to extend this circulation for the originally intended clientele on the continent and elsewhere. [...] If we succeed in brokering average circulation of £500,000 maintained with the G.[erman] B.[ank], we would already be satisfied with the commission profit of £5,000 (this is how much we paid the German B[an] k) because when forming our branch there, we did not initially place any higher demands than to cover our expenses in order to see that our London-based business was represented there in an appropriate manner.[97]

The point was to secure the acceptance business of the Berlin headquarters and the two domestic branches via Deutsche Bank's own London Agency. For this, Wallich planned for a volume of £50,000 for the Berlin headquarters, £200,000 for Bremen and £50,000 for Hamburg. Only when this was guaranteed were customers also to be allowed to take out acceptance credit directly from the London branch. Consequently, Deutsche Bank's agency in London took on a central role in its foreign trade financing from the first day of its existence since it was possible to profit through it from the more favourable conditions of the London money market.[98]

Despite the differences, Deutsche Bank's investment in the German Bank of London was maintained for a while purely as a financial asset. In 1877, Deutsche Bank sold its shares with a loss of about 117,000 marks.[99] The London branch, by contrast, was a success from the beginning because it managed to refinance itself under favourable conditions in London as a financial centre and, thus, to successively expand its own lending business. Although, as a branch of a foreign bank, it did not gain access to the Bank of England's rediscounting facilities, it was, nonetheless, able to open an account there with a relatively generous line of credit. The tight spots it had experienced in providing sterling credits up to that point, in any case, were quickly overcome, and the troublesome commissions that the German Bank had demanded from Deutsche Bank and even increased after the opening of the London Agency[100] were a thing of the past. The London Agency remained the only branch of a major German bank in London – a position that Deutsche Bank consistently knew how to put to its advantage. Only in 1895 did Dresdner Bank and in 1900 Disconto-Gesellschaft open agencies in the

Letterhead of Deutsche Bank's London Agency from 1876.

leading financial centre of the world. The Management Board was only too aware that this deprived Deutsche Bank of its unique quality, so that the board called upon the London Agency to engage in even better reporting:

> We would, thus, like to ask you, in order to maintain our reputation as those best informed about the conditions there, to tell us as promptly as possible about everything that happens there that is of interest to us, especially at the moment, concerning the money market there. We will, of course, only pass on to others what seems right to us, but we must firmly expect competition from Disconto-Gesellschaft also in this direction, particularly since the latter is working very intensively as far as attention to already acquired or to be acquired customers is concerned.[101]

The branches in Bremen, Hamburg and London experienced good business development. There they had the strengths for which they were created, namely in the area of foreign trade financing: 'It was pleasant for us to note from your worthy letter of the 30th of the month [...] that the business sectors there, especially the lending business

George Yard/Lombard Street: from 1889 to 1914 the London Agency of Deutsche Bank was located here.

Merchant Ludwig Knoop (1821–1894) was considered the Bremen branch's most important customer during the first decade. Photograph from c. 1875.

for overseas locations, are experiencing a delightful boom and present the prospect of favourable results for the future', Management Board members Mölle and Wallich wrote, praising the Bremen branch in late 1871, which was continuously expanding its circle of business clients.[102] Bremen merchant Ludwig Knoop soon became the branch's most important client; his companies were connected through the purchase, production and sales of raw materials worldwide. Knoop had begun work in the cotton factories of de Jersey & Co. in Manchester and had expanded into Russia beginning in the 1840s, where he built up a textile industry with English machines and English know-how that soon dominated the market in the Russian Empire. Since 1861, he had been running his worldwide businesses from Bremen, which developed into the leading trade centre for cotton.[103] He often owed the Bremen branch vast sums for his purchases of raw materials in the United States and India. When the Administrative Board in Berlin declared 'Lex Knoop', formulating 'the strict resolution that loans over £100,000 should not be granted at all',[104] the branch management reacted with incomprehension. In its estimation, this was a matter of an 'extremely pleasant, highly lucrative a[nd] also probably beyond any doubt noble connection with Knoop & de Jersey. […] to our knowledge, there is no more extensive a[nd] at the same time better founded business'.[105] Meanwhile, the decreed credit limit remained in place. Hermann Wallich responded to the lament of those in Bremen that they were losing business with his usual reference to the tight controls placed on the management by the Administrative Board, emphasising, however, that they could not be changed: 'We have told you repeatedly that we, too, profoundly object to the overly rigorous views of our highest authority & have tried in vain to convert the gentlemen to another point of view.'[106] The Administrative Board reserved the right to make operative decisions not only in questions of the capital markets business but also in the small day-to-day transactions of foreign trade financing, which sometimes tested the patience of the members of the Management Board and branch managers and certainly also cost the bank some business.

From the beginning, the bank did not restrict itself just to financing trade; it also pushed forward into precious metals and foreign currency trading (FX business) early on. Siemens's good connections with high-ranking individuals in the Reich leadership, namely, in the Reich chancellery under the cousin of the chairman of his Administrative Board, Rudolf Delbrück, and, through that, to the finance department located there, where his university friend Otto Michaelis was in charge,[107] provided the still new Deutsche Bank with one of its most lucrative businesses, which, meanwhile, had serious consequences for its newly founded Asian branches. With the transition to the gold standard, the large quantities of silver for making coins available in Germany became superfluous except for a small number of silver coins that remained in circulation. Added to this were the stores of silver French francs in Alsace-Lorraine, which had been part of the German Empire since 1871. Georg Siemens arranged for Deutsche Bank to handle silver sales because it was the only German bank with agencies in London and Asia, the main sales areas for silver. Hermann Wallich took care of this so efficiently that both the Reich and the bank itself made considerable profits and commissions, respectively. Of total silver sales amounting to about 3,500 tonnes and a value of 567 million marks, Deutsche Bank managed the sale of 1,100 million tonnes of silver with a value of 180 million marks before the newly founded Reichsbank took this segment over for itself. This business raised Deutsche Bank, and especially its London branch, to one of the top-ranked international banks in precious metal and foreign currency trading.[108] Wallich was *persona non grata* at least temporarily at the Reichsbank because people there resented Deutsche Bank for profiting from a business that would actually have been a perfect fit for the Reichsbank. From the beginning, then, Wallich kept quiet about the position he held, also as a trusted representative of Rudolf Delbrück: 'In order not to spur the jealousy of the competition, we enjoyed our triumph quietly. … We could only operate in secret. Yet I did attract the personal hatred of the then president of the Reichsbank, Dechend, upon myself; because the operations could not remain hidden from him, and he bore a grudge against me because I had prevented him from reaping the benefit for his institution.'[109] Nevertheless, this did cost Hermann Wallich the title of privy councillor, as he later found out. He coped with it.

The success of the precious metals business, however, came at a high price because it was the real reason for the failure of the branches in Shanghai and Yokohama, which had been founded in 1872. The capital that the two East Asian branches were provided with consisted of silver endowments – this made sense in China and Japan – but these lost considerable value in the course of the sale of the German silver reserves in these markets, and they had to be written off accordingly. In addition, there were losses in the financing of trade because the goods which were pledged in the bill business also lost value and sometimes could no longer be sold, which had a serious effect not only on the Asian branches but also on the Hamburg branch, which primarily conducted the Japan and China business.[110] Since things were going well for Bremen, the traditional German port for Atlantic trade, it was only a matter of time before the funds tied to the Asian business would be recalled – with considerable losses – in order to end those losses and to utilise the capital more profitably elsewhere. As it was not possible under the present conditions to enter into the Asian lending business and to engage in suitable interest arbitrage in connection with the financial centres of Europe, as Wallich had dreamed of given his own Asian experiences, the bank closed its branches there in 1875, only to return to China and Japan in the late 1880s, but then as investors in Deutsch-Asiatische Bank.[111] The loss caused by the devaluation of the operating capital endowed with silver – amounting to 435,000 marks – was tremendous, and undoubtedly one of the reasons why Hermann Wallich, who had led the way in this, tended to be more risk averse in the future.[112] After all, word of the losses got around and Deutsche Bank was also suspected of having made a very bad deal with the silver, which Wallich vigorously denied: 'All that babbling about the supposed losses of D.[eutsche] Bank on silver is incomprehensible to us. You cannot repudiate every silly rumour. We can give you the firm assurance,' he wrote on 21 July 1876 to the Bremen branch, 'that we did not acquire a single pound at our own expense in the entire significant silver deals that we made. We work for the Reich exclusively on a commission basis & the pittances that we receive from Freiberg's cottages we immediately pass on to the best positioned markets.'[113] Deutsche Bank's first venture into Latin America was also a failure. For the opening of the Latin American market to German financial relations, Disconto-Gesellschaft, together with its own partners, had founded Deutsch-Belgische La Plata Bank with branches in Buenos Aires and Montevideo, with the branch in Montevideo receiving the right to print money in order to grant generous loans to the Uruguayan state. From the beginning, this was a dubious matter, and Disconto-Gesellschaft made an effort to quickly sell the shares of the bank to the public, with only limited success, of course.[114] Georg Siemens's initiative to not only buy up a third of the shares but also to take over the operative management of the business right away pleased sellers but also met with scepticism from Hermann Wallich, who was quite concerned about the fact that Disconto-Gesellschaft wished to get rid of its shares. In any case, he found it difficult to understand how the branch in Montevideo would maintain its solidity. Siemens prevailed, and Wallich turned out to be right. In this case, it was not normal setbacks that caused the bank difficulties but, rather, the fall of the government in Montevideo and the end of the interest and principal payments on the loans it had issued, which the new government did not resume. Only in 1876 were the loans serviced again, and the government repaid its loans through the transfer of government bonds, which Deutsche Bank then immediately sold. In 1885, La Plata Bank was finally liquidated, albeit without losses overall.[115] The bank had escaped with nothing more than a black eye. Along with the branches and the foreign banks, Deutsche Bank's limited partnerships in Paris and New York also helped it to develop a network for financing German (and, when possible, all international) trade. The successes varied according to the economic situation, but all in all, they were not very encouraging. The bank's investment in Weissweiller, Goldschmidt & Co. in Paris, which generated little profit, had already been halved in 1876, only to be given up completely in 1877.[116] The New York limited partnership founded in October 1872 deserves a little more attention because the financing of transatlantic trade, particularly with companies that were located in the United

States, played an important role in the bank's foreign trade business. Since attempts to found a branch encountered legal hurdles, the bank decided to found a private bank located in New York and acquired a limited partnership share of $500,000 of the $600,000 capital stock. The decisive impetus for this came from the founding shareholder and member of the Administrative Board Hermann Marcuse, who had been a partner of a successful private bank in New York before retiring to the Rhine district. Marcuse was not only extremely familiar with New York as a financial centre but also had important personal connections and brought his nephew Paul Lichtenstein in on the deal, together with ethnic German bill broker Charles Knoblauch, to manage the limited partnership. Lichtenstein came from Frankfurt am Main and had emigrated to New York at the age of 21 in order to join his uncle's banking business.[117] Shortly before the founding of the New York limited partnership, which was given the name Knoblauch & Lichtenstein, Lichtenstein married Clara Kapp, the daughter of the German-American politician Friedrich Kapp, who, like Marcuse, was a member of Deutsche Bank's Administrative Board and, furthermore, was one of Georg Siemens's close political and personal friends. Thus, the bank's Administrative Board and Management Board were not turning the New York business over to someone unknown to the bank. Nevertheless, there was no guarantee of success on account of personal connections. Even though the limited partnership agreement stipulated that the New York affiliate was to regularly inform the bank in Berlin about all business transactions, the actual supervision of the New York business proved to be difficult. The German partners had to depend on Knoblauch & Lichtenstein strictly checking applicants for loans, especially in the petroleum business, 'because companies that work intensely with petroleum cannot be assessed at all'.[118] This is precisely what would cause the downfall of the limited partnership in New York. In 1877, Knoblauch & Lichtenstein suffered heavy losses in some of their bank acceptances

New York 1872: the Great East River Bridge between Manhattan and Brooklyn.

and through their credit involvement in petroleum deals that had to be offset by reducing the limited partnership's capital.[119] Ongoing losses generated by Knoblauch & Lichtenstein, 'who, contrary to the previous business practices, invested heavily in securities', prompted Deutsche Bank finally to write off its investment completely in 1882 and to liquidate the New York bank.[120]

If the managers of Deutsche Bank had been called upon to draw up a balance sheet for the foreign business after one decade, the results would probably have been rather mixed. In Asia and Latin America, the bank had failed in its attempts to expand and had sustained losses; the limited partnerships in Paris and New York were obviously flops. By contrast, the London branch had performed brilliantly; it had become the centre of the bank's foreign trade financing and an important station for international precious metal and foreign currency trade, consequently forging the important bridge to the financial centre of London and the international money and capital markets for the bank's Berlin headquarters. The branches in Bremen and Hamburg fulfilled their purpose, serving the German trade companies that did business with Asia (primarily Hamburg) or America (primarily Bremen), although Bremen especially proved to be of value since the Atlantic trade turned out to be more stable than the Asian business. But both branches were successful overall.

However, a quantitative balance measured by this mixed picture clearly would have turned out positive. Whereas Bremen only contributed a little more than 10 per cent of the bank's turnover with 36 million thalers (108 million marks) in 1871 as the only existing branch, the two domestic branches, as well as those in London and East Asia, had already reached a share of more than 40 per cent of the total turnover, with 550 million thalers (1.65 billion marks), by 1873, with the largest share deriving from cash trans-actions, bills of exchange and current accounts business, followed by bill acceptances and lombard loans, with which the branches sometimes reached a higher volume than the headquarters.[121] The branches, however, did not engage solely in financing foreign trade but gradually began offering a variety of financial services. For example, early on the Bremen branch also sought to finance railway projects and provided loans or entered into securities trading, naturally always in close co-operation with the Berlin headquarters. The latter kept a sharp eye on the business practices of its branches, whose business policies had to secure the agreement of the directorate for larger sums on account of the business regulations anyway.[122] The local committee in each place was very helpful in this process; it was comprised of Bremen businesspeople with the approval of Berlin and was supposed to fulfil locally a task similar to the one the Administrative Board did for Berlin. At least as seen by Carl Fürstenberg, the long-time head of Berliner Handels-Gesellschaft, which co-operated closely with Deutsche Bank on numerous projects, it was the branch system that gave Deutsche Bank its special dynamic in the years before 1914:

> His [Georg Siemens's] greatest achievement was, however, probably the develop-
> ment of the branch system, likewise modelled on Western European circumstances,
> within Germany itself, which contributed not least to securing the position of
> Deutsche Bank. Others could only catch up with the advantage it obtained at that
> time gradually and with considerable effort.[123]

8. The Beginnings of the Domestic Business

Even though the domestic business was not intended to take on a prominent role in the founding of Deutsche Bank, the early players were probably aware that only the success of the domestic business would create the basis for a self-confident performance on the international markets. As the banker and bank theoretician Jakob Riesser later stated, Deutsche Bank was the first major institution that regarded deposit banking as having a significant function – indeed, even to some extent, an essential one.[124] What is certain is that Deutsche Bank, at Georg Siemens's instigation, accepted deposits for interest from 1 July 1870. Since the Preußische Bank and later the Reichsbank did not pay interest on deposits, this offer triggered a large wave of customers moving to Deutsche Bank, which 'at the same time [comprised] a firm and constantly increasing circle of buyers for the issuances of the bank'.[125] In the first business premises of the bank on Französische Straße, there was no counter dedicated to accepting cash deposits. Only in the autumn of 1871, when the bank moved its headquarters to Burgstraße 29, was a counter put in after some time exclusively for handling the deposit business. When the central headquarters then moved to Behrenstraße 9–11 in 1876, the customer base had already grown so much that the Burgstraße location continued to exist as the first Berlin 'deposit-taking branch' (*Depositenkasse*). At the same time, the 'main deposit-taking branch' (*Hauptdepositenkasse*) at the headquarters acquired the character of an independent department.[126] As a matter of fact, the intention of winning customers lay behind this; the bank could offer a comprehensive service to these customers, that is, not just deposit accounts, but also current or giro accounts and securities or custody businesses. In Berlin alone, there were 47 'deposit-taking branches' by 1914. There and in the other

Deutsche Bank's first deposit-taking branch was located on Burgstraße, near the Berlin stock exchange, from 1876.

Deposit account book from the year 1876 for the Privy Senior Government Councillor Otto Michaelis. Director of the Reich chancellery at that time, Michaelis was the earliest verifiable private customer of Deutsche Bank.

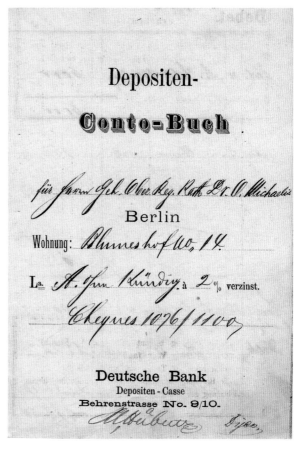

major cities, where deposit-taking branches were also opened, these functioned as very visible shop windows for Deutsche Bank.

The deposit business, along with current account deposits and the loans of other banks, became the core of Deutsche Bank's debit operations (*Passivgeschäft*), upon which it built up its lending business, which continued to grow in size and importance. Because deposits could possibly be withdrawn after the agreed upon withdrawal notice, the bank was forced to structure its risk clearly. Siemens was aware of this because, as he astutely pointed out, the bank had to be able to liquidate all of its assets within 12 months to keep from falling into existential crises.[127] Deutsche Bank always had good arguments for repudiating widespread criticism for having fused its deposit and credit businesses, on the one hand, and capital markets transactions, on the other – criticism accompanied by the demand for a separate banking system similar to the one that predominated in Great Britain. But it was also always aware of the explosive nature of this combination.

The universal bank as a type, as developed over time in Germany, can be traced back to this combination of businesses, which was encouraged by circumstances – behind it was an approach that essentially called for the bank to take responsibility for the clientele of the bank on both the asset and liability side of the balance sheet, something that was foreign to the Anglo-American banking system, for example. Jakob Riesser spoke of the major German banks, certainly not only as typified by Deutsche Bank but with it in mind, as the

> maid of all work. Except such tasks as came within the sphere of special banks, such as note banks, the provincial co-operative land mortgage associations (*Landschaften*), the mortgage banks, or the co-operative societies, the credit banks had to take upon themselves all or nearly all the tasks which in England are apportioned as a rule under a strict division of labor among deposit banks (with a further subdivision between city, west end, and suburban banks), merchant bankers, colonial banks, and even bill and stock brokers.[128]

Hermann Wallich had already set his sights on this broad range of banking activity for Deutsche Bank's domestic business in the report he presented to the Administrative Board when he joined the bank: he recommended not only the deposit business that Siemens had already started up, but also taking up the current accounts, bill, arbitrage and underwriting business, as well as the granting of unsecured loans, customs loans, and the buying and selling of government bonds and securities on behalf of third parties.[129] Deposit banking turned out to be the catalyst for other business sectors. On the one hand, it generated means for financing short-term bills of exchange, especially as the basis for lombard loans and discount credits; on the other hand, extensive banking activities could be transacted via the deposit accounts, which Siemens was quite interested in, having also dealt intensively with chequing transactions in England. It was not far from a deposit account to a current account, which the owner could transact by writing a cheque 'without previously giving notice'; this was primarily interesting for business customers, whereas private individuals had little demand for accounts of this kind in the 1870s. Siemens strove in the following years to expand chequing transactions in Germany.[130] Before the chamber of commerce, he gave a programmatic speech in 1882 advocating chequing transactions and that they should not be hampered by a requirement for stamps; that is, they should be tax-free.[131] If every single cheque were to be taxed, it would have made this means of payment, already unpopular in Germany,

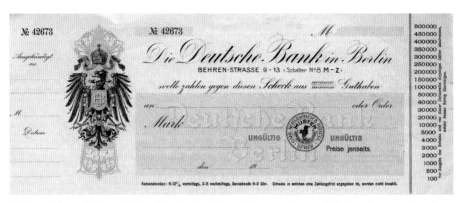

A cheque form of Deutsche Bank in Berlin: Georg Siemens advocated the implementation of cheques for payment transactions as early as the 1880s.

even less attractive. The corresponding legislation was only passed in 1908; nevertheless, the Reichsbank functioned from the 1880s as a clearing house for the cheque transactions of the private banks.[132]

Through this connection between deposit and current accounts, the bank was not only able to gradually take on ever greater shares of its business customers' transactions; there were other advantages as well. The balance of current accounts, which only earned very little interest, if at all, provided another advantageous source of liquidity. Moreover, the bank was well informed about the financial status of 'its' customers, which simplified the lending business as well. There was, thus, a simple, pragmatic reason for there being a relationship with one's Hausbank – a relationship that was later praised but was sometimes also notorious. In addition, there were advantages in the placement of shares and other securities because it made sense that the bank's own customers, to the extent that they had liquidity, would be open to investment tips. Siemens's vote for deposit accounts, therefore, had considerable consequences for the banking business because the customers' tie to the bank also tied the bank to its customers: if it sold them securities that did not produce or rapidly lost value, it not only risked its good reputation but also was in danger of alienating its customers, on whom, after all, it was dependent. Above all, in the rapid expansion of the bank's capital markets business that Siemens had in mind, there were considerable latent challenges that would soon become apparent. The bank did little in the business of issuance or founding new businesses, which was booming in Germany between 1870 and 1872. The restrictive requirements of the Administrative Board kept the new bank from getting involved in the speculative transactions of the exhilarating industrial boom after the victory over France. Partly for this reason, Deutsche Bank was only indirectly affected by the Panic of 1873, which impacted many of its competitors severely. Mostly, Georg Siemens's or Adelbert Delbrück's personal connections prompted the bank's investments; for example, in March 1871 it invested in the founding of Berliner Bank-Verein, with both Delbrück and Siemens joining the latter's Administrative Board. This was a consequential step because Berliner Bank-Verein and Wiener Bankverein had mutually invested in one another. When Wiener Bankverein had to be restructured in the wake of the Panic of 1873, Deutsche Bank made an international investment for the first time, purchasing shares worth 1.45 million guilders, and it contacted the other major shareholders of the Viennese company.[133] Similarly, the takeover of shares in Mecklenburgische Hypotheken- und Wechselbank in the summer of 1871 followed a personal decision on the part of Siemens, and quickly turned out to be a 'serious problem child'.[134] Other investments were not necessarily successful either, but the investment in the founding of the Internationale Baugesellschaft gave Deutsche Bank initial connections to the Frankfurt construction company of Philipp Holzmann – connections that would become particularly important from the beginning of the 1890s. There were also investments in the Union-Allgemeine Versicherungs AG, in the shipbuilder AG Weser in Bremen-Gröpelingen via the branch in Bremen,[135] as well as the Deutsche Jute-Spinnerei und Weberei AG in Meißen. The Panic of 1873 led to large write-offs in Deutsche Bank's investment portfolio, too. The reserves it had built up, however, were more than sufficient to cover the losses in the securities business, which were determined at about 285,000 marks.[136] Consequently, the bank was initially extremely cautious in this sector, a strategy that would pay off as well. Siemens felt the effects of this when he advocated that the bank invest in the company founded by his relatives for the construction of an undersea cable between Ireland and Newfoundland (the Direct Cable Company). His loyalty to a family company lay behind this, as did a certain desire to engage in speculative investing, but the Administrative Board and the Management Board were against it so Siemens invested in it personally in the end, to his detriment. The bank had correctly regarded the business as being too risky.[137] In addition to its direct investments, Deutsche Bank was quite interested in syndicate business, that is in financing companies or public establishments for which its risk of loss was low. In this process, a friendly network of banks in Germany gradually formed that later made it possible for Deutsche Bank to expand its regional presence. Among its early syndicate partners, the most important were Schlesischer Bankverein in Breslau, Bergisch Märkische Bank in Elberfeld and Württembergische Vereinsbank of Siemens's friend Kilian Steiner in Stuttgart. Other important syndicate partners were Wiener Bankverein, Deutsche Vereinsbank and Frankfurter Bankverein in Frankfurt, Mecklenburgische Hypotheken- und Wechselbank and Oldenburgische Spar- und Leihbank. The syndicate structure also suggested itself because most of these banking companies were themselves shareholders in Deutsche Bank. In later years, Deutsche Bank then purchased shares of these companies in return.[138] In late 1875, however, the syndicate account only held nine current investments, including in a property business, in railways, public bonds, covered bonds (*Pfandbriefe*) and an industrial company.[139]

9. Crisis, Revolts and Takeovers

At the end of 1873, Max Steinthal transferred from A. Padersteinscher Bankverein, located in Berlin, to Deutsche Bank, a position Hermann Wallich had interested him in on a trip they took together to Sylt. He was surprised when he took up his new position: 'I expected … to encounter a small and quiet business and was more than a little astonished at all that had already occurred, and what I encountered in terms of quality and quantity, and of highly regarded names in the world of merchants and of brisk sales.'[140] In Steinthal's view, Deutsche Bank's ability to withstand the Panic of 1873, unlike other banks that failed, had to do with, among other things, Wallich's 'nose for crises'; Wallich had truly sniffed out the major crisis: 'He had kept his powder dry and held together his funds, whereas other new banks had got heavily involved in undertakings that were, in part, directly weakened by the crisis, and, in part, had become long-sighted.'[141] Of course, this was a retrospective view long after the crisis had passed. Between 1873 and 1875 the bank did get itself into deep water even though it did not experience an existential crisis. After the crisis began, numerous banks had to stop making payments, stock prices plunged and dividend payments were drastically reduced. The annual report for 1873 stated concisely and clearly that the crisis forced 'us to be extremely cautious in the cultivation and expansion of our business relationships'. Moreover, the bank needed to reduce already existing risky business relationships or sectors. This was also surely another reason why the unprofitable Asian branches were closed.

The Management Board and Administrative Board had already let caution and reserve prevail before the Panic of 1873 in the matter of dividends, which hovered in the lower level among the major banks. Whereas Disconto-Gesellschaft distributed dividends of 24 per cent for 1871 and 27 per cent for 1872 on its capital, and the other major banks paid dividends of between 10 and 17 per cent, Deutsche Bank and Commerz- und Disconto-Bank brought up the rear with about 8 per cent. In the year of the panic, 1873, Deutsche Bank reduced its dividend from 8 to 4 per cent; in 1874, it was raised only slightly to 5 per cent. In 1875, the bank deposited more than a third of the surplus it earned into its loss reserve, and the dividend was once again reduced, this time to 3 per cent. This put it well behind Disconto-Gesellschaft (1875: 7 per cent), but, unlike Berliner Handels-Gesellschaft or Schaaffhausen'scher Bankverein, it did not have to temporarily discontinue dividend payments altogether.[142] After the dividend reductions, many a shareholder who himself was in need of liquidity may have asked himself whether his money was well invested at Deutsche Bank, which had once again increased its share capital in late 1872, now to 15 million thalers (45 million marks), particularly since the press repeatedly reported on difficulties within the company. Wallich sought to calm unsettled shareholders: 'All that blathering on [in Bremen] about big losses at Deutsche Bank is simply exaggerated and unjustified,' he wrote on 25 June 1873 to the Bremen branch, and continued: 'Nevertheless, like all banks, we have had failures, yet such as we have had are not significant enough to cut the total dividend considerably.' This was not entirely true because the dividend had to be significantly cut for 1873, although of course

Stock certificate of Deutsche Bank from 1873. These newly issued stocks for 5 million thalers (15 million marks) raised the equity capital to 15 million thalers (45 million marks). After the Panic of 1873 began, there was some opposition to the high capital base of the bank.

the capital increase that occurred in late 1872 needs to be taken into consideration, which impacted dividends in 1873; yet Wallich wanted to calm his Bremen colleagues, also emphasising that the London branch had lost nothing at all, even though it bore the losses in the Asian market.[143] These efforts at appeasement did not help, however: some shareholders in Bremen demanded that the bank limit itself to its core business of financing foreign trade and reduce its 45 million marks in capital by one-third.[144]

The uncertain situation as well as the high equity diminished not only the profit expectations; in general, during the crisis it seemed advisable, wherever possible, to reduce the share capital in order to stabilise share prices. The Bremen consul Heinrich Plenge suggested something to this effect to the Administrative Board in April 1874, but the board rejected it after a lengthy discussion. Adelbert Delbrück informed Plenge that, although one could not deny that the share capital was too high, and that a reduction would stabilise the share price and increase the dividend, a capital reduction would nonetheless 'do more damage to the credit of the bank … than the increase in the share price would be beneficial to its credit'. In other words, Delbrück feared for the bank's reputation. He openly admitted that he could not prove this with numbers: 'It is a matter of instinct, and it does not merely come down to viewpoints in Germany but altogether to England and foreign countries.' Such a move would put the bank on the same level with a whole range of failing banks and, at the same time, send out a signal that the bank could only continue to pursue its own programme with a more limited scope. But Delbrück did not want this simply because a number of large projects were in the works. Consequently, he made an appeal to Plenge: 'I thus ask you, Honourable Sir, to oppose this motion, which is aimed at a reduction of capital, in the interests of the bank and, indeed, in the best interests of the shareholders and to seek to use your great influence to thwart this same [motion].'[145] Of course, this by no means put the matter to rest because many of the Bremen shareholders continued to wish for this and, in May 1875, took up the cause once again after the situation concerning the branches in Asia had become critical, the La Plata Bank project had essentially failed and Deutsche Bank's share price dropped further. The management of the Bremen branch reported to Berlin that a group of local shareholders were pushing for an extraordinary general meeting of shareholders in order to bring about the reduction. Although this had been discouraged, it was not clear what would happen now.[146] In the summer of 1875, the leading merchant Alexander Georg Mosle, the chairman of the local committee of the Bremen branch, also took up with those agitating for the reduction, whose numbers had by now grown into a regular committee. Although Mosle, the Bremen branch management told Berlin, rejected the reduction, even larger shareholders had begun to get involved in the matter so that the managers were already considering how to reduce the votes of the advocates. A proven method seemed to be not to issue ballots for pledged shares, that is, to take away the voting rights of shareholders who had pledged their shares.[147]

Siemens found all of this 'very uncomfortable, because [these initiatives] limit us a great deal in our freedom of action in concluding various contracts'.[148] Siemens's view derived from his fear that negotiations to take over bankrupt banks, which the Berlin Management Board had been engaged in for some time in an effort to utilise the crisis, would be hampered because currently available capital was needed for this. Put simply, it was about the acquisition of the two Berlin banks, Deutsche Union-Bank and Berliner Bank-Verein, which were sitting on a large quantity of debt claims that could not presently be collected because of the Panic of 1873 and had to write off large parts of their investment portfolios in light of the drastic decline in their share prices. Deutsche Bank had owned shares of Berliner Bank-Verein since it had been founded in 1871; it also had good contacts among the members of Deutsche Union-Bank's management board. Since it was possible to realistically assess these banks' situation and be aware that their difficulties had resulted not from a deficient business model but, rather, from crisis-related liquidity problems, it made good sense to use Deutsche Bank's own capital to liquidate both banks and take over their business.[149] Bank managers had been pursuing this idea for some time, but it did not initially find favour with the chairman of the Administrative Board, Adelbert Delbrück, as he believed that this sort of a merger would transform Deutsche Bank overnight into a serious competitor of private bankers in the German financial market.[150] In the circumstances, Siemens's friendship with Stuttgart

Members of the directorate of the Bremen branch from 1871 to 1911.

banker Kilian Steiner was very helpful. Steiner, who was a member of the Administrative Boards of Deutsche Bank and Berliner Bank-Verein, was able to persuade Delbrück that the merger made sense. A takeover of the illiquid banks would expand Deutsche Bank's business to such an extent that its profitability would have to increase and it would, in the future, be able to more than compensate for the looming cut in the dividend for 1875. Delbrück was persuaded by these considerations, and in the second half of 1875 Georg Siemens, who was leading the takeover negotiations and was drafting the contracts, was granted the necessary freedom of action.[151]

Consequently, the Bremen shareholders' demand that the share capital be reduced came at a bad time. Those agitating to lower the capital were unfazed by appeasement efforts and threats; rather, they hired a lawyer, Johannes Wilckens, who promoted the campaign to reduce the share capital by means of targeted press initiatives. Siemens and Wallich were alarmed and feared that Deutsche Union-Bank and Berliner Bank-Verein could break off the negotiations if the plan for an extraordinary general meeting became known to the public. That would have been devastating, especially because Deutsche Bank had bought up the shares of these banks in the meantime, and would then probably only be able to sell them again with losses. In addition, they pointed out that, if the capital were reduced, the business would contract and 'our branches in Bremen, Hamburg and London [would have to] be recalled';[152] then one would only be able to work from Berlin. The threatening tone that Siemens and Wallich adopted had the desired effect. On 18 September 1875, the Bremen branch management wrote that the shareholders involved had, after much discussion, declared their willingness to cease their agitation for the time being: 'The reason for the agitation is the desire on the part of the agitators to disburden the market of a part of – in the view of the agitators – an excessive number of bank shares.' Since the merger of Deutsche Bank with the two Berlin banks would achieve exactly this, the gentlemen from Bremen were 'temporarily willing' to remain silent. However, the Bremen managers made it very clear that if the merger negotiations were not successful the 'agitation' would in all probability be resumed.[153] Two days later, however, any hopes that the agitation would cease were dashed when a further decline in Deutsche Bank's share price provoked speculation that the merger negotiations were difficult or even bound to fail.[154] This was not the only reason. The agitating to reduce the capital began once again, partly because one Bremen shareholder who had discussed the situation with Delbrück and Siemens in Berlin, and had been convinced that the merger would take place, nevertheless urged that the reduction campaign should continue, something Wilhelm Platenius, meanwhile, was also 'energetically' pursuing.[155] Wallich was 'unpleasantly affected' by the fact that the annoying business was to begin anew, but especially because Platenius, too, who was obviously fed up with his former employer, was now participating in the campaign: 'That Platenius, forgetting our earlier relationships, is conspiring against us is sad, but it shines a poor light on him.' The merger negotiations were proceeding well, Wallich told the Bremen management, while also touting the positive prospects in the hope of diverting well-meaning shareholders from taking an action 'that could only be devised by our bitterest enemies or by people who have not sufficiently recognised the facts'.[156] Consequently, Wallich himself travelled to Bremen, something Siemens would also have done had he not been attending his doctoral graduation ceremony in Heidelberg at the same time. Consequently, Wallich met with the Bremen shareholders alone. However, this meeting was not really successful because the Bremen management suggested after Wallich's return that the shareholders there, even after a successful merger, would insist upon a reduction of the share capital as 'compensation'. If Berlin were to signal that this sort of reduction would be undertaken in about a year, the 'agitation [could] be subdued'.[157]

Berlin responded swiftly and robustly. A reduction was out of the question. A repayment of the shares at the desired price would, in the best case, only be possible if Deutsche Bank did not wish to acquire the two Berlin banks. Now it could not be considered, and those sorts of implications must not be made and needed in some cases to be corrected. 'We cannot get around characterising the behaviour of the Bremen agitators right at this time as a suicidal beginning,' the Berlin directors Max Steinthal and Rudolph Koch wrote.[158] After Berlin's clear refusal to give in to the wishes for a reduction, the two sides dug their heels in and the campaign expanded to Hamburg as well. In Bremen, there was scepticism that anything could still be achieved at all: 'The main leaders hold very fixedly to their project and go so far as to regard the liquidation of Deutsche Bank as not a bad thing.'[159] As a result, the branch management in Bremen resorted to winning back potential supporters of the campaign and to deny voting rights to those who had supported the campaign but had lent out their shares: 'We have not yet declared a war to the finish, but we are quietly working hard to secure votes for ourselves or to prompt the shareholders to temporarily remain neutral.'[160] Above all, however, it was now a matter of taking the edge off the 'agitation' through a suitable resolution in a regular meeting of the entire Administrative Board of Deutsche Bank, which was scheduled for late October.

Up to this point Bremen's attempt had only been rejected by the Committee of Five in the Administrative Board and by the Management Board. There was still uncertainty as to how the entire Administrative Board would act with regard to the issuing of an equity reduction, since some of its members were, after all, mainly shareholders from the fields of banking, trade and industry, including George Albrecht and Alexander Georg Mosle, two Bremen merchants, among others, who liked the idea of a capital reduction. In a memorandum addressed to the Administrative Board, the Management Board made its position clear: after the setbacks in Asia, the bank would not be able to maintain its previous course without a strong position in the domestic market. The opportunities for expansion abroad were not favourable, it stated, but in the domestic market there were chances that should not be risked by an imprudent action.[161] If the Bremen campaign were to be publicly successful, and, more to the point, if there proved to be strong resistance in the Administrative Board, this would call the entire project into question and make the work of the preceding months worthless. The Management Board argued with suitable decisiveness by presenting the merger and, thus, simultane-ously the rejection of the Bremen initiative, as a question of survival for the bank. The result was a complete victory. The Administrative Board unanimously (that is, includ-ing its Bremen members) backed the Management Board, which now pushed to have the contracts drawn up with the two banks that were to be acquired. The contracts were already drawn up when, in January 1876, an extraordinary general meeting, which had been called for by the still dissatisfied Bremen committee that favoured the capital reduction, voted on the question. Thanks to Delbrück's support, Steiner's campaigning and targeted efforts to influence vacillating shareholders, the Management Board was successful beyond all doubt. Of the 8,000 or more votes cast, 6,169 were for the Management Board's plan, whereas 1,902 were for a capital reduction to 30 million marks.[162] This now also formally cleared the path for the acquisition of the two Berlin banks. A syndicate led by Deutsche Bank withdrew the shares of Union-Bank and Bank-Verein from the market while Deutsche Bank itself took over these banks' business dealings and personnel, running them under its own name. Prior to this, the two banks were restructured by means of the necessary balance sheet reductions and their stock prices were stabilised so that Deutsche Bank could later acquire these without excessive losses for the former shareholders and, thus, complete the merger. The Management Board's strategy paid off, and the harsh manner of dealing with the Bremen initiative to effect a capital reduction proved to have been justified.

For the bank itself, the merger really was a tremendous leap forward since, in terms of the sum of its balance sheet and its turnover, it became the largest bank in the German Empire overnight. Its total assets, at 190 million marks in 1876, exceeded even Disconto-Gesellschaft, which had 136 million marks on its balance sheet. Nevertheless, Disconto-Gesellschaft still had more than 15 million marks in capital and a considerably higher reputation than its young competitor.[163] Deutsche Bank's domestic business benefited especially from the merger because both of the acquired banks had possessed an extensive clientele that Deutsche Bank succeeded in retaining. Deutsche Union-Bank, for example, had been very active in deposit banking. After it had been integrated, Deutsche Bank changed the structure of its deposit banking segment by creating an independent department for this, which later came under the management of Gustav Schröter, who had come from Berliner Bank-Verein. With Berliner Bank-Verein, Deutsche Bank's foreign contacts expanded because the former had not only invested in the founding of Wiener Bankverein, but also had close connections with Paris. The chairman of the supervisory board of Deutsche Union-Bank Wilhelm Herz and its management board member Wilhelm Kopetzky transferred into the Administrative Board of Deutsche Bank, with Herz later becoming the chairman of this committee.[164] The prestigious building of Deutsche Union-Bank on Behrenstraße was also taken over by Deutsche Bank and henceforth used as its headquarters.

As to the burning question of Deutsche Bank's future business policies, the successful merger of 1876 thus constituted an essential step but was not yet the final culmination of Georg Siemens's strategic ideas, who had long pushed for expanding the domestic business. After all, it was not only the Administrative Board that debated the question of how to utilise the newly emerging possibilities; the Management Board also repeatedly resisted Siemens's initiatives, some of which seemed arbitrary and idiosyncratic, and his tremendous tolerance for risk. It was by no means just plucked out of thin air when he spread word of Hermann Wallich's constant reminder 'Just no ideas' on the occasion of the tenth anniversary of the bank.

But Siemens did not wish to be slowed down. In the summer of 1876, things came to a head. Only a few months after the merger, in July Georg Siemens once again requested

With the acquisition of Deutsche Union-Bank in 1876, Deutsche Bank came to own the building at Behrenstraße 9, which then served as its headquarters and was expanded with additions and new buildings in the following decades.

that he be released from his position on the Management Board of Deutsche Bank. For the chairman of the Administrative Board Adelbert Delbrück, who very much appreciated Siemens and thus always strove to maintain a balance in all the conflicts, this request must have felt like a bomb going off because, up to that point, Georg Siemens had been the driving force behind the development of Deutsche Bank's various business segments. Although Wallich and Steinthal set the tone in the areas of foreign trade financing and foreign business, Siemens was the one who wanted to take the bank to the top of the German financial world, at the cost of a great deal of personal sacrifice. He had experienced plenty of self-doubt in doing this, but he believed above all that he lacked the strength to prevail against resistance.[165] Up to this point, Siemens had always managed to assert himself despite significant conflicts, with his zeal for his work and a reluctance to spare himself helping him achieve this. He was one-sided to 'excess', he declared to his bride; anything other than the bank hardly interested him, and he was of little use in the company of ladies 'if one has had hours-long discussions with people one wishes to push one's plans on'. There was 'a lot of annoyance and scorn in this way',[166] an attitude that also had something to do with Siemens's pushy manner. 'If I am not mistreated, then I easily mistreat others,' he told his mother in March 1872,[167] and his wife told her parents-in-law in 1873 that he got up early, spent the entire day at the bank, spent his free time in political activity – Siemens had been elected to the Reichstag as well as to the Prussian House of Representatives for the National Liberal Party – and even on a good day was only at home for a brief lunch at midday.[168] Siemens himself admitted that he had 'loaded' himself up with 'perhaps too many different sorts of work. But if one wants to make progress, one simply has to do more than other people; Berlin is a ruthless patch in this regard. Since I can no longer go walking, I have helped myself by smoking.'[169] His working style, in any case, was considered uncompromising and not always amiable. He tended to speak his mind, talking about the need to kill off all bank managers when they reached the age of 50,[170] and only slowly began to change his gruff manner under the influence of his wife, who wrote to her parents in early February 1878 that her husband had given up 'the drastic expressions he usually favoured'.[171] There was a good reason for his brusque and homespun manner. Neither the Administrative Board nor his colleagues on the Management Board found Siemens's political involvement justifiable; nonetheless, he managed to push it through, albeit at the cost of all of his free time.[172] He even felt that having a certain degree of cynicism in the process even seemed to help matters:

> And concerning cynicism, this is a language that can easily be understood by everyone in this earthly world. One gains clarity by means of it; and he to whom the matter is of prime importance may make use of this language whereas he does not care what other people think of him. To act in a cynical manner is shameful, but to speak in a cynical manner means saving a lot of time in business.[173]

But now, in the summer of 1876, everything seemed to be failing because the remaining managers of the bank were not following his lead; so he wanted to throw in the towel. He used a brief stay in the Black Forest as an opportunity to draft a letter outlining his reasons for this, which, although he did not then send it to Adelbert Delbrück, clearly expressed his motivations.[174] Siemens was firmly convinced that the bank could only be successful in foreign business in the long term if it had solid domestic banking business at its disposal, and investments in financing large projects and capital market transactions were a part of this business. The lending business the bank had engaged in on the basis of its deposit banking was far from sufficient for this, he believed: in future, only an expansion of the domestic business would help to maintain such a course, but his colleagues on the Management Board rejected this idea. In the financing business, 'I mostly encountered a passively disapproving attitude on the part of my colleagues, [and] in some cases they worked against me. … I willingly admit that I am not blameless in this', because he did stay out of the 'regular business' and concentrated on 'establishing new connections and preparing new deals. […]. Since I […] frequently came with new suggestions, one believed finally one could view me as a sort of "swindler" that one could not be careful enough around.'[175] He often continued on his own, but this had not been successful, he wrote. Now, after the merger with the other Berlin banks, he had hoped things would change. That had not happened. Consequently, Siemens requested that he be released on 1 October 1876, and he recommended that the bank reduce its capital and downsize its business.

Helfferich's belief[176] that Siemens was entirely serious in requesting this was no doubt correct, but his aim was not to end his employment with Deutsche Bank but, rather, to change the course of the Administrative Board in his favour. He had already done this by threatening to resign in 1872, and he could be confident that he would also be able to assert himself this time; after all, he knew how much Adelbert Delbrück and his colleagues on the Management Board valued him; they tried to slow him down, but they did not wish to be rid of him. Although he prepared to take up work on his father's estate, it is difficult to say whether he intended this as a sort of last resort. Hermann Wallich's reaction, in any case, was completely in Siemens's interests; Wallich launched a massive bid for him to remain and demanded that the Administrative Board keep him. And this is exactly what happened: Siemens henceforth became the 'man of the house', both as an individual and as a strategic figure. His behaviour was certainly not irrational, quick-tempered, or rash. He knew the Administrative Board and his colleagues far too well to let himself get taken in by an angry quarrel. Only a year earlier he had written to his father: 'The trick is not that one beats one's head against the wall but that one finds the door.'[177] Things had now reached that point: the door to the development of a full banking business as Siemens imagined it had been pushed open. Siemens's determination to make the most of the new opportunities and, lest there be any doubt, to prevail over resistance with ruthlessness had already become obvious in the conflict over the capital reduction. Now the Administrative Board and the Management Board were also at least fundamentally like-minded.[178] This was no secret in the financial centre of Berlin. At Deutsche Bank, Carl Fürstenberg remarked in his memoirs that Georg Siemens 'always implemented […] what he thought was right in the end'.[179]

II. Consolidation in a Difficult Time: The Era of Wallich, 1876–1887

1. The Consequences of the Panic of 1873

After the strategic development of the bank had been clarified, there were no more obstacles to it going on the offensive. Even so, the following decade was not easy for Deutsche Bank's development. Above all, this pertained to the economy, which was recovering, albeit sluggishly, and the repeated setbacks, which made it seem as though the crisis would continue.[1] Although it is generally accepted today that the German economy did not stagnate and that the world economy recovered relatively quickly, with the United States driving this trend, the years between 1873 and the early 1890s were difficult ones in which there were repeated crises and boom phases always slowed down relatively quickly.[2] The effects of this recovery process were also contradictory. Initially, after the preceding massive expansion of production capacities, the weakness of the respective home markets resulted in excess capacities. At the same time, international competition grew more intense, particularly in the agricultural sector, but also in the iron and steel industry and in the textile sector.[3] These industrial branches were already suffering from low prices, which depressed companies' profits both in Germany and in general, and significantly curbed their ability to invest. Demands for protection for the national markets from foreign competition were little more than an attack on consumer income, but they were successfully sold throughout almost the whole of Europe as a sort of 'national task'; from the late 1870s, most continental European countries adopted a system of modest protective tariffs, one which traditionally existed in the United States.[4] Only Great Britain, which was more than able to compensate for a negative trade balance in Europe over the course of time with revenues from its colonial business, and the Netherlands, which had hardly any advantages from tariff borders as a location for trade and shipping, remained free trade zones, a concept that continued to be widely appreciated into the early 1870s. In the words of Joseph Schumpeter, a 'neomercantilist epoch' began in which the economic successes of one's own country became the measure of politics, even if it was only, as was the case with Bismarck, thereby to gain the support of parliament, which otherwise would not have been so easy to get.[5]

The consequences of the Panic of 1873, the low prices, the minimal investment propensity, the protectionist atmosphere: all of this had a curbing effect and precipitated a phase of low interest until the end of the 1880s. The climate remained bad. Even if Deutsche Bank's Management Board did not regard the protective tariffs as a serious problem for the overseas business, those at the top levels of the bank were quite sceptical about a sort of protectionism in which 'injustices' were perpetrated 'deliberately and systematically', favouring 'unnecessarily some classes of the population at the expense of all taxpayers'.[6] Since trade activities increased considerably in the run-up to the protective tariff legislation, the bank initially profited from the transition to moderate protective tariff policies, particularly since this led to an improvement in the business conditions for the bank to get involved early in industrial financing, in the Deutsche Jute-Spinnerei und Weberei AG. All in all, the protective tariff was not a big deal for the bank. Rather, it was concerned with the continuing restrictive stock-market legislation and the state's reluctance to modernise the German money market, in which cashless payment trans-action options were still underdeveloped – something Siemens repeatedly and forcefully advocated.[7] Even though the Administrative Board and Siemens's colleagues on the Management Board were sceptical about his political involvement, they must certainly have welcomed his advocacy on behalf of a suitable design for the Reichsbank and later on the issues of the development of the money market and stock-market legislation, particularly since his parliamentary initiatives were primarily restricted to these matters. However, he was not very successful in this; the Stock Market Stamp Act of 1881, which raised the taxation on stock-market transactions, had an additional 'curbing' effect on the already depressed economic climate, as the bank noted in its annual report for 1882.

This did not augur well for the stock markets and stock-market trading; stock prices barely recovered. The public's critical mood towards the stock market and banks only gradually settled down in the years after the Panic of 1873.[8] Various state measures did provide the banks with opportunities, particularly in the finance ministries' and the municipalities' practice of using the low-interest phase to convert old bonds with high interest rates, for which they needed the banks' help. But the rest of their business was either weak or significantly riskier. After the Panic of 1873, and until 1875, the bank's profit only recovered temporarily. In 1877 and 1878, it collapsed again. Only from the end of the decade did profits stabilise, but then they stagnated until 1887 at the pre-crisis level of about 7 million marks annually. In light of the simultaneous drop in the price level, this stagnation needs to be put in context, but the temporarily dramatic volatility of prices, share prices and profits pushed the bank towards engaging in a very careful business strategy. This foregrounded the consolidation of the bank itself, which meant, among other things, that relevant adjustments to the reserve fund had to be made. Even though Siemens had struggled for greater room to manoeuvre in 1875–6, the decade after the Panic of 1873 was nevertheless shaped by Hermann Wallich's careful strategy, which kept the bank on a short leash – undoubtedly mostly with the approval of the Administrative Board.

All this was anything but easy, because, in addition to the consequences of the crisis, the bank's business was hampered from the 1870s by the nationalisation of the railways in Prussia. The domestic market for railway stocks and railway bonds, which had been tremendous and, all in all, also profitable up until then, gradually dried up.[9] This had conflicting consequences for the bank. Prussia financed the railway nationalisation by issuing state securities at a low interest rate, which was easy to effect because of the low interest rates of that time. Many railway shareholders were also willing to accept these securities but, at the same time, quite a few of them seemed to think this was not a very good deal. They were interested in higher returns and expected their banks to make offers along these lines. It was not easy to find or create such offers because the interest rates remained depressed as a result of the weak investment demand and the high liquidity. In its annual reports of the 1880s, Deutsche Bank repeatedly emphasised that it faced an investment crisis; there were large sums of capital that needed to be invested, but hardly any profitable investment opportunities in the domestic market. In the report for 1886, the bank was still reporting, for example: 'The abundance of money has continued to exist unchanged.' Only at the end of the 1880s did the low-interest phase show signs of coming to an end, and conditions for banking shifted once again. Up until this 'interest-rate reversal', all the major Berlin banks were faced with the problem of not being able to offer their wealthy domestic clients enough profitable investment opportunities. If Deutsche Bank's business model were to prove itself, and if the deposit banking and current accounts business, in which large sums of potential investment capital came together, were to continue to be successful, ways out of this crisis had to be found, and they certainly were not to be found exclusively in the domestic market. In its annual report for 1887, the bank wrote that the 'necessity … of the introduction of foreign securities' had essentially presented itself, whereupon the bank resumed an activity it had taken up in the late 1870s. Thus, at this time, business proceeded in a manner similar to the squaring of a circle: on the one hand, risks were strictly limited in light of the sensitive economy, and, on the other, the bank actively sought international investment opportunities for the public that was interested in this, and all this occurred within the framework of stiff competition among the major Berlin banks.

2. Pitfalls in Everyday Banking

In the second half of the 1870s, what Siemens called the 'regular business' was very clearly in the foreground because it continued to develop in a stable manner in the years of the 'money flood' and the low interest rates as well, even though the profit margins were not very high in this highly competitive business segment. Deutsche Bank successfully and seamlessly navigated the acquisition of the two Berlin banks and the consolidation of the business volume this entailed. Consequently, the bank was able to expand its own bill business significantly, even in a market that was only expanding slightly overall. Deutsche Bank primarily cultivated business with long-term bills of exchange, and was thus able to provide relatively generous loans, which was both well received by the public and gave the bank an edge over the competition, although it required an appropriate loss provision. Along with the headquarters in Berlin, the branches in Bremen, Hamburg and above all in London became much more significant in this regard, even though the newly founded overseas banks contributed to the boom in this segment from the mid-1880s, which largely comprised the financing of (cross-border) trade by providing advances on goods and import loans. The bank followed the principle of only accepting bills of exchange drawn on it with great caution; managers were already talking about the credit volume limit of a maximum of £100,000 per customer that the Committee of Five from the Administrative Board had decreed in March 1876. This credit cap was uncomfortable for the branches, who knew their customers and considered it necessary to have greater flexibility in foreign trade financing. Nevertheless, Berlin reacted vehemently to repeated 'violations' of the strict rules, particularly when branches exceeded the limits for unsecured loans: 'The conditions of the time are [...] of such a nature that they demand the strictest measure in the acceptance of risks', the Bremen branch was informed in April 1876 and cautioned about the consequences bad loans would have on the bank's share price: 'In addition, would you kindly consider that one is more and more accustomed recently to criticising the balance sheet of a bank from the point of view of how many unsecured debtors it has, and that the summary of such an assessment undoubtedly influences the share price.'[10]

The directorate in Berlin was even willing to forego business if necessary and thus to disappoint its own customers, and in some instances even to offend them. Hermann Wallich was implacable in this respect because, after all, there could be serious consequences for the reputation and the value of the bank's shares and, thus, potentially, renewed unrest among dissatisfied shareholders. The Bremen branch was impelled always to check the creditworthiness of even good customers in order to be allowed to maintain loans it had already granted.[11] Yet Berlin did not see any wriggle room because the bank was publicly criticised for the large amounts of its acceptances and many observers even speculated about payment defaults. Wallich admitted that the strict risk provision was also a consequence of the fact that the boom in banking activities following upon the mergers had created 'enviers and enemies ... & since acceptances are our most sensitive segment, where our enemies can harm us, we must attempt to prevent an unnecessary spread of this'. He did not only insist upon very strict checking of creditworthiness: 'This will result in the question of the reduction of our loans. I thus ask you to get used to the idea now & to see which companies we should initially cause to suffer under this reduction.' For Wallich, it was also clear who should be affected: 'I proceed in this on the principle that companies that use us solely for accepting deserve less consideration than those who also occupy us in other ways.'[12] He was not the only one saying this: that same month, the Committee of Five of the Administrative Board ordered that the headquarters as well as the branches in Bremen and Hamburg present the lists of loans and the committee went through the lists of debtors and agreed on principles by which the credit lines were to be settled each year. Unsecured loans over 300,000 marks were to be reduced and account overdrafts (*Giroobligo*) were not to be permitted at all if they were not covered by the prime securities (bills of exchange of the

The Management Board of Deutsche Bank in Berlin around 1880: from left, Georg Siemens, Rudolph Koch, Max Steinthal and Hermann Wallich.

highest quality).[13] As the following example makes clear, this restrictive stance on the part of the Management Board and the Committee of Five led repeatedly to conflicts with the branches. The time delay alone that resulted from branches having to check with Berlin caused irritation: 'Because of the absence of the members of your finance committee, extremely important points like the present one [it pertained to a loan for a partner of Knoop & Jersey, which Berlin had initially refused with reference to the £100,000 limit] cannot remain unprocessed for 6 weeks without significant damage to our entire business operation; if they do remain unprocessed, then you restrict our movements so that we lose any inclination to move at all.' In particular, they insisted, one could not treat good clients like Knoop & Jersey in this manner.[14] In this case, Wallich and Steinthal shared Bremen's criticism, but they had no wriggle room to make changes; up to this point they had tried in vain to correct 'the overly rigorous viewpoint of our highest authority', that is, the Committee of Five, but they wanted to continue trying.[15] Nevertheless, Berlin only minimally accommodated the Bremen branch, which had traditionally provided Knoop & Jersey with unsecured loans. The Bremen branch had to be more restrictive in granting loans, which was also problematic because these sorts of restrictions could be very damaging to the reputation and creditworthiness of the loan recipients, in this case Knoop & Jersey.[16] Consequently, the Bremen branch had the goods collateral for its loans carried out in secret in order not to damage its business relations with Knoop, but first it had to have the commercial bill Knoop presented approved in Berlin before it could grant the loan. Bremen pushed for speed, 'because we would like to avoid anything that would cause us to come into serious conflict with Mr Knoop, as the latter describes the bill of exchange as good and solid security &, in the end, we cannot ask for more than that.'[17] The Bremen bankers were actually afraid that Berlin would reject the request, because 'if, on account of the quest. bill of exchange there are difficulties on your end, K.[noop] would break off with us!'[18] But the Berlin directorate remained unconcerned: Knoop would not break off relations so quickly with the bank 'if his wishes are not granted. A loan of £100,000 can't, after all, be obtained every day!' It only approved the loan after carefully reviewing the bill of exchange.[19] To the Bremen bank managers, this meant that they had to dance to Berlin's tune and rely increasingly on collaterals for loans on bills of exchange. These collaterals, moreover, provide a good example of the bank's range of business, since wool imports from South Africa received advance financing, as did deliveries of hides from Latin America, tea from India and China, petroleum from the United States and grain exports from Germany.[20] Despite such caution in the granting of loans, the Bremen branch performed well; it earned ½ per cent commission on discounted bills of exchange, as well as a discount rate of 4 per cent per annum. Its profits were satisfactory, the Bremen branch management emphasised: even though the low discount rate was a cause for concern, the first half of the year had ended with a positive balance and 17.3 per cent net profits[21] had been earned on the utilised capital.[22] The situation at the Berlin headquarters and in the Hamburg branch was not really different from this; however, the Hamburg branch's rate of profits was mostly lower. Financing trade was a good, solid business especially in the difficult economic time, particularly if it was conducted with the necessary caution.

Berlin did not relax its restrictive stance following the Panic of 1873 and the rebellion of the Bremen shareholders the following years, either. The Administrative Board's attitude had nothing to do with the bank's business segments. It was not about keeping Deutsche Bank small as a potential domestic competitor. Rather, it was foreign trade financing and its risks, which certainly needed to be contained. This required hard work and strict controls. Only by being meticulous about granting loans, by securing them with pledges and deposits, could large losses be avoided. This was by no means always the case. Some business partners proved to be untrustworthy despite intensive controls. Furthermore, the Bremen and Hamburg branches repeatedly became involved with dubious business partners or in speculating on intransparent goods deliveries through their co-operation – for example, with the Antwerp bank August Block or the New York limited partnership Knoblauch & Lichtenstein[23] – that did not turn out well, as with the bankruptcy of W. Pustau in Hamburg. Therefore, Berlin repeatedly and forcefully called for strict controls and caution: 'We repeat our frequent verbal instructions that the supervision of all loans should be strictly and meticulously managed & that overdrafts not be permitted of these.'[24] But because the branches did not want to be restricted, conflicts erupted again and again. Finally, in December 1878, a series of bankruptcies and losses at the Hamburg branch prompted the Management Board to restructure the business completely. The branches were now limited to local transactions only. Basically, the rule applied

> that the branches should focus on local business, that these non-local transactions and loan issuances, which could be granted just as well by the headquarters, should [be] referred there if possible, that in any case when such a loan is granted, if it does not fall within the framework of local business, it should only be transacted by a branch if the Berlin headquarters has been notified about this beforehand. That the limits, which are to be determined for each place, in case a company works with several establishments of Deutsche Bank, must always be adhered to very precisely a[nd] no overdrafts of any kind are to be permitted.[25]

This had consequences, above all for Hamburg and London. The Hamburg branch had to reduce numerous credit lines, and the London branch had to abstain thereafter from all independent transactions: 'The London branch should mainly deal only with the procurement of transactions allotted to it from Berlin, Bremen, Hamburg.'[26] These sorts of restrictions did not really work well in everyday business because they would have forced the branches to reject even good customers or to limit their credit. Bremen, in any case, continued to violate the regulations with regard to the Knoop company; only in response to tremendous pressure from Berlin did it recall its credit lines in March 1882 as a result of obvious uncertainties in the Russian market. Still, the Bremen bankers showed their unwillingness, because they once again feared that they would lose Knoop and, thus, their best customer.[27] Had the branch in Bremen followed Berlin's instructions precisely, it would only have been able to assist the Knoop company again in its ongoing business when its credit volume had shrunk considerably, which would have completely soured relations with it. Consequently, Bremen repeatedly requested special

In 1891 the Bremen branch moved into a new building in the Cathedral Court of Bremen. It was the first domestic branch to be opened in 1871.

permissions, and also received them after the Committee of Five had made the relevant decisions.[28] Strict guidelines were obviously not very helpful by themselves. In order to implement a risk-conscious business policy overall, without hampering everyday business, the Management Board and the Committee of Five finally decided on another path: the monthly conferences in Berlin of the management of both the headquarters and the branches with the members of the Committee of Five, which had been taking place since late 1876, became the forum in which all major transactions were discussed.

When the Panic of 1873 had run its course in the late 1870s, the money market problems – the surplus liquidity with few opportunities for investment as well as the depressed interest rates – did not disappear, but fear that the temporarily overcapitalised institution would not survive gave way to the conviction that the crisis had been overcome with some success. The annual reports of the years between 1877 and 1886 are not overwhelmingly exuberant, but they make the bank's consolidation clear. The growth in statutory and extraordinary reserves very clearly demonstrates the bank's efforts to comprehensively cover possible risks. The public criticism of the payment obligations the bank had entered into gradually subsided:

> If we were subjected in earlier years to some attacks on account of the size of our acceptance account, now in broad circles it has been recognised that, since overseas transactions are brokered by means of acceptances, it is unavoidable and not a matter for concern to have a sizable acceptance account with those businesses that Deutsche Bank takes care of as its area of specialisation.[29]

Now the time seemed to have come for the bank to once again pursue the failed project of founding a bank of its own in Latin America. Whereas the bank management had been quite cautious and had gradually extricated itself from the Paris and New York limited partnerships in the late 1870s, in 1886 it founded Banco Alemán Transatlántico (Deutsche Ueberseeische Bank) and announced the opening of a branch in Buenos Aires. In a similar vein, the annual report for 1886 reported that the bank had forged connections with Zanzibar, but that was just the first step. The bank supported the efforts Berlin took up shortly thereafter to establish a bank-like agency in Asia and invested accordingly in the founding of Deutsch-Asiatische Bank in early 1889. The headquarters were located in Shanghai, so the bank was returning after an interruption of 14 years. In the years of consolidation between the mid-1870s and the mid-1880s, foreign trade financing thus became a pillar of the bank's business both in terms of volume and reach, and it was finally being expanded again on a large scale. In the 1880s, Deutsche Bank had thus fulfilled its founding mission. It had carved out a strong position for itself in foreign trade financing. With its branches in Bremen and Hamburg it was well represented in the centres of German foreign trade. Its London branch not only made it easier for the bank to access the London money market but also gave it a

The Hamburg branch, opened in 1872, together with Bremen, was the centre of German foreign trade financing.

unique quality that enabled the bank to provide its customers with the sterling loans they much preferred in a considerable volume. The foreign trade financing thus made possible, meanwhile, spanned the globe because the bank by no means limited itself to the financing of German foreign trade but also supported German merchants when they conducted business transactions between Asia, Africa and America. At least the national competition was hardly equal to Deutsche Bank in this business segment.

As the economy picked up, so the domestic business began to grow rapidly. This segment already had a broad basis after the consolidation of the acquisition of the two Berlin banks. In the lending business, the current account loans were especially dynamic in their growth, whereas the domestic business in bills of exchange experienced only average growth. This is indicative of the average economic development. Many customers financed their trade transactions with bills of exchange or made use of short-term current account loans, which was a rather profitable business for the bank on account of the commissions and interest it earned from it.[30] The current accounts business eventually contributed about one-third of the bank's overall results. Particularly noticeable in the balance sheet structure, though, was the strong expansion of the securities business. Whereas ownership of securities or securities loans only played a small part in the asset side of the balance sheet for 1877, by the mid-1880s their share of the overall balance sheet had doubled. The liabilities side during these years was shaped by another capital increase from 45 to 60 million marks, a doubling of the deposit funds from 10 to more than 22 million marks, a strong rise in the current account balances and the circulating acceptances not yet redeemed, as well as a strong expansion of the reserves. Thus, the bank was easily able not only to refinance its assets but also to build up considerable buffers against risk. The earnings trend was solid overall. The bank's dividends, which had to be halved in 1873, gradually increased again, exceeding the pre-crisis level in 1879 at 9 per cent, and reaching 10 per cent in 1880 – a level they were able to roughly maintain in the following years as well. Thus, the years of consolidation were also reflected in the only modest dividends, which aligned with the strategic intentions of the bank leaders. The bank preferred to utilise its financial resources for targeted expansion of the lending business, for which the accumulation of the relevant reserves seemed indispensable.

The bank's lending business acquired new motivation above all by participating in larger issuances and the financing of industrial projects. There had already been movement in this direction early on, but from the late 1870s the contours became clearer. These sorts of transactions had not been carried out in a systematic way, but, rather, only when an opportunity arose or when Georg Siemens happened upon a supposedly good deal. The successive, initially unspectacular expansion of this business was not something the Berlin headquarters specialised in either; it also took place in the branches, namely the early domestic ones in Bremen, Hamburg and, from 1886, in Frankfurt am Main. The business that began to emerge from this could derive from the export and import trade, but could also be completely independent of it. The fact that Deutsche Bank had already invested in a joint-stock company for a jute-spinning mill in 1872 shows the close connection between trade financing and industrial financing: the import of cheap raw materials from India had reached a certain volume, but it was apparent that the market for jute products would increase sharply. However, one could not earn much from the import of raw materials itself; the added value came in the processing and the manufacture of end products, which prompted a German merchant and an English manufacturer to found a yarn-spinning mill in Germany to supply the industry in Silesia and Saxony. In the summer of 1872, Georg Siemens was willing, when asked, to finance this and, in light of the supposedly minimal financial commitment, the Administrative Board and his management colleagues did not try to thwart him. Logically, Deutsche Bank acquired a larger sum of shares, which could not, however, be offered on the stock market after the onset of the Panic of 1873 and the apparent start-up difficulties the company experienced. Instead of now trying to liquidate its shares as it ordinarily would have done, the bank held on to its portfolio until the company had consolidated, and, indeed, the bank even pushed it not to distribute its first profits but, rather, to use them for restructuring. All in all, the company managed to do this in the early 1880s, so that these experiences later became decisive in Deutsche Bank's stance towards industrial financing – that is, not always to bet on rapid success or the highest possible dividend but, rather, to provide help and guidance to the companies it had an interest or investment in. This may have been the view once the matter of Deutsche Jute-Spinnerei und Weberei AG had turned out well; previously, it was one of Siemens's risky deals, which had caused furrowed brows among his Management Board colleagues.

By no means did the bank initially want to take on long-term risks in the industrial financing segment because it had seen what that could lead to in other banks following the Panic of 1873. If one got involved at all, a clear aim was not to take the acquired securities into one's own portfolio but, rather, to offer them to the public as rapidly as possible in order to minimise the risk of a possible fall in price. In the simple financing of a company flotation, the bank derived its advantage from the commission and agiotage in order to then divest itself of the newly founded company as rapidly as possible. But this could not always be carried out so easily, which shaped the bank's cautious business conduct in the following period. Only when the bank's reserves seemed to be high enough did it also set its sights on the financing of large-scale industrial projects or more voluminous issuances, and now, too, only after serious consideration and with the appropriate debates in the Administrative Board and the Management Board. From the late 1870s, Deutsche Bank was more heavily involved in initial public offerings (IPOs), for example, with Farbenfabriken vorm. Friedrich Bayer & Co. (now Bayer AG), Harburger Vereinigte Gummi-Warenfabriken and other companies, and in these cases it typically managed to carry out the public offerings rapidly and only to keep small blocks of shares for a longer period of time. Not all plans were fulfilled, particularly since the Administrative Board examined each deal meticulously and occasionally thwarted the Management Board's aims. But gradually Deutsche Bank became the go-to address when the goal was to introduce new companies to the stock market or to support a company expansion through bond issues and debentures. In this, it was rather a matter of course that the bank urged the companies it served to transact at least a portion of their business through accounts at Deutsche Bank, be it in relation to domestic payments, or relevant to the import and export of goods. Arranging IPOs, capital increases and bond transactions thus often resulted in

Stock certificate of Farbenfabriken vorm. Friedrich Bayer & Co.: Deutsche Bank managed the firm's transformation into a joint-stock company in 1881 and, four years later, its initial public offering on the Berlin stock exchange.

Deutsche Bank becoming a sort of 'Hausbank' for the companies for whom it arranged these matters. In this banking relationship, in the end these companies conducted all or certainly a large portion of their ongoing payment transactions through the bank. To give one example: an agent of Hoffmann's Stärkefabriken in Bad Salzuflen was searching for a mortgage-backed loan of millions in February 1880 and, at the same time, he presented the prospect of the company conducting its voluminous financial transactions through the bank. Thereafter, the Management Board made inquiries in Bremen, where the owner, Eduard Hoffmann, maintained business (and family) ties, about the starch factory's financial situation. When the answer turned out to be positive, Deutsche Bank not only granted the loan but also stood by the starch factory with support and guidance in its expansion in the following years, and also finally organised its transformation into a joint-stock company.[31]

With industrialisation, the centres of industry also grew – those initially small cities that got bigger and bigger, whose own development could itself become a lucrative financing deal. Construction companies, infrastructure developers and project sponsors typically had to secure advanced financing for their projects since they could only bring in earnings after the projects were completed. Mortgage-backed loans or corresponding bonds became the financing tool of choice for this, with Deutsche Bank also being able to take over Berliner Bank-Verein's already existing business. The bank was initially able to acquire a very prestigious investment in the development of the land surveyor company for the Kurfürstendamm and then a little later in the village colony of Grunewald in the early 1880s. These were showcases of Berlin and Charlottenburg city development and, at the same time, residential and commercial areas of the higher echelons of Berlin society.[32] These business dealings, which were initially hard to develop, prompting Georg Siemens repeatedly to contemplate getting out of the property company,[33] were tarnished by rapid speculative gains, which Siemens wanted to keep his distance from; he was convinced, at least according to Helfferich, that Deutsche Bank would only be able to gain long-term benefit from these projects if they also provided a general benefit to all.[34] The bank also got similarly involved in tram projects – for example, under the leadership of the Bremen branch, which had already gained experience with the horse track of Bremerhaven-Geestemünde, as well as with the tram from Nuremberg to Fürth.[35] In this way, the business volume grew ever larger.

3. America

As important as the expansion of the 'regular business' was, it did not promise tremendous leaps forward because of the depressed economic situation. But above all, expanding the regular business was hardly sufficient for utilising the great liquidity that had existed since the nationalisation of the railways. The search for alternatives may also have been interesting because it freed one, at least for a time, from the routine of 'regular business'; that is, from the frequent meetings in Berlin at which every sizeable loan was thoroughly analysed in terms of its chances, risks and security. This routine must also have been oppressive because the Committee of Five insisted on having the last word and thus had every matter, large or small, submitted to it, and Siemens or his colleagues on the Management Board were subjected to a round of questioning. This may well have suited the temperaments of Steinthal and Wallich; at least, that is what was later said. Georg Siemens, however, visibly suffered from the routines and restrictions arising from this way of conducting business, which is probably why he himself suggested that he pursue international business connections, giving him the opportunity to at least temporarily escape the narrow world of the Berlin office. He often reported enthusiastically about the trips he took on behalf of the bank. It is also likely that he increasingly enjoyed being regarded as a promising financier for whom doors seemed to open on their own. His visit to Bucharest in 1882 was notable also because the local press had heralded him as the 'wealthy uncle' from Berlin, whereupon the project managers and 'knights of industry' lined up in his hotel 'in order to lift the hidden "ressources de la Roumanie" with our money'.[36] On such trips, Siemens certainly tended to take on too much at once – to set his sights on electrification in Vienna, to discuss projects in Romania, and, at the same time, to attempt to acquire Serbian government bonds, not to mention the individual discussions that accompanied all of this because he always wanted to lead important negotiations himself. This stretched him to the limit: 'My nerves are getting considerably worse,' he complained in September 1882, 'situations like this [simultaneous negotiations in Vienna, Belgrade and Bucharest] get me worked up.' But by no means did he wish to give up his activities, nor did he want to surrender any of his responsibility: 'I wanted to be the sole wise one and burdened myself with a workload that I will have to spend years digesting and with which nobody can provide me with help.'[37] Of course, it would not come to 'years'; things had to be worked through more quickly than that. Just under a year after his lament, he wrote to his wife from the steamship *Elbe*, which he had recently boarded for a trip of many months' duration to the United States. The frequent business trips continued to be part of his daily affairs; in addition, though, holiday trips also gradually entered the picture – above all, to the Alps and lakes in northern Italy. Naturally, on these trips, as on the trips to Greece, the Ottoman Empire and to the Middle East, business matters always played a role. In sum: Georg Siemens undertook the internationalisation of the business for a variety of reasons, and in the process it became a sort of way of life for him.

The opportunities for greater involvement abroad, above all in brokering foreign assets with good interest in the German money and capital markets, were quite favourable in the late 1870s, although they were not the same in all sectors. Projects awaiting financing were everywhere, as were project managers who were wringing their hands looking for financing. This was not always serious, but it was usually rather promising. The railway boom, in any case, had by no means run its course from a global perspective; indeed, railway assets triggered grand fantasies, whether pertaining to the shares of railway companies or to their high-interest bonds. The availability of these sorts of assets was quite good, but the markets, particularly the gigantic, gradually developing Russian market, was difficult for Deutsche Bank to access. Other banks were ahead in this. But the large American market, which was veritably exploding after the Civil War with its numerous railway projects that could not be financed from the internal capital accumulation of the country, was promising. The appetite for capital there drew European capital across the Atlantic, as it had in the years before and during the Civil War. Some of this capital was provided through money market loans, and, above all, it went into the securities of American companies that could easily be sold on the European stock markets.

New York, Wall Street, around 1900. American railway securities, which were also very popular with German investors, were traded here.

Various railway projects in Central and South America were also interesting; indeed, the opportunities of the vast continent seemed tremendous in general since access to the markets there was much easier for Deutsche Bank than in Russia, Asia, or the British Empire. The previous attempts to gain a foothold in these markets, of course, had either failed completely (Knoblauch & Lichtenstein) or had generated only modest results.[38]

How was this to be carried on? Executives in Berlin had long considered founding an office or branch of Deutsche Bank in New York, but they finally gave up on this idea because of the all but insurmountable legal hurdles. Since no such hurdles existed in Latin America, the bank founded Deutsche Übersee-Bank (from 1893 Deutsche Ueberseeische Bank) or Banco Alemán Transatlántico in 1886 as a fully owned subsidiary to take over financial services in South America controlled by Berlin. Naturally, this did not help with North America. Without a firm, trustworthy and influential connection in the United States, the bank would hardly be able to enter into the money and capital markets business there. Nonetheless, it succeeded in doing this relatively quickly thanks to a coincidence that would have great significance for the North American business. On a European trip, the German-American businessman Henry Villard, born Heinrich Hilgard in Speyer, stopped off in Berlin and met with many representatives from the banking and business worlds. His aim was to procure German capital for various projects, including the expansion of his own railway company in the American Northwest, but also for Thomas Alva Edison, with whom Villard had close business relations, to use for his electrical engineering patents. Villard was not completely unknown in Berlin. The career he had behind him was similar to that of Deutsche Bank Administrative Board member Friedrich Kapp.[39] After quarrelling with his father, Villard had left Germany in 1853; he then worked for a long time as a journalist in New York and had finally got involved in a railway project in the American Northwest that he now wanted to roll out on a grand scale. He had already financed his 'Oregon Railway und Navigation Company' in the 1870s with German capital (including capital provided by the Frankfurt bank Stern) and had managed to expand it to a certain size in the American West. However, the Northern Pacific Railway, which had been founded as early as 1864 and owned the rights for the expansion of the railway from Michigan to the Pacific, now seemed poised to dominate the lucrative market. Villard thus forged a plan, successful in the end, to acquire a majority share of the Northern Pacific Railway and to merge it at some point with the Oregon Railway. Until then, of course, a lot of capital needed to be procured for the rapid expansion of the stretches in the American Northwest so that the railway connection from the Great Lakes to the Pacific could be completed and transformed into a lucrative source of income. For this, Villard was also searching for financiers in Germany, and he found them at, among others, Deutsche Bank, to which he probably gained access through Friedrich Kapp. The bank invested a large sum in the expansion of the Northern Pacific Railway, thus helping to make it possible for the connection from Mississippi to the Pacific to be inaugurated with great fanfare in September 1883.

Georg Siemens, at the invitation of Henry Villard, used the inauguration of the Northern Pacific Railway to undertake a long trip to North America; he had always been fascinated by the continent's economic prospects. Villard, of course, had spared no effort to impress his German guests. Invitations, 'grand breakfasts' and excursions occurred

In September 1883, the last rails of Northern Pacific Railway were laid in Montana.
Georg Siemens himself travelled there from Berlin in order to participate in the inauguration,
celebrated with great fanfare, of the transcontinental railway.

in quick succession; the 'programme of enjoyments,' Siemens wrote to his wife on 2 September 1883, hardly left him any time to write letters. A trip to Niagara Falls that Villard and Siemens took was a veritable celebrity tour, attended also by the Prussian envoy to the United States, and, above all, Carl Schurz ('who administers to the needs of the entire party with wonderful graciousness and politeness'), who was the American Secretary of the Interior from 1877 to 1881, as well as other prominent emigrants, but also American politicians.[40] Later on, too, Siemens met with important politicians or local bigwigs. Overwhelmed by the impressions he experienced during this trip, he wrote: 'Only here has the size of America become clear to me.'[41] He had already known before that Deutsche Bank had good prospects in America, but the trip showed him that the opportunities were greater than he had expected.[42]

The trip lasted several months and fulfilled its purpose to the extent that Villard had sought to secure Siemens's financial support. Villard's enthusiasm made it possible to overlook the difficulties the young railway company was obviously having, its high debts and initially only low earnings. Despite apparent profitability problems, a growing scepticism that the Northern Pacific Railway could be successful and falling share prices, Deutsche Bank once again acquired a large share of a mortgage-backed bond in the autumn of 1883, but this only delayed the company's problems. After all, the Northern Pacific was on the brink of bankruptcy and Villard had to leave the company against his will. Instead, a syndicate led by JP Morgan took control and restructured the Northern

Pacific.[43] Deutsche Bank nonetheless maintained its ties and also continued to finance the restructured company, whose securities it placed on European capital markets. In the meantime, Henry Villard did not give up his ambitious plans but, rather, returned to Germany in 1884 with the intention, but probably only for show, of raising German capital to regain his position with the Northern Pacific. It is not known in detail why Siemens welcomed Villard with open arms. People speculated that Siemens admired him on account of his way of life and his success in the United States, but it's impossible to be certain of this. In any case, Villard not only won Siemens's support; later, in September 1886, he also formally became the agent of Deutsche Bank in the United States, and the bank simultaneously revised its business practices there. Whereas previously it had primarily acted as an intermediary for American securities to the European money and capital markets, it now planned to enter into the American investment business with an equity interest of its own in the Northern Pacific Railway. Siemens justified this by arguing that this was the only way German bondholders could be protected from negative price developments.[44]

As it was, Deutsche Bank financed Henry Villard's return to the top of the Oregon and Wisconsin Railway as well as the Northern Pacific. In return, Villard brokered business transactions worth $64.3 million in his time as the agent of Deutsche Bank, primarily railway securities that Deutsche Bank sold to the European public. This obviously provided some consolation for the ever-growing risks involved in the financing of the Northern Pacific, to which Deutsche Bank remained loyal in spite of ever-worsening news, not least because Siemens was able to prevail over his sceptical colleagues on the Management Board of Deutsche Bank, who nevertheless capped the bank's quantitative US investment. Conversely, the bank's investment up to this point was not enough for Villard. He planned a comprehensive reallocation of land in the region of the Northwest railways in America, including the merging of various railway lines with the North American Company and a transfer of all of its debts, a transaction estimated to cost $24 million, a sum that threatened to put Deutsche Bank in over its head. When the North American Company finally went bankrupt, Deutsche Bank, as its *de facto* share-holder, was in the same boat and had to decide whether the dropping prices of its American railway securities meant that these should be written off or kept, not to mention that the bank also had to answer to its German customers, to whom it had sold these products.

Villard had put the bank in a similar situation in the financing of Edison's businesses in the United States. Villard and Edison were friends. From the beginning, Villard had harboured an interest of his own in the use of Edison's patents in Europe and was able to gain more influence on Edison after JP Morgan had lost interest in utilising Edison's patents. Villard wished to build up a company

Henry Villard (1835–1900) around 1890.

in the United States that would promote the production, sale and use of electricity. This was obviously a giant market, but it required considerable capital advances in order even to begin development. Once again, Villard managed to interest Siemens in the business. Siemens was familiar with the opportunities for electrical engineering from his own home, and with this deal he had a chance to kill two birds with one stone. Along with revenues from the financing of the company, America was an enticing market where Siemens & Halske could sell their goods; moreover, the use of the patents of his uncle Werner there was also attractive. The involvement itself then turned out to be much more difficult than expected because the shares acquired in the poorly performing Edison company could not initially be listed on the stock exchange but had to remain in the bank's portfolio. Nor did the economic performance of Edison General Electric, which had to assert itself against considerable competition, proceed very well. When Edison General Electric was finally merged with one of its main competitors to become the General Electric Company, Deutsche Bank withdrew from the financing of the company and liquidated its shares. Its first experiences in investing in US business, therefore, were rather mixed. With and through Henry Villard, it managed to get into the lucrative flotation of American railway and industry securities; his interests in the development and control of companies in the United States for which he used Deutsche Bank as a sort of financier of his own ambitions clearly put the bank into a difficult situation. Only in the 1890s did a scandal erupt. The beginning of business in Latin America was anything but spectacular after Banco Alemán Transatlántico had been set up. Although Deutsche Bank did invest in an Argentine gold bond as early as 1888, the underwriting business and project financing were not initially the focus of the South American subsidiary. However, Deutsch-Ueberseeische Elektricitäts-Gesellschaft founded towards the end of the century for the electrification of Latin America was then the biggest pre-First World War German foreign industrial investment. But in the 1880s this was just a vision for the future, albeit one that was quite realistic because projects for lighting cities, for local public transportation and, in general, for the use of electricity were springing up everywhere, especially in the larger cities. Latin America, particularly Argentina, was regarded as extremely attractive. It was not least for this reason that the head of the Reichsbank was pushing German merchants and bankers to get more involved there.[45] From the beginning, Latin America was an important market for Deutsche Bank, above all in trade finance and its associated business opportunities. Thus, the initiative to found Banco Alemán Transatlántico, which will be discussed more below, did not need a political push in the end.[46] Whereas the early business in Latin America was comprised primarily of bill credit and arbitrage in bills of exchange in the financing of foreign trade, say, in furs and hides or raw material exports from Chile (saltpetre, guano), which all brought good returns, industrial financing was later added, especially in Argentina and Chile. But local deposit banking also played a role because it enabled the bank to limit its foreign-currency risk since this usually provided sufficient liquidity in local currency. In this way, the bank managed to secure a presence in Latin America and, all in all, to make money from it, even though it did have occasional setbacks, particularly resulting from the wrong or disappointing choice of personnel or problems in public finances.[47]

4. The Issuing Business

The issuing business, which the bank initially undertook only here and there and on a smaller scale, had grown considerably more important primarily as a result of the extensive placement of American securities on German and European stock markets or with its own ever-expanding clientele. It was clear that the bank's executives would try to become more involved in its home market. After all, this was the point of the discussions about the business policy in 1876. The bank certainly did tap the German money and capital markets, even though it did so to a lesser extent in the crisis years and after the long deflation phase of the early 1890s had come to an end. In this, municipalities, real estate financiers and, to an ever-greater extent, once again industrial companies were also keen to sell their stocks and bonds to the public. According to its annual reports, Deutsche Bank invested in individual projects from the 1870s, but typically it did not do this alone. Instead, it became a member of syndicates that were formed for the handling of individual issuances, thus keeping its own involvement manageable, and, above all, limiting its risks. A typical example of this was the involvement in a bond issue of the Krupp company. In April 1879, together with other Berlin and Cologne banks, Deutsche Bank underwrote a 22.5 million mark bond of the Essen steel manufacturer, which Krupp wished to use to convert a loan granted in 1874 by the Prussian Seehandlung during the crisis.[48] Thus, the bank gradually established itself in the highly competitive national underwriting business. This could be difficult, as the example of an 1883 bond

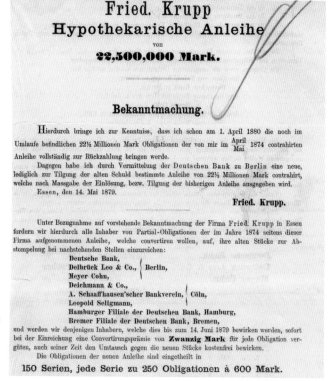

Deutsche Bank first came into contact with the leading steel production company Krupp when it took a pre-eminent role in the issuance of the Krupp bond for 22.5 million marks in 1879.

Fried. Krupp
Hypothekarische Anleihe
von
22,500,000 Mark.

Bekanntmachung.

Hierdurch bringe ich zur Kenntniss, dass ich schon am 1. April 1880 die noch im Umlaufe befindlichen 22½ Millionen Mark Obligationen der von mir im April / Mai 1874 contrahirten Anleihe vollständig zur Rückzahlung bringen werde.

Dagegen habe ich durch Vermittelung der Deutschen Bank zu Berlin eine neue, lediglich zur Tilgung der alten Schuld bestimmte Anleihe von 22½ Millionen Mark contrahirt, welche nach Massgabe der Einlösung, bezw. Tilgung der bisherigen Anleihe ausgegeben wird.

Essen, den 14. Mai 1879.

Fried. Krupp.

Unter Bezugnahme auf vorstehende Bekanntmachung der Firma Fried. Krupp in Essen fordern wir hierdurch alle Inhaber von Partial-Obligationen der im Jahre 1874 seitens dieser Firma aufgenommenen Anleihe, welche convertiren wollen, auf, ihre alten Stücke zur Abstempelung bei nachstehenden Stellen einzureichen:

Deutsche Bank,
Delbrück Leo & Co., } Berlin,
Meyer Cohn,
Deichmann & Co.,
A. Schaaffhausen'scher Bankverein, } Cöln,
Leopold Seligmann,
Hamburger Filiale der Deutschen Bank, Hamburg,
Bremer Filiale der Deutschen Bank, Bremen,

und werden wir denjenigen Inhabern, welche dies bis zum 14. Juni 1879 bewirken werden, sofort bei der Einreichung eine Convertirungsprämie von **Zwanzig Mark** für jede Obligation vergüten, auch seiner Zeit den Umtausch gegen die neuen Stücke kostenfrei bewirken.

Die Obligationen der neuen Anleihe sind eingetheilt in

150 Serien, jede Serie zu 250 Obligationen à 600 Mark.

of Norddeutscher Lloyd shows. The company wanted to consolidate and redeem older bonds and debts with it. Georg Siemens and Hermann Henrich Meier led the negotiations directly, but Meier was also simultaneously speaking with Disconto-Gesellschaft.[49] Pointing to the competition, Meier demanded better conditions. The negotiations could only be concluded after Georg Siemens had made concessions concerning the amount of interest and payment offices. Only now was he able to complete the issue of a bond for a Bremen syndicate under the leadership of Deutsche Bank's branch there.[50] There were quite a few similar transactions: Deutsche Bank also participated in bond issues of HAPAG, the Schlesische Aktiengesellschaft für Bergbau und Hüttenbetrieb, it supported efforts to consolidate the jute industry market and provided advice on capital increases of aspiring industrial companies like Agfa or BASF. It was by no means able to directly assert its own ideas in these deals. These were all matters for negotiation.[51]

The data in the annual reports unambiguously reflect this development. The syndicate account had a meagre portfolio of 1.7 million marks for 1876, but this had risen by 1878 to 3.8 million and by 1880 to 7 million marks. In 1886, the bank finally listed 12 completed syndicates and 35 current ones, and the syndicate account had a value of around 20 million marks. Whereas these accounts reflected almost exclusively public bonds and railway securities in the 1870s, over time they included a much larger number of industrial financing loans and mortgage transactions. In 1886, there was finally a broad mix of issue transactions, which clearly displayed both the bank's national and international involvement. The shift that Siemens had demanded had thus taken place both in terms of volume and business partners. Deutsche Bank had reacted successfully to the situation of low interest and excess capital, among other things, by helping customers convert older bonds into new, low-interest ones.[52] In this sense, the low interest rates were not only a burden but also contributed to new business opportunities, particularly since it was not the interest rate in and of itself but, rather, the relevant spread of interest rates that mattered.

The bank's rise into the premier league of issuing houses was by no means easy. To be sure, in the 1870s the bank already had solid syndicate partners, above all banks with whom it had other close ties as well. But for the attractive larger government bond issues, the ad hoc syndicates proved to be unwieldy, as Deutsche Bank discovered in one of its first major initiatives on the market for Austrian government bonds in the 1870s. In addition, tedious syndicate negotiations with different interests could benefit the competition. But the sheer task of mobilising the necessary sums of capital could also take up so much time, despite the tremendous personal engagement of the Management Board members, that good opportunities could not be utilised. For example, in the summer of 1876, the Rothschilds snatched a Viennese gold pension right out from under the nose of a group including Deutsche Bank because Siemens was not able, despite his considerable involvement, to raise the necessary amount of silver in order to provide the advance for the bond.[53] Although Deutsche Bank's group lost the advance business with the Viennese government in this way, it was still able to successfully take part in the placement of the bond that the other group had made possible. This was already instructive as the bank's leadership saw in detail the difficulties that could accompany the formation of a syndicate of different partners with different interests.[54]

In this attempt, the bank must also have recognised which obstacles had to be overcome for it to advance in the sector of state financing for Prussia and the German Empire. For a time, the Prussian Seehandlung had organised this alone, but from 1876 the Prussian

Bond of the German Empire from 1878. The previous year, Deutsche Bank had fought to attain a position in the so-called Prussian Consortium, an exclusive circle of German banks that issued bonds for Prussia and the empire.

Consortium was active once again; in it, the Seehandlung, Disconto-Gesellschaft, Berliner Handels-Gesellschaft and some private banks set the tone. Siemens sought to change this, but Management Board members Steinthal and Wallich, who had also urged caution in the Viennese bond issue, were reluctant.[55] Siemens, for whom the issuing business was the core of banking, managed to prevail. He finally broke through the blockade of the Prussian Consortium by suggesting a bond floated by Deutsche Bank alone to the Seehandlung. Although the Seehandlung rejected this proposal, this did open the path to the Prussian Consortium – albeit with a small quota of 7.5 per cent. For Georg Siemens, this was in the best case a beginning. He repeatedly attempted to raise the quote in accordance with the importance Deutsche Bank had attained, but he failed because of the phalanx of Seehandlung and Disconto-Gesellschaft, which had no intention of upgrading Deutsche Bank. Only after 1880, when the Seehandlung's president Rudolf von Bitter, who had been closely associated with the head of Disconto-Gesellschaft Adolph von Hansemann, died and Max Rötger assumed the presidency, did the alliance with Disconto-Gesellschaft start to fray; still, it would take some time before Deutsche Bank would acquire a position in the syndicate that it felt was appropriate to it.[56]

Judging by the annual report for 1887, the contours of the completed issuing projects and the future issuing activity could already clearly be discerned at this point, when the bank's consolidation phase was winding down after the Panic of 1873. In 1887, the bank completed a total of 14 syndicate deals, the majority of which were domestic and foreign government bonds as well as conversion bonds of German and foreign cities and regions. However, Austrian and Swiss railway bonds, as well as at least one industrial security, were also among these. Thirty-five other projects were also factored into the report from ongoing syndicate deals – two real estate transactions, 19 government, municipal and railway bonds and 14 participations in share issues. The 'account of [the bank's] own rated securities', that is of shares that the bank held permanently or long term in its portfolio, had increased significantly in the meantime to more than 6.7 million marks in value. In addition to public bonds, these were comprised of, above all, equity interests in other banks with which the bank co-operated closely and in whose capital increases it participated, namely Bergisch Märkische Bank, Schlesischer Bankverein and other similar banks. Thus, a lucrative domestic and foreign field of business had opened up, and the annual report for 1887 left no doubt that the bank would continue to be proactive in accordance with market conditions wherever favourable business opportunities emerged:

> The mass of invested funds in the individual branches of economic exchange has apparently not changed. A decline in the newly emerging assets could not be discerned, probably because neither in agriculture nor in industry was there any impetus for a particular development: for the construction of railways even fewer funds were utilised since the introduction of the state railway operation compared to the average of the previous years. The necessity of further introducing foreign securities resulted from this for the stock market. We attempted to meet this need by introducing Spanish annuities, various Italian securities and North American railway debenture bonds.[57]

This made it clear that the bank would stick with this strategy while market conditions remained subdued. But then things turned out differently after all.

The period from the mid-1870s to the mid-1880s was one of consolidation, despite all the crucial developments that began at this time; the bank's focus was primarily to assert its status within the complicated conditions of the national and global economy. After all, the market conditions were difficult not only for Deutsche Bank. All the major Berlin banks had to look around for lucrative alternatives given the weakness of the domestic market. The competition, accordingly, was stiff. Deutsche Bank consequently had considerable difficulty in gaining a foothold outside of its core business segment, in becoming a member of the important consortia and in showing its presence on the promising international markets, particularly since the issuing business in Germany was effectively stagnating at that time. The number of issuances hardly rose from 1883 to 1887, although the balance between domestic and foreign assets remained roughly the same; for a short time – that is, in 1884 and 1885 – the value of issued foreign securities was even higher than that of domestic ones.[58] It was only natural that the various major banks would watch each other closely and attempt to snatch away shares of business, whereas dispensing with the stiff competition that damaged the profit margins was out of the question. No banks could behave in a passive manner in this difficult situation; all of them had to make competitive offers on the market – that is, if necessary with low commissions and more favourable interest rates – and fight for their customers. Deutsche Bank approached the market in a rather aggressive manner, as competing banks claimed, but it managed to do so quite successfully.[59] Yet it had little alternative: it had meanwhile become a major deposit and current accounts bank, so it was not only forced to offer ongoing payment transactions at competitive prices, but also had to transact the day-to-day business of its growing customer base in a cost-effective manner and, lastly, to offer its affluent clientele lucrative investment opportunities. By participating in large and small issuances, it thus expanded its own offers, which its customers emphatically wanted. And fulfilling these wishes suited Georg Siemens perfectly; he regarded his 'international excursions', and also asserting the bank's position in the national syndicate business, as a personal challenge. He was happy to take up this challenge at times, and thus got into conflicts, occasionally personal ones, so that these quarrels tended to be equated with him as an individual, whether at his own bank, where Hermann Wallich, for one, always feared 'new ideas' from Siemens, or in competition with other banks, although a special rivalry gradually crystallised with Disconto-Gesellschaft. This challenge to be top dog in the Berlin financial market had its personal nuance, for, as Siemens's son-in-law and biographer pondered concerning Georg Siemens's relationship with Adolph von Hansemann: 'Every great business competition is, in the end, a fight between two individual personalities.'[60]

III. The Expansive Years: The Era of Siemens, 1887–1900

1. The End of the Depression and the Transition to a Booming Economy

The last 13 years before Georg Siemens withdrew from the company for health reasons in 1900 turned out to be completely different from what might have been expected in 1887. The bank's annual report for 1887 was not able to find 'anything remarkable […] in the development of economic conditions of the year 1887'; surplus capital was still available, it reported, and interest rates were low. Thus, Deutsche Bank continued to broker interesting foreign securities to the German investment-seeking public and otherwise devoted itself to taking care of the 'regular business'. This business had grown ever more extensive and now employed a large staff in Berlin and the other German cities as well as in its most important foreign branch, the London Agency. But business picked up again in the next couple of years so that the bank even determined with some relief that the economic momentum had begun to slow down.[1] This would just be an episode. Soon, another economic boom set in not only in Germany but also worldwide, which the discovery of gold in Alaska and South Africa strengthened. The long deflationary phase after the Panic of 1873 was finally over. Once gold was discovered, feverish speculation had spread through the world's stock markets by the first half of the 1890s, leading to exaggerations, and caused setbacks. However, in the opinion of the bank, these did not justify the restrictive German stock-market legislation, which largely prohibited trading in futures in 1896. Under the temporary drop in prices, the management argued, only a few had really suffered; development overall continued to be positive. Rather, the bank found the temporary shortage of capital remarkable, which made funding for banks more difficult and caused Deutsche Bank to raise its equity capital in 1895 from 75 million to 100 million marks.[2] The restrictive stock-market legislation, which resulted from the speculative trend, was not ineffectual but, in light of the fact that the international money and capital markets had long been connected, could achieve little of what its advocates believed it could. The annual report noted that

> Widespread international circumstances cannot be regulated by national laws limited to a relatively small area. The public's appetite for speculation is neither diminished by restricting the number of objects for speculation nor by changing the form in which speculation occurs; nor does the reduction in the number of dealers associated with the prohibition of futures trading ensure stable prices for

the products; nor does it change the quality of the debenture bonds or shares that manage to become offers if one makes it more difficult or even prevents their issuances in German territory.

That did not help anyone, they argued; it accelerated the structural change of banking because the smaller banks had an ever-more difficult time asserting themselves.[3]

What prompted the stock-market legislation was, in fact, only partly fear of speculation running off the rails. With the rising economy, industrial expansion and infrastructure development, especially in the major and middle-sized cities, the money and capital markets were used to such an extent that the investment crisis of the 1880s was soon forgotten. In fact, the situation was the opposite. Now the German financial market repeatedly reached the limit of its capacity, which caused the agricultural sector – where it was difficult to obtain credit – to heavily criticise capital export. Deutsche Bank, however, regarded this criticism as unjustified and wrong. Its counter-argument not only pointed to the ineffectiveness of national steps to regulate the international financial markets; it also defended its capital export very confidently, arguing that it was only the profits from foreign investments, foreign bonds, as well as the gold imports made possible by the banks, that kept the German balance of payments on an even keel despite chronic trade deficits and made it possible to maintain the gold standard without endangering the domestic economy. This tension remained in the coming years. Relative scarcity of capital, significantly higher interest, but above all competing desires for credit set the stage. Only in 1900, the year Siemens left the bank, did the situation settle down for economic and political reasons – in the United States the demand for steel had collapsed and in the Transvaal the First Boer War was raging. The world economy slipped into a crisis, which the bank observed with a certain relief.

As a result of this, the years after the end of the long deflationary phase up until Georg Siemens left were of a totally different nature than before. The bank's consolidation strategy, namely to shore up capital and reserves and to establish a strong position in the current account and deposit businesses, now really started working. And also, somewhat coincidentally, the competencies Deutsche Bank had gained in international precious metal and foreign currency trading from the silver sales of the 1870s started to pay off in a big way in the international precious metal imports it handled through its London Agency.

2. The 'regular business'

The 'regular business', as Georg Siemens called the daily banking operations, started to boom in the late 1880s and also changed its character. Whereas it had initially consisted primarily of foreign trade finance, current accounts and deposit banking, underwriting had been added in the mid-1880s, and after the first more or less spectacular beginnings it likewise quickly became routine. Unlike during the long deflationary phase, the global economic expansion was now financed, above all, by capital markets, which now began to play an ever-greater role. And it was the (major) banks which acted as a sort of door opener, less in the sense that they tied themselves to certain projects long term than that they functioned as guides helping the states, municipalities and companies to sell their securities to a broad public. Different from, say, in Britain, where independent brokers played a big role, in Germany it was the major banks that controlled the stock-market business, strengthened by the legislation there.[4] A prerequisite for a bank to fulfil this function was for it to have placing power, and in this Deutsche Bank gradually developed almost unheard-of capacities, as Jakob Riesser respectfully noted.[5] Its balance sheet structure reflects, on the one hand, the bank's ability to raise the necessary capital: in 1900, at the end of the Georg Siemens era, it had paid-up capital of 150 million marks and had various reserves set aside amounting to 48 million marks. Deposits totalled a good 191 million marks; the current accounts balances added up to 340 million marks, counter-balanced by current account loans of 285 million marks. In addition, there were circulating acceptances totalling 141 million marks as well as several smaller items.[6] These sums determined the room to manoeuvre of the lending business; in some segments, specifically in the use of deposits and current account monies, the bank also established a cautious business policy, but its capital strength around 1900 was far superior to that of all the other major banks. A comparison of Deutsche Bank's most important competitors shows how high its deposits were: Disconto-Gesellschaft, with 48 million marks, Dresdner Bank with 94.5 million marks and Darmstädter Bank with 43.2 million marks altogether could not match this amount.[7]

The bank now also stuck consistently to its cautious business policy because the few poorer years showed how quickly a large lending business could become a problem if, for example, deposits or current account balances were withdrawn. Payment defaults and withdrawals on short notice, however, never occurred on a dangerous scale, so the bank was well equipped for the capital markets business. Looking at the bare facts, it

The deposit-taking branch on Lutherstraße in Berlin's Schöneberg district: one of the 47 Berlin deposit-taking branches in the capital city around 1914, which collected deposits for the bank, forming the basis for its business with private customers.

is possible to see that it was tremendously successful. Whereas the bank was participating in 45 syndications in 1888, which tied up about 21 million marks at the end of the year, their number continually increased, finally reaching 168 syndicates in 1900, with a sum of 32.8 million marks paid in to them at the end of the year. The bank had obviously succeeded in expanding its underwriting business, without at the same time having needed to significantly increase the shares it kept or held in its own portfolio. On the contrary, the funds tied up per investment even grew smaller on average, which shows that the bank typically managed to sell the shares it acquired rapidly to the public. The syndicates in which the bank participated were just as varied as the transactions it handled this way. In 1900 the bank was participating in eight property syndicates, it had 33 investments in government or municipal securities as well as railway securities, and reported on 127 current industrial financing projects. The amount of securities sold to the public was correspondingly high. The sales volume in the bank's securities account amounted to more than 3.3 billion marks. The monthly inflows and outflows of the headquarters alone reached about 454 million marks.[8] These sums were breathtaking.

In the late 1890s, when Georg Siemens and his Management Board colleagues recalled the difficult beginnings in the 1870s and early 1880s, they must have been astonished at the extraordinarily dynamic development. What they had had to develop through tedious petty work and to push through with a rather sceptical Administrative Board now seemed to fall into the bank's lap almost on its own. In any case, the bank could hardly escape offers brought to it from inside and outside the country, not least because it had for some time been improving its position with the use of favourable conditions, namely acceptance credits with longer terms – much to the distress of the competition, which accused Deutsche Bank of engaging in a sort of fee dumping.[9] That said, it also used the position of power it had earned in the German money and capital markets to upgrade significantly its symbolic position. The competition would have preferred to prevent it from joining the circle of the Prussian Consortium in the late 1870s. Since it could not do so, Deutsche Bank's share was kept low. Siemens tried repeatedly to gain a better position for the bank. This failed because the other syndicate partners resisted, so that the bank finally took the bull by the horns and bypassed the Prussian Consortium, offering Prussia and the empire to underwrite 125 million marks for 3 per cent Prussian consols and 75 million marks of 3 per cent German imperial bonds at a rate of 91.5 per cent (later 92 per cent) which Deutsche Bank would offer to the public on its own.[10] However, Prussia and the empire, both of which entered into this deal, specified the conditions in the contract in such a way that no one could get the impression that a bank was, in this case, benefiting unilaterally at the expense of the state and the general public. The effect of this contract being concluded was, nevertheless, tremendous, because it sent a clear signal to the public about who was number one in the German money and capital markets. Members of the Prussian Consortium were surprised by this development, and the mood was correspondingly downbeat, at least among those who were not experiencing Schadenfreude in the expectation that Deutsche Bank would choke on the deal. The head of the Seehandlung, Emil von Burchard, had to listen to numerous accusations that he had not made Prussia's and the empire's bond plans sufficiently clear. He ultimately resigned. Nevertheless, the hopes of those who had bet on the bank failing to sell the shares and getting stuck with a portion of the bonds, or having to sell them at lower rates, also went unfulfilled. On the contrary: the bonds were heavily oversubscribed and Deutsche Bank successfully offered them to the public. These bond issues, of course, significantly burdened the German money and capital markets' capacity as it was already being used for numerous other projects. Consequently, the bank did not make a grand announcement about its success, particularly since, in addition to the bonds' financial benefit, it had achieved its further aim of breaking apart the fixed structures of the Prussian Consortium and underscoring its leading status.

3. The Development of the Bank's Presence at Home and Abroad

The bank's expanding significance and concomitant greater financial power – this was what all the talk was about – made it the financier of choice, and one that was also in demand where it had not previously been prominently represented. To this extent, improving the bank's regional presence in the most important German industrial centres was a challenge that arose naturally from the expansion of its business. In addition to Bremen and Hamburg, the bank had initially refrained from spreading to further regions and instead bet on co-operating with institutions it was on friendly terms with and in which it had already participated financially here and there or with which it had personal connections. The bank's own Supervisory Board member Hermann Marcuse also sat on the supervisory board of Frankfurter Bankverein, which Deutsche Bank acquired in 1886, transforming it into a branch in its own right. The bank wanted to be directly represented in Frankfurt because the city was a traditional financial centre – only recently overtaken by Berlin – with its numerous banks and the relational structures associated with that position. What is more, Siemens tried to organise the takeover of Frankfurter Bankverein by mutual agreement in such a way that there would be no bad blood. Along with the buildings and properties, Deutsche Bank took over Frankfurter Bankverein's customer base and relationships.[11] The founding of the branches in Munich and Leipzig in 1892 and 1901 took place in a similar fashion.[12] In addition to Frankfurt am Main, Saxony and, above all, Silesia and the industrial centre of Rhineland-Westphalia were undoubtedly very important for the bank's business. In the east as in the west, there were connections to regional joint-stock banks, some of which had already participated in the founding of Deutsche Bank, such as Schlesischer Bankverein in Breslau. When, in 1897, in light of a capital increase from 100 to 150 million marks, there was an opportunity to get the shareholders of Bergisch Märkische Bank in Elberfeld and of Schlesischer Bankverein to buy shares of Deutsche Bank and, thus, to substantially shore up the 'friendly relations', the Management Board of Berlin did not hesitate.

> The advancing concentration of the business in Berlin, which has already prompted a range of rural institutions to establish branches in Berlin, made it seem necessary to solidify our connections with the rural areas. As a result, we suggested to the shareholders of Bergisch Märkische Bank and Schlesischer Bankverein, which cultivate

the same business segments with us and pursue the same programme, that they exchange their shares for new shares to be created. This suggestion was taken up by more than three-quarters of all the shareholders. This procedure will not affect the independence of the relevant banks in any way: however, we have assured ourselves that the relevant connections will be maintained to the same extent as heretofore by adding to the same simultaneously the further tie of the solidarity of interests.[13]

This was quite a clever manoeuvre because the rapid growth of the bank meant that the different institutions could grow ever closer by this means as a sensible division of labour emerged between the branches and the headquarters without further bloating Berlin or intensifying the competition there as in the rural areas. To the other banks with which Deutsche Bank had allied itself in the Berlin money and capital markets, it was now able to offer all the necessary services and its international connections just as these banks ultimately brought their regional customer base into the broader purview of Deutsche Bank. Later, when Carl Fürstenberg lamented the lack of regionalisation of Berliner Handels-Gesellschaft, but then pointed out that one had possessed a sort of decentralised infrastructure as the 'bank of banks', Deutsche Bank was able to lay claim to this even more.[14]

As Deutsche Bank's regional presence grew stronger, so its foreign footprint also improved. Domestically, the bank was no longer exclusively concerned with the question of trade finance. The economic boom in Latin America, and especially in Argentina, seemed to be so significant that the bank wished to play a role in infrastructure development and company financing while it also strove to open doors for German companies seeking to gain a foothold there.[15] Deutsche Übersee-Bank (Banco Alemán Transatlántico), which was founded as a subsidiary of Deutsche Bank in Berlin, opened a branch in Buenos Aires as early as 1887. In order to obtain the right to print money, it acquired an Argentine government bond to the amount of 1 million pesos, but it became distressed relatively quickly. The reserves were soon used up; in 1890 and 1891 it stopped paying dividends.[16] A capital increase was needed, but this was not possible within the framework of the bank's statutes because in German law the existing capital had to be fully deposited before a capital increase could be undertaken; Deutsche Bank had avoided this and did not plan to pay up capital in full in the future either, so that it would be able to remain sufficiently flexible. Consequently, it made sense to found a new company and to provide the new institution, Banco Alemán Transatlántico, with higher equity capital. Of the 20 million marks intended, 40 per cent was initially paid up.[17] Banco Alemán Transatlántico expanded its branch network beyond Argentina initially into Chile and Peru. Conditions were favourable; the institution's contribution to the bank's income was satisfactory. However, the difficult situations in the individual Latin American countries, in which governments repeatedly had difficulty paying their bills, rendered it far from easy. And something Wallich later described in detail made itself readily apparent: what, in the end, was decisive as to whether the bank managed to establish a position of trust and thus a sufficient basis for its business in the various Latin American cities was the competencies, qualifications and characteristics of the responsible personnel on site.[18]

The Buenos Aires branch of Banco Alemán Transatlántico moved into the building at Calle Reconquista 31 in 1894.

Deutsch-Asiatische Bank (DAB),[19] with headquarters in Shanghai, did not have these problems when it began operating in 1890. It was founded in 1889 at the diplomatic behest of a banking syndicate led by Disconto-Gesellschaft (16.1 per cent); Deutsche Bank owned an 11.1 per cent share, and 11 other banks were also involved. The Chinese financial market proved to be rather closed off, particularly towards a new institution. Doing business there depended on so-called compradores. These compradores, which every foreign, and especially European, undertaking made use of in order to be able to do anything in China, were more or less independent Chinese businesspeople working for themselves who would contractually bind themselves to one or several foreign companies and work for them. The companies paid these brokers a fixed salary, but of course they also earned money from the transactions themselves in a manner that the companies could hardly control.[20] All the major European banks had to learn this the hard way. Shortly before the First World War, DAB even brought to trial a compradore who had illegally traded the bank's stamps to its detriment. The bank served the various German trading companies active in China and East Asia, in particular, and built up a business network for this purpose with branches in Tianjin, Hankou, Qingdao, Jinan and Beijing. Thus, the network was primarily located on the Chinese mainland but also extended to Japan and the British colonies in Hong Kong, Singapore and India. In 1896, DAB also managed to place a Chinese bond in the German capital market for the first time as a junior partner of the Hong Kong &

Shanghai Banking Corporation, followed by even further issuances. The forced lease of 1898, which granted the German Empire the use of Shandong peninsula with its capital city of Tsingtao for 99 years, opened up another lucrative business segment for DAB. It became a sort of state bank for the colony and became involved in the founding of Shantung Railway and Shantung Mining Company.

In the 1880s and 1890s, Deutsche Bank became so well established in Latin America, North America and East Asia – three important regions in the global economy – that it was gradually able to function as a comprehensive provider of banking services. In the United States, opportunities to establish its own operations were severely limited due to legal restrictions. In Europe, too, the bank sought opportunities to expand its business with the intention of strengthening its presence. From 1889, it was represented in Spain through its investment in Banco Hispano Alemán (together with the bank Arthur Gwinner & Co.); this later became a branch of Banco Alemán Transatlántico. In Italy,[21] where Georg Siemens had enjoyed close ties with the government from the early 1880s and worked as financial adviser of sorts, later bringing important Italian railway transactions to Deutsche Bank,[22] it participated in numerous government, municipal and railway bonds in the 1880s. In the case of the Italian railways, the result was not satisfactory. This was especially so because an open conflict erupted between Georg Siemens, who pushed for the investment, and the former railway president Paul Jonas, who had joined the Management Board shortly before this. According to Siemens, the bank lost important railway business to Disconto-Gesellschaft because Jonas hesitated.[23] The major difficulties in the promising but difficult Italian market prompted the interested German parties finally to join together in an Italian syndicate in 1890. This only occurred with the assistance of the German Empire's foreign policy, which sought to keep Italy on its side and thus supported any help in the financing of the Italian state.

Headquarters of Deutsch-Asiatische Bank in Shanghai around 1900.

Stock certificate of Banca Commerciale Italiana from 1914. Deutsche Bank participated in the founding of the leading Italian joint-stock bank in 1894.

Berliner Handels-Gesellschaft and Deutsche Bank led the syndicate. This syndicate was quite successful subsequently. It initially sold Italian government bonds on the German market and later also managed much of Italy's public borrowing needs, namely for its municipalities and railways.[24] Italy's extreme dependence on the German capital market had a great deal to do with the fact that French loans, which had traditionally played a major role in Italy and had always formed a part of French foreign policy, became harder to come by after the Triple Alliance of 1882. The German Empire's foreign policy interest and the banks' business policies coincided here. In order to gain even greater influence and perhaps bind Italy to it even more firmly, the syndicate founded Banca Commerciale Italiana in Milan in 1894, but the optimism for this was unfounded. Rather, interested parties in Italy succeeded in systematically pushing Deutsche Bank out of the institution over the course of several capital increases. Whereas Deutsche Bank had controlled three-quarters of the capital in 1895, its interest had become insignificant in 1914 while the Italian share had become dominant and French shareholders, too, developed a much greater importance.[25] Yet this also resulted from the German public's interest in Italian securities not being great enough, so that the bank's engagement was disappointing in the end, in Georg Siemens's opinion.[26]

Deutsche Bank's attempts to gain a foothold in Austria, and especially in Vienna, where, after all, it had participated in Wiener Bankverein since the 1870s, did not go much better.[27] Southeast Europe, and Austria as the gateway to this region, had certainly been important to the bank since the beginning of the project of the Anatolian Railway, but the conditions had to be right. When Bernhard von Bülow as the state secretary of the Foreign Office pointed out to Georg Siemens in May 1899 that the German envoy in Belgrade had made him aware there was an opportunity for a railway licence there, Siemens declined it. Although there was interest in principle in Serbian railway projects to close the last remaining gap in the oriental railways, the risk was not calculable because of the absence of institutional guarantees. The bank therefore decided not to invest in Serbia.[28]

4. Major Projects

The bank's 'regular business', which mostly took place quietly and unspectacularly, has long since faded in the memory, even if, at its core, it contributed more to the bank's success than the spectacular projects that drew the interest of the financial press and, indeed, the broad political public at that time.[29] The bank's involvement in the Anatolian Railway, followed by the construction of the Baghdad Railway, perhaps Deutsche Bank's most prominent project prior to 1914, caught the imagination of the German public early on, since this made it sound exotic and connected it with the desire for economic and political expansion. A popular caricature bearing the caption 'Full steam ahead towards Baghdad' portrayed Georg Siemens as an Anatolian Railway signalman indicating that the way forward was clear 'for German cultural work in the Orient'. Nevertheless, Deutsche Bank, as shown, above all, by its defensive behaviour on colonial initiatives, had fundamental reservations about political business before the turn of the century, but also beyond then if it could not be justified from a business point of view. In this, it was not so different from the British banks and financial agencies of the time, which were likewise always more interested in the use a potential deal could have for their company than in the colonial or foreign policy expectations of the respective government.[30] In colonial politics, Siemens long remained quite reserved, even if he did personally support colonial policy initiatives. Only after Germany's colonial power had been somewhat consolidated[31] did Deutsche Bank show openness towards attractive business opportunities, and specifically the construction of a railway in East Africa built along the lines of its experience in the United States and the Ottoman Empire;[32] this project began in the mid-1890s. Together with Wilhelm Oechelhäuser, Siemens explored the possibility of building a railway in East Africa in the mid-1890s and concluded that it was a worthwhile project.[33] However, his ambitions met with only modest interest from the colonial administration; a long battle ensued pertaining to the question of how much money and time should be put into it and, above all, which route the stretch of railway should take. This conflict was only resolved in 1900 when it was decided that a large railway line would be built. At this point, Deutsche Bank assumed the leadership of a syndicate for the newly founded Ostafrikanische Eisenbahngesellschaft (OEG), which was to build a railway from Dar es Salaam to the

'Full steam ahead towards Baghdad!' – Georg Siemens as a railway signalman in a caricature from the year 1900.

Great Lakes region of Africa and make a considerable contribution to connecting the giant territory. This was quite an attractive prospect, not least because it involved various sources of income (railway construction, construction financing and the operation of the railway) and friendly companies like the construction company Philipp Holzmann could likewise profit from it, but there was no great enthusiasm for the deal, which developed only slowly.[34] Support for the colony in south-west Africa developed along very similar lines; Deutsche Bank had participated early on in the colonial company for south-west Africa and remained loyal to it despite all its concerns. It would only pay off later.[35] Thus, Deutsche Bank was rather cautious overall in its colonial ambitions, which contrasted sharply with, say, Disconto-Gesellschaft, which was much more active in this field. But even the latter's involvement did not seem sufficient to contemporary observers, since 'the banks had restricted themselves up to this point primarily to the tasks that lay within the actual banking business for the colonies as well'; that is, they had geared their involvement soberly towards business prospects. Consequently, it was argued, a state or state-brokered colonial bank was needed.[36] This was something Deutsche Bank would definitely have had no interest in at this point (nor did it later).

Conditions in South Africa, in turn, were very different. There, the discovery of gold on the Witwatersrand had been attracting business since the 1880s. Nevertheless, their qualities required a very capital-intensive gold-mining operation, whereas in

California and Alaska it was still usual to acquire gold from individual gold-diggers, an 'inexpensive' process. The rapidly growing gold production in the Transvaal drove investors' expectations to such heights that, almost as a necessary consequence, the market for gold assets, overheated by speculation, declined sharply in the early 1890s. But it was exactly this situation that gave Deutsche Bank an opportunity. It had supported an expedition to South Africa that was to explore the South African terrain under the leadership of Siemens's brother-in-law, the metallurgist and mining engineer Adolf Görz. The expedition was promising so the bank financed a company in the name of Adolf Görz with £100,000 whose goal was to manage the 'acquisition of transactions concerned with the extraction of gold and other mining products'.[37] When prices for gold assets dropped in London and Johannesburg in 1890, the syndicate led by Deutsche Bank used the opportunity to acquire mines or shares in gold mines. In early 1893, the syndicate consolidated its extensive investments in gold mines in the company Adolf Goerz & Co. GmbH, into which, alongside German capital, British and French capital also flowed.[38] The company's headquarters was Berlin, and Adolf Görz ran the branch in Johannesburg. In 1895, Deutsche Bank's share of the company was worth 476,000 marks.[39] The company's capital amounted to 3.2 million marks, with an obligation to pay up the same amount later on.[40] Whereas Berliner Handels-Gesellschaft sold off most of its shares in the Goerz company 'in light of the tense political situation' before the Boer War began in October 1899,[41] Deutsche Bank took another path towards reducing the risk in case of a war between Great Britain and the Boer republics. It sought to develop closer relations with British investment groups in southern Africa. This also took into consideration that almost all the gold extracted in the Transvaal, and particularly the gold that came from German mines, passed through the British harbour Cape Town and the Bank of England to London. Consequently, co-operation with England was a necessity. The most important step in this co-operative endeavour was the transformation of the company into A. Goerz & Co. Ltd., with headquarters in Pretoria. The new company's capital amounted to around £1 million, and a part of it was deposited in early 1898 in London. The sale of the shares was largely completed in the first half of 1899. Deutsche Bank remained heavily invested in the company, even if its interest was smaller.[42] This company was more a financing company than a mining operation of its own, but already it failed to meet the financial expectations of the bank before the beginning of the Boer War. 'These sorts of difficult developmental transactions cannot be taken care of "on the side",' Siemens admitted with resignation.[43]

The 'African adventure' of the 1890s generated rather mixed results. The bank had already gained similar experience in the second half of the 1880s with its Argentine business. Georg Siemens and his colleagues on the Management Board regarded Argentina's boom – 'clearly discernible' from the figures for exports, customs, railway revenues, and so on – as 'just great'.[44] The bank's first endeavours at financing companies, therefore, were also quite successful. A gold bond of the regional bank of Buenos Aires, which had been acquired by an international group centred around Deutsche Bank, was heavily oversubscribed. Other similar transactions with the national bank, other regional banks, railway companies and property companies were added, with Deutsche Bank finally succeeding in pushing its way into the domain that had previously been exclusive to the British banks and co-operating with them. In the end, a large syndicate of sorts emerged including other European competitors as well, with Deutsche Bank and Disconto-Gesellschaft taking turns in taking the lead among German banks.[45] Yet just as the South African gold rush had rapidly led to speculative ventures, so the story of Argentine success began to unravel after a few years, eventually turning into a veritable crisis. The crisis that erupted in late 1890 became an existential one for the leading London bank Barings Brothers when Argentina ceased servicing its debt. Deutsche Bank participated in the bailout for Barings, but it hoped that the payment difficulties would only be temporary. Yet this was unrealistic, not only because the crisis grew more severe on account of other payment defaults but also because the European creditors had come into conflict with one another. In the end, the British side managed to prevail: it succeeded in ensuring that the restructuring measures undertaken primarily contributed to maintaining solvency for the benefit of British creditors by means of additional loans, whereas the other European payment demands came to be of secondary importance. Only in 1898 did it become possible to consolidate the older bonds and convert them into new ones that now granted German creditors certificates of 740 marks per 1,000 marks owed in the new Argentine debentures, which were at least regularly serviced in the period that followed. This did not fulfil all Siemens's wishes, but he did seem to find it 'acceptable'.[46]

These mixed results, if one is to take a positive view, were only made possible by means of countless negotiations, conferences and associated business trips, so they put a considerable strain on the bank's leadership, and especially on Georg Siemens, particularly because the situation in North America was growing critical at almost the same time. The restructuring of the Northern Pacific, which was tumbling into an existential crisis in 1892–3, became a question of fundamental significance for Deutsche Bank. After all, the bank's reputation and standing as a financial institution that could invest customers' assets safely and be a reliable adviser was at stake.[47] Moreover, the bank itself was no doubt also in danger of having to deal with significant losses. Thus, it was not possible for the bank to reach a decision about how it should proceed after the actual bankruptcy occurred in September 1893. On the one hand, avoiding losses would have suggested that the company's still considerable portfolio be sold to satisfy its creditors to the extent that this was possible; on the other hand, restoring the company, that is, maintaining it and restructuring it, could have been much more advantageous in the medium to long term. But this would require very differentiated insights into the situation in the United Sates and the ability to exercise the necessary influence over the restructuring of the company. Without yet having precise information, the bank initially tried to soothe German owners who possessed substantial debentures and assure them that everything that needed to be done in their interest was indeed being done. This bought time during which a direct intervention could be undertaken. Initially, the deputy chairman of the Management Board, Ludwig Roland-Lücke, travelled to New York, sending not very encouraging reports back to Berlin. Later, Georg Siemens himself travelled to the US, where he encountered a rather intransparent situation. The Northern Pacific, quite an impressive formation in terms of the length of its route, the property ownership and the companies and institutions that belonged to it, was heavily in debt. The profits, which were subject to strong fluctuations in any case, were not sufficient to bear the extensive interest and principal payments to service the debt. In addition, this situation lacked transparency because many individual transactions and contracts had been made on a credit basis or under conditions that did not make sense but, rather, fed the suspicion that the Northern Pacific had been prompted to take on unfavourable business by Villard himself out of greed. Although Siemens initially refused to disparage Villard in public, the bond between them had been broken. There was no longer a basis for trust. In conversations with Villard, the amicable tone that had been maintained, at least on the exterior, gave way. Accompanying her husband, Siemens's wife repeatedly reported in letters to her parents of serious conflicts and loud words being exchanged that were unmistakable even from the next room. 'A few days ago, here at the hotel,' Elise Siemens wrote to her father on 18 October 1893, 'there was a mean and also interesting discussion. Villard was here, and the gentlemen for once stated very clearly what they thought of him.'[48] In the autumn of 1893, Henry Villard was shown the door.

Still, his departure did not help much because the creditors and shareholders involved in the restructuring were of very heterogeneous natures. There was a danger that the Argentine experience would repeat itself. In addition to Deutsche Bank, the Rockefeller Group played an important role, but a Rothschild agent also took part, whereas the appointed receivers maintained close contact with the group centred on Henry Villard, who, though no longer active in operations, remained a substantial shareholder or creditor, respectively. In October 1893, these men agreed to establish a new management in which the various interested groups were to be represented. One of Georg Siemens's trusted associates was also given his position. At the same time, a replacement for Villard needed to be found who would act in the interests of Deutsche Bank in the future. People at the Berlin headquarters had to be able to trust that this representative would not combine his own business interests with those of Deutsche Bank in a risky manner. To express it in contemporary language, with Villard there had been a principal–agent conflict the entire time because Villard had by no means limited himself to representing the interests of Deutsche Bank in the United States, to arranging new and attractive projects for it and to handling these transactions in a proper manner. Villard had always also done business in his own name – business he neither lost sight of nor subordinated to the interests of the investors in Berlin when they were also in play. By contrast, he had obviously used his connections in Berlin to stabilise his own position in the United States and to shore up his risky way of doing business. In the end, there were individual transactions for which one could no longer tell whose concerns they were. Villard's successor, carefully chosen, would have to be scrutinised much more closely. The choice, following a suggestion Ludwig Roland-Lücke had made as early as October 1893, was for banker Edward D. Adams, a businessman who also had relevant banking experience and was very interested in co-operating with Deutsche Bank. He took up the position Henry Villard had held for the next 20 years – obviously a lucky find. With Adams, the bank for the first time had a real agent in New York who was also institutionally bound to its interests and was also now sufficiently compensated for his services.[49] Adams also arranged numerous underwriting deals for the bank; among others, Deutsche Bank underwrote portions of a government bond issue negotiated by JP Morgan.[50]

With this, the restructuring of the Northern Pacific Railway was far from complete, of course; rather, now a long, complex restructuring began. The battle between the various interests in the north-western American railways, which the participating companies and banks carried out utilising all available means, would intensively occupy Deutsche Bank employees for some time yet to come. Edward Adams was now a key player, dispatched to the Management Board of the Northern Pacific up to 1901, but this did not change the fact that Deutsche Bank was not able to participate successfully in the acquisition and competitive battles from Germany, even if Management Board members repeatedly travelled to the United States. Finally, the bank settled for 'the role of an observer'. This made sense. Practically, there was nothing anyone could do anyway. The restructuring of the railway and the sale of the shares in the Northern Pacific, whose price sometimes shot up on account of various acquisition battles, brought in good profits – $3.1 million after all, according to more recent calculations.[51] As Christopher Kobrak concluded, 'Northern Pacific was a seminal experience for Deutsche Bank. Perhaps the saddest aspect of the whole story is what it said about the characters of many of the people involved. [...] After the Northern Pacific saga, the reliability and good character of those with whom they worked played an even greater role in the investment analyses of Deutsche Bank managers.'[52]

American banker and industrialist Edward D. Adams (1846–1931) represented Deutsche Bank's interests in the United States until the First World War.

5. The Anatolian Railway

If Deutsche Bank's Argentine and North American experiences had already been influential in the second half of the 1880s, who knows whether its most spectacular project ever up to the present would have come about? This was surely a case of good luck because the bank's involvement in the Anatolian Railway, that is, incorporating western Asia Minor into the railway network, was probably one of the most successful projects that Deutsche Bank had financed and supported since the late 1880s. Because its history, but particularly the history of the project that succeeded it, the Baghdad Railway, is discussed extensively in the literature and in the previous anniversary writings of the bank,[53] it can be reported on here fairly briefly. It came about, like most of the major projects of the time, without the bank taking the initiative; rather, it fell into the bank's lap. Alfred Kaulla, a Management Board member of Württembergische Vereinsbank

who also worked for Mauser-Werke, visited Constantinople in 1887 in order to negotiate weapons deliveries for the Ottoman army.[54] During these negotiations, railway
projects were also mentioned, and Kaulla was left with the impression that the Ottomans
were not only very interested in these projects but also preferred to get financing from
German rather than British or French banks because the latter two's domination of the
administration of Turkish government debt was perceived as oppressive and one-sided.
Kaulla kept Kilian Steiner, the head of Württembergische Vereinsbank, apprised of these
negotiations. However, Steiner thought the deal was too big for his bank and recommended it instead to Georg Siemens, laying claim to only a reasonable investment for
his own bank in it. Siemens found the project interesting and thought too about a
possible syndicate, but leaned in the end towards a more reserved stance since he did not
wish for, say, Berliner Handels- or Disconto-Gesellschaft to participate. Yet he believed
that Deutsche Bank on its own would not be able to do it: 'After long consideration,
we have concluded that the employees we have available would not be sufficient for
carrying out an undertaking that would be so difficult and complicated, both in the
acquisition of the licence and in the supervision of its implementation,' Siemens wrote
to Kilian Steiner on 22 June 1888.[55] Moreover, Siemens was afraid of the challenges
posed by the Ottoman Empire, where the bank had no agency. This was a persuasive
argument that finally led to a peculiar division of labour between Württembergischer
Vereinsbank and Deutsche Bank: 'Vereinsbank brought the business, organised it, led
the negotiations – naturally in agreement with Deutsche Bank – this primarily took care
of the financing, a task that was certainly of decisive importance and could only have
occurred in a financial centre like Berlin.'[56]

The prospective task was indeed a major challenge. The Oriental Railway, which
connected Vienna to Constantinople, already existed. This was the field of interest of
the legendary Baron Maurice de Hirsch, who had financed the construction of a railway
in the European part of the Ottoman Empire and had also run it with an operating
company of his own. The repeated squabbles between the operating company and the
Ottoman government were put aside in the end; the Vienna–Constantinople line was
finally opened in the summer of 1888.[57] The length of time construction had taken
and the recurring conflict gave an indication of what Deutsche Bank could expect with
a railway in Asia Minor that was to extend from Constantinople to Ankara and, if
possible, beyond. Bismarck responded coolly to an inquiry in the Foreign Office that
petitioned the government to provide political backing for the project. Although he
gave assurances 'that [there are ...] no political concerns about the application for a
licence', he made it clear that the bank would exclusively bear the economic risk.[58]
Going it alone – this was also evident from Kaulla's negotiations – did not seem at all
advisable. An international financial syndicate that would control a construction and
operating company was to be favoured above all, which is also how the German ambassador in the Sublime Porte saw it.[59] In the negotiations it became apparent that the
Ottoman government did indeed prefer a German solution, but Kaulla was negotiating
simultaneously with the Turkish side and – underhandedly – with potential British and
French financiers. Georg Siemens, who favoured a joint German–British–French initiative anyway, found this entirely suitable, but the co-operation of the French-controlled

Telegram Alfred Kaulla sent from Constantinople to Georg Siemens in Berlin on 4 October 1888: The licence for the construction of the Anatolian Railway has been granted.

Ottoman Bank fell through – and very quickly this time. Kaulla came to an agreement with Vincent Caillard, an Englishman who behaved in Constantinople as if he were the representative of the City of London, but one could not tell how serious Caillard's assurances were. In any case, the Porte wished to have German leadership for the project, and when Deutsche Bank approved the underwriting of a railway bond for 30 million marks, a licence was finally granted on 4 October 1888. Shortly before this, the question of the short stretch that had already been built from Haidar-Pasha, the harbour on the Asian side of Constantinople, to Izmit was clarified. Deutsche Bank acquired this piece from a British syndicate in order to extend the line from Izmit to Ankara.

When the time came to put together an international financial syndicate, however, it became apparent that Vincent Caillard's claims to having British capital to back him were baseless. The City of London had no serious interest in the project. Thus, Deutsche Bank had to do something it had really not wanted to do, namely to take the project forward on its own. It negotiated a subscription/redemption price for the bond that was favourable for it and successfully sold it by itself or through its syndicate banks to the public. It passed on the Haidar Pasha–Izmit line it had purchased for 6 million marks to the newly founded Anatolian Railway Company for the actual price of 10 million marks. It founded construction companies for the Izmit–Eskişehir–Ankara line and later for the extension of the Eskişehir–Konya line, estimating construction costs to be so expensive that it profited in the end from the fact that the actual costs were considerably lower but the railway company paid the full price. Construction proceeded apace: the line initially extended to Eskişehir and then forked into routes to Ankara and Konya, which were completed in late 1892 and the summer of 1896 respectively: 'The commission was fulfilled to the centimetre.'[60]

The Anatolian Railway was a complete success not only because Deutsche Bank had been able to negotiate favourable conditions in the founding process and the construction proceeded according to plan; the operation of the railway itself also proved to be lucrative despite fluctuations. The experience was so positive that in October 1890 the bank took the initiative to push for the construction of the railway from Salonica to Monastir in the European part of the Ottoman Empire in a now proven manner, and it even acquired Baron de Hirsch's shares of the Oriental Railway. Consequently, Deutsche Bank at least financially controlled large parts of the railway connection from Central Europe to Constantinople and beyond to Asia Minor. Only in Serbia was there a gap, but conditions there were too uncertain for Deutsche Bank to make an investment.[61] The bank finally consolidated its railway interests in south-eastern Europe and in the Ottoman Empire in the financial holding company Bank for Oriental Railways located in Zurich, controlling it together with Credit Suisse, with whom it had developed friendly relations. The Bank für orientalische Eisenbahnen gradually acquired all Deutsche Bank's shares in the Asia Minor and European railways of the Ottoman Empire.

All this was successful, which is why Deutsche Bank seemed almost to be the natural financial partner when the question of extending the railway to Baghdad and the Persian Gulf came up towards the end of the Siemens era. Nevertheless, Siemens was not necessarily enthusiastic about the idea. It was clear to him that it might be difficult to obtain the international financing for the project he had in mind. However, he could not resist the project's attractions from a business perspective and the political expectations associated with it. Finally, the positive business outlook, which would also include the exploitation of mineral deposits found along the railway, as well as the bank's experiences with the construction of the Anatolian Railway, were decisive. Siemens did not see this deal through to its conclusion; this occurred in the era of his successor Arthur Gwinner, who shared Siemens's scepticism in light of the tremendous challenge it presented.

6. Industrial Financing in Germany

In the end, Deutsche Bank tended to pursue lucrative business opportunities in its international investments. There is no doubt that political factors played a role in this, as in the case of Italy or later the Baghdad Railway, and Deutsche Bank always regarded itself as a German institution that neither denied nor ignored the foreign policy interests of the empire. Nevertheless, it did not follow political demands nor was politics alone in a position to have a considerable influence on the bank in its business activity. In this sense, Deutsche Bank was no different from its international competition, which proceeded in a similar manner. Within Germany, nothing different would have been possible anyway. It was exclusively about pursuing business prospects.[62] In the late 1880s, the circumstances fundamentally changed because, after years of recession and a depressed mood, 'imagination' returned. German industry witnessed a rising cycle that persisted with short interruptions up until the First World War and brought the German Empire up to second place in the ranking of important economic nations. It caught up with and surpassed Great Britain, which had seemed so over-powerful for so long, at least in terms of the important data, and France even fell substantially behind.[63] Although the empire did not achieve the dynamic of the United States, the economy had a similar feeling. For the banks, this meant that project opportunities multiplied rapidly, and being well represented in the important industries of the future was now what mattered. The conditions for Deutsche Bank were favourable because it hardly had any holdover liabilities. In the end, however, coincidence also played a part in this. That Deutsche Bank became a key player in the emerging electrical engineering industry had little to do with Georg Siemens's family connections to the company Siemens & Halske. Rather, the opposite was the case because Werner von Siemens had long rejected the idea of financing his company and plans through capital markets. In some way, Deutsche Bank owed its entry into this lucrative business to Henry Villard because in 1884 he not only sought financiers for the railways of the north-western United States, but also represented the interests of Thomas A. Edison in selling his patents on the European market. Through the contact with Henry Villard, the management of the bank discovered electrical engineering's tremendous potential for the future after, among other things, inventions like the dynamo generator by Werner von Siemens[64] brought technology that much closer to making the use of high-voltage current possible. For Siemens & Halske, however, the national and international telegraph business and the laying of cable associated with that continued to form the core of its business, even if it did also experiment with some high-voltage technologies. Attempts to make advances in the question of lighting (cities) remained half-hearted; the technological solutions that were found were hardly able to compete with traditional gas lighting.[65] There was no interest in the use of Edison's patents. Consequently, Emil Rathenau was even more interested in them; he had a machine factory that had failed in the Panic of 1873 and was now looking for lucrative business opportunities.[66] Rathenau visited the Paris electricity exhibition at which Edison's lighting system was presented in 1881, and as an unemployed electrical engineer it fascinated him. Without thinking too hard about it, he acquired the rights to the German use of Edison's patents, which the Paris-based Compagnie Continentale Edison had owned, and went in search of people who would finance a company based on the use of the patents. Although he found financiers, these wished to sell the shares of a newly founded company directly on the stock market, which Rathenau considered too risky. He did, however, manage to get the banks to finance a study association to demonstrate the economic potential of Edison's inventions with various projects at the Munich electricity exhibition, among other places. This was also successful because Siemens & Halske had a rather imperious attitude towards Edison's process and was not even represented in Munich at this stage.[67] Werner von Siemens explicitly rejected the idea of co-operating with Rathenau, although he was clever enough to discuss the matter with Compagnie Continentale. Siemens & Halske undertook to recognise the patents in Germany and to refrain from entering into the lighting sector, and thus to give Rathenau a free hand.[68] In exchange, Siemens & Halske was granted the 'exclusive right to supply an Edison company' in Germany.

This cleared the way for the founding of a German Edison company focusing on the sector for expanding the lighting infrastructure in cities; in the end, a financial syndicate was found for this as well.[69] It was definitely advantageous for the new company that, in the division of labour fixed in the founding contract, Siemens & Halske also gave up the construction of electrical power plants and licence payments, settling for merely supplying the equipment.[70] Although there were disadvantages to this because Rathenau gave up parts of the construction of devices – in particular, that of dynamo generators and the lucrative business of manufacturing cables – this enabled him to avoid getting into what would have been a hopeless competition from the outset with the much larger company Siemens & Halske. Only later did the contract lead to considerable conflict, but in the beginning it at least allowed the project to get off the ground.

Deutsche Edison-Gesellschaft was founded in May 1883 by 11 natural and four legal entities, with Nationalbank für Deutschland as well as the banks Sulzbach and Landau providing more than four-fifths of the seed money, which they submitted for subscription just a short time later. Emil Rathenau assumed the directorship and also subscribed to a large block of shares. Felix Deutsch received power of attorney. In the same year, the engineer Oskar von Miller joined; Werner von Siemens had alienated von Miller at the Munich electricity exhibition organised by the latter, so the company was not only based on Rathenau's strategic leadership but also on the commercial competence of Deutsch and the technical expertise of Oskar von Miller. The new company rapidly took up its work. After a few quite prestigious projects involving the lighting of theatres, factories and business premises, the first public power plant was opened in 1885 in Berlin's Markgrafenstraße, and from there lighting for the surrounding district was started by means of underground cables and Edison lamps. Deutsche Edison-Gesellschaft did not manage this electrification itself but instead founded the Berliner Städtische Elektrizitätswerke for this purpose. However, its capital base quickly proved to be too small, particularly since the income situation fluctuated dramatically. This was because the supposed monopoly in the manufacture of light bulbs and use that was formally associated with Edison's patents could not be maintained in practice. New variations of light bulbs were constantly appearing on the market that could be legally challenged but with uncertain prospects of success, but this was not an economically viable path for the future. In the circumstances, only a tremendous expansion in the provision of electricity would have been helpful, but this is precisely what failed to happen as a result of the weak capital base of the Berliner Elektrizitätswerke,[71] which Deutsche Edison-Gesellschaft could not eliminate with subsidies either, especially since this would have created an imbalance between the parent company and its subsidiary. Rathenau refused to consider turning the power plant into a public work of the municipality as well, and instead went in search of sponsors in order to fundamentally rectify the situation. In part due to Henry Villard's mediation, Deutsche Bank now got involved, declaring itself willing to participate in a syndicate for a capital increase.[72] After the division of labour between Deutsche Edison-Gesellschaft and Siemens & Halske had been improved in that both had agreed to acquire the Edison patents for Germany (previously, Deutsche Edison-Gesellschaft had only possessed licences) and arranged for their joint use in accordance with the co-operative agreement from before, a path was opened for Georg Siemens to become personally involved. He assessed the prospects for the electrical industry strategically differently from his uncle and found the business model of the company to be founded, Allgemeine Elektricitäts-Gesellschaft (AEG), more attractive, telling his brother-in-law this in May 1894: 'Personally, I fall into a rather unpleasant conflict in this because my business interests lie on the side of A.E.G. whereas my sentiments pull me more towards the side of Siemens & Halske.'[73]

The founding of AEG, which replaced Deutsche Edison-Gesellschaft with a higher capital base, was not necessarily the work of Georg Siemens; but the ground for it had been prepared by Siemens's visits to America and his contact with Henry Villard, who, after all, had participated in the Edison companies. And it was Georg Siemens who took the initiative and, as will be shown below, did not orientate himself towards the interests of his cousin Werner von Siemens, who wanted to turn Deutsche Edison-Gesellschaft into a dependent subsidiary of Siemens & Halske.[74] Georg Siemens assessed the development of the electrical industry in a much more strategic manner than Werner von Siemens, who at least in the initial years of AEG still found himself very much in the tradition of low-voltage technology, with which Siemens & Halske had grown big. In the negotiations prompted by Henry Villard about the future of the German electrical industry between Werner von Siemens, Georg Siemens, Emil Rathenau and the American Edison Company, which was also interested in settling the situation in Europe, Georg Siemens consistently pursued the aim of creating a new, efficient player in the field of high-voltage technology. Only by means of these negotiations did it first become possible finally to separate from the French Compagnie Continentale, to formally transfer the patents to Siemens and later to AEG, as well as, in the end, to divide the labour between these two companies, which at least temporarily alleviated the competitive relationship. AEG was finally founded in 1887, constituting an independent actor with a large capital base that divided the high-voltage segment with Siemens & Halske. The latter company continued to function primarily as a supplier of equipment, whereas AEG operated the electricity business in a real sense (manufacture, supply, operation) and now even acquired certain rights in the construction of power plants.[75] Georg Siemens, the head of the financial syndicate, became a member of the Supervisory Board of the new company, taking over the chairmanship in 1890 from Rudolph von Sulzbach.[76] It was here that he probably got to know Carl Klönne quite well, who represented Schaaffhausen'scher Bankverein and who was later lured to Deutsche Bank.

Siemens & Halske, too, participated in financing AEG and was represented on its Supervisory Board, so it experienced AEG's tumultuous development in the following years first-hand. Major technological projects (rotary current, long-distance electrical lines, etc.) were a part of this success story, whereas the turbulent expansion of the electro-technological infrastructure in the cities in Germany and abroad, as well as the breakthrough of electricity as an everyday source of energy in industry, made up the other side. At this point, Siemens & Halske's representatives would have recognised that they had underestimated not only Emil Rathenau but the entire field of high-voltage technology as well, and they would also have noticed that Werner von Siemens's way of running the company, which was critical of the capital market, had reached its limit. By contrast, AEG Group that gradually emerged from Berliner Handels-

Allgemeine Elektricitäts-Gesellschaft (AEG) resulted from the transformation of Deutsche Edison-Gesellschaft in 1887.

Gesellschaft under the leadership of Rathenau, Georg Siemens and Carl Fürstenberg made corporate history.[77] The system of constructing a group was not new, but it was utilised in a particularly consistent way with AEG. Unquestionably the way Deutsche Bank had organised its involvement in the Anatolian Railway was a pattern that could be copied. And AEG's international expansion, especially, proceeded according to the same pattern. For example, a licence was acquired for constructing and operating a tram system in Genoa, with financing having been previously secured via a syndicate for that purpose. Then, a local operating and possibly also construction company was founded, which in turn was financed by the syndicate. Meanwhile, its shares were given to the licence owners or sold on the stock market by the syndicate. As long as the banking syndicate held together, AEG itself only needed a relatively small share to control the company. If the local company expanded, AEG in turn invested in the capital increases in accordance with its original share, which, after the acquisition of new shares at the parity price, were then sold at current – usually significantly higher – rates, so that AEG, while maintaining its absolute share, even managed, under some circumstances, to earn considerable additional profits. Besides this, it profited, above all, from the dividends of its affiliated subsidiaries, but both Georg Siemens and Emil Rathenau were by their own accounts not motivated by personal profit. They were concerned with forming and controlling groups that were intelligently financed – and also wished to gain personal recognition. The foreign undertakings were supposed to protect AEG and its banking syndicate from the consequences of international conflicts. As a result, they incorporated the group of companies into Bank für elektrische Unternehmungen (Elektrobank) in Zurich, which was created for this purpose in 1895. This became a financial holding company controlled by Deutsche Bank and Berliner Handels-Gesellschaft for AEG's foreign electrical business.[78] There were similar attempts to consolidate business in Germany as well, primarily driven by the desire to divide the risk of the extremely rapidly expanding industry and make it controllable. Gesellschaft für elektrische Unternehmungen founded in 1894 is a salient example of this: it was created by Ludwig Loewe & Co. and AEG together with a banking syndicate – this time without Deutsche Bank.[79] The principle was the same as in the case of the organisation of the Oriental and Anatolian Railways: Deutsche Bank had not invented it then, either, but up to the founding of a Swiss financial holding company it had perfected it. Emil Rathenau took up this concept and also implemented it so consistently, according to his biographer Felix Pinner, because he had become very pessimistic since his bankruptcy during the Panic of 1873 and wanted to keep AEG's capital as untouched as possible by the subsidiary structuring, not to mention the tremendous build-up of reserves he almost neurotically engaged in. In the end, the corporation not only had enormous reserves but also tremendous cash deposits at various banks, so that it could handle any possible crisis.[80]

The development of a nested 'deep trust', as the business journalist Felix Pinner calls it, enabled AEG not only to grow very rapidly; it also allowed it to participate in the 'markets game'. From the second half of the 1890s at the latest, the purchase and – when possible – successful sale of blocks of shares was considered on a par with the electricity business, although Rathenau always made sure that he maintained his controlling position in the latter. AEG was so successful in the end that the ceasefire with Siemens & Halske negotiated in 1887 collapsed. This was because Siemens & Halske abandoned its antipathy towards the capital market after Werner von Siemens's death so that it could grow rapidly on its own. In 1894, the contractual division of business with AEG, now perceived as obstructive, was ended. AEG and Siemens & Halske entered into open competition, which meant that Georg Siemens had to take a side. He resigned his seat on the Supervisory Board of AEG and another Deutsche Bank representative took it up, whereas Deutsche Bank relinquished its leading role in Berliner Handels-Gesellschaft.[81]

AEG could now expand freely and did so.[82] Yet now the transformation of Siemens & Halske also accelerated. The rivalry between the two 'ruthless and pitiable fellows', as Georg Siemens put it,[83] increased decisively both in Germany and abroad, which, in Georg Siemens's words, again, bore the seed of a severe crisis since both companies and other companies in the sector as well were expanding too much, building up considerable excess capacities. The number one man at Deutsche Bank was by no means innocent in this. He had helped put AEG on track, and Siemens & Halske, too, had opened itself to the capital market with his energetic assistance. In 1897, the company was transformed into a joint-stock corporation, which, although the family maintained its ownership, could now be more aggressive. In the following years, Georg Siemens always made an effort to steer the competition into orderly paths and to improve co-operation among the companies, which also succeeded, for example, in the Russian and Latin American markets. But in Germany the conflict was merciless. Georg Siemens was not successful, either. Although the dialogue with AEG was never broken off, Siemens &

In 1897 Siemens & Halske was transformed into a joint-stock company with the help of Deutsche Bank: stock certificate from the same year.

Halske did not wish to come to an agreement. Siemens regarded Rathenau as the 'most hard-working electric businessman',[84] but he had to disappoint him when Rathenau invited him to return to AEG's Supervisory Board. This was a bitter pill to swallow not only on a personal level; he also viewed the lack of an agreement as a serious business mistake because the bloated electrical industry was imperiously calling for a structural adjustment that would come one way or another. As an alternative to the competition, Georg Siemens envisaged a large trust of electrical companies in which AEG and Siemens & Halske would invest:

> It is a matter of making preparations to find the best way to arrange the great liquidation in electricity for the fatherland, how one arranges it so that the factories and companies endangered in this liquidation are taken up so that general despondency and general ruin will not occur. I had hoped that Siemens & Halske would understand this without any more being said. Now the opposite has occurred. I received letters from Carl Siemens and from you [his brother-in-law Hermann Görz, who worked for Siemens in Russia] that would be quite reasonable if we were facing a normal future, but they just prove that none of you understand at all what this is about. But I have finally thought the matter over. I am over 60 years old and have no obligation to make people happy against their will. I was a fool when I left A.E.G. in order to help Siemens & Halske out of the situation it was in. I would be a fool a second time if I got involved again to build

bridges that would have given Siemens & Halske the opportunity to participate in the upcoming adjustment of the electrical market. That is why I explained to Rathenau that I am going back on my promise.[85]

Georg Siemens was noticeably discouraged and pessimistic, which may well have made his resignation from the bank's Management Board shortly thereafter at least easier to bear. His efforts to mediate had been well meant, he said: 'But in this case, too, my old bad luck has struck that I see things that must of necessity occur two or three years too early and am regarded as a fool by all the people if I make the necessary preparations.'[86] This was in October 1900; mere weeks later he gave up his responsibilities on Deutsche Bank's Management Board and resigned from the company. His prognosis concerning the structural adjustment in the electrical engineering industry would come to pass in the following years, although the restructuring proceeded differently from how he had wished. Despite all the conflicts, the financing of the electrical engineering industry counts among Deutsche Bank's greatest success stories prior to 1914. The major foreign projects that kept it closely associated with AEG will be discussed elsewhere.[87]

By contrast, the experiences in another case were less good. In the industrial boom of the time, the need for efficient pipes grew exponentially. Seamless pipes were a major future project for which the brothers Max and Reinhard Mannesmann, who had studied with Franz Reuleaux at the Technische Hochschule in Charlottenburg, had a solution – supposedly the right one – patented in 1886. It was then a trusted friend of Reuleaux, Werner von Siemens, who not only heard about the Mannesmanns' idea early on but who also secured the licensing rights for the process of manufacturing one's own pipes in Great Britain. Entering into the industrial – that is, electrical engineering – use of these patents made sense; it was probably not difficult for Werner von Siemens to gain Deutsche Bank's support for initiatives along these lines. In 1890, Deutsch-Österreichische Mannesmannröhren-Werke was founded with equity capital of 35 million marks, largely provided by Deutsche Bank; the Mannesmann brothers' inclusion of the patents in this was valued at 16 million marks. In order to pre-empt possible criticism in his own company, Georg Siemens personally invested, according to his biographer Helfferich, 'for his financial circumstances rather considerable sums' in the founding.[88] This had already turned out badly once before, namely in the case of the Direct Cable Company, and there were already signs of a similar disaster shortly after the founding because finding a way to use the patents in major industry proved rather difficult. In fact, it was only possible to produce marketable pipes after numerous connector improvements were made, yet these met with serious competition and were even boycotted by other pipe manufacturers. The management also proved to be commercially in over its head; the factory lost money, and a quarrel – which did not remain hidden from the public – erupted between the sponsors and the management of the Mannesmann brothers.[89] Siemens's involvement hung in the balance, particularly since Werner von Siemens was only kept on board after much pleading. Operations in Bohemia and in the Bergisches Land did not start up, the share price dropped and there was no realistic prospect of selling the shares without considerable losses. The bank faced the question of whether to break off the project with significant losses or to finance it until a technically satisfactory operation could be guaranteed as the basis of exploiting the economic opportunities. The bank chose the second option. Max Steinthal devoted himself to this for a considerable time. The final result was then reasonably satisfactory, but it had required a long, nerve-racking involvement which, at its core, did not really fit into the banking business. In 1893, the Mannesmann brothers were forced out of the management, and after that construction began on a new factory in Düsseldorf where pipes could be produced profitably with an improved process. Hostilities with the other pipe manufacturers were put aside, and the company proceeded to develop peacefully. In 1896, the company started to become profitable, and in 1900 the Mannesmann brothers were paid off. Later the capital base was reduced whereby the company bought up the shares of its shareholders at a discount. Only for 1905–6 could a dividend be paid, and only in the following year were the shares first publicly offered on the Berlin stock exchange. Georg Siemens had been dead for six years by then.

7. Criticism of the Banks' Involvement

Most market participants, and especially also the interested political public, still remembered clearly the Panic of 1873 when stock prices declined and many equities and bonds sank below their initial prices again in 1892–3. The strategy of the preceding years – to get around the domestic investment crisis by investing more abroad – did not seem to be reaching a successful conclusion. Rather, many Germans who had bought foreign securities prepared themselves for bitter losses and now blamed the banks because they had pushed these securities on to the German market on a grand scale particularly in the late 1880s. While Siemens and his colleagues on the Management Board concerned themselves with the bank's reputation, which was further burdened[90] by a scandal involving a bank employee's forging of brokers' certificates,[91] they also kept the interests of their customers in mind, whose trust was vital to the bank's economic success. However, the interested German public had very different concerns. In the end, it was all the same to the bank whether the poorly performing assets were domestic or foreign, but the German public – not least those interested in inexpensive loans – eyed the foreign securities, above all, with suspicion. During the period when capital appeared to be abundant, many projects had proceeded without comment, but now the banks with international involvement came under severe criticism, being accused of squandering German capital abroad instead of utilising it for the really 'patriotically important' financing of, say, agriculture or public works. Ostensibly, the criticism of capital export seemed justified, particularly since numerous foreign investments were associated at least temporarily with considerable losses. Such criticism missed the mark because the share of exports on the total issuances of the German capital market had declined drastically in the economic boom of the 1890s anyway.[92] Consequently, the bank could calmly point to the figures and repudiate the relevant accusations with regard to its business policy, in which loans and issuances for government entities, be they the empire, individual states or various municipalities, played a growing role.[93] This was the point that was not to be underestimated when repudiating the propaganda against the squandering of German national wealth, which was presented by the agriculturalist side and often carried anti-Semitic overtones.[94] When the extension of the Reichbank's mandate was negotiated in 1899, the conflict revolved precisely around the question of the extent to which the Reichsbank should orientate itself towards the logic of the international money and capital markets, the gold standard or, rather, towards the interests of German borrowers like agriculture, which Deutsche Bank believed would have been fatal.[95]

Still, from this point on the problem would remain acute. There were recurring shortages in the German money and capital markets, which simply were not in a position, despite all the growth, to simultaneously stem the tide of important capital exports, to finance rapidly expanding domestic industry and to satisfy the increasing financial needs of the public sector. These shortages would become a constant theme. Especially risky foreign business came under considerable pressure to prove its legitimacy. Even though one could repudiate the public criticism of dangerous, damaging foreign investments by giving good reasons, there was still the problem of determining the options for dealing with payment defaults. This was because what could initially be dealt with in the everyday business as an individual problem – that is, the solidity of individual major financial investments – presented itself as a fundamental challenge of the international business sector in light of the limited possibilities of the German money and capital markets: how could one adequately calculate the risks of major investments in order to be able to make responsible decisions? Moreover, how should the interests of the banks and the investors be protected when individual, and especially major, debtors turned out to be untrustworthy or when major investments failed and the bank as well as its customers were threatened with tremendous losses?

Consequently, the question of necessary information was also crucial. This was nothing new, but now it took on new dimensions. In the older bank practice, the majority of banks had reacted to this challenge by developing informal information networks. The relevant correspondence about the solidity of individual borrowers or certain transactions became a cornerstone of the banking business, both in order to avoid mistakes in the granting of loans and also to be prepared for fluctuations in stock prices. Partly for this reason the relevant information networks were also jealously maintained and kept from the public in order to give one's own bank an informational advantage in case of doubt and, thus, important room to manoeuvre in relation to the competition. Rothschild bank was absolutely legendary with regard to this.[96] From the beginning, Deutsche Bank, too, had relied on informal structures of this sort, and over time it managed to effectively hedge its own decisions by this means, as the business correspondence and the friendly ties to important people at other banks, companies and in the political realm show. But these networks, as complex as they became over time, were almost amateurish in light of the tremendous abundance of projects at that time, particularly since the capital market segment had actually gone global, but the information networks were not at all so, at least in the beginning. Structures of this sort had to be established gradually with the branches of Banco Alemán Transatlántico, for example, in Latin America, which could not always be achieved without ruffling feathers. It only seemed as if the situation was easier in the United States, not to mention Africa and Asia. Deutsche Bank never managed to penetrate the market in China despite its investment in Deutsch-Asiatische Bank; the bank remained dependent on the mediation of the local compradores, whose honesty and reliability, even in the best cases, could only be hoped for.[97] In addition, the banks suffered from the fact that the book-keeping in the companies they co-operated with (and *had* to co-operate with) was often anything but complete, let alone transparent. False or incomplete figures did not always entail a fraudulent intention. Often project leaders and company managers either did not know the actual financial status of their own companies, or they had lost track of the revenues and obligations as well as their relevant timelines. Book-keeping in companies only gradually began to be carried out professionally in the last third of the nineteenth century. It would take even longer in some countries for clear legal regulations to be drawn up and for critical invoice auditing to emerge.[98] In a way, Henry Villard and the Northern Pacific Railway summed up all these faults to a tee: mismanagement, dishonesty, an overactive imagination and outright deficiencies in the book-keeping formed a toxic mix, which, in the end, threatened to ruin a business idea that was actually both promising and profitable. Georg Siemens summed the problem up himself in another case, that of Deutsche Bank's South African gold mine interests, in 1899:

> [We] were not up to the technical leadership because all the information and aids that one can easily obtain in London were almost unattainable for us. Thus, we always only had the choice of entrusting the management of our money to people we did not sufficiently know or managing it ourselves and making mistakes and omissions in the process that held up or even damaged development.[99]

In 1890, Deutsch-Amerikanische Treuhand-Gesellschaft was founded as a subsidiary of Deutsche Bank and the Frankfurt bank Jakob S. H. Stern, the first of its kind in Germany. It was initially supposed to actively act, above all, in the interests of German investors when investments in America were performing poorly,[100] but this new institution rapidly expanded its sphere of activity, which was not surprising in light of the circumstances described. Representing investor interests quickly faded into the background whereas another function became more important – the auditing of companies in the context of capital market activities.[101] There certainly was a willingness among companies to subject themselves to this sort of procedure because the management of many a company hoped, with good reason, to gain favourable financing conditions if the assessment was positive. Gradually, Deutsch-Amerikanische Treuhand-Gesellschaft became a general monitoring and auditing company whose services were primarily utilised by domestic businesses. At the same time, Deutsche Bank strategically sought to expand its customer base. Through the institution, which soon shortened its name to Deutsche Treuhand-Gesellschaft (1892), it was discovered that the recommendations of the company's own Supervisory Board members from Deutsche Bank and other participating banks and companies were what prompted new candidates to seek an audit. The Supervisory Board of the Treuhand-Gesellschaft was consequently expanded to include bankers from whom the relevant network effects promised to arise. This succeeded so well that the number of audits rose sharply and important companies even allowed themselves to be monitored without demur. As Arthur Gwinner later admitted, the trust did not earn any money through this; it paid its rather substantial dividends out of

Registered share of the Northern Pacific Railway Company from 1897 issued to Deutsche Bank.

the profits from syndicate and speculative business that was carried out on the coat-tails of Deutsche Bank.[102]

The major advantage of auditing balance sheets derived from the systematic acquisition of information, which was complemented by the collection of facts that had heretofore been gathered by the Archive, which was later transformed into the Economics Department. Although the monitoring and auditing reports were confidential, the mere fact that employees of the trust company would routinely review the commercial and technical working process of a company must have prompted a considerable push toward professionalisation. In any case, the trust company's success was so sweeping that almost all of the major banks followed Deutsche Bank's example after the turn of the century, creating similar institutions. Meanwhile, this extended the trust's activities systematically to southern Germany and beyond the borders of the empire to Austria and Switzerland. In doing so, the bank consistently utilised the procedure of putting interested bankers on the trust's Supervisory Board. This expansion was so successful that it provoked critics among the public who questioned the legitimacy of this sort of institution in the hands of a major bank because, they claimed, this situation did not guarantee either objective monitoring or the necessary secrecy. Alfred Lansburgh, the editor of the trade journal *Die Bank*, ultimately regarded the trust as 'an office of the major bank behind it'.[103] The bank might have formally disputed this, but in fact the declared aim of the formation of the trust company was the procurement of information for the benefit of bank decisions. This connection was most compellingly expressed in the fact that decisions about 'large loans and also capital market transactions were made dependent on a preceding audit of the company in question'.[104]

As a result, the trust company also signalled a break in the bank's decision-making tradition. When Arthur Gwinner (who was ennobled in 1908) took over Georg Siemens's position as the 'foreign minister' of the bank in 1901, this shift constituted more than a mere change in personnel. Up to the end of the Siemens era, even though staff size increased dramatically, the bank had basically been run by a small cadre of managers, with experience, business sense and energy being the decisive criteria. Until the stock law of 1884, the four-man Management Board had nevertheless still been integrated into the Committee of Five of the Administrative Board, which did more than just curb activity but also gave more than competent advice. After the formal authorisation of the Management Board in 1884–5, but above all when the economy began to pick up in the late 1880s, business expanded dramatically, initially in foreign securities projects and later in a much more pronounced way as a consequence of the dynamic development of industry and infrastructure in Germany itself. The limits of this kind of leadership quickly became apparent in the struggles of the previous Management Board members to stay on top of everything, and they quickly gave up – first of all, Hermann Wallich, then Georg Siemens, and finally Max Steinthal. They were replaced not only by more people; rather, more than anything, the numerous internal processes, and especially the procurement of information and the division of labour, were professionalised. This happened not only at Deutsche Bank. All the major banks had to react to the massive expansion of business because the risks were growing and it was no longer possible to decide whether to enter into them or manage them purely instinctively, even if that instinct – a sense of promising business prospects – would continue to be of major and even central importance.

IV. On the Path to Success: The Gwinner Era, 1901–1914

1. In the Wilhelmine Economic Miracle

At the turn of the century, the Siemens era had come to an end. At the same time, many other things came together that were weighing on the German economy. Due to sinking prices in the US, a sure-fire indication of a downturn in the economic cycle in the late nineteenth century, recessionary phenomena could be observed around the world.[1] As Georg Siemens had already suspected, in light of exaggerated speculation in the electrical industry, an economic downturn was also bound to have grave consequences, because it was linked to a structural correction of the entire industry. The electrical industry was not the only booming sector in the second half of the 1890s. Things were quite similar in the chemical industry. Even the 'old' heavy industries – mining as well as iron and steel – were still experiencing exceptional rates of growth. Amid the crisis, these industries were only able to maintain their position inasmuch as corporate mergers – and especially the cartelisation of Ruhr coal mining in the Rhenish-Westphalian Coal Syndicate – were keeping prices stable; these had fluctuated sharply in the past as the economy moved forward.[2] However, the crisis was also directly impacting the financial sector since, due to population growth and robust urbanisation, the construction industry was one of the most dynamic sectors of the economy, its expansion having been made possible chiefly by real estate credit. The collapse of Deutsche Grundschuldbank, part of Preußische Hypotheken-Aktienbank, came as a major shock to the financial sector, and it was compounded by the payment problems of nine other mortgage banks.[3] Once again confidence in the soundness of German money and capital markets had been undermined. The problems of the German financial sector not only caused a stir domestically but also abroad, where they were most accurately registered. Even though the mortgage sector, made more restrictive by legislation in 1899, succeeded in restructuring fairly quickly,[4] the financial shock to banking was considerable: securities backed by real estate were an extremely popular form of investment among the public at large. Many Deutsche Bank customers had acquired securities from the mortgage banks as well and were now faced with price slumps and interest shortfalls. Deutsche Treuhand-Gesellschaft proved a success when it came to restructuring the mortgage banks and representing the interests of investors who had acquired appropriate securities.[5] Similarly, Deutsche Bank played a pivotal role in the structural adjustment of the German electrical industry that was eventually divided into two large groups under the leadership of AEG and Siemens. This was because, completely consistent with its times, the bank viewed the gradual emergence of 'industrial duchies' not as a danger but a rational response to technological change, as well as a meaningful correction of competition that had been tending towards excessive speculation.

From the crisis of 1900, following upon the best year in the economic history of the nineteenth century in 1899, the bank itself emerged relatively unscathed. In its 1901 annual report, Deutsche Bank saw the economic downturn as having passed, yet the expected economic recovery did not really take off until 1902. According to the bank, this was also because a further increase in stamp duties had once again made it more expensive to conduct business on the stock exchange. At the same time, a dispute over customs levies had been raging in trade and customs policy, and it was not clear which tariffs would determine German foreign trade policy going forward. Consequently, the prime interest rate was also low, as was demand in the money markets; the bank's business opportunities suffered as well. Deutsche Bank's profits had been stagnating since 1900 and would only visibly improve in the 1903 fiscal year. At that point, interest rates began to increase, as did the demand for credit. Business in the following years was excellent. In 1905, the Management Board even spoke of one of the 'best years ever' and the bank was able to distribute a total of 12 per cent in dividends on its nominal capital.[6] In 1907–8, as a result of an American crisis, Germany experienced an economic slump as well. That said, the economic climate remained positive for almost the entire decade prior to the war. The money and capital markets were heavily utilised. The crisis of 1907–8 did little to alter this situation, as the Bank of England and the Reichsbank kept their interest rates high during the downturn in order to avoid large outflows of gold to the US. The high interest rates, in turn, restricted the refinancing capability of many institutions whose liquidity sometimes seemed to be in a rather critical state. The utilisation of money and capital markets was therefore repeatedly a subject of discussion. While Deutsche Bank rejected foreign rumours about weaknesses in Germany's financial markets, it was also critical of the German public sector's utilisation of those markets as it alleged that this sector was engaged in unnecessary government spending.

Nonetheless, none of this called the bank's own position into question. In 1913 Deutsche Bank achieved a net profit of about 36 million marks, compared to around 20 million marks at the beginning of Gwinner's tenure. Between 1900 and 1913, the bank consistently paid dividends of between 10 and 13 per cent on registered share capital, which then rose in the same period from 150 million to 200 million marks. In 1914, that capital increased finally to 250 million marks in the course of the acquisition of Bergisch Märkische Bank. The reported reserve assets had grown from around 50 million to 115 million marks in that same period, i.e. to 57.5 per cent of the share capital. The growth of Deutsche Bank was also reflected in other indicators, such as the number of clients and account holders, the number of employees and the number (and geographic reach) of its transactions. Moreover, the bank was clearly at the top of the German financial world in 1913 in terms of its number of Management Board members and authorised representatives, as well as its functional organisation and regional agencies. It was not only admired but greatly envied as well; it similarly garnered criticism for supposedly pursuing expansion aggressively. There were certainly reasons for this, but the fierce competition was not just being promoted by the bank itself. Rather, domestic and international financial markets served as the field of play for an array of highly competitive institutions. Even if Deutsche Bank had behaved more cautiously, it would hardly have minimised the larger rivalries; other banks would have jumped into the fray. Nor was there anything on the horizon to suggest that the world would soon be facing a great catastrophe, much less a military one, on account of these conflicts. Today there is scholarly consensus that the banks had an interest in maintaining positive, stable conditions for business but not in pursuing war or major conflicts, because doing so might put at risk everything they had achieved up until then.[7] To the bankers involved, it was clear that their institutions, their competitors and the diplomacy of international finance were all part of politics on the global stage. Georg Siemens had already proclaimed that 'the times are forever past when it would have been considered possible to maintain pleasant political relations between two governments at the same time as their nations were moving toward economic conflict'.[8] Yet the converse was equally true.

In everyday banking in the Gwinner era, such escalations of financial diplomacy were not unheard of. Nor should they in any way be seen as a warning sign of the First World War, because such an interpretation would suggest a logic that in retrospect was simply not discernible before 1914. Still, it was not 'business as usual' either; things were not merely being continued under Gwinner that had been commenced under Siemens. By the 1890s, the bank's organisational and personnel structures had begun to change, a process that would only accelerate after the turn of the century. The bank's upper echelons grew larger as well as more complex. As the number of Management Board members increased, so too did the number of departments assigned to them, something that was not necessarily caused by the internationalisation of the business itself. Of the 13 members of the Management Board in the final pre-war years, five of them had a clear connection to business conducted abroad. There was Arthur Gwinner himself and – at his side since 1908 – Karl Helfferich, whose particular bailiwick was the railways in the Ottoman Empire. At times, Ludwig Roland-Lücke was in charge of the American business as well as Morocco and trade finance. Then there was Elkan Heinemann for foreign investments, and finally Paul Millington-Herrmann, who was responsible for the foreign branches in addition to the German ones.[9] In the 1890s, the bank's business in domestic industry had grown considerably; for that, the credit went to Max Steinthal and later Carl Klönne, along with Oscar Schlitter, who had come from Bergisch Märkische Bank. There was still no clear individual responsibility for certain tasks. In principle, the bank adhered to a 'strict collegial charter', according to a 1910 issue of the financial newspaper *Plutus*, citing an informant connected to the bank on why the public impression that the bank was led by a few men was not accurate. In the bank's 'decisions and transactions … the publicly lesser-known members were much more involved than the outside world assumes'.[10]

The workload at the bank was enormous, what with its international presence and a domestic one about to go nationwide. (In addition to seven domestic branches, Deutsche Bank had 15 permanent stakes in other banks.) Since a technical rationalisation of operations seemed neither possible nor (really) desirable,[11] the volume of work at the bank could only be managed by greater industriousness, improved organisation and – if not otherwise feasible – by expanding the number of employees. All three of those factors

Arthur Gwinner (1856–1931, ennobled in 1908) joined the Management Board of Deutsche Bank in 1894; in 1910 he became its Spokesman. Since the major foreign projects were in his hands, he had already been considered Georg Siemens' real successor even before that.

were essential; if nothing else, it appears that Gwinner played an instrumental role in keeping up the pace of the work. The inefficiency that seemed to have reigned under Georg Siemens quickly came to an end under Gwinner. The more precise structuring of the so-called 'Secretariat', which oversaw the syndicate business, and the office work was obviously his doing. It can also be traced back to his demands inasmuch as he also found himself at the limits of his own resilience. After all, due to nervous strain, he was absent for several months in 1904–5, spending that time being treated at a spa in the Black Forest. His contact with colleagues on the Management Board was maintained during that period by Emil Georg Stauß, Georg Siemens's former assistant. After Gwinner returned to work in Berlin, further steps were taken at restructuring the work. Above all, additional or deputy Management Board members were called upon to manage certain tasks. Among them was the aforementioned Karl Helfferich, who initially led operations in Constantinople and was formally promoted to the Management Board after 1910; he was followed by Emil Georg Stauß, who took over the bank's oil interests from Gwinner. It was no later than at this point that Gwinner modified his own work routines. He no longer appeared early for work at the bank but had his personal secretary come to his home in the morning to help with important tasks, and there he was able to dictate his first responses or statements on matters. Gwinner would then not show up at the bank until the 'board breakfast', as the late morning meal was referred to. After a (much later) midday meal, he would take appointments or hold smaller meetings.[12] He would not return home before 7.30 p.m. However, this way of arranging his work day meant more space to work uninterrupted, thereby allowing him to devote himself to matters other than the daily business of Deutsche Bank, matters such as monetary, currency, or banking policies.

This restructuring of office work and the expansion of personnel at the top level were therefore intended to relieve the individual Management Board members of excessive obligations. In the case of Siemens, Gwinner thought he had witnessed what could happen if an individual lacked organisational skill or was chronically overburdened. Following that midday meeting of the Management Board, of course, the 'treadmill' would really commence for the clerical staff, something which many of them evidently complained about. When *Plutus* praised Gwinner on the occasion of his appointment to the Prussian parliament in spring of 1910,[13] a member of the secretariat or another well-informed insider sent a long letter to the editor (Georg Bernhard), highlighting a side of Gwinner omitted by the article. Not only was Gwinner 'petty-minded' in money matters, but he also possessed that 'trait shared by many with abundant energy [who] expect their employees to work at the same pace. Gwinner is quite stressed; he has been known to work at home for several mornings in a row. If he arrives late in the afternoon at the bank, i.e. when the most serious work time begins for those employees who must work directly under him, then the workday does not end at the usual time. His subordinates rarely get an opportunity to leave early, especially on Saturdays. I am primarily writing these lines to you,' concludes the anonymous informant, 'in the quiet hope that if Mr von Gwinner reads them he may be persuaded that they are not entirely unjustified. Then again, I am also aware that you care about distributing light and darkness as justly as possible. For ultimately, the glowing portrait that you have painted of Mr von Gwinner can also tolerate some more shading without losing its appeal.'[14] The existence of this letter is not only important because it shed light on everyday work in the bank; it is also significant that its author apparently could not think of another way to impress upon Gwinner the problematic side of his work behaviour than by writing an anonymous letter. Apparently, it was not possible to express reservations or criticisms at a business workplace that deemed itself so 'democratic'. For well-informed outsiders, the impression was reinforced that '[t]he Deutsche Bank may be one of the largest organisations in Germany, but it is also one of the biggest treadmills in the country. Its directors never get to rest, day or night. Some of the best have collapsed while working, and others have only avoided this fate by retiring early or restricting themselves to semi-managerial activities.'[15]

2. Global Perspectives

The link between Europe, America and Asia was the main focus of the global economic division of labour before 1914, as it continues to be today, albeit clearly on a different scale. Before 1914, the US was the world's most dynamic economy, yet the real power of the global economy was still centred in Europe, whereas Asia and its regions derived their significance more from a mixture of political and economic factors. In Asia, as would later be the case in Africa, the 'imperialists' could not avoid each another in their hunger for commodities or ambition for power; Britain continued to hold a dominant position in South Asia (India) while other areas were still subject to dispute.

In the Near East, the competing interests of Russia and France clashed (along with those of Great Britain) since these nations were struggling over control of the waning Ottoman Empire. This was initially manifested in the Crimean War and later on in the fiscal control over the bankrupt Ottoman Empire exercised by the debt administration of the European powers (Dettes Publiques Ottomane). In Central Asia, Great Britain and Russia were pitted against each other in the Great Game. Britain, France and the Netherlands were directly involved in Southeast Asia. All the European powers wanted their piece of the Chinese pie made available through the Opium Wars. In this instance, the British economy and British banks once again stood to benefit the most. Even though Japan had been forcibly opened up to the West, it had nonetheless been able to retain its autonomy.[16] America, by contrast, was inaccessible to such imperialist designs on the part of the great European powers. The UK held nominal sovereignty over Canada, but British supremacy had been cast off much earlier by the US, which was not only much more significant economically but was also strictly pursuing its own interests. The influence of Europe, especially of the UK, was considerable in Central and Latin America, though it was neither dominant nor undisputed. The economic expansion of the US to countries to the south of it was only a matter of time. Politically, its claim to leadership had already been declared in the Monroe Doctrine of 1823, a policy that was later to be repeatedly affirmed: the US would not countenance any further colonial penetration of South America by European powers.[17]

In the years prior to the First World War, the evidence actually favoured the European economies. Before 1914, Europe accounted for well over 60 per cent of all exports, while North America and Asia each achieved a respectable 10 per cent; the rest of the world registered well below those figures. Of those exports, about 60 per cent consisted of food or natural resources and 40 per cent of industrial goods (understood in the broadest sense).[18] This was not just an expression of the hunger for raw materials in the rapidly industrialising nations; it was in equal measure an attempt to finance that hunger by driving up exports or, where this was not possible, by using other income from abroad as capital export. In 1913, the big four of the global economy – the US, Great Britain, Germany and France – accounted by themselves for about 70 per cent of industrial production worldwide. Half of it derived solely from the US which, thanks to its prodigious domestic market, was noticeably less involved worldwide in economic activity than Britain and Germany. Participating in the global economy on favourable terms was nothing less than an existential question for those two countries, the strongest exporting nations on earth – something repeatedly emphasised by Deutsche Bank in its annual reports before 1914. And, in view of the rapid rate of growth in this epoch, it became even more urgent to ask: where would the raw materials come from for industry to continue to expand? Where would the food come from for a growing population? And from where would the means come to pay for all this, if not from the balance of trade?

From the outset, Deutsche Bank demonstrated its commitment to German foreign trade, the financing of which it still regarded as key. However, prioritising such investment was only possible if the bank was strongly positioned at each foreign location – and that, in turn, required that comprehensive financing be available. There is no complete list available of the bank's international projects in the years before 1914. However, a later compilation of preserved files indicates the truly global character of the bank prior to 1914.[19] The bank's activities were clearly focused in: the US, Latin America, southern Europe (Spain, Italy), south-eastern Europe and the Ottoman Empire, to an extent in Africa (Morocco, colonial enterprise), and less so in Asia, where the presence of Deutsch-Asiatische Bank was evident. In addition, types of business conducted by Deutsche Bank were more or less clearly structured. Its emphasis was on trade financing, followed by the issuing of public and private bonds (government, rail and corporate bonds), and finally investments in industrial and infrastructure projects, such as the Madrid Electric Company (which it co-founded) or sugar plantations in Peru. In that process, the bank's efforts were by no means always successful. Nonetheless, it did not seize every opportunity offered but instead proved rather particular in its choices.

This can all be illustrated nicely using the example of Deutsche Bank's branch in Brussels which was established in January 1910, resulting from the acquisition of the private bank Balser & Co. Before the First World War, Brussels was considered Europe's most important financial centre after London, Paris and Berlin. It was an extremely attractive site due to Belgium's neutrality, the local clientele's significant level of savings and its comparatively liberal tax laws. Many companies that were financing streetcars or in the energy business had their registered headquarters in Brussels; German and French capital in particular looked for investment opportunities there.[20] It is difficult to say what exactly moved Deutsche Bank to seek a foothold in Brussels. Up until then, the bank had only maintained loose contacts to Belgium through Essener Credit-Anstalt, to whom it was close.[21] What most likely played the decisive role was the local German-speaking population, which provided a potential customer base. In addition, there was the prospect of doing business via Brussels in Belgium itself and especially in its colony of Congo.[22] Until the war broke out in 1914, Deutsche Bank actively sought to participate in trade in and with Congo. That was the primary motive behind its establishment of the 'Société Commerciale Belgo-Allemande du Congo' in 1911–12, and how the Brussels branch was able to acquire a mining licence in Katanga in April 1912.[23] In turn,

Blank cheque of the Brussels branch for payment transactions with the affiliated branch in Constantinople.

such capital market transactions favoured ties with German corporate clients such as the Hamburg-based Woermann-Linie which had substantial interests in Africa.

Deutsche Bank's 'Succursale de Bruxelles' was active in all areas of the banking business, thereby having the character of a universal bank. The staff grew from at least 60 employees to more than 200 before the war began, though total assets and profits actually stagnated. The office premises also expanded rapidly.[24] Especially in its early years, the branch displayed its strength in the public offerings and securities trading. For that reason, the Berlin office instructed the Brussels branch not to 'immobilise' itself; that is, it should not make capital investments that were too large. Nor did it need to take advantage of every opportunity: 'Deutsche Bank should always remain only an intermediary.'[25] Even so, it was already helping to establish banks in Belgium at an early stage.[26] On the whole, however, the Belgian branch did not develop adequately. Some of this can be traced back to the staff that had been taken on from Charles Balser who, according to a later report, were accustomed to 'the quiet Balser way of working'. For when it came to the 'complicated requirements that fundamentally transformed the organisation and its book-keeping, a set of operations implemented by Deutsche Bank Group with elemental force, [these employees behaved] as though they had been taken by surprise'.[27] There were also communication problems between the German and French-speaking employees, especially since the latter were in the majority and since – much to the disappointment of the Allgemeiner Deutscher Sprachverein (General German Language Association) – they also tended to correspond with German customers in French.[28] Eventually, the Brussels branch was subjected to intense criticism in the local financial press. Although it was treated similarly to its French counterparts, those banks offered less cause for protest since (in the opinion of the Brussels branch management) they had been less visibly involved in new issuances and public offerings than Deutsche Bank. The press campaign was deemed 'in part a result of the latent animosity of the Francophile party in Belgium against all things German, and we have reason to believe that its campaigns are sustained practically (and in principle) by France. Deutsche Bank in Brussels, as a visible representative of Berlin high finance and a veritable symbol of German commercial and industrial power, is therefore a welcome target for attacks by such journalists, who are reaching new levels of spiteful invention and outright fabrication.'[29]

Along with these difficulties, the local business did not itself develop as had been initially expected. As part of a rather unsuccessful campaign undertaken by the branch in the spring of 1910 to lobby new German business customers, it became clear that the bank's Berlin office was not holding out hope that the Brussels branch would bring in much business. Companies whose business the Brussels branch tried to win gave various reasons for not utilising its services: the company being approached stated that it did not do (significant) business via Belgium or Brussels; it was already well served by another local bank; it was already quite satisfied with the bank's Berlin office; or it was actually conducting its business via Antwerp or Hamburg.[30] Branch director Hermann Dufer complained in March 1914 that the bank had neglected its business in Antwerp, the main trading centre of Belgium, for many years. To that extent, the branch's problems were wholly of its own making, as Dufer conceded.[31] What is more, no German financial

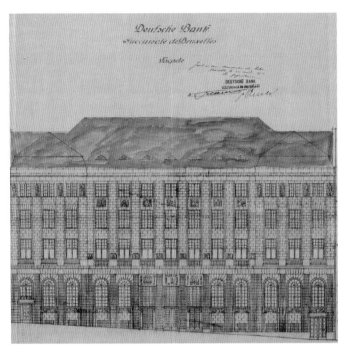

Design drawing for the façade of the Brussels branch at Rue d'Arenberg, 5, 7 and 9, from 1912.

institution besides Deutsche Bank had established an office in Belgium. Only Disconto-Gesellschaft decided in May 1914 to set up a new branch in Antwerp, not least because the costs there were significantly lower than in Brussels.[32]

Generally speaking, the Brussels branch had only limited decision-making powers. For larger transactions, it always needed to obtain the approval of the Berlin headquarters, something that at times seemed like a reprimand to their Belgian colleagues. In addition, there were disputes over authority with the bank's London Agency.[33] The Brussels branch had been repeatedly urged by Berlin 'to limit as much as possible large loans, not to speak of using our acceptance, especially since conditions in Belgium are so modest, and we in England, for instance, receive for our acceptances – which we cannot extend any further – twice as much commission as you do in that country'.[34] Ferdinand Kautz, co-director of the Brussels branch, even had to ask Gwinner for financial assistance from the Berlin office in December 1911 since the second half of the fiscal year was projected to 'turn out very bad'. After all, it had been 'pretty much common practice to support those entities which were unable to excel in their early days,' recalled Kautz, referring here to the youthful phase of Banco Alemán Transatlántico.[35] In the end, the Brussels branch retained its character as a subsidised endeavour until the outbreak of war in 1914.

3. The Ecstasy and Agony of the Bank's Business in the Americas

It can be seen that the extension of German economic interests into the global economy was not just influenced by economic competitors, who typically had the advantage of having been in place much longer. Rather, it was also shaped by political envy, something which Deutsch-Asiatische Bank in China was to experience quite painfully. That bank was only able to participate in lucrative business there in the most gradual manner; even on the eve of the First World War it still had to carry out larger projects almost exclusively within the German colony in north-east China. Nor were the Americas an easy playing field by any stretch of the imagination. In Latin America, though, Banco Alemán Transatlántico managed to gain an early foothold. The problems that might accompany such success were revealed in the disastrous Argentine gold loan of 1888 and in the difficult situation of the Buenos Aires branch during the Barings crisis of 1890. That said, other branches of the bank developed quite promisingly, above all in Chile. Latin America steadily became a success story, not least because Banco Alemán Transatlántico managed to offer all the important banking functions on-site. This Berlin-based bank was not limited to trade finance but also managed public issuances and industrial operations, maintaining current accounts and receiving deposits. In Peru, Chile, Bolivia, Argentina and Uruguay, Banco Alemán Transatlántico eventually had branches in all major locations and paid out respectable dividends to its Berlin parent company; these dividends, with slight fluctuations, stayed around 9 per cent.[36] However, all this was not a matter of course. The Brazilian branches, which had been opened between 1911 and 1913, never really got up and running, despite all the efforts made. Brazilian loans were regarded as uncertain and business in São Paulo as difficult:

The branches of Banco Alemán Transatlántico in South America and Spain in 1911.

'The situation in Brazil really worries me,' Elkan Heinemann wrote on 16 July 1913 to Paul Richarz in Rio de Janeiro. Richarz was the colleague who had been granted general authority over the Brazilian branches:

> Rubber and coffee continue to develop to the disadvantage of Brazil. Their retroactive effect on general Brazilian conditions can only be unfavourable. We've also been informed that this is especially true in São Paulo and in Santos. I'm convinced that you are already exercising the utmost caution, but I cannot hide my impression that we've been working in São Paulo almost entirely with smaller, weak partners to this point; it's to be feared they will have to be the first to suffer in any crisis. In any event, it's better that we start out by limiting our expenses and staying cautious in our selection of loans and liabilities.[37]

Banco Alemán Transatlántico did not achieve any major success either in individual financing or loan transactions but only when – after lengthy negotiations – it obtained a licence for AEG to construct a power plant in Buenos Aires. This was the origin of the most successful foreign entity of a German corporation in the pre-war period (and the largest in terms of volume): Deutsch-Ueberseeische Elektricitäts-Gesellschaft (DUEG) (German-Overseas Electricity Company). After 1898, that company was continuously able to initiate and operate major electrification projects in Latin America, projects undertaken jointly by Deutsche Bank, AEG, Berliner Handels-Gesellschaft and other

Stock certificate of Deutsch-Ueberseeische Elektricitäts-Gesellschaft with the signature of the chairman of the supervisory board, Arthur Gwinner.

lenders. Here also, the now well-established nesting principle was used, limiting capital expenditure but permitting the operative companies to effectively exercise control.[38] This also included the very successful business of Banco Alemán Transatlántico in Spain, whether by expanding the Iberian network of branches, by issuing Spanish government bonds or by financing extensively the construction and development of infrastructure for electrical engineering in Spain.[39]

In the US as well, the bank's business was developing better since it had found in Edward D. Adams a representative whom the management in Berlin could trust. However, it cannot really be said that the bank performed well in the US over the following years.[40] The shock of having been involved in the Northern Pacific Railway was still deeply felt, and the founding of Deutsche Treuhand-Gesellschaft was an enduring sign of this distress. The restructuring of Northern Pacific went off reasonably well since it was possible to entrust that risk to others, notably JP Morgan, to whom Deutsche Bank was also linked in financing other projects.[41] The bank had succeeded in withdrawing from Edison's electrical engineering ventures in a timely fashion. An attempt to establish a subsidiary of Siemens & Halske in Chicago failed because of strong US competition. All the more astonishing was the fact that the bank once more embarked on an economic (and engineering) adventure by building a coking plant on behalf of the American steel industry. It chose to provide venture capital for the construction of Lehigh Coke, something which then hung like a millstone around the bank's neck inasmuch as the unprofitable company could not be floated on the stock exchange.[42] What appeared especially encouraging were syndicate business deals in the issuance of US bonds, either by the public or the private sector; examples included the railway companies but also Niagara Power Falls Company. In such cases, Adams usually facilitated the contacts and syndication rates (which were not always high). Nor did he confine himself to US business but also focused on Central America. And Adams represented the interests of Deutsche Bank on the administrative board of Guatemala Railway, to which the bank had granted an advance loan in 1905.[43]

Arthur Gwinner also sought close co-operation with his relatives who owned the banking houses of Speyer in New York and London, yet those relationships were not without their problems from the outset.[44] It was not difficult to arrange syndicate business deals with one another, but Deutsche Bank soon began to feel it was not being treated fairly by Speyer & Co. in New York, although that institution had in turn expected preferential treatment by Deutsche Bank. As early as May 1904, Gwinner complained of a 'certain feeling of dissatisfaction with our business relationships'. Despite its strength, Deutsche Bank felt it had not been given its due: 'The dissemination of such a perception [that an exclusive partnership existed between Speyer & Co. and Deutsche Bank] can only be pleasing to Deutsche Bank if an equivalent is found for it. We've actually missed out on many opportunities in deference to our relations with you.'[45] James and Edgar Speyer tried to appease Gwinner, but now Deutsche Bank turned to Kuhn, Loeb & Co. – which after JP Morgan was the most important New York bank of the era[46] – with which it likewise had close personal ties. The head of that banking house behind the boss Jacob Schiff was Otto Kahn. He was a brother-in-law of AEG director Felix Deutsch and had worked for five years as a manager at Deutsche Bank in London; that was before he relocated to New York in 1893 to work first for Speyer & Co. and then for Kuhn, Loeb & Co., where he became the boss after the death of Jacob Schiff.[47] In the autumn of 1904, a first major deal was concluded: the joint acquisition of a $25 million loan (at a rate of 4 per cent) for Missouri Pacific Collateral Trust. The initiative evidently went back to Jacob Schiff, who proposed a business relationship with Deutsche Bank 'for short-term, high interest-bearing securities', to which Gwinner assented.[48] Later on, the bank entered into syndicate business deals, such as with the company that built the Niagara power plant.[49] These good relationships in turn bothered James Speyer, who eventually asked his brother Edgar, the head of Speyer Brothers in London, to complain to Gwinner about the un-co-operative behaviour of Deutsche Bank. Gwinner answered quite unambiguously:

> If we count the Speyers among our closest, best, and most important friends, then it's completely out of the question for us to dispense with other American busi-nesses and relationships when we compare how much the Speyers are doing for us. I think I've told you of the significance of the figures we've earned in Northern Pacific in a few years, and the benefits we're getting from other relationships, especially those with Adams. If, for example, we wanted to limit ourselves to Speyer & Co. for stock exchange and arbitrage, we'd have lost our clientele long ago and would no longer be well positioned in the market. The information we receive from Speyer & Co. is almost zero. However, such information is just as valuable and even more valuable than large syndicate participations and deals.[50]

Edgar Speyer then tried to mediate: his bank did not want an exclusive relationship but was hoping for 'most intimate relations'.[51] Edgar Speyer's desire to see one of the Frankfurt-based Speyers on Deutsche Bank's Supervisory Board was ultimately agreed to by Gwinner, who was just as averse to conflict as Speyer; for the first time, the bank's 1906 annual report listed Eduard Beit (von Speyer) as a Supervisory Board member.

Relations with Kuhn, Loeb & Co. soon grew worse once more. When Max Warburg asked about relations with Kuhn, Loeb & Co. in 1909,[52] Gwinner reacted equivocally; he considered it fundamentally possible to advocate for doing 'business with Kuhn and Loeb', but was not definitively ready for it.[53] Another context for this restraint, which had become even greater since the crisis of 1907, was probably the experience of the German public with American assets, which were far from being deemed good or secure forms of investment. As late as 1906, Gwinner had argued that, in the event of a major war, the US was the safest haven: 'A cautious capitalist will invest at least part of his fortune in America.'[54] But as he called on his Management Board colleagues, stock exchange chief Paul Mankiewitz and head of the deposit business Gustav Schröter, to market American bonds more aggressively, Mankiewitz challenged him. He considered it 'not at all advisa-ble [...] to approach the deposit-taking branches [...] in such a way. [...] The reason for the unpopularity of American bonds is that they all declined in value right after they were issued; then, there is the considerable mistrust that we here have towards the American conditions, the wild, clique-based economy over there.' The public, he claimed, was inter-ested in solid dividends and industrial assets; any other advice was of little help. Although he maintained that the bank would continue to recommend US assets, it was not clear whether they would be profitable. Furthermore, the bank had more than enough 'irons in the fire' domestically: 'we can only deal them one at a time.'[55]

On the one hand, the problems in the bank's US business resulted from (not always conflict-free) co-operative arrangements with American partners, on whom the bank was dependent as long as it did not have its own presence in the US. On the other, the American capital market itself was highly competitive, and players there did not pull any punches, something not really understood from the vantage point of Germany. In fact, the news from the US was as sensational as it was sordid, with numerous cases of fraud, speculation and the unscrupulous business practices of the 'robber barons', not to mention trusts which had grown so big in deals ranging from the uncertain to the highly risky. Even in the US, such business practices were becoming less and less acceptable. There a dedicated political movement was beginning to contest these monopolistic syndicates and their business practices while also seeking to break up the big trusts.[56] None of this really made US business more attractive to Deutsche Bank, especially since what had been achieved elsewhere since the 1880s, i.e. dropping the role of financier and becoming entrepreneurial, had not been possible with the Northern Pacific or the Edison companies or even at Lehigh Coke. In the US, Deutsche Bank remained limited to the rather successful financing transactions; even in such cases it only got to deal with major companies in exceptional cases. Instead, the bank had to make do with the little morsels which occasionally fell from the tables of the syndicates or which were handed to it directly. It was almost inevitable that other projects ended up looking more attractive.

4. The Baghdad Railway

The most famous project Deutsche Bank operated before the First World War was undoubtedly the Baghdad Railway. This was the continuation of the railway line across Anatolian Konya through the Taurus Mountains to Mesopotamia, first to Baghdad and then all the way to the Persian Gulf (its crowning achievement). In contrast to the US, there was no serious competition in this case; however, the political and diplomatic situation was highly strained. The British Empire regarded a land connection to the Persian Gulf under German control as a provocation because it felt the development would impinge on its interests in India and Egypt. Beyond that, the construction of this railway required that the Ottoman Empire be financially stabilised. Yet doing that was not at all in the interests of Russia, which was further disturbed by the potential boost to German prestige. In addition, France and the UK controlled the tariffs and revenues of the Ottoman Empire in order to ensure that the country was meeting its international payment obligations in a timely fashion. In financial terms, then, the Ottoman state was by no means sovereign. The big question was whether it was even going to be able to guarantee the pre-financing of this gigantic project, that is, whether the risk of constructing the railway would be measurable for the operating company and the financial syndicate associated with it.[57]

Nonetheless, after the Anatolian Railway was finished and more or less up and running in the mid-1890s, it was clear that the question of its further development would come up sooner or later. Deutsche Bank remained cautious. Given the high cost of constructing such a railway in technically difficult terrain, along with the weakness of Ottoman finances and the political volatility of such a project, the bank chose not to act. However, political pressure mounted because German foreign policy supported the continuation of the railway line desired by the Ottoman government. There were various reasons for this, foremost among them the stabilisation of friendly relations between the two states.[58] Wilhelm II's second trip to the Orient in autumn 1898 was expressly intended to realise this objective. A part of his itinerary included taking a short journey on the Anatolian Railway. The German delegation, which Wilhelm II welcomed at Hereke railway station on the Sea of Marmara, included Georg Siemens as well.[59] In the ensuing negotiations, Siemens remained open-minded but left no doubt that he believed only an international financial syndicate was capable of building the railway. After the preliminary licence was granted in November 1899, a commissioned study that estimated the cost of construction all the way to the Persian Gulf at 568 million marks reinforced the call to form such a syndicate. This was a sum that Deutsche Bank neither wished nor was able to finance on its own.[60] Intensive negotiations with French and British banks did not seem to preclude joint financing; thus, after consulting with the Ottoman side on the design of the licence, the contract could finally be signed. The holder of the licence granted was Anatolian Railway Company, which was to set up an independent company for constructing the line to Basra. It was estimated that it would take eight years to construct the railway from Konya to Basra by way of Adana–Mosul–Samarra–Baghdad. The Ottoman government guaranteed an annual income of 16,500 francs per kilometre and reserved the right to buy back the railway. Moreover, the licence granted the company the right to exploit natural resources within a corridor of 20 kilometres along the railway line; this point would later have significant repercussions, given that the railway passed through the oil-rich

Receiving the German emperor at the train station in Hereke on 20 October 1898; in the middle of the delegation was the Spokesman of Deutsche Bank's Management Board, Georg Siemens.

area of today's northern Iraq (Mosul). Yet the rights granted to Anatolian Railway Company were of limited duration. It would have to make practical use of them in a fairly short span of time, otherwise these rights would revert back to the Turkish government. As the initial exploration for oil deposits did not yield any definitive results, the bank was reluctant to become involved in this.[61]

This licence limited the financial risk of constructing the railway itself, but a substantial sum had to be advanced nonetheless. Thus, in April 1903 Anatolian Railway Company, with the participation of Deutsche Bank and the French-dominated Ottoman Bank, founded the 'Société Impériale Ottomane du Chemin de Fer de Bagdad' whose shares and loans were to be placed broadly throughout the world.[62] The share ownership of the company was structured accordingly: the Ottoman government held 10 per cent of the 15 million francs in capital; Deutsche Bank and Ottoman Bank each had 27 per cent; and Wiener Bankverein and Credit Suisse each took 4 per cent. The remaining shares were distributed among a variety of investors in Germany, the Ottoman Empire and Italy. In February 1904, a first Baghdad Railway bond of just under 45 million marks was offered internationally, but it quickly became apparent that – for a number of reasons – neither the British nor the French capital markets would absorb a significant portion of the bond. The French government closed off the French capital market after the Ottoman Bank failed to acquire an influence comparable to that of the German side. Talks with interested British circles fell apart after politicians sharply criticised the plans for constructing the railway and they were veritably scandalised in public. Although it was by no means intended that way, the Baghdad Railway was perceived quite quickly as a 'German' affair, something that likewise manifested itself in the practical organisation of the railway's construction.

Following on the example of the Anatolian Railway, the first phase of construction was transferred to a company based in Frankfurt am Main that had been specially established for the purpose. This was no coincidence, for, apart from Deutsche Bank, two Frankfurt construction companies were particularly involved: Philipp Holzmann and Internationale Baugesellschaft. The 200 kilometres of track from Konya to Burgulu could already be completed by 1904. The financing of the next section of the line proved difficult, though, as the Ottoman government was unable to guarantee the financing of further construction through the Taurus Mountains to Adana. After complicated negotiations, Deutsche Bank finally succeeded in unifying and restructuring Ottoman government debt.[63] It thus expanded the Sublime Porte's financial scope of action so that the next licence could be finalised for completing the route from Burgulu to Tel-El-Helif, allowing construction to be resumed in 1908. Negotiations in Constantinople, meanwhile, were in the hands of Karl Helfferich, whom Deutsche Bank had lured away from the Imperial Colonial Office after he had gone to the Bosporus in 1906 as director of Anatolian Railway Company.[64] Helfferich's vigorous supervision of the negotiations, as well as the willingness of Deutsche Bank and Anatolian Railway Company to repeatedly advance substantial funds to the Ottoman government, were the reasons for the success of a financing plan that earmarked 'using the government's share of the surpluses from the revenues from underwriting the old government debt' to build the railway.[65]

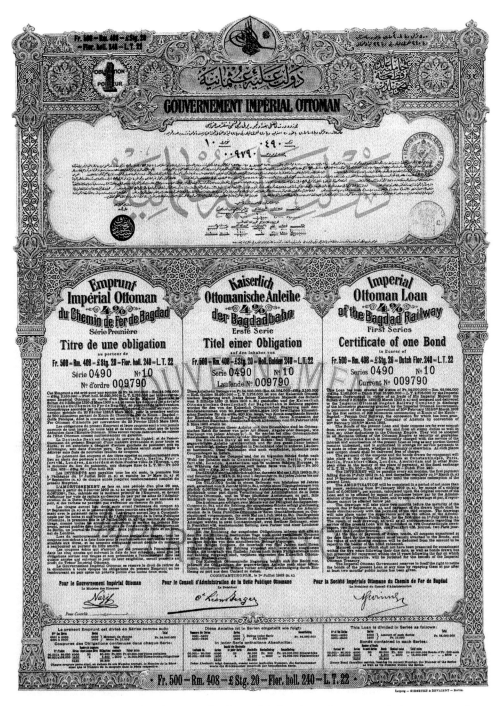

Debenture bond issued in four languages for the Baghdad Railway Company with the signature of the chairman of the administrative board, Arthur Gwinner.

Helfferich's detailed reports for the bank's Management Board in Berlin reveal an extremely complex negotiating situation that became even more complicated with the proclamation of Bulgaria's independence and the annexation of Bosnia-Herzegovina by Austria in 1908.[66] This was because oriental railways on Bulgarian territory in Eastern Rumelia were now in danger of being lost. The annexation humiliated the Ottoman government, which also had consequences: The 'Young Turk' Revolution veritably swept away the government of Abdul Hamid, a sultan who was generally on amicable terms with Germany. For Deutsche Bank and its railway interests, this was quite catastrophic: apart from the problems it was having in Bulgaria, its helpful ties to the Ottoman government had now been suddenly cut.[67] To improve relations with the new political elites in Constantinople, the bank's Management Board in Berlin had to jump over its own shadow. As late as 1902 Arthur Gwinner had explained to Edward Adams, the bank's New York confidant, that he was reluctant to open foreign branches:

Karl Helfferich (1872–1924) was a member of Deutsche Bank's Management Board from 1908 to 1915. In 1920 he married a daughter of Georg Siemens and, in the years that followed, wrote a three-volume biography of his father-in-law, who had died two decades previously.

We have […] never contemplated opening a branch at Constantinople. You will have observed that Deutsche Bank has adhered to the policy of not going beyond the German frontiers, although the temptation to do so has been strong, particularly in Italy. […] The only exception we have made, our London Agency, was a necessity for our transoceanic business, and you will also have observed that our London Agency has always kept away from other than purely commission and banking business.[68]

Even in Constantinople, where the bank's economic and financial interests were concentrated, it had taken a long time to launch a new branch. The head of the bank explained that it finally opened one on the Bosporus in 1909 due to the political circumstances that had arisen after the Young Turk Revolution: 'If Deutsche Bank has now decided to set up its own branch, then it was doing so in connection with the political upheaval that has occurred in Turkey. […] Deutsche Bank's move is a sign of the hopes and sympathies of German business for the new regime.'[69]

In all foreign policy matters, Helfferich thus stood on the side of the Ottoman Empire, which he did not wish to see weakened in any way.[70] Deutsche Bank found little support from the imperial government, since Berlin was by no means orientated towards its material interests but instead preferred to muddle its way through things while doing nothing to offend Austria, Russia, Bulgaria, or even the Ottoman Empire. Some tangible support of the bank's claim for compensation from Bulgaria after the East Rumelian Railway had been seized was as about as unexpected as unequivocal criticism of Vienna's foreign policy. This state of affairs called especially for the skills of Karl Helfferich, who successfully manoeuvred his way through the intensive negotiations that took place in Constantinople. After lengthy talks, he managed to overcome the resistance of some groups of Young Turks who had been critical of developing railways with foreign capital; in June 1910 a further bond was issued to continue the construction. It was designed to be similarly international, like the one that had preceded it, yet it was once again placed almost exclusively on the German capital market.

Nonetheless, in 1909, after five years of interruption, construction was finally resumed. But the question now emerged of who would build and operate the rail link from Baghdad to Basra and whether the route should continue beyond Basra all the way to the sea. It was impossible to think of a solution for this that did not involve a trade-off with Great Britain, which would have been necessary even earlier because the railway traversed large-scale oil deposits found north of Baghdad. Deutsche Bank had not exercised its rights of use to these for quite some time. It was only in 1913–14, when Turkish Petroleum Company was founded with major contributions of British capital, that the bank took the initiative and was finally prepared to take on the risk of drilling in co-operation with British investors. In finally utilising its rights, the bank received a 25 per cent stake in Turkish Petroleum Company. But it was also now clearly a junior partner of UK investors who were pursuing their oil interests – not least to ensure that the British navy would be supplied with fuel – much more determinedly than their German counterparts. Gwinner had no problem with this since he always sought a balance with British interests on the question of the Baghdad Railway.[71]

Just as an agreement had been reached on utilising the oil reserves, so, too, was there a settlement on building the railway following lengthy negotiations between the various national groups in the months just before the First World War. French interests in northern and eastern Anatolia, as well as in Syria, were respected by the German side; the latter had enjoyed a *de facto* monopoly in western Anatolia and along the railway to Baghdad ever since the Ottoman Bank had decided to leave the railway syndicate. The settlement of interests with Great Britain stipulated that railway construction stop just before the Persian Gulf, that access to the sea remain under British control and that the British side would also be represented in the railway company linking Basra to Baghdad. In return for these stipulations, the French and British money and capital markets would be opened up to finance the additional construction, which had been borne almost exclusively by the German capital market up to that point. After another customs bond for the Ottoman Empire was issued in 1910, amounting to 160 million francs, the placement options in Germany were regarded as exhausted.[72] However, the conclusion of the negotiations came too late. The onset of the First World War prevented the Baghdad Railway from becoming a major international project. The construction work was continued during the war from a military standpoint, though the route to Baghdad was not completed. The remaining gaps in the network were not closed until 1940.

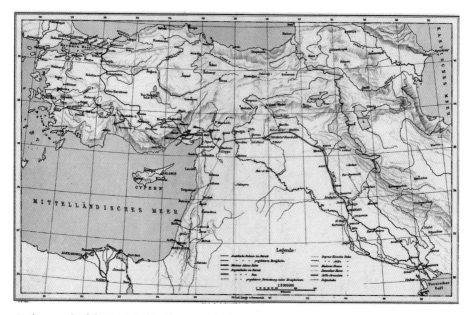

Rail network of the Baghdad Railway in 1915.

From the vantage point of the bank, the Baghdad Railway project was extremely complex and difficult to steer through the storms of political and diplomatic differences. Nonetheless, Deutsche Bank was able to carry out the project to a fairly large extent and (more or less) on its own, thanks chiefly to the energy and negotiating skills of Karl Helfferich. It was less surprising that all these steps, which were not easy to implement in the face of British and Russian resistance, are what determined the image of the bank in the eyes of its critics. Economically speaking, the bank's involvement in railways was quite successful, from the Balkans to Anatolia as well as in Mesopotamia. The Oriental railway lines, i.e. the Balkan lines, had been cast aside by the bank in 1913 since the political risks were unforeseeable; it was able to do this by selling its shares at a profit to an Austrian syndicate.[73] For all the economic fluctuations, its revenue from railway lines in the Ottoman Empire had increased. The bank's annual report of 1913 stated:

> The Turkish railway companies we are interested in, have worked out satisfactorily in the year under review, even though the difficult political conditions still persist. The Anatolian Railway on the Haidar–Pasha–Angora main line has exceeded the amount of revenue guaranteed by the Turkish State for the third time, while the Eskişehir–Konya line has made minimal use of the guarantee. The Baghdad Railway, in the year under review, has [...] helped to further develop its main line so that it's likely that the stretch of about 136 km from Baghdad to Samara about 200 km east of the Euphrates will become operational this year.[74]

The bank earned money on profits and dividend distributions from the construction and operating companies, from Turkish guarantee payments, and from commissions and gains in the acquisition and placement of the issuances. In the end, the railway construction and the rights attached to it were accompanied by high hopes for related projects, especially for exploiting oil wells in present-day northern Iraq, utilising Turkish coal deposits together with Krupp and Stinnes, or expanding the railways linking Syria to the Mediterranean. Corresponding project ideas were discussed intensively in Berlin, and these were in part carried out, for example, in the founding of Turkish Petroleum Company.[75]

Consequently, Deutsche Bank acted with the utmost caution, at all times seeking to distribute the risk among several partners. After much hesitation, the bank was only prepared to finance the Turkish coal mining industry (in Heraclea) once Ruhr industrialist Hugo Stinnes himself got involved in it.[76] There was a simple reason for Deutsche Bank's restraint beyond the usual economic reservations. The general conditions of doing business in the Ottoman Empire had increasingly forced the bank into the reviled role of a player who had to act politically even if he himself had never been a political player. The bank therefore had an interest in not being very visible in politically volatile transactions. Therefore, the bank signalled its approval towards Stinnes while at the same time making it clear: 'It's certainly in the interest of business, and in that of German policy as well, that Deutsche Bank – an institution that frankly makes all our political opponents and rivals see red – stay in the background as much as possible. You are not suspect if you show an interest in coal.'[77] The actual backgrounds involved did not stay hidden for long, of course. The British quite swiftly became familiar with the details, even suspecting that Stinnes intended to bring the coal trade in Constantinople and all Turkish ports under his control in an effort to replace British coal with its German equivalent.[78] While that assessment was not accurate, it serves as a striking demonstration of the politicised banking environment, which greatly irritated those in the business – with one exception. The only one who felt suited to the role of politician was Karl Helfferich. For him, the situation represented both a personal challenge and an opportunity. Helfferich was in his element when it came to these complicated negotiations over financing the Baghdad Railway and later – after the Balkan Wars and the Ottoman Empire's loss of its European territories – when it came to stabilising the finances of what remained of Turkey as well as clarifying the issue of the Ottoman Empire's debt.[79] These were highly political matters within the framework of national rivalries.[80] In this context, the financial experts of the banks could not help but act politically, and Helfferich also seems to have increasingly savoured this role.[81] Understandably, the tenor of the corresponding passage in the bank's annual report for 1913 had a semi-official character:

> Negotiations with Turkey, England, and France over Turkish railway and financial issues have been fostered considerably in the year under review; we confidently hope that their pending completion will secure the foundations of our Turkish ventures and guarantee peaceful cooperation with both great Western European nations on Turkey's economic and financial development.[82]

The fact that Helfferich got formally involved in politics after war had broken out is therefore something that some of his colleagues on the bank's Management Board might have lamented. In his eyes, after having already been so actively involved in the matter, it may only have been a small transition.

5. The Steaua Română

Deutsche Bank's ambiguous reputation also resulted in large part from another southeast European project that, like the Baghdad Railway, caused it a great deal of trouble. Specifically, it was the bank's entry into Romania's 'Steaua Română', an episode that deserves a more detailed look as an example of how the bank overextended itself.[83] The acquisition of this company, the largest Romanian oil producer, was so important because Deutsche Bank's role was not limited solely to the financial restructuring of the troubled oil company, but also involved actively intervening in its corporate governance. There were many reasons for the bank to become active in this area. On the one hand, the petroleum market was extremely lucrative, even though it was largely controlled in Germany by John D. Rockefeller, i.e. Standard Oil. But as the use of electric lighting expanded, it became apparent that the growth market in lighting oil (or kerosene) would bottom out. On the other hand, there appeared to be considerable growth opportunities in other oil products (gasoline, diesel, heating oil) and lubricants as well as, more generally, in the use of petroleum in the chemical industry.[84] The petroleum market was therefore only a small detail in a rapidly growing marketplace, albeit the most interesting single item at the turn of the century. In any event, German imports of lamp oil (kerosene) rose from 267,000 tons in 1880 to 989,000 tons in 1910, yet then fell back to 745,000 tons in 1914. The share of imports from the US, which arrived primarily in Bremen, was initially 100 per cent; it then dropped every ten years by about 10 per cent

Stock certificate of Steaua Română from 1897. Deutsche Bank acquired the Romanian oil company in 1903.

but still amounted to a good 77 per cent in 1913.[85] US petroleum had maintained its market dominance, and Deutsch-Amerikanische Petroleum-Gesellschaft (DAPG), or German-American Petroleum Company, founded by Rockefeller's Standard Oil specifically for the German market, left no doubt that it planned to defend its market by hook or crook, relying on the quality of its distribution network and the virtues of its product. Nonetheless, European competitors such as Shell Transport and Trading Co. in London repeatedly tried to contest the Americans' sales territory, thereby chancing upon the (not disinterested) goodwill of Deutsche Bank. Together with Shell, the bank went on to finance Petroleum Producte Aktiengesellschaft (PPAG), which intended to compete in Germany with Standard Oil and its DAPG.[86] The German public welcomed this development, yet PPAG's chances of success were not very promising when compared with DAPG's efficient distribution channels and pricing power. If petroleum seemed to hold little promise, the prospects were quite favourable for developing other oil-derived products, especially fuels and lubricating oils. After 1900, a number of German syndicates went beyond organising competing sales channels and worked on opening up additional sources of oil for the German economy.

Deutsche Bank entered the oil business at a relatively late juncture. Apart from Russia, Galicia and Romania were the primary suppliers of raw materials in Europe, with Russia (notably in the Caucasus) dominated by the combined interests of Nobel and Rothschild as well as by Russian firms. At the same time, neither Austria-Hungary nor Romania had to face such robust competition. Consequently, there was a realistic chance of entering this market, which was already being taken advantage of in Austria-Hungary (Galicia) by a group including Disconto-Gesellschaft and S. Bleichröder's bank. In Romania, the largest company involved was Steaua Română, which was financed by Ungarische Industrie-Bank, which was itself backed by Wiener Bankverein. Due to a host of problems, but especially its poor (and technologically inadequate) structuring of oil extraction, Steaua found itself in straitened circumstances in 1902–3. It was a situation that overwhelmed the Hungarian bank, in spite of the promising oil deposits. Accordingly, a buyer was sought, one who naturally had to comply with the 'national expectations' of the Romanian government. It was out of the question for Romania to allow Standard Oil to enter the market, and especially not on terms that the American company would dictate. This was because the Romanian government wished to be neither disadvantaged nor utterly dependent on foreign interests. Deutsche Bank, closely associated with Wiener Bankverein, expressed its interest, not least in an attempt to catch up with other banks which were already investing. Between the two groups around Deutsche Bank and Disconto-Gesellschaft, there was an intense dispute. In the end, Deutsche Bank took the lead – not least owing to its better contacts with Wiener Bankverein – much to the frustration of Disconto-Gesellschaft.[87]

Even so, for Deutsche Bank the restructuring of Steaua was hardly painless. It called for substantial investments. Moreover, the possibilities for future expansion were uncertain since the Romanian state vacillated between more liberal rules and a licensing system orientated strictly around Romanian interests regarding land use. But the core of Steaua was evidently still salvageable. After acquiring that bank's shares in 1903, Deutsche Bank resorted to the already well-established nesting principle by first establishing Deutsche Petroleum-Aktiengesellschaft (DPAG). Deutsche Bank thus held 50 per cent of its shares; Wiener Bankverein, 25 per cent; and smaller syndicate partners owned the rest. DPAG, in turn, became the owner of Steaua, which was run from Campina, Romania, even though its administrative (or supervisory) board was based in Berlin. At least at the start, Gwinner assumed the chairmanship of both boards. Emil Georg Stauß, Gwinner's right-hand man on questions of oil production, became a director of DPAG in 1906. He was supposed to help modernise the operations while also dealing with the marketing of Romanian oil. Yet this landscape was full of pitfalls because decisions in Berlin were made too far away from Romania for interventions to be specific. The actual responsibility would therefore have to fall to the management of Steaua. Consequently, the first restructuring step of the new owner was to replace the previous managers and appoint new ones. Steaua was freed of debt and concurrently received new senior management under Georg Spies, an ethnic German who had previously worked in the Caucasus oil industry.[88] His first charge was to shake up the previous management and to replace some of the employees with new ones. Spies got to work immediately and with great earnestness, keeping Arthur Gwinner up to date on every detail. He did not wait to address the weaknesses he observed in Steaua. Nor did he hesitate to resort to decisive measures: 'You have in Campina an invaluable bonanza, one which will produce very gratifying results for your company if managed rationally and reasonably,' he wrote to Gwinner on 8 June 1904. However, Steaua had not been managed well: 'I hope that I will be able to carry out these tasks and in so doing not only justify the trust you have in me but also gain the confidence of the officials under my supervision. A firm and just hand is clearly needed here.' Above all, 'S.[teaua] R.[omână] has thus far been an open field for suspicion and intrigues. [...] There are undercurrents here which do not serve the best interest of the company and whose instigators can be named for you by Mr Zeller [Steaua's agent in Berlin]. [...] It will be my duty to distinguish truth from fiction here, and I hope that the task will be made easier for me because of my experiences in Russia, where I had to handle such elements with a touch of the oriental, i.e. that mastery at fishing in murky waters.'[89] Yet his proposals for (and assessments of) personnel did not meet with complete approval in Berlin, thereby upsetting Spies: 'With the way Steaua is organised, only the general director resident here can be the eyes and arms of the company, while the administrative board – to further express myself figuratively – is the brain. If my eye is not sharp enough or my judgement unclear, it will be necessary for

Georg Spies (1861–1926) came from a German entrepreneurial family that had worked in Russia from 1845. From the 1890s he was involved in the Russian oil business. In 1904 Deutsche Bank appointed him general director of Steaua Română.

Steaua to send a better man than me to Romania; for under no circumstances should Berlin prolong its failed attempt at centralization, which has only resulted in confusion.' He then added unequivocally: 'Not in Campina – but in Berlin – lie the roots of the malady from which Steaua suffers.'[90]

It was precisely this question that repeatedly triggered the conflicts that were to come. As late as the summer of 1904, Spies submitted a restructuring plan for Steaua; at the same time, he took charge of gradually replacing its 'rotten officials'.[91] Gwinner granted him relatively generous leeway in this. To his colleagues on the Management Board, he made the following observation concerning a letter from Spies: 'Here is an illustration for the directorate of the satisfactory work done by G.[eorg] Spies: Ever since he has been in Bucharest, I have hardly had to work on Steaua. In every important decision, he asks for our approval or for advice: failure is his to claim.'[92] Gwinner, meanwhile, was also deluding himself, for Spies was also making the most of the leeway granted him to reject demands made by Berlin. In the spring of 1905, he insisted – in what was virtually an ultimatum – that Steaua's Berlin office be closed: 'I'd be lying,' he wrote to Elkan Heinemann, who was representing Gwinner while the latter was recuperating in the Black Forest, 'if I did not confess that I've never in my life confronted such a mess, such a slapdash mishandling and confusion of immature and amateur notions as in Behrenstraße 8 [the address of Steaua's Berlin office]. Two-thirds of the gentlemen there are little more than an expensive adornment – I'm talking about the indirect costs, not their direct compensation – and an adornment that interferes with the sound development of the business, so that I – if you were emperor of Russia and I were you – would neutralise it in the "Imperial Council" without any hesitation.'[93] Spies was right, as demonstrated by his success in restructuring Steaua in terms of its personnel and procedures, and this was probably what Gwinner's positive impression of him was based upon. His personnel and technical restructuring of the company was succeeding gradually; and its oil production had risen from about 185,000 tons in 1903 to more than 400,000 in 1913. Steaua was soon able to resume paying dividends.[94] But this was deceptive, for Steaua's product was not always of high quality. The expansion of oil extraction was proceeding more slowly than desired owing to the ongoing dispute with Disconto-Gesellschaft.[95] The drilling techniques were not being updated rapidly enough, and refinery capacities on-site were too low. In short: Steaua may have been producing a lot more than before but not always at prices that were competitive in the (already) highly contested European market.[96]

Furthermore, precisely these successes in improving Steaua led to an almost insoluble problem. While the firm was greatly expanding its production, a corresponding increase in sales was by no means certain. Nor were sales really in the hands of Steaua, which sent its oil or processed products on to PPAG, whose task it was to sell them. Yet PPAG, from which Shell had already withdrawn in 1906, was not making progress in its desperate attempts to compete with Standard Oil. It was unable to guarantee a certain quantity of sales or revenue for Steaua. Spies attributed that, in turn, to ill will and incompetence at PPAG, which he alleged was making an excuse of the market difficulties and the (occasionally) poor quality of the Romanian products. The tone between Steaua and PPAG deteriorated, though Spies was wholly aware of the situation: 'We're telling PPAG: "You don't seem to understand your business." PPAG replies: "Why are you delivering us a shoddy product!?" Steaua is indignant, saying: "People always liked buying the product from us in the past. You've also never told us which one you'd like," and so on.'[97] Gwinner found it increasingly difficult to mediate but was still not willing to give up. That did not help much since little could be done to challenge the market power of Standard Oil. Whenever there were attempts to make inroads with Romanian products, Standard Oil answered with a regional price war, one which PPAG could only lose – and did.

For Georg Spies, who was accustomed to leading with zeal, all these were only excuses or attempts to hold on to bad or incompetent personnel. Even Gwinner eventually accommodated him and embellished Steaua's balance sheet at the expense of the numbers of PPAG, so that Steaua did not slip into the red on account of poor sales revenue. On the other hand, the Management Board in Berlin was absolutely clear that PPAG's policies were not at fault for the lacklustre performance of its oil business. Elkan Heinemann made it clear

Elkan Heinemann (1859–1941) was a member of Deutsche Bank's Management Board from 1906 to 1923. Deutsch-Ueberseeische Elektricitäts-Gesellschaft, along with Steaua Română, counted among his most important work responsibilities.

vis-à-vis Gwinner: 'Mr Spies has simply underestimated the extent and impact of the price war being waged by Standard; he was too optimistic yet again.'[98] Heinemann also insistently opposed Spies's expressed wish to Gwinner that he relocate to Berlin and take the sales organisation into his own hands. Gwinner, in contrast, favoured the idea. Having Spies in Berlin would be useful 'for our general petroleum interests,' he replied to Heinemann.[99] '[I]t's better if the wheels creak a little at Steaua [because of Spies's possible transfer] than if the entire PPAG cart gets bogged down.' In addition, 'If Spies is often in Berlin, it will be our best opportunity to curb his optimism.' Heinemann thought that was out of the question, partly because he judged Spies very differently:

> On the contrary: more and more I'm getting the idea that Spies is still too much above the fray and isn't sufficiently involved in the individual branches of the business to fully master them or really guide them pragmatically. Even less can we say that everything is organised so well that it's running on its own; a lot is still not running well under Spies. [...] Our interests in Romania are far too large to be perceived from here in Berlin as anything but imperfect.[100]

Spies remained in Romania and continued to work to enlarge Steaua, hoping that its revenue problem would eventually be solved by improving the sales organisation. Yet Deutsche Bank, DPAG and PPAG had too far to go and eventually realised they did not have a realistic chance on their own against Standard Oil-DAPG. Deutsche Bank therefore attempted to pool together all the European oil interests and lead them in the struggle against Rockefeller's Standard Oil and its European offshoots. What they could not do alone might succeed if they all pulled together: the Russian group around Nobel and Rothschild, Royal Dutch and Shell and, finally, the despised Disconto-Gesellschaft and S. Bleichröder. And their efforts succeeded. In the summer of 1906, European oil interests merged their sales companies into the European Petroleum Union (EPU), which operated out of London and provided the respective national supply companies with petroleum and its by-products. In Germany, DPAG arranged for the merger of PPAG with a German-Russian group in order to form Deutsche Petroleum-Verkaufsgesellschaft, headquartered in Bremen. This syndicate ultimately intended to compete with DAPG with some hope of success, yet Steaua was primarily annoyed since Russian petroleum was also to be sold.[101] Even this was not enough to impress DAPG, which instead ramped up its price competition against the new supplier to such a degree that EPU finally had to reach an understanding with it.[102] Standard Oil was granted a 75 per cent share in the German petroleum market while Deutsche Petroleum-Verkaufsgesellschaft acquired only a 20 per cent market share for itself. In addition, the business had been pooled. Deutsche Petroleum-Verkaufsgesellschaft was not itself active in the market but got its petroleum from EPU and then passed it on, in the agreed-upon amount, to DAPG; the latter then sold the petroleum and paid each a share of the proceeds.[103] For Steaua this was bad news, especially since Berlin had also committed itself to the non-cartel sector of fuels and lubricants, as stipulated in its contracts with the Romanian companies of Disconto Group. From the outset, Steaua was sceptical of plans for forming EPU and of co-operating with Disconto Group. Between Campina and Berlin, the dispute eventually became public, with Gwinner getting caught in the middle between the fronts. For business reasons, he supported Steaua's position, focused as it was on Deutsche Bank's interest in crude oil; he thus stuck with Spies as a technical expert, realising that Steaua could not be run from Berlin. Yet Gwinner also defended the course of EPU, which had to be prepared to make various compromises in London. His appeals to compromise, though, made both orally and in numerous letters, were ineffective. As early as the summer of 1906, Gwinner sounded almost desperate in a letter to Spies:

> Dr Herz [who represented the interests of Deutsche Bank and Steaua while concurrently heading EPU] has proven himself a useful, energetic, and loyal employee in very trying circumstances. The relationship between EPU and Steaua will become tolerable, and especially beneficial to Steaua, only if you and Dr Herz can restore a good enough mutual understanding to work to each other's advantage.[104]

The conflict lasted from 1906 to 1908. Arthur Herz sought to balance the interests pooled in EPU, from Shell to Nobel/Rothschild and Disconto Group, while Spies was solely interested in the position of Steaua, where extensive investments in modernisation had not yet paid off. The financial problems of Steaua were disguised through manipulations in the accounting of Steaua and Deutsche Petroleum-Verkaufsgesellschaft. Gwinner undertook such manipulations at the risk of jeopardising his own reputation, so that Steaua would look good even if it meant that PPAG was unable to pay out dividends: 'The main thing is that our financial statements are sound and that we have nothing to hide.'[105] But none of that helped Steaua. As a result, Spies sought to remove all the contractual obligations in order to have a free hand to conduct sales in Germany.[106] And, ultimately, he wanted to call the shots in Deutsche Bank's petroleum business. Subsequently, Spies released a hail of long letters to Gwinner, complaining about EPU and the incompetence of its staff in Berlin and London. With that, he increasingly got on his boss's nerves; Gwinner had earlier griped: 'On a personal level, I can thank this petro business for my bad health and grey beard.'[107] He was losing patience with Spies:

> I can't help but add that the ongoing friction between Dr Herz and yourself is a source of worry and annoyance to me. It's in the vital interests of our companies that you and Dr Herz be on reasonably good terms, and we're justified in expecting that any personal sensitivities be overcome in line with this broad perspective.

Herz was certainly more to blame, he wrote,[108] 'but you, too, Mr Spies, are by no means free of any reproach; I'm appealing here to your manliness and compassion.'[109] Spies, of course, did not let the matter lie; he insisted on a free hand for himself, claiming that the business could not at all be supervised from Berlin:

> Sadly, you and Mr Heinemann, as you once said, 'are also managing a small banking business'. Thus, you do not hear or see what is an open secret. The view of everyone outside the Deutsche Bank building, all of them, without exception, is that Dr Herz is merely an amusing, highly adept juggler, and none of us [...] really takes him seriously as a businessman.[110]

This massive attack on Gwinner was not ameliorated by Spies also recommending that Herz be replaced by Emil Georg Stauß, with whom Spies was still cooperating at this time. Lastly, Spies basically denied that the bank's management in Berlin was competent. Gwinner would not have disputed this, and Spies knew it. As late as the spring of 1908, Gwinner lamented: 'We [Gwinner and Heinemann] are too busy to work through these extensive reports in detail and, quite frankly, too unfamiliar with the matters addressed to understand the results of the numbers correctly.'[111] That said, Gwinner took Spies's intervention as the occasion to make it clear to Herz where the bank stood:

> We must constantly recall that the main purpose for which we took a sole and exclusive interest in EPU was to create the most favourable opportunity for selling Steaua's oil. We should never lose sight of this, and I'm asking you to make all your decisions based on this key consideration.

Since Steaua was only able to sell to EPU and did not have a home market, it had to be guaranteed that its oil be treated no worse than Russian or other oil. 'EPU should never be in a position *not* to accept Steaua's oil. Otherwise, we will have missed the main point of our involvement in EPU, where we've invested such huge amounts.'[112]

Despite all these appeals, the war between Herz and Spies continued unabated. Gwinner slowly resigned himself to it, asking them 'to occasionally show me […] some consideration'.[113] Spies withdrew from the management of Steaua; his post was to be taken over by Emil Georg Stauß.[114] After further discussions, it turned out that Herz's position in London was noticeably less certain, whereas Spies had been able to score points through his restructuring of Steaua. As a result, after finding a successor for himself in Romania, Spies was supposed to take over Herz's job in London – his office as head of EPU.[115] Gwinner was also relieved because Spies was not coming to Berlin but going to London instead.[116] The administrative board of Steaua signed off on the transition on 29 September 1908. At that point, Spies, who had been hired to serve as general director of Steaua until March 1909, was supposed to move to London to join EPU's executive committee.[117] Yet even in his last months at the head of Steaua, Spies clashed with Stauß. Spies had the impression that he had become subordinate to Stauß, whom he disparaged for lacking expertise and discretion. This is when Gwinner, whom Spies had now accused of spinelessness, lost his cool:

> You're way off track and almost pathologically so. If Mr Stauß weren't such an intel-
> ligent and positive fellow, we'd again have a conflict à la Herz. […] But the blame
> lies with me, not with Mr Stauß, if it has truly got so bad. You regard me and all
> of us as a lot more complicated than we are. I haven't time to spin such fine webs,
> and I've always done better to approach things with some clarity and openness, in
> the Bismarckian sense.

Gwinner was absolutely clear about prohibiting any 'irritated tone towards Mr Stauß'.[118] Spies countered that he was not yet sick; however, his health would not be able to endure the conditions at Deutsche Bank's petroleum group in the long term. He there-fore called off prolonging his contract with EPU,[119] which he had just signed and which was to expire in May 1910:

> As he that will not hear must feel. […] My letter of 12 October 1908 informed
> you that I cannot be drawn into a renewed dualism, this time of Stauß v. Spies. Yet
> you apparently established it again, since it's asserting itself once more. You created
> it by being averse to further clarifying personnel positions, stemming from your
> agreeable, conciliatory nature and perhaps from your habits as a banker as well.

Spies claimed that he no longer wanted to endure the most arduous struggles to imple-ment his ideas of a well-run oil company. He was therefore now going to make room for Stauß.[120] This letter was followed by his official termination of his contract on 30 April 1910 'for health reasons'.[121] Gwinner accepted his resignation, observing that 'Deutsche Bank [has to] remain master of its own business at all costs'. That, in turn, brought

Spies back to reality. He then attempted to schedule a meeting with Gwinner while at the same time signalling that he wanted to continue working for Steaua and EPU going forward.[122] Nonetheless, he tied any further cooperation to his ideas being endorsed on the structural reform of EPU – something that clearly did not take place.[123] The definitive break ensued once his contract ended formally in the early summer of 1910.

A lengthy dispute followed, accompanied by an assortment of legal filings. Here, in order to legitimate his position, Spies reached out to German politicians, the Foreign Office and the Imperial Treasury with internal information about a possible imperial petroleum monopoly. Ultimately, he would claim to have always acted solely in the public interest of the nation. Deutsche Bank challenged his account, accusing him of disclosing an internal memorandum on the proposed petroleum monopoly;

Emil Georg Stauß (1877–1942, ennobled in 1918) began as an assistant to Georg Siemens. Later he worked under Gwinner, who transferred the petroleum business to him. In 1915, he was appointed to the Management Board.

moreover, the bank insisted that he release all the files he still possessed from his time at Steaua. Spies complied with the demand but took nearly a year to do so.[124] In his correspondence with Steinthal, Heinemann speculated that there were very tangible motives behind Spies's behaviour: 'His appeal to patriotism is, of course, only a pretext. His driving motivation is vanity but also – indeed most of all – a self-serving interest in recommending himself to the Foreign Office and the Imperial Treasury as the future director of any monopoly administration.'[125]

This was therefore something the bank could simply not tolerate. It had been considering the idea of an imperial monopoly on petroleum in more than an academic way for quite some time.[126] After all, up until then, the modernisation of Steaua had involved a great deal of work without garnering much of a return. Max Steinthal was likewise critical that the bank had been 'putting far too much more effort into petroleum transactions than should be required by a complicated syndicate business; two of its managers have now had to spend most of their time on it for years'.[127] Such work would have paid off only if a market in Central Europe could have been secured for the increased production of Steaua. Yet Deutsche Bank was further away than ever from achieving that. The price of Steaua stock had necessarily had to be kept up for quite some time. It was therefore not possible to exit from Steaua by selling the bank's shares on the stock market – a way out that suggested itself and had, in fact, been successful in the past. One possible way to remove oneself from the situation was to establish an imperial monopoly on petroleum that might be able to limit the market power of Standard Oil by setting price guidelines. Although Standard would not be so easily crowded out of the market, in view of its sheer quantitative significance, the ruinous price wars would become a thing of the past. The imperial monopoly did not come to fruition since it was obviously too much in the interest of Deutsche Bank. At the same time, interest in a monopoly was significantly less among other interested German parties such as Disconto-Gesellschaft and Deutsche Erdöl AG (DEA), which had been formed in 1911 from various other, predecessor firms. Neither of these companies wished in any way for such a monopoly or its sales organisation to come under the dominant influence of Deutsche Bank. All these conflicts, waged fiercely on occasion, ultimately prevented a corresponding monopoly from being formed on the eve of the war.[128] Such a development would no longer have been so important given the structural changes affecting the demand for petroleum. This shift in demand eventually brought the desired success, as announced in 1912 by the private Berlin bank A. E. Wassermann, which Deutsche Bank was doubtless aware of:

> Since 1909, business in heating and fuel oil has grown tremendously. While earlier, kerosene and gasoline were the main factors in the petroleum business, there has recently been a great demand for the residues from the distillation of crude oil. These are being used not only as heating oil for boilers, especially on warships, merchant vessels, and locomotives, but also as motor oil for engines designed for the diesel system. The naval forces of Britain, Italy, Austria and (more recently) France are preparing to use fuel oils instead of coal, and most of them have signed contracts with Steaua Română, the only major supplier of fuel oil in Europe.[129]

Just before the war commenced, Deutsche Bank's earlier involvement in the oil industry came to a quiet close. However, the quarrels over Steaua and its sales had left behind a negative impression. The bank's executives were understandably no longer interested in getting into another adventure, much less in taking on responsibility for developing a production operation. In any case, the history of Steaua revealed quite clearly that it was nearly impossible for a bank to independently take charge of extracting and processing oil while also distributing its products. Such a venture depended on foreign personnel and their capabilities, thereby hampering a bank's ability to make informed decisions. In pursuing the nesting principle typical prior to 1914, the bank's directorate believed it could solve such problems by establishing financially dependent special-purpose vehicles, entities that had also worked for railways in the Ottoman Empire and for Deutsch-Ueberseeische Elektricitäts-Gesellschaft. But in each of these cases, the market position was relatively undisputed, having depended primarily on the financing and the fulfilment of licensing requirements. When a market was fiercely contested, as was generally the case in the US, or when it was not possible to quickly sell off the individual nesting entities, as was the case in the European oil market, by contrast a bank needed to be able to do much more than professional financing. Even an organisation as large as Deutsche Bank could not accomplish such things. The nesting principle was therefore more something for the bank when it came to financing than serving as a model for its own business behaviour. The history of Steaua is also typical for this experience. Its clearest manifestation was the 'oil fatigue' that gradually worked its way through the top levels of the bank. Gwinner left no doubt about it in his memoirs, where he noted that the problem was not extracting the oil but selling it when one was not up to the task: 'As a banker, if I had to do it again, I'd never touch the petroleum business again.'[130]

6. Morocco

German industry expanded rapidly after 1900 and was immensely starved for raw materials. In such a context, Steaua Română became increasingly important, as did the question of other natural resources in the Ottoman Empire. Considerations such as these also determined the Scramble for Africa, at least in part. More specifically, Deutsche Bank's financing of infrastructure development also served to make attractive resource projects economically possible in the first place. At the same time, the interests of a variety of companies, financial groups and governments were mostly at odds in those parts of the world that were rich in resources but not yet clearly dominated by other nations. Especially in Morocco – a sultanate on the north-west coast of Africa that had maintained independence at least formally – these assorted interests finally clashed, leading to two major crises in which the German Empire participated but was unable to prevail against Britain or France. The Moroccan Crises of 1904–5 and 1911 have been broadly addressed in the historiography on the origins of the First World War. As seen from Germany, the issue was ultimately about access to Morocco's reputed wealth of resources, while the UK and France shared a strategic interest in controlling the maritime routes in the region. This 'open door' policy was guaranteed by the Madrid Convention of 1880, an international treaty that simultaneously recognised Morocco's autonomy. In subsequent years, Morocco experienced *de facto* colonisation at the hands of France, which always justified its actions on the grounds that there was internal unrest in the country. In two instances, this elicited increased German opposition, which was not enough ultimately to upset France's position, backed as it was by the UK.[131] In fact, Germany was really only interested in having open access to Morocco's economic potential. That attraction can be traced back to the beginning of the 1890s, when newspaper articles assessed the value and importance of establishing a German bank in the sultanate of Morocco that would invest in its foreign trade and infrastructure development. At first, this notion remained purely speculative.[132] Even at the start of the twentieth century, the economic weight of German businesses was not yet that pronounced. At that point, however, Reich Chancellor Bernhard von Bülow clearly articulated the interests, especially of German heavy industry, in having access to Moroccan ore mines.[133] The issue regularly showed up in the business and financial press in the years that followed. A number of rumours circulated about possible projects, alleged stakeholders and strategic objectives.[134] Yet the German government likewise called on the banks to get involved accordingly. At Deutsche Bank, such ideas met with little favour since it seemed unrealistic to finance ventures like the Moroccan railways using the German capital market. In this, the stock exchange laws in Germany were simply too restrictive, as had already been demonstrated in the case of the South African Goerz corporations, when it became impossible to trade a company founded under British law on the Berlin stock exchange. 'We must therefore give up on pursuing this idea further', the bank let the government know.[135] Deutsche Bank thus remained very aloof in the following years. It kept track of the financial situation in Morocco but shied away from the risk of getting involved. Even when there were direct inquiries as to whether Deutsche Bank could make advance payments to the sultan against pledges on customs duties – as the French or British backers had been doing – the bank reacted equivocally, 'because the desirable conditions for such business are not really attractive'.[136] Most of all, though, the members of the bank's Management Board shied away from the political risk. They knew that the sultan believed he was most likely to maintain Morocco's independence by inviting in a variety of competing powers. Yet they also realised that any gains would be minor in the face of the 'great hue and cry' that would immediately ensue if Deutsche Bank were to display serious interest.[137] As late as November 1903, the bank was 'too uneasy about conditions in Morocco' to get involved.[138] Yet the bank – and more specifically in this case Management Board member Ludwig Roland-Lücke, in whose jurisdiction Morocco fell – was now closely following the growing activity of German merchants and companies in Morocco. With regard to project proposals, though, the bank remained unconvinced. Roland-Lücke remarked to the Leipzig branch, which had repeatedly sent project ideas to Berlin, that:

> In general, we'd like to note that it doesn't seem at all practical if, in this current boom, all German businessmen with relations to the country hound the Moroccans with loan projects and the like. […] Despite the current trend, one has to anticipate the prevailing sentiment in France, making it unlikely that the German financial community will have an opportunity to make any major financial transactions on a sound basis. In any event, such efforts are not served well by cooking up ill-defined projects.[139]

Gradually, especially after the First Moroccan Crisis and after the open-door policy was sustained, the bank nonetheless demonstrated that it was more interested. Yet it unfailingly tried to stay in the background. This camouflaged approach had obviously been determined – at least outwardly – by the financing struggles over the Baghdad Railway. In that case, Deutsche Bank, despite striving to develop international syndicates, had always been blocked along the way, especially by the British side. In April 1905, another request was made to establish a bank in Morocco. Roland-Lücke took it as the occasion to become informed in detail about the situation. In his background discussion with Joachim Graf von Pfeil, an expert on Africa who had long been campaigning for increased involvement in Morocco, Pfeil talked about four business opportunities in Morocco, immediately ruling out the first one: settling German colonists there. The second, to construct harbour projects, was more interesting given the lack of good ports; the necessary land could be purchased fairly inexpensively from the Moors, he claimed. Third, there was a considerable need to build a wireless telegraph network. Fourth, and finally, it would be 'quite advantageous … to establish a German bank' that could do good business by financing trade with the Moors. Roland-Lücke was sceptical: he too considered German colonisation a futile idea. But he was also rather reserved about port construction projects because of the political situation there because, as the case of Turkey showed, 'none of the powers […] [were going to] yield something of Morocco to the others'. On the telegraph question, Roland-Lücke had been informed that efforts were already underway to obtain a licence, and he indicated that Deutsche Bank might potentially be prepared to participate in the financing. By contrast, establishing a German bank in Morocco, even a branch of Banco Alemán Transatlántico, did not make much sense to him. Any promising businesses could be financed from Germany. Little could be expected from doing business with traders there; above all, the bank would have to wait to see how things developed politically. Yet Roland-Lücke showed great interest in the natural resources of Morocco and asked Pfeil targeted questions about them. Pfeil gave some hints about ore deposits, but, even so, he maintained, the situation in the interior was too uncertain to launch any projects. In this context, Roland-Lücke also kept a low profile while still agreeing 'to

Ludwig Roland-Lücke (1855–1917) managed the Morocco projects. He was responsible for the American railway investments before he joined the Management Board in 1895; he remained a member until 1907.

have friends in the industry send an expert to those deposits which might be reached without special effort or danger'. Overall, he deemed Pfeil's proposals worth considering and recommended also getting an Arabic-speaking representative of the bank with good relations to Moroccans to make inquiries about starting a branch there.[140]

In 1905, despite some initial hesitation, Deutsche Bank began drafting specific plans for building two ports at Tangier and Larache (El Araish) together with the construction company of Philipp Holzmann. The bank wanted to finance these projects using loans, which the Moroccan government could guarantee through pledges of customs revenue.[141] Holzmann had already made inquiries on the ground and was quite encouraging about the opportunities in Morocco.[142] That, in turn, made Gwinner more confident, especially since he was 'on friendly terms' with the German chargé d'affaires in Morocco, Christian Graf von Tattenbach, whose wife came from the Frankfurt-based banking family of Metzler.[143] When a German company based in Tangier contacted Deutsche Bank in the summer of 1905 about the port construction venture, the Berlin headquarters showed its cards, telling a representative of the company that the bank was 'in principle ready […] to make a specific credit available to his company that will make it possible to conclude a business deal with our friend, the construction company Ph. Holzmann & Co. of Frankfurt/M'.[144]

Word got around. At the end of May, Max Warburg approached Paul Mankiewitz, confirming that he had heard about the bank's Moroccan activities and that he, too, was attracted by the prospects, being interested in a possible collaboration.[145] The bank reacted equivocally: it would get back to him if business there 'could be realistically pursued', which was not the case at the moment.[146] The reason for such evasiveness was plain: Deutsche Bank did not want to co-operate with Warburg and Norddeutsche Bank, as Roland-Lücke let Beit von Speyer know, since the other group had sought to establish a German-French bank in Morocco at the start of July 1905.[147] He openly expressed his reasons for abstaining from such bank projects:

> We ourselves have not wanted to take an initiative in this direction because creating such small banks is all too often a questionable pleasure. If, as reported, Messrs Ballin [the general director of the Hamburg America Line] and Max Warburg are pursuing the matter, then it means, of course, that the circle surrounding Norddeutsche Bank and Disconto-Gesellschaft is involved. It does not seem advisable to me in this instance to disrupt that group or to offer our co-operation.[148]

Deutsche Bank pressed forward with harbour construction yet got caught up in the details because Holzmann was dependent on the sultan's middlemen, whose sincerity was not easy to assess.[149] After a great deal of toing and froing, the contract for expanding the Tangier port was finally signed in August 1905, much to the chagrin of the French public and political class. Even so, Deutsche Bank, at the request of the Foreign Office, had made intensive efforts to postpone its signing in response to the criticism.[150] The construction of the port could therefore begin. Deutsche Bank supported Holzmann in building the quayside in Tangier and continued its support later on as well, when it came to expanding the port and adjacent land and planning the construction of a railway line.[151] Making a deal for a potential port in Larache turned out to be more difficult, however. Roland-Lücke and Holzmann initially agreed on a proposal that would set up a port-operating company. That entity would receive a loan to expand one of the sultan's ports, and it would operate that port until the guaranteed revenue completely repaid the loan amount; after that point, the port would revert to the Moroccan government at no further costs.[152] Yet the Moroccan government – clearly under the influence of potential French interests opposed to German involvement in the construction and operation of ports – not only proved a less than reliable partner but was unable to prevent itself from asking for new advances. Deutsche Bank did not want to provide these, nor was it willing to issue a large Moroccan loan.[153] Hence, it became increasingly clear that the business environment in Morocco was so politicised that there was almost no leeway to develop normal projects. According to Roland-Lücke, that is also why Deutsche Bank was still indisposed: 'I said to Mr Goetsch [a representative of the Foreign Office] that we were absolutely not hot on Morocco and that we still thought it advisable to proceed with great caution in the present moment.'[154] Above all, it was, in fact, politicians who were pressing to expand business activity, not only towards specific businesses they were backing but also towards a merger of German interests, particularly by establishing a Moroccan-based syndicate that would be as broad as possible and would enable the financing of large-scale businesses through risk diversification. Yet such a group would only be valuable to Deutsche Bank if it were to remain small and select, as explained by Roland-Lücke to a representative of the Foreign Office:

When we got to the topic of forming a syndicate, it turned out that Goetsch assumed that we would more or less unite all the local banks into one, at which point I straight away told G.[oetsch] it was utterly out of the question. He claimed that these kinds of sensitive matters really only required a simple table where one could work quietly – today with the French, tomorrow with the British – and that would, hence, not be prevented by the problems of a larger table, at which none of those involved had a proper interest.[155]

However, Deutsche Bank was able to envisage 'an association of companies from our group' but not much else. Then, however, the Foreign Office insisted on a large syndicate and requested a meeting at the Hotel Continental in Berlin to bring all interested German parties together. Deutsche Bank responded by refusing to enter a syndicate under anyone else's leadership and recommended that the meeting be postponed. Only after the bank had further discussions with the Foreign Office and came to a mutual understanding with Berliner Handels-Gesellschaft did it finally consent to a syndicate of limited duration, to be operative until 30 December 1907 under the heading of 'exploring economic conditions' in Morocco. At the same time, this was not a syndicate that would be making itself known in public.[156] Deutsche Bank clearly had no interest, after its trying experiences in the Ottoman Empire, in once again being a player in challenging political circumstances.

And further developments proved the bank was right. In 1907, the political situation in Morocco came to a head after its customs administration was put under the control of a French citizen. This resulted in a popular uprising which already disapproved of the French port construction project in Casablanca. The ensuing riots were suppressed by France's military – in some circumstances without direct orders. The consequences were devastating.[157] Similar disturbances in 1911 had given France a pretext to occupy the country militarily and to place the sultan effectively under its supervision; that eventually led to the Second Moroccan Crisis after the failed 'Agadir Incident' in which the German Reich experienced a humiliation that was more than just diplomatic. At that point (at the latest), German investors also finally realised that Morocco was a difficult place to do business and would remain that way. German 'parties interested in Morocco' submitted a complaint on 4 September 1911 to Alfred von Kiderlen-Waechter, a state secretary at the German Foreign Office, that the Reich was not adequately looking out for them in Morocco and demanded that the Reich intervene to ensure that German companies were being treated equally.[158] This statement was as symbolic as it was meaningless. When, just a few weeks later, the Hamburg branch of Deutsche Bank proposed a railway project in Morocco, the bank's headquarters in Berlin issued a sober response: not interested.[159] And that was a line it would stick to. In February 1913, Gwinner observed that Deutsche Bank had only kept 'its familiar very small share rate quite low via Holzmann'. There were some interesting projects otherwise, but, as he noted, the bank would then lag behind the dominant French and Spanish investors.[160] More might have been possible in Morocco under different circumstances. But, from the outset, Deutsche Bank gauged the situation there realistically and avoided any grander risky ventures.

7. Nothing But Aggravation in Vienna and Only Good Business on the Limmat

In his memoirs Arthur Gwinner furnished his own – ultimately bitter – views on the history of Wiener Tramway.[161] Together with Siemens & Halske, Deutsche Bank received a licence in 1898 from the city of Vienna to set up a construction and operating company there with a share capital of 50 million crowns. Its goal was to electrify Vienna's 160 kilometres of streetcar lines.[162] The project was from the outset marked by difficult negotiations with the Viennese city government. And soon after it was completed, the city and its dynamic mayor, Karl Lueger, attempted to get the bank out of the venture and to put the city in control. The city administration of Vienna found it possible to do so because it approved the prices for using the streetcar; it left no doubt that it intended to exploit precisely this means in order to get the streetcar company into its own hands. By charging low ticket prices, the city managed to drive the streetcar company into the red, thereby causing the value of its shares to decline. The Vienna streetcar project thus became a bad deal for Deutsche Bank. The bank became more willing to sell the company to the city, but only at a price that would cover the expenses already incurred. Yet city officials did not concede even that, instead wanting to reduce prices even further. Deutsche Bank found itself in a tight spot, as Gwinner saw it. Siemens, who had been repeatedly undiplomatic in Vienna and wanted the Viennese financiers to take more of a German approach to things, had generously tried to help out his friend Moritz Bauer at Wiener Bankverein by taking on the majority of shares in Wiener Tramway at 'highly inflated prices'.[163] Nevertheless, the operation had not become profitable because the city of Vienna constantly communicated new expectations. And, as already mentioned, it was unwilling to approve any higher fares to cover the costs. Selling the streetcar company to the city of Vienna was therefore the only way out for Deutsche Bank. The sales negotiations, described in detail by Gwinner, proved challenging – and not only because of the mediator who had insisted on substantial commissions for his work. Rather, the city of Vienna itself, in exchange for setting a reasonable purchase price, demanded that Deutsche Bank take on a municipal bond – something the bank found difficult to swallow. Gwinner ended up doing what he always did: he sought to share the risk on the loan. He thereby managed to get Crédit Lyonnais on board. Hence, it only became a question of getting approval for the sale at the general shareholders' assembly of the company. At that gathering, however, 'all the shysters, muckrakers, and hacks – of whom there were many – registered their shares […] and [showed up] as indignant investors who were losing money, seeking to declare the management or the banks or anybody else at fault'.[164] It was only thanks to Gwinner's personal efforts, he noted, that the mood of the meeting suddenly changed: 'I never again experienced a meeting that was so raucous.'[165]

In Vienna, Gwinner had little room for manoeuvre. It was clear that he would no longer pay amicable prices under any circumstances. Business in Austria was utterly uninteresting for the Berlin Management Board after these experiences, particularly since the annexation of Bosnia had made the bank's operations in Turkey very difficult. In any case, Wiener Bankverein opened itself up to criticism after presenting its figures in September 1908, where it claimed that it had been very useful to Deutsche Bank in

Stock certificate of the construction and operating company for the municipal trams in Vienna from 1899.

recent years. Mankiewitz put it in clear terms to Bernhard Popper, managing director of Wiener Bankverein:

> On this occasion, though, I'd like to ask you to take a look at the list of transactions we've brought you in the last few years – which consistently yielded quite sizeable profits for you – and compare them with the transactions you've provided Deutsche Bank. You will see quite astonishing numbers there, all the more so since none of your transactions have yet to be settled other than your bank's shares. I know that you can probably tolerate such honesty, which is why I didn't avoid making the comparison.[166]

Gwinner was so infuriated by the Viennese response to Mankiewitz's point that he instructed one of his employees to closely review the numbers from Vienna. Deutsche Bank, he maintained, had not actually profited from its association with Wiener Bankverein; on the contrary, the Viennese partner had only been able to conduct much of the business it was now claiming on its financial statements because it could rely on Deutsche Bank.

> In fact, besides Mannesmann – which is at last a decent business thanks to Mr Steinthal's dedicated efforts – Bankverein has got big gifts and smooth and amicable investments from Deutsche Bank year in, year out. By contrast, we've only got

difficult commissions from Bankverein (Oriental Railways, the streetcar, petroleum, Bulgaria) in addition to business failures and losses such as the Ungarische Industrie-Bank […] etc.

Gwinner concluded his memorandum expressing his outrage: 'The only thing Bankverein hasn't done yet is take the credit for Wiener Tramway, as something it did for Deutsche Bank.'[167]

Gwinner became downright hostile towards any further involvement in Austria. Why, he asked himself, should the bank invest its money in a country 'that we're already on friendly political terms with? Even if the power of our capital and savings there has fortunately increased, the surplus is nonetheless reaching its limit, and these moderate quantities could be used much more appropriately by distributing them to a number of foreign countries in smaller amounts and at good terms; instead, we've been giving ourselves away to simple-minded Austrians who have severely compromised our entire political situation.'[168] In the years to come, Deutsche Bank repeatedly refused to participate in Austrian bond syndicates, having had to take a loss with a syndicate in 1909:

> We're in the unpleasant situation of having to collect this loss from our numerous secondary partners. It's the first time since 1 January 1894 that Deutsche Bank has been in such a position. Apart from a few ventures in gold mining and exploration, in which only a very small group of our employees was involved, Deutsche Bank has not had to take a loss in syndicate business deals since at least 1894. The present case ought to teach us not to let the Austrians get the better of us each time.[169]

This attitude would harden in the coming years until the beginning of the First World War. Although Deutsche Bank was still involved in financing individual companies, it nonetheless was reserved when it had opportunities to finance the Austrian state, as shown by Elkan Heinemann's rejection of an informal request made by the k. u. k. Postsparkasse (Imperial and Royal Postal Savings Bank) just a few days before war broke out.[170] In the decades prior to the First World War, Austria had not been a good place for Deutsche Bank. There, as in the US, the domestic competition ultimately prevailed whenever it was necessary to put down rivals from abroad. Deutsche Bank's services were welcomed if they benefited Austrian commerce, yet in the end the bank was not allowed to act independently there.

While Deutsche Bank's relationship with Wiener Bankverein, and with Austrian business per se, had become difficult once Georg Siemens's close ties no longer existed, its cooperation with Credit Suisse developed quite constructively. Deutsche Bank was a key part of the syndicate that implemented the capital increases in the Swiss bank in the 1890s. Yet, beyond that, the two banks also undertook strategic projects together. The Swiss had interests in the petroleum business but also wanted to participate in Ottoman railway projects. And they had similar plans for electrifying the Mediterranean railway: 'That would, of course, be an immense deal for AEG, and [Julius] Frey [general director of Credit Suisse] has high hopes for it,' observed Paul Mankiewitz after a visit to Zurich in 1903.[171] This trusting relationship between the banks continued up to the war. Each involved the other in major financing deals such as Bank für elektrische Unternehmungen (Elektrobank) and Bank for Oriental Railways, both of which had their headquarters in Zurich. Deutsche Bank also deliberately avoided conflicts of interest. In 1904 it relinquished the Basel branch of the allied Oberrheinische Bank to Credit Suisse without protest, wishing to avoid a competitive situation in which there was little to gain anyway.[172] Deutsche Bank also readily agreed to Swiss plans to jointly establish a bank in Paris and to support a London branch of Credit Suisse.[173] Gwinner was also upbeat about establishing a joint Paris institution; his bank had refrained from getting involved on its own because it expected the French public to have reservations about it.[174] Even though such a mutual institution never materialised, Credit Suisse remained a key link to France. All in all, it was a very important partner and was treated accordingly 'as a friend' by Deutsche Bank. The tone was encouraging on both sides,[175] and it certainly helped that the German side generally went out of its way for Credit Suisse so that the latter did not risk becoming completely dependent on the extremely liquid money and capital markets in France; these were already much more influential in Switzerland than the German capital markets ever could have been, if only due to the diverging interest rates. Max von Thielemann, the state secretary in the Reich Treasury, urged Deutsche Bank (and Disconto-Gesellschaft) to be more involved in Switzerland so that the Swiss would not end up even more dependent on France.[176] Roland-Lücke was able to explain this well: the lower French interest rate made its money and capital markets highly attractive, circumstances that would have been even more one-sided if the stamp duty legislation in France had not discouraged foreign investors.[177] That comment was likewise a dig at the laws regarding the Berlin stock exchange, though that issue played only a marginal role in this case. Ultimately, Deutsche Bank could not ignore the prevailing conditions in Switzerland. Yet, its co-operation with Credit Suisse was also successful because the leaders of the respective banks knew and liked each other.

8. The 'Fürstentrust' (Princes' Trust)

Even if Disconto-Gesellschaft still possessed a greater aura, Deutsche Bank came to be the pivotal player in the German financial markets in the years leading up to the First World War. In this respect, it is not surprising that Emperor Wilhelm II turned directly to Arthur Gwinner when one of the largest financial scandals of the late empire needed to be kept under wraps. It was the collapse of Handelsvereinigung AG, informally referred to as the 'Fürstentrust', in which the princely houses of Hohenlohe and Fürstenberg had pooled part of their financial interests. These aristocrats had aimed to conduct financial transactions using assets that were not committed to trusts so that they might participate in the economic boom of the years prior to the First World War.[178] The nesting principle, already mentioned above, was also something the princes intended to make use of. Thus Hohenlohe-Öhringen, after failed attempts to gain a foothold on Madeira, founded Handelsvereinigung to pursue real estate and building projects in Berlin, to which Fürstenberg then contributed his Berlin real estate assets. Through its shady general director, Handelsvereinigung developed a variety of project ideas primarily directed at real estate and trading companies in Berlin. These projects, which eventually comprised Berlin companies that were nested together for construction, real estate and commercial transactions, could then be financed through mortgage loans to which Deutsche Bank also contributed. In addition, the 'Fürstentrust' made use of the Berlin-based Deutsche Palästina-Bank (German Palestine Bank), established in 1889, that operated branches with moderate success in Jerusalem, Haifa, Jaffa and Beirut.[179] Half of Palestine Bank's shares were held by the Hohenlohe Group. To buttress its financial strength, the bank's capital was initially increased to 5 million marks and its management transferred to Hermann Witscher, a successful banker from Niederrheinische Bank in Düsseldorf.[180] The broader public did not fail to notice that these moves were not exclusively concerned with financing trade in the Levant:

> It's well known that the institution is completely dominated by the princes' trust of Hohenlohe-Fürstenberg, as is already evident in the composition of its supervisory board. Hohenlohe's interests are by far the predominant ones here. Although this bank maintains vigorous relations to the Orient even today, having just recently expanded its number of branches there by establishing an office in Tripoli, its name is really only of historical interest for us today inasmuch as transactions within Germany have increasingly moved to the centre of the bank's business.[181]

This was a more than accurate assessment. Palästina-Bank was, above all, financing the Berlin transactions of the princes' trust; the core of these transactions was developing a large, already mortgaged property on Oranienburger Straße where a huge department store was to be built under the direction of the youngest of the Wertheim brothers.

This development was closely watched by Deutsche Bank, which was interested in the business of Palästina-Bank and knowing whether it could develop into a competitor in the Ottoman Empire. In the course of some property transactions in Berlin, in which a new office was sought for Handelsvereinigung, there was open discussion about splitting up the actual activity of Palästina-Bank. This Orient-focused trade bank

Stock certificate of Deutsche Palästina-Bank, which belonged to the Hohenlohe Group, from 1912.

was to be relocated to Hamburg while an 'asset management office for the Hohenlohe family' would stay behind in Berlin. In the course of this split, the bank's capital was to be increased to 20 million marks, which is why Witscher and Klönne wanted to have a meeting to prepare the capital increase for 1 January 1911. Prince Hohenlohe, it was claimed, wanted to increase that capital to 10 million and take over 2.5 million from the other 10 million 'while the other half would be at the disposal of Deutsche Bank,' noted Klönne. He did not find it unattractive to participate since that meant that he would also be named on the supervisory board of Palästina-Bank:

> We would have to occupy a position on the supervisory board to represent our interests in Asia Minor, to get the bank to go to the places we want, [and] to keep it away from Constantinople. One must also consider whether, over time, the bank should go to Alexandria, or whether that site should instead be reserved for Deutsche Bank.[182]

In the subsequent internal consultations, Deutsche Bank quickly realised that the whole matter could cause considerable trouble. Evidently, none of it had to do with the Orient. Deutsche Levante-Linie, which was also controlled by Palästina-Bank, did well,[183] but inquiries made in Deutsche Bank's Constantinople branch suggested that capital increases for it or for Palästina-Bank's network of branches were completely inflated: 'So, it almost seems to me,' said the head of the Constantinople branch, 'as if D.[eutsche] P.[alästina] B.[ank] had mainly earned its dividends from managing the assets of the princes' group, and not from its branches.'[184] Most of the bank's loans were to be used for the department store project on Oranienburger Straße, although it was not certain whether those loans were sufficiently covered. Deutsche Bank was therefore hesitant about participating in the capital increase and waited for additional information.[185] The recommendations made eventually pointed towards investing in the Oriental business of Palästina-Bank – indeed, Witscher was considered a serious banker[186] – yet also advised that this business be detached from Handelsvereinigung's dealings in Berlin.[187] That is, in fact, what transpired, but Deutsche Bank was in no way putting distance between itself and the princes' group. After a rift had emerged between the Hohenlohe Group and its Hausbank, Berliner Handels-Gesellschaft, Deutsche Bank got closer to this parent company of Handelsvereinigung when Carl Klönne took over the chairmanship of the supervisory board previously held by Carl Fürstenberg. Deutsche Bank was thus involved in several respects: as a mortgage holder, as a partner co-operating with Palästina-Bank and as a supervisory authority reporting to the Hohenlohe Group. It is an open question whether the bank was completely able to see through the interlocked and heavily indebted structure of Handelsvereinigung. This itself depended entirely on whether the Passage Department Store project would be profitable. For it was hedging its bets that revenue from that project would repay the interest and the credits received and result in at least a minimal yield on the capital invested. The collapse of Handelsvereinigung undoubtedly involved fraud, yet representatives of Deutsche Bank must have realised that the institution was already on shaky ground.[188] In any event, the bank had ensured that its claims against Handelsvereinigung were adequately covered by 'good collaterals'. And, when Handelsvereinigung did fall apart in 1913, Deutsche Bank was not at risk but was able to collect key assets from the bankruptcy estate, such as the construction company Boswau & Knauer. As Gwinner remarked, 'The only losers here must be the two wealthy aristocrats, Prince Hohenlohe and Prince Fürstenberg, who will be several million marks poorer – yet richer as well for having learned that high-ranking gentlemen should stay away from commerce.'[189]

9. 'Irons in the fire'

All in all, Deutsche Bank's experiences in foreign capital markets provided a mixed bag. Even if the bank's foreign syndicate financing deals were almost all successes, it was not unusual for it to end up high and dry in its own business activities, as had been the case in the US and in Austria. Likewise, the bank's oil transactions in the Balkans and Turkey had been anything but trouble-free. And it was said that Paul Mankiewitz ultimately deemed the chances of placing American securities to be unpromising. More interesting, however, was his point that Deutsche Bank had enough 'irons in the fire' in its home markets to be able to thrive splendidly. This point came to be gradually acknowledged by the bank's other Management Board members as well. The costs and proceeds from foreign investments did not always have to be better than corresponding activities in the domestic market: 'Why should we,' contended Arthur Gwinner vis-à-vis Mankiewitz at the end of 1908, 'have to stoop to sending large sums of German capital abroad at interest rates that our own industries would very much approve of.'[190] In fact, domestic demand in the money and capital markets was rising sharply due to cyclical factors. Not only were there countless industrial projects to finance, but the public debt of the empire, its states and its municipalities also continued to rise steadily.

But Deutsche Bank did not relinquish its engagements abroad, which it had good grounds to defend against its critics. However, the actual weight of its business shifted in favour of financing domestic projects since these also became increasingly prominent. Only in special cases did the annual reports of Deutsche Bank tally the individual businesses it dealt with separately, such as the Baghdad Railway or Steaua Română. A similar status was also achieved in 1913 by a few domestic projects in which the bank played a leading role. These investments included Gesellschaft für elektrische Hoch- und Untergrundbahnen in Berlin, a business that was controlled by both Deutsche Bank and Siemens & Halske and that, in accordance with the usual nesting principle, promoted the expansion of public transport in the rapidly growing metropolis of Berlin. Without this expansion, it would not have been possible for the city's population to grow from about one million people (in the Greater Berlin of 1870) to more than three million prior to the First World War.[191] It was therefore pivotal for Deutsche Bank to draw attention to this contribution in a way that made for good publicity, especially since the investment proved entirely successful:

In the year under review, Gesellschaft für elektrische Hoch- und Untergrundbahnen in Berlin has placed these new lines into operation as planned: Spittelmarkt–Alexanderplatz–Schönhauser Allee, Wittenbergplatz–Nürnberger Platz (with a connection to Dahlem), and Wittenbergplatz–Uhlandstrasse. Expectations for these new routes have been entirely fulfilled; the increase in revenue has been so substantial that it has ensured a reasonable return on the capital newly invested by the company.[192]

When examined on their own, the syndicate transactions documented in Deutsche Bank's annual reports reflect a strong increase in volume, from around 45 issuances, capital increases and real estate transactions in 1900 to more than 300 such transactions in 1913,[193] divided in roughly equal numbers into domestic and foreign activities. Not only had real estate transactions expanded robustly; in this period, the bank was also involved in almost all large capital increases of major companies in Germany while also serving the credit needs of the public sector to a significant extent. Between 1900 and 1913, Deutsche Bank was becoming one of the leading banks in the Rhenish-Westphalian industrial region, a special accomplishment attributable to Carl Klönne. In this, too, the bank was catching up with Disconto-Gesellschaft, whose real strength had been its good relations with heavy industry in western Germany for some time.[194] The capital increases by large and important companies denote clearly what Mankiewitz meant when he talked about 'irons in the fire': the capital needs of up-and-coming German industries were so prodigious that they nearly entirely claimed large portions of the German money and capital markets, and specifically at interest rates and conditions that could scarcely have been achieved abroad. One way these circumstances were manifested was in the solid rise of appointments of Deutsche Bank's own Management Board members to the supervisory boards of

Deutsche Bank advertised in the subway station at Wittenbergplatz in 1918 with its contribution to the construction of Berlin's elevated and underground railway.

other companies. Carl Klönne alone held 25 such seats on supervisory boards[195] while Elkan Heinemann also managed to make it on to 15 boards including at Siemens & Halske and Mannesmann.[196] The case of Heinemann, whose importance in the bank's petroleum business was already identified above, demonstrates the idea of having many 'irons in the fire' even better than the case of Klönne, whose sphere of activity was chiefly limited to the Rhenish-Westphalian industrial area. By contrast, Heinemann had been involved in financing transactions in Bolivia, Java, Russia (Petersburg Streetcar) and Japan; in the Ottoman Empire, he had looked after German pipe mills and electrical businesses. He also handled the affairs of Shantung Mining Company and Shantung Railway Company in China, on whose boards he was a member. He supervised power plants in Alsace as well as oil fields in Germany and was deputy chairman of the adminis-

Carl Klönne (1850–1915) began his career at A. Schaaffhausen'scher Bankverein in Cologne, where he took care of the industrial business. In 1900, he transferred to the Management Board of Deutsche Bank in Berlin, where he continued to deal with industry in the Rhine and Ruhr area.

trative board of Gesellschaft für elektrische Beleuchtung in St Petersburg until 1914. In addition, he organised loans for Victoria Falls Transvaal Power & Co., launched Deutsche Bank's equity stake in London's Underground Electric Railway and played a significant role in Aktiengesellschaft Elektrische Kraft of Baku. Yet he also served on the board of Ungarische Localeisenbahnen and was a key figure in international financing transactions conducted through the Brussels branch of Deutsche Bank.[197]

Since the other members of the Management Board besides Klönne and Heinemann held diverse seats on other boards, Deutsche Bank was also a kind of spider in the web before 1914. Yet that hardly justifies the argument of 'financial capitalism', postulated at this time by Marxist theorist Rudolf Hilferding and today still considered relevant by a number of social scientists conducting research on supervisory board networks.[198] Such an impression, for which something might be said, does not do the matter justice, because one can hardly speak of the banks being dominant in their relationships with industry. Rather, the banks played a kind of service role because they had little control over the businesses they financed. Nor did most of them want to have it. Anatolian Railway Company or Steaua Română were the exceptions, not the rule.[199] And as Volker Wellhöner has shown, the banks by no means dominated the industrial enterprises they financed and on whose supervisory bodies they were represented. Rather, large-scale industry was usually successful at maintaining its autonomy despite growing ratios of debt financing.[200] As Paul Mankiewitz soberly stated: 'The large industrial companies generally dominate the banks and not vice versa.'[201]

To be sure, the profusion of supervisory board mandates helped the bank preserve the information necessary for conducting its increasingly extensive business, both at a relatively low cost and in a reliable manner. Together with information compiled by Deutsche Treuhand-Gesellschaft, the management of Deutsche Bank, based on the economic research of its Archive, may ultimately have had a good overview of the German corporate landscape, especially because it had unrestricted access to the banks in 'its' group at all times. Deutsche Bank Management Board members were therefore sought-after and sometimes even feared figures in every respect. This was because the bank's high level of informedness often made it reluctant to deal with certain businesses.[202] Yet the information base of Deutsche Bank not only included its knowledge of projects, supervisory board mandates and audit reports; it was also well informed about current economic transactions in Germany on the basis of its 'regular business'; in addition, it was quite well acquainted with the wishes and concerns of the investment community due to its large deposit business. Owing to its nearly 290,000 managed accounts in 1913, the bank could make a reasonably realistic assessment of the German market and its capacities at any time. This was an essential issue for any bank, if it wished to adequately assess the prospects of risky issuance transactions. It should come as no surprise that the voice of Deutsche Bank attained special significance in the disputes over the liquidity of the banks and possible bottlenecks in the German money market in the years prior to the First World War, above all, the voice of Arthur Gwinner, who was appointed to the Prussian parliament in 1910 in recognition of the bank's importance.[203]

One specific feature of Deutsche Bank should not be disregarded, which distinguished it at least quantitatively from other major German banks. Unlike Disconto-Gesellschaft, Deutsche Bank did not primarily make its money from its financing business. Although this undoubtedly contributed to the results despite all the variability, the backbone of Deutsche Bank's profitability was its 'regular business', as Georg Siemens had dubbed it. Since the 1870s, the bank had enjoyed a certain advantage in the deposit business, which it gradually expanded by extending its network of branches. Then, in the 1890s, Deutsche Bank took a big step forward, rendering the difference between itself and the other large banks ever greater. In the years after 1900, the bank's deposits were already much larger than those of Disconto-Gesellschaft and kept growing rapidly.[204] In 1910 they reached 558 million marks, whereas Disconto-Gesellschaft had only 313 million and Dresdner Bank 268 million.[205] This basis enabled Deutsche Bank, at least in the eyes of the competition, to have an aggressive lending business in the areas of short-term trade finance and general lending, both unsecured and against collateral. The bank developed into a veritable 'suction pump', turning its ever-growing number of creditors into a highly active business so that, as early as the mid-1890s, a number of observers such as Paul Model regarded Deutsche Bank's balance sheets as inflated to an almost unhealthy extent. In Model's eyes, this deficit could be attributed to business practices that were unfair or just too aggressive, but also to excessive deposit rates and veritable credit dumping; he thus deemed liquidity problems as highly likely. But such negative predictions never materialised.[206] On the contrary: a clever mixture of debit and credit business was the secret of Deutsche Bank's remarkable success. An astute policy of maturity transformation between creditors and debtors, as well as forming reserves and strictly limiting risk, kept the bank from having liquidity problems even in the challenging period following the outbreak of the American financial crisis in 1907. At that point, the Reichsbank had to raise the discount rate radically and on short notice, due to the threat of gold outflows. The 'suction pump' that also served its purpose in the opposite direction – by placing issuances publicly – instead remained intact for the entire period before 1914, thereby giving Deutsche Bank a decisive competitive advantage.

V. The Group: Organisational Structures, Personnel Development and Regional Form, 1870–1914

1. Organisation[1]

At least until the stock corporation laws were amended in 1884, the organisational structure of Deutsche Bank was based on the Statute of 1870, which, strictly speaking, only provided for two major bodies of a joint-stock company: an Administrative Board and a general meeting.[2] The Administrative Board, or its smaller Committee of Five presided over by Adelbert Delbrück, was the bank's actual control centre; the annual general meeting had no major operational significance.[3] The Management Board, or 'directorate' (as it used to be called), was, at least on paper, an executive body of the Administrative Board that lacked the authority to act on its own. This was the background to Wallich's bitter comment that he was treated like a clerk at first – and a poorly paid one at that. In point of fact, the Administrative Board's Committee of Five took its duties very seriously. It met weekly, making all the major decisions itself. As a result, whenever important strategic planning was to be done, there was invariably protracted conflict – especially when the Management Board had its own ideas about something. This was also the context in which Siemens remarked sarcastically that 'when 24 people try to run a bank, it's like a wench with 24 suitors. None of them marries her. But she still ends up with a child!'[4] A formal emancipation of the Management Board from the Administrative Board did not take place until 1884.

The composition of the Administrative Board was therefore of enormous importance, especially before 1884. First and foremost, the bank's founding parties were represented on it. In 1880, the Administrative Board, which had 25 members at the time of incorporation, still included 24 people from the sphere of initiators, i.e. its first underwriters and customers. By 1913, the Supervisory Board had 27 members, who still included representatives of the most important founding shareholders and customers but also earlier members of the Management Board and branch managers. In the years prior to 1914, Deutsche Bank remained true to itself when recruiting Administrative or, later, Supervisory Board members. Above all, this practice served to stabilise business relationships and was undoubtedly intended to signal the bank's solidity. Occasionally, there were also political gestures, such as appointing the German-American journalist Friedrich Kapp, a good friend of Ludwig Bamberger and a liberal politician with an early socialist past. After the failed Revolution of 1848,

Kapp had emigrated to the US. However, he returned to Germany in 1870, where he represented the National Liberals in the Reichstag and in the Prussian House of Representatives.[5] Kapp, who had likewise been in business with the founders of the bank during his time in New York, remained on the Administrative Board until his death in 1884. Incidentally, his son Wolfgang, who went on to play an inglorious role in 1920 as the namesake of the Kapp Putsch, succeeded his father on the bank's Supervisory Board in 1912. Such cases, though, were the exception and not the norm. The leading members of this board were businessmen, industrialists and shareholders. Hermann Marcuse, for example, was a member for the entire period between 1870 and 1899. Besides him, there were other significant initial subscribers on the Supervisory Board, albeit not for long periods. A change on the Supervisory Board, typically when a member had died, usually indicated that the bank's business relationships had changed. Although the board initially consisted primarily of bankers and business-men, they were later joined by industrialists. Ernst von Eynern, also the chairman of the supervisory board at Farbenfabriken Bayer & Co., served until his death; Ernst von Borsig was added, too, as were industrialists from Düsseldorf and the Ruhr at the turn of the century. In addition, there was always a strong presence of members from Frankfurt am Main. Non-Germans did not play a role again until shortly before the war, when the Belgian Charles Balser found his way to the Supervisory Board in connection with the founding of the Brussels branch.[6] Adelbert Delbrück presided over the supervisory board until 1889, yet none of his successors claimed a prominent role in the management of the bank before the First World War. Neither Adolph vom Rath, who chaired the board from 1889 to 1907, nor Wilhelm Herz, who chaired it from 1907 to 1914, were particularly important in the bank's operations. As distin-guished members of Berlin society, they undoubtedly helped to promote the bank's reputation while also symbolising its importance, although it would be hard to over-estimate the import of Anna vom Rath's salon (see below). In practice, however, the significance of the Supervisory Board did not go beyond its legally mandated tasks of supervision and auditing.

The organisational structure of the banking operation, as it gradually materialised, plainly had a clear hierarchy ranging from the Supervisory Board and the Management Board, down through the secretariat and other departments, all the way to the day-to-day operations. Yet, in some respects, this structure could be broken down into two main areas, as reflected in Deutsche Bank's traditions as they have been passed down. The basis of the bank's work was the functioning of a technical apparatus, which had to deal with ever-increasing daily business smoothly and efficiently. In its details, however, this work was so unspectacular that it is largely forgotten today, apart from a few fragments. At the same time, it constituted the beating heart of the banking oper-ation. Besides the general cash desk operations, this operation consisted mainly of: transactions in current and exchange accounts, the lending business, foreign currency and the performing of routine securities transactions. Each of these areas had separate offices, held together by the correspondence office and the respective accounting departments. Separate from the others was the deposit business. Orders and requests came in through interactions with the public and incoming mail. These were then processed by the sorting office and forwarded to the responsible 'bank officials'. After a subsequent internal audit, orders and requests were executed and registered; finally, the client received notification via the correspondence office.[7] These business areas engaged the bank from the very outset, though only on a limited scale at first. Consequently, the assorted departments, which were slowly becoming established, were initially able to get by with a minimal number of bank officials. Karl Wichmann described this early organisation of the workflow in some detail while recalling his apprenticeship at Deutsche Bank in Berlin's Burgstraße.[8] Even though the hours were demanding and the offices were open seven days a week – Wichmann recalled that the staff was in the office on Sunday mornings as well – the 30 or so bank officials who initially performed the day-to-day labour were soon no longer sufficient. Yet a rationalisation of banking operations in the sense of mechanising certain work processes was a very limited possibility in technological terms before 1914. Moreover, at the banks, employees were convinced that technological rationalisation was not at all desirable.[9] Only the typewriter managed to conquer the bank's offices by the 1890s. Until that time, according to Max Fuchs, long-time chief economist and archivist of the bank, 'the components of our craft were [...] ledgers, paper, quill and ink'.[10]

The number of employees swelled considerably over the years, a development paralleled by the increase in exchange and current accounts plus in deposit transactions. Clearly, the bank's merger with Deutsche Union-Bank and Berliner Bank-Verein in 1875–6 may have driven those numbers upward. By the same token, the total number of accounts mushroomed, as did incoming and outgoing exchange transactions and the amount of general correspondence. For the first time in 1879, an annual report documented the number of current account customers, which had reached 1,923. Together with the deposit customers, the total number of accounts was probably still under 5,000 at this point. By the start of the 1890s, however, the number of current and deposit accounts was well over 25,000. In 1900, almost 77,000 accounts were registered; by 1903, the 100,000 mark had been surpassed, and, in 1913, in the last regular financial year before the war, almost 290,000 accounts were recorded.[11] For 1908–9, Max Fuchs summed up the range of the bank's operations as follows:

> In the bills of exchange department this year, there were around 3,580,000 bills coming in and going, i.e. considering a working time of 300 days a year, that makes approximately 12,000 bills per day. That figure rose considerably in the year 1909. Now the daily input alone is approximately 7,000 items.[12]

The volume of incoming and outgoing mail was correspondingly high, at 11,000 pieces shipped in 1908. In 1913, that means that there were almost 4.3 million bills distributed throughout the year; at 300 working days annually, that resulted in 14–15,000 pieces per day, each having to go through several hands before processing was completed.[13]

With its labour productivity stagnating or only marginally increasing, Deutsche Bank's elasticity of supply depended largely on whether the necessary personnel could be recruited and retained. The ensuing numbers indicate a high degree of success. In

1880, a decade after the bank was established, the number of employees had reached c. 550; in the early 1890s, that figure exceeded 1,000. An exact number of employees was mentioned for the first time in the annual report of 1894: 1,072 people were recorded as working for the bank. This trend accelerated in the years to come: thus, in 1900, the 2,000 mark was exceeded, and in 1904 there were more than 3,000. By 1906, there were already more than 4,000 employees. In 1914, including the employees of Bergisch Märkische Bank, which had just been acquired in March 1914, that number finally reached 8,607, thus marking the end of the dynamic development of the pre-war period. During the First World War, employee numbers continued to rise. However, this expansion had other causes than the growth of the pre-war period, which clearly was attributable to regular banking business. After the war had broken out, regular business was no longer possible.[14]

The bulk of the personnel were employed at the Berlin headquarters of Deutsche Bank. A quarter of them were at the branch deposit banks, which were based mostly in Berlin and had possessed their own organisational structure since the mid-1870s. The heaquarters was divided into several large divisions with corresponding departments, each of them headed by senior authorised representatives, and later on by departmental managers.[15] These divisions, departments and subdepartments included a correspondence office, a department for bills of exchange and foreign currency, a securities department and a cash office. Yet, in addition to these, there were numerous accounting operations, including

> the accountant who maintains clients' current accounts, the securities accountant who keeps the deposits ledger, the securities order book in which accounts are listed (not by the individual names of customers but by those of the securities themselves), the auditor who examines the invoices, and the controller of settlement notes who monitors usage of the stamp (so that the tax office, when it has occasion to audit those stamps, has no reason to deduct any funds).[16]

Close co-operation and mutual control over the varied work areas were essential; accordingly, the general atmosphere at work was rigorous and serious. From their clothing to their general appearance, the bank officials embodied this spirit of propriety, something that the bank methodically promoted in its expectation of how employees should behave. This requirement even extended to the large number of messengers and servants, a total of 420 people in 1908. Just like the 100 or so porters and guards, they were 'provided by the bank with dress uniforms'.[17] The only ones without uniforms were the approximately 200 women who cleaned the bank every day between 5.00 and 8.30 a.m. in the years before 1914. At the same time, however, they cost the bank more than 100,000 marks in wages and cleaning supplies: order and cleanliness were indispensable, especially when dealing with the public.

This well-oiled 'calculating machine', which by and large handled the extensive day-to-day business smoothly and efficiently, operated very differently from the actual leadership at the bank. This was because the top management was only partially involved in organising and guiding daily business, being involved instead in handling major non-everyday tasks that (in hindsight) were more spectacular. The charts below reflect the bank's organisational structure as described here quite well, even if they suggest a clarity that did not really exist. Nonetheless, these figures may provide a decent outline of the state of the organisation in the 1870s:

Figure 1: Organisational structure of Deutsche Bank in the 1870s.

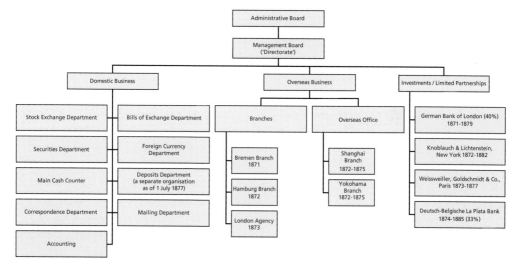

Source: Dahlem, *Professionalisierung*, p. 37.

Compared to this 'calculating machine' numbering thousands of staff, the department referred to as the 'Secretariat', remained quite small into the 1890s. Closely aligned with the Management Board, it was in charge of the syndicate business. That would change in the Gwinner era. Max Fuchs, to whom we are indebted for inside perspectives on the bank, likewise commented on the period of the mid-1890s:

> In light of the number and extent of the bank's financing transactions at that time, the secretariat had a comparatively small staff of officials. In exactly the same room, along with three correspondence clerks, sat the bank's legal counsel; he was the only one in the organisation back then, and he had no assistants. The next room housed the three members of the secretariat's team of accountants, and a third room housed three officers who were also registrars. The only one who had a small room off to the side, separated by a glass wall, was the deputy Management Board member who ran the secretariat. Gwinner had brought a number of employees over from his own bank (which he led until moving to Deutsche Bank in 1894) when he arrived; two of them who were especially attuned to his needs were assigned to the secretariat. That was in some ways symbolic of the upsurge in work that was about to commence under his leadership. In the nineties, the bank's business expanded so rapidly that every attempt at enlarging the staff soon proved inade-

quate. New and renovated buildings were almost always being worked on. Nor did every Management Board member get his own office space. Gwinner worked with Dr von Siemens at the same double desk, although that enabled them to have a quick chat about a matter and thus to work quite harmoniously.[18]

This portrayal from 1931 is one of the rare pieces of information about how the bank's leaders carried out their work, because they were otherwise disinclined to let the competition know what they were up to. Max Fuchs evidently exercised a great deal of restraint when he characterised the organisation of Deutsche Bank in 1909 as the source of 'its strength and distinctiveness as well as its trade secret'.[19] The leadership of the bank consisted initially of four Management Board members but later grew to more than 10. Their labour, in turn, was supported by a secretariat that also expanded; it did much of the legwork for the Management Board and took care of its correspondence. That legwork was performed, above all, by authorised representatives and later by departmental managers; immediate assistance was ultimately provided by the deputy Management Board members, whose number in the 1890s fluctuated between one and four. Similar to Disconto-Gesellschaft, for instance, whose organisational structure was the basis for Deutsche Bank's (according to information provided by Hansemann's biographer Hermann Münch),[20] there was a kind of informal cabinet at the top. At the beginning, this cabinet decided on the bank's strategic orientation in consultation with the Administrative Board; later on, the cabinet exercised more autonomy. The decisions were made in close (and often disputatious) communication between the initial four Management Board members, and then after the 1890s in an extended round. Nonetheless, it all continued to occur in a kind of informal voting that was effectively shaped by mutual discussions of business opportunities and proposals. In these discussions, the Management Board dealt with the entire range of capital market transactions. The respective weight of an individual Management Board member depended, above all, on his personal qualifications and inclinations; on this Management Board, there was no formal hierarchy.

Organisationally as well, the leadership of the bank had long been rather uncomplicated. The Management Board members were responsible for all business appropriations, something which, in practice, was limited by certain specialisations. Only with the robust growth of certain business areas in the 1890s did the undifferentiated structure of the secretariat turn out to be too simple, although it had previously been adequate for directing the bank's syndicate business. Therefore, certain work areas were spun off from the secretariat and given their own organisational structures. There was, for instance, the 'Oriental Office' in which, prior to 1900, the very extensive business in and with the Ottoman Empire – especially railway construction – was concentrated. Together with the office overseeing the bank's branches, which also co-ordinated all correspondence with those branches, the Oriental Office remained the only organisational innovation made by the top management. The organisational structure in the years before 1914 reveals this kind of differentiation, even though it suggests a greater level of organisation than was actually the case. Nonetheless, the internal differentiation of functions was made very transparent:

Figure 2: Organisational structure of Deutsche Bank in the 1880s.

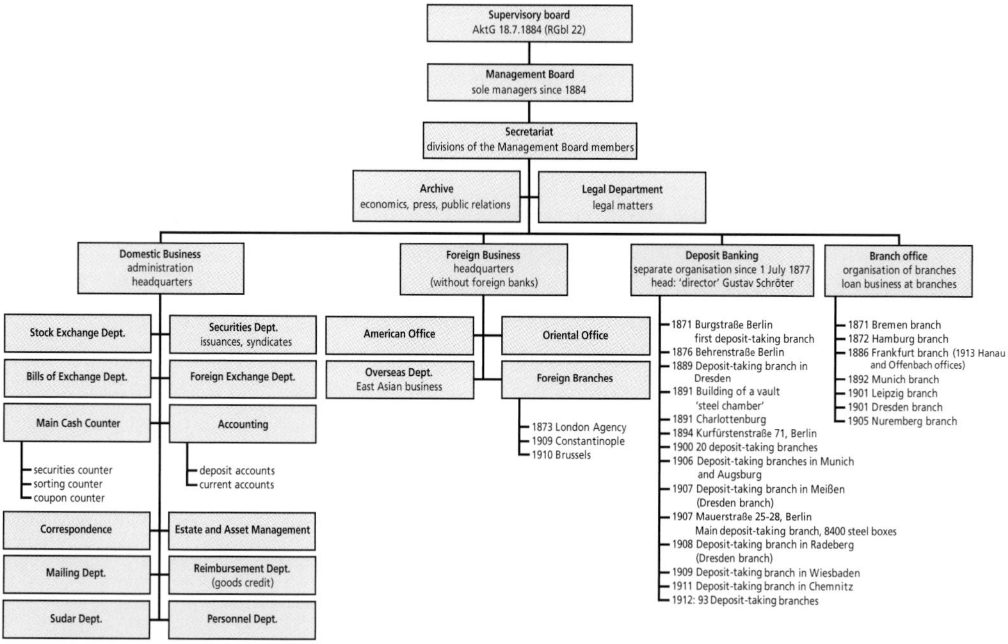

Supervisory board
AktG 18.7.1884 (RGbl 22)

Management Board
sole managers since 1884

Secretariat
divisions of the Management Board members

Archive
economics, press, public relations

Legal Department
legal matters

Domestic Business
administration
headquarters

Foreign Business
headquarters
(without foreign banks)

Deposit Banking
separate organisation since 1 July 1877
head: 'director' Gustav Schröter

Branch office
organisation of branches
loan business at branches

Stock Exchange Dept.

Securities Dept.
issuances, syndicates

American Office

Oriental Office

Bills of Exchange Dept.

Foreign Exchange Dept.

Overseas Dept.
East Asian business

Foreign Branches

Main Cash Counter

Accounting

- securities counter
- sorting counter
- coupon counter

- deposit accounts
- current accounts

- 1873 London Agency
- 1909 Constantinople
- 1910 Brussels

Correspondence

Estate and Asset Management

Mailing Dept.

Reimbursement Dept.
(goods credit)

Sudar Dept.

Personnel Dept.

- 1871 Burgstraße Berlin
  first deposit-taking branch
- 1876 Behrenstraße Berlin
- 1889 Deposit-taking branch in Dresden
- 1891 Building of a vault 'steel chamber'
- 1891 Charlottenburg
- 1894 Kurfürstenstraße 71, Berlin
- 1900 20 deposit-taking branches
- 1906 Deposit-taking branches in Munich and Augsburg
- 1907 Deposit-taking branch in Meißen (Dresden branch)
- 1907 Mauerstraße 25-28, Berlin Main deposit-taking branch, 8400 steel boxes
- 1908 Deposit-taking branch in Radeberg (Dresden branch)
- 1909 Deposit-taking branch in Wiesbaden
- 1911 Deposit-taking branch in Chemnitz
- 1912: 93 Deposit-taking branches

- 1871 Bremen branch
- 1872 Hamburg branch
- 1886 Frankfurt branch (1913 Hanau and Offenbach offices)
- 1892 Munich branch
- 1901 Leipzig branch
- 1901 Dresden branch
- 1905 Nuremberg branch

Source: Dahlem, *Professionalisierung*, p. 53.

The growth of the bank, the expanding of its personnel, the launching of a solid departmental structure and particularly the upsurge in customer traffic – all these ultimately demanded that the bank update its physical presence in terms of its architectonic construction on an ongoing basis. In this, it was equally important to address the requirements of prestige, i.e. for the bank to draw (aesthetic) attention to itself in the Berlin financial district south of the boulevard Unter den Linden and thereby to highlight its architectonic claim to being one of the leading German banks.[21] After very modest beginnings on Französische Straße and later Burgstraße, Deutsche Bank in 1876 came to own the building of Deutsche Union-Bank, which it gradually expanded into a coherent complex built up between Französische Straße, Mauerstraße, Behrenstraße, and Kanonierstraße. In the first decade after 1900, the phase of development had been largely completed.[22] In 1909 Max Fuchs described this office complex with its large counter areas and distinct building structure not without pride, especially the new counter area for deposit accounts that customers seemed to like:

The public enters the new building in its round centre section through three portal openings. The subsequent oval vestibule is especially subdued in its colour effects by the tone of the blue-grey stone of the walls. All the more powerful, then, is the incursion of light from the immediately adjoining [...] great banking hall. The large glass roofs covered in opal glass allow the light to flow through freely to the very last workspace. The large room is divided into a central domed hall 15 metres in diameter and structured into two axially connected side halls, each 19 metres in length. The domed hall and central aisle of the side halls extend through the two stories.[23]

Customer traffic merged there, so customers would have to take greater notice of the building. The entrance to the large customer hall was designed accordingly:

> The exterior of the building is executed in sandstone in forms of the Italian High Renaissance. Standing figures of the parts of the world, modelled by Brütt, decorate the portal construction […] Above the entrance are reliefs by the sculptor Carl Reinert, who has also created the figures of Germania and Berolina that crown the roof. The middle relief depicts the traffic of the world flowing across a bridge connecting Europe and Asia. The keystone of that bridge is formed by a bust of the late Dr Georg von Siemens, thus referring to the timeless contribution of this brilliant man to the history and significance of Deutsche Bank.[24]

Main building of Deutsche Bank on Berlin's Mauerstraße in the year 1909.

The great banking hall of the main deposit-taking branch, 1909.

The entry portal to the great banking hall on Mauerstraße with the statues of the four continents and the reliefs on commerce and worldwide trade.

The actual design by architect Wilhelm Martens was not particularly original; indeed, it was probably not at all intended to be. Rather, its conventionality was mostly meant to embody solidity.[25] The sculptor Adolf Brütt was certainly a celebrity of the Berlin art scene of his time, and his work was valued by both the Munich Secession and Berlin officialdom. He was involved with several works in the design of the Berlin Siegesallee, opened in 1901; moreover, he fashioned the statue of Theodor Mommsen in front of the main entrance to the Friedrich Wilhelm University. The Kaiser ultimately awarded him the Order of the Red Eagle Medal, second class, which was quite remarkable.[26] Carl Reinert could not quite match the status of Brütt, yet both sculptors demonstrate how Deutsche Bank wished to present itself in both an appropriate and quite extravagant manner. Consequently, the total expenditure by Deutsche Bank on its real estate was very high. The property of the headquarters and the branches alone had a book value of at least 28 million marks in 1910; however, the market value, which the bank did not have assessed, must have been significantly higher.[27] Together with the buildings, which had a thoroughly prestigious character, an estimated value of 40 million marks would not have been unrealistic – an enormous sum for that period.

2. Personnel

The 'bank officials' and the messengers and servants

The staffing question was an absolutely crucial one for the expansion of the bank, given the obvious barriers which it posed to productive operations.[28] Without sufficient – and, above all, without *sufficiently qualified* – staff, the bank was not going to be able to compete effectively. The leaders of all major banks were aware of this. Therefore, the struggle for appropriate human resources was extremely fierce, yet it did not endanger their existence. For, throughout the Wilhelmine era, the influx of applicants was always large enough to meet the needs of all major banks in a reasonably satisfactory way.[29] A job in one of the large banks in Berlin, especially, was considered financially attractive and offered good opportunities for advancement. Formal study was not a prerequisite. Instead, bank employees qualified for their profession differently, by serving as an apprentice and as a journeyman for a shorter or longer time in different banks. Although Deutsche Bank itself also trained bank officials from the very start, it did not necessarily see this as an ideal solution to its own workforce needs: 'I would like to reiterate here as well,' wrote Carl Michalowsky, the Management Board member responsible for staff, in 1909,

> what I have always said, that someone who truly wants to learn banking should under no conditions go to work for a major bank, because the large division of labour there renders the work in the individual positions one-sided and uninter-esting, while working in a smaller bank means that one can observe everything that might happen on a daily basis. For this reason, Deutsche Bank does not, on principle, accept any trainees or apprentices.[30]

When Michalowsky spoke of Deutsche Bank in this context, he was referring to the Berlin headquarters, whose employees, as he himself said, 'are so heavily made use of that there is no time left for the training of apprentices'. Moreover, the large volume of transactions performed required a trainee to be led through a large number of depart-ments, 'each of them having a very special, well-defined area for its activity so that it is not really possible for an apprentice to circulate through all of these departments in the course of an ordinary apprenticeship'.[31] This assessment was by no means implausible. And the impression that not all facets of the business could be learned in a large-scale operation by (participant) observation was confirmed by Hermann Wallich's son Paul, who had experience in a variety of banks.[32] Further, there was one more reason for appearing to be inaccessible: in the final years before the First World War, Deutsche Bank was virtually overwhelmed with requests and appeals for employment, internships and job shadowing, as the head of its London branch complained:

> Not a day goes by that we do not receive […] highly recommended applicants. A variety of excellencies, both ladies and gentlemen, almost constantly pester us to accommodate their sons or other charges, and we hardly know how to fend them off. Now, of course, the applicants are always people who deserve our complete confi-dence and have been completely tried and tested. But it just doesn't work, nor is it a pleasant task, to have to constantly explain that there are no vacancies and that there is a binding waiting list that should meet our needs for the next year and beyond.[33]

Therefore, such requests were mostly rejected, although granting them was occasionally unavoidable, especially when hiring interns at the London branch. Yet such a practice was anything but popular there.[34] Even a request by Gwinner, who wished to accommodate an acquaintance with a position there in the summer of 1910, was rejected by the branch: 'We have complete understanding for the gentleman's request, but we are unfortunately already too busy with such training, thanks to the very large number of young people who come to us for a brief period year after year & leave us when we hope they might become of service to us.'[35] Nevertheless, the bank's eight branches (at the time), whose organisation was not as sizeable or differentiated as that of the headquarters, definitely did train apprentices; Michalowsky himself offered to recommend a candidate in 1906.[36] Personal requests, however, certainly did not determine personnel policy at the bank, especially not when it came to leadership positions.

Carl Michalowsky (1862–1941) joined Deutsche Bank in 1900 as a legal adviser; in 1908 he was promoted to the Management Board, where he was responsible especially for the internal company organisation, as well as for legal and personnel questions.

The Berlin headquarters of Deutsche Bank relied much more upon fully trained bank officials since it was possible to get a fairly accurate sense of their previous education. The future employee was supposed to be well acquainted with practical banking and ready to fit into the existing work organisation. Evidently, it depended less on their schooling than one would expect from certain remarks made by Michalowsky. He had stated quite clearly in 1906: 'Generally speaking, banks – at least the larger ones – are used to requiring that apprentices have the one-year certificate; often primary education is a prerequisite. Even high school graduates in many cases devote themselves to banking without such a level of education being required.'[37] At the same time, it is by no means certain that the general public claim (also made by Lothar Gall) was correct[38] in that banking apprenticeships were confined to 'middle-class children'.[39] Although banking apprenticeships had been formalised in the 1870s, and there was already talk of a one-year examination,[40] the hurdle was not always that high in practice, not least because the training was often done in regional banks, ranging in size from the small to the very small. By contrast, the robust flow of applicants to the Berlin banks made it possible for them to make a precise selection, and even at times to choose according to social criteria. But the head of the London branch of Deutsche Bank, Otto Roese, denied the importance of school completion in a letter to an association of bank officials. He regarded it as a German tendency to 'put everything in the form of a template'. However, such a tendency was to be avoided 'when it comes to finding the right education for the next generation in the banking industry. [...]. For what is primarily needed are banking skills and abilities, and

Rudolf Freericks, an employee of the London branch, around 1900.

these cannot be acquired anywhere better than in practical work at a bank office.' The apprentice ought to begin as young as possible, he claimed, because

> it doesn't really have any special significance in the banking profession what kind of school he attends; any school where he can learn and truly learn something competent among knowledgeable teachers will be the right one, as long as it's more about acquiring knowledge than about certifying it. Further, it's irrelevant whether he stays at the school until he's passed the school-leaving exam since this exam is intended to prove that he has the necessary abilities for certain state offices or certain learned professions. Whether he has the ability to work in the banking industry, however, doesn't depend on a school exam but on whether he proves himself at the position in which he's placed.[41]

In the everyday recruitment of new staff, a probationary period was likely to be the determining factor, since it was difficult to predict how suitable individuals were when initially hiring them. This image is confirmed by examining selected personnel files of bank officials born predominantly in the 1880s, whose common feature was having worked for a time at the bank's London branch before 1914. In point of fact, none of them ever left the bank before they retired. The exception to this rule was almost always military service or internment during the First World War. In a few select cases, there were also some employees who had worked temporarily for other companies. If their school qualification was even noted – a rare occurrence in such personnel files – then it was for Realschule or Oberrealschule [secondary modern or upper secondary modern]. More often, though, nothing was entered, so that one can only speculate about the educational background of (at least) this group. Usually, employees who entered service around 1900 either as apprentices or trained bank officials then went on to complete careers in various branches of the bank or in departments at the Berlin headquarters. If the employees investigated here were still too young to advance to the top ranks prior to 1914, it very frequently transpired that they would rise from chief agent to authorised representative and finally to Management Board member after they had passed through various departments at the bank. To take just one example, Paul Vernickel (born in 1884) completed an apprenticeship at the A. H. Müller bank. In 1906 he started at the Leipzig branch of Deutsche Bank and moved from there to the London Agency, where he remained until its closure, transferring to the Berlin headquarters after the war. In 1919–20 he received power of attorney at the bank's Elberfeld branch where he became an authorised representative in 1920 and then a deputy branch manager in 1922. In 1931 he took over the management of the Leipzig branch for eight years; from 1939 to 1945 he headed the Reichenberg branch with general power of attorney for all bank branches in the Sudetenland. Then, after the Second World War, he returned to Berlin, where from 1949 to 1956 he served as a Management Board member of Berliner Disconto Bank, a newly founded subsidiary of Deutsche Bank.[42] This kind of career was not exemplary but quite typical, even if most employees did not manage to advance to the highest level at the bank or its branches.

The salary system was tailor-made for such careers. What is typical about them is not a coincidence. The starting salaries, which Karl Wichmann extolled in the early days of Deutsche Bank and which were initially generous at other banks,[43] later declined. However, they could also rise gradually following a probationary period. In this way, the bank aimed for a specific form of personnel selection, i.e. hard-working candidates whose loyalty to the company would increase over time as much as their salary would. Accordingly, apprentices did not receive any bonuses at all – like all other people employed at Deutsche Bank – while also starting out at a relatively low salary. For 1876, the salary structure of the Bremen branch is known to us: apart from the management, 14 officials and three apprentices were employed there. The only authorised representative, cash officer J. H. C. Corssen, earned 3,500 marks, quite a respectable figure for

The employees of the Bremen branch in the year 1892.

the mid-1870s. The salary of the four accountants ranged between 1,500 and 2,500 marks; however, the assistant accountants only made 1,000 marks. The loan agent and the correspondence clerk got between 1,800 and 2,000 marks. The first cashier's assistant earned 1,700 marks, but the second cashier's assistant was paid only 1,000 marks (which, incidentally, was how much the bank servants earned).[44] In the years to follow, these salaries did not change much in nominal terms; instead, they were raised in keeping with each probationary period. The managers of the branches and the subsidiaries were also integrated into a system of performance-based pay, as had already become commonplace at many major German companies of the era.[45] Like the Berlin Management Board members, these managers received large shares of profits and revenue whereas the 'simple' employees received substantial annual bonuses. The incentives were clearly structured according to length of service and probationary period. Carl Michalowsky advocated actively for this and put it succinctly to a father recommending his son to the bank:

> You shouldn't be surprised if, in the event your son is hired, Deutsche Bank would consider a salary which is likely below his expectations. In this, it is a matter of principle to have newly hired gentlemen start small and then rise quickly through the ranks, depending on their probationary period. In addition, your son, although he trained in the banking profession, went on to work for companies in certain specialised industries where he wasn't able to do much for his further development in banking.[46]

The essential career drivers at Deutsche Bank, thus, were credentials and competence, probation at various points, diligence, a willingness to fall in line and loyalty to the firm. Social background, however, or even the 'cultural capital' that Pierre Bourdieu so strongly emphasised, did not play a recognisable role, at least in the hiring process. It may well be that a type of corresponding 'habitus' was produced solely by the long period on the job after a corresponding banking apprenticeship. From the perspective of the bank's management, a certain esprit de corps was probably desirable, but that by itself was by no means sufficient for accomplishing something noteworthy at the bank.

The nominal wage structure did not adequately reflect the internal structuring of careers at Deutsche Bank. While the bank officials at the start of the 1870s were still at the top of the bank's income pyramid, they most likely lost their former predominance over time due to the persistent throng of strong applicants, because the growth in their salaries was below average. Even in the years before 1914, the entry-level annual salary at Deutsche Bank was 1,200 to 1,500 marks,[47] thus amounting to little more than the income of a skilled worker in the Berlin steel industry, and at times even less.[48] Yet that was just the starting salary, which could grow quickly by means of rises and allowances. The aggregate of wages and salaries cannot be deduced directly from the profit and loss account since it also included all the bank's expenses. In any case, we know that the sum of the general overhead – of which the salaries of bank officials were the most essential proportion – increased sharply from 421,896 marks in 1876, following the takeover of the two Berlin banking companies, to over 1.8 million marks in 1896 and finally

Bank agents, apprentices and messengers in the book-keeping department of Hannoversche Bank in the year 1904. The regional bank was already within Deutsche Bank's sphere of interest. After the First World War it was acquired and transformed into the Hanover branch.

to 21.7 million marks in 1913. At the same time, the individual bank officials earned salaries averaging 2,056 marks in 1876, 2,284 marks in 1896 and 2,625 marks in 1913.[49] These are approximate figures; however, they demonstrate that the average wage amount increased. And, together with allowances and salary increases, materially employees at the bank must have felt quite secure, at least if they had worked in the company long enough and proved their value.[50] The salaries were supplemented by company social benefits for illness, disability and death, in addition to a canteen subsidy and legally mandated social benefits. Yet the bank was different from other large companies in that it did not build its own housing for employees before the First World War. However, symbolic gestures played a role in this more than tangible material assistance, as Carl Michalowsky was to affirm. In writing to his cousin in 1911, he emphasised 'that Deutsche Bank's subsidies for the canteen and for its club[51] are very substantial, because the prices on the menu – along with the fact that only the highest quality meat is used – will make you see that people in Berlin cannot afford what's on the menu unless it is subsidised'.[52]

A job at Deutsche Bank was therefore quite attractive and became increasingly rewarding (at least materially) in the course of one's employment. Nonetheless, there were differences because bank employees did not form a homogeneous group. Women were not paid less than men for the simple reason that the bank did not employ them before 1914. 'The Central Office of Deutsche Bank does not employ ladies,' Carl Michalowsky informed a member of the Reichstag in 1910.[53] Apart from cleaning ladies, Deutsche Bank's Berlin office was a masculine preserve; and even at the branches only a few women were employed, for example, as telephone operators. In that respect, the bank was quite different from other major banks in Germany, including its arch-rival Disconto-Gesellschaft. Generally speaking, female employment in the banking sector had increased from a marginal level of 0.76 per cent in 1873 to 4.59 per cent by 1907.[54] The circumstances were far clearer in the large banks when compared with the banking sector as a whole. In 1875, the owners and managers of the mostly smaller banks still accounted for 33 per cent of all employees while bank officials only comprised 67 per cent. In the occupational census of 1907, the proportion of owners and managers in the entire industry had dropped to 12.5 per cent whereas bank officials now accounted for 74 per cent and auxiliary workers for 13.6 per cent.[55] Of the more than 8,000 employees at Deutsche Bank in 1913, only 150 were in management (i.e. Management Board members, branch managers, departmental managers, or authorised represent-atives). They represented under 2 per cent of all personnel, as compared with 7,850 bank officials who, in turn, differed distinctly in rank as well as compensation from the approximately 500 unsalaried employees, messengers, servants and doormen. The bank officials were by far the dominant group, accounting for around 90 per cent of the bank's personnel. Their salient feature was less their heterogeneity than their age struc-ture. The overwhelming majority had been with the bank since the turn of the century and were correspondingly young. Even if it is difficult to quantify, it can be assumed that the average age of employees before 1914 was low, given the recruitment policy of the bank and its recruiting periods; the strongest personnel growth was after the turn of the century. Hence, those born in the 1880s were highly overrepresented. The differences in status among bank officials may therefore have resulted mainly from their respective ages and degrees of seniority. There was a large group of young and relatively inexpensive bankers in training, on the one hand, and a relatively small group of older, experi-enced bank officials on the other. Their material situations varied accordingly, yet the younger cohorts' opportunities for advancement compensated for the difference. The messengers, servants and porters, in turn, found themselves in a very different situation; however, in view of their lesser credentials, it cannot be said that wearing the Deutsche Bank uniform lowered their prestige.

The 'council of the gods'

This expression was coined at I. G. Farben in 1925 in reference to the administrative council of its supervisory board, which was regarded (at least formally) as the company's centre of power. In the case of Deutsche Bank, this 'council of the gods' was initially comprised of the Administrative Board. That was soon to change. The Supervisory Board lost its centrality in the mid-1870s when the *de facto* management of the bank was taken over by the Committee of Five as well as the Management Board, branch managers and a handful of authorised representatives. Over the years, the 'council's' numbers contin-ued to grow but never became unmanageable. Ultimately, the bank's 1913 annual report mentioned 67 individuals entitled to bonuses, specifically members of the Management Board, deputy Management Board members, departmental managers, and finally 11 branch managers. All these individuals, along with their regular salaries for the year 1913, received performance related bonuses averaging approximately 58,000 marks.[56]

This was rather a large group when compared to how things were at the outset. At first, apart from the Committee of Five, the only ones who really exercised leadership were Platenius, Wallich and Siemens, and occasionally Friedrich Mölle. Platenius left the bank at the end of 1871, and Friedrich Mölle threw in the towel in 1872. That same year, Rudolph Koch, who had just turned 24, was appointed deputy director. A year later, in 1873, Hermann Wallich arranged that Koch was followed by Max Steinthal, who, at 23, was even younger. In 1878, the bank had a four-man Management Board: Hermann Wallich, who at 45 was the most senior member; Georg Siemens at the age of 39; and two young men, aged 28 and 30.[57] That was a pretty daring assemblage, given the limited experience of two younger board members; however, Wallich and Steinthal had at least completed bankers' training, and Wallich had also acquired a great deal of experience in foreign business. Yet the Administrative Board, which was responsible for the composition of the Management Board, did not object to this configuration. These four men turned

Max Steinthal (1850–1940) joined Deutsche Bank's Management Board as early as 1873 at only 23 years of age and remained a member until 1905. The stock exchange and issuance business were his domains, but he also worked on the restructuring of Mannesmann and the construction of Berlin's elevated and underground railways.

out to be a genuine stroke of luck for the bank. All of them remained in leading positions at Deutsche Bank until the end of their working lives – and some of them beyond that – thereby laying the foundations of the company into the early twentieth century. When he finally became deputy chairman of the Supervisory Board of 'Deutsche Bank und Disconto-Gesellschaft' in 1930, Max Steinthal was able to look back on 57 years of uninterrupted service in the management of the bank.[58] That constellation – along with the related self-recruitment of the board and its commitment to performance – had proven so effective that the bank had basically adhered to it for the entire period before 1914. Likewise, a structure of collective leadership had now been established that eventually came to characterise itself as 'democratic'. On the Management Board at least there was no formal hierarchy, and decisions were also to be made by consensus, not by majority principle, thus leading on occasion to major arguments and lengthy debates. As late as 1912, Arthur Gwinner refused to accept the title of 'general manager': 'Deutsche Bank has never had one and won't get one, as long as I'm a member of the Management Board. Our company's charter is a democratic one.'[59]

Just as there was no hierarchical structure, so there was no formal division of labour among the Management Board members either. To be precise, individual managers worked on certain business areas that suited their talents, temperaments and inclinations. Wallich thus worked on foreign-trade financing and ongoing banking operations as well as overseas activities,[60] Steinthal concentrated on securities and foreign exchange, and Koch focused on the more obscure issues of organisational development. Finally, Georg Siemens was something of a jack of all trades, yet he was particularly responsible for the major projects he had himself initiated. That was the origin of Siemens's early leadership role. He thus wrote to his fiancée on 8 March 1872 that he was 'pretty much the number one here', although that was determined by the 'matter at hand' and not by a formal hierarchy.[61] The role of Management Board Spokesman, though never formally fixed, fell to Siemens as events unfolded, then stabilised as a result of his long-time managerial activity. The recruitment of new Management Board members continued to be governed by these loose, informal procedures, presumably because they allowed for greater flexibility.

Rudolph Koch (1847–1923, ennobled in 1908) was a Deutsche Bank employee from the company's first day. In 1878 he became a member of the Management Board and succeeded Georg Siemens as its Spokesman from 1901 to 1909.

There were only two career paths for acquiring a leadership position at Deutsche Bank. The first was for a young banker to attract the attention of a senior member of the management, who then brought him into the bank and sponsored him if he proved himself worthy. This was the case, for instance, with Arthur Gwinner, who was recruited to succeed Hermann Wallich, whose duties he assumed in 1894. Gwinner would then grow into Siemens's role after the latter's departure in 1900, and at that point Rudolph Koch became Spokesman of the Management Board in accordance with the principle of seniority. Other examples in this category were Carl Klönne and Karl Helfferich. Klönne arrived in 1900 from Schaaffhausen'scher Bankverein and built up relationships with West German heavy industry; Helfferich had been specifically recruited to relieve Arthur Gwinner on matters concerning the Anatolian and the Baghdad Railways. The second career path was a more standard one in some sense. Trained bank officials were recruited while relatively young and went through an inhouse probationary process, which could lead from simple to greater responsibilities and then on to becoming an authorised representative; the final stages were departmental manager and eventually a position on the Management Board. Paul Mankiewitz, who took over the stock market business from Max Steinthal, or Carl Michalowsky, who succeeded Rudolph Koch in the domain of internal organisation, may be seen as examples of individuals who followed this path. Others who followed this career path were Ludwig Roland-Lücke and Elkan Heinemann, both homegrown products of the bank.

All things considered, an inhouse career was the more likely path. Of the ten Management Board members in the last pre-war year of 1913, four were 'lateral entrants' while six had started their careers at Deutsche Bank. For a long time, Siemens was the only university graduate on the Management Board and incidentally one of the few lawyers in the house. Another graduate was Carl Michalowsky, who became legal adviser to the secretariat in 1900. And then there was Karl Helfferich, who had completed his habilitation in Berlin in the field of economics and who, deep down, had always wavered between academia, politics and business. He ultimately moved from the bank into the Reich administration in 1915, thus pursuing a career in politics.[62] Neither university graduates nor their alleged attitudes were held in great esteem at the bank. On the contrary, Paul Millington-Herrmann, a later appointment to the Management Board, could even joke that he had not read a book since his apprenticeship.[63] Practitioners were much more respected, especially those who showed a knack for the business. As one employee remembers, Paul Mankiewitz – who had joined the bank in 1878 and gradually worked his way up to deputy manager and on to the Management Board in 1898 – was 'an uneducated man but very experienced in the stock market, believing that you could run a large bank the way you ran a stock brokerage'.[64] Co-operation on the board, as a result, cannot have been smooth. Mankiewitz and Gwinner evidently had frequent conflicts and disagreements, and Siemens and Heinemann did not get along well. But the issue was more about personalities than formal qualifications. In depicting them, you do not have to use the words of Maximilian Müller-Jabusch. As a former press secretary, he knew each member of the Management Board and characterised them, particularly in reflecting on Carl Klönne, as a 'generation of strongmen'.[65] Yet he was quite right when

Paul Mankiewitz (1857–1924) was a stock exchange expert. He became a member of the Management Board in 1898 and its Spokesman in 1919. Max Liebermann painted this portrait of him that same year.

viewing bankers of the era before 1914 more as practitioners, who may have needed a feel for business but certainly not a theoretical education; the latter did no harm but was of little use in the end. 'That generation had a healthy and natural sense of business. If Klönne's employees gave him long reports to read, he replied that he was not interested in the legal details, merely asking: "Where does it say what our commission is?"'[66] Klönne's sometimes harsh tone was recalled by some much later. For example, when the original Hertie firm was being transformed into a joint-stock company, Klönne dealt severely with young Georg Tietz: 'Either you obey, you young badger, or you'll have to pay back the loan within eight days. Then I won't redeem your cheques any more. Your stupid phrases like "not authorised" don't impress me: you have general power of attorney and you're an authorised representative. I expect to receive your answer within three to four days.'[67] Those may not have been his exact words; nonetheless, it was extraordinary that he said anything of the sort. Klönne's comparatively simple beginnings and tough manner were not the norm at Deutsche Bank; many senior men there came from quite privileged backgrounds and were already somewhat familiar with the banking milieu. Nonetheless, one's social pedigree was not a key criterion for a career at the bank.[68]

Georg Siemens was the only one who had completed academic studies, in his case in law, and had finished his doctorate while starting out in banking. That was not all that was atypical. Siemens grew up in the household of a lawyer and civil servant; his father, who looked down on the banking business, mockingly observed that his son had chosen a career as 'a clerk'. In short, Georg was not from the 'same stable' as the others. The *Neue Freie Presse* in Vienna put it quite straightforwardly in March 1870:

> However solid the bank may be, its main difficulty lies in finding capable leaders and representatives for its foreign, i.e. overseas, agencies. Those elected directors were: Platenius in Stuttgart and the lawyer Siemens in Berlin; their elections were received with some head shaking; you have to ask if the decision was based on patronage or credentials. Certainly, it is not likely that a Prussian lawyer had acquired skills that would enable him to manage an overseas banking business.[69]

The fact that Siemens had to struggle initially to gain recognition in the financial world was clearly one of the reasons he worked so tirelessly; he had always aspired to leadership at the bank as it matched his ambitions. He had deliberately rejected employment opportunities in government administration or at the company belonging to his uncle Werner, neither of which would have been as feasible. His ambition may have had its price, but it was bound to enhance his self-confidence in the event of success. From day one, Siemens displayed a tremendous passion for work, and his discipline was so exacting that it became tacitly mandatory for the rest of the top managers. After a good nine months in the bank, he penned a letter to his fiancée with his signature sarcasm: 'Believe me, my business claims more of my time than your seamstress claims of yours. When I leave the office, most of our people have nothing left to do. I am always the one who gives them something new to work on, thus keeping them in suspense.'[70] His future wife would have to accept his enormous workload, and his first successes altered his image of himself. Shifting to the leadership of a small bank was out of the question:

Georg Siemens (1839–1901, ennobled in 1899), was at the helm of Deutsche Bank for 30 years.

You may well think that I will never be able to take on the management of a regional bank if I'm effectively the number one at a global bank. The staid Kilian [Steiner had suggested such a thing to him] has not seen me for 1½ years, and so I've changed somewhat, even if my bank hasn't yet paid me for having done so. I am on the way to becoming influential, and if you [Elise Görz] help me out, then in the next ten years you can become a very respected woman whom people will work hard for – not only for your sake but also for mine. What would you think of that?[71]

Until then, it was clear to Siemens that he wanted to succeed at virtually any price, both out of desire and a sense of duty: 'If people give me their money, then they have a right to my work at any hour of the day and night.'[72] Later on, though, he came into

conflict with the Supervisory Board again and again because the board did not appreciate him repeatedly running as a candidate for the Reichstag. Yet in this matter, too, he
prevailed. After the government shifted to a protective tariff policy in 1878, Siemens
found himself frequently clashing with the conservative lobby of large landowners,
thanks to his advocacy for the gold standard and the newly founded Reichsbank, as
well as for ending protectionism and aligning Deutsche Bank with the requirements of
the global capital markets. Yet the Junkers' responses mattered little to Siemens: to the
end of his days, he remained faithful to his economic liberalism – indeed, to his liberal
convictions as a whole.[73]

Consistent with Hermann Wallich's own reports, it is clear that he, a much more
cautious man, occasionally had to put the brakes on Siemens. Nonetheless, the older
banker and the self-made younger one co-operated well over many years, despite their
different temperaments – and portfolios. The same went for Max Steinthal, whose work
ethic nearly exceeded that of Siemens, though Steinthal conducted negotiations almost
exclusively from his Berlin office whereas Siemens was constantly on the road while doing
so. Steinthal was regarded as a hard worker, who was systematic and very precise and

> treats his business like a mathematical problem that has to be solved so that there
> are no uncertainties remaining. Yet it would be just as correct to say that his work
> method resembles that of a philologist. In each longer letter or article that he
> dictates, the sharp lucidity of his thinking matches his clarity of expression – some-
> thing he doesn't hesitate to revise until hitting the mark. The effect of his speech is
> so great, not least because one gets the impression of hearing someone who's always
> practised self-criticism and self-restraint. His example teaches one that something
> can only succeed if it's been fully prepared from the start. He doesn't go into a
> meeting without having fully mastered the material, because that's the only way to
> have the presence of mind and persuasion to deal with the unforeseen.[74]

Steinthal withdrew from the Management Board in 1905 and moved to the Supervisory
Board, observing that he would now be able to have dinner at home at least once a week.[75]
He was only 55 but had served the bank loyally for more than 30 years. Rudolph Koch
(who was ennobled in 1908) remained a member of the Management Board as long as
Steinthal, serving until 1909. Koch then joined the Supervisory Board, which he chaired
from 1912 until his death in 1923. At first, Steinthal took care of the foreign exchange
and current accounts business, monitoring the securities business and looking after key
industrial clients, in particular. By contrast, the 'calculating machine' described above,
namely, the current accounts and deposit business, was the domain of Rudolph Koch,
who had also served on numerous supervisory boards at other banks, specifically at those
in which Deutsche Bank had acquired shares over the years.[76] Koch was probably the
least powerful of the four Management Board members from the bank's early years. On
account of his seniority, the position of Spokesman reverted to him after Siemens died.[77]

In the mid-1890s, a generational change took shape when Hermann Wallich, who
was apparently overburdened by the heavy workload, withdrew from the main business
of the bank. In addition, repeated conflicts with Georg Siemens may have made him

weary of the office: 'Having recognised the weaknesses of the system, I was too tired to participate any longer in this eternal trapeze game,' he affirmed in his memoirs. 'Making money had never been my ultimate purpose in life. Without exactly becoming rich, I had amassed enough money to safeguard an income for my loved ones. [...] I thus decided, after genuine internal struggle, to give up my cherished position at the bank.'[78] After 24 years as a Management Board member, Wallich moved to the Supervisory Board in 1894 at the age of 60; there he remained responsible for the annual audit into his old age. He died in 1928 after turning 94 – an age that Georg Siemens came nowhere near reaching. Although Siemens managed to survive long enough to be ennobled, he died in 1901 at the age of 62, much earlier than Wallich and having had to give up his Management Board activities in late 1900 for health reasons.[79]

The generational transformation at the top of the bank thus began with the search for a successor to Hermann Wallich. One was found quickly: the private banker Arthur Gwinner, who, based on his wealth of experience abroad, commenced by taking responsibility for the areas that had mainly been Wallich's. But in time Gwinner also assumed many of Siemens's duties, who had already been taken ill and whom he succeeded formally in 1900. Gwinner mainly assumed responsibility for Siemens's major projects, ranging from the electrical industry and the railways in North America and the Ottoman Empire all the way to the major issuances of government bonds. All these tasks demanded a great deal of him. As a result, in 1904–5, Gwinner suffered a nervous breakdown owing to his excessive duties and had to stay away from the business for several months.[80] That accelerated the generational transformation because Gwinner now needed some relief from these responsibilities more urgently than ever. The career of Emil Georg Stauß, who had started as a personal assistant to Georg Siemens,[81] was thereby advanced: he was chosen to assist Gwinner during his half-year sojourn at St Blasien.[82] Gwinner left a deep impression on the recruitment of staff, as Max Steinthal noted when Gwinner died, not only because he had brought along former employees when he moved to Deutsche Bank but also because he rewarded loyalty and performance: 'This was a salient trait of his: he clung tenaciously to employees whom he had deemed capable and reliable, supporting them in every way possible. Among his close associates, no less than three have become members of Deutsche Bank's Management Board.'[83]

Even though Arthur Gwinner was a banker who had trained from the ground up, he was a completely different sort of banker from the other Management Board members. This was because he was the son of a Frankfurt lawyer who had not only practised law in that city but was also closely associated with its intellectual milieu, not least with Arthur Schopenhauer. Gwinner, who quite liked to talk about his background and was not averse to mentioning that Schopenhauer was his godfather, was admired for his approachability, communications skills and worldly demeanour. In these respects, he was already a different kind of Spokesman for Deutsche Bank than Georg Siemens had been. Gwinner's demeanour was also more formal as Siemens was often sarcastic, smoked cigars and did not spend too much time on his appearance. In this respect, Gwinner differed from his predecessor and, as Kurt Weigelt recollected, he 'felt very much that he was "a member of the House of Lords" and therefore a "statesman". He was therefore sensitive when something seemed to limit his position or need for recognition.' According to Weigelt, the (at times) pointed antagonism of the bank towards Disconto-Gesellschaft had a lot to do with such personal issues.[84] The work ethos of Siemens was shared by Gwinner, which is precisely why Deutsche Bank was known as a 'treadmill' under his spokesmanship, which lasted until 1919.[85]

In 1895, the Management Board acquired a fifth member: Ludwig Roland-Lücke. Having started his career in 1877 at the Hamburg branch of the bank, he became a deputy Management Board member in 1894 and then a full member in 1895. He initially took over from Georg Siemens on the restructuring of the American railway business,[86] yet Roland-Lücke was more important as a *de facto* successor to Wallich. He displayed a keen commitment to the overseas business, especially to Banco Alemán Transatlántico; however, his true metier was the acceptance business. Overworking repeatedly forced him, too, to take time off, and in 1908 he finally left the Management Board.[87] The impression he left on his employees was a mixed one since he was 'as one said back then, a hard worker with a strong will; he insisted on his point of view. Roland-Lücke made sure that everything was very well thought out. On a personal level, he was not as affable as Gwinner.'[88]

There had been deputy Management Board members since 1890, starting with Carl Hundrich, and then a total of four the following year, when Erich Breustedt, Paul Mankiewitz, and August Schulze were added to Hundrich. But this number fluctuated: in 1902 there were two, then in 1913 at least 10 deputy Management Board members alongside 11 department managers. A deputy could eventually move up to the regular Management Board, but that was by no means automatic. In 1898 Paul Mankiewitz succeeded in making such a move, and in 1900 Carl Klönne was welcomed as the sixth member of the Management Board, which ultimately grew to 10 members by 1913. Compared with the small group of four Management Board members and some men who assisted them in the Siemens era, the management of Deutsche Bank expanded significantly in accordance with the bank's expanding volume of business, numbering 31 including Management Board members, deputy Management Board members and departmental managers. Nonetheless, it still adhered closely to many of the old traditions. New members of the Management Board did not receive any responsibility over a specific area but instead were tasked with certain business fields and regional priorities. Accordingly, Klönne was entrusted with heavy industry in western Germany, Mankiewitz with the stock exchange business and Michalowsky with the bank's organisational, personnel and legal questions. It was already a remarkable mix, what with the irascible, casual Paul Mankiewitz, the brusque Carl Klönne, and Karl Helfferich, whom others characterised as a pedantic know-it-all.[89] The Management Board was ultimately joined by Elkan Heinemann as well, who had come to Deutsche Bank in 1885 and was promoted to authorised representative in 1893. Yet he only became a deputy Management Board member in 1902 (and a regular one in 1908) after Siemens had taken ill because the latter had been sceptical about his abilities.[90] To relieve Gwinner, Heinemann initially took on duties in the Romanian oil business and the oriental railways, but his main assignment would later be South American operations.[91] Some Management Board members were hardly noticed by the public in comparison to colleagues who had been tasked with the big projects that could sometimes get highly volatile. One such little noticed member was Gustav Schröter, who came from Berliner Bank-Verein and then stayed at Deutsche Bank for 56 years, becoming an authorised representative in 1881 and serving on the board between 1906 and 1925. The development of the bank's system of deposit-taking branches would have been unimaginable without Schröter's work, however.[92] Paul Millington-Herrmann, for a time a deputy Management Board member and then branch manager in Leipzig, served too briefly at the top to have had any formative influence before 1914. In the (mostly) well-informed financial newspaper *Plutus*, the following apt characterisation of the bank's Management Board appeared in 1910, on the occasion of Arthur Gwinner's appointment to the Prussian House of Representatives:

Gustav Schröter (1852–1931), the 'father' of the deposit-taking branches, was a member of the Management Board from 1906 to 1925.

The election of the king did not turn out badly, and Gwinner is undoubtedly the most important of the present Management Board members at Deutsche Bank. If one wanted to include Steinthal on the Management Board – he is officially a member of the Supervisory Board but, in reality, works even harder than top managers at other banks – then he is perhaps the number one businessman and revenue producer. And Klönne can be seen as at least equal to Gwinner in his success at attracting new clients. Yet Gwinner is a businessman of an entirely different ilk. He has accepted the legacy of Siemens, who had a large-scale conception of the bank's purview. Gwinner is thus responsible for the major financial transactions abroad, the railway businesses in Anatolia and Macedonia, and probably those in America too. Yet Gwinner is additionally endowed with […] other qualities: the first is his considerable skill at diplomacy. Klönne may be intelligent, but he's an awkward Westphalian. Steinthal may be intelligent, but he has a nervous and slightly irritable nature. Mankiewitz may be shrewd on the stock exchange, able to drum up business with brokers but not so much with ministers and other excellencies. Except for Koch, who heads the internal administration, that leaves only Helfferich, and while he may be dubbed a 'substitute-Gwinner' even today, he is still too young to be counted here. Nonetheless, Gwinner is the bank's diplomat, always outwardly calm and measured; he not only represents the bank but takes action on its behalf, something made possible by a certain cosmopolitanism. He has been in all sorts of countries, knows their languages and customs, and is as much at home in Madrid as in Constantinople, in New York as in London and Paris. Gwinner has had a rather unusual education.[93]

The following chart shows quite precisely the division of labour in the Management Board before the First World War:

Figure 3: Management structure of Deutsche Bank beginning in 1900.

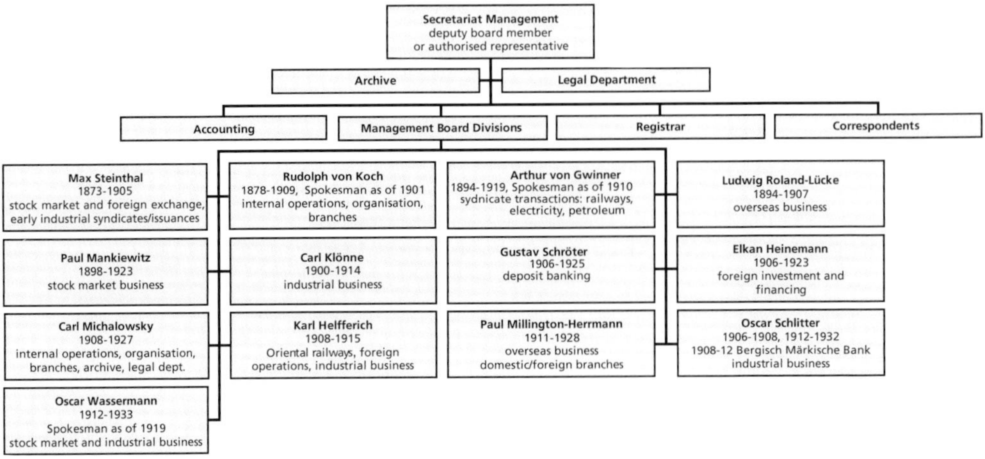

	Secretariat Management deputy board member or authorised representative	

Archive	Legal Department

Accounting	Management Board Divisions	Registrar	Correspondents

Max Steinthal 1873-1905 stock market and foreign exchange, early industrial syndicates/issuances	Rudolph von Koch 1878-1909, Spokesman as of 1901 internal operations, organisation, branches	Arthur von Gwinner 1894-1919, Spokesman as of 1910 sydnicate transactions: railways, electricity, petroleum	Ludwig Roland-Lücke 1894-1907 overseas business
Paul Mankiewitz 1898-1923 stock market business	Carl Klönne 1900-1914 industrial business	Gustav Schröter 1906-1925 deposit banking	Elkan Heinemann 1906-1923 foreign investment and financing
Carl Michalowsky 1908-1927 internal operations, organisation, branches, archive, legal dept.	Karl Helfferich 1908-1915 Oriental railways, foreign operations, industrial business	Paul Millington-Herrmann 1911-1928 overseas business domestic/foreign branches	Oscar Schlitter 1906-1908, 1912-1932 1908-12 Bergisch Märkische Bank industrial business
Oscar Wassermann 1912-1933 Spokesman as of 1919 stock market and industrial business			

Source: Dahlem, *Professionalisierung*, p. 56.

The aforementioned board members headed a larger group of senior employees who were almost all banking practitioners. According to internal correspondence of 1913, 'besides two members of our Management Board, twenty of our employees currently have a higher education. Most of these gentlemen are lawyers, a minority are economists; almost all of them work in the secretariat and archives, and, of course, in the legal department.'[94] These managers usually stayed with the bank longer because of the young age at which they had assumed Management Board tasks; furthermore, hiring managers away from the competition appeared to be at odds with an unwritten code of conduct. Before 1900, the average age at which members joined the Management Board was well below 40; only from that time did it slowly increase. Carl Klönne was the first person to be promoted who was over 50, but he set a precedent because he had previously been a director at Schaaffhausen'scher Bankverein for a long time. Only Gustav Schröter and Paul Millington-Herrmann were older than Klönne when they were appointed to the Management Board at the respective ages of 54 and 53, but both had already served as deputy Management Board members.[95]

It can therefore be assumed with a great deal of certainty that shared experiences, mutual loyalties and an intimate knowledge of processes at Deutsche Bank came to be absolutely key over time, especially since the members of this group had – with few exceptions – each been similarly professionalised through banking apprenticeships. By the same token, there were major differences between the two generations on the Management Board, that is, between the Siemens/Wallich generation of the period from 1870 to 1895 and the Gwinner one between 1895 and 1914. Wallich, Steinthal, Koch, and, above all, Siemens had had their formative experiences during the boom time of early industrialisation. Yet the Panic of 1873, the consequences of which were felt for a long time, had left a significant mark on these men. It meant that they were not inclined to exaggerate or brag. They knew that the success of the banking business depended on circumstances that were largely beyond their control. At the memorial service for Hermann Wallich, Max Steinthal was probably not wrong in highlighting the scepticism that Wallich had acquired from those earlier crises: 'A tremendous lesson for him was the Panic of 1866, which just happened to occur on Good Friday of that year; it was an experience that contributed greatly to his later wariness and ability to sense a crisis coming.'[96] Georg Siemens was by no means so cautious; indeed, he repeatedly displayed an interest in ostensibly risky ventures. Yet, over the years, he became more self-confident as the bank became more successful: 'So, what are "banks"? We do not take the view that the Conservative Party has of us, i.e. that we are small securities dealers or stock exchange jobbers. Instead, we have always availed ourselves of the view, and will continue to do so, that we are a kind of leader in this nation's spirit of enterprise.'[97] To have been a genuine 'Wilhelminer', though, Siemens was not merely too old. Rather, everything deemed 'colossal' – a favourite word of Emperor Wilhelm II – was as foreign to him as were the agriculturalist and conservative circles which had such a penchant for criticising the big Berlin banks.

If these kinds of self-critical experiences predominated in the Siemens generation, a Wilhelmine spirit was more noticeable in the Gwinner generation. Members of that cohort already began with a large and established bank and were highly aware of Deutsche Bank's import; indeed, they proclaimed that major banks had a responsibility for the entire national economy.[98] And, in fact, the numbers alone justified this self-assurance. The bank's deposits were so large that Arthur Gwinner could proceed quite confidently on the question of banking regulation on the eve of the war.[99] The journalist Felix Pinner at *Berliner Tageblatt* emphasised in retrospect that it may not have been a particular individual who had tipped the scales, especially since those involved each had their weaknesses and shortcomings. 'Not all these men […] loom at the heights of genius. Instead, they produce a concert in which fine-tuning and ensemble playing have successfully cultivated the giant organism of Deutsche Bank, both actively and organically shaping its inventive transactions and business methods.'[100]

3. Head and Limbs: The Regional Structure of Deutsche Bank

The core of Deutsche Bank's business was conducted from Berlin, even though the city concentrated on foreign business from the outset. Yet domestic business had effectively gathered a great deal of momentum, not least because of the bank's founding during the Franco-Prussian War; this fact goes a long way towards explaining how operations in Berlin expanded. Enlarging the bank's presence had not actually been the original goal of the Management Board. Before 1914, this only took place if it was essentially required, especially when an international network had to be established to enable the smoothest possible financing of foreign trade in German currency. In this context, as in the launching of its domestic branches, Deutsche Bank was a trailblazer, outperforming competitors such as Disconto-Gesellschaft or Berliner Handels-Gesellschaft. This undoubtedly gave the bank a major competitive advantage. Altogether, the bank used three methods to build and consolidate its regional and international representation before 1914, methods that were definitely in competition with one another and capable of shifting over time.[101]

The first method had to do with establishing branches, first in Bremen and Hamburg – the most vital German sites for export and import. Branches were then built in 1872 in Shanghai and Yokohama, in 1873 in London, and later on in Frankfurt am Main, Leipzig, Munich, Dresden and Nuremberg; moreover, deposit-taking branches were founded in Augsburg, Chemnitz and Wiesbaden. Additional foreign branches followed, specifically in Constantinople and Brussels. The bank did not systematically pursue German branches, but, rather, these emerged over the course of time; this happened especially whenever there were problems with banks that Deutsche Bank had co-operated with or invested in. In Frankfurt am Main, for example, Frankfurter Bankverein had failed; and in Leipzig, Leipziger Bank had collapsed. Establishing branches was not the ideal solution, as had been demonstrated in the cases of Shanghai and Yokohama, where branches had to be liquidated soon after they were set up. The risk of branch offices was fully reflected in the parent bank's balance sheet. This also applied to foreign branches, which were not easy to control. In addition, Deutsche Bank had long shied away from possible entanglements created by its foreign branches.

In foreign countries, Deutsche Bank was much more interested in investing in or establishing legally independent subsidiaries. Yet that approach was not without its problems, as shown by the investment in the German Bank of London, founded in 1871. Deutsche Bank possessed a large share of the capital in that bank, but its equity investment did not perform well enough to compete in the rapidly growing sector of foreign trade. What was needed instead was a separate branch that would enable it to get things done. Deutsche Bank had not had good experiences with its investment in Deutsch-Belgische La Plata Bank in South America, either, because La Plata had got into trouble due to payment difficulties that the Uruguayan government itself was having; ultimately, that bank had to be liquidated, having only barely broken even.[102] Nonetheless, Deutsche Bank made a second attempt to do business in Latin America by founding a wholly owned subsidiary, Deutsche Uebersee-Bank (and later on, Deutsche Ueberseeische Bank, or Banco Alemán Transatlántico), which was legally independent but entirely under Berlin's control. In the end, Banco Alemán Transatlántico was represented in almost all the important sites in Latin America. It was generally able to position itself convincingly there, especially in Argentina and Chile, whereas its outreach to Central America and Mexico was unsuccessful.[103] In its Asian dealings, the bank participated in the founding and operation of Deutsch-Asiatische Bank, which primarily operated in China, above all, in the territory colonised by Germany. In this instance, the bank's successes were very impressive, especially since it finally managed to penetrate the highly attractive business in Chinese government bonds. In Africa, Deutsche Bank eventually made pivotal investments in Deutsch-Ostafrikanische Bank, primarily in financing infrastructure projects in German East Africa.

But even this form of international expansion was not necessarily the rule. In most of the countries in which Deutsche Bank had interests, it chose the path of 'limited partnerships', i.e. equity investments in local banks, such as in Paris, Vienna and New York. In this way it could safeguard trustworthy and efficient partner institutions on site. Occasionally, as in the case of Banca Commerciale Italiana, Deutsche Bank also participated in establishing a bank, thus being able to exercise some influence at least for a time.[104] However, the bank built up enduring 'friendly' relations especially with foreign banks where it (not infrequently) already had personal or sometimes even family relationships, as was the case with the Speyer family's banks in Frankfurt, London and New York. In these cases, confidential information as well as shared investment and syndicate memberships proved to be a bond that might occasionally crack but mostly held up.[105] Similar relationships existed with Credit Suisse in Zurich and with Wiener Bankverein in Vienna, to name but two banks with which Deutsche Bank co-operated closely.

Within the German Empire, friendly investment was the path most taken by Deutsche Bank. After 1908, the bank's 'group'[106] included at least 29 partially large investments in domestic banks, including major banking companies such as Bergisch Märkische Bank in Elberfeld, Essener Credit-Anstalt,[107] Rheinische Creditbank in Mannheim, or Schlesischer Bankverein in Breslau. As Deutsche Bank generally participated in capital increases, just as the named banks also participated in *its* capital increases, the relationships became ever closer over time and soon went beyond representation on supervisory boards. Only in the case of Bergisch Märkische Bank was there a formal merger before the war broke out; in other instances, mergers did not take place until the war or in its aftermath. Deutsche Bank's operations thus underwent regional diversification for a simple reason: the bank was (at least indirectly) present in all pertinent locations within Germany. It was likewise able to attract customers and offer them services, something particularly vital in the economic regions of western Germany[108] and Silesia, which were its priorities. The route of investing in already established banks was much more promising than creating its own branches, which would then have had to compete with these established banks. Investing in such banks meant that the risk of losses could also be limited.[109]

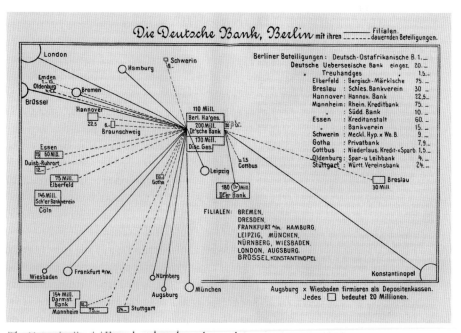

The Deutsche Bank 'Group' with its branches and participations in 1909.

Consequently, before the First World War, a Deutsche Bank *group* had developed. It had a large and resourceful headquarters in Berlin, direct or indirect representation in all important German cities, a strong presence in London, Latin America and – to a lesser extent – in East Asia and parts of Africa. Lastly, the bank maintained good relations with the US and almost every European financial centre. Maintaining such a network required great effort. Gwinner and other Management Board members devoted a considerable amount of their time to making contacts and agreements with friendly or co-operating banks. This process was not always conflict-free, but, for the most part, the outcome was satisfactory for both sides.[110] In the process, Deutsche Bank managed to successfully cultivate fairly lucrative relationships despite political tensions, as was the case with Crédit Lyonnais in France. By contrast, the bank's relationship with Paris Société Générale – a bank that was ruining business everywhere – was exceedingly bad, as highlighted by Rudolph Koch. He rejected the idea of Deutsche Bank making any investment in the Berlin subsidiary of Société Générale, founded in 1909. Koch thus wrote to Gwinner, who was already conducting negotiations on the matter in Paris, that such an investment would be 'directly supporting competition that we should try to keep as far away as possible from ourselves'; in effect, he argued, it would provoke 'the alienation of Crédit Lyonnais, a partner of much greater importance to us'. Plus, if Deutsche Bank were to begin investing in foreign banks situated in Berlin, then imitators would be likely, 'and that would, of course, be an unpleasant prospect'.[111] The only place Deutsche Bank was hardly involved was Russia, with the exception of oil investments in the Baku area. However, there were special reasons in play here: other German banks – in particular Mendelssohn, Warschauer and Disconto-Gesellschaft – already occupied a strong, unassailable position there.

But the bank's regional differentiation created a new problem for it: how much control would be needed? This was not a central issue when it came to investments and friendly co-operative endeavours, even if Deutsche Bank was always careful not to be taken advantage of, for example, with syndicate rates or issuances that looked promising. But that was a matter of one's skill in making business deals. At remote branches and subsidiaries, however, it was not clear how Berlin's claim to be running the bank could be practically enforced. The form of corporate governance that came into being combined strict controls and guidelines with financial incentives. At first, the branches acted very much like the individual departments at the Berlin headquarters, subject to instructions just as individual departments were in the Berlin central office. There were clear rules to be followed on current accounts, export credits and the deposit business, particularly with respect to deadlines and prices (on interest and commissions). As long as there were no abnormalities, the branches could act fairly autonomously within this given framework. But in all capital market transactions and larger loans as well as issuances and related investments, the Berlin headquarters reserved the final decision for itself – a stipulation that was by no means a mere formality. In the early days, for instance, it had to be made very clear to the branch in Bremen that its lending practices were being closely monitored from Berlin.[112] In addition, the branches were persistently asked to submit lists of their debtors and to review their individual loans. If these were questioned in terms of their amount or collateral, then the branches were referred back to Berlin's Management Board, which had reserved the right to decline specific transactions. This proviso extended so far that Berlin could prohibit a branch from making transactions that it may have deemed lucrative. To give another example: the Berlin headquarters declined the request of the Frankfurt branch to invest larger sums in financing a certain company.[113] Besides these regulations and required correspondence, the Berlin headquarters also introduced monthly conferences in mid-1876. That meant that the managers of the branches in Bremen and Hamburg were required to travel to Berlin 'in order to discuss items of general interest as well as special circumstances at the branches (specifically, the granting of credit). In these regular meetings,' cautioned Georg Siemens and Max Steinthal, 'we are expecting positive results from a lively, face-to-face exchange of opinions & are asking to have this new practice instituted immediately.'[114] In the final analysis, the monitoring was essentially enforced by Berlin's authority to make staffing changes. The headquarters decided on any managerial promotions at the branches, along with any dismissals or firings. Berlin, therefore, wished to remain well informed on personnel matters.

The decision-making process between Berlin and London was structured quite similarly. It was not so easy, though, to implement these procedures at the other foreign branches, especially those of Banco Alemán Transatlántico. Its Berlin headquarters could be managed on a tight leash, but it was extremely difficult to control its branches in Spain and even harder to do so in Latin America. Above all, the success or failure of those branches depended not only on the local economic conditions or (sometimes barely predictable) currency adjustments but also on the individuals who had been recruited to manage the foreign agencies.[115] The risks remained substantial, no matter how carefully these managers had been selected or how closely their banks were being watched from Berlin; nor did it matter how precise their business reports were supposed to be or how often the bank's leading representatives chose to visit them in Latin America. Hermann Wallich's assessment of the development of Banco Alemán Transatlántico, which he had carefully monitored when he was chairman of its supervisory board, was correspondingly mixed; he concluded that the development of the respective branches was closely linked to the performance of their respective managers. The bank might get lucky in this, as was the case in Chile; or it might be less fortunate, as was the case in Peru and Brazil.[116] What Franz Urbig noted in the 1930s, even though it was from the perspective of Disconto-Gesellschaft, was not far off the mark with regard to Deutsche Bank's international operations: 'The personal element is much more pronounced in overseas banking than in Europe, and the history of overseas banks is – perhaps for that reason – not lacking in disappointments and incidents that have led to the brink of catastrophe.'[117]

* * *

The organisational structure, staffing and branch formation of Deutsche Bank were, compared with other major German banks, generally in good shape when the First World War broke out. Fewer large differences proved to be decisive, especially since routine bank operations predictably involved many similarities in organisational and personnel structures. At the same time, it is worth acknowledging how Deutsche Bank managed to differentiate itself functionally and regionally so that, inevitably, it was able to keep up with the robust expansion of its business. It managed to keep the costs of banking operations at a level so that it was competitive at all times without having to reorganise workflows, something that might have compromised social integration within the bank. There is no mention in the preserved files of high turnover among employees, as was characteristic of large-scale industrial operations in the years prior to the First World War, with rare exceptions. This had a great deal to do with how staff were selected and what was expected of them. And then there was the actual working behaviour of the bank's employees, who apparently never objected to following the example set by their indefatigable managers. In spite of the invariable 'grind' and their rather average starting salaries, Berlin's major banks were popular employers before 1914, consistently attracting a large supply of appropriately pre-trained workers. Deutsche Bank was not the only bank to benefit from this, but it probably benefited to a remarkable extent as a dynamic institution. This was because the bank proved to be all of the following: an organisation managed not along dogmatic lines but constantly changing according to situations and events; a network – differentiated according to the task at hand – of branches, subsidiaries and connections to friendly banking companies; and, finally, an institution overseen by a cadre of disciplined and competent bank officials. Each of these features contributed significantly to the bank's competitive strength on the eve of the First World War; none of them protected it against setbacks and failures, or against inhouse struggles and disputes, but it sufficed for the bank to be able to assert itself nationally and internationally and even stand out in a number of respects.

The differentiation of its organisation and personnel did not follow a master plan or similar considerations. Instead, it was more the product of a sort of 'muddling through', as recommended by modern organisational theory – that is, a company should respond situationally rather than getting fixated on certain models or variants. Max Fuchs therefore proclaimed quite confidently that '[t]he organisation of a bank represents a sum of experiences, along with attempts and improvements'.[118] Maintaining the organisation's performance was a major challenge, and on balance it was a challenge the bank mastered impressively. And yet the bulk of the work was not performed by the Management Board with help from its secretariat or from the special offices created for the Orient and later for the Americas. While this was certainly where issues were dealt with such as organisation, relationships with the branches, or company policy on personnel or benefits, the Management Board by itself was unable to guarantee the smooth operation of such a large organisation. It had influence insofar as it determined the principles of the company's personnel policies, that is, who was employed by the bank and who took on more responsibility in the course of time. The top management, which really had to focus primarily on the bank's capital market business, had to be able to rely blindly on its 'middle management', not least the departmental managers at the headquarters as well as the branch managers and authorised representatives. That was where the bulk of the business had to be performed, where the revenue was generated and where the profits were earned. And it was only because of such successes that the bank's Management Board was able to devote itself to the national and international capital markets with such virtuosity in the 1880s and 1890s. Thus, Deutsche Bank's categorical adherence to the principle that only people who really understood the banking business should have influence and control there was not some gratuitous social protectionism on the part of bank officials. Neither was the bank's scepticism towards university educated staff, especially lawyers but also civil servants attempting to transfer to the private sector. Rather, this was truly a matter that went straight to the core of the business, which only seemed to be in safe hands when real bank officials were on the job. When eulogising Paul Mankiewitz in 1924, Max Steinthal quoted him as having said: 'The main asset of Deutsche Bank is the trust we have in it, and preserving that trust must remain our highest task.'[119] Prior to 1914, that must have been applied to all members of the Management Board, indeed, to the senior employees of the bank if not to the staff as a whole. To put that trust at risk would have been negligent.

VI. From Troublemaker to Top Dog: Deutsche Bank in Politics and Society before the First World War

In the years before the First World War, Deutsche Bank could always be certain that it would attract criticism whenever it did something in public, particularly concerning major international economic issues. In Germany, it was regarded as a 'roughneck' because of its tough behaviour towards the competition, and outside Germany it came to be seen as the epitome of what was deemed to be German imperialism. This no doubt had to do with the fact that, as a young institution, it had much in common with the history of its own nation-state. Just as the young German Empire jumbled up the previously accepted rules and principles of the international order, so Deutsche Bank seemed little inclined to stick to its status as a newcomer and outsider. It, too, jumbled up the seemingly established relations of Berlin as a banking centre and then of the German money and capital markets as a result of its remarkably rapid development from the mid-1870s. At the latest from the time it essentially single-handedly financed the construction of the Baghdad Railway, it also cast doubt on the international ranking that had heretofore prevailed. Just as the established powers regarded the upwardly mobile German Empire as a troublemaker, so the competing banks viewed Deutsche Bank with great mistrust, especially institutions like Disconto-Gesellschaft or S. Bleichröder, whose standing the new institution gradually displaced. The challenge of Deutsche Bank, as a parvenu, pushing its way into an already crowded business and seeking to assert its power was by no means limited to Germany. Its founding mission explicitly consisted of improving the international financing opportunities for German foreign trade. This was at least implicitly a declaration of war against those who had been top dogs up until then, who did take this challenge quite seriously and reacted accordingly. The reactions were by no means all hostile or only negative; Deutsche Bank became and was a sought-after partner in the national and international world of finance, but even that always remained a fragile combination of co-operation and competition. The choice of name itself, 'Deutsche Bank' – certainly to be interpreted within the context of its founding when the semantics of nationalism appeared to be promising – must have seemed like a provocation since it made a claim to leadership both within and outside Germany; that is, not only as a German bank, but, rather, as *the* German bank, Deutsche Bank. The bank's relationship to politics cannot be understood without this constantly changing space of experience and expectation of both its protagonists and its critics. This was a space in which the bank's attempts to position itself took place in an ongoing and changing dialectic of self-description and the perception of others; within this space, economic and political moments merged into an inextricable package which can only be disentangled through its transformation over time rather than through fundamental aspects. The centre of gravity of this space of experience and expectation lay in the bank's economic success, which formed the core of what allowed the bank to become over time ever more of a political entity.

1. Political Influences

The mere fact that Deutsche Bank was the only joint-stock bank (except for Schaaffhausen'scher Bankverein) licensed by the state prior to the approval of the joint-stock law of 1870 already gave its founding a political quality. The new bank had to be presented by its founders as being in the national interests of Prussia, and, thus, from the beginning, its self-understanding had a national characteristic, albeit a rather pragmatic one. The founders were mostly internationally networked bankers with a liberal bent, who had close ties to the liberal emigration of the years after 1848 and whose expertise gained in France and the United States was of major importance in the bank's initial steps. This liberal influence, at least in the first years after the founding of the bank, was not at all opposed to the liberal economic policies of the empire, but this would change after the empire turned away from economic liberalism in the late 1870s and transitioned to a moderate neomercantilism with its social and protectionist policies of the 1880s. Georg Siemens, who was a member of the Reichstag almost continuously throughout these years, remained a liberal – and, more precisely, a left-leaning liberal – parliamentarian throughout his life, and he was by no means swayed by the opinion of the government but consistently represented his political views and the interests of the bank, which were committed to a liberal monetary and financial policy. Among his colleagues on the Management Board no one else had this sort of closeness to politics. In Siemens's case, this even extended to a certain position of trust with the German Chancellor Chlodwig of Hohenlohe-Schillingsfürst. They also viewed Siemens's political engagement with scepticism because they believed that one could not reconcile a political mandate with a bank manager's extensive duties. Siemens's political stance and his distance to the authoritarian state associated with that were, no doubt, also a consequence and expression of his fundamental tendency towards sarcasm, in which he preferred to caricature any sort of ostentatious behaviour rather than adopt it as his own. As the statements on the occasion of the bank's twenty-fifth anniversary in 1895 show, Siemens's political involvement heavily influenced the public perception of the institution he led. As a result, Deutsche Bank was not regarded as close to the state or even as being a major entity within it in its first decades. Rather, Disconto-Gesellschaft[1] and S. Bleichröder, Bismarck's bank, but also other established banks like Mendelssohn & Co., were seen in this role; some of them could even look back on a long history with and close ties to the Prussian bureaucracy.[2] For the history of Deutsche Bank, its competitive position, present from the start, was of more crucial importance; after all, its aim was to rise to the same level as the established banks. When it had achieved this around 1900, its self-image also gradually shifted as a result: it was now on an equal footing!

Georg Siemens (standing sixth from right) in 1888 in the circle of representatives of the Freisinn Party in the old Reichstag building.

What made itself felt over time to an ever greater extent, however, was the fact that three events all came together – the founding of the bank, the Franco-Prussian War of 1870–1, in which Georg Siemens had participated from the first day to the last as an officer, and the founding of the German Empire in January 1871 – or they could be pulled together into a sort of unique memorial site. After the Panic of 1873 and the subsequent crisis had been overcome, and the enduring Wilhelmine economic boom had begun, one could not help but draw parallels between these events.[3] Deutsche Bank became a key support in the German economic boom, just as the economic boom of the German Empire was a condition of Deutsche Bank's success. Deutsche Bank's annual reports, largely edited by Karl Helfferich, finally took on an almost official character, extensively addressing Germany's position in the global economy in their opening remarks and then transitioning seamlessly to the presentation of Deutsche Bank's business activities. It almost seems as though Helfferich's grand presentation of Germany's national wealth from 1888 to 1913[4] was also an homage to the success of Deutsche Bank, emphasising their mutual connectedness. A liberal national economist and a financial politician, though personally quite wilful, Helfferich became an embittered German nationalist after the downfall of this supposedly unique model of success, and he persecuted the Weimar Republic with his hatred. Although this should not be excused, it seems understandable against the backdrop of this sort of identification of imperial splendour with financial greatness. Gwinner's memoirs, too, completed in 1926, have the same bitter taste, lamenting the destruction of a unique rise by enemies and by the envious.

Prior to 1914, the bank's leadership was by no means comprised of German nationalists. After the turn of the century, its understanding of itself changed from the occasionally sharply ironic and cynical position of being on the attack with little regard for conventions or rankings into a more established self-image that was expressed perhaps most clearly in Arthur Gwinner's successful striving to be granted a seat in the Prussian House of Lords.[5] Managers of Deutsche Bank were also willing to accept ennoblement, which Arthur von Gwinner (1908), Rudolph von Koch (1908) and – though with self-ironic reserve – Georg von Siemens (1899), as well as Emil Georg von Stauß (1918) shortly before the end of the war, all achieved. Of the four representatives of the major banks who were ennobled prior to 1914, three came from Deutsche Bank alone, which was noteworthy in itself. The only representative of a major bank who did not come from Deutsche Bank, but who had been ennobled several years earlier, was Adolph von Hansemann, the legendary head of Disconto-Gesellschaft.[6] This did, indeed, also signal the bank's closeness to the state because although the quota of ennoblements among private bankers was much higher, it was quite rare in the rest of the banking world and in major industry. Moreover, some industrialists like August Thyssen even rejected ennoblement because he regarded the nobility as not capable of much.[7] Of course, all this was supposed to signal social success much more than political approval, even though it can certainly be assumed that the high-finance world of Berlin did not call the political system of the German Empire into question. Some people were occasionally annoyed by the emperor and his real or supposed failures, they criticised the dominance of the parties in the parliament and they sought to minimise political intervention in how their own institutions were organised and led. There were close, amicable relation-ships with individual politicians, though. In 1900, Georg Siemens, for instance, was one of the few confidants, whom Chancellor Chlodwig of Hohenlohe-Schillingsfürst asked for advice before resigning from office.[8] Still, genuine political interest is hard to find in the bank's debates or among the bankers. It was quite different for the bank than for major industry, which had been affected since the 1890s by ever-increasing strikes, which led to interventions in the companies, whether it concerned co-determination in operations, working conditions and protection from accidents, or, finally, the inspection of the facilities, which were often dangerous and bad for the environment. Berlin's world of high finance was, in principle, spared these sorts of conflicts. Although there were attempts by various employee associations to gain a foothold among 'bank clerks' as well, these sorts of organisational attempts foundered. They achieved at best moderate success among the technical employees; the financial world remained closed to them prior to 1918.[9] 'Bank clerks' were largely immune to these issues on account of their social standing, their prestige and their self-confidence. Nevertheless, Deutsche Bank was sceptical about the expansion of social insurance for employees in 1911, particularly since it had already taken internal measures to provide security for its employees in old age.[10] Still, there is no evidence of a decisive political rejection of the Social Democratic Party, as was typical in heavy and major industry. The problems of the class struggle were simply too insignificant in the financial sector.

The general political orientation of banks or their management personnel prior to 1914 followed conflicts about state monetary and financial policy. The organised labour movement did not play an important role in this. The conflicts in this branch occurred primarily between the conservative-leaning representatives of agricultural interests who simultaneously wanted to keep the tax burden low for their clientele, on the one hand, and, on the other, the advocates of a modern banking, stock exchange and tax system who pushed for reducing taxation on capital market business and liberalising payment transactions. From the 1890s, the question of capital export generated conflict; agricultural lobbyists criticised it whereas the bank representatives believed it made business sense. Even if a majority of the management personnel of Deutsche Bank purchased estates primarily in the Mark of Brandenburg prior to the war, these leading bank representatives were anything but conservative Junkers (landed nobility). The financial circles of Berlin strenuously resisted the restrictive stock exchange legislation of the 1890s and 1900s benefiting agriculture as well as the shift in the tax burden in 1908–9 to the banking sector and stock trading in order to protect agriculture from an increase in the inheritance tax. They participated in large numbers in the founding of the Hansabund für Gewerbe, Hansel und Industrie (Hansa League for Commerce, Trade and Industry), a collective anti-agriculturalist movement. Even though Deutsche Bank held back in this matter, it provided one of the members of the constitutive executive committee in the shape of Rudolph Koch.[11] It is not known whether Arthur Gwinner shared Riesser's – head of the Hansabund (Hansa League) – flirtation with opening the political spectrum from the left liberals to moderate social democrats. Nevertheless, it is a fact that the bank did not belong in the conservative camp in the German Empire. In this sense, there is a line of continuity from Georg Siemens to Arthur Gwinner and their respective colleagues. Even though the bank may have changed its social status and social self-image, it essentially retained its understanding of the state and the economy – a liberal core that followed the material interests of the bank.

Deutsche Bank's position regarding the emergence of 'organised capitalism' in the crisis after the turn of the century was determined less by considerations of principle than by pragmatic calculation. This phenomenon concerned the emergence of so-called industrial duchies in heavy industry, the electrical industry or the chemical industry with the formation of the precursors of I. G. Farbenindustrie AG, to name just a few outstanding German examples. In general, it appears that the great financial capitalism debates of the time provoked little response from the banks, and particularly Deutsche Bank. These debates were associated with Hilferding's publications on the theme, and later provided fodder and supposed historical evidence for the scholarly debates about 'organised capitalism' and the 'interventionist state' in the 1970s and 1980s.[12] Whereas an academically trained national economist like Helfferich may have found them significant, everyday bankers were always more concerned with finding solutions to problems close at hand and hardly at all with academic deliberation. The idea that the bank and its competitors adopted a key role in controlling the German economy and influencing state action might have flattered one or other Management Board member of the bank, but they would hardly have been able to reconcile this with their own practical experiences. The banks' complaints usually went in the opposite direction: in important questions of monetary, tax and stock exchange policy, nobody listened to them, they claimed. Rather, state policies seemed to follow a bureaucratic logic that was foreign to the economy and showed little respect for the conditions of its functioning, instead subordinating these to the special interests of certain privileged groups such as large-scale agriculture. The tendency for large company units to form did not go unnoticed. But the banks knew all too well that this tendency was not commonplace but remained limited to certain sectors. The development of company structures, particularly the principle of nesting, which it carried out to perfection, was much less an abstract than a pragmatic question for dealing with the problems of rapidly expanding industrial sectors. Citing numerous facts, Jakob Riesser noted the tendency towards concentration in the German banking system,[13] the dynamic core of which was Deutsche Bank itself. In Riesser's opinion this had little to do with abstract banking power and more with economic growth and the well-developed competition among Berlin's major banks, which were far from forming a power bloc. As the saying goes, there is calm in the eye of the storm, and one could regard bank managers' lack of awareness of the tendencies of 'organised capitalism' as a problem of perception at Berlin's major banks. However, there is now documented criticism of Rudolf Hilferding and the analyses associated with him or historically based on his work; this criticism has left hardly a hair of his head untouched. In fact, there was no 'organised capitalism' grouped around a supposedly dominant financial capital. Moreover, no political system could be identified that was acting in the interests of this capitalism, either; that is, the modern interventionist state could not be shown to have emerged at that time.[14]

Taking all this together, the relationship between Deutsche Bank and politics in the first 40 or so years of its existence shifted, above all because its economic position changed. It went from being an outsider and a rising force to being a 'top dog' by the 1890s, at the very latest. That is, it became a decisive factor in the German money and capital markets, which largely determined its weight but also its self-confidence and its perception of others. Its own political stance – taking a liberal position in all questions of monetary and financial policy and, thus, automatically opposing conservative agriculturalist circles – was hardly affected by this. However, overall it did become a constitutive 'state-supporting' part of the political system in the German Empire; it never called the state into question but dealt with it in a very pragmatic manner in all individual questions. The German Empire, which was rather rigid with regard to rank and status, may also have been conducive to this given the well-developed hierarchies within the company. Nevertheless, the men at the top of Deutsche Bank were not typical 'Wilhelminers'.[15] Arthur Gwinner was not afraid of picking an argument with the Prussian government and attacking the stingy financial policy of the Prussian finance minister in his rare appearances before the parliament.[16] Men like Carl Klönne or Paul Mankiewitz would hardly have allowed members of the bureaucracy to dictate regulations to them. The bank managers themselves, although they did not necessarily have contempt for trained lawyers, tended to be rather condescending towards them, not trusting their ability to judge financial matters at all. This may have been different in dealings with the Reichsbank, but this was a half-state institution in which bank representatives were able to share important ideas. In short: the German Empire as a political order was basically accepted, and the respective form it took was an object of pragmatic considerations; the conflicts – for example, with the agricultural lobby or with authorities sceptical of the stock market – followed the usual trajectory. This was nothing special, particularly in an international comparison. Thus, it is possible to eliminate the idea that the representatives of Deutsche Bank looked longingly beyond the German borders or hoped for fundamental changes. On the contrary: the Gwinner generation suffered severely from the downfall of the German Empire.[17] When war broke out in 1914, suddenly everything the bank had worked hard for in its over 40 years was called into question and finally became the irretrievable past.

2. Deutsche Bank and International Financial Diplomacy

It is far more difficult to position Deutsche Bank within international financial diplomacy than within its domestic political sphere, particularly since the change in this field over time was also very dramatic. In general, it is also true of this sphere that the bank's actual founding phase up to the early 1890s was calmer than the period that followed, which was characterised by a double movement of increasing successes and growing tensions. Various larger studies in recent years, including those by Boris Barth[18] and Jonathan Kirshner, the latter of which appeared under the telling title of *Appeasing Bankers*,[19] have drawn a complex picture of this. There is no doubt that the banks were part of international financial diplomacy in the pre-war period and their behaviour contributed at least indirectly to the intensifying of international conflicts, although this indirectness is of decisive significance. Whereas the banks themselves relied on a peaceful business environment, and, indeed, profited considerably from that, their respective successes were in turn interpreted as evidence of national strength or weakness. This was because the intensive structural shift of the pre-war decades, of course, entailed more than just a general economic boom. It was also associated with shifting weight between the European states, which had consequences for the system of political alliances. In this respect, the shift in the economic structure itself, which the banks supported and even pushed through, was a political matter, whether the financial players wished for it to be so or not. And in this regard, the respective states were consequently interested in influencing and using this structural shift and, with it, the behaviour of the banks, to achieve their political aims. To a certain extent this had long been the case. Paying subsidies or financing military projects was only possible by means of an efficient banking system. The rise of the Rothschild bank was a symbolic and highly regarded expression of this. However, when capitalism prevailed and generated a worldwide boom in the second half of the nineteenth century, things reached new dimensions. Now it was no longer about mobilising financial means for particular situations but, rather, entire domestic economies faced off, believing that they had found the appropriate measure of their respective strength in their economic and financial indicators. And the roles in publishing were also distributed in accordance with one's participation in the structural shift. Whereas German publications stressed their country's rapidly growing economic successes and strove to highlight whenever it caught up with or surpassed Great Britain and France, which had previously been ahead, British and French publications tried to contrast these successes with their own strengths, but, above all, to question the permanence of Germany's financial capacity. On the one hand, the country was admired;

on the other hand, its arriviste qualities and unsolid foundations were heavily emphasised.[20] Above all, in the final pre-war years, veritable press wars recurred around these
questions, which were often closely associated with the international conflicts such as
the Boer Wars and the Moroccan Crises.[21] Deutsche Bank also participated in this war
of words. Its annual reports were frequently read outside Germany and translated into
English and French, and, once Karl Helfferich exerted an influence over them, they
constituted one thing above all: a comparison between the way in which the German
Empire performed internationally and, of course, came out looking good, and the way
international scepticism about the capacity of the German money and capital markets
was regularly repudiated.

For Deutsche Bank all this was neither exclusively nor primarily a question of
prestige, although it had identified with the German view of things since its founding:
how else *could* it have been since it had to accept financial diplomacy as a precondition
of its own actions without being able to change much about it? It never welcomed the
predicaments associated with this; instead, it almost always perceived them as a burden
to be eliminated or minimised as much as possible. Yet this did not depend on the bank
but, rather, much more on the state and the development of international relations, with
the difficult relationship with France and the French market virtually being a part of the
bank's inheritance. It had arisen in the context of the Franco-Prussian War of 1870–1, a
conflict that strained relations with the second most important European financial centre
for a long time. On the one hand, as Hermann Wallich and other German employees
of Comptoir d'Escompte had themselves experienced, the former border-crossing co-
operation among bankers broke down. On the other hand, financial diplomacy came to
be instrumentalised in a targeted way by the governments in their efforts to push through
their respective political interests and damage their political competitors.

From the beginning, Deutsche Bank operated in international waters, but in the
early years it perceived this political dimension of its business as being only marginal.
It even managed to successfully sell the French silver francs it had collected in Alsace-
Lorraine in the financial centre of Paris without heavy losses. The limited partnership
in Paris, of course, was not doing well and was terminated early on. In the following
period, the bank also avoided direct involvement in Paris, for example setting up a
branch there analogous to the one in London.[22] When the suggestion came from the
Swiss side in the years after the turn of the century to open a joint agency in Paris,
Gwinner was interested but he pointed out that this was a difficult place for the bank
and it was better to lie low. Nevertheless, relations with Paris were not bad. They just
had to occur with or by means of a partner who represented the matter externally in
order to avoid resistance from the French public or politicians. Since the bank had built
up good relations with Crédit Lyonnais and then with Banque de Paris in its first years,
this was usually successful, particularly since Arthur Gwinner also had a good network
in Paris. But France was not an easy territory, particularly since the Rothschilds in Paris
worked with S. Bleichröder and Disconto-Gesellschaft in Germany. When the bank
had agreed to participate in the financing of the Baghdad Railway in the 1900s with
interested French parties, the authority in charge of supervising the French stock
exchange prevented the respective bond from being issued in Paris. This had an effect;

later, too, when French parties were actually or supposedly involved, Berlin banks preferred to stay in the background. This did not mean that lucrative business opportunities were dismissed, for example, in Morocco; but it always seemed more appropriate to proceed discreetly, which, incidentally, only reinforced the mutual mistrust once such involvements became public knowledge.

But this could not always be avoided. The alliance between Italy, Austria and Germany (the Triple Alliance) had serious consequences for capital flows in Europe. Notoriously cash-strapped Italy had until now primarily found financing on the French market. When the so-called Triple Alliance was initially concluded in secret in May 1882, the sources of money temporarily dried up there. The German government, in turn, was very interested in German banks jumping into the breach and called upon the Berlin banks to step up. Deutsche Bank's efforts to be involved in the Italian market were successful from the 1880s, which was not only, and indeed, not even primarily, a consequence of the German government's wishes. From the 1880s, there was a fundamental need to seek attractive investment opportunities, which is why Deutsche Bank took advantage of these sorts of opportunities wherever possible, and Italy seemed quite attractive. Why not combine something useful with something politically advantageous, Georg Siemens may well have asked, as he accordingly participated in syndicates for financing the Italian state. The political connections, in any case, were obvious.[23] Thus, it was not Deutsche Bank that was vying for political transactions; it was the circumstances that turned normal transactions such as underwriting government bonds into a political matter – and for the banks on all sides. Deutsche Bank was only an exception to the extent that it had its headquarters in a country that was mixing up the previous rules on account of its rapid expansion, which almost of necessity pushed the bank into the role of troublemaker – a role it was well suited to because it was pursuing its own expansion so energetically. Its success in Italy was by no means a resounding one. Although Italy utilised the German money and capital markets more heavily than before for a while, this shifted again, particularly once the Italian government realised that it had some room of its own in which to manoeuvre so that the courting of various sponsors only increased. The country, its economy and its financial world were, thus, certainly not simply victims of the imperialist financial desires of Germany and France and their respective players. Foreign investors never did manage to control Banca Commerciale Italiana, which Deutsche Bank had co-founded.[24]

The engagement in Austria-Hungary was not problematic politically, and after the Dual Alliance it was even politically desirable. Siemens had got involved there early on and later also participated in the stabilisation of Wiener Bankverein and other businesses. Austrian business, at the same time, opened doors to southern Europe and finally to the Ottoman Empire, which – at least in retrospect – became a prime example of the supposedly financial imperialist activities of Deutsche Bank and its close collaboration with the expansionism of the German Empire. Like all simple theses, this one, too, as shown above, is false, but there is something to it. Initially, Bismarck had welcomed the construction of the Anatolian Railway, but he refused to provide any sort of political loan-loss guarantee if the project should go wrong. The construction of the railway to Ankara and Konya was, in the opinion of the Ottoman

In 1910, the Spokesman of Deutsche Bank's Management Board Arthur Gwinner (in the right foreground) met the Turkish minister of finance Djavid Bey for talks in Berlin.

government, a political project because it wanted to free itself from the clutches of British and French financial interests. In this sense, Deutsche Bank slipped into a sort of 'political game' from the beginning because competing British and French interests had to be factored in. The entire history of the railway's construction, however, only makes logical sense when one considers that it was never in the bank's interest to build the railway on its own. It wished to have a strong voice, particularly in the railway's construction and operation, but it always sought international financing and was thus trying to avoid a confrontation! It did not really succeed in this with the Anatolian Railway, although the project did not become explosive. This changed in the case of the construction of the Baghdad Railway, which had the character of a political project from the beginning. Up to the end, it remained unclear whether the bank would be sufficiently interested in taking on this technologically challenging project, which led into the very heart of competing geopolitical interests. In the end, it decided on a pre-licence, which was undoubtedly doing the Ottoman government a political favour, but especially also, and above all, the German government and

Emperor Wilhelm II. The exact designs required a financial outlay that neither the bank nor the German capital market believed it could bear on its own. Negotiations were immediately initiated with prospective British, French, Dutch, Austrian and Swiss partners, but they turned out to be tricky. In light of public resistance, no capital at all could be obtained from Great Britain. French participation was negotiated, but only on paper because the French government did not allow the Baghdad bond to be traded in Paris. The bond was finally offered in Austria and also the Netherlands alongside Germany, but the German capital market bore the main burden – and in an astonishingly smooth manner. Thus, Deutsche Bank, whether it wanted to or not, found out that going it alone could be rather successful, at least for the first construction section of the Baghdad Railway.

But this by no means marked the end of the difficulties. For further construction guarantees, the Ottoman government needed greater access to customs revenues, which, in turn, depended on the structure of its national debt, and this could not be changed without international consensus. The unification of Turkish national debt now became a veritable act of financial diplomacy in which the respective governments and their representatives in Constantinople wished to have some say. Deutsche Bank, therefore, was of necessity pushed into being a political player who proceeded in close co-operation with the Foreign Office. This succeeded, in the end, against strong British resistance, but the Young Turk Revolution and Austria-Hungary's annexation of Bosnia-Herzegovina completely upended the political constellation on the Bosporus which up to that point had been stable. In order to stabilise relations with the new government in Constantinople, as well, Deutsche Bank was obliged to be quite accommodating in the granting of loans (also because of political pressure from Berlin). Consequently, the bank became a sort of allied power of the new Turkey orientated towards the European nation-states; the bank viewed Turkey's expulsion from Europe in the Balkan Wars with rather mixed feelings. After the Balkan Wars, the bank, represented by Karl Helfferich, became a diplomatic entity in the regulation of the national debt and ownership rights of the former Turkish and international railways. The relatively satisfactory solution to the question of assets was down, not least, to the bank. It ultimately managed to finance the further construction of the Baghdad railway by itself. Moreover, it balanced out French and British interests in the final section of construction through Mesopotamia to the Persian Gulf including stub lines to Syria and the Mediterranean Sea.

Close co-operation with (German) politics was unavoidable in this transaction. The bank, however, did not act under a sort of commission from the Foreign Office, nor did it uncritically accept everything the Foreign Office did or wished to do. It was unavoidable that the bank perceived itself as a *German* player solely because it was made into just that by the British and French competition. It pursued related commercial projects in the areas now connected to the infrastructure by means of the railway construction, yet this was quite usual; in North and South America, for example, such business was always an accepted part of all railway projects. What was special was not so much the idea but the way in which it unfolded and the jealousy or the competition among other interested parties that it provoked. When financial and economic imagination or positive expectations for the future were lacking, Deutsche Bank was much more reserved even then – indeed, it refused outright to pursue ambitions in this direction when its own government would have liked to see it get involved. Deutsche Bank's colonial involvement was rather limited, despite its basic agreement with colonial policies. Where there were interesting railway and mining projects, it got involved – and in German South West Africa even though this generated no profitable revenues for a long time. However, it kept its distance from plans that did not seem very promising, as the example of Morocco shows. In general, the bank was more of a latecomer in the question of colonial involvement, whereas Disconto-Gesellschaft and S. Bleichröder had already engaged in active 'colonial politics' from the 1880s and got heavily involved in the question of New Guinea, for example.[25] Deutsche Bank was not familiar with these sorts of endeavours, and in the case of Morocco it was even happy that it had only participated in a minimal way despite pertinent political expectations. And the bank also rejected the financing of the Bulgarian state in 1913–4 that the government advocated on account of alliance considerations.[26] In the end, economic calculation always dominated: how could it have been any other way since Karl Helfferich was the only individual there who perceived himself as a politician at all? Political advances were made towards Siemens, who was offered the Prussian finance ministry, and Gwinner, who was supposed to get a leading position in the Imperial Colonial Office, but they declined these.[27] All the other members of the Management Board would probably have considered these sorts of expectations to be an imposition in light of the burden of their work. That Siemens dismissed rumours he was to become the finance minister as 'stupid talk'[28] may sufficiently express this stance. In addition, Siemens's long-term activity as a liberal member of the parliament, Gwinner's activity in the Prussian House of Lords and Roland-Lücke's parliamentary mandate for the National Liberal Party, which he only took up after his active period on the Management Board had ended, do not point to these men as being politicians; their contributions in the parliaments were always expert ones. In an eminently political sense, the Management Board members of Deutsche Bank were all dilettantes.

The members of the Management Board were, nevertheless, only too aware that the bank operated within a difficult political environment, and they were by no means indifferent to it. Of course, not much could be changed about the configuration within which the bank had to act; consequently, the difficult relationship with France, above all, was regarded as almost a given, whereas the German–British conflicts that flared up again and again were almost invariably perceived as an unnecessary burden. The London branch functioned as a sort of local bank there. The relationships with most of the players in the British financial market were as good or as bad as the competition allowed. But this was also true in Germany, in which the rivalry with Disconto-Gesellschaft was regarded as an ongoing problem, whereas the bank was on good terms with Carl Fürstenberg's Berliner Handels-Gesellschaft. In the British case, it was less the business competition that caused concern than the endlessly hostile attitude of the public, which Deutsche Bank energetically sought to combat. From the Krüger telegram and the Boer Wars to the *Daily Telegraph* interview of the Emperor,[29] there were many instances of press hostility that were acted out in both countries maliciously and acrimoniously,[30] Deutsche Bank almost always tried to maintain a moderate tone and employed its foreign agencies to try to counteract rumours or any spitefulness or apparent hostility in the British press.[31] For example, Roland-Lücke advised the bank's own branches to try to have a mitigating influence on the local British newspapers when rumours arose about the exclusion of German firms from British business; such rumours had surfaced after Austen Chamberlain had given a speech on German warfare in 1870 in reaction to criticism of British warfare in the Boer War. Berlin's business circles sought to make a visit by a particular British journalist in Berlin an out and out success. The committee receiving him had representatives from Disconto-Gesellschaft and AEG, as well as Deutsche Bank, which provided two Management Board or Supervisory Board members.[32] The management of Deutsche Bank continuously pursued the aim of improving the press and intensifying personal contacts to important businessmen and public figures in the following years. It supported the formation of an Anglo-German Union Club, it fostered the so-called Anglo-German Conciliation Committee and it generally sought to find forces that would improve the public mood. In the perception of Deutsche Bank's management, the main concern was the London press, which it accused of having a more or less spiteful view of Germany. But this was only successful to a limited extent. As much as certain actions seemed to have positive effects, German global economic expansion would just as regularly prompt a correspondingly harsh reaction in the British press. When this happened, the London branch always informed Berlin immediately.[33] There was no improvement in the respective mutual perception of the two countries, even though personal relations in the international world of high finance were decent and even friendly. At Deutsche Bank, the perception was that one was dealing with unfair criticism, and that the more successful one was the less fair that criticism became. In the end it seemed that the principle motive behind the negative press reports was always something like trade envy. This impression would finally take on self-reinforcing significance since no decisive action was taken to combat it. In any case, it made it much easier to explain Great Britain's entry into the war in 1914, even though both sides had previously sworn again and again that a war would not be advantageous to anyone.

In general, *Appeasing Bankers* gets it right; but it would be too easy to model the behaviour of the banks solely on the basis of the expectations of stable markets. On this side of the threshold of war, too, there are some remarkable variations. The war was a disaster for Deutsche Bank that it really did not need.[34] The bank would not forgo its international success, which was, whether justified or not, part of foreign reservations. Deutsche Bank was a winner in terms of importance, business volume and reputation following the intensive structural changes of the pre-war world economy. It profited from having its home in the most rapidly growing market in Europe. It was a peculiar dilemma to have to see in its own success likewise a factor contributing to increasing international tension. Strictly speaking, there was no way out.

3. Monetary, Trade and Financial Policies

In Germany, as well, competition, criticism and jealousy prevailed. Before Deutsche Bank had achieved an equal standing in the Prussian Consortium, it had long felt that it was unfairly treated by its leading competitors and, before that, by the cartel which long controlled the state bond market in the empire and in Prussia. However, it became obvious when the demand for government loans increased sharply that it was not possible to permanently exclude the bank that was potentially the strongest financially, particularly since the bank had showed its muscle sufficiently when it single-handedly acquired about 200 million marks in imperial and Prussian bonds in the late 1890s. In the following years, the relationship was reversed. Whereas Deutsche Bank had long been kept at a distance, now it could go its own way in the knowledge that it was strong enough to be able to represent its pertinent interests. In the formation of groups and associations, which occurred much later in the financial sector than in industry, Deutsche Bank demonstratively held back. In the Central Union of German Banks and Bankers, which was founded in response to the empire's 1901 legislation that was hostile to the stock market, Deutsche Bank largely remained in the background,[35] just as it did in the Hansa League founded in 1909, which came into being as a result of financial reforms the empire enacted in 1908 that were likewise hostile to banks and the stock market.[36] Just as if it wished to provide a monument to Friedrich Schiller's William Tell in his conviction that 'the strong man is strongest when alone', Deutsche Bank did not subordinate itself to any party discipline or the interests of any association but, rather, represented its views sometimes in the parliaments and sometimes in corporations, committees and institutions alone or made ad hoc agreements with other players about a potential joint procedure. Nevertheless, it did not do this in a vacuum. Even Georg Siemens was well 'connected' in Berlin in the 1870s and 1880s. From 1882 to 1901, he could be counted among the oldest Berlin merchants, so he belonged to the executive board of its chamber of commerce, where, above all, he maintained business contacts but was also able to have an impact far beyond that. For the banker's reputation in the city, this office was just as important as his being anchored in influential Berlin circles, not least because the meetings of the oldest of them frequently ended in informal gatherings.

> Thus, the leading heads of the group – namely, Eduard Arnhold, Georg von Siemens, Isidor Loewe, Emil Rathenau and Louis Ravené – typically went to a nearby wine bar in order to talk about their business experiences as a 'small imperial economic council'. Being a member of the group of the oldest thus meant, above all, having an information edge over the other Berlin companies.[37]

However, Siemens was by no means a regular guest; but when he did attend he carried weight.[38] This was also true of Siemens's successor, Arthur Gwinner, who was a prominent figure in Berlin society and its political scene, just as Deutsche Bank, in general, was present wherever it mattered, even if not always in the front row.

The topics that interested the bank as an institution were limited. Initially, it was concerned with the implementation of the gold standard and securing it with the establishment of the Reichsbank as its protector. The position favoured by the bank, both in the establishment of the Reichsbank and in the extension of the Banking Act in 1899, was successful.[39] In later years, the items on its agenda dealt almost exclusively with questions concerning the organisation of payment transactions and restrictions on and control over stock trading. Conflicts concerning trade policies paled in comparison.

Participants of the first German Banking Convention organised by the Centralverband (Central Union) in Frankfurt am Main. At the left-hand table, at the front and second from left is chairman of the Central Union Jakob Riesser.

Although Georg Siemens regarded the moderate protective tariff policy[40] pursued from the late 1870s as a redistributive measure for the benefit of agriculture that could hardly be justified, trade policy was seldom a prominent topic. Trade wars were not in the bank's interest, but the reciprocal trade policies that were finally implemented and sought to balance out the various interests of agriculture and foreign trade to some extent met the bank's expectations. This was, in any case, no cause for great excitement.[41] This was not the case with regard to the empire's stock market legislation. The bank's position, however, was not dogmatic in these matters either, but, rather, related to the significance the respective provisions had for the functioning and liquidity of the money and capital markets. In the 1870s and 1880s, the situation was still relatively calm in light of the rather high liquidity and the low average interest rates. At this time, Georg Siemens was already leading a struggle to make cash-free payment transactions more favourable – that is, to make cheque payments as tax- and commission-free as possible. Although this struggle was rather unsuccessful,[42] it was motivated not by the needs of the time but by very basic considerations about a modern payment system. This effort failed both because of the hostile attitude of the time towards the stock market and banks and, equally, because of the fiscal interest of the government, which taxed stock and other security transactions (cheque transactions were also part of this) by means of the Stamp Act of 1881. This was later called the Stock Exchange Turnover Tax and was not got rid of until 1991 when the Financial Market Promotion Act was passed. Not only was this tax increased twice in the German Empire (1889, 1908), but also, in 1896, under pressure from the agricultural lobby, futures trading on the stock market was prohibited for numerous goods and stock trading in general was made more expensive and more difficult, which hurt the efficiency of the German money and capital markets. This, at least, was the unanimous assessment of the banks. Whereas the criticism of the 1880s primarily focused on pointing out that the taxation of the stock market drove business to foreign stock exchanges, the tendency to do so was now different. Domestic and foreign demands on the efficiency of the German money and capital markets were constantly increasing, but politics was disrupting stock trading, propped up by narrow-minded agricultural interests. Deutsche Bank forcefully repudiated criticism of capital export, which the agricultural side fired up and large-scale agriculture utilised to present itself as patriotic while filling its own boots. If, Deutsche Bank maintained, the German national economy did not have the revenues from its foreign assets, the rapidly growing economy would not be able to afford either its trade balance deficits or maintain its current account balance, and, consequently, it would be in danger of getting caught in severe currency upheavals. With this argument, the bank also clearly criticised the conservative agricultural positions which demanded that agriculture be strengthened at the expense of Germany's integration into the global economy – and thus simultaneously advocated the illusory possibility of Germany being able to wage war autonomously.[43] By contrast, Deutsche Bank always understood that the disintegration of the world economy would be extremely damaging to the German national economy – and, incidentally, would also permanently destroy its own business model.

The focal point of Berlin as a centre of high finance: the Berlin stock exchange on Burgstraße, around 1900.

As if to confirm exactly this, the fallout from the American financial crisis in 1907 generated considerable difficulties for the German money and capital markets. Deutsche Bank was not particularly affected by the liquidity shortfalls of the post-crisis period; on the contrary, it even offered generous help to the American financial system in its crisis.[44] But the Reichsbank had to raise the discount rate dramatically in order to limit the outflow of gold from Germany. This led to significant refinancing problems among numerous banks that only had small liquidity reserves. As a consequence, the balance structures of many banks came to be questioned as many critics felt that they had stretched their lending too far. Thereupon, a banking inquiry took up the issue, but, as had recently happened, for example, to the cartel inquiry, it did not manage to come up with clear recommendations for the appropriate regulation of the financial sector, which would have forced the banks to maintain larger liquidity reserves.[45] In the following years, there was intense discussion about the extent to which banks should be forced to maintain liquidity reserves and to publish short-term balance figures to keep them from granting too much credit. Yet this was not primarily a problem for Berlin's major banks, which entirely understood the imperatives of the Reich Treasury and the Reichsbank. Rather, it affected above all the smaller and medium-sized regional institutions that had experienced repeated funding difficulties. Deutsche Bank, which did not think much of the legal regulations, thus pushed the banking world to voluntarily comply with the Reichsbank. Gwinner, in particular, welcomed the declaration of many banks to present balance sheets every two months to the Reichsbank, enabling the central bank to assess the liquidity of the German money market at any time. There should be no recurrence of the unpleasant surprises of 1907–8. This was similar to a self-imposed obligation to do so, which Deutsche Bank found easier to bear not only because it had impressive reserves but also because it had considerable refinancing potential. This, in turn, derived from its extensive deposit business and also from the fact that it already regularly utilised cash-free payment transactions. In the following years, the Reichsbank pushed again and again for the banks to improve their liquidity as the country would, after all, be dependent on this in case of war, and shortly before war broke out it once again contemplated possible measures it could impose. Thus, it was important for Deutsche Bank not only to maintain the self-imposed obligations but also to put pressure on delinquent banks to behave in the same way. When Commerzbank in Lübeck did not uphold this obligation in early 1913, Deutsche Bank admonished it to do so in order to avoid a conflict with the Reichsbank and the minister for trade and commerce. Even if Commerzbank might prevail in a court of law, it would be inopportune for it to engage in a conflict in this case, Deutsche Bank warned.[46] And Arthur Gwinner also argued in a similar vein in relation to this self-obligation later at a meeting at the Reichsbank when he explained that the other banks could not get out of behaving in a similar manner if Deutsche Bank, which had strong deposits, set the appropriate example.[47] Consequently, the financial sector managed to avoid any further regulation even in the final days before the outbreak of war. This was also a sign that people expected anything except what actually happened.

4. Deutsche Bank in Wilhelmine Society

Taking Berlin's 'good' society of the years prior to 1914, bank managers had become conspicuous figures, but they were not at all part of the top echelon of society. Their nobility was, without exception, a relatively recent phenomenon. Courtly aristocracy and Berlin's high financiers were worlds apart, both in attitude and self-image. When the princes' trust collapsed in 1913, Gwinner snidely remarked that they should have stayed out of such explosive financial transactions, expressing the financial expert's clear sense of superiority over the aristocratic dilettantes. No matter how much the heads of all Berlin's major banks, along with the head of Deutsche Bank, may have yearned for prestige, they were bourgeois in their self-perception; a model comprised of work, industriousness and competence. No one any longer speaks of a 'feudalisation' of the bourgeoisie; this long-harboured conception alluded to a supposed weakness of the German bourgeoisie in comparison to the traditional nobility, and the reverse now appears to have been the case.[48] The members of Deutsche Bank's Management Board had all become wealthy over the years. From the turn of the century, their incomes and assets rapidly increased in step with the bank's success, and they utilised their new wealth more or less conspicuously. The houses and apartments of the most important bankers were almost all impressive and newly constructed buildings in the prestigious Tiergarten district.[49] Most of Deutsche Bank's Management Board members also acquired country estates from around the turn of the century. Although they differed little from their counterparts at other banks in this regard, none of them matched the achievements of Adolph von Hansemann, who built Schloss Dwasieden in the neoclassical style near Sassnitz on Rügen Island.[50] Their country estates were more modest but no less remarkable for all that, from Wallich's house in Potsdam to Gwinner's manor house in Krumke. Georg Siemens had already inherited the country estate of Ahlsdorf in Brandenburg from his father and repeatedly toyed with the idea of settling down as a farmer after quitting Deutsche Bank. For the younger members of the Management Board, agriculture was no longer a serious alternative. For them, rather, the manor houses and impressive country estates were accessories which allowed them to showcase their commercial success in the manner of other successful industrialists. Although such estates were neither unloved nor unused, they were not the expression of a special relationship with the land that they were for the aristocracy; if they expressed any sort of relationship at all, it was at best a kind of investment with which to secure their assets.[51]

These external commonalities with the world of the German aristocracy should not disguise another point concerning the crisis this group supposedly experienced in the German Empire – a point that is usually overlooked. According to Rudolf Martin's yearbook of millionaires, prior to 1914 industrialists and bankers were by no means among the richest people in Prussia. In terms of the number and size of their assets, the old aristocratic families were typically still significantly richer than industrialists. This was especially true if important raw materials had been found on their lands, as in the case of the Silesian magnates. Bertha Krupp, August Thyssen, Hugo Stinnes and members of the Borsig family were the exceptions that prove the rule. Among bankers as well it was the old money of the Rothschilds and the Speyers that was very highly ranked. Of the employed managers, it was, however, the members of the management boards, specifically those of Disconto-Gesellschaft and Deutsche Bank, who succeeded in rising to the top, thus putting themselves in the class of rich industrialists like Wilhelm Merton of Metallgesellschaft and Friedrich Bayer Jr. The numbers that Rudolf Martin compiled for 1912 are rather impressive and also give an indication of where the leading gentlemen of Deutsche Bank stood. First place among employed bankers went to Arthur Gwinner (13.86 million marks in assets; 865,000 marks in annual salary), followed by the head of Berliner Handels-Gesellschaft (12.64/1,005,000), Disconto-Gesellschaft (12.6/805,000) and Dresdner Bank (12.2/845,000). Gwinner's position as front runner on account of his wealth was also due to his wife's dowry; otherwise, the heads of the major Berlin banks did not take much for themselves. Beyond that, it was quite conspicuous that Deutsche Bank's Management Board members, starting with Max Steinthal and extending from Paul Mankiewitz, Ludwig Roland-Lücke and Carl Klönne all the way to Rudolph Koch, were wealthier or had a greater income than the representatives of competing banks. Gustav Schröter, the manager of the deposit business, was the only one who lagged behind, but his wealth, too, was still estimated at 3–4 million marks, although his income, by contrast, was estimated to be 'only' 210,000 marks a year, a sure sign of how the remuneration scheme at the bank was structured, but also of the level of appreciation various positions in the bank enjoyed. Compared to the average incomes of employees in high-level bureaucratic, scholarly, or administrative positions, all these incomes and assets were astronomically high, not to mention how they compared to the average yearly income of a labourer, which would hardly have exceeded 2,000 marks a year for a skilled labourer in 1914.[52] A Prussian minister earned 36,000 marks a year in 1910, a ministerial director's salary amounted to 17,000 marks a year and a chancellery secretary took home 4,000 marks and a housing allowance of 800 marks. The Prussian senior presidents – that is, the heads of the respective administrations in the various provinces – made 21,000 marks a year and had housing provided, which, in all likelihood, put them below the level of the bank's authorised representatives. Consequently, there was hardly a unified middle class to speak of, at least in a material sense. High finance had already become a world of its own. And the real meaning of these numbers only becomes clear when one takes the tax burden of the era into consideration. Prussia only had a rather effective income tax from when Finance Minister Miquel, a former owner of Disconto-Gesellschaft, had restructured investments and the top rate of tax had been set at 4 per cent. Municipal surcharges, which varied from one town to another, were added to this,[53] and they were higher in the major cities. Thus, one could expect an effective tax rate of 25 per cent of one's invested income in Berlin. Consequently, taxpayers had a large number of options for private patronage and social engagement, and the expectations of rich people were, of course, commensurately high.

Even though they still ranked far below the great wealth of the aristocracy, bank managers embodied the highly visible top level of income and wealth of the newly emerging mercantile middle class.[54] Their social prestige was, of course, still fragile:

In Germany, the upward rise of such far-sighted merchants is still made particularly more difficult by various prejudices of a military and civil servant state that has not yet really found its role as an economic world power. The lieutenant and the assessor – and certainly above all the cavalry lieutenant and the government assessor – are much more distinguished than the young merchant or industrialist who comes into direct contact with the stock market or sooty labourers, not merely in their own eyes but also within the dominant philistine view of the social order

wrote liberal politician Theodor Barth in the autumn of 1901 in an obituary to his friend Georg Siemens,[55] and not without a certain irony. For Siemens had been all of these things – assessor, lieutenant, decorated war veteran, lord of the manor and successful bank manager. Barth attributed a remarkable asynchronicity to his world; the ruling *juste milieu* had not yet realised that the age of the global economy had arrived and that one not lived a backwater existence any more. A proper portion of self-worth was surely expressed in this, and even though it did not yet set the tone, it was at the height of the time, which was no longer true of the traditional provincial elite.

Despite all successes, a political, social and cultural gulf continued to exist between the old upper class and the leading groups of the newly emergent mercantile middle class. Bank managers now separated from the general middle class, from which most of them had come, not least in their daily professional life. In Georg Siemens's generation, and even more in the case of his significantly older great-uncle Werner von Siemens, the differences were minimal. However, they began to expand gradually, which had something to do both with the dramatically increasing salaries of the mercantile middle classes as well as with the development of their careers, which gradually precluded them from living their lives as educated middle-class citizens simply because of lack of time.[56] The work demanded as the head of AEG or of Siemens & Halske, the activity as a Management Board member of Deutsche Bank or on the executive council of Disconto-Gesellschaft simply no longer allowed for the rich life of an educated middle-class citizen, as much as Georg Siemens may have appreciated that or how much the turn towards science corresponded with Werner von Siemens's inclinations. Extensive reading, house concerts, literary salons and regular attendance at concerts or plays, which were a way of life for the educated middle classes, as paradigmatically demonstrated by the example of the educated middle-class Karl Hampe,[57] were out of the question for there was simply no time to enjoy them, and they did not fit, either, with the constant stress of leading a global company.[58] Georg Siemens or his wife at least tried: For a while, the Fontanes would visit them and they would meet figures from cultural Berlin at the residence of their brother-in-law, the publisher Ferdinand Springer, who lived in the same house by the zoo. Siemens admitted that he was simply no longer capable of making conversation after a long day at the bank.[59] As a result, the salons that gradually became established in certain houses of high finance were not primarily meeting places of the financial elites themselves. Rather, their houses became sought-after conversation circles in which the old social divisions also became fluid. In this process, the salon in the house of the chairman of Deutsche Bank's Supervisory Board Adolph vom Rath became tremendously important; Rath's wife Anna turned it into the leading middle-class-liberal meeting point of the city between 1880 and 1914. Anna vom Rath was the daughter of one of the protagonists of the Revolution of 1848, and so it made sense that initially, above all, liberals like Rudolf von Bennigsen and Max Forckenbeck could regularly be seen in her house. Over time, the salon was opened up to Berlin's aristocratic world. In her memoirs, Marie von Bunsen marvelled at the transformation of the house. 'A certain comical aspect' could not be missed, she wrote, 'that the daughter of a barricade fighter raved later on about monarchs and royalty the way Frau vom Rath did.'[60] In the end at the Rath household you might come across founders of Deutsche Bank like the Delbrücks, Ludwig Bamberger and Otto Wesendonck, and famous middle-class people like Hermann von Helmholtz and Theodor Mommsen rubbing shoulders with members of high society such as Countess Maxe Oriola, the daughter of Bettina von Arnim.[61] Consequently, a salon finally emerged that brought together 'for over thirty years […] the courtly society, politicians, scholars, artists and writers', who clearly felt secure in the generous atmosphere.[62] Bankers themselves remained in the background in this and mostly only participated as occasional guests in the life of the salons their wives formed. The active shaping of social life, as Carl Fürstenberg openly states, was a task but also an inclination of the bankers' wives.[63] Without the generally known financial success and influential position of their husbands, these salons could, of course, hardly have become as important to the top tier of middle-class, liberal Berlin society as they were in the end. To be sure, the bankers themselves also played an important role now and then, maintaining contacts and making connections, and, indeed, not least, increasing their aesthetic credentials by supporting Wagner's music. Yet they did not really play a part in these groups. Responsible company managers simply had too little time for this. Emil Rathenau, whom Siemens admired, did not even begin to try to develop an educated middle-class or cultivated air. To the chagrin of his wife and his son Walther, he was entirely consumed by managing the company.[64] This may have seemed extreme, but it was typical of the character of the successful entrepreneur during these years.[65]

Nevertheless, Rathenau's personal thriftiness, which bordered on stinginess, similar to that of August Thyssen[66] and Ernst Abbe,[67] was more the exception that generated acerbic gossip. In the majority of cases, an individual's lifestyle changed as his income increased, and it became much more elaborate.[68] That began with the expensive houses, the country estates, and extended to everyday life with numerous receptions and dinners, as well as to trips that became ever more impressive, soon encompassing all the continents in a colourful social and private mix. You could meet figures from high finance in the Swiss Alps, on the Italian lakes, on the Côte d'Azur or in select German and Bohemian spas where the world of high finance permanently met in grand hotels.[69] The life of bank managers took on a glamorous quality that could easily be discerned, say, in Arthur Gwinner's trips and the places he stayed, but also in Georg Siemens's desire to own a house in Stresa, on Lago Maggiore, where the family frequently stayed. All this certainly had both an official and a private side: Carl Fürstenberg, the head of Berliner Handels-Gesellschaft, observed the custom that he saw all around him in the years before the war of hosting expensive dinners and receptions, summing it all up rather scathingly: it was boring, one ate too much and was hardly entertained and, when being seated at the table, and so on, was over, the hosts mostly signalled that it was time to go, he said. Unadulterated pleasure it was not, but in taking part in such activities that showed you were part of high society you could not afford to fall below certain standards – standards

Arthur Gwinner acquired Schloss Krumke near Osterburg in the Altmark in 1911; his family used it as a holiday home.

that even the upper middle class could no longer take part in (let alone wish to do so).[70] The reports of 'country life' are then also mostly less formal, less forced, more personal. Gwinner even relates that he had finally had 'enough of holiday trips and staying in over-crowded inns' and longed for a 'place of his own', which he eventually found in the shape of the country estate of Krumke. He never regretted the purchase; for him there was 'no better place to stay' than the estate, and he wished to be buried in its parklands one day.[71] His children took a more rational view; after Gwinner's death, the estate was sold.

Nevertheless, the opposites that can be distinguished here demarcate the life of a member of Berlin's high finance world prior to 1914:[72] wealthy, but strongly shaped by the self-image of a middle-class elite based on achievement, not at the top of the social pyramid but still very high; availed of all the conveniences of modern life, moderately cosmopolitan, internationally and, indeed, globally connected, very fixed in everyday life with a tendency (that grew stronger as one got older) towards escapism, which was perennially fulfilled by trips and temporary escapes (stays at spas, vacations, retreats to the countryside). The burdens of having a management position at a bank in which one was 'only' an employee and was always assessed in terms of one's contribution to its business success were extreme. They essentially precluded anything like 'dynastic forma-tion', which many who had made it to the top aimed for at that time. This was out of the question for Georg Siemens in any case: He 'only' had daughters, who for the most part married into the educated middle class. But otherwise, there is little sense of the 'bequeathing' of management positions to the next generation; when such a thing did occur it was an exception, as with Hermann Wallich's son Paul, it was a rather complicated story.[73] Deutsche Bank's way of structuring careers precluded such bequeathing of positions, just as much as its corporate governance as a joint-stock company without dominant shareholders rendered the 'old boy networks' that might have enabled this improbable. Finally, the fierce competition among the German big banks made selecting personnel for other than professional reasons seem at least explicitly to be far too great a risk for it to be intentionally pursued. In this question of selecting personnel, Deutsche Bank was, indeed, highly sensitive. Georg Siemens himself lacked the weight within this realm that Adolph von Hansemann at Disconto-Gesellschaft or Carl Fürstenberg at Berliner Handels-Gesellschaft made use of for themselves. On Behrenstraße there were never even the rudiments of a 'personality cult' despite a certain veneration for Siemens; in this respect, the management of the bank was actually quite 'democratic'.

This was also true in another respect. Anti-Jewish resentment and occasional anti-Semitism were part of everyday life in the German Empire, but a sharp distinction in social life, like the one that existed in New York between the Christian partners of JP Morgan and the Jewish ones of Kuhn, Loeb & Co.,[74] was unknown in Berlin. There has been plenty of speculation concerning the 'glass ceiling' that Jewish individuals repeatedly came up against and which it was extraordinarily difficult to break through concerning the example of Walther Rathenau.[75] The world of German high finance was *de facto* not familiar with these sorts of 'ceilings'. Nevertheless, one repeatedly had to deal with anti-Jewish resentment, which prompted Elkan Heinemann, for one, to more or less dispense with writing out his given name.[76] Paul Wallich also engaged in a sort of 'avoidance behaviour', knowing full well that his Jewish heritage might make access to the social circles he sought to join more difficult. But there were also many Jews within the management of Deutsche Bank who gave the appearance of caring little about this, or who, like the later Spokesman of the Management Board Oscar Wassermann, consciously and methodically lived their Jewishness.[77] Wassermann's biographer Avraham Barkai thus soberly concludes that 'at Deutsche Bank [...] members of the Management Board and directors who were Jews or descended from Jews [took] up central management positions from its founding',[78] circumstances that would not change until Jewish leaders were forcibly displaced under National Socialism. Despite all the possible resentments, as long as Deutsche Bank was not forced or prompted by political pressure, it did not influence or even steer the careers of its employees by criteria that were not related to the job.[79] Anyone who could prove himself in everyday operations had an opportunity for advancement, whether he was Jewish, Christian, or a member of any other faith community. Anything else would have been highly irrational, as well, because selecting one's business partners on the basis of their faith would almost have amounted to a sort of retreat from business, since European high finance was now populated to a considerable degree by Jews or people of Jewish descent. Arthur Gwinner had married a woman from a wealthy Jewish family, and the contacts with the 'Speyer Empire' that opened up to him through his new relatives were extremely useful, quite apart from the personal familiarity they provided. Consequently, selecting business contacts on the basis of their faith was out of the question. The thesis that the bank purposefully selected personnel according to 'ethnic' viewpoints by, for instance, utilising Jewish employees for stock market business,[80] is, nevertheless, not very likely;

in this matter, the fact that Jewish Management Board members occasionally promoted young up-and-coming Jewish bankers does not say much. That could have simply been a coincidence since a precise observation of confessional divisions within the bank itself must have been difficult. Adelbert Delbrück was married to a woman of Jewish heritage, just like Gwinner. Hermann Wallich was a Jew, though not a practising one; his son and daughter were baptised. Steinthal and later Wassermann got involved in Jewish welfare work. Wassermann supported Zionist organisations in the interwar period. The Chairman of the Supervisory Board (1907–14), Wilhelm Herz, was an old Jewish gentleman, related to the parents-in-law of Max Liebermann; in 1913, he was appointed by Wilhelm II to the Real Privy Council with the title 'Excellency'. Finally, at the very end of the German Empire, Berthold Naphtali advanced on to the Management Board; his brother Fritz later became an important trade union theorist and eventually one of the first labour ministers of Israel.[81] Consequently, it was simply not possible to distinguish between Jewish and non-Jewish employees and to orientate one's behaviour accordingly in the case of Deutsche Bank prior to 1914 – nor was this desired, except by notorious anti-Semites. The war, inflation, and, finally, the political crises of the Weimar Republic changed the climate and contributed to Elkan Heinemann's immediate departure from the Management Board and emigration abroad in 1923. Prior to 1914, this would have been unimaginable.

Similarly, political considerations do not seem ever to have played a major role at the bank either. It was a matter of course that individuals who were considered for leadership roles did not call the contemporary social system into question but were fundamentally loyal to the German Empire.[82] A certain national- to left-liberal political bent was probably characteristic of the vast majority at the bank, although there was no politicisation, as was typical of industry, which was shaped by major social conflicts. The bank – this is how it was seen – fulfilled its socio-political obligations to its employees, but it did not fall into any explicitly political fighting position. The bank and its success – this was what everything was measured by. Anything that fell below this was not on anyone's radar.

Before 1914, the bank hardly made a collective social, political, or cultural appearance, largely keeping its distance from public involvement. A part of its Management Board members and directors did occasionally involve themselves, but this tended to be for their own private enjoyment. Social or cultural engagement was by no means required, although it was certainly expected. Siemens had already taken such initiatives upon himself and sometimes also failed at them, as evident in the staff's poor response to the reward he offered for an endowment fund to benefit Theodor Mommsen after his library burned down. Gwinner donated money to Kaiser-Wilhelm-Gesellschaft (the precursor of Max-Planck-Gesellschaft), and he remained its senator until his death in 1931.[83] In acquiring this position, he had reached the Mount Olympus of those who supported German scholarship and met key figures from business, society as well as science and scholarship there. By contrast, Gwinner was not very cultured. Rather, he possessed collections related to science and the history of money and supported the relevant scholarly and scientific research. The cultural and social engagement of Deutsche Bank's Management Board members manifested itself perhaps most obviously in the example of long-serving director Max Steinthal. Steinthal was of key significance not only to the bank's business development; he was an important proponent of the bank's social activities (orchestral and singing groups at the bank, company sports), and also a supporter of Kaiser-Wilhelms-Gesellschaft to the same extent as Arthur Gwinner. In addition, he was involved in the field of municipal development as well as in Jewish welfare work, and after the turn of the century also put together a remarkable art collection.[84] Regardless of his individual motives, he thereby fulfilled almost perfectly the expectations that were put upon industrialists and bankers who had grown rich in the pre-war years: that is, they were expected to provide visible evidence of their success by fulfilling certain social requirements and legitimatising it in this way. The directors of Deutsche Bank were no exception. This was also true of Hermann Wallich. Little is known about his aesthetic interests, but they were certainly quite well developed. That he had the renovation of his Potsdam house (Villa Schöningen) carried out by the architect Ernst von Ihne alone attests to this. Wallich was also a member of the Kunstgeschichtliche Gesellschaft founded in 1887, whose aim was to bring together 'the art historians, friends of the arts, and collectors of Berlin'. This association was not only active in art patronage but also organised presentations and exhibitions from private collections, and, moreover, advised wealthy private collectors. Hermann Wallich was probably also the person who brought Eduard Arnold to the Kunstgeschichtliche Gesellschaft. Arnold, who temporarily lived in Wallich's house at Bellevuestraße 18a, was later an important patron.[85] No Management Board member at Deutsche Bank came close to matching his importance as a patron, but that is not what their social engagement was about. It was about representing a successful major bank at the top of Wilhelmine society. The bank, in turn, found its fulfilment in this without disguising the fact that successful banking was at its core.

Conclusion: Deutsche Bank, 1870–1914

A bank's balance sheet is naturally comprised of a more or less complicated set of numbers, and the structure and shift of these numbers tells us a lot about its strategic and tactical actions and its business success. This success surely does not depend solely on the bank's actions. Economic and structural factors determine the surrounding environment, which is not always an easy one. Moving within this setting at Deutsche Bank demanded a great deal of finesse on the part of its leadership, but, in addition, success also frequently depended on luck and chance coincidences. Thus, a very complex history is hidden behind the numbers, yet what it tells us in itself is mostly absolutely obvious. Deutsche Bank began in 1870 as a small institution for financing foreign trade boasting an impressive capital of 15 million marks. But it had only a few employees and a very small balance sheet, thus it was heading into an uncertain future. Although the young bank did not have a share of the industrial boom, it nevertheless got sucked into the Panic of 1873. Already in its fourth year of business, its dividend was halved. Moreover, the rapid increase of its capital to 45 million marks garnered considerable criticism, and the stock price dropped, only reaching its par value again at the end of the decade. The 1880s saw a consolidation of the numbers, the stock price recovered, total assets tripled and the dividend could be raised to an average of 9–10 per cent. By the end of the decade, the number of domestic and foreign connections and staff (about 1,000) had reached a substantial size. In terms of the numbers, Deutsche Bank had finally caught up with its competition; indeed, it took an insurmountable lead in the following decade because it was the only institution in Germany that offered really comprehensive banking services almost across the board and, at the same time, displayed an international presence. This presence was also due to the bank's expansion into the capital market business starting in the 1880s, which it pursued in an effort to compensate for the stagnant German market. Despite all the criticism of this move, the bank stuck to this course. It ran its 'regular business' on the offensive in combination with an aggressive presence on the international capital markets, thus utilising all forms of financing. Its success proved that it was right to do so: in 1900, it had equity capital of 150 million marks, total assets of nearly 900 million marks, more than 2,000 employees at its headquarters, seven domestic branches and an agency in London, as well as large investments in institutions and other banks it was on friendly terms with. This made it more of a universal banking institution than any other German bank, a development that continued consistently in the following years of the Gwinner era up to the outbreak of the war, despite some fluctuations and lots of difficulties. The stock price alone shows this: in 1900, it was twice the nominal value, and in the following years, with fluctuations, it rose on average, reaching 264 per cent in 1911, whereas in the same period the dividend distributions remained stable at between 10 and 12.5 per cent. This, too, demonstrates the bank's secure position and the market's solid trust, particularly since the stock price experienced none of the speculative exaggerations typical elsewhere. At the end of 1913, the bank's equity capital reached 200 million marks, 2.25 billion marks in total assets and the number of employees had expanded to a solid 6,600: Deutsche Bank was indisputably Germany's number one bank. Internationally, Deutsche Bank perceived that 'great clamour' started whenever the bank turned up as a competitor since its almost single-handed financing of the gigantic Baghdad Railway project had shown what achievements it was capable of.[1]

From its founding, a mere 40 years had passed, which makes this success story all the more remarkable. Of course, not every success was due to the achievements of the bank itself. After the Panic of 1873 had been overcome and the long deflationary phase had ended in the early 1890s, the bank was acting in a favourable economic environment. The structural shift of the global economy, too, but especially the so-called Wilhelmine Economic Miracle of the years between 1892 and the First World War, were beneficial to the bank. This was because this miracle was brought about by the unfolding of new technological possibilities and the bank had not bound itself early on to the industrial business of the old sectors but, rather, without older burdens, had been able to support the new industries that were expanding from the mid-1880s. The bank's success was not a foregone conclusion because the fluctuating economic and structural conditions subjected the German money and capital markets repeatedly to severe 'stress tests'. One such test was when the great liquidity met with only minimal demand; another was when the boom very quickly reached the limits of its capacity. Deutsche Bank also managed to perform well in these crises, whether it was the crisis of the mortgage banks around the turn of the century or the liquidity crisis of 1908, because it had gradually professionalised its operations and structured its risk in a very cautious and strict manner. Above all, though, it had generated refinancing options for itself by maintaining its 'regular business' (deposits, clearing transactions and current account, acceptance and collateral credit). Other banks could only dream of such options, which carried the bank securely through the depths of liquidity shortages. Its balance sheet structure, compared to Disconto-Gesellschaft, for example, was not only different in terms of volume. Deutsche Bank, vividly characterised as a financial 'suction pump', also earned its money to a much greater extent from its 'regular business' and was far less dependent on the financing of major projects, such as major issuances. In this way, the bank also crucially contributed to mobilising the German money and capital markets – a fact Gwinner and others never tired of stressing later on. The German capital market, for its part, managed to develop dynamically despite all the shortages and – after British capital – ranked second in foreign investments prior to the First World War. Only this quite aggressively advertised and operated 'suction pump' enabled the bank, to the consternation of its critics, to get involved with such confidence in the international economy and in the financing of domestic public and private capital needs. The bank carried out its foreign investment business – which took place, above all, against the backdrop of only weak domestic capital demand in the 1880s – in a manner very similar to its British competitors, primarily in accordance with business calculations; it sought to avoid political transactions when they did not align with good business sense. It countered critics of this pragmatic benefit calculation with the compelling argument that, without this involvement, Germany would not be in a position to stabilise its current account balance or balance of payments given its ongoing trade balance deficits. The bank was doing something that benefited both it and, at the same time, the German economy. While generating self-confidence, these actions did not necessarily make the bank well liked because they took place under tough competition or gave the bank something of the character of constantly being the best pupil in the class who, for this very reason, was not particularly popular with his fellow pupils.

That Deutsche Bank was able to combine its 'regular business' and its involvement in the (international) capital markets business in such an astonishing way can doubtlessly be attributed to the course Georg Siemens was responsible for and implemented in the 1870s and 1880s. In any case, the spectacular projects, not all of which were successful, were not at the centre of this course. Precisely because Deutsche Bank became a universal bank without ever planning for that, it was able to afford setbacks in individual sectors. The profits it gained in its 'regular business' and its reserves were always sufficient to withstand major setbacks, too; indeed, they were the condition for the bank's legendary and frequently vaunted placing power. A consistent policy of risk structuring was behind this from the beginning. Hermann Wallich and Max Steinthal, above all, stood for this, with Elkan Heinemann acting as their successor. Although he was regarded as a ditherer, he managed to spare the bank severe losses precisely because of his hesitation. Probably the bank's rise can be attributed ultimately to the smooth functioning of its organisational apparatus combined with management that was simultaneously cautious and aggressive. This, after all, is exactly what contemporary observers like the editor of *Plutus*, Georg Bernhard, also emphasised: the peculiar mix of different characters who complemented one another leading the bank, not a single one of whom failed to fulfil his duties in a strict sense, and when one did fail, he left the bank very quickly, as Andreas Friedrich Mölle did in the early years and Paul Jonas later on. There is no statistical significance to the fact that 75 per cent of the bank managers who were ennobled prior to 1914 came from Deutsche Bank because the group of ennobled bank directors in general is too small. However, it nonetheless speaks volumes, as does the fact that Emperor Wilhelm II directly approached bank leaders when the scandal concerning the collapse of the princes' trust needed to be ended as quietly as possible. While this made sense because the bank was close to the princes' trust anyway, at the same time it shows the high reputation that Arthur Gwinner, at least, had among the 'highest circles', as one said at the time. And this reputation was not a consequence of the merchant cosying up to the aristocracy; it was the result of a 40-year success story which had not just taken place on the national level.

Many feared the great European war, but no one expected it to emerge when it did, nor, above all, did anyone expect its severe consequences. Shortly before it began, Deutsche Bank had reached a settlement with interested French and British parties concerning the construction of the Baghdad Railway. This successful negotiation shows that international conflicts could still be solved in 1914 without necessarily leading to war. Just a few days before the outbreak of war, Elkan Heinemann expressed to his Austrian colleagues the hope that the conflict could be resolved and that the swirling cauldron of a great war would pass. But his hopes deceived him, and his concern, in contrast, turned out to be justified. The war destroyed everything that the bank had worked so hard to build up in its international business since 1870.

BETWEEN STATE
AND MARKET,
1914–1989

ALEXANDER NÜTZENADEL

Introduction

With the start of the First World War, the international financial system, which had remained stable for over 50 years, collapsed.[1] The event represented an existential threat to the 'largest bank in the world', as the *Frankfurter Zeitung* had described Deutsche Bank in early 1914.[2] Branches and subsidiaries throughout Europe and overseas were either closed completely or restrained in their operations; all at once, the bank lost its most important business fields: trade finance, which had traditionally been a significant source of income, and also the entire international capital market business, which had grown steadily in the years prior to the war. How did Deutsche Bank face these changes? What strategies did it develop to compensate for the losses? What impact did this 'European civil war' have on banking and finance as a whole?

There are five key characteristics that stand out in terms of Deutsche Bank's development in the decades after the First World War.

First, the war brought to an end the long era of political and economic stability that had shaped banking for nearly half a century. Since the foundation of Deutsche Bank in 1870, there had been no major military conflicts between the great powers in Europe. The continent had, since the Panic of 1873, also been spared any major economic turbulence or political revolution. All of this would change dramatically in 1914. Economic crises, military conflicts and political regime changes made banking more unpredictable: in addition, political uncertainty compounded the usual business risks; wars and revolutions cannot, for the most part, be anticipated, nor can their effects be predicted. 'Exogenous shocks' such as these presented major challenges, even for banks – institutions that should have been accustomed to dealing with risk.[3]

Second, state and politics became increasingly important for Deutsche Bank. Until the First World War, bankers had mostly abstained from engaging in politics. In the economically liberal climate of the German Empire, the state merely set the legal framework, while banking remained a private activity. If individual bankers did choose to become involved in politics, they did so out of personal conviction, not in their role as representatives of the leading German bank. With the First World War, this attitude fundamentally shifted. The state was increasingly involved in the economy and gradually became an important economic actor itself. Private companies – and banks in particular – were more frequently called on to assume public responsibilities and operate in an environment regulated by the state. As a consequence, political lobbying increased in importance, as did the cultivation of contacts with the state and bureaucracy through informal channels. Often, bankers served as experts and political advisers without being formally engaged in public office. They also became more involved on the international political stage, and the First World

War ushered in a new era of banking diplomacy, one in which the representatives of Deutsche Bank frequently played a central role.

Third, in the decades after 1914, the business model of Deutsche Bank had to adapt itself to a new economic and financial environment. Only then did Deutsche Bank become a truly universal bank, offering a full array of financial services. It built an extensive network of branches and acquired new client groups, including medium-sized companies, tradesmen and private savers. The role of the bank in financing large-scale industry also changed. While access to international capital markets became more difficult, industrial corporations depended increasingly on credits from banks. This also meant that customer support and supervision became a more important factor, in that the bank's default risks grew considerably.

Fourth, starting with the First World War, the bank turned into a corporate group with numerous holdings and subsidiaries. Whereas until 1914 Deutsche Bank grew primarily on its own internal momentum, the driving force now became external growth through mergers and acquisitions. This change carried with it new organisational challenges. In general, internal growth is more organic and does not demand extensive restructuring, while mergers often require an enormous organisational effort. In addition to direct integration costs, the bank was faced with new problems such as opportunistic behaviour from staff and managers and asymmetric information.

This points to the fifth core element of development after 1914. The major transformations that took place at Deutsche Bank complicated its corporate governance. While tensions grew between shareholders, the Management Board and the Supervisory Board, the bank had to face new organisational challenges due to the sheer number of its holdings and its wide network of branches. Deutsche Bank simply did not have a strategy to cope with this new situation. While many industrial corporations had, by the 1920s, implemented a multidivisional structure, the internal organisation of the bank remained largely unchanged until the 1970s. Unlike how the Chandlerian theory suggests, the structure of the bank did not follow a coherent business strategy, but adapted late to market transformations[4] and in a completely unsystematic fashion.

These five core elements shaped Deutsche Bank's development for the entire 'short twentieth century,' which stretched from the First World War until German reunification. However, they are also an indication that, despite all the ruptures and crises that occurred, there were crucial elements of continuity in the history of the bank during this period.

I. The End of the World Economy: War, Revolution and Inflation

1. Losing the Foreign Business

The outbreak of the First World War represented a deep caesura for the foreign activities of all German banks. Until that time, nationalist rivalries had exerted a limited impact on the international financial system. The military escalation changed this dramatically. Banking experts soon warned about the effects of war on financial business. In the early days of August 1914, the journal *Die Bank* wrote that the country stood 'at the start of a war that is unprecedented in the history of humanity, one that, unless a miracle happens, will throw civilised Europe into disarray to its very core'.[1] Georg Bernhard, the publisher of the financial newspaper *Plutus*, emphatically warned of the potential economic consequences: 'If it becomes a struggle between nations, the entire European economy will be shaken to its very foundations, and no one can say today how the map or the distribution of wealth will look after such a battle ends.'[2]

The management of Deutsche Bank began to prepare themselves for an uncertain future. In August, Management Board members Arthur von Gwinner and Karl Helfferich described the situation in Germany to the managers of the Anatolian Railway in Istanbul:

All thinking is dominated by the great war. All regular work has as good as completely stopped. We are nearly fully cut off from the outside world; not only is our entry and exit interrupted, but communication via telegraph or regular mail is possible only with difficulty, and with some countries is not possible at all.

For Gwinner and Helfferich, however, these serious changes were merely temporary in light of the swift victory that they expected for Germany:

We can report from here that everyone in Germany has unlimited trust in our army and our navy. We see this as a battle for our existence; and precisely because everyone is pervaded by this feeling, we are all convinced that we will surely be victorious.[3]

However, it soon became clear that the war would not just affect the foreign branches but would also cause changes to the business in Germany. As Max Schinckel, the head of Norddeutsche Bank, wrote on 8 August 1914:

The area around Hamburg is currently in an even more difficult situation than Germany as a whole. Since 1870, the Hamburg business world has increasingly done business abroad. [...] All of a sudden, we are fully cut off from all foreign markets with the exception of Scandinavia. Beyond the fact that all the countries that Hamburg works with, England above all, are currently under legal moratoria and great payment difficulties, remittances can no longer come to Germany from most countries, and even the North and Austria, which are still open for business, are not sending any more remittances because of their moratoria.[4]

Were there plans in place for reorganising the bank's business activities in the event of a war? Everything that we know suggests that such plans were completely absent in the German business world. Indeed, the war was not fully unexpected. It ensued after a long-standing political-imperial polarisation of Europe and the world, as also manifested by the martial rhetoric of the early days of the war.[5] By the second Morocco Crisis of September 1911, banking circles had begun thinking about the financial aspects of a possible war.[6] However, no one expected such a long, destructive and constantly expanding conflict, which could only be brought to an end by the utter defeat of one side. German elites envisaged a conflict along the lines of the Franco-Prussian War of 1870–1. No one predicted a 'total war' that would involve more than three dozen countries across the world and affect the entire global economy. If Deutsche Bank had no plan in the summer of 1914, it is clear that it adapted relatively rapidly to the new situation. Herfried Münkler argued that the First World War was characterised by a 'fluid and continuous learning process' in which the various actors constantly had to face changing situations.[7] Deutsche Bank, with its wide-ranging business interests, applied a twofold approach: first, it retreated, in as ordered and noiseless a fashion as possible, from those countries in which it no longer saw promising business opportunities; second, the bank moved its business activities to other countries and regions by activating informal channels and connections, often through allied banks and neutral states. Despite the increasingly hostile atmosphere, its connections with financial institutions outside of the country often still functioned well and – paradoxically – even gained importance under wartime conditions.

One of the greatest sources of concern for the bank in the summer of 1914 were events in London. With 300 employees, Deutsche Bank's London branch was the most important foreign branch office. Its balance sheet of 218 million marks represented about one-tenth of the entire bank's total assets in 1913. In addition, the majority of all foreign trade financing, and trading in foreign exchange and precious metals, was carried out there. If the London branch were to close down, a large part of the international operations and money market business was in danger of breaking off.

Developments gained momentum over the course of summer 1914.[8] By 27 July, Deutsche Bank could no longer discount bills in London, and within days the bank's money at call had shrunk to less than £50,000.[9] After the London Stock Exchange temporarily ceased trading on 31 July, the banks of the City were ordered on 3 August to close for four days to prevent a bank run.[10] After the British declared war on 4 August, German banks[11] were barred from further business transactions by order of

The hope was still entertained that a European war was avoidable: telegram from Deutsche Bank's London branch to Berlin headquarters of 27 July 1914.

the British government. Behind the scenes, representatives of Deutsche Bank worked intensively to acquire a new licence in order to resume business. At the very least, open credits and liabilities had to be settled. The British government hired a chartered accountant to wrap up all contractual commitments. One of the accountant's key tasks was to prevent the assets of branches of German banks from flowing out of the country. British government officials suspected that the London offices of German banks had significant assets and substantial holdings in gold, an assumption that proved to be mistaken.[12] A report submitted in early 1917 by Sir William Plender, the British chartered accountant, made clear that the liabilities of the German branches in London at the start of the war were actually much higher than their assets. Deutsche Bank's assets and liabilities balanced almost perfectly.[13] Ultimately, the British government also had an interest in an orderly wind-down of remaining business, and a government decree allowed the German banks to collect existing receivables and to meet their payment obligations to British, allied and neutral clients. The latter proved difficult, however, as monetary transactions with the states at war had been suspended in most countries.[14] Only in September 1916, when most liabilities had been settled, did the Treasury provide instructions to dismantle the branch offices.[15] Deutsche Bank's office building on Old Broad Street was eventually acquired by Barclays in June 1917 for the sum of £230,000.

These events illustrate that, although the war had far-reaching consequences for the world of finance, business questions were handled in a relatively level-headed manner. Neither the British nor the German banks wanted to let the military escalation damage their connections to institutions in enemy states. All involved knew that they would at some point in the future be working together again. Nevertheless, the likelihood of reopening the London branch in the medium term was viewed at Deutsche Bank with scepticism. Despite its nearly comprehensive settling of all liabilities, an internal report from Max von Rapp, who had been head of the London branch for many years and would not be able to leave Great Britain until 1917, argued that business could not resume as normal due to the experiences of the war:

> Because hate, mistrust, and contempt have seeped into the flesh and blood of the population, it is entirely possible that the English will break with all traditions of commerce and disregard their material interests. Aside from the draft legislation that would prevent banks from enemy countries from carrying out business for a number of years, this animosity should be expected to continue after the war as well, a situation which will hardly be conducive to the promotion of new business. In a country in which so much is based on loyalty and trustworthiness, the yellow press's incitement has resulted in such a lack of sympathy and reasonableness towards Germans, that, in my opinion, it will take decades to regain the goodwill and trust that form the basis of fruitful commerce. [...] The utilisation of credit in any form would be met by major resistance; our acceptances would find no takers. A branch would therefore need to be equipped with far greater capital than previously, and the use of this capital would for the most part be possible exclusively through the goodwill of individuals and only by means of commission.[16]

Von Rapp's report of course also referred to the expected loss in influence of London as a financial centre: 'I am inclined to think that London will not return to its previous position. England, which had previously been the creditor of the entire world, has now become a debtor country after its ejection of a large sum of foreign assets.'[17] Von Rapp also viewed Great Britain's role in international trade sceptically. He recommended that the bank set up connections through friendly banks or through a representative office and that it refrain from founding a branch: 'A branch will always be seen as a competitor, a representative office as an alleviating linkage.'[18]

This sceptical assessment would prove true after the end of the war. In a similar way, Robert Bassermann, the director of the Hamburg branch, came to the conclusion after visiting London, Edinburgh and Manchester that the reopening of branches should not even be considered.[19] The experiences of the war and its severe financial and political repercussions had placed too great a strain on former business connections. Moreover, after the war, London did not regain its previous position as the global centre of finance and trade. Great Britain depended increasingly on capital imports, and the value of the British pound dropped continuously. New York became the most dynamic centre of the international capital markets, even though the instability and imbalances of the interwar era made global finance more difficult.[20]

The transfer of many financial activities from London to New York had become apparent as early as the middle of 1914. The United States gained a significant amount of importance for German bankers and businessmen after the start of the war; the country's neutral stance seemed to allow for the continued promotion of business abroad and to compensate, at least partially, for the closure of the London branches. In mid-1914, the US embassy in London also played an important role in protecting German financial interests. However, the increasing engagement in the United States was not by itself a consequence of the war. Business in America had taken on momentum even before 1914.[21] As the largest economy in the world, the United States was of great interest to German investors and exporters, and Deutsche Bank's involvement in North America had grown continuously for a number of years by this time. Shortly before the war broke out, its assets and securities in the United States amounted to approximately $3 million.[22] Still, the American financial sector was viewed as murky and particularly risky – there were no national banking laws or regulations in place to protect investors, and the management had long been wary of founding an office in North America. Deutsche Bank therefore carried out business quite reliably via agents or allied correspondent banks, such as National City Bank; Kuhn, Loeb & Co.; and the New York offshoot of Speyer & Co. Representatives of Deutsche Bank frequently travelled to the United States for larger investment projects, particularly if they were asked to provide venture capital for new technologies. This applied, for example, for the bank's investment in Lehigh Coke, an American coke plant, which was co-ordinated by board member Paul Mankiewitz. After the start of the war, the bank briefly considered opening its own branch, propelled in particular by Edward Adams, who had long served as a business partner and agent of the bank in New York. The bank even sent Hugo Schmidt, a member of the management board of Banco Alemán Transatlántico, to New York in October 1914 to co-ordinate activities there.[23] Schmidt was also given the responsibility of managing business in Latin America from New York after the Atlantic cables were cut off by British warships shortly after the outbreak of the war.

German banks were able to remain active in the United States without legal limitations until the end of 1916. However, the political mood of the population, which turned against German activities of any form early on, proved to be a challenge. 'Public sentiment is not favorable, I am sorry to say, to the German interests in the present hostilities,' Adams wrote to Gwinner in September 1914.[24] After a German U-boat sank the Lusitania, a British passenger ship, in May 1915, anti-German sentiment in the United States reached a new pitch. One thousand one hundred and ninety-eight people (including 128 US citizens) died. Deutsche Bank's representative in New York reported to Berlin that 'the newspapers are positively howling with anger'.[25] By the summer, Hugo Schmidt reported very pessimistically about relations with the United States:

Though no one seriously thinks of going to war with Germany, a breaking off of diplomatic relations is considered to be within the realm of the possible [...] This would create very inopportune circumstances, which could possibly make all trade relations with Germany – and by association, what I do here – impossible.[26]

The New York banking world split into pro-German and pro-British camps.[27] National City Bank and JP Morgan, with both of which Deutsche Bank had maintained good relations prior to the war, positioned themselves firmly on the side of the Entente. Goldman Sachs and Speyer & Co., the latter traditionally closely connected with Deutsche Bank, were more pro-German. Despite the political tensions, Deutsche Bank continued to achieve high turnover in the United States until 1916. After the New York Stock Exchange resumed trading on 12 December 1914, the Germans were particularly interested in tapping the American capital market to finance German war loans. By July 1915, the Central Powers and the Ottoman Empire had been able to market government debt to the amount of $5.3 billion in the United States, though this was only half the volume of that marketed by the Entente powers.[28] German investment in US firms also remained high. As in Great Britain, a rapid withdrawal of investment and credit proved complicated and in many cases was neither economically nor politically desirable. American firms in which Deutsche Bank had a stake (including Bethlehem Steel and General Electric) experienced high returns during the war, and investment in Lehigh Coke was even increased in the hopes of boosting the supply of hydrocarbons needed for the war effort, such as benzol and toluol.[29] German capital was therefore still extensively tied up in the United States when the country entered the war in April 1917 and, in October, established the legal basis for expropriating the assets of investors from Germany and other enemy countries. This was acted on a large scale: by December 1918, the share of German investment in the United States had fallen to zero.[30]

The bank's business in South America was also significantly impeded by the war. In 1914, Deutsche Bank's operations in Latin America comprised its subsidiary, Banco Alemán Transatlántico (BAT), which operated 25 branches in Argentina, Brazil, Mexico, Uruguay, Chile, Bolivia and Peru. Including the Spanish offices, BAT had a turnover of nearly 22 billion marks during the final year of peace and achieved net profits of 12.2 million marks. Both of these figures represented approximately 17 per cent of the balance sheet of the parent bank. This side of the business was in danger of being lost, a painful consideration in light of the high dividend of 9 per cent that BAT brought in.[31] At first, however, the Latin American countries remained neutral and did not place restrictions on German banks.[32] However, when the Atlantic cables were interrupted, BAT's branches were left largely to their own devices.[33] Trade between Latin America and Germany was also brought to an almost complete standstill by the British embargo. Because the London banks no longer accepted trade bills from German companies, there was an attempt to establish New York as a new financial hub for business in South America, which predictably never fully succeeded.[34] After the United States entered the war, this path was definitively closed. Argentina, Germany's most important trading partner in South America, remained neutral until the end of the war, whereas Brazil declared war on the Central Powers in October 1917 and placed all German banks under state control. While Deutsche Bank's involvement in Latin America was not fully terminated by the war, it did suffer a major setback, especially because most of the countries there faced serious economic difficulties after the war due to a drop in worldwide prices for agricultural goods and raw materials.

German banks' business in Asia was also brought to an almost complete standstill after the outbreak of the war. In the British sphere of influence, all branches of Deutsch-Asiatische Bank (DAB) were forced to close, their assets confiscated and their employees detained. The impact was especially significant in the key bases of Hong Kong, Singapore and Calcutta. Co-operation agreements with other banks in the region – especially with the British-influenced Hongkong and Shanghai Banking Corporation (HSBC) – were shut down. Nor was DAB management's suggestion to trade its branches in the British sphere of influence to HSBC in exchange for its subsidiaries in Hamburg and Tsingtao pursued further.[35] After Japan declared war on the Central Powers, the branches in Kobe and Yokohama also had to severely limit their operations, and were closed in 1916. Conditions in China were more favourable for the bank due to its stronger business connections and the emerging Sino-Japanese conflict. With the backing of the German embassy, representatives of DAB initiated talks about issuing a loan to the Chinese government. The bank paid an advance of 14.5 million marks to the Chinese during the war, which the German government guaranteed.[36] In light of the military situation, this was a highly risky decision, but the Germans hoped by these means to win over the Chinese as allies.[37] The branches on the mainland did in fact remain open for business until China entered the war in 1917. However, trade with Germany was mostly interrupted, and communication via regular mail and telegraph became nearly impossible. After Japanese troops conquered Tsingtao in late 1914, the DAB branch there was closed and all its assets confiscated. As with BAT, there was an attempt to do some business via the United States, and two members of DAB's management board were even sent to the United States for that purpose.[38]

Deutsche Bank's overseas business had all but ground to a halt by 1917. How did it attempt to compensate for this loss? One important strategy consisted in generating business in the neutral, allied and occupied European countries, and using informal channels to enable business activities, at least on a modest scale, in enemy countries or countries sealed off due to sanctions. This was the case in the Ottoman Empire, where Deutsche Bank had been financing trade as well as major investment projects for decades.[39] Whereas the branches of the competing Deutsche Orientbank in British-influenced Egypt were closed, its branches and both of Deutsche Bank's offices in the Ottoman Empire were able to continue operations through the end of the war. They were responsible for the financial and organisational management of German raw-material and food imports from the region. Deutsche Bank's branch office in Istanbul, which had been opened in 1909 and had approximately 250 employees, played an especially important role. A product section (*Warenabteilung*) was even set up in Istanbul under the management of Rudolph Brinkmann, a long-time bank employee, in order to arrange the risky transport of goods to Germany across the Balkans.[40] Deutsche Bank also supplied the Turkish army with gold from its branch's reserves in Istanbul. Turkey did not just receive cash loans from Germany; it also received gold for purchases critical to the war effort in regions that did not accept paper currency.

At the same time, the years-long contractual negotiations over the construction of the Baghdad Railway were brought to completion in 1916. In light of the financial difficulties associated with the project, an increasing number of voices within Deutsche

The Hong Kong (top) and Singapore branches of Deutsch-Asiatische Bank, lying within the British sphere of influence, were closed at the start of the war in 1914.

Bank had criticised the enterprise. The fact that the agreement was nonetheless signed, even during the war, was due above all to military considerations: the finished railway would, the Supreme Army Command hoped, provide a strategic advantage to the Central Powers by allowing troops and supplies to be quickly transported to the Middle East and even to India.[41] An internal bank memo from early 1915 explained,

> His Excellency Falkenhayn considers it possible that the transport of supplies to Aleppo and even farther south can be assured by means of the Hedjaz Railway by October 1915, if [...] transportation over the Taurus mountains is carried out by truck and over the Amanus Mountains by extending the narrow-gauge service railway. His Excellency Falkenhayn also considers that the rapid creation of such a high-capacity, continuous connection in Asia Minor in the direction of the Suez Canal to be important for the pursual of future objectives.[42]

These imperialist fantasies soon proved unrealistic, however. They were quickly overtaken by the course of events: the Ottoman Empire progressively unravelled and in October 1918 surrendered to the Entente.

Railway construction in the Ottoman Empire also brought the leadership of Deutsche Bank into contact with the Armenian Genocide. The management of the Anatolian Railway sent shocking reports to Berlin, gathered from visitors and railroad engineers. Arthur von Gwinner, the Spokesman of the Management Board, provided funds for aid. This was carried out anonymously in order to avoid giving the impression that the bank was opposed to a government that was allied with Germany. The leadership of the bank intervened with the Turkish government in order to ensure that nearly

In late October 1915, the management of the Anatolian Railway Company informed Berlin that its cattle cars had been used to deport Armenians.

all of their Armenian salaried employees and their families were spared deportation.[43] However, the attempts of leading engineers to prevent deportations at the construction sites of the Baghdad Railway in the Amanus Mountains were unsuccessful. In June 1916, several thousand Armenian men, women and children were forced on death marches or were massacred.[44]

In November 1918, German banks in the Ottoman Empire were placed under Allied control; they were shut down the following year. After complicated negotiations, however, they were reopened from 1923 onwards after the reinitiation of the German–Turkish relationship by the newly founded Republic of Turkey.

Deutsche Bank's connections to the neutral countries of Europe were of even greater importance than those with Turkey. In addition to Denmark and Sweden, these included Switzerland and the Netherlands. Shortly after the outbreak of the war, Deutsche Bank had sent representatives to these countries in order to explore opportunities to continue its international business via allied banks. The Swedish banker Victor Wallenberg was an important contact in Stockholm; since raw materials and food could be imported to Germany from Sweden, this connection was to be of vital importance. Many of the purchases of imports were carried out via German financial institutions. Capital transactions with banks and companies in Russia could also be carried out via the Scandinavian countries.[45] In Zurich, Bruno Axhausen, an authorised representative of the Berlin headquarters, was able to secure a co-operation agreement with Credit Suisse. From then on, a portion of the bank's international transactions were handled through Switzerland, and Credit Suisse also served as a cover for communication with branches abroad. The path through Switzerland was lost, however, after the Entente threatened Credit Suisse and all other Swiss banks with major sanctions.[46]

Deutsche Bank's connections to the neutral Netherlands therefore gained importance, and the country played a central role in the supply of food and raw materials to Germany as well as being an avenue for carrying out international money transfers. After the loss of the London acceptance market, Amsterdam also grew in importance for trade finance. A lively money and capital market developed in the Netherlands in light of its high trade surpluses and the strong flight of capital to financial centres in neutral countries. The British news magazine *The Economist* remarked that 'the position of the London exchange market is encroached upon by Amsterdam, so that Dutch currency has for the time being become a standard of value for other countries'.[47] Substantial sums of money probably flowed to Amsterdam from Germany, as the German government did not prohibit the outflow of capital until August 1916.[48] Irrespective of these undesirable capital flows, the Netherlands was crucial for the German war economy. Imports were financed through direct transfer of currency or gold from the Reichsbank, but in practice carried out by private importers. The 'Decree on Trade with Foreign Currencies' of 20 January 1916 increased government control, but left foreign exchange trading completely to the leading private banks (in addition to Deutsche Bank, these included Disconto-Gesellschaft, M. M. Warburg & Co., S. Bleichröder and Mendelssohn & Co.). This was not only intended to ensure a more targeted and careful use of increasingly scarce gold and foreign currency reserves. Private-sector banks with their long-standing international connections were considered to handle international payments more effectively and, above all, more discreetly than state institutions such as the Central Purchasing Company (*Zentral-Einkaufsgesellschaft*) or the Reichsbank.[49] The banks in Amsterdam were indeed an important source of credit for German importers; by the end of the war the total credit offered to German companies amounted to 308 million guilders, making Germany the most important credit partner of the Netherlands. Finally, Dutch banks provided brokering services. They were tasked with transferring securities from Germany to the United States in order to obtain foreign currency that could be used for imports. Because all overseas shipping was under the close control of the British Ministry of Blockade, banks from the Netherlands and other neutral states (above all from Switzerland, Denmark and Sweden) took on commissions on behalf of German banks and government offices, albeit it in return for high fees.[50] Deutsche Bank was well connected in the business world of Amsterdam, but preferred to act from behind the scenes and was mainly involved in clearing operations, as it did not want to alienate its Dutch competitors by behaving too brashly.[51]

In addition to the Netherlands, neighbouring occupied Belgium also played an important role in the German war economy. Both Deutsche Bank (in Brussels) and Disconto-Gesellschaft (in Antwerp) had, as has already been shown, only become active in Belgium in the immediate lead-up to the First World War. The war, which had been looming since July 1914, strengthened German business interests in owning offices in a neutral trading centre. Thus, the Hamburg insurance company Bleichröder & Co. asked the Brussels branch of Deutsche Bank for support in applying for a commercial licence in Brussels in late July 1914 in order to be able to continue its international business (with British clients, among others).[52] However, only a few days later, the German bank employees in Belgium were expelled and the branches were provisionally closed. After Brussels and Antwerp were occupied by German troops, the German banks quickly restarted operations, as Belgium was expected to become an important financial hub after the war.[53] Georg Solmssen, who travelled to occupied Belgium in early December 1914, wrote to his colleagues at the directorate of Disconto-Gesellschaft:

> If one regards the war as a conflict between us and England for an equal position in global trade, it is of the essence that the base we have acquired on the English Channel in Belgium be expanded, if possible, to Calais, that it be turned into the point of departure for free access to the ocean, and that Antwerp be developed into a site for acceptance credits that will free us from our reliance on London.[54]

However, the German branches in Brussels and Antwerp could only carry out business to a limited degree. The lending and capital markets business ground to an almost complete halt during the war, especially because the few Belgian companies that were still in operation showed little readiness to work with German banks. Deutsche Bank therefore focused on providing credit to the war corporations (*Kriegsgesellschaften*) that operated under the German military administration.[55] The bank also helped the Reichsbank to acquire foreign currency and gold reserves.[56] In November 1918, the German bank offices in Belgium closed. The Brussels branch remained active as a settlement agency in Berlin for some years, as it had been able to unload most of the assets of its German clients in time. Disconto-Gesellschaft evacuated its Antwerp branch to the premises of A. Schaaffhausen'scher Bankverein in Düsseldorf. The Belgian government sequestered the branches, which were eventually liquidated after a protracted lawsuit.

The First World War led to the closure of many branches abroad and to the withdrawal from numerous large international investment projects. This was the case, for example, with Deutsche Bank's financial interest in Deutsch-Ueberseeische Elektricitäts-Gesellschaft (DUEG) in Latin America.[57] The company had played a decisive role in the electrification of the continent and had received large capital investments from Deutsche Bank. The loss of this investment was particularly painful; John Maynard Keynes was not alone in seeing the company as 'the fine and powerful German enterprise in South America'.[58] By the end of 1918 the management of Deutsche Bank knew that it could not hold on to the company. Neither could the divestment of the holdings be avoided, as foreign investors were taking advantage of the weakness of the mark to buy large quantities of shares. Based on some calculations, half of the shares were already under foreign ownership, with Swiss investors playing a particularly important role. It was also feared that the remaining German shares would be confiscated by the victorious powers. Deutsche Bank therefore began negotiations with Elektrobank, a Swiss bank, although these ultimately failed because, from the perspective of the Swiss investors, incipient inflation posed too many unpredictable risks. Exploratory talks with a Spanish bank group were more successful, however. Neutral Spain had become a haven during the war for capital on which investors wanted to make a profit after the end of the war. Due to their close relationship with Latin America, Spanish banks also had a strong interest in DUEG. After extensive negotiations, the parties agreed in early 1920 to transfer all shares in DUEG to the newly founded Compañía Hispano-Americana de Electricidad (CHADE), which was based in Madrid. CHADE, in turn, issued shares and bonds to compensate the shareholders. This proved to be a good business decision for Deutsche Bank, since the holders of preferred shares in particular received high payments. This did not signal a permanent withdrawal from Latin America, however. When CHADE shares were officially traded in Germany in 1927, its Supervisory Board included Arthur von Gwinner and Elkan Heinemann, two former members of Deutsche Bank's Management Board.[59]

In the case of other similar major investments, there was an attempt after the end of the war to settle things in an orderly manner to keep the bank's losses to a minimum. In only a few cases was this impossible. Deutsche Bank's involvement in Africa, for example, ended without a settlement of assets. This applied in particular to the Deutsch-Ostafrikanische Gesellschaft and its associated bank, which had been undergoing a silent liquidation process since the start of the war. Its legal construction as a colonial business made both its continuation and a wrapping-up of business operations impossible.[60] The same applied to the investment in the Société Commerciale Belgo-Allemande du Congo.[61]

Deutsche Bank's investments in railways and property in Mosul, Mesopotamia and Syria were lost without compensation. Far more important, however, was the fact that Deutsche Bank was able to end its long-standing involvement in the Baghdad Railway without causing much noise. Its shares in the Anatolian Railway were first transferred to a Swiss company – Bank for Oriental Railways in Zurich – and then sold to an English consortium.[62] Overtures from the new Turkish government, which invited Deutsche Bank to pick back up its railway investments, were declined in 1922. As long as Constantinople was under Allied control, German investment in Turkey seemed too risky.[63]

Divesting from another foreign investment project, Deutsche Petroleum AG (DPAG), founded in 1904, proved much more complicated. Deutsche Bank did not just have a financial interest in DPAG, it had also become actively involved in the management of it as a subsidiary. From 1904 onward, DPAG's chief executive was Emil Georg von Stauß (ennobled in 1918), who quickly rose through the ranks in Deutsche Bank and by 1915 was a member of the Management Board. Unlike other international holdings, DPAG had risen in significance over the course of the war because of its strategic importance to the Central Powers' energy supplies. In particular, the Romanian oil fields of Steaua Română, which belonged to DPAG, delivered oil to Germany throughout the entire course of the war, despite the constant movement of the front lines, and represented a highly profitable business for Deutsche Bank. In fact, the bank wanted to expand further into this sector in the expectation of growing oil markets around the world after the war. The bank's private interests and Stauß's market-oriented position, however, did not conform to the ideas of the representatives of the German government, who were interested in a state takeover of the Romanian oil industry.[64] After the war it did not seem entirely out of the question that the Germans would be able to continue to pursue their oil policies in the Balkans and the Middle East. In late 1920, representatives from both Deutsche Bank and Disconto-Gesellschaft looked at the possibility of melding DPAG with Deutsche Erdöl AG (DEAG). These negotiations failed, however, over the conflicting visions of the two major banks. Whereas Disconto-Gesellschaft, which had increasingly fallen behind in the oil business, wanted equal managerial powers in the planned holding company, Deutsche Bank believed it should have the leadership role. In addition, the difficult international environment led to Deutsche Bank withdrawing from the oil business. This, too, involved complex manoeuvring via foreign financing companies. To prevent its assets from being confiscated by the Romanian government, Deutsche Bank merged with DPAG in 1922 and then sold its shares to Erdölsyndikat (EOS), which had been founded for this purpose in Switzerland. An international banking consortium finally acquired the share package. As a result, Deutsche Bank brought in earnings of 72 million Swiss francs; the shareholders of DPAG were compensated with shares in Deutsche Bank.[65]

This deft operation makes it clear how rapidly and comprehensively Deutsche Bank was able to react to the changed international situation. The bank's withdrawal from its large international investment projects was not just a reaction to the defeat and threats to its assets, however. Decision-makers at the bank recognised that the era of large international business was over. In addition to the high political and legal risks, German financial institutions' material capacity for capital exports had shrunken considerably. Due to the war and the reparations, Germany had changed from a creditor to a debtor state and now had to import capital itself. In this, Deutsche Bank would once again play an important role, as the German government faced major difficulties in securing foreign credit. As we shall see, Deutsche Bank somewhat involuntarily took on the role of an institution in charge of opening the paths that many German companies and domestic households would have to take in order to access global markets. Its connection to the world of international finance paid off for Germany after the First World War, even if the consequences for the German economy, which was becoming increasingly encumbered by debt, were ambivalent.

2. Walking on Eggshells: War Finance and Government Bonds

As in much of the German population, a wave of patriotism swept through Deutsche Bank in July 1914. Though the bank made considerable efforts at damage control in its relationships with foreign business partners and actively sought compromise solutions, when it came to the military conflict, the bank stood publicly and unconditionally behind the Kaiser and the German government.[66] Blame for the outbreak of the war was placed solely on the Entente, with the argument that Germany and the Central Powers had no other choice but to defend themselves militarily. There existed 'full clarity', as Karl Helfferich, a member of the Management Board, wrote in December 1914 in the *Norddeutsche Allgemeine Zeitung*, 'that Germany did not want the war and did not cause it, and that the egregious guilt for this global catastrophe is exclusively on the shoulders of our band of enemies'.[67]

The positive stance on the war was a result of the expectation that Germany would quickly turn the conflict in its favour and that any setbacks to international business would be brief. The greatest perceived losses in the war – from a military as well as an economic standpoint – were expected to fall on Great Britain. Arthur von Gwinner was already 'very sure' in November 1914 that 'serious and irreparable damage to London's position as the world's clearing house' was in the offing.[68] Deutsche Bank expected that in the future, foreign investors would invest their assets elsewhere, and that Germany was not least among the parties that stood to profit.[69]

It was therefore not patriotism alone but also a hope for new areas of business that motivated the bank's leadership to support the war with all the means at its disposal. In late January 1915, Karl Helfferich was appointed state secretary of the Reich Treasury (*Reichsschatzamt*) and from then on organised with great success the financing of the ever-greater financial burdens of the war. Helfferich seemed predestined for this office; he had served in the colonial department of the German Foreign Office prior to joining Deutsche Bank in 1908 and enjoyed a wide network of political contacts.[70] He had been a member of the Central Committee of the Reichsbank since 1911 and so was heavily involved in day-to-day matters of monetary policy.[71] Helfferich also had excellent international contacts: he had lived in Constantinople for many years as director of the Anatolian Railway Company and had undertaken numerous trips to Africa on behalf of the bank. It was generally known in Berlin that, in addition to his well-paid employment on the Management Board of Deutsche Bank, Helfferich also had political ambitions, and his appointment to a high position in the Reich Treasury therefore was not wholly unexpected. Though Helfferich officially resigned from Deutsche Bank in late January 1915, he informally maintained his contacts in the finance community. On the matter of financing for the war, he did in fact represent the interests of the banks, opposing the introduction of new taxes and speaking strongly in favour of raising finance through bonds. The banks not only prevented a high tax burden, they were also able to bring in high fee income by selling the bonds, which compensated, at least temporarily, for the collapse of international business. Like its fellow leading financial institutions, Deutsche Bank worked closely with the Supreme Army Command and the newly created institutions of the war economy.

In the summer of 1914, most financial analysts underestimated both the length and the costs of a war. It was taken for granted that Germany's 'organisation in the financial field is superior to that of our opponents', as Helfferich emphasised in August 1914.[72] The German banks considered the government's financial plans to be sound and, in light of the Reichsbank's high gold reserves, no one feared a dramatic currency decline. This was also Gwinner's attitude, despite the fact that he had always supported conservative budget principles in the Prussian House of Lords.[73] For him, too, however, the war represented an exceptional situation, and his expectation that Germany's war opponents would be made to pay after his country's certain victory seemed to suspend the rules that would have applied under normal circumstances.

The ostentatious optimism that the banks exhibited over that summer was of significance in another respect as well. During the July Crisis, major unrest had developed in the money and securities markets, and many customers began to withdraw their funds, although the situation calmed down again shortly after war had been declared. According to internal calculations by Deutsche Bank, contributions already exceeded withdrawals by mid-August.[74] In order to prevent a bank run, the Reichsbank had blocked all gold payments on 31 July – like all the other countries, Germany withdrew from the rules of the international gold standard. Removing the obligation to redeem in gold created new opportunities for the creation of money and credit, which the Reichsbank only intermittently used at the start of the war; they sought to avoid a rampant decline of the currency at all costs.[75] The war, so went the slogan, was not supposed to be financed by printing money but instead with the help of the domestic capital market.

German banks were indeed more deeply involved in financing the war than were banks in other countries.[76] In contrast to the Entente powers, Germany could rely only to a limited extent on credit abroad. However, the German banks succeeded in the first phase of the war in marketing a portion of the bonds in the American capital market. The good business contacts that Deutsche Bank had built up over the course of many years in the United States were of great advantage in this effort.[77] Access to the American capital market began to shrink over the course of the war, however. Financing the war through taxation also initially appeared unfeasible, as Germany relied almost exclusively on indirect taxes and revenue from customs duties and monopolies. The German government also feared that increasing taxes would lead to substantial domestic resistance.

Even the country's substantial financial reserves – in which, at the beginning, much confidence was placed – were entirely insufficient in light of the daunting costs of the war. The 'imperial war chest', which was based primarily on French payments from 1871, amounted to 205 million marks and was only enough to cover a few days of the war; in consideration of the total war costs of 165 billion marks, it was an essentially trivial sum. Since financial needs continued to increase over the course of the war, the German government decided to use its gold reserves to increase the reserves of the Reichsbank in order to prevent a decline in the currency. Another problem that Germany faced was that its money market had a lower capacity than, for example, Great Britain's, where banks had long been taking treasury bills into their portfolios to a large extent, thereby providing the state with greater short-term liquidity. For this purpose, loan bureaux that could issue certificates to finance short-term credit were founded in Germany. Like the rediscountable Reich Treasury bills (*Reichsschatzwechsel*) and trade bills, these certificates were considered a secure cover for the issuing of notes by the Reichsbank. In late 1914, war credit banks (*Kriegskreditbanken*) were also established, in order to ensure supplies for the armament industry through credit. Max Warburg, a Hamburg banker, seems to have been the driving force behind this initiative, though he worked with the support of the other big banks. Deutsche Bank also became involved by providing nominal capital of 2.3 million marks by 1914 in a total of 12 war credit banks.[78] Of course, this was barely used – the established credit institutions would prove to be fully capable of providing the economy's investment needs, especially because the companies' self-financing rates were already quite high.[79] Unlike the war corporations, which were created for armament production, the war credit banks played only a marginal role.[80]

The banks were increasingly limited by legal ordinances and special requirements intended to support the war effort. In order to ensure that the capital market was entirely available, the private trade in securities was mostly shut down. After the Hindenburg programme was introduced in 1916, corporate bonds and preferred stock could no longer be issued. New joint-stock companies could only be founded with state approval. At the same time, new pricing requirements aimed to suppress inflation, as any decline in the currency could have endangered the sale of war loans. The money and capital markets' orientation towards the war required the active involvement of the banks, a development which they engaged in out of necessity, but also to their own advantage. After the beginning of the war, not only did stock trading cease to exist, almost all private business with bills of exchange ended. For Deutsche Bank, this meant that a large portion of the bank's usual turnover disappeared from one day to the next. Acceptance credit fell from 312 million marks in 1912 to 59.4 million marks in 1916.[81] The bank registered an increase in advance payments for goods, however, by means of which the bank helped, in the early phase of the war, to cover the war corporations' temporary lack of capital. Unlike the other big banks, Deutsche Bank could maintain stable advance payments for goods at least through the end of 1916. This was because the bank took over the financial support of numerous war raw materials corporations (*Kriegsrohstoffgesellschaften*) and clearing houses, which meant the bank had a substantial increase in turnover starting in 1915. While nominal turnover increased from 106 to 244 billion marks between 1915 and 1918, the number of customer invoices increased from 360,000 to 578,000 and the sum of deposits increased from 2.5 to 6.7 billion marks. Even if, at least in the last year of the war, inflation was mostly responsible for this increase, this development was perceived in a positive light. Even American newspapers were impressed by this growth and reported that Deutsche Bank 'continued to grow at a rate commensurate with the progress of the big American institutions'.[82]

War loans and Reich Treasury bills made up a growing proportion of turnover. Deutsche Bank issued, by its own assessment, war loans in the amount of 6.5 billion marks throughout the war, which corresponded to just under 7 per cent of all war loans, but only held a very small proportion in its own portfolio. In general, the bank kept the war loans only for short periods and attempted to sell them off at a profit as soon as rates went up.[83] Bringing in profits in this manner became increasingly difficult, however, because the willingness of investors to buy went down considerably over the course of the war. Deutsche Bank succeeded, however, in selling most of the bonds to its customers. This would prove to be a great advantage after the war, as the bank's balance sheet was not weighed down by worthless securities, and in the meantime its brokerage business was bringing in considerable commission revenue. At the same time, the bank's holdings of short-term Reich Treasury notes (*Reichsschatzanweisungen*), which, depending on maturity, yielded interest rates of 4 to 4.5 per cent, increased.[84] Even though the yields of the Reich Treasury notes were somewhat lower than those of private commercial bills, they proved to be popular with banks. They could be rediscounted with no limits at the Reichsbank and were considered risk-free and easy to process, since they were standardised and did not require a credit assessment.[85]

Deutsche Bank was thus able to compensate, at least temporarily, for the loss of international business. Earnings on both interest and securities, as well as revenue from fees, increased significantly during the war, even if inflation, especially in the final year of the war, immediately neutralised this growth. Nevertheless, the bank increased its dividend payments from 12.5 to 14 per cent in late 1917 – the highest dividend payout to that point. Through the end of the war, the bank sought, at least outwardly, to spread optimism.

Keeping investors and clients happy was not only for business reasons; it was also highly important for financing the war, with the result that only a small portion of

Figure 4: Deutsche Bank's profits from 1914 to 1918 in marks (nominal).

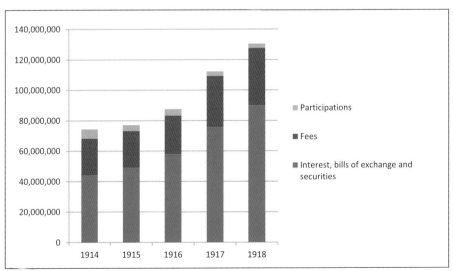

Source: Deutsche Bank, Annual Reports 1914–18.

An advertisement by the Frankfurt branch promoting the purchase of the 8th War Loan in March 1918.

Germany's enormous state debt had to be financed by printing money. As economic historian Albrecht Ritschl has shown, Germany's monetised debt only amounted to 15 per cent of new debt even in the final year of the war, far below the proportions experienced in other countries.[86] This was not just because of the German state's successful propaganda campaign promoting the purchase of war bonds; it was also due to the efficient organisation of Germany's money and capital markets through its big banks, which handled more than 50 per cent of all bonds.[87] The enormous wartime debt of 98.2 billion marks was raised primarily through war bonds, which had been purchased by approximately half of all German households .[88]

In no other country was the campaign for the purchase of war bonds as successful as in the German Empire. Of course, this also had far-reaching effects that went far beyond the monetary and fiscal spheres. Political scientist Herfried Münkler has argued that the manner in which the war was financed caused large portions of the population to believe in a 'victorious peace' for Germany until the very end of the war – or at least to indulge in the illusion. Many people also rejected the idea of a negotiated peace on these grounds, fearing that their bonds would become worthless. 'The financing of the war,' writes Münkler, 'thus became the force driving the continuation of fighting.'[89] This argument may be slightly overstated, but there do seem to be indications that many representatives of high finance repressed reality for a long time.[90] On the other hand, it also seems that, from early 1918 onwards, the upper management of Deutsche Bank was more aware than most that defeat was inevitable. Its maintenance of close contacts in neutral countries – not least to gather information – allowed it a much more objective assessment of the course of the war than was available to most of the general public. At any rate, Deutsche Bank began significantly reducing the number of long-term government bonds in its portfolio by 1917. Almost all remaining war bonds were sold over the course of 1918 and replaced with short-term Treasury bills. The largest German bank wanted at all costs to minimise the risks of a government default.

3. Domestic Expansion

From the First World War onwards, Deutsche Bank began systematically expanding its branch network within Germany. Until 1914, Deutsche Bank had a direct presence in only a select number of locations. For various reasons, it had opened its own offices in only a few central sites (Bremen, Hamburg, Frankfurt, Munich, Nuremberg, Wiesbaden, Leipzig and Dresden). It also owned a series of city deposit-taking branches, in particular in Berlin, which did not offer the full range of bank services, but instead focused on deposit and payment transactions for local customers. In many locations the bank co-operated with regional banks in order to avoid the costs of operating its own branches. With this goal in mind, Deutsche Bank formed a community of interest with Schlesischer Bankverein in Wrocław and with Bergisch Märkische Bank in Elberfeld in 1897, and gradually increased its shares in both banks. The bank also acquired shares in numerous smaller regional banks, in which Deutsche Bank Management Board members held supervisory board positions.[91] These co-operative frameworks were usually governed by loose contractual agreements, which regulated the distribution of profits and shared administration. Despite this array of co-operation agreements, the Berlin headquarters was of tremendous importance for the business as a whole and brought in close to half of all turnover until the First World War.[92]

However, the beginning of the war brought with it a fundamental reorientation. Whereas the bank's core business had been focused on Berlin and other international centres, its weight now shifted to its growing number of domestic branches. The expansion of Deutsche Bank's branch network followed a variety of strategies. In only a few select locations were entirely new branches founded, due mainly to a lack of suitable candidates for takeover. It was far more attractive to purchase, mostly through stock swaps, regional banks that were already known entities. In this manner, the bank could acquire not just these banks' buildings and employees, but also their customer bases. In pursuing this path, Deutsche Bank succeeded in significantly expanding its presence in Germany over a relatively short period of time.

Carl Michalowsky, who had joined the Management Board in 1908 along with Karl Helfferich and was considered an organisational specialist, was the strategic thinker behind the expansion of the branch network.[93] Prior to his career with Deutsche Bank,

Michalowsky, a trained lawyer, had worked as a civil servant; he joined the bank in 1900 as a company lawyer and quickly rose through the ranks. As head of the legal section and the Secretariat, he was responsible not only for contract negotiations in takeovers and communities of interest with other banks, but he was also in charge of internal administration and personnel. While Arthur von Gwinner, Karl Helfferich and Oscar Wassermann served as the public face of the bank, Michalowsky played a major role in the company's strategic reorientation.

The first big merger occurred shortly before the start of the war with Bergisch Märkische Bank, which had been part of a community of interest with Deutsche Bank since 1897.[94] Bergisch Märkische Bank was one of the most influential financial institutions in the industrial area of Rhineland-Westphalia and had financed numerous large and mid-sized companies in the region, particularly within the textile industry. The joint-stock bank, which had been founded in 1871, had gradually expanded its presence in the years prior to the takeover and had opened a series of new sub-branches as far away as Saarbrücken and Trier; at the time of the merger it had a total of 38 offices. Co-operation with Bergisch Märkische Bank was of vital importance to Deutsche Bank because of its strong network in the region and because its customer base was an excellent fit with Deutsche Bank's business profile. Bergisch Märkische Bank had also become increasingly dependent on Deutsche Bank, since it could not single-handedly meet the large industrial companies' growing need for capital and had repeatedly run into payment difficulties. Deutsche Bank had needed to intervene back in 1908 to help 'Bergbank', as it was called, out of a difficult spot caused by failed investments in the company Boswau & Knauer's construction business. Restructuring the bank took several years. In 1906, there had already been rumours of an impending merger, which had been successfully denied. Due to the fact that Bergisch Märkische Bank's balance sheet had already been cleaned up by the time of the merger, a relatively small capital increase of 50 million marks was sufficient to finance the takeover. In fact, Deutsche Bank already owned 40 per cent of the shares of Bergbank by this time. Because of the bank's large reserves, the merger ultimately proved to be a positive business decision, allowing Deutsche Bank to increase its hidden reserves by 63.5 to 178.5 million marks.[95]

In 1914, Deutsche Bank also expanded into the area around Frankfurt and opened branches in Darmstadt (through the takeover of Ferdinand Sander bank) as well as in Hanau and Offenbach. Even though these were smaller mergers, they demonstrated the bank's strategic interest in opening its own branches in dynamic industrial regions.

The second wave of takeovers took place in the eastern regions of the German Empire, where the bank saw as yet unrealised business potential. By late 1916, the big banks had already begun looking eastward, where the defeat of Russia seemed imminent, and new opportunities for influence and new business interests seemed to be opening up. Here, too, Michalowsky was the driving force for Deutsche Bank. In his assessment, a stronger presence was:

of ever greater importance, due to the political and economic changes that the war will presumably bring to the east. [...] We lack direct representation at all along the coast of the Baltic from Szczecin all the way up to Königsberg and Libau, and yet the Prussian ports of Szczecin, Gdańsk, and Königsberg, and after the annexation of Courland, Libau, will be of enhanced importance for business.[96]

Michalowsky did not just have business relationships with the Polish and Baltic regions in mind; he was also thinking of the broader trade relationship with Russia and the other Eastern European countries. Russia, in particular, was expected to play a far greater role in German foreign trade and thus also for Deutsche Bank. It was therefore important, in his opinion, to act quickly, as other big German banks might also be looking to expand into the region. It was 'the chief thing' that 'we are the first to go east'.[97] In fact, the intensifying competition between the big banks meant that they were under greater pressure to expand than before the war.

Deutsche Bank had long had close connections with many of the potential candidates for mergers in the east. Norddeutsche Creditanstalt in Königsberg and Schlesischer Bankverein in Wrocław had both been co-operation partners of Deutsche Bank, so their takeovers did not come as a surprise. Deutsche Bank had been a majority shareholder in Schlesischer Bankverein since 1897, so taking it over was simple. One year prior to the merger, Schlesischer Bankverein itself had acquired a number of small regional banks, including Kattowitzer Bankverein and Oberschlesischer Credit-Verein in Ratibor. This gave the regional bank a network of branches across 21 cities throughout the Silesian industrial belt, including five sub-branches in Wrocław alone.

Norddeutsche Creditanstalt also had a large number of sub-branches in eastern and western Prussia and held a strong position in the region. However, the banks were not reciprocal shareholders, and so its connection to Deutsche Bank was much weaker. Deutsche Bank merely had a seat on the supervisory board of Norddeutsche Creditanstalt, albeit one that had been occupied since 1905 by the influential Carl Michalowsky. Michalowsky made active use of his position and frequently intervened in fundamental business decisions being made by the Management Board. Deutsche Bank had considered a possible merger with Norddeutsche Creditanstalt as early as 1912, though it had not pursued it actively at the time. Negotiations were initiated in 1916, in part because the other big German banks wanted to gain a foothold in the region. Mergers were generally preceded by a recommendation from the supervisory board of the bank being acquired; hostile takeovers were not common, even if resistance had to be overcome in the run-up to the merger. In this case, for instance, Deutsche Bank's offer to Norddeutsche Creditanstalt was highly contentious and required lengthy preparatory work.[98] There were also other cases in which substantial resistance had to be overcome.[99] The 1920 merger with Hannoversche Bank, for example, was delayed by numerous disagreements. Hannoversche Bank had planned a capital increase prior to the merger in order to buttress its working capital. However, Paul Mankiewitz, by then Deutsche Bank's Spokesman of the Management Board, opposed this, as it would increase the cost of the takeover. There was also a difference of opinion on the appropriate exchange rate for the shares. The merger then nearly foundered over the salary requirements of Paul Klaproth, Hannoversche Bank's chief executive. Only after long negotiations and substantial pressure from Berlin was the merger finally brought to completion.[100]

Königsberg i. Pr. — Grüne Brücke

With the acquisition of Norddeutsche Creditanstalt in Königsberg (Kaliningrad) and Schlesischer Bankverein in Breslau (Wrocław), Deutsche Bank expanded its network of branches into Eastern Germany during the war in 1917.

Paul Klaproth (1862–1947), the head of Hannoversche Bank, negotiated Deutsche Bank's acquisition of his bank and subsequently joined Deutsche Bank's Supervisory Board.

By contrast, a planned merger with Hildesheimer Bank in the early 1920s failed over insurmountable differences and could only be finalised in 1928.

Takeovers were generally financed by a capital increase. In large takeovers, the transaction (in particular the financing of the capital increase and the share swap) usually occurred via a consortium or syndicate, while for smaller mergers Deutsche Bank acquired the shares directly, avoiding a capital increase.[101]

Despite the resistance and the conflicts that occurred during the run-up to mergers, Deutsche Bank always attempted to carry these out as quietly as possible and to find solutions that were also acceptable to its negotiating partners. The success of a takeover also depended on whether the acquired bank could be successfully integrated into Deutsche Bank's own structure. The process was much easier with banks with which Deutsche Bank had a long-established business relationship and in which it already owned shares – in these mergers, costs were kept under control, as there were generally no conflicts or structural differences that had to be overcome. One of the many measures that the bank would take as part of the merger process was to bring a portion of the members of the acquired bank's supervisory board onto Deutsche Bank's own Supervisory Board and to found local committees in which those who had been in leadership positions at the predecessor institutions could be involved.

Why did the bank abandon the community of interest model that it had previously favoured? It is clear that the Management Board had become convinced that loose co-operative agreements of this type were no longer sufficient to systematically promote Deutsche Bank's interests. While Deutsche Bank was liable for the growing volumes of 'non-performing loans' of regional banks, it had little influence over the operations side of the business. In general, supervisory board seats were inadequate for this, and reciprocal positions on management boards were not common practice in communities of interest. To the degree to which loose co-operation began to develop into something more like a corporate group, questions of control and the separation of spheres of interest became more problematic. Deutsche Bank was contractually barred from opening branches in its own name in many regions because of communities of interest with other banks.

The merger wave that had begun with the start of the First World War was not unique to Deutsche Bank. It reflected a general process of concentration that was underway in Germany's heterogeneous banking system as a whole.[102] The war was not the only reason for this change, but it did accelerate the process considerably. It quickly became clear that the generally undercapitalised regional banks were no longer able to meet the growing capital demands of their corporate clients. They were therefore constantly under pressure to increase their capital, making them reliant on the big banks, which used the situation to expand their influence over the smaller banks or even take them over. Mergers were driven by a number of other factors as well: inflation increased the banks' liquidity and led to more opportunities for purchases; at the same time, the sinking value of the currency was a motivation to quickly invest capital in real assets such as highly valuable commercial properties. In addition, banking circles were expecting a change in the tax regulations pertaining to mergers. This explains the decision in many cases not to wait until the end of the war to finalise these difficult negotiations, but instead to hurry them along to a rapid conclusion.[103] Mergers did, in fact, become far less attractive from a taxation standpoint when the Corporate Income Tax Law was passed in 1920, which led many companies to prefer different types of co-operation, such as cartels and communities of interest. This was especially true of industrial firms, while mergers continued in the financial sector. Despite the higher tax burdens, further concentration was considered unavoidable even in political circles, as many small banks faced major difficulties during hyperinflation. Their integration into the big banks seemed to be a necessary step in the direction of stabilising the German financial sector, especially because a rescue of the banks on the part of the government was not expected.

Deutsche Bank pursued its efforts to build a comprehensive network of branches more systematically and aggressively than the other big banks. In 1920, after a robust capital increase, it acquired Hannoversche Bank, Braunschweiger Privatbank and Privatbank zu Gotha; in 1924 Württembergische Vereinsbank in Stuttgart and its branch network; and in 1925 Siegener Bank as well as Essener Credit-Anstalt, with its numerous offices in 25 locations throughout the industrial region of Rhineland-Westphalia. By the mid-1920s Deutsche Bank had a network of branches that covered nearly all of Germany, including more than 186 offices and 102 deposit-taking branches.[104]

The lean and dignified big Berlin bank with its handful of offices in strategically important locations had suddenly become a German branch bank represented almost nationwide. What advantages did the bank seek to gain from this new organisational structure, and how did its business profile change as a result? What strategic considerations did this involve?

For one, the bank's leadership had come to recognise that most of its business would no longer take place internationally, but in Germany. The war had not created a temporary, exceptional situation; it had permanently altered the bank's business model. The bank had withdrawn from most of its major international investment projects. The significant fall in German industrial exports reduced the importance of export finance. The trade in acceptances, which had collapsed in 1914, resumed after the war at a much lower level. The international securities and foreign exchange business showed little potential for growth. It was therefore a logical decision for the bank to focus to a greater degree on the domestic market with a more wide-ranging array of services and a greater local presence. In the wholesale business, the focus was now on lending; capital markets, in contrast to the situation before the war, now barely played a role in corporate financing. The market for corporate bonds had already collapsed in 1914 and did not recover much after the end of the war. Companies were therefore increasingly dependent on loans to finance investments. While it was easiest to issue bonds and arrange initial public offerings from Berlin, investment loans required intensive on-site discussions. The bank itself also had an interest in more thoroughgoing knowledge of its borrowers' business backgrounds, as the risks associated with these loans were much higher than with bond issues or capital increases. Even in trade finance, default risks for banks were relatively low, so a prior assessment for creditworthiness was generally unnecessary. If a company went bankrupt – and this occurred more frequently during the interwar years due to the instability of the economy – the banks had to write off a large portion of the loan. They therefore had a great interest in being in regular direct contact with their industrial clients. The Hausbank principle therefore became not just to connect corporate clients to the bank for the long term, but also to reduce transaction costs, as a lengthy test of creditworthiness was not necessary for every loan.

The expansion of the bank's branch network was also aimed at bringing in new sources of funding, given the newly limited capacity of capital markets to provide these services. The deposit and current accounts business became even more important to the bank than before. The bank's leadership was clear about the fact that decentralised deposit-taking branches were not by themselves enough to gain new clients and investors. This applied especially to the many small investors and savers who had not previously been Deutsche Bank's target client base. These deposits did, in fact, form a growing proportion of the liabilities on the bank's balance sheet. Whereas retail deposits had only represented 40 per cent of liabilities in 1880, by the start of the war they had increased to around 70 per cent. In the years after the war this proportion increased to over 90 per cent, reducing slightly after stabilisation.[105] Especially after 1924, when capital became increasingly scarce, the banks began competing more intensely for deposits with the savings banks and the co-operative banks.

The big banks also became increasingly involved in the strategic decision-making of the companies in which they invested.[106] Here, too, the war was a catalyst. Because of their essential role in financing the war, the banks had been brought into numerous committees (the war committees, for example) and decision processes. Deutsche Bank had become involved in a number of state initiatives. This involved, for one thing, the financing of railway and shipping companies critical for the war effort. In November 1915, Deutsche Bank and Norddeutscher Lloyd co-founded Deutsche Ozean-Reederei (DOR) in Bremen. The sole objective of this company was to provide merchant U-boats that could evade the British naval blockade in order to enable the exchange of goods

Steamships belonging to Bayerischer Lloyd on the Danube.

with the United States.[107] Deutsche Bank also controlled, either directly or indirectly via Deutsche Petroleum AG, more than 80 per cent of the shipping company Bayerischer Lloyd in Regensburg, in which the Bavarian state and numerous southern German cities also had a share. An expansion of shipping on the Danube between south-eastern Europe and Germany was supposed to make the Balkans more accessible for the German war economy. This was intended to guarantee oil deliveries, in particular, to Germany, which in turn suited Deutsche Bank's oil interests in Romania.[108]

One of the bank's important projects during the war years was its involvement in founding the Mitteleuropäische Schlafwagen- und Speisewagen-Aktiengesellschaft (Mitropa) (Central European Sleeper Car and Dining Car Joint-Stock Company) in Berlin in November 1916. The collapse of relations between allied and enemy states raised the difficult question of how companies with international capital participation were supposed to carry on. One prominent case was that of the Internationale Schlafwagengesellschaft, which was based in Paris and Brussels and in which both French-Belgian and German-Austrian investors held an interest. Mitropa resulted from the Central Powers' attempts to displace the Internationale Schlafwagengesellschaft, which had continued to operate in continental Europe up until that time. Mitropa was founded for this purpose on 24 November 1916 in the Berlin headquarters of Deutsche Bank, which served along with Dresdner Bank as the leader of the consortium. Deutsche Bank had agreed to finance the politically motivated initiative 'not without a heavy heart', as it feared reprisals against German property abroad and future damage compensation claims.[109] Nonetheless, in the end Arthur von Gwinner even accepted the chairmanship of the supervisory board. The company was given a monopoly on the operation of dining cars and sleeper cars in Germany, Austria and Hungary.

The energy and substitute goods industries also played an important role in the Central Powers' war economies, which were suffering under the Entente's blockade, and represented a new field of business for Deutsche Bank. Shortly after the start of the war, the Hungarian government commissioned Deutsche Bank to develop its natural gas reserves in Transylvania. Deutsche Bank, along with the Hungarian state and several other financial institutions, founded the Ungarische Erdgas-Aktien-Gesellschaft in Budapest. Deutsche Bank also played a significant role in the chemicals industry, becoming involved in the expansion of Bayerische Stickstoffwerke AG, based in Munich, which had already been founded in 1908. The production of calcium cyanamide gained importance during the war because of its role in producing nitric acid, which was needed in ordnance and gunpowder factories. Starting in 1915, the company also began investing in the production of aluminium and expanded other production sites in Chorzów und Piesteritz (in Upper Silesia) that were important for the war effort. In May 1916, the Reich Naval Office signed a contract with Deutsche Bank in which the latter committed to building and operating a factory for the production of tetralin. Tetralin was a newly tested substance for operating diesel engines, which the navy's U-boats depended on. To fulfil the contract, Deutsche Bank led the consortium and founded Tetralin GmbH, which had capital of 5 million marks. Bayerische Stickstoffwerke and Deutsche Petroleum AG were among the biggest investors.[110]

One of the bank's more spectacular initiatives was the founding of the Universum-Film Aktiengesellschaft (Ufa) in Berlin, which was finalised in late 1917 after long preparations

Registered share of Mitropa issued by Deutsche Bank with the signature of supervisory board chairman Arthur von Gwinner.

through a consortium of Deutsche Bank and Dresdner Bank. The exigencies of the war played an important role in this initiative as well: Erich Ludendorff of the Supreme Army Command was convinced that German film propaganda could be significantly improved and ought to be co-ordinated by a central company.[111] Ludendorff hoped, through the targeted use of film, to create new opportunities for psychological warfare and build stronger support within the general public. By 1916, a film and media office had been created in the Foreign Office's news department, eventually resulting in the creation of the centralised Bild- und Filmamt (Bufa) in January 1917. However, the opinion prevailed that a large private film conglomerate was in a better position to catch up on the lead that the film industries in other countries had already established. Ufa was finally founded with a seed capital of 25 million marks with the secret involvement of the German government and the Ministry of War; Emil Georg von Stauß, a member of Deutsche Bank's Management Board, was selected as chairman of the supervisory board.[112]

Deutsche Bank also increased its involvement in numerous companies and consortia, including the Frankfurt construction company Philipp Holzmann, which was merged in 1917 with the Internationale Baugesellschaft and transformed into a joint-stock company.[113]

These examples illustrate the changes that were underway in corporate financing, which, in turn, led to major changes for Deutsche Bank. The bank's business model was no longer based only on managing IPOs for companies and providing the resources and advisory services for this process. Instead, a much more comprehensive involvement was now expected, which incorporated Deutsche Bank to a greater degree into the leadership structures of industrial companies and frequently led to long-term investments. If this was a result of the First World War, the crises and defaults of the 1920s and 1930s only further intensified the process. The structural changes in the big banks were therefore only partially planned and could not be directed in the way that its management might have hoped.

4. Revolution and Inflation

The First World War brought an irrevocable end to a dynamic era in the history of German banking, one which since the turn of the century Arthur von Gwinner had, in his role as a financial diplomat, played an important role in shaping. Gwinner understood the consequences of this change in circumstances: he resigned from the Management Board in spring 1919 and transitioned to the bank's Supervisory Board, of which he served as deputy chair from 1923 until his death in 1931. His successor as Spokesman of the Management Board was Paul Mankiewitz, until then the head of the stock market operations. His years in office were marked by unprecedented challenges. The bank found itself newly reliant on the domestic market; instead of ambitious projects, a pragmatic approach was now necessary to rescue what could be saved from the ruins of the bank's foreign assets. Political chaos gripped Germany, and the new Weimar Republic could not find peace. Mankiewitz had no illusions about the gravity of the situation or its causes: 'Germany succumbed because it overestimated its power and believed that it could do its work and wage war from the Caspian Sea to the Baltic Sea, from the Daugava to the English Channel. This proved to be a disaster.'[114]

If the war created enormous challenges for the banks, in many respects the post-war years were even harder.[115] One of the main problems was the degree of uncertainty that prevailed about the future. During the winter of 1918–19, it was entirely unclear under which political and legal conditions private banks would be able to carry out their business at all – or whether they might even be completely abolished. With the beacon of the Russian Revolution, Germany and many of the other European countries were shaken by political unrest and social conflict. Would the revolutionary unrest lead to the collapse of the capitalist economic system, as had happened in Russia? Or was there reason to fear an authoritarian dictator who would steer the economy towards

As Spokesman of the Management Board from 1919 to 1923, Paul Mankiewitz (1857–1924) guided the bank through the difficult post-war years and the years of inflation.

dirigisme and autarky, as had happened in many eastern and southern European countries? And what financial pressures would Germany face after a war that had stretched the country's economic and financial resources to breaking point?

The transition from a wartime to a peacetime economy brought with it enormous economic difficulties. The big banks had acquired large quantities of shares and industrial obligations in 1918 – these had mostly been supporting purchases, which did not, however, prevent the collapse of share prices following the end of the war. These securities were now transitioned to a holding company, which was linked with major write-offs.[116] It was also not clear what effect the high level of state debt would have on the monetary and financial system. Deutsche Bank only held a small number of government bonds, but as a result even more Treasury bills and other short-term money market securities, which inflated its balance sheet. Even though the bank was able to prevent losses by deftly restructuring its own portfolio, banking circles were concerned that the large excess of liquidity would eventually push the German monetary system beyond its limits.

One of the reasons why inflation had not got out of control during the war were the numerous price requirements that had been issued, especially during the late phase of the war. This was, however, a pent-up form of inflation, which, as those in banking circles were fully aware, would lead sooner or later to a major devaluation of the German currency. It was also unavoidable that the banks would be particularly affected by a currency decline of this kind. By 1918, the bank's annual report referred openly to 'monetary depreciation' as a major reason for its large increases in turnover, and, a year later, the bank looked even more pessimistically at the 'heightened inflation' which had set off a veritable 'passion for playing the stock market'.[117]

Foreign capital and currency speculation

The bank was also greatly concerned about the turbulence in the securities markets. This was compounded by the fact that many foreign investors had invested in Germany after the end of the war. The high volatility in exchange rates prompted speculation and arbitrage, a business in which the banks eagerly participated. During the war, Deutsche Bank had been part of a select group of financial institutions that managed foreign exchange transactions under the supervision of the Reichsbank. It had also arranged loans from banks in neutral countries, in particular the Netherlands, Switzerland and Scandinavia. These foreign exchange credits had to be insured through guarantees and sureties, which was highly risky because of the ongoing fluctuations in the exchange rate. This official role ended when it was decided in July 1919 that the Foreign Exchange Decree would be phased out. The strict regulation of foreign exchange and capital transactions was not completely lifted, but foreign investors were now allowed to open accounts in Germany more easily. A veritable boom in speculation did in fact begin. After the strong decline in the value of the mark in 1919, many investors expected the German currency to recover, as it seemed undervalued considering its real purchasing power. According to Reichsbank estimates, the mark balances of foreigners in Germany amounted to approximately 36 billion marks by summer 1921.[118] In 1922, more than one-third of all bank deposits came from foreigners. Deutsche Bank, due to its strong international connections, was one of the first banks that investors turned to; by 1920, half of its deposits came from outside Germany.[119] After the London Ultimatum of 5 May 1921, the German currency came under significant pressure, and, as hyperinflation set in, a large number of foreign investors withdrew their money again. Deutsche Bank was also indirectly impacted by speculative foreign currency transfers. In December 1921, the relatively small Pfälzische Bank experienced a serious crisis after a bank employee lost 340 million marks in unauthorised currency speculation. Because Pfälzische Bank was part of Deutsche Bank's broader co-operative framework of banks through Rheinische Creditbank, Deutsche Bank felt obligated to save the bank through a takeover and to compensate its shareholders for a portion of their losses. The continued depreciation of the currency allowed Deutsche Bank to recoup these costs, and the move in fact fitted well into Deutsche Bank's strategy of domestic expansion at the time.[120]

Internal conflicts

In addition to the economic problems that it faced, the ongoing political unrest and social conflicts were cause for major worry at Deutsche Bank. The November Revolution was not just an abstract threat; it also had concrete manifestations at the bank. Though bank employees were not leading the revolutionary charge, they did express self-assured demands for higher salaries, greater social protections and, in particular, more co-determination rights. These demands, particularly those pertaining to salary, were not baseless: bank employees' incomes had declined significantly relative to those of other income groups during the war. The modest wage increases that they did receive were consumed by inflation.[121] Deutsche Bank had indeed offered a 'cost of living bonus' to employees with salaries under 12,000 marks, and on 1 January 1919 had even offered a salary increase of 5–25 per cent based on income group.[122] However, these increases were

Memorial to the fallen employees of Deutsche Bank's Elberfeld branch, part of Wuppertal after 1929.

not sufficient to compensate for the employees' increased cost of living. Whereas those in industry were paid high allowances, the incomes of those in banking, and those of salaried employees in general, stagnated. Money aside, the bank officials, who saw themselves as the elite of the commercial field, perceived this to be a decline in social status.

At the same time, the bank's personnel structure had gone through a major transformation during the war, involving the hiring of employees unfamiliar with the industry, and also, for the first time, women. This had been necessary because, in the first months of the war, around 2,500 Deutsche Bank employees, amounting to around 30 per cent of the bank's payroll, had been drafted into military service. Over the course of the war, 1,023 bank employees died at the front, and many others were severely injured and could no longer return to their workplaces, or could do so only after a long period of recovery. They had to be replaced with temporary workers, many of whom had no intention of spending their entire careers at the company, as many pre-war bank officials had. As this new group of employees felt less of a sense of loyalty, it was much more willing to enter into conflict with the company management or even to go on strike.

The varying loyalties and interests of the workforce quickly became apparent during the revolution and led to heightening tensions.[123] While the newly elected white-collar workers' council had ties to the Socialist General Organisation of German Bank Officials (*Allgemeiner Verband der Deutschen Bankbeamten*), and in November 1918 forcefully vied for its interests against the Management Board, the longer established employees were linked to the more moderate German Bank Officials' Association (*Deutscher Bankbeamten-Verein*) and avoided making radical demands:

Closely linked for years, even decades, with the bank's fate, the original staff received the unexpectedly far-reaching demands with indignation and strongly disapproved of the version that was submitted to the Management Board. The longer serving officials are also in favour of negotiations with the Management Board to improve conditions for all employees, but they cannot support the form and content of the measures taken by the white-collar workers' council, which go far beyond the goal of appropriate and needful requests. Many of the officials who have been prevented from voting due to their military service will likewise react to the actions of the Company Employees' Council with sincere regret and even open resistance.[124]

The white-collar workers' council was not, in fact, primarily interested in material improvements. On this matter, the bank management was willing to compromise in full. The Management Board, for example, agreed in January 1919 to provide 3 million marks of transitional assistance for its employees, 'despite unfavourable business conditions'.[125] They were less enthusiastic, however, about the white-collar workers' council's demands for extensive co-determination rights in hiring and firing and in general matters pertaining to the running of the business. A conflict was building, in which the bank's paternalistic business model was increasingly being called into question.

In the revolutionary climate of the months following the end of the war, the atmosphere at the bank became increasingly conflictual. The employees of the big Berlin banks took part in long internal discussions during the general strike of April 1919. Karl Emonts, the head of the General Organisation of German Bank Officials, was

Bank employees went on strike in Hamburg in August 1919 for higher wages, but without success. Military posts were set up in front of the building on Adolphsplatz.

the driving force behind these talks; he would be arrested in June 1919 on the charge of having engaged in communist agitation. The strike involved heated discussions, but did not lead to a permanent radicalisation of the workforce. In the end, the Berlin bank strike was brought to an end by an arbitration ruling that gave employee representatives a limited number of co-determination rights in hiring and firing decisions; salary demands would be solved in the future through a collective bargaining process. State-controlled wage arbitration also no longer had to be taken into account. In October 1920 the Reich collective agreement for bank employees was completed, which staked out the framework for further collective wage agreements.

The question of employee representation at the management level and on the Supervisory Board, which was introduced when the Factory Council Law (*Betriebsrätegesetz*) was passed in January 1920, remained controversial, however. The bank's leadership was concerned about this law, not least because it feared that it would allow confidential information about the bank's internal workings to fall into the wrong hands. The bank did, in fact, make multiple attempts to request an exemption from the German government, proposing that employee representation of the kind required by the law be waived in cases where 'important state interests' made this necessary.[126] The bank made reference to the many responsibilities that it now carried out on behalf of the Reichsbank and other government agencies. The German government rejected the request, however, on the grounds that it would have created a precedent that most of the other banks could have invoked. Employee representation on the Supervisory Board proved to be unproblematic in practice, however – and unlike in many other industries, the employee representatives' influence remained small. The general Supervisory Board meetings also increasingly lost importance as decision-making on important matters was shifted to committees in which employee representatives did not have a seat.[127]

Even though the conflicts from the revolutionary era could eventually be put to rest, matters pertaining to personnel policy and the management of intra-company politics gained in importance during the Weimar Republic. The bank leadership was fully aware that personnel management required more attention than previously. One important step was to improve communications within the firm. The *News Bulletin*, the company newsletter that had been introduced in autumn 1914 in order to maintain a line of communication with the new employees, ceased production in 1920 for cost-saving reasons. In October 1927, a new publication appeared: the *Monthly Journal for the Officials of Deutsche Bank*, which featured comprehensive information about important company matters, as well as regular announcements of dates and events that provided opportunities for a direct exchange with the workforce and an improved work atmosphere. The system of internal bonuses and social benefits was also substantially expanded after the war. The 'gifts' to the bank's employees at the front were of a primarily symbolic nature – of greater importance were the social protections provided to disabled veterans and their families. The bank's spending on war relief had already reached 5.2 million marks by 1915 and increased to 16 million marks by the end of the war. Its spending on welfare services and its contributions to the Employee Welfare Association also increased significantly. In 1918, the bank's social services amounted to nearly one-third of all staff expenses.[128] In addition to providing financial support, these measures were

Deutsche Bank acquired the Johannaberg spa in the Teutoburg Forest in 1918.

also aimed at improving leisure and convalescence activities for the workforce. After Management Board Spokesman Arthur von Gwinner in 1917 donated 300,000 marks for the establishment of a convalescence home in Caputh, near Potsdam, the bank in 1918 acquired the Johannaberg spa near Detmold and another compound in Sellin, on the island of Rügen, as vacation and convalescence sites for its employees. Company sports, which until then had been limited to a small number of activities (fencing and rowing, for instance) were expanded. In 1924, Deutsche Bank formed a sports association and acquired or built numerous sports facilities in and around Berlin, where its employees could engage in activities including track and field, boxing, tennis, rowing, fencing and gymnastics. The association also arranged competitions and attempted to integrate physical training and other health measures into the everyday activities of the bank's employees. Donations from members of the Management Board often provided funding for this. Management Board Spokesman Paul Mankiewitz, who died in 1924, donated 45,000 RM for the expansion of the sports facilities in Berlin during the last year of his life; Oscar Wassermann and Carl Michalowsky provided further contributions. The company also sought to improve the food options for its employees. Deutsche Bank opened a new casino in a large building on Behrenstraße in the vicinity of the company headquarters in 1925. This building included a series of cafeterias in which the bank's employees – with senior bank officials, officials, female employees and other employees all strictly divided by group – could eat for a reasonable price; there were also rooms for social activities, including a music room, where the bank's choral society (*Gesangverein*) held its rehearsals. In the same year, the orchestra of the Berlin headquarters, founded in 1898 and disbanded during the war, was revived.

The bureaucratisation of banking

Measures such as these, intended to improve the work climate and engage employees, proved to be increasingly difficult, however: personnel turnover increased considerably, reducing the bank's original staff to a small portion of the workforce. The number of employees had, in fact, continued to increase during inflation. The bank had 13,529 employees in late 1919; by the height of the inflation in 1923, it had more than 2.5 times as many – a total of 35,868. This trend of growth, which had begun during the war, continued without interruption. It was connected with the bank's many mergers and the expansion of its branch network. The bank also had to hire a large number of employees to manage its growing bureaucratic challenges. The large number of new regulations and requirements, for example in capital and foreign exchange transactions, made the everyday aspects of banking exceptionally challenging. Many new laws and decrees had to be complied with, and the banks' documentation requirements grew considerably. Inflation also led to an enormous increase in cash transactions. Because clients were no longer interested in investing money long term, the number of transactions sharply increased. The daily operations of the branches and deposit offices became limited almost entirely to keeping up with payment transactions. During hyperinflation, this took on a dimension that was nearly impossible to manage, as conversion rates were changing daily and the banks themselves had an interest in prompt settlement. There was hardly enough room in the cashier counter areas and vaults for the ever-increasing quantity of paper money. In late 1920, the bank complained about the remarkable 'increase in unproductive work'. Due to the general 'lack of personnel trained in banking' it was necessary to hire untrained employees, which made day-to-day operations much more difficult.[129]

Personnel costs thus increased tremendously, causing profits to shrink, especially with the addition of other cost factors, such as higher taxes. Whereas taxes had still been manageable before the war, the banks now faced a heavier burden. In a continuation of a wartime practice, for example, a special Reich Emergency Levy (*Reichsnotopfer*) was imposed on property between 1919 and 1922. Of greater consequence were the fundamental changes to the financial system enacted during the Weimar Republic, which gave the state comprehensive access to earnings and property. The Erzberger finance reforms of 1920 led not just to the establishment of a Reich financial administration (*Reichsfinanzverwaltung*), it also imposed a variety of new taxes on earnings, implying a considerable burden on companies. These included the general corporation tax of 10 per cent, the income tax, the property tax and numerous other levies (earnings tax, payroll tax, contributions to unemployment insurance, etc.). Whereas the tax burden had been 9.2 per cent of profits in 1913, by 1918 it was 20.3 per cent.[130] Between 1919 and 1923, this rate increased to 25.8 per cent. The new taxes did not just result in a direct fiscal burden, however; they also involved a considerable administrative burden, as in the case of the capital gains tax, which the banks had to pay as a withholding tax. In total, the cost/income ratio worsened considerably in the post-war years. Expenses were already 57 per cent of total earnings by 1918, and increased to 86 per cent in 1923. Deutsche Bank's average was significantly worse than that of the other big Berlin banks.[131]

Mountains of paper currency at a Berlin bank during hyperinflation.

Inflation had negative effects for Deutsche Bank in another respect. The erosion of assets was considerable, as the banks only had limited opportunities to invest their capital in real assets. Through the sale of DEAG, Deutsche Bank had nonetheless gained substantial foreign currency assets and had invested a portion of its capital in dollar Treasury bills and German gold loans as well as other inflation-resistant securities. In 1919, in addition to its Berlin buildings, it owned its own property in 62 cities.[132] Compared to the tremendous loss of capital caused by hyperinflation, this was a mere drop in the ocean. Foreign investors abruptly withdrew their capital from Germany, and many German customers emptied their accounts in order to invest their money in real assets or to use it for other purposes. While the stock of deposits rapidly decreased, the demand for loans went up. By 1922, however, the bank was already pursuing a very cautious course, and was reluctant to fund loan requests even from long-established clients. Starting in 1922, the bank ceased giving out loans for long-term increases in operating capital, securities or foreign currency mortgages, or longer term loans. In addition, the bank ceased providing loans to non-German clients, and foreign banks were put under pressure to reduce their debit balances.[133] The bank also attempted to base company financing more heavily on commercial bills, which was not suffi-cient, however, to satisfy the companies' high demands for capital.[134] The fact that the Reichsbank would fully rediscount commercial bills (and at good rates) created a series of new problems and fuelled inflation further, however. Many companies and banks – including Deutsche Bank – took advantage of this situation to borrow against trade bills in order to lend out the capital at much higher interest rates. Despite short-term profit opportunities such as these, however, the banks felt that the massive reduction in their capital ratios had put their very existence at stake. Recent research on the history of banking estimates that Deutsche Bank's loss in assets amounted to 258 million gold marks between 1919 and 1923, corresponding to 46 per cent of its adjusted equity in 1913.[135] Against this background, the bank pressed vehemently for a rapid restructuring of the currency. Oscar Wassermann advised the Cuno government on the matter of currency reform, and the definitive draft for the introduction of the Rentenmark on the basis of all agrarian and industrial property values was supposedly the work of Karl Helfferich, a former member of Deutsche Bank's Management Board.

The massive write-offs that went hand in hand with the currency reform of 1924 were only one aspect of a much larger set of losses that Deutsche Bank incurred due to war and inflation and from which it recovered only with great difficulty. While the financial consequences were serious, the loss of trust was just as costly. It affected not only Deutsche Bank, but the monetary and financial system as a whole. Who was still willing to deposit their money at a bank, and where was investment capital even supposed to come from, after the great inflation, the most extensive loss of capital in German history? Another challenge was that the general public counted the banks as among the parties responsible for the general misery. They were pilloried not only by the radical political forces, namely the communist left and right-wing nationalist groups: a growing number of voices in the middle-class centre also voiced their criticism of the banks' alleged power and the destructive role that they had played, pursuing their own financial interests while savers and wage-earners lost out.

The bank's actions during inflation, such as its restrictive loan policy and its high commissions, were, in fact, not always felicitous, giving many Germans the impression that it was profiting from the situation – which was, for a time, true, since the big banks involved in the short-term loan and capital market businesses were certainly able to earn profits over the course of inflation. After the introduction of the Rentenmark in 1923 as well, Deutsche Bank charged high interest rates of 20–50 per cent; not until late

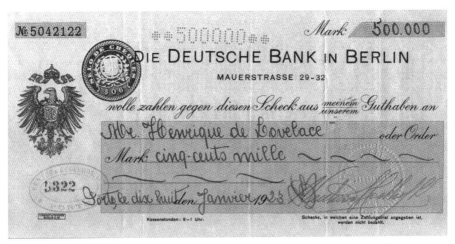

This cheque for 500,000 marks, written on 18 January 1923 in Porto, was equivalent to just under $2.70 due to inflation.

1924 was this gradually reduced again. Moreover, the bank stopped granting long-term loans – a precautionary measure, from the bank's perspective, but one which gave the general public the impression that the bank was taking advantage of the general lack of capital after stabilisation. These in some respects unfortunate choices led to frequent accusations that Deutsche Bank was a 'usurer', followed by ever-more frequent charges that it had broken usury laws. Even though the bank won all legal disputes, this caused substantial damage to its image and further fuelled the latent anti-Semitic resentment against the banks with their connections to international finance.[136]

Deutsche Bank also emerged from inflation in a generally weaker position. This manifested itself especially in comparison to the large industrial companies, which for the most part did not face a similar erosion of their assets, as a large portion of their capital consisted of fixed assets. The process of industrial concentration also had unfavourable consequences for the banks, since they were less able to bring their strength into play effectively against the large corporations and frequently had to accept the other side's conditions. Even worse, the large industrial firms attempted to increase their influence over the banks, or even created their own financing structures, which were intended to reduce their dependence on external financing. There was also another growing threat to the position of Deutsche Bank: competition from the savings banks and the co-operative banks, which found in the Weimar Republic a favourable political climate. They increasingly emancipated themselves from their marginal positions and confidently asserted themselves in the banking sphere.[137]

What conclusions did Deutsche Bank draw from this crisis? What strategy did it pursue in the years following inflation? As we shall see, a combination of instruments was now put to use. On the one hand, the bank continued to work on reducing costs, which involved redoubling efforts to reduce its workforce and rationalise workflows through the use of technical banking innovations. On the other hand, it attempted to gain advantages in spheres in which other German financial players had few opportunities to compete: access to international capital markets and international business.

5. Precarious Internationalisation

The 'Russia business'

Deutsche Bank's relations with Eastern Europe and Russia improved considerably over the course of the First World War. Not least for political reasons, new expansion opportunities also seemed to present themselves.[138] Paradoxically, it was the October Revolution that set off these developments. In the peace treaty of Brest-Litovsk of March 1918, Soviet Russia had made major territorial concessions to the Central Powers for internal political reasons. As a result, Germany now occupied not just the Baltic States and the Russian regions of Poland, but also large portions of Ukraine reaching all the way to the Caucasus; it even briefly gained control over the oil fields in Baku. From the perspective of Deutsche Bank, which had just acquired a branch network in the eastern provinces of Germany through mergers, this development fitted seamlessly into its own expansion goals. 'Today,' claimed the 1917 annual report, 'we can already see the evidence that our expansion into the eastern regions of Germany was a step in the right direction.'[139]

Representatives of Deutsche Bank had, in fact, played an important role in planning the economic expansion process into Russia and the successor states of the Tsardom. It had been involved, for example, in the development of a new currency system in the republic of Georgia.[140] Helfferich, a former board member, was even considered as the new ambassador in Moscow in summer 1918, and Deutsche Bank participated in the negotiations over the additional agreement of 27 August 1918 on Russia's foreign debts.[141] In this agreement, Soviet Russia committed to meet all payment obligations to Germany, totalling 6 billion marks. A quick solution, and one that was also satisfactory for German financial interests, seemed to have been found.

Because the Treaty of Brest-Litovsk became moot with the defeat of the Central Powers in November 1918, the issue of how to settle Imperial Russia's old debts remained unresolved. Foreign investors wondered whether business relations would even still be possible with revolutionary Russia. The German banks' old networks and connections in Russia no longer existed, and it was still unclear how the new state, which had just expropriated all private banks and companies, would meet its payment obligations. Mendelssohn & Co., which had been one of the most important financiers of the Russian Empire prior to the war, had fallen into disfavour with the new rulers, and from then on would only act in the 'Russia business' behind the scenes.[142]

For Deutsche Bank, this presented new opportunities to win the 'Russia business' for itself. For Soviet Russia, which desperately needed foreign capital to finance reconstruction and to import industrial products and capital goods, access to international financial backers was especially important. By summer 1920, a Soviet economic delegation had already begun talks with the German Foreign Office and German companies in order to negotiate the delivery of around 800 diesel locomotives from Germany. A German bank consortium, which included Disconto-Gesellschaft, Mendelssohn and Deutsche Bank, was set up to settle the deal financially. The diesel locomotives were to be paid for with the Russian gold reserves, which the consortium would use to trade for foreign exchange in the London market. When this turned out to be impossible for political reasons, the deal ground to a halt. Deutsche Bank seemed to have continued the negotiations on its own. Using its good relations with Stockholm, it convinced the Swedish Riksbank to take on the delivery of gold from Soviet Russia and to settle it with foreign exchange for the German suppliers.[143]

Both Disconto-Gesellschaft and Mendelssohn, which led the consortium, saw this as an affront and demanded both a share in the deal and a statement 'that Deutsche Bank acknowledges that its involvement in this transaction, which was carried out mistakenly and in contravention of our agreement, implies no preference for later business ventures with the Russian government'.[144] This formulation, and the conflicts that carried on for months between the three Berlin banks, show that more was at stake than just the envisaged project. The banks were positioning themselves for a power struggle over the lead position in the 'Russia business'. Disconto-Gesellschaft and Mendelssohn considered Deutsche Bank's actions to be a serious violation of the unwritten rules of the consortium business. Deutsche Bank's unauthorised actions were not an accident, in fact, but the expression of a new, aggressive strategy in its foreign business. The competition for new international markets had become much fiercer.

Deutsche Bank did, in fact, succeed in the following years in gaining a position of undisputed leadership in Eastern Europe. Whereas Mendelssohn and Disconto-Gesellschaft continued to insist that Russia settle its old debts,[145] Deutsche Bank was prepared to relinquish its debt claims and build up the loan business with the Soviets under new conditions. The Bolshevik government in Moscow proved to be a highly reliable partner, in fact, since the pressure to build a reputation as a creditworthy country motivated it to meet its financial obligations on time. Soviet Russia was also an important partner for Germany in light of the Allies' isolation of Germany through trade policy. Many German companies, such as Siemens & Halske, Krupp, or AEG, saw an opportunity to revive their export business and rebuild their previous connections in Russia as the wartime situation ended.[146]

The Treaty of Rapallo, which was signed in April 1922, marked the beginning of a new era in the economic relationship between Germany and the Soviet Union. Both countries agreed to mutually renounce reparations payments and to establish a most-favoured nation clause for the bilateral trade relationship. Germany agreed to send the Soviet Union a large number of capital goods, including industrial equipment for exploiting the oil fields of Baku, and recognised the Soviet Union's state monopoly on trade. A series of legal measures regulating foreign exchange transactions and the trade in goods followed in the German–Russian trade agreement of October 1925.

Trade with the Soviets entailed a number of organisational and legal challenges for the German economy. For example, the Soviet side insisted that the Germans recognise the state's monopoly on all trade and renounce all claims for compensation for the expropriation of German companies after the revolution. The Germans also had to follow the bureaucratic rules governing socialist trade. Soviet foreign trade mostly operated through licences. These were granted to mixed companies which were created for this sole purpose, and in which the Soviet Union was required to hold at least a 50 per cent share. By 1922, a number of German companies had set up a consortium led by Otto Wolff, a Cologne-based iron trading company. Deutsch-Russische Handels-Aktiengesellschaft (Russgertorg) transacted early export deals in co-operation with the Soviet People's Commissariat of Foreign Trade.[147] This was followed by a series of similar consortia, although in the context of hyperinflation the volume of trade remained small.

Not until the currency had stabilised did foreign trade with the Soviet Union gather momentum. The essential question in nearly all delivery transactions was how these would be financed, since the Soviet Union generally financed its imports via long-term bills of exchange but also often needed bridging loans.[148] After the Reich Association of German Industry (*Reichsverband der Deutschen Industrie*) created a Russia committee in 1925, Deutsche Bank took the initiative in founding Ausfuhrvereinigung Ost GmbH, in which a number of large German industrial firms joined forces in order to receive assurance that Deutsche Bank would discount Soviet commercial bills. Deutsche Bank also provided the State Bank of the USSR with a loan of 100 million RM to finance imports of food and other consumer goods that Moscow desperately needed. In summer 1926, again on the initiative of Deutsche Bank, the Russia Loan Consortium was created. It controlled a loan volume of 300 million RM to finance German–Soviet trade projects. This consortium had 27 members, including all the big Berlin banks

The State Bank of the USSR in the mid-1920s.

and Preußische Staatsbank, which also offered a 35 per cent rediscount.[149] At the same time, the Industry Finance Corporation East (IFAGO) was founded in July 1926 to serve as an interface between industry and banks. IFAGO was, inter alia, responsible for processing loan requests, but could not grant loans without prior approval from the consortium. An important role in all this was played by the fact that Germany and its regional governments took on a deficiency guarantee of up to 60 per cent of the total amount of export loans to the Soviet Union.[150]

Deutsche Bank not only provided the greatest volume of financing, it also led all negotiations between the Russian ministry of trade, IFAGO and the Preußische Staatsbank. While more than half of the Russians' delivery orders were for mechanical engineering products, the electrical industry and the shipbuilding industry were also well represented. From the perspective of the German government, this was not just an economic stimulus for German industry, which was suffering from a lack of orders; it was also good business for the banks. For bills with a maturity of two to four years, the banks charged rates of 7 per cent plus fees of 3.25 per cent per year. Deutsche Bank also received a commission for leading the consortium.[151]

The bank consortium and IFAGO, the deficiency guarantee by the state and the rediscounting of commercial bills by the Preußische Staatsbank had created a new basis for foreign trade with the Soviet Union. By 1941, a total of 12 consortium loans adding up to more than 1 billion RM had been provided for German–Soviet trade.[152] From 1927 onwards, foreign investors could also be won over for the 'Russia business'. For example, a Dutch bank consortium under the leadership of the Amsterdam Bank invested 30 million guilders in the 'business with the Russians'. The initiative seems to have come from the branches of Darmstädter und Nationalbank and Deutsche Bank in Amsterdam, as both banks also joined the Dutch consortium, which of course led to sharp criticism by the other German consortium banks. American investors also sought to take part in the German–Russian loan programme under the leadership of Dillon Read & Co.[153] The 'Russia business' thus indirectly led to the opening of the German capital market for foreign investors.

The close economic relationship did not lead to the German financial institutions being able to enter the USSR themselves, however. Deutsche Bank had opened an account in 1923 with the Soviet State Bank. Since all transactions took place via the Soviet trade commissariat, however, a branch in Moscow was not necessary, and in fact would not have been legally permitted.

Breaking new ground in Central and Eastern Europe

The situation was very different in the other eastern and southern European countries, in which Deutsche Bank could continue to operate some of its branches.[154] The territorial changes brought about by the Versailles Treaty, especially the creation of new autonomous nation-states, required major adaptations on the part of Deutsche Bank as well.[155] Above all, this affected the regions that were ceded to form the new republic of Poland. Deutsche Bank had to liquidate its branches in Poznań and Toruń in the now Polish parts of the provinces of Poznań and western Prussia in 1921, as well as its newly established agency in the Latvian port city of Libau. For political reasons it also distanced itself from the planned founding of a branch in Riga. In contrast, it reinforced its involvement in the Silesian industrial belt. Its branch in Katowice, which was in territory that had been ceded to Poland, could continue operations due to the Geneva Agreement of 15 May 1922 and was allotted capital in the amount of 2.4 million marks. With the support of the local heavy industry, Schlesischer Bankverein was refounded in a different form in January 1920. It had a capital endowment of 50 million marks. The bank hoped, by this strategic move, to further develop its business in both the German and in the Polish regions of Upper Silesia. The Bankverein thus acquired Deutsche Bank's branches in Chorzów and Rybnik, and ran a branch in Opole, which was granted to Germany after the referendum of 1921. The fact that Deutsche Bank and Schlesischer Bankverein had double representation in some locations (Bytom, Gliwice, Zabrze and Głubczyce), was accepted or even seen as an advantage in light of the complicated political and ethnic situation in the region, as it allowed for business with a variety of clients. Polish companies and municipalities did in fact sound out opportunities to work with Deutsche Bank in order to get funding for large investment projects.[156] Schlesischer Bankverein also began in 1921 to co-operate with Schlesische Escompte Bank in Bielsko, with the two banks agreeing to divide business areas. Schlesischer Bankverein committed not to open branches in the old Polish regions, and the Escompte Bank agreed to abstain from expanding into Upper Silesia.[157]

Deutsche Bank pursued a similar double strategy in the Free City of Gdańsk. Its branch there, which it had acquired from Norddeutsche Creditanstalt in 1917, expanded significantly in the 1920s and founded multiple sub-branches in the area around Gdańsk. At the same time, much as in Upper Silesia, a subsidiary, Danziger Bank AG, was founded, since the existing branches' future legal status seemed uncertain. The bank also hoped thereby to obtain access to Polish companies and clients who might have reservations about working with a German bank. Gdańsk, which was under the control of the League of Nations, was considered a 'hole in the East' in the early 1920s and attracted many international investors. The free city had its own stock market and was one of the few eastern and Central European financial centres where free trade in securities and foreign exchange was possible. Much of the Baltic Sea trade was carried out via the port of Gdańsk as well.

The complicated territorial conflict situation in Eastern Europe required regional solutions and new alliances. It was often necessary to avoid operating under one's own name, instead carrying out operations via subsidiaries or investments in existing banks. Deutsche Bank thus abstained from founding a branch in Vienna, despite the city's great importance for business with south-eastern Europe. Here, too, the bank preferred to continue its long-established co-operation with Wiener Bankverein and Rosenfeld & Co. Deutsche Bank also invested in autumn 1920 in the founding of Tiroler Hauptbank in Innsbruck, thereby expanding its business radius into the region bordering Italy.

The Balkans and south-eastern Europe also continued to play a central role in Deutsche Bank's strategy outside of Germany. The bank thus decided to hold on to its branch in Sofia. This branch had been founded in 1917, when Deutsche Bank had been financing government bonds for Germany-allied Bulgaria; moreover, Bulgaria had offered promising investment opportunities as an oil-supplying country. The branch had to close in September 1918. However, it was reopened in 1921 with a reduced staff, and was not, of course, able to continue its previous role. Its main task was now simply wrapping up former deals and catering for the few German companies still in the area.[158]

Deutsche Bank's Kattowitz (Katowice) branch was in Polish territory from 1922 onward.

The bank also maintained a presence in Constantinople (which became Istanbul in 1930). The Deutsche Bank branch and its sub-branches were placed under forced Allied administration in January 1919 and their German and Austrian personnel were expelled. In order to continue payment transactions, an alternative location for the Constantinople branch was established at the Berlin headquarters in early 1919.[159] This decision was also calculated to wait out political developments in the region in order to preserve the ability to quickly resume operations in this formerly important location, should the possibility arise. The threatened liquidation of the branch in Istanbul was, in fact, avoided, after Deutsche Bank management intervened on numerous occasions with Allied leaders at Versailles with the help of the Foreign Office.[160] The branch in Istanbul was reopened after Turkey became independent in 1923, though the political circumstances remained difficult. While Turkey under Kemal Atatürk was very much interested in economic relations with Germany, its modernisation programme involved pursuing its own interests in a muscular fashion and building up a Turkish money and banking system that was intended to be independent of international influence. Foreign banks were controlled by the state and could no longer act as freely as they had under the sultanate.[161] Deutsche Bank adapted to this new situation. It no longer became involved in financing investment projects or government bonds, instead focusing on serving the many German companies and businessmen in Turkey. The majority of the branch's turnover was in trade finance and the purchase and sale of foreign exchange and securities.[162]

Latin America and Asia

Whereas Deutsche Bank pursued a systematic expansion strategy in Central and Eastern Europe, it did not perceive much opportunity to regain its once excellent business connections overseas. This was connected with the fact that German exports to these regions now played a much smaller role than they had before the war, and that careful limitations had been placed on capital exports, as Elkan Heinemann had forthrightly remarked upon in late March 1917 to the German Economic Association for Central and South America:

> The German capital market will be needed well into the future for domestic requirements on a scarcely imaginable scale, and it is clear that under such circumstances only a small part of German capital can be invested abroad, and in particular overseas, and only if immediate political or economic advantages might be expected. With regard to our currency as well, it is necessary for the time being that we avoid too much German capital flowing out of the country. [...] How long it will be before all of these factors unfavourable to financial investment outside of the country are overcome is of course impossible to predict. But it certainly seems clear that this will not be just a short period of transitional difficulties.[163]

Deutsche Bank decided nonetheless to maintain its presence in the region in order to preserve the opportunity of expanding at some point in the future. Banco Alemán Transatlántico (BAT) still had a good reputation in Latin America, even if their opportunities for active business were substantially reduced.[164] This was not only due to

Germany's situation: the South American states also faced major economic challenges after the First World War. They had brought in substantial earnings during the war from exporting agricultural goods and raw materials to the belligerent countries, but were now confronted with a highly challenging trade environment, which involved a drop in the prices for agricultural goods and raw materials and higher tariffs.

One result was that these countries drew back from the international division of labour and increasingly pursued nationalist economic policies. This did not allow for

In 1926, a new headquarters for Banco Alemán Transatlántico was opened in Buenos Aires's banking quarter.

high imports of capital from outside the country, as had been the norm before the First World War. These countries were nonetheless still interested in co-operating with foreign banks and authorised BAT to continue its operations or reinitiate them. This applied even to Brazil, where the German banks had been placed under state supervision after Brazil entered the war in October 1917. BAT's branches in Rio de Janeiro, São Paulo and Santos could already be reopened by mid-1919, and another branch opened in Curitiba. Even though Argentina was not able to revive its previous export boom during the 1920s and even registered a trade deficit in 1925, it remained the leading economy on the continent. On 2 November 1926, BAT moved into a grand new building in Buenos Aires; the Argentinian president Marcelo de Alvear and former Reich Chancellor Hans Luther were present for the dedication.[165]

At the same time, Brazil gained importance for BAT. Here as well, the bank moved into a new building in 1926 in Rio de Janeiro on the prestigious Rua Alfándega. BAT went through another expansion phase in early 1930 when it acquired Banco Brasileiro Alemão, which belonged to Disconto-Gesellschaft. BAT was also represented in Bahia and Porto Alegre and had a total of 28 branches in Latin America and Spain. Deutsche Bank opened a third branch in the Andalusian city of Seville in December 1928, following the branches in Barcelona (1904) and Madrid (1907).

During the years of inflation, BAT's status as a subsidiary proved advantageous. By leaving its capital in its branches in Latin America, BAT was mostly spared the consequences of the devaluation of the currency in Germany.[166] On the ground, the bank itself functioned increasingly independently. Its operations no longer centred on financing trade or large investment projects, focusing instead on loans for local companies, many of which had German connections. The branches' greater degree of autonomy was also reflected in changes in the employee roster. Whereas the Berlin headquarters of BAT halved its staff from 745 in 1924 to 356 in 1925, its number of local employees increased slightly. By 1925, the bank's offices abroad employed more than 2,000 people in total.[167] In fact, BAT did experience a slight expansion of its business activities over the second half of the 1920s. Between 1924 and 1927, turnover increased from 34 to 41 billion RM and profits increased from 2.3 to nearly 2.9 million RM.[168] After 1924, the bank paid its shareholders annual dividends of 7 per cent. By 1928, however, there were already signs of cooling, starting with Argentina. Argentina had tried unsuccessfully in 1927 to introduce the gold standard and suffered above all from the major decline in international prices for raw materials. All the countries in which BAT did business faced tremendous currency declines from 1931.

The situation in Asia was much different. Due to the political-territorial conflicts there, business for German banks after the First World War was very challenging, barely allowing for regular foreign trade.[169] The basis for future economic and political relations with China, which had not signed the Versailles Treaty, had to first be settled through protracted negotiations. All German assets had been confiscated after China entered the war in 1917, and the bank concessions – including that of Deutsch-Asiatische Bank (DAB) – had become defunct. Nearly all German citizens, including most of the bank employees, had had to leave the country, and the branches were placed under forced Chinese administration. Though the German–Chinese Treaty of May 1921 prohibited further liquidations and held out the prospect of settling property issues, it was not until June 1924 that the mutual financial claims were settled and DAB could resume its operations in China.[170] However, due to the fact that DAB was no longer considered extraterritorial and had been placed under Chinese jurisdiction, it lost some of its standing and could not 'bring in deposits from Chinese sources' to the same degree as it had done before.[171] The German government had provided DAB with financial aid in 1922 to save it from bankruptcy and keep a critical business running.[172] However, as DAB supervisory board chairman Franz Urbig claimed in late August 1924, it was impossible to see 'how the bank is supposed to be competitive abroad if it has to pay a big commission and high debit interest rates on every transaction', while HSBC or the Chartered Bank continued to profit from their own branch networks. The difference was that DAB had been able to refinance at a good rate through the London branches of German banks prior to the First World War, something that was no longer possible.[173] The bank's branches in the British sphere of influence – Calcutta, Hong Kong and Singapore – were confiscated, the proceeds going towards the payment of reparation costs. But not until seeing DAB's final balance sheet in 1925 was Urbig aware of 'what major losses the bank suffered due to the war and all the measures that resulted from it'.[174] Deutsch-Asiatische Bank estimated that its total loss of assets amounted to more than 10 million Shanghai taels; its capital had shrunk greatly, declining from 25 million RM (1913) to 16 million RM (1927), and then to 6.5 million RM by late 1932.

Even though the branches in Shanghai, Canton, Hankou, Beijing, Qingdao and Tianjin could resume operations, business volume was far below pre-war levels, especially because the situation in China, as the 1928 annual report put it somewhat euphemistically, remained 'confusing'.[175] Irrespective of the continuing civil war and the tense security situation, China's economy in the 1920s was on the verge of collapse. German companies returned only gradually, expecting business relations to improve under Chiang Kai-shek. Germany was still an important trading partner for China,

The Beijing branch of Deutsch-Asiatische Bank was closed by allied troops in 1917.

The customer lobby of Deutsch-Asiatische Bank in Shanghai in 1930.

and DAB made energetic efforts to 'expand relations with our old clientele'.[176] Much as in the case of the Soviet Union, this involved above all the financing of railways and machines for industrial facilities. The bank did not want to underwrite Chinese government bonds, however, because the German capital market did not have sufficient capacity and because, after the write-offs of the war and the post-war era, no bank wanted to take these risks into their own portfolios. Nonetheless, DAB brought in small profits again in 1929, which were, however, nullified by the large decline in the value of the Chinese currency.[177] This brief economic recovery ended with the Great Depression, of course, when DAB's refinancing opportunities suddenly deteriorated due to the withdrawal of American capital. Beginning in 1931, DAB was posting losses in China and, in light of the banking crisis, could barely issue any loans.[178] Not until Chiang's Nationalist government consolidated power in 1934 and a currency reform was carried out did business take a turn for the better.

DAB found itself confronted with a confluence of economic and political problems in Japan as well. While the Japanese economy recovered significantly, its nationalist politics created difficult conditions for foreign investors. The bank's Japanese branches had gone back into business shortly after the end of the war, but did not have much turnover. After the violent earthquake of 1923, the Yokohama branch was closed, followed in May 1932 by the official closure of the branch in Kobe, which had been in existence since 1931, a decision that Kurt Meißner, one of the highest profile German businessmen in Japan and a client of DAB, had trouble understanding: British, Dutch and American banks had also had to reduce the loans they offered due to the worldwide lack of capital, but 'the international and native businessmen would have good reason to doubt the importance of German firms and trade with Germany if they saw that a German bank, the only German bank in Japan, could not hold fast'.[179] Not until the late 1930s would economic relations with Germany improve again in the context of the Axis alliance.

In autumn 1926, Franz Urbig had reported to the management board of DAB on the business malaise that, due to previous asset erosion, the bank's profits had to be 'exclusively achieved through current business'. It was, at the time, 'not clear what path lies ahead for us. Our hope is that we can keep the bank as an economic and political instrument in the East.'[180] This hope would not be fulfilled; from 1928 onwards, business – also due to cases of fraud – was once again on the decline. By late autumn 1933, according to Urbig, DAB resembled only a 'torso', and had been in 'a state of unmistakable self-destruction for two years'.[181]

The United States

The United States' financial dominance, which set in with the First World War, was a reflection of Europe's weakness. Almost all European countries had deficits after 1918 with the United States, which had now become the largest economy in the world and which had switched from its pre-war position as the world's largest debtor to become the largest global creditor. For Germany, this situation was especially precarious, because its access to the American capital market was initially limited for political and legal reasons. In light of its trade deficit, it was also unclear how its capital imports would be financed. From the perspective of Deutsche Bank, its loss of the US business was especially grave because it had been able to achieve a high turnover prior to the war. Because the United States was not a signatory of the Versailles Treaty, Germany, as in the case of China, first had to clear up unresolved asset claims.

Politically, the question of reparations was the biggest obstacle, as the representatives of Deutsche Bank knew only too well. Arthur von Gwinner, Paul Mankiewitz and Oscar Wassermann had regularly advised the German government during the reparations negotiations and had pushed for an agreement with the United States. Access to the American capital market was premised on Germany being capable of stabilising its currency. In November 1922, Wassermann submitted a comprehensive plan for stabilising the mark. According to this plan, Germany would issue gold bonds at a fixed rate, which would be guaranteed through customs receipts. A portion of these bonds would be given to the Allies as compensation for a two-year moratorium on payments, and a portion would be placed on the German domestic market and its proceeds would go to the German state in order to balance its budget and stabilise its currency. By issuing these inflation-proof obligations, so Wassermann hoped, German and foreign investors would be motivated to invest their capital in Germany over the long term instead of destabilising the currency through arbitrage or withdrawing their capital via circuitous routes.

German chancellor Wilhelm Cuno did in fact suggest to the Allies in late 1922 that the country's reparations payments be financed through a gold bond which would be issued both inside and outside Germany. The Wassermann plan was rejected by the Allies, however, and also seemed unrealistic in light of hyperinflation.[182] Nonetheless, initiatives consistently came from Deutsche Bank and its circle intended to clarify the complicated international financial and currency issues. In 1919, Carl Bergmann, a former employee of Deutsche Bank, became the German representative on the Reparations Commission and head of the War Burdens Commission.

Like Helfferich, Bergmann was part of a group of bankers who took on public office and advisory roles and often acted as experts on central questions of international monetary and financial policy. In contrast to Helfferich, who had gained a reputation as an opponent of the Weimar Republic and was not considered for other roles, Bergmann did not become politically active. While Helfferich had to watch Hjalmar Schacht being selected as Reichsbank president after Rudolf Havenstein died in November 1923, Bergmann played more of a background role.[183] Trained as a lawyer, he had begun his career with the Anatolian Railway in Constantinople, and after study trips to the United States had transitioned to Deutsche Bank, where he was promoted as far as deputy member of the Management Board. In the First World War, he joined the diplomatic service and was the financial delegate of the German mission in The Hague. In July 1919, he was appointed undersecretary of state in the Reich Ministry of Finance and led the German Reparations Commission until September 1921, after which he joined the Supervisory Board of Deutsche Bank and travelled to the United States to settle property issues.[184] At the same time, he continued to advise the German government on reparations matters until the Dawes Plan came into force in 1924. Like Wassermann, Bergmann considered financing the reparations through international loans as the only way for the economy to handle the burden of their high costs.[185]

Bergmann's double role as banker and financial diplomat was typical of a new generation of bankers, who moved on the international stage as political officials, external advisers or even delegation leaders. Their technical expertise and contacts abroad were highly valuable in consideration of the complex international financing and currency problems to be resolved; German politicians, meanwhile, faced difficult conditions abroad after the war. Deutsche Bank hoped, in turn, that Bergmann, who had gained a reputation for his objectivity on the Paris Reparations Commission, even among those on the opposing side, would help bring about as rapid a solution as possible to the open property issues in the United States. The bank also opposed suggestions, which had been made by M. M. Warburg and other German banks, of using the seized German assets as security for American loans.[186] This would have led to considerable losses for the bank and its customers. The bank's involvement in international negotiations such as these was therefore never entirely selfless, as would be proven in the coming years, for example in the standstill negotiations after the banking crisis and the debt conferences after the Second World War. Representatives of Deutsche Bank always had a front seat in such negotiations.

After the German–American Peace Treaty was signed in August 1921, Deutsche Bank first attempted, via its New York representative Hugo Schmidt, to be reimbursed for its assets in the US, which, based on its own estimates, amounted to $4.3 million ($3 million belonged to Deutsche Bank; the remaining $1.3 million were customers' assets).[187] Schmidt's efforts did not bear fruit – the bank's interests diverged too much from those of its American trustee, the Alien Property Custodian (APC), and Deutsche Bank's former business partners, such as JP Morgan and the other American banks. Bergmann, who travelled to the United States in 1923, was able to resolve only a few matters, and returned shortly thereafter. Alfred Blinzig, a member of the Management Board, continued the negotiations with American banks as his replacement; most discussions on restitution were drawn out until the late 1920s.

The patience with which Deutsche Bank carried out the negotiations in New York reflected the decisive importance the bank placed on merely regaining a foothold in the American capital market. By autumn 1924, it had already succeeded in selling a large packet of common shares to American investors via an English–American bank consortium under the leadership of J. Henry Schröder & Co. These were shares with a total value of 40 million gold marks (20 per cent of the bank's total common equity).[188] Deutsche Bank also succeeded in placing smaller numbers of securities in the American market with the help of American banks. Deutsche Bank also underwrote a modest number of American bond issues (a small portion of a Standard Oil bond of $50 million, for example) and placed them in the German market. By spring 1929, the bank was even considering getting a licence for the New York Stock Exchange, but this plan was soon dropped.[189]

More promising than German investments in the United States, from the bank's perspective, was gaining American investors for the German market. The Dawes Plan of 1924 had not only settled the reparations issue, it had also set the foundation for major capital imports from the United States. Many German industrial companies contacted American banks directly or founded, like Stinnes in 1924, their own financing companies in the United States. Deutsche Bank concentrated at this point on those companies that faced difficulties in founding such financing businesses: mid- and small-scale companies that were only offered operating and investment loans at unfavourable terms in Germany and were desperately searching for external capital. Thanks to Alfred Blinzig's negotiating prowess, Deutsche Bank was able to issue its own large bond in the amount of $25 million.

Blinzig had travelled to the United States in April 1927 and had not only settled many of the open asset conflicts with American banks, including the bank's long-established partner JP Morgan, but had also made new contacts on Wall Street. The bank Dillon, Read & Co., in particular, proved highly interested in working with Deutsche Bank, whose business practices were seen as more reliable than that of many other German institutions, which had been repeatedly involved in risky speculation in the United States. The dollar bond did in fact garner great interest in Germany, not only because it was one of the largest German bonds in the United States since the war, but because it also had a relatively long-term payback period of five years. Most German companies and banks committed themselves to very short-term loans, which Reichsbank President Schacht had frequently sharply criticised.[190] Schacht's concern would prove to be well founded only a few years later, when American investors withdrew a large portion of their money from Germany in just a few days during the banking crisis of summer 1931 – with devastating effects for the German financial system.

From the perspective of Deutsche Bank, the 1927 bond, which was used primarily for loans to mid-sized companies, was a great strategic success. It could be seen as a sign of the leading German bank's successful return to the international capital market. The great importance that was attached to a comparatively small deal, however, exposed a series of fundamental problems: for some time, Deutsche Bank had no longer been the top address in the international credit and capital market business; it now faced growing competition from other German banks and financing companies, which could

$25,000,000

Deutsche Bank

(BERLIN)

Five-Year 6% Note

(Represented by American Participation Certificates)

To be dated September 1, 1927   To mature September 1, 1932

Principal amount of note $25,000,000. Interest payable semi-annually on March 1 and September 1 at the rate of 6% per annum. Principal and interest payable in United States gold coin without deduction for any taxes, present or future, levied by German governmental authorities.

American participation certificates in the aggregate principal amount of $25,000,000 are to be issued by The Equitable Trust Company of New York, trustee, against the deposit with it of the above note of Deutsche Bank. The certificates are to be in coupon form, in interchangeable denominations of $1,000, $5,000 and $10,000, registerable as to principal only. Payments received by the trustee on account of principal and interest are to be payable in New York at the principal office of Dillon, Read & Co. Also collectible in London at the office of J. Henry Schroder & Co., in pounds sterling; in Amsterdam, in addition to the office of Deutsche Bank Filiaal Amsterdam, at the offices of Mendelssohn & Co. Amsterdam and Nederlandsche Handel-Maatschappij, in guilders; in Zurich at the office of Crédit Suisse, in Swiss francs; or in Stockholm at the office of Stockholms Enskilda Bank, in Swedish kronor; in each case at the buying rate for sight exchange on New York on the date of presentation for collection.

From their accompanying letter, Mr. Alfred Blinzig and Mr. Oscar Wassermann, Managing Directors of Deutsche Bank, summarize as follows :

COMPANY AND BUSINESS

Deutsche Bank was organized in 1870 with its principal office in Berlin. With the exception of the Reichsbank, it has for more than forty years been the largest bank in Germany with respect to volume of business and deposits. Deutsche Bank has always enjoyed a particularly high standing, internationally as well as in Germany.

The bank conducts a general domestic and foreign banking business in the broadest sense, including deposits, discounts, commercial credits and an extensive investment banking business. It has been instrumental in the development of many important industries in Germany and is closely connected with most of the leading industrial and commercial enterprises in that country. Deutsche Bank maintains offices in 174 cities, many of which in turn have a number of branch offices.

CAPITALIZATION AND EQUITY

This $25,000,000 Five-Year 6% Note is to be the direct obligation of Deutsche Bank and will comprise, upon issuance, its only funded debt (except $201,879 of revalorized mortgages on certain office buildings of the bank).

The present authorized and outstanding par amount of the bank's share capital is $35,700,000. Current quotations on the Berlin Stock Exchange indicate a market value for this capital of more than $55,000,000.

DIVIDENDS AND EARNINGS

Dividends have been paid for each year since organization of the bank in 1870, with the exception of the inflation year 1923, and, with that exception, since the year 1895 have never been less than 10% per annum.

Profits as reported by the bank, after deduction of interest, all taxes, and payments to the Supervisory Board, for the years 1924, 1925 and 1926, were $4,346,409, $3,996,319 and $5,773,518, respectively.

PURPOSE OF ISSUE

The proceeds of the note will be used by the bank in the general conduct of its business.

Conversions of German into United States currency have been made at par of exchange.

A substantial portion of this issue has been withdrawn for offering in Europe.

Information herein contained has been received in part by cable.

We offer these American participation certificates for delivery if, when, and as issued and accepted by us, subject to the approval of legal proceedings by counsel. It is expected that delivery will be made on or about September 30, 1927, in the form of temporary or definitive certificates, or interim receipts of Dillon, Read & Co.

Price 99½ and accrued interest. To yield over 6.10%

Dillon, Read & Co.

In 1927, Deutsche Bank issued a bond of more than $25 million in the American market. This allowed it to refinance loans to medium-sized German companies that were unable to raise capital in the US themselves.

easily acquire American venture capital. At the same time, the bond was on a small scale in comparison to the large number of short-term loans or deposits, which could be immediately withdrawn. As those in Reichsbank circles also noted with concern, Deutsche Bank's short-term liabilities added up to nearly 2 billion RM.[191] To this was added another problem: how would the mid-sized companies, in light of the foreign currency shortage, find the dollars needed to pay back these loans? Deutsche Bank could not solve the basic dilemma of the German economy, which had a weak foreign trade balance and a high need for capital. This problem would of necessity backfire on the banks sooner or later.[192]

6. Consolidation and Concentration

Deutsche Bank was not able to profit much from the economic upswing of the 'golden years' between 1924 and 1928. The opening balance in gold marks presented in spring 1924 laid bare the degree of asset erosion that had taken place. The bank's capital and reserves had shrunk, and Deutsche Bank, measured by its share capital, was no longer the top German company. It had fallen to ninth place behind the large industrial conglomerates.[193] Though turnover developed satisfactorily in the following years – increasing from 133 billion RM in 1925 to 225 billion RM in 1928 – profits remained at a relatively low level of 18–22 million RM.[194]

There was a variety of reasons for the restrained nature of the bank's business development: even though deposits grew considerably, the lending business remained below expectations. Growing liquidity caused by the inflow of capital from outside Germany led many companies to choose not to take loans from German banks or to repay them ahead of time after borrowing money in other countries at lower interest rates. The annual report of 1926 therefore confirmed a major 'shift in accounts receivable' to the disadvantage of the German banks, which was connected with a reduction in interest income and commissions. The fact that the bank was still even making a profit was thanks not to its core business but to income from investments and foreign assets.[195] The securities markets were expected to recover, but the bank did not predict a sustainable future from a stock boom. There was also a certain degree of concern about the increase in the proportion of creditors outside Germany, which had grown to 35 per cent of all creditors by 1928.[196] Michalowsky therefore warned Deutsche Bank's branch directors in spring 1926 to keep an eye on the 'serious economic crisis', because it 'has unfortunately been seriously underestimated'.[197]

The bank's business woes to some degree reflected the brief economic recovery of 1925–8, which was unsustainable because it was based on major imbalances. The bank reflexively connected the 'interior weakness of our economy' to external, i.e. political forces:

It is weighed down and overburdened by taxes, as required by the far too expensive state, by excessive social expenditures, and especially by the reparations which are expected to be collected in their full amount, so that healthy growth is impossible. Development will only be possible to the extent to which these chains are loosened from their chokehold.[198]

Involvement in industry and venture capital

These statements hid the fact, of course, that problematic developments could be seen within the business landscape itself – developments in which the banks also played a part. An astonishing process of concentration was taking place in industry, which the big banks not only supported, but also assisted and shaped. Deutsche Bank not only had a share in the Stinnes empire, it had invested in the other large heavy industry and chemical conglomerates (Vereinigte Stahlwerke, I. G. Farben) with major loans. In general, all sectors of industry were impacted by the process of concentration. Cost pressures and the tax benefits for mergers that had been introduced in 1926 drove the formation of multiple consortia and cartels, often involving high financing costs.[199] Increases in capital, public offerings and the issuing of stock were almost always carried out through bank consortia, many of which Deutsche Bank led. The book value of such consortium transactions increased between 1924 and 1928 from 10 to 38 million RM.[200] This figure does not reflect, however, the full extent of the transactions; in reality it was probably much higher.[201]

At the same time, the risks involved in financing such enterprises, which were highly dependent on external capital to finance their rapid growth and often had opaque business structures due to a high degree of cross-shareholding, quickly became clear. The payment problems of the large empire that Hugo Stinnes left behind after his sudden death in 1924 also demonstrated the dangers that these enterprises' bankruptcies brought for the banks.[202] Other industry holdings, including some that were considered quite prestigious, also increasingly proved to be burdens during the second half of the 1920s. Often these were in new industrial branches, which were not operating profitably yet and whose continued existence in the market was difficult to envisage. This was the case with Ufa, which had been founded for propagandistic reasons in 1917, was privatised after the war, and was supposed to become a purely commercial company. Emil Georg von Stauß of Deutsche Bank was chairman of the supervisory board and exerted influence over the restructuring of the firm. The goal was to create a vertically integrated film company, which would unite production, sales and presentation under one umbrella and was supposed to compete with the French and above all the American film industries. Stauß ensured that Deutsche Bank took on the state's share of 30 per cent of Ufa in 1919. Even though Ufa produced numerous successful films in the 1920s, its financial situation was very troubled. Especially after currency stabilisation, the German film industry fell into serious crisis.[203] Competition with the large American studios in Hollywood became increasingly intense. After long negotiations, Ufa was acquired by Alfred Hugenberg in 1927, which did not entirely end Deutsche Bank's involvement, but dialled it back considerably. Stauß remained deputy chairman of the supervisory board.

Deutsche Bank's attempt to create a German 'automobile trust', in which, in addition to Daimler and Benz, other manufacturers such as Opel or BMW would be involved, was also rife with challenges. The goal was – based on the model of the Ford company in the United States – to produce compact vehicles on a large scale in order to supply the German and European markets. Through its merger with Württembergische Vereinsbank in Stuttgart, Deutsche Bank had become Daimler's Hausbank; in this case as well, Stauß served as chairman of the supervisory board, playing a central role in restructuring the firm. After Daimler and Benz formed a community of interest in 1924, the two companies merged in 1926. However, Deutsche Bank's efforts to found a large German conglomerate with the inclusion of BMW and Opel failed – Opel in particular, which was doing best economically, showed little interest in such a consolidation.[204]

Deutsche Bank had greater success in the aviation industry. This sector was seen as promising and also had political support. At the same time, investment costs were very high and profits difficult to achieve. Almost all German airlines were under severe cost pressures during the Weimar Republic, so banks and the state had to lend them financial support on multiple occasions. Deutsche Bank had already been involved in the inception of Deutsche Luft-Reederei (DLR) in the First World War, which had been founded in January 1917 on the initiative of Walther Rathenau and AEG in order to create capacity for military transports. The adjustment to civilian air transport was possible only with great difficulty after the end of the war. Few airlines could establish themselves, and the passenger volume was far too low from the point of view of profitability. DLR merged

In 1926 the Daimler-Motoren-Gesellschaft in Stuttgart and Benz & Cie. in Mannheim merged to form Daimler-Benz AG.

with Lloyd Luftdienst GmbH on these grounds in 1923. Deutsche Bank had a majority share in Deutscher Aero Lloyd, which resulted from the merger, with Stauß again serving as chairman of the supervisory board. Stauß was interested in consolidating the chronically unprofitable aviation branch and therefore pushed for its merger with the aeroplane manufacturer Junkers, which was on the brink of bankruptcy in the mid-1920s and had to be acquired by the state. Germany had an interest in the continuation of the aviation branch for political, economic and also military reasons, and subsidised it heavily. The founding of Lufthansa in January 1926, which resulted from the combination of Aero Lloyd, Junkers and a number of other aviation companies, was therefore the final point of a process of consolidation that would be of critical importance for the further development of the German aviation industry. The new company was also the paradigm of a public-private partnership. It received a large number of public subsidies, and its supervisory board included, in addition to representatives from banks and other industrial firms, numerous representatives from ministries and local government.[205]

Linkages and governance

As the above examples show, Deutsche Bank was actively involved in the process of industrial concentration and attempted to use it to further its own interests and ideas. The bank wanted to act as a type of venture capitalist in promoting new industries. Often the bank not only financed the companies' restructuring, but also acquired shareholdings for itself and included them in its portfolio over the long term.[206] Of course, in many cases the bank did not intend to establish long-term interests in industrial companies, but hoped, rather, to sell its shares later on at a higher price. In the years of the Great Depression, the bank acquired a large number of shares in troubled companies because of loan defaults and ended up keeping many of them for years.

The bank's actual influence over the companies often went far beyond direct holdings and the associated voting rights. Like any other big bank, Deutsche Bank's holdings included a large number of private investors' shares; the bank often had the voting rights for these transferred as well. Legally, there were a number of ways to deal with this. Shareholders could, on their own initiative, transfer their votes to an agent (proxy voting). This occurred often with minor shareholders who did not want to attend general meetings. Of far greater importance was the widespread practice of investors automatically transferring the voting rights for shares they had purchased to Deutsche Bank after opening a securities account with the bank. These 'securities account voting rights' gave the bank – even in cases where it had no shares or only a small number of shares in a company itself – a major influence in shareholders' meetings, often even holding a blocking minority.[207]

Another instrument of control was Supervisory Board membership. Some members of the Management Board and directors of Deutsche Bank had seats on dozens of other companies' supervisory boards. According to a list from 1930, Alfred Blinzig sat on 17 supervisory boards, Paul Bonn on 21, Oscar Wassermann on 24, Gustaf Schlieper on 27, Werner Kehl on 41 and Emil Georg von Stauß on 53. It was not just the Management Board members but also the bank directors at headquarters and the branches who held multiple supervisory board seats. Wilhelm Schaefer, the director of the Düsseldorf branch, sat on 30 supervisory boards, and Felix Theusner from the Wrocław branch on 39. Representatives of Deutsche Bank often played a leading role in the supervisory committees. Paul Millington-Herrmann, for example, who was a member of Deutsche Bank's Management Board from 1911 to 1928 before switching to its Supervisory Board, was active in 56 other supervisory boards in 1930, of which he served on 24 as chairman and 10 others as deputy chairman.[208] This accumulation of supervisory board postings frequently drew criticism and contributed to the introduction of a limit of 20 appointments during the banking crisis of 1931.[209] The main argument for this was that supervisory board members often could not fulfil their monitoring functions because of their profusion of appointments. The fact that the positions were paid and considerably boosted board members' earnings also drew heavy public criticism.

Even if these monetary incentives may have played a role, the bank also had practical reasons for wanting the right to supervise firms to which it had provided larger loans or in which it held a share. The unstable conditions of the interwar years led to a desire on the part of the bank for a greater degree of control over its large clients. Even after currency stabilisation, and despite the fact that economic conditions had improved, many companies were in financial trouble. In 1926, the bank expressed concern about the large number of bankruptcies, oversight responsibilities for at-risk companies and bill protests it was facing, which increased default risks tremendously.[210] Representation on their supervisory boards allowed the bank direct insight into companies' business activities, allowing it to more effectively predict possible loan defaults or bankruptcies – and, if possible, to fend them off.

The bank's increased interconnection with industry was therefore also aimed at lowering risk and reducing informational asymmetries. Recent research into sociological networks does, in fact, show that Deutsche Bank had particularly close personal connections in the large industrial companies and that it began systematically growing its networks starting in the First World War. Through appointments to management boards and supervisory boards, the bank (not counting its branches) had connections with 338 companies. These links were also very stable: many continued for a number of decades.[211]

Another component of the bank's networks was its numerous local and regional committees. The rosters of these committees were generally filled by representatives of the important companies in the region as well as representatives from chambers of commerce, economic associations and politics. These committees had only an advisory role, but were very important for networking within their respective regions. Prior to the First World War, there had only been local committees in Bremen, Hamburg and Constantinople, and these had only a handful of members. The wave of mergers that began with the First World War led to the establishment of many more committees. In 1914, a 21-member committee was founded for the Rhineland-Westphalia branches, drawing its personnel mostly from heavy industry. Beginning with the First World War, many decentralised regional committees were also formed. By the late 1920s, Deutsche Bank had local committees in Bremen, Hamburg, Harburg-Wilhelmsburg, Lübeck, Siegen, Essen, Saarbrücken, Königsberg, Gdańsk, Szczecin, Braunschweig and Hanover. There were also regional committees for Rhineland-Westphalia, Württemberg, Bavaria, Thuringia and Silesia. In addition to the number of committees, the number of members on these committees also increased considerably, beginning with the war. In total, the local and regional committees included more than 200 members by the late 1920s.[212]

With its 24 members until the First World War, Deutsche Bank's Supervisory Board also grew as mergers occurred and new branches were founded. The members of the management boards of acquired banks often joined the Supervisory Board, unless they could be hired as branch directors. By 1920, the Supervisory Board had 51 members. By 1923, this number increased to 59 and by 1928 to 75. The merger with Disconto-Gesellschaft in 1929 increased this number still further to 115. With these numbers, the active participation of the entire board was, of course, impossible. Some members seem to have been free riders motivated primarily by the bonuses and prestige that came with the position and who appeared at meetings only infrequently or carried out their roles passively.[213] Conversely, it also seems that many prominent individuals were selected for the Supervisory Board in the hope of boosting the company's prestige or building strategically important connections.[214] In addition to economic leaders and financiers, Deutsche Bank's Supervisory Board also included a number of politicians, including Cologne Mayor Konrad Adenauer. In addition, their co-determination rights also gave employee representatives a vote.[215]

That said, important decisions seem to have been made by a small group of influential figures. The Supervisory Board was, in fact, at quorum with just seven members, and after revisions to the statute in 1923, written votes were allowed, making the decision-making process much easier. The fact that its approval was acquired for the bank's many capital increases and mergers meant that the Supervisory Board played an increasingly active role. The committees (such as the financial oversight committee) became ever more important, and the chairman of the Supervisory Board played a particularly prominent role. Rudolph von Koch, who was appointed in 1914, was the first chairman who had formerly been on the Management Board, and his successor Max Steinthal, appointed in 1923, had also served on the Management Board for many years.[216] His deputy, Arthur von Gwinner, had served on the Management Board, too. This practice of co-opting former members of the Management Board to leadership roles on the Supervisory Board would continue for many decades at Deutsche Bank. One effect was that the Supervisory Board chairman worked more closely with the management and was more involved in the strategic and personnel-related decisions of the company than had been the case during the Wilhelmine empire, when the Supervisory Board had acted as more of a counterweight to the Management Board and as a powerful monitoring body.[217] The fact that, from 1931 onward, balance sheet audits of joint-stock companies had to be carried out by an external body led to the Supervisory Board seeing itself as more of a partner in the business.[218]

The greater degree of integration of the Supervisory Board and the management of the company did not mean, however, that management now acted in an uncontrolled and arbitrary manner, heedless of the interests of the owners. Rather, as recent studies have shown, shareholder protections at Deutsche Bank were assured, and – in contrast to many other big banks – fulfilled the legal requirements in almost exemplary fashion.[219] The role of the general meeting had been strengthened since the turn of the century. Shareholders had to agree to any planned dissolution of the company or increase in

Members of the Supervisory Board and shareholders participate in the extraordinary general meeting of October 1929, held in the bank's large assembly room on Mauerstraße in Berlin.

capital. There were also minimum dividends and generous rules for superdividends, which gave the owners financial security. At the same time, share ownership was widely distributed. There was no controlling shareholder who dominated general meetings. Even the bank's largest shareholders controlled less than 5 per cent of the capital.[220] They could increase their influence through proxy voting, which did frequently occur. However, the large shareholders were mostly allied private Berlin banks (Jacquier & Securius, E. J. Meyer, A. E. Wassermann, Wilhelm Kuczynski) as well as the Frankfurt bank Lazard Speyer-Ellissen. Two institutions outside Germany, Niederösterreichische Escompte-Gesellschaft and Wiener Bankverein, which Deutsche Bank had been working with for many years, also had large share packages. These banks were in many cases not actually the owners of the shares, but represented private investors. When Deutsche Bank increased its capital, these banks often took on large quantities of the newly issued shares and sold them to their customers.[221]

Since the reform of the New Company Act of 1884, there had been a clear separation between the ownership and the management at Deutsche Bank. This delineation became further accentuated after the First World War. After the reforms to the statute in 1923, Supervisory Board and Management Board members no longer had to own a minimum number of shares. The proportion of shares owned by the members of the Management Board was, in fact, low, and lay well below 10 per cent in the 1920s. This was presumably also linked to new members in leadership roles and increasing turnover. The bank found itself confronted with organisational challenges caused by a high rate of growth and the assumption of numerous new functions. In addition to a further professionalisation of the central administration through the development of the Secretariat and the specialist departments, the size of the Management Board was increased in 1914 from six members to 10. After the war, the number was reduced, but from the mid-1920s the bank began adding more deputy members to the Management Board, members of the broader leadership circle of the bank who would generally later be promoted to full membership on the Management Board.

In general, there was an effort to maintain a high degree of continuity in the bank's leadership personnel. A lifelong career at the bank was the goal not just of the low-level employees, but also of the management; promoting this was an express goal of the bank. Careers like that of Max Steinthal, who was active on the Management Board and the Supervisory Board for a total of 62 years before he was forced to resign because of his Jewish heritage, were certainly exceptional. But others such as Elkan Heinemann (a member of the Management Board from 1906 to 1923), Arthur von Gwinner (1894–1919), Paul Mankiewitz (1898–1923) or Alfred Blinzig (1920–34) were a part of the Management Board over the long term. Many members of the board had served as authorised signatories (*Prokuristen*), directors or department directors before being promoted to the bank's top levels. Such in-house careers from employee to director or Management Board member were common. Many executives also came from banking or business families. While apprenticeships were common until the turn of the century, more people with academic backgrounds were now joining the bank, most (like Carl Michalowsky, Paul Bonn, or Werner Kehl) holding a law degree and some even a doctorate. In some cases, they had combined an apprenticeship with study at a university. Karl Kimmich, a member of the Management Board from 1933 to 1942, for example, had completed an apprenticeship at a private bank in Ulm before attending university and earning a doctorate in political science (*Staatswissenschaften*). Those who had studied business administration or economics were less common in the leadership ranks. Banking was considered a career that required many years of practice or strong legal knowledge. The bank placed great value on international experience. Almost all those in senior management had spent a long period of time abroad, either during their studies or in an early stage of their careers.

Though a rise through the ranks and lifelong tenure at the bank was the primary model for advancement at the bank, there were repeated examples of careers that ended abruptly. Even at the top levels of management, difficult personnel decisions sometimes had to be made. Werner Kehl, who had joined the bank in 1919, who was responsible for the securities department starting in 1926 and was promoted to the Management Board in 1928, had to resign after some failed financial transactions and a breach of trust on the part of the director of the Düsseldorf branch, which fell under his regional responsibilities. Kehl, who was known to be ambitious, was afterwards given special assignments within the bank from time to time, but was not able to resume his promising career. A similar fate befell Selmar Fehr, who had joined the Management Board as Paul Mankiewitz's successor in 1923. After major price slumps at the Berlin stock exchange in May 1927, Fehr was accused of having personally enriched himself through insider trading and of having partially caused price drops through short selling. Even though these accusations were never proved, he was forced to vacate his position on the Management Board in mid-1930. Paul Bonn, who had built up the branch in Sofia and, after it had been closed, was responsible for the 'Russia business' at the Berlin headquarters, was dismissed in 1930 after major losses in his business sector. Bonn had been promoted to the Management Board only two years earlier, and great hopes had been pinned on him at the company.[222] Stauß's resignation from the Management Board in 1932 was also due to a series of losses and scandals in his area of responsibility. Most recently, Stauß had, in his position as chairman of the supervisory board of the Berlin Schultheiss-Patzenhofer brewery, not recognised quickly enough that the company was engaging in fraud.

Interrupted careers such as these were no longer rare by the late 1920s, when substantial profits could be made very quickly from arbitrage on the turbulent stock and foreign exchange markets. At the same time, they were evidence of the growing organisational and personnel-related challenges with which the bank was confronted after currency stabilisation. The bank's tremendous growth through the expansion of its branch network had not led to changes in its organisational structure. The Management Board still operated under a collegial model with a Spokesman who was essentially primus inter pares. The Spokesman's position of prominence was mainly relevant with regard to external communications. Internally, the long-standing collegial system remained in place, which gave each member of the Management Board a business segment in which he could act relatively autonomously. Each member of the Management Board also had a regional responsibility area for a region of branches in Germany. There were nonetheless informal hierarchies within management that resulted from length of employment, personality and the relative importance of the various business segments.

Oscar Wassermann, who had been brought on to the Management Board from his family's private bank in 1912 as a specialist in securities, was also responsible for other important business segments, such as mortgage banking, investments in ship-building and the bank's international relationships. In particular, Wassermann had made a name for himself during the period of inflation as a political adviser for the German government on currency matters and reparations. He was not only active in numerous professional associations, for example as deputy chairman of the Central Union of German Banks and Bankers, but was also a member of the General Council of the Reichsbank. In 1923, he succeeded Paul Mankiewitz as Spokesman of the Management Board. Besides Wassermann, two other members of the Management Board played an important role in the 1920s. One was Oscar Schlitter, who, like Wassermann, had joined the Management Board in 1912, and, as Carl Klönne's successor, was responsible primarily for business with the industrial

Oscar Wassermann (1869–1934) came from a private banking family. In 1912, he joined the Management Board of Deutsche Bank, and in 1923 he succeeded Paul Mankiewitz as Spokesman of the Management Board. In 1933, he was forced out of office.

firms of Rhineland-Westphalia. The region's economic importance for the bank, not least after the merger with Bergisch Märkische Bank, gave Schlitter prominence, as he was primarily involved in its restructuring. After resigning from the Management Board, he joined the Supervisory Board, which he and Franz Urbig alternated in leading between 1933 and 1939. Emil Georg von Stauß, who also played a prominent role, had close political connections and was elected to the Reichstag as a member of the Deutsche Volkspartei (DVP) in 1930. Other members of the Management Board were more active in the background, serving an important internal role. Gustav Schröter, who was responsible for cash management and payments from 1906 to 1925, was considered an introvert and rarely made public appearances. However, his time at the bank coincided not only with the challenging expansion of the branches and deposit side of the business, but also the transition to cashless payments and cheque transactions.

Management Board members and their employees were all but given carte blanche in their areas of responsibility, making it easier to abuse power, as in the case of Selmar Fehr.[223] The actual problem was that the bank, with its new activities and the expansion of its branches, had grown to such a scale that central control was increasingly difficult. This was the case, above all, with the branch activities, which were held under an unsatisfactory sort of control by a branch office at headquarters that had been created before the war and by regional 'head branches'. The branch office was responsible, above all, for creating guidelines on the issuing of loans and other requirements, but it was, of course, unable to effectively supervise day-to-day business on site. The branches did, in fact, interpret these rules quite generously, especially when they were working with large and long-established industrial clients, for most of which the bank did not carry out a strict credit assessment.[224] Carl Michalowsky had already criticised the 'branches' autonomy, which had got out of hand' in 1926 and saw it as one of the causes of many of the bank's loan problems. Often, loans were given to old customers for the simple reason that 'the client needed the money'. 'The general pattern is that branches, once something has gone wrong, stand there bewildered and helpless, and it is up to headquarters to make amends for an investment that has usually been carried out against its will.'[225]

Only for very large loans did the branches have to receive authorisation from Berlin headquarters. In general, this also applied to loans outside Germany. Often, though, headquarters was presented with *faits accomplis*. In March 1926, Carl Michalowsky criticised along these lines the 'dangerous desire for autonomy of some branches' and warned against centrifugal forces within the bank:

If the degree of autonomy continues to grow in the same way it has until now, fruitful co-operation will be impossible. The bank is a unified organisation, and this cannot be changed. The necessary precondition for co-operation is that branches follow headquarters' principles.[226]

The relationship between headquarters and the branches continued to present the bank with one of its greatest challenges, which time and again would lead to internal conflicts and power struggles. The question of how autonomously the branches could act and which control structures were necessary would remain highly contentious into the 1980s.

Lean years

The process of consolidation not only changed the power relations in the banking sector, where the private banks and regional institutions lost while the big banks became ever more consolidated. Within the bank conglomerates, too, there was plenty of conflict, as consolidation was always linked with the goal of reducing costs. Since nearly 80 per cent of the bank's day-to-day operating expenses were personnel expenditures, this also represented a major opportunity to improve the bank's profit margin.[227]

In 1924, Deutsche Bank began a comprehensive laying off of the excess number of staff that had built up over the course of the war and the era of inflation. At the height of inflation in late 1923, the bank had nearly 40,000 employees; one year later, this number was reduced by half. However, the cost savings – at only 17 per cent – were initially less than had been hoped.[228] As bank management emphasised, the layoffs mostly affected the temporary assistance staff.[229] This was also an accommodation of the workers' councils' demands that social factors be taken into account in the reduction of the workforce. Long-serving employees were also generally more expensive for the company. The company's co-determination rights did mean, in practice, that personnel decisions could not be made as freely as before.[230]

In the years that followed, the management nonetheless proceeded determinedly in its efforts to reduce personnel expenses, which was seen as essential in reducing the bank's ballooning expenditures. By early 1927, the workforce was further reduced to 14,800 employees.[231] The layoffs affected administrative staff most heavily, but also impacted on approximately 1,000 directors and high-level employees, mostly older ones who were sent into early retirement. While it was emphasised that the 'staff reduction could now be seen as pretty much complete', internally, attempts were still underway to further reduce the number of employees, affecting above all the branches of newly acquired banks.[232] Wage increases were the main reason cited for the layoffs; these in turn to a certain degree cancelled out the savings achieved. Expenditures on contract employees even increased between 1925 and 1927 by 7 per cent.[233]

Of course, these numbers hid the fact that employees' salaries did not significantly increase. Michalowsky had already admitted in 1936 that the 'purchasing power of bank officials' income is even lower today' than in the pre-war era. In light of the economic conditions at the time, however, this could not be remedied. The conditions, according to Michalowsky, were 'stronger than our goodwill'.[234] Nor did this stance change much in the years that followed. According to internal statistics from March 1929, only the salaries in the lower income brackets had even slightly increased in comparison to 1914, while the salaries of mid- to high-level employees had actually worsened. An employee in the highest pay scale group, pay scale group 3, with 15 years of employment at the company, earned 400 RM per month in 1929 in comparison to 509 RM per month in 1914. This was partly due to the fact that employer social contributions had grown in the lower wage groups but had gone down for those in the upper income brackets. The trend towards a levelling of income differences, which had begun with the war, continued over the course of the 1920s.[235] At the same time, branch directors complained that salary reductions made it harder than before to carry out the representative duties on behalf of the bank that were necessary in the branch regions.[236]

By early 1929, the bank's staff had been reduced to 13,200; taking into account changes within personnel categories, this amounted to 26,800 fewer than in 1924 and only 1,300 fewer than before the war.[237] How were these cuts in personnel brought about in terms of company structure? One important step was the systematic reduction of the bank's many accounts with very low turnover. Some of these had been taken over from the newly acquired regional banks; in other cases, customers had opened accounts with low turnover at the bank during the war and inflation, when payment transactions had increased significantly. According to the Management Board's assessment, these did not fit into the bank's business profile, especially because the effort involved in payment transactions did not justify the costs. Whereas the average amount of a transaction was 3,213 marks in 1913, it had fallen to 952 RM by 1926. The number of transactions in the current accounts segment was twice as high as before the war.[238] Approximately half of the bank's employees were involved in carrying out payment transactions.

The bank did succeed in greatly reducing the number of its accounts from 800,000 to 280,000, about as many as before the merger with Bergisch Märkische Bank.[239] Many smaller customers transitioned to savings banks, co-operative banking institutions, or postal savings banks, which attracted new client groups by offering better conditions and an expanded range of investment opportunities.[240] While this loss of customers was actually desired in the mid-1920s, it would prove to be a problem during the banking crisis of 1931, when the bank was frantically attempting to increase its deposits.

Cost concerns also played a role in the introduction of new technology and rationalisation. This led to a far-reaching technological revolution in banking, which had functioned almost without any technical assistance for decades, with the exception of the typewriter, introduced in the 1890s. In 1924 the bank launched a campaign to 'reduce the cost of operations by introducing machines'.[241] By using accounting machines and calculators, including Hollerith tabulating machines with punched cards, the bank aimed to accelerate workflows across the board. The comprehensive introduction of account numbers and the standardisation of transfers and other bank transactions with

By introducing modern accounting machines, like the ones used in the Berlin headquarters in 1927, payment transactions were to be streamlined and costs cut.

standard forms were also aimed at this goal. Payment transactions had changed significantly regardless of these changes – bills of exchange were barely used as a means of payment any longer, in contrast to the practice prior to the war, and most transactions were carried out in cash or transfers. Because cash transactions at the bank counter involved high personnel costs, cashless payment methods were to be expanded, especially in the high-volume business, where turnover was generally lower. By increasing the number of apprentices and founding a banking school through the Berlin Chamber of Commerce, the bank sought to build up a new cohort of younger bank employees who not only knew stenography and other banking methodology, but could also use calculators and had a basic knowledge of foreign languages.[242]

The success of these innovations was not immediate, however. The annual report of 1927 confirmed that 'rationalisation measures up to now […] do not yet sufficiently reduce expenditures'. Therefore, according to the report, the bank 'still had to devote special attention to the time-saving operation of our business'.[243]

The merger with Disconto-Gesellschaft

How this was to be achieved had already been discussed intensively by this time behind closed doors. It was foreseeable that this would involve another realignment of the banking landscape. At the time, however, it was entirely unclear which banks would combine. The preferred merger partner for Deutsche Bank would have been Danat-Bank, the second largest bank in Germany and in many respects an ideal partner with a similar business profile. However, early exploratory talks between the two banks had already failed because of personal differences, above all the 'excessive demands' of Jakob Goldschmidt, Danat-Bank's managing partner.[244] Disconto-Gesellschaft, with which the bank merged in 1929, was in some respects the second choice, even though talks had been underway at least indirectly since 1926, through Oscar Schlitter and Robert Pferdmenges. It is not clear at what point the exploratory talks turned into more serious negotiations, as there are few sources about the secretive discussions. In order to avoid merger rumours, initial negotiations were held in Pontresina in the Swiss Engadin and were later continued at the Berlin bankers' private villas.[245]

There were good reasons for merging the two banks, which held large business portfolios and, with a share capital of 285 million RM, had a higher capitalisation than the three other big German banks combined.[246] Both had achieved success above all in the industrial and capital markets business and had been involved in numerous mergers and in the public offerings of large conglomerates. Together, they would have enough capital to finance more large projects and to meet the industrial conglomerates on an equal footing. According to Deutsche Bank's estimates, the 'D[eutsche] B[ank]-D[isconto-]G[esellschaft] bloc would quickly achieve profits of [R]M 20,000,000 and be in a position to develop such strength that it would be an unopposable force in the underwriting business and in the reconstruction of the German economy both domestically and abroad'.[247]

But there were also weighty arguments against a merger. The banks had long been competitors, Deutsche Bank having displaced the older Disconto-Gesellschaft from the position of largest German financial institution at the turn of the century at the latest. In many markets – especially abroad – the two banks were in competition with each other, a rivalry that had intensified in recent years. At the same time, there were chances for the banks to co-operate in a number of syndicated loans, which indicated that tensions might diminish again. The two big banks also realised that, on their own, they could barely come out of their defensive posture. Not only were their earnings reduced by high costs, turnover was also in danger of collapsing due to new competitors in the credit markets.[248] Disconto-Gesellschaft was under even more pressure than Deutsche Bank, having been overtaken by Dresdner Bank in 1925 and Danat-Bank in 1926. And Disconto-Gesellschaft, which was known for its high salaries, had profitability problems that were much more serious than those at the other big Berlin banks.[249]

Disconto-Gesellschaft's main building, located in Berlin on the corner of Unter den Linden and Charlottenstraße, pictured here in the 1920s.

There were other obstacles, too. Though Deutsche Bank was a full joint-stock company, Disconto-Gesellschaft, an older company, was a partnership limited by shares. This was a hybrid entity between a partnership and a joint-stock company with a group of personally liable proprietors at its head. In addition to the different legal statuses of the two companies, there were also major differences in company culture. Disconto-Gesellschaft embodied to a greater degree the traditions of the old-established, dignified banking profession. Their business practices were less aggressive. The bank acted more cautiously both in the lending business and in the capital markets business, and was careful not to engage with dubious business partners. Disconto-Gesellschaft had acquired numerous private and regional banks, including A. Schaaffhausen'scher Bankverein and Norddeutsche Bank. However, these companies had been given a greater degree of autonomy, and Disconto-Gesellschaft co-operated with them in a community of interest, even though it controlled their entire share capital. Deutsche Bank had long given up this model, instead fully integrating the banks which it had acquired.

In light of these differences, the merger discussions carried on for several years. Disconto-Gesellschaft, in particular, reacted cautiously at first to Deutsche Bank's overtures, fearing that it, as the smaller institution, would be swallowed up by the other bank. At Deutsche Bank, in turn, there were reservations that Disconto-Gesellschaft would introduce new problems into the company. It was considered to be bureaucratic and not as profit-oriented as Deutsche Bank. Therefore, an initial comprehensive analysis of costs and profitability was carried out at Deutsche Bank under the leadership of directors Peter Brunswig and Hans Rummel, who were responsible for the organisation of the bank and matters pertaining to accounting and cost management. Rummel, who had led the Munich branch until 1927 and had been brought to Berlin for merger planning, was considered a particular expert in the field and, as the author of numerous publications, had made a name for himself in the newly emerging field of bank management.[250] Like many other managers at the bank – in 1930 he became a deputy member of the Management Board and in 1933 a full member – he had completed a bank apprenticeship, but never went to university; he had taught himself the technical side of the banking business.

Though little is known about the merger negotiations, it seems relatively certain that no clear agreement was in place until summer 1929. Deutsche Bank seems to have even considered combining with Dresdner Bank in the meantime. In the spring, Commerz-und Privat-Bank had combined with Mitteldeutsche Creditbank, and rumours were circulating of a merger between Danat-Bank and Berliner Handels-Gesellschaft.[251] Further motivation for prompt action resulted from the fact that the reduction of the merger tax expired on 1 October 1929. The Law on Tax Mitigation and to Ease the Economic Situation which had been passed on 31 March 1926 had reduced capital transfer taxes to 1 per cent, presenting considerable incentives for merging.

In the summer, Oscar Schlitter and Eduard Mosler of Disconto-Gesellschaft met in Pontresina in Switzerland and clarified the final outstanding questions, clearing the way for the merger to be announced on 26 September 1929 at a joint Supervisory Board meeting. Even for Deutsche Bank, which had experience with mergers, this consolidation process was technically complicated; not only did it involve two big banks, it also drew in both of Disconto-Gesellschaft's formally autonomous subsidiary banks

Group picture of Deutsche Bank's Management Board and the heads of its Supervisory Board after the merger agreement of October 1929: Alfred Blinzig (1), Arthur von Gwinner (2), Supervisory Board Chairman Max Steinthal (3), Management Board Spokesman Oscar Wassermann (4), Oscar Schlitter (5), Emil Georg von Stauß (6), Paul Bonn (7), Otto Sperber (8), Fritz Wintermantel (9), Werner Kehl (10).

in Hamburg and Cologne. Two additional regional institutions in Mannheim, in which both big banks had long had majority shares, were also acquired in the merger: Rheinische Creditbank and Süddeutsche Disconto-Gesellschaft.[252]

In a general meeting of both banks that took place in late October 1929, Management Board Spokesman Oscar Wassermann again presented a detailed case for the merger. The tremendous cost pressures, the difficult financial situation in Germany as a whole and the 'extraordinarily intense competition' in German banking, according to Wassermann, made the merger of vital importance. Wassermann emphasised that this was not a one-sided acquisition, but the mutual coming together of two equal partners.[253] Although Disconto-Gesellschaft, including its four subsidiaries, was legally transferred to Deutsche Bank, it was a merger of equals, as indicated by the company name 'Deutsche Bank und Disconto-Gesellschaft'. The shares and share certificates of both merger partners were exchanged for new shares of Deutsche Bank und Disconto-Gesellschaft on a one-to-one basis. This resulted in a joint share capital of 285 million RM. At the same time, the new bank took on most of the members of the management boards and supervisory boards of both institutions. In consequence, the leadership committees increased considerably in size. The new Management Board consisted of all seven representatives of Deutsche Bank (Emil Georg von Stauß, Oscar Schlitter, Selmar Fehr, Werner Kehl, Alfred Blinzig, Paul Bonn and Oscar Wassermann), and five of the eight proprietors of Disconto-Gesellschaft (Eduard Mosler, Franz A. Boner, Georg Solmssen, Theodor Frank and Gustaf Schlieper).

A share of the new Deutsche Bank und Disconto-Gesellschaft from November 1929.

Just a year later, the Management Board was reduced to 10 members, however, with equal representation from both banks. Max Steinthal and Arthur Salomonsohn jointly led the Supervisory Board. Their deputies, likewise following the principle of parity, were Arthur von Gwinner and Ernst Enno Russell, and the former chairman of the supervisory board of Disconto-Gesellschaft, Max von Schinckel, was made honorary chairman. At least on the leadership level, therefore, Deutsche Bank did not take a dominant position. On the contrary: the most prominent representatives of Deutsche Bank drew back from operations after the merger, thereby making room for a generational change in management. Thus there was a surprising amount of young talent at Disconto-Gesellschaft promoted to leadership roles: by late 1932, four of the now only seven members of the Management Board were previous proprietors of Disconto-Gesellschaft, and until 1945, all the spokesmen of the Management Board – Georg Solmssen (1933–4), Eduard Mosler (1934–9), Karl Kimmich (1940–2) and Oswald Rösler (1943–5) – were from its ranks. Many of Disconto-Gesellschaft's principles also prevailed in the management of the company The central credit department, for instance, played a much more active role at Disconto-Gesellschaft. This centralised process was introduced in the newly merged bank in 1930, not least because Deutsche Bank had found itself confronted again and again in the years before with the consequences of many of its offices' generosity in the offering of loans.[254]

What was the result of the merger? As Wassermann emphasised, the consolidation led to a 'strong structure, the capacities of which went beyond the simple summation of the two'. The economic power of the new big bank was in fact impressive. Its assets amounted to more than 5.5 billion RM, thereby getting close to the big American and British banks. In Germany, the new company had a dense network of branches and had offices in 289 different locations, as well as 177 deposit-taking branches. The number of accounts amounted to 800,000 by late 1929, 72,000 more than one year earlier. The second largest bank in Germany, Dresdner Bank, had by comparison only 338,000 accounts at this time.[255] This expansion of creditors was certainly a goal of the merger, along with a more active wooing of 'small savers'. As Brunswig and Rummel urged their branch directors in the autumn of 1929, the bank could 'not wait until the customers bring the money to us', it had to 'seek the customers', for example through appropriate marketing measures and by founding more smaller-scale deposit-taking branches. They also encouraged winning over the wealthy through targeted 'investment advice'.[256]

One of the more important goals of the amalgamation of the banks was that of reducing personnel and operating costs. Under Rummel's leadership, financial accounting was expanded and a first form of price-performance analysis was established. Rummel hoped this would more efficiently steer the bank's resources and organise all activities according to profitability calculations.[257] This also meant reducing redundancies and consolidating where possible. Branches were merged in many locations in order to save infrastructure and personnel costs.[258] At headquarters, too, many positions were done away with. By late 1932, the number of employees had been reduced by about a quarter. This did not just affect those involved in the basic technical and business activities of the bank, but also high-level officials (*Oberbeamte*) and directors. The membership of the Management Board was reduced to seven, and in 1931 the rank of deputy member was phased out. Many leading employees were given early retirement, some with substantial severance packages and redundancy pay.

The overall result of cost savings was, in fact, sobering. Not counting the immediate costs of the merger, which amounted to 3.5 million RM, resulting from capital transfer taxes and property transfer taxes as well as notary invoices,[259] many of the savings did not materialise for a long time. This was not only down to personnel costs, but also because of the many buildings that were maintained for years – in many locations next to one another, or standing empty. The main building of Disconto-Gesellschaft on

Figure 5: Cost/income ratio of Deutsche Bank und Disconto-Gesellschaft, 1928–38 (in %).

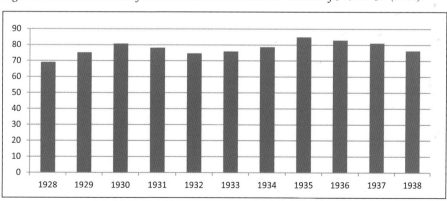

Source: Annual Reports by Deutsche Bank und Disconto-Gesellschaft 1928–38. Note: without taxes or retained earnings. For 1928 the numbers from both banks were added.

Unter den Linden could not be sold until 1933 – not least in order to increase the firm's capital, which had been eroded by the banking crisis. There was even a short-term increase in operational costs. Whereas the sum of the total expenses of both banks in 1928 was 141.4 million RM, these increased in 1929 to 155.9 million RM and did not go down until 1930, when they totalled 134 million RM. However, much of this seems to have been due to deflation and layoffs during the Great Depression, rather than an improvement in profitability. On the contrary: adjusted for taxes and retained earnings from the previous year, the ratio of costs to income of both banks increased from 69 per cent in 1928 to more than 80 per cent in 1930 and remained at this level, with some fluctuation, until the late 1930s. While this was due in part to the decrease in profits during the economic and banking crisis, even after the crisis was over the cost–income ratio remained unsatisfactory.

As cost-cutting had only little effect, this may be just one indication of the major difficulties connected to the consolidation of the two big banks. When the annual report of 1929 explained that it was 'a quick success, welding both organisations into a homogenous whole that draws on two pasts', this was only wishful thinking.[260] Into the 1950s there were differences in the workforce between employees from Disconto-Gesellschaft – the 'Hansemanns', named after the bank's founder – and those from Deutsche Bank. Even though the double name was abandoned in 1937, with only 'Deutsche Bank' being used, internal differences remained. What was then the largest merger in German banking history made it clear that the costs of integration were far greater than the short-term savings. Nonetheless, the 1929 merger and the harsh cuts associated with it meant that Deutsche Bank und Disconto-Gesellschaft was better prepared for the effects of the banking crisis of 1931 than its competitors.

The headquarters of the merged Deutsche Bank und Disconto-Gesellschaft on Mauerstraße in Berlin in 1930.

II. Age of Extremes: Crisis, Dictatorship and Expansion

1. The Banking Crisis of 1931

When, just a few weeks after the merger of Deutsche Bank und Disconto-Gesellschaft, stock prices in the United States dived by around 25 per cent, most observers were unaware of the momentousness of this event. On the Management Board of Deutsche Bank, for instance, Selmar Fehr assumed that after years of a bull market, current developments were merely an overdue 'stock market correction' that would have no negative effects for the real economy.[1] This assessment was widely shared at the time. On 23 November 1929, *The Economist* wrote,

> Can a very serious Stock Exchange collapse produce a serious setback to industry when industrial production is for the most part in a healthy and balanced condition? … Experts are agreed that there must be some setback, but there is not yet sufficient evidence to prove that it will be long or that it need go to the length of producing a general industrial depression.[2]

The 1929 annual report, published in April 1930, emphasised that, despite all the symptoms of crisis in the labour market, the German economy rested 'on a solid foundation'. The newly merged bank had earned a decent profit of 34 million RM that year, based above all on high earnings from fees and interest.[3] Nor did 1930 bring any sharp fall in business; the reduction of net profit to 20 million RM was primarily a consequence of necessary write-offs of losses in the securities and syndication departments, while interest and fees brought in satisfactory earnings.[4] The number of accounts even rose slightly. In comparison to other German companies, things were going relatively well for Deutsche Bank und Disconto-Gesellschaft.

The signs of a crisis of the German financial sector could not be overlooked, however. The American stock market crash of October 1929 quickly made its effects felt in Europe and caused difficulties for many German companies. Despite all protectionist tendencies, the global economy was still too strongly interconnected for a crisis to be limited to one country.[5]

In Germany, many highly indebted industrial companies found themselves in payment difficulties or even had to declare bankruptcy. This could not fail to have an effect on a bank so heavily involved in industrial financing. In the years before, Deutsche Bank had already had to accept significant losses because of defaults and restructurings,

Figure 6: Price of the Deutsche Bank share on the Berlin Stock Exchange, 1923–42 (as a percentage of par value).

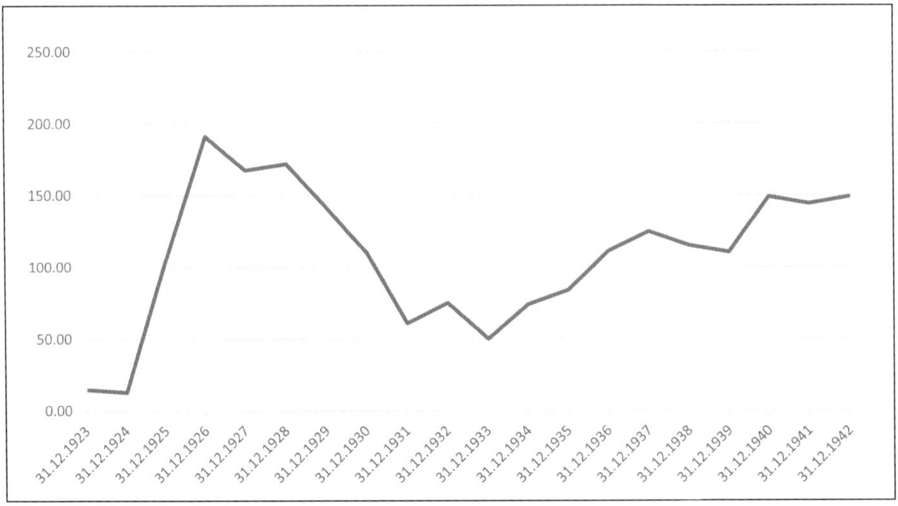

Source: Handbuch der deutschen Aktiengesellschaften, 1923–42 (year-end figures).

such as a significant write-off in 1927 related to its engagement with Universum-Film Aktiengesellschaft (Ufa), which, however, the bank had been able to offset with especially high earnings in the securities trade. The next warning signs came in summer 1929, when the Frankfurter Allgemeine Versicherungs-AG (FAVAG) had to declare bankruptcy. The company had engaged for years in speculative investments that had nothing to do with insurance, its core business. A special audit by the Reich Insurance Supervisory Office revealed that the conglomerate had, moreover, falsified balance sheets and had constructed a non-transparent conglomeration of holdings and subsidiaries in order to obfuscate its business dealings. Three members of FAVAG's management board were given long prison sentences. Both Deutsche Bank und Disconto-Gesellschaft had for years been creditors of the insurance company, which had been founded in 1865 and ranked second only to Berlin's Allianz AG in Germany. Only through a standstill agreement that pooled the company's domestic liabilities to the amount of 66 million RM and its foreign loans of over 37 million RM could a domino effect be avoided. For Deutsche Bank und Disconto-Gesellschaft, this implied not only high write-offs but led to the justifiable question of whether the creditworthiness of the business had been sufficiently examined, especially because both banks had long been represented on FAVAG's supervisory board.[6]

Numerous other insolvencies followed in the subsequent months, bringing the merged bank into difficulties. The high losses of the Aktiengesellschaft für Osthandel, which Deutsche Bank had founded along with Britain's Eastern and Overseas Products Ltd., were particularly sensational. The collapse in the prices of raw materials and agricultural goods was fatal for the trading company. The fact that Paul Bonn, the member of the Management Board responsible for the Aktiengesellschaft für Osthandel, had to resign his post over these losses shows how nervously the bank responded to events such as these. The next big scandal was to cost Emil Georg von Stauß his seat on the Management Board: as chairman of the Schultheiß conglomerate's supervisory board, he had failed to notice that the company's general manager, Ludwig Katzenellenbogen, was a swindler. He had falsified stock exchange prospectuses and taken out loans at numerous banks, without informing them of his other liabilities.[7]

Fraud of this type was, of course, commonplace in the Weimar Republic, and no bank was immune from becoming entangled in such scandals.[8] In the politically charged climate of these years, scandals like these offered a welcome chance to pillory not just individual companies, but the capitalist economic system as a whole. People tended to be especially critical of the role of the banks. Parties and press organs of every stripe ramped up their criticism of the corrupt and speculation-oriented financial system, which was concerned above all with quick profit at the expense of the common good.[9] As the largest and most prominent bank in Germany, Deutsche Bank was especially subject to these attacks, and responded nervously, fearing that 'bad business methods and morals' would provoke a 'general mistrust' in the financial sector.[10] Partly for this reason, in 1927 the bank established a press division, directed by the journalist and long-time *Berliner Tageblatt* columnist Maximilian Müller-Jabusch. The professionalisation of the bank's publicity reflected an ever-intensifying domestic political polarisation into which the banks found themselves inevitably drawn.

Public relations in 1930: a transmission on the radio station Funk-Stunde from the Berlin headquarters of Deutsche Bank und Disconto-Gesellschaft. From left: the reporter Zeiz, director Mehrhardt, and press officer Müller-Jabusch.

At the leadership level of Deutsche Bank und Disconto-Gesellschaft, a widespread fear emerged that the FAVAG and Schultheiß conglomerate scandals were just the tip of an iceberg whose true dimensions could not yet be determined. While there were 4,893 bankruptcies in Germany in 1929, there were 7,052 in 1930 and 13,599 in 1931.[11] A large proportion of these insolvencies ended in settlements between the companies and their creditors. One frequent problem was that loans had been extended for investment, and as such were committed for the long term. Many short-term loans were also continuously renewed, and many businesses had taken out loans at multiple banks – even banks abroad. If the companies were unable to service their debts, banks often took shares in these companies into their portfolios. When, for example, the machinery manufacturers Lanz and Maffei found themselves in difficulties, Deutsche Bank und Disconto-Gesellschaft obtained a majority stake in the company in compensation for loans granted.[12] The acquisition of industrial holdings was, as mentioned earlier, an unintended side effect of specific combinations of crisis circumstances, not the strategic expansion of the portfolio. As a result, the bank found itself linked, for better or for worse, to the economic development of these companies, a situation which would turn out to be disastrous during the banking crisis of summer 1931. If Deutsche Bank und Disconto-Gesellschaft's losses in 1929 and 1930 amounted to 125 million RM in total, its write-offs in 1931 added up to 240 million RM. They originated overwhelmingly in industry.[13]

Moral hazard?

The collapse of the German banking system in summer 1931 did not come as a surprise. In early May 1931, Österreichische Creditanstalt had reported a loss of 140 million schillings, and shortly thereafter announced its insolvency. The company, which dated back to 1855, was not only the largest Austrian bank, but had numerous industrial holdings and was systemically important in every sense.[14] Only with the help of a foreign emergency loan and a co-ordinated rescue operation on the part of the Austrian state and numerous banks was a complete collapse of the European financial system prevented that spring.

The crisis nevertheless spread rapidly to Germany. In early May it became known that the Karstadt conglomerate had suffered great losses, followed by signs that Nordstern Versicherung was in a precarious state. By the end of May, investors had withdrawn nearly 300 million RM from their accounts in German banks. At the beginning of June, Danat-Bank refused to extend a loan to the City of Berlin. Shortly thereafter it became known that Nordwolle, one of the largest European textile companies, was highly indebted and had been brought by dubious business deals to the edge of insolvency, which put its creditors – above all, Dresdner Bank and Danat-Bank – in great difficulty. It was not only the large Berlin financial institutions, but also the regional banks and central savings banks (*Girozentralen*) that found themselves in distress. Landesbank der Rheinprovinz, which was involved in numerous municipal bonds, was considered doomed. And no one knew what the balance sheets of many other public and private-sector banks looked like. The political situation escalated when, on 5 June, German Chancellor Heinrich Brüning announced that Germany could no longer pay its war reparations. The moratorium announced two weeks later by American President Herbert Hoover barely eased tensions, underlining instead how serious the situation was.

It is nevertheless unclear when exactly the withdrawal of foreign investors started, whether it triggered the banking crisis of July 1931, or whether the capital flight merely strengthened an endogenous crisis.[15] For the banks, the development was disastrous. They could not prevent the withdrawal of these funds, but had instead to actively support the transfers through foreign exchange payments to the accounts of foreign correspondent banks. Representatives at the Reichsbank were frustrated to note that the commercial banks were acquiring foreign exchange for this purpose at the central bank and saving their own reserves.[16]

There has long been scholarly debate about whether the banking crisis was primarily a result of political or market failures.[17] While there is consensus that the interplay of economic distress, currency imbalances and banking crises was particularly disastrous and led to a prolonged economic depression,[18] the causality of these factors are disputed. While Peter Temin and Gerd Hardach hold politicians primarily responsible in that they held on to the gold standard too long and refrained from expansionary monetary policy even after its abolition,[19] Karl Erich Born, Harold James and Isabel Schnabel emphasise the failures of the big banks, which took irresponsible risks in the expectation of government bailouts. Since the banks were aware of their systemic importance, Schnabel argues, they could trust in the fact that the state would not stand back and watch as they collapsed. On these grounds she identifies moral hazard on the part of the banks as the central explanation for the crisis.[20]

This view was widespread at the time. In fact, Deutsche Bank und Disconto-Gesellschaft were themselves accused by representatives of the Reichsbank and the Brüning government of having largely caused the banking crisis of July 1931. Management Board Spokesman Oscar Wassermann, Brüning would later stress in his memoirs, had not actively supported the rescue of Danat-Bank and had knowingly accepted its insolvency in order to get rid of a fierce competitor.[21] Of course, the Reichsbank, and especially Brüning himself, were also targets of public criticism, and were attempting to divert attention from their own mistakes. These mutual recriminations ought to be viewed in the context of the tense political situation of summer and autumn 1931. Deutsche Bank und Disconto-Gesellschaft were concerned with limiting losses and sent Brüning a long report in October 1931 justifying their behaviour during the crisis.[22]

The controversy between banks and policymakers makes a detailed and nuanced analysis of the banking crisis complicated, given that both sides tried to justify their own behaviour. Moreover, the situations of the banks varied considerably, and they pursued different strategies. German banks were not a homogenous bloc with common interests, and they were competing heavily with each other. This might explain their often hostile and non-co-operative behaviour during the crisis. What were the banks accused of, and which of these attributions of blame are accurate?

Firstly, the banks were blamed for having recklessly extended loans to private companies and public institutions and thus contributed to an increase of commercial debt. This accusation is, as we have seen, true of Deutsche Bank. Many loans were not subjected to sufficient scrutiny and, in retrospect, should never have been approved. Of course, the big banks were not solely responsible for the expansion of credit in the late 1920s, since many large industrial companies and state agencies also borrowed considerable

On 13 July 1931, Darmstädter und Nationalbank (Danat-Bank) had to close its counters. The run on this and other banks prompted the Reich government to impose banking holidays on 14 and 15 July and shortly thereafter to place strict limits on payment transactions.

sums of money abroad. In addition to the big private-sector banks, public institutions as well as the savings banks were active in the lending and bond business with the help of the newly founded *Landesgirozentralen*. Gerd Hardach has argued, moreover, that the growth in liquidity of the second half of the 1920s was by no means disproportionately high, and that the banks were only responding to economic demand.[23] On the other side, even the management of Deutsche Bank und Disconto-Gesellschaft was worried about the lax lending practices of some of their branches, and made efforts to establish central controls to reduce default risk. From spring 1930 onwards, stricter guidelines governed the allocation of large loans.[24] From September 1930, the auditing commissions of the regional committees began to subject loans over 50,000 RM to detailed examination. Regional head branches could independently give loans up to 150,000 RM and only had to report loans above 20,000 RM to headquarters.[25] However, even with these precautionary measures, existing loans could not be reversed – and many losses resulted from the bank's older loans. In any case, none of the company insolvencies threatened the existence of Deutsche Bank und Disconto-Gesellschaft. In contrast to Danat-Bank, which had extended loans to Nordwolle to the tune of 48 million RM, almost the value of its entire share capital, Deutsche Bank had only loaned Nordwolle 8.7 million RM.[26] In other words, the cluster risk was not so great that the bank could be thrown into the abyss by the insolvency of a few large clients.

The second accusation was that the capital buffer of the banks was not sufficient to absorb the losses. Here, too, Deutsche Bank und Disconto-Gesellschaft was in a better position than the other big banks. While its total losses in 1930–31 reached 275 million RM, its equity, including reserves, amounted to 445 million RM. Dresdner Bank's losses totalled 371.5 million RM; Commerz- und Privat-Bank's totalled 106.7 million RM. Both banks, however, had far lower equity endowments.[27] Deutsche Bank had undoubtedly profited from its merger with Disconto-Gesellschaft, which had rather high capital reserves. The equity ratio of Deutsche Bank und Disconto-Gesellschaft in late 1930 was still 9 per cent, while all the big banks on average came only to a ratio of 6.2 per cent.[28] The comparatively solid capital resources allowed Deutsche Bank und Disconto-Gesellschaft to handle a large portion of the losses on their own, not depending on government aid to the same degree as the other big banks.

The third accusation was that the banks were attempting, by repurchasing their own shares, to contain the slump and to regain the trust of the public.[29] Here, too, there were significant differences. Between January 1929 and July 1931, the price of Deutsche Bank und Disconto-Gesellschaft's stock fell by 41 per cent. Dresdner Bank suffered a similar drop in price, while Commerz- und Privat-Bank registered losses of 49 per cent and Danat-Bank of 62 per cent. To prevent further slumps, all the big banks acquired their own shares. Though the repurchase of issued shares was not forbidden until September 1931, engaging in this behaviour increased the risk structure of the banks considerably in that it decreased equity.[30] In early 1931 Danat-Bank acquired about half of its share capital, Commerz- und Privat-Bank about the same proportion and Dresdner Bank about one-third of its own shares. At Deutsche Bank und Disconto-Gesellschaft, the amount was only 12 per cent. Over the summer, however, the bank acquired further blocks of shares, albeit to a lesser degree than the other big banks.[31]

The fourth accusation related to the banks' low liquidity. In order to maximise profits, the banks had continuously reduced liquidity in the form of cash and central

Figure 7: Equity ratio of Deutsche Bank (1924–8) and Deutsche Bank und Disconto-Gesellschaft (1929–32).

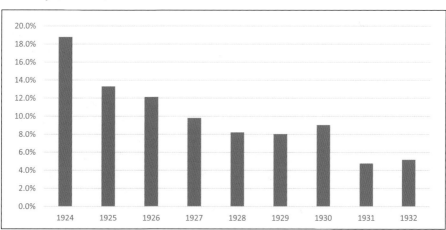

Source: Deutsche Bank, Annual Reports 1924–8; Deutsche Bank und Disconto-Gesellschaft, Annual Reports 1929–32. Equity ratio = share capital and reserves in relation to total assets.

bank balances. There were also differences between the banks in this respect. Whereas Deutsche Bank und Disconto-Gesellschaft's liquidity buffer had been eroded, it was still somewhat higher than that of their competitors.[32] This probably also had to do with the fact that they had lost fewer creditors than the other big banks and also had successfully attracted new customers and savers since 1929.[33] Whereas the liquidity ratio of the big banks was still at 6–7 per cent during the mid-1920s, it had sunk to 1.7 per cent by August 1930.[34] The banks could only deal with this drop because the Reichsbank permitted an unlimited discounting of the bills held by the banks. In an emergency situation, bills could be temporarily cashed in with the Reichsbank in order to increase liquid assets. Aside from the fact that the number of these bills fell significantly during the crisis, the commercial banks were thereby displacing the problem of low liquidity reserves to the Reichsbank. But what would happen if the Reichsbank no longer had enough funds because of an outflow of foreign exchange over an extended period? It was precisely these questions that arose in summer 1931, when the Reichsbank's currency reserves were depleted and it transitioned to discounting the banks' bills only to a limited extent.[35]

The high proportion of foreign deposits, especially from the United States, was the big German banks' fifth structural problem.[36] While most long-term foreign bonds were issued by public enterprises and municipalities,[37] the banks had pushed short-term loans. This division of labour was now becoming fatal for the banks. In 1931, these short-term foreign loans amounted to 15.3 billion RM. By late 1929, over 40 per cent of the big banks' creditors were foreigners, though Deutsche Bank und Disconto-Gesellschaft, with only 38 per cent, was in a somewhat better position than Dresdner Bank and Danat-Bank, 44 and 45 per cent of whose respective creditors were foreigners. The private banks were especially exposed (with 58 per cent foreign creditors), as were Reichs-Kredit-Gesellschaft and Berliner Handels-Gesellschaft (51 and 69 per cent, respectively), which had no domestic branches.[38] From mid-1929 onwards, foreign

Figure 8: Deposits of Deutsche Bank und Disconto-Gesellschaft, 1929–33 (in RM million).

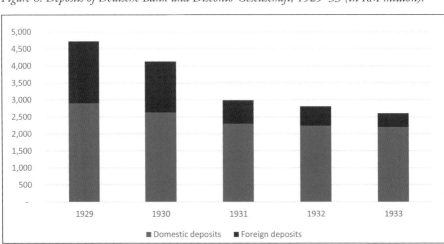

Source: Deutsche Bank und Disconto-Gesellschaft, Annual Report 1933, p. 12.

creditors began to withdraw their deposits from Germany for a variety of reasons.[39] After the downturn on Wall Street, capital had become scarce in the US as well, so many banks and companies began liquidating their assets abroad. Another large withdrawal in the amount of 900 million RM followed in autumn 1930. A good half of this amount was accounted for by Jewish clients who were alarmed by the success of the NSDAP (Nationalsozialistische Deutsche Arbeiterpartei) in the elections of September 1930.[40] Deutsche Bank und Disconto-Gesellschaft could not stop the capital flight, but only try to maintain their own foreign exchange reserves – which they clearly did at the cost of the Reichsbank during the crisis of summer 1931. In June and July 1931, they bought 586 million RM in foreign exchange from the Reichsbank, of which they used 266 million RM to cover short-term foreign debts, the other 320 million RM being used for transactions in the context of capital flight.[41] The complaints of the Reichsbank that the commercial banks had preferential access to the foreign exchange reserves of the central bank are therefore hard to dismiss. Deutsche Bank und Disconto-Gesellschaft clearly made especially heavy use of this opportunity to save their own reserves.

In summer 1931 Deutsche Bank und Disconto-Gesellschaft were in a significantly better position, all things considered, than most of the other big banks. They had expended considerable energy to compensate for loan defaults and other losses without entirely depleting their own capital and liquidity reserves. The lender had already pursued strict cost-saving measures since 1930. In 1931 alone 21 branches and sub-branches were closed or consolidated and the number of employees reduced from 21,600 to 20,051. At the same time, in Deutsche Bank there were linear salary cuts from 1 January 1931 onwards at all levels of the pay scale. The remuneration of directors and board members was also substantially cut (to a total of 1.1 million RM in 1932, and to 593,000 RM in 1933).[42] In 1931 the position of deputy board member was abolished and bonuses for the Supervisory Board were suspended for three years. Shareholders also had to accept considerable setbacks. With dividends already having been cut from 10 to 6 per cent in 1930, from 1931 onwards distributions were suspended for four years. It was not until 1935 that shareholders again received a dividend of 4 per cent.[43]

In view of the consolidation that had already taken place, there was little willingness at Deutsche Bank und Disconto-Gesellschaft to carry the burden of the losses of other banks. This was especially true regarding Danat-Bank, which had barely cut costs and had paid out generous dividends to its shareholders to the last. Its managing partner Jakob Goldschmidt was the *enfant terrible* of the German financial sector.[44] He had begun his career as a broker, and after his entry on to the management board of Nationalbank für Deutschland, which merged in 1922 with Darmstädter Bank to become Danat-Bank, had made a name for himself with his risky financial practices. Hjalmar Schacht withdrew from the leadership of Danat-Bank in 1923 over differences with Goldschmidt, who had become involved in numerous large industrial financing ventures. Goldschmidt himself had held positions on 123 supervisory boards and was involved in the foundation of almost all industrial conglomerates of the 1920s. His demeanour was not particularly diplomatic. It was known in banking circles that Oscar Wassermann and, above all, Georg Solmssen thought little of Goldschmidt and saw him as a competitor of the first rank. Solmssen had complained in early 1930 about

Management Board member Georg Solmssen led the committee meeting of the Central Union of German Banks and Bankers on 27 June 1931 in the context of the emerging banking crisis. Reich Chancellor Brüning and Reichsbank President Luther spoke as well.

Goldschmidt's 'megalomania'. With him one 'could not reach a reasonable agreement until we are ready to go on the attack'.[45]

Beyond such personal differences, over the course of summer 1931 the well-established solidarity among the big German banks eroded. Wassermann had hinted to Reichsbank President Luther that his bank might involve itself in providing financial support to Danat-Bank. He soon dialled back this commitment, however, as Luther was not willing to offer a default guarantee from the Reichsbank. The bank finally agreed to take over Danat-Bank's loans to Hapag and Norddeutscher Lloyd and a few other industrial companies, since it did in fact have a strong interest in securing these loans. However, Wassermann refused to consider either a guarantee of all liabilities or the offer of a merger that Goldschmidt made to him on 8 July 1931. A few days later, first Danat-Bank and shortly thereafter Dresdner Bank and Landesbank der Rheinprovinz had to close their counters and acknowledge their insolvency.[46]

Soon word began to circulate that Wassermann had actively pursued the bank-ruptcy of Danat-Bank in order to get rid of an irritating competitor.[47] Deutsche Bank und Disconto-Gesellschaft was accused of having spread rumours in the Swiss press about the dire straits in which Danat-Bank found itself in order to stoke speculative attacks on the bank. Accusations were also made that the bank had engaged in the short selling of Danat-Bank's shares, contributing to its downfall. Georg Solmssen and Theodor Frank vehemently rejected these accusations. They even invited the German government to audit the bank's accounts in order to dispel any suspicion.[48] Even though this transparency offensive was part of a political strategy in order to prevent further accusations, there is little reason to believe that Deutsche Bank und Disconto-Gesellschaft had purposely worked to bring down Danat-Bank. A further escalation of the situation would not have been in its own interest. At the same time, though, Wassermann was not willing to save Danat-Bank through a joint action.[49] Like representatives of the other big banks, Wassermann pursued a strategy in July of keeping the damage that Danat-Bank's expected insolvency might cause to his own institution to a minimum and preventing the entire financial system from falling into the abyss.

Of course, it was difficult to predict how high the costs of a Danat-Bank bankruptcy would prove to be for Deutsche Bank und Disconto-Gesellschaft as no one had a full overview of Danat-Bank's balance sheets. One advantage was that the bank was not particularly interconnected with the other big banks. Even though the banks frequently co-operated in consortia and sat at the same table on supervisory boards, direct financial business relationships were less pronounced. Deutsche Bank und Disconto-Gesellschaft held few deposits or shares in the other big German banks. Most of its nostro accounts were in foreign banks and served to settle international payments and hold reserves of foreign exchange.[50] Interbank trading in securities or foreign exchange played a minor role. There was therefore reason to hope that Danat-Bank's insolvency would not prove so contagious that it would threaten Deutsche Bank und Disconto-Gesellschaft's own existence.

In conclusion, there is little evidence that moral hazard characterised the behaviour of Deutsche Bank und Disconto-Gesellschaft during the crisis of 1931. According to Isabel Schnabel there was a positive correlation between the size of a bank and its risk exposure. The largest German commercial bank, however, had a better risk structure – measured by equity ratio, liquidity and foreign exchange reserves, credit concentration and share buyback rate – than the other big banks. It had also reacted more quickly to the crisis and had attempted to fend off potential threats of insolvency. In so doing it used all legal options to preserve its own capital. Above all, the bank, by falling back on the reserves of the Reichsbank, saved its own foreign exchange buffer to cover withdrawals of capital abroad.

In light of its relatively strong position, Deutsche Bank und Disconto-Gesellschaft refused to save the stricken Danat-Bank in summer 1931. In this situation, it was still not clear whether the government might decide to save the bank in the end. Under such conditions of uncertainty, it is rather unlikely that the banks relied on a strategy of moral hazard, given that nobody could predict the political reactions.[51]

Restructuring and regulation

In any case, the costs of the crisis for Deutsche Bank und Disconto-Gesellschaft were daunting. Adjusting the balance sheets in February 1932 resulted in losses and write-offs to the sum of 275 million RM in addition to the losses of the two previous years. Whereas the German government took on most of the costs of the merger between Danat-Bank and Dresdner-Bank and put large sums towards the restructuring of Commerz- und Privat-Bank, Landesbank der Rheinprovinz and the savings banks, Deutsche Bank und Disconto-Gesellschaft did not require state assistance. The bank was able to carry out its restructuring mostly on its own due to the fact that it still had high reserves. In addition to its 1931 operating profits of 23.2 million RM, 145.6 million RM from the bank's reserve funds was used to compensate for the losses. The bank made another 108 million RM in paper profits by combining share capital.[52] In addition to this, the bank also held 105 million RM worth of its own shares. Since these could not be sold at a profit on the stock exchange, 33 million RM worth of shares were retired, while allied industrial companies committed to making 22 million RM worth of supporting purchases. Deutsche Golddiskontbank, a subsidiary of the Reichsbank, took on a share package of nearly 50 million RM. After this, Deutsche Bank und Disconto-Gesellschaft's share capital fell from 285 million to 144 million RM, while its reserves dropped from 160 to 25.2 million RM. The bank was nonetheless already buying back its own shares by late 1933, purchases that were financed, inter alia, by the sale of Disconto-Gesellschaft's former headquarters. From the bank's perspective, its 'full private-sector independence' had to be preserved at all costs.[53] Deutsche Golddiskontbank's recently acquired minority share of 35.3 per cent was reduced to 6.5 per cent by spring 1935; by February 1936, Deutsche Bank und Disconto-Gesellschaft was again fully reprivatised.[54]

The bank's decision mostly to eschew state assistance was – in contrast to the other big banks – not motivated by purely commercial calculations. It also related to a domestic situation that in autumn 1931 was menacing for the banks. State Secretary of the Reich Economics Ministry Ernst Trendelenburg spoke of a 'crisis of confidence in capitalism' and former Reich Finance Minister Rudolf Hilferding called for a separation between capital markets and deposits business.[55] Brüning likewise spoke in favour of a break-up of the big banks, which in his opinion had taken on a dominant position in Germany by entering into branch banking. A separation of investment and commercial banking based on the Anglo-Saxon example would have deeply shaken the German banks' business model, however, especially since deposits were becoming increasingly important in light of weakened capital markets. An abandoning of the universal banking system would have been an enormous blow to Deutsche Bank und Disconto-Gesellschaft.

Against this backdrop, the state supervision of banks introduced in autumn 1931 was not the worst-case scenario, even though it had far-reaching consequences. The standstill agreement of 1 September 1931 – which Gustaf Schlieper, the Deutsche Bank board member responsible for foreign business, had negotiated on behalf of the Reichsbank – prevented

Gustaf Schlieper (1880–1937) belonged to the top management of Disconto-Gesellschaft from 1914 onwards and was on the Management Board of the merged bank beginning in 1929. He became known to a wider audience starting in 1931 as the head of the German delegation in the standstill agreement negotiations with foreign creditors.

a further outflow of foreign capital. However, this agreement also limited the access of German banks to international capital markets.[56] The emergency decree significantly restricted foreign exchange transactions – and thereby the bank's options for acting independently abroad. Deutsche Bank und Disconto-Gesellschaft's business abroad, already severely limited, practically came to a halt. The big banks were increasingly sidelined into an advisory role in helping their clients in the complicated arrangement of transactions under foreign exchange controls.

Over the course of the banking crisis, the state established new financing institutions intended to re-establish payment transactions. The Akzept- und Garantiebank was created in July 1931 to provide the banks with short-term liquidity. Deutsche Bank und Disconto-Gesellschaft did not make use of this refinancing facility. Nor did it take advantage of the option of transferring holdings in restructured industrial companies to the Deutsches Finanzierungsinstitut AG (Finag).[57] The less state support the bank made use of, the more easily it could avoid state-imposed constraints and preserve its status as a private company.

The regulation of the banks had not, in fact, limited the bank's business operations as much as had been feared. The Reich Commissioner of Banks, whose position had been instituted on 19 September 1931 by emergency decree, carried out his supervisory role only to a limited extent. It was advantageous for the banks that the German government focused in the autumn of 1931 on immediate rescue measures and announced a political assessment of the crisis in the form of an investigation of the banks. The establishment of this commission was delayed, however, due to political turbulence, and it was not set up until summer 1933, by which time the banks had stabilised somewhat. That the investigative committee, which included the Nazi economic ideologue and Reich Economics Ministry State Secretary Gottfried Feder, did not take more decisive action against the banks was thanks not least to Hjalmar Schacht, who again became President of the Reichsbank in March 1933. Schacht was less critical of the banks than his predecessor Hans Luther and belonged to the more business-oriented wing of the Third Reich. In April 1933, he took the initiative and launched the long-planned investigation. He ensured that the committee was filled mostly with experts from the Reichsbank and academia, with only a few representatives of the NSDAP. Though Wilhelm Keppler, the commissioner for economic affairs in the Reich Chancellery, and Gottfried Feder took part in the meetings, they played only secondary roles in the discussions. Keppler demanded a decentralisation of the banks and restructuring along the lines of the leader principle (*Führerprinzip*), while Feder reiterated his criticism of the private-sector banks and the economic system. According to Feder, the system, like 'a critically ill body', had to 'receive a camphor injection, as it were, through state-imposed measures'.[58] Schacht conceded that there were 'deficiencies in our banking system' that had to be fixed by government regulations; however, he argued that it was important at the same time to 'clearly establish the borders between the two elements'. A 'confused and conflict-ridden co-operation between the private and public sectors', according to Schacht, would necessarily 'lead to dangerous disruptions'.[59]

Schacht had ensured that Deutsche Bank und Disconto-Gesellschaft, with Franz Urbig as Chairman of the Supervisory Board and Eduard Mosler and Hans Rummel as members of the Management Board, had three representatives in the hearings. Whereas Urbig kept a low profile, Eduard Mosler vigorously defended the role the bank had played in summer 1931. In particular, he rejected the claim that the banks should collectively bear liability for the mistakes of individual institutions.[60] Rummel also served as an expert for financial reporting on the committee, preparing two written reports on the banks' profitability problems.[61] After months of international discussions with numerous subject area experts that resulted in a three-volume publication, the investigation committee came to the conclusion that, despite all its missteps and defects, the banking system was basically sound. A break-up of the banks was thus off the table, and the numerous emergency measures of 1931 and 1932 were brought together into a unified legal framework.

While the Reich Credit Law (*Reichsgesetz über das Kreditwesen*, KWG) of 5 December 1934 further strengthened state supervision of banks, it did not lead to a fundamental, or even Nazi-specific, reordering of the German financial sector.[62] It is best characterised, according to Christopher Kopper, as 'a long-overdue modernisation, independent of the system […] which primarily responded to the crisis of 1931'.[63] In comparison to bank regulation in the United States or Italy, where the state engaged in wide-ranging interventions in the financial system, the KWG was a strengthening of existing controls. For example, special safeguards for savings deposits were introduced, accounting rules were tightened and auditing requirements were established for loans of more than 5,000 RM. A Supervisory Office for Credit (*Aufsichtsamt für das Kreditwesen*) was set up at the Reichsbank and given comprehensive auditing rights over the banks. The law also required that banks maintain reserve and liquidity minimums, a requirement that was not upheld in the years that followed because the requirements themselves were not further defined.[64] The law also introduced the regulation of interest

In the hearings of the banking investigation convened by Reichsbank President Hjalmar Schacht in 1933, Deutsche Bank und Disconto-Gesellschaft was represented by (from left) Supervisory Board Chairman Franz Urbig (1864–1944) and members of the Management Board Eduard Mosler (1873–1939) and Hans Rummel (1882–1964).

rates, thereby sanctioning a long-existing practice. The savings banks were now included in the 'interest rate cartel'. One of the long-term consequences of the law was that the regulatory divide between the savings and the co-operative banks on the one side and the credit banks on the other was narrowed.

In addition to the new supervisory office, the law named Friedrich Ernst, who had been appointed banking supervisor in September 1931, Reich Credit Commissioner, and gave him wide-ranging powers. All banks were required to hold an operating licence from the Reich Commissioner. His decisions had to be put into effect immediately and could not be legally contested. The commissioner also had significant sanctioning authority over the banks in that he was able to impose fines or even rescind banks' licences for not following requirements. Rescinding a licence required no great justification and could occur merely because the leadership of a credit institution was determined to be 'not honourable' or 'not sufficiently trained' or the organisation seemed 'unnecessary with reference to local or macroeconomic needs'.[65]

In practice, rigid sanctions such as these were seldom enforced. This was partly because Reich Commissioner Friedrich Ernst – an administrative lawyer who had begun his career in 1919 in the Prussian Ministry of Trade – was a pragmatist.[66] Despite not having joined the NSDAP, Ernst was able to continue his career in 1933 thanks to Schacht's protection. When the Reich Commission was abolished in 1939 and banking supervision was transferred to the Reich Supervisory Office for Credit under the control of the Reich Economics Ministry, Ernst served as Reich Commissioner for Enemy Property (*Reichskommissar für das feindliche Vermögen*) for two years, after which he switched to the proprietorship of the bank Delbrück Schickler & Co. in 1941. Ernst, like Schacht, was an important defender of the commercial banks and prevented excessive political involvement in the structure of the banking system. No one could foresee, however, whether the instruments created through the KWG would eventually be used against the banks.

In addition to the KWG, another law was passed in the aftermath of the banking crisis which would have long-term consequences for the big banks: the German Stock Corporation Act (*Aktiengesetz*) of 1937. This law took up substantial elements of the emergency decrees of 1931 and moulded them into a legal framework that would remain in force until the law was amended in 1965. Inter alia, its provisions strengthened the position of the management board with respect to shareholder meetings and, along the lines of the leadership principle, gave the chief executive or general director considerable authority. The supervisory board could no longer become involved in operational matters, but instead was given stronger supervisory powers.[67]

How did Deutsche Bank react to the new regulations introduced after the banking crisis? Even though the legal requirements of the KWG and the Stock Corporation Act were mostly aimed at better regulating accounting and capital market requirements, they also led to fundamental changes in corporate governance. While the number of members of its Supervisory Board was reduced according to the new rules, the Management Board's collegial model was not abandoned, even though this had been the intention of the law. The prevailing view at the bank was that the traditionally equitable positions and division of duties on the board level had proven themselves successful and that the Spokesman would only play an enhanced role in representing the bank.[68]

For one, the bank significantly expanded its internal accounting system, a step in which Hans Rummel played a decisive role. This was intended not only to adapt the bank's operations to the new statutory accounting rules, but also to establish a more efficient internal controlling system. Rummel was responsible on the Management Board for accountancy and organisation. Second, the branch and credit office was expanded and the Supervisory Board was tasked with carrying out special audits of all major loans of 1 million RM or more. The body responsible for this was the Supervisory Board's credit committee, which had been given more authority with regard to strategic planning in general. The Supervisory Board was considerably reduced in size in accordance with the amended Stock Corporation Law.[69] Third, economic experts were to be involved to a greater degree in order to predict economic crises and market risks for the bank. However, political considerations seem to have played a role in this decision as well. By making the debate more objective, the bank hoped to counterbalance the economic ideas of 'extremists of various tendencies'. In autumn 1930, Solmssen initiated the idea of 'starting up a movement to call the German economics profession into action in order to pick apart the economic aspects of the National Socialist programme'.[70] Nothing came of these plans, so the bank established its own 'scientific advisory board' led by the Hungarian monetary policy expert Melchior Palyi. Palyi had been teaching at the Commercial College (*Handelshochschule*) of Berlin and had been the director of the Berlin Institute for Currency Research (*Berliner Institut für Währungsforschung*) since 1931. While the scientific advisory board does appear to have played a very active role, Palyi had to leave his post in 1933 due to his Jewish heritage and emigrate to the United States, where he was able to continue his academic career.

Moreover, the economics department of the bank gained importance by transforming the so-called Archives of both Deutsche Bank and Disconto-Gesellschaft into a powerful division.[71] At Deutsche Bank, this department had originally collected the annual reports of other banks and companies and extensive analyses of the business press. It was also responsible for the bank's public relations and for preparing its annual reports until the press department was created. This department gained in status after the economic and banking crisis; it now included five economists, two editors and one statistician. While the department remained responsible for documentation, the company library and interest rate and commodity price reporting, it was also given more economic assignments. It was led by Ernst Wilhelm Schmidt, an economist with a doctorate, who prepared comprehensive reports on economic matters for the Management Board, many of which took up prognostications of the market and economic research institutes.[72] Unlike the later 'chief economists', Schmidt served a more internal role, despite the fact that he also had many contacts in academia.

While the banking crisis did not lead to a comprehensive reform of the bank, it did cause readjustments in its internal control structures and led to an increased incorporation of economic expertise. As in economic policy, the Great Depression had led to greater professionalisation and scientific sophistication in the banking sector as well. Whether this would actually help to avoid further crises could, of course, not yet be seen. However, it was clear that political risks were now of much more concern for the bank than those that emerged from its everyday business.

2. Deutsche Bank under National Socialism

From the crisis of 1931 onwards, private-sector banks were under great pressure to justify themselves to the public; this pressure intensified significantly after 30 January 1933. From the perspective of Deutsche Bank und Disconto-Gesellschaft, Hitler's 'seizure of power' posed new risks. Politically, the bank was particularly exposed due to the fact that it had traditionally had strong international networks and that many of its leading employees were of a Jewish background. Nor did the management, with the exception of Emil Georg von Stauß, have any connection to the leading representatives of the NSDAP. As far as can be determined, most of the other members of the Management Board favoured either the conservative wing of the German People's Party (*Deutsche Volkspartei*, DVP) or the moderate faction of the German National People's Party (*Deutschnationale Volkspartei*, DNVP). They presumably favoured a business-friendly, politically conservative government with a strong executive, without giving up the solid ground of the constitution.[73] Solmssen, for example, was one of the founders of the Conservative People's Party (*Konservative Volkspartei*), which had broken off from the DNVP in 1930 because it rejected Alfred Hugenberg's anti-republican trajectory. After the electoral success of the NSDAP in autumn 1930, Solmssen had called a number of his colleagues to 'create a front against the dangers that the National Socialist program brings. This reaches across economic, and especially financial matters in such a tense, unsophisticated, and inflammatory manner that, in my opinion, something must happen.'[74]

Solmssen and Wassermann strongly supported Hindenburg for Reich President and Franz von Papen for Reich Chancellor in the election of 1932.[75] Though there is no extant evidence, most of the members of the Management Board must have looked at Hitler's takeover of power on 30 January 1933 with great scepticism. From the bank's perspective, it was not at all clear how the National Socialists would act with regard to the private-sector banks. The NSDAP's smear campaigns, which linked traditional anti-Semitic accusations of usury with conspiracy theories about 'global Jewish finance capital', implied scathing criticism of the big banks. For private and commercial banks whose top leadership included individuals of Jewish heritage, the situation was especially serious. At Deutsche Bank und Disconto-Gesellschaft alone, three of the seven members of the Management Board – Solmssen, Wassermann and Frank – were Jewish according to Nazi racial ideology.

Georg Solmssen (1869–1957) came from one of the leading German-Jewish banking families. He had pursued a career at Disconto-Gesellschaft and prepared the merger with Deutsche Bank. He was on the Management Board of the merged bank from 1929 until 1934 and was Spokesman of the Management Board during the final months of his tenure.

Forcing out the Jewish bankers

In April 1933 there was concerted action throughout Germany against Jewish account holders. Local NSDAP groups put pressure on bank managers to divulge the names of their Jewish clients and to lock their accounts. Wassermann attempted, through his connections with the Catholic Church, to intervene with Reich President Hindenburg to counteract these actions, but without success.[76] This campaign did not end until Reichsbank President Hjalmar Schacht intervened. Schacht also hindered all attempts by Reich Economics Minister Hugenberg to put the credit sector under rigid state control. When Schacht himself took on the position of Reich Economics Minister in August 1934, the radical bank critics increasingly lost influence. Gottfried Feder, for instance, had to leave his position as State Secretary in the Reich Economics Ministry in December 1934. Schacht had the support of Hermann Göring, who likewise did not believe that the banks should be placed under full state control, being of the opinion that private-sector banks could be more efficiently be harnessed to further the economic goals of the regime.[77]

Schacht, whom Hitler granted the unofficial function of general plenipotentiary for credit, monetary and banking policy, prevented the dissolution of the banks, but at the same time insisted that they dismiss their Jewish management personnel. For this reason, Solmssen had to resign as spokesman of the Central Union of German Banks and Bankers (*Centralverband des Deutschen Bank- und Bankiergewerbes*) in April 1933. His successor was Otto Christian Fischer of the Reichs-Kredit-Gesellschaft. Solmssen and other Jewish bankers such as Max Warburg and Paul von Mendelssohn-Bartholdy could still be involved on the board committee of the association, but in February 1934 the union was formally dissolved. Its members were shortly thereafter forced to gather in the Private Banking Group (*Wirtschaftsgruppe Privates Bankgewerbe*), which formed a sub-unit of the Reich Group Banks (*Reichsgruppe Banken*).[78] Within the Reich Group, Deutsche Bank und Disconto-Gesellschaft was no longer prominently represented. Schacht appointed Fischer the leader of the Reich Group, while Friedrich Reinhart from Commerz- und Privat-Bank took over the leadership of the Economic Group Private Banks. Both Fischer and Reinhart were believers in National Socialist policy and had strong connections in the party and the SS, though they resisted a dissolution of private-sector banks.[79]

At Deutsche Bank und Disconto-Gesellschaft, the reaction to the anti-Semitic slogans of the NSDAP were 'quite hasty and speedily obedient' – there was a rapid and quiet separation from the Jewish bankers.[80] Oscar Wassermann, as Spokesman of the Management Board, was particularly exposed. Wassermann was particularly hated in the NSDAP for his role in the banking crisis and for his long involvement in Zionist causes. However, it would also prove to be the case that even within his own bank Wassermann had enemies. After the Nazis came to power, old conflicts stemming from the conflicting loyalties of associates of Disconto-Gesellschaft and Deutsche Bank were resurrected. This seems to have been less for political reasons, though the board members of Disconto-Gesellschaft were a little more right-leaning than the former board members of Deutsche Bank.[81] Personal rivalries seem to have been the decisive factor. Franz Urbig, the co-chairman of the Supervisory Board, played an important role in the expulsion of Wassermann and the other Jewish bankers. He used the situation to criticise not just Wassermann, but also Deutsche Bank's collegial system, which, he claimed, had given the individual board members too many powers and had been responsible for many of the losses in the previous years.[82] This showed once again that the merger of the two banks with their quite different cultures had had significant after effects.

In the dismissal of the Jewish board members, the bank attempted to avoid the impression that it had caved in to the anti-Semitic pressures of the NSDAP; after all, the bank still had many Jewish clients. Nor did anyone know at this point how much longer Hitler would be in power. In January 1934, Urbig wrote to a colleague on the Supervisory Board:

> Other times can come, and we must avoid the possibility of the reproach being made at any time that the bank's decision-making body or its representatives played a role in making the non-Aryan members of the Management Board leave.[83]

Though a press statement stressed that Wassermann would not be resigning until the end of 1933 and referenced, in this context, the fact that he would soon reach the retirement cutoff of 65 years in any case, the Spokesman of the Management Board was no longer active at the bank by May and was not appointed to the Supervisory Board either. He left the bank a broken man and died in September 1934.[84] The other Jewish board members also had to leave their posts. Theodor Frank served only in the honorary role of deputy chairman of the Berlin-Brandenburg advisory council until he emigrated in 1936. Solmssen, who had already converted to Protestantism at the turn of the century, was able to hold out a little longer. After serving as Wassermann's successor as Spokesman, he resigned from the Management Board in mid-1934 after reaching retirement age and switched to the Supervisory Board before emigrating to Switzerland in 1938. In internal discussions, he had expressed his deep-seated pessimism about the future of the Jewish economic elite as early as April 1933: 'I fear,' he wrote to Supervisory Board chairman Franz Urbig, 'that we are only at the beginning of a conscious and planned development, which is aimed at the indiscriminate economic and moral destruction of all members of the Jewish race living in Germany.'[85] In light of these fears, Solmssen submitted a proposal to Göring's press officer Martin Sommerfeldt of establishing a national council that

Theodor Frank (1871–1953) came from Disconto-Gesellschaft and was in charge of the trading business on the Management Board of the merged establishment. Like Oscar Wassermann and Georg Solmssen, he was forced to resign from the Management Board after the Nazis took power due to his Jewish heritage.

would 'examine all complaints against Jews and organise the emigration of those who prove to be harmful or undesirable'.[86]

The bank's personnel decisions prove the opportunism that took place after 30 January 1933 in many companies. There is no evidence that the bank's leadership resisted the Nazi regime or attempted to avoid the new rules. The restructuring of the bank was more than a pure external adaption to the new political circumstances. By no means did the bank swim 'against the political tide' after 1933, as the bank's former chronicler Fritz Seidenzahl once put it.[87] The frequently employed term 'entanglement' (*Verstrickung*)[88] is likewise highly euphemistic and implies a passive role and as such does not appropriately express the proactive nature of Deutsche Bank's actions during the Third Reich.[89]

Though the bank neither actively supported nor seems to have desired the National Socialist seizure of power, over the years it became more and more an important pillar of the Nazi economic system.[90] In the process, not only did the bank reorganise its Management Board, it also increasingly collaborated with the regime in its business operations, as will be shown later. At the same time, there was no complete political and economic 'co-ordination' (*Gleichschaltung*). Despite the dismissal of Jewish personnel and the promotion of politically advantageous candidates, a full-scale purge or even internal restructuring of the bank did not take place. The organisational form of the bank remained mostly unchanged, and it could still make its business decisions autonomously, even if the pressure to conform and the degree of Nazi domination throughout state and society was growing. Paradoxically, the growing demands of the Nazi armament economy created new room for manoeuvre for the bank. The bank operated according to a different logic, which manifested itself not least in a distinctive time horizon: whereas the regime's political leadership, the farther the war progressed, barely planned for the future (despite its rhetoric about the 'thousand-year Reich'), the bank carried out its transactions and acquisitions with a longer-term perspective and increasingly attempted to separate its own survival from the current political and economic situation.

The fact that Deutsche Bank und Disconto-Gesellschaft's upper management lacked good connections in Nazi circles turned out to be an enormous disadvantage after 1933. Whereas banks like Dresdner Bank had strong contacts in the NSDAP and the SS, at Deutsche Bank und Disconto-Gesellschaft only Emil Georg von Stauß had strong political ties. However, Stauß at that time served only on the bank's Supervisory Board. He kept an office in the Berlin headquarters, however, and represented the bank on the supervisory boards of numerous industrial companies. In November 1933, he ran successfully for the German parliament, became a guest of the NSDAP parliamentary group and was elected vice-president of the Reichstag. In 1934, Göring appointed him Prussian state councillor. Though Stauß never joined the NSDAP, he had good connections with leading Nazi politicians and was thus an important intermediary for Deutsche Bank until his death in 1942.[91]

The bank looked for further opportunities to build its networks with the regime. The Supervisory Board, which had been decimated after the banking crisis, was expanded again in 1933: numbering only 16 in 1933, by 1935 it had grown again to 35. Businessmen loyal to the Nazis, such as the Hamburg cigarette manufacturer

Philipp Reemtsma, or Albert Pietzsch, the head of the Reich Economic Chamber, were targeted for inclusion on the board. Two members of the National Socialist Factory Cell Organisation (*Nationalsozialistische Betriebszellenorganisation*, NSBO) were also given seats on the Supervisory Board.

After the Nazi seizure of power, the change in personnel on the Management Board, which had already begun with the dismissals of Stauß, Fehr and Kehl during the banking crisis, was continued. However, the bank initially avoided hiring in a politically opportunistic manner from outside the bank, holding instead to its established principle of recruiting from within. In addition to Solmssen, Frank and Wassermann, Alfred Blinzig resigned in 1934 due to old age, and Peter Brunswig transitioned to the Düsseldorf bank Trinkaus in 1934. With the exceptions of Gustaf Schlieper and Eduard Mosler, the entire Management Board was replaced over the course of 1933 and 1934: Karl Ernst Sippell took over the legal and personnel departments, Fritz Wintermantel the management of the Berlin headquarters and Hans Rummel organisation and accounting. Oswald Rösler, who would play an important role in the acquisition of numerous Eastern European banks and companies from the late 1930s onwards, also joined the Management Board. Karl Kimmich, who had worked for A. Schaaffhausen'scher Bankverein until 1929 and had taken on various special assignments and reconstructions after the merger, assumed responsibility for large segments of the business with

A parade of Berlin companies on 1 May 1934: At the head of the 'Betriebsgemeinschaft Deutsche Bank und Disconto-Gesellschaft' (Works Community of Deutsche Bank und Disconto-Gesellschaft), in civilian clothing, marches Karl Ernst Sippell, who was responsible for personnel on the Management Board from 1933 onwards.

industrial clients. Kimmich was the only new member of the Management Board who was said to be close with the NSDAP; he had family connections to the Nazi leadership: his brother was married to Joseph Goebbels's youngest sister. He also became chairman of the Reichsbank's Credit Committee. After Kimmich resigned from his post for health reasons in spring 1942, he took over the chairmanship of the Supervisory Board, which he held until his death. Kimmich was one of the central figures in the widespread Aryanisation measures that began in 1936.

The spokesman role was filled from 1934 onwards by Eduard Mosler, who had joined Disconto-Gesellschaft in 1911 and had been in charge of stock market transactions there. He was also considered an expert on rationalisation. Mosler was vulnerable to anti-Semitic attack due to his mother's Jewish heritage; he nonetheless continued to serve as Spokesman of the Management Board until 1939 and afterwards was elected chairman of the Supervisory Board of the bank shortly before his death.[92]

The replacement of almost the entire Management Board around 1933 was the largest reshuffle in the bank's upper management since its founding. One effect of this transformation was that the management from the former Disconto-Gesellschaft gained a stronger position. This group benefited from the fact that they had not become as heavily involved in scandals and business mistakes, in contrast to many members of the Management Board of Deutsche Bank.

However, the bank's personnel policy also changed in another respect. With the appointment of Karl Ritter von Halt and Hermann J. Abs in 1938, the principle of internal careers, which had been mostly upheld since the turn of the century, came to an end. This also had consequences for the social composition of its management. Many new board members did not have an upper-middle-class background, coming instead from more humble origins. Karl Kimmich's father was an art teacher, Fritz Wintermantel's a postman and Hans Rummel's a brewer, while Oswald Rösler and Karl Ritter von Halt came from craftsman families. None of the eight members of the Management Board of 1939 had a business background or came from a banking family. However, all had the relevant training. With the exception of Karl Ernst Sippell and Johannes Kiehl, both of whom held doctorates in law, all had completed bank apprenticeships and worked for many years in finance.[93] Despite the political concessions that were granted to the Nazi regime, a professional background in banking was a prerequisite for a successful career.

Jewish employees were forced out of not only the Management Board, but many other leadership positions at the Berlin headquarters and the branches from 1933 onwards. This often occurred by means of early retirement. Whereas employees who had been associated with the company for more than 10 years received a pension, younger employees were let go without retirement. Another wave of purges followed the passage of the Nuremberg Laws in 1935, affecting mid- and low-level employees as well.[94] Though no reliable statistics are available, by late 1938 it seems most likely that, with only a few exceptions, all the bank's Jewish employees had been dismissed.[95] This was caused not only by pressure from the outside; it also came from inside the bank. By late 1932, by some estimates 10 per cent of the bank's employees were members of the NSDAP.[96] After 30 January 1933, this percentage seems to have further increased significantly. The NSBO representative Franz Hertel frequently intervened with the bank leadership

Robert Ley, the head of the German Labour Front (Deutsche Arbeitsfront), visited the Berlin headquarters of Deutsche Bank und Disconto-Gesellschaft on 24 October 1934; behind him stands Factory Cell chairman Franz Hertel.

to pressure it to crack down on Jewish employees and ensure that the bank continued to pursue the ideal of a National Socialist 'works community' (*Betriebsgemeinschaft*). He demanded that a National Socialist orientation be of paramount importance in hiring and promotion decisions. Hertel claimed that preference had to be given to the 'old fighters' of the NSDAP.

In addition to the political pressure from the party and the NSBO, there also seem to have been numerous denunciations from employees themselves against Jewish co-workers or political opponents. In reaction to the continued attacks, in 1935 the bank hired Karl Ritter von Halt, a prominent National Socialist and sports official, to be director of the Berlin headquarters.[97] Halt had completed his professional training at Deutsche Bank and had served as head of personnel for many years at the Munich bank H. Aufhäuser. He took on this same role at Deutsche Bank. Due to his political background and connections, Halt had enough authority to counter Hertel and the NSBO's demands, being no friend of the National Socialist trade union wing. After long negotiations with the German Labour Front (*Deutsche Arbeitsfront*, DAF) he was able to bring about the dismissal of Franz Hertel in 1936. In other situations, as well, the bank was able to force out leaders of the NSBO.[98] In general, Halt responded cautiously to demands from the party that the bank protect the old fighters and give them good positions.[99] He also rigorously cracked down on established party and SA members if it was in the best interests of the bank.[100] Otherwise, there is little evidence that Halt became involved in the bank's business policies or was on a collision course with other members of the Management Board. However, he did maintain contacts with the top Nazi leadership, was part of the 'Himmler Circle of Friends' (*Freundeskreis Himmler*) and made financial contributions in the bank's name to a special fund that Himmler could use for his own purposes.[101]

The bank also appointed other NSDAP members to the Management Board, but not until war had broken out. In May 1943, Robert Frowein, the head of the Frankfurt branch, was promoted to the board, where he was responsible primarily for the offices and business in Silesia. In September 1943, Heinrich Hunke, a prominent Nazi economic ideologue, was co-opted by the Management Board. Hunke had been a member of the NSDAP since 1928 and had acted in a variety of roles since 1933, serving inter alia as honorary professor on the military engineering faculty of the Technical University (TU) of Berlin and as

Karl Ritter von Halt (1891–1964) became a director at headquarters in 1935 and a member of the Management Board of Deutsche Bank three years later. As an NSDAP party member and high-ranking sports functionary, he had good contacts with the top leadership of the Nazi party and state.

president of the Advertising Council for the German Economy (*Werberat der deutschen Wirtschaft*). He was made leader of the foreign department of Goebbels' propaganda ministry in 1941, and began promoting the concept of a European continental economic zone (*Großraumwirtschaft*) under German rule. Though Hunke had been in favour of nationalising the big banks in 1934 and was a member of the banking committee of the Party Chancellery of the NSDAP, Abs and Rösler had begun attempting to win him over to the bank by 1942. It is possible that in doing so they wanted to deflect the NSDAP's attacks on private-sector banks, which had been increasing since 1942. In any case, Hunke only began working for the bank in April 1944 and did not have a specific area of responsibility on the Management Board. He therefore does not seem to have had a major influence over the bank's strategic decisions.[102]

Party members could also increasingly be found in the top positions of the sub-branches of the bank. By the end of the war, according to an internal assessment, 44 of the bank's 84 branch directors were members of the NSDAP, although all seem to have joined the party after 1933.[103] It does not seem likely that headquarters put pressure on the branch directors to join the party. Rather, in most cases they joined due to the intervention of the local NSDAP offices.[104] On the other hand, there were also examples of resistance and criticism of the Nazi regime in the bank, which some paid for with their lives. Hermann Koehler, the director of the Stuttgart branch, was executed on 8 November 1943 because of disparaging remarks he had made about the regime on a train. Koehler was denounced by the director of another bank who was travelling with him and was sentenced to death by the People's Court (*Volksgerichtshof*) in Berlin. The same fate befell Georg Miethe, the director of the Hindenburg branch, whose secretary reported him to the Gestapo in August 1943 for making statements critical of the regime. In both cases the leadership of the bank attempted to intervene with the political leadership to prevent execution, without success.[105] One year later, Management Board Spokesman Oswald Rösler narrowly avoided conviction. He had been arrested in September 1944 for supposed knowledge of the failed assassination attempt on Hitler of 20 July 1944, but was released in November 1944 by the People's Court due to a lack of evidence, on the condition that he resign from all of his offices.[106] Rösler did in fact know about the assassination plans through the Leipzig businessman Walter Cramer. Rösler, along with Hermann J. Abs and Clemens Plassmann, were the Catholics on the Management Board, thus belonging to a group which the party already viewed with suspicion.

Banking in the Nazi economic boom

How did Deutsche Bank und Disconto-Gesellschaft deal with the political and economic changes that took place after Hitler acquired power in January 1933? How did the bank assess the consequences of the 'National Socialist revolution' in terms of its own business activities? In light of the constant risk of reprisals, few leading representatives of the bank openly expressed their opinions about the Nazi regime. An internal report of May 1933 from Ernst Wilhelm Schmidt, the head of the Economics Department, is one of the few extant documents that give insight into the reasoning of bank managers.[107] Most had little sympathy for National Socialism, but hoped that the political and economic situation would stabilise after Hitler's seizure of power. Schmidt saw advantages over the 'ever more hotly contested domestic political power battles' of the late years of the Weimar Republic, which had paralysed the economy. He thought a certain advantage could be gained if the economy did not 'ignore' the new regime's 'plea for trust'.[108]

> It would be a misjudgement of the magnitude of political events in recent weeks and months to harbour serious doubts about the future because of individual disturbances in economic life caused by the regime change. Large political upheavals, which are justifiably referred to as revolutions, are always followed in history by a period of a certain irregularity. This irregularity has manifested itself in the German economy in the form of a series of arbitrary interventions, which have in some instances set off major uncertainty and nervousness [...] Today we seem to be past this first stage of uncertainty. The government has made it unmistakably clear that it will not be undertaking boundless and adventurous experiments in the field of economic policy or in monetary or trade policy and that it not only will not seek to hinder the development of private initiatives, but even views these initiatives as a quintessential element in the reconstruction of our economy.[109]

Like many other political observers, Schmidt was convinced of the fact that the radical forces within the NSDAP would quickly be disempowered and that a dictatorship on the model of Italian fascism would result. In April 1933, Schmidt prepared a longer report on the 'Economic Policies of Italian Fascism'.[110] This report included a positive appraisal of fascist Italy, which had overcome political infighting and retained a 'private capitalist economic model' within its co-operative order. According to Schmidt, it was 'unmistakable that the German National Socialists' position is substantially influenced by the Italian model'. In his view, this included not just 'similar worldviews' but also the 'details of political actions, means of fighting, and methods of fighting'. He also expected 'certain tendencies towards Mussolini's example' in economic policy.[111]

Like many observers, Schmidt underestimated National Socialism's ideological radicalism and capacity for violence.[112] In 1933, however, it was vital that the bank attempted to adapt to the new political circumstances as quickly as possible. Just two years since the great banking crisis, business had by no means been consolidated. Profits were completely devoted to write-offs and the repurchase of Golddiskontbank's shares until 1934. Rapid reprivatisation was important to the bank, since the state held a blocking minority through the shares held by Golddiskontbank. In 1934 and 1935, the bank once again reduced salaries, especially those of management personnel.[113] In 1935, the bank had small net profits again for the first time to the amount of 5.3 million RM and could pay out a dividend of 4 per cent. The improved economic situation could also be seen in deposits, which increased again for the first time in 1935. This was due solely to the increase in domestic creditors. Foreign deposits went down between 1932 and 1936 from 402 to 301 million RM and by then represented only 11 per cent of all deposits. These were mostly the blocked funds of foreigners, which fell under the stipulations of the standstill agreement of 1931, which had been extended multiple times.

Figure 9: Income statement of Deutsche Bank 1932–44 (in RM million).

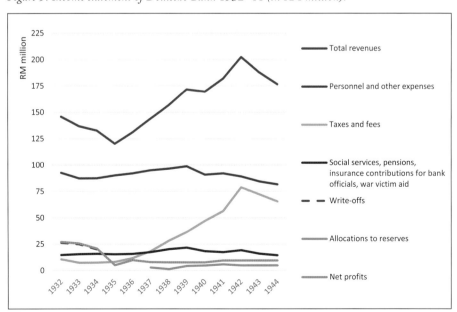

Source: Deutsche Bank, Annual Reports 1933–44.

Figure 10: Composition of income of Deutsche Bank, 1932–44 (in RM million).

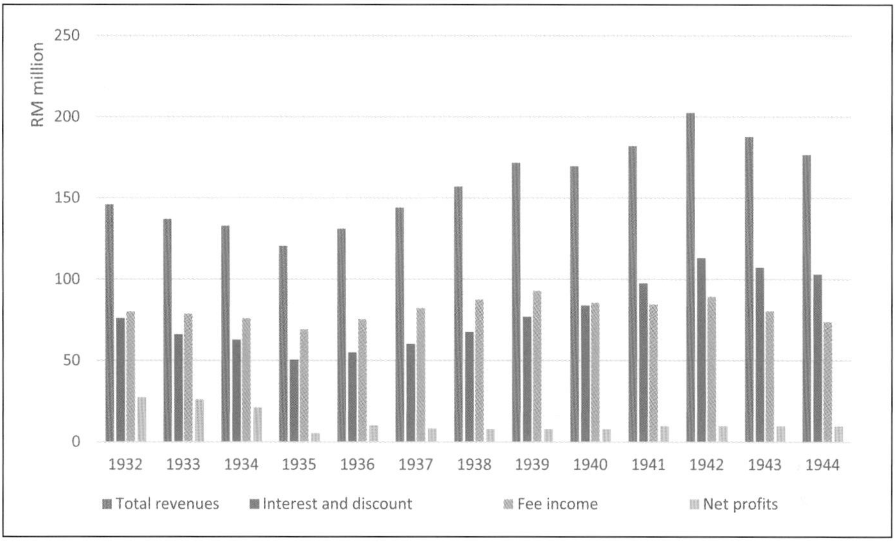

Source: Deutsche Bank, Annual Reports 1933–44.

Deutsche Bank also profited from the economic upswing that had been set off in 1935 by the regime's growing expenditure on armaments. Looking at the bank's revenues (Figure 10), a significant rise is noticeable between 1935 and 1942. In the final years of the war, earnings collapsed again, however, though the published balance sheets for this period were no longer particularly informative and earnings might not have been fully disclosed. It is interesting to note that income from fees, interest and bills of exchange showed a similar increase at the beginning of the war. Commissions stagnated from 1940, however, whereas interest income continued to grow. Though the bank's total revenues were satisfactory, net profits looked far worse. Overall profits stagnated at a very low level during the Third Reich, much lower even than they had been at the height of the banking crisis. Whereas the bank had average profits between 1929 and 1933 of 25.2 million RM per year (some of which went towards write-offs), this had gone down to 5 million RM by 1935 and only recovered slightly after that. With the exception of 1936, profits were consistently well under 10 million RM per year.

How can this be explained? Irrespective of possible distortions of the balance sheet, the allocations to reserves played a particular role – these reserve contributions amounted to approximately 5 million RM per year starting in the late 1930s and took up a portion of net profits. However, the bank's contributions to its reserves were small in comparison to its total assets, and the bank's equity ratio sank between 1933 and 1944 from 5.1 to 2.2 per cent. By involving the banks in the state's expansion of credit and the resultant inflating of the balance sheet, the legal reserve requirements of the KWG were contradicted. With its growing financing demands, the Nazi state, instead of making the banks more secure, increasingly forced them to shrink their capital and their reserves in proportion to their total assets.[114]

Unlike in the 1920s, the lag in profits was not due to higher operating costs for the bank. The bank's expenditures on social welfare contributions and salaries even went down. The main cause for the weak development of net profits was the bank's high tax burden. Due to a war surcharge, the corporate income tax increased in 1941 from 25 per cent to a nominal rate of 50 per cent. An excess income tax of 15 per cent was also introduced on the increases in profit that the bank achieved in 1938 over those of 1937, and in late 1939 the Reich Commissioner for Pricing introduced a transfer of profits of 20 to 30 per cent of added profits. Since opportunities for write-offs were also limited, companies' tax burdens – in particular those of the large joint-stock companies – increased, on average, to more than 70 per cent.[115] As can be seen in Figure 9, the bank's taxes and duties increased by a factor of 10 between 1933 and 1943, with the result that its pre-tax profits were almost completely skimmed off by the regime.

Deutsche Bank's business development during the Third Reich presents an ambivalent picture. Whereas total assets, turnover and earnings increased significantly from the mid-1930s, the bank's profits stagnated. The bank employees' salaries and social welfare benefits also stayed low. Though the DAF and the NSBO frequently called for higher salaries, the Reich Ministry of Labour (*Reichsarbeitsministerium*) and the Reich Trustees of Labour (*Reichstreuhänder*) insisted that wages not be increased. Over the course of the armaments boom that began in 1936, many employees attempted to push for better working conditions – the competition for workers strengthened their negotiating position – but narrow limits were set on wage increases by the regulations of the Trustees of Labour and the Office of the Four-Year Plan.[116]

Moreover, the bank's room for manoeuvre in business operations was increasingly limited by the state. From 31 May 1933, the Capital Market Committee of the Reichsbank controlled the selling of new shares and the issuing of corporate and public bonds.[117] In December 1934, the Dividend and Bond Law (*Anleihestockgesetz*) was passed, setting upper limits for dividends. The ownership and issuing of shares were not just strictly regulated by the two laws, but had also become financially unattractive because stock exchange trading had been limited. The Stock Corporation Act of January 1937 increased minimum capital requirements from 100,000 to 500,000 RM, with the intention that the legal status of a joint-stock company be reserved for large businesses.[118] The regime presented all these legal interventions as measures against companies' and banks' supposed obsession with profit. In reality, these measures were intended to focus the capital market exclusively on financing the state. The Reichsbank also acquired a powerful instrument through its open-market policy, by means of which it could direct the money and capital markets towards armaments financing. The banks were forced to take state treasury bills and bonds into their portfolios. State securities, which had amounted to 20 per cent of assets in the early 1930s, had increased to nearly 60 per cent by 1940.[119] This was refinanced mostly through the deposits of workers, whose assets were used, via the banks, to finance the state. This 'silent' form of war financing was the crucial difference between the Third Reich and the German government of the First World War, which sold war bonds to the general public with major propaganda efforts.

Table 1: Balance sheet figures and personnel of Deutsche Bank, 1933–44.

Year (on 31 Dec.)	Share price (in %)	Dividend (in %)	Market capitalisation (in RM)	Equity (in RM)	Total assets (in RM)	Personnel
1933	50.00	0.00	65,000,000	155,200,000	3,038,550,838	16,789
1934	74.00	0.00	96,200,000	155,200,000	2,962,755,696	17,588
1935	84.00	4.00	109,200,000	154,901,760	3,017,100,229	17,619
1936	111.00	5.00	144,300,000	158,000,000	3,064,789,477	17,282
1937	124.50	6.00	161,850,000	161,000,000	3,300,725,012	17,462
1938	115.50	6.00	150,150,000	175,500,000	3,748,158,384	17,947
1939	110.25	6.00	143,325,000	182,000,000	4,184,225,822	19,265
1940	149.00	6.00	238,400,000	226,500,000	5,314,964,522	20,605
1941	144.25	6.00	230,800,000	232,500,000	6,573,274,637	20,929
1942	149.00	6.00	238,400,000	237,500,000	7,503,776,783	21,004[a]
1943	152.50	6.00	244,000,000	242,500,000	8,702,572,485	20,741[b]
1944	150.00	6.00	240,000,000	247,500,000	11,299,902,264	20,743[c]

[a] 1 Oct. 1942 [b] 1 Oct. 1943 [c] 1 Oct. 1944.

Source: Deutsche Bank, Annual Reports 1933–44; Workforce 1939–44, HADB, B237.

Whereas until 1935 many of the bank's loans went to the Nazi state's work-creation programmes, with the start of the Four-Year Plan in 1936 loans for armaments and raw materials came to the fore. They were mostly financed via Mefo bills, of which Deutsche Bank und Disconto-Gesellschaft held a total of 285 million RM in October 1936, corresponding to approximately 20 to 25 per cent of all bank-held Mefo bills.[120] The bank also played a significant role in the issuing of Reich bonds, which first appeared in 1935 (in some cases acting as the consortium leader with a share of 16 per cent).[121] The Nazi regime wanted to use these bonds to find new sources of funding and simultaneously consolidate its short-term debt. Deutsche Bank und Disconto-Gesellschaft placed around a quarter of all German government bonds in the first half of 1936, not only thereby expanding its share in the issuance business, but also expressing its political loyalty. 'Success in this,' according to Mosler in October 1936, was 'enormously important for our relationship with the authorities.'[122]

The placement of industrial bonds only gained importance with the onset of the Four-Year Plan, when many companies involved in armaments production began to seek financing through the capital market. Here, too, the bank played an important role in numerous projects, despite the fact that by 1938 at the latest it had become clear that the German capital market was highly overburdened. Both corporate bonds and government bonds were difficult to sell in the market. The interest rate conversion (*Zinskonversion*) of 1935 created the opportunity to turn high-interest-bearing public and private debt securities into long-term loans with a low interest rate of 4.5 per cent. These interest rates were hardly attractive for private investors, however, in light of growing inflation. Nonetheless, the bank became involved in the placement of government and private bonds and also carried out numerous conversions, which to some extent cancelled out the growth in its commission income. It was important to its public image for the bank to underscore its significance in the new economic system: 'We have discovered once again,' read the annual report for 1936,

> that our large circle of business allies, which extends across all parts of the country and all sectors of the economy, gives us the opportunity to play an important role in the issuing of any form of share or bond. We hope we have proven once again [...] through our placement work, that the German banking structure, which combines the activities of loans and deposits with those of an investment bank, is the best answer to German needs.[123]

Aryanisation

The banks, through their networks of business connections and contacts and their experience with the quiet settlement of complex asset transactions, became institutions that played a major role in 'Aryanisation', as the elimination of Jewish participation in the economy was euphemistically termed.[124] The scholarship of Harold James provides a comprehensive analysis of Deutsche Bank's role in this process and refutes the older assessment that the bank was only responding to external pressure and did everything it could to 'enable Jewish bankers and businessmen to carry out the unavoidable Aryanisation of their companies without too much difficulty or to many losses for those involved'.[125] The bank was actively involved in a large number of Aryanisations. In spring 1938, the Management Board asked the branches to create lists of Jewish client companies that might be for sale. This information was collected in the branch office of the Berlin headquarters and passed along to the offices through special circulars. The goal for the bank was to find appropriate buyers within its own organisation that could acquire the companies slated for Aryanisation. By these means, the bank could provide a service to its clients and at the same time earn a commission.

However, bringing in high commissions earnings was not the main focus; against the background of the increasingly radical anti-Semitism of the Aryanisation process, a veritable competition was developing between the banks. In the process, a division of responsibilities developed which reflected the different clientele and expertise of the various credit institutions. Whereas savings banks were often involved in the expropriation of smaller companies and commercial businesses, big banks took on the larger Aryanisations, in which complex ownership structures had to be addressed. Deutsche Bank also took on multiple international cases. Many Aryanised companies and assets had foreign holdings and complex legal claims that had first to be settled. In these cases, Deutsche Bank could use its global connections and, as an international bank, had different options than, for example, the savings banks, regional banks or co-operative banks. In many cases, Deutsche Bank also transferred abroad the small remaining balances that were left to the former Jewish owners after they had been expropriated. On average this amounted to 1 to 2 per cent of the original value.

There is no definitive figure regarding the number of Aryanisations in which Deutsche Bank was involved. It was significant, however, and probably put the bank under great time pressure, because it could be assumed that 'private Aryanisation was prohibited

[…] and the entire economy was supposed to be free of Jews by 1 January 1939'.[126] In late August 1938 Kimmich confirmed that of the '750 large-scale Aryanisations reported by our bank, […] 250 companies have by now been transferred into Aryan hands'.[127] According to another internal analysis carried out by Gerhard Elkmann, the deputy director of headquarters and the manager of Kimmich's office, the bank had 'dealt with' 569 cases by November 1938, of which 363 had been 'transferred to Aryan ownership or liquidated'.[128] The wave of Aryanisations that set in after the November pogrom was not even counted in this case, nor were the Aryanisations that were carried out by the bank's branches, presumably on their own initiative. There was in fact – unlike at Dresdner Bank[129] – no central department in charge of Aryanisations. Rather, they seem to have been carried out as normal business transactions by the responsible bodies. While Kimmich and Abs played a significant role in this on the Management Board – Abs in particular in Aryanisations in the occupied territories – the individual transactions were often carried out by the branch directors.

Harold James has shown that the economic advantages that Deutsche Bank gained through these Aryanisations were not as high as previous research had frequently claimed. This was, in particular, the case for many instances of smaller-scale Aryanisation as well as numerous dispossessions of industrial firms, in which Deutsche Bank carried out the financial transactions but did not benefit from the transfer of assets. In general, the bank earned a commission of 1 to 3 per cent of these transactions. In some cases, the bank was also able to realise substantial capital gains from the shares of Aryanised companies and private assets. According to an internal calculation prepared for the tax balance sheet, the bank had 'special profits and brokerage fees in connection with Aryanisations, sales of securities and real estate' to the sum of 936,812 RM in 1938. To this were added special items from certain business transactions that had been carried out separately. In 1938, this amounted to 213,310 RM, which was declared 'special profits from shares' from the Aryanisation of the Essen-based private bank Simon Hirschland.[130] Deutsche Bank also brought in revenue from loans that it provided to other investors for Aryanisations and which presumably are not included in the lists. In most cases, the bank acted solely as a broker, looking for buyers for the companies to be Aryanised, making the contractual arrangements and providing the necessary financial means. In the years that followed, these earnings continuously fell, as Aryanisation in the *Altreich* – those territories that were part of Germany prior to the Nazi expansion in 1938 – had been brought to a close. However, the subsidiary banks outside Germany, which carried out a significant number of Aryanisations over the course of the Nazi expansion, also brought in further revenue. These profits are not reflected in Deutsche Bank's accounts, but, of course, benefited the group as a whole.

In light of these factors it is not possible to reliably estimate the total profits that the bank gained from Aryanisation. To this can be added the fact that the short-term profits probably carried less weight than the long-term growth in value of the company and its improved market position. By August 1938, Kimmich could confirm that 'we have expanded our holdings as a result of the Aryanisations', without, of course, giving precise numbers.[131] The participations reported on the balance sheet doubled between 1937 and 1940 from 37 to 70 million RM, but these numbers probably do not reflect

In October 1938, Essen bank Simon Hirschland was 'Aryanised' and renamed Burkhardt & Co.

real growth.[132] The bank's growth in revenue over the course of the late 1930s thus seems also to have been a result of Aryanisation. This path allowed the bank to gain more clients, increase its holdings and expand its market share by purchasing banks.

Strategic considerations such as these played an important role, for example, in the incorporation of the business and the non-Jewish employees of Mendelssohn & Co.[133] The Aryanisation of Mendelssohn & Co., the largest German private bank, was complicated as well, as the bank, which specialised in sovereign bonds and international trade finance, was heavily engaged in foreign business. Until 1938, the bank had been operating actively in Germany and was a member of the consortium that issued German government bonds. Among the many issues that had to be settled before the bank was liquidated were the high liabilities abroad that fell under the standstill agreements. These loans, for which the owners were personally liable, needed to be settled as foreign creditors would otherwise be able to access the bank's foreign exchange assets. Though Mendelssohn had a branch in Amsterdam, this could not become involved in settling foreign transactions because the head of the branch, Fritz Mannheimer, had been implicated in a fraud scandal. Deutsche Bank's international expertise came into play here. Because Hermann J. Abs, who had just joined the bank, was trusted by Mendelssohn's partners, Deutsche Bank won the bid and was able to edge out the government-owned Reichs-Kredit-Gesellschaft, which was also interested.[134]

68 million RM in assets and liabilities were thus transferred to Deutsche Bank. Some of Mendelssohn's capital, as well as its foreign holdings and real estate, were otherwise liquidated. No major immediate profits were therefore to be gained from the Aryanisation of Mendelssohn & Co. Over the long term, however, it was a strategically important acquisition for Deutsche Bank, especially as it could barely

expand further within Germany in the 1930s. Deutsche Bank was also able to acquire another important private bank, Simon Hirschland in Essen, which had 84 million RM in capital and standstill credits worth 38 million RM in 1937. In this case as well, Deutsche Bank's international contacts helped it to earn the bid to handle the Aryanisation process.[135]

These and other cases show that Deutsche Bank adeptly took advantage of the business opportunities that arose in the context of Aryanisation. In the large international operations in particular, the regime required a big bank experienced in business abroad and which, as a private institution, could carry out the transactions more discreetly than the Nazi government or the state-owned banks. If the break-up of the big banks, which parts of the NSDAP had called for, never took place, this was also due to the fact that, from the regime's perspective, the disadvantages of such a fracturing outweighed the advantages. Deutsche Bank's importance to the regime would become especially apparent after the outbreak of war, when a rapid creation of economically sustainable structures in the occupied territories was necessary to finance Hitler's war.

The banks did not follow a consistent pattern in implementing Aryanisation. In fact, they had considerable room for manoeuvre. The competition that this unleashed was a unique feature of National Socialist polycracy which culminated in a process of radicalisation. The banks aimed at improving their position, using political contacts and cutting out rivals. As historian Frank Bajohr argued, the various banks applied different strategies towards the 'victims of Aryanisation'.[136] Beside the 'active and unscrupulous profiteers' who aggressively used their positions to their own advantage, there were the 'sleeping partners' who proceeded more passively while still benefiting from Aryanisation. Bajohr also identified a third group, which attempted to create prices that were as fair as possible and to give the Jewish owners the opportunity to transfer some of their assets abroad. In the case of Deutsche Bank, all three strategies can be identified. Some cases of Aryanisation seem to have fallen to the bank without it taking any initiative, whereas in other circumstances it acted proactively and did everything possible to take advantage of the situation. As will be shown, the bank acted particularly recklessly in the Eastern European countries, where it mainly pursued its own profit interests. Especially in the *Generalgouvernement* (the German-administered part of Poland) and in the Protectorate of Bohemia and Moravia, Richard Gdynia and Walter Pohle represented the bank in an unscrupulous manner and showed it had no qualms about working with the SS, the Gestapo and other occupation authorities.[137]

This was different in Germany, where the bank was frequently dealing with long-established business partners, often involving close personal connections. In these cases, though Deutsche Bank had its own interests at heart as it carried out the Aryanisations, it attempted to give the dispossessed companies at least reasonably fair compensation. For this reason many of the dispossessed Jewish business families, such as the Petscheks and the Mendelssohns, maintained good relations after 1945 with the representatives of Deutsche Bank and even gave them 'clean bills of health' (*Persilschein*) during the denazification process. The timing of the Aryanisation also played an important role. The early cases were often carried out on the initiative of the owners of Jewish firms whereby they would contact a bank they trusted and attempt to assert their own interests in the negotiation. This was related not just to the purchase price and a possible transfer of the proceeds abroad along with the relevant tax liabilities, but also the question of how the continued existence of the company would be assured and whether the workforce could still be employed. After the pogroms of November 1938 at the latest, however, their options became increasingly limited as pressure from the state agencies and the party grew. The later the Aryanisation, the more radical and reckless the proceedings against the Jewish owners were. By that point, they had to accept any offer.[138]

For the banks, however, Aryanisation also represented a risk. For one, it was possible that Jewish companies might no longer be able to service their debts due to the boycotts and expropriations that they faced; in addition, the valuation of the companies was challenging, in particular in the case of complicated ownership structures. The process, from initial contact to pricing and finally to the contractual settlement process, was often protracted.[139] Because the banks did not acquire many of the industrial companies for themselves, but acted on behalf of clients who often needed loans themselves, there were additional risks.[140] Historian Ludolf Herbst has emphasised that the banks pursued a rational risk strategy in the Aryanisation process and in particular attempted to avoid loan defaults.[141] The political implications notwithstanding, this was above all an attempt at running an efficient business.

To summarise, the role of Deutsche Bank under the Nazis was characterised by two-faced opportunism. The bank not only adapted itself politically to the regime, it also attempted to make optimal use of the business opportunities that the Nazi regime created for it. This applied above all to business abroad, which presented unforeseen opportunities for growth for the bank over the course of the Nazi expansion.

3. Nazi Continental Economic Zones

International business and foreign exchange regime

From the summer of 1931, banks involved in international business must have wondered if their operations abroad had any future. German foreign trade volume in 1932 stood at only a third of its 1929 levels and remained at this low level thereafter.[142] Trade finance thus lost considerable importance. Nor could the banks bring in much revenue from foreign exchange and forward transactions. International capital movements were limited from 1931 onwards, and the ban on transfers imposed in autumn 1933 led to more permanent limitations.

How did Germany's leading foreign trade bank deal with this situation? At first it did not seem to have made an immediate decision to change its business model, especially because it was not clear how long the interruption to international finance would last. At this particular time, the bank was fully engaged in dealing with the consequences of the banking crisis. Above all, settlements had to be made with foreign creditors in order to prevent further losses. Gustaf Schlieper took part in numerous rounds of negotiations with international creditors and the Bank for International Settlements in Basel in summer 1931 and played an important role in the finalisation of the standstill agreement of August of that year, which stipulated a six-month deferment of the payment of short-term German debts abroad to the amount of 6.3 billion RM.[143] In autumn 1931

Schlieper was confident that normal conditions would soon be resumed, as 'our bank enjoys great trust abroad, as it always has, and on its own could probably have come to better agreements'. It would not have been possible for the bank to act unilaterally for political reasons, but one could 'certainly expect that in practice the other side will soon show a more relaxed treatment and greater willingness to accommodate'.[144]

However, this would prove to be a delusion. By 1939, a total of nine standstill agreements had been made. In addition, the banks had to come to individual settlements with creditors abroad. Of particular importance were the American banks, which held a large proportion of German foreign loans. The legal settlement of these obligations was a lingering process, and Deutsche Bank ended up keeping its office in New York until 1938. After Hugo Schmidt, the long-time Deutsche Bank representative in the United States, resigned in 1930 due to old age, Adolf Koehn, who had already represented the interests of Disconto-Gesellschaft in New York, temporarily took over the office. In 1933, Deutsche Bank und Disconto-Gesellschaft sent Herbert Waller from the Berlin headquarters to New York.[145] In addition to the final clarifications of property issues dating to the time before 1914, the New York office was involved in repurchasing dollar obligations (in particular the $25 million bond from 1927). In light of major markdowns, it was attractive for the bank to reduce its foreign exchange obligations in the United States. By 1935, many of the dollar bonds could be bought.[146] The office also assisted American clients who had blocked accounts at Deutsche Bank and were interested in selling their assets to German companies. Until the late 1930s, there was also still direct American investment in Germany. On the books of Deutsche Bank und

The Bank for International Settlements in Basel, 1931.

Disconto-Gesellschaft alone, American companies still held accounts in 1936 amounting to 27.5 million RM, mostly through Germany-based subsidiaries.[147] Nor did German investors withdraw all their capital from the United States. In 1937, this still amounted to approximately $124 million – only a fraction of the money that German banks and companies had invested in the United States prior to the First World War.

In fact, by the Banking Act of 1933 at the latest, it became clear that the German universal banks had no future in the United States. The introduction of a separate banking system and other regulatory measures made it practically impossible for Deutsche Bank to continue to be active in the American capital market.[148] This made the bank's existing connections to other countries even more important. It shifted activities, along the lines of the 'New Plan' that Hjalmar Schacht announced in autumn 1934, to Europe – particularly to states with which Germany had clearing agreements. Trade without foreign exchange concentrated on the southern and Eastern European states, which the Nazi regime increasingly worked to infiltrate economically.

Outside Europe, Latin America, with its abundant agricultural produce and raw materials, loomed large in Germany's economic strategy. Banco Alemán Transatlántico (BAT) had also been hit hard by the banking crisis, but business started to recover in 1935.[149] Profits increased considerably, and in 1937 the company was able to pay a dividend again for the first time. Through the merger with Disconto-Gesellschaft, the latter's subsidiary, Banco Brasileiro Alemão, could be merged with BAT, after which

Advertisement by Banco Alemán Transatlántico for trade in the most important foreign notes and coins.

business in Brazil increased significantly. The upswing was not permanent, however, as with the outbreak of the Second World War and the Allies' naval blockade, trade with Latin America immediately became severely limited.[150] BAT could, in 'contrast to the overly nervous, in some cases even panicked, atmosphere' that had predominated in August 1914 in South America, continue to operate quite calmly.[151] In May 1940, however, BAT's management board confirmed that 'the problem of shifting business relations that has existed until now is reaching its full effect'.[152] In January 1942, Peru, Uruguay and Brazil broke off relations with the Axis powers, and a few months later the governments in Brazil and Peru arranged the closure of the BAT branches there.

In Spain, the outbreak of civil war in July 1936 had already significantly shifted the bank's room for manoeuvre along the political lines of the conflict. Business had 'come to an almost complete standstill'.[153] While the branches of BAT in Madrid and Barcelona, which were under Republican influence, were seen as hostile and quickly lost authority, business in Seville, which was governed by the right-leaning Nationalists, proceeded 'at full blast'.[154] In Seville, BAT, which was active primarily in the olive export business, was the only foreign bank in the area that originated in a country with which the Francoist camp had friendly relations. The Seville branch also took in many employees who had been let go in Madrid and Barcelona as a result of the civil war. Despite Franco's close ties with Nazi Germany, the strictly regulated nature of Spanish trade and foreign exchange transactions prevented a more intensive exchange of products between the two countries, even after the end of the civil war and the outbreak of the Second World War in 1939.[155]

In Argentina, the bank could continue to work relatively freely until the declaration of war on 7 March 1945. A decree of 8 June 1945 revoked the bank's authorisation to do business and prescribed its liquidation by the Banco Central. In August 1945, the Argentinian central bank took over BAT. In Uruguay as well, BAT's activity came to a halt at the end of the war.

Figure 11: Yearly profits of Banco Alemán Transatlántico (Deutsche Ueberseeische Bank) and Deutsch-Asiatische Bank (without accounts carried forward), 1931–43 (in RM thousands).

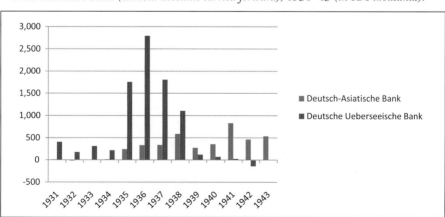

Sources: Annual reports of BAT and DAB; Müller-Jabusch, *50 Jahre*, p. 330.

In Asia the situation for German companies had become very challenging after the outbreak of the Sino-Japanese War in summer 1937.[156] Deutsch-Asiatische Bank (DAB) had withdrawn almost completely from Japan in the 1920s to concentrate entirely on the Chinese market, but had suffered losses not least due to lending policies that had been 'unfortunately too liberal'.[157] Business developed tolerably for a few years after the consolidation of the Chinese Nationalist government under Chiang Kai-shek, despite continued currency turbulence. But the Chinese banks themselves had also gained ground since the First World War by offering more attractive interest rates on deposits than foreign banks could.[158] Until 1941, Germany had direct access to the Chinese market through the Soviet Union, and temporarily even became China's most important trading partner. However, the advantages that Deutsche Bank gained from being DAB's largest shareholder were negligible, and it even faced significant losses in some of its investment projects.[159] At the same time, the foreign exchange controls in Germany and the requirements of the standstill agreements did not allow DAB to take out new foreign currency loans, which, with its slim capital base, it desperately needed. Nor were the Reich Economics Ministry or the Reichsbank willing to subsidise DAB. Hjalmar Schacht would 'personally not have considered a closure of the bank under the given circumstances a tragedy', Franz Urbig bitterly discovered in January 1935.[160] DAB's scope of business therefore remained strictly 'within the limits of its own funds'.[161]

After the Japanese army occupied a large portion of China, the activities of DAB were further limited. Direct business with Chinese partners was now nearly impossible. The branches in Shanghai, Hankou, Canton, Beijing, Tianjin and Qingdao continued to operate, but could not acquire new orders. After the Tripartite Pact of September 1940 between Germany, Italy and Japan, German companies' room for manoeuvre in China

Headquarters of Deutsch-Asiatische Bank in Shanghai in the 1930s.

became ever smaller. Though the Third Reich and Japan had agreed to greater economic co-operation, and DAB had even been encouraged by German government agencies to rebuild its presence in Japan and in occupied Manchuria, it responded cautiously to plans such as these: in the opinion of DAB's supervisory board, an office would only be economically profitable in peacetime. The bank had also had bad experiences in Japan in the past and not been able to compete with Japanese banks.[162] Due to political calculations, Deutsche Bank für Ostasien was founded in November 1942 with its headquarters in Berlin; Deutsche Bank held a 20 per cent share in the new bank. In June 1943, it opened a branch in Tokyo. The bank's main role was to carry out German–Japanese trade clearing and to finance trade with German companies and importers. Given the military situation, this was only a small volume of trade, however, and Deutsche Bank für Ostasien remained a short episode.[163]

Autarky, trade finance and clearing

Interestingly, Deutsche Bank's acceptance credit, which was primarily used in foreign trade, remained at a relatively constant level of 200–230 million RM per year after the banking crisis.[164] Not until the war broke out did it decline. Deutsche Bank also increasingly played the role of a 'clearing bank', discreetly carrying out complex foreign trade transactions on behalf of the Nazi regime. German companies faced many obstacles, especially in foreign trade with long delivery periods and the necessity of pre-financing.[165]

There were mixed feelings about this development at the bank. On the one hand, the bank could use this to justify its existence as an international bank. Deutsche Bank itself frequently emphasised its many contacts abroad and its wide-ranging expertise in cross-border transactions. The bank, as Schlieper stated in a public address in March 1936, was an important player in the 'hard-fought battle to maintain our sales markets and our supply of the raw materials that our own country does not provide us with'.[166] The annual report of 1938 stated:

> In keeping with the traditions of our bank, we pay especial attention to the support of foreign business. By arranging foreign currency loans and putting large sums into the financing of long-term foreign business ventures, we have successfully strengthened exports and eased imports. To ensure the continued supply of raw materials in future years, it is especially important for the national economy that the banks work together in financing medium-term export transactions. In addition to our entire domestic organisation, which is up-to-date on all developments in foreign business and in currency legislation through a comprehensive business intelligence service, our own branches […] are available for our clientele to carry out business abroad.[167]

This as well as other statements prove that Deutsche Bank had not entirely cut itself off from its international business during the Third Reich. Nazi autarky policy was viewed critically. Mosler emphasised in October 1936 that though 100 million RM per year in foreign exchange could be saved by these means, little more could be achieved without leading to 'serious sacrifices of capital'.[168] It was clear to those at the bank that autarky was connected with a tremendous loss of prosperity for the German economy,

At the Berlin Transfer Conference in 1937, Reichsbank President Hjalmar Schacht (second from left) negotiated with the representatives of Germany's creditor countries over German foreign debt.

which was dependent on products from abroad – not to mention the administrative complexity of the policy. Schlieper complained in March 1936 that the bureaucratic requirements caused a 'perceptible additional burden to expenditures'.[169] The 'complication of the requirements' had 'gradually reached such a level that only officials [i.e. bank employees] who knew the most intricate details of the material could carry them out'.[170] The Private Banking Group made similar statements. According to their assessment, German exports in particular suffered from the restrictive regulations. It was often impossible to acquire loans to finance orders, and the 'numerous formalities' were 'very obstructive', especially for small companies.[171] 'The new methods,' Schlieper argued in 1936, 'do not correspond in any way to the business ideal.'[172]

Credit business with the Bolshevist enemy

One of the paradoxical aspects of the Nazi economic system was that business contacts were maintained even with ideological opponents, insofar as they corresponded to the Nazis' own interests. This opportunism was particularly striking with respect to the Soviet Union, with which Germany had close connections dating back to the 1920s. As a socialist economy, and one that was mostly disconnected from the international economic cycle, the Soviet Union had suffered less during the banking crisis than most of the capitalist states. However, Stalin's empire faced major economic challenges with the devastating famine that followed the collectivisation of agriculture and therefore relied on foreign economic assistance. Between 1925 and 1933, 10 loan consortia for the 'Russia business' had been formed under the leadership of Deutsche Bank and were used to give loans to German companies via IFAGO. During the economic crisis, the loans served as an economic boost for German industry. In 1931 alone, approximately 1,100 applications by 639 companies were approved. This enabled the protection of around 150,000 jobs in Germany at the height of the crisis; exports to the Soviet Union, meanwhile, had risen to more than 10 per cent of Germany's total.

After the Nazi seizure of power, it was unclear whether the special trade relationship with the Soviet Union would survive the two regimes' stark ideological differences. Moscow was very wary of Hitler's acquisition of power and had also reacted sceptically to the German–Polish liquidation agreement of October 1929, which settled the two countries' financial claims from the First World War. Germany nonetheless remained the Soviet Union's preferred trade partner, especially since the Soviets' negotiations with the American government were not very promising. American products were cheaper, but the Soviets valued the quality of German industrial products and the support that its technical staff provided.[173] Germany primarily exported machines and other high-value investment goods, which the Soviet Union answered with raw materials. Between 1926 and 1932, orders from the Soviet Union amounted to 2.9 billion RM, though these were not fully equalled by Soviet deliveries. The 'Russia business' was also attractive for Germany, therefore, from a balance-of-payments standpoint, especially since the Soviet Union paid for its trade deficits in gold. In 1931 alone, gold payments amounted to 230 million RM. However, the Soviet Union could no longer pay its foreign debts in full. In late 1932, they had added up to 2.4 billion RM, half of which was owed to Germany.[174]

While the overall balance was positive, German–Soviet trade found itself at a tipping point in spring 1933. In that year alone, the Soviet Union had 650 million RM of debt fall due. Not until Deutsche Bank und Disconto-Gesellschaft pushed for continued loans to Russia and a settlement of its debts in spring 1933 did Reichsbank President Schacht agree to continue to discount 'Russia bills' and thereby provide a default guarantee. Export credits were ensured from then on by a Hermes export credit guarantee.[175] Thus, the eleventh consortium for the Russia business under the leadership of Deutsche Bank und Disconto-Gesellschaft could be commissioned in summer 1933, and the Soviet Union was given a debt deferral. This was followed by another consortium credit of 200 million RM in 1935, this time under shared leadership with Dresdner Bank.

German expectations had completely changed, however. In light of the economic upswing, the Third Reich was no longer interested in exports, though demand for raw materials from the East continued. The balance of trade had in fact changed significantly from in 1934: Germany started to have a trade deficit with the Soviet Union, with the result that the latter could reduce its own deficits; the discovery of gold in Siberia also made repayment easier. The Soviet Union, however, was not willing to agree to the German desire for currency-free trade, which Schacht had called for in his 'New Plan' of 1934.[176] The German–Soviet economic agreement of spring 1935 was therefore ended without any compensation and gave no further boost to trade. 'Business with Russia is practically over,' Schlieper confirmed in autumn 1936.[177] Whereas German exports increased slightly in the years that followed – though they were still significantly below their levels during the Weimar Republic – imports from the Soviet Union contracted considerably starting in 1936.[178] In 1939, Germany made one final loan transaction, though it was not used in full.[179]

From Deutsche Bank's perspective, the 'Russia credits' of the Nazi era were nonetheless of great importance. Not only did it provide 26.5 per cent of the total loan in the 'special transaction' of 1935, it was also able to bring in additional commissions as the leading bank in the consortium. Based on its own assessment, this agreement alone allowed the bank to broker orders for its industrial clients to the amount of 182 million RM. The 'Russia business' also had an important political function for Deutsche Bank, which was the only bank represented on the Interministerial Committee for Taking on Russian Default Guarantees (*Interministerieller Ausschuss für die Übernahme von Russen-Ausfall-Garantien*).[180] The negotiations were led by Helmut Pollems, who, inter alia, operated a 'little Russian circle' in Berlin in party circles.[181] The bank used this position to defend its leadership role in business with the Soviet Union against other banks (especially against Dresdner Bank and Reichs-Kredit-Gesellschaft).[182] From 1939 onwards, however, trade with the Soviet Union played a numerically minor role.

Aryanisation and the European large-area economy

Eastern and southern European countries gained considerably in importance in Deutsche Bank's international strategy from the 1920s onwards, although expansion in this region was complicated. Besides the economic problems of most countries, many of the newly formed nation-states had been taken over by authoritarian military dictatorships that seldom showed interest in economic openness. Access to domestic markets was often restricted and only possible via state agencies. In Bulgaria, for example, Deutsche Bank's branch in Sofia, founded in 1917, continued to exist, but it had low turnover. Merging the branch with Deutsch-Bulgarische Kreditbank, which had been founded by Disconto-Gesellschaft, strengthened the bank's position in Bulgaria.

In other countries the situation was not much better. In Turkey, the bank was unable to return to its long-standing business relations. The Kemalist state was pursuing a policy of nationalist development and gave preference to domestic financial institutions. The branch in Istanbul continued operating, supporting German clients in particular, but large investment projects were not an option, especially since negotiations to compensate Deutsche Bank for the newly nationalised Anatolian and Baghdad Railways dragged on. During the Second World War, though, Istanbul again increased in importance as a hub for international financial transactions. Deutsche Bank also hoped to build up business connections with northern Africa and the Near East via Turkey.[183]

The banking crisis of 1931 had the paradoxical effect that trade between Germany and many eastern and south-eastern European states gained in importance, as bilateral clearing agreements facilitated economic exchange. As we have seen, Deutsche Bank was frequently involved in these payment transactions. With the annexation of Austria and the occupation of Czechoslovakia, new opportunities opened up in these regions. The Nazi expansion allowed Deutsche Bank to build a continental European banking empire, which at its apex reached from the Baltics to Greece. The dispossession of Jewish companies provided the bank with the opportunity in many locations of acquiring strategically important holdings, to open up new markets and to expand its branch network.

This process of expansion followed approximately the same pattern everywhere. Following military conquests, Deutsche Bank would acquire majority shares in strategically important financial companies and place its own representatives on management and supervisory boards. In many cases, the existing institutions were not dissolved, rather being formally integrated into Deutsche Bank. Care was taken to preserve the appearance of autonomy, and, in cases of acquisition, the bank operated under the guise of contractual legal property transfers. The hope was that this would create a legally secure entity that would survive the war.[184] In fact, these transactions were by no means voluntary, but occurred under significant pressure from the occupying authorities, which aimed at a rapid economic infiltration of the conquered regions.[185] The purchase prices paid by the bank were also often significantly lower than the actual value of the companies. The latter often agreed to the contracts because they expected to be better protected by collaborating with a private bank than by being directly subject to the Nazi authorities.

From the perspective of the Nazi regime, there were good reasons for preserving the existing financial institutions of the occupied states rather than simply destroying them. An intact money and banking system was essential to the continuation of payment transactions with the occupied territories, and only in this way could economic production in the occupied areas be maintained. Local industries also needed loans to be able to continue to operate, or even – if they were involved in the armaments industry – to expand. One of the specific features of war waged by the Nazi regime was its enormous capacity for destruction that went hand-in-hand with a stealthy economic integration of the captured countries. This involved not only the civilian administration of the *Altreich* (employment offices, tax officials, etc.), but also the private banks.[186]

To what extent was Deutsche Bank involved in the war economy of the Third Reich? The range of its holdings abroad and the revenue that resulted from it can only be identified in the case of direct investments, rather than those that occurred through subsidiaries.[187] Its investment in Creditanstalt-Bankverein (CABV), which in 1942, for example, brought in earnings of 1.4 million RM, was especially remunerative.[188] Abs is known to have benefited personally from some business activities. These included the acquisition of shares of the Aryanised Petschek concern, but also a large part of the gold transfers with neutral Sweden, which he arranged in 1940 on behalf of Göring's Four-Year Plan agency.[189] The long-term strategic goal of expanding Deutsche Bank into a European financial and industrial conglomerate and thereby reacquiring its leading role on the international stage seemed to have greater importance. Its great competitor in this was Dresdner Bank, which was politically far better connected with the Nazi regime (in particular with the SS economic empire) and which was likewise attempting to gain a foothold in the occupied territories.[190] Both the sense of competition and the fear of falling behind in the political game were important motivations for the bank's determined and at times aggressive acquisition of foreign banks and industrial holdings.[191]

Who was the driving force behind this expansion? Deutsche Bank had reorganised in the autumn of 1937 when it appointed Hermann J. Abs to succeed its head of international business Gustaf Schlieper, who died suddenly in August that year. As Abs left his lucrative position at Delbrück Schickler & Co. and moved to Deutsche

Bank in early 1938, he probably expected to play a defining role in German finance in this new position.[192] The transition was more than risky for the 37-year-old banker, as Deutsche Bank was a far greater focus of public criticism, and there were hints from within party circles that it intended to break up the big banks. From the perspective of Deutsche Bank, too, the appointment of Abs, who was from the Catholic Rhineland and was not a member of the NSDAP, represented a certain risk. However, Reich Economics Minister Schacht in particular supported his nomination to the Management Board, partly with an eye on the standstill negotiations that Schlieper had up to that point largely directed. Abs's long years of experience abroad and his good contacts in the international banking world were decisive for his nomination. Abs had worked in London, Amsterdam, Paris and various parts of North

Hermann J. Abs (1901–1994) at his entry into Deutsche Bank's Management Board in 1938.

and South America, and was fluent in English, French, Spanish and Dutch. His skilful and sympathetic demeanour opened doors for him abroad, and many foreign bank leaders in Nazi-occupation territory hoped that a collaboration with Deutsche Bank would allow them to save at least a part of their business.

Abs was the architect of a banking group that dominated a large part of the financial business in Europe for a number of years. He acted as strategic head at the Berlin headquarters, and also travelled extensively throughout Europe to carry out many negotiations himself. Abs spent around half of his working days travelling. He was on the supervisory board of nearly all of Deutsche Bank's foreign subsidiaries, often serving as chair. At the same time, he built up a staff of loyal employees who often had the strong connections with the Nazi Party that he himself lacked. One of his closest employees was Franz Heinrich Ulrich, who had joined Deutsche Bank in 1936 after studying law and since 1941 had worked as a department head under Abs, co-ordinating his many supervisory board positions. Ulrich was a member of the SS from 1933 to 1939 and joined the NSDAP in 1937. Helmut Pollems, the director of Berlin headquarters, was another central figure in Abs's team. He was responsible for international operations in the Secretariat.[193] Pollems, who had a doctorate in economics and was himself fluent in a number of languages, was at Abs's side almost everywhere where important decisions for the bank were being made. He was also a specialist on bank relations in Eastern Europe and the Soviet Union.

Indeed, Abs was not solely responsible for the international expansion of the bank. On the Management Board, Karl Kimmich played an important role, too. Particularly influential was Johannes Kiehl, who had joined the board in 1938. As head of the Secretariat, he was in charge of the syndicated and the issuing business, and was also responsible for the bank's branches in eastern Germany. After the invasion of Poland, he played a vital role in the expansion of the branches in the German-administered zone. Kiehl persistently sought contact with political decision-makers and was thus able to ensure that Deutsche Bank established itself more rapidly and effectively in the Upper Silesian industrial region than its competitors.[194]

The business expansion in Upper Silesia led the bank into a direct link with the Holocaust. Its branches in Katowice and Bielsko were each only about 25 kilometres from Auschwitz. A few smaller companies among the branches' clients were involved in the construction of the concentration camp, about which the loan divisions of the branches were informed in detail by guarantees from the contracting authorities, including the SS.[195] The furnaces of the crematoria in Auschwitz were also delivered and installed by one of Deutsche Bank's borrowers, the Erfurt-based Topf & Söhne. A severe liquidity crisis in spring 1941 would have prevented the company from fulfilling the orders without loans from Deutsche Bank, which were provided by the branch in Erfurt.[196] The Katowice branch, meanwhile, was the most important bank for the Buna-Werk, which I. G. Farben built in Auschwitz-Monowitz with prisoners from the nearby concentration camp. After a visit to the large construction site in April 1943, a branch employee reported, not without pride, that '80 per cent of the current financial operations' were carried out via Deutsche Bank.[197]

Another eminent manager was Walter Pohle, who played a key role in the Protectorate of Bohemia and Moravia. Pohle had begun working at Deutsche Bank's Berlin headquarters in 1934 on the recommendation of the Reich Economics Ministry, had already been granted power of attorney (*Prokurist*) by 1937 and would become a deputy director a year later. After playing an important role in Aryanisation in the *Altreich*, he represented the interests of Deutsche Bank in the Protectorate of Bohemia and Moravia as a member of the management board of Böhmische Union-Bank (BUB) from 1939 onwards, distinguishing himself by a particularly aggressive approach. In 1942, however, he came into conflict with the authorities of the Four-Year Plan and had to resign.[198]

Another member of the circle of leading international experts at the bank was Kurt Weigelt, who over his many years as a director at the Berlin headquarters not only managed numerous industrial investments (including in Deutsche Petroleum AG and Lufthansa) but was also a prominent supporter of a colonial-style expansion policy.[199] Weigelt was a member of the SS and the NSDAP. He was also the leader of the Office of Colonial Policy within the party.[200] After the German occupation of France, he made a concerted effort to acquire investments in French companies.[201] Among the international managers who also featured was Alfred Kurzmeyer, who had worked for Mendelssohn & Co. until 1938 and after its Aryanisation became a director at Deutsche Bank.[202] He was responsible for the acquisition of Banca Comerciala Romana and was involved in many other activities in the occupied territories. In some cases, important positions abroad were also filled by managers from the branches. For instance, the director of the Saarbrücken branch, Ludwig Rohde, was appointed to the management of BUB in Prague, and the director of the Leipzig office, Walter Tron, joined the board of Creditanstalt-Bankverein (CABV) in Vienna in 1942.

Austria and south-eastern Europe

The acquisition of CABV, however, shows that Deutsche Bank's international strategy was met with considerable resistance. In Austria, Deutsche Bank had to assert itself against the tremendous political and economic interests of the NSDAP. From Deutsche Bank's point of view, the big Vienna bank was the key to the Austrian economy. Österreichische Creditanstalt had been rescued by the Austrian government during the 1931 banking crisis and in 1934 had merged with Wiener Bankverein. Thirty-five per cent of the shares of the post-merger bank were held by the Austrian government. Its numerous industrial holdings made CABV an extremely interesting target for acquisition; it would also enable numerous 'Aryanisations'.[203] Perhaps even more important was the fact that CABV had offices, equity participations and other commercial connections throughout southern and eastern Europe. For Deutsche Bank, CABV was thus an ideal acquisition target in its goal 'to make Vienna a bridge to the south-east from a banking perspective as well'.[204] Just a few days after Germany's invasion of Austria in March 1938, Mosler made Deutsche Bank's interests known to Reich Commissioner for Credit, Friedrich Ernst, referring to the bank's long-established relationship with both Creditanstalt and Bankverein.[205] Shortly thereafter, Abs went to Vienna with a team that included Walter Pohle and Helmut Pollems to sound out the possibilities of an acquisition. A 'treaty of friendship' was envisaged: CABV would continue to exist, at least externally, as an independent bank, a configuration that would allow expansionist goals to be better pursued.[206] 'Precisely the special tasks that Creditanstalt must perform within the Austrian economy and above all in foreign trade with the south-east mean that it must be independently managed and capable of making decisions on its own authority.'[207]

These ideas, however, did not come to fruition. Not until December 1938 did Deutsche Bank manage to acquire 25 per cent of CABV's share capital. Any investment beyond that, however, foundered on the opposition of Hans Fischböck, the new Nazi Economics Minister in Seyß-Inquart's regional government, as well as that of Reich Commissioner for Austria Wilhelm Keppler. Both wanted to direct the process of Aryanisation to a greater extent themselves and also preferred Dresdner Bank, which had already acquired shares in the Austrian Mercurbank.[208] Furthermore, the German industrial conglomerate Vereinigte Industrie-Unternehmungen AG (VIAG) had shown interest in acquiring industrial holdings in Austria on a grand scale, which Reichs-Kredit-Gesellschaft, as VIAG's affiliated bank, supported. In response, Deutsche Bank called for the founding of its own branches in Vienna and elsewhere in Austria should CABV not agree to an acquisition.[209] Perhaps this threat was not meant seriously, as it was not carried out even though the acquisition initially did not succeed and the majority of the shares went to VIAG and its banking subsidiary. It would be more than three years before Deutsche Bank's intentions would be realised. Only after complicated negotiations, and after CABV had sold off its industrial holdings, could Deutsche Bank acquire the majority stake in May 1942.[210] It had previously acquired CABV shares from Société Générale de Belgique and Compagnie Belge de l'Étranger, which had to sell off their equity investments in south-eastern Europe after the German invasion of Belgium.

According to Abs's plans, CABV ought no longer to concentrate on business in Austria, instead 'dedicating its powers fully and completely to tasks in the south-east'. This

The main building of Creditanstalt-Bankverein at Vienna's Schottentor in the late 1930s.

concerned, above all, Hungary, Serbia and Croatia, where the bank had been building up a strong position for decades.[211] In Budapest, it had a large branch, which had considerable turnover. CABV also acquired a minority interest in the Hungarian Commercial Bank of Pest. In Croatia, it founded Bankverein für Kroatien in Agram in 1941.[212] In Slovakia, it acquired the branches of Böhmisch-Mährische Bank and in Serbia it acquired shares in Allgemeiner Jugoslawischer Bankverein. At the same time, CABV extended its activities to Romania and Bulgaria, where it had previously barely been present.

The entire zone played a central role in Nazi expansionist plans, not least because of its importance as a source of raw materials and agricultural goods. Deutsche Bank, for its part, had long pursued commercial interests in these countries. In Romania, it had invested primarily in the financing of oil fields through Kontinentale Öl AG and, as we have seen, it acquired the majority of Banca Comerciala Romana, which had branches across the entire country, from French and Belgian shareholders.[213] Abs was president of the Deutsch-Rumänische Gesellschaft, which aimed to promote co-operation between the industries and banks of Germany and Romania.[214] In Bulgaria, Deutsche Bank already held a strong position with Deutsch-Bulgarische Kreditbank.[215]

In countries where CABV was not present, Deutsche Bank entered directly into negotiations with local banking institutions.[216] This included parts of the Balkans, where

Deutsche Bank co-operated with the Landesbank für Bosnien und Herzegowina. After the occupation of Greece, Deutsche Bank, with the backing of the Reich Economics Minister, secured a majority stake in Banque Nationale de Grèce. As in many other cases (such as those of Allgemeiner Jugoslawischer Bankverein and Böhmische Union-Bank), Abs had already taken over shares from French and Belgian banks.[217] Abs was the chairman of the supervisory board of Greece's largest bank.[218] While the expectation on the Greek side was that Germany would bring investment to the country and help it in its economic reconstruction, these connections were increasingly put to use for the processing of trading and foreign exchange transfers. Deutsche Bank thus acquired not only interests in other banks, but also in industrial companies; its existing subsidiaries were also used for this purpose. German companies like Siemens & Halske envisaged large infrastructure investments in the tradition of classical pre-1914 economic imperialism, which, as it happened, never came to fruition. Far more important was the rapid exploitation of local raw materials. In Greece, for instance, a joint-stock company was founded in 1941 for the extraction of lignite deposits in the region.[219]

In principle, Deutsche Bank did not want to act under its own name when making these purchases, but sought to penetrate the individual countries locally through majority participations. According to Abs, it was 'better to set up banking operations in south-eastern Europe with national circles than to try to establish distinctly German establishments'. This struck him as a possibility because 'in these countries there are a sufficient number of domestic institutions under mainly German influence'.[220] Activities on site were frequently co-ordinated through provisional agencies set up in hotels or apartments that would be closed as soon as local subsidiaries commenced operations.[221]

The fact that the bank attempted to expand, to the degree possible, through legally formalised transfers of ownership reflected Abs's goal of creating a conglomerate that could endure after the war. This included the involvement of local elites, insofar as it did not contradict the bank's own plans. Even in the case of the reorganisation of property relations, attention had to be paid to the local populace, since 'we have a fundamental interest in promoting the industrialisation of the south-eastern European countries'. As Abs stressed, 'if we want to be successful in the south-east, the only source of support we can rely on is the voluntary co-operation of the countries of south-eastern Europe'.[222]

That Abs's vision would be repeatedly frustrated was already evident in summer 1939, when he spoke out against politically motivated personnel placements in leadership positions in Allgemeiner Jugoslawischer Bankverein. Göring had pushed for Franz Neuhausen, Germany's consul general in Belgrade, to be placed on the administrative council of the bank, and for the bank to serve primarily German customers. After the 'departure of the Belgians', the bank should 'end up being a fully German bank'.[223] According to Fischböck, Abs, by contrast, was of the opinion that Göring's plan to place Neuhausen in the bank's leadership could result in the 'exodus of a certain part of its clientele'.[224] On these grounds, he pleaded with Belgian shareholders to vote the former president of the Jugoslawische Nationalbank, Milan Radosavlievic, into the position. On this occasion, Abs also stressed his interest in keeping Belgian investors in the bank.[225] He was unsuccessful with regard to both the personnel issue and the Belgian shareholders, but his intervention shows that he aimed at co-operation with local elites in south-eastern Europe.

In the Protectorate of Bohemia and Moravia and the *Generalgouvernement*, Deutsche Bank secured a grip on the banking system shortly after the invasion by German forces. The Protectorate, thanks to its highly developed industries and the large number of German-Jewish financial institutions, was of great interest. Immediately after the Munich Agreement, the Reich Commissioner Friedrich Ernst had authorised the management of Deutsche Bank to begin negotiations with Böhmische Union-Bank (BUB) and Deutsche Agrar- und Industriebank to take over their branches in the Sudetenland. At the same time, the banks were provided with lists of companies that needed to be 'Aryanised'. After the Nazi invasion of Czechoslovakia, the process was all but seamless. Deutsche Bank took over 90 per cent of BUB's share capital and charged Walter Pohle with restructuring the bank. Pohle initiated not only the purge of almost the entire management and advisory boards of BUB but also vigorously pursued the Aryanisation of numerous Czech industrial companies. As Harold James has shown, BUB played a major role in the seizing and exploitation of cash, shares and other assets from the deposits of Jewish clients, many of whom were deported to Nazi concentration and extermination camps.[226] It also financed the expansion of the Reichswerke 'Hermann Göring' in the east on an increasing scale.

In the occupied areas of Poland, too, Kimmich and Kiehl, who led Deutsche Bank's negotiations, preferred an expansion that incorporated local banks.[227] An internal memorandum of 7 September 1939 expresses a preference for 'continuing the operations of existing institutions and then restructuring them as necessary'.[228] A few days after Germany invaded Poland, the director of Deutsche Bank's Wrocław branch, Felix Theusner, drew up a long list for the Reich Economics Ministry of Polish banking institutions that might be of interest for Deutsche Bank.[229] The military administration and the Reich Economics Ministry, however, viewed this initiative with scepticism, particularly as an administrative agency for Polish assets already existed, namely the Main Trustee Office for the East (*Haupttreuhandstelle Ost*). The banks were operating in Poland on their own initiative and were engaged in real competition.[230] Through its branches in Katowice, Gdańsk and Upper Silesia, Deutsche Bank occupied a good initial position from which to begin business activities in the occupied Polish cities.[231] Shortly after the German attack on Poland, sub-branches opened in Bielsko, Cieszyn and Bogumin (all three in the Karviná coal-mining region), followed by branches in Łódź, Poznań and Kraków. In October 1939 Kiehl stressed that it was 'of greatest importance [...] to establish our claim on these individual sites in an objective manner, whether by reference to earlier business relationships or to the realities that have since unfolded'.[232] Not least, the ends pursued by these means was to pre-empt Dresdner Bank and Commerz- und Privat-Bank, which likewise wanted to gain a foothold in Poland. CABV – not yet at this point controlled by Deutsche Bank – made considerable efforts on the initiative of its director, Fischböck, to pursue business in this region as well.[233]

Deutsche Bank's office in Kraków actually had to be surrendered to CABV in April 1940. After the attack on the Soviet Union, the Viennese establishment was also allowed precedence in Lviv. Deutsche Bank could not gain a foothold in the rest of the annexed Soviet zones either. The Reich Economics Ministry showed a preference in these cases for Dresdner Bank, which held, in Poznań and the Reichsgau Wartheland, a better

The Kattowitz (Katowice) branch shortly before the outbreak of the Second World War.

starting position. For the most part, the ministry looked rather sceptically on the idea that 'it was possible to rebuild private industry' in the formerly Soviet areas that had been seized during the war.[234] The only exception was the Baltic, where Deutsche Bank strenuously pursued the authorisation to open a branch in Riga.[235] Deutsche Bank also indirectly took part in the exploitation of Soviet oil fields via Kontinentale Öl AG.[236]

After the German invasion of Poland, German banks enjoyed a 200 million RM credit guarantee from the Reich Economics Ministry and thus did not enter into any of their own obligations. This changed with the consolidation of the occupation.[237] Deutsche Bank therefore tried to transfer part of its active business to a regional credit institution or to take over a Polish bank.[238] The goal, as Abs emphasised in 1943, was 'to limit the possible risks to the capital to be invested in the new regional bank'.[239] By autumn 1939, Deutsche Bank was looking into a takeover of Schlesische Kredit-Anstalt[240] and the possibility of also taking over a larger Polish bank in Warsaw.[241] The efforts in Silesia came to nothing, and the negotiations with the biggest Polish credit bank, Bank Handlowy – in which Dresdner Bank also had great interest – were never concluded. Nor did the plan to found a general Polish regional bank along with other German banks ever materialise. After protracted negotiations, however, Creditanstalt AG was founded in May 1944 in Kraków. Of course, German troops were by this time in retreat on all fronts, so the bank never had the chance to initiate activities of any magnitude.[242] As in Austria and the Protectorate, planning was complicated. As Kiehl wrote to Felix Theusner in August 1941, it was difficult to direct the restructuring of the Polish banking system in any organic manner, as party leadership, banking supervision authorities, the Reichsbank and the Reich Group Banks (*Reichsgruppe Banken*) were all involved, and all had differing interests – 'so that there are already four cooks in the kitchen'.[243]

France and the Benelux countries

In Western Europe, too, Deutsche Bank faced a complicated situation that made it difficult to expand according to a unified plan. The Reich Economics Ministry had instructed the German banks on 10 September 1940 'that German capital be invested in economically significant Dutch, Belgian, and French businesses'. Foreign businesses should also be acquired by German institutions, especially those 'that work in the Balkans'.[244] Deutsche Bank operated in annexed Alsace-Lorraine under its own name and opened branches in Strasbourg, Mulhouse, Thionville and Metz. It also took over the business of Crédit Industriel, which played a prominent role in the industrial financing of the region.[245] In Brussels, Luxembourg and Paris, meanwhile, it maintained offices, which served primarily for the acquisition of numerous holdings. In the annexed French regions, it was most interested in Paribas and Union Parisienne.[246] In fact, Deutsche Bank's offices in Brussels and Paris managed to 'execute all commercial transactions with the help of allied banks'.[247] As with CABV in Vienna, Société Générale de Belgique in Brussels played a key role. This was the biggest Belgian universal bank, which also had holdings across all of Europe that were of strategic importance for the expansion of Deutsche Bank. It was with increasing alarm, therefore, that Deutsche Bank reacted when Joachim Riehle of the Reich Economics Ministry promised Dresdner Bank the takeover of Société Générale. This proposal stemmed from the idea of dividing up the occupied territories and assigning Amsterdam to Deutsche Bank and Brussels to Dresdner Bank. Deutsche Bank was to be offered the takeover of Rotterdamsche Bankvereeniging, which it in fact turned down, primarily because it already held a strong position in the Netherlands with its subsidiary H. Albert de Bary & Co.[248] With reference to the 'manifold pre-war interests' that linked Deutsche Bank to Société Générale, Kimmich suggested that Dresdner Bank was hardly in the position to sort out the complex relationships in the Belgian coal and steel industry. Furthermore, Société Générale had a clear preference for Deutsche Bank, with which it had long co-operated.[249]

In the following months, Deutsche Bank tried hard to argue that Brussels should be its base. Abs and Kimmich engaged, among others, Hjalmar Schacht, who, as Minister without Portfolio, however, had little influence.[250] In fact, Société Générale would have preferred to subordinate itself to Deutsche Bank and was ready to sell off many of its holdings in occupied Europe; at the same time, however, it had transferred its extra-European property to London. In light of these difficulties, Deutsche Bank decided to establish its own offices in Belgium and Luxembourg, as co-operation with banks in those countries was not possible simply through majority shares.[251] It was able to avert the plans of Reich Economics Minister Walther Funk to apportion specific zones of influence to the big banks as well as the idea of founding a regional community bank. Both solutions would have considerably reduced Deutsche Bank's room for manoeuvre.[252]

While numerous acquisitions occurred on this basis – in Luxembourg, Deutsche Bank acquired Banque Générale and other holdings[253] – considerable delays interrupted the planned acquisition of the Arbed group, the second largest European steel conglomerate, whose free float shares were largely held by French and Belgian investors, with the result that a temporary state administrator was involved.[254] Here, too, the competing interests not only of the German banks but also of the different occupation authorities prevented a rapid liquidation.[255] This was compounded by the fact that the military leadership, in light of the intensifying war, urged a rapid seizure of industrial resources and would no longer allow time-intensive transfer-of-ownership processes to work themselves out.[256] It was not until September 1943, in an agreement with the Reichswerke 'Hermann Göring', that Deutsche Bank succeeded in acquiring a portion of the shares of the Arbed group.[257]

Gold and foreign exchange transfers

Until the end of the regime Deutsche Bank played an important role in international payments. It was assigned the processing of complicated transactions that the Reichsbank and other government agencies could not carry out themselves. This was particularly true of the use of the gold that had been stolen in the occupied zones. In autumn 1940, Deutsche Bank carried out a transaction that was as delicate as it was significant. Göring tasked Abs with buying German government bonds in Sweden on a large scale, financing the purchase with gold reserves seized from Belgium and the Netherlands. The so-called Kreuger Bonds were the remainders of a foreign bond issue from the Weimar years that was now supposed to be bought back at a low rate. Germany had carried out similar transactions since the beginning of the war all over Europe; in most cases, Reichsmark assets from clearing accounts and blocked mark accounts were used. Outside German-controlled territory, these assets were, of course, not accepted, so the acquisition of these new stocks of gold presented a welcome opportunity to pay off these debts. Abs's excellent connections with the Swedish banker Jacob Wallenberg allowed him to conduct these transactions relatively easily. Via his bank, Stockholms Enskilda Bank, Wallenberg sold Abs $40 million worth of bonds. Both Abs and Wallenberg were able to pocket considerable commissions on these transactions. A repeat deal that Abs tried to set up, however, did not come to fruition, as the Reich Finance Ministry vetoed it.[258]

In any case, the German war economy had more pressing problems than the paying off of foreign debts. During the war, Germany desperately sought avenues through neutral countries to import the raw materials that it could not acquire – or could not acquire enough of – in the areas it occupied. Tungsten was imported via Spain and Portugal, iron ore via Sweden and chrome via Turkey. In light of Germany's shortage of foreign exchange, in 1942 the SS began to amass gold by brute force through 'Operation Reinhard', including gold from Jews murdered in concentration camps.[259] The precious metal was transported to Germany, bought by the Reichsbank on behalf of the Reich Treasury, refined by Degussa (a precious metals smelting and refining company) into central bank-quality gold and delivered back to the Reichsbank.[260] In order to exchange the gold for foreign exchange, the Nazi regime relied on Deutsche Bank and Dresdner Bank to make these transactions via their manifold channels and foreign branches. Until summer 1944, most of these gold sales were transacted by Deutsche Bank via its branch in Istanbul, where there was a largely free gold market and many businessmen and diplomats who would willingly accept ingots and coins. Germany reduced its gold reserves in Switzerland at an increasing rate, partly because of the restrictions that the Swiss government imposed. Although Deutsche Bank's Istanbul branch had set up a gold sight account at the Reichsbank for the settling of transactions in August 1942, the deliveries were initially made at CABV in Vienna, which then sent them on to Turkey or Switzerland.[261] It was evident that this arrangement should obscure the origin of the gold. In light of Allied boycott measures, gold and foreign exchange transactions had to be carried out as secretly as possible and via private channels. When Turkey broke off political relations with Germany in August 1944, neutral Switzerland gained once again in importance for gold and foreign exchange trade. In autumn 1943, Abs sent Alfred Kurzmeyer, who held Swiss citizenship, to Zurich to administer the foreign exchange reserves of Deutsche Bank and its subsidiaries BAT and DAB that had been moved there. With his excellent contacts in the Swiss banking world, Kurzmeyer organised a large part of Deutsche Bank's gold trade from Switzerland, as well as that of the SS's economic empire.

All the same, the significance of Deutsche Bank's gold and foreign exchange trade should not be overestimated. Even if the bank realised profits from gold arbitrage, these transactions were limited to relatively small amounts. Between 1941 and 1944, Deutsche Bank sold around 5,000 kg of fine gold, then valued at around $5.6 million. This value lay well below 1 per cent of the total quantity of gold traded during the war.[262] In terms of Deutsche Bank's revenues, the trade in gold, profitable as it may have been, was rather small. This does not affect the moral responsibility of the bank, all the more that the management was probably fully informed about the transactions. Since around one-third

The Deutsche Bank branch in Istanbul was the destination of most of the bank's gold transports during the war.

of the gold bullion traded by the bank came from concentration camps, there are reasons to believe that the board members were not only well informed about the gold transactions as such, but also about the provenance of the precious metal. The fact that Abs left Deutsche Bank's gold reserves untouched in the vaults in Switzerland for decades after 1945 indicates that he knew perfectly well that the gold came from the concentration camps.[263] Abs himself emphasised after 1945 that he was one of 'those who do not deny' that they had known about the 'awful events in Majdanek or Auschwitz'.[264] With that in mind, the provenance of the stolen gold could hardly have been unknown to him either.

A European conglomerate

The Nazi expansion gave Deutsche Bank the chance to build a European conglomerate with numerous subsidiaries and industrial holdings. Its special strength was that it used its existing cross-holdings with strategically important banks, especially CABV in Vienna and Société Générale de Belgique, to rapidly expand its business in the various countries and occupation zones. Like all German banks, it profited from the Germanisation policies of the racist National Socialist state, which seized property all across Europe to use for the war. The banks played an important role in this process, which could be quickly and efficiently realised only with their help. With their international networks and expertise, they were able to arrange the clearance needed to conduct foreign exchange and gold transfers with neutral states and to provide the necessary loans to the occupied zones. The banks also played a central role in the Aryanisation of Jewish property and the displacement of economic elites in the occupied countries. That said, Abs in particular was more restrained than other bank managers and made an effort to arrange the construction of the conglomerate structure via contractual transfers of ownership. Even if these acquisitions occurred under duress, Abs did not want an unrestrained raid. He presumably hoped to make the bank, as a private group, independent of the political fate of the regime – a goal which, of course, was illusory.

The expansion in the occupied zones was determined by the logic of the war economy, with its monstrous need for resources and increasingly destructive dynamic. The banks competed against each other fiercely and operated in a chaotic landscape in which they had to hold their ground against rival occupation authorities and political-economic institutions. This meant that all banks were anxious to be on the ground as quickly as possible and to secure their commercial positions by any means necessary. Thus, they themselves became actors in the National Socialist polycracy, which as the war progressed became more and more radical.

4. Survival Strategies

Between war and reconstruction

The winter of 1942–3 not only marked the turning point in Hitler's war, but also the end of an era of expansion at Deutsche Bank. By now, the bank's business activities were becoming increasingly focused on financing the conflict. Its total assets rose from 7.5 billion RM to 11.4 billion RM between 1942 and 1944, a product of the rampant growth in the money supply driven by war and military spending.[265] By the time the conflict ended, some 70 per cent of all the bank's assets consisted of bonds or treasury notes.[266] 'We are increasingly turning into a broker for the financing needs of the Reich,' noted Rösler at a board meeting as early as spring 1941.[267] Industry's demand for lending was increasing, too, and was often tied to requests for special terms and more lenient collateral requirements.[268] This put the bank in a politically difficult position, as the armaments firms in particular had the backing of Albert Speer and therefore a strong negotiating hand. Kimmich had already complained in 1938 that the bank was 'being greatly exploited by industry'. For Kimmich, this meant that the bank should 'apply stricter standards and seek to improve the quality of our debtors'.[269] In reality, however, the bank's authority to do so was increasingly limited; banks' lending decisions were no longer autonomous, but politically guided. The same applied to the deposit-taking business. The Third Reich's rapacious demand for capital was

Karl Kimmich (1880–1945) became a member of the Management Board in 1933 and served as its Spokesman from 1940 until 1942.

financed in no small part by savers, whose deposits it devoured without hesitation. Here, too, the bank played an important role. Increased advertising and a dense network of branches successfully attracted savings deposits, raising their share of total assets from 6.9 per cent to 19.2 per cent between 1934 and 1944.[270]

Despite its central role in financing the war, there was no let-up in the political pressure.[271] In February 1942, Martin Bormann complained to Reich Economics Minister Walther Funk about excessive borrowing costs and the increase in banks' earnings since the beginning of the war. Deutsche Bank alone, he noted, had quadrupled its profits between 1939 and 1940. In 1942, Bormann installed a 'bank committee' in the Reich Chancellery. As well as greater infiltration of management positions, this set its sights on the old idea of regionalising the major banks.[272] Similar demands came from the NSDAP's *Gauleiter*, who attempted to gain greater control of the banking sector with the aid of the *Gauwirtschaftsberater*, the Nazi Party's economic advisers in the party districts.[273] The Management Board members Abs and Plassmann found themselves increasingly under fire, with their 'Catholic orientation' attracting the suspicion of many in the NSDAP.[274] Karl Heinrich Heuser, the deputy *Gauwirtschaftsberater* in Berlin, demanded Abs be removed from his post for criticising, in his trips abroad and in front of foreign audiences, the German economy's lack of efficiency and for seeking contact with Catholic circles (Abs had indeed met the Pope in Rome on several occasions). Heuser also pushed for the Brandenburg *Gauwirtschaftsberater* Hellmut Börnicke to be made Management Board Spokesman at Deutsche Bank.[275]

In the end, no such drastic measures were taken. At this stage of the war, neither Göring nor Hitler was greatly interested in restructuring the banking sector.

Nevertheless, the bank took a substantial hit from the growing political hostility. Calls for greater 'rationalisation' of the lending industry led to privately owned banks being ordered in May 1942 to close 10 per cent of their branches. That year, Deutsche Bank shut 21 branches and 24 city deposit-taking branches. The following year, it closed a further 61 branches and 30 deposit-taking offices.[276] With fears rife that the bank would be broken up, directors even discussed making the largest branches more autonomous and geographically aligning branch divisions with the Nazi Party districts.[277] In October 1943, the Reich Economics Minister issued directives stipulating that stock corporations should reduce the size of their supervisory boards and cut the number of bank representatives back to 'essential' levels. Deutsche Bank responded to the pressure by recommending that bank representatives should make up no more than a third of supervisory board members, though this policy had in fact already been implemented in many cases.[278] It also co-opted Heinrich Hunke, a civil servant (*Ministerialdirektor*) and important Nazi Party member, on to the Management Board, having already appointed the *Gau* economic adviser Otto Fitzner to the Supervisory Board in April of that year.[279] Karl Ritter von Halt also continued to play an important role in defending the bank against attacks from the Nazi Party.[280]

Of far more long-term consequence than the political pressure were the military developments. As the German armies retreated, the bank had to steadily relinquish its recently acquired presence and investments in the occupied countries. The Allied bombing campaign that began in 1943 led to the destruction of numerous Deutsche Bank buildings in Germany, too, including the branches in Cologne, Mainz, Lübeck and Bremen. The Berlin head office was heavily damaged in an air raid in November 1943. Some 3,000 employees had to relocate to temporary quarters on the Hausvogteiplatz, which were themselves destroyed just a few months later.[281]

By this time the scale of conscription was making it almost impossible for the bank to handle day-to-day business. In 1940, 3,356 bank employees had left for military service. The number increased to 5,901 by January 1941 and 7,300 by January 1942. In October 1944, 9,705 employees – almost half the bank's permanent staff – were away at the front.[282] Temporary employees and women could replace only some of them. Between 1939 and 1944, the number of temporary staff rose from 243 to 1,400 and the number of women from 2,655 to 3,007. It is worth noting that this trend was invisible at management level; women were confined to ordinary roles and probably to the lower pay grades in the vast majority of cases.[283]

The bank also employed several hundred foreign workers.[284] These were mainly involved in foreign transfers at the Berlin head office, where the bank had established a dedicated department with some 200 staff members to transfer the wages of the new employees it had acquired in other countries. The complex foreign exchange regulations meant that these payments were associated with considerable bureaucratic burdens. In many cases, foreign language skills were also required. Some 150 to 200 French employees worked daytime shifts at Berlin factories followed by evening shifts at the bank's headquarters. Political prisoners and other detainees were used for cleaning, clearing rubble and other tasks in Berlin and at the branches. Opportunities for the deployment of foreign workers at the bank were far fewer than in the industrial firms critical to

The bank's permanent staff, drafted into the war effort, were replaced by female and younger workers like those seen here in 1943 in the Homburg/Saar branch.

the war effort, many of which covered up to half of their labour needs in this way.[285] However, given the bank's industrial interests, its management was well aware of the scale and conditions of forced labour in Germany and had also received relevant information from the Reich Ministry of Labour.[286]

By autumn 1943 at the latest, Deutsche Bank's management had begun to brace itself for a military defeat. While speaking openly on the subject was punishable by death, as the tragic fates of Hermann Koehler and Georg Miethe showed, managers such as Abs were very well informed of the military situation thanks to their contacts and numerous trips abroad. Internally, they now started to plan for the end of the war. In September 1943, the bank awarded general power of attorney for the whole institution to its 10 most important branch directors. The intention was to ensure the bank's survival in the event that parts of Germany were occupied by the enemy or the head office destroyed.

Abs began preparing in August 1943 to move his family from Berlin to the estate he had acquired in Remagen in 1939. With bombs raining down on German cities, carbon copies of correspondence belonging to the Foreign Department at the Berlin head office were moved to Görlitz, beyond the reach of Allied air raids.[287] Abs himself and the remaining directors stayed in Berlin until March 1945, when the Management Board decided to establish regional evacuation centres in Wiesbaden, Erfurt and Hamburg. Once American troops had taken Wiesbaden on 28 March and Erfurt on 12 April 1945, Abs moved on 13 April from Berlin to Hamburg, where he joined Erich Bechtolf and established a senior management office. They were joined from Erfurt in early June by Clemens Plassmann, while the other Management Board members remained in Berlin. Karl Ernst Sippell did not survive the final days of the war. Others, like Karl Ritter von Halt, Robert Frowein and Oswald Rösler, were imprisoned by the Soviets.[288] One

The destroyed main building of Deutsche Bank in Berlin at the end of the war.

hundred million RM worth of securities made it to Hamburg before Soviet troops took Berlin, as did some of the other important documents. The majority, however, remained in the capital and were confiscated. The old Deutsche Bank, with its headquarters and much of its business in Berlin, was history.[289]

Continuities

If 1945 marked the biggest turning point in the history of Deutsche Bank, there were nevertheless some strong elements of continuity. While Germany's political and economic circumstances were changed at a stroke, which inevitably affected the bank's activities, elements of the organisational structure, workforce and business orientation remained surprisingly intact. This is not necessarily as astonishing as it may at first seem. In fact, it mirrors important findings of research into business resilience, which has shown that companies attempt to stabilise their internal structures in periods of upheaval and crisis in a bid to ensure their continued existence. From the perspective of the bank after 1945, rebuilding earlier networks and relationships was thus an important survival strategy. After all, little of the old Deutsche Bank was left: many buildings had been destroyed, deposits and securities had been lost or rendered worthless, customers and investments were gone for ever.[290] What remained was the bank's human capital – that is, its management and staff, including their knowledge and business relationships – along with the Deutsche Bank name and the institution's history as the most successful private-sector bank since the turn of the century.

One need not buy into the idea that employees' post-war reconstruction efforts were an act of heroism[291] in order to acknowledge that the strong continuity of personnel ensured the bank's survival beyond 1945. While the Berlin head office and all premises in the Soviet occupation zone were closed, many branches in the zones occupied by the Western Allies resumed business soon after the war had ended, though often only to handle deposits and withdrawals. The Allies were well aware that even a rudimentary monetary system could not function without banks. They also wanted to help avert any further expansion of the black market. 'To utilise, in so far as it is consistent with Military Government politics, the financial machinery already operative in Germany' was an official policy of the American military administration.[292]

Deutsche Bank's management attempted to maintain emergency operations from Hamburg in order to prevent the break-up of the bank. For a time, they had to cope without the entire Management Board. Those members who had not been killed in the war or subsequently arrested were forced to temporarily give up their work and could do no more than provide advice in the background. The members of the Supervisory Board and regional advisory committees (*Beiräte*) were also suspended.[293] Two experienced branch directors, Max Jörgens from Wuppertal-Elberfeld and Ludwig Kruse from Essen, now took over the management of the Hamburg headquarters. They were joined by Franz Heinrich Ulrich, who had already worked very closely with Abs. The decision in September 1943 to award four directors from the head office and 10 from the major branches with a general power of attorney now paid off. Only two of these directors were unavailable – Alfred Kurzmeyer, who had remained in Zurich, and Kurt Weigelt, whose former role in the Nazi Party now left him unable to work for the bank. The others, nicknamed the '12 Apostles' by Abs, provided the bank's management in Hamburg and elsewhere with a considerable degree of continuity. Kurzmeyer continued to act as

Closed branch of the dormant Deutsche Bank in Berlin. The façade served as an informal exchange site in 1946.

an intermediary in Switzerland,[294] while Weigelt began in the 1950s to represent the bank again in various supervisory board functions (including Lufthansa). The remaining, temporarily suspended board members gradually returned. In spring 1946, Fritz Wintermantel became head of the Hamburg management office. In 1947 and 1948, the denazification process categorised Abs, Plassmann, Rummel and Bechtolf as 'exonerated', allowing them to officially return to work for the bank. A schedule of responsibilities dating from January 1948 put Wintermantel in charge of foreign business, the cash office and organisational duties. Plassmann was assigned to human resources and Bechtolf to securities trading and the legal department. Joachim Kessler, one of the Berlin directors with general power of attorney, was responsible for the Corporate Secretariat and for the economics department, which continued to be headed by Ernst W. Schmidt.

A degree of communication with the branches was maintained using circular letters from the Hamburg head office as well as couriers and visits by individual managers. Transfers took place through clearing accounts of the main branches, while larger amounts were handled by a dedicated centre in Hildesheim. Accounts had been set up here for all major branches based on the balances as at 30 June 1945. While this allowed payment transactions to continue – only transfers from the Soviet zone were frozen in blocked accounts – the lending and securities business returned only very gradually. All assets were subject to Allied banking controls. Only small loans with short maturities were issued, with larger amounts requiring approval from the Hamburg head office. Rudimentary securities trading was conducted by telephone. In Hamburg, the stock exchange reopened for controlled unofficial trading. In Berlin and the Soviet zone, all branches and their assets were liquidated. In the Western occupied zones, however, the majority reopened. Of the bank's 227 branches that had existed at the beginning of 1944, 153 remained in spring 1946 (30 in the American zone, 88 in the British zone and 35 in the French zone). The movement of cash and securities from the Berlin headquarters to Hildesheim saved an estimated two-thirds of the bank's total assets, though a considerable portion of them were later rendered worthless by the currency reform of 1948. At the time of the currency reform, 68 per cent of the bank's assets consisted of treasury bonds, treasury bills and bonds issued by the Reich. These, along with the balances at the state central banks and postal cheque offices, were initially cancelled without compensation, reducing the total assets of the Western branches to approximately DM 650 million. The compensation later paid by the Federal Government offset these write-downs to some degree and allowed the bank to create opening balances denominated in Deutschmarks.[295]

Fragmented unity

During the war, American policy based on the New Deal held the ambition of destroying German industrial corporations and major banks. In the US, the government had taken action against monopolies and trusts and enforced a strict separation between commercial and investment banking. By fragmenting the West German economy along similar lines, it hoped to prevent the emergence of a new authoritarian regime.[296] In 1947–8, this vision began to have implications for Deutsche Bank, Dresdner Bank and Commerzbank. With the British and French authorities replicating the American approach, this was felt even outside the American occupation zone. In September 1948, Deutsche Bank's Hamburg management office was disbanded and its activities divided up between 10 regional institutions.[297] This division took place largely along political lines. For instance, around half of the business therefore went to the Rheinisch-Westfälische Bank in Düsseldorf, while other regional banks such as Württembergische Vereinsbank in Reutlingen received a much smaller volume.

The regional banks were legally independent and subject to the supervision of a trustee appointed by one of the occupying powers.[298] In practice, however, the impact of the bank's break-up was less serious than feared. The trustees avoided rigid checks in most cases and did little to interfere in operational business. Moreover, the regional banks maintained close ties through an informal network. The management of the 10 banks managed to co-ordinate the work of their branches. All 10 banks retained direct payment transactions and used consortia to co-operate on large projects. In the British zone, the occupiers were reluctant to follow American policy given their own tradition of large banks. In any case, the British zone of occupation, in which Germany's heavy industry was concentrated, relied more heavily on strong lending banks than the farming businesses and light industries in the American-controlled south of the country. The banks managed to establish new companies specialising

The logos of the ten successor banks into which Deutsche Bank was divided in 1947–8.

in certain business areas. GEFA Gesellschaft für Absatzfinanzierung, for example, was founded in Wuppertal in 1949 to handle the instalment business of Deutsche Bank's successor institutions. At management level, former Deutsche Bank Management Board members and directors were active in nearly every part of the regional banks. The Hamburg management office moved almost in its entirety to Düsseldorf, where the Rheinisch-Westfälische Bank became Deutsche Bank's informal headquarters. The management board of the dormant 'old bank' (*Altbank*) in Berlin continued to meet regularly to make important decisions on the activity of the individual banks. This contravention of the Allied rules was tolerated, allowing remnants of Deutsche Bank-wide control to survive. As Plassmann reported to the old bank's Supervisory Board on 19 December 1949, a 'balkanisation' of the bank had been successfully averted: 'I can report with satisfaction that the network of sister banks is up and running smoothly and has proven itself.'[299]

Faced with the threat of liquidation and prosecution by the Allies, the three major banks – once fierce competitors – now co-operated closely. They even developed a joint defence strategy in the Nuremberg Trials.[300] In addition, they co-ordinated with each other on all negotiations with the Allies and compiled joint memoranda aimed at the formal restoration of the big banks. One thing in their favour was the fact that the introduction of the regional banks had not put in place any arrangements for the 'old banks'. Important questions regarding the compensation of shareholders or the treatment of foreign liabilities had not been settled. In this respect, time was on the banks' side. The banks did everything they could to prevent the Allies from rapidly and irrevocably breaking them up, and opened fresh negotiations after the Federal Republic was founded.

The new, old bank

At the end of 1949, the three banks started to re-enter negotiations with a long memorandum drawn up by Ernst Wilhelm Schmidt which called for a return to the major banks of old for economic reasons.[301] Abs, however, having good contacts with the Allied administration and with many British and American bankers, thought that such a demand was premature. Instead, he recommended proposing that the regional banks initially be combined into three larger institutions, with the option to call upon an overarching 'banque d'affaire' in specific business areas. Abs pointed out that an arrangement needed to be reached in any case on the issues of tax and shareholdings, and that the 10 regional banks, arbitrarily organised to correspond with the boundaries of the federal states, were not suited to the task.[302] Abs's proposal was not only supported by the boss of the Bank deutscher Länder (BdL), Wilhelm Vocke, but also by the Economics Minister Ludwig Erhard and two major industry associations that were in the process of re-establishing their presence: the Federation of German Industries (BDI) and the Association of German Chambers of Industry and Commerce (DIHT). On a trip to the US in late 1949, Abs also succeeded in convincing American politicians and financiers of the merits of his plan. He argued that the now 11 regional banks (following the opening of the Berliner Disconto Bank in West Berlin in 1949) were effectively 'excluded from international business transactions from the outset'.

> Banks without their own legal personality, articles of association or supervisory board, that publish neither balance sheets nor profit and loss, and that share liability for one another without reciprocal oversight will not find any foreign institution willing to enter into a close business relationship with them.[303]

After long negotiations with the Allies and various political players in West Germany, Abs's preferred solution became reality. On 25 September 1952 it was decided to establish three regional successor institutions: Norddeutsche Bank in Hamburg, Rheinisch-Westfälische Bank in Düsseldorf and Süddeutsche Bank in Munich. Criticism came especially from the federally minded southern German states, which wanted to maintain a regional banking system. The move also raised tax questions concerning the free reserves. Under the tax system of the day, 70 per cent tax would have been payable on the hidden reserves released by creating the new banks, which would have reduced the

The headquarters of Deutsche Bank's three successor institutions (from top): Norddeutsche Bank in Hamburg, Rheinisch-Westfälische Bank in Düsseldorf and Süddeutsche Bank in Munich.

already low levels of equity even further. A tax exemption was therefore agreed. A series of conditions was designed to ensure the three banks remained independent from one another. These banned them from integrating through equity investments or mandates, for instance. Yet, in practice, the rules did not prevent Deutsche Bank from operating as a single unit to an even greater extent than it already had.

The creation of the three banks in 1952 was a boon to the existing shareholders. The shares – still traded in Reichsmarks – had already risen considerably in value and were now translated into new Deutschmark-denominated shares in the three banks at a favourable ratio of 10:6.5. By now, the successor banks, which were also benefiting from the Federal Republic's export boom, were in an even better position than before the war. A comparison of balance sheets between 1937 and 1953 shows that, despite the territorial losses, the reduced number of branches and the smaller workforce, total assets were a third higher than before the war.[304] Admittedly, the inflation-adjusted data also show that, in other respects, the recovery was incomplete. At the time of founding, the three banks had equity capital of DM 100 million and reserves of DM 40.5 million.[305] The equity ratio was just 3.4 per cent. The risk structure, including in terms of the lending portfolio, had worsened – there were far fewer small loans and considerably more large customers. Given the strength of the economy, this was no cause for concern, yet it nevertheless showed how highly profit oriented the bank's business had become as memories of the banking crisis faded.[306]

By 1952, then, seven years after the end of the war, the bank had largely rebuilt. In practice, the three banks acted together on important matters despite their formal independence. In 1955 they prepared a joint annual report, describing themselves as the Deutsche Bank 'Group'. The three banks also committed themselves to offsetting profits and losses among themselves in line with their share capital.

Süddeutsche Bank decided in its annual general meeting on 30 April 1957 in Munich to merge into Deutsche Bank, the last of the three successor institutions to do so. From left: Erich Bechtolf, Hermann J. Abs, Hans Rummel and Clemens Plassmann.

On 2 May 1957, 'Deutsche Bank AG' was formally reunified with its registered office in Frankfurt. In other respects, however, the internal structure created in 1952 remained largely intact. The decentralised organisation with three headquarters (Frankfurt, Düsseldorf and Hamburg) and relatively independent branches continued. Frankfurt and Düsseldorf looked after 114 and 118 branches respectively in 1957, while 75 branches and deposit offices were assigned to the Hamburg office. As the home of Banco Alemán Transatlántico und Deutsch-Asiatische Bank, Hamburg was more strongly integrated into the international business.

Alongside the three headquarters, the 24 main branches also held considerable autonomy. The Allied banking policy thus reinforced the centrifugal forces within the bank that had been a common cause for complaint in the 1920s. With its forced move from Berlin to the West, from centralism to regionalism, Deutsche Bank mirrored the federal principle of the new West German state. However, this was not a radical change, but part of a longer-term trend that had already begun with the expansion of the branch network between the wars.

The elements of continuity also dominated when it came to the bank's workforce and business activities. There was no change in direction in the banking business itself, and most branches and departments retained their existing personnel. This was particularly striking at senior management level. The management boards of the three banks were entirely comprised of long-serving senior figures who had worked for Deutsche Bank during the Third Reich. The Süddeutsche Bank management board comprised Hermann J. Abs, Robert Frowein and Walter Tron, as well as Heinz Osterwind, who had worked for the bank as a *Prokurist* (officer with power of attorney) since 1937 and had also managed the Munich branch. Management of the Rheinisch-Westfälische Bank was in the hands of the former Deutsche Bank Management Board members Clemens Plassmann and Oswald Rösler, along with the long-standing directors Fritz Gröning, Hans Janberg and Jean Baptist Rath. Norddeutsche Bank was headed by Erich Bechtolf, Karl Klasen and Franz Heinrich Ulrich. Other former managers also took on new functions. Hans Rummel became deputy chairman of Süddeutsche Bank supervisory board, on which Karl Ritter von Halt also served following his release from Buchenwald

Oswald Rösler (1887–1961) joined the Management Board of Deutsche Bank und Disconto-Gesellschaft in 1933 and was Spokesman of the Management Board during the final two years of the war. After five years in a Soviet prison camp, he joined the Management Board of Rheinisch-Westfälische Bank in 1952 and served as the first Supervisory Board Chairman of the refounded Deutsche Bank from 1957 to 1960.

concentration camp.[307] Fritz Wintermantel became supervisory board chairman at Rheinisch-Westfälische Bank. Following its reunification in 1957, Deutsche Bank recruited its Management Board from those of the three successor banks: the new board comprised Abs, Bechtolf, Frowein, Gröning, Janberg, Klasen, Osterwind, Plassmann, Rath, Tron and Ulrich. The Supervisory Board, too, was home to many individuals who had held mandates during the Nazi era and was chaired by Oswald Rösler.

Although no reliable data are available, it is likely that there was also a high degree of continuity at mid-management (e.g. head of department, senior bank official) level.

Table 2: Changes in the successor banks' staff and Deutsche Bank staff, 1952–1960 (1 January of each year).

	1952	1953	1954	1955	1956	1957	1958	1959	1960
Total number of staff:	31 Dec. 1938 = 17,947								
	21 June 1948 = 6,299								
Management Board	9	11	12	12	12	12	11	9	11
Directors (head office, main branches)	70	75	76	79	80	84	81	88	89
Deputy directors (head office, main branches)	44	40	48	52	54	58	60	58	45
Directors below head office/main branch level	116	130	131	126	124	136	136	133	141
Deputy directors below head office/main branch level	31	29	32	39	40	36	41	42	45
Heads of department	62	72	73	75	79	89	94	107	117
Staff holding power of attorney ('Prokuristen')	297	329	338	368	399	420	442	446	450
Senior bank officials ('Oberbeamten')	521	545	658	672	736	777	821	856	899
Commercial staff on standard wages	9,348	10,360	11,208	11,990	12,342	12,484	12,614	12,918	13,418
Temporary staff	232	170	196	233	123	63	41	58	52
Trade-related/technical staff	356	384	449	637	729	794	868	935	978
Apprentices	798	826	869	1,028	1,271	1,397	1,379	1,278	1,240
Semi-skilled workers	37	28	21	20	23	13	5	1	1
Messengers ('Jungboten')	159	216	234	265	254	234	246	210	230
Total number of staff	12,080	13,215	14,345	15,596	16,266	16,597	16,839	17,139	17,716
of whom men	8,130	8,674	9,155	9,792	10,142	10,300	10,386	10,437	10,601
of whom women	3,950	4,541	5,190	5,804	6,124	6,297	6,453	6,702	7,115
percentage of men: women	67.3: 32.7	65.6: 34.4	63.8: 36.2	62.8: 37.2	62.3: 37.7	62.1: 37.9	61.7: 38.3	60.9: 39.1	59.8: 40.2

Source: HADB, ZA2/199.

Due not least to the lack of available skilled personnel, the majority of the Nazi-era management staff were retained or re-employed after a few years. If they did not have an official function in the bank, as was the case with the heavily implicated Kurt Weigelt, for example, they were at least given other work at companies with which the bank maintained a close business relationship.

It took until the late 1950s for the workforce to return to its pre-war level. The size of the workforce increased evenly across the board, though slightly more sharply at senior levels than for ordinary employees. The booming labour market drastically reduced the number of temporary staff, as few people were willing to work on such unattractive terms. The number of trainees increased sharply, indicating that the bank's internal training structures were becoming increasingly professionalised. The rapid expansion of the workforce and the technical requirements of banking operations in the post-war world meant that the bank increasingly trained its own new generation of staff.[308] An even bigger change in this decade, however, was the rapidly increasing proportion of women in the bank's workforce, which rose from just 13 per cent in 1937 to 24 per cent in 1948. By 1952, it increased to 32 per cent, and in 1958 it exceeded the 40 per cent mark. The bank's growth and the lack of male applicants quickly transformed the gender composition of the workforce, though this change was largely confined to the lower- and medium-paying jobs. Management, meanwhile, remained an exclusively male domain.

Return to normality

The fact that Deutsche Bank was able relatively quickly after the Second World War to return to normality and restore its status as Germany's leading major bank was also a product of the political and economic environment of the post-war period.

First, the banks' top executives had emerged unscathed from the Nuremberg Trials. While the US in particular had pushed for legal proceedings against the bankers and also prepared charges against Abs, the economic trials in Nuremberg concentrated on the major industrial companies (I. G. Farben, Krupp, Flick).[309] Even proceedings against board members of Dresdner Bank, which had been closely interlinked with the SS business empire, were dropped. Instead, a largely symbolic case was brought against the former Dresdner Bank director Karl Rasche, who was convicted to seven years' imprisonment in the Wilhelmstrasse Trial in April 1949.[310] The proceedings against Rasche had the paradoxical effect of quickly rehabilitating those bank managers not put on trial and of dissociating the major banks themselves from the Nazi crimes in the public mind. The conviction of a few principal offenders unintentionally fostered the narrative of a largely apolitical business elite who had been forced to adapt to the regime against their will and had supported the war economy for purely patriotic motives. However, this did not prevent Abs, on whom extensive material had been collected in the OMGUS (Office of Military Government for Germany, US) investigations by the American Military Government, becoming a target for repeated media attacks in relation to his Nazi past. These came, not least, from the German Democratic Republic (GDR).[311]

Second, the economic and political environment had changed dramatically since 1947–8. Faced with the Cold War, the Western Allies abandoned their plans to disrupt the German economy. They now supported a rapid economic recovery and the reintegration of West Germany into the world market.[312] In May 1950, the French foreign minister Robert Schuman had floated the idea of a European coal and steel union to help Western European countries rebuild their heavy industry together. The European Coal and Steel Community (ECSC) founded in 1952 urgently needed functioning banks to meet the industry's demand for credit. Though the ECSC was permitted to issue its own bonds in order to finance investments, the weak capital market rendered this impossible. The presence in Germany's Ruhr region of both the largest coal reserves and the largest steel companies of any of the six ECSC members meant an important role for German banks, and one which regional institutions would have struggled to fulfil given the scale of financing required.

Third, the banks played an important part in settling international payments. In the absence of freely flowing capital and foreign exchange, and, given the need for cross-border transactions to combat supply shortages, banks were essential as international financial intermediaries. For one thing, the complex international debt obligations pre-dating the end of the war needed settling. This meant dealing with old clearing accounts from the Third Reich as well as the still-existing standstill debts dating from the 1930s. The American occupation directive JCS 1067 of April 1945 called for a resumption of debt servicing at the earliest opportunity.[313] As the German banking sector was devoid of significant assets after inflation and currency reform, it was impossible to satisfy foreign creditors' claims straight away. This gave the American and British financial sectors a vested interest in strong, well-functioning, large German banks. In 1950, German debt under the standstill loans amounted to approximately DM 425 million: DM 293 million was owed to banks in Britain, DM 114 million to America and DM 15 million to Switzerland.[314]

The question of Germany's foreign debts came to a head at negotiations in London in 1953. It was here that Abs would once again be a decisive figure, fulfilling a key foreign policy role in the rehabilitation of the Federal Republic. In so doing, he would restore his bank's leading role and his own position as the most important banker in Germany and perhaps anywhere in the Western world.

5. 'Commercial and moral guilt'

In the years after 1945, Deutsche Bank faced the task not only of rebuilding its business relationships, but also of restoring its international reputation. Hermann J. Abs understood this better than probably any other business leader in the early days of the Federal Republic. Nobody could rival his ability to use old contacts in the business and political worlds to rehabilitate the bank – and himself – in the public eye. Though officially suspended from all functions until the end of the denazification process in February 1948, he participated in key decisions and remained in close contact with numerous leaders, politicians and Allied representatives, who, despite their political reservations, valued his proven financial expertise. He was also adept at seeking out new relationships where he saw opportunities for the bank, quickly making contact in the summer of 1945 with the soon-to-be founder of the Christian Democratic Union and future first Chancellor of West Germany, Konrad Adenauer. Though they both hailed from the

The chancellor and his financial adviser: Konrad Adenauer and Hermann J. Abs met not just on the political stage, but also privately, like this 1957 meeting over coffee in Kronberg with Abs's wife Inez (left) and Adenauer's daughter Libet Werhahn.

Catholic Rhineland, it was the first time these two prominent men had met.[315] Through intensive correspondence, numerous conversations with visitors and the travel involved in his remaining supervisory board mandates, Abs used the period of his forced suspension to prepare the ground for a post-war career. He continued to see his professional future at Deutsche Bank, quickly recognising that public office would remain closed to him given his former position in the Third Reich.

In fact, despite his past, Abs had been considered in spring 1948 as a potential president of the Bank deutscher Länder. Citing a lack of sufficient assurances concerning the independence of the bank's central council, however, he turned the post down. He criticised the requirement for the council to take unanimous decisions and demanded the right to veto the expansion of lending to the public sector. While there was substance to these concerns, especially given the experience of National Socialism, they are unlikely to have been the only reason for Abs's reluctance to entertain the role. Suspecting that the Americans would veto his appointment, he appears to have pre-empted their rejection.[316] History repeated itself the following year when Adenauer offered him the post of secretary of state for the new foreign service. This time, reservations were expressed by both the French and the Americans, and Abs once again steered clear.[317] Though he sought contact with politicians, then, he had little desire to tie his own fate to public office. As had been his *modus operandi* during National Socialism, Abs avoided expressing political views in public and never joined a party. As a banker, he preferred to remain a background figure and avoided the risks of political engagement.

Abs and the Kreditanstalt für Wiederaufbau

Abs was able to put his reputation as an international financial expert to good use in the early 1950s in two roles: he not only headed the German delegation sent to London to settle the country's foreign debts, but was also an important figure in the establishment of the Kreditanstalt für Wiederaufbau (KfW). Created in 1948 to distribute Marshall Plan aid, KfW became the most important development bank in the Federal Republic.

British and American experts approached Abs as early as autumn 1947 to discuss ways of financing the rebuilding of the West German economy. More specifically, they wanted to know how the US Marshall Plan funds, as well as GARIOA (Government Aid Relief in Occupied Areas) funds received by German importers in return for deliveries of American goods, could best be used. Though the idea of establishing a publicly owned development bank to distribute funds to investors efficiently and unbureaucratically was not his own,[318] Abs had a considerable influence on the shape taken by KfW. The Kreditanstalt für Wiederaufbau, or 'Credit Institute for Reconstruction' (its name deliberately avoided the word 'bank'), was to direct the use of incoming foreign aid without itself playing the role of a bank in the narrower sense of the word. Rather than issue its own loans, it would leave this task to the commercial institutions. It was also forbidden from providing other banking services (securities, deposit and current account business). This was doubtless an important structural decision, with which Abs intended to strengthen the role of the private banks. With economic planning in vogue after the Second World War and no consensus on whether a market-based lending system would survive long term, the legal status of KfW was no mere side issue.

In December 1948, Abs was appointed together with Otto Schniewind to KfW's board of directors, before joining the management board a few months later.[319] This put him in a position to exercise considerable influence over lending policy in the early days of reconstruction in the Federal Republic. With capital in short supply, the approximately $3 billion Germany received through the Marshall Plan was a substantial sum. Abs ensured that KfW also financed itself by issuing bonds, thereby mobilising the capital market for German industry once again. Though there was little demand for the first bond issue, for which Abs founded a guarantee consortium of leading German banks, it nevertheless served to set an important example, signalling to banks and businesses that they should seek capital market funding wherever possible.[320] Abs also had a considerable influence over KfW's operational business, not least where the distribution of loans and communication with American creditors were concerned.[321] Alongside his management board activities, he was also a member of four committees of the board of directors and held key positions in KfW's management together with some old familiar faces. He persuaded Walter Tron, for example, the former CABV director in Vienna, to join the management board. When Tron moved to Süddeutsche Bank three years later, Richard Gdynia, former director of Deutsche Bank in Katowice, took his post.[322] Other confidants of Abs also took up leading roles at the bank, including Bruno Bauer and Hans Erich Bachem.[323] Paul Krebs, an economist and former member of the Reich Economics Ministry who had edited the *Handelsblatt* newspaper since 1945, became another important figure in KfW's management. In 1952, Krebs accompanied Abs to the negotiations in London on German debt and subsequently became director of the

Corporate Secretariat and Foreign Secretariat at Deutsche Bank.[324] For Abs and many other senior managers of Deutsche Bank, then, KfW was an important step on the road from National Socialism to the Federal Republic.

Primarily responsible for financing corporate investment loans, KfW was also involved in trade financing for West German industry amid soaring exports in the early years of the Federal Republic. Given the importance of trade financing, however, Abs was reluctant to leave it to a public bank. For one thing, the rediscount line provided to Bank deutscher Länder for this purpose was not particularly high, amounting to just DM 600 million in 1952. Moreover, KfW generally only provided loans with Hermes guarantees.[325] On the initiative of Abs and Oswald Rösler, multiple private sector German banks therefore founded the Ausfuhrkredit-Aktiengesellschaft (AKA), a consortium bank based in Frankfurt. This provided a broad basis for medium- and long-term export promotion. The founding consortium was convinced that further export financing should be the domain of the private sector alone, enhancing the prestige of German banks abroad.[326] In Rösler's eyes, the aim was to spread risks across the consortium members and to liberate the member banks' balance sheets from reserve obligations, allowing greater leeway for the equally important short-term lending business.[327] The creation of a private sector export financing institution, calculated the Rheinisch-Westfälische Bank, would 'create a lasting positive impression in public opinion and prove that the banks are ready to promote exports under their own steam', despite the lack of refinancing opportunities.[328] Nevertheless, KfW continued to increase its activities abroad in the years that followed, especially through its promotion of investment in developing countries. In 1961, it became officially responsible for realising West Germany's financial co-operation with 'third world' countries.[329]

The London Debt Agreement

His work at KfW quickly restored Abs's reputation in the financial world. Among politicians, however, concerns remained. In 1950, Abs once again missed the opportunity to win nomination to high office when Jean Monnet vetoed the German proposal for Abs to lead the country's delegation in negotiations on the European Coal and Steel Community. For Monnet, Abs represented the wartime pillaging of the French economy and could not be considered a credible partner.[330] When Adenauer toyed with the idea of proposing Abs as foreign minister in 1952, he was met with reservations not only from the opposition but from within government. These reactions show how markedly his reputation was still tainted by his work for Deutsche Bank in the Third Reich.[331]

When it came to the negotiations on Germany's foreign debt, Abs was better placed, though other individuals were also being considered. They included the former Reichsbank chief Hans Luther, finance minister Fritz Schäffer and the president of the Nordrhein-Westfälische Landeszentralbank Walter Kriege. In opting for Abs, Adenauer particularly had the foreign policy implications of the debt issue on his mind, as its final settlement was a prerequisite for the sovereignty of the Federal Republic.[332] His position was that the Federal Republic should be declared the legitimate legal successor of the former German Reich and recognise all the rights and liabilities this entailed.[333] This largely politically motivated position had already been set out before the talks in

London had begun and before it was clear what financial costs the Federal Republic could expect to incur. This put the German side in a weak negotiating position from the start, necessitating considerable diplomatic skill on the part of its delegation.[334]

Few people understood the complex legal, financial and political aspects of Germany's foreign debt better than Abs. He had been involved in negotiating the numerous standstill agreements since 1931, initially for Bankhaus Delbrück Schickler & Co. and, from the end of 1937, for Deutsche Bank. During the war, which had interrupted the standstill agreements with the Allies, he had travelled regularly to Switzerland to continue the bilateral negotiations. No other German bankers in the years after 1945 could rival his expertise in this area. What was more, as chairman of the Deutscher Ausschuss für internationale finanzielle Beziehungen (German Committee for International Financial Relations), Abs had taken soundings from foreign creditors and was thus best prepared for the official negotiations themselves.[335]

Abs's mission faced numerous pitfalls, however. Financial claims from various different creditors had to be settled in a single process: First World War reparations, the loans and bonds of German companies, banks and public bodies from the interwar period (which from 1931 onwards largely fell under the standstill agreements) and the repayment of Allied aid after 1945. Reparations for the Second World War were also up for debate, though the Federal Republic took the view that these could not, under international law, form part of the negotiations in London. Another question was how to value the German foreign assets confiscated by the victorious powers. Finally, there was the separate and politically sensitive issue of how to atone for the persecution and annihilation of the Jews by the Third Reich. The entanglement of 'commercial and moral guilt' did not lend itself to finding a quick solution.[336]

After preliminary discussions in June 1951 to clarify the process ahead, the real negotiations, divided between four committees, began in November. Alongside the 30 members of the German delegation, 40 delegations from 65 creditor states attended. Compromise on post-war debt proved quickest to reach, partly because only a small number of creditors were involved, and partly because the US reduced its claims for repayment of Marshall Plan funds and other aid (GARIOA) from $3.2 to $1.2 billion. Generosity was also forthcoming from the other creditors. The UK reduced its claims from £240 to £150 million, and France from 15.8 to 11.84 million francs. This favourable settlement from the German perspective was subject, however, to all sides agreeing a satisfactory solution for the other debts.[337]

After this smooth start, the rest of the negotiations would prove far more complex. In December 1951, Adenauer had promised the newly elected chairman of the Jewish Claims Conference, Nahum Goldmann, comprehensive moral and material reparations for German crimes against the Jews.[338] The negotiations with the Jewish Claims Conference and the State of Israel thus overlapped the debt issue from the outset. This contradicted the original German negotiating position, which had been to settle the country's debts without reaching a resolution on reparations and other compensation for the Second World War. Abs himself had entered the negotiations with this position and now felt undermined by Adenauer. In this, he sided with the finance minister Fritz Schäffer, who wanted to avoid accepting reparations, fearing Germany would be financially overstretched.[339] Despite threatening to resign as the head of the delegation, Abs was unable to change Adenauer's mind; Adenauer's calculations were primarily political rather than economic, and he was in any case less knowledgeable about Germany's economic situation. Abs also failed in his bid to take charge of negotiating the Reparations Agreement with Israel, with Adenauer choosing instead to entrust the economics professor and CDU politician Franz Böhm with this task.

In the London debt negotiations, too, Abs had to retreat from some of his demands. He could not persuade the creditors to offset confiscated German assets against the amounts owed – though, given the low total value of the assets involved, this would not have made a substantial difference in any case. Nor could he convince them to forego reparations in return for debt settlement. Nevertheless, the German delegation did succeed in postponing any final resolution until after the signing of a peace agreement. There was little serious prospect of such an agreement at the time, and no such formal treaty has been signed to this day.[340] This deferral proved advantageous to the Federal Republic, as it meant that the question of reparations did not return to the political agenda until reunification in 1990.

As a banker, Abs placed special importance on reaching a settlement in London for the loans included in the 1930s standstill agreements. The fact that agreement was rapidly achieved in this area was partly thanks to the small number of countries on the other side of the table: Switzerland, the UK and the US.[341] Dating from 1939, the final standstill agreement, to which all sides still considered themselves bound in principle, served as the template. The new arrangements, on which the parties reached an accord in June 1952, were as follows: German banks could repay their debts in Deutschmarks and the frozen loans could be 'recommercialised'. The repayment deadline was set at one year to ensure rapid settlement of these liabilities.[342]

The wider results of the negotiations were also respectable from a German perspective. Abs's delegation successfully persuaded the other parties not to insist on a gold clause when calculating pre-war debt. This reduced the total from DM 13.5 to DM 9.6 billion. Interest and compound interest were calculated favourably from the German standpoint, allowing the parties to agree on total debts of DM 7.3 billion. The creditors also agreed to reduce post-war debts from DM 15 to DM 7 billion. This took the total amounts owed to approximately DM 14 billion, a manageable amount considering the long repayment period. Abs had always been adamant that Germany must not be financially overstretched given that it had only a small current account surplus and a severe lack of foreign exchange.

The German delegation argued against heavy payment obligations, pointing to the potential political problems this might store up.[343] One lesson learned from the years that had followed the First World War was the inclusion of a transfer clause. This meant that the amounts to be paid by the Federal Republic were tied to the country's trade surplus, which amounted to roughly half a billion DM in the first half of 1953. Though the German side could not persuade the other parties to forego reparations altogether, the reparations question was postponed until after the signing of a future peace agreement. In subsequent years, the West German government was unable to escape demands from Western European countries for compensation of the victims of

The signing of the London Debt Agreement at Londonderry House on 27 February 1953. At the table, from left: Werner Kroog, Georg Vogel, Gerd Weiz, Hermann J. Abs and Bernhard Wolff.

National Socialism. Instead of reaching a single agreement, however, it negotiated separately with each of the 11 countries concerned, resulting in 11 bilateral treaties between 1959 and 1964 in which Germany agreed to one-off payments.[344] Millions of Eastern European forced labourers, meanwhile, were left empty-handed until the early twenty-first century. For German businesses, this was a beneficial outcome.[345] The agreement reached with Israel and the Jewish Claims Conference was also economically sustainable for the new German state. The payments to Israel – which, at over DM 3 billion, comprised the principal component of total reparations – could be made in the form of goods, which provided an additional stimulus to the German economy and took into account the lack of foreign exchange.[346]

Following the conclusion of the London Debt Agreement, Abs toured Germany 'like an itinerant priest',[347] attempting to reassure business leaders. This was not without self-interest given his own role in the process. Abs succeeded in presenting the agreement as a diplomatic success and a product of common sense – an essential step towards achieving Germany's foreign trade ambitions.

The London Debt Agreement not only created the basis for recognition of the Federal Republic in international law but also for German industry's ability to borrow. It was thus a prerequisite for the economic growth of the post-war era.[348] Before the agreement, importers had generally had to pay for their goods directly upon delivery rather than within the usual 90-day window.[349] Pending a solution to the country's outstanding liabilities, it had also been almost impossible to borrow from foreign banks.[350] For

Deutsche Bank's successor institutions, which wanted to quickly resume their international activities, the agreement was thus an important step. In 1955, Abs was tasked with another international mission: securing the return of confiscated German assets abroad or compensation for their German owners. The obstacles to these negotiations were far more complex, however, as there was little political pressure to reach an all-encompassing agreement.[351] In the years that followed, Abs worked repeatedly on behalf of Deutsche Bank for the return of confiscated German property and pushed – albeit without success – for an international convention to protect foreign investments.[352]

For Abs, the London Debt Agreement was perhaps the most important task in the transition from the Third Reich to the Federal Republic. He had proved the value of his foreign connections and his ability to solve complex international financial problems that might have defeated politicians. With this work, he performed a great service to his bank and to the banking industry as a whole. Whenever major banks were able to participate in international financial policy in the decades that followed – for example during the debt crises of the 1980s – it was thanks in no small part to the diplomatic success of this German banker.

With his mission in London, Abs had become a central player in Germany's efforts to deal with its past.[353] Though he considered it a strategic error to have linked the issues of foreign debt and material reparations, he ultimately backed the (domestically controversial) Luxembourg Agreement of 10 September 1952.[354] The fact that Abs personally sought to restore relations with the former owners of companies that had been Aryanised during the Third Reich shows that he, more than many others at the time, understood the connection between financial reparations and a new economic beginning.

6. The Return to the World Market

The London Debt Agreement of 1953 was the prerequisite for German banks to return to the world market and resume their business activities abroad. However, cross-border foreign exchange transactions remained subject to a series of conditions and controls. These were initially governed by the payments agreement under the Marshall Plan and, from 1950, by a system of multilateral clearing for cross-border trade in goods: the European Payments Union.[355] A considerable advance on the bilateral system of the 1930s, this allowed clearing between 14 countries to take place at European level through the Bank for International Settlements.[356] Balance of payment deficits were balanced out by loans from the IMF and World Bank. The member states of the European Payments Union also undertook to gradually liberalise trade in goods.

Until 1958, this tightly woven system of foreign exchange and capital controls greatly limited the banks' business opportunities, but did not inhibit them completely. An important task of the banks was, just as it had been during National Socialism, to handle international payment transactions. Initially, this also included checking their customers' export declarations, a task that passed to the customs authorities in 1951. The banks also provided travel money and monitored incoming payments in the export business.[357] An internal report shows that the three successor institutions to Deutsche Bank also generated considerable income through currency switch transactions. The branches in southern Germany alone generated some DM 1 billion of turnover through currency business in 1951.[358] Aside from this, however, there was little money to be made from foreign exchange business in the post-war fixed exchange rate regime, and banks soon cut back their activities in this area after 1953.[359]

Apart from foreign exchange business, the largest proportion of the international activities of Deutsche Bank's successor banks in the early 1950s consisted of pre-import and pre-export finance. Long-term loans or foreign investments were barely possible given the lack of deposits and were still largely the preserve of KfW and the Ausfuhrkredit-Aktiengesellschaft (AKA).[360] However, this did not leave Deutsche Bank entirely without a role in this business. Its three successors held a 26 per cent share in AKA, and the AKA supervisory board was chaired by Oswald Rösler, who had played a major part in the organisation's creation. AKA also took over the remains of the now defunct Exportkreditbank AG, in which Deutsche Bank had held a majority stake prior to 1945.[361]

From the beginning of 1952, German banks were once again legally permitted to make direct investments in other countries. They could open branches abroad and acquire equity interests in foreign companies. Even before this, the Bank deutscher Länder had permitted the opening of 'concentration accounts' with foreign banks in order to handle payment transactions. For example, at the end of 1949, Rheinisch-Westfälische Bank already held accounts with banks in the UK, France, Denmark, Belgium, the Netherlands, Luxembourg, Finland, Sweden, the Saar region (at that time partitioned from Germany) and the US.[362] In some cases, the foreign accounts also contained older foreign currency deposits that were now accessible again following the London Debt Agreement.[363] As Osterwind noted, the network of correspondence banks and nostro accounts attracted large transaction volumes and was systematically expanded in the years that followed.[364] By 1953, it had already outgrown that of the old Deutsche Bank.[365]

The three successor banks were delighted by the 'extremely respectable' performance of their trade financing business.[366] Exports by the banks' customers had already reached DM 7.1 billion by 1953 and rose further to DM 12.7 billion in 1956. For imports, business volume was slightly lower, but also grew sharply from DM 5.4 billion to DM 8.9 billion. The trade surplus Germany had already developed by the early 1950s was clearly reflected on the balance sheets of the three successor banks.

Deutsche Bank advertisement from 1957 highlighting its worldwide business connections.

Figure 12: Exports and imports by customers of Deutsche Bank's three successor banks 1953–6 (in DM millions).

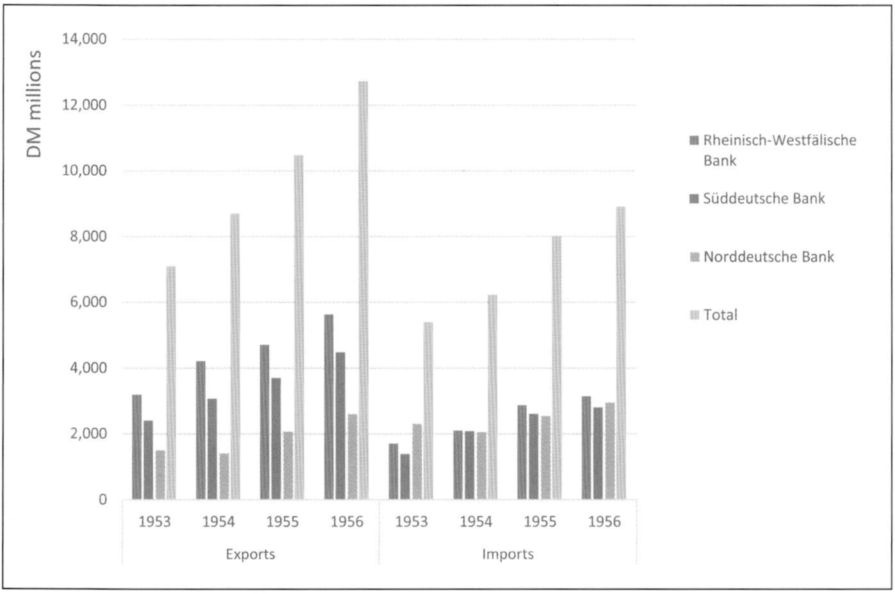

Source: Regling, Dezentrale Bearbeitung des Auslandsgeschäftes nach durchgeführter Fusion, 4 April 1957, HADB, ZA1/146.

Organisation of international business

The bank's decentralised nature meant that the branches were handling a growing share of international business. Their ability to offer local companies bespoke solutions proved to be an advantage during reconstruction, when Germany's foreign trade needed to be revived amid difficult circumstances.[367] German industrial businesses turned in their droves to their local banks for help with financing cross-border trade and for advice on the latest rules of commerce and foreign exchange. The major banks faced growing competition from savings banks and co-operative banks, which had large numbers of local branches and could finance foreign trade on often favourable terms.[368]

The international activities of the regional banks were only loosely co-ordinated, for example through the monthly meetings of the 'foreign trade experts' (*Außenhandels-fachherren*), information events and regular circulars. In 1952, the creation of the three successor banks, which had the legal status of stock corporations, allowed for a more streamlined organisation of international business. Süddeutsche Bank created a 'Central Foreign Department' to handle large transactions with other countries and to set the rules for, and where possible oversee, foreign business.[369] The department was split between the two head offices of Süddeutsche Bank – Munich and Frankfurt – with different regions and countries assigned to each location. Frankfurt was responsible for business with the UK, the Netherlands, Scandinavia, North and South America and Australia, while Munich co-ordinated the other European countries along with Asia

Deutsche Bank's first post-war Frankfurt headquarters on the Roßmarkt and Junghofstraße, 1957.

and Africa.[370] The Central Foreign Department was responsible for all international syndicated business, major loans and general issues in relation to KfW financing, for handling foreign debts and standstill loans and for currency trading. It served large foreign customers and maintained contacts in ministries, associations and chambers of commerce. Abs's own residence in Bonn, for example, was home to a liaison office. Regular reports on individual countries, which were often based on the travels of the bank's leading experts, also played an important role.[371] As well as 'overseas news' and 'country reports', the bank also published its own 'foreign trade information' series. Norddeutsche Bank and Rheinisch-Westfälische Bank both created similar organisational structures for their international business.

Despite the legal division into three successor institutions, the banks were determined that their representatives should present themselves during foreign travels as part of 'Deutsche Bank'. This reflected the tendency, as Karl Klasen from Norddeutsche Bank noted following a trip to South America in 1953, for foreign institutions to perceive the three banks 'as a single entity – Deutsche Bank'.[372] Klasen called for the banks' 'propaganda material' – i.e. their publicity and information brochures for foreign customers and their advertisements in international newspapers – to share a similar design where possible, while still bearing the name of the individual bank. He also demanded that the three banks should all offer foreign customers the same terms.[373] As these and other efforts show, ensuring that the main branches took decisions which were aligned with at least the overarching objectives of the three banks was a major exercise in co-ordination. The decentralised nature of the banks' international business would lead to repeated conflict as the autonomy of the main branches undermined the ability of head offices to manage the business effectively. The hybrid structure of international business that emerged after the war and persisted (despite multiple reforms) into the 1980s made management and oversight exceptionally difficult. It was barely possible to obtain reliable data on the scope of international business, let alone monitor it effectively.

The main branches in particular had little interest in relinquishing their newly won autonomy. Upon recentralisation in 1957, they argued that the established system was far better able to meet the service-intensive requirements of the bank's international business. The director of the Düsseldorf head office, Wilhelm Regling, stated that:

> The regional system forced on us by the war [...] has proven itself in international business. It has been possible with the greatest efficiency, and while avoiding a mammoth apparatus or an unwieldy, dirigiste approach, to achieve what customers normally expect only from the private banks: first-rate advice and swift service.[374]

Indeed, following the merger of the three banks in 1957, the international business changed little in terms of its organisation. The three head offices in Düsseldorf, Frankfurt and Hamburg retained their foreign departments, while the branches were largely free to conduct their own international activities.[375] Very large lending and securities transactions required approval by one of the branches or the full Management Board, but there was otherwise little central interference on either a commercial or practical level.[376] The branches also retained their own nostro accounts at correspondent banks abroad and conducted their own international lending and securities business. The general intention was to handle transactions with large foreign customers in Frankfurt – in a sense, the Foreign Department and Secretariat there were 'the bank's Foreign Ministry' – and to leave the branches to look after the international business of German customers.[377] In practice, however, this distinction was often difficult to maintain. The head offices in Düsseldorf and Hamburg retained their role in international business and each continued to specialise in certain countries: Hamburg was responsible largely for South America and Asia, Düsseldorf for the Middle East and Frankfurt for the rest of the world. Individual countries were not, in reality, always allocated as rigidly as this suggests. An internal discussion in 1958 concluded that the aim was not to be 'perfectionist' or to neatly 'divide up the world', but, rather, to gradually assign countries to the different offices 'in a way that matches business circumstances and staff availability'.[378]

The particular challenges of internationalisation included recruiting suitable personnel. Given the environment of the interwar period, most of the banks' own employees had little work experience abroad or in-depth knowledge of a foreign language. To remedy this, the banks began in the early 1950s to exchange officials with partner institutions abroad.[379] In most cases, the employees were sent abroad for a year to co-operate with local banks and acquire 'specialist knowledge' of securities and foreign exchange trading.[380] The later Spokesman of the Management Board, Hilmar Kopper, for example, completed a trainee programme from 1957 to 1958 at the J. Henry Schroder Banking Corporation in New York.[381] Foreign language courses were also offered and 'ambitious young people given the opportunity to gather experience at representative offices and friendly banks overseas'.[382] The programme proved popular among German bankers.[383]

By contrast, it was rare for foreign trainees to be hired for long-term positions – in most cases, non-German participants were from developing countries and returned home after completing the placement.[384]

Old networks, new business

The division into regional and, later, successor banks may have gradually increased the importance of the main branches, but it did not create a true interregnum. Even before he joined the management board of Süddeutsche Bank in 1952, Abs had informally pulled the strings at the regional banks and participated in all important decisions. Now, he officially set the international strategy for the three successor banks. Abs built systematically on the contacts and networks he had established all over Europe during the National Socialist era. A point of insistence in Abs's efforts to re-establish the bank's presence was his conviction that the bank was still the rightful owner of the holdings it had acquired in other European countries during his time in office.[385] In building a European bank in the Third Reich, he had used contracts to secure new long-term ownership interests and had intended these, if necessary, to outlast the war and even the Nazi state.[386]

In the case of the Austrian Creditanstalt-Bankverein (CABV), Deutsche Bank did, in fact, consider claiming reimbursement for its shares following the company's nationalisation in 1946, and eventually benefited from the government bonds paid as compensation by the Austrian state to former shareholders in the mid-1950s.[387] Abs maintained a good relationship with the managing director of CABV, Josef Joham, until the latter's death in 1959. The two men had co-operated closely between 1938 and 1945, and Joham remained at the helm of CABV after the war.[388]

Abs had more success with efforts to reacquire shares in the Amsterdam bank Albert de Bary. This bank, too, had been nationalised in 1945, with the long-standing managing director Eugen Max Brändlin remaining in post. Its activities were largely international. Upon reprivatisation in 1954, Abs managed to acquire a 20 per cent stake through a European consortium agreement, having waived any claim to compensation on the part of Deutsche Bank. Abs became a member of the supervisory board of de Bary, on which he had previously served from 1938 to 1945. Brändlin remained managing director. During the negotiations, Abs successfully persuaded Société Générale de Belgique, a company with which Deutsche Bank had maintained close relations in the Third Reich, to join the consortium.[389] Société Générale had a representative office in Frankfurt, which reopened soon after the war and was headed by the former director of Deutsche Bank in Istanbul, Hans Weidtman.[390] This was another clear indication of how valuable Abs's old networks remained.

Relationships with a number of other banks were also reactivated in the 1950s. In 1958, for example, co-operation was agreed, on Abs's initiative, with Banque Nationale de Grèce in Athens.[391] Representative offices were even opened in some foreign cities, including Istanbul. The city's branch had closed in 1945. However, there were efforts to retain at least an unofficial local presence. The branch's former director Edmund Goldenberg, who had been sacked in 1938 as a result of his Jewish heritage, returned to a senior position. When a representative office was officially opened in 1954, Goldenberg was chosen as its head. The close economic relationship between Turkey and West

Germany that began in the 1950s[392] created lucrative opportunities for Deutsche Bank, though the rules on representative offices meant that the business activities themselves had to take place in Germany. Istanbul was also a useful strategic location for expanding business relationships in nearby countries such as Iran and Greece.[393] Operating in Turkey was not without its problems, however, given the country's shortage of foreign exchange and large balance of payments deficit. The bank itself described the situation as 'far from rosy'.[394] Goldenberg, too, speaking in 1956, expressed scepticism about the opportunities for trade in what he still regarded as a developing country. Goods traffic with Turkey thus remained limited, despite the country's integration into the Western European economic sphere through NATO membership and its association agreement with the European Economic Community (EEC) in 1963.[395]

Beyond Europe

While Deutsche Bank held back from opening foreign branches under its own name, it re-established business relationships around the world after 1952.[396] The bank did not generally lend to foreign businesses. Loans for short-term commercial transactions were only granted to select foreign banks, mainly in the state socialist countries of eastern and south-eastern Europe, including Poland, Bulgaria, Yugoslavia, Hungary and Czechoslovakia. Deutsche Bank usually provided the foreign trade banks and state banks in those countries with fixed lines of credit to enable them to finance trade with German industry.[397]

Business with the eastern bloc states was admittedly 'quite complicated and unappealing in terms of profitability', but the bank took the view that it should co-operate with these countries for strategic reasons.[398] Responsibility for activities in the USSR continued to lie with Helmut Pollems, who also represented the Deutsche Bank Group in the Russia working group of the *Ostausschuss der deutschen Wirtschaft* (German Committee on Eastern European Economic Relations).[399] Abs pushed for an expansion of trade with the Soviet Union and pointed out that the latter could make up for its trade deficit with gold payments, as it had in the 1930s. There are clear indications that Abs did indeed aspire to return to the consortium financing of the interwar period. In 1955, for instance, he asked Pollems to produce a substantial study of the 'Russian business' and sounded out other banks on opportunities to expand trade financing to the USSR and its satellite states.[400] Such plans ultimately fell victim to growing Cold War tension, particularly with the US pushing its allies to participate in an economic boycott of eastern bloc countries. It would not be until the detente of the 1970s that the bank would once again be able to build on the business relationships of decades past.[401] For now, its role in the region was limited to financing small-scale export business by selected German companies.[402]

In the 1950s the bank also began to explore the options for trading with the People's Republic of China. Deutsch-Asiatische Bank (DAB) began operating again at the end of the war in May 1945. However, the six branches in China (Beijing, Hankou, Shanghai, Tianjin, Qingdao and Canton) were closed by the Chinese authorities in the autumn of 1945 and the German employees repatriated.[403] With the Berlin branch sequestered by the Soviets, DAB moved its German headquarters to Hamburg. It was licensed as a foreign trade bank in 1949 and regained its full autonomy in 1952. In 1953, it officially moved the head office from Shanghai to Hamburg and converted its capital from yuan to Deutschmarks.[404] Abs had already successfully recovered almost 5 million francs of assets that had been frozen in Switzerland.[405]

With Abs expressly advising in 1953 against the 'inclusion of other East Asian countries' in DAB's business, DAB continued to concentrate on the Chinese market despite the difficult political situation after the revolution of 1949.[406] Trade between Germany and China had fallen sharply in 1937 with the outbreak of the Sino-Japanese War. Now, however, it began to recover despite the communist takeover in mainland China. In the early 1950s, China became West Germany's most important trading partner in the communist world.[407] As a report produced in 1953 makes clear, DAB believed that the German and Chinese markets complemented one another perfectly.[408] In 1952, the German Committee on Eastern European Economic Relations created a China working group with the help of the West German government. Its members included the director of Norddeutsche Bank in Bremen, Paul Witting, who prior to 1945 had been the Deutsche Bank Management Board member responsible for East Asia. The working group quickly bore fruit. In May 1953, it met with a Chinese trade delegation in Berlin and agreed to intensify trade between the two countries to an annual volume of approximately DM 200 million. With the US having imposed an embargo in 1950 and the UK and France gradually withdrawing from China, Germany had high hopes of continued growth in business. In 1955, further banks were persuaded to join a 'China consortium', and in 1957 a German business delegation travelled to Beijing to conclude

By 1959, Deutsche Bank was advertising its 'world-wide banking service' in Chinese as well.

a trade agreement.[409] It quickly became clear, however, that foreign trade with this market was reaching its limits. China was suffering from a severe lack of foreign exchange and primarily exported agricultural goods, whereas German industry supplied machinery, steel and chemical products. Settling transactions was an extremely complex undertaking for DAB and involved negotiating foreign exchange controls in both China and Europe. Most transactions were handled through the Bank of China, in whose London branch both DAB and Norddeutsche Bank held a correspondent account. DAB financed German exports in the early 1950s using standard credit facilities such as reimbursement and post-shipment credits. Transactions were settled using both DM- and sterling-denominated accounts.[410] Despite this positive start, a planned agreement between DAB and the Bank of China, which would have allowed the German bank to lend directly to the Chinese market, did not come to fruition.[411] This partly reflected the new political realities. The forced industrialisation, or 'Great Leap Forward' in the People's Republic, which began in 1958, ended in an economic disaster and caused widespread famine, leading the communist government to put a stop to further trade with foreign countries.

Despite these difficulties, DAB attempted from the mid-1950s to regain a foothold in Asia by opening branches. A partnership with the Dutch company, Nationale Handelsbank NV, which already had several Asian branches, had been briefly considered but never implemented.[412] DAB therefore explored the option of establishing its own branches in the region.[413] The first of these was opened in Hong Kong in 1958, a city which was quickly becoming an Asian financial hub.

In Japan, too, Deutsche Bank began in the 1950s to rebuild old business relationships. Due to Sino-Japanese tensions, it created its own network of correspondent banks instead of utilising DAB. This approach proved highly effective and by 1954 had secured some 50 per cent of the Japan business in West Germany for the Deutsche Bank Group.[414] In 1957, the bank also began to explore options for a representative office in Japan. It finally opened one in Tokyo in 1962.[415]

In terms of business volumes in the post-war years, North and South America were even more important than Eastern Europe and Asia. In the US, the bank soon resumed old customer relationships. Abs was met with a friendly reception by the American business community on his trip to negotiate Germany's foreign debt in 1949.[416] He even established good relations with Arnhold and S. Bleichroeder, a Jewish-owned bank that had moved to the US to escape Nazi persecution.[417] Relations with the US proved complex, however. While large American banks were increasingly asserting themselves in European markets and represented serious competition for Deutsche Bank, the US market remained largely closed to German institutions.

Despite German companies' close economic relationships with the US, Deutsche Bank therefore refrained – just as it had in the days of the German Empire and in the interwar years – from opening its own US branches. Instead, it decided that leading Deutsche Bank representatives should 'regularly visit US banks in New York and the provinces as well as US companies with an interest in Germany'.[418] The first person to take on this task in 1958 was the manager of the Bremen branch, Paul Witting, whose responsibilities already included business with the whole of Asia. This reveals how few of the bank's managers had adequate international experience to accept such a role.[419]

In Latin America, meanwhile, Banco Alemán Transatlántico (BAT) recovered its presence relatively quickly. At the outset of war, BAT had employed 2,358 members of staff in 21 branches. It continued to exist after 1945 as a 'dormant bank' with zero turnover, before finally reopening in 1953 once securities and accounts had been converted to Deutschmarks. The head office moved from Berlin to Hamburg. BAT's total assets on reopening were relatively modest (DM 14.8 million compared to the RM 190 million on the last official balance sheet in 1942). However, it managed to bolster these by recovering its former premises and confiscated securities in various Latin American countries. BAT was headed by Johannes Feske, former manager of the Foreign Secretariat at Deutsche

Announcement of the reopening of Banco Alemán Transatlántico in Buenos Aires on 12 May 1960.

Bank's Hamburg management office, and Hans Joachim Wolff, a figure with years of experience at Deutsch-Südamerikanische Bank (a Dresdner Bank subsidiary) and Banco Nacional do Comercio de São Paulo.[420] They were joined on the management board in 1960 by Paul Witting and Louis Rodenstein, the latter also serving as director of the Buenos Aires branch. Abs chaired the supervisory board, just as he had prior to 1945. In 1959, he stepped down and was succeeded by Karl Kasen, but still maintained a background presence as honorary chairman and travelled frequently to the region.[421]

In 1954, BAT and Deutsche Bank's successor institutions jointly opened the first representative offices in Buenos Aires and Mexico City. Joint offices followed in São Paulo and Caracas in 1955, and Rio de Janeiro and Santiago de Chile in 1956. A further office opened in Bogotá (Colombia) in 1962.[422] After protracted negotiations with the government of Argentina and restitution of the original building, BAT's Buenos Aires branch reopened in 1960.[423] Argentina and Chile in particular were considered attractive locations given the large numbers of German businesspeople and émigrés, including many who had fled Europe after the fall of the Third Reich. In Spain, meanwhile, where the bank had also run three branches prior to 1945, the bank was unable to recover its assets. BAT therefore decided not to open any branches of its own, but instead to continue its Spanish business through a shareholding in Banco Comercial Transatlántico.[424] The country's political isolation under Franco also made it inadvisable for the bank to operate in Spain under its own name.[425] Deutsche Bank would not begin to build its own branch network on the Iberian peninsula until after the transition to democracy.

In Latin America, by contrast, BAT noted its early performance with satisfaction. By 1958, the bank already boasted total assets of DM 57.8 million and since reopening had increased turnover from DM 26 to 813 million.[426] As BAT was increasingly financing exports by German industrial firms, it established branches in Cologne and Düsseldorf in 1958 and 1960.[427] The encouraging growth of business in Latin American countries themselves also gave grounds for optimism. There were great expectations for the region's economic potential, as BAT's 1960 annual report demonstrates: 'It is to be hoped that tensions and even crises in various countries are soon overcome. For the Western world, there are opportunities for extensive international economic cooperation, of which these countries are also in urgent need.'[428]

German companies invested some DM 1.5 billion in Latin America between 1953 and 1963, primarily in Brazil, Argentina and Mexico. Though BAT chiefly regarded itself as an 'export bank' for German business, it also participated in direct investment in the region. The continent's growing demand for long-term loans soon outstripped BAT's means, however.[429] The parent company Deutsche Bank thus became increasingly involved in such lending – often through syndicated loans with BAT or other banks.[430] In 1958, Deutsche Bank co-financed two steel works built by Deutsche Maschinenbau Aktiengesellschaft (DEMAG) in Argentina.[431] In 1961, Deutsche, together with other European banks, placed an Argentinian government bond with a volume of $25 million. By 1963, however, concerns about the region's economic problems were mounting. In that year's annual report, a resigned BAT management concluded that neither business investment nor development aid had 'brought about anything more than a rudimentary improvement in the situation'.[432] While domestic industry stagnated, most countries in the region had a trade deficit and relied heavily on commodity exports. The warning signs of the 1980s debt crisis were already emerging.

Financing development projects in the postcolonial world

From the mid-1950s onwards, the bank was increasingly involved in postcolonial developing nations, despite the risks this entailed. As the new countries established themselves, Deutsche Bank proved open-minded not only to trade financing but also to direct investment, particularly given the support offered by the West German government to German businesses and banks willing to work with these regions. Abs became a member of the government's *Beirat für Entwicklungspolitik* (Council for Development Policy) and travelled to many countries in the southern hemisphere on behalf of the Federal Foreign Office and World Bank. In spring 1960, for example, he took a three-week trip to Pakistan and India to explore the opportunities for foreign aid.[433]

For privately owned banks, business with these countries was often highly risky. Abs therefore urged restraint when acquiring new business and advised the bank, in case of doubt, only to award loans backed by KfW or Hermes cover. Assessing the political and economic circumstances of the various countries was an often difficult task. To help it better evaluate the situation on the ground, the bank therefore acquired shares in local development banks in a wealth of countries. The aim was to gain access to investment projects related to development assistance. These often involved a lower level of risk as they were backed by international organisations. Returns on such business were only modest, and the bank regarded its 'shareholdings in developing countries not as profit-making investments', but first and foremost as 'practical development aid'.[434]

Abs urged caution in many potential investments. Deutsche Bank chose not to help finance the Aswan Dam, for example, despite the project's backing from Ludger Westrick, state secretary in the Economics Ministry. Abs considered the risks incalculable, particularly after the nationalisation of the Suez Canal in 1956 and the looming conflict between Egypt and Israel.[435] The bank was wary of doing business in Iraq and other countries in the region, too, as conditions there were 'opaque in every respect'.[436] It did not lend to countries where there were unresolved disputes concerning the assets of foreign banks. This was the case in many states of Africa and Southeast Asia that had confiscated property from Western companies after the fall of colonial regimes. Abs repeatedly advocated an international convention obliging signatory nations to give 'fair and equal treatment' to the rights and interests of foreign companies and to 'refrain from direct or indirect intervention in such interests'. Alongside such a 'Magna Carta to protect the rights of foreigners', he called for the establishment of an international arbitration court to intervene in cases of conflict.[437] Though no such institution was ever created, this initiative shows the extent to which Abs was determined to avoid credit defaults and the loss of assets in developing countries. It was only once the West German government began to issue guarantees for foreign investments and loans by German companies that the bank started to engage more strongly in development finance. Even then, it did so only in countries 'where there is certainty as to the law, and where an economic policy is pursued which resists the temptation to be immoderate and to strive for autarky'.[438]

Table 3: Deutsche Bank AG's shareholdings in foreign banks in 1963.

Banco Español en Alemania SA, Madrid	15.00%
Banque Nationale pour le Développement Economique, Rabat	1.00%
Consafrique Consortium Européen pour le Développement des Ressources Naturelles de l'Afrique SA, Luxembourg	16.60%
Corporación Financiera Colombiana de Desarrollo Industrial, Bogotá	0.50%
Deltec Panamerica SA, Panama/Nassau	3.20%
Deltec S. A. Investimentos, Crédito e Financiamento, Rio de Janeiro/São Paulo	7.80%
Euralliance Société de Gestion d'Investment Trusts, SA, Luxembourg	32.70%
Foreign Trade Bank of Iran, Tehran	14.50%
Handel-Maatschappij H. Albert de Bary & Co. NV, Amsterdam	19.90%
Industrial and Mining Development Bank of Iran, Tehran	2.30%
Malaysian Industrial Development Finance Ltd., Kuala Lumpur/Malaysia	1.00%
Nationale Investitionsbank für Industrieentwicklung AG, Athens	5.30%
Private Development Corporation of the Philippines, Makati, Rizal	1.80%
Société Camerounaise de Banque, Yaoundé	5.00%
Société Dahoméenne de Banque, Cotonou	10.00%
Société Européenne de Developpement Industriel SA, Paris	49.90%
Société Ivoirienne de Banque, Abidjan	16.00%
Teollistamisrahasto Oy, Helsinki	1.10%
The Industrial Credit and Investment Corporation of India Ltd., Bombay	1.50%
The Pakistan Industrial Credit and Investment Corporation Ltd., Karachi	5.50%
Union Gabonaise de Banque, Libreville	10.00%

Source: Deutsche Bank, Annual Report 1963, p. 28f.

The bank had no particular reservations, however, about doing business with authoritarian states. This applied not only to state socialist countries but also to the many military dictatorships in Latin America and Africa. By 1958, business had also resumed with South Africa. That year saw Deutsche Bank float a DM 50 million bond on behalf of the Anglo American Corporation of South Africa Ltd.[439] Founded to mine gold in the East Rand in 1917, the company had previously relied on the Swiss capital market. So large was this bond issue, however, that it approached Abs instead. The bond enjoyed strong sales in Germany and was oversubscribed several times within just a few days. At 5.5 per cent, the coupon was considerably higher than that offered by domestic bonds. This was the first bond denominated in German currency to be issued by a foreign company on the German capital market since 1914 – a milestone so prestigious that Deutsche Bank placed the bond alone without the usual consortium. Abs was determined that this success would belong to his bank alone and celebrated the occasion with a reception at his home in Kronberg near Frankfurt. The bond's

The first foreign bond issue in German currency on the German capital market since 1914: Deutsche Bank placed the partial debenture of the Anglo American Corporation of South Africa in the German capital market in 1958 without forming a consortium.

admission to the Frankfurt Stock Exchange also coincided with the issue of the company's ordinary shares in spring 1959. The bond marked the start of a close business relationship between Deutsche Bank and South Africa.[440] Abs himself maintained close contact with businessmen and politicians in the apartheid regime and travelled to the country on several occasions.[441]

Deutsche Bank succeeded in claiming its position as Germany's leading foreign trade bank. By 1962, it handled a third of German foreign trade (equivalent to approximately DM 35 billion) and 3.5 per cent of world trade. This was as much as two of its competitors – Commerzbank and Dresdner Bank – combined.[442] It had a global network of 2,600 correspondent banks, numerous international shareholdings and representative offices in a wealth of countries. Though its activities spanned the globe, its business had a clear regional focus on Europe and North America. Seventy-five per cent of turnover came from Europe (including 2 per cent from the eastern bloc), 10 per cent from the US and Canada and 5 per cent each from Asia, Africa and Latin America. The majority (75 per cent) of turnover stemmed from the payments business, while the remainder was split roughly equally between letters of credit and collections. Around 8 per cent of time deposits and 35 per cent of bank deposits came from outside Germany. Approximately half of foreign turnover was transacted together with 25 European and US banks with which Deutsche Bank often co-operated in consortia. Deutsche Bank's financial exposure abroad was estimated at DM 600–700 million and thus considerably exceeded its equity.[443] Despite this boom, there were mounting warnings from within the bank that growing competition threatened the strong international business. Osterwind noted as early as 1960 that 'while we have been able to maintain our share of the Federal Republic's increased volume of trade, neighbouring banks are to some extent catching up'.[444] Trade financing alone would thus barely suffice to grow the business. A report produced by the bank on its international business insisted 'we cannot rest on our laurels'.[445] In the years that followed, Deutsche Bank would therefore reorient its international activities back towards the very thing that had made it so successful prior to the First World War: the international capital markets business.

III. Deutschland AG: Rhenish Capitalism and the World Market

1. Structure Follows Strategy?

The strong growth in business following the re-establishment of Deutsche Bank in 1957 presented the institution with major organisational challenges. Within the space of three decades, the workforce nearly trebled, while the number of branches increased approximately eightfold and total assets roughly twentyfold. However, even these figures do not give a complete picture of the organisation's true growth. In addition to developing its own business, Deutsche Bank evolved into a corporate group by acquiring a wealth of investments and subsidiaries in Germany and abroad. How did the bank master this rapid expansion and what structural changes were entailed?

The merger of the successor banks in 1957 created a hybrid structure. On the one hand, the bank returned to its old tradition as a national universal bank with a unified organisation. On the other hand, however, the new Deutsche Bank retained many features of the decentralised architecture that had emerged during the first post-war decade. These included the strong position of the main branches, which conducted their business largely independently and were used to a high degree of autonomy. The three head offices of the successor banks in Düsseldorf, Hamburg and Frankfurt also remained in place. Departments covering areas such as currency trading, stock markets and securities, international business and economic research were therefore replicated across each of these locations. Meanwhile, bank-wide responsibilities were divided up between the three offices, as were support services for the 23 main branches. The board members were also split across the three locations and met only for the regular meetings of the full Management Board.[1]

Despite this careful division of responsibilities, the three head offices were not created equal. The Frankfurt headquarters, which was the registered office of Deutsche Bank AG, had a particularly prominent position from the outset. This developed further over the course of time. As the home of the Bundesbank, the largest German stock exchange and a multitude of German and international banks, the city steadily gained importance. It was here that Abs, the Management Board Spokesman, had his office. Frankfurt also housed several important bank-wide functions such as the main book-keeping department and the Corporate Secretariat, which was in charge of co-ordinating the bank's boards and its annual general meeting. Major international capital market operations and lending were based here, too.

Figure 13: Deutsche Bank workforce, 1957–89.

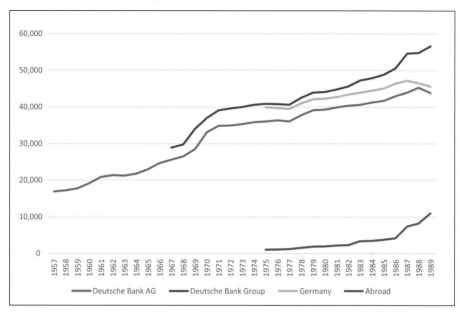

Source: Deutsche Bank, Annual Reports 1957–89. NB: Data available on the Deutsche Bank Group since 1967, broken down into Germany and other countries beginning in 1975.

Figure 14: Deutsche Bank total assets, 1952–89, in DM billions.

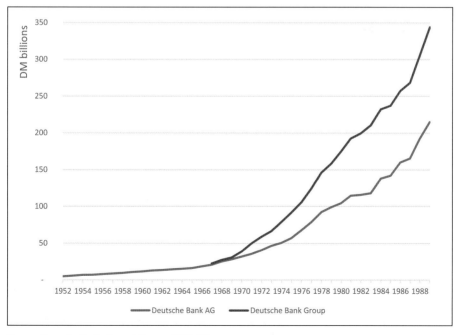

Source: Deutsche Bank, Annual Reports 1952–89.

From 1967, managerial functions were further centralised in Frankfurt. The Hamburg head office closed altogether, while Düsseldorf lost most of its bank-wide departments and was only saved at all thanks to the economic importance of the local Rhine-Ruhr region. The main aim was to achieve 'more efficient organisation as a whole' and avoid 'unnecessary expense'.[2] Mounting operating expenses and weak earnings were an increasing source of concern for the bank's management. As Franz Heinrich Ulrich, the then Management Board Spokesman, explained to the Supervisory Board in early 1971, operating profit had been 'falling constantly' in relation to the volume of business since 1957. Since 1962, the workforce had grown by 60 per cent and personnel expenditure by 191 per cent. With the bank's interest income on the decline (by 1970, the average interest margin was just 2.6 per cent, compared to the 3 to 4 per cent typical of earlier years) and a lack of significant income from fees in the retail business, the bank's earnings situation was on a continuously deteriorating trend.[3]

More than a decade after the reunification of Deutsche Bank, then, it was clear that the bank's expansion had not brought the desired growth in profits. The competition between banks beginning with the liberalisation of interest rates in West Germany in 1967 had put considerable pressure on margins and vastly increased administrative expenses. The standard terms and conditions that had long dominated the traditional current account business had been swept away by increasingly complex new products that were more costly to support. Credit and deposit rates changed constantly, making both the administration of bank accounts and the company's own accounting processes enormously expensive. In 1965, the bank processed some 26 million cheque transactions and 82 million transfers, deposits and other payments. Information technology had the potential to greatly rationalise data processing but entailed vast investment that would take years to pay off in the retail banking business.[4] Punch card computing was still commonplace in the early 1960s, while mainframe computers with magnetic storage media were only used for account and portfolio management afterwards. The technical and financial outlay for the new IT structure was considerable. By the end of the 1960s, the bank had successively replaced three generations of IBM mainframes at its offices in Eschborn, Düsseldorf and Hamburg. Digitalising the company's book-keeping and the management of all accounts held with the bank was also a gradual process. All current accounts were moved to computer systems in 1963 followed by savings accounts in 1965 and instalment loans in 1967. Automated administration and processing of payment transactions only became possible in 1970 with the nationwide introduction of bank codes in Germany. Now, for the first time, a standardised customer number was introduced, enabling cross-selling in the personal banking business.[5]

Though costs were high and implementation time-consuming, the new technology brought considerable labour savings. This was especially important given the difficulty in attracting new qualified staff in an era of full employment. The disproportionately small increase in the bank's workforce compared to its expanding balance sheet shows that labour productivity was rising rapidly in response to the technological transformation of the financial sector. The use of electronic data processing across the board was also designed to improve central book-keeping, allowing the bank to record and analyse every single transaction for accounting purposes. Comprehensive cost and results accounting in the banking industry would have been almost impossible without the use of IT.

IT enabled cost and results accounting in unprecedented detail. This was also a central aim of the organisational reform that began with the strengthened position of the Frankfurt head office in 1967 and continued from 1974 with the gradual reform of the branch network in line with the 'OM model' ('Organisation and Management'). At Management Board level, the more centralised approach and emphasis on management planning were made possible by a new generation heralded by the arrival of Alfred Herrhausen in January 1970. Herrhausen held a doctorate in business administration and was a former manager of the Dortmund energy supplier VEW. He was an advocate of long-term corporate planning based on the comprehensive calculation of costs and efficiency. An industry outsider whom Abs teasingly referred to as 'the electrician', he was also fascinated by the latest theories of business management from the fields of operations research, cybernetics and linear programming. This set him apart from his more practically minded colleagues on the Management Board. Herrhausen had responsibility at board level for the economic research department and economic reporting. In 1971, he also initiated the creation of a new 'planning department', which he turned into an engine of organisational reform. The idea proved controversial among the other Management Board members. Crucially, however, Herrhausen gained the support of Ulrich, who was well aware of the bank's cost problems and was convinced of the necessity for organisational change.[6] It was Herrhausen's influence that now finally led Deutsche Bank to avail itself of the services of McKinsey and other management consulting firms – a step other major banks had taken much earlier.[7]

The presence at the Frankfurt head office of a group of experienced and reform-minded experts in organisational theory – Herbert Zapp, Klaus Mertin and Horst Burgard, who had arrived in the early 1970s – played to Herrhausen's advantage. Zapp, a doctor of law, had begun his career in the finance ministry of the state of Baden-Württemberg before moving to Deutsche Bank in Mannheim, where he rapidly rose within the hierarchy. In 1972 he joined Herrhausen in Frankfurt and established the 'corporate planning' department, joining the Management Board in 1977. After a banking apprenticeship, Mertin had initially studied business administration and later completed a doctorate on the topic of lump-sum provisioning. He joined the Frankfurt head office in 1957 and in 1969 was made responsible for accounting across the entire bank. From then on, he began to turn the accounting system into an instrument of corporate planning. Mertin was appointed to the Management Board in 1971 and worked closely with Herrhausen in the planning department. Horst Burgard held a doctorate in business administration and joined the Management Board in 1971 as board member for human resources, a position he would hold for the next two decades. For a time, Burgard was also responsible for credit control, which he expanded into a comprehensive mechanism for risk management. While Herrhausen's various operational duties in the industrial banking business prevented him from fully immersing himself in administrative concerns, Zapp, Burgard and Mertin had a considerable influence on the bank's organisational reform.[8]

In the late 1970s, the bank greatly increased its Group-wide accounting and controlling activities and turned the main book-keeping office into an 'accounting and planning' department. This was, not least, a response to the exploding costs in the branches. The bank thus sought to streamline the organisation of branches in Germany with an emphasis on efficiency and profit. The main branches were to be strengthened in order to limit the power of the 'dukes' in every bank branch, whose *de facto* local authority came close to that of board members.[9] The OM model put in place divisional managerial structures in the main branches. Dedicated departments were set up within these branches for personal and commercial banking, investment consultancy, lending, international financing and the securities business. With this move, the bank intended to create a system of key account management and to increase its profitability at local level. In order to make the income and cost structures of the individual branch districts more transparent, the number of main branches was reduced from 23 to 14 and the districts aligned more closely in terms of their size, total assets and business structure. The effect of this was to give major branches greater ownership of their results and greater regional authority. Revenue was broken down by customer group and business area. The operating results of the lending and deposit businesses were determined separately through the calculation of interest and unit cost.[10]

The reorganisation of the German branch network took considerable time and failed to deliver the cost savings hoped for. It was therefore followed a few years later by another reform with a new regional structure designed to reinforce the principle of local accountability.[11]

Organising international business

At head office level, too, the organisational reform that began in the early 1970s entailed considerable difficulties. This was evident in the fast-expanding international business, a particular focus of Deutsche Bank's management given the increasingly multinational nature of the industries the institution served. A memo prepared for a Management Board meeting in 1979 concluded as follows: 'A hundred years ago, major German banks set out to lead the way for industry. Today, it is the other way around.'[12] Hans-Otto Thierbach, the primary figure on the Management Board responsible for international business, stressed in 1976 that the domestic market in Germany had already been largely divided up between the banks. In the long term, 'above-average growth' would be found solely in the international business.[13] According to figures presented in 1978, business in Germany had grown by a factor of only 1.5 since 1973. The international business had more than trebled in size over the same period to reach 36 per cent of the Group's total business volume. This was unevenly distributed, however. The head offices in Frankfurt and Düsseldorf now handled around half of international business. With the foreign branches and investees accounting for another third, only a relatively small proportion was the domain of branches in Germany. There were major differences between these branches, too: while business volumes in Düsseldorf, Hamburg and Bremen remained high in the international segment, many smaller branches lost ground.[14] The largely branch-based export financing business declined in importance.

As part of the reorganisation at the top of the bank, the international business was transferred to a 'Central Foreign Department' in Frankfurt in 1969, while Düsseldorf retained only a smaller 'central foreign office'. The new department in Frankfurt was headed by Thierbach and a long-time confidant of Abs, Otto Georg Pirkham.[15] The new set-up did not deliver the strategic integration that had been hoped, however. An internal report in summer 1973 complained of 'unclear roles and responsibilities' and a 'confusing organisational structure'. Authority, it added, was often assigned at random, and many people were appointed to positions to which they were unsuited. There was a complete lack of 'tightly organised, robust leadership',[16] and the majority of managers lacked a business- and profit-oriented mentality. Finally, the report complained that flow of information between head office and the various departments was inadequate, with little use made of information technology. The criticisms were aimed primarily at the head office in Frankfurt, but applied in essence to the branches, too. Almost a fifth of the bank's approximately 1,100 branches in Germany had their own international departments. These operated largely independently of one another and were poorly integrated into the strategic plans produced by head office.[17]

It was in this context that the bank moved to extend its OM model to the international business. The aim was a more streamlined organisation and improved customer focus, with special attention being paid to the German exporters whose business the bank was steadily losing to the competition. Both other German banks and European competitors such as Amrobank, Midland Bank and Crédit Lyonnais had long introduced industry-oriented account managers to systematically provide customer support. Deutsche Bank, meanwhile, had taken a largely passive approach, relying on business customers to turn to their regular branch when they required help with international transactions. Now, it was proposed that account managers based at head office should regularly visit companies and advise them comprehensively so as 'to sell as many of our services to each customer as possible'.[18] The bank also set its sights on visiting and winning the business of major companies abroad.[19] Introducing these proposed reforms was a slow process, however. The long-desired account managers would not become a reality until the 1980s.

In the international business, where the bank focused heavily on individually supporting commercial clients, digitalisation came later than in the personal banking segment, which was dominated by standardised products. It was only in the late 1960s, once management of bank accounts in Germany had been fully computerised, that the bank began to consider the use of IT in the international segment.[20] Ulrich warned in 1969, however, that 'use of computers is costly and should pursue specific business objectives' before any blanket transition to electronic processes.[21] The complexity of such an undertaking was quickly apparent: 'Due to the shortage of personnel and technical capacity in the IT department, we have so far been unable to realise any of the envisaged projects,' concluded the head of planning in the Foreign Department, Wilfried A. Hollenberg, resignedly in December 1971.[22] In April 1973, computer-based international transactions were still the preserve of the main branches.[23] At small branches it would be many years before IT infrastructure would be in place to implement the international SWIFT system for example.

Many at the bank increasingly regarded international business as a problem area. A customer survey conducted by the Institut für Demoskopie Allensbach in 1975 revealed a series of deficiencies in Deutsche Bank's international services. Among small and medium-sized enterprises in particular, both Commerzbank and Dresdner Bank scored more highly, especially in terms of customer relationships, while Deutsche Bank was criticised for 'shortcomings in relation to decision-making authority and customer support'. Increasing numbers of German companies were moving activities abroad and wanted to maintain contact with their Hausbank when they arrived there. Instead of establishing its own foreign branches, Deutsche had entered co-operation agreements with local banks. These were no substitute in customers' minds for the bank's own presence, as a special working group led by Hilmar Kopper, then executive vice-president in the Düsseldorf head office, concluded: 'A pure branch network would be best placed to offer the flexibility demanded by customers as well as the benefits of an internal system for linking banks and settling payments. The US banks have clearly shown us in Germany how this system can generate competitive advantage.'[24]

The working group suggested a series of further improvements, which mainly comprised organisational changes. One problem was that no fewer than seven different departments were responsible for international business. Their roles were not clearly differentiated. The Central Foreign Department was responsible for the interbank market, country assessments, business with international non-banks and the affiliates

Franz Heinrich Ulrich (1910–1987) served on the Management Board of Deutsche Bank starting in 1957. In 1967, he and Karl Klasen became the Co-Spokesmen of the Management Board, succeeding Hermann J. Abs. Ulrich served as sole Spokesman from 1970 to 1976 and led the Supervisory Board from 1984 on.

and investees. It also oversaw the international activities of branches in Germany. Meanwhile, money market, foreign exchange and precious metal trading were combined in a central currency trading department and project finance activities in a central foreign trade financing department. The 'foreign branch main office' oversaw BAT and all other Deutsche Bank Group branches abroad, while Düsseldorf ran its own separate 'central foreign office'. The 'secretariat' was responsible for capital market financing and the bank's increasingly important foreign equity investments. The 'branch office' was responsible for overseeing lending with non-banks in other countries and had established an 'evidence centre' in 1957 to avoid risks in the international lending business. Finally, a steering committee established in 1972 was responsible for evaluating major loans and driving long-term strategic planning. This appears, however, to have lacked the authority it needed to get to grips with the many parallel structures. What was more, the system was additionally complicated by the (largely random) assignment of a different international region to every Management Board member.

As Thierbach and Kopper concluded in a dossier prepared for the Management Board in March 1977, 'overlaps in organisation and customer service' had resulted from years of growing fragmentation. 'This hinders the bank's ability to adapt to the constantly growing requirements of international business and, in light of the efforts of competitors in Germany and other countries, fails to do justice to DB's potential or leadership ambitions.' The authors therefore called for international business to be organised under a single management.[25] It recommended that the bank bring together the activities of the Foreign Department and foreign branch main office at Management Board level and combine their competencies in a 'Central International Department'. The bank additionally decided to appoint 'co-ordinators', whose responsibilities included approving major international loans.[26]

Deutsche Bank was constantly preoccupied in the 1970s with creating a coherent organisational structure to reflect the highly complex and fast-growing international business. The international corporate structure also created considerable problems of information. The statistical and financial recording of all international activities presented an enormous workload. The foreign branches, which the bank began to establish from 1976, generally had more urgent things to do, especially in their early years, than to prepare extensive business documentation and balance sheets. In any case, they often lacked the necessary staff and technical resources.[27] Bound both by legislation in the host country and the rules of the parent bank, they often had to prepare two sets of accounts. Time-consuming though these accounting processes were, the bank was determined that each department should have a greater awareness of and responsibility for its profit contribution. This was rarely straightforward, as winning and handling new business was generally a collaborative effort between multiple departments. In practice, the bank's approach to apportioning interest and commission income was usually to split the margins. A branch initiating international business for one of its counterparts abroad, for example, would receive a 'commission' of 50 per cent.[28] Though pragmatic, such calculations very rarely reflected the true contribution of the various departments. They became increasingly problematic in a global financial corporation required to demonstrate its profitability in its every field of activity.

The tower with the so-called 'cappuccino cap' was the home of the Frankfurt headquarters from 1972 to 1984.

Personnel and international business

The bank's international growth also necessitated a rethink of its human resources policy. The first restructuring efforts in this area in 1970 were intended to improve efficiency, reduce costs and free up staff, including in international business.[29] The bank hoped 'to make better use of the experienced staff in the Foreign Department while also providing better advisory services to customers'.[30] This proved unrealistic. As quickly became apparent, qualified personnel were in short supply. Considering its growing importance, the international side of the business was heavily understaffed. Branches had barely anyone with international experience, as Heinz Osterwind complained in 1969. One goal at this time was to have a junior employee with international expertise in every main branch as reinforcement for the 'international experts', but even this seemed ambitious.[31] The Foreign Department in Frankfurt and the smaller 'central foreign office' in Düsseldorf together employed just 239 people in 1972, 202 of them in Frankfurt. In 1978, the newly established 'Central International Department' had a workforce of only 306.[32] Put together, foreign branches employed 1,336 people or approximately 3 per cent of the Deutsche Bank workforce in late 1978, most of whom were locals. Only 113 had been seconded from Germany – a figure just as low as five years earlier.[33]

The bank's working group for the international business had already pointed to the expected staffing shortfalls in 1975 and called for 'systematic human resources development' in this area.[34] Employees, it noted, often lacked the training for an international role. Few had language skills or experience abroad. Moreover, the lack of professional development prospects made postings abroad unattractive to managers, many of whom feared their careers would suffer from such a move. The working group noted that there were considerable 'psychological barriers to choosing a career in the international business'.[35] While the group no longer ruled out greater recruitment of foreign experts at management level to overcome the shortages, it still favoured the employment of German staff. The bank therefore took measures to create a 'reserve' of potential international staff in Germany. It instructed all departments and branches to nominate employees who could be considered for a post abroad and who would be able to move at short notice. It also set out plans to improve training provision, for example through seminars for managers and ordinary employees, and considered increased training on the job, in which apprentices and professionals would be temporarily posted abroad. As in the past, it also sought to encourage the exchange of staff with partner banks abroad.

The implementation of these measures had limited impact, however. Though the bank organised a considerable number of professional development seminars – 21 events in 1977, attended by 374 participants – their content was rather basic and largely covered simple letters of credit and collections. There were few events at management level.[36] The reserve of potential international staff attracted little interest and its membership fell well short of expectations.[37] The lack of an internationally qualified workforce thus remained one of the bank's largest problems. In 1985, Wilfried Guth, Co-Spokesman of the Management Board, complained that employees were still insufficiently 'willing to move'.[38] Now, the bank finally began to systematically recruit international managers. The proportion of managers with non-German nationality more than doubled from 6.3 per cent in 1983 to 14.1 per cent in 1988.[39]

Management and corporate governance

International recruitment was long uncommon at the most senior management level, too. It was not until the takeover of Morgan Grenfell and the appointment of John A. Craven to the Management Board in 1990 that this began to change. For their part, German managers rarely made the move abroad to work in a foreign branch or subsidiary. Those with international experience tended to have gathered it during their training or in the early stages of their career. Rolf-E. Breuer, for example, completed internships during his degree at financial institutions in London and Paris. Ulrich Weiss spent short spells in Milan, Buenos Aires and New York.[40] To most of the bank's managers, moving abroad later in their career was an unappealing option and one that could even hamper their prospects. Weiss, for instance, had been ready to move to the New York branch during its build-up phase in 1977, when he was persuaded to remain in Germany where a higher calling awaited.[41]

Directors and Management Board members tended to spend their entire career at the bank. They often began a bank apprenticeship in a small branch and either worked their way up to the position of branch manager or switched to a main branch or even the head office. These promotions were dependent on further training. As well as a bank apprenticeship, many top managers at Deutsche Bank had completed a degree in law or – increasingly commonly – economics, and in more than a few cases had earned a doctorate. A banking apprenticeship followed by degree studies remained the best way into a career at the bank. As the experiences of Hans-Otto Thierbach and Hilmar Kopper showed, though, it was still possible to reach the top even without a university degree. The in-house training centre opened in Kronberg im Taunus in 1973 enabled employees to make up for their lack of university qualifications through ongoing professional development. Despite this, banking was increasingly and inexorably becoming a graduate occupation, including at Deutsche Bank. In the 1980s, the bank began to train graduates for leadership positions, and many students now found their way to the company by completing internships during their degree course.

A career on the Management Board was not something that could be planned. Nevertheless, there were clear similarities in the paths taken by later board members. Almost all top managers had mentors or sponsors high up in the bank. Many had been assistants to board members or worked in a strategy department, giving them access to influential people and the opportunity to prove their personal effectiveness.[42] The support of a main branch director could also be of considerable importance, particularly to those in the middle phase of their career. To succeed at head office, candidates needed to have spent time at a branch getting to know the basics of the banking business, ideally in a lending department and in a managerial function, for instance as a sub-branch director.[43] Rolf-E. Breuer was a model example. After a bank apprenticeship, he studied law in Munich and completed a doctorate in Bonn. He first spent several years at the Karlsruhe branch, where he was responsible for the lending business, before quickly making a name for himself at the stock exchange department in Frankfurt. He joined the Management Board in 1985. Georg Krupp joined the bank's legal department at the Frankfurt head office in 1965 after graduating with a law degree. In 1968, he became head of the Heilbronn branch before returning to Frankfurt in 1970 where he worked for Abs in preparing the case against the East German historian Eberhard Czichon (as we shall see, Czichon had spread false allegations regarding the bank). Michael Endres, also a law graduate, began his career in the credit department at the main branch in Munich. His manager there helped secure him a new position as assistant to the Management Board member Robert Ehret in Frankfurt. From 1985 onwards, after spells in Ulm and Mannheim, Endres worked for several years in the management of Deutsche Bank's newly founded investment subsidiary in London. These examples show that a top career consisted of relatively few different stages. Working abroad for a period, as Endres had done, was still very much the exception to the rule. A branch management function was a vital step on the path to the Management Board, but it was rare for directors at the main branches to make the move to head office. This was because they generally reached this position only late in their career. Promotion within the same branch was the norm, and the title of branch director attracted enormous prestige in this hierarchical, status-conscious world. Looking back in 2013, the long-time head of personnel, Ulrich Weiss, bemoaned the 'rigid traditions in the personal banking business regarding titles, the cumbersome system of promotion, and the correlation between title on the one hand and payment and even office size on the other'.[44] Among staff not subject to collective wage agreements, the title of 'senior bank official' – in German, the title *Oberbeamte* was reminiscent of the civil service – remained commonplace in the 1980s.

Candidates did not apply to managerial positions but 'received a call', remembered Kopper. 'It was always quick; in fact, you only found out where you were going after the decision had already been made.'[45] These promotions were not offered at random but emerged from a sophisticated system within the bank. Workforce planning was centralised in Frankfurt in 1969, where Horst Burgard and Axel Osenberg turned it into a professionalised human resources management apparatus. This was particularly true at managerial level. Here, the aim was to nurture potential future managers so that for every vacancy the bank already had around 10 suitable candidates who had been regularly discussed by the management and supervisory boards.[46]

Even at the most senior management level, positions were filled by internal candidates with only rare exceptions. Between 1952 and 1989, just two Management Board members came from outside the bank: Wilfried Guth and Alfred Herrhausen. Guth's appointment in 1968 can be regarded as symptomatic of a cautious opening up, driven not least by the need for an experienced expert in the international capital market business following Abs's departure. After studying economics, including in Geneva and at the London School of Economics, Guth began his career at the Bank deutscher Länder – the forerunner of the Bundesbank – in 1953 before being appointed as an executive director at the International Monetary Fund in Washington in 1959. In 1962 he returned to Germany, where he joined the board of the Kreditanstalt für Wiederaufbau (KfW). Guth was one of the few German bankers with an international profile. In the turbulent years following the end of the Bretton Woods system, the proven currency expert was a valuable asset to Deutsche Bank. Thanks to his work at the Bundesbank and at KfW, he also had long-standing contact with the Deutsche Bank management. The more unorthodox appointment was that of Alfred Herrhausen, who had no prior banking experience at all. Nevertheless, his arrival bolstered the bank's industrial business

The Management Board of Deutsche Bank at the press briefing on annual financial statements in March 1972: front row, from left: Wilfried Guth, F. Wilhelm Christians, Andreas Kleffel, Wilhelm Vallenthin, Manfred O. von Hauenschild, Management Board Spokesman Franz Heinrich Ulrich, press officer Walther Weber, Hans Feith, Hans Leibkutsch, Alfred Herrhausen and Robert Ehret; back row, from left: Eckart van Hooven, Horst Burgard, Hans-Otto Thierbach and Klaus Mertin.

given his previous work in the energy sector. The vacancy for Herrhausen was opened up by Karl Klasen's sudden move to the Bundesbank, where he became president. Though significant, these two appointments did not mark the start of a fundamental shift away from the model of internal promotion. This change would come only in the 1990s.

Continuity and a high degree of personal consensus were also evident in the bank's leadership culture. However, the Management Board's principle of collective responsibility did not, in practice, create a collaborative environment. Instead, the members managed their board divisions independently. An overly sociable atmosphere was frowned upon. On a personal level, the relationships among board members and directors were distant. First-name terms were unusual, as were extended shared leisure activities. A conservative spirit ruled – Endres later described Deutsche Bank's management style even in the 1980s as 'akin to that of a religious order'.[47] Board members were expected to have an impeccable reputation and, as representatives of the bank, to keep their private affairs in good order. Herrhausen's divorce in 1977 was considered such a scandal that it jeopardised his entire career at the bank. Abs, whose Catholic, conservative attitudes long shaped the climate inside the bank, was particularly outraged by the demise of Herrhausen's marriage and attempted to convince him to return to his wife.[48] Eventually, the Management Board reluctantly took note of Herrhausen's separation without accepting his formal offer of resignation.[49]

All Management Board members were formally equal and took votes on over-arching issues. Decisions generally required unanimity and could be vetoed by any member, though the 'sledgehammer' of a veto was rarely used.[50] The board frequently spent hours attempting to resolve differences of opinion at its Tuesday meetings. In seeking to avoid open partisanship or prolonged confrontation, it sometimes failed to solve long-standing problems, or simply kept revising proposals until it found the lowest common denominator.[51]

In keeping with the bank's pre-war tradition, there was no formal chairman. Instead, the members elected a board Spokesman, who continued to perform this role until his departure. As in the past, the Spokesman did not receive higher remuneration than the other board members, nor was he any more prominent in the bank's official public image. Nevertheless, the role of the Spokesman had changed significantly with Abs, whose personal authority, years of service at the top of the bank and diverse contacts in the political and business worlds gave him a special position of power that made him a 'first among equals'. What was more, a large proportion of the management staff had been promoted under his aegis and felt a strong loyalty to him. The principle of unanimity probably increased his power still further, as it intensified the pressure to reach consensus and made it essential to come to informal arrangements in advance of board meetings.[52] This played into the hands of the well-networked Abs, while leaving those with a smaller power base like Herrhausen at a disadvantage. Though Herrhausen found acceptance at the bank, he would always remain an outsider, and many of his proposals and reform efforts met with opposition.[53]

After Abs's departure, Ulrich and Klasen shared the role of Spokesman on the grounds that the position was too important for a single person to fill.[54] Ulrich cannot have been overly convinced of this reasoning, however, as he became sole Spokesman from 1970 onwards following Klasen's departure. When Ulrich moved to the Supervisory Board in 1976, the bank returned to the system of dual Spokesmen, with Wilfried Guth and F. Wilhelm Christians sharing the role. The persistence of this model hints at back-stage rivalries that could only be solved by such a compromise. It certainly points to a lack of clearly structured hierarchy, which meant that managers had to rely on alliances and co-operation in order to assert themselves.[55] Guth and Christians co-operated well, discussing many issues together and speaking at length every Sunday by telephone. As Christians later admitted, however, the arrangement demanded 'a high degree of self-restraint'.[56] Once Herrhausen succeeded Guth in 1985, the system of dual Spokesmen was doomed to fail. For one thing, Herrhausen and Christians were two very different personalities.[57] More importantly, the younger man had a keen instinct for power and a desire to lead the bank alone. When Christians retired in 1988, Herrhausen finally became the sole Spokesman of the Management Board.

The Management Board usually comprised 10 to 12 members including deputies (new members were normally appointed initially as deputies for a two-year period before being entrusted with full responsibility). Appointing new board members was a drawn-out process. The Management Board regularly discussed an internal list of 'papable' candidates, and successors were chosen long before vacancies arose.[58] The actual election by the Supervisory Board was thus often merely a formality.

Directors at branches and head office were generally recruited internally. Rotation within Deutsche Bank, let alone a move to another institution, was a rarity. The stability of this in-house recruitment and promotion system with its old boy networks not only hindered the appointment of managers from outside the bank, but probably also explains why so few women found their way into senior positions, despite comprising more than half the bank's workforce by the early 1970s. In 1975, there were only three female directors and just 16 women with *Prokurist* (officer with power of attorney) status. In 1988, Ellen R. Schneider-Lenné became the first woman to be appointed to the Deutsche Bank Management Board. Like her male colleagues, Schneider-Lenné had learned the banking business from the bottom up and was regarded as assertive and compatible with the male-dominated management culture at Deutsche Bank. As Hilmar Kopper later recalled, she was appointed not as a token woman but because she was 'our best man'.[59] After two and a half years as an assistant to Franz Heinrich Ulrich, Schneider-Lenné had established the new London branch and proven her expertise as a specialist for trade finance and the capital markets business. In 1980, she was named head of the 'central foreign office' in Düsseldorf and in 1985 became head of the international trade finance department in Frankfurt. Her appointment to the Management Board three years later was a proposal of Herrhausen's.[60]

Each Management Board member was responsible for one to two departments that covered either domestic business (lending, construction and mortgage financing, stock market business or personal banking customers), international business (money markets, currency trading, foreign trade financing, international issuances, etc.) or organisational matters (HR, legal, tax, economics, etc.). There was also a deputy for each of these divisions. In addition, the board members were responsible for up to two domestic branch districts and subsidiaries and, in the international business, for specific country groups and regions. Responsibilities were set out in a business allocation plan,[61] but were not permanently fixed. Often, they reflected personal interests or were merely coincidental. Despite its many overlaps and ongoing debate about its merits, the bank did not change this organisational structure until the early 1990s. It was only then that the system was revised in an effort to strengthen board members' responsibility for their departments and release them from operational duties.

The Management Board at the 1988 press briefing on annual financial statements. From left: Ellen R. Schneider-Lenné, Rolf-E. Breuer, Ulrich Weiss, Hilmar Kopper, Horst Burgard, press officer Walther Weber, Spokesmen F. Wilhelm Christians and Alfred Herrhausen, Eckart van Hooven, Herbert Zapp, Ulrich Cartellieri, Georg Krupp and Michael Endres.

Compared to the powerful Management Board, the Supervisory Board was relatively weak. Though Germany's two-tier board system, unlike the Anglo-American model, required a formal separation between governance and operational management, the Supervisory Board at Deutsche Bank did not perform a true oversight role. Open conflict was unusual as the post of Supervisory Board chairman was always filled by the bank's former Management Board Spokesman and was thus part of the company's extended managerial team. Following Management Board meetings, the Spokesman kept the Supervisory Board chairman fully abreast of the most important matters. The regular Supervisory Board meetings, then, which took place three to four times a year, were generally peaceful affairs. Though the two boards still had to reach a degree of consensus, the unwritten rule was that the Supervisory Board would look favourably on the work of the Management Board, asking occasional questions but very rarely intervening in operational or strategic decisions. As a rule, the Supervisory Board also took no active part in personnel-related decisions. Conflicts arose only where there was controversy about the refusal to let employee representatives participate in the credit committee.

With the high free float of Deutsche Bank shares, the annual general meeting was also unable to serve as an effective counterweight to the Management Board. The number of small and private shareholders rocketed in the 1960s, and by 1973 the bank could count more than 120,000. This figure doubled again by the end of the 1980s, reducing the relative weight of institutional investors. With their high dividends of 16 to 20 per cent, the shares were popular with small investors.[62] From 1974, the bank also regularly issued employee shares to its staff. These enjoyed high demand and further enlarged the shareholder base. The dispersed share ownership and issue of employee shares, which employees could only sell after holding them for several years, contributed to stabilising the share price and helped the bank's management control the annual general meeting. Most investors held Deutsche Bank shares for purely financial motives and had little particular interest in corporate policy. Shareholders were – if they attended the annual general meetings at all – generally loyal and approved the Management Board's proposals with large majorities. What was more, the bank's management could exercise its proxy voting rights and, if necessary, count on the support of friendly banks. From 1975 onwards, the bank limited the voting rights of individual shareholders to 5 per cent of the share capital. Its aim was to restrict the influence of large shareholders. This was purely a precautionary measure as not even the large institutional investors at that time owned anything close to a 5 per cent stake. It was true, however, that the shareholder structure was rapidly becoming more complex and international as Deutsche Bank shares began trading on important foreign stock exchanges from the mid-1970s. The bank therefore held fast to the maximum voting right despite this restriction undermining its claim to be a true public corporation subject to free market principles.[63]

Endless reforms

The emphasis on harmony, the interwoven nature of the Management and Supervisory Boards, the continuity of management personnel and the fragmented ownership structure were central to Deutsche Bank's stability. They probably also go some way to explaining why organisational changes were slow to take hold. Although the shortcomings of the bank's international business were a regular topic for discussion from the late 1960s onwards, thorough efforts to reform it or introduce a multi-divisional system of management were not forthcoming. The OM reform of the 1970s restructured the branches while changing little at central management level.

This shows that the functionalist theory inspired by Alfred D. Chandler, in which a company's organisational structure adapts dynamically to its business strategy, did not apply to Deutsche Bank.[64] Despite its strong growth, the bank remained rigid, conservative and wary of radical institutional innovations. In terms of many organisational changes, it lagged behind other major banks in Germany and Europe.[65]

The bank was certainly aware of its own shortcomings in relation to strategic planning. Hans-Peter Ferslev later recalled that the management were implicitly aware of the need for the bank 'to evolve and to identify new trends'. However, in practice, he observed, 'strategy was and still is an essentially uncoordinated, sometimes intuitive process. Unlike much of industry, Deutsche Bank's strategy largely escaped a system of ongoing institutionalised revision and oversight.'[66]

The tendencies Ferslev identified can be illustrated by the co-ordination group set up in autumn 1982 to formulate an overall strategy for Deutsche Bank's development. This consisted of four experts from different areas, including the future Management Board member Michael Endres. The group failed to act as the 'catalyst' that had been hoped, however, and its output made little impression. While it discussed numerous problems at the bank, it did not present a coherent overall plan. In its closing report presented in early 1985, the group admitted problems with data collection and the lack of innovative theoretical approaches. It therefore concluded that 'working on individual projects' was 'more suited to our bank' than 'drawing up an overall strategy' or even a 'master plan'. The group clearly lacked the necessary influence over the Management Board, its report conceding that it 'had not always found the right format to persuade the Management Board of its findings and results'.[67]

The co-ordination group was therefore broken up and some of the staff integrated into the Group Strategy (Abteilung für Konzernentwicklung, AfK) department, which emerged out of the shareholdings department in January 1986.[68] The AfK was the brainchild of Herrhausen, who wanted to 'flesh out and improve the Deutsche Bank Group's future business potential using strategic guidelines for the Management Board's corporate policies'.[69] The AfK now developed a holistic approach to strategic corporate planning. It noted in October 1986 that American banks were far ahead of Deutsche Bank and had systematically expanded strategy development work for planning purposes since the 1960s. The banking landscape, it concluded, was in the midst of 'dramatic change' triggered by the technical revolution on the financial markets, growing global risks and increasing international competition. The AfK proposed a distinction between operational and strategic objectives, an alignment of business policy with future trends of economic development and a reduction of internal bureaucracy. The report also recommended embedding comprehensive risk management processes into every part of the company and integrating them with corporate controlling. Given the increasingly complex corporate structure, the AfK called for greater segmentation, in which individual divisions would be given full responsibility for their results. This would involve giving the 'strategic business units' full autonomy over their operational targets while still integrating them into overall planning at group level.[70] One proposed practical solution for this was to transform the group into a holding company with fully independent subsidiaries. Nothing less than the renunciation of the universal bank model, which Deutsche Bank had embodied since its creation, was now up for debate.[71]

The idea of a holding company was soon rejected. Nevertheless, the reform announced by Herrhausen in 1986 still entailed far-reaching changes to management. The various fields of work were organised into 11 areas and placed under the direction of 'co-ordinators'. As senior figures, the co-ordinators acquired responsibility for income from the operational business so as to allow the Management Board to concentrate solely on strategy. A decentralised organisational structure, delegation of responsibility and a comprehensive focus on profit were now to be the guiding principles of the Deutsche Bank Group's development.

Like its predecessors, this reform took years to get off the ground and was less revolutionary than originally planned. The new structure did not, in fact, radically alter responsibilities. Herrhausen himself had emphasised that the initial aim was not to seek a 'grand solution' but to stick to what was 'familiar and trusted wherever possible'.[72] Important tasks such as organisation and HR, controlling and refinancing (Treasury) remained in dedicated departments. The Group's subsidiaries did not receive full autonomy but continued to be controlled through Management and Supervisory Board appointments. The maxim 'as local as possible, as centralised as necessary' pointed to the dilemma of the reform, which had to reconcile competing goals and interests.[73]

Moreover, considerable opposition was forming within the bank and was now being directed increasingly openly against the Spokesman. Many older staff perceived Herrhausen as elitist and aloof. Among younger colleagues, meanwhile, his reform mindedness and distinct aversion to hierarchies and vested interests was well received.[74] The controversy surrounding Herrhausen's reforms thus partly reflected a generational conflict that was heightened by the planned restructuring, especially with Herrhausen pressing for speed. As Breuer recalled, Herrhausen was very 'demanding' and it was 'clear that the general had rushed far ahead of his troops. There was a gap there; the contact was gone.'[75]

Following the assassination of Alfred Herrhausen on 30 November 1989, the new Management Board Spokesman, Hilmar Kopper, attempted to push on with key elements of the reform while fitting them even more closely into existing structures.[76] In a speech to managers in December 1989, he emphasised that the reform simply implemented 'what was *de facto* already in place and common practice'. There were no plans, he added, to partition the bank or abandon the universal bank model, and no prospect of a revolution from above: 'We are no Jacobins, no self-destructive *Directoire*. We know what we owe to the traditions of this company. Nobody wants to break this bank up.'[77]

Kopper recognised that the opposition to the reforms was partly an expression of the widespread resistance to cultural change throughout the company. On the Management Board, for example, there was criticism of the growing use of Anglicisms. The powerful main branch directors had to be reassured that their privileged access to the Management Board members would remain. Unions and the works council feared job cuts, greater wage inequality and internal redeployment of staff. Given that the bank's enormous cost problems were the motive behind the reforms, the latter fears were not unfounded.[78] In 1988, the bank had already implemented a 'pronounced reduction of personnel' in Germany, while creating new jobs in other countries.[79] It was clear to all parties that the bank's reform would turn its familiar structures on their heads.

The reform thus remained a balancing act. Kopper, who had stayed loyal to the company since completing his training, was perceived as more down to earth than Herrhausen and was far better able to sell the necessity for reorganisation. He also reduced the pace of change and sought to better communicate the objectives at all levels of the bank. Internal strategy papers had, in any case, already recognised that a radical reorganisation in one fell swoop was hardly realistic. The Group Strategy department's report in October 1986, for example, argued: 'Just as there is no sure formula for strategic planning, experience shows that single leaps forward are rare. We will make quicker progress by taking small, robust steps in the right direction and taking stock at regular intervals to correct any deviations from course.'[80]

The question was, however, whether incremental organisational change ('small, robust steps') would be enough to keep pace with the 1990s. This question quickly arose again when the integration of foreign investment banks into the Deutsche Bank Group brought completely new organisational challenges.

2. 'Troubles of the plains'

Discovering savers

The interwar years showed that commercial banks without branches were at a structural disadvantage compared to the savings banks and co-operatives, which boasted extensive branch networks. Savings and demand deposits were becoming increasingly important to refinancing the lending business. No longer the leading player in the deposit business it had been in decades past, Deutsche Bank therefore sought from the late 1920s to bolster the number of savers and small investors banking with it.[81] These efforts yielded a substantial increase in savings deposits, which reached almost 20 per cent of total assets in 1944.[82] Political turmoil intervened and the bank lost many of its deposit holdings between the end of the war and the currency reform. From the early 1950s, however, deposits began to grow again. The three successor banks saw their total volume of deposits increase from DM 197 million to 1.15 billion between 1952 and 1957. As a proportion of the three successor banks' total assets, savings deposits grew from 5.2 per cent at the beginning of 1952 to 13.8 per cent at the end of 1957. By then, customers held no fewer than 550,000 savings accounts.[83]

Tax benefits for private savings and the rocketing disposable household income of the post-war era (disposable income trebled between 1950 and 1960) made the 'retail' or 'personal banking' business increasingly attractive to the commercial banks.[84] Though Abs, so legend has it, still mocked this 'business with housemaids and allotment holders', the successor banks began by 1953 to lay specific plans to attract ordinary working households with novel new products. The initiative for this came from Franz Heinrich Ulrich, who developed a series of ideas with his Management Board colleagues Karl Klasen and Manfred O. von Hauenschild in Hamburg. From 1959 onwards, von Hauenschild was also the board member responsible for the retail customer business at the reconstituted Deutsche Bank and played a major role in the institution's domestic expansion.

Entering the retail banking business required the bank to aim its advertising efforts at customers who had so far been catered for primarily by the savings banks and co-operatives. With companies, freelancers and wealthy private clients still the mainstay of its business, the bank also needed to change both its mentality and image. This was no easy feat. The era when the bank could consider, in a genteel way, whether it wanted to 'go among the people', as an internal report put it in 1956, 'belonged to history'.[85] Initially, this recognition translated only into rather half-hearted action, which was limited to donating money boxes to charities and associations or awarding savings vouchers to customers on occasions such as weddings or the birth of a child. It is unlikely that these campaigns had a major impact. The same applied to efforts to attract rural customers using 'mobile branches' and to the opening in Hamburg of the first drive-in counter in 1959.[86]

Of far greater importance, however, was the development of standardised products that customers could use without the need for time-consuming advice and creditworthiness checks. Ulrich and his planning team in Hamburg modelled their approach on the US, where many renowned institutions such as First National City Bank in New York – which later became Citibank – had already entered the retail banking business in the late 1920s.[87] In one of the numerous discussions on strategy, Ulrich pointed to the 'great successes of big American banks' and, with the competition from savings banks in mind,

The drive-in counter was a novelty adopted from the United States. Deutsche Bank's first counter was opened in 1959 in Hamburg-Hammerbrook.

called for an end to the 'apathy towards small loans'. The bank, he added, should put 'every effort into intensifying [its] deposit business'.[88] Even though, as research has shown, there was no wholesale 'Americanisation' of the West German retail banking business in the post-war years, the US was an unmistakable source of inspiration.[89] Observing the American market was important for another reason, too: US banks were moving into Europe and represented a growing source of competition for Deutsche Bank.[90]

The most important prerequisite for the bank to become an established player in the retail business was a comprehensive Germany-wide local presence. This only became possible in 1958 with the abolition of the *Bedürfnisprüfung* rule dating from 1934, which had prevented banks from opening branches except where there was officially deemed to be a local need for one. Now, all German banks were free to expand across the country.[91] In the space of 10 years, Deutsche Bank almost trebled the number of its branches from 364 in 1959 to 1,000 in 1969.[92] After this early surge, the pace of growth then slowed and the number of branches reached a temporary peak of 1,132 in 1976.

Despite the strong growth in its branch network, Deutsche Bank was a latecomer to the retail business and lagged behind the savings banks and co-operatives. Whereas customers at the savings banks had already opened 1.5 million salary accounts by 1956, it took until 1960 for Deutsche Bank even to launch its first such product.[93] The bank was also relatively late to begin offering loans for working households. Social acceptance of consumer loans was slow to emerge in Germany compared not only to the US but also many other Western European countries. Consumer lending retained a certain stigma even in the 1960s, with most households relying on their savings and only taking out loans in case of emergency. Despite the historical experiences of hyperinflation, the savings rate in Germany was one of the highest in the world.[94]

Public attitudes shifted only gradually. Deutsche Bank launched attractive loan products in an attempt to overcome popular reservations. In May 1959, it mirrored the strategy of Dresdner Bank and Commerzbank by introducing a small personal loan (*Persönlicher Klein-Kredit*) of up to DM 2,000. This was followed in 1962 by the medium-sized personal loan (*Persönliches Anschaffungs-Darlehen*) for amounts between DM 2,500 and DM 6,000, which had a term of up to 36 months. Despite multiple increases in the credit limits for these loans, however, they failed to meet expectations. In the first 10 years, Deutsche Bank's branches issued approximately 3.3 million small loans with a volume of around DM 5 billion.[95] Given a total business volume of DM 29 billion in 1969 alone, this did not represent a resounding success.

In fact, there was even a substantial decline in demand for small personal loans in the late 1960s.[96] In 1968, the bank consolidated its marketing and sales activities in Frankfurt and provided staff training to improve sales of its own products. It also further expanded its range of loans. In 1968, for example, it introduced a personal overdraft facility as well as cheque cards to facilitate cashless payment.[97] From 1969 onwards, customers were offered eurocheque cards that could be used abroad. This was not only a response to the growth in foreign tourism, but also an attempt to break the dominance of US banks in the traveller's cheque business. From 1977, customers travelling in Europe could make use of the Eurocard credit card. In this segment, the German and European markets proved stubbornly sluggish, however. Unlike in the US, where

| | | Konto-Nr. | | | Bankleitzahl **354 700 32** |

DEUTSCHE BANK KAMP-LINTFORT
AKTIENGESELLSCHAFT Moerser Straße 259

Zahlen Sie gegen diesen Scheck aus meinem/unserem Guthaben

DM

Deutsche Mark in Buchstaben

an _____ oder Überbringer

Ausstellungsort/Datum   Unterschrift des Ausstellers

Eine Streichung des Zusatzes »oder Überbringer« gilt als nicht erfolgt. Die Angabe einer Zahlungsfrist auf dem Scheck gilt als nicht geschrieben.

| Scheck-Nr. | x | Konto-Nr. | x | Betrag | x | Bankleitzahl | x | Text |

26973949   0924084   35700329 014

New paths in European payment transactions for private clients. In 1969, Deutsche Bank initiated and introduced the eurocheque.

consumers widely used credit cards to fund their purchases, German customers tended to regard them simply as a means of cashless payment.

Where Germany's growing market for real estate financing was concerned, Deutsche Bank was a relative latecomer. Although it held shares in various mortgage banks and sold their products through its branches, these banks operated largely independently. Moreover, they did not offer the *Bauspar* products (savings plans for future home buyers) favoured by German consumers but were instead primarily involved in financing commercial real estate. Recognising the importance of residential construction, Deutsche Bank finally introduced its own mortgage loan in 1968. In 1970, it launched its own real estate investment company, Deutsche Grundbesitz-Investmentgesellschaft, and also jointly established Deutsche Grundbesitz-Anlagegesellschaft together with Wüstenrot. In 1971, the investments in mortgage banks were consolidated. Deutsche Bank sold its shares in the mortgage bank subsidiaries of Dresdner Bank and Commerzbank. In return, it obtained majority shareholdings in Frankfurter Hypothekenbank and Deutsche Centralbodenkredit-AG.[98] In 1975, the bank combined its various forms of building financing into the 'BauKreditSystem' and began to co-operate more closely with building and loan associations.[99] The bank now expanded its real estate financing activities through further subsidiaries and, by 1980, achieved a market share of 5 per cent in the residential market.[100]

The deposit business performed even more strongly. In 1957, the bank was home to 550,000 savings accounts with a volume of DM 1.1 billion. By 1970, this had risen to 3.4 million accounts holding total deposits of DM 7.6 billion. Savings made up almost a third of total deposits and were the largest item on the liabilities side of the balance sheet.

A nation of shareholders?

As was clear in the bank's early strategy discussions in the mid-1950s, Ulrich regarded the task of making the bank more attractive to retail customers not as an end in itself but as a means of funding the bank's entire lending business. He also saw the potential to integrate the deposit business with one of the bank's traditionally most important segments: securities. Ulrich described these 'close functional relationships' as a 'dualism': savings deposits could be converted into securities so as to invigorate West Germany's rather weak capital market at that time.[101] This strategy was all the more important given that competition was inhibited by the lack of interest rate liberalisation, making it almost impossible to build market share using traditional savings products. Developing securities products specifically for small savers was therefore an opportunity for the bank to take advantage of its capital market experience when competing with the savings banks and co-operatives.[102]

One of Ulrich's first initiatives was to develop new products for securities savings. Together with 12 other institutions, Deutsche Bank founded its own fund company – Deutsche Gesellschaft für Wertpapiersparen (DWS) – in May 1956. Despite Deutsche Bank holding only 30 per cent of the shares in DWS, its branches contributed 90 per cent of the certificate sales.[103] Rivals had already established the Union Investment GmbH and Gesellschaft für Wertpapieranlagen mbH investment funds that same year. Launched in December 1956, DWS's 'Investa' fund consisted exclusively of equities issued by solidly performing German companies and sold for an initial issue price of DM 100. Investa performed well in the brief stock market boom of the late 1950s and, with a market share of over 20 per cent, rapidly became the largest German investment

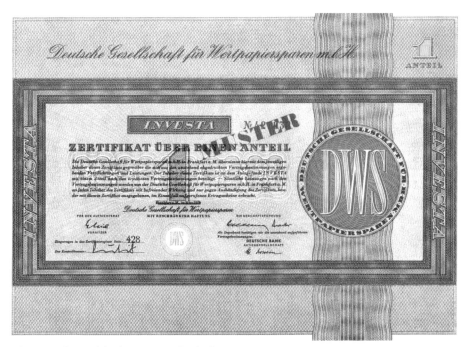

Share certificate of the first 'Investa' fund of DWS.

fund. From 1960, DWS introduced savings plans for the acquisition of its investment fund certificates. These were aimed at small investors and enabled customers to benefit from government-subsidised savings bonuses. A further equity accumulation fund – 'Akkumula' – followed in 1961. This time, however, success proved more elusive. With the equities market stagnating after 1960, sales of the DWS share savings plans were underwhelming. Already in 1956, the bank had worried that among Germans, unlike in the US, there was 'still a certain distrust of this form of saving'.[104] Fund-based saving failed to keep pace with more conservative savings products (savings books, life insurance and *Bauspar* schemes) and interest in investment certificates was modest.[105]

In view of the lack of demand for equity-based products, DWS therefore began in the mid-1960s to focus on fixed-interest securities.[106] 'Inrenta', the first bond fund, was launched in 1966, and a fund consisting of international bonds followed three years later. In its equity funds, too, DWS was also relatively quick to incorporate international stocks into its portfolio. The Frankfurt Stock Exchange permitted over-the-counter trading of foreign shares for the first time in autumn 1956. In May 1959, DWS launched a new fund called 'Intervesta', which was designed to open up the international capital market to German investors who only rarely had the opportunity to invest directly in financial centres abroad. The fund was well received by the bank's German customers. Within six weeks of the launch, more than a million certificates with a total value of DM 80 million had already been sold.[107]

In December of that year the European fund company 'Euroalliance' was founded jointly by Deutsche Bank, Amsterdamsche Bank and Société Générale de Belgique. Partly for tax reasons, it elected to locate its registered office in Luxembourg. This financial centre was thus already playing a major role for the Group long before 1970, when Deutsche Bank moved a large part of its international issuing business to its Luxembourg-based subsidiary Compagnie Financière de la Deutsche Bank AG. The importance of tax considerations to the structuring of international securities transactions at this time is indicated by a dossier, dating from November 1966, prepared by an expert panel of the EEC Commission. Euromarket issues, this concluded, were 'particularly attractive to savers' as the bonds were issued in countries where non-residents were not subject to withholding tax. The same applied, it added, to issues by American-owned subsidiaries in Europe. These were able not only to overcome the 'complex formalities concerning reimbursement of withholding tax' but also, the authors warned, to create the 'opportunity for tax evasion'.[108]

The ferocity of competition to attract investors was another factor making tax aspects relevant. American banks and investment companies were asserting themselves ever more strongly on the German market and achieving considerable success with their aggressive approach. One example was Investors Overseas Services (IOS), founded in 1960 as a Panama corporation headquartered in Switzerland. IOS launched a highly successful equity fund in Luxembourg under the name International Investment Trust. The fund's door-to-door and telephone sales methods, which it borrowed from the US, proved extremely effective with small savers. The certificates, which the company combined with long-term savings plans, promised very high returns. Other foreign providers, too, successfully established themselves in the German market. Net sales of foreign fund certificates rose from DM 20.4 million in 1964 to DM 297.6 million in 1967 and DM 354.5 million in the first half of 1968. By this time, there were 106 foreign investment funds in West Germany (compared to 29 domestic funds) with a collective market share of 37.6 per cent of total sales. A projection by the Federal Ministry of Economics predicted that foreign products would outstrip German certificates by as early as 1969.[109]

For Deutsche Bank, which had launched its own securities savings products just a few years earlier, this competition was a bitter setback. The bank responded by instructing its branches not to provide accounts for investment sales companies, over-the-counter business or paying agent services. Meanwhile, the Arbeitsgemeinschaft deutscher Investmentgesellschaften, an association of German investment companies, pushed for stricter regulation and oversight of foreign funds. In the eyes of the German financial sector, these were pushing their way into the German market using aggressive and sometimes dubious sales methods.[110] The Foreign Investment Act (*Auslandsinvestmentgesetz*) passed by the Bundestag in 1969 imposed a series of constraints on foreign companies, including the obligation to keep assets in a custodian bank, the prohibition of funds and stricter publication requirements. Foreign funds also had to submit to an audit by Germany's West Berlin-based bank regulator, Bundesaufsichtsamt für das Kreditwesen. The aim was to bring supervisory requirements on foreign fund providers into line with those already in place for German funds.[111]

The new law was unable to prevent the spectacular insolvency of IOS, which was triggered by a bear market in 1970 and cost many small investors their savings. The collapse seemed to vindicate the reservations about American methods held by many in the German financial sector. However, this first major financial scandal of the post-war era not only caused foreign companies to lose market share but damaged the reputation of fund-based saving more generally, probably inhibiting sales of German certificates. Worse still, poor share price performance in the 1970s also rendered equity-based savings plans unattractive, leading many households to favour fixed-interest bonds, *Bauspar* contracts and endowment policies instead.

Efforts to spread share ownership more widely among the population, including numerous initiatives by Deutsche Bank, also had only muted success. Ulrich participated in the Arbeitskreis zur Förderung der Aktie (Task Force to Promote Shares), for example, which was founded in 1953. From the late 1950s onwards, Germany privatised several state-owned companies. This was regarded as an opportunity to use share ownership to promote wealth formation among ordinary employees.[112] The first 'Volksaktie', or people's share, was issued in 1959 during the part-privatisation of Preussag (at that time a mining company). Volkswagen shares followed two years later and the privatisation of the state-owned energy company VEBA in 1965. Deutsche Bank played a central role as lead manager in all three cases. Despite the ability for low earners to acquire shares in the first two privatisations at a discounted price, the results of these initiatives were disappointing. Though many working households acquired shares for the first time, they usually soon sold them again in response to rising stock prices.[113] And while the number of share portfolios at the bank increased sharply from 284,000 in 1959 to over 400,000 by as early as 1961, the bank was forced to admit at the end of the 1960s that most of these accounts contained very low volumes and saw almost no transactions. In the case of 90 per cent of custody account customers, the bank was unable to recoup the cost of providing the service.[114] A change in popular attitudes towards investing in securities would finally come in the late 1980s, when DWS began to experience strong demand and was able to substantially increase sales of its investment funds.[115]

Competition from savings banks and the interest rate liberalisation in 1967

Until the late 1960s, true competition did not exist in the lending business in the Federal Republic. The Bundesaufsichtsamt für das Kreditwesen set bank rates, forcing banks to attract new customers mainly through their products and local presence rather than by competing on price.[116] This explains Deutsche Bank's decision both to constantly expand its branch network and bring a range of new offerings to the market. The strong position of the savings banks and co-operatives in the retail business represented a considerable challenge, as these institutions already boasted a large customer base and considerable deposit volumes. They also enjoyed a range of privileges and were largely tax-exempt. What was more, the savings banks were often well connected with local politicians, giving them a competitive advantage in many public contracts. They also benefited enormously from the maintenance and guarantee obligations known as *Anstaltslast* (institutional liability) and *Gewährträgerhaftung* (guarantor liability), through which the owners – state governments and municipalities – were required to bear any losses.

In the 1960s, the business profiles of commercial banks, savings banks and credit co-operatives increasingly converged. While the major banks entered the retail banking segment, the savings banks and co-operatives began to move beyond their traditional role as deposit takers. Having long served only as municipal banks, the savings banks now expanded with the help of the Landesbanken and giro institutions into all segments of the lending and securities business and increased their activities abroad. Westdeutsche Landesbank, for example, advanced under the leadership of Ludwig Poullain in the 1970s to become one of the largest German banks with numerous foreign investments and branches. Deutsche Genossenschaftskasse and BHF-Bank jointly opened a subsidiary in Luxembourg in 1972. They followed this a year later by founding London & Continental Bankers Ltd. with S. G. Warburg.[117] The public sector and co-operative institutions grew at a disproportionate rate to the wider German banking industry. The savings and giro banks increased their total assets sixteenfold between 1950 and 1966, from DM 12 billion to 186 billion. Meanwhile the big banks achieved only sevenfold growth, from DM 7 billion to 46 billion.[118]

Deutsche Bank watched this development with great concern and criticised the many privileges afforded to non-privately-owned institutions. The Association of German Banks (Bundesverband des privaten Bankgewerbes, later Bundesverband deutscher Banken), which represented the privately owned banks, lobbied for an end to the special status of public sector institutions, especially following the 1967 decision by Economics Minister Karl Schiller to liberalise interest rates and the termination that same year of the *Wettbewerbsabkommen* (competition agreement) – an agreement between the banks to limit competition and restrict advertising. These policies made the banking sector considerably more competitive and posed a threat to the big banks.

So large was the savings banks' share of total deposits, feared the major banks, that lifting the interest rate caps would effectively grant them a monopoly and allow them to set prices.[119] Despite their lobbying efforts, the big banks were unable to prevent the liberalisation of interest rates. Nevertheless, they did persuade the government to end the tax-exempt status of the savings banks in 1968.[120] This was insufficient to create full equality with the privately owned banks as the savings banks and co-operatives continued to enjoy special privileges.[121] Nevertheless, the savings banks were required, from 1969, to produce comprehensive financial reports and agreed to establish their own voluntary deposit guarantee scheme alongside the existing state guarantees.

While this partly overcame the distortion of competition, a basic problem of the West German banking market was increasingly evident: Germany's banking sector was becoming highly concentrated and, by the early 1970s, had reached saturation point as far as domestic business was concerned. Deutsche Bank's growing workforce and branch network was also generating excessive costs that were only partially brought under control by organisational reform and rationalisation.[122]

The limits of growth?

Where had the dramatic expansion of retail banking during Germany's post-war 'economic miracle' left Deutsche Bank? Despite the strong growth in this business segment, the situation was far from satisfactory. In 1974, the bank was forced to admit that 'the lending business was no longer making any money'. In fact, only 30 per cent of the bank's revenues were coming from the entire customer business, while resting assets and proprietary trading accounted for the remainder. Deutsche Bank's profit ratio, which measured the bank's operating result relative to its volume of business, had fallen sharply from 2.5 per cent in 1957 to just 1.03 per cent in 1973.[123] Deutsche Bank's market position in the personal banking business continued to worsen in the years that followed. A report by the head office planning department in 1979 painted a gloomy picture.[124] Though the business volume had more than doubled from DM 33 billion to 82 billion since 1970, revenues were going backwards.[125] Moreover, growth in the bank's domestic business was considerably slower than that of its international activities. The 'convergence of balance sheet structures'[126] between the various banking institutions, and particularly the aggressive expansion of savings banks and credit co-operatives, had led to a further loss in market share in the lending business just as in the deposit business. Whereas the bank had assumed in the early 1970s that new branches would attract sufficient deposits 'to fund our growing lending business',[127] it was forced to recognise by the end of the decade that this strategy was not working. While savings still made up around a third of total deposits, there was little prospect of increasing this further.[128] On the contrary, the bank was losing ground to Dresdner Bank and Commerzbank, which were sharply expanding their domestic businesses. Between 1970 and 1978, Deutsche Bank's market share for deposits by non-banks fell from 4.1 per cent to 3.8 per cent.[129] By the end of the 1970s, its branch network had been overtaken in size by Dresdner Bank.

Weaknesses were also becoming evident in the commercial banking business, where the structural transformation of the German economy and the relative decline of the industrial sector was reflected in the bank's results. This was little surprise given that medium- and large-sized industrial companies were still its most important customer group. The bank's market position was worsening here, too.[130] Its share of lending to German businesses and individuals fell from 6.8 per cent in 1970 to 5.7 per cent in 1978.[131]

This trend would intensify in subsequent years. In the traditional lending and deposit business, Deutsche Bank continued to shed market share and faced the loss of its traditional role as Germany's largest and most influential bank.[132] The trend was reinforced by the fact that many services were now also offered by companies outside the banking sector. Foremost among them was the German Post Office, which was systematically expanding its banking activities and, like the savings banks and co-operatives, making inroads into the lending and securities business. Many retailers also offered consumer loans, and strong competition emerged from the insurance industry, too, which absorbed 21 per cent of all savings by 1981.[133]

The bank responded to these challenges with a two-pronged strategy. Not only did it, as already shown, overhaul its branches, introduce the comprehensive use of IT systems and expand its range of financial services, but in the mid-1980s it also began to internationalise its retail banking business through the acquisition of foreign banks.

Branch overhaul and automation of customer service

The restructuring of the retail business began in the mid-1970s with a branch redesign based on the American-inspired 'Mannheim model'. Von Hauenschild and Eckart van Hooven had travelled to the US in 1965 to get an insight into the far more customer-oriented American banking culture. Among the most important changes introduced was the abolition of traditional, imposing bank counters in favour of open-plan 'branch landscapes', in which customers could enjoy a more personalised service. Instead of having separate counters for cash payments, lending business and account management, branches were now designed around an integrated customer service. This new service philosophy entailed higher personnel costs and was therefore only gradually implemented. The full refurbishment across the branch network also required considerable time and took until the early 1980s to complete.[134] Van Hooven, who joined the Management Board in 1972 to replace von Hauenschild, was the driving force behind the redesign.

The branch redesign came at a time when information technology was radically changing customer administration and transaction processing. One aspect of this was the rationalisation of processes with the aim of saving costs. As van Hooven noted in 1981, the bank handled some 2.5 million transactions a day. This generated considerable expense that was not covered by account maintenance charges. In the domestic business, the bank put the resulting deficit at several hundred million marks a year.[135] New standardised procedures were therefore designed to 'effectively channel the costly escalation of payment traffic'.[136]

Internal accounting and administration had already switched to computerised data processing in the 1960s. In the second half of the 1970s, electronic cash management finally began to find its way into customer service. The Eurocard – introduced in 1977 in partnership with the savings banks and co-operatives – enabled customers to make payments in 13 European countries. By 1981, no fewer than 15 million Germans and 39 million consumers from elsewhere in Europe had this credit card. The partnership with other banks was designed to avert a 'costly fragmentation' in European payment traffic and provide a counterweight to the US credit card companies.[137]

Deutsche Bank's management was under no illusions about the time-consuming nature of moving the entire front-of-house business to IT systems. At the time it made the decision in 1975, it estimated that this technological transformation would take 10 years.[138] Computer terminals were introduced to branches in three stages, beginning with the savings business in 1977. The use of terminals for general cash transactions followed from 1980 and for current account transactions in 1983. From 1981, the branches also used terminals to process securities transactions. This meant that branch staff could now accept and forward orders directly.

Herbert Zapp, the Management Board member responsible for the commercial banking business, regarded the new terminals as the most important innovation of the post-war era and anticipated a competitive advantage over other banks: 'With the new terminals, we are putting in place the technical and organisational means of communicating with customers electronically. How and when we enter electronic banking will be decisive to the success of our bank.'[139] At least in the short term, however, the rationalisation measures did not have the transformational effect that had been hoped. Procuring IT equipment was associated with major capital expenditure despite the prevalence of lease agreements. One fundamental problem was the mixture of different IT components. While Siemens and IBM provided the equipment for the main data centres, the in-branch computers came from Nixdorf.[140] The bank's reluctance to make itself dependent on a single supplier was a sound business reason for using hardware from different manufacturers. It came at a cost, however. Even without the use of multiple providers, the bank would have had a complex IT landscape. The branch terminals were

Transfer transactions in 1975 at the Frankfurt branch with the first generation of terminals.

connected to 16 regional data centres, which in turn served the mainframes in Eschborn, Düsseldorf and Hamburg. All systems were laboriously programmed in machine code or assembler language. In the early days of this new technology, there were neither standard routines nor universally defined interfaces. Meanwhile, for customer transactions, a common metalanguage with bank-specific interfaces had been developed, for which all manufacturers had to design their own interpreters. The diversity of systems thus increased the complexity of the bank's IT structures still further. Each area using the new technology tended to become locked into its existing system.[141]

In terms of the planned timeframe, meanwhile, the introduction of the terminal technology was a clear success. The first generation of terminals was replaced again beginning in 1982, and by 1987 the bank's more than 1,300 branches were equipped with around 15,000 sophisticated devices.[142] Alongside the initial investment – a very substantial figure in the 1980s given the computing power and storage capacity required by the banking industry – the bank had to spend considerable sums on training courses and the recruitment of computer experts.[143] For many older employees, the terminals necessitated different work processes and a new mentality. There was also a range of problems in monitoring transactions and preventing fraud.[144]

To reduce personnel expenses and augment its customer service, the bank began in the early 1980s to introduce automated teller machines (ATMs). Deutsche Bank was a latecomer here compared to the savings banks, which had been much keener to introduce the new technology. In 1983, it still had only 800 ATMs. The main obstacle was not the technology itself (reliable and fairly secure cash machines had existed since the 1970s), but, rather, the fear of losing customers through automation. This was especially true in the case of older – and often wealthier – customer groups, many of whom were not well versed in using the new devices and still preferred personal customer service. Board member Ulrich Weiss pointed to this dilemma in a presentation on the 'problems and limits of technology' in 1981:

> What we are dealing with is the decision on which tasks carried out by our employees so far – predominantly concerning monetary transactions – can be expected to be carried out by customers using a self-service terminal. A bank has to pay attention to not losing its individual customer service standard by exorbitant automation. On the other hand, automation offers the opportunity to improve the terminal's quality of advice and above all to use employees that have been relieved from routine tasks for qualified customer advisory services.[145]

This conflict would escalate in subsequent years. The bank sought to counter rising cost pressure and growing competition from other institutions with standardised services. In 1986, it introduced an early form of online banking using a videotex service that transmitted information through the telephone network. As a result, the personal service that had set Deutsche Bank's branches apart from other providers increasingly became a thing of the past. Automation in the 1980s dramatically raised competitive pressure in the retail banking business and meant that the bank had to offer ever more new financial services.

Becoming an all-round financial services provider

Despite the shortfalls associated with account management and payment transactions, which generated considerably more costs than revenue, the bank continued in the 1980s to expand the retail business for strategic reasons. Eckart van Hooven argued in 1981 that 'good market share in terms of bank accounts' meant good market share in more 'profitable services', too.[146] These particularly included building and real estate finance, which made up a rising proportion of the bank's overall business. In 1982, when the bank's total business volume fell for the first time since the war, property financing was the only area of growth.[147] The expansion of the Group's own mortgage banks (Frankfurter Hypothekenbank, Lübecker Hypothekenbank, Centralbodenkredit and Europäische Hypothekenbank in Luxembourg) was rapid. In 1987, the total lending volume in the building loan segment hit DM 58 billion. Building financing amounted to almost 10 per cent of the bank's total lending.[148] At this time, some 58 per cent of mortgage loans were issued by subsidiaries, while Deutsche Bank branches sold only a small proportion. In order to consolidate its mortgage offering under its own brand, Deutsche Bank therefore established Deutsche Bank Bauspar AG in 1987 and terminated long-standing co-operation arrangements with other institutions.[149] By 1988, it already ranked sixth out of 19 privately owned building and loan associations in West Germany in terms of the number of new contracts.[150]

A year later, the bank further expanded its portfolio by entering the insurance business. Until then, it had only offered insurance products (such as life insurance policies to cover mortgage loans) in partnership with existing insurance companies. In 1983, it launched 'Berlinische Leben', a savings plan with built-in insurance cover. Customers could also use Deutsche Bank branches to purchase products from other companies such as Allianz AG. Given the enormous expansion in private pension plans through endowment life insurance policies, the bank decided after lengthy internal debate in December 1988 to establish its own dedicated subsidiary: Lebensversicherungs-AG der Deutschen Bank ('db-Leben'). This threw down the gauntlet to the insurance industry and was met with a hefty response. The chairman of the Allianz board of management, Wolfgang Schieren, left his advisory board post at Deutsche Bank and numerous insurers announced that they would withdraw their funds. The bank had anticipated this reaction, but there was nevertheless confidence especially on the part of Alfred Herrhausen and Wilfried Guth that 'the project would be a financial success for Deutsche Bank'.[151] This hope proved well founded. Deutsche continued to push its banking-related financial services segment. While a minority stake in the Gerling insurance group was conceived purely as a financial investment, the bank completed its portfolio of insurance products by acquiring a majority shareholding in Deutscher Herold Group in 1992. This turned Deutsche Bank into an all-round financial services provider able to offer the full spectrum of financial products under its own brand and through its own branches – a philosophy that relied, not least, on efforts to give employees an affinity with the insurance business.[152]

The internationalisation of personal banking

Until the 1980s, Deutsche Bank's retail banking business largely concentrated on Germany. While international financial services – especially investment and securities products – had been available to German investors from an early stage, and Deutsche Bank had also used special offers to lure wealthy foreign clients, the bank's international branches were not designed with ordinary customers in mind. In 1987, however, this began to change. Van Hooven cited the strategic 'expansion of the international personal banking business' as an important component of the Group's development.[153] Unlike in investment banking, where the bank had genuinely global ambitions, this growth would concentrate on markets in which the personal banking business was not already saturated. There was also no intention to supplant subsidiaries by competing in countries where these had existing branch networks. After all, as Ulrich Weiss noted in January 1989, retail banking took place largely within the parameters of national markets, which foreign banks often found difficult to penetrate. The bank, he argued, therefore needed to closely examine existing financial institutions and customer structures and work out how best to 'adapt to local markets'.[154] Another problem was how to recruit suitable personnel from Germany to build a large-scale branch network in another country. Van Hooven had already warned in 1986 of the staff shortages affecting the work of branches in the US and Asia.[155]

Regulation had long prevented such expansion in many countries. Until the 1980s, strict rules had greatly limited market access for foreign banks. Though gradual deregulation was now taking place, the situation in many countries, such as France, remained difficult. A further complication in Western Europe was that the rules of the European Banks' International Company (EBIC), of which Deutsche Bank was a member, did not permit extensive business activities in the home countries of partner banks. Only once this era of 'club banking' had come to an end could Deutsche Bank expand its retail business into other European countries under its own brand (see chapter III.4).[156]

In Luxembourg, the 'dramatic decline in the traditional Euroloan business and the changing market structures' in the mid-1980s led the bank to turn its attention, following its competitor Dresdner Bank, towards high-net-worth private individuals. This approach, it believed, was also in line with DB Lux's official status as a universal bank. Strict banking secrecy, an 'investor-friendly tax system' and the stable political environment promised strong earnings prospects. The bank's hopes that 'German customers interested in Luxembourg' would compensate for the declining Euromarket business with institutional clients were quickly realised.[157]

Before the 1990s, then, the international personal banking business was usually provided through existing investees rather than by Deutsche Bank directly. A case in point was Argentina, where Deutsche Bank had always served personal banking customers in Buenos Aires through BAT. In 1997, however, the bank sold its Argentinian subsidiary Deutsche Bank Argentina SA to BankBoston NA for $250 million and exited the personal banking business here. Maintaining it would have necessitated 'considerable investment and a doubling of the number of branches'. No fewer than half of the subsidiary's approximately 1,200 employees worked in 48 branches serving retail banking customers. Despite this, the total market share in loans and deposits was barely

3 per cent. Deutsche Bank now shifted its focus in Latin America to large customers and investment banking.[158]

Back in Europe, Deutsche Bank tentatively entered the Spanish market through Banco Comercial Transatlántico (BCT) from 1969 onwards. Following the end of the Franco regime and Spain's entry into the European Community, Deutsche Bank repeatedly increased its stake in BCT, but did not gain a controlling interest until 1989. The country's rapid economic growth provided a strong foundation on which to build, especially as Spaniards already held large deposits and securities portfolios.[159]

In Italy, too, Deutsche Bank became established in the personal banking business through the purchase of existing banks. It had long had a close relationship with Banca Commerciale Italiana and, in addition, had opened a representative office in 1977 and a branch in Milan in 1979. The latter was mainly responsible for commercial banking with industry in northern Italy. Given its size and close integration with Germany, Deutsche Bank's management regarded the Italian market as particularly important.[160] The country had one of the world's highest saving rates and private households held considerable assets. However, with Italians not yet permitted to acquire foreign securities (this restriction would not be lifted until 1988), 60 per cent of their securities holdings in the late 1970s consisted of Italian government bonds. Domestic banks were underdeveloped in the personal banking business and, by German standards, rather 'archaic'.[161] The state-owned bank of the Italian postal service handled a large proportion of transactions. An internal market analysis in the late 1980s thus concluded that there was 'considerable potential' in Italy. At this time, only 28 per cent of the population held their own personal bank account. This compared to 84 per cent in Germany, where the market had nearly reached saturation point.[162]

In 1984, Deutsche Bank therefore began to explore options for expanding into branch-based business in Italy by acquiring shares in an existing bank. Efforts concentrated initially on Banca Cattolica del Veneto. However, as this was largely a regional institution, it did not seem a suitable vehicle with which to tap the wider Italian market.[163] A far more serious takeover candidate was Banca d'America e d'Italia (BAI), owned by Bank of America. With 98 branches and 3,000 employees, this was the eighth largest privately owned bank and biggest foreign-owned bank in Italy. Originally active in the financing of small and medium-sized industrial companies and in business with the Americas, this was one of the first Italian banks to introduce consumer loans in the 1960s and one of the country's largest providers of credit cards.[164] Due to the growing financial problems of its US owner, however, BAI was put up for sale in the mid-1980s. Italy's banking system, which until then had largely been state-controlled, was undergoing a sea change characterised by privatisation, loosening of state supervision and openness to the capital market. A thorough audit by Deutsche Bank showed that BAI was financially sound and a purchase price of $603 million well justified in view of the strong market potential.[165] Although it was then the largest ever takeover by a foreign bank in Italy, the purchase of BAI in December 1986 was relatively easy to absorb from Deutsche Bank's perspective. BAI was, in fact, roughly equivalent to a medium-sized branch district in Germany. The acquisition was largely financed from equity.[166]

Milan headquarters of the Banca d'America e d'Italia, which was acquired in 1986.

BAI continued to present itself as an independent bank, and the old management and most of the existing staff continued in post. Initially, the old name was also retained for fear of alienating customers. Deutsche Bank Group's management thus had only indirect oversight of the company. This was exercised primarily through the supervisory board and 'appointments to key positions vital for monitoring purposes'.[167] The main aim, 'from the beginning', was to 'improve' BAI's market position and branch network 'in selected regions', which proved to be a sluggish process.[168] In 1993, BAI took over Banca Popolare di Lecco, which had a strong presence in northern Italy. With its 230 branches and 4,200 employees, BAI was now the largest foreign-owned institution among Italy's 25 largest banks. A year later, both institutions were renamed Deutsche Bank SpA and integrated more closely into the Group. In summer 1995, DWS (70 per cent) and Deutsche Bank SpA (30 per cent) jointly acquired the Italian fund manager Finanza & Futuro, making Deutsche Bank the second largest player in the Italian fund business.[169]

The acquisition of BAI marked a fundamental reorientation of Deutsche Bank's international business. As Christian L. Vontz (Central International Department) and Hans-Peter Ferslev (Group Strategy) emphasised, the aim of the takeover was to allow Deutsche Bank 'for the first time to offer a nationwide full banking service abroad' and thereby take the 'first step' into 'multinationalism'.[170] Italy thus served as a test case for exploring the options for international expansion of the personal banking business.

In other European countries, the bank did indeed take a similar approach to that used in Italy. In Spain, it acquired Banco de Madrid in 1993 and merged this institution a year later with BCT. With its 250 branches, the company operated from 1994 onwards under the name Deutsche Bank SAE. Though its high branch density made it the country's largest foreign bank, it came under heavy competitive pressure from the mid-1990s in what was a rather overbanked country.[171] In Belgium, Deutsche Bank took advantage of the opportunity presented by financial difficulties at Crédit Lyonnais, which was 'under pressure from the European Commission' to sell its Belgian subsidiary. In 1997, this was Belgium's sixth largest bank. Amid strong concentration in the Belgian banking industry, Deutsche Bank acquired Crédit Lyonnais Belgium for DM 1 billion at the end of 1998. This gave it access to high-net-worth personal banking customers and corporate clients in the Benelux region.[172]

In Poland, Deutsche Bank established its own subsidiary in October 1995, which proved to be too late, however. Deutsche had expended a great deal of energy in expanding into the new eastern states of Germany following reunification in 1990. Meanwhile, other foreign institutions such as ING and Citibank had established themselves in Poland and many other Eastern European countries. Measured in terms of equity, Deutsche Bank was not even among the top 10 foreign banks in Poland in 1996.[173] Attempts to gain a foothold in France also fell flat. Strict regulation meant that Deutsche did not establish its own branch bank here until 1999. This was sold just two years later. Large parts of Banque Worms SA, acquired from AXA in April 2001, were sold off in as early as spring 2003. In the Netherlands, too, where Deutsche Bank had long held a strong position in the corporate and institutional client business, intense competition from domestic banks and a relatively small market prevented this success being replicated in the retail banking business. The bank withdrew from the personal banking segment again in 2005.[174]

Overall, the results of the internationalisation of the personal banking business were mixed. Successes were achieved in countries with relatively weak local banks and low market saturation. Long-established shareholdings in local institutions, such as those in Spain and Latin America, were an advantage in many cases. In Italy, Deutsche Bank's well-balanced strategy succeeded in gaining market share for the Group. In this case, the recipe for success was the gradual integration into the Deutsche Bank Group of an already sound, established bank with its own international profile and solid position in the local market. It is clear, however, that Deutsche Bank's international expansion in the personal banking business did not follow an overarching plan. As Hilmar Kopper put it in 1990, this was a 'strategy of opportunistic, selective acquisition'.[175]

3. The Bank and Society

Politics, networks and the public

In the early days of the Federal Republic, maintaining good relationships with politicians and performing a social role that extended beyond the business of banking itself was integral to Deutsche Bank's own self-image. Germany's economic model of 'Rhenish capitalism', in which business and politics were closely interwoven, provided space for a wide range of political activities and social engagement at Deutsche Bank. This extended beyond traditional lobbying and participation in industry associations, advisory bodies and specialist organisations. In some cases, the bank's board members even became public figures in their own right and achieved an unprecedented level of prominence. However, this role as figureheads could also leave them dangerously exposed. Growing criticism of banks and their seemingly limitless power could quickly turn personal. In West Germany's fast-changing media landscape, the ground rules of press debate were increasingly unforgiving. Deutsche Bank therefore now sought to shape its own media image through targeted public relations work. This involved developing a professional apparatus for corporate communication and expanding the activities of its cultural and social foundations.

Deutsche Bank's most publicly recognisable figure in the first two post-war decades was Hermann J. Abs. His successful work in negotiating the London Debt Agreement had made him one of Adenauer's most trusted advisers on economic and financial matters along with Robert Pferdmenges from the Cologne-based bank Sal. Oppenheim. Having steered clear of political office, Abs was a powerful background figure in the early years of the Federal Republic. In addition to his activities in banking associations, he was involved in numerous advisory bodies and economic policy committees. He regularly participated in meetings of the Cabinet Committee for Economic Affairs (*Kabinettsausschuss für Wirtschaft*) established by Adenauer in spring 1951 to work on important economic policy decisions.[176] As Germany's most important banker and one of the most powerful men in the world, Abs indisputably provided the bank with valuable social capital. While his influence on Deutsche Bank's business activities gradually ebbed away after his departure from the Management Board in 1967, his reputation continued intact. No other German businessman remained so influential even after his career had ended.[177]

Although none of Abs's successors achieved comparable prominence, maintaining close relations with leading politicians remained an integral part of the Management Board Spokesman's role. In 1967, the bank jointly appointed Karl Klasen and Franz Heinrich Ulrich to share the position of Spokesman. The intention was presumably for the more personable Klasen to act as the bank's public face while the more reserved Ulrich played a largely internal role. Only three years later, however, Klasen was appointed president of the Bundesbank. While Deutsche Bank no doubt hoped that his position at the top of the monetary and currency policy apparatus could play to its advantage, this was nevertheless a significant blow: the bank had lost one of its most high-profile and experienced managers. The importance of the Spokesman as Deutsche Bank's primary representative appears to have diminished somewhat after Klasen's departure. Instead, the job of representing the bank was increasingly divided between a number of different individuals. Wilfried Guth, for example, was involved in a range of international bodies set up to discuss economic and monetary policy, while F. Wilhelm Christians was a key figure in economic relations with the Soviet Union and other COMECON countries and was regarded as Deutsche Bank's foreign minister.[178] In addition to his Management Board role at Deutsche Bank, he served simultaneously as president of the Association of German Banks from 1975 to 1979. The charismatic Alfred Herrhausen also systematically built his relationships with important political figures in Bonn, even before his

Five Spokesmen of the Management Board at the annual general meeting of 1979, from the left: Hermann J. Abs, Karl Klasen, F. Wilhelm Christians, Franz Heinrich Ulrich and Wilfried Guth.

appointment as the bank's Management Board Co-Spokesman in 1985. Herrhausen had soon established close contact with representatives from all parties, including Helmut Schmidt, Otto Graf Lambsdorff, Hans-Jochen Vogel and Franz Josef Strauß. After the change of government in 1982, he became a close confidant of Helmut Kohl. Despite their very different personalities, he was best placed to replicate Abs's prominent position.[179]

Deutsche Bank's growing status as a symbol of 'Deutschland AG' – the country's distinctive interweaving of industry, the financial sector and the state – could sometimes put it in a difficult position. Its prominent role made it a focus of public attention whenever the shortcomings of the lending sector were discussed. With the banks among other industries in mind, Ludwig Erhard had repeatedly warned against the concentration of economic power.[180] Following the recentralisation of the big banks and the political controversy surrounding the introduction of the Act Against Restraints of Competition (*Gesetz gegen Wettbewerbsbeschränkungen*) in 1957, this criticism never entirely went away. Erhard regarded powerful banks as inimical to a competitive market economy.[181] Another bone of contention concerning the concentration of economic power was Abs's numerous supervisory board mandates. In 1960, he was a member of no fewer than 30 supervisory and administrative boards of major privately and publicly owned companies. On 21 of these boards, he served as chairman.[182] Abs also had numerous seats on the supervisory boards of foreign banks and businesses. Strictly speaking, this contravened the Stock Corporation Act (*Aktiengesetz*) of 1937, but was enabled in practice by a string of exceptions and general lack of legal clarity. After extensive preparation, the government revised the law on stock corporations in 1965. The changes limited board members to five supervisory board posts in the corporate sector and five bank mandates and also imposed restrictions on the exercise of proxy voting rights and the creation of hidden reserves.[183] At the time, Abs held 25 seats, but was able to make use of transitional provisions to avoid reducing these at a stroke.[184]

Coming to terms with history

In the late 1960s, the student movement and the rise of neo-Marxist criticism of the capitalist system began to stoke controversy about the power of the banks. This was also fuelled by the debate on the role of large industries and the banking sector during the Nazi era. Following the publication in 1970 by Pahl-Rugenstein Verlag of a book entitled *Der Bankier und die Macht. Hermann Josef Abs in der deutschen Politik* (Power and the Banker: Hermann Josef Abs in German Politics), attention came to focus increasingly on Deutsche Bank. The study was written by East Berlin historian Eberhard Czichon, who had spent years in GDR archives collecting material on Deutsche Bank's ties with the Nazis. Czichon used these incriminating documents to push his conspiracy theories about the all-pervasive power of the bank and its leading representative in the Third Reich. These arguments contrasted sharply with a commemorative book commissioned by the bank to celebrate its 100th anniversary. Written by the journalist Fritz Seidenzahl in the same year as Czichon's publication, the quality of this work was far higher than that of a typical corporate history of the time. It did not, however, claim to be an academic study; the content and style were aimed at a broad readership. What was more, Seidenzahl's book largely ignored the bank's role under National Socialism and, not untypically for a commemorative publication, was something of a hagiography. By comparison, Czichon's study, with its extensive references and keen moral judgements, was regarded by many as the first critical portrayal of the bank's actions during the Nazi years. Many readers were probably unaware that Czichon, and the East German Ministry for State Security, which lay behind the publication, were not interested first and foremost in genuine historical research but determined to draw lines of continuity between the Third Reich and the West German economic system. Abs took successful legal action against the author and publisher and prevented further publication of the study, which contained numerous factual and methodological errors. However, this did not stop Czichon's ideas finding a wide audience. Worse still, Abs's legal action created the impression among some observers that Deutsche Bank was unwilling to face up to its historical responsibility and wanted to stop uncomfortable facts from reaching the public. The context of these debates on corporate responsibility and historical guilt, which also affected other large German corporations such as Krupp, Thyssen and Flick, is well known.[185] In 1976, Deutsche Bank's commitment to historical research led to the creation of the *Gesellschaft für Unternehmensgeschichte* (Society for Business History). More recently, to mark the bank's 125th anniversary, a group of independent historians were asked to compile a historical study of the company in which the National Socialist era would be explored in depth. These initiatives were motivated partly by the recognition that legal battles were not an adequate strategy for dealing with the past.[186]

Philanthropy, social engagement and corporate image

In the early 1970s, Deutsche Bank began increasingly to promote science and the arts through a range of activities without neglecting traditional forms of patronage. Abs, for example, who had a large private art collection, donated a considerable share of his fortune to cultural projects and institutions after he left the Management Board. Artists, museums and classical musicians were among the beneficiaries.[187] Alongside these private initiatives, however, Deutsche Bank also began systematically to use its support for art and culture as a form of corporate communication. In 1979, Herbert Zapp was tasked with developing a plan for the bank's art collection. This coincided with the planned construction of the new premises for the Frankfurt head office, which were to feature works of modern art. The artworks were not to be selected at random but, rather, integrated into an overall interior design in keeping with the modern skyscraper complex. Zapp proposed that the collection should turn its attention to contemporary German art and move away from its existing focus on older works and classic modernism. This refocusing would also enable systematic support for young artists – Zapp proposed an annual budget of at least DM 5 million for art purchases. In his view, the concentration on the German art market would complement rather than conflict with the bank's growing activities abroad. After all, he argued, 'when we do business, we present ourselves as a German international bank'.[188] Zapp also suggested showcasing the newly acquired artworks not just at the head offices in Frankfurt and Düsseldorf but in foreign

Herbert Zapp (1928–2004), the trailblazer of Deutsche Bank's art collection, at the unveiling of the granite sculpture 'Continuity' (Kontinuität) in front of Deutsche Bank's Frankfurt headquarters on 7 October 1986.

branches, too. He also envisaged loans to German and international museums. From 1980 onwards, the Frankfurt offices hosted annual exhibitions of works by young artists. The Management Board also created an 'art committee' comprising leading experts from the art and museum worlds in Germany. They included Peter Beye from the Staatsgalerie Stuttgart, Klaus Gallwitz from the Städel Museum in Frankfurt and patron of the arts Peter Ludwig. The committee took stock of the existing works, developed plans for a new collection and, working with Zapp, acted in effect as a purchasing commission for the bank. The new collection focused on works on paper mainly from the German art world or by international artists with a connection to Germany. As well as supporting little-known, innovative artistic currents, the collection also promoted the vision of art in the workplace.[189] From 1981, artworks featured as illustrations in the annual reports. In addition, the bank published calendars featuring art from its own collection and sent them to customers as gifts.[190]

The integration of the contemporary art collection into the bank's public image was intended to emphasise the Group's cultural openness and modernity. The bank therefore deliberately also supported socially critical artists such as Joseph Beuys. This programme marked a decisive break with traditional patronage. Instead, the bank now sought to develop a new corporate identity and fundamentally overhaul its old-fashioned image. This was also reflected in other areas such as the design of customer areas in bank branches and the use of professional marketing. The logo, which dated from the 1930s and no longer seemed to represent the bank's modern, cosmopolitan image, was redesigned. Inspired by the French bank Société Générale, Eckart van Hooven had in fact already developed the idea in 1972 of creating a new logo to stand at the heart of a new marketing concept.[191] The new symbol, chosen through a competition, came from the well-known pioneering Stuttgart graphic designer Anton Stankowski. The 'slash in a square' was designed to be highly recognisable and expressed the bank's basic philosophy. The slash stood for economic vitality, while the square represented stability and trust.[192] Introduced in 1974, the new logo drew occasional criticism – the *Bild* newspaper ran an article headlined 'Painter draws five lines and earns DM 100,000' – yet soon became a successful trademark and an essential part of the bank's new image.[193]

This logo, designed by Anton Stankowski, was introduced in 1974.

In the 1970s, the bank expanded its support for science and academia. As with its art collection, these initiatives were intended to be an expression of the bank's engagement with social issues and the big questions for the future. In 1970, to mark its 100-year history, the bank established an anniversary fund endowed with DM 10 million to support education and research. This was set up under the auspices of Stifterverband für die Deutsche Wissenschaft, with the bank largely free to decide on how the funds should be used.[194] Alfred Herrhausen was keenly involved not only in the Stifterverband but also in the Senate of the Max Planck Society and on the advisory boards of several academic and art foundations. On his initiative, Deutsche Bank supported a wide range of institutions in the humanities and social sciences, including WZB Berlin Social

Science Centre, the Historisches Kolleg in Munich and Witten/Herdecke University, a private university with an interdisciplinary approach to teaching and research.

The financial commitment to these projects was considerable. In 1986 alone, Deutsche Bank donated DM 9.1 million to cultural and academic projects. The annual donation to political parties at this time amounted to just DM 400,000.[195] That same year, Herrhausen was instrumental in the creation of the foundation 'Helping People to Help Themselves'. This was endowed with DM 100 million to support private self-help initiatives.[196]

Though Abs, Zapp and Herrhausen were the most prominent figures in the bank's support for art, culture and science at this time, almost all Management Board members at Deutsche Bank were involved in some form with private foundations, academic associations and state-led initiatives. In many cases, they intensified their philanthropic activities later in life to an even greater extent than during their active careers. F. Wilhelm Christians, for instance, worked to promote German–Russian cultural exchange in the 1990s, while Horst Burgard spent a long spell on the board of Freies Deutsches Hochstift (one of Germany's oldest cultural organisations) and was also involved in the Association of Friends and Sponsors of the Goethe University, Frankfurt. Wilfried Guth dedicated time to the Society of Friends of the Alte Oper Frankfurt (the city's opera house) and the Society of Friends of Bayreuth. Long before the term corporate social responsibility entered the lexicon, then, Deutsche Bank had developed a diverse programme of social and cultural activities that helped to shape the company's image.

Industrial shareholdings and bank power

The image campaigns and the work of the foundations with which the bank was associated also served to counter the recurring criticisms of the bank's power and focus on profit.[197] Representatives of the bank such as Guth and Herrhausen did not deny the bank's social and economic weight, but pointed to the responsibility arising from it and the company's efforts to live up to this through wide-ranging social engagement.[198] They pushed back against suggestions that the bank was abusing its position. Speaking to *Capital* magazine in 1970, for example, Ulrich argued that banks 'are not power-hungry, nor are they constantly seeking to win control over industry'. In principle, the bank avoided acquiring majority shareholdings in industrial companies, he stressed. Acquisitions in this sector were not systematic, but usually only a 'transitory item' in the balance sheet and thus essentially an advantageous 'by-product'. Though they boosted the bank's earnings, industrial shareholdings were not designed to give it extensive control over other businesses.[199] In 1979, Herrhausen addressed public concerns directly in an interview with *Der Spiegel* magazine: 'Of course we have power. But I object to the term "uncontrollable" and I object to the term "great". Our power is controlled by legislation, competition and the public, and it is not as great as some assume.'[200]

What was the scale of Deutsche Bank's ownership interests in reality? The bank was largely silent on this question and provided no more than the information demanded by law. It was only required to disclose shareholdings where it held at least 25 per cent of the share capital and the tax relief under intercorporate privilege applied. Deutsche Bank kept the remaining equity interests falling below this threshold a secret, citing the lack of disclosure obligation. This led in 1970 to criticism from the Federal Ministry of Economics.[201] The bank's own documents reveal that at the end of 1969 the carrying amount of its direct and indirect cross-shareholdings in industrial companies was DM 1.04 billion. The market value was even higher, amounting to approximately DM 3.4 billion.[202] By August 1975, the industrial portfolio had a stock market value of around DM 4 billion, a figure that represented almost 75 per cent of Deutsche Bank's market capitalisation.[203] Deutsche also held shares in many other banks, for example in several mortgage lenders and regional institutions. An internal document shows that in 1965 the bank held equity interests of more than 25 per cent in 73 German banks and non-banks, including numerous majority shareholdings.[204] While the interests in other banks were strategic acquisitions intended to expand Deutsche Bank's own business, many of the equity stakes in industrial businesses had been acquired in the course of restructuring measures or in response to a request for financial assistance.[205] Most of these shareholdings were soon sold off again, although a proportion remained in the bank's hands.[206] The most significant holdings in 1970 included Hapag-Lloyd (83 per cent), Philipp Holzmann (35 per cent), Karstadt (25 per cent), Didier-Werke (25 per cent) and Daimler-Benz (28 per cent).[207]

The bank drew a variety of benefits from such shareholdings. They enabled it to influence companies' strategic decisions or at least to gain a deeper understanding of their financial position through representation on the supervisory board. This knowledge was often invaluable to creditors in assessing risks and compensating for a lack of information. In the 1970s, corporate insolvencies increased sharply, prompting banks to look more closely at risk structures where large exposures were concerned. The bank constantly emphasised that it did not seek an active role in other companies' operations. It could not deny, however, that in practice it wielded considerable influence. This power was also manifested in the bank's ability to exercise proxy voting rights at annual general meetings.

Shares in other companies also had a strategic function. They helped to attract new customers and to consolidate relationships with regular clients and make it harder for them switch to another bank. They were also a product of the frequent competition between the major banks to win restructuring assignments – this was not just about new customers but also prestige, particularly in large and difficult cases. With the self-confident Dresdner Bank, then headed by Jürgen Ponto, challenging Deutsche Bank's leadership position in the 1970s, there ensued a growing battle for mandates, restructuring projects and – linked to this – the acquisition of new equity interests.[208]

Aside from these strategic concerns, the industrial portfolio also represented a considerable source of income, and one which the banks did not want to forego given the fluctuations in interest and commission. Between 1957 and 1969, Deutsche Bank achieved net profits of DM 404 million from German industrial cross-shareholdings alone, representing over 25 per cent of its net profit in this period. This proportion rose constantly over the years and by 1969 had already reached 41.8 per cent.[209] Against this backdrop, any notion that equity interests in industrial businesses should be sold or moved to a dedicated holding company was quickly rejected.[210] While a holding company in the form of a closed-end investment fund would have continued to generate income for the bank, there would have been considerable drawbacks. The carrying amount of the shareholdings increased the bank's equity.[211] Losing these shareholdings, warned Ulrich in spring 1970,

> would unacceptably reduce the bank's equity and therefore its lending and business opportunities. Losing the income subject to intercorporate privilege would also diminish the earnings basis to such an extent that we would lack the necessary foundations to run the business in a dynamic way and address the new tasks that will face us in the future. If the ideas and plans fomenting among government bureaucrats, various business journalists and others were to begin to take concrete shape, we would be bound in the interests of shareholders, our customers and the wider economy to oppose them vigorously and fight back with all means, including examining the constitutional implications.[212]

The government was indeed considering tightening the rules on cross-shareholdings. Political pressure on banks rose sharply in the mid-1970s, especially after the collapse of Herstatt-Bank in 1974. Regardless of the fact that this was a special case involving a degree of criminal intent, the insolvency of the Cologne-based private bank seemed to prove that irresponsible business practices were widespread in the lending sector. Although the demands from parts of the Social Democratic Party (SPD) and unions for full nationalisation did not pose a serious threat, government intervention in the structure of the private banking system could no longer be ruled out. In summer 1973, for example, finance minister Helmut Schmidt announced the abolition of tax advantages for banks' industrial cross-shareholdings.[213] After consultation with Jürgen Ponto, Ulrich responded by offering the government a gentlemen's agreement. The banks, said Ulrich, were prepared to treat such shareholdings simply as a form of 'investment' to bolster their equity and would refrain from exercising any influence over the companies concerned. Moreover, they would not seek any majority shareholdings in non-banks.[214] For the Finance Ministry, however, these proposals did not go far enough. State Secretary Karl Otto Pöhl argued that the practice of including such shareholdings in equity was incompatible with the principles of the Banking Act (*Kreditwesengesetz*). He also considered the bank's promise not to seek majority shareholdings in industry to be insufficient, as enormous influence could result even from an interest of just 10 to 15 per cent. Pöhl wanted the banks to be required, within a specified deadline, to sell shareholdings acquired in the course of restructurings.[215]

Political action now seemed to be on the cards. In 1974, the Federal Ministry of Finance appointed a study commission for 'Grundsatzfragen der Kreditwirtschaft' (Fundamental issues in the banking industry), which was tasked with taking stock of how much power the big banks wielded and developing reform proposals accordingly.[216] However, the 11-member commission also included five representatives from the banking industry, including Alfred Herrhausen, who successfully put up a united front against a tightening of legislation.[217] Representatives from the Bundesbank and two generally bank-friendly academics were also on the commission. It was little surprise, then, that the final report, presented in 1979, did not propose in-depth reform of the banking sector. It neither questioned the German universal banking system in principle nor recommended a ban on shareholdings or an end to proxy voting rights. The report did, however, call for shareholdings to be limited to 25 per cent, allowing banks to hold a blocking minority but no majority stake in companies. This fell well short of the suggestions of the Monopolies Commission, which had proposed a 5 per cent limit on bank shareholdings. Otto Graf Lambsdorff, the West German Economics Minister, had suggested a limit of 10 to 15 per cent.[218] In other respects, too, the report was an exercise in moderation. It proposed that the number of supervisory board mandates be limited to six to eight per person and called for more precise criteria for calculating share owner-ship, though without recommending a fixed equity ratio. The commission rejected any further tightening of regulations, for example in relation to proprietary trading or the issuing business.[219] Far from paving the way for legislative reforms, then, the report was soon forgotten.[220] The Commission, wrote *The Economist* in May 1979, had given the banks a 'pretty clean bill of health' and the 'panic' of the banks was 'over'.[221]

By this time, the enormous public criticism of the banks had abated. After the murder of Jürgen Ponto by the Red Army Faction in July 1977, the strident attacks increasingly gave way to more measured tones. The difficult economic situation in Germany also put a lid on the hostility towards the banking sector. The structural crisis in industry made it clear that the banks were indispensable to turning around the fortunes of large companies. Deutsche Bank had also earned considerable credit for its role in the Flick controversy, which involved its acquisition in 1975 of a block of shares in the Flick conglomerate. Following the death of Friedrich Flick in 1972, the heirs to his company decided to sell a large portion of their shares in Daimler-Benz AG. In 1974, working on behalf of the Quandt family, Dresdner Bank had already sold a stake in the automotive group to Kuwaiti investors. These shares also originated from the Flick fortune. The circumstances of this deal, which Dresdner Bank initially kept secret, created a consid-erable stir in the press. The sale, on terms that were unclear and in the midst of the oil crisis, of large parts of one of the most important German manufacturers to the Middle East prompted popular fears that German interests were being sold out.[222] When Ulrich became aware of another intended sale, which would have transferred an entire block of Daimler-Benz shares to Iran, he used all his leverage to prevent the transaction. He not only contacted Friedrich Karl Flick, the son of the company's founder, but also informed the German government. The subsequent discussions with the Chancellor in January 1975 were extremely advantageous to Deutsche Bank. In a one-to-one meeting, Chancellor Helmut Schmidt encouraged Ulrich to acquire the Flick shares and promised the bank the full support of his government in completing the transaction. Daimler-Benz – said Schmidt, according to Ulrich's notes on the conversation – was not only one of Germany's largest employers but a 'flagship of the German economy' that should not be sold to the 'megalomaniacal Persians' under any circumstances. Such a sale would be inimical to the 'self-respect of the German people'.[223]

Given the widespread view that this transaction – worth DM 2 billion and at the time the biggest in West Germany's history – was in the public interest, there was little concern about the fact that Deutsche Bank temporarily acquired the majority of the company. In addition, Ulrich had given an assurance that the bank would quickly resell the shares to a German investor.[224] Ulrich used his discussions with the Chancellor to reiterate Deutsche Bank's position on the general issue of shareholdings. The aim, he stressed, was not to gain power over industry but to act as an intermediary in a difficult economic and foreign policy situation. Ulrich also communicated the bank's interest in resuming confidential talks on a voluntary agreement in relation to bank shareholdings.

The acquisition of the Daimler shares was not only financially lucrative but also a clever political move to get the bank off the defensive. Press coverage of the transaction was consistently positive, and the bank received encouragement from other German companies.[225] The boost to Deutsche Bank's image was considerable. The Group was able to present itself as the defender of the national interest and deliberately distance itself from Dresdner Bank's Quandt deal. Such was the reputational windfall for Deutsche Bank that the Dresdner press officer Walter Vielmetter accused Ulrich of 'deliberately orchestrating the Flick/Daimler transaction as an anti-Dresdner Bank campaign'.[226]

New directions in corporate planning

Deutsche Bank had succeeded in the mid-1970s in fending off the considerable number of political attacks. The long-prepared amendments to the German Banking Act (*Kreditwesengesetz*), which came into force in 1985, did not impose the expected limit on shareholdings. *Wirtschaftswoche* magazine wrote of a 'victory for the banks'. The accounting rules in the revised legislation were also favourable.[227] The consolidation requirement for banks was limited to wholly owned subsidiaries. Only these shareholdings needed to be reported on the balance sheet and counted towards equity. As the Banking Act allowed banks to lend only up to 18 times their equity, these rules carried considerable practical significance. They meant that foreign subsidiaries such as DB Lux were included in the Group's accounts, whereas smaller shareholdings continued to be omitted.[228]

Organising the Group's shareholdings in compliance with the multitude of tax, competition and regulatory rules was becoming increasingly complicated. Ulrich had already suggested in 1975 that they be centralised and integrated more closely into the Group's strategic planning. Until this time, responsibility for equity investments lay with various departments, including book-keeping, the Corporate Secretariat and the individual Management Board members. This meant that the bank did not even have a clear overview of all its existing shareholdings, let alone an overarching plan for them. In 1977, it therefore established a new 'Shareholdings Department'. This was led by Johann Wieland, who had long worked in building financing and real estate and had taken on many special tasks for the bank, including the VW privatisation in the early 1960s. The new department was staffed by an expert team, many of whom came straight from university with training in specialist areas such as tax and company law, corporate financing, valuation and merger control. The department served as a sort of 'mobile task force' for various mergers and restructurings.[229]

From 1985 to 1986, the department was responsible for the winding up of the Flick empire, a major undertaking for the bank that also temporarily increased its shareholdings. This transaction, too, was politically charged. It came in the wake of a scandal involving the Flick manager Eberhard von Brauchitsch, who, for the 'cultivation of the political landscape', had bribed politicians from all parties. Those caught up in the Flick Affair included the former Economics Minister Hans Friderichs, who had granted a tax break of almost DM 1 billion on the sale of the Daimler shares in 1975 on the grounds that the reinvestment of the proceeds from the sale would benefit the German economy. Not only Friedrich Karl Flick himself, but the entire German government thus wanted to wind up this economic empire as quickly and discreetly as possible. The industrial core of the old Flick Group comprised the companies Feldmühle, Buderus and Dynamit Nobel. There were also large equity interests in Daimler-Benz, the Gerling insurance group and the American conglomerate W. R. Grace & Co. The transaction required considerable negotiating skill and discretion, especially as Friedrich Karl Flick wanted to sell off his entire shareholdings of approximately DM 5 billion at a stroke. He was also determined to negotiate only with a single party, which ruled out partnering with other banks.

The Shareholdings Department worked for months in top secrecy on a complex structure that needed to take account of a series of tax, regulatory and competition law considerations.[230] Flick demanded extensive tax exemptions for the transfer. However, applying intercorporate privilege required Friedrich Flick Industrieverwaltung KGaA – a partnership limited by shares – to be converted into a stock corporation. The tax implications of this first had to be discussed with the authorities in the states of Hesse and North Rhine-Westphalia. Prior discussion with the financial regulator, Bundesaufsichtsamt für das Kreditwesen, was also required as the financing volume of DM 5 billion exceeded the applicable threshold. With the regulator having rejected the initial request for an exemption, the bank was forced to implement an alternative solution in which it acquired the assets in multiple instalments through a specially established subsidiary. Friedrich Flick Industrieverwaltung KGaA was converted into a stock corporation and – in order to avoid wealth tax and trading capital tax burdens – was acquired by Deutsche Bank with effect from midnight on 31 December 1985. For regulatory reasons, the individual assets then had to have left the bank's balance sheet by the end of 1986 so that they did not appear in its annual accounts for either 1985 or 1986. In order to 'pre-empt public debate', the bank reported the merger in advance to the Federal Cartel Office, which issued its approval on the same day, albeit with the condition that voting rights in the acquired companies could only be exercised where necessary for the placement of the shares.[231]

The bank sold its shareholdings in several tranches – some directly on the stock market and some through an international consortium. It gained approximately DM 1 billion on the sale, which made a considerable contribution to the bank's exceptionally high operating profit in 1986.[232] This, the second major deal involving the Flick Group, once again brought considerable prestige for Deutsche Bank, despite suspicion in some quarters that the bank had deliberately undervalued the stocks. This accusation did not hold water as Flick's own asset managers had undertaken the valuation and submitted their offer on this basis.[233] A dossier dating from November 1985 shows that Johann Wieland and Jürgen Bilstein from the Shareholdings Department expected a gain of just DM 250 million on the placement. The fact that the profit was ultimately much higher was attributable to strong increases in stock prices that could not have been foreseen when the contract was signed.[234]

With the Flick transaction in 1985–6, Deutsche Bank had definitively confirmed its leading position in the restructuring of industrial assets. In the years that followed, it organised a series of large transactions, such as the restructuring of Klöckner (a steel and metal distributor) in 1988 and the merger of Messerschmitt-Bölkow-Blohm (MBB) with the Daimler-Benz subsidiary DASA in 1989. However, the Flick deal marked a break from previous restructurings not only in terms of its financial volume but in the very nature of the business itself. Unlike the first Flick deal in the 1970s, this was not a reorganisation dictated by industrial policy and the national interest, but essentially a capital transaction in which both sides sought to profit from the sale of shares. It reflected the growth of the German stock market, which just 10 years earlier would have been unable to absorb such volumes (the placement of large share packages abroad would probably have been ruled out on regulatory grounds in any case). Instead of the six years required to sell the shares in the 1970s transaction, the second Flick deal took just a few months. It was a happy coincidence for the bank that the shares were sold before the international stock market crash in October 1987.

The bank was also involved with increasing frequency in large international transactions. In 1986, in a consortium with Mediobanca, it organised the sale of FIAT shares held by the Libyan state. The sale of the share package, worth over $3 billion, was handled by the recently founded Deutsche Bank Capital Markets in London. Amid falling stock prices, however, this transaction proved to be a loss-maker. The bank was forced to absorb large parts of the share package into its portfolio and accept a considerable drop in value. This illustrated the risks of such large-scale transactions.[235]

These activities once again increased the size of Deutsche Bank's industrial portfolio substantially. Its market value exceeded DM 20 billion in October 1986, up by a factor of six since 1970. The Shareholdings Department was therefore greatly expanded and, in 1986, renamed Group Strategy (AfK). It now reported directly to the Management Board. Group Strategy's role was to enter new business areas, push ahead with the Group's strategic development and diversify the bank's shareholding and financing portfolio.[236] This did not mean fully dismantling the bank's industrial shareholdings, which were still needed for reserves and to offset the bank's risks. Nevertheless, the AfK suggested in autumn 1986 that the bank should diversify its shareholdings and gradually reduce them to less than 20 per cent of each company's total share capital.[237] Longer term, it proposed a reduction to just 10 per cent. This was a response to renewed political criticism of banks' industrial policies, which had reignited after the second Flick deal. In spring 1986, for example, Otto Schlecht, state secretary in the Federal Ministry of Economics, expressed concern about banks' industrial shareholdings and pointed to possible implications under competition law.[238] Similar concerns came from the Federal Cartel Office and the Monopolies Commission, which produced a special report in 1988 on regulatory guidelines for a viable financial system.[239] The report did not name specific banks, but it was clear that the Commission had Deutsche Bank in mind given the large shareholding in Daimler-Benz. The criticism was of all the more concern, warned Wieland and Ferslev from the Group Strategy department, because it came not from socialists but, rather, 'from the conservative camp'.[240]

The bank thus now began gradually to reorganise its industrial portfolio. It set out to reduce its large shareholdings in Philipp Holzmann, Südzucker, Hapag-Lloyd, Karstadt and Didier. The reduction in the tax-relief threshold (intercorporate privilege) from 25 to 10 per cent with effect from 1 January 1984 provided an additional incentive. The bank responded by reducing large industrial shareholdings while increasing smaller equity interests – for example in Munich Re and Allianz – to 10 per cent.[241]

Deutsche Bank increasingly regarded its shareholdings as a financial investment. While still important to its earnings and capital structure, they were thus no longer integrated into an active industrial policy. The days of Deutschland AG were numbered. While not immediately reflected on the balance sheet, this was, in strategic terms, a considerable change in direction.

4. Euromarket and International Financial Business

Prior to 1957, Deutsche Bank's international business concentrated largely on trade financing and the handling of payment and foreign exchange transactions in the European Payments Union. This reflected the restrictive nature of the wider European economy in the early post-war years. It was only in 1957–8 that currency convertibility was restored, allowing the free movement of capital to resume. The founding of the European Economic Community (EEC) injected strong momentum into the international money and capital markets by removing many of the obstacles to trade and commerce between member nations. West Germany's large export surplus ensured high liquidity but also brought the risk of inflation. With the Bretton Woods system of fixed exchange rates making it difficult for Germany to increase the value of its currency, and given vehement opposition from the German export industry to such a move, capital exports served as an alternative means of balancing out the large current account surplus. These largely took the form of short-term investments abroad by German banks – transactions made profitable by the interest rate differential. The banks thus made a considerable contribution to 'evening out exchange reserves on a worldwide commercial basis', as the Deutsche Bank annual report put it in 1959.[242] This earned the bank considerable interest income and was also in the interests of Germany's foreign trade balance. In 1960, 'for the first time in almost half a century, Germany once again became a capital-exporting country'.[243] Abs joined efforts both in Germany and abroad to bolster capital exports and was a member of the Central Capital Market Commission, which was established by the major German banks in 1957 as a self-regulatory body for the banking industry. He also participated in international committees calling for a reanimation of cross-border capital flows. In Paris in 1957, for example, as a member of the Institut International d'Études Bancaires, he initiated a new committee to promote the international capital market business.[244] Even more significantly, however, he used his many international contacts to open up the German market for foreign bonds and, in just a few years, turned his bank into Europe's leading issuing house.

International issuing business

From 1958 onwards, Deutsche Bank placed numerous foreign bonds on the German capital market, where it benefited from relatively low bond market rates and keenness among local investors to subscribe. A convertible bond issued by the Anglo American Corporation of South Africa in October 1958 served as a test case for the receptiveness of the German capital market and was the first in a long line of bond issues. In 1959, net sales of foreign securities already stood at DM 1.4 billion, exceeding the previous year's figure by a factor of five.[245] Most issuers, however, were not corporations like Anglo American, but public sector institutions and international organisations. In April 1959, for instance, Deutsche Bank acted as lead manager for a DM 200 million bond from the World Bank. Given the large volume and the wishes of the issuer, Deutsche Bank underwrote the bond issue together with other West German institutions. Things did not go entirely to plan, however. Although the World Bank's excellent creditworthiness ensured the issue itself passed smoothly, weaknesses soon became apparent in the secondary market. These put downward pressure on the bond's price to such an extent that Deutsche Bank was forced to intervene with supporting purchases. For a time, it held two-thirds of the total bond issue in its own portfolio. So determined was the bank to raise its profile as a top-class international issuing house and to showcase the German capital market, however, that it was prepared to accept such risks in return for prestige and potential future business. In the years that followed, Deutsche Bank repeatedly floated large bonds for the World Bank and, from 1963 onwards, for the European Investment Bank, the Inter-American Development Bank and the EEC.[246] Many municipal governments in other countries, which urgently needed funds in the post-war era, also financed themselves through the German capital market. Business with governments, international organisations and public bodies thus proved highly lucrative. In 1959, the bank placed a bond for DM 30 million for the city of Oslo. A bond worth DM 100 million on behalf of the Japanese prefecture and city of Osaka followed in 1962. This was the first of many for Japanese issuers. The bank also increasingly acquired foreign treasury bonds with strong rates of return, for example from the Dutch and Belgian governments. For international corporations, though, the West German capital market did not begin to grow in importance until the mid-1960s. Here, too, Deutsche quickly took a leading position among the German banks and placed large bonds for companies such as Transocean Gulf Oil, DuPont, British Petroleum, IBM and the Italian energy firm ENEL. The customers were often energy companies seeking to fund expensive explorations.[247]

Within just a few years, Deutsche Bank had successfully earned a reputation as an efficient and reliable issuing house and was involved in ever-larger projects. By 1963, it had already placed a total of 15 foreign bonds with an overall volume of DM 700 million. In the years that followed, business took off in earnest. In 1964 alone, Deutsche Bank headed 10 (of a total of 12) bond syndicates in Germany involving foreign issuers. These had a total volume of DM 895 million.[248] Given the high levels of commission they generated, these issues were not only highly lucrative but led the bank back to a business area in which it had historically been highly active. Abs also took the view that financing businesses and public entities via the capital market was far more efficient – and less risky for the bank – than lending to them directly. Though Abs was not opposed to loan financing per se, he was adamant that this should be limited in view of the high demand for capital from abroad.

Initially, the majority of issues were denominated in German currency. For the most part, the bank refrained from participating in foreign currency bonds or international syndicates.[249] The exceptions included a bond issue worth $25 million by the Belgian oil company Petrofina AG in 1957, on which the bank collaborated with Société Générale de Belgique. In July 1961, a European syndicate led by Credit Suisse and Deutsche Bank placed an Argentinian sovereign bond for $25 million. In general, however, Abs was sceptical of bonds denominated in foreign currency and saw little necessity for involvement in them given the strength of the German capital market and healthy subscriptions even for very large international bonds.

Abs's reluctance was somewhat out of step with the times. The new era of currency convertibility was sharply accelerating the influx of dollars into Europe. The US current account deficit and the restrictive rules of the American capital market, which had been introduced in the early 1930s, caused American money to stream across the Atlantic. The centre of the so-called 'Eurodollar' market was London. Aspiring to restore the status of the City as an international financial centre and to compensate for the weakness of sterling, the British government sought to attract foreign investors. Here, investments earned high returns and the financial industry was free to develop without stringent restrictions.[250] Abs remained wary, regarding this market as extremely risky. Deutsche Bank thus kept its distance from London's money and capital markets and, for a long time, did not extend any Eurodollar loans.[251] The risk of a sudden withdrawal of this American 'hot money' was too great in Abs's eyes, especially given the capital hunger of the US itself in the context of the Vietnam War. Abs also pointed out that Eurodollar loans were often initiated by brokers rather than by the debtor or lender themselves, making oversight extremely difficult. Moreover, loans were frequently replaced upon maturity with further credits, creating ever-larger loan pyramids. With their true volume difficult to assess, these structures posed considerable risk to creditors.[252] By Abs's estimate, 95 per cent of all Eurodollar loans in 1965 served the repayment of existing borrowings. This was a risky state of affairs. Some banks, noted Abs, generated turnover of $100–200 million a day through Eurodollar loans, which therefore made up a large proportion of their total activity. As there was often no real underlying transaction, he argued, the Eurodollar business artificially inflated the market and created a dangerous imbalance: 'If everybody is happy in a market,' he commented, 'something must be wrong with the market.'[253]

Abs's criticism of the Euromarket did not stop at the risk to individual banks. Eurodollars accounted for an ever-larger share of foreign capital flows, especially in West Germany.[254] In the space of just a few years, the Euromarket's volume increased by a factor of 10.[255] Given that it was beyond the reach of the central banks, unlike national financial markets, Abs also regarded it as a threat to monetary stability itself. These fears materialised in the foreign exchange and balance of payments problems that triggered the demise of the Bretton Woods system in the late 1960s, which were partly attributable to the growing inability of central banks to control liquidity with their traditional policy tools. This development increasingly elevated the commercial banks into important international monetary policy players in their own right.[256]

Objectively speaking, Abs's scepticism of the Euromarket was well founded. In business terms, however, staying away from the most important financial market of the post-war era was not a credible long-term position. In 1963, when the US introduced an interest equalisation tax on foreign securities to prevent further capital exports,

The Autostrade bond of 1963, aimed at financing Italy's highways with an issuing volume of $15 million, was the first Eurodollar bond.

and Switzerland followed suit with its own restrictive measures, Germany became even more attractive to foreign investors. Deutsche Bank thus now gave up its resistance and began to play a more active role in the Eurodollar business. In the summer of 1963, it participated in a $15 million bond issue by the Italian state-owned motorway operator, Autostrade.[257] In 1964, the bank lead-managed a syndicate for the issue of a Japanese government bond, which was placed in several currencies and worth over DM 200 million. This was the first occasion on which non-Japanese banks participated in such a bond issue. The bank was also increasingly involved in parallel bonds, which were issued in multiple countries and denominated in the respective national currencies. Here, different issue prices were used to compensate for different national interest rates.[258] Constructing such complex bonds necessitated a high degree of co-operation with foreign banks, especially at European level.

European club banking and the American challenge

The post-war Deutsche Bank long avoided opening foreign branches or acquiring large shareholdings in other companies. Despite its increasing international exposure, this was a principle to which the institution held firm until the late 1960s. Abs repeatedly cited the experiences after 1945, when 'German private property was confiscated in contravention of the rule of law', as justification for this stance. The bank therefore 'made a virtue of necessity': in its relationships with other banks, it sought merely loose collaboration that would preserve extensive autonomy. For Abs, the absence of branches and ownership interests in other countries also had the additional advantage of preventing 'true competition' from arising. Even within the EEC, the 'regional principle' still applied, and the banking market was organised predominantly along national lines within a federal system.[259]

Despite these general principles, the bank still faced the question of how to co-ordinate co-operation with other European banks. The network of correspondent banks was sufficient for handling payments, but fundamentally unsuited to structuring large capital market transactions.[260] While Deutsche Bank had co-operated extensively with Amsterdamsche Bank and Banque de la Société Générale de Belgique since 1958, this had been informal and not widely communicated. There was a good reason for such discretion: the banks wanted to avoid the impression of a cartel so as not to alienate other friendly institutions.[261] In 1963, however, the three banks went a step further and created the 'European Advisory Committee' together with Midland Bank, thereby beginning to formalise their co-operation. The committee comprised senior managers (Deutsche Bank was represented by Abs and Ulrich) and met several times a year. It deliberately avoided setting itself specific objectives. The members gathered to share experience, co-ordinate flows of information and create 'a common basis for the handling of specific transactions, especially major international financing operations'.[262] This loose co-operation stopped short of creating the 'European issuing syndicate' some banks had called for.[263] Representatives from Deutsche Bank also emphasised the absence of preference clauses or similar arrangements.[264] Nevertheless, the frequent press description of the committee as merely an 'information circle' was a gross understatement.[265] In reality, the new grouping created a core of leading Western European banks with similar interests, who would work together ever more closely through bond and lending syndicates.

The European Advisory Committee also served as a vehicle for developing strategies to counter the growing dominance of American banks in the European market. The US competition was in the ascendancy thanks to global branch networks, refinancing opportunities on the international capital market and experience in the investment banking and advisory services business.[266] As Hans-Otto Thierbach told Ulrich in December 1964, Deutsche Bank would not be able to rely solely on a 'largely defensive' strategy, but would have to advance proactively into new areas of the international financial business. He suggested that it take advantage of its European grouping in order to compete with American institutions on an equal footing. Thierbach therefore proposed that the European Advisory Committee create its own bank to offer specific products such as multiple-currency loans to multinational businesses.[267]

This vision became reality in 1967 when the Committee members agreed, together with the private London-based bank Samuel Montagu & Co., to create a specialist bank for the issue of medium-term loans. Founded in Brussels in 1967, 'Banque Européenne de Crédit à Moyen Terme' (BEC) focused its lending on companies seeking funding from outside sources with terms of up to seven years for major international investments. As such loans were considered particularly risky, Deutsche Bank was keen to outsource this business to an international subsidiary bank of the Advisory Committee. The existing BEC shareholders were also subsequently joined by Banca Commerciale Italiana in Milan and by Société Générale and Crédit Lyonnais in Paris.[268]

The creation of BEC was part of an important new development in Deutsche Bank's international organisation. Subsidiaries now became the lead players in certain segments of the international business, and these companies soon began to expand beyond their originally conceived roles. In addition to corporate lending, BEC, for example, began extending credit to public entities and also issued long-term loans. In 1968, it founded a subsidiary in Amsterdam – BEC Finance – to advise and fund large corporate mergers. BEC also expanded beyond the European market and opened foreign branches in Latin America, the Middle East, Japan, Indonesia, South Africa and New York.[269]

Luxembourg, the Euromarket and the beginnings of offshore banking

While the European Advisory Committee proved to be an important vehicle with which to quickly gain a foothold in other countries, Deutsche Bank went one step further in 1970 and founded its own subsidiary in Luxembourg: Compagnie Financière de la Deutsche Bank AG (CFDB). In the space of just a few years, this would grow into one of the largest Eurobanks anywhere in the world. The location seemed a natural choice. Deutsche Bank had already selected the Grand Duchy of Luxembourg as the headquarters for the fund company Euroalliance. The Autostrade bond – the first true Eurodollar bond ever issued – had been listed in Luxembourg in 1963. During that decade, the country had raised its profile as Europe's up-and-coming financial centre with pragmatic admission rules and a lack of any minimum reserve requirements. What was more, foreign investors enjoyed enormous tax advantages here. Interest income, dividend income and capital gains were tax free, and foreigners were not required to pay inheritance tax.[270] There was neither a stock exchange tax nor a rule preventing off-exchange trading of securities. West Germany, by contrast, had introduced a 25 per cent coupon tax on foreign-owned fixed-interest securities in 1965, thereby making its previously flourishing bond market a less attractive proposition to international investors.[271]

Within Deutsche Bank, the establishment of a subsidiary in Luxembourg was not without controversy. There were fundamental objections, which were primarily brought forward by Abs in his role as Supervisory Board chairman and rested on the potential risks.[272] Board Spokesman Franz Heinrich Ulrich expressed doubts about the sustainability of the Eurobank business in Luxembourg and also saw problems with capitalisation.[273] On the other hand, however, the soaring demand in the German issuance business was exhausting the bank's capacity for underwriting and placement and had already forced it to introduce a 'waiting list'. In November 1969, Wilfried Guth expressed concern that the German market was no longer adequate to meet the high demand for financing and that issuers would respond by turning to other institutions.[274] The risk of losing custom stemmed not only from German competitors but increasingly also from American banks, which were enticing a growing number of business customers in Germany.[275] To add to the difficulties, the Bundesbank introduced a 30 per cent minimum reserve for all foreign liabilities in 1970. This imposed major costs on German-based banks working in the international capital market business.[276]

In fact, Deutsche Bank was relatively slow to set up a Luxembourg subsidiary. Dresdner Bank and Commerzbank had already made this move in 1967 and 1969 respectively. CFDB's earnings prospects appeared excellent and its expenditure fairly low. Deutsche Bank was confident in light of the tax situation and lack of reserve requirements that time deposits of DM 80 million would be more than sufficient to cover the annual operating costs of DM 230,000. Extensive capital backing by the parent company would therefore be unnecessary. Instead, the subsidiary's capital would 'earn its own interest through investment in short-term money transactions'.[277]

Geographical proximity was another factor that made Luxembourg a more attractive location for Deutsche Bank than offshore Caribbean locations or the City of London. CFDB was modest in scale. The 250m² office initially had just a dozen staff, who could be supported at short notice by employees from the nearby Trier branch across the German border. The head of the Luxembourg subsidiary for almost three decades was Ekkehard Storck, who had prior experience of international banking from his work in the branch network and at the Düsseldorf head office. In other respects, too, the new company was closely integrated with its German parent. The board of directors consisted of three Deutsche Bank Management Board members.[278] The largest capital market transactions were managed by the Secretariat in Frankfurt, while loans to German companies were the responsibility of the main branches in Germany.[279] For a large proportion of the transactions, Luxembourg thus served merely as a settlement venue. At DM 10 million, CFDB's share capital was on the low side and soon had to be increased on multiple occasions. Deutsche Bank also transferred deposits of DM 250 million, comprising term money from friendly foreign banks.[280] However, this was nowhere near enough to cater for CFDB's fast-growing lending business. The company therefore increasingly refinanced itself on the Euromarket. Total assets doubled between 1971 and 1973 from DM 2 billion to DM 4.1 billion. By the end of the 1970s, they exceeded DM 15 billion. This made Compagnie the largest bank in the financial centre of Luxembourg. Despite this size, the bank's capital was still relatively low at around DM 500 million in 1979, and 85 per cent of refinancing therefore came from the interbank market.[281]

Though the Luxembourg subsidiary had been founded for the securities and foreign exchange business and to issue international bonds, it was increasingly lending to German companies, too. These customers preferred to borrow in Luxembourg thanks to the more favourable tax rules and a considerable interest rate differential.[282] CFDB's lending generally comprised medium-term rollover loans with a minimum volume of DM 1 million, which were largely used by medium-sized businesses. Many German industrial companies such as BASF, Siemens, AEG and Thyssen had already established holding companies in Luxembourg and used CFDB in order to finance themselves through Euromarket bonds.[283] From the mid-1970s, Deutsche Bank also used its Luxembourg subsidiary to offer numerous loans to emerging markets and developing countries. Luxembourg additionally played a central role in petrodollar recycling after the 1973 oil crisis.

In many respects, the founding of CFDB marked the start of a new phase in Deutsche Bank's international business activities. The bank now emphatically joined the Euromarket, which it had previously resorted to for only a few individual transactions. For a long time, the high returns available in the German capital market had

Figure 15: Deutsche Bank's share of the Eurobond market by issue volume (in %).

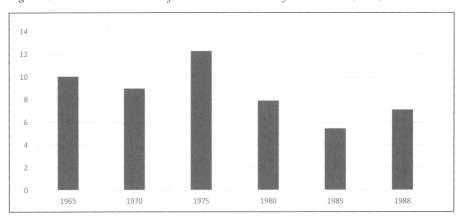

Source: Michael von Brentano, Investment Banking Activities in Europe, presentation at the Investment Banking Conference 1989, HADB, B733.

rendered this move unnecessary. In 1965, German companies sourced just 5 per cent or $3 billion of their total borrowing from the Eurodollar market.[284] By the end of that decade, however, the heyday of the German capital market was over.[285] With demand for lending growing at home and abroad, Deutsche Bank – since 1968 the world's largest issuing house[286] – was forced to embrace the Euromarket.[287] Pure DM-denominated foreign bonds did not disappear entirely, but increasingly lost ground to dollar-denominated Eurobonds. The consolidation of the US dollar from the mid-1970s onwards made fixed-interest securities in dollars highly attractive. In 1976, the issue volume surpassed the $10 billion mark for the first time.[288] Deutsche Bank scored some notable achievements here, winning the hard-fought contract for the issue of an EEC bond for $1 billion in 1976. That same year, it lead-managed a bond issue worth $300 million by the Commonwealth of Australia. Yet despite the size of the market, competition was fierce. The big American banks also wanted to claim this segment as their own, and not only prestige but considerable commission were at stake. Moreover, with DM-denominated bonds losing their traditional importance and international market share – they declined to just 5 per cent of all bond issues in 1980 – Deutsche Bank's position in the bond issuing market was gradually eroded.[289]

From 1970 onwards, Deutsche Bank moved large segments of its international business abroad. By the late 1970s, a third of the bank's international business (measured by business volume) went through its Luxembourg subsidiary.[290] In the Euroloan business, 95 per cent of which was based in Luxembourg, this proportion was even higher. The Grand Duchy's tax and investment laws made it highly attractive to customers and helped CFDB to turn a large profit. The risks to the Group increased considerably, however.[291] CFDB's equity and reserves were negligible, amounting to just 2–3 per cent of total assets in 1980.[292] Compagnie also participated extensively in syndicated loans with other banks, which had the advantage of keeping this lending off the books and avoiding breaches of internal country exposure and maturity transformation limits. The tightening of the reins by Deutsche Bank in the early 1980s, which bound

Meeting of the administrative board of Compagnie Financière de la Deutsche Bank AG in Luxembourg in 1975. Clockwise from the left: Franz Heinrich Ulrich, Robert Ehret, Hans-Otto Thierbach, Klaus Mertin, Jean Louis Schrader and Ekkehard Storck.

CFDB more closely to the risk management rules set by the Group, was a measure of just how far the subsidiary had moved from the principles of Abs's tenure.[293]

Finally, the new company in Luxembourg also marked Deutsche Bank's entry into offshore banking. For the first time the bank began systematically to handle part of its business through subsidiaries and holding companies in countries with highly favourable tax environments, strong client confidentiality rules and light-touch banking regulation and supervision. These were increasingly to be found outside Europe, for instance in the Caribbean, the Middle East and Asia. As the bank would discover, however, these locations were far harder to control from Frankfurt than the Luxembourg subsidiary.

EBIC and US subsidiaries

Like Deutsche Bank, the other members of the European Advisory Committee were also increasingly in the process of building up their international shareholdings. Société Générale and Creditanstalt-Bankverein joined the Committee in 1971 and Milan-based Banca Commerciale Italiana in 1973. The organisation was already evolving into an international banking corporation in its own right. In autumn 1970, the members founded the European Banks' International Company SA (EBIC) and chose Brussels as the location for its headquarters. At $2 million, the new company's share capital was low, leaving it unable to conduct real transactions under its own steam. Instead, EBIC's primary task was to establish and co-ordinate other international subsidiaries, helping them to enter risky business sectors or expand into countries and regions where European banks were underrepresented. This often involved overcoming regulatory barriers or establishing regional partnerships to gain market entry.

Seat of the European-American Bank & Trust Company on New York's Park Avenue, 1969.

Foremost among the target markets was the US, where existing banking regulations made access difficult for European universal banks like Deutsche. The European Advisory Committee founded its first regional subsidiary bank in New York in May 1968: the European-American Banks (EAB) group.[294] EAB emerged from a subsidiary of Société Générale de Belgique, which had been operating in New York since the 1950s but was no longer profitable.[295] To maintain the strict separation of different banking activities required in the US, EAB consisted of two separate companies: the European-American Banking Corporation (for lending) and the European-American Bank & Trust Company (for the deposit business and portfolio management). Deutsche Bank held $20 million of the total share capital of $70 million and played a leading role within the organisation.[296] EAB established a 'German desk' to serve the bank's 'business friends'. This was responsible for 'handling and financing their business and generally attending to their banking transactions on the spot'.[297]

It was quickly clear, however, that the new enterprise was more than just a US liaison office for European businesses. EAB soon grew into a major banking group in its own right, offering a growing range of financial services such as investment advice and property financing. In 1974, it took over part of the failed Franklin Bank in New York, thereby establishing a presence in the personal banking business.[298] With total assets of $4 billion, it was already among the 25 largest banks in the US and would soon open branches and subsidiaries in Los Angeles, San Francisco, Chicago, Baltimore and Miami. It also had an offshore presence in the Bahamas and a branch in Luxembourg for the Euromarket and foreign exchange business. In 1982, EAB acquired a stake in Banque Européenne pour l'Amérique Latine in Brussels and worked extensively in public sector financing for Latin American countries.[299] This was clearly a high-risk strategy. In fact, however, these loans were far from the bank's largest problem. Rather, EAB's primary weakness from the outset was that it had neither sufficient equity capital nor adequate deposits and thus largely resorted to the Euromarket for its own refinancing.[300] This created strong dependence on the capital markets. In the 1980s, when the international debt crisis broke out and interest rates rocketed, EAB found itself in an increasingly precarious position.

As regulations prevented the two EAB banks from conducting any investment banking in the US, Deutsche Bank had to seek another solution for this business area. In 1971, Union Bank of Switzerland offered the bank a $4 million stake as an equal partner in American UBS Corporation, its recently founded investment subsidiary in New York.[301] For Deutsche Bank, this was an extremely attractive prospect, as gaining admission to the American stock exchanges was no easy feat. While Deutsche Bank was a leading player in the Eurocapital market, Union Bank of Switzerland was strongly positioned in the foreign securities business. Jointly operating an American securities bank was thus an opportunity for the two institutions to 'perfectly complement one another'.[302] In addition to its primary task of expanding its securities and foreign exchange trading on Wall Street, the new bank – UBS-DB Corporation – was also involved in real estate financing and asset management.[303] It quickly built relationships with American financial institutions. In 1972, for example, Chase Manhattan Bank offered to collaborate on market research.[304] Two years later, Merrill Lynch approached the chairman of the UBS-DB Corporation, F. Wilhelm Christians, to propose a bond issue worth $650 million as part of a syndicate with other US institutions. Christians ultimately rejected the deal in light of the bond's long maturity and the sizeable currency risk. Nevertheless, the offer showed that UBS-DB had rapidly become a respected player in the American investment banking industry.[305]

In its first year, the new bank proved to be a loss-making enterprise.[306] Securities trading was sluggish. The target of handling 25 per cent of the two parent banks' order business on Wall Street through UBS-DB was missed by a wide margin.[307] What was more, there were growing American efforts to restrict the access of foreign banks to the US stock market. These came from the Advisory Committee on International Capital Markets and from US issuing houses and brokers.[308] While this climate did not result in any new concrete measures, the protectionist mood in the US banking sector made it difficult for foreign institutions to gain a foothold.

UBS-DB was able to position itself far more successfully in an area that had not originally been intended as part of its main remit: the international bond business. With the reduction in interest rates in 1974 and high petrodollar liquidity, the importance of the Eurodollar business in the US began to grow again. As this was Deutsche's core area of expertise, however, the bank ended the joint venture with Union Bank of Switzerland in 1978 by acquiring the remaining shares. The investment subsidiary now continued under the name Atlantic Capital Corporation and, from 1985, as Deutsche Bank Capital Corporation.[309]

Asia and Euras

Deutsche Bank used EBIC to gain access to regional capital markets in other parts of the globe, too, especially the Arab world, Asia and the Pacific. In 1972, EBIC joined forces with 14 Arab banks to found European Arab Holding S.A. (EURAB) in Luxembourg. EURAB in turn opened its own subsidiaries based in London, Brussels, Frankfurt and Manama (Bahrain). Deutsche Bank initially had a 5.7 per cent stake in the group and increased this in subsequent years to over 10 per cent. Swiss Bank Corporation and two Japanese institutions also joined the holding company in 1975.[310] EURAB's most important function was to channel the enormous liquidity surpluses of the oil-producing countries into the European and international capital markets. In 1982, Deutsche Bank opened a representative office in Bahrain – the centre of offshore banking in the Arab world – to expand its business with high-net-worth private clients in the Middle East.[311]

EBIC was active in the Pacific, too. Together with other banks in the region, it founded the Euro-Pacific Finance Corporation Ltd. in Melbourne in 1970.[312] Here, too, EBIC proved to be a useful vehicle with which to establish regional operational structures, which were later assimilated into the Deutsche Bank brand. Deutsche Bank opened a representative office in Sydney in 1973 and subsequently acquired a majority stake in the EBIC subsidiary.

In Asia, the situation was somewhat different, as Deutsche Bank had long had a presence in many Asian countries – albeit often only through relatively small shareholdings in national development banks, for example in Bombay, Karachi, Kuala Lumpur and Seoul. Overall, business volumes here were relatively low until the late

The Tokyo branch of Banco Alemán Transatlántico, 1971.

1960s. Activities mainly comprised export finance for German companies and loans for development projects. In addition, Deutsche Bank placed large numbers of Japanese municipal bonds on the German market.[313] Japan's rapid industrialisation and strong export industry made it increasingly important to the German economy. In Japan itself, however, market access for Deutsche Bank remained difficult.[314] Foreign financial institutions were not admitted to the Tokyo Stock Exchange, nor could they participate in Japanese underwriting syndicates. They were also barred from selling European stocks and investment funds. What was more, Japanese companies overwhelmingly preferred to use their own domestic banks.[315] Deutsche Bank had thus long concentrated on serving German businesses in the country. The bank had maintained a representative office in Tokyo since 1962. In 1971, it converted this into a branch of Banco Alemán Transatlántico,[316] despite the latter's focus on Latin America. Abs's stipulation that the bank should not open foreign branches under the 'Deutsche Bank' brand evidently still held sway at this time.

The second pillar of Deutsche Bank's activities in the region was Deutsch-Asiatische Bank (DAB). In 1970, this had branches in Hong Kong, Karachi, Kuala Lumpur, Jakarta and Singapore, and was owned by a consortium of German banks. From Deutsche Bank's perspective, however, DAB was not a success story. While its business volume had increased from around DM 10 million to DM 200 million between 1953 and 1970, 60 per cent of this was attributable to the head office in Hamburg. Elsewhere, the picture was one of relatively weak turnover, except at the long-established Hong Kong branch, which had opened in 1958 and generated a further 20 per cent of DAB's business. Moreover, DAB barely turned a profit; in 1970, it produced net income after tax of just DM 600,000.[317]

In view of the great economic potential especially in Japan, Hong Kong, Singapore and South Korea, Deutsche Bank's management redoubled their efforts to expand activities in this part of the world. There were additional factors behind this decision, too. Other German and international banks were pushing into the Asian market.[318] Moreover, the management had long been dissatisfied with the collaboration within the DAB Group, believing that the other consortium banks had invested too little in the region and simply wanted to join the bandwagon. DAB was regarded as heavily under-capitalised and understaffed.[319] Beginning in 1970, Deutsche Bank therefore attempted to acquire shares from the other owners. This was far from straightforward. Dresdner Bank in particular was pursuing its own interests in Asia and would not be bought off with a simple financial offer. The Dresdner head Jürgen Ponto claimed the Singapore branch for his own bank and demanded heavy compensation.[320] At the same time, Deutsche began negotiations with its EBIC partners to establish a consortium bank for Asia similar to EAB in the US. The plan was for this to become the successor to DAB. The outcome of these discussions was the new European Asian Bank (Eurasbank), which was created in January 1972 as a stock corporation under German law. German interests dominated from the beginning. Wilfried Guth was appointed supervisory board chairman, and the headquarters remained in DAB's home city of Hamburg.[321] In terms of the pace of expansion, however, Euras was a very different beast from the old DAB. It benefited from the explosive economic growth of Southeast Asia and Japan and gradually expanded its branch network across the entire region. Japanese banks were particularly interested in co-operation with Euras, seeing it as a means of accessing the European capital market.[322]

European Asian Bank

EURASBANK combining the banking experience of

Amsterdam-
Rotterdam
Bank

Banca
Commerciale
Italiana

Creditanstalt-
Bankverein

Deutsche Bank

Midland Bank

Société
Générale
(France)

Société Générale
de Banque
(Belgium)

The partners of the Eurasbank from 1972 on.

As in the US, Deutsche Bank did not want to rely on EBIC subsidiaries alone to establish its presence in the Asian capital market business. In 1973, it therefore began to explore options for establishing its own merchant bank.[323] The Asian market was still highly fragmented and difficult for foreign investors to penetrate. Internal reports pointed to a 'different mentality' among investors. In Hong Kong, the bank noted, 'short-term profit orientation' ruled the day.[324] Placing international bonds – Deutsche Bank's specialism – or engaging in long-term lending business with local industry both appeared equally implausible strategies.[325] Moreover, provision of other financial services – whether in investment advice or the capital markets – was almost impossible given the access restrictions. There were thus 'narrow economic limits' to Deutsche Bank's commercial opportunities.[326] Despite these complications, the region held great appeal. From the early 1970s onwards, Asian countries enjoyed high export surpluses and an influx of international liquidity, leading to the emergence of an Asian dollar market. Hong Kong and Singapore became established financial centres. Already doubtful by 1973 about the future of the co-operation with EBIC, Deutsche Bank laid plans for its own representative office in Hong Kong. This opened in 1976 and was upgraded to branch status three years later.[327] In 1978, the bank also founded its own subsidiary in Singapore – Deutsche Bank (Asia Credit) Ltd. – to expand the lending, money market and foreign exchange businesses.

Going it alone

Deutsche Bank regarded the co-operation with EBIC as little more than a temporary solution. It was clear early on that the collaboration had considerable downsides and could be more of a hindrance than a help to Deutsche Bank's ambitious international business objectives. What was more, it was not regarded as particularly profitable.[328] Internally, there had always been reservations about tying Deutsche Bank so closely to other institutions. Particularly where the international capital market business was concerned, Abs, for example, had taken the view that Deutsche Bank should not rely on fixed partners. He had therefore rejected the idea of an international issuing syndicate, instead favouring a looser co-operation. In 1967, he had negotiated with a group of US, French and Swiss banks on ways of working together in the international capital market business.[329] Given its existing position of strength, the bank was not tempted to engage in cartel practices.

Thierbach, too, noted in as early as 1971 his belief that Deutsche Bank was putting more into the EBIC group than it got out in return. This applied 'both to the provision of staff and expertise and to the ongoing acquisition of new business'. In the case of EAB, for example, Thierbach claimed that Deutsche Bank accounted for 60 per cent of business – far more than its 20 per cent ownership stake would suggest. Furthermore, this ratio was even more unfavourable in the case of the other subsidiaries. The prospect of 'the cake always being divided between six', he argued, 'can only be described as extremely unsatisfactory. One cannot say that the income we forego through this agreement will be compensated for by the potential benefits, which are a long way off and still quite vague.'[330] Irrespective of this, the bank also felt that EBIC was increasingly acting as a brake on its own internationalisation efforts. Deutsche considered opening its own branches in London and Paris in the early 1970s, but held back due to the collaboration with Midland Bank and the French partners.[331] Plans to set up a branch in New York were also initially rejected for fear that the partner banks would have regarded it as damaging to EBIC.[332] It was only in 1976, after long negotiations, that Deutsche Bank persuaded EBIC to allow the member banks to open branches outside their home region.[333]

In October 1976, the Co-Spokesman of the Management Board Wilfried Guth defined four objectives for the bank's international business:

1. Expansion in the provision of trade financing to German industry. Deutsche Bank's position had continuously weakened in this area. Between 1971 and 1977, for example, its market share fell from 25.1 per cent to 21.5 per cent due to strong competition, especially for small and medium-sized business customers, from other major banks, savings banks and co-operatives.[334]
2. Deeper business relationships with foreign banks through comprehensive key account management so as to enable improved customer service and correct accounting and hedging for all exposures.
3. The issue of sovereign loans, including in Eastern Europe, Southern Europe and the 'Third World'.
4. A further increase in foreign issuing business, especially in the dollar segment.[335]

These four goals were only achievable with an extensive international presence. Beginning in 1976, the bank thus opened its own branches in all the main financial centres around the world. In many places, it expanded existing representative offices, starting in London. Here, the representative office opened in 1973 was converted into a branch in 1976. London at this time was still the world's most important international financial centre and home to 47 per cent of the Eurodollar market. That same year, Deutsche Bank took over BAT's Tokyo presence. In 1978, Deutsche Bank went a step further and absorbed BAT altogether, taking over the latter's branches in São Paulo, Buenos Aires and Asunción. Deutsche Bank branch openings followed in Paris in 1977 (a representative office had already opened there in 1970), Brussels and Antwerp in 1978, and Madrid and Milan in 1979. The bank opened its first US branch in New York in 1979, followed by representative offices in Chicago and Los Angeles in 1982. In 1980, it took over the EBIC representative office in Johannesburg and founded Deutsche Bank (Suisse) in Geneva. A Zurich branch opened a year later. By October 1978, the bank was referring to its foreign branches, together with the Luxembourg subsidiary, as the 'main pillars of the expansion of the international business'.[336] This was not without justification: the EBIC banks were by now contributing less to Deutsche Bank's operating profit than its own branches abroad. Though the bank did not yet put an end to its twin-track strategy, in which EBIC and its own international business operated side by side, the writing was on the wall for European club banking.

In 1985, Wilfried Guth concluded that the EBIC partnerships 'had all been unsuccessful, to put it mildly'.[337] The only option was thus an orderly withdrawal. In legal and accounting terms, this meant lengthy restructuring, which initially led to a rise in Deutsche Bank's shareholdings. In 1983, the bank gradually acquired a majority

In the second half of the 1970s, Deutsche Bank returned to the most important international locations under its own name: In rapid succession, it opened branches in (from top) London (1976), Paris (1977) and New York (1979).

stake in Euras and absorbed the latter's branches into its own network. Rebranding as Deutsche Bank (Asia) took place in 1986. In 1988, the Asian subsidiary was merged with the parent bank and its senior management moved from Hamburg to the regional head office in Singapore. Although this reorganisation necessitated considerable write-downs, the former Euras branches proved useful to strategic expansion in the region. Divesting from EAB, which had lent extensively to Latin American countries, was an even longer process. EAB's large portfolio of subprime loans meant that this process was not completed until 1988.[338]

Becoming a global corporation

In contrast to the first wave of internationalisation prior to the First World War, the internationalisation of Deutsche Bank from the late 1960s onwards was associated with an extremely complex global corporate structure that required constant restructuring. The international financial system in the 1970s was still highly fragmented and characterised by a multitude of regional regulatory regimes that made a consistent overarching strategy very difficult to achieve. While the financial markets globalised rapidly, a process of deregulation only gradually took hold at political level. At the same time, new regional trading and monetary alliances began to emerge in Europe, Africa and Asia following the collapse of the Bretton Woods system. This context explains why Deutsche Bank made use of various different strategies and tools, adapted itself to regional circumstances and constantly changed its approach. The numerous branches, investments and subsidiaries created parallel structures that were rarely very profitable and made centralised management extremely difficult. Collecting statistics and accounting data on the Group's own international activities was far from straightforward and relied heavily on estimates. The enormous momentum of the bank's international growth should not be underestimated, however. By 1980, the scale of Deutsche Bank's international presence was unprecedented in its corporate history. It was not only represented in every region of the world but generated some 40 per cent of its operating profit from the international business.[339]

5. Public Finance and the International Debt Crisis

In the years after 1945, sovereign borrowing proved to be a lucrative business area for the banks. Public spending on the rebuilding of cities, expansion of infrastructure and provision of social services was growing all around the world. In the 1960s, Deutsche Bank was already a leading player in the underwriting and placement of large bonds issued by local and national governments and international organisations. The growth in industrial bonds, meanwhile, was much more modest. In 1968, the private sector accounted for just a quarter of the DM-denominated foreign bond issues lead-managed by Deutsche Bank. This paled in comparison to public sector bonds, which represented an enormous 50 per cent of all such bond issues. International organisations comprised the final quarter.[340] With the stock market stagnating and share issues sluggish in the 1960s and 1970s, the public sector bond business was of fundamental importance to the bank.

During Abs's tenure, the bank considered it too risky to lend directly to foreign governments. In terms of free market principles, too, financing via the capital market was considered the better option as it meant that governments had to pay the going market price for their debt. From 1970 onwards, the bank gradually gave up its reluctance with regard to direct lending. By now, Abs's influence over the bank's business decisions was waning. Riskier forms of financing such as forfaiting transactions, issuance of bonds in foreign currencies and direct loans to foreign governments now began to gain ground. The state socialist countries proved particularly important in this business segment.

The USSR and the gas pipeline business

Deutsche Bank's once very intensive business relationships with the USSR continued after the war, albeit on a much diminished scale. They primarily involved the financing of trade with the Soviet Union and other COMECON countries.[341] The bank did not initially finance large investment projects, especially in light of the trade embargo imposed in 1963 by the German government on NATO recommendations. With the lifting of the embargo in 1966, a gradual economic detente began. Deutsche Bank now started to explore opportunities to expand business with the USSR and to build on the history of the interwar period.[342] Given the continuing political tensions, the bank turned to the Austrian institution Österreichische Kontrollbank (a specialist bank founded to support Austrian exporters) to help it with a gas pipeline transaction in 1968. This was the first of several pipeline transactions over a 10-year period. Voest AG in Linz, Austria, supplied pipes from the manufacturer Mannesmann to the Soviet Union. Formally speaking, Österreichische Kontrollbank was the lender and the Soviet Gosbank (the USSR's central bank) the borrower. Österreichische Kontrollbank then received a matching refinancing loan from Deutsche Bank.[343] Though an ingenious solution, this lending structure had some drawbacks, including the lack of Hermes cover. The following year, in May 1969, the Soviet trade minister Nikolai Patolichev used the Hanover Fair to announce the Soviet Union's interest in expanding trade with West Germany. That December, the Deutsche Bank board member F. Wilhelm Christians travelled to Moscow to negotiate financing for major investment projects involving German industry.[344] These consultations were the starting point for a German–Soviet economic agreement concluded in February 1970, which reopened the door to larger projects. Negotiations centred on a major delivery of pipes by Mannesmann AG to build a natural gas pipeline network connecting the Soviet Union and the other COMECON countries and enabling gas imports into Western Europe. A consortium consisting of 17 German institutions led by Deutsche Bank was created to provide the DM 1.2 billion loan. Deutsche Bank's share of 18.4 per cent was the largest of all the consortium members.[345]

This was the biggest loan yet between Germany and the Soviet Union. It required a slew of concessions from the German side. The loan had a term of 12 years and an interest rate of 6.25 per cent. Given the high rates of inflation, this was not especially favourable for the German banks.[346] The lengthy term was a particular headache for the German negotiators given that the EEC countries, in accordance with the rules of the Berne Union, had agreed to impose a five-year limit on guaranteed loans in international business.[347]

The signing of the first gas pipeline contract in Essen's Hotel Kaiserhof, 1970.

The political importance of this project and the skill with which the Soviets conducted the negotiations put the German side in a weak position, as soon became apparent. The most fundamental problem was that the Soviet government was not prepared to pay the usual market rate of interest and instead insisted on preferential treatment.[348] It cleverly played the German consortium partners and the industrial firms involved in the project off against one another. The Soviet negotiators refused to pay for Hermes cover, arguing that the USSR was not a developing country and should not be liable for such additional costs. In 1969, Dresdner Bank promised the Soviet government that it would waive the requirement for Hermes cover, further adding to the pressure.[349] Deutsche thus declared itself willing to assume half the risk arising from the loan and accepted an interest rate 2–3 per cent below what it considered the going market rate.[350] The usual practice at that time, in which suppliers contributed an interest rate subsidy of 2.5 per cent and bore a portion of the Hermes costs, was not realistically negotiable for the gas pipeline project.[351] Franz Heinrich Ulrich had already predicted in 1969 that 'though business with the Soviet Union was interesting from a broader perspective, it would hardly be especially profitable'.[352] The low margins and long-term nature of this lending could only be justified by the fact that the USSR was a 'first-class borrower' that always serviced its debt on time. The country's creditworthiness, stated an internal report, was built on 'vast reserves of gas, oil, gold and diamonds'.[353] Three further loans worth billions of marks and again led by Deutsche Bank followed in the period up until 1978.[354]

The reasons for agreeing such large loans on relatively poor terms were largely strategic. Deutsche Bank wanted to position itself as the leading international institution in the lending business with the Soviet Union. According to UN estimates, the USSR accounted for an eighth of global output in 1970, and its economy was forecast to grow by as much as 6 per cent a year.[355] The bank hoped that leading the consortium for the pipeline loans would help it expand its market position in Eastern Europe, particularly given Soviet assurances that 'sporadic contact' could be turned into 'ongoing collaboration'.[356] From 1971, the bank negotiated on the establishment of a representative office in Moscow. This opened in March 1973 in the Hotel Metropol, located opposite the Bolshoi Theatre in close proximity to the Kremlin.[357] In the words of the Central Foreign Department, the aim of the representative office was not only to 'underline our leading position in terms of business with the USSR' but also to offer German customers 'effective support in initiating and conducting their transactions'.[358] While large German industrial corporations such as AEG, Siemens, Krupp and BASF had already concluded co-operation agreements with the Soviet State Committee for Science and Technology, it was difficult especially for medium-sized German firms to do business with the USSR and other COMECON countries.[359] According to the department, there were a 'considerable number of large and medium-sized industrial businesses that had often not yet been able to gather experience and build up contacts in the way that they had recently done with countries in Western Europe'.[360]

By 1972, Deutsche Bank's share of West German trade financing with the COMECON countries amounted to approximately DM 2 billion, representing 18.6 per cent of West Germany's foreign trade with these states. As far as West German lending to the COMECON banks was concerned, Deutsche's position was even stronger. These loans amounted to DM 641 million, or a 30 per cent share. The bulk of this lending (DM 555 million) went to the USSR. According to Deutsche Bank's own estimates in 1972, almost 10 per cent of its total foreign exposure was attributable to the COMECON banks and 6 per cent to Soviet institutions alone.[361]

Efforts to finance Soviet capital needs through bonds were less successful. This was largely because the state socialist countries were not regarded as viable issuers on the free capital market. While loans were generally provided with Hermes cover, no such protection was available for bonds, meaning that the risks to creditors were far higher. Moreover, syndicated lending with variable interest rates, fixed interest ceilings and very long terms was on conditions so favourable to the Soviet side that there was little interest in alternative forms of financing.[362] One change, however, was that lending was increasingly financed through the Euromarket. An initial Euroloan of $25 million to the USSR's foreign trade bank was organised in 1973, with CFDB in Luxembourg leading the lending syndicate.[363] Euroloans to the 'state-trading countries' totalled approximately $18 billion between 1973 and mid-1980, making up around 6 per cent of this lending market.[364]

Deutsche Bank continued to expand its lending business with the Soviet Union throughout the 1970s. This was no easy feat given the competition from Dresdner Bank, which also had strong interests in Eastern Europe.[365] Competition from businesses and banks in other European countries was also stepped up. Subsidies for loans and exports allowed Italy and France to compete on particularly strong terms.[366] This challenge from foreign rivals was evident in the Yamal project initiated in 1978, which set out to exploit the enormous gas reserves in western Siberia and install new gas pipelines leading to Western Europe. The project, for which a financing volume of DM 10 billion had been estimated, soon hit setbacks. The plans were overshadowed by the Soviet invasion of Afghanistan in 1979 and the nuclear armament debate, and were also greatly delayed not least by US government sanctions. Despite this, after long negotiations led by Christians, and several trips to Moscow, a framework agreement between the USSR and German banks was signed in July 1981. Given the involvement of other Western countries in the Yamal project, however, the total lending volume from Germany of DM 2.1 billion was considerably less than had been hoped.[367]

Nevertheless, the Yamal project was an important success in the eyes of Deutsche Bank. As the head of the Moscow representative office, Axel Lebahn, underscored in July 1981, the bank had achieved an 'unrivalled leading position in business with the Soviet Union'. It had now surpassed 'Dresdner Bank, which had often had its nose ahead in recent years'. For the Soviet authorities, it had also 'become the clear "number 1" among all the Western banks represented in Moscow in terms of real financing strength and prestige'. Lebahn also believed that the Yamal project would set a 'precedent' for co-operation on other major projects such as the exploitation of oil and gas reserves in the Caspian Sea and Barents Sea, the supply of coal-refining technology to the Kansk–Achinsk coal basin and the planned construction of nuclear reprocessing facilities.[368] The increasing international tensions between the Soviet Union and the Western nations put a stop to such major projects, however.[369] Though German and Soviet politicians expressed their wish to continue the economic relationship despite the political differences, the main beneficiaries were now smaller companies. Deutsche Bank was less strongly positioned in this SME (small and medium-sized enterprises) sector than in the financing of major energy projects.[370]

In the debt trap

While the Soviet Union began to improve its international credit rating in the late 1970s thanks to its high oil revenues, the other COMECON countries increasingly found themselves in financial difficulties. Deutsche Bank's Foreign Department watched this development with grave concern. Since the early 1970s, the bank had greatly expanded its credit lines to Poland and the GDR. Low-interest Euroloans, medium-term investment loans (via BEC in Brussels), forfaiting transactions for trade financing and even the issue of long-term bonds had all been among the products offered.[371] Poland had already drawn upon Euroloans of around $500 million, second only to the Soviet Union's borrowings of $750 million.[372] Deutsche Bank's lending policy had been motivated not least by political considerations. The economic relationship with Poland and the GDR was an important element of Bonn's *Ostpolitik*. In 1973, the West German government used an interest rate ceiling to subsidise lending to Poland.[373] Meanwhile, the GDR was offered a DM 600 million interest-free credit line referred to as the 'swing'.[374]

International debt in the COMECON countries swelled to dramatic levels in the 1970s. Between 1971 and 1981, it increased by a factor of 12 from $8 billion to $95 billion. The annual cost of debt servicing rose from $1.6 billion to $24 billion over the same period. This was an alarming figure given that the COMECON states had a combined trade deficit of $4 billion in 1981. High interest rates were also worsening the position of the debtor nations still further.[375] In 1980, the German banks alone had exposures to COMECON countries of approximately DM 18 billion on their books.[376] In Poland, where the government introduced martial law in December 1981, the economic situation deteriorated especially dramatically.[377] In 1981, Polish national output fell by 13 per cent. The country accounted for approximately 30 per cent of all foreign debt in the COMECON. Deutsche Bank's economic research department had already highlighted Poland's impending insolvency in 1980, when an internal risk assessment had placed the country in the most at-risk group.[378] With Poland's gross foreign debt standing at $23 billion at the end of 1980, only Brazil and Mexico had a worse ranking among the less-developed economies. Settling its foreign liabilities would have cost the country two years' worth of its entire economic output. Deutsche Bank had considerable exposures in other COMECON states too, such as Romania and Yugoslavia. In Hungary and the GDR, meanwhile, the situation was regarded as less problematic, partly thanks to a higher economic output.[379]

A further reason for the disquiet at Eastern Europe's large foreign liabilities was the indication that the COMECON countries could no longer be regarded as a single unit when it came to their borrowing. In the 1970s, the long-held 'umbrella theory' had led many Western banks and governments not to examine the individual countries' creditworthiness too closely. Instead, they relied on their belief that the USSR would intervene as the 'lender of last resort'. With the growing disintegration of the eastern bloc, this assumption was beginning to look questionable.[380] What was more, a large portion of the loans to COMECON states had gone directly to these countries' national banks. Trade loans financed from AKA funds had, meanwhile, declined in importance.[381] When Poland suspended payments to foreign creditors in 1981, Deutsche Bank was forced to recognise considerable write-downs. Although guarantees from the German government and other Western states averted the country's insolvency, loss allowances on around half a billion marks of exposures in Poland were required.[382]

Poland's solvency problems marked the start of a global debt crisis that would primarily hit the developing nations of Africa and Latin America.[383] The affected countries had similar problems. Many of them had borrowed heavily in the 1970s, when excess liquidity from oil-producing countries found its way into the international financial system and made capital available on favourable terms.[384] Low interest rates and, in many cases, lax lending practices by European and American banks had played a significant part in this development. The banks had granted large loans to Asia, Africa and Latin America, where many developing economies were growing at a rapid pace and found themselves on the cusp of industrialisation.[385] In the early 1980s, however, with interest rates rising and the second oil crisis putting the brakes on economic growth, large numbers of these countries found themselves struggling to repay their debts. Those without oil reserves, and whose balance of payments was adversely affected by high imports and persistent currency depreciation, landed themselves in irresolvable difficulties. Not only had they amassed enormous dollar-denominated foreign debt, which was rapidly increasing as the dollar appreciated, but they also tended to have a high balance of payments deficit. Between 1971 and 1981, developing countries' gross debt rose from $87 billion to $524 billion. Debt servicing payments alone in 1981 amounted to $112 billion.[386] A host of African countries were affected, with multiple rounds of debt restructuring required in Ghana, Liberia, Tanzania, Zaire and Chad. Turkey and many Eastern European countries were also considered at risk. The most serious situation, however, was to be found in the Latin American countries of Mexico, Brazil and Argentina. These nations had amassed enormous mountains of debt. Worse still, as large open economies, their difficulties were considered a threat to global growth. Deutsche Bank had increased its activities in Latin America since the early 1970s and had therefore closely examined the risks, especially in Brazil and Mexico.[387] Nevertheless, it had participated in several major loans. In November 1977, for example, it was involved in an international consortium, comprising a total of 113 financial institutions, created to provide a $1.2 billion loan to Mexico.

International risk management and country ratings

Deutsche Bank watched the ballooning international debt levels and growing risks with increasing alarm. In spring 1977, the bank set up a 'country limit' working group. The brainchild of Wilfried Guth, this was led by the head of the Central International Department ('ZIA') Werner Blessing and the chief economist Franz-Josef Trouvain. Its mission was to create a comprehensive rating system for developing countries.[388] The judgement of the Central Foreign Department, previously responsible for setting country exposures and assessing the risks, had evidently been excessively swayed by potential business opportunities, resulting in assumptions that were far too optimistic. Guth accused it of 'wishful thinking'.[389] It also lacked the statistical and economic expertise to undertake systematic risk assessment. Its country documentation was based on a rather eclectic set of data and the travel reports of the bank's representatives. A first step in the new system was thus to bring together the expertise of the economic research and ZIA departments.[390] An idea to create a shared risk system for the entire German commercial banking sector, which would have been based within the Association of German Banks, was soon dropped. The data provided by the Bundesbank were also considered far too vague for risk assessment purposes, as was that of the World Bank, the IMF and the Bank for International Settlements.[391] The latter organisation only included long-term loans in its reporting and only took into account the data reported by the commercial banks on a national basis. In the case of Deutsche Bank, this excluded loans by the subsidiary banks in Luxembourg and America, despite their importance to the Group as a whole.[392] A further problem was that of recording the activities of foreign branches. The newly created Central International Department and its 'Accounting and Planning' subdivision pointed out in mid-1978 that foreign branches had 'hit considerable difficulties with reporting'. These branches lacked both the 'technical means' and the staff to deliver the requisite accounting data.[393]

The bank's internal rating system, created in autumn 1977, concentrated on 47 'developing' nations, including the state socialist countries and the whole of south-eastern Europe. These 47 states accounted for approximately 40 per cent of the bank's total foreign exposure. For each country, a new indicator system recorded information on the debt servicing burden, borrowing requirements, currency reserves, balance of payments and economic policy to calculate an overall risk. Countries were then assigned to five risk categories. This system was designed both to identify countries in particular danger and to limit systemic risk for the bank as a whole. This meant it not only had to look at the countries individually but also at the cluster risk that would arise from a multi-country default. New ground rules were also established for future lending. From now on, an individual country's liabilities to the bank would no longer be allowed to exceed 5 per cent of the total foreign exposure. Limits would ensure that a complete national default on interest payments would not exceed 20 per cent of the bank's prior-year operating profit. Total foreign exposure was capped at half the bank's total lending. The bank used the risk categories as the basis for a broad risk diversification.[394] The exposure rules, meanwhile, were treated as a general guideline and could be exceeded on a case-by-case basis. Ultimately, there was an acceptance that the bank was often forced to 'accept inconvenient risks from the financing of export business' in order to prevent rivals from targeting existing customers with a more lenient approach. Instead of being excessively rigid about country exposures, Deutsche Bank therefore had to 'endeavour to put itself in the leading position in all upcoming major projects'.[395]

Over the following years, the bank expanded its risk management system.[396] It became apparent that the rating system did not adequately capture the structural problems in the countries worst hit by the crisis – Mexico, Argentina and Brazil. All three regularly fell within category III – the medium risk category – which resulted in an increase in exposure to these countries.[397] Mexico was even upgraded in June 1980 and remained in category II until shortly before the crisis broke in August 1982.[398] Guth later admitted in October of that year that the bank had 'not foreseen the confluence of many negative factors in the case of Mexico'.[399]

Following the onset of the debt crisis, the bank redoubled its efforts to improve the international country rating system. In 1982, it increased the number of risk groups to seven and expanded the number of countries covered to 129.[400] A much stricter approach was also taken to measuring the risks themselves. Category VII – the highest risk category – thus included not only Brazil, Mexico and Argentina, but a host of other states. By 1987, there were 29 category VII countries, making this by far the largest category.[401] The new rating system was designed to take into account not only the current threat potential but also the long-term trends. It thus gave greater weight to political factors. Static risk analysis was to be turned into a dynamic 'early warning system' in order to identify long-term threats several years in advance so that the bank's lending policy could be adjusted accordingly.[402]

The bank's economists were now given their own independent economic research centre. In addition to producing a quarterly breakdown of all country risks with detailed individual reports, this also conducted analyses using complex macroeconomic models, often with a time horizon of several years. In 1984, the economic research department produced a joint study with the Central International Department. This calculated the borrowing requirements and loan loss provisions for 27 at-risk countries up to the year 1990. The forecast was linked to projections of key macroeconomic parameters such as interest rates, commodity prices and the balance of payments. The results were used to estimate the potential impact on the bank of various macroeconomic scenarios.[403]

Such analyses were not merely of academic interest, but increasingly served as the basis for operational decisions by the bank's management bodies.[404] They were a manifestation of the increasingly research-based planning approach pushed by Alfred Herrhausen.[405] In Management and Supervisory Board meetings, Herrhausen frequently referred to the analyses of his economic research department. He also quoted them extensively in international negotiations, public speeches and interviews. The international debt crisis showed that extensive information on the structural links between different parts of the world economy was of fundamental importance to recognising and swiftly responding to systemic risks. It was also an important tool in helping the bank to implement its own strategies in the complex international negotiations that took place during the debt crisis.

New responsibility: debt crisis and debt relief

The crisis in Latin America revealed the extent to which governments relied for their financing on international banks. A large portion of the loans taken out by developing countries had been provided through the private financial sector. [406] The flipside to this growing importance was the implication that it was incumbent on the banks themselves to actively seek a solution to the international debt problem. This was a matter not just of political responsibility but of self-interest, as a default by one or more states could put them in a highly precarious position.

During the Polish crisis Deutsche Bank began to build reserves and reduce its international exposure. The large write-downs in Eastern Europe later proved a blessing to the bank, as they forced it to respond earlier than other institutions to the international warning signs. At the end of 1980, the bank decided to transfer a 'substantial portion of the operating result to risk provisions'. In that year alone, the bank moved DM 120 million from hidden to open reserves.[407] Given that the bank was in a strong earnings position and had increased its profit by 23 per cent year on year in 1980, it could easily afford this risk provisioning.[408] Guth reported to the Supervisory Board in January 1982 that Deutsche Bank had 'adequate risk provisions in light of the Polish situation'.[409]

It soon became clear, however, that the crisis in Latin America would require loss allowances on a completely different scale. In October 1983, the bank had a 'basic exposure' – consisting of loans without Hermes cover and local loans (i.e. by local branches in local currency) – of around DM 7.6 billion on its books. Three countries accounted for the largest share of this debt: Brazil (DM 1.7 billion), Mexico (DM 1.1 billion) and Argentina (DM 0.8 billion). The bank also had exposures ranging from DM 300 million to DM 600 million in Iraq, Poland, Venezuela, Yugoslavia, Chile, Nigeria and Turkey. These were substantial amounts, though still less than 1 per cent of the total foreign debt of all developing countries. They also represented a relatively small exposure compared to that of other German institutions. At this time, Deutsche Bank's share of the risky lending by German financial institutions was around 15 per cent. Dresdner Bank, West LB and Commerzbank were more exposed almost everywhere in Latin America.[410] Even so, the amounts Deutsche Bank had to set aside for loan loss provisions were considerable. The bank recognised allowances for loan losses of DM 2.6 billion at the end of 1983 alone.[411] Internal estimates put the number of countries with payment difficulties at around 50. Debt restructuring agreements had already been instigated for some 30 of these in autumn 1983 with the involvement of the IMF, the banks and various governments.[412] Nobody involved was under any illusions, however, that the situation had been rectified. As Wilfried Guth admitted to the Supervisory Board in October 1983, there was no straightforward way out of the crisis for the bank.[413] The economic research department predicted in 1984 that by the turn of the decade the net demand for financing in developing countries would grow by as much as 40 per cent.[414] Such a rise would further increase Deutsche Bank's exposure by approximately DM 1.6 billion from DM 6.95 billion to DM 8.55 billion, even ignoring potential losses by foreign subsidiaries.[415]

In fact, the Group's interests in banks in the US, the UK, Belgium and Saudi Arabia, posed a significant problem given their heavy involvement in Latin America. An internal Deutsche Bank report in April 1983 described these indirect exposures as a 'grey area with considerable risk potential'.[416] At the end of 1982, Deutsche had unsecured loans of around DM 10 billion on its books, which, under its own rules, would have necessitated provisions of approximately DM 2.7 billion. Loan loss allowances by subsidiary banks at this time amounted to just DM 411 million. Liquidity shortages especially at New York-based EAB meant, however, that Deutsche did no longer rule out intervening with support measures. Internal recommendations therefore suggested creating a portfolio of $300–400 million in US Treasury Bills to ensure 'foreign currency liquidity at our international branches and subsidiaries at all times'.[417] The bank also planned to scale back the particularly risky Euromarket business as well as currency and gold trading. For the first time, it also proposed the introduction of a clearing limit for the American correspondent banks and the New York branch. Interbank business was to be restricted so as to reduce Deutsche Bank's own risk exposure in the event that a foreign bank were to fail. In the long term, the recommendations continued, intragroup monitoring structures needed considerable expansion, while investments in other banks were either to be sold off or a majority shareholding acquired so as to exert greater influence over lending and risk management.[418]

The recommendations reflected the increasingly precarious position of US banks since 1983. Continental Illinois, the eighth largest American bank with total assets of $42 billion, only narrowly avoided collapse at the last moment. The Manufacturers Hanover Trust Company, whose outstanding loans and receivables of $1.3 billion made it Argentina's largest creditor bank, found itself with considerable liquidity shortages and only avoided insolvency thanks to support from the US Federal Reserve. These difficulties were not only the result of a much higher exposure to Latin America than that of the German banks, but also reflected a general lack of risk provisions. The 'crisis of trust in the interbank market,' said Guth in July 1984, could only be overcome by a 'change in American methods of risk provisioning'. For its part, the Management Board of Deutsche Bank decided to 'reduce money market investments placed with foreign banks to a greater extent than previously planned'.[419]

The situation appeared increasingly unsustainable. Deutsche Bank's management were becoming highly reluctant to participate in further bridging loans in Latin America. They were losing their willingness to pay the price for the risky lending practices of American banks and of the Japanese financial institutions also heavily exposed to Latin America. The bank's strategy was thus increasingly one of damage limitation.

The '"fresh money" method born of necessity', Guth told the Supervisory Board in October 1983, would reach its limits sooner or later and devastate international solidarity between banks. Deutsche's own shareholders and depositors, he added, could no longer be expected to accept a situation in which 'exposures in the countries affected by debt rescheduling grow higher and higher in relation to equity'.[420]

In reality, however, there was little realistic prospect of the bank charting its own course in splendid isolation.[421] Exposed to markets all around the world, Guth admitted in resigned manner, it 'could not simply extricate itself from the mess'.[422] Deutsche Bank was involved in various international committees of the IMF, World Bank and Paris Club. In the important Bank Advisory Committee, it represented not only the interests of all German banks but also those of Dutch, Austrian and Scandinavian financial institutions. It therefore had little option but to participate in the multiple debt restructuring measures pursued under the leadership of US Treasury Secretary James Baker in 1985.[423] His comprehensive economic restructuring programme known as the Baker Plan brought a new approach to lending policy and made financial aid conditional on the implementation of economic reforms. This was associated, however, with high adjustment costs and political conflict in the countries affected. In the short term at least, it failed to reduce debt. On the contrary, the financing requirements of Latin American countries continued to grow, just as Deutsche Bank had predicted in 1984.[424]

In light of this development, the voices calling for a rethink of international debt policy began to multiply. Alfred Herrhausen repeatedly brought new ideas into play, such as the introduction of an interest compensation fund in which private-sector banks, the IMF and the World Bank would all participate. More generally, Herrhausen called for governments and international organisations to share responsibility instead of placing the burden mainly on banks as the Baker Plan had done.[425] It is unclear whether Herrhausen seriously expected his suggestions to be adopted or whether they were largely intended to set the scene for Deutsche Bank to withdraw from new lending commitments. The international solidarity between banks, which had enabled drastic rescue measures for Mexico, Brazil and Argentina in the early 1980s, had by now become fragile. In this context, Herrhausen now decided on a solo initiative that would earn him publicity and widespread recognition but was met with disbelief by the international banking community – including by his counterparts at other German banks and even some of his Deutsche Bank colleagues.[426] In September 1987, at the annual meeting of the World Bank and IMF in Washington, he proposed that highly indebted countries be granted debt relief. Herrhausen continued to repeat this call openly, for example at another World Bank and IMF meeting in September 1988, until his assassination in November 1989. He pointed out that the highly indebted countries' bank liabilities had increased further from $270 billion to $290 billion between 1982 and mid-1989 and that the countries involved were in a deep economic plight. The liquidity crisis had developed into a 'solvency crisis' that only extensive debt forgiveness was capable of solving. Herrhausen also recommended specific aid measures tailored to each country using a 'menu approach' and supported the idea of exchanging outstanding debts for equity (debt-to-equity swaps) to provide the affected countries with new capital. In addition, he emphatically called for the securitisation

Management Board Spokesman Alfred Herrhausen (1930–1989, right) at a press conference on the occasion of the World Bank meeting in late September 1989 in Washington. On the left sits Hellmut Hartmann, Deutsche Bank's press officer.

of liabilities in the form of internationally tradable promissory notes that would be channelled, after a discount, into the international capital market in the form of zero bonds or other warrants.[427]

In fact, these ideas were largely in line with the new strategy launched by the new American Treasury Secretary, Nicholas Brady, in 1989. The 'Brady Plan', too, involved the banks granting a partial debt moratorium. Mexico, which in 1989 still had medium- and long-term unsecured liabilities to foreign banks of $53 billion, was once again the focus of the restructuring measures as in previous rounds of negotiation. Deutsche Bank's share of this debt was calculated for the purposes of the debt restructuring at DM 170 million. From the menu of measures provided for by the Brady initiative, the bank opted in summer 1989 for capital reduction. Mexico's existing debt was converted, after a discount of 35 per cent, into relatively high-interest Mexican sovereign bonds ('discount bonds'). These were then collateralised using US zero-coupon bonds and sold on the international capital market.[428] There were also new loans from the World Bank and IMF. Similar measures in other Latin American countries allowed these countries to regain their international creditworthiness and the debt crisis to be defused. For Deutsche Bank, the discounts on the value owed were bearable given the loan loss allowances that had already been recognised.[429] The specific design of the Brady bonds created a new form of collateralised derivatives trading and led to a surge of innovation in the international financial business in which Deutsche Bank would play a major part. Paradoxically, the debt crisis thus gave considerable impetus to the process of 'financialisation' that had begun in the 1970s.[430]

All in all, Deutsche Bank survived the consequences of this crisis without serious damage. Given the tax implications for the Group and the timely recognition of

On 18 April 1985, only a few weeks after assuming the office of General Secretary of the Communist Party, Mikhail Gorbachev met F. Wilhelm Christians (1922–2004, left), the Co-Spokesman of the Management Board of Deutsche Bank, in Moscow.

provisions, the financial impact was probably less severe than the years of uncertainty that threatened to paralyse the international capital markets and forced the bank to temporarily restrict its activities abroad. By the end of the 1980s, the situation had been turned around. The bank consolidated its position on the international money and capital markets and boosted its involvement in the Eurocapital market once again. This documented a record of more than 1,500 bond issues in 1989. In that year alone, Deutsche Bank was involved in 563 Eurobond issues with a volume of $108 billion. It acted as lead manager for the World Bank's first global bond issue totalling $1.5 billion.[431]

Despite considerable write-downs, then, sovereign lending remained an attractive business area for the bank. The high debt levels – which in developing and industrialised countries alike were increasingly financed on the secondary market using new financial products – created new investment opportunities for investors. The stock market boom of the 1980s gave this business an additional boost. In Eastern Europe, too, the bank was able from the mid-1980s onwards to revive old lending relationships. Deutsche Bank played a leading role in the DM 950 million loan granted to the GDR in 1984 and led the West German syndicate with a contribution of DM 150 million.[432] After the election of Mikhail Gorbachev as General Secretary of the Communist Party of the Soviet Union in March 1985, the bank managed to revitalise the economic relationship between Germany and the USSR. This was thanks especially to Christians' excellent Soviet contacts. Christians was invited to accompany state visits to the Kremlin and was received personally by Gorbachev.[433] Deutsche Bank was clearly still an international force in the lending and issuing business and a company that foreign heads of state wanted to do business with.

6. 'First class or no class': Becoming a Global Investment Bank

On 30 March 1988, Alfred Herrhausen gave a widely noticed speech to the directors of Deutsche Bank. Comprehensively taking stock of the company's position, he painted a picture of strengths and weaknesses. Deregulation, technological innovation and rapid global market integration had revolutionised the financial industry. Despite an 'impressive performance' over the preceding decade, these were challenges to which Deutsche Bank had not yet found an adequate answer. While it was a leading player in the international bond business, Herrhausen argued, it was losing the race in investment banking to American, British and Swiss rivals. In many other business areas, too, earnings were far from outstanding; meanwhile, costs were exploding. 'Spoiled by ten years of plenty,' he added, the bank had indulged in a 'diffused feeling of general euphoria' while neglecting to thoroughly reorganise the Group. There remained a sharp organisational divide between domestic and international banking, and there was little continuity between traditional commercial banking on the one hand and investment and consulting banking on the other. Herrhausen regarded this as 'a big mistake, which results from our having developed the habit of thinking along the lines of a split banking system'. The speech concluded with a reaffirmation of the global expansion strategy launched earlier that decade. 'First class or no class' – insisted Herrhausen – must become the Group's new 'slogan'.[434]

Herrhausen's view was typical of the atmosphere among Deutsche Bank's leading managers. This sense of crisis, which was tinged, in seeming contradiction, with euphoric optimism, emerged from closely watching the competition from both German institutions and leading international banks.[435] There was no dismissing the observation that global competition had considerably intensified in the financial sector. Whereas Deutsche's main rivals had once been the other big German banks, the savings banks and the co-operatives, the primary threat now came from American and British investment banks, which sought to claim the international capital market for themselves through aggressive methods and rapid expansion abroad. The full liberalisation of capital flows and the opening up of national banking markets heightened the competitive pressure dramatically. The financial sector became ever more complex as new players such as insurers and fund companies joined the market and made life difficult for traditional banks.

The late 1980s thus represented a transition period that marked the limits of Deutsche Bank's old business model and heralded a comprehensive reorganisation. Five structural problems for the bank were evident during these years. These were not entirely new but were certainly deepened by the growing competition.

Growth or profitability?

If the volume of business is taken as an indicator of commercial success, the bank's performance in the 1980s was nothing short of brilliant. The Group's total assets grew by a factor of almost two and a half in the space of a decade and reached DM 400 billion by 1990. Internal forecasts predicted that they would hit approximately DM 900 billion by 1995.[436] What was more, even these figures did not fully reflect the scale of the bank's business activities, as the Group's balance sheet excluded the numerous minority shareholdings. Off-balance-sheet transactions (futures, swaps, options, derivatives) also increased sharply during this period and amounted to half of the total business volume of German commercial banks by the end of 1990.[437]

Figure 16: Total assets of Deutsche Bank, 1980–90 (in DM billions).

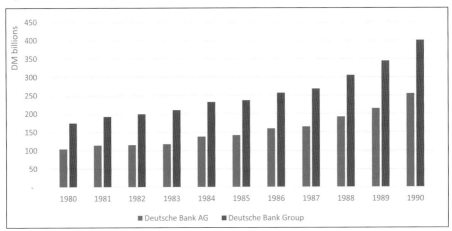

Source: Deutsche Bank, Annual Reports 1980–90.

Figure 17: Deutsche Bank's return on equity (after tax), 1970–89 (in %).

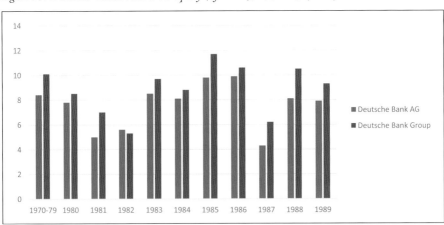

Source: Deutsche Bank, Annual Reports 1970–89; own calculations.

Figure 18: Income statement of Deutsche Bank Group, 1980–89 (in DM millions).

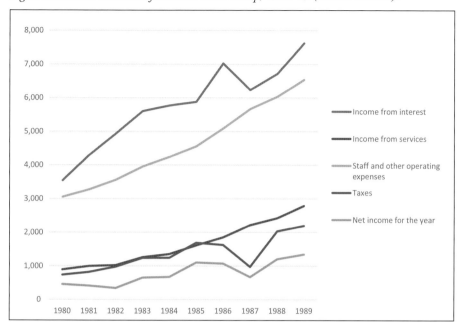

Source: Deutsche Bank, Annual Report 1989, p. 129.

The strong increase in business activity did not lead to a corresponding rise in profits, however. Although interest and commission income both grew in the 1980s, this was partly due to the very high one-off returns from the Flick transaction in 1985–6. All in all, commission from the securities and custody business and fees charged for savings, real estate and loan agreements made up just a quarter of total income. Net interest income, meanwhile, represented by far the most important source of receipts, helped by persistently high rates of interest. With doubts about how long the period of high interest rates would continue, the bank feared that this income was unsustainable.[438]

An even more immediate concern was that rising personnel and operating expenses, along with a growing tax burden, were absorbing an increasing proportion of revenues.[439] The average return on equity after tax between 1980 and 1989 was 7.5 per cent for Deutsche Bank AG and 8.76 per cent for the Group. This was lower than the equivalent figures for the 1970s (8.4 per cent and 10.1 per cent). A considerable portion of these returns came from Deutsche's industrial shareholdings rather than its banking operations. In purely mathematical terms, around half of Deutsche Bank's stock market value was attributable to its holding in Daimler-Benz,[440] meaning that, in most years, these shares alone effectively funded the bank's dividend distribution. It was clear, then, that although the bank's balance sheet looked healthy, its core business was not especially profitable.

Stagnating domestic business

Despite the international expansion, the German market remained vital to the bank, continuing to account for more than two-thirds of lending and deposits. Even

Herrhausen did not question the importance of the domestic business when considering the Group's global objectives. He regarded it as a 'physical underpinning for everything we do outside' the country.[441] With the market highly saturated, however, further growth in Germany appeared virtually impossible. The country had one of the highest concentrations of bank branches of any nation. Given the pressure on margins, this pointed long term to the necessity for a reduction in capacity, and not only in retail banking but

Figure 19: Market shares of Deutsche Bank in lending to personal and corporate banking customers in West Germany (in %), 1982–87.

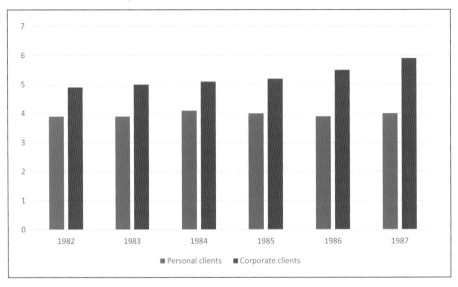

Source: Die Deutsche Bank im Markt, ZRP-Planung 1987, HADB, ZA4/x877.

Figure 20: Market shares of Deutsche Bank in foreign trade financing in West Germany (in %).

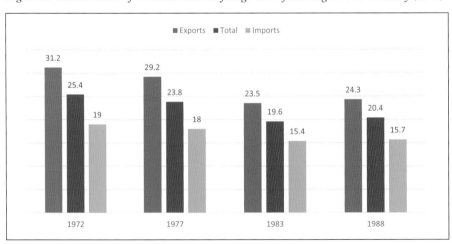

Source: Internationales Geschäft – Konzernentwicklung und -koordination, 19 April 1988, HADB, ZA18/2.

in the traditionally important corporate banking business, too. Deutsche Bank's market share in both segments fell to around 5 per cent in the 1970s, where it then stagnated. Even more worryingly, the German branches' share of the international business fell continuously from the mid-1970s onwards. In trade finance, Deutsche Bank was no longer such an important player as it had once been – this lending increasingly went to small and medium-sized enterprises, which were not Deutsche Bank's core clientele.[442]

The bank's strategic answer to this development was product diversification and cross-selling. It would now aim to offer the gamut of financial and advisory services under one roof. As part of this strategy, Deutsche Bank had already expanded its real estate financing in the 1970s. In the 1980s, the product range was further diversified through strategic acquisitions in the insurance, management consulting and project finance segments. The bank also sought to improve customer orientation, with Herrhausen issuing an urgent call for 'far more committed and aggressive salesman-ship'.[443] The success of this strategy was far from certain, however. Possible synergy effects in terms of sales were offset by potentially higher costs. In a branch network that was already in chronic deficit, the more sophisticated approach to providing services tied up considerable human resources. Internal analyses showed that Deutsche Bank's cost structure at branch level was far less favourable than that of the competition. Their higher customer numbers and lower advisory workload allowed the savings and co-oper-ative banks to work more cost-efficiently than Deutsche. Building and loan associations and life insurers also had the edge in their own markets. These companies were able to make better use of resources and, in many cases, to offer products on more favourable terms. Other banks, too, used the advantage of specialisation by limiting their activi-ties to specific financial services (e.g. investment advice or credit cards), thereby greatly reducing their costs compared to the big banks. Frankfurter BHF-Bank, for instance, decided to concentrate exclusively on the capital market business and gave up most of its branches. A similar trend had long been seen in the US, encouraged by the traditional separation of deposit and lending business from investment banking.

The dangers of these changes in the banking sector – which were also emerging in other countries – were certainly recognised at management level.[444] 'As a universal provider,' wrote the Group Strategy (AfK) department, the bank would be up against 'a varied landscape of competitors who steer clear of the onerous payments business'.[445] Nevertheless, Deutsche Bank lacked an original strategy with which to counter the competition's advantages in terms of costs and specialisation. It was unwilling to disman-tle inefficient business segments or pool resources, despite calls for greater awareness of costs and profit contributions for each activity. Instead, it responded to problems in the market with its familiar strategy of growth and diversification.

Dynamics and risks of internationalisation

This growth path based on an ever-larger portfolio of services was particularly pronounced in the international business, where it was combined with the ambition of conducting activities under Deutsche Bank's own brand. In the mid-1980s, the bank finally parted company with EBIC and other strategic partners. Its stated aim was to have its own premises in all major economic centres and offer a comprehensive range of financial services.[446] The focus was on asserting a stronger presence in the big cities central to the financial industry, such as London, New York, Hong Kong, Zurich and Tokyo.[447] With the German capital market nowhere near strong enough to accommodate the large international bonds now being floated, the bank created Deutsche Bank Capital Markets, London, in 1985. Its primary aim was to expand the bank's position in the Eurodollar segment amid the decline in importance of the German issue market. In the US, too, there was a desire to strengthen the bank's position on the capital market. The New York branch, which was supplemented by others in Chicago and Los Angeles, limited itself for regulatory reasons to serving German and American commercial clients, while DB Capital Corporation operated the securities business. In 1988, Deutsche also considered the purchase of an American bank but chose not yet to pursue this given the substantial market risks.[448] Meanwhile, in Canada, Japan, Hong Kong, Italy, Belgium, Australia and Switzerland, the bank founded new subsidiaries for the capital market business or created them from existing investments.

Deutsche Bank now also expanded its branch presence across various countries. From the mid-1980s, it systematically acquired branch-based banks especially in Europe, where it hoped to penetrate national markets and establish a broad-based business serving commercial and retail customers. It was drawn in particular to countries with less developed banking systems, such as Italy and Spain. While Banca d'America e d'Italia and Banco Comercial Transatlántico both expanded and proved highly profitable,[449] attempts to build branch networks in Belgium, the Netherlands and France were largely unsuccessful. The personal banking business was generally confined to Europe. In other regions of the world, the bank limited its activities to commercial clients and the capital market business. In 1987, Deutsche Bank had 29 branches, 17 representative offices, 17 subsidiary banks and 22 associated companies abroad. To these could be added the branches of its subsidiaries in Spain and Italy. This international presence was far greater than that of Dresdner Bank or Commerzbank, but did not come close to the big US, British and French institutions. Barclays had 706 foreign outlets, Citibank over 479 and Banque Nationale de Paris more than 285. In international terms, Deutsche Bank thus ranked mid-table.[450]

The global expansion strategy initiated in 1985 had mixed results. Deutsche Bank's share of foreign trade financing stagnated in the second half of the 1980s. In other business areas, the bank even lost ground. Deposits from foreign customers, for example, shrank from DM 76.6 billion in 1984 to DM 72.6 billion in 1987, partly due to exchange rate changes. Lending to foreigners declined from DM 38.4 billion to DM 34.7 billion. Of even greater concern, the operating profit of the foreign branches tumbled from DM 146.9 million to 83.9 million over the same period. This was only partly due to falling revenues. Rising operating costs and (in the case of the New York branch) unfavourable exchange-rate effects had a bigger impact. The payments business via the approximately 4,000 correspondent banks abroad barely turned a profit any longer, despite the bank fully embracing international cash management in 1984. In 1987, the payments business generated an earnings contribution of just DM 36 million.[451]

The high risks and associated provisions were also a heavy burden on the balance sheet. Unsecured exposures in at-risk countries had risen from approximately DM 1.1

billion in 1980 to DM 7.9 billion in 1984. Despite a gradual reduction in debt-to-equity swaps and a weaker dollar from the mid-1980s onwards, they still amounted to DM 5.2 billion in 1987 (the coverage ratio, however, had increased from 41 per cent in 1984 to 76 per cent in 1987). Deutsche Bank had been consistent in recognising impairments and provisions during the international debt crisis, despite the unfavourable impact on earnings.[452] In general, risks in the international business rose over the course of the decade. This included export finance. In 1984, 88 per cent of this business still comprised buyer credit and refinancing for suppliers. By 1987, the figure had fallen to just 40 per cent. The remainder consisted of forfaiting transactions and lease agreements, which entailed a considerably higher risk of default.[453]

Corporate integration

Risks were growing in other respects, too. As a result of the numerous international acquisitions, Herrhausen recognised that the 'complexity of the entire Group' was 'increasing steadily'. Managing this complexity meant creating an IT landscape to reflect it, which in turn entailed 'coming to grips with an unbelievable volume of data'.[454] This statistical information was essential for accounting and regulatory purposes as ever more subsidiaries had to be included in Deutsche Bank's financial statements. In 1980, Deutsche Bank had presented its first global corporate balance sheet. The control and monitoring of foreign branches and subsidiaries was also increasingly difficult, especially as the transaction-intensive financial services sector was far more prone to information asymmetries than the traditional lending business.

As part of the corporate reform initiated in 1985, the bank decided to integrate international growth into its strategic planning. At the same time, it appointed coordinators to 'vertically and horizontally unite' all central departments.[455] Long-term planning, however, proved difficult precisely in the international business, where the majority of acquisitions were opportunistic. The conglomeration of branches, investees and subsidiaries would not easily coalesce into a coherent whole. The rapid international growth and increasing diversification thus indirectly elevated risk levels and presented the bank with considerable organisational challenges. This pointed to a fundamental problem that was rearing its head at many German financial institutions. While the bank had largely hedged its business and market risks, it was increasingly difficult to gain a clear picture of operational risks within the highly fragmented Group. In Herrhausen's eyes, this problem was partly rooted in an outdated mentality, with many of the bank's staff continuing to think solely in national terms. There was still a sharp division between domestic and international business. He therefore called for a new organisational culture to instil his global strategy.[456]

Strengthening investment banking

While the bank faced increasing pressure on margins in the traditional lending and borrowing business, major growth still appeared possible in investment banking.[457] The bank was thus able to maintain its traditionally strong position in international bond issuance. With Deutsche Bank Capital Markets in London, it established itself as the top address in the competitive Eurobond business.[458] Proprietary trading and the foreign

In early 1985, Deutsche Bank opened its new headquarters at Taunusanlage 12 in Frankfurt am Main.

exchange business also performed well.[459] By the end of the 1980s, securities products accounted for over half of commission income.[460] This was clear evidence of a major change in strategy. In fact, the new approach had already been initiated internally in 1983 with the creation of a co-ordination group to develop a comprehensive plan for expanding the investment banking business.[461] In its strategy paper presented in June 1984, this argued that Deutsche Bank's existing approach could, at best, maintain a niche position in the Euro-DM market. To keep pace with the international competition, however, an active role especially in dollar-denominated financial products was necessary, which required rapid expansion abroad.[462] In an indication of the time pressure under which the global investment banking strategy was implemented, less than a year passed between this diagnosis and the development of foreign investment subsidiaries.[463]

It is perhaps unsurprising, then, that the anticipated success did not come immediately. The main obstacles, as in the past, included problems finding the right staff. The bank lacked internationally proven experts in securities and derivatives trading, asset management, mergers and acquisitions (M&A) and (importantly not least from a risk assessment perspective) controlling. A possible solution began to emerge when Deutsche Bank acquired a majority shareholding in the management consulting firm Roland Berger in 1987. With this step, the bank hoped to gain expertise in those segments of the finance and advisory business in which it did not have its own sufficiently strong position. However, these acquisitions were also associated with considerable integration costs and could only go some way to alleviating staff shortages.[464] Herrhausen's appointment of the communications adviser Gertrud Höhler, who was tasked with developing a comprehensive plan for a new corporate culture, was a sign of the growing internal frictions created by the Group's rapid expansion.[465]

In October 1989, Hilmar Kopper, who was responsible for the issuing and syndicated lending business, gave a damning verdict of Deutsche's international investment banking strategy. This had been far too tentative, giving the bank only a modest presence in many international financial centres. Top global talent could no longer be afforded, and Japanese, British and American big banks were set to capture the lion's share of the market, leaving Deutsche lagging behind in every region of the world. Instead of truly diversifying, the bank had 'simply fanned out geographically and replicated what we have always been able to do'.[466]

Kopper gave this verdict a month before the takeover of the British merchant bank Morgan Grenfell, in which Deutsche had already held a minority stake since 1984. The acquisition was an admission that Deutsche Bank was unable to build a strong position in the international investment banking business solely under its own steam. For Deutsche's management, the risks of such a takeover appeared to pale in comparison to the danger of becoming no more than a provincial player.

Like Herrhausen, Kopper cherished the hope that the acquisition of Morgan Grenfell and other foreign investment banks would not come at the cost of giving up Deutsche Bank's own identity. He was determined to continue Deutsche's history as a universal bank. According to Herrhausen's vision, Deutsche Bank would combine the 'best of the continental European and Anglo-Saxon models'.[467] However, the difficulties of such a synthesis in a fast-changing financial world would soon become apparent.

GLOBALISATION AND CRISIS, 1989–2020

CATHERINE R. SCHENK

I. The Acquisition of Morgan Grenfell

The acquisition of Morgan Grenfell in November 1989 marked a significant shift in Deutsche Bank's global strategy. It also provoked one of the deepest and most prolonged schisms within the bank as it struggled to find its way in the new era of globalised investment banking. Two key aspects of this struggle during the 1990s were the clash of cultures and the lack of understanding between London and Frankfurt on the one hand, and, on the other, efforts in Frankfurt to smooth over differences among senior staff rather than resolve them. The story of Morgan Grenfell's acquisition itself reflected the compromises necessary for the Management Board to come to consensus, and the way that this process left key aspects of Deutsche Bank's strategy unresolved.

In the wake of the announcement in 1983 that the structure of the London Stock Exchange would be opened up for competition, there was a flurry of mergers and acquisitions in the financial industry. Merchant banks sought to buy up brokers and jobbers to compensate for the loss in margins by increasing the scale and scope of their business in this more competitive environment. British merchant banks were particularly threatened by the large US banks that gained entry to the market directly and through acquisition. The business model of banking in London seemed destined to follow the US model where fee generation, deal making and trading culture would replace the traditional relationship banking that had characterised the cosy post-war City of London.

Alfred Herrhausen (1930– 1989) in his Frankfurt office in 1986. He was Spokesman of the Management Board from 1985 until his death in November 1989.

On 30 November 1989, Alfred Herrhausen was the victim of a terrorist attack that remains unexplained to this day.

But other opportunities also drove conglomeration in the 1980s: corporate IPOs, the wave of pending privatisations across Europe, interest rate volatility and the surge in bond market trading all increased demand for investment banking services. The European White Paper on completing the internal market published in 1985 signalled the looming single market scheduled for 1992 and financial institutions sought to position themselves for this new world. In 1986 alone, London merchant banks acquired stakes in 11 brokers and three jobbers, while 45 foreign institutions acquired stakes in London-based firms.

Throughout the 1960s and 1970s, Deutsche Bank had built a significant overseas presence mainly through representative offices and branches, and the emphasis remained mainly on traditional commercial banking. But in the mid-1980s, Alfred Herrhausen, as Spokesman of the Management Board, led Deutsche Bank's turn towards becoming a 'global player' in response to changes he perceived in international and domestic financial and banking markets. The traditional German universal banking business, which had been built so successfully by Deutsche Bank, now threatened to leave the bank behind in the revolution of global investment banking. Aware that Germany did not have the talent pool to penetrate the global banking system, and in particular investment banking, expansion into this area would have to be through acquisition, either of teams of people or entire institutions. At the same time, the profitability of Deutsche Bank's traditional German business had stalled and it was clear that organic growth in the home market was going to be limited. Moreover, the bank's major industrial clients would increasingly seek out the services and products offered by the major investment banks to tap global markets – the bank needed to shift gear to meet the competitive environment. Within the bank's Management Board, the need to change the business model outside Germany was explicitly not extended to the domestic market where the universal bank, and Hausbank relationship to customers was preserved.

The acquisition of Morgan Grenfell in November 1989 took place just as Deutsche Bank lost its charismatic leader, Alfred Herrhausen, to an assassin's bomb and it was left to his successor, Hilmar Kopper, to complete the transaction and absorb Morgan Grenfell into the Deutsche Bank Group. Although Herrhausen led the origination of the bank's transformation through acquisition, Kopper was an enthusiastic disciple of this ambitious vision. But the process of convincing the rest of the Management Board was slow. The costs of this strategy were high both in financial terms and for the preservation of the soul of Deutsche Bank as a decentralised but closely managed German bank, albeit with international interests. In the end, the acquisition did not go smoothly, partly because of the failure to adapt to each other's structures, and the ongoing struggle for control over the new investment bank business between London and Frankfurt. This episode clearly exposed a lack of consensus about the best direction for the bank and the tension between traditional German banking and global investment banking cultures. While often viewed in hindsight as a rash mistake, the acquisition of Morgan Grenfell was not a hasty leap in the dark. Plans to use Morgan Grenfell as a route into London-style European investment banking evolved over a period of seven years and were highly contested among the Deutsche Bank leadership. This prolonged struggle is crucial to understanding the Deutsche Bank strategy, its approach to its own development in a rapidly changing market and the unusual foundations of the merger.

1. Early Steps, 1983–1987

In her history of Morgan Grenfell, Kathleen Burk describes how a close business relationship between Deutsche Bank and Morgan Grenfell grew from 1983, when Morgan Grenfell was asked to advise on an equity participation in a London merchant bank.[1] The outcome was consideration of a joint venture or other form of co-operation with Morgan Grenfell itself. This did not materialise, but Deutsche Bank's interest continued and the relationship was reassessed. In April 1984, the Management Board took the decision to take a 4.99 per cent equity stake in Morgan Grenfell and to begin a programme of staff exchange to transfer skills. The focus was on co-operation in securities, corporate finance, export and project finance. Deutsche Bank was among the top 10 players in the London Eurobond market and Morgan Grenfell had strong London merchant banking expertise so the relationship was a complementary one at a time when Morgan Grenfell was seeking capital injection to expand its scale.[2] The liberalisation of capital markets, the surge in high-yield corporate bonds and the new era of fee-based advising no doubt inspired this effort to learn and to co-operate with a respected London merchant bank.

In the midst of the wave of mergers in London, in July 1984 Morgan Grenfell made a rights issue for £45 million at 400 pence per share to fund the acquisition of a broker and to build gilt trading (government securities), but it needed further capital to realise its ambitions to compete with American investment banks.[3] With Big Bang approaching (in 1986 the stock market was dramatically changed by removing the distinction between brokers and jobbers) in the City of London, Morgan Grenfell was following other traditional merchant banks by acquiring brokers and jobbers to be able to compete in terms of scale. After Deutsche Bank decided in principle to the equity participation, there followed months of haggling about the price at which Deutsche Bank would buy these unlisted shares.[4] In the end, Deutsche Bank succumbed to Morgan Grenfell's hard bargaining and agreed to a price of 494.5 pence per share (compared to their initial offer of 388p) thus pricing the 4.99 per cent stake at £14 million. The deal included an option to increase Deutsche Bank's participation to 10 per cent in the future, but an opportunity soon arose for an even greater stake.

Deutsche Bank acquired Morgan Grenfell by the end of 1989. The headquarters of the long-established London merchant bank were located on Great Winchester Street and is still used today as the guest house of Deutsche Bank in London.

In 1986, Morgan Grenfell & Co. advised Guinness brewers in a takeover of the whisky manufacturers Distillers that included illegal share manipulation to strengthen Guinness's position. This prompted a huge scandal when it was discovered at the end of the year. A court case found four traders guilty and there was a government inquiry into the affair that reported in 1987. This debacle prompted Herrhausen to consider whether the moment might be right to take over Morgan Grenfell now that it was weakened. In London in late January 1987 Herrhausen met the incoming chair of Morgan Grenfell, Sir Peter Carey, at the home of Lord Stephen Catto (former chairman of Morgan Grenfell Holdings) to discuss the future of the bank. In a carefully worded letter, Carey wrote later that 'the natural reaction of Morgan Grnefell [sic] staff to the recent events is that we should, if possible, remain independent', but he acknowledged that this might not

> make the best use of Morgan Grenfell's resources in the circumstances following 'Big Bang': an association with a larger group might benefit both them and us. In such an event we should naturally wish that association to be with an institution within which we believe we could work harmoniously and effectively. The Deutsche Bank is such an institution. There may indeed be others, and as we told you some have been expressing an interest in us. Some of these might be acceptable; others distinctly not.[5]

He was thus somewhat noncommittal, but he did remark that 'decisions may be forced upon us at short notice' and hoped that he and Herrhausen would 'keep in close touch as our thinking and yours develops'.[6] Herrhausen also met officials at the Bank of England to gauge their views on the possibility of a takeover by Deutsche Bank.

In Frankfurt there were mixed opinions on the benefits of Deutsche Bank becoming more involved with Morgan Grenfell. Hans-Peter Ferslev, a director of Group Strategy (AfK), and Frank Heintzeler, the head of the Corporate Finance Department (Sekretariat) in Frankfurt, advised caution on proposals to acquire a majority stake in the weakened Morgan Grenfell: on the positive side, they remarked that '[o]verall, it can be noted that the acquisition of MG would considerably strengthen our position in the international investment banking sector and improve our chances as the European investment bank to compete with the strongly expanding US houses and Japanese banks'.[7] The London branch of Deutsche Bank was in favour of the acquisition but, as Heintzeler and Ferslev remarked: 'In order to realise the above-mentioned business policy advantages, the following organisational requirements arise from our view: preservation of the independence and identity of MG; this is the only way to preserve the loyalty of employees and customers.'[8] Here we see the concept that underlay the eventual merger in the need to preserve and exploit the London-based traditional merchant banking skills that Morgan Grenfell offered. But this distinct culture would also be the major obstacle to the successful exploitation of the merger in the years that followed.

Heintzeler and Ferslev agreed that if Morgan Grenfell became the basis of Deutsche Bank's investment banking operations, the existing Deutsche Bank Capital Markets unit could be integrated. This would leave Frankfurt with the Deutschmark (DM) business and the domestic market. They suggested that one or two representatives from Deutsche Bank should join the management of Morgan Grenfell 'in order to ensure on the one hand control and on the other hand the realisation of synergies'.[9] The acquisition thus required a fundamental reorganisation of Deutsche Bank to realise the advantages, and they doubted whether Deutsche Bank could cope with the integration and significant management burden such a deal would require. The legacy of the Guinness affair was a further concern; would staff and customers remain loyal to Morgan Grenfell after a takeover by Deutsche Bank? Would a takeover reverse the loss of trust in the bank arising from the Guinness affair? Was there still the possibility of outstanding claims for damages from the Guinness investigation? They concluded:

> The acquisition of the majority interest in MG represents a potentially unique opportunity to achieve a leading position in international investment banking with one step. The capital to be used for this purpose is significant (up to 25 per cent of the current capital). It must be taken into account that the funds used will not generate any adequate profit in the short term even if the investment develops positively. […] This is to be seen against the background of a rather declining interest margin and probably considerably reduced provisional income. Before such a step, we must therefore answer the question whether we, in view of the funds to be used here, could achieve the goal to gain a leading position in international investment banking not in other ways – e.g. through the purchase of appropriate personnel capacities. However, we should then at least expect a longer period.[10]

Clearly, Group Strategy (AfK) and the Corporate Finance Department (Sekretariat) were not sold on the prospect of Morgan Grenfell as the ideal target (or acquisition as the ideal strategy) to expand Deutsche Bank's investment banking business. At the Management Board meeting on 26 January 1987, the memorandum was discussed and it was agreed that no action was currently required. Herrhausen had signalled that the initiative would now need to come from Morgan Grenfell. If they expressed interest, Deutsche Bank could 'enter into a detailed examination of the opportunities and risks and, if necessary, set conditions'.[11]

Despite this holding message, on 3 February 1987 Rolf-E. Breuer, who was in charge of securities, secondary trading and asset management on the Management Board, met John Craven, CEO of Phoenix Securities Ltd., and two of his colleagues to discuss 'Project Bulldog'.[12] Craven had founded Phoenix Securities as a boutique London company in 1980 after leaving senior positions first at White Weld and then at Warburgs. Breuer asked Phoenix to conduct an analysis of Morgan Grenfell and provide a recommendation on the advisability of a potential takeover. Craven expected this to take three to four weeks and proposed to charge £75,000–100,000; the work would be undertaken by his partners. The task was to assess organisational fit, valuation, synergies, potential spin-offs, contingent liabilities, regulatory issues and strategy/tactics. Deutsche Bank was given the code name 'Eagle' in the proposed work programme.

An external review dated 20 February on 'Bulldog/Eagle' was submitted to Deutsche Bank, which confirmed the Management Board's cautious stance.[13] The report suggested a valuation of 525p–550p per share (the eventual price was 550p) representing a premium of 30–35 per cent over the market price. But the strategic fit with Deutsche Bank's ambitions to be a global investment bank were not promising except in the securities business, which was 'the smallest and least developed of Bulldog's four major businesses'.[14] Morgan Grenfell Securities employed about 410 people and lost £4.8 million on UK revenues of about £17 million in the first half of 1988.[15] The Corporate Finance group was predominantly UK-focused and Investment Management did 'not appear vital to Eagle's [Deutsche Bank] requirements'. On the basis of 'Catalyst Theory', however, there might be a strategic justification if Morgan Grenfell were 'to become the focal point of the bank's international investment banking organisation' based on

> the premise that, with Eagle's non-Anglo-Saxon DM-centred base, its complex decentralised structure, and its current relatively limited range of products and markets, it will prove difficult and may take a very considerable time for Eagle to achieve its international investment banking objectives. This is of particular concern, given that Eagle's major competitors are already considerably ahead.[16]

But success on this basis required 'full and authoritative support of Bulldog's management, and the appointment of an outstanding CEO'.[17] Moreover, 'successful commercial bank-owned and -backed investment banking businesses' required strong central management, globally integrated organisation, excellent working relationships between investment and commercial bankers, ability to commit the balance sheet quickly and flexibly and strong product orientation of investment bankers. This could only be achieved either by fully integrating Morgan Grenfell into Deutsche Bank, which would not be approved by Morgan Grenfell's staff or its senior management, or transferring *all* of Deutsche Bank's 'non-German investment banking activities plus the corporate side of its London commercial banking business into Bulldog and make Bulldog/Eagle the global investment banking flagship'.[18] The report concluded that 'Expanding financial services business, especially ones characterised by complex, integrated global matrix organisations, by means of acquisition is a hazardous business' and they were unable to identify any fully successful cases. Any progress should happen 'with the greatest caution' and a focus on 'long-run benefits' possibly after 'a considerable toll on both organisations in the process'.[19]

With these uncertainties and the large financial burden, the Management Board decided not to pull the trigger on the acquisition. At this point it seemed there was some benefit to be had through a shallower co-operation between Deutsche Bank's London branch and Morgan Grenfell to consolidate a range of services for customers, although Manfred ten Brink, the head of Deutsche Bank's London branch, concluded: 'The harmonisation of the systems, on the other hand, should create considerable transitional problems.'[20] There the proposal rested until there were further changes in London.

2. Negotiating the Deal

In a rather surprising about turn, the board of Morgan Grenfell invited John Craven to be the CEO of Morgan Grenfell and he took up this role in May 1987, becoming

In 1981 Deutsche Bank's London branch moved into the building located at 6-8 Bishopsgate. More than 250 employees worked there.

chairman in October 1989.[21] Craven later recalled that Morgan Grenfell approached him to replace the outgoing CEO soon after Christopher Reeves resigned on 21 January. Craven held out for two to three months before finally appointing Warburgs to act for Phoenix in a £15 million merger with Morgan Grenfell in May 1987. This left him as CEO of Morgan Grenfell and a large settlement from selling his firm. On 27 April, Breuer wrote to Craven offering his congratulations on his appointment, noting:

> Since my first contacts regarding the future of Morgan Grenfell and the potential role Deutsche Bank could possibly play, we shared the common feeling that the most important question Morgan Grenfell had to solve was to find an outstanding Chief Executive. I am fully convinced that this is now the case.[22]

He concluded, 'I wish you all the best and much success – not only for [the] sake of our participation in the future wellbeeing [sic] of Morgan Grenfell's.'[23]

In a later interview, Craven claimed not to have arrived with a plan for Morgan Grenfell and asserted that he was initially not very comfortable there since he was not a very 'English Englishman' and Morgan Grenfell was very traditional.[24] Morgan Grenfell had left itself particularly weak in the UK equity markets, waiting too long after Big Bang to expand in the expectation that they would be able to acquire either Rowe & Pitman (which went to Warburgs) or Cazenove (which remained independent) so Morgan Grenfell's business model did not suit the post-Big Bang environment in London. In his opinion, Morgan Grenfell had good corporate relationships and asset management, but these were not the growth areas in the City. This left Morgan Grenfell vulnerable to acquisition, but, before accepting his post, Craven received verbal assurances from its largest outside shareholder, Willis Faber insurance brokers, that they would not sell their almost 22 per cent of the bank to a buyer that Craven and Morgan Grenfell did not like. This assurance lulled Craven into some sense of complacency when IndoSuez, a relatively minor French bank, hired David Scholey at Warburgs to acquire Willis Faber's shares and more to take control of the bank. Morgan Grenfell initially rejected IndoSuez's proposals but Scholey came back later to tell Craven that they were beginning a hostile takeover.[25] Michael Dobson, who had become deputy chief executive of Morgan Grenfell in January 1988, later recalled that he would have preferred Morgan Grenfell to have remained independent and to have built organically rather than being sold, but the Guinness affair had weakened the bank and Craven was more of a 'deal guy' than a long-term manager.[26] For this reason Dobson, alone among Morgan Grenfell's board members, had voted against taking Morgan Grenfell public in 1986 and against buying Phoenix (and Craven) in 1987.

Near the beginning of November 1987 a memo was faxed from Morgan Grenfell setting out the bank's strategy and 'the reasons for supporting the acquisition by DB of MG to create Europe's premier investment bank'.[27] The memo quoted a Statement of Group Objectives agreed at Morgan Grenfell's board meeting of 1 July 1987. The board aimed at a compound annual rate of growth in earnings per share of 15 per cent and set out Craven's priority of 'development of an integrated investment banking function and, for defensive reasons, to protect the Group's established corporate finance

Deutsche Bank's Management Board at the 1988 annual general meeting in Düsseldorf. Front row, from left: Georg Krupp, Herbert Zapp, Spokesman Alfred Herrhausen, Ellen R. Schneider-Lenné, Eckart van Hooven and Ulrich Weiss. Back row, from left: Jürgen Krumnow, Ulrich Cartellieri, Horst Burgard, Michael Endres, Rolf-E. Breuer and Hilmar Kopper.

business'. These goals were inhibited by 'the relative weakness of MG's capability in the international debt capital markets', which a merger with a partner would overcome 'if that partner had a significant capability in the debt market'. To this end 'MG believes that, overseas markets apart, its and DB's home market, Europe, will present significant business opportunities for such a combined investment banking group'. Such a trans-action would bring 'stability of ownership and enormous financial strength', 'a major presence in the euromarkets', 'increased capacity to build a substantial international equity securities business' and 'potential for synergy internationally', although it might require selling C. J. Lawrence in the US to conform with Glass Steagall. At the same time, Morgan Grenfell would enhance its 'leading position in Corporate Finance inter-nationally' so that 'DB will be able to help exploit the European market fully'. Morgan Grenfell's 'major position in international asset management' would also present 'the potential to float the business when better market conditions return'. [28] A week later, *The Economist* ran a story from 'a highly placed source' at Morgan Grenfell that the bank and Deutsche Bank were in discussions for a takeover.[29] But this report was premature. The Management Board at Deutsche Bank was still not ready to commit – perhaps taking more seriously the advice offered by Craven's firm Phoenix at the start of the year. Moreover, the global stock market crash in October 1987 had created more uncertainty in London and the investment banking business generally.

Seven months later, in late June 1988, Frank Heintzeler spoke with John Rawlings (head of the Banking Division, Morgan Grenfell) in London to review the situation.[30]

Rawlings told him that the situation at Morgan Grenfell had calmed down and the profit outlook looked promising as Craven focused the company on its domestic business of M&A and MG Asset Management. But the possible sale of Willis Faber's share equity was alarming and 'Craven is apparently looking for a quiet partner who does not want to get an operational influence on MG'. At this point, Rawlings noted that Craven had a close relationship with Piet-Jochen Etzel, a management board member at Dresdner Bank as another former customer of Phoenix Securities. Nevertheless, Rawlings reported growing interest in Morgan Grenfell for a connection with Deutsche Bank and he recommended that, if this was of interest, Herrhausen should contact Group chair Peter Carey (not Craven as CEO). In response, Ferslev and Heintzeler identified three alternatives: first, 'a theoretical takeover by DB on friendly basis is currently not considered due to the large-scale order. At a takeover price of £4.50, we had to raise some DM 2.3 billion (including preferred stock).' Secondly, buying the Willis Faber equity would amplify Deutsche Bank's stake without obtaining control. Thirdly, creating joint ventures for particular areas of business such as European M&A would only create ongoing delineation problems. Their conclusion was that 'we should sell our stake in MG and we will be able to make a profit for strategic investments in investment banking, e.g. M&A'. As the bank's deputy Management Board member responsible for both international operations and the United Kingdom region since January 1988, Ellen R. Schneider-Lenné agreed with this suggestion (noting 'Ja' in red ink). She had worked in the London branch in the late 1970s, so she had some knowledge of the market there, although this experience was now almost 10 years in the past. Ferslev and Heintzeler suggested aiming to sell at a block price of 400 pence per share (compared to the current price of 317). The book value of Deutsche Bank's holdings was DM 79.6 million, but at 400 pence per share they could earn c. DM 14 million. But Board member Hilmar Kopper was not ready to abandon the plans and Heintzeler was tasked with continuing discussions.

Heintzeler spoke to Craven on 1 September 1988 in London. At this point Kopper appeared to hope that they might be able to purchase the parts of Morgan Grenfell that they could fit into their strategy without committing to the cost of a complete takeover. But Heintzeler reported that 'MG's talks with their attorneys led to a clear conclusion that a sale of individual parts of the company for legal and business policy reasons was not considered. Except for the field of Securities, which, however, is not of interest to us.'[31] Heintzeler asked Craven how a friendly takeover by Deutsche Bank was viewed within Morgan Grenfell and Craven answered 'clearly positive', even in their Corporate Finance Division, subject to a convincing overall concept ('Gesamtkonzept'). Craven suggested a price of DM 1 billion, with some parts, such as the US operations, to be sold off later. Heintzeler wanted to discuss the following issues with Management Board members: given the huge price, was a takeover still to be considered at all? If so, Deutsche Bank should try, together with Morgan Grenfell's lawyers, to get a sense of the likely future liabilities related to the Guinness affair, find out whether Willis Faber wished to retain its shares and determine what parts of Morgan Grenfell could be sold.

The project found strong support in Deutsche Bank's London branch. On 12 September 1988, the new co-head of the London branch, Charles Low, reported to Schneider-Lenné on talks he had had with Morgan Grenfell's CEO John Craven and expressed his view that Bulldog could be part of Deutsche Bank's 'worldwide investment banking strategy'.[32] Low was fluent in German, trained in the traditional way within the bank at a regional branch (Duisburg) before taking up his post as head of the Deutsche Bank London branch in 1988. The London branch was relatively small, with only 250 members of staff located next door to the Deutsche Bank Capital Markets subsidiary that comprised a further 180 staff. The branch was mainly a funding centre for Deutsche Bank, operating in money markets and building business with British corporates.[33]

Low noted that after the Guinness affair and the stock market crash of October 1987, Morgan Grenfell was struggling and had gone to the market with a public share issue in 1986.[34] In these changed circumstances, Low saw potential for an acquisition.[35] His concept was that Morgan Grenfell would become the main Deutsche Bank vehicle in London (although the Deutsche Bank AG branch would need to remain open for regulatory purposes – e.g. Basel I, Bank of England capital rules). Importantly, he insisted that 'Bulldog retains its own name'. Low noted that 'this is a selling job' for Morgan Grenfell's staff who would need to be convinced to stay after a takeover by Deutsche Bank. On the plus side, 'Bulldog's staff have lost confidence in themselves' and '[w]e offer a way out' but 'it must also make clear what Bulldog is not responsible for (e.g. European merchant banking)'. He asserted that Deutsche Bank was viewed in London merely as a commercial bank and 'we have to explain what a Universal bank is (their CEO doesn't understand) by reference to our history and the type of business we have always done'. Staff at Morgan Grenfell might 'assume that our approval systems make it impossible to do deals' and that compensation systems would be changed. Without delegating considerable management authority to Morgan Grenfell 'there would be little point in buying their knowledge and experience'. The distinctive operational systems in London and the need to preserve them were clearly recognised, although, as we shall see, the Deutsche Bank Management Board found it difficult to come to terms with them in the decade after the acquisition.

Heintzeler met Craven again in Berlin on 26 September 1988.[36] This time Craven reported that discussions were continuing with Mitsubishi Trust and two Japanese insurance companies to take 5 per cent each of Willis Faber's shares and gain a seat on the Morgan Grenfell board. If the plans became more concrete, Deutsche Bank would have about four weeks to decide whether to come in as a buyer. Heintzeler reported again that 'internal discussions at MG have shown that it is indeed not possible to take over individual parts of MG. Even a takeover of the asset management site alone, which is of interest for us, is out of the question. Overall, everything has been internally invested in a fully integrated investment banking system.' Craven expected another fall in income in the second half of 1988 and advised: 'If we [Deutsche Bank] were interested in a total takeover, he would consider a takeover price of £3.50 realistic.' This is pretty surprising since the ultimate price paid was £5.50 a year later. Heintzeler also reported Craven's view that 'a friendly takeover by us was very much welcomed by the management level of MG'. But he advised that the full Management Board should only discuss an acquisition when there was a need for a decision in two to three weeks' time. Meanwhile, in the last week of November 1988 Deutsche Bank bought 20,000 shares in Morgan Grenfell, which were then sold at a slight profit the following week.

Morgan Grenfell's losses mounted in the second half of the year as Craven had predicted and, in December 1988, the bank announced that it would be the first big investment bank to close its loss-making securities business (both equities and gilts) in London and laid off 450 staff, although it would continue its smaller operations in New York. The losses being sustained were too large and there seemed no prospect that the market would recover soon.[37] To the date of withdrawing from securities trading, operating losses amounted to about £21 million and subsequent rationalisation cost a further £52.4 million (£39.3 million after tax).[38] Concentrating on its core businesses of corporate relations and asset management brought the bank back into profit through 1989.

In summary, the Morgan Grenfell acquisition did not happen suddenly, as earlier accounts have suggested.[39] Deutsche Bank recognised the need to increase its facility for investment banking in the new global financial environment and took a cautious but tangible decision to explore growing that capability though its relationship with Morgan Grenfell. But the pace of change through organic growth in talent was slow. Deutsche Bank management returned repeatedly to the prospect of taking over Morgan Grenfell and the deliberations over these years revealed some of the key parameters for an acquisition; importantly, Deutsche Bank would not be able to stamp its brand or culture on this traditional merchant bank and would have to share managerial responsibility. Human capital was the most important resource in finance, but it was expensive and mobile. The fluid market for Morgan Grenfell's main assets, its staff, made this strategy of expanding into investment banking through acquisition particularly risky since key people could simply move on if they were dissatisfied. However, during the 1980s, the pace of global finance accelerated and Deutsche Bank risked being left behind with its strong foundations in Germany and Europe but limited scope in the most important financial markets in the world: London and New York. It also risked losing its customer base in Germany and Europe if it were not able to service their increasingly complex international needs. On the other side, Morgan Grenfell needed an injection of capital to restore its position after major scandals and itself needed to be of a scale and stature to attract and retain the key skills in new markets to compete with US investment banks and to rebuild an integrated international investment house. It seemed like a good fit between institutions, but the good intentions at the outset were not in the end delivered.

The historical milestones of Morgan Grenfell since the founding of the bank in 1838 as George Peabody & Co., as seen on the plaques outside its London headquarters.

3. Taking Over Morgan Grenfell – The Decision is Made

In February 1989, after Morgan Grenfell had abandoned its London securities business, an acquisition was again under consideration in Frankfurt. This time Hans-Peter Ferslev and Peter Thelen from Group Strategy (AfK) noted that 'the company is severely weakened', but the cost would still be high, the return slow to come and the 'manpower' to bring Morgan Grenfell quickly and sustainably back to success was 'not present in our group' so Deutsche Bank would need to rely on a small group of key people at Morgan Grenfell who might not be tempted to stay (including CEO John Craven).[40] Nevertheless, in London, Low continued to press for the acquisition to be considered and his lobbying fell upon receptive ears – those of Rolf-E. Breuer and Hilmar Kopper.

In April 1989, the code name had changed from Bulldog to 'Magic' and Kopper was exceptionally positive about the complementarity of Morgan Grenfell with Deutsche Bank: 'Magic is strong, where we are weak and will remain insignificant without buying' especially in corporate finance and European M&A.[41] Now that Morgan Grenfell had withdrawn from primary and secondary securities trading, 'we could continue to play the Deutsche Bank card exclusively' in this area: complementarity had increased. Kopper believed that the 'too aggressive and controversial' managers had now left the company. With profits low, the leadership seemed willing to lean towards Deutsche Bank but this might change if Morgan Grenfell's income rose and prospects improved, so there was a sense of urgency about making a decision. Kopper estimated the price at DM 2 billion (twice the valuation of a year earlier despite the loss of the securities business) of which about 50 per cent would be goodwill. He expected Craven to leave and a new CEO to be appointed. He anticipated that no profit would be repatriated to Frankfurt for the first three years and earnings would mainly come from the M&A and Asset Management businesses of Morgan Grenfell. In line with Low's analysis from September 1988, Kopper argued that the name and self-sufficiency of Morgan Grenfell must be retained. On this basis he made a powerful case for the acquisition to the Management Board on 18 April 1989. But it took a further six months to come to fruition.

In July 1989 J. O. Hambro Magan & Co. were commissioned to produce a recommendation and valuation.[42] They valued Morgan Grenfell at £790–940 million or 462p–550p per share, with about 75 per cent of the value coming from the Banking and Asset Management divisions. Corporate Finance, they thought, represented only 8.5 per cent of the total value of the company. Hambro Magan considered that Morgan Grenfell's share price was undervalued on the market so Deutsche Bank could offer a premium while still getting a good deal, but success would require the 'full support of Magic's Board' as well as middle management and professional staff, partly by offering 'appropriate incentives' to key people. Most of the benefit would derive from the 'unique opportunity to obtain immediate critical mass in the international fund management markets'.[43] Three days after this document was completed, Dewey Warren announced that it was selling its 4.9 per cent stake in Morgan Grenfell and the share price surged from its level of 292p on 21 July to 475p by 24 November 1989, the last trading day before the announcement of the Deutsche Bank offer.

Deutsche Bank's own valuation of Morgan Grenfell was considerably lower at £589–725 million, with most of the difference from Hambro Magan in the valuation of Asset Management.[44] Hambro Magan responded, confirming that they stood by their valuation in a further report on 4 August 1989.[45] They argued that asset management businesses rarely came on the market and that, while the cost was high, the marginal returns from scaling up the size of managed funds would be large, particularly with access to Deutsche Bank's German customers.

On 17 August 1989, Charles Low reiterated his views of the benefits of Magic: depth of corporate relationship and specialist product knowledge, 'relationship management, market and government contacts and, to some extent the team building necessary for successful product development are all dependent upon culture. I assume that we would want to retain the Magic name as a symbol of our wish not to disturb that culture.'[46] Hambro Magan's analysis was discussed in a meeting in Frankfurt called by Kopper on 2 September 1989 with Low, Schneider-Lenné and Heintzeler as well as the bank's deputy general counsel, Klaus Kohler, the head of Deutsche Bank (Suisse), Richard Steinig, and one of the managing directors of Deutsche Bank Capital Markets, Alexander von Ungern-Sternberg.[47] Key questions included what areas Morgan Grenfell would strengthen, where its units were to be integrated into Deutsche Bank or Deutsche's units in Morgan Grenfell, who should take on the integration tasks and 'Are alternatives to Magic imaginable?'[48] It seemed that Deutsche Bank was coming inexorably closer to buying Morgan Grenfell even as the cost of the deal began to rise.

In a later interview, Craven claimed that the merger with Deutsche Bank came from a chance late-night encounter with Rolf-E. Breuer on a bench at a party during the first day of the IMF meetings in Washington DC, which took place from Tuesday 26 to Thursday 28 September 1989.[49] But clearly Deutsche Bank had been considering the British bank as a target of acquisition for years. In the interview, Craven recalled that Breuer asked what help Deutsche Bank could offer and what outcome Craven was seeking from its discussions with IndoSuez. Craven told him confidentially that the merger with a 'second rank' French bank would not create a powerful combination in investment banking. Breuer assured Craven that Deutsche Bank was a well-intentioned and supportive shareholder and offered to speak at the Management Board meeting the following Tuesday to see what Deutsche Bank might do. On 3 October 1989 (the day of the Management Board meeting) Kopper and Schneider-Lenné were to report on the discussions of an internal working party on the Magic plan, noting that this was 'possibly the only realistic opportunity for a long time to build a larger DB position in UK wholesale business and asset management'.[50] That very afternoon, Breuer telephoned Craven to report that the Management Board was willing to see if there was 'anything for us to do with you' and they agreed to explore a basis to move forward together.[51] The news that Willis Faber was selling 10.6 per cent of its holding in Morgan Grenfell to IndoSuez broke three days later, on 6 October, so the time was suddenly right. Herrhausen and Kopper arrived in London to discuss the commercial 'dream' of Deutsche Bank and their ambitions for the bank in international capital markets. Craven later noted that Morgan Grenfell was 'like a bird with one wing down', still not recovered from the reputational damage of the Guinness affair.[52]

Back in Frankfurt, the proposal continued to be controversial. Most difficulties focused on the high price and the questionable value that could be achieved by leaving Morgan Grenfell autonomous. Some, such as Thomas R. Fischer and Tilo Berlin from the Accounting and Controlling Department in Frankfurt, argued that synergies could only be achieved through integration but this was expressly rejected as part of the strategy of the acquisition.[53] Ferslev and Thelen worried that Deutsche Bank was set to pay perhaps DM 750 million above a 'reasonable' valuation of Morgan Grenfell based on the sum of its parts.[54] They pointed to alternatives including Yorkshire Bank, a bank in Liechtenstein or James Capel. They also highlighted the danger of a lack of integration if the acquisition was left as a standalone entity. For them 'the risks seem clearly disproportionate to the strategic opportunities' offered by the deal and they consistently lobbied against it.[55]

On the other hand, at the end of October Kopper expressed passionate enthusiasm for the acquisition, arguing against false economies and openly criticising the existing investment banking strategy of Deutsche Bank as incremental and ineffective.[56] Deutsche Bank had taken tentative steps internationally, but these had been piecemeal and not strategic. Kopper recalled the historical origins of Deutsche Bank as a universal bank and its prominent position in international investment banking in the nineteenth and early twentieth centuries alongside JP Morgan and Rothschilds. After 1945, he continued, 'thanks to Mr Abs, we quickly gained ground again at home and, in the wake of the strong DM and the "economic miracle", first nationally, but then also internationally in the underwriting business'. In the wake of globalising markets Deutsche Bank had expanded internationally, but not boldly enough. Its international banking business was focused on small offices in major centres like London, New York, Zurich and Tokyo that provided a presence but not leadership or scale, and in a range of peripheral centres in Australia, Europe and Asia. For Kopper, the major weaknesses were:

- the shortage of suitable <u>own</u> executives
- the reluctance to transfer this (off-balance sheet) business to (local) managers
- the urge to direct everything from a single location (headquarters) 'in the culture of the DB', although business requires ever faster, decentralised decisions in time zones and market cultures
- lack of support in the area that we have been able to provide as the most important element in building up our business abroad <u>locally</u>: the strong position and competence of the bank in German bond and equities trading
- too short-term and small-scale ideas when setting up your own business, which prevented the emergence of local economies of scale combined with attractiveness for first-class local employees.

The threat was not only in the international sphere: 'The advancing globalisation is increasingly threatening our position in the domestic market.' The range of competencies that the bank needed were primary and secondary trading, structured finance, currency, interest rate and cash flow management, asset management and M&A/consulting. Deutsche Bank was a market leader in these areas domestically, but not internationally, and the logical first step for expansion was into Europe through a new initiative in London. 'Magic offers an excellent approach. With one leap we would for the time being have covered our lack of capacity and international competence in the areas of M&A and asset management. This would also create the conditions for securing the worldwide expansion with a broader basis in the business and personnel areas by integrating an Anglo-Saxon "Center of Competence".' The skill pool in Germany was not sufficient to grow this expertise organically and the best staff could not be recruited to the offices that Deutsche Bank had scattered throughout global financial centres: 'We are not attractive for top investment banking professionals outside Germany.' To combat the arguments about the high price, Kopper noted, 'If you build up from your own resources, you need more time but, cumulated over a number of years, it is highly likely that you will need the same amount of money as would have been required from the outset for an acquisition of the "right" size.'

He concluded his memorandum with the observation that 'International merchant banking thinks, speaks and acts Anglo-Saxon. We must accept this "culture" for ourselves, integrate it as a multinational element, allow it to develop and make use of it. This is the only way we can live up to our claim to be the "Deutsche Bank Group" and avoid the danger of being seen as a German bank.' The distinction between his vision for a diversified international Deutsche Bank Group rather than merely a German universal bank is particularly striking in Kopper's analysis.

The very next day, George Magan of Hambro Magan & Co. wrote to Kopper to urge him to act quickly and make contact 'face to face' with Craven that very week 'to ensure that you have the best possible opportunity of securing the position of the most favoured "white knight"' given that Morgan Grenfell had other offers of support.[57] The Management Board debated the proposed acquisition on 7 and 19 November 1989 and Kopper, Breuer and Herrhausen were able to persuade their colleagues to proceed with Morgan Grenfell to secure a deal for final approval.[58] On Friday 24 November, Herrhausen returned to London and the terms were more or less finalised. Herrhausen then went directly to the Deutsche Bank's Munich weekend retreat (a regular event where board members also met with clients) where he brought the proposal to the Management Board and then to the Supervisory Board and gained final approval, but the battle for Deutsche Bank's future was not yet over.

The discussion at the extraordinary meeting of the Supervisory Board extended for almost two hours. Herrhausen pitched the plan not only at gaining essential skilled personnel and business areas, but also as part of the bank's wider European strategy, which found favour with some Supervisory Board members. Kopper, Breuer and Jürgen Krumnow, who was responsible for accounting and controlling, followed Herrhausen in making the case. Kopper described Morgan Grenfell's history, 'excellent' reputation and business lines and announced the price at 550p per share or a total of DM 2.6 billion, taking into consideration the 5 per cent participation already acquired. Breuer especially stressed the value to be gained through enhancing asset management that would bring Deutsche Bank into 'the leading group of asset managers in the world'.[59] Reflecting the internal debate, the Chairman of the Supervisory Board, Wilfried Guth, noted that 'the Management Board had not taken this decision lightly. The price for the takeover is high; however, the acquisition of Morgan Grenfell is an important investment for the

John Craven (left) and Alfred Herrhausen announced the acquisition of Morgan Grenfell by Deutsche Bank at a 27 November 1989 press conference in London. On the same day, Herrhausen invited Craven to join Deutsche Bank's Management Board.

future, and it is hoped that the returns will develop favourably, not least through synergy effects'.[60] Afterwards, 'the strategic component, individual accounting issues, the impact of the investment on the profit situation of the group, the chances of success of the takeover, the costs in case of failure and the eventual impact on the parent company's own dividend policy were discussed in detail'.[61] The Supervisory Board then decided unanimously to go ahead with the deal to acquire the shares of Morgan Grenfell.

Alfred Herrhausen returned to London the next day to sign the legal papers and to confirm the draft press release. At this point Craven warned Herrhausen that Morgan Grenfell's 70 or so board members would be shocked and would need reassurance about the continuation of the Morgan Grenfell name, the role of individuals and how they personally would be affected financially.[62] There were 10–15 key people who would need to be 'treated with kid gloves' to ensure that they would not oppose the merger; Craven had only taken four to five individuals into his confidence throughout the negotiations.[63] As Craven and Herrhausen walked to the board room annex to sign the papers, Herrhausen invited Craven to join the Deutsche Bank Management Board. In an interview in 2013 Craven recalled he didn't really understand the responsibility that this honour conferred.[64] The press release was made on Monday at 7 a.m. and Herrhausen and Kopper addressed the full board of Morgan Grenfell about an hour later, successfully convincing them all to accept the deal. After the months of uncertainty over Guinness and IndoSuez they were ready to 'grasp onto something really solid'.[65]

Herrhausen's notes for the press conference emphasised that 'Deutsche Bank is not just a commercial bank but is also an investment bank', 'one of Europe's largest stockbrokers, domestically we manage funds in excess of £25 billion and internationally we are one of the top securities houses'.[66] To the Morgan Grenfell staff he reiterated 'there may be some of you who see us principally as a very large commercial bank. That impression would not be correct', while recognising that 'you will represent within Deutsche Bank a core of Anglo-Saxon culture which has become an essential element of M&A, international funds management and indeed all forms of international finance'.[67] Executives of the Bank of England and several other CEOs from the City were then invited to a lunch to meet Herrhausen. As he got into the car to take him to the airport, Herrhausen invited Craven to dinner the following Monday night and to attend the Management Board meeting the following day. Three days later, Herrhausen was assassinated by a roadside bomb on his way to his office in Frankfurt.

4. Building Walls

A controversial and secret aspect of the deal was a 26-page 'Memorandum of Understanding' setting out the governance of Morgan Grenfell. This document was drafted in London and considered by the Management Board in Munich on Sunday 26 November. At this meeting it was described in the English translation as a 'constitution', and it was unanimously approved although 'it was noted that this document would not be legally binding'.[68] Although it was later described as ensuring Morgan Grenfell's 'autonomy' for five years, there was no reference to any time limits in the document itself.

The Memorandum confirmed that 'Deutsche Bank attaches importance to the retention of the British character of Morgan Grenfell and believes that this will best be preserved by retention of the existing corporate name', although the banks' names might be linked in some parts of the world, or Morgan Grenfell business might be done in Deutsche Bank's name alone.[69] There would be no change to the management of Morgan Grenfell and

> Ultimate responsibility for the conduct of the business of Morgan Grenfell will rest with the Morgan Grenfell Board as reconstituted (including four Frankfurt-based members of the Vorstand). This, amongst other things, means that while there will be the statutory requirements of the German authorities, responsibility for credit decisions, trading limits, client adoption decisions, compliance and the general prudent conduct of the business will be in the hands of the management reporting to the Board in London.[70]

Deutsche Bank's Management Board would approve an annual budget and three-year rolling plan but would not review the monthly performance of each business unit.[71] Deutsche Bank would control the board and therefore be able to replace management but would only do so to protect its investment or to meet regulatory requirements. In terms of business, Morgan Grenfell could continue with its 'leading reputation in contested takeovers, although inconsistent with Deutsche Bank's domestic tradition' but there would be a short list of Deutsche Bank clients 'which for various reasons are not legitimate targets for hostile takeovers by clients advised by Morgan Grenfell'. All the bank's M&A activities would 'in due course, report to London but Morgan Grenfell will be sensitive and patient about the actual implementation of this strategy'. In particular Deutsche Bank M&A would remain as a subsidiary in Germany with London representation on its board. The M&A capability in the US would be strengthened by hiring new senior staff. Morgan Grenfell Asset Management (MGAM) 'must be seen to be at arm's length from Deutsche Bank' to avoid the appearance to investors of conflict of interest and Morgan Grenfell intended to seek a separate listing within two to three years, i.e. to spin it out through an IPO. 'Equally important, obviously, is the retention and motivation of key staff which will depend both on operational autonomy and appropriate financial incentives.' For remuneration, Morgan Grenfell paid discretionary cash bonuses to directors and executive staff (MGAM had a formula) which amounted to 17 per cent of Morgan Grenfell Group profits in 1990, and they proposed to pay 20 per cent of Group profits in future years and not less than a pool of £15 million. An additional retention bonus would be payable in 1990, 1991 and 1992 on a discretionary basis to 'key directors'. The areas for Morgan Grenfell's business were agreed to be three core activities: international M&A and other corporate transactions; globally integrated investment management; and specialised banking. There was a recent addition of development finance related to management buyouts.

Craven later judged the Memorandum to be a mistake since the model of running two separate organisations would not achieve the synergies that motivated Deutsche Bank's investment. By June 1992 he was privately ready to revoke it in return for greater control from London over Group asset management and integrating Group M&A with primary and secondary debt and equity business, also to be run from London.[72] Michael Dobson, however, recalled that the idea for such a document originated with Craven. After the upheavals of the previous two years, in late 1989 the bank needed stability and certainty rather than further restructuring and realignment. For Dobson, the Memorandum was a success since Morgan Grenfell returned to profit and client relationships were restored.[73]

Morgan Grenfell Group's preliminary results from 1990 were discussed at a Morgan Grenfell Directors Meeting on 21 March 1991.[74] It was a successful year, 'partly the result of the tough decisions taken in 1988' and 'Deutsche Bank ownership had given the Group stability and credit backing without interfering with its flexibility of operation, owing to Deutsche Bank's broad adherence to the Memorandum of Understanding and its autonomy provisions'. Senior staff and client defections had not materialised as feared and, indeed, Morgan Grenfell rose from sixth to third in number of corporate clients in *Crawford's Directory of City Connections*. Craven reported that the Management Board's view was that 'while our result was not sparkling, it was extremely good compared to our peers'. Moreover, as part of trying to curtail cost inflation the bank introduced a salary freeze for those earning over £100,000 per year.

From 1990 to 1993 pre-tax profits for Morgan Grenfell grew from £46.6 million to £235.8 million, representing a return on average equity capital employed of about 55 per cent. At the same time they developed an Emerging Markets Division.[75] Nevertheless, the marriage between the two institutions was not a happy one because of continued conflicts over jurisdiction between Frankfurt and London and the lack of progress in pushing forward Deutsche Bank Group's presence in the lucrative equities (IPO and distribution) business that had inspired Herrhausen's strategy of acquisition in the first place. In a later interview Craven recalled a Management Board meeting he attended around this time, when Morgan Grenfell's positive results were reported. He expressed his pride but was surprised that Kopper and other Management Board members were less enthusiastic. For them the profits were gratifying, but Morgan Grenfell was not delivering its mission of accelerating investment banking within Deutsche Bank through transfer of skills and capacity.[76]

5. Conclusions

The acquisition of Morgan Grenfell exposed clear conflicts within the management of Deutsche Bank over how the bank should respond to the changing external competitive environment. The move into investment banking through acquisition was certainly not a hasty one, nor was it merely opportunistic. The focus on Morgan Grenfell as the only serious target, however, was taken quite early. The drive of Herrhausen, Breuer and Kopper to pursue their target over two years finally won the battle over the more conservative members of the bank's Management Board. But it was also not just a one-sided pursuit, as we have seen from Craven's early involvement and the views of the Morgan Grenfell board by November 1987. The process was also buffeted by the storms in the international financial markets in these years, in particular the stock market crash of October 1987.

Ellen R. Schneider-Lenné was a key protagonist in resolving the question of how to fit investment banking into Deutsche Bank. She is of particular interest as the first woman on the Management Board, and the last for 20 years, until Sylvie Matherat and Kim Hammonds joined in 2016. She spent her entire career in the bank, rising from a

Ellen R. Schneider-Lenné (1942–1996) in conversation with John Craven. Schneider-Lenné was the first woman on the management board of a German big bank. She served as a Board member from 1988 to 1996 when she died at only 54 years of age. She was responsible for international business and credit risk management.

position as loan clerk in the Hamm branch in 1967. What made her career distinctive was her facility with English and her experience in New York and London, where she helped to evolve the London representative office into the bank's first post-war foreign branch in 1976 and remained there until 1980. She joined the Management Board in 1988 with responsibility for credit risk just as the direction of the bank was about to change; her international experience was put to good use as the Management Board member responsible for the UK. She was thus perfectly placed to understand both sides of the divide and she had strong views on the different natures of German and British business cultures. In 1992 she wrote to Sir Adrian Cadbury, who was chairing the UK Committee on the Financial Aspects of Corporate Governance, that 'corporate govern-ance is a subject which I find extremely interesting, not least because the approaches to basically the same types of problems are at first glance so different in the UK and in Germany'.[77] She gave several lectures and published articles on this topic in the early 1990s that help to identify the cultural gulf as well as addressing criticisms of the German system. Her key messages were, firstly, that the universal bank system made the German banks more resilient since they could internalise shifts in product demands. She also challenged the claim that German banks had too much control over industry by pointing out the limited participation on supervisory boards and the declining bank ownership of industrial shares.[78] Secondly, for her 'the essence of good business is long-termism. But long-term success sometimes can only be bought at the expense of short-term profits'.[79] She regretfully observed 'a certain lack of long-term orientation' among British companies from the second half of the 1980s.[80] In Britain the focus was on shareholder returns while in Germany it was about the longer term success of the company and a wider group of stakeholders: customers, employees, suppliers and the community.[81] The emphasis on short-term quarterly results in Britain was also driven by managerial bonuses in the form of stock options and by the threat of hostile takeover. In the context of the Morgan Grenfell acquisition it is worth quoting her public view expressed in 1994, which defended the distinctiveness of Deutsche Bank's operations in Germany:

> When it decided on the takeover [...], the bank was particularly interested in the access that such a move would give it to distinctive Anglo-American banking philos-ophies, which are a major formative force behind many innovative developments in banking. Deutsche Bank sees Morgan Grenfell as its 'centre of competence' for the areas of corporate finance (especially mergers and acquisitions business), and institutional and international asset management. It wanted this additional compe-tence in order to better defend and develop its leading position at a European level. The bank has, however, no intention of transferring British financing techniques wholesale to Germany.[82]

Schneider-Lenné made an enormous contribution to the bank's strategy in this key moment in its evolution. It is clear from the evidence presented in Chapter II that she continued to struggle with the blending of the two systems. She died prematurely in 1996 from cancer, before the acquisition of Bankers Trust pushed forward the bank's full transformation.

II. Building the Investment Bank, 1991–1998

As discussed in Chapter I, one of the motivations for embarking on investment banking was the prospect of a surge in fee income as governments across Europe moved away from the post-war model of state ownership and sold off national assets. In 1996 the German government sold its first major tranche of Deutsche Telekom through an IPO for the equivalent of about €10 billion in a landmark privatisation. But rather than Deutsche Bank, Goldman Sachs was identified as the co-ordinator of the foreign sales for the new issue at the end of November 1994, having built up a 250-strong staff in Frankfurt and developing close links with the German government.[1] According to Anshu Jain (later the head of Deutsche Bank's sales and trading business) in a 2006 interview, this decision left Kopper 'upset' and prompted a fresh initiative to transform Deutsche Bank into an investment bank that could compete on the global scale, despite some opposition from the Management Board.[2] Herrhausen's vision in the 1980s that Deutsche Bank could no longer rely complacently on its home market but must engage in Anglo-American investment banking seemed to have been confirmed. But the development of investment banking expertise proved much more challenging than either Herrhausen or Kopper had imagined. Acquiring Morgan Grenfell was clearly not enough and, throughout the 1990s, the Management Board struggled to come to terms with the much more profound changes needed to realise this vision.

The debates were sometimes heated and certainly complex. This is understandable given the existential nature of the reorganisation of the bank's business to align with the trend in global banking and finance. The transformation was especially challenging because of Deutsche Bank's history and position in the German market. Deutsche Bank had long been identified as the quintessential German universal bank, so the development of a distinctive investment bank within the larger Deutsche Bank Group threatened Deutsche Bank's very DNA. The debate also heralded the shift in the bank's emphasis from interest income to fee income, in line with the conglomeration of its competitors and the nascent globalisation of the financial system. The German market for corporate finance, equity and other aspects of investment banking was no longer secure, as was made clear in the Deutsche Telekom privatisation, but at the same time the bank's ability to extend itself successfully into the wider European market through London or further afield in New York or East Asia posed even greater challenges. The arguments over how investment banking would fit into the bank's overall structure were therefore much more than merely a cosmetic organisational strategy. It marked a distinct turn in the bank's business orientation in a process that had begun with the Morgan

Hilmar Kopper in his Frankfurt office in 1992. He joined Deutsche Bank's Management Board in 1977 and became its Spokesman in December 1989. In 1997, he transitioned to the Supervisory Board, which he chaired until 2002.

Grenfell acquisition but was not completed until six years later with the integration of investment banking into the new 'Deutsche Morgan Grenfell (DMG)' entity.[3] The bank's new orientation also affected how the bank was viewed in Germany, coming as it did at the same time as the retail offering was slimmed down. On the one hand having a national champion in global financial markets was desirable, but stakeholders also identified the cracks in Deutschland AG and the erosion of the particular German business practices of co-determination, consensus decision-making and local civic engagement.

1. Local Scandals: Metallgesellschaft and Schneider

It is important to bear in mind that Deutsche Bank's reputational issues did not begin with the move into international investment banking. The attitude of the German public to their banks was already changing by the early 1990s after a rash of scandals undermined the traditional public admiration for the relatively small group of bankers that ruled the financial system in Germany and the 'bank officials' (*Bankbeamte*) who worked for them. The *Spectator* cited a poll from 1993 in which 82 per cent of the respondents said they did not entrust their money to banks.[4] Two of these scandals are worth discussing in detail as they had lasting effects on the bank.

The near-collapse of Metallgesellschaft AG in December 1993 as a result of a potential $1.3 billion loss from complex oil futures hedging rocked confidence in the probity of German big business. Metallgesellschaft AG was the country's most important commodity trader, having expanded rapidly in the years after 1989. Deutsche Bank was both a major shareholder (holding 11 per cent) and a major creditor, and Deutsche Bank's Management Board member Ronaldo Schmitz had in parallel been chair of

Metallgesellschaft's supervisory board since March 1993. When it became clear that the hedged position of a US subsidiary of Metallgesellschaft was deeply negative, Schmitz pushed for the hedges to be liquidated and the losses realised, bringing the company to the brink of bankruptcy.[5] Schmitz then co-ordinated a $2.2 billion bailout of the company by German banks and other major shareholders. Metallgesellschaft's ousted CEO Heinz Schimmelbusch moved to the US, from where he and another US executive, Arthur Benson, tried unsuccessfully to sue Deutsche Bank. In particular, Schmitz came under criticism for closing out the hedged positions too soon and thereby exaggerating the company's losses. It also raised questions about the potential conflicts of interest of bankers on the supervisory boards of their customers. The way that a relatively small New York subsidiary could almost bring down such a large and prominent industrial conglomerate in Germany, with more than 100 years of history, shocked the German public and led to debates about the nature and risks of derivatives trading on both sides of the Atlantic. In particular, the case sparked an academic debate about how to interpret hedging positions and whether the firm's problem was insolvency or merely illiquidity. Nobel Prize-winning Chicago economist Merton H. Miller entered the fray on the side of the derivatives traders, arguing that the position was retrievable when Schmitz closed the hedges precipitately. Even if it was a liquidity rather than a solvency problem, however, the parent company was in a weak position to provide liquidity to its hedging subsidiary in New York, having expanded quickly over the previous three years and suffering from a cash flow problem of its own.[6] Deutsche Bank and Schmitz were never found guilty of any wrongdoing from their actions, but doubts were raised about their understanding of these new complex hedging strategies and the derivatives market.

A few months later, the bank was caught up in another scandal arising from the collapse of commercial real estate company Schneider Group. Alarm bells began to ring over the quality of the group's loans in early 1994 after reports reached the bank that the group was not paying its bills to suppliers. Ulrich Weiss, Deutsche Bank's Management Board member responsible for the Mannheim area, where the loans originated, met with the group's owner, Jürgen Schneider, in February and was satisfied for the time being; but on 7 April, before the next appointment was due, Schneider wrote to Weiss that he had to go overseas for health reasons and asked Deutsche Bank for a further line of credit. This was refused, and the company filed for bankruptcy just over a week later.[7] Schneider disappeared, and it became clear that the group's portfolio of mortgaged properties was overvalued and the loans were unlikely to be fully repaid. Deutsche Bank was a major creditor, having loaned DM 1.2 billion (or almost a quarter of Schneider's outstanding loans) mainly through one of its mortgage banking subsidiaries, Deutsche Centralbodenkredit-AG, for eight commercial property developments including shopping malls and office buildings. The main question for Deutsche Bank was how its controls could have allowed the loans to be made (and extended) against inadequate collateral. An internal investigation and an independent audit revealed no 'systemic flaws' but processes for valuation and approval of mortgage lending were tightened and four members of staff left the bank.[8] Provision was made for losses of at most DM 500 million, which were expected to be easily absorbed and the bank's credit rating was not affected.

The fact that Hilmar Kopper described the 50 million DM losses that contractors faced as a result of the collapse of the real estate company Schneider Group in 1994 as 'peanuts' was criticised as arrogant by media and politics. Five years later, Kopper posed on a pile of peanuts for the Frankfurter Allgemeine Zeitung*'s ad campaign 'Dahinter steckt immer ein kluger Kopf' (There's always a smart head behind it).*

The bank's sanguine attitude to the fraud and also to the collapse of the group, which resulted in many job losses, drew the ire of the German public. An off-the-cuff remark by Kopper at a lengthy press conference on 25 April 1994 referred to the DM 50 million in unpaid bills to contractors and suppliers as 'peanuts'. This was intended to offer reassurance that these debts would be honoured by the bank. But Kopper's comment served instead to illustrate the gulf between the rich banking community and the small firms and workers that it was meant to serve.[9] The remark haunted Kopper for the rest of his career, being quoted regularly in the press for the next 20 years.

In May 1995 Jürgen Schneider was arrested in Miami and brought to Frankfurt for trial. He was a colourful character with a trademark toupee. Just before his arrest Schneider recorded a video, released on ZDF television, blaming Deutsche Bank for encouraging him to take on more debt to complete projects in eastern Germany.[10] In addition to his own failings, the case focused on why banks had made loans to Schneider in the first place and whether this had been reckless. When the debacle finally found its way to court in 1997, Georg Krupp, chair of the supervisory board of Centralbodenkredit and member of the Deutsche Bank Management Board, testified that Deutsche Bank had become concerned about Schneider as early as 1990 when it became aware that the group was increasing its borrowing from a wider range of lenders, but the bank continued to lend to ensure that the existing projects were completed (and thus revenue generated) so that the debt could be repaid.[11] Deutsche Bank's Management Board and Centralbodenkredit's supervisory board relied on the risk assessment of the mortgage banking subsidiary so their decisions were, properly, based on the brief reports from the mortgage bank's Credit Control Division.[12] These attempts to deflect the public's impression that the bank's senior management had been irresponsible in its lending were met with scepticism, but the court case concluded without finding anything actionable against the bank. In December 1997, Schneider was found guilty of credit fraud and forgery and sentenced to serve six years and nine months in prison.[13]

These two episodes had lasting effects on the bank. The legal proceedings took years to unfold, which meant that the media reports repeatedly brought doubts about Deutsche Bank management into public debate. The image of senior bankers denying responsibility in court or caught up in legal wrangles did little to support Deutsche Bank's public reputation at a time when the German economy was struggling. Secondly, the Metallgesellschaft debacle highlighted the growing transatlantic cultural divide in global finance in the context of markets in complex derivatives. Thirdly, it must be remembered that these high-profile scandals, although primarily domestic in nature, developed as the Management Board struggled to define and structure the investment banking business within the bank after the acquisition of Morgan Grenfell in 1989. It is to these debates which we now turn.

2. Early Initiatives in Investment Banking, 1991–1993

As noted in Chapter I, the bank's management hoped that Morgan Grenfell would prompt a culture change as well as enhance the bank's expertise and market share in Anglo-American investment banking. In the end, however, Morgan Grenfell mainly delivered M&A business but little equity origination or distribution, and its corporate finance was limited to secondary firms. The Guinness scandal had driven the largest FTSE100 companies out of the bank's client list. Part of the reason that culture and expertise were not transferred effectively originated in the Memorandum of Understanding that guaranteed Morgan Grenfell's independence for an unspecified time. Another barrier was competition between Morgan Grenfell and Deutsche Bank's London branch since the two were not well integrated.

In May 1992 the Deutsche Bank Group set out its long-term strategic plan, which included a range of stretching targets. The target for return on equity within the Group as a whole was set at 15 per cent after tax, and the non-German part of the Group was to increase its contribution by cutting costs. By the end of 1998 the investment banking business was to be one of the leaders in its cohort, which was identified as including Credit Suisse First Boston, JP Morgan and Goldman Sachs. This was an ambitious aim from the rather modest base in 1992, and Craven became increasingly concerned that the targets would not be met. An internal review confirmed that 'Morgan Grenfell is unlikely to achieve pre-tax return on capital after all compensation much in excess of 15% in the foreseeable future'. A key phrase, of course, is 'after all compensation', which was much higher in London than in Germany. On the other hand, high returns on capital could be achieved by reducing capital intensive business rather than increasing net revenue. After the May Management Board meeting, Craven approached Group Strategy's (AfK) Hans-Peter Ferslev to ask how he viewed the future of Morgan Grenfell. Ferslev recommended the following to Kopper: integrating German M&A back to Frankfurt, and creating a new Corporate Banking business division that included M&A business and structured finance as well as the existing corporate banking business. He also suggested a new business unit for primary and secondary markets. The UK-related activities of the London branch should be transferred to Morgan Grenfell in the short term but, ultimately, the Morgan Grenfell name would be lost and the domestic business in the UK would be branded Deutsche Bank.[14] After this conversation, Craven felt concerned enough to make proposals for a dramatic reorganisation of the London operations and the role of Morgan Grenfell in corporate finance, equities and M&A. These included moving away from the Memorandum of Understanding that underpinned Morgan Grenfell's independence.

In June 1992 Craven wrote confidentially to Kopper alerting him of the 'somewhat depressing' prospects for Morgan Grenfell and setting out a set of radical proposals that he considered necessary to meet the Group's targets.[15] He thought his ideas were potentially so controversial that he urged Kopper to keep any discussion strictly between the two of them and purposely left the document in draft and unsigned, 'so that if you would prefer it, it can be ignored'.[16] The note referred obliquely to others on the Management Board who would find his proposals particularly disruptive. The first suggestion was to revoke the Memorandum of Understanding to allow Morgan Grenfell to become 'a wholly integrated part of the Deutsche Bank Group subject to all the controls and procedures emanating from the centre to which all other affiliates, both in Germany and abroad, are already subject'. He insisted that the Memorandum had been useful at the start in protecting Morgan Grenfell's reputation with clients, but 'it is now reaching the end of its useful life and is becoming a positive irritant within the Group' and an obstacle to achieving synergies. But if the Memorandum was to be abandoned, then structures needed to change in ways that would strengthen Morgan Grenfell's position in London.

First, he advised combining the corporate advisory work (including M&A) of Morgan Grenfell and the corporate business of Deutsche Bank's London branch and integrating this business with primary and secondary debt and equity business. This would bring the London operations closer to the structure of its rivals, able to offer 'full service corporate finance'. It was important to include 'to the greatest extent possible' the capital market and other corporate finance services of the Group as a whole. This would make it easier for Deutsche Bank Morgan Grenfell to penetrate the German market. He recommended these activities be brought under common management and a common brand name. The London branch should be merged with Morgan Grenfell and 'the surviving entity should be Morgan Grenfell' because of its relative size (1,500 employees compared to the branch's 600) and name recognition/reputation. He complained also about 'market gossip' that the London branch was about to relocate to an office that would not be big enough to combine with Morgan Grenfell and asked that this project should be suspended for the time being until the ultimate space requirements were known. Moreover, he 'would have liked to have been consulted at an early stage about the alternatives since optimum location, even within the narrow confines of the City, calls for the best possible local knowledge'. Clearly he felt sidelined from decision-making about operations in his own backyard.

He also had plans to identify Morgan Grenfell as the Group's 'centre of competence' in international asset management in Germany, Europe and beyond while exploiting the potential to market asset management services to retail customers through the Deutsche Bank network in Europe. This would solve another problem, which Craven identified as a potential conflict of interest. He was surprised that primary debt and equity business were separated from secondary market activities, which he claimed never to have seen before in any institution he had worked in or advised: 'Ideally the man responsible for deciding what we buy should be the man in control of the sales force.' On the other hand, combining asset management with secondary market trading 'look[s] anomalous, at least viewed from the Anglo-Saxon world and in the light of heightened concern about compliance'. Finally, he offered to 'relegate myself to a Co-Chairman or Deputy Chairman position in London' or to relocate to Frankfurt if this was required by restructuring.

This was an extraordinary memorandum from Craven, setting out a clear agenda and identifying what he saw as the weaknesses in investment banking that needed to be overcome for Deutsche Bank to realise its ambitions. It also reflected the challenges of unintegrated and overlapping business, gaps in equity origination and distribution and tensions between Frankfurt and London. But it also proposed solutions that anticipated the eventual reforms over the next few years, such as consolidating investment banking under a single management structure shared between Frankfurt and London but located in London, and the common branding of London and international investment banking that retained the Morgan Grenfell name. Craven followed up this campaign in the autumn of 1992 by offering to make a presentation on Morgan Grenfell to the Management Board.[17] Although the final outcome was similar to Craven's suggestions, the battle was prolonged.

In November 1992 the Management Board discussed proposals to reorganise Corporate/Institutional Banking.[18] They agreed that the identity of Morgan Grenfell as a merchant bank should be retained but the German M&A business would be transferred to Deutsche Bank Corporate Finance Division led by Ronaldo Schmitz. This followed Ferslev's advice to Kopper in June; Craven's suggestion of integrating the German and non-German corporate finance was not followed through. Moreover, the Management Board removed Morgan Grenfell's exclusive responsibility for 'the entire Anglo-Saxon region and Japan' to allow Deutsche Asset Management to compete in the North American and UK markets.[19] The questions over where the locus of investment banking should be, under what name and the division between German and non-German business were clearly identified as the key battlegrounds.

3. The Road to Madrid, 1994

As well as challenging the universal banking identity, creating an investment banking facility within Deutsche Bank challenged the bank's 'matrix' managerial structure, which was deliberately built with overlapping constituencies and responsibilities, with cross-cutting lines of business and control on a regional as well as functional basis. This was anathema to the Morgan Grenfell management who anticipated that such a structure would lead to a lack of clarity and disincentivise their lead personnel, so-called 'prima donnas' who were highly mobile and likely to be lost to the bank. Their skills and personal networks were Morgan Grenfell's main assets and it seemed that Deutsche Bank was on a course to destroy this intangible value. In Deutsche Bank, the matrix structure was seen as a way to preserve the close local relationships of bankers with their customers and the shared responsibility of the Management Board for the bank's operations as a whole. But the globalisation of international capital markets in the 1980s, and the financial innovation that accompanied it, required more streamlined, efficient and speedy decision-making. Deutsche Bank was a less agile institution than many of its competitors and this was becoming increasingly costly as a wave of European privatisations swept across global capital markets. If Deutsche Bank did not have the capacity to take part in this fees bonanza it risked being left behind.

Acquiring Morgan Grenfell alone failed to create the ability to engage with the fast changing business model in international capital markets. Five years after Herrhausen's initiative to launch the bank as a 'global player', it was evident that Deutsche Bank was falling behind its competitors. An internal report on the bank's investment banking expertise in March 1994 noted that 'Despite the efforts undertaken by Deutsche Bank over the past 10 years to develop international investment banking expertise, the international – as opposed to German – peer group has overtaken us and the gap is widening. This observation applies not only to certain large US banks (Morgan Guaranty, Bankers Trust and the top investment banks) but also to all three major Swiss banks and even Paribas.'[20] There was a consensus that stronger investment banking capabilities needed to be built quickly, but debate over the management implications revealed the cultural and strategic obstacles for a traditional universal bank such as Deutsche Bank to enter this quickly growing global market. In early 1994, Breuer tasked a small committee of five senior executives (two Germans, two British and one educated in the US with experience in New York investment banks) to review the management approach to investment banking in the Deutsche Bank Group as a whole.[21]

The Investment Banking Review Committee's first report landed on the desks of Ulrich Cartellieri and Breuer (both responsible for Trading & Sales) and Craven in early March 1994. It recommended a 'radical' consolidation of non-German investment banking activity into 'one global investment banking "shop" in Deutsche Bank'.[22] Management would 'pull together the various regional investment banking operations into one global division organized along product lines with an assertive entrepreneurial philosophy'.[23] Primary management would be structured on product lines with supporting regional management structures forming the axes of the matrix management system, 'focusing mainly on ensuring collaboration and cross-selling […] as well as developing and servicing local corporate and institutional clients'. The unit would have its own distinct organisational and legal framework and be based in London, likely a subsidiary of Deutsche Bank AG, reflecting 'the reality that London, rather than Frankfurt, is the centre of European investment banking and likely to remain so for the foreseeable future'. Consolidating investment banking risk in an expanded Morgan Grenfell could require 'excessive re-capitalisation' to get an adequate long-term credit rating, so the Committee recommended that some credit risks (e.g. medium-term OTC derivatives) should be booked in the name of Deutsche Bank AG, although the management reporting line for these products would continue to be within the investment banking team. This way the bank's large balance sheet would be put to best use.

Leaving German investment banking in Frankfurt reflected 'the perception that the problems to be solved in Germany and abroad, although fundamentally similar, derive from different commercial environments and require different treatment'. In Germany, Deutsche Bank's investment banking operations were 'superimposed on an ingrained commercial banking structure with multiple branch trading units, a concentration on plain-vanilla products, a distinct quality of customer relationships and a special professional ethos'. In contrast, an important requirement for global investment banking was the distinctive human resource: performance/profit-related remuneration and incentives, flat hierarchy, short reporting lines, 'high levels of individual responsibility, innovation and entrepreneurism' and 'a proactive attitude toward risk-taking and risk-distribution'. Sequestering the German market would preserve the universal banking character of Deutsche Bank in Germany.

Hung Tran, co-head of Deutsche Bank Research, offered a minority opinion that the Investment Banking Division needed to be located in Frankfurt both to enhance its authority through proximity to the Management Board and to promote the 'modernization' of the whole of Deutsche Bank to be 'made more efficient and competitive, first and foremost to be able to defend its position in its home market'.[24] For Tran, 'one can never clearly separate investment banking from commercial banking'. Thus, 'a separate legal entity represents a move away from the concept of universal banking towards the concept of a financial conglomerate as the investment banking unit, separately capitalized, will require all functions appropriate to its activities and thus will tend to minimize its interface with the commercial bank'. It would also 'be seen as a blow against the effort to enhance Finanzplatz Deutschland [a government initiative to promote Frankfurt as a major international financial centre]. Since the Bank is a premier finance institution in Germany, it has to think carefully about this decision' particularly since the European Monetary Institute was coming to Frankfurt. In retrospect much of what Tran predicted came true as the investment banking business came to dominate the focus and profits of the bank in the 2000s.

Craven viewed the report's recommendations as 'interesting' but 'probably too radical' although he agreed with the need for some kind of unit to consolidate equity and equity-related business of the bank, and that it should be located in London.[25] Tension persisted between Frankfurt and London. For example, in late March 1994, Hans-Werner Voigt and Bernd von Maltzan from the Trading & Sales Division in Frankfurt complained about Morgan Grenfell's business in the new issues market. Voigt was trying 'to get the Vorstand to lay down a rule that all equity or equity-related issues other than those which are to be placed wholly in the domestic market of the issuer should be led by the Deutsche Bank and that the Deutsche Bank syndication unit in Frankfurt take responsibility for syndication'.[26] Breuer tried to reassure Craven that fees would be reallocated to Morgan Grenfell where they had originated the business, but Craven rejected this as inadequate both on principle and because it would undermine incentives for senior staff. Craven's suggestion was to 'create a strategic road map to bring together of [sic] all our equity businesses to form a significant global business (while not necessarily rebranding or changing the management of purely domestic businesses) over a period of, say, 3–5 years'. Existing regional responsibilities needed to be overridden and a common branding could be introduced gradually, but it would only be successful and competitive with 'the kind of non-hierarchial [sic] management, short lines of communication and flexibility on compensation issues which were features of all investment banks (not just Morgan Grenfell). This pointed in my mind the need for some new entity to take on the international equities business.' For Craven, leaping to a full investment banking unit was too ambitious and he focused instead on consolidating international equity into a single London-based unit.[27]

Craven and Michael Dobson as CEO of Morgan Grenfell both feared that the proposals of the Investment Banking Review Committee were an existential threat to the future of Morgan Grenfell and consulted a high-level business consultant, Dennis Stevenson, for advice on how to proceed with the Management Board.[28] Stevenson advised that 'sense will probably prevail to the extent that Morgan Grenfell will end up not being interfered with' but 'Mike's [Dobson] gloomier forecasts **could** be fulfilled whereby in the rush towards one global all singing all dancing investment banking unit they force Morgan Grenfell in to a straitjacket from which it never emerges'. He recommended that Craven and Dobson should 'recognise the limitations of your power base' and prepare to accept it if the Management Board members agree 'to do something unbelievably stupid and against the interests of their business' but in the meantime they could 'lay the right "trip wires"' by setting criteria for the new scheme that would protect Deutsche Bank's investment in Morgan Grenfell and finally to set out a paper trail 'so that any withdrawal by you and other senior managers is clearly an honourable with-drawal'. Stevenson enclosed a draft communication to be used by Craven emphasising that 'proposals which seriously dismember the corporate whole of Morgan Grenfell run the very real risk of forcing the disappearance of the greater part of our investment in Morgan Grenfell in a very short space of time' since '80% of our investment in Morgan Grenfell is goodwill (perhaps now with a value of £.75bn)' of 'highly marketable highly self-confident and prima donnaish' human assets. Secondly, 'the most successful invest-ment banking organisations evolve and cannot be set up on the basis of blue prints'; they relied on long-term relationships and retaining 'highly paid prima donnas' who appreciate continuity and a long-term outlook. Morgan Grenfell should expand in its securities business to protect Deutsche Bank's investment.

In mid-June 1994 the Investment Banking Review Committee revised its proposals but persisted in its recommendation to have a single integrated 'world ex-Germany' management structure based in London, although not a separate legal entity or subsid-iary.[29] They retained the matrix structure of management that combined cross-cutting regional and product/functional responsibilities. Thus Deutsche Bank's regional legal entities, including subsidiaries and branches, would continue to operate; 'the role of regional Chief Executives and their local general managers is that of an integral – but not independent – part of the management process of the Deutsche Bank Group's range of operations as a universal bank in the region. As a team they are the Group's local cross-divisional universal bank managers' and report directly to the regionally respon-sible Management Board member.[30] An important element was that 'the coverage of institutional investors in Germany will continue to take place primarily from Germany' and the local German product heads would 'work closely' with the regionally responsi-ble Management Board members and branch managers since 'without this arrangement the Deutsche Bank universal bank advantage in Germany will rapidly erode […] this is Deutsche Bank's relative advantage in Germany'.[31]

This effort to create a compromise between an 'Anglo-American' investment bank and continuing existing reporting responsibilities through regional managers met with particular resistance from Morgan Grenfell's group finance director, Jonathan Asquith. He was a dissenting member of the Investment Banking Review Committee, declaring,

'I do not believe that the investment bank can be set up in an effective fashion without giving it a proper legal identity.'[32] For him, devising another layer of co-ordination as 'a sort of "super division"' would leave the leadership of the investment banking business with the same problems as experienced by the existing team: 'perceived as remote, [they] will spend their time (and dissipate their energies) in endless political battles with local management and will ultimately lack the genuine authority which is a combination of respect and control' which would not only undermine effectiveness, but also hinder recruitment.[33] What was needed was 'a direct chain of command […] which crosses a minimum of matrix structures or legal entity divisions'. For Asquith, 'the efficiency of management structure is inversely proportional to the number of lines that cut across it. It is difficult to see how a solution could have been devised with more "fault lines".'[34]

There was also disquiet among the German members of the Management Board. Ferslev and Schmitz discussed the issues on a flight from Barcelona to Frankfurt and Ferslev passed on his private and confidential views to Kopper on the eve of an important meeting in Madrid on 24 June. He noted, 'Our preference for complex matrix-organisations no longer meets the requirements of modern investment banking' but 'we' still wanted to remain a universal bank.[35] 'Organisational independence of the investment banking area, for example under the umbrella of Morgan Grenfell, would *de facto* lead to a splitting of the bank and thus to the abandonment of the universal banking character.' Moreover, 'It cannot be our goal to copy successful American systems so far that the European character of the bank is lost. Our chance is to become the European alternative to the American market leaders.' His solution was to combine all investment banking into a sub-group within Deutsche Bank with operating units in London, New York, Asia and Frankfurt. But the global leadership ('Global Coordinator') of each product group would be located where the existing competence was, e.g. London for equity, Frankfurt for fixed income. The investment bank would thus have no single location, but four equal centres. He recommended a full assessment of where the capabilities for investment banking were located before making a decision about where investment banking functions should be located.

The momentum in favour of locating in London, however, was strong. After considerable discussion and debate, a sub-group of the Management Board met in Madrid on the afternoon of Friday 24 June 1994. The German newspaper *Die Welt* reported that Kopper later (in 2003) described this meeting as 'the breakthrough on our way to becoming a global investment bank […] we grabbed each other by the shoulders and said: let's risk it'.[36] The archive record tells a rather more hesitant story. The outcome of the Madrid summit was a decision in principle that left the details unresolved. And, as always, the devil was in the detail. Present were Craven, Schneider-Lenné, Breuer, Cartellieri, Kopper and Schmitz. Before the meeting, Craven circulated a paper that reflected the advice from Stevenson. Thus he pointed out that 'of the DM 2.7 billion invested some 60% related to goodwill or, in stark terms, the loyalty of the top, say, 400 people of Morgan Grenfell and the clients to whom they relate'.[37] But 'in the last few months a number of disturbing developments […] are beginning to undermine the confidence of the Morgan Grenfell people'; some 'high fliers' were leaving and it was difficult to recruit stars since, unlike competitors, the Deutsche Bank Group had virtually no European equity capability. 'We are thus seen as a 1980's style merchant bank rather than a 1990's investment bank with too narrow a product range.'[38] Craven pointed to some minor checks to Morgan Grenfell's ambitions to expand operations in Singapore and the US and internal competition from Deutsche Bank in Treasury operations that was unsettling his staff, but the major disturbance was the radical suggestion to restructure Morgan Grenfell into Deutsche Bank as part of a new integrated investment bank. The Investment Banking Review Committee report had 'been given fairly wide circulation within the Deutsche Bank and the contents of which are known to a wide audience within Morgan Grenfell'. Craven's fears for morale and staff retention were influenced by his experience as CEO of Credit Suisse First Boston where a radical restructuring aimed at integration had 'the result that the entire top team in London left within 18 months'. Craven concluded that 'at the heart of this is the conflict between two wholly different and perhaps incompatible management structures – the matrix system which serves the Deutsche Bank Group very well and the linear system which has served Morgan Grenfell well for some 150 years. This is a real challenge for us all.'

The group meeting in Madrid finally agreed to a 'holding' statement to the effect that 'We have decided to propose to the rest of the Board to unite all investment banking activities of the Deutsche Bank Group under one divisional roof centred in London. This complex endeavour needs careful legal, fiscal and organisational planning' and they promised a 'blueprint' at the end of September 1994.[39] It was left to Craven to draw up the minutes of the meeting in Madrid.[40] The modified plan would create a new Deutsche Bank Investment Banking Division, although not a new legal entity. Morgan Grenfell would retain its name and regulatory reporting to the Bank of England and many lines of business would continue along existing reporting lines. The investment banking businesses would be 'brought within the management orbit of the new Deutsche Bank Investment Banking Division'. Morgan Grenfell Asset Management (MGAM) would remain outside the new division and perhaps take over the Group's global institutional investment management business. The new Investment Banking Division would be supervised by a committee of four to five Deutsche Bank Management Board members. Below them, a new Investment Bank management board in London would have five to six members drawn from both Frankfurt and London. A formal regional structure would be avoided, but 'all concerned would have to come to terms with and embrace a matrix management structure in which global product and relationship management interacts with an appropriate degree of local and regional management authority'. Below the new board were global product heads and a group of coverage officers run from London. The Madrid sub-group also discussed Craven's plans for building up a global equities business with research and origination operations in a single physical unit. This business might operate in the name of and for the account of Morgan Grenfell (emerging markets) or Deutsche Bank (Germany) but they would share a single management structure. After the meeting Breuer reasserted the importance of the German business as the 'very corner stone of our p[rofit] and l[oss]' and so he insisted that the new division must continue to have a centre in Frankfurt as well as in London.[41] He also reinforced the matrix reporting scheme with more explicit reporting lines from regional boards. Clearly, the geographic and managerial issues were still unresolved.

A few days later Craven set out how he viewed the cultural gulf between Deutsche Bank in Germany and Morgan Grenfell in London.[42] For him, the key elements for successful investment banking were 'partnership rather than hierarchical bases, with flat management structures, open access between management layers and short lines of communication'. This required 'partners' to consider themselves stakeholders in the business, 'a strong bottom line orientation, coupled with a conservative approach to risk', consensual management structure 'with a strong emphasis on fairness and shared responsibility' and delegation of 'the strategic direction of the business and the resolution of conflicts' to a Management Committee 'selected on merit, whose members command the respect and trust of their colleagues'. The 'partnership' model allowed high levels of delegation and individual empowerment that were needed to promote the innovation required to retain competitive advantage. Craven still insisted that the best way forward was to start with building up the European equity capacity and then encourage links with Morgan Grenfell M&A and other corporate service functions, leading to 'a natural growing together and perhaps eventual formal integration of the relevant parts of Morgan Grenfell and Deutsche Bank'. If 'radical change' was necessary then it should be based on the existing Morgan Grenfell structure, bringing in key people as partners. He particularly regretted the way the discussion had concentrated on the structure and organisation charts and not on the 'vision, business plan and competitive environment'. Dobson agreed that it would take at least three years to put together the elements for a single global force in investment banking and 'the right way and probably the quickest way to achieve that objective is via an evolutionary process which does not put in jeopardy the existing strengths in Deutsche Bank and Morgan Grenfell'.[43] If structural changes were deemed necessary from the outset, however, Dobson advocated a small management team charged with running the business on a day-to-day basis with substantial delegated authority to flatten the hierarchy and be closer to linear management, facilitating individual responsibility and innovation.

The Frankfurt side, meanwhile, had hired its own consultant, Klaus Droste from McKinsey. His vision for restructuring was more ambitious based on the matrix structure and management by committee, which would entail downgrading most of Morgan Grenfell's businesses except Morgan Grenfell Asset Management.[44] Anthony Richmond-Watson, deputy chairman of Morgan Grenfell Group plc, put it even more starkly as 'an irreconcilable conflict between the profit ethos of Morgan Grenfell people and Deutsche Bank's desire to protect market share'.[45] Craven shared these views with Breuer, Kopper, Schmitz and Schneider-Lenné.

On 23 August 1994 the Madrid group met again to consider the competing visions from Deutsche Bank and Morgan Grenfell as expressed in proposals from Droste and Dobson.[46] Droste's record of the meeting was refuted by Craven, but some essential points appear to have emerged. In particular, a high level and small team of one or two chief executives should be appointed to drive the agenda towards integration. This would include Dobson and Alexander von Ungern-Sternberg (Trading & Sales) and possibly Hans Beck, managing director of Deutsche Bank's London branch. A day after the meeting, Craven was contacted by the *Evening Standard* newspaper in London and the press officer of a competitor institution in London with reports that Deutsche Bank

Michael Dobson began working at Morgan Grenfell in 1973 and succeeded John Craven as CEO of the London-based merchant bank in 1989. He served on the Management Board of Deutsche Bank from 1996 until 2000.

was about to acquire a firm of stockbrokers in London because they were so disappointed and fed up with Morgan Grenfell. Moreover, there were rumours that Deutsche Bank managers found Craven and Dobson 'obstructive and recalcitrant'.[47] The atmosphere was souring further. Dobson and Craven arranged to meet Kopper the following Monday, noting, 'I am very concerned that we are now reaching a point where irreconcilable differences are emerging which, unless we can resolve the situation, will lead to irreversible damage.'[48] A proposed meeting on Tuesday 6 September was then postponed for a week to allow more constructive discussion.[49] Craven and Dobson used the time to come up with a compromise to embrace the Deutsche Bank 'desire to establish immediately a structure which will bring together the investment banking activities of the Deutsche Bank Group'.[50]

At this point Craven conceded much to Frankfurt but tried to cling to a clear linear management structure: management would be in the hands of two individuals responsible to an investment bank board, and the Deutsche Bank Group's Management Board would give 'unequivocal downward delegation' to the management so their mandate could not be undermined from above or below. This was especially aimed at stopping any direct appeals to the Management Board that bypassed the management of the investment bank. It would be up to the two co-executives of the investment bank to evolve a unified structure, optimum remuneration arrangements for senior officers and to build a worldwide equities business. At the meeting on 13 September 1994, Droste made a final effort at a more elaborate scheme but the group only agreed to expand the management to four: drawing two each from Morgan Grenfell (Dobson and another) and Deutsche Bank (von Ungern-Sternberg and von Maltzan). Breuer noted that he 'had already had certain telephone calls from senior people in the Bundesbank and the German Finance Ministry (based upon the rumours which are circulating) concerned about the Deutsche Bank moving its deutschemark [sic] securities centre from Frankfurt to London. It was clear that in order to maintain its position with the authorities in Germany and in order to protect and enhance Finanzplatz Deutschland that those activities must remain there.'[51] The authority of the Investment Banking Management Committee was generally agreed, although Craven did not believe that Cartellieri (Asia) and Schmitz (US) were really ready to give up their regional responsibility for investment banking. At this point, it was agreed that the details would be written up with a view to a proposal going to the full Deutsche Bank Management Board on 27 September 1994 to meet the deadline of the end of the month promised in June's Madrid communique. But the final form of how investment banking would be embedded in Deutsche Bank remained unresolved.

In late October 1994, the Management Board announced its intention to develop an investment bank in London. This marked an important departure and seemed to open up the possibility that Deutsche Bank itself could move its headquarters out of Germany, although this threat was mainly discounted in the German press. The bank's press release stressed that the new arrangements were explicitly 'evolutionary' with the 'strategic intent to integrate the investment banking businesses of Deutsche Bank and Morgan Grenfell over time'.[52] Rather than a legal entity or physical relocation, they created an Investment Banking Board chaired by Schmitz, including Breuer, Cartellieri, Craven and Dobson. Although London was to be the seat or 'nerve-centre' there was no full scale consolidation in London.[53] From here, Michael Dobson as CEO chaired the Investment Banking Management Committee (IBMC) which was responsible for the day-to-day business of investment banking.[54] The IBMC in turn included senior Deutsche Bank (Beck, von Maltzan and von Ungern-Sternberg) and Morgan Grenfell executives. German business and customers continued to be serviced from Germany, Deutschmark business would be centred in Frankfurt and Kopper pledged the bank's continued support of Finanzplatz Deutschland.[55] As part of this reorganisation, Deutsche Bank's chairman of the Risk Management Committee Thomas R. Fischer (who had opposed it) quit Deutsche Bank. Finally, it seemed a decision had been made, but the strength of this consensus was soon tested as expenditure on expertise, office space and allocating capital resources advanced rather more quickly than the 'evolutionary' strategy agreed at the Management Board. In the meantime, a set of no fewer than 16 working parties was set up to hammer out the details of the nature and structure of the new entity over the next three months.[56]

4. Creating Deutsche Morgan Grenfell, 1995–1996

At the end of 1994 and the beginning of 1995, when the final shape of the investment bank was being debated, there were several developments inside and outside the bank. First, the Management Board agreed at its meeting on 30 January 1995 to build an independent online direct bank under the name Bank 24. The aim of this transformational restructuring, discussed in greater detail in Chapter V, Part 3, was to reduce costs in the highly competitive retail banking operations of the bank while at the same time offering its customers access to innovative and time-saving facilities. Meanwhile, in the investment banking sphere, 28-year-old Nick Leeson brought down the venerable Barings Bank through his derivatives trading, a catastrophic fraud exposed in February 1995. Thirdly, Warburgs' failed merger with Morgan Stanley in December 1994 demonstrated the risks of quickly losing morale and the need for a clear strategy in a business where 'the main assets have legs and can walk'.[57] The lessons from these developments were that, on the one hand, the domestic German market was highly competitive and generated low profits, but, on the other hand, investment banking could be operationally risky and indeed if mismanaged could prove an existential challenge for banks even with strong historic reputations in this business. Deutsche Bank was also not alone in its ambitions in London: Dresdner Bank acquired Kleinwort Benson in June 1995, forming Dresdner Kleinwort Benson and building a leading presence in London under the leadership of Hansgeorg Hofmann. The controversy about the investment bank needs to be viewed in the context of these domestic and international developments.

The deal carefully brokered in October 1994 quickly unwound over operational details of what business would happen where. This prompted fresh conflict in the Management Board. Craven and Schmitz each prepared papers on the remit of the investment bank respectively for the Management Board and the Supervisory Board at the end of January/ early February 1995 but they were seen as an affront by several senior members.[58] The Management Board was split between supporters (Breuer, Cartellieri, Craven, Schmitz) and what Anshu Jain later labelled 'recidivists',[59] including Schneider-Lenné, Carl L. von Boehm-Bezing, Michael Endres, Jürgen Krumnow, Ulrich Weiss and Tessen von Heydebreck, who resisted the shift towards investment banking. For this latter group, the creation of the investment bank based in London threatened Deutsche Bank's heritage as a German universal bank.[60] Ferslev, as head of Group Strategy (AfK), wrote directly to Craven that his 'paper "downgrades" the Deutsche Bank from a proud Universal Bank to a bulky Commercial Bank. This is – I admit – somewhat polemic and it is clearly not your intention' but 'to make a long story short: the present paper does not give Frankfurt any role in the investment banking business apart from the money market and FX-activities'.[61] He noted that 'Deutsche Bank AG was founded – if you so will – as an investment bank and became a wholesale bank only many years later. The retail business was a stepchild of our activities until Mr van Hooven took care of it. The bank always felt that it was the number one partner of German industry in all financial respects.'[62] The new plans for the investment bank threatened the foundations of the bank's historic mission.

Meanwhile, Schmitz's report drew criticism from von Boehm-Bezing who wrote that what had been discussed at the Supervisory Board meeting on 31 January 1995 went well beyond what had been agreed at the Management Board.[63] He was concerned that the reports from the investment bank working groups had not yet been considered and yet 'facts' were being 'concluded'.[64] Having received this procedural criticism from von Boehm-Bezing (and in expectation of a hot debate at the Management Board) Schmitz asked Craven to circulate a paper to the Management Board meeting scheduled for 14 February 1995.[65] Craven noted that the paper had not yet been discussed by the Investment Banking Board, but agreed to take it first to the Management Board because he was aware of 'a certain amount of concern amongst those of you who have not been directly involved in the implementation of the Investment Banking Initiative about what is going on and what the implications are in relation in particular to large elements of our business in Germany'.[66] It was crucial to keep all decision-makers abreast of developments in order to build consensus.

The paper set out Craven's team's preferences for the structure of the new entity and the division of responsibilities between London and Frankfurt.[67] The evolutionary reform should be speeded up. The paper endorsed the Management Board's earlier decision to unite all of Deutsche Bank's investment banking under a single management structure but went further to promote a 'one firm concept' to establish a subsidiary company with its own capital allocation. This would be a clearer target for clients and staff to adhere to, particularly facilitating the adoption of a 'single culture' and 'investment banking ethos' including credible remuneration models appropriate to the business.[68] Management would be more transparent, as would performance. There were several reasons why Morgan Grenfell Group plc was the obvious platform for the new subsidiary, although the name would be changed to reflect its new status. Moreover, since it had been agreed that the investment bank would be managed from London, it made sense to use a UK-based company. Morgan Grenfell's constitution could easily be adapted and this solution would retain the 150-year-old name of a venerable London merchant bank. The new entity would thus be governed under English law by a unitary board, rather than the dual German structure. But the Deutsche Bank Management Board would have ultimate control as the full shareholder. Craven's report concluded with an emphatic statement:

> There exists a dangerous management vacuum which puts us all at risk because, although the announcement made on 28th October 1994 stated that there would be no changes in management responsibility or lines of reporting until a new structure was announced, de facto in certain parts of the Group considerable uncertainty prevails. It is imperative that decisions are made on the structure and businesses to be included in the I[nvestment] B[ank] as soon as possible.[69]

One of the key issues still outstanding was what business lines would continue to be run from Frankfurt and what would be managed from London. This seemingly technical issue had considerable implications since some activities required large amounts of regulatory capital to be held, which reduced profitability. Craven wanted to restrict the London operations to lucrative equities and fixed income and not take on the capital-heavy treasury operations such as foreign exchange and money markets, but in late January 1995 the Treasury Working Group recommended that the investment bank should have responsibility for all foreign exchange and money market activity in all Deutsche Bank branches not only in Germany but also globally.[70]

These plans were met with some hostility in London.[71] Together these businesses comprised about 700 staff and 'ceding the management of these activities to the I[nvestment] B[ank] would remove a central pillar of DB's wholesale banking capability'.[72] Moreover, these areas would be a distraction for the new investment bank that had quickly to develop an equities business. On the other side, fixed income, equities and derivatives needed to be co-located to take advantage of synergies in origination and distribution and overlapping relationship building. For OTC derivatives and Exchange Traded Derivatives, the Deutsche Bank name with its AAA rating would be beneficial, but the trading and risk management should take place in London. A system of credit fees would compensate Deutsche Bank for the credit risk it took on these businesses and there would be 'service agreements' between the investment bank and Deutsche Bank in Frankfurt to cover the terms of co-operation.

Craven remarked to Schmitz and Breuer after the Management Board and Investment Banking Board meetings on 14 February 1995, 'it seems to me that we are now faced with one fundamental issue: is there in fact a common view as to the vision we have about the creature that we are trying to create and its characteristics?'.[73] He noted that 'The Morgan Grenfell view is effectively an enlarged homogenous investment bank of a quasi-partnership character meeting the criteria set out under the "One Firm" concept above. Placing the whole of FX/MM [foreign exchange/money market] activities under common management with the I[nvestment] B[ank] activities causes us to be deeply concerned that the vision DB has for this business is seriously at odds with our own.' The 'overwhelming view in Deutsche Bank' was that foreign exchange, money markets, fixed income and derivatives was a single global business. But the Morgan Grenfell management believed that including all foreign exchange/money market business would overwhelm the investment bank and make it difficult to develop 'the culture of an investment bank'.[74]

Craven's proposed revisions included text suggested at the Management Board meetings, including, 'we believe that the German domestic I[nvestment] B[ank] businesses that trade in the name of DB A.G. should continue to do so, in order to preserve the pre-eminent position of DB as a universal bank in Germany' but that 'we assume that the domestic German I[nvestment] B[ank] businesses will report to global product heads in London'.[75] The revised text also made the first reference to 'Deutsche Bank Morgan Grenfell'. Craven's amendments included that 'in the long run, all the I[nvestment] B[ank] activities (except the German domestic businesses, Morgan Grenfell's asset management and Channel Islands businesses) should operate under a single name', although 'in the short term, the use of this name at the operating level could damage businesses'.[76] This draft obviously left many issues still to be resolved.

After discussion and minor amendments and clarifications, the proposed revisions were sent to Schneider-Lenné and Kopper as members of Morgan Grenfell Group board and copied to Breuer, Cartellieri and Schmitz on 20 February 1995.[77] Craven asked Schmitz also to put his name to this version, but this was not in the end agreed.[78] Two days later Schmitz reported on discussions with Kopper and Cartellieri that reasserted that foreign exchange and money markets businesses must be conducted within the investment bank in London. They also insisted that not all investment banking activities outside Germany and Europe should be legally transferred to the investment bank immediately, but, rather, over time and only after further consideration on a case-by-case basis. But they did agree with the name change. By this time Craven was worried that a compromise would prove 'a serious corporate embarrassment'.[79] Yet further drafts for the Management Board were devised on 23 February and again on 2 March 1995.

The 2 March draft circulated to members of the Management Board reiterated that 'the position of Deutsche Bank AG as Germany's foremost universal bank will in no way be prejudiced'. All investment banking activities outside Germany could be transferred to the new legal entity 'on a pragmatic basis over time'.[80] But foreign exchange, money markets, derivatives and German-based fixed income and equities would continue to be booked in Deutsche Bank AG while fixed income underwriting outside Germany would be in the new investment bank entity. The investment bank would manage foreign exchange and money markets only in key geographic hubs rather than across the bank's entire operations. This draft also suggested that it was possible that different models (as yet unspecified) would be needed for Germany, Europe, North America and Asia. The vision was blurring under the pressure to compromise.

On 3 March six sceptical members of the Management Board (half the total membership) produced a paper setting out their core principles and proposals for the investment bank.[81] First was that a new structure 'must not destroy the benefits of the universal bank, but should complement it sensibly. In our home market and the European centres where we can offer our full range of services, the universal bank has priority over the predominantly product-oriented investment bank.' Capital intensive products that relied on the bank's AAA rating such as foreign exchange, money market and precious metals would be supplied 'under the legal umbrella of the AG'. All Deutschmark products would be distributed out of Germany and in particular 'the German equities business is an inalienable constituent of the Universal bank as well'. Corporate Banking (not the investment bank) would control structured products, leasing, trade finance and project finance. The investment bank would include M&A, international privatisations, international advisory business and international equities including trading and sales. Fixed income would remain with Deutsche Bank. Moreover, managers of German businesses 'should have a special and strong influence on the development and fixation of global strategies in the individual products within the I[nvestment] B[ank]'. A separate Corporate and Institutional Banking division would manage corporate finance and corporate clients. This formal circulated joint paper revealed a serious division within the Management Board.

Given the divergence of strongly held views, it was agreed to reach a final decision at a special in camera meeting of the Management Board in Frankfurt on 25 June 1995. As the deadline for the meeting loomed, Kopper had to send a note to all Management Board members warning that 'I have been receiving signals from many areas of the Bank leading to the conclusion that opinion still exists among several of our management staff that a decision to establish an Investment Bank in the Group has in principle not yet been made' despite the collective announcement at the end of October 1994 that this was the bank's aim.[82] Craven urged that 'creating an effective global integrated investment bank is not a strategic option for the Deutsche Bank Group. It is a strategic **imperative**.'[83] But Ulrich Weiss warned the Management Board, 'I am concerned that we do not only have the right vision but that we also take the right path which leaves those who are not part of the investment bank not only on board but which makes them active supporters and players in this development.'[84] This issue still seemed to have the potential to pull the bank apart.

In a meeting on 25 June 1995 lasting eight hours, the Management Board finally approved the Investment Bank Board, the change to Morgan Grenfell's name and the distribution of product lines after a presentation by Dobson, who was to be the new CEO supported by an Investment Banking Management Committee (IBMC).[85] In the end, the structure was very similar to what had been agreed nine months earlier; a board in London, chaired by Schmitz with Breuer, Cartellieri, Craven and Dobson (CEO) and an Investment Banking Management Committee (IBMC) for day-to-day management. The Group Management Board members on the Investment Bank Board would represent the interests of the whole Group Management Board so that the latter's responsibilities and oversight were not eroded through the delega-

Ulrich Weiss served on the Management Board from 1979 to 1998. He was responsible for personnel, compliance, audit and southern Europe.

tion to London.[86] The goal was to build the leading European investment bank and one of the top global investment banks in just three to five years and that 'with our Investment Bank as a global Group Division, we are decidedly pursuing an integrated approach and are determined to create a "unified culture" over time between it and the other divisions of the Group'.[87] The business would be organised into seven global product groups, which would each have a global head and a management committee. Dobson reassured the Management Board that the focus on product organisation did not preclude regional involvement in establishing strategies and implementation. He also promoted Deutsche Morgan Grenfell (later abbreviated to DMG) over Deutsche Bank Morgan Grenfell as the brand name for investment banking, although it did not signify a separate legal entity. Dobson remarked that 'Deutsche Morgan Grenfell has the advantages of relative brevity, it is therefore unlikely to be abbreviated and Deutsche Bank is widely referred to as Deutsche in the market-place, certainly outside Germany'.[88] There was to be a final vote on the draft proposal at the Management Board meeting of 4 July 1995 once a few minor amendments had been completed.

But even the public announcement exposed ongoing confusion. Dobson complained that the German version left the impression that 'a German investment bank' was being established separately within the global investment bank.[89] Even more importantly, Craven noticed that the internal announcement 'dramatically' changed the arrangements for credit risk by separating out credit and risk management and also removing them both effectively from the investment bank.[90] Craven threatened that if the announcement did not instead suggest that these arrangements had yet to be final-ised, 'a number of names appearing in the announcement will have to be removed' (i.e. people would resign).

The final approval of the investment bank primarily based in London was, there-fore, achieved only a few days after the target of the end of June 1995. The most obvious change was the new name for the investment bank, Deutsche Morgan Grenfell, which marked the formal end of the terms of the 1989 Memorandum that had secured Morgan Grenfell's distinctive name and management. The management structure replicated part of Deutsche Bank's cross-cutting regional and functional responsibilities as shown in Figure 21 below. There were also separate leaders for German Investment Banking and Corporate Finance.

This final approval occurred at exactly the same time that Dresdner Bank acquired Kleinwort Benson for £1 billion. In announcing this takeover, the spokesman of the management board of Dresdner, Jürgen Sarrazin, stressed that there would be no changes in management structures or job losses in London. Hansgeorg Hofmann from the management board of Dresdner, with his experience of US investment banking, became deputy chairman and executive director of Kleinwort Benson. He promised, 'We are now seeing a new Dresdner Bank. Everything we do in the future with regard to investment banking will be done with Kleinwort Benson.'[91] This was a rather more concrete statement than Deutsche Bank's solution. It is not conceivable that Deutsche Bank's Management Board was unaware of Dresdner's plans while they were quarrelling over their own investment banking presence in London. The takeover by Dresdner was described in the *New York Times* as 'one of the worst-kept secrets in Europe for several months'.[92] Also, in March 1995 ING bought up the remnants of Barings and in May 1995 Swiss Bank Corporation bought the wounded S. G. Warburg. The evolution of Deutsche Bank was thus part of a general move of European banks into London to embark on global investment banking. Five years after acquiring Morgan Grenfell, it finally seemed ready to begin to fulfil Deutsche Bank's ambitions. But there were yet more hurdles to come.

Figure 21: Management structure of Deutsche Morgan Grenfell in July 1995.

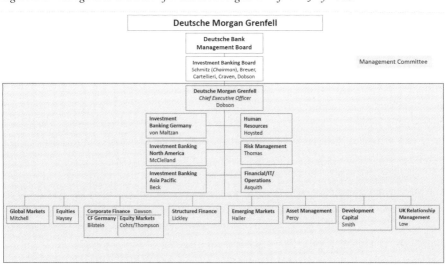

Source: *Forum* (International), Special, July 1995.

5. Transforming Deutsche Morgan Grenfell, 1996–1998

While the structure and leadership of the investment bank was being debated, the Investment Banking Board made progress with building the bank's capacity. An important part of the initiative was to capture the human resource that they had hoped to have acquired with Morgan Grenfell in 1989 and they found an opportunity with a failed takeover of S. G. Warburg that unsettled key staff there. The recruitment of Maurice Thompson, Michael Cohrs and Edson Mitchell, who came from Merrill Lynch, filled the places for Craven's focus on equity capital markets and fixed income.

At the end of 1994 S. G. Warburg was shaken by the failed takeover by Morgan Stanley. This merger of the two largest investment banks in the world was announced in December 1994 but promptly cancelled a week later since Mercury Asset Management (of which Warburg owned 25 per cent) had excluded itself from the deal.[93] After Morgan Stanley pulled out, Warburg's shares plummeted. Swiss Bank Corporation was able to take over Warburg for about £100 million less than Deutsche Bank had paid for Morgan Grenfell six years earlier. The failure of the deal left Warburg's senior staff demoralised, particularly Maurice Thompson, the 36-year-old originator of their equity capital markets business. He approached Michael Cohrs and suggested that they both plan to leave Warburg. Inspired by a published interview with Kopper in which he promoted Deutsche Bank's ambitions for creating a global platform for investment banking in London, Thompson quietly approached Craven's adviser Nicholas Berwin and then Craven and Dobson themselves in January 1995. Schmitz and Breuer met with Thompson in London in January 1995 before the two met with key management in Frankfurt. Attracting such a high-profile team of equity market experts was viewed as a signal to the market that Deutsche Bank had credible ambitions for building its investment banking business. Thompson and Cohrs resigned from Warburg in early February, followed almost immediately by about a dozen colleagues, to move to Morgan Grenfell.[94] The press reported salaries of £1.7 million over two years for each.[95] But this was just the start.

Two months later, in April 1995, Edson Mitchell (then 41) was recruited from Merrill Lynch, where he had co-headed the fixed income division, for a two-year compensation package (reported to be worth between £3 million and £6 million) to head what became Global Markets in London.[96] In March, Craven had advised Schmitz, 'As I see it we need somebody who is charismatic and energetic and a clear leader who can build a team over a period of three to five years.'[97] Mitchell was disenchanted with Merrill, which was pushing him towards equities and away from fixed income, so he took little persuading from Dobson who recruited him.[98] Mitchell started at the bank in May 1995 and he quickly leased new premises to create a trading floor, and brought in about 200 people from Merrill Lynch and elsewhere. More than 20 years later, Michael Philipp, another Merrill Lynch executive who followed Mitchell to Deutsche Bank, told the *New York Times*: 'I remember Edson called me up and said, "I have just been given the keys to the kingdom at Deutsche Bank — we can do whatever we want," […] 2,500 people in 18 months — it has never been done since.'[99] The momentum was building fast.

In mid-May 1995, Edson Mitchell briefed the Investment Bank Board on his assessment of the business after his first two weeks. OTC derivatives were 'all right' in New

Edson Mitchell (1953–2000, far left) switched from Merrill Lynch to Deutsche Bank in 1995 in order to lead the Global Markets division. In early 1996, he celebrated the 20th anniversary of Deutsche Bank's London branch together with (from left) Jonathan Asquith, Claus-Werner Bertram, Charles Low and Rainer Stephan.

York, Frankfurt and London but weak elsewhere and it 'was imperative to put in place a Debt Capital Markets capability able to serve the origination needs of Fortune 500 companies in bonds and private placements' in North America. It was at this meeting that he suggested hiring Michael Philipp for Global Sales and Anshu Jain for Derivative Sales from Merrill Lynch.[100] At its meeting in July the Investment Bank Board 'was in agreement with the strategy of building an Equities business through the hiring of high calibre though expensive individuals, capitalising on our unique position to attract such people at the present time. The cost was compared to the alternative of acquiring a business.'[101] New premises in Winchester House with a link to 72 London Wall were also approved at this meeting to accommodate staff numbers in excess of 3,200 by 1998.

This scale of hiring caused tension over compensation, which had to be financed from other parts of the bank until the profits were generated to cover them. Deutsche Bank's hidden reserves based on their industrial shareholdings offered a cushion to take on this expensive gamble.[102] In early May 1995, just after Mitchell had joined Deutsche Bank, Schmitz reported that his aggressive recruitment campaign had been noticed at Merrill Lynch and that 'I got a very sharp reaction from them today. Allegedly Mitch[ell] is talking to people who do not want to leave Merrill Lynch. On balance, I think he should move decisively and quickly so that we can control the damage.'[103] Deutsche Bank was disrupting the local labour market in London with its ambitious and expensive campaign to attract talent. Many of the new recruits were loyal to their own remuneration and their line managers rather than to their employer bank itself. Secure short-term contracts and bonuses also increased the appetite for risk among these traders. Mitchell reported 'unrest and uncertainty prevailing amongst senior I[nvestment] B[ank] staff in Germany. There was a recognition that their salary and compensation levels generally were below those being offered by the competition.'[104] The base salary of selected senior staff was increased and a bonus target set, but it is clear that the debates about governance, streamlining decision-making and tensions between Frankfurt and London continued through the early years of the Investment Banking Division.

'Investment Banking' became a separate division of DMG in a general restructuring in January 1996.[105] Personnel and resources were distributed across five global functions: Coverage, Industry Groups, Advisory/Execution (including M&A), Equity Capital Markets and Support. Maurice Thompson (with Jürgen Bilstein and Peter Espenhahn as deputy heads) presided over a Management Committee for the new Investment

Winchester House at the corner of London Wall/Great Winchester Street was finished in 1998, uniting Deutsche Bank's investment banking under one roof in London.

The Group Executive Committee of Deutsche Bank, May 1997.

Source: *Forum,* May 1997.

Committee of Deutsche Bank

Michael Endres | Michael Dobson | Ronaldo H. Schmitz | Michael Endres | Ulrich Weiss | Josef Ackermann | Ronaldo H. Schmitz

Heads of Divisional Boards

Regional CEOs

te and I Banking

Investment Banking

Group Services

Overseas Regions

Jürgen Bilstein
*MNCs**** and Public Sector Entities*

Jonathan Asquith
Chief Operating Officer

Edson Mitchell
Global Markets

Peter Gerard
*IT**/ Operations*

Heinz Fischer
Personnel

Simon Murray
Asia/ Pacific

W. Carter McClelland
North America

Lutz Mellinger
Commercial Real Estate

Maurice Thompson

W. Carter McClelland
Investment Banking Division

Marc Sternfeld
*IT**/Operations Investment Banking*

Klaus Kohler
Legal

Michael Philipp
Equities

Robert Smith
Institutional Asset Management

Rick Haller
Proprietary Trading (Emerging Markets)

Eisele
*Compliance**

Schuricht
*Auditing**

FORUM

rises   ****MNC=Multi-national corporations   ** IT= Information Technology

Banking Division (IBD) within DMG, consisting of Heads of Function and Heads of Region who jointly reported to Thompson.[106] There was, therefore, a continuation of cross-cutting lines of reporting rather than the fully integrated Investment Bank that Craven and Asquith had hoped for.

At the end of March 1996, the Supervisory Board accepted Craven's resignation from the Management Board of Deutsche Bank effective as of the end of May and Dobson replaced him. In a later interview Craven reflected that after the creation of Deutsche Morgan Grenfell, he was more or less managing a brand within the larger organisation, which did not suit him. He was also tired of the constant travel and felt ill-equipped linguistically for his Management Board role, which included responsibility for the Ruhr Valley region of the bank's activities.[107] In any case, he had never committed to staying for a second five-year term and he resigned as chair of Deutsche Morgan Grenfell a year later in June 1997. Meanwhile, an ambitious Swiss banker, Josef Ackermann, joined Deutsche Bank's Management Board in October 1996 after leaving Credit Suisse where he had a dispute with the chairman, Rainer E. Gut. Kopper moved from the Management Board to be chair of the Supervisory Board in May 1997, while Breuer succeeded him as Spokesman.

The debates over the operational and managerial responsibilities in the investment bank prompted a general restructuring to reflect the internationalisation and greater complexity of Deutsche Bank Group. By July 1996, Deutsche Bank's structure was organised into four Group Divisions, each with its own management board; Corporate and Institutional Banking (CIB), Retail and Private Clients, the Investment Bank (Deutsche Morgan Grenfell), and Group Services. This lifted the Group Management Board out of direct operational responsibility and at the same time eliminated the tradition of Management Board members having specific responsibility for operations in the German regions. A new Group Services Division took over operational management of IT, personnel, etc. As part of the effort to manage the Group on a global basis across all of its divisions, a new Group Executive Committee included members of Divisional Boards, selected Heads of Staff Divisions and the CEOs for Asia/Pacific and North America (Cartellieri and Schmitz). This rather large advisory committee brought together operational and strategic matters and met only four times a year.[108]

6. Disappointment and Fresh Restructuring, 1997–1998

In its first full year, the investment bank was not as successful as was hoped. Morgan Grenfell Asset Management (MGAM) was hit by a fraud scandal in September 1996 when Peter Young, a 38-year-old fund manager, voted 'Fund Manager of the Year' by *Investment Week*, was fired for 'gross misconduct' and Deutsche Bank had to pay £400 million to bail out 180,000 clients.[109] Young had apparently been boosting the value of the funds by investing in unlisted securities whose price could not be verified, which was against the rules for these mutual funds.[110] After internal investigations, the CEO of MGAM, Keith Percy, was fired, as were several other senior executives. This scandal was followed in mid-January 1997 by the spectacular mismanagement of the suspension of Nicola Horlick at MGAM for allegedly planning to take her successful team to a rival. Her bosses in MGAM in London refused to meet with her, so in the glare of substantial international press publicity she flew to Frankfurt to confront Deutsche Bank senior management, and subsequently quit.[111] These episodes seriously damaged Morgan Grenfell Asset Management, Deutsche Morgan Grenfell and CEO Michael Dobson's reputation in Frankfurt.[112] In the wake of the Young scandal, in December 1996 Moody's reduced the bank's long-term debt, counterparty and deposit ratings from AAA to Aa1 due to the increased risks and intensive competition associated with its commitment to global investment banking. Dresdner Bank and Union Bank of Switzerland, on the other hand, retained their top ranking. But there were more fundamental questions over Thompson's Investment Banking Division (IBD).

At the beginning of 1997 Craven drafted a paper on the way forward for the IBD, asking whether the record to date was 'a glass half full or a glass half empty', noting that 'there exists internally within DMG and increasingly within the Deutsche Bank the perception that the IBD is not living up to our expectations and that radical change is necessary'.[113] He pointed particularly to the failure to develop competitive industry expertise to allow the investment bank to become an attractive adviser for corporate restructurings and how a deteriorating reputation would make it difficult to retain existing talent. This time, the problem was not only 'continuing cultural and management problems between London and Germany' but also between the '"old" Morgan Grenfell advisory corporate finance division and the new seasoned professionals that have joined us in London and elsewhere in the Equity Capital Markets Group'. Indeed, Schmitz expected that most resistance to change would come from the 'traditional middle market focus of Morgan Grenfell. This must not be allowed to stand in the way.'[114] To overcome these managerial and strategic shortcomings a single management team led by Craven himself and located together in an open-plan office in London was planned to 'hopefully become a constantly inter-active team which will give the IBD a central focus and direction that it has hitherto sadly lacked'.[115]

There were also continuing tensions with Germany. In March 1996, Philipp as head of Global Markets Sales noted that the German section had low morale: 'In Germany, the business was very decentralised and there was a major overlap between sales and trading. It was necessary to separate sales from trading, prioritise accounts and appoint one relationship manager for each client', since 'there were sometimes 15 people calling on one account'.[116] By November the German fixed income business had been restructured, including the gradual closure of trading activities in branches.[117] But the headcount overall in Germany for fixed income, at 230, was deemed too high.[118] Global Markets trading centres in Amsterdam, Brussels, Lisbon, Madrid, Paris and Stuttgart were scheduled to be closed and the German headcount was to be reduced by about 100. Another important turning point was the decision taken at the April 1997 meeting of the Investment Banking Board that Morgan Grenfell Development Capital Holdings should lead on private equity investments for larger deals. This would be done from a base in London and included 'opportunities in German speaking Europe'.[119] There was also tension between Corporate and Institutional Banking (CIB) and the Investment Bank (DMG), with CIB seeking to take over Structured Finance and unwilling to agree revenue sharing on various activities in Germany such as export finance and leasing.

CIB rejected overtures to create a joint venture of closer management links to resolve the question.[120] Schmitz offered a robust defence, stating 'it was out of the question that S[tructured] F[inance] would be transferred into the CIB since it contributed over DM100m to the net performance of the Investment Bank'.[121]

In mid-February 1997 the Group Executive Committee (GEC) met to discuss Strategic Planning for 1997–2001. Each of the four Group Divisions presented their plans, which the GEC discussed in detail.[122] In preparing their presentation, the Investment Banking Board noted that 'a number of key issues should be openly debated with members of the Vorstand [Management Board]'[123] in order to clarify the Investment Bank's business model. These included the allocation of capital and risk-weighted assets through the Deutsche Bank Group, the special relationship in the Investment Bank between costs and revenues because of the labour market, relationship management models and the Investment Banking Division's strategy and role in the US.[124] Jonathan Asquith, the Chief Operating Officer of DMG, presented the Investment Banking strategy, emphasising that some key resources which were 'a sine qua non to being a global investment bank' were weak, including 'relationship management, M[anagement] I[nformation] S[ystems], risk management, integrated culture'.[125] He reported that the strategy for 1997 was 'a year of consolidation' with no new major business initiatives.

Despite this call for a pause in restructuring, the discussion at the GEC meeting focused on how to achieve better market penetration in the US. Acquisition was dismissed as an option since no target was likely to be available for less than $15 billion and it was expected that 'the relative global significance of the U.S. capital market would decline anyway, since stronger growth was evident in most other markets'. Emerging markets in East Asia, in particular, were a booming target for international capital flows. The Group Investment Banking Division was asked to draw up a 'supra-divisional relationship management concept for MNCs [multinational corporations] outside Germany in collaboration with G[roup] D[ivision] CIB', review the Investment Banking Division's strategy with the aim of breaking even 'soon' and, thirdly, to develop ways to improve market position in the US, Latin America and Asia. This opened up the overlapping interests between CIB and the Investment Bank (e.g. Deutsche Financial Services [DFS] was under CIB), but also emphasised that different models were required for German customers compared with the rest of the world. Thus 'For Germany, the continued importance of "house banks" was emphasised, based primarily on the bank's function as lender and provider of payment services' even for MNCs.

The discussion on Human Resources dwelt on the cultural changes within the Group and 'the need to improve the cross-border exchange of staff [...] as a way of contributing to the integration of "different cultures" (Germany and abroad)'. Some suggested that in recruitment 'priority should be given to people with international experience, as this would promote a global corporate culture. Developments over the past ten years from a largely patriarchal corporate culture increasingly towards a culture built on partnership were noticed positively. However, the divisionalisation of the bank, enforced by the market, also had negative cultural implications (segregation). Group Board and Group Executive Committee were called upon to set an example in terms of a holistic awareness of Group concerns.'[126]

7. Crisis and Further Restructuring

From 1996 to 1999 a wave of currency and banking crises struck emerging market economies in Latin America, East Asia and Russia. Through the late 1980s and 1990s the prospects for high returns from rapid growth had drawn investors from around the world, but the abrupt collapse of currencies led to substantial losses. At Deutsche Bank, the squeeze on profits gave added impetus to the agenda to reform the investment banking business in the US and Europe. Within DMG, Global Markets and Equities were flourishing but the Investment Banking Division (IBD), which focused on corporate finance, was weak. Maurice Thompson's strategic plan in mid-1997 noted that the IBD lagged well behind its competitors due to high costs in London (cost/income ratio was 121 per cent in 1996) and lack of presence in key corporate client relationships.[127] The problems arose partly from overlap with von Boehm-Bezing's Corporate and Institutional Banking (CIB) Group Division, which held the bulk of the bank's large MNC customers, and partly from the internal accounting procedures that booked the labour costs of the global salesforce in London against revenues from M&A and primary equities only. In November 1997, the Management Board rejected Thompson's and Carter McClelland's budget for 1998 and asked that they come back with a more radical plan to turn the business to profit. As part of this new strategy, the Management Board directed the division to run a profit in 1998 by focusing on Europe and North America and by leveraging the other product groups in Deutsche Bank AG. A week later, the Investment Banking Board agreed to a proposal to break up the IBD into three components: M&A, Equity Capital Markets and Relationship Management, with a significant reduction in staff and offices.[128]

At the end of the November, the Management Board set up a working group to reflect on the structural relationship between Corporate and Institutional Banking (CIB) and the Investment Bank. The result was that in December 1997 Bilstein, Jürgen Fitschen (both CIB), McClelland, Mitchell and Philipp together developed a concept for the creation of a 'corporate bank' or wholesale bank.[129] Such a bank would cover all investment banking and CIB products delivered to MNC clients, financial institutions, middle market corporates and the public sector. The aim was to streamline the delivery of services under a single management structure by combining commercial and investment banking business. The working group recommended that the structure be set up quickly, within 100 days, in order to limit the transition costs and uncertainty for staff and clients. The communication would need to be clear – that the bank was responding to the changing external environment in the financial sector and avoid 'misinterpretation that Deutsche Bank has failed with its engagement in Investment Banking'.[130] The reorganisation was announced in late January 1998 and took effect in April. The main innovation was the new Global Corporates and Institutions (GCI) wholesale banking division led jointly by Josef Ackermann and Ronaldo Schmitz. As Management Board Spokesman Breuer explained to employees in February 1998, combining commercial and investment banking into GCI would 'make us a leading global wholesale bank'.[131] DMG was absorbed into GCI and the Deutsche Morgan Grenfell name disappeared. Thompson and McClelland both left the bank as Ackermann's ascendancy began.

Table 4: New Group Division structure 1998.

Group Division	Retail and Private Clients	Corporates and Real Estate (CORE)	Global Corporates and Institutions (GCI)	Asset Management (MGAM and DWS)	Global Technology and Services
Management Board Member	v. Heydebreck	v. Boehm-Bezing	Ackermann (Schmitz for Relationship Management)	Dobson	Endres
Main Focus	Germany/ Europe	Germany/ Europe	Europe/ Global	Global	Global
	Retail	Corporate Clients	Investment Banking Division	Institutional Asset Management	Payments
	Private	Real Estate	Global Markets	Retail Asset Management	Securities Processing
		Financial Services	Global Equities	Private Equity	Custody Services
			Global Banking Services		Electronic Banking
					IT
					Site-Based Services
Corporate Center: Audit, HR, Controlling, Corporate Strategy, Press, Treasury, Research, Credit and Market Risk Management, Marketing, Holdings, Legal, Taxes (Breuer [Spokesman], Krumnow, Fischer)					

Source: Breuer letter to staff, February 1998. *Forum.* Annual Report 1998. Schmitz was responsible for relationship management for the Americas, Germany and Switzerland and Bill Harrison was brought in by May 1998 to oversee relationship management for the rest of the world. Global Corporates and Institutions Division, fax dated 20 May 1998, HADB, V50/354.

Along with GCI, another new unit, Corporates and Real Estate (CORE) was focused on SMEs and the domestic market. The Global Technology and Services Division aimed to consolidate the technical and IT support for global payments, settlement and custody across the bank. Morgan Grenfell Asset Management (MGAM) and DWS were grouped together to meet the needs of institutional investors. The Management Board launched the restructuring in February 1998 as a three-year plan that would cost up to DM 2.5 billion. They aimed to recoup these costs by setting a target to achieve return on equity of 25 per cent across the Group as a whole. As Breuer explained in the in-house magazine, the target 'should be seen as a landmark. Nobody is obsessed with generating a 25% return on equity down to the last decimal point, but it must substantially increase.'[132] He reminded his colleagues that the bank had achieved this target in 1993 and warned that if 'we plod along as before and do not set an ambitious target, then we endanger existing jobs, never mind being able to create new ones'.[133] This target was later most closely associated with Ackermann as he took over *de facto* leadership of the bank. It received harsh treatment in the German press and among employees whose jobs had become uncertain. Critics argued that the target was too ambitious and paid too little attention to the quality of revenue rather than just the amount.[134] In the end, the target proved elusive and the Group reported only 3 per cent return on equity in 1999. Although return on equity rose in

Figure 22: Global Corporates and Institutions, May–June 1998.

Global Business Area Management Josef Ackermann	Client Relationships **Americas, Germany & Switzerland** Ronaldo Schmitz **Rest of the World** Bill Harrison

Credit Risk Management – Credit International Hugo Bänziger	GCI-IT/Operations Marc Sternfeld	Global Banking Services/Structured Finance Jürgen Fitschen/ Gavin Lickley	Emerging Markets Proprietary Trading Rick Haller	Equities Michael Philipp	Investment Banking Division Equity Capital Markets Michael Cohrs	Global Markets Edson Mitchell

Asia
John Ross

Americas
Barry Allardice

- International Leasing & Asset Based Finance
- UK Relationship Management
- Syndicated Loans
- Leveraged Finance
- Special Products
- Project & Export Finance
- Principal Contacts in Countries

- Forfaiting
- Proprietary Trading
- Illiquid Debt & Sourcing
- Financing & Local Currency Fixed Income
- Special Situations
- Finance & Administration

- Cash Equities
- Equity Derivatives
- Equity Financing

M&A
Norbert Reis
Coverage Teams
Edward Chandler
Simon Ellis

- Equity Capital Markets
- Advisory
- Industry Groups
- Origination
- Operations

- Mortgage-Backed Securities
- Government Bond Trading
- Credit Bond Trading
- Research
- Proprietary Trading
- OTC Derivatives
- Metals & Commodities
- Money Markets/Repo worldwide
- Institutional Client Group
- Foreign Exchange Management
- Emerging Markets
- Debt Capital Markets
- Exchange Services

Source: Global Corporates and Institutions Division, fax dated 20 May 1998, HADB, V50/354.

2001 to 19 per cent it then subsided to about 5 per cent and then 4 per cent in the next two years.

Internally, the bank's approach was dubbed a 'Dual Focus' strategy aimed at European asset gathering and distribution on the one hand and on global wholesale banking and the global finance franchise on the other. In this way the bank straddled its traditional European strength in retail and corporate banking with a global reach into the burgeoning financial markets in the US and Asia. The so-called 'safe' funding based on deposits and traditional commercial banking protected the strong credit ratings needed for the riskier trading and sales businesses on the other side of the bank.

At the annual general meeting in Frankfurt in May 1998, Breuer reiterated the bank's commitment to being the leading bank in Europe but that 'Our motto is: "Europe first, but not only Europe."'[135] At the same time he introduced the new structure of five divisions in addition to the corporate centre, partly to 'remove organizational confusion'.[136] Breuer's speech was somewhat defensive, noting that Deutsche Bank had fallen behind its competitors in terms of market capitalisation, which prompted the need for a new strategy. Traditional lending over the past three years had risen, but the value of such credits fell from 59 per cent to 43 per cent of total assets. The balance sheet was becoming more focused on assets held for dealing and repo business, which together were almost at the level of regular lending. Asset management and securities business accounted for the largest share of the increase in income while net interest income fell from 61 per cent of total revenues in 1994 to 46 per cent in 1997. This underlined the importance of capital markets business for the bank's strategy. The process of leveraging the bank's balance sheet to increase return on equity had begun.

8. Conclusions

Deutsche Bank's transition from a German universal bank primarily focused on its domestic and regional market to an institution bent towards global investment banking was fundamental to its performance in the twenty-first century. The path to this transformation took almost a decade to travel and was bitterly contested among the bank's most senior leaders. It also posed fundamental challenges to the culture of the bank's business and brought in a new generation of traders who came to dominate operations in London and New York. The cultural shift profoundly influenced the management of the bank's entire operations and created damaging tension between Frankfurt and London. The new generation of leadership that emerged was less embedded in the German traditions of corporate-bank relations or the sensitivities of the German public towards the attitudes reflected by 'their' bank.

We must remember, however, that the changes taking place at Deutsche Bank reflected the experience of global banking more generally. From the mid-1980s financial conglomerates struggled in a battle for the scale and scope required to succeed in increasingly globalised financial markets. The pace of financial innovation and the liquidity of the market combined with increased fee and trading revenue created a global banking culture in the 1990s and 2000s that was clearly reflected in Deutsche Bank's own performance and strategy. The heightened competitive atmosphere – for talent, for ratings, for ranking, for reputation – meant that the world of investment banking became highly charged, and highly lucrative for the right individuals and the right business model. But it also sowed the seeds of short-termism, excess, greed and irresponsibility that would ultimately bring the world to the brink of crisis by 2007.

For Deutsche Bank, as the millennium drew to a close, the next chapter was about to begin. Five months after an acquisition in the US had been dismissed as a route to global markets because it would be too expensive, circumstances in the global financial markets had changed dramatically. Craven had left Deutsche Bank, and the Asian financial crisis in July 1997, the rouble crisis of 1998 and the Russian sovereign bond default in August 1998 ended the dream of the emerging markets overtaking the US. At the same time, the weakness of global financial markets reduced the costs of potential targets in the US and encouraged another look for acquisition targets.

III. The Bankers Trust
Acquisition, 1999

The Morgan Grenfell acquisition provided several lessons for the Deutsche Bank management. First was the need for deeper analysis of synergies, overlaps and gaps so that the target firm fitted in with the bank's strategy; secondly, the danger of underestimating the gulf between German universal banking and London or New York trading and investment banking cultures; thirdly, the need to integrate a new acquisition quickly into the bank in order to reap the benefits of synergies and to adapt the cultures of the two entities to create a coherent business model. The Morgan Grenfell acquisition had not resolved the cultural and organisational distinctions between German and Anglo-American banking as had been hoped.

By the late 1990s the cultural gulf between German universal banking and global investment banking seemed almost as large as in 1989. But it was also clear that competing effectively with the large American investment banks would require a direct and strong presence in the US market. Deutsche Morgan Grenfell (DMG) might eventually deliver the investment banking and equities expertise for the European market, but bigger players were wolfing down the huge market potential of the IPO, fixed income and M&A business in the US. In the 1990s, the Federal Reserve relaxed regulatory barriers and opened up a hugely lucrative investment business in the US that Deutsche Bank could not afford to miss. A small US brokerage (C. J. Lawrence) had come with the Morgan Grenfell acquisition in 1989, but Deutsche Bank had greater ambitions and by 1996 they were looking for a new target in New York. Schmitz claimed in a later interview that the idea to acquire Bankers Trust was his.[1] Indeed, in early 1997 he was quoted as telling an international bankers' forum that he was 'firmly convinced that the Europeans do not have any long-term chance to establish themselves among the world-wide leading investment banks if they do not also achieve a critical mass in the U.S.A.'.[2]

1. Strategy: Grow, Build or Buy?

Deutsche Bank explored three different strategies for its American adventure. It could seek to grow on the base of its DMG and Deutsche Bank North America (DBNA) holding, which was the umbrella for the bank's US activities, by hiring talent and expanding the range of business, but this would be a slow process. At the other extreme of ambition was an acquisition of an entire US securities company or investment bank for a faster leap into the market. In between was the possibility of building the US presence by buying in targeted teams to fill gaps in Deutsche Bank's expertise, or taking a significant equity interest in a specialist firm. The bank pursued all these options, sometimes in overlapping ways. By mid-1998, however, the decision to acquire had come to the forefront after the failure of the 'build' strategy.

The operations in the US had grown somewhat haphazardly, but they were focused on the New York branch. In May 1993 the decision was taken to rationalise the US operations of DBNA by creating a distinct securities company and moving the C. J. Lawrence operations into the Deutsche Bank branch. This was achieved by October 1993 when DB Securities Corporation (DBSC) was announced. By this time, it was clear that to remain competitive in the US the bank needed to enhance the technological infrastructure and personnel in securities, derivatives and trading. In spring 1994 John A. Rolls as CEO of DBNA proposed growing DBNA's capacity.[3] He preferred incremental growth rather than expanding through acquisition because it was cheaper, avoided 'integration issues' (product/skill overlap and threat to culture) and allowed more discretion in targeting business gaps. The risks of this strategy included the expense of recruiting top talent and the lack of a sophisticated technology infrastructure to attract that talent. If it could be achieved, DBNA leadership expected to raise their return on equity from 10.2 per cent in 1993 to 15.5 per cent by 1996. Asset-backed securities (ABS), mortgage-backed securities (MBS) and high yield were 'potential new other business' at this point, and it was proposed to grow the business by 'react[ing] to opportunities that may arise when talent from other firms become available'.[4]

Meanwhile, the US investment banking business was languishing. Carter McClelland was recruited from Morgan Stanley in August 1995 to head the investment banking business of DMG/C. J. Lawrence Inc. In October he reported to the Investment Banking Board that 'financial performance was poor; the business was uncoordinated' and the lack of capability to originate equity issues was a major gap.[5] He identified a comparative peer group of 8–12 firms in the US which each had twice the staff of DMG in the US (2,500 compared with DMG's headcount of 1,000). But the solution was not clear. Craven and Dobson suggested that taking on more staff would increase the cost base too quickly and that DMG should instead focus on a narrower range of business rather than competing with the larger US firms. But Schmitz 'queried whether it was possible to build a global investment banking business without a major presence in North America' and that the next year 'should be used as a learning curve'.[6] The US base was also weak in fixed income, where revenues were dominated by Germany, although the US Treasury market was the

Ronaldo H. Schmitz had come from BASF to join the Management Board in 1991. He was a Board member until 2000 with responsibility for, among other things, business in North America.

largest fixed income market in the world. DMG's presence was inadequate and the sales and trading staff were weak.[7] Schmitz, who was responsible for North America on the Management Board, clearly had ambitions for his regional remit.

McClelland took over as CEO of DBNA at the start of 1996 and immediately began to make changes, including a shift in the strategy from 'grow' to 'build'. He identified an opportunity to make a step change in DBNA/DMG's corporate finance presence in the US market by hiring a leading technology group of 20–25 staff from Morgan Stanley, led by Frank Quattrone.[8] The IT sector was booming with new start-ups and established firms launching IPOs, but this sector required specialist knowledge that DBNA did not have. McClelland had been instrumental in founding Morgan Stanley's IT group in the early 1980s and so Quattrone and his team were well known to him.[9] The proposal, code-named 'Cardinal', ambitiously expected to grow the group to 70, based in California's Silicon Valley. Preliminary negotiations began at the start of 1996 and followed a new model for Deutsche Bank.[10] The structure of the deal with Quattrone created a ring-fenced business in which the participants would have their own personal stake; they would be paid an agreed proportion of the business they generated as well as a base salary. The projected costs to compensate the leaders of the group quickly skyrocketed from $15 million to $45 million over the first three years.[11] Once again, Deutsche Bank was entering unfamiliar territory with a business culture foreign to the bank's core business, but the framework of a semi-independent unit operating on performance-related compensation was not unusual in investment and corporate banking.

McClelland's plan for Schmitz to bring to the Deutsche Bank Management Board identified DMG's 'principal strategic shortcoming in North America is Corporate Finance' but overcoming this gap posed some challenges.[12] The US Glass–Steagall Act of 1933 prevented commercial banks from dealing in securities and so separated investment banks from commercial banking, so buying an entire existing securities firm would be difficult. Building capacity through incremental growth 'would be time consuming and expensive and would take at least ten years to accomplish' and so the plan for Schmitz advocated a third option of acquiring 'successful groups of people on somewhat unique terms and "jump start" our Investment Banking presence in North America'. Tempting successful leaders and their teams away from other investment banks to join Deutsche Bank would create pockets of excellence and build reputation, but would be expensive. An area to start with was the information technology sector, where new business was booming, the US was the market leader and where Deutsche Bank itself had little core expertise. DMG identified Frank Quattrone's Technology Group at Morgan Stanley, which could be offered a $10 million bonus to move plus guaranteed compensation to the leaders of the Tech Group for the first three years (at $15 million per annum). DMG proposed to provide $50 million of venture capital for the leaders to manage for five years. They would also take an equity share in this business and the principals would be entitled to a long-term 20 per cent profit participation. Group Strategy's (AfK) opinion was rather cautious, noting that the team would be 'very much independent' and if replicated there was the risk of 'building a "warehouse of investment bank boutiques" contrary to the concept of building an integrated global Investment Bank'. The compensation terms 'could set a precedent that has negative implications for both future hiring and some previous key hires'. Despite these misgivings, in April 1996 DMG Technology Group was duly set up in Menlo Park, California, with Frank Quattrone as CEO. By November 1997, DMG Tech was forecast to incur a loss and the cost/income ratio was considered 'unacceptable' by the Investment Banking Board.[13] The 'build' strategy was an expensive experiment.

The issue of bonuses was crucial for the culture of the investment bank and integrating the German, London and New York operations. To compete for talent with US banks there needed to be higher gearing for incentives: rather than just cash, they should also include cash, Deutsche Bank shares and warrants.[14] At this point, bonus accruals were over DM 200 million above budget (equivalent to 35 per cent) with three-quarters attributable to Global Markets, Emerging Markets and IT due to the rapid growth in the number of senior staff.[15] Table 5 shows the rising cost/income ratio for DBNA as the number of employees grew rapidly from 1994, more than doubling in two years as a trading floor was built in Midtown Manhattan. The Commercial Bank part (including Deutsche Financial Services) was the only profitable division and offset small losses in the Private Bank and the much larger losses of the Investment Bank, which made a cumulative pre-tax loss of over $200 million from 1995 until June 1998. At the end of 1996 Carter McClelland told the Management Board that the strategy of a 'universal bank approach to corporate coverage' rested on a strong Commercial Bank but that gaps would need to be filled in Equities and Global Markets as well as building industry group expertise.[16]

Even Schmitz began to lose confidence. At the February 1997 meeting of the Investment Banking Board, he complained that 'it was not acceptable that North America should be run at a loss or be subsidised by the rest of the investment bank' and cut the planned expansion of staff from 400 to 200.[17] Despite his efforts, DBNA made substantial losses in 1997, and in early 1998 Carter McClelland resigned 'in a huff' according to *The Economist* and was followed a few months later by the entire Quattrone team.[18] In the meantime, the bank had undergone a major reshuffle in its leadership and restructuring.

In June 1998, Credit Suisse First Boston hired 132 staff from the Deutsche Bank Technology Group in Menlo Park (95 per cent of the team) including the leaders Frank Quattrone, George Boutros and Bill Brady. Ackermann reportedly remarked that

Table 5: Deutsche Bank North America financial performance, 1990–1998.

	1990	1991	1992	1993	1994	1995	1996	1997	1998 1/2
Total Revenues (in $ million)	273	339	364	420	441	712	1,041	1,335	792
Total Expenses (in $ million)	235	249	290	339	358	614	1,038	1,399	740
Pre-Tax Income (in $ million)	39	90	74	81	83	98	4	-63	51
Cost/Income Ratio %	85.8	73.5	79.8	80.6	81.2	86.2	99.6	104.7	93.5
Headcount	n/a	1,192	1,369	1,437	1,779	3,444	3,766	4,434	4,529

Notes: Excludes Morgan Grenfell Asset Management (MGAM), includes restructuring charges. 1998 is January to June 1998. Source: HADB, V50/364.

'Deutsche Bank Technology could not be integrated into the GCI structure. It was a US business with its own management structure and compensation systems. Our Europe-first strategy requires a focused approach to integrated wholesale banking.'[19] The *New York Times* reflected that this debacle 'stoked long-lingering speculation that it [Deutsche Bank] might be among the next of the world's financial giants to announce a big-bang merger with a Wall Street investment house'.[20] The experiment with organic growth or hiring teams seemed to have failed. The acquisition of Bankers Trust thus needs to be seen as part of a general readjustment in Deutsche Bank's strategy and prospects, including changes in leadership and other experiments in strategy.

2. Identifying a Takeover Target

Entry into the US market was a risky and technically difficult enterprise due to the heavy weight of incumbent US competitors and the complexity of regulation. Section 20 of the Glass–Steagall Act of 1933 prohibited affiliations between banks and securities firms, but only if the firm was 'engaged principally' in underwriting and dealing. This seemed to open up an opportunity to have subsidiaries that were not fully devoted to these activities, but it was not until 1987 that three banks were approved to set up affiliates under Section 20. The condition was that the subsidiaries' revenue from underwriting and dealing in securities that banks were not allowed to deal in amounted to less than 5 per cent of total revenue (later raised to 10 per cent).[21] The so-called 'three dwarfs' that embarked on this strategy were Citicorp, JP Morgan and Bankers Trust. From September 1996, the revenue limit from bank-ineligible business was increased to 25 per cent and the firewalls between Section 20 affiliates and the parent firm were reduced, which opened up the possibility for bank holding companies to have subsidiaries that dealt more in securities. This liberalisation prompted a series of mergers and acquisitions in the US market. At the start of 1997 the rules allowing foreign banks to participate were clarified to include the requirement that the parent banks were 'well capitalised', although the meaning of this was somewhat obscure.[22] By March the thresholds defining 'well capitalised' were set at 10 per cent capital ratio and 6 per cent Tier 1 capital. Deutsche Morgan Grenfell Inc., New York (formerly C. J. Lawrence Inc.), was a Section 20 company within Deutsche Bank from 1998.

The gradual changes to the Glass–Steagall Act prompted strategic investigations within Deutsche Bank. In May 1996, DBNA identified PaineWebber as a possible target for DMG in North America, in a project code-named 'Penguin'.[23] PaineWebber was a large supplier of retail investment banking services, with particular strengths in US equities, employing 16,000 people. Such an acquisition would pull Deutsche Bank into the US major bracket. At this time, though, the restrictions on Section 20 firms still meant that the combined entity would have to massively increase its non-investment banking business to $70 billion to stay within the 10 per cent overall limit on revenues from proscribed trading. But DBNA anticipated that the Fed would soon raise the limit and suggested that some other arrangement could help, such as a special-purpose vehicle. The acquisition thus seemed technically possible, but, on the other hand, Donald B. Marron, the chair and CEO of PaineWebber, was believed to be reluctant to sell.

Meanwhile, the plans for the Investment Banking Division of DMG, which focused on M&A and equity capital markets, were highly dependent on achieving scale in order to reach the target of top 10 ranking in North America and global top seven ranking by 2001.[24] At this point 1996 revenues were only about 15 per cent of major competitors like Morgan Stanley, JP Morgan or Goldman Sachs, while the cost/revenue ratio was twice as high as for these banks. Likewise, Deutsche Bank's headcount in this business was only about a third of that of the major US investment banks. The bank was just too small to compete in the US market and, without a significant presence in the United States, it was unlikely to be able to retain its competitiveness with European customers.

Ronaldo Schmitz's statement at an investment bankers' forum in February 1997, quoted at the beginning of Chapter III, that Deutsche Bank (in common with other European banks) needed to 'achieve critical mass in the USA', was reported in the *International Herald Tribune* on the day of the DBNA board meeting in New York.[25] At this point, the focus on PaineWebber was renewed after its prospects (and share price) increased. Schmitz agreed to explore purchasing a 25–35 per cent block of PaineWebber shares with a view to moving to a full acquisition after a period of collaboration. If PaineWebber's owners were not satisfied with the trial and did not want to proceed with a full merger, they would retain an option to buy back Deutsche Bank's equity at a guaranteed minimum price, which limited the risk. Marron, PaineWebber's CEO, was involved in discussions at this point, and McClelland was keen to proceed quickly with a decision by the Management Board in order to retain his trust. The DBNA team were asked to prepare more detail on the implications of either a partial participation in equity or a full acquisition, as well as an analysis of how PaineWebber compared with other potential targets.[26]

Schmitz and McClelland had a conference call in the evening of 26 March 1997 to discuss how and whether to proceed. From DBNA's point of view the consolidation of the US securities industry in the wake of the changes to regulation offered opportunities, but also competitive pressure as other banks were moving quickly. This meant that the number of desirable targets might quickly contract, and Deutsche Bank would be left behind with a gap that was 'not closeable through "build" strategies'. Schmitz and McClelland also believed that DMG was 'not ready to fully integrate a large North American acquisition at this stage of its own organizational development'.[27] The two-step proposal for acquisition allowed Deutsche Bank to establish a foothold with relatively low risk while providing opportunity for fuller engagement later. They could benefit from the existing management and structures while building relationships in the US market. PaineWebber was deemed a good fit for Deutsche Bank because of its focus on retail, which was growing quickly in the US. This sort of pairing of retail and wholesale had underpinned the recent Morgan Stanley Dean Witter merger. PaineWebber had negligible international presence so there was no overlap in Europe but there were synergies which could be achieved in equities, fixed income and administration in New York. On the other hand, PaineWebber was not strong in investment banking, but the combination with DMG in New York could be an attractive platform to attract talent and PaineWebber's New York infrastructure was big enough to accommodate DMG's New York business. While the two-step process had some advantages, however, it also introduced uncertainty over the final outcome, which could affect the US build strategy in the meantime. and the cost savings from synergies would be delayed. Buying an interest of 25–35 per cent would cost about $0.8–1.4 billion based on a market valuation of $3.1 billion. But McClelland considered Marron's willingness even to consider such a deal as 'a windfall set of circumstances'.[28]

A major problem with the deal was the effect on Deutsche Bank's balance sheet. Under Bundesbank rules, buying a minority interest in PaineWebber would be expensive in accounting terms because it would not be possible to write off 'goodwill' against earnings. The entire value of the equity investment would thus be netted out of the capital adequacy limits for the Bundesbank's regulatory requirements. So, either core capital would need to be increased, or 'historical assets' (other industrial holdings) replaced with PaineWebber shares. On the other hand the upfront cost was lower than that for the other potential targets being considered; Merrill Lynch, Goldman Sachs, Lehman Brothers, DLJ (Donaldson, Lufkin & Jenrette) and Alex. Brown. Table 6 below sets out some of the data underpinning the comparison. While Deutsche Bank was much larger in terms of total assets and book value than these narrower institutions, the return on equity was much lower.

DBNA's assessment of the options was that deals with Merrill Lynch and Goldman Sachs would create a premier global securities firm but Deutsche Bank would have to cede control of its Investment Banking to its new 'partner' in each case. A deal with PaineWebber offered retail distribution, while DLJ would create leadership in high-yield securities, merchant banking and middle-market investment banking. Lehman Brothers offered strength in global markets but had overlaps with DMG. Alex. Brown mainly offered research and reputation to channel future investment banking business.

The meeting in late March 1997 left the discussion open. Tessen von Heydebreck (head of retail banking) wrote to Breuer and Schmitz that Penguin (PaineWebber) was 'interesting' but there were outstanding issues that required further investigation both on strategy and financing.[29] Triggered by Breuer, the Management Board discussed Project Penguin on 15 April in Schmitz's absence. Von Heydebreck reported to Schmitz that the reception had not been completely negative and that most Management Board

Table 6: Deutsche Bank compared to potential US targets: financial summary 1996.

$ billion	Deutsche Bank	Merrill Lynch	Goldman Sachs	PaineWebber	DLJ	Lehman Brothers	Alex. Brown
Net Revenue 1996	11.9	13.12	6.14	3.68	3.5	3.44	1.0
Total Assets (June 1996)	551.3	207.0	105.0	52.8	54.4	128.6	2.6
Book Value of Common Equity	27.2	6.0	5.25	1.7	1.5	3.4	0.64
Return on Average Common Equity (%)	9.2	28.1	25.9	19.6	21.7	13.1	27.2

Notes: Goldman Sachs based on estimates. Source: Memo from Carter McClelland to Ronaldo Schmitz, including presentation on Project Penguin, 24 March 1997, HADB, V37/x142c.

members believed the proposal was at least worth considering. Von Heydebreck's suggestion of financing the deal through an asset exchange sparked particular interest.[30] Further discussion was planned for early May. In the meantime, Frank N. Newman, chair and CEO of Bankers Trust, wrote to Schmitz (as an institutional customer) to let him know about his bank's takeover of Alex. Brown.[31]

Barry Allardice and Carter McClelland at DBNA continued to be enthusiastic about a deal with PaineWebber. They held further meetings with Marron and prepared papers aimed at taking a final decision at a Management Board meeting in early June.[32] Marron visited Frankfurt on 23 May 1997 to lunch with Breuer, Schmitz, Dobson and von Heydebreck.[33] Following the lunch, all the relevant divisional heads took part in a workshop with the PaineWebber team to discuss developments in private and institutional asset management.[34] But the potential to bring Deutsche Bank and PaineWebber closer was abruptly dismissed, because neither side would consider a full takeover. The plans for a two-stage process were rejected. Instead the conversation turned to how to deal with press speculation that a deal was imminent. It was agreed to get the message across that the two institutions intended to co-operate in the distribution of products, but nothing else. The talks with Marron were over. Afterwards, Schmitz defended the entire exercise to Breuer by asserting that it was his duty as regional head of North America to conduct such discussions on the strategic orientation of his region but the foundations needed to be better researched.[35] In response, Breuer stated: 'I share your opinion: Business units and regions must do their homework. Unfortunately, such exercises in our company regularly create such a stir that everyone thinks they have to muscle in.'[36]

3. Crisis and Fresh Opportunities

In the midst of these deliberations, in July 1997 the Asian financial crisis struck. During the period of high-speed growth from the 1960s onwards, most Asian currencies had been pegged to the US dollar, giving a sense of security to outside investors. By the 1990s, however, it became clear that many of these currencies had become overvalued as they followed the US dollar in a sustained appreciation. In July 1997 the Thai baht fell precipitously. Speculation then spread to other countries in the region; devaluations caused debt servicing problems for borrowers and a rapid withdrawal of foreign capital. Growth was abruptly reversed and financial markets tumbled. For Deutsche Bank, falling asset values and depreciating currencies meant that what had seemed good investments when East Asia was growing suddenly lost value as this growth was abruptly reversed. Extra provisioning for losses cut deeply into the bank's operating profits in 1997 and emphasised the risks of operating outside the core advanced economies in Europe and North America.

The bank's operating profits fell by about one third in 1997, partly as a result of the need to make greater provision against risk (DM 1.4 billion). Immediately after the Asian financial crisis Mitchell and Jain recruited David Folkerts-Landau from the International Monetary Fund, where he had worked on the Fund's surveillance of emerging market economies. He quickly built up an emerging markets research team, drawing many staff with him from the IMF. But another emerging market crisis was on its way.

In 1997, as the Russian economy seemed poised for recovery and growth, Deutsche Bank prepared to set up a subsidiary in Moscow. Deutsche Morgan Grenfell had offices there and Corporate and Institutional Banking (CIB) was the leader in the finance of German–Russian trade. DMG provided a range of investment banking services during the period of economic reform in the mid-1990s including fixed income, trade finance and advisory services associated with equities. In 1995 Morgan Grenfell Securities LLC, Moscow, entered the local market in trading and execution for equities and fixed income while CIB offered services through correspondent banking. Business opportunities in the oil, gas and metals industries meant that CIB took a greater interest in Russia, although business was carried out through Frankfurt. In October 1997 Deutsche Bank submitted the final documents for a full banking licence with the aim of consolidating these activities in Deutsche Bank OOO, Moscow. Unfortunately, the timing of the official opening on 29 April 1998 was especially poor. In November 1997, the rouble came under pressure, but was successfully defended. However, falling oil and gas prices at the end of the year drove Russia to seek support from the IMF in February and March 1998, but negotiations could not be concluded. Four months after the Moscow branch opened, the rouble was devalued, the government defaulted on domestic debt and declared a moratorium on payments to foreign creditors. By the end of 1998 real output had fallen 4.9 per cent. Deutsche Bank's share price fell by 50 per cent in the wake of this turmoil.[37]

4. Returning to the Hunt

The disappointment over PaineWebber and the shock to global markets in 1997–8 coincided with a fundamental restructuring of the bank into four Group Divisions and the reorganisation of the investment banking business. The search for a target in the US resumed in the middle of 1998 after the Quattrone group left the bank.[38] In mid-July Corporate Strategy (Strategische Konzernplanung, SKPL) and DBNA proposed that a merger between the new Global Corporates and Institutions (GCI) Division and Bankers Trust should be considered. This could launch Deutsche Bank into the top five in asset management and custody and top 10 in other areas as well as delivering a 'credible and sufficient' presence in the US.[39] Their proposal argued that the strategy of creating a 'fully fledged universal bank' based in Europe but also serving customers overseas was too unfocused, with targets across all divisions but 'no convincing proposition for sustainable value creation'. Instead, they suggested that the bank needed a clearer product/regional market focus. Bankers Trust fitted Deutsche Bank's strategic orientation to create an integrated retail and wholesale bank and a leading European provider of global financial services/wholesale banking products. This required a shift away from the 'GCI-approach' by adding custody/payments, a credible presence in the US in investment banking and a high-yield securities team in Europe. Bankers Trust offered complementary attributes in asset management while bridging the gap in global finance and delivering 'state-of-the-art technology and knowhow' to Deutsche Bank in the US.

Like Morgan Grenfell in 1989, Bankers Trust had been weakened by scandal and it was then hit hard by the emerging market financial crises in Asia and Latin America. In a court case reminiscent of what was to come after 2008, lurid audio tapes of traders

The headquarters of Bankers Trust on Liberty Street in New York. The 158-metre building was opened in 1974 as Bankers Trust Plaza. Following the acquisition of Bankers Trust in 1999 it was transferred to Deutsche Bank.

discussing how they could exploit their customers through complex derivatives formed the cornerstone of a case brought against the bank by Procter & Gamble in 1995. In November 1993 Bankers Trust entered into complicated leveraged derivatives transactions (including interest rate and DM swaps) with Procter & Gamble that lost value when interest rates rose sharply in 1994. Bankers Trust contended that they were owed $200 million while Procter & Gamble claimed they had been mis-sold. In the end, Bankers Trust settled on receiving a payment of $35 million in May 1996. The *New York Times* reported that Bankers Trust had charged off about $300 million for losses related to disputes with clients over derivatives.[40] As part of the evidence to be brought to trial, Procter & Gamble forced Bankers Trust to produce 6,500 taped conversations between its traders, some of which hinted at misleading their customers through the complexity of the deals; for example, 'Kevin Hudson, the trader who sold Procter & Gamble the two contracts, saying, "It's like Russian roulette, and I keep putting another bullet in the revolver every time I do one of these."'[41] The case was highly publicised as it illustrated potential conflicts of interest in high fee transactions, the perils of complex financial instruments that blurred the border between hedging and speculation and the question of where responsibility lay for understanding the nature of risk: between the seller and the client.[42] The tapes also revealed the often juicy language and aggressive attitudes of bankers about the market and their customers. In 1996 a new CEO, Frank Newman, was hired to turn the bank around, but the reputation of aggressive and unethical Wall Street practices stuck.

In May 1996 Bankers Trust acquired Wolfensohn, a leading mergers and acquisition firm, bringing Paul Volcker, former chairman of the Federal Reserve, onto the board of Bankers Trust.[43] A year later, they followed this up by buying Alex. Brown & Sons in Baltimore to create a subsidiary investment bank/brokerage (BT Alex. Brown) that offered services in equities, high-yield securities, leveraged lending and M&A. The message for analysts on the deal warned investors that 'banks that have yet to develop fully an investment banking culture or acknowledged leadership in core investment banking capabilities face serious challenges in entering the equities business through acquisition or merger'.[44] This certainly seemed to reflect Deutsche Bank's experience with Morgan Grenfell. By 1997, therefore, Bankers Trust had quickly diversified itself into a range of investment banking and advisory businesses that increased its scale and scope in the US market.

But the deliberations in Frankfurt continued as other targets were examined. At the start of September 1998 Axel Wieandt and Tillmann Lauk of Corporate Strategy (SKPL) completed an 'outside-in' analysis of Lehman Brothers, which suggested that it could also be a good target for GCI, although this route would focus more closely on investment banking and fixed income business than the scheme for Bankers Trust.[45] Lehman had no presence in asset management so would not enhance Deutsche Bank's profile in this area. However, Wieandt and Lauk warned that 'the cultural challenges of possible integration are not to be underestimated'.[46] Lehman Brothers was the best option only if Deutsche Bank wanted to 'reposition itself as a bank with strong investment banking capabilities and credible US presence'. Lehman was also 'one of the last available targets in the US' valued at about $9.9–10.3 billion compared to market capitalisation of $4.7 billion. On the other hand, if Deutsche Bank sought to build global finance/wholesale banking instead, to aim at 'bulge bracket status', then Bankers Trust was the better target given its wider breadth of strengths in asset management, debt and investment banking areas.

The place of investment banking was still somewhat opaque, with a distinctly titled 'Investment Banking Division' (IBD) embedded within GCI. At the time, Wieandt and Lauk described the Investment Banking Division's strategy within GCI as confusing to stakeholders, threatening the loss of key staff and industry teams as well as goodwill.[47] The IBD really concerned only M&A and equity capital markets rather than a broad definition of investment banking. Meanwhile, the strategy of rolling out Deutsche Bank across Europe as a fully-fledged universal bank, aiming to be top five in each division, was ambitious, but also lacked focus. Deutsche Bank was particularly behind in asset management (number six in Europe and 14 in the world) and M&A/advisory (number 10 in Germany and 15 in the world).[48] The choice between Lehman and Bankers Trust was a choice between reinforcing the existing GCI or widening the scope of business to global finance/wholesale banking. Acquiring Lehman would bring the bank into the top five 'bulge bracket' in M&A, equity capital markets (ECM), investment grade debt, high-yield debt and mortgage-backed securities. Bankers Trust would bring the bank into the top five in asset management and custody and global top 10 in M&A and ECM. These options are illustrated in Table 7 below. The broader strategy was opted for, Lehman Brothers was dropped as a target and plans with Bankers Trust acceler-

Table 7: Strategic choices for target selection: ranking 1994–8.

	Deutsche Bank		Deutsche Bank + Lehman Brothers		Deutsche Bank + Bankers Trust	
	North America	Global	North America	Global	North America	Global
Mergers & Acquisitions	26	16	5	4	11	10
Equity	22	6	7	4	7	6
Investment Grade Debt	15	6	5	1	15	6
High Yield	36	6	7	4	9	5
Syndicated Lending	20	12	14	10	7	6
Mortgage-Backed Securities	14	8	1	4	14	8
Equity Research	14	n/a	9	16	14	n/a
Custody	n/a	7	n/a	7	4	4
Asset Management	n/a	Top 15	n/a	Top 15	n/a	Top 5

Source: 'Lehman Bros, Short Profile, For Discussion', Memo by SKPL/Corporate Strategy, 1 September 1998, HADB, V37/x501.

ated. It is interesting to speculate about how events would have unfolded a decade later if Lehman Brothers had been absorbed into Deutsche Bank, with Lehman's greater focus at the time on mortgage-backed securities.

As noted above, in April 1997 Bankers Trust had bought Alex. Brown, which increased its investment banking business. This business was the major source of pre-tax profits ($857 million in 1997 of an overall pre-tax profit of $1.239 billion).[49] In the wake of the emerging market financial crises the bank recorded a pre-tax loss of over $700 million in the third quarter of 1998. Bankers Trust's CEO Frank Newman, who was appointed in 1996, had moved the bank away from transaction banking, derivatives and financial engineering towards relationship management so that 'while proprietary trading accounted for 50% of total trading income in 1993, this has now been reduced to 25%'.[50] The risk in the bank's balance sheet was reduced somewhat but it remained high.

Breuer and Newman made contact in early October and Deutsche Bank announced its intention of taking over Bankers Trust on

Frank N. Newman was Deputy US Treasury Secretary in 1994–5 before becoming CEO of Bankers Trust in 1996. He negotiated the acquisition and then left the bank with a large severance package.

18 November 1998. Two rounds of due diligence identified the potential for large synergies.[51] Teams of senior staff travelled from Frankfurt to investigate the business of their Bankers Trust counterparts in New York and Baltimore. The conclusion was that the acquisition, code-named 'Project Circle', would provide the foundation for a credible Dual Focus strategy of focusing on corporate customers and retail banking in Germany and Europe alongside a focus on wholesale clients' global financial business in Europe, Germany, the Americas and Asia.[52] The initial investigations confirmed that Bankers Trust boasted 'a solid US wholesale presence and strong management team across business lines'. A week later, Deutsche Bank's business heads and teams had completed reviews of a range of activities.[53] Bankers Trust's Emerging Markets division had suffered considerable losses and had a much higher risk profile than Deutsche Bank, but all functional areas recommended moving ahead with the deal. The cost savings would come mainly from reducing staff by 5,700 (about half from IT/Operations and 20 per cent from Global Equities). On 24 November Hilmar Kopper called for an extraordinary meeting of the Supervisory Board: 'The only item on the agenda at the meeting is the approval of the Supervisory Board to acquire a 100 per cent interest by DB AG in BT.'[54]

Breuer recommended the deal to the five-hour extraordinary meeting of the Supervisory Board in Munich on Sunday evening 29 November 1998.[55] Breuer began with the purchase price of $10.1 billion in cash ($93.00 per share) to be paid in April or May 1999. The combined balance sheets of the merged bank would make it the largest in the world at $850 billion, leapfrogging Citigroup and UBS. Breuer based the case for approval on the strategic importance of gaining a leading position in Global Markets/Structured Finance, US equity issues and global equity research, as well as strengthening the leading position of Global Banking Services, Asset Management and Private Banking. He described several of Bankers Trust's recent high-profile mandates on either target or buyer side, including Walt Disney, ICI and Labatt Breweries. They also had a high-tech industrial group, which 'closes the gap created by exit of the Quattrone group'.[56] The main strategic benefit within Deutsche Bank would be for GCI.

Unlike the Morgan Grenfell acquisition, this time the plan was to maximise the synergies quickly with the aim of fully exploiting them by 2001. Breuer himself chaired the Integration Committee, although Ackermann played a key role. In discussion, Breuer reassured Supervisory Board members that the deal would not be an obstacle to further expansion in Europe, so there was no conflict with the Dual Focus strategy. Moreover, Bankers Trust employed only 60 people in Germany so there would be no direct synergy-related loss of jobs in the home market. Some members worried about the risks from the merger given the problems arising from other bank mergers. Breuer reassured them that the provisions made against risks were adequate and indeed were perceived by the Securities and Exchange Commission (SEC) as cautious and conservative. In the end, Breuer's proposal to acquire Bankers Trust was passed by a majority of the Supervisory Board. After the vote was concluded, Kopper announced that the Supervisory Board unanimously approved the acquisition of Crédit Lyonnais Belgium for $1 billion by written procedure, confirming the Dual Focus strategy.

The offer price for Bankers Trust was 20 per cent above the pre-acquisition market value and 2.4 times book value, 'making it the largest acquisition of a US banking company by a foreign firm', although the bank ranked only thirty-fifth in the US in terms of market capitalisation.[57] The final offer was $93 per share, entailing a goodwill charge of c. DM 9.4 billion ($5.6 billion) amortised over 15 years through the profit and loss accounts. The final goodwill was written off in October 2015. The total cost including 'in-the-money' options and restricted stock rights of management was $10.1 billion (just over DM 17 billion). The deal required $9 billion of financing of which 70 per cent was by Deutsche Bank AG Frankfurt and 30 per cent by Deutsche Bank AG New York branch. This financing included a capital increase of €3.3 billion for Deutsche Bank AG, sold mainly to institutional investors (about two thirds) in Germany and UK. In addition, both entities issued floating rate notes and senior debt. The deal was a 'reverse triangular merger' between Deutsche Bank AG, Bankers Trust Corporation and Circle Acquisition Corporation.[58] In the Annual Report Meeting on 18 March 1999, Breuer noted that the Bankers Trust acquisition was almost finalised. About 60 per cent of the purchase price had been raised on international capital markets, and there were plans to raise DM 4 billion from existing shareholders through pre-emptive rights and a further DM 2 billion placing equity without pre-emptive rights.[59] Breuer stressed the dual approach of European business and global business and was able to confirm the expansion into Belgium through the acquisition of Crédit Lyonnais Belgium as well as new initiatives in Spain, Greece and Poland at the same time as he confirmed progress on the Bankers Trust acquisition.

The proposed merger of Bankers Trust and Deutsche Bank was announced at the end of November 1998 but not completed until 4 June 1999. In the meantime, there was an elaborate integration process, including negotiations with US regulators and with Jewish representatives in the US and the World Jewish Council to acknowledge the bank's role during the Second World War. The role of Deutsche Bank under National Socialism had already been examined publicly in the bank's commissioned anniversary book from 1995, but concerns remained in New York about a German bank taking over a historic US company.[60]

5. Bankers Trust Acquisition: The Final Hurdles

The initial market response to the merger was not positive and Deutsche Bank's stock price dropped 2.2 per cent after the deal was announced at the end of November 1998. JP Morgan, for example, predicted, 'we believe that Deutsche's proposed acquisition of Bankers Trust is likely to be a value destroying deal' and identified 'the key risks as Deutsche's ability to manage the integration process successfully and the vulnerability of Bankers Trust's portfolio to further market corrections'.[61] JP Morgan also reminded its customers of 'Deutsche's poor track record on melding the Corporate and Investment Banking cultures' in DMG, and that Breuer had admitted that lessons would need to be learned from the Morgan Grenfell experience.[62] John Paulson, the leader of the famous Paulson and Co. hedge fund (which correctly predicted the US subprime housing crash and made $5 billion), wrote to Breuer directly 'to express our dissatisfaction' with the acquisition because 'Bankers Trust is the wrong partner. Bankers Trust is the weakest of the majors in either investment banking or commercial banking' and was barely profit-

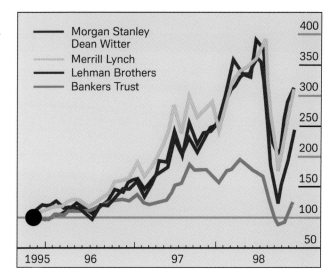

Underperforming banks. Share prices, 31 December 1995 = 100.

Source: 'The battle of the bulge bracket', *The Economist*, 26 November 1998.

able.[63] By 21 May 1999, the main ratings agencies had all downgraded Deutsche Bank (Moody's to AA3 from AA1; Standard & Poor's to AA negative outlook from AA+; Fitch IBCA to AA from AA+).[64]

The image above shows the weak performance of Bankers Trust compared with its peers from early 1997 onwards and also the dramatic impact of the emerging market financial crisis on all the bulge bracket banks in the US. Just as the takeover was finalised, in March 1999, Bankers Trust was fined $60 million for making false entries that diverted over $19 million in unclaimed cheques and other credits owed to customers onto the bank's own balance sheet to enhance financial performance for the three years leading up to 1996. In total 13 officers and employees resigned or were dismissed over the scandal.[65]

Deutsche Bank came to this second major international acquisition in a more deliberate way than it had with Morgan Grenfell. Thus, Deutsche Bank announced at the same time as the original offer that the Group's combined Global Markets, Global Equities and Global Corporates would be headed by Deutsche Bank executives, while Investment Banking and Global Institutional Services would be headed by executives from Bankers Trust.[66] In order to monitor Bankers Trust's OTC equities derivatives business closely, it was transferred to Deutsche Bank at the end of January 1999 on an 'arm's length' basis to limit the direct exposure of the bank's capital to this portfolio, using PricewaterhouseCoopers for price verification.[67]

The intention of being more deliberate and organised over this acquisition was also signalled by the establishment of an Integration Steering Committee (ISC) that was replaced by an Implementation Review Committee (IRC) at Management Board level in June 1999. A major priority was to retain key staff in the wake of 'aggressive poaching attempts from competitors'.[68] Table 8 shows the distribution of personnel as of April 1999. Bankers Trust had about 16,000 employees, of which 69 per cent were located in the Americas, and 4,000 in Europe (mainly in the UK). Deutsche Bank Group (excluding retail banking and CORE for comparability) had 34,500 employees, of which only 13 per cent were located in the Americas and 42 per cent in Germany.

Table 8: Staff numbers as of 12 April 1999.

	Bankers Trust	Deutsche Bank
Germany	0	14,500
UK/Ireland	3,500	6,500
Rest of Europe	500	4,500
Americas	11,000	4,500
Asia Pacific (excl. Australia)	1,000	4,500
TOTAL	16,000	34,500

Notes: Deutsche Bank figures exclude staff in retail banking and CORE. Australia excluded because it was not part of the acquisition (BT Australia was sold off). Source: Human Resources presentation to Integration Steering Committee Meeting, 15 April 1999, HADB V37/x657.

As in the case of Morgan Grenfell it was clear that individual talent was the key to successful global banking. Using a special bonus pool of close to $500 million to be paid over three years, retention letters were sent to 842 Bankers Trust employees to be signed and returned. Investment bankers were the largest single target for retention bonuses, comprising just under half of the total. The amounts reflected strong 'poaching' efforts by competitors and the risk of losing entire teams that would make it difficult to keep Bankers Trust operations profitable. The other major departments were Equities (22 per cent) and Global Markets (15 per cent). These retention bonuses were on top of the $231 million paid out as the normal 1999 pro rata bonus.[69] The effort appeared successful since at the end of August 1999 it was reported that 'far less than 10 per cent of the targeted 500 Bankers Trust key players have left the bank so far' although it was anticipated that more would leave. The specific Bankers Trust retention pool was then closed.[70]

The Implementation Review Committee was tasked to deliver DM 1.7 billion in savings from cost reductions and headcount reduction (targeted at a reduction of 5,500 by 2001) as well as DM 2.5 billion in Group Restructuring begun in January 1998 (including a reduction in headcount across the group of 8,600 by 2001).[71] As the months passed, it proved challenging to meet net headcount targets as layoffs were offset by new hires (particularly in CORE and Private Banking). By November 1999 there had been 5,800 terminations and 3,300 new hires. Nevertheless, in the first week of December 1999, Breuer announced that 'recognizing the fact that the overall integration of Bankers Trust went remarkably smoothly and successfully and that all divisions benefitting from it are meanwhile changing gear towards business-as-usual, I think it is now appropriate to terminate the managerial structure of the IS/IRC committees'.[72]

Meanwhile, there were efforts to try to engage the workforces of the two banks, for example through regular integration newsletters. Three months before closing day, Human Resources at Deutsche Bank hired Towers Perrin to undertake a 'cultural assessment of each former company, separated by geography and business line, to help understand the key issues the "new Deutsche Bank" faces'.[73] The methodology was interviews with executives and senior managers, focus groups from each bank (separately) aiming for a 3–4 per cent sample size overall.[74] The outcome was quite negative, finding that 'many employees are still confused about the logic of the deal', 'employees in both companies have a poor and inaccurate perception of employees in the other company' and '[e]mployees everywhere feel that clear, united and visible leadership from the top of Deutsche Bank is lacking'.[75] Furthermore, 'staff in both companies perceive big gaps between what is said and what is being done'. On the other hand, 'Most Deutsche Bank clients do not feel strongly impacted by the acquisition, Bankers Trust's clients have mixed feelings'.[76] The Management Board proposed a range of communication and engagement initiatives including a Senior Leadership Forum and an integration review conference scheduled for December 1999.[77]

As part of the terms of Deutsche Bank's takeover of Bankers Trust, the US authorities required the bank to confront its role during the Holocaust of the Second World War. The deal came at a time when other German companies had taken over or merged with US firms, including Daimler-Benz with Chrysler and Bertelsmann with Random House, which raised public attention concerning the role of German business during the war. Alan Hevesi, the financial Comptroller of New York City and a Democrat politician, pledged to stop the deal unless Deutsche Bank paid compensation. The controversy prompted German Chancellor Gerhard Schröder to announce the 'Foundation Initiative of German Industry: Remembrance, Responsibility and Future' in February 1999.[78] This was the official route for German business and government to provide some financial recompense for forced and slave labour and other outstanding claims under the Nazi regime.[79]

In order to compensate forced labourers of the Nazi era, (from right) Federal Chancellor Gerhard Schröder, Deutsche Bank Management Board Spokesman Rolf-E. Breuer and Thyssen-Krupp management board head Gerhard Cromme announced to establish the Foundation Initiative of the German businesses on 16 February 1999.

The Deutsche Bank management were committed to being as open as possible about the bank's history. In late 1997 Deutsche Bank appointed a commission of independent historians to investigate the bank's wartime gold transactions.[80] They reported in July 1998, before the merger was announced. In February 1999, in the midst of the final negotiations with the US authorities, Manfred Pohl, the head of Deutsche Bank archives, released fresh evidence that the bank had helped to finance the construction of Auschwitz concentration camp.[81]

In order to defuse the issue, Breuer was due to meet Hevesi in mid-April 1999, but in the end it was Schmitz who attended the Executive Monitoring Committee chaired by Hevesi.[82] Schmitz expressed the bank's firm commitment to the 'Remembrance, Responsibility and Future' initiative and convinced the Committee of the bank's commitment to recognising its history. Breuer followed up two weeks later to make this commitment in writing and Hevesi and the World Jewish Council withdrew their objections to the acquisition of Bankers Trust on 5 May.[83] In the general reshuffle, Frank Newman was shown the door. After admitting publicly that 'the role originally envisioned for me will not be necessary', he left the bank with a large settlement package, reportedly amounting to about $100 million.[84] The Federal Reserve gave its formal approval at 23.30 on 20 May 1999.[85] The final legal and financial details were concluded on 4 June 1999, at last fulfilling Deutsche Bank's long-term dream of a major presence in the US market.

The acquisition of Bankers Trust closed on 4 June 1999 and was celebrated with a live video link between Frankfurt and New York.

6. Conclusions

In 2012, at his last annual general meeting, Josef Ackermann recalled proudly: 'At the end of the 1990s, more than 20 banks around the globe wanted to advance to be one of the five best investment banks in the world. Deutsche Bank is the only non-U.S. financial institution to have achieved this objective.'[86] Certainly, the acquisition of Bankers Trust was a major step along this path. Kobrak's history of Deutsche Bank in the US finishes in 1999, and he concluded that 'the acquisition [of Bankers Trust] brought the bank a platform, an identity, an innovative spirit, and a perception on the street that it was committed to being cutting edge'.[87] In the longer term, the bank's US operations may be judged more harshly and there was some controversy at the time about whether Bankers Trust was a good target given its weak balance sheet, its reputation for weak compliance and expensive overheads.

It is clear that the management tried to learn lessons from its adventure in the London market with Morgan Grenfell. The bank's strategy for the American market took some years to develop; from growing organically, building through targeted team hires, partial equity participation and finally acquisition of an entire firm. The range of target banks was carefully compared to determine which fitted best with Deutsche Bank's Dual Focus strategy and competencies. Compared to Morgan Grenfell, the analysis of the business areas in Bankers Trust was much deeper and involved a wider group of senior staff who personally attested to the strengths and weaknesses before the final decision was made. But there is also a sense of time running out and competitive pressures prompting quick decisions in the end. The mergers and acquisition wave prompted by regulatory changes and financial innovation in the US clearly created challenges as well as opportunities for a large German bank with a relatively unprofitable domestic market and there was a sense of urgency to find a target quickly before they were all snapped up by other banks.

Deutsche Bank's ambition to acquire scale and scope in the US through acquisition was certainly shared by other European banks. In 2000 two of Deutsche Bank's early targets were taken over by Swiss banks for even more than the Bankers Trust deal; UBS bought PaineWebber in 2000 for $10.8 billion ($73.50 per share or a 47 per

Table 9: Major purchases of investment banks or broker dealers in 1999–2000.

	Target	Acquirer	Value (USD billion)	Premium (%)
July 2000	PaineWebber	UBS	15.8 (10.8)*	52 (47)*
Aug 2000	DLJ	Credit Suisse Group	11.5 (+1.9)	36
1999	Paribas	BNP	5.9	n/a
1999	Safra Republic	HSBC	5.1	62
1999	Hambrecht & Quist	Chase	1.2	22
1999	CIE Belge	BNP	1.1	23
2000	JP Morgan	Chase	38.6	23

Source: Memo for Management Board discussion, 19 September 2000, HADB V38/x6. Note: *figures in brackets from SEC filing, others from the original Deutsche Bank memorandum.

cent premium over the market price). In the same year Credit Suisse bought DLJ for $11.5 billion. Table 9 shows some other high-profile acquisitions noted by the Management Board in 1999 and 2000.

The Bankers Trust deal must also be viewed within the context of new leadership in the bank with Breuer replacing Kopper as Spokesman of the Management Board in May 1997, and the reorganisation into five functional divisions that brought corporate and investment banking together in GCI. Moreover, the management remained committed to its Dual Focus Europe/Global strategy despite spending over $10 billion on a US bank. Even as the funds were being raised to complete the purchase of Bankers Trust, Breuer was planning the merger with domestic rival Dresdner Bank.

IV. The Failed Merger with Dresdner Bank, 1999–2000

The rash of bank mergers across Europe and North America in the 1990s sparked a large academic literature debating the advantages and disadvantages both for the resulting bank's own performance and for financial stability on a systemic level.[1] Overall, the verdict at the time was that the measurable benefits were at best mixed, although CEO compensation tended to increase. Creating value from a merger required so-called 'synergies', which in practice meant cutting staff and overlapping competencies to reduce overcapacity. But achieving synergies was a huge managerial task that could be costly in the short term and the benefits were often rather slow to materialise. Despite the lack of clear evidence about the advantages, bankers continued to search for mergers and the industry was increasingly consolidated, particularly in the US as regulatory barriers were relaxed. Some banks found comfort in size to avoid being taken over themselves, while others sought to increase their balance sheets as financial innovation created new opportunities for leverage. Deutsche Bank was a prominent player in this global game, but it also had experience of the risks. The lessons from Morgan Grenfell were that crossing cultures was difficult and that it was important to have good knowledge of the target's competencies. A merger within its home market of Germany promised to avoid these challenges.

The failed merger with Dresdner Bank in 2000 had two main outcomes. Firstly, it undermined fundamentally the power and influence of the Spokesman of the Management Board Rolf-E. Breuer, who led the campaign. Secondly, it reinforced the dominance and power of the group of high-flying investment bankers in London who helped to block the merger. The collapse of the merger therefore marked a crucial turning point in Deutsche Bank's domestic and international position. Deutsche Bank had to find other solutions for its retail banking, such as moving more of its customers to online platforms. The attempt to make a step change in the German market came at a time of reorientation of the bank after the creation of Deutsche Morgan Grenfell (DMG) in London and the acquisition of Bankers Trust in New York as well as restructuring within the bank in Germany. It therefore reflected internal pressures for change as well as a response to the external environment.

The last-minute reversal was viewed as a victory for the investment banking stars in London over the bank's Frankfurt leadership and a signal of the eclipse of the German business by the bank's global focus. In its analysis of the debacle, for example, *Süddeutsche Zeitung* reported that Edson Mitchell's 'success and power were enough to bring down the merger with Dresdner Bank'.[2] The article reported: 'From London, the securities stars said it was just an expensive merger to reorganise retail banking business. Under no circumstances would they join forces with the people from Kleinwort Benson, the alleged jewel of Dresdner Bank.'[3] This victory enhanced the power and reputation of the 'investment banking clique.' This diagnosis of the reasons for the collapse of the deal is somewhat ironic since Breuer's aim for the merger was to spin off the low-margin retail business of the bank in Germany in order to focus on investment banking and other financial services. A closer look reveals a more complex story of mismanagement and misapprehension in Frankfurt as well as in London.

1. First Attempt

Dresdner Bank was the second largest German bank with a long tradition, but it lagged far behind Deutsche Bank both in terms of size and international profile. Dresdner was 21.7 per cent owned by Allianz and it was between Deutsche Bank and Allianz that the terms of the merger were forged.[4] Allianz viewed the deal as a way to increase its access to retail customers for its insurance products and increase the scale of mutual fund management along the lines of its bancassurance model, which focused on co-operative sales partnerships rather than providing banking and insurance from within one firm.[5] The aim was to get rid of the low-margin retail banking business and focus on investment, corporate and high-net-value customer banking as well as increasing scale to allow the new bank to become the second largest European bank and to compete globally. The ability of Allianz to sell its products through the retail customer base as well as increasing its scale in asset management was critical to their acceptance of any merger scheme.

Retail banking had long been a challenge to Deutsche Bank's overall strategy because of its high cost base, including physical property of branches and high staff costs, and low margin for most of the customers on average or lower incomes who used a narrow range of retail products. In 1995, the launch of Bank 24 (see Chapter V) marked an effort to reduce costs by moving customers to more efficient online services, but more radical proposals ensued as part of the reimagining of Deutsche Bank. For example, at the end of March 1998 Management Board member Tessen von Heydebreck proposed a radical idea to spin off the whole retail business of the bank while keeping high-wealth private clients.[6] The margins on retail were low compared to the private banking clients who could be linked to other parts of the bank's businesses through their investments. A separate legal entity for retail banking, initially wholly owned by Deutsche Bank, could streamline the management and cut costs through merging branches and other efficiencies, particularly in labour costs. The goal was to create an economically viable retail bank with a return on equity of 25 per cent, in line with later targets for the bank as a whole. An important benefit of the separate legal entity would be the ability to impose new contracts on staff that focused on performance and sales and that 'the new retail bank should not be a member of the employers' association'.[7] In the end this proposal did not go ahead, but the question remained how to move Deutsche Bank out of low-margin retail and more firmly into an investment bank model such as Morgan Stanley or Merrill Lynch.

The German retail banking market, with its combination of savings banks, credit co-operatives, postal banking offices and private sector commercial banks offering retail services was overcrowded, and in the mid-1990s there were calls for consolidation. If Deutsche Bank's retail business could gain a greater market share it could be more viable, so attention turned to the potential for combining the retail operations of Deutsche Bank with another bank to gain scale. This planning took place in a general environment of consolidation in the German banking system, which is still characterised by high competition, low prices for products and services and a branch density that makes for high fixed costs. In the 1990s three pillars of German banking – private sector banks, co-operative banks and savings banks – also competed with the state-owned Post Office savings bank for low-margin retail business. These features meant that the return on equity in retail banking was generally low. During the 1990s and early 2000s there was a strong process of consolidation so that the number of banks fell from 4,177 to 2,160 between 1991 and 2003, mainly due to M&A among savings banks and among co-operatives.[8] The big commercial banks also sought to achieve cost efficiencies through M&A but the process of blending the banks' interests often proved intractable. One example was the HypoVereinsbank that was created by a merger of Bayerische Hypotheken- und Wechsel-Bank and Bayerische Vereinsbank in 1998. Two years later, it acquired Bank Austria in Vienna, and it was then taken over itself by the Italian bank UniCredit SpA in 2005. But Commerzbank, Dresdner and Deutsche Bank, with their wider portfolio of core services, struggled to take part in the consolidation wave.

In August 1999 Deutsche Bank finalised plans to merge Deutsche Bank 24 (DB24), which was to start operating on 1 September 1999, with Dresdner's entire retail banking business to prepare it for an IPO within three years.[9] The rationale was that both partners could benefit from a joint venture to secure customers on a larger scale to distribute other products like insurance or retail asset management. A separate management board would be responsible for maximising these links, and the joint venture would soon become an attractive prospect as the market leader in Germany with a significantly higher market share. As always, valuation was difficult to pin down: at the last minute Axel Wieandt of Corporate Strategy (SKPL) feared that Dresdner's valuation of its retail business as a standalone concern was inflated (more realistically DM 2 billion rather than DM 3.6 billion).[10] But Deutsche Bank still thought the merger could be salvaged if Dresdner transferred all of its retail business to Deutsche Bank 24 in exchange for shares. The joint venture would then be 65–70 per cent owned by Deutsche Bank (Dresdner, meanwhile, hoped to retain 35–40 per cent of the shares). A key part of the deal was how partnership agreements for selling insurance to retail customers would be shared between Allianz and Deutsche Bank's insurance subsidiary, Deutscher Herold. Allianz would expect wide access to agree to the scheme, and this could require Deutsche Bank to sell or transfer Deutscher Herold to Allianz. Unfortunately, with only a 74.77 per cent share, the disposal of the insurance company was not in Deutsche Bank's control. The other shareholders were older members of the family that had previously owned the company, and it was expected that they would be reluctant to sell. So, there were still many obstacles to overcome within a tight timescale for the management boards of each bank due to be held on 21 September.[11] What would be the balance of ownership between Deutsche Bank and Dresdner and what would it take to get Allianz to agree to the scheme? It seems that, at this stage, negotiations were suspended by Dresdner. A week later, in Washington at the IMF/World Bank summit, Bernhard Walter, the Dresdner Spokesman, was quoted as asserting: 'we will not merge. Whether the institutions fit, is not the question. We both don't want it.'[12] Dresdner then entered into merger negotiations with HypoVereinsbank, Germany's third largest bank, in which Allianz also held 18 per cent of shares. The view of the press and analysts was that this partnership would not deliver the internationalisation strategy needed by Dresdner.[13] The first attempt was over.

2. Second Attempt

In a later interview, Paul Achleitner recalled that the next stage began through his long-standing collegial relationship with Ulrich Cartellieri. As head of Goldman Sachs in Germany from 1994 to 1999, Achleitner had helped Deutsche Bank with the Bankers Trust acquisition and he and Cartellieri had also begun to discuss a merger of Dresdner and Deutsche Bank. The time wasn't right at that point, but when in September 1999 it became clear that Achleitner would become CFO at Allianz from the start of 2000, Cartellieri came back to him.[14] Within two months, Breuer had opened negotiations again, this time directly with his counterpart at Allianz, Henning Schulte-Noelle. Thus began six months of negotiations that exposed publicly the internal conflicts about the direction of Deutsche Bank's future and brought about the downfall of Breuer's influence at the bank.

In the post-mortem of the debacle in April 2000, Breuer set out the chronology of events for the more ambitious but equally doomed merger, which began on 11 November 1999 with a conversation between Breuer and Henning Schulte-Noelle, CEO of Allianz.[15] There were two proposals: merging only the retail businesses or embarking on a full merger of the two banks. A week later the two had a telephone conversation and agreed to set up a working group under the leadership of Axel Wieandt of Deutsche Bank and Paul Achleitner to identify alternatives. The very next day, 19 November 1999, Wieandt and Achleitner devised a deal with three components:

1. Allianz would receive DWS (without DIT, the asset management company of Dresdner Bank) and Deutscher Herold and shares in Deutsche Bank 24 against shares in Dresdner Bank.
2. Dresdner's retail business would be brought into Deutsche Bank 24 and there would follow an IPO for the new Deutsche Bank 24 to spin it out of the new combined bank.
3. There would be a full merger of Deutsche Bank and Dresdner Bank.

Clearly the motivation for the merger was to create the conditions to sell off the retail part of Deutsche Bank's operations and also to divest itself of the insurance business. DWS was/is the retail asset management group within Deutsche Bank while DIT was the investment trust business of Dresdner Bank. The new deal was more ambitious than the summer plans and would leave the commercial, investment, asset management and corporate banking activities as the main parts of the 'New Bank'.

At the start of December, Breuer and Achleitner spoke on the sidelines of a Siemens banking conference and this was followed up on 11 December 1999 when Schulte-Noelle and Breuer had a substantive discussion setting out:

1. The strategic importance of DWS and DIT for Allianz and 'Deutsche Bank New'.
2. The long-term competitiveness of Deutsche Bank 24.
3. The strategic importance of Eurohypo and Deutsche Hyp[16] for Allianz.
4. The distribution of insurance in Italy and Spain.
5. The external perception of the influence of Allianz.
6. The reconciliation of the strategic interests of Deutsche Bank and Allianz.

A few days later Deutsche Bank set up a wider working group of 12, divided into a functional team and a divisional team representing all Group Divisions (except Asset Management) although only the functional team members were named at this point. The slow engagement with divisional heads in Global Corporates and Institutions (GCI), Deutsche Bank's investment banking arm, was to prove fatal to the deal. Through the rest of December and into mid-January there were five working group meetings with Allianz to discuss the structure of the transaction. Allianz's first structural proposal was discussed on 13 January 2000. The next day Breuer and Schulte-Noelle discussed on the phone several points that still had to be resolved, including comparing DWS with DIT, valuation differences, substitution of payment in shares by cash for part of the deal. They then tasked the working group with drawing up a basic agreement and valuation ranges.

The integration into 'Deutsche Bank New' was discussed on 19 January, but this meeting related mainly to accounting issues. The next day the working party discussed valuation and the gap was significant: the evaluation of the relevant Deutsche Bank companies by Allianz was €5.3–5.8 billion, while Deutsche Bank valued them at €10.3–12.4 billion (each for 100 per cent). Wieandt and Achleitner spoke on 23 January about the mechanics of the deal including more payment to Deutsche Bank in cash rather than Dresdner Bank shares and how the joint venture would be structured. Asset Management remained an open question, as did the inclusion of Deutsche Bank's Italian financial advisory subsidiary Finanza & Futuro (F & F). A follow-up meeting with KPMG confirmed the impact of the planned merger on core capital and the resulting goodwill. The working party had two more meetings to discuss the plan in principle and the question of valuation, and then at the end of January 2000 Breuer and Achleitner spoke about the state of the negotiations in Davos. The discussions had been underway secretly for almost three months and there

Rolf-E. Breuer was Spokesman of Deutsche Bank's Management Board from 1997 to 2002 and had been a member since 1985. From 2002 to 2006, he was Chairman of the Supervisory Board. He spent his entire career at Deutsche Bank, beginning with his banking apprenticeship in 1956.

were still many outstanding issues. However, the integration of Dresdner Kleinwort Benson (DKB) with GCI had not yet loomed large in the negotiations.

On 31 January, Wieandt wrote to Breuer questioning whether the discussions should be terminated given the ongoing disagreement over valuation. He also noted that in particular GCI and Corporates and Real Estate (CORE) had to present a strong willingness to integrate and a conclusive integration concept.[17] Clearly the integration of the investment banking, corporate and asset management activities of the two banks was crucial to the final outcome, which was a larger, internationally competitive investment bank. If there was no clear vision as to how this would be achieved, the deal on retail banking would not achieve its goal. The disputes over valuation also indicated the gulf between Dresdner's view of the deal as a merger of equals and Deutsche Bank's implicit sense that this was a strategic takeover executed to transform the shape and business model of Deutsche Bank itself. Wieandt's warning was not heeded and the working group meanwhile continued to discuss details in the basic agreement. Achleitner and Wieandt continued their negotiations of the valuation, plans for the IPO and corporate governance of Deutsche Bank 24. Breuer, Tessen von Heydebreck and Herbert Walter (CEO of Deutsche Bank 24) went to Munich to make a presentation about Deutsche Bank 24 to Allianz representatives.

On 3 and 4 February 2000 the Allianz management board approved the transaction on the basis of a valuation of the relevant Deutsche Bank companies of €5.15–6.25 billion (excluding F & F) so they had widened the range of their valuation, but the lower bound had not shifted significantly. Achleitner called on Wieandt a few days later suggesting that some of the open questions could be resolved. This included the contribution ratio from Dresdner Bank Retail (35 per cent) and Deutsche Bank 24 (65 per cent) that met Deutsche Bank's original concept. Allianz agreed that F & F should be taken out of the basic agreement if no agreement could be reached on the purchase price. By this time Allianz assessed the Deutsche Bank companies within an even wider range of €4.9–6.4 billion while Deutsche Bank's assessment had been reduced to €7.8–8.4 billion. The gap was narrowing, but still persisted.

Telephone calls between Bernhard Walter, Breuer and Schulte-Noelle failed to overcome the impasse over valuation and Walter called on Breuer on Tuesday 8 February to ask if he was still interested in a merger.[18] The discussions then turned to governance. Breuer later reported that a co-spokesmen model 'was absolutely necessary as a transitional solution for successful integration' so it was agreed that Breuer and Walter would share the leadership of the new bank.[19] On the Friday, they spoke again and Walter was more positive about the merger, although his board colleagues had not yet been involved and not all would transfer to the management board of the new bank. In the final format, Dresdner was to have six management board members and Deutsche Bank eight, with plans to reduce the number to four and six respectively by 2002.[20] Meanwhile, talks between Dresdner Bank and HypoVereinsbank had not yet been broken off, but Walter did not advocate this combination and Albrecht Schmidt, the spokesman of HypoVereinsbank's management board, had also spoken out against their merger. The same day, Achleitner spoke with Wieandt and agreed on the open points to be settled between Breuer and Schulte-Noelle or within the working group. The first meeting of a formal working group between Dresdner and Deutsche Bank took place on 13 February to discuss the basic agreement, three months after talks with Allianz had started. Subsequent meetings debated the balance of shareholding between Dresdner and Deutsche Bank in the new bank as well as the name and colour of the corporate identity. Breuer, Schulte-Noelle and Walter met in Munich on 24 February to clarify the remaining points including the valuation of Deutsche Bank companies at €7.1 billion.

The Deutsche Bank Management Board unanimously approved the proposed merger on 26 February, but they also agreed that no divisional board members were to be informed until the beginning of March 2000.[21] The Management Board specifically approved the sale of 75.1 per cent of the shares of Deutscher Herold and the DWS Group, 70 per cent of F & F and 49 per cent of the shares of Deutsche Bank 24 to Allianz. Since the first attempt, Deutsche Bank had managed to increase its control of Deutscher Herold. Allianz would then be the preferred insurance sales partner for 'Deutsche Bank New' and Deutsche Bank 24, and DWS would be the preferred product supplier for retail asset management. A teleconference with Allianz and Dresdner Bank representatives was held the next day in order to clarify some of the remaining questions in the basic agreement, including the valuation of F & F, the involvement of Allianz and Deutsche Bank 24 as well as the financing commitment.

The Dresdner management board then approved the merger on 1 March and Morgan Stanley Dean Witter were commissioned to prepare a fairness opinion and a due diligence report within a week.[22] Breuer and Walter met again on 3 March, invitations were sent out for an extraordinary meeting of the Deutsche Bank Supervisory Board and the two sides began to exchange information. Everything seemed on track. The communications and press team at Deutsche Bank began to prepare to make the deal public on 9 March, but at 11 p.m. on 6 March, *Bild-Zeitung* broke the story early online followed quickly by reporting from *Manager Magazin*.[23] The initial market reaction was positive and the share price of all three participants jumped significantly. Dresdner and Deutsche Bank quickly issued their own press releases the next morning confirming that discussions on closer co-operation between the two banks were at an advanced stage. The final terms of the basic agreement were agreed by teleconference among the three participants.

The document setting out the principles of the agreement stated at the very start that the two banks had agreed to a model of 'a merger between equal partners'.[24] The goal was to realise this partnership as a 'strategic advantage' to strengthen competitiveness on a global platform, increase profitability and be more attractive to customers. The new bank would thereby play an active role in the consolidation of the German banking sector, particularly in retail banking. The specification of a merger among equals meant that the agreement was not a takeover and that both parties would have shares in the new entity, even if not on a strictly balanced basis. It is clear in this case that Deutsche Bank and Dresdner viewed this commitment differently. There was evidently something of a myth about 'equals' from the outset since Dresdner was considerably smaller and this was reflected in the anticipated distribution of shares in 'Deutsche Bank New' in the document, with a range of 60–64 per cent for Deutsche Bank and 36–40 per cent for Dresdner.

Breuer presented the merger to a three and a half hour extraordinary meeting of the Supervisory Board on the afternoon of 8 March, although by this time they all had a clear idea of the deal from the newspapers.[25] The chairs of the supervisory boards of Dresdner and Deutsche Bank had already met in the morning.[26] Breuer first described the sale to Allianz of 75.1 per cent of Deutsche Bank's insurance business (held in Versicherungsholding der Deutschen Bank AG), all of DWS and 70 per cent of Finanza & Futuro. Allianz would pay cash for DWS at a price of at least 4 per cent of assets under management at the end of 2000 (about €3.8 billion on 1999 basis). Allianz would also acquire 49 per cent of Deutsche Bank 24 (including Deutsche Bank Bauspar AG) at a valuation range of €2.7–2.8 billion. Dresdner would subsequently transfer its entire retail operations to Deutsche Bank 24, thus diluting Allianz's stake in the new retail bank to 32 per cent. The newly expanded Deutsche Bank 24 would be a subsidiary jointly governed by Allianz and Deutsche Bank New.[27] An IPO of the combined retail bank was planned within three years and Allianz had the option of acquiring a majority within six months after the IPO. At the end of the full merger of Deutsche and Dresdner Bank (expected on 1 July 2000), old Deutsche Bank shareholders would hold about 62 per cent of the total shares of 'Deutsche Bank New' (+/- 2 per cent). At the same time, Allianz and Deutsche Bank agreed to reduce their own existing reciprocal shareholdings to below 5 per cent. The deal thus allowed Allianz to expand its insurance operations and distribution channels and Deutsche Bank to concentrate on high-value private and corporate clients, GCI, Asset Management and Global Technology and Services (GTS). 'Deutsche Bank New' would be Europe's second largest bank in terms of a pro-forma market capitalisation of about €80 billion, allowing it to compete in the consolidated global investment banking environment. Figure 23 shows the impact of the planned merger of Deutsche and Dresdner Bank on the involved entities.

There was no mention at the Supervisory Board meeting of Dresdner Kleinwort Benson (DKB), which soon became a major stumbling block. But Breuer did highlight

Figure 23: Group structures before and after the planned merger between Deutsche and Dresdner Bank.

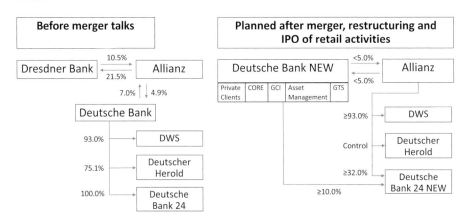

Source: Presentation 'Merger of Deutsche and Dresdner Bank – International Analyst Meeting', 9 March 2000, HADB, SG8/35-1.

that the merger would strengthen the bank's position in the European M&A/global equities business 'especially in the UK'.[28] Cost synergies estimated at €2.9 billion p.a. from 2003 would require about 16,500 staff cuts, 85 per cent in Germany. The gains were mainly in combining the IT business processing (estimated at €1 billion) and synergies in private and business customers and CORE (€0.5 billion). The one-off cost of the restructuring would be slightly more than €3 billion. Additional goodwill was set at €9.7 billion.

The deal was always subject to the approval of the management and supervisory boards of the participants and the global supervisory authorities, 'in particular the EU Commission'. Confirming Deutsche Bank's dominance, the new bank would be called Deutsche Bank AG, although a new logo in Dresdner's trademark green was being designed. Deutsche Bank's Supervisory Board discussion mostly focused on the cost synergies and staff cuts.

3. The Deal Unwinds

The joint announcement of the merger was made the following morning, 9 March, in a press conference with the tag line 'European Champion with Global Platform'.[29] Meanwhile the press had been speculating about job losses, reporting a concerned statement by Margret Mönig-Raane, chair of the HBV trade union and a member of Deutsche Bank's Supervisory Board. Initial market euphoria about the merger quickly turned to pessimism. Most crucially, the *Financial Times* reported on the day of the press conference that Deutsche Bank was considering closing Dresdner Kleinwort Benson (DKB).[30] Sources 'close to the situation' were quoted as saying, 'It might be sold, but

Deutsche Bank Management Board Spokesman Rolf-E. Breuer (left) and Dresdner Bank management board spokesman Bernhard Walter at a 9 March 2000 press conference in Frankfurt.

it is more likely to be torched' although a decision had not yet been taken. Breuer was forced to respond at the joint press conference and was drawn into making a very forceful rebuttal, describing Dresdner Kleinwort Benson (DKB) as 'a precious jewel and a valuable addition to the investment portfolio of Deutsche Bank. […] We can only win if we keep this jewel.'[31] This turned out to be ill-advised hyperbole since the decision was soon taken that DKB could not be integrated fully into the new bank. To pour salt on the wounds of Dresdner, the *Financial Times* also characterised the deal as a takeover rather than a 'merger of equals'.[32]

The reaction of market analysts was also negative and the share price of both banks fell after an initial post-announcement bounce. The internal report of Deutsche Bank on market reactions on 14 March 2000 took an upbeat line on the change of rating by most analysts from buy to sell, blaming it on the short-term execution risks but asserting that the market believed the bank was 'doing the strategically right thing' for the longer term.[33] Reports of 'frictions' between management teams in GCI and DKB made the prospects for integration unclear to the market. Analysts found the synergy targets too optimistic and the goodwill too high at almost €10 billion.[34] Meanwhile, the share price kept falling, particularly as the struggle over the future of DKB continued. By 5 April 2000, when the deal was finally called off, Deutsche Bank's shares had fallen 17 per cent since the announcement on 9 March, and Dresdner shares had fallen 16 per cent in the same period.[35] On 17 March, there was a spike in trading of Deutsche Bank shares to 32 million from an average of about 2–3 million per day. Public opinion was also negative about the merger, mainly because of anticipated loss of retail banking jobs and changes in branch services. Importantly, they did not view the plan as a 'merger of equals', but, rather, as a takeover of Dresdner by Deutsche Bank.[36]

As the mood in the market soured, a joint meeting of the management boards of Dresdner and Deutsche Bank was called and on 14 March both supervisory boards approved the outline merger proposal.

Breuer presented the scheme in two parts to his Supervisory Board: first, the decision on the merger to form the new Deutsche Bank AG, and, second, approval of the deal with Allianz, Deutsche Bank and Dresdner about the transfers of business that would allow the deal to take place.[37] Members raised concerns mainly about the treatment of employees and about the loss of the branch-based business. Employee representatives met outside the meeting for 10 minutes before the two proposals were put to a vote. Unusually for the Supervisory Board, neither decision was unanimous, but both passed on the basis of majority with several members abstaining.[38]

In a later letter, Bernhard Walter claimed that Deutsche Bank first proposed the sale of Dresdner Kleinwort Benson (DKB) on 14 March 2000, the day the two supervisory boards approved the merger package.[39] Certainly, planning moved quickly. By 16 March Josef Ackermann (then leading GCI) had prepared a draft discussion paper on potential options for DKB in London.[40] The paper noted that Deutsche Bank's Global Markets and Global Equities were strong enough to take a leading position in Europe without integrating DKB, and DKB would add almost nothing to the bank's strength in the US market (where Deutsche Bank had just acquired Bankers Trust). On the other hand, DKB's expertise in M&A advisory and Primary Equity would be useful and could be retained.

Table 10: Comparison of DKB and GCI.

	DKB	GCI
Net Income Before Tax (full year 1999)	€983 million	€2,325 million
Contribution to total bank income (1 January to 30 September 1999)	33%	54%
Total Headcount*	6,987	14,467
Global Markets	1,052	2,825
Global Equities	1,295	2,300
Global Corporate Finance/Global Investment Banking	823	3,825
Global Finance/Global Banking	663	1,727

Notes: Total bank income calculated differently for each bank means figures are approximate.

* Headcount for DKB is year end 1999, for GCI year end February 2000.

Source: GCI Integration Preparation, Background Material, 22 March 2000, HADB, V27/x7.

In a comparison of DKB and GCI, it was clear that GCI was bigger both in absolute terms and in terms of the contribution to the revenue of their respective banks. Table 10 shows some of the indicators used by GCI at the time. Full-scale integration would result in about 1,600 job losses and potential defections of key staff in areas where Deutsche Bank was strong, so would be value-destroying, particularly at a time when the integration of Bankers Trust was underway. The report asserted that the synergy targets in the merger plans were too optimistic. On the other hand, selling off DKB's Global Markets and Global Equities businesses as independent units would raise funds to reinvest in the US or elsewhere. Selling all of DKB would save integration costs, but also risked strengthening their competitors. If DKB was sold as a sum of its parts, it could be valued at as much as €6.5 billion, or about 10 times earnings. Moreover, there were potential buyers in the market, including Commerzbank, whose spokesman of the management board, Martin Kohlhaussen, had already contacted Deutsche Bank to express his interest. Chase Manhattan Bank was also considered a likely customer as it sought an expansion platform in Europe. To execute a sale either on a 'cherry-picking' or an entire basis, 'speed, speed and speed matters most' to avoid major defections.[41] The next day Edson Mitchell and Gurdon Wattles (the chief of staff for GCI) in London revised the valuation and agreed that full integration of DKB should be ruled out.[42] But cherry-picking would only be possible if the DKB Global Markets and DKB Global Equities could be carved out as separate legal entities.

At the first meeting of the joint Integration Committee on 17 March, Breuer announced the resignation of Michael Dobson, whose duties were taken over by Sir Robert Smith, who reported to Josef Ackermann.[43] Dobson had led the bank's asset management business and been with the bank for 10 years, since the acquisition of Morgan Grenfell. Breuer also backtracked somewhat on his earlier statement about DKB, commenting that he had been misquoted in the press that morning and that all options were open with regard to the integration process. This was not quite the same as asserting that DKB was a jewel to be kept, but somewhat better than the *Financial Times* report that he had remarked after a meeting of the German–British Chamber of Industry and Commerce in London that Deutsche Bank 'would consider offers for

Dresdner Kleinwort Benson'.[44] Discussion of DKB was postponed to the next meeting to allow Ackermann and Leonhard ('Lenny') Fischer, the head of Dresdner's investment banking, to consult.

Meanwhile, GCI commissioned Morgan Stanley Dean Witter (MSDW) to consider the full or partial sale of DKB.[45] Their view was that a full sale would not be well received by the market. The experience of Barclays de Zoete Wedd (BZW) and Schroders showed that it was 'extremely difficult to conduct a sale of a people-intensive business such as investment banking without severely disrupting the ordinary course of business' and racking up large retention costs. They recommended that retention bonuses be offered to key DKB staff now to protect the value of the franchise and that the sale of selected parts of the business could be considered 'at a later stage'. Nevertheless, Deutsche Bank asked MSDW to quickly undertake a 'sum-of-the-parts' analysis of DKB and seek out 'discreet investors'.[46]

The MSDW 'inside-out' evaluation of DKB estimated the business to be worth about €5.5 billion compared to the GCI estimate of €6.4 billion.[47] MSDW's conclusions reflected the preferred option for GCI, i.e. disposing of DKB's Global Markets and Global Equities. Significant overlaps in Global Markets and Global Equities meant that full integration was 'sub-optimal' while on the other hand complete disposal was not 'strategically sound' for the reasons mentioned above. MSDW suggested quietly disposing of the Global Markets and Global Equities parts of DKB directly to identified buyers, without starting a public auction, and integrating only the departments of Global Finance (valued at c. €2.4 billion) and Global Corporate Finance (valued at c. €0.4 billion). For legal reasons, the decision on this disposal had to be taken by the Dresdner Bank management board, so there was going to be a huge challenge of persuasion.

As GCI pushed for the break-up of DKB, discussions at the second Integration Committee meeting on 21 March became more controversial and the issue was adjourned to a third meeting a week later. The 28 March meeting also ended in stalemate with Deutsche Bank pressing for partial sale and Dresdner arguing that this was contrary to the original strategy and created problems of credibility.[48] On the margins of the meeting, Ackermann expressed his view that the merger was really a takeover of Dresdner by Deutsche Bank, which further provoked the indignation of Dresdner's leadership.[49] Later that day Deutsche Bank's Management Board reflected on the implications of the merger for GCI and GTS, after which Breuer stressed to Walter that Ackermann's statement did not reflect the Management Board's opinion.[50] Walter was not reassured.

On 29 March 2000, Dresdner's management board sent a letter to their counterparts at Deutsche Bank to express their growing concern that the discussions were diverging from the merger of equals, or at least a balanced partnership, as set out in the 13 March agreement in principle.[51] In particular, they were offended by the treatment of DKB: selling all or part of DKB was 'not feasible, not in the interest of Dresdner Bank and does not comply with the spirit of the agreement in principle'. The Dresdner board called for the full integration of Global Equities and Global Markets as per the agreement. Since it was clear that senior staff in Deutsche Bank's GCI were not willing to integrate, they wanted this process to be led by a respected, independent investment banker employed for the purpose. In a pointed attack on Ackermann the letter went on that 'employees who question the contractual principles of integration should have no place in our combined business'.[52] The letter concluded with a threat that 'we would regret it if the step to merge our two houses in partnership that both our houses sought and which was closely followed in the world were to fail'.[53]

Once again, the dispute leaked to the press and on 3 April the *Financial Times* reported that Ackermann had criticised Breuer for not consulting his colleagues before announcing the merger.[54] That day, Wieandt advised Breuer, 'Although the sale is basically feasible, Dresdner Bank insists on integration. However, in view of the high overlaps, integration is not likely to create value for the new bank.'[55] On 5 April, *Bloomberg* reported that 'most of DKB would be shut' and T. J. Lim, global head of fixed income, quit DKB due to the uncertainty and moved to Merrill Lynch.[56] Lim later told *Euromoney*: 'People said I should have been relaxed because I used to work for Edson [at Merrill] but the overlap is huge. I wasn't prepared to go through all that downsizing again.'[57] The deal was clearly creating reputational damage and needed to be finalised quickly.

The Deutsche Bank Management Board met on 4 April to discuss the DKB problem and resolved to offer only the partial integration of DKB along the lines of proposals developed by GCI and MSDW. Breuer told Achleitner, Schulte-Noelle and Walter, who considered the offer overnight. The next morning at eight o'clock the management boards of Deutsche Bank and Dresdner Bank met together to discuss Deutsche Bank's final offer.

The Deutsche Bank Supervisory Board reconvened at 9.30 the same morning of Wednesday 5 April in Frankfurt along with the nine members of the Management Board and two representatives of KPMG to discuss the bank's regular balance sheet outcome. At the start, Hilmar Kopper asked for approval for Dobson's early resignation from the Management Board, which was agreed with good wishes. There is no record of a discussion of the merger in the official minute. The minute records only that Breuer reported on the state of the merger talks.[58] By this time, however, the talks were called off. Breuer's chronology of the debacle notes that at 1.15 in the afternoon Walter informed Breuer that the talks were over and he immediately informed Deutsche Bank's Supervisory Board. Two hours later trading in the shares of both banks was suspended for just under an hour while an ad hoc release by Dresdner Bank asserted that the management board of Dresdner Bank 'has unanimously decided to discontinue the merger process with Deutsche Bank AG with immediate effect'.[59]

Unlike Deutsche Bank, the collapse of the merger had an immediate effect in the leadership of Dresdner Bank: Bernhard Walter resigned on 6 April and his deputy, Andreas Bezold, and two other members of the management board followed a week later. *Reuters* reported that Kopper had tried in vain to replace Breuer with Ackermann.[60] Clearly Breuer's position was under threat in the press and from some members of the Supervisory Board, although the Management Board stood behind him, at least publicly. All members of the Management Board, and Kopper, signed a letter to all bank employees on 11 April expressing satisfaction with the 1999 results and stating:

> The Board of Managing Directors, with Dr. Breuer as its Spokesman, intends to
> sustain the momentum of this success jointly with you and make Deutsche Bank

the world's leading financial services provider. Here, the Board has the unrestricted support of the Chairman of the Supervisory Board.[61]

But not all within the bank were as supportive. Two employee representatives, Gerhard Renner and Margret Mönig-Raane, called an extraordinary meeting of the Supervisory Board for 20 April to discuss the debacle.[62] Renner made several statements to the press casting doubt on Breuer's future and it seemed that this meeting would be an opportunity to challenge him.[63] At the meeting, Breuer presented the chronology of the negotiations, including informal discussions with Allianz. He then reviewed the criticisms of the process and presented examples of other failed mergers. The discussion focused mainly on the impact on employees, shareholders and customers, although there was some discussion of the sale of DKB. Breuer survived the meeting unchallenged.

In terms of the bank's reputation, Deutsche Bank's surveys of the impact of the failed merger showed that employees were disappointed but that the markets had a more positive reaction.[64] A key challenge was how to retrieve reputation, particularly with retail customers and employees, who had been prepared to be spun out of Deutsche Bank but now needed to be retained.[65]

4. Conclusions

The collapse of the Dresdner–Deutsche Bank merger was clearly a managerial failure and, while Breuer did not lose his job (as Walter did), he was definitely severely weakened for the rest of his time as leader of the Management Board. Six months later, Josef Ackermann was already publicly acknowledged as Breuer's successor two years before Breuer's tenure was up. But how much is this judgement merely the benefit of hindsight?

The scheme cooked up with Allianz seemed to be a win-win proposition for Deutsche Bank and Allianz, although Dresdner's interests were less well defined. The focus on getting rid of the weight of retail banking, combined with government and market encouragement for consolidation in the German domestic market, must have made it irresistible to try to find a scheme to strengthen Deutsche Bank's retail division enough to spin it out of the company. All merger negotiations needed to be discussed secretly to avoid undue publicity, but there were clearly problems in the conception of the plan caused by not bringing Ackermann and other key leaders of Global Corporates and Institutions (GCI) into the discussions at an early stage. Increasing the scale of the Global Markets and Global Equities by absorbing Dresdner Kleinwort Benson (DKB) was in the end not desirable for GCI, as they risked losing their own senior talent in the process. If they took all the staff from DKB, this would also have significantly increased the dependence of 'Deutsche Bank New' on volatile trading and fee income. There was also the ongoing challenge of integrating Bankers Trust, which had been acquired only months before the start of the negotiations with Allianz, so there was extra pressure in terms of timing. All these weaknesses could have been anticipated.

The deal with Dresdner was very different from the earlier experiences with Morgan Grenfell or Bankers Trust. For one thing, Deutsche Bank management was more familiar with the market both for customers and labour in Germany than in the UK or US. Yet, the gulf between Frankfurt and London was still an important factor, as it had been in the case of Morgan Grenfell 10 years earlier. The debacle over DKB reveals continued misunderstanding or mismanagement of talent in global corporate and investment banking. But it wasn't just a problem of different national cultures. Deutsche Bank also seems to have mismanaged the relationship in Germany with Dresdner, by underestimating the value Dresdner placed on the merger of equals concept. This was despite the failure of the first set of negotiations between the two banks earlier in 1999. Breuer's about-face on the integration of DKB meant that relations between Dresdner and Deutsche Bank deteriorated almost immediately after the announcement of the merger. Despite being the largest shareholder, Allianz was unable to force Dresdner to sell off parts of DKB and take the deal cooked up with Deutsche Bank. When Allianz took over Dresdner a year later, in April 2001, for more than €20 billion, the bank's name was retained and it was able to resist efforts at restructuring to conform to Allianz's vision for a more customer-oriented multiple product service.[66] In 2008, on the eve of the Lehman collapse, Allianz tried again to strengthen its bancassurance strategy of selling through bank branches, exchanging 60 per cent of Dresdner to Commerzbank for €9.8 billion and taking a 30 per cent share in the new larger Commerzbank. The Dresdner name finally disappeared just as the global financial crisis struck.

This case can also be compared to the JP Morgan-Chase merger in September 2000, which was also a merger between a larger and smaller bank that created a third new entity: the third largest bank in the US by assets. Chase dominated, filling most of the positions of the combined board and retaining the Chase name for retail operations. The motivation from Chase's side was to gain a major investment banking house. It was partly a defensive move in the period of consolidation: the new CEO, William B. Harrison from Chase, told analysts, 'I think there will be less than a handful of end-game winners in this space. This gives us [a] platform to be one of those winners.'[67] Although the two companies were more complementary than overlapping, as was the case for Deutsche Bank and Dresdner, execution costs and cultural gulfs were still large and the new bank struggled through difficult market conditions in the early 2000s. The deal was negotiated by senior staff in 'two or three weeks', which contrasts with the five months spent on the Dresdner deal. This speed may have been facilitated by the fact that there were only two parties in the negotiations, rather than the three in the case of Deutsche Bank–Dresdner–Allianz. JP Morgan Chase chose and embedded its top 40–50 executives in advance so the new management teams were already set and committed to the new strategy.[68] Chase also had considerable merger experience, having absorbed Chemical Banking Corporation in 1996.

As noted above, the press interpreted the failure of the merger as a victory for the investment bankers in London, particularly Edson Mitchell. Certainly, it is clear from the archival record that Ackermann and other members of Global Corporates and Institutions (GCI) in London were opposed to the integration of Dresdner Kleinwort Benson (DKB). It was their insistence on the 'cherry-picking' option that finally proved unacceptable to Dresdner, but their position was also supported by outside advice from Morgan Stanley Dean Witter (MSDW). Ironically, Dresdner had arguably been stronger than Deutsche Bank in investment banking when Hansgeorg Hofmann, a high-profile investment banker with Wall Street experience, led Dresdner to the acquisition of Kleinwort Benson in 1995. But the integration of London investment banking into a Frankfurt-based German bank was as fraught for Dresdner as it was for Deutsche Bank. In February 1997 the chairman of DKB, Simon Robertson, was pushed out over the strategy to integrate DKB. Like John Craven, he wanted the investment banking business managed out of London.[69] A few months later Hofmann admitted tax irregularities and left the bank in December 1997. When the merger discussions were underway, therefore, the mood at DKB was not bright.

Rather than merely an ideological battle between London and Frankfurt, the wake-up call coming from GCI about the risks inherent in the deal might be viewed more positively. Until the merger was announced, Breuer's planning was mainly focused on the solution for retail banking and how to meet Allianz's needs, with little substantive consideration of investment banking. Ackermann and his colleagues were no doubt right to highlight the risks to the bank's overall agenda from dramatically increasing the scale of trading-based income as well as taking on expensive personnel in DKB who would not add value. Despite the fact that the ultimate goal of the merger was to reorientate the bank towards investment, corporate, asset management and private banking, the failure to give due consideration to how these parts of the two banks would be integrated was clearly at the foundation of the failure of the merger.

After the collapse of the negotiations, Deutsche Bank had to find another solution for its retail banking. Instead of divesting, in November 2000 the lower cost retail Deutsche Bank 24 subsidiary was relaunched with ambitions to extend the model across European platforms. The strategy was aimed particularly at identifying higher income customers in order to sell them the investment products from other parts of the bank. Rather than providing a channel for Allianz, therefore, Deutsche Bank sought to turn its retail network into a (less expensive) pool of customers for its own products.

V. The Retail Bank: Cinderella or Fairy Godmother?

The domestic retail business was a constant challenge for the bank's management. The highly competitive and crowded environment for retail deposits and lending in Germany meant that margins were low while costs remained high. Until the 1990s, the governance and management of the bank's domestic business was decentralised, with considerable power and influence vested in the regional and local branch managers. This followed the traditional emphasis on relationship banking between bankers and their local customers, including the Mittelstand, which forms the heart of German industry. Retail was important to gather funds and to generate income through interest margins, but the costs of this form of funding increased relative to money markets as the bank expanded out of German regulatory barriers in the early 1990s. The extensive branch system, with its high fixed costs in terms of property and relatively inflexible labour force, proved an enduring challenge in the bank's strategy. On the other hand, the 'safe' side of the bank's funding allowed it to achieve better risk ratings, which lowered the cost of raising funds on the investment banking side of the business. The two halves of the bank were thus interdependent.

The market for deposits was unusually crowded in Germany with a variety of institutions so that the private sector competed with publicly owned banks that did not have the same drive for profit. The German system is usually described as a three-pillar banking system comprised of public sector banks, co-operative banks and commercial banks (including specialist mortgage banks and Postbank). The Landesbanken and Sparkassen (savings banks) were publicly owned and operated with a government guarantee until 2005, while the co-operatives were owned by their depositors and borrowers. This pattern was not unusual in Europe, but the German system was less profitable than those of Italy, France or Spain.[1] This was of less concern to the pillars for which profit was not a main objective, but left commercial banks with a weaker base for their retail operations. Thus, the 'Big Four' commercial banks – Deutsche Bank, Dresdner Bank, Commerzbank and HypoVereinsbank – competed with institutions with public guarantees and a lower profit motivation.

Table 11 shows some comparative data on banking structures in 1999 where it is clear that Germany had a larger number of banking institutions and a higher reliance on interest income than many other European countries (particularly France, the Netherlands and Switzerland) even when taking into account GDP and population.

Figure 24 shows the changing distribution of assets in the German banking system from 1989. The big banks' share was below 10 per cent until Bayerische Hypo- und Vereinsbank AG was included from 1999, which added a further 5 per cent. There was

Table 11: Comparative data on selected European banking structures in 1999.

	Number of Banks	Branches	Employees	Net Interest Income (in € million)	Net Non-Interest Income (in € million)	Ratio of Interest to Non-Interest Income	Branches per billion GDP	Branches per million population
Germany	2,833	40,934	722,950	70,663	22,517	3.14	20	499
Italy	876	27,134	341,311	36,759	21,449	1.71	23	477
France	543	25,501	379,355	26,675	37,504	0.71	18	436
Switzerland	334	2,922	115,075	22,719	37,816	0.60	11	410
Netherlands	85	5,493	122,677	21,960	16,292	1.35	13	349

Notes: 'Banks' includes commercial banks, savings and co-operative banks and other miscellaneous monetary institutions such as mortgage credit institutions. France population, metropolitan only. Source: Population and GDP from Eurostat. OECD (2019), 'Structure of the financial system', OECD Banking Statistics (database), https://doi.org/10.1787/data-00271-en (accessed on 24 June 2019). OECD (2019), 'Income statement and balance sheet', OECD Banking Statistics (database), https://doi.org/10.1787/data-00270-en (accessed on 24 June 2019).

Figure 24: Balance sheet total of different categories of German banks as a share of total banks' balance sheets, January 1989–April 2019.

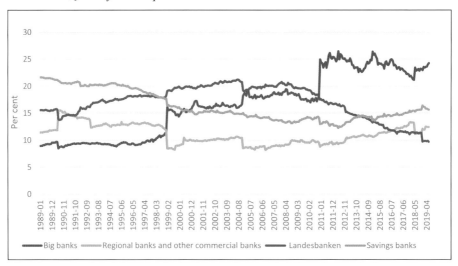

Source: Deutsche Bundesbank. Notes: From 1999 onwards, 'big banks' includes Bayerische Hypo- und Vereinsbank AG. From 2004 onwards, 'big banks' includes Deutsche Postbank AG (up to then in banking category 'Regional banks and other commercial banks'). Owing to the Act Modernising Accounting Law (Gesetz zur Modernisierung des Bilanzrechts) of 25 May 2009, derivative financial instruments in the trading portfolio (trading portfolio derivatives) within the meaning of section 340e (3) sentence 1 of the German Commercial Code (HGB) read in conjunction with section 35 (1) No 1a of the Credit Institution Accounting Regulation (RechKredV) are classified under 'Other assets and liabilities' as of the December 2010 reporting date.

another leap at the end of 2010 when derivative financial instruments in the banks' trading portfolio were included in total assets and liabilities. The dominance of savings banks at the start of the period and the rising share of the Landesbanken until the global financial crisis is also clear in the data. In the retail market, this pattern was reflected in the big banks' share of total deposits, which stayed below 10 per cent through almost all of the 30 years to 1995, before increasing sharply to almost 25 per cent by 2011 after consolidation of Postbank into the category of big banks.

It is also striking, as shown in Figure 25, that the big banks were nearly as reliant on net interest income as the credit co-operatives and savings banks until the mid-1990s when the expansion into investment banking began to generate fee and other income. Moreover, Deutsche Bank was not alone among the big German banks in pursuing this strategy; it was also a feature of savings banks and credit co-operatives.

The structure of the German banking system had profound implications for Deutsche Bank's strategy. We have seen in Chapter I that the constraint on its ability to generate profit from domestic retail business was an important impetus for the bank's push into foreign markets and investment banking. The adjunct to these developments was a series of strategies to reduce costs while retaining a competitive presence in the local German retail market. These initiatives proved to be among the more innovative, but also most controversial, changes to the bank's presence and branding.

Figure 25: Interest margin – net interest received as a percentage of the average balance sheet total in German banks, 1968–2014.

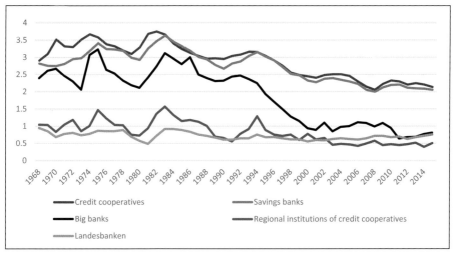

Source: Deutsche Bundesbank. Notes: From 1999 onwards 'big banks' includes Bayerische Hypo- und Vereinsbank AG (up to now banking category 'Regional banks and other commercial banks'). From 2004 onwards, 'big banks' includes Deutsche Postbank AG (up to then banking category 'Regional banks and other commercial banks'). Owing to the Act Modernising Accounting Law (Gesetz zur Modernisierung des Bilanzrechts) of 25 May 2009, derivative financial instruments in the trading portfolio (trading portfolio derivatives) within the meaning of section 340e (3) sentence 1 of the German Commercial Code (HGB) read in conjunction with section 35 (1) No 1a of the Credit Institution Accounting Regulation (RechKredV) are classified under 'Other assets and liabilities' as of the December 2010 reporting date.

1. Integration of Eastern German Banking

The fall of the Berlin Wall in November 1989 marked the most dramatic political event of post-war German history. The images on TV screens shared simultaneously in living rooms across Europe and the world inspired an abrupt shift in German identity from a divided to a unified state. Immediately, planning for the reintegration of Eastern Germany with Western Germany began, and formal reunification was accomplished within a year. Even before the political systems were aligned, the monetary and economic systems were integrated. Lower living standards, wages and productivity in the Eastern regions had a profound impact on the West and contributed to the end of the 40 years of high-speed growth that had established West Germany as the engine of the European economy. The new enlarged Germany also took shape in the context of broader European economic and monetary integration. Deutsche Bank played a leading role in the construction of the new Germany, reflecting the bank's dominant national profile and close political connections. By the end of January 1990, Deutsche Bank had opened 10 representative offices and assembled small teams of employees to get in touch with East German industry and public institutions.

Deutsche Bank's commitment to the German Democratic Republic (GDR) and Eastern Europe predated the collapse of the Berlin Wall. In summer 1989 Alfred Herrhausen signed an agreement jointly with Mikhail Gorbachev, Hans-Dietrich

Under the gaze of German Foreign Minister Hans-Dietrich Genscher, Federal Chancellor Helmut Kohl, and General Secretary of the Communist Party of the Soviet Union Mikhail Gorbachev (standing in the middle ground, from right), Deutsche Bank Management Board Spokesman Alfred Herrhausen signed a German-Soviet economic agreement in June 1989.

Genscher and Helmut Kohl to promote economic co-operation. Among Herrhausen's last initiatives before his death was the establishment of a special task force led by Georg Krupp to consider the opportunities and challenges in the GDR. Once the Wall had come down and labour could move, the prospect of integrating the two economies became especially pressing. In early February 1990 Chancellor Helmut Kohl made an abrupt (and for many surprising) announcement that the Deutschmark would be extended into East Germany and a currency union created. This was achieved on a 1:1 basis for bank deposits up to fixed limits, which reflected political but not economic realities of the purchasing power of the two currencies, i.e. it strongly overvalued the East German currency.[2]

The banking sector in the GDR was a state monopoly vested in the Staatsbank (which performed the functions of a central bank as well as a commercial bank) and the German Foreign Trade Bank (*Deutsche Außenhandelsbank*) that controlled foreign currency business. In addition, as in West Germany, there were specialised savings banks and co-operative banks. The infrastructure was poor, with branches in bad condition and, while there were about 12,000 bank employees, they lacked experience in capitalist banking practice. Deutsche Bank faced two options: either create new bank offices under the Deutsche Bank name or engage in a joint venture within the existing banking system. Very quickly, Deutsche Bank offered training to East German bank employees and provided technical support for fund transfers, and this brought them into co-operation with the Staatsbank.[3] They became the preferred partner as the Staatsbank began to manage the privatisation of banking.

In March 1990 the Staatsbank separated out its commercial, retail and mortgage business into the Deutsche Kreditbank, ready to create joint ventures. Due to concerns expressed by the Federal Cartel Office (*Bundeskartellamt*), Deutsche Kreditbank sought to conclude contracts with more than one Western partner. It thus created two separate joint ventures. Finally, Dresdner Bank took one third (72 branches) while Deutsche Bank took the other 122 branches. Hilmar Kopper later explained that he hoped to avoid charges of profiteering or trying to create a monopoly out of weak East German institutions; when Allianz took over 100 per cent of the East German insurance business, it suffered a backlash in public opinion.[4] The new joint venture Deutsche Bank-Kreditbank was 49 per cent owned by Deutsche Bank and opened on the day of the Monetary, Economic and Social Union, 1 July 1990. A main advantage of the co-operation with the subsidiary of the Staatsbank was the ability to secure office space and local staff, both of which were scarce at the time; Deutsche Bank inherited about 8,500 staff. In addition to the old Staatsbank branches, Deutsche Bank rushed to create 18 offices around the country so that, on 1 July, there were 140 Deutsche Bank branches for customers to access. But the only branch opened at midnight was at Berlin Alexanderplatz, and it was inundated with anxious and jubilant East Germans seeking to collect their new Deutschmark. On that first day, the Alexanderplatz branch gave out DM 10 million amid chaotic scenes in which 13 people were injured, windows were broken and the world's press recorded the evidence of the gap between East and West. By the end of the year, Deutsche Bank acquired the rest of the capital of Deutsche Bank-Kreditbank and it was subsumed into Deutsche Bank AG. The number of Deutsche Bank branches in Eastern Germany and united Berlin had grown to 240.[5]

On 1 July 1990, the West German mark arrived in the GDR. The first bank branch to open was Deutsche Bank's branch in Berlin's Alexanderplatz, which opened its doors at midnight to let in the crowd. For hours people had waited for the first exchange of East German marks for Deutschmark.

Deutsche Bank's participation in the reunification was not without controversy. In August 1990 the press leaked Kopper's proposal that the agency designated to privatise East German industry (the *Treuhandanstalt*) should take over the legacy of bad loans to unprofitable enterprises, and this sparked public outrage.[6] Moreover, while the modern West German banks expected to be able to take over the market, local East German savings banks retained a dominant position in deposits. By 1993 Deutsche Bank had a 7 per cent share of deposits in the new federal states compared with 6 per cent in the old West Germany. There were also complaints about the quality of the offices and services provided by Deutsche Bank, and it lacked the historic local identity of Dresdner Bank.[7] The outdated technological infrastructure required a DM 1 billion investment in electronic data processing and other operational requirements in 1991.[8] Training remained a challenge and in 1991 the bank transferred about one thousand staff from the West to branches in the new federal states to support local staff. Under the GDR, the tasks had mainly been clerical payments operations rather than selling and managing loans and providing other services for customers. Indeed, some staff approached their new employers with trepidation since Deutsche Bank had been the epitome of evil capitalism.[9] Nevertheless, Ulrich Weiss (the member of the Management Board responsible for personnel) later pointed out the particularly positive contribution of local employees.[10] The transformation was remarkably swift given the scale of the challenge.

In the short term, reunification had a detrimental effect on the former GDR economy and output and employment fell sharply in 1990. Nevertheless, there was a

Mobile service: In the first few months after the start of business on 1 July 1990 in eastern Germany, bank buses replaced the missing branches in some places, such as in Mühlhausen/Thuringia.

strong demand for credit for new start-up companies and the bank used the Leipzig Trade Fair in spring 1990 to make contact with potential customers. Contrary to original expectations, business with corporate customers was strong in the first few years after reunification, which prompted renewed efforts to gain market share with private customers. Georg Krupp, who oversaw the business, reported in 1997 that market share in loans and deposits with private customers was 'significantly higher' than in the old federal states, while total revenues had first risen until the abolition of guaranteed loans in 1994 and then stabilised by 1996. Kopper added that Deutsche Bank was the biggest investor in the new federal states.[11] Despite the challenges, Deutsche Bank's commitment to a united Germany did not falter and the extension into the old GDR proved an important element in the reimagining of domestic banking services over the following decade.

2. Reorganising Retail Branch Banking in Germany

A key challenge in retail was to try to reduce the ratio of costs to income, which was persistently high in this part of the bank's business. In 1998 costs absorbed 84 per cent of income in Retail and Private Banking compared with 70.2 per cent for the bank overall.[12] Fixed costs in terms of property as well as a large workforce meant that expenses were relatively inflexible. In the competitive German banking environment, a careful balance needed to be made between slimming down the workforce or closing branches, and protecting the bank's reputation as an embedded part of the communities that the bank served. A range of IT solutions was tried to economise and rationalise the provision of back- and front-office services but these met with mixed results, as we shall see below. The margins achievable from providing daily retail banking services were restricted by the competition from savings banks and co-operatives, which have a less intense profit requirement. An alternative was to try to increase revenue by targeting clients with higher value-added products such as consumer credit, insurance, brokerage and investment services. For example, there were efforts to exploit the bank's insurance subsidiaries, especially Deutscher Herold, to sell insurance to the retail customer base. This combination of cross-selling between banks and insurance companies was at the foundation of the German retail financial market as evidenced, for example, in the co-operation and eventual merger of Allianz and Dresdner Bank discussed in Chapter IV. But this strategy proved a challenge since it often required creating a demand among customers for new fee-based services.

In an effort to boost profits and retain the bank's competitive position, in 1991 the retail customer base was divided into relatively low income (Private Customers I/ Retail) 'who generally make use of standardised, less advisory-intensive services' and higher net worth individuals (Private Customers II/Private Banking).[13] Lower income customers were offered standardised services while higher income customers had access to individual account officers who could tailor their portfolio of higher fee- and inter-est-generating products.[14] Understandably, the introduction of this discrimination was met with some disappointment among loyal depositors. But for Kopper this segment orientation was necessary as a way to focus attention on costs and revenues, while rewarding 'creative initiatives'.[15] The year 1991 also saw the launch of Deutsche Bank's mobile sales activities. By 1994 the bank had engaged a battalion of 200 self-employed financial advisers as agents to market services to customers on an incentive basis. It was hoped that if employees became more responsible for results, there would be more inno-vation, higher quality service and more revenue.[16]

The Mittelstand or SMEs were a particular feature of the German industrial land-scape, but Deutsche Bank lagged behind other banks in market share for this sector. In spring 1991 the bank launched an aggressive campaign to meet the Mittelstand's needs more effectively through branches, providing a programme of events, networking and educational lectures locally to create a demand for corporate services.[17] The emphasis was on building customer relationships by exploiting the regional and local branch network. The public relations campaign was also partly designed to counter the percep-tion that Deutsche Bank was primarily a bank for large and international companies, and to bring in more local business.

Meanwhile, the reintegration of the former GDR prompted an opportunity to rethink how the domestic retail bank was structured. In November 1991 the Management Board began the process of reorganising the regional structure of the bank with the intention of centralising more activities.[18] This would include larger regional administrative centres for some business segments while retaining a local presence throughout the country to be close to customers – the aim was to create 10 regions focused around the main cities.[19]

The restructuring and rationalisation of management and delivery of services to retail customers proved almost as controversial and difficult as the investment banking business during the bank's transformation in the 1990s. At the end of 1991, the Management Board set up a commission that included members from head office and from the branches to investigate how to organise the activities of the domestic bank.[20] But the approach was cautious; proposals would only be meaningful if they provided 'decisive advantages in terms of market penetration and costs'.[21] In March 1992 the Management

Board considered the commission's report but it agreed to take no action at this point despite the poor performance in the Retail and Private Clients division. While business volume was stable at DM 11 billion (after accounting for risk), this business produced a loss of DM 220 million because of the extremely weak lending portfolio.[22] Instead, the bank embarked on a cost-cutting exercise aimed at reducing the workforce of the Group as a whole. In 1993 alone the number of staff in Germany was reduced by 3,000, or 5 per cent, even as the number of domestic offices increased by 21 to 1,734. In contrast, the number of staff employed outside Germany increased by 2,000, or 13 per cent.

Over the next few years, the retail structure continued to be debated by the Management Board, leading to new 'Guidelines for the Updating of the Structure' at the end of July 1994 and further reforms at the end of August.[23] The reorganisation of the Group's overall structure in July 1996 prompted yet another reassessment. The number of regions was reduced to eight in November of that year, folding Bremen, Hanover and Hamburg into one northern region.[24] Within the eight regions there were 21 main branches located in core cities, while sales and operations were separated from processing functions to increase efficiency. The bank's employees were reassured that the strategy remained aimed at keeping the bank close to its customers and providing autonomy for local decision-making while centralising clerical back office functions. The reforms were expected to generate DM 100 million in additional revenue per annum over the following three years plus a net synergy gain from lower costs of DM 330 million, creating an ambitious benefit of DM 630 million over three years.[25] At the same time, the Retail and Private Clients division was also reformed to move from the two Retail Banking and Private Banking areas to add an area for New Distribution Channels and Business Processing and a specialist Marketing and Product Management area. In 1997 small businesses from Corporate and Institutional Banking were transferred to Retail and Private Clients to boost this division.

By this point, technological changes and competitive pressures were transforming the delivery of retail banking across Europe and North America as banks and customers sought to exploit the advantages of cheaper and more secure IT services. While the full-service branch was not completely eclipsed, these technologies offered new possibilities for cutting costs by further segmenting the market into higher value-added and lower yielding customers. At the same time, a new generation of depositors was keen to avoid time-consuming contact with branches and did not value the personal connections offered under the traditional model. It seemed like a win-win

The domestic regional structure introduced in 1996 featured eight regions and 21 head branches. In 2019 the domestic bank is divided into seven regions.

opportunity, but, as discussed below, the implementation turned out to be more challenging than developing the vision behind the innovation.

3. Transition to Direct Banking: Bank 24

Direct banking was, of course, reliant on the spread of computer technology and software protocols that allowed customers to bank securely from their telephones and home computers. The first attempts were made in the US and the UK in the early 1980s: *Pronto* by Chemical Bank in the US and *Homelink* by Bank of Scotland for their Nottingham Building Society, both launched in 1983. From 1995, Wells Fargo offered full account services through its website and Presidential Bank offered customers the opportunity to open bank accounts over the Internet. In terms of offering complete branchless banking, FirstDirect in the UK was a leader, using the telephone in 1989, PC banking in 1997 and full Internet banking in 2000. It started life as a subsidiary of Midland Bank and then of HSBC (when Midland was taken over by HSBC in 1992). In Sweden, Skandinaviska Enskilda Banken launched its online subsidiary, Sesam, in 1994.

The unusual structure of the German retail market described above provided a strong incentive for Germany's biggest commercial bank to innovate, but other banks were already moving into this area. In 1994 Bayerische Hypotheken- und Wechsel-Bank opened Direkt Anlage Bank, the first discount telephone brokerage service, and in 1996 Bayerische Vereinsbank launched its direct banking subsidiary, Advance Bank. Commerzbank also deliberated over direct banking models and launched an online retail broker in January 1995 called Comdirect Bank, which was first noted by Deutsche Bank's Management Board in November 1994.[26] While intuitively attractive as a way to reduce the high fixed costs of a physical branch and at the same time to reduce labour costs by introducing lower skilled and more flexible working patterns, the actual results proved more challenging to achieve. This is to some extent confirmed in empirical analyses of Internet-only banks in other jurisdictions where costs tended not to be reduced as much as was hoped, at least in the early years.[27] In essence, the direct-bank concept created a competitor to the bank's existing offering that would gradually take over the least profitable part of that business and deliver it more efficiently.

In the autumn of 1994 Deutsche Bank's Retail and Private Clients Division began to discuss 'Alternative Distribution Channels' to reconsider how retail banking could be delivered in the changing customer environment. An important decision was whether these alternatives should be integrated with Deutsche Bank's traditional branch banking, or better served through an independent direct bank, whether through telephone or computer. The bank had already experimented with a 24-hour telephone banking service in the Essen district in 1994 and in July the Management Board agreed to roll it out across the country.[28] Part of the impetus was that competition was already evident in this area from other direct banks in the market.[29] But the details took another year to be ironed out.

After months of debate, the proposal to create a direct bank was put to the Management Board at the end of January 1995. An independent subsidiary under the name 'Bank 24' would offer a range of retail banking products and brokerage services at a discount of 30 to 50 per cent compared with branches.[30] The goal was to attract half a million customers over five years and to generate a return on equity of over 20 per cent. It was anticipated that the exercise would cost about DM 100 million and would open up for business on 1 September 1995.[31] The German banking market had a growing younger or 'young feeling' clientele with higher income and education, which was expected to appreciate phone and online self-service. These customers could be serviced with 40 per cent lower costs because the products available would be simpler (requiring less advice and having more efficient forms of settlement) and staff could be centralised without the administrative and real estate expenses of a bank branch. By structuring the new bank as an independent subsidiary, it was hoped that introducing cost-saving shift work and different management cultures would be facilitated. The Management Board urged the Bank 24 management to 'focus its business policy decisively on gaining market share from the outset in order to achieve the economy of scale as quickly as possible'.[32] The operative break-even should be reached after four years in 1999.[33]

The Management Board finally approved the proposal to set up an independent direct bank on 30 January 1995, and in May agreed to 'become participants on the Internet with immediate effect'.[34] Tessen von Heydebreck, in charge of Private Banking on the Management Board, made the case for locating Bank 24 in Bonn where there was the largest supply of part-time and multilingual staff (partly due to the location of a large university) that could eventually allow expansion to other countries.[35] The project had to be carefully tested on the market and the technical aspects had to be robust. Bank 24 built on the branches' existing framework for telephone banking with some additional functionality for call centres, so the investment in IT was about DM 17.3 million in 1996.[36] Much more costly than the IT platform was the marketing budget including press and television. DM 55 million was budgeted for 1996, but by October this budget was expected to be expanded to DM 90 million for the year.[37] The new venture needed to build up the customer base quickly to test whether this channel was actually profitable at scale.

There were initial teething problems. In November 1996 Georg Krupp, who was responsible for retail clients, announced that Bank 24 was attracting 500–600 new customers per day, but there were delays in processing applications.[38] The next month the Management Board noted that Bank 24 would reach over 60,000 customers by the end of the year and that the systems problems had been resolved.[39] At the start of 1997 von Heydebreck confirmed that only 11 per cent of Bank 24's 80,000 customers had come from Deutsche Bank branches, so they were tapping a new customer base.[40] But almost two thirds of existing customers believed that a branch was 'indispensable', suggesting that the prospects for further cost-cutting through branch closures would lead to loss of customers rather than transferring them to lower cost outlets. Instead there would be changes within the structure of the 1,480 domestic branches to reduce costs. Nevertheless, Bank 24 seemed to be on its way to success with a break-even point in 1999–2000, and von Heydebreck expressed his hope to achieve the target 25 per cent return on equity for the Retail and Private Clients division as a whole through further cost-cutting. Kopper, however, pointed out that almost all the profit for the entire division came from private asset management services sold to retail customers rather than through net interest income.

Advertisement for the direct bank 'Bank 24'. It was founded in 1995 to offer retail customers a range of products and brokerage services at a discount of up to 50 per cent compared with branches.

Despite the innovation of Bank 24, in 1998 Deutsche Bank's market share in German retail banking still hovered at about 5 per cent and had to be supported by high infrastructure and overhead costs.[41] About six million customers were generating a loss of some DM 100 million after risk provision. Given this profile, in March 1998 von Heydebreck proposed creating a retail bank that could be spun off out of Deutsche Bank AG. As noted in Chapter IV, this was a proposal that appealed to several members of the Management Board, including Spokesman Breuer, and it formed the basic rationale for the proposed merger with Dresdner Bank in 1999–2000. Von Heydebreck's vision was to retain high-net-worth customers in Deutsche Bank AG's Private Banking, to whom revenue-generating complex services and asset management could be sold. At the time there were 250,000 Private Banking customers and perhaps a further 140,000 could be migrated from Retail and Private Clients. By reducing the number of branches (from 1,450 to 1,250) and narrowing the range of services provided to households, small business and self-employed retail customers, costs could be cut and management streamlined. This could make the retail business ripe for a spin-off, initially as a fully owned subsidiary. Separating retail operations in this way would make it easier to make the required cost-cutting, with the goal of achieving a return on equity in line with the 25 per cent target for the bank as a whole. In particular, von Heydebreck anticipated that the new retail bank would not be a member of the employers' association and contracts could be concluded with new employees that put more emphasis on performance-related pay.

At the supervisory board of Bank 24 at the start of November 1998, von Heydebreck confirmed that Bank 24 was 'the innovation leader' in Deutsche Bank's private customer business and the meeting agreed that 'it is important to maintain this "speedboat character" [of Bank 24] in the emerging new retail bank as well'.[42] In October the management had agreed to investigate whether to blend the traditional branch business with Bank 24 to provide a mixed service for customers by January 1999. Von Heydebreck noted that 'a particularly important task is to convey to employees that the planned bank is not a cost-cutting programme, but a clear opportunity to safeguard existing jobs and create new ones'.[43] He expected that retail banking would increase its profit contribution from DM 200 million in 1998 to DM 1.1 billion in 2003 and return on equity before taxes from 6 to 26 per cent, while the cost/income ratio was to improve from 89 to 71 per cent.[44] These were certainly ambitious targets.

After much debate, eventually Bank 24's direct banking ('clicks') and Deutsche Bank's branch-based ('bricks') retail operations were merged into 'Deutsche Bank 24' as a separate legal entity based in Frankfurt. The new subsidiary began operating on 1 September 1999. Meanwhile, Private Banking focused broadly on retail asset and portfolio management, offering a bespoke product range catering for high-net-worth individuals. They were charged a flat fee for their accounts and serviced through a smaller number of branches. This unit remained part of Deutsche Bank AG. But the strategy with two brands in personal banking was resisted, particularly by customers who believed they were being forcibly 'downgraded'. The result was a public relations disaster.[45]

After the failed merger with Dresdner Bank, in November 2000 Deutsche Bank 24 shifted strategy to aim at more affluent customers for cross-selling higher margin services and to serve as a distribution platform for the parent company's investment banking and asset management products.[46] The online Brokerage 24 was rebranded as maxblue in April 2001 and Deutsche Bank 24 was extended to the rest of Europe, targeting Deutsche Bank's existing clientele in Italy, Spain, France, Portugal, Belgium

In September 1999, at the launch of the new Deutsche Bank 24, most of Deutsche Bank AG's existing branches had their signs changed. Three years later the signs disappeared again.

and Poland. Despite the brand issues in Germany, the profit that Deutsche Bank 24 transferred to its parent company grew from €38 million in 1999 to €344 million in 2001.[47] This was still rather far from the predictions in 1998.

When Ackermann gained formal control of the Management Board in 2002, one of his early steps was to rebrand private and retail banking and turn it into a channel for more stable retail-based investment banking. In October 2002 the Deutsche Bank 24 brand ceased to exist, as all of Deutsche Bank's retail operations, including Private Banking, parts of Corporate Banking and the online broker maxblue were merged under the umbrella of a new corporate division named Private & Business Clients (PBC) and headed by Rainer Neske. About 30,000–40,000 SMEs were transferred from investment banking to this new division where they would be offered simpler services through branches. The new

Swiss citizen Josef Ackermann joined Deutsche Bank's Management Board in 1996 and became its Spokesman in 2002. In 2006 he was appointed as the first Chief Executive Officer in the bank's history.

retail division would also take in the lower end of the private wealth management customers.[48] The bank also reduced its retail footprint with a renewed focus on Spain and Italy and selling off Banque Worms in France, which had been acquired in 2001. The goal was to reduce the number of German branches by about half to 770 along with about 4,000 job cuts. 'Deutsche Bank Privat- und Geschäftskunden AG' was set up as an independent legal entity for retail, private and commercial banking operations.[49] Private & Business Clients (PBC) now served customers all across Europe, while Private Wealth Management (PWM), established in 2003, offered products for high-net-worth individuals.

These restructuring efforts were confusing for the bank's customers and employees, but they did help to reduce the cost/income ratio in PBC from 84 per cent in 2002 to 72 per cent in 2004, partly through a sharp decline in workers. From a meagre 13 per cent return on equity in 2001, the PBC Division was the leading contributor on this metric by 2004 with a massive 60 per cent underlying return, meeting its target of €1 billion in pre-tax profit. But Neske warned the Supervisory Board: 'Restructuring and repeated changes of client advisory services have a negative impact on customer perception in local markets.'[50] The next phase would seek to achieve balanced growth with a focus on remotivating and training workers.

4. Domestic Expansion: Berliner Bank and Norisbank

Growing the bank's market share in Germany through acquisition was a persistent concern. In 1996 the Management Board and Kopper supported the acquisition of shares in Munich-based Bayerische Vereinsbank partly through a foreign private bank to avoid alerting the market. Ferslev later recalled that 10 per cent of the bank's shares were acquired quickly in this way.[51] As a target for acquisition, it had fewer overlaps with the Deutsche Bank branch network because of its concentration in the south of Germany. Vereinsbank also held a 10 per cent interest in each of Allianz and Munich Re, which could have been sold to finance the purchase. In mid-1996 Deutsche Bank announced that it had acquired directly 5.2 per cent of Bayerische Vereinsbank's voting shares, which Edmund Stoiber (then Bavaria's Minister-President) found 'alarming'.[52] Stoiber later said he was 'electrified' by the prospect that Bayerische Vereinsbank 'was in danger of becoming a branch' and Deutsche Bank withdrew its interest.[53] The following year Vereinsbank merged with Bayerische Hypotheken- und Wechsel-Bank, prompting Deutsche Bank to sell off its shares in autumn 1997.[54] The combined Bayerische Hypo- und Vereinsbank became the second largest bank in Europe for a time (after Deutsche Bank).[55] In 2005 the Bayerische Hypo- und Vereinsbank was itself taken over by Italy's Unicredit; there was clearly competition and consolidation in Deutsche Bank's home market.

Planning for the acquisition of Berliner Bank began at the end of 2005, code-named 'Project Bandeon', and led by Frank Strauß, head of PBC in Germany since 2006.[56] Berliner Bank was founded in 1950 to promote the reconstruction of West Berlin and by 2006 had almost 1,200 employees and 60 branches. Of the more than 300,000 retail customers, 20 per cent were considered 'affluent' (i.e. earning more than €6,000 per month) and therefore ripe for cross-selling lucrative products. Moreover, the bank had a nationwide credit card business that could double Deutsche Bank's share of this market to 8 per cent. A key rationale for the deal was that 'an acquisition would reinforce DB's commitment to Germany, sending a strong growth message to the public' and the bank was one of the few available targets left in the home market.[57] On 21 June 2006, after a competitive bidding process against six rivals, including Citigroup and Société Générale, Deutsche Bank agreed binding contracts to take over Berliner Bank at a cost of €680.5 million. Another bidder, Mittelbrandenburgische Sparkasse, had given an employment guarantee to strengthen its bid; Deutsche Bank also promised that there would be no mandatory redundancies as a result of the buyout (at least until 2010) on the basis that there was no substantial overlap with the bank's existing services. Berliner Bank had a market share of 6 per cent in Berlin and increased the number of Deutsche Bank's domestic retail customers to 15 per cent of the Berlin market.[58] The strategy was to retain the bank's corporate identity and brand name to meet the preferences of local customers for continuity. The 'new' Berliner Bank began operations on 1 January 2007. It was legally integrated into Deutsche Bank Privat- und Geschäftskunden AG in 2010, but the branches still used the old brand until November 2016.

A few months after this acquisition, in October 2006, a rather more complicated purchase of Norisbank for €420 million from DZ Bank marked the takeover of a nationwide retail bank with an attractive consumer credit business but offering a distinctive segment of low-cost or 'quality discounter' banking facilities compared to Deutsche Bank's standard offering.[59] Norisbank had more than 300,000 customers and 98 branches with total deposits of €1.6 billion. The deal included branches and customer accounts, but no staff or IT platform. As in the case of Berliner Bank,

Table 12: Branch network development of Deutsche Bank Group (including Deutsche Bank AG in parentheses until 1992), 1989–2018.

Year (as of 31 December)	Total (DB AG)	Domestic/Germany (DB AG)	Foreign (DB AG)
1989	1,640 (1,200)	1,330 (1,124)	310 (76)
1990	1,894 (1,334)	1,514 (1,257)	380 (77)
1991	1,944 (1,449)	1,539 (1,374)	405 (75)
1992	2,146 (1,518)	1,713 (1,440)	433 (78)
1993	2,431	1,734	697
1994	2,483	1,722	761
1995	2,494	1,691	803
1996	2,417	1,627	790
1997	2,355	1,584	771
1998	2,310	1,566	744
1999	2,374	n/a	n/a
2000	2,287	n/a	n/a
2001	2,099	1,254	845
2002	1,711	936	775
2003	1,576	845	731
2004	1,599	831	768
2005	1,588	836	752
2006	1,717	934	783
2007	1,889	989	900
2008	1,950	961	989
2009	1,964	961	1,003
2010	3,083	2,087	996
2011	3,078	2,039	1,039
2012	2,984	1,944	1,040
2013	2,907	1,924	983
2014	2,814	1,845	969
2015	2,790	1,827	963
2016	2,656	1,776	880
2017	2,425	1,570	855
2018	2,064	1,409	655

Source: Deutsche Bank, Annual Reports 1989–2018.

Notes: Method of counting branches changed from 1991. In the 1990 Annual Report, the total number is 1,856. There is a conflict between the numbers given in the annual reports for 2009 and 2008 regarding the numbers of branches for 2008. Data is from the 2009 Annual Report. From 1999, numbers for 'foreign branches' are no longer reported separately. The table shows the difference between Total and Domestic/Germany.

the brand name and identity of Norisbank was retained as it catered for a different clientele than did Deutsche Bank's retail branches.[60] By 2008, the bank turned from loss-making to profit and in 2012 all branches were closed, transforming Norisbank into a pure direct bank.

Table 12 shows the changes in the number of branch offices of the Deutsche Bank Group as a whole. The number of offices in Germany peaked in 1993 and then declined after the 1994 reforms while the number of foreign offices continued to expand. By 2008 the bank had more offices outside Germany than it had domestically. After the global financial crisis the bank's strategy returned to focus on the domestic German market (see Chapters VII and VIII) and retrenchment of its international operations so the balance was reversed. Indeed, the number of domestic offices grew quickly in the late 2000s due to local acquisitions including Postbank, Berliner Bank and Norisbank.

5. The Introduction of the Euro

On 28 September 1995 Helmut Kohl wrote to Hilmar Kopper:

> For the people of our country, the introduction of a common European currency far beyond its great economic importance will have a special symbolic character for the integration of Europe. Therefore, we must do everything in our power to ensure that the Economic and Monetary Union is a success and is accepted by both the people and the economy.[61]

But he asserted that the euro would only be successful if it were as strong as the Deutschmark, which depended in turn on a strong interpretation of the Maastricht stability criteria. He urged that this position should be conveyed to the public through banks. Kohl also argued, 'The nature and pace of the introduction of the common European currency should not lead to a change in the competitive landscape in the German banking industry, to the detriment of those institutions which bear the brunt of supply in the area.' Kopper replied, 'I can assure you that the Management Board and staff of Deutsche Bank will continue to work hard to bring the idea of the currency union closer to the people of Germany.'[62] He had confidence that the 'Finanzplatz Deutschland' would indeed face challenges by the removal of the 'home advantage' in DM financing, but the large banks with international reach would be resilient.[63] The publicly owned and co-operative banking sectors were more likely to face challenges from the introduction of the euro. For larger banks, Kopper considered globalisation and electronic banking to be a more important challenge to the banking industry than the currency union. He also steered Kohl away from any possibility of interfering with free competition in the German market to protect smaller banks, which 'contradicts the basic principles of a federal government that has always upheld the banner of competition as the main pillar of our economic system'.[64] Kopper was also insistent that the introduction of a common currency should not be delayed. Deutsche Bank's position from the start, therefore, was enthusiastic about the opportunities of further European integration from the Economic and Monetary Union.

The bank's preparations for the introduction of the euro were prolonged and technical, but in the end the transition was smooth and relatively inexpensive. This benign outcome reflected the general experience across the Eurozone when the euro was introduced at the start of 1999. As the market leader in European corporate banking (based in no small measure on the strength and resilience of the Deutschmark), Deutsche Bank was well placed to leverage that expertise into a dominant position in euro-business. In July 1989 the regulations restricting medium term DM-commercial paper were lifted, leading to a boom in this business. On the eve of the introduction of the euro 10 years later, the Deutschmark was the second most frequently traded currency in the world after the US dollar at almost $250 billion per day on average (compared with $455 billion for the US dollar, $143 billion for the yen and only $67 billion for the British pound).[65] Three years later, when the next data are available, the euro had taken over the Deutschmark's second place, where it has remained ever since. The location of the European Central Bank in Frankfurt signalled the importance of Germany and the German financial markets in the new system.

Deutsche Bank as a whole began to plan for the euro in 1995, particularly focused on system and operations and the IT infrastructure needed to service clients and manage the transition. But identifying and confronting the strategic opportunities and challenges for the bank in its established markets was slower to develop. Deutsche Morgan Grenfell (DMG), the investment bank entity, for example, only began to plan in 1997 and took on a consulting firm, Gemini, to help lead the campaign.[66] At the end of that year, the Management Board found the DMG efforts too complex and was concerned that this part of the bank was lagging behind in its preparations.[67] Board member Ronaldo Schmitz became quite exercised that the issue needed to be given priority even though there were important restructuring initiatives underway, including the creation of GCI (Global Corporates and Institutions).[68] He urged the equity capital markets division that 'we need urgently to learn how ECM (Equity Capital Markets) should position itself to develop a competitive advantage from the advent of the Euro', noting that 'some of our peers (foreign!) are well advanced'.[69] New products needed to be developed since older products based on national currencies would be obsolete, and both clients and staff needed training and education in the implications of the single currency. In March 1998 Ackermann and Schmitz wrote jointly to the new board of GCI warning that, while some progress had been made on developing 'action plans', 'unfortunately, this is only the beginning, we need to follow up this initial effort by taking the following next steps; initially to achieve compliance, then to achieve a competitive position and finally to position ourselves as world-wide leaders on the Euro issue'.[70] The next month the DMG EMU (European Monetary Union) project team complained that, unlike their competitors, there was no specific budget for marketing euro services to global customers.[71] These frictions over the process expressed the bank's anxiety over its ability to move itself into a strategically strong position with its customers to provide the euro services that would allow it to become dominant in the new market. In the end, the anxieties about the process of transition were overcome despite the competing preoccupations of restructuring the bank in 1999–2000, the absorption of Bankers Trust and the failed merger with Dresdner Bank. By the end of 1999 Deutsche Bank was able to claim that 'with the introduction of the Euro, we graduated from being the leader in DM issues to the leader in Eurobond issues'.[72] As the largest bank in the European economy with the strongest currency, Deutsche Bank had a strong advantage that it was able to transfer to the euro.

6. The Bank's European Retail Strategy

In January 1994 Hilmar Kopper explained his vision for the bank in a major interview with *Euromoney* magazine, where he set out clearly the balance between the domestic and European market and the place of retail banking in the overall strategy.[73] Reflecting on the unification of Germany, he noted that 'we have seized a wonderful opportunity to grow our home base by 17 million people over the last three years' but at the same time he explicitly rejected the prospect of becoming a retail bank in Europe.[74] His strategy was to be market leader in Germany and a European corporate bank. More specifically, 'we want to be a retail bank in Italy and Spain, and to be a corporate bank across Europe where we want to be strong on corporate finance, and in trading money, currencies, fixed-income, equities and derivatives. We want to do asset management and distribute mutual funds in these countries.'[75] He aimed positively to avoid becoming a European retail bank like Crédit Lyonnais: 'We don't want to be the 10th largest bank in some European country where we never make any money.' '[…] I look around the world today and I cannot identify a country where I wish to be a retail banker.' Italy and Spain were exceptions, where no bank dominated the retail sector and Deutsche Bank offered an advantage in 'professionalism when it came to retailing'.[76] By 1993 over half of the bank's profits came from outside Germany, mainly in Europe through corporate banking and capital markets. The bank was the second largest international bond underwriter because of the strong demand for Deutschmark bonds.

Soon after Kopper's confident interview, the looming single market and anticipation of the euro suggested that the European banking system would become more integrated and this prompted a reconsideration of the bank's localisation strategy in Europe. As in the rest of the world, a process of consolidation in the financial sector washed across Europe in the second half of the 1990s. At Deutsche Bank most of the late 1990s was spent debating the integration of DMG, but in 1999 the acquisition of Bankers Trust put the capstone on the major investments in the global investment bank. Attention turned to the other part of the Dual Focus strategy – the bank's presence in Europe. In July 1999, the Management Board took stock of the bank's existing portfolio and assessed how to move forward. Investments to date were a piecemeal rather than strategic expansion, mainly focused on taking over local banks opportunistically while initially retaining their brand and identity. In part this reflected the fragmented nature of the European banking system with its strong national characteristics and regulatory frameworks.

Deutsche Bank tended to insist on majority or 100 per cent ownership of its European operations to get market share, which prompted retail acquisitions in Italy, Spain and corporate franchises in the Netherlands and Portugal.[77] Acquisitions in 1993 included the Banco de Madrid in Spain (with 300 branches) to add to the Barcelona-based Banco Comercial Transatlántico (1989), and the Banca Popolare di Lecco (BPL) in Italy to add to the Milan-based subsidiary Banca d'America e d'Italia (BAI) (1986). From 1995 to 1999 the main new investments were in Germany's neighbour Poland, and in Greece, Belgium and France, but the book value of these investments was rather modest except for Italy. In 1998, in a departure from the majority ownership model, a new strategy was employed to buy 10 per cent of the rapidly expanding Eurobank, based in Greece. With the end of the Cold War Deutsche Bank established representative offices across Eastern Europe and some corporate banking offices in Prague (representative office in 1990, full office 1993), Warsaw (representative office in 1990, subsidiary 1995), Budapest (representative office 1990, subsidiary 1995) and Moscow (representative office 1973, subsidiary 1998). But most of the bank's energy was focused on global investment banking or wholesale banking after the creation of DMG in 1995. Table 13 shows the relatively higher returns in established markets in Italy and Spain, and also the relatively low cost/income rations in Europe (except for the new investment in Hungary). The net income reported in Table 13 amounted to about 5 per cent of total pre-tax profits for Deutsche Bank AG.

The review of the European strategy in mid-1999 considered the different options open for the bank.[78] The most ambitious was to create an integrated European banking group by merging with two to four national champions at a cost of up to €170 billion, or to focus on a single country to create a 'second home market' either through acquisition or merger between equals, which would reduce the cost to perhaps €50 billion. The targets suggested in either case were Barclays, Société Générale or Unicredito Italiano (UCI). Both of these suggestions were discounted as 'unfeasible'.[79] Alternatively, the bank could spend up to €25 billion to acquire a range of second-tier local banks, which was similar to the current strategy. A fourth alternative would be to abandon the control element and take 5–10 per cent participations in national champions, as had been done in Greece with Eurobank. Another set of options would be to abandon the universal bank concept and the physical branches and focus on particular products rather than full-service operations.

In the end the strategy remained opportunistic and eclectic with minority and entire acquisitions in both established and new markets. The core focus continued to be on existing markets in Italy, Spain, Portugal, Belgium and Poland in the early 2000s with the aim of becoming 'a leading European Bank for the retail and small business client'.[80] Acquisitions included Crédit Lyonnais Belgium in 1999 and Bank Wspolpracy Regionalnej SA in Poland in 2000. Retail business in Poland was launched in July 2001 with Deutsche Bank PBC SA. The bank's overall operations in Poland met with mixed success; in 2002 all eight Corporate and Investment Banking (CIB) branches outside Warsaw were closed to focus on wealthier clients with the highest cross-selling potential.[81] Nevertheless, the retail part of the operations expanded. In 2005 the bank embarked on a major investment to add more than 80 branches in Poland and 50 new branches in Portugal. There were also initiatives in emerging markets in Turkey, China and the Middle East. By the first quarter of 2008, Spain and Italy still accounted for more than 75 per cent of the revenues from Europe for the Private & Business Clients Division, and Italy generated about half of the consumer finance revenue for the division through its Prestitempo and credit cards brands.[82] The bank also launched a retail investment in Mumbai in India in 2005 and credit cards in 2006, opening 10 branches by 2007. By 2019, India was the only non-European country in which Deutsche Bank had retail operations. In the aftermath of the global financial crisis, the bank also concentrated its

Table 13: Selected Deutsche Bank investments in Europe, 1998.

Country	Acquisitions	Total assets (€ million)	Branches	Employees	Net income before tax (€ million)	Pre-tax return on equity in %	Cost/ Income ratio in %
France	DB SA	9,364	2	343	15	n/a	68
Belgium	Crédit Lyonnais Belgium	9,852	38	955	47	13	60
Greece	Eurobank, Ergo	4,312	166	3,581	47	13*	70
Poland	DB Polska	321	8	166	7	10	59
Hungary	DB RT	133	1	52	0	0	124
Czech Republic		1,066	1	100	4	n/a	56
Italy	F & F, BCI, UCI	26,664	261	4,175	219	28	66
Spain		10,750	281	2,849	90	22	71
Portugal		3,582	3	139	9	14	46

Source: Die Bank in Europa, presentation by AfK for Closed Meeting, 17 July 1999, HADB, V27/x215. *After acquisition in 1998. Operations include CORE, GCI, and Asset Management as well as Private and Commercial Banking.

Table 14: PBC's retail franchise in developed markets, 2007.

	Germany	Italy	Spain	Poland	Portugal	Belgium
Invested Assets (€ billion)	152.7	24.4	11.5	1.8	0.7	11.8
Loan book (€ billion)	60.2	12.9	12.6	1.8	0.9	0.0
Clients (million)	9.7	2.5	0.7	0.2	0.02	0.2
Branches	932	250	267	129	36	30
Financial Agents	c.1,500	952	130	c. 205	91	-
Employees FTE	15,040	2,730	2,167	1,357	256	353

Notes: 'Branches' includes loan shops in Poland and DB Credit in Spain. Presentation by Rainer Neske, head of PBC at the Goldman Sachs Annual European Financials Conference, Berlin, 12 June 2008. https://www.db.com/ir/en/download/Neske_GS_Conf_Berlin_12_June_2008_final.pdf

European operations; in 2014 the Polish retail bank was merged with Deutsche Bank Polska and at the end of 2018 the bank sold its private and commercial banking and securities brokerage operations in Poland to Spain's Santander.

Overall, the European retail operations remained small relative to Germany, as Table 14 illustrates. This snapshot also shows the reliance on agents to sell products to customers; in Germany this form of contract accounted for about 10 per cent of the number of full-time jobs, while this was closer to 20 per cent in Poland and 35 per cent in Italy. This form of employment increased the flexibility of the workforce and the focus on sales. At this point, in the midst of the global financial crisis, the German domestic retail presence was about to expand dramatically with the acquisition of Postbank.

7. Acquisition of Postbank

The weaknesses in the retail side of the bank and the need to balance funding sources between the 'safe' and the risky halves of the bank encouraged further efforts to grow the deposit base domestically through acquisition. The largest and quickest way for Deutsche Bank to gain market share would be for it to take over Postbank with its 10 million clients and over 10,000 employees. Postbank was formed in 1990 and 100 per cent owned by Deutsche Post, which repeatedly considered selling off all or part of the banking operations. The prize for Deutsche Bank would be to become the market leader in Germany and the third largest bank in Europe.

In summer 2001 discussions began between Deutsche Bank, Deutsche Post and Postbank, but at that time Deutsche Post was not ready to sell a majority stake and so Deutsche Bank withdrew. By 2003, the CEO of Deutsche Post AG and chairman of Postbank's supervisory board, Klaus Zumwinkel, was believed to be again considering selling part or all of Postbank. There were two options for Deutsche Bank: offer either to buy 100 per cent of Postbank or to act as the IPO manager if only a minority interest was to be sold. Acquiring Postbank represented a unique opportunity to improve Deutsche Bank's ratings by taking on €53 billion of deposits and balancing the Group's more volatile operating profits from trading and fees. Secondly, the scale of the contemplated acquisition would have established the bank as the market leader in Germany. The timing was ripe for PBC, which was implementing a programme of 'scale and scope' to deliver a wider range of services to a larger customer base. Postbank customers presented large potential for such services. Some considerations were that other banks were likely to be interested, which could lead to a bidding war or higher purchase price, and that there was a high proportion of civil servants (about 40 per cent of employees) which could not be reduced easily to realise synergies. Finally, the deal would reduce regulatory capital so measures would have to be taken to mitigate this, either through reducing the bank's share buyback programme (see chapter VI.3), a capital increase or paying for part of the deal in shares rather than cash.

In the end, the second round of discussions went a bit further than the first, but they were ultimately abandoned. There remained a significant gap of about 25 per cent in the value placed on Postbank by Zumwinkel compared to Deutsche Bank's estimate.[83] The lower valuation offered by Deutsche Bank was leaked to the press in early June 2004 just weeks before Postbank's IPO, which further soured relations. Deutsche Bank reflected that Postbank customers were not a good 'fit' for Deutsche Bank at this stage in its transformation into an investment bank; customers mainly used Postbank as their second or third banking outlet, which made them less profitable for cross-selling. Further obstacles included the physical link of branches to post office premises, which constrained flexibility. Instead, Postbank launched its IPO for 49.9 per cent of its equity on 23 June 2004 at a share price of €28.50 in a deal partially brokered by Deutsche Bank.

Having failed to arrange a merger, the Postbank management set about growing through acquisition. In 2005, Postbank acquired mortgage lender BHW and in 2006 formally took over 850 branches from Deutsche Post and became a member of the DAX German share price index. The Postbank of 2008 was thus a very different proposition than in 2004. Postbank had three million more customers, customer deposits had grown from €57.3 billion to €112.9 billion and loans had more than doubled from €43 billion to almost €100 billion. Clearly Postbank was a much larger entity for Deutsche Bank to absorb than any of its other retail acquisitions. When Norisbank was taken over in August 2006 it had 98 branches and 334,000 clients. In 2007 Berliner Bank had 1,400 staff and 341,000 clients served through 60 branches in Berlin compared to Postbank's 21,470 workers (FTE) and 855 branches across Germany.[84]

Second approach: 2008

In early November 2007, the Deutsche Post CEO Klaus Zumwinkel hinted that he anticipated selling off its controlling interest in Postbank (50 per cent plus 1 share), sending shares soaring.[85] Both Commerzbank and Deutsche Bank informally expressed their interest.[86] Speculation that Postbank would be sold as part of a deal with both Commerzbank and Dresdner Bank prompted a renewed surge in the share price in the spring of 2008 (after Zumwinkel was forced to resign due to a charge of personal tax evasion).[87] Ackermann publicly confirmed his interest in acquiring Postbank in February 2008,[88] and by June the *Financial Times* reported that Deutsche Bank was among the leading domestic contenders in negotiations with Deutsche Post.[89] At the end of May 2008, Deutsche Bank was approached on behalf of Deutsche Post to solicit an offer to buy Postbank. This initiative came after the shudder in the markets in spring 2007 and the de-risking of Deutsche Bank's investment banking business during that summer, but before the financial meltdown prompted by the collapse of Lehman Brothers on 15 September 2008.

The strategic rationale for taking an interest in Postbank in 2008 focused on several of the same concerns as four years earlier, but additionally reflected changes in the domestic competitive environment. By this time Postbank had 14 million customers, of which about four million were believed to hold their main or sole account with Postbank, thus providing a customer base for cross-selling profitable products. Secondly, such a large acquisition would not be so overwhelming after the integration of Norisbank and Berliner Bank since 2006. Moreover, the acquisition of Postbank would prevent any competitor from acquiring Postbank and challenging Deutsche Bank's leadership.

On the other hand, on 1 September 2008 the supervisory boards of Commerzbank and Dresdner Bank announced the merger of these two historic banks in a takeover by Commerzbank worth €9 billion. This was much less than the €24 billion Allianz had paid for Dresdner after the failed merger with Deutsche Bank in 2000. The combination created a larger competitor in the domestic German market for Deutsche Bank. Table 15, below, shows that Postbank and Deutsche Bank together would have by far the largest reach in retail banking, and beyond the combined client base of 12 million at Commerzbank and Dresdner Bank. In July 2008 Citibank announced that its retail operations in Germany would be taken over by French co-operative bank Crédit Mutuel for €5 billion, a deal concluded in December 2008. The first half of 2008 was therefore a time of general restructuring in the German market and jockeying for position among the suppliers of retail services.

In September 2008, Postbank was too big for a complete takeover by Deutsche Bank. Therefore, Deutsche Bank aimed to acquire a minority stake with the option to acquire the majority at a later point in time, if this should turn out to be feasible

Table 15: Distribution of retail customers in Germany: end 2007.

	Number of Clients (million)	Share (per cent)
Savings banks	50	38.6
Co-operative banks	30	23.1
Postbank	14.5	11.2
Deutsche Bank	9.7	7.5
Dresdner Bank	6.5	5.0
ING DiBa	6.1	4.7
Commerzbank	5.5	4.2
HypoVereinsbank	4	3.1
Citibank	3.3	2.5
Total	129.6	100

Source: Analyst Call by Stefan Krause (Deutsche Bank Management Board), 12 September 2008. https://www.db.com/ir/en/download/Analyst_Call_Postbank_final.pdf

and strategically advantageous. Initially, the deal was structured so that Deutsche Bank would buy a 29.75 per cent stake for a total of €2.8 billion (€57.25 per share) but had an option to acquire a majority stake for the next three years at a price of €55 per share. Moreover, Deutsche Bank had first refusal on all remaining shares of Postbank.[90] In the meantime, Deutsche Bank and Postbank would explore co-operation in cross-selling insurance and retail mortgages. If Deutsche Bank exercised the option to buy the rest of Postbank (at €55 per share) then Private & Business Clients (PBC) would be the market leader in German retail banking. Even more importantly, perhaps, the deal prevented any competitor from acquiring Postbank and challenging Deutsche Bank's leadership. The acquisition could be financed through issuing new equity of about €1.7–2 billion plus subordinated debt. The final agreement was confirmed and announced on Friday 12 September, a mere three days before the collapse of Lehman Brothers in New York drove the global banking system into its existential crisis. In this time of turmoil the deal signalled Deutsche Bank's commitment to the domestic German market and economy as well as rebalancing its global activities between retail and investment banking. Moreover, Deutsche Bank's cautious approach of starting with a minority interest limited their initial exposure. But the timing did create challenges.

At a joint press conference on 12 September 2008, Josef Ackermann and Frank Appel, chief executive officer of Deutsche Post, announced Deutsche Bank's shareholding in Postbank.

In the wake of the financial crisis of September 2008, Postbank's share price fell dramatically from €60.75 at the end of 2007 to €26.66 at end September and €15.50 by the end of 2008, making the price of €57.25 in September 2008 seem, in hindsight, a huge overvaluation. In light of the changed circumstances, Deutsche Bank and Deutsche Post amended the transaction structure in January 2009. The fresh structure comprised three tranches and enabled Deutsche Bank to complete the transaction in more capital-efficient manner.[91] Postbank reported pre-tax losses of about €1.5 billion combined in financial years 2008 and 2009, but a profit before tax of €315 million for 2010. It was fully consolidated as a subsidiary in December 2010, as Deutsche Bank increased its position to a majority stake. Postbank would remain an independent brand. At the time, Ackermann and Neske told staff that the integration 'makes us the undisputed market leader in the retail banking segment of Europe's most powerful economy'.[92] The move was also meant to match the 'remarkable achievements in investment banking' since the takeover of Bankers Trust 10 years earlier. By developing the retail business 'into a strong second pillar', Deutsche Bank felt 'now ready for the new era in banking'.

8. Conclusions

The retail business of the bank was the most visible to the German people, but for much of the period under review it was also a challenge to generate profits. In the German context, retail banking was even more challenging than in most markets because of the elevated level of competition from not-for-profit enterprises. As the corporate and investment banking expanded in the 1990s and 2000s, however, retail remained the anchor of Deutsche Bank's business model. The 'safe' funding streams from deposits, the reach into customer pools for cross-selling higher profit-generating products and the protection of the bank's footprint and influence in Germany required a continued commitment to its retail customers. The tension between the two sides of the bank generated a series of restructurings until the two halves were finally clearly distinguishable from each other by 2000. Within the retail network there was a constant revolution during the 1990s and 2000s of job cuts, regional restructuring and attempts to segment the market by customers' wealth and mode of service delivery in order to try to boost net revenues and to cut costs. These efforts did not deliver the hoped-for results and often damaged the bank's domestic reputation. While under constant pressure to prune costs, this division also embarked on substantial acquisitions to try to capture market share both domestically and in Europe. The highest levels of management were committed to trying to sustain and, if possible, increase retail deposit-taking, even if losses in this business needed to be offset by retail asset and wealth management. While something of a 'Cinderella' as the target of repeated economy drives and restructuring, the retail sector was crucial for the bank's strategy: a sort of 'fairy godmother'. Without the retail business, the ambitions for corporate and investment banking would be undermined by an unbalanced risk profile that would reduce the bank's credit rating. Finally, on the eve of the global financial crisis, the Private & Business Clients Division seemed poised to lead the international and cost savings strategies for the bank as it slimmed down the workforce, enhanced its IT provision and embarked into promising new markets in India and China. But the ensuing decade was set to be one of retrenchment.

VI. The Road to 2007

The astonishing rise of trading in asset-backed securities linked to the real estate market in the US has been widely documented, notably through two official US investigations in 2010 and a bestselling book by Michael Lewis, later made into a Hollywood feature film, *The Big Short*. Deutsche Bank was attributed a prominent part in how the financial crisis was allowed to occur. As noted in Chapter II, the emergence of investment banking at Deutsche Bank in the 1990s was highly contested and strategically challenging for the bank as it sought to rush forward into markets with which most of the senior management and the Supervisory Board were unfamiliar. The acquisition of Bankers Trust in 1999 provided a foundation for the rapid expansion of Wall Street operations, but the bank's businesses there initially struggled amid strong competitive pressure from the big US players such as Goldman Sachs, Citigroup and Merrill Lynch. However, during the early 2000s Josef Ackermann, as Breuer's heir apparent, strengthened his leadership of the bank's strategy, giving more resources to the investment banking arm. This pulled the bank deliberately into a competitive position with the top US financial conglomerates. It must be remembered, however, that Deutsche Bank was not the only bank pursuing the strategy of seeking high returns from the securitisation boom – it was part of an industry-wide pursuit of revenue, profit and scale during these decades.

In the short term, Deutsche Bank appeared to survive the 2007–08 US subprime mortgage market meltdown relatively unscathed despite being among the most prominent banks during the boom. Deutsche Bank Group was involved in the entire life cycle of mortgage-backed securities that were at the heart of the increased risk in the market. At the foothills of the debt mountain, the bank owned or part-owned several commercial and retail mortgage providers in Germany and the US. Deutsche Bank also engaged in financing transactions that turned bundles of mortgages into tradeable assets through asset-backed securities (ABS) and collateralised debt obligations (CDO).[1]

Figure 26 shows the life cycle of a mortgage through the securitisation process. Mortgages and their claims on the homeowners' payments of capital and interest were sold on by the original lender to specialist entities that combined them into retail mortgage-backed securities (RMBS). The RMBS were then divided into tranches that were assessed by independent ratings agencies (e.g. Moody's or Standard & Poor's) as to their risk and then sold to investors. The higher risk tranches were sometimes then bundled together into collateralised debt obligations with their own ratings and then sold to other investors or bundled up again into CDO Squared. In the process, the details of the thousands of individual home mortgages became obscured, but the fees associated with each round of securitisation created an appetite for retail mortgages to feed the machine.

Figure 26: Life cycle of a mortgage through the securitisation process.

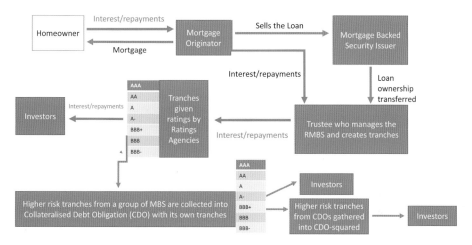

Between 2004 and 2008 Deutsche Bank Securities Inc. (DBSI), the Group's US broker-dealer subsidiary, built and sold 47 different CDOs that securitised about $32.2 billion worth of assets.[2] Much of the securitisation business was recorded off the bank's own balance sheet through specialised conduits that Deutsche Bank controlled directly, or through third-party conduits. One of the characteristics of such special-purpose vehicles was that if certain conditions were met they could help reduce the precautionary regulatory capital that had to be set against these assets. But the bank's senior management recognised the dangers and reduced the exposure as the first cracks appeared in the mountain of debt from 2005 to 2007, so that the short-term impact of the collapse in the mortgage-backed securities (MBS) market was relatively modest. Thus, the bank's warehouse of subprime mortgage-backed securities waiting to be bundled into CDOs was reduced from €2.4 billion at the start of 2007 to about €1 billion by June and a mere €8 million by September 2007, a year before Lehman Brothers collapsed.[3] By this time Deutsche Bank was net short €1.4 billion of US subprime exposure (i.e. they stood to gain if the price of US subprime assets fell) while net default risk for US subprime was estimated at €1.7 billion. But to understand how the bank was drawn into this business, we first need to look further back. Deutsche Bank began its trading and sales in mortgage-backed securities in the mid-1990s and the next section traces the evolution of this business line.

1. Building the Trading Business in the USA

In early May 1994, while the structure of the investment banking business was still being hotly debated, the Management Board approved a proposal to create a new department specialising in the creation and trading of securities collateralised by real estate mortgages and other forms of asset-backed securities (ABS).[4] The strategy was to establish a niche market based on advanced technology (to enhance customer service), product innovation (new types of securities) and high-margin capital-intensive businesses 'that require exper-tise possessed by few organizations in the marketplace'.[5] This was to be achieved by taking on a leader in the field – the proposal was developed with Howard B. Hill who had led the team at Daiwa Securities. Daiwa closed Hill's unit at the end of March 1994 after Fed interest rates began to rise and the market in collateralised mortgage obligations (CMOs) plummeted after homeowners slowed the pace of refinancing. This turn in the market also caused the collapse of David Askin's Collateralised Mortgage Obligation hedge fund, sending ripples through the system.[6] This might have seemed an inauspicious time for Deutsche Bank to launch a mortgage-backed securities (MBS) unit, but John A. Rolls (CEO of Deutsche Bank North America), Bernd von Maltzan (Trading and Sales) and Jürgen Bilstein (Corporate Finance) believed that regulatory changes, including new capital regulations for banks and insurance companies, would soon require banks to sell on their mortgage portfolios and invest instead in MBS. Hill was to lead a team of 30–40 staff, of which about a quarter would come with him from Daiwa. The US subsidiary Deutsche Bank Securities Corporation (DBSC) agreed to employment contracts that paid a base salary, minimum bonus guarantees for up to three years and profit-sharing of one third of the department's net income before bonus and taxes. If an individual's bonus exceeded $1 million in any year, a proportion would be vested in a fund and the employee would need to remain with DBSC for three years to get this portion.[7] The unit also required an IT system that would cost about $5–8 million and take up to six months to be up and running, but Hill's expertise and experience were deemed to mitigate the risk of these upfront costs. This was clearly an expensive commitment with a compensa-tion scheme that conformed to US rather than German norms.

The core business for the new department was 'trading in, and acquiring for the purpose of restructuring for sale, securities consisting of certificates of interest in pools of mortgage loans (on single-family residences) insured by US government agencies' such as Fannie Mae and Freddie Mac.[8] Since the Fannie Mae and Freddie Mac mortgages were insured, and there was 'substantial history on which to base loss projections', the risk was considered easily manageable. The proposal noted that 'there have been occa-sional examples of severe economic conditions in a given locality having a widespread effect on single-family home mortgages; therefore, the risk management policies would limit or preclude any substantial exposure to a concentration of uninsured mortgages in a single geographic area'.[9] The potential for an industry-wide collapse was not part of this assessment. The main target market was institutional investors such as pension funds, banks and corporate treasurers, with which Hill's team already had good contacts. The Management Board was advised that there was a highly liquid market for such secu-rities, which would be mainly investment grade using a senior/subordinate structure to enhance the rating. Thus, lower quality mortgages could be bundled up to create higher rated (and higher valued) securities. Specialised staff were recruited to market the less liquid subordinated tranches. The proposal asked for $100 million in equity capital to start, rising to a further $200 million by 1996. In addition, as mortgages were collected and inventoried before sale, the department would need $2–3 billion in credit lines. This was a substantial amount given that Deutsche Bank Group's net income after taxes in 1994 was the equivalent of less than one billion dollars. Manfred Timmermann, head of Controlling at Deutsche Bank headquarters, urged caution and also questioned why Daiwa was closing off this branch of activity if it was so promising, but the enterprise went ahead and grew quickly.[10] Hill left the bank two years later in 1996 to open his own firm. John A. Rolls also left in February 1996 and was replaced by Carter McClelland, who had been recruited from Morgan Stanley to head the investment banking business of Deutsche Morgan Grenfell (DMG)/C. J. Lawrence Inc. in August 1995.

The predictions of the size of the market turned out to be correct and the unit grew quickly; too quickly, indeed, for the bank to hold on its own balance sheet. In October 1997, the Management Board agreed to set up a special purpose vehicle (SPV) conduit to support the growth of MBS trading off the bank's balance sheet. This solution reduced the regulatory capital that had to be held against the assets of this business and thereby increased the possible scale and profitability of trading.[11] Aspen Funding Co. would be nominally owned by a third party called Amacar but would be managed by Deutsche Morgan Grenfell (DMG). Aspen provided warehousing facilities for assets while they were being gathered for securitisation or refinancing, essentially providing up to $2 billion in financing facilities.[12] It was exceptionally successful, generating about $30,000 per day in fee income and was 'a key factor in securing approximately $7 billion of DMG underwriting mandates (as lead- and co-manager) for 1998'.[13] By May 1998, Aspen had met its warehousing target and the Management Board was asked to approve a second SPV conduit, Newport Funding Corporation (incorporated in the low tax state of Delaware), with a capacity of up to $5 billion in asset-backed commercial paper. In order to ensure that Newport Funding Corporation did not need to be consolidated into Deutsche Bank's balance sheet, Newport needed to buy about $3 billion of up to 10-year AAA-rated ABS and MBS on its own account to hold until maturity. This kept the financing part of its business below 40 per cent for regulatory purposes, leaving $2 billion for financing warehousing through repurchase (repo) agreements with Deutsche Bank's New York branch. Newport was also nominally owned by a third party, Cornish Holdings Corp., but managed by DMG under contract. These entities generated income for the bank (Aspen generated $18 million in 1998) from bridge refinancing and bond underwriting, but they also provided vital market knowledge about portfolios to be securitised which helped to win mandates.

The rapid growth of the US operations also raised IT and other technical challenges to build the infrastructure to support the new business. In March 1998, Deutsche Morgan Grenfell (DMG) acquired NatWest's Asian and US equities derivatives business, partly to provide a platform for processing DMG equities trade through the ADP Brokerage (the largest third-party provider of securities processing, which serviced over 30 per cent of US broker dealers).[14] The deal was announced in December 1997 with DMG paying £50 million for these parts of NatWest Markets (Bankers Trust bought NatWest's European cash equities for £129 million at the same time). In early 1998 DMG also moved to a new clearing system to process fixed income deals, but there were glitches that left liabilities on the balance sheet and required a further capital injection from head office. In May 1998 Deutsche Bank AG channelled $250 million to support the balance sheet of Deutsche Morgan Grenfell Inc. in the US.[15] But the technical problems attracted the attention of regulators such as the Securities and Exchange Commission

(SEC), which put Deutsche Bank North America on a 'watch list' to ensure that it was adequately capitalised. This led Ronaldo Schmitz (in charge of the US region) to ask Ackermann to 'impose volume limits on trading in NY immediately'. '[…] We must not wait for limits to be imposed by regulators, as undoubtedly they will.' '[…] I do not trust product groups to react to our very difficult situation adequately and in time.'[16] Clearly there were issues over controlling the business, which attracted the attention of regulators as well as senior management.

The SEC wrote to Robert Lynch, managing director of Deutsche Bank Securities Inc. (DBSI), New York, at the end of July 1998 to report a range of DMG's infractions of SEC rules. These included unreconciled ledger balances (some exceeding $1 billion) and 'improper posting of MBS repurchase principal and interest payments', delayed notifications and 'significant and startling weaknesses' in DMG's internal management reporting policies. The faults in trading risk and credit risk management related to MBS and collateralised mortgage obligations (CMOs) amounted to several billions of dollars.[17] Hugo Bänziger, head of credit risk management in GCI, also noted that there were issues raised by the Federal Reserve over credit risk management in the MBS businesses related to documentation.[18] At the end of January 1999 the New York Stock Exchange (NYSE) accepted Deutsche Bank's offer of $170,000 to settle enforcement actions related to their examinations of the broker DBSI so long as 'the proposed settlement will not specify any individuals nor involve any letters of admonition'.[19] The fast-growing business in New York clearly created fresh challenges for the bank's operational risk.

On the other hand, the MBS group in the US was also a source of pride for DMG. It was the first dealer successfully to market and trade with an automated trading system for products known as MBS Pass-Through. Pass-through was the term used when individual mortgages were bundled into pools and shares in the pool were sold to customers. The owners of these securities then received revenue from the interest and mortgage repayments that 'passed through' to the holders of the securities. In 1998 the volume of pass-through sold by Deutsche Bank increased 400 per cent, increasing market share and profitability so that DMG was ranked fourth in commercial mortgage-backed securities (CMBS) underwriting in the first quarter of 1998.[20] DMG was also underwriter for over $4 billion home equity loan transactions in the first quarter of 1998. In April 1998 the MBS group's pipeline exposure in the US (i.e. holdings of mortgages waiting to be securitised) was almost $10 billion, 60 per cent of which was with the bank's special purpose subsidiary German American Capital Corporation (GACC).[21] Hans-Dirk Krekeler, counsel of the investment bank, became concerned and penned a note to Schmitz, Barry Allardice (CEO for the Americas) and others warning:

> As Deutsche Bank most painfully experienced in the past, our concern should be that due to a sudden change in the US real estate markets, we get stuck with a largely illiquid real estate portfolio. Falling real estate values could force us to make high provisions on our portfolio. A 30% drop in values would not be unprecedented. Our concern should also be whether we have the management capacity to deal with work-outs in an extremely large geographical area.[22]

To clarify the situation, Schmitz asked for a special presentation on MBS in New York on 1 May 1998. He noted that the discipline controls on MBS operations were more numerous than almost any of the bank's other businesses, but 'it appears no event risk discipline was put in place' to prepare for a market downturn.[23] The discussion pointed to historic events such as 1989–94 when property prices had fallen 30–50 per cent as a 'worst case scenario' and concluded that the current workout infrastructure would not be sufficient in such circumstances.

Edson Mitchell reassured Schmitz in a lengthy memo a few days later, copied to Ackermann and Krekeler.[24] He calculated the total balance sheet for MBS was $8.5 billion. This excluded an additional $4 billion off balance sheet with Aspen, most of which were AAA, were insured by MBIA (Municipal Bond Insurance Association) and were match-funded in the commercial paper markets.[25] Of the $8.5 billion, $3.5 billion was 'extremely liquid, highly rated securities (82% AAA, and AA rated)' and marked to market to determine a realistic value on a daily basis if they had to be sold. A further $1.7 billion was 'fully secured with collateral which use haircuts provided by credit and are marked to market daily. The counterparties include such highly regarded firms such as Banc One and UBS.' A further $3 billion were loans held in advance of securitisation that were valued according to rating agency credit enhancement models that accounted for recession scenarios. Mitchell noted that 'the holding period for this inventory has shrunk from close to one year to three to four months'. Holding these loans for a year was a risky prospect given the potential for property prices to fall sharply and unexpectedly. But Mitchell reassured Schmitz by citing 'an interesting example of securitization of mortgages in the face of a steep drop in the underlying real estate value' of a $200 million portfolio of Hong Kong mortgages whose value had fallen 25 per cent during the six months they were held by Deutsche Bank 'yet we were able to successfully complete the securitization and earn $7–8m' in fees. In this business much depended on the sales force identifying potential buyers. Mitchell attached a DMG report which concluded that both commercial and residential real estate had low levels of risk and that this was reinforced by the 'discipline of mark to market' that further protected the bank. Bänziger suggested to Ackermann in October 1998 that 'given the high volume of work with some of our mortgage originators, I consider setting up a small work-out group which can dedicate 100% of their time to manage the exposure. In general, I am not overly concerned with our exposure, however it is vital for our success to get all documentation and collateral valuation right. I consider the risk for DB at this moment in time to be rather of operational nature' rather than market risk.[26]

2. Structural Changes – Realigning Investment Banking

The infrastructure for the securitisation boom in the US described above was built during perilous times in international banking markets. The Asian financial crisis of the second half of 1997, and the other emerging market crises that followed in the late 1990s, created a risky environment for investment banking and hit the profitability of many global financial institutions.

During these challenging times, Josef Ackermann built his reputation and influence through his leadership of the GCI Division and his strategic influence on the debates over the bank's future. As noted in Chapter IV he was a key player in the cancellation of the Dresdner merger of 1999–2000 that weakened Breuer's position as head of the Management Board and, with Mitchell's support, he was nominated as Breuer's successor for the final 18 months of Breuer's term of office. Until January 2006, the Management Board selected its own 'spokesman' but after this point the Supervisory Board took on this responsibility. On 21 September 2000 Hilmar Kopper informed the Supervisory Board about the decision, confirming: 'Together with the Management Board, I regret that this decision has to be made known so early. But it seemed to us to be the right measure, so that there is no room for further public speculation and insinuations. The harmful insecurities associated with them inside and outside the bank make a clear statement already necessary.'[27] This was unprecedented and left Ackermann in a particularly powerful position even though Breuer continued as Spokesman of the Management Board until May 2002. Meanwhile, the integration of Bankers Trust in 2000 and the revenue generated by Mitchell's Global Markets division changed the shape of the bank's operations. The dual strategy soon prompted another formal restructuring to exploit the growth in financial markets and rapid pace of financial innovation in the US and elsewhere. In June 2000, Edson Mitchell replaced Ronaldo Schmitz as co-leader of Global Corporates and Institutions (GCI) along with Ackermann on the Management Board, while equities' chief Michael Philipp succeeded Michael Dobson to head Asset Management. This marked the promotion of the first Americans to the bank's Management Board.

A month later, Breuer presented the refreshed vision to shareholder representatives on the Supervisory Board.[28] The plan was to create two major sides of the bank to reflect better the bank's sources of revenue. Breuer claimed that the Dual Focus strategy had paid off; the Bankers Trust acquisition had pushed the bank into a number three global ranking in investment banking (by revenues in 1999) and number four for asset management, private banking and custodian services. The share price had outperformed the Bloomberg European Banks Index by 85 per cent since the announcement of the Bankers Trust acquisition in November 1998. An astonishing 95 per cent of the net income before tax in 1999 had come from GCI, Asset Management and Private Banking.[29] The challenge was that Deutsche Bank was still very small compared to its competitors, which had grown faster through acquisition, so that Deutsche Bank ranked only fourteenth overall among US and EU financial services companies in July 2000. Deutsche Bank had a market capitalisation of €60 billion compared with €68 billion for ING, €69 billion for Chase, €201 billion for AIG and €252 billion for Citigroup. In the new and lucrative business of trading and sales, size mattered.

Breuer advised the Supervisory Board that a quick boost could be achieved by selling more of the bank's considerable industrial holdings, which had been accumulated over the years as part of the German universal banking model. The book value of industrial holdings reported in the annual balance sheet for 1999 was just €6 billion but the market value was €26 billion. Allowing for a liquidity discount of 15 per cent or €3 billion (for lower market prices as the shares were sold), there was still €17 billion of added value to be realised. The Management Board expected that there was likely to be further consolidation of the banking industry driven by deregulation, internationalisation and economies of scale from IT in transactions and distribution. As a relatively small firm, Deutsche Bank was likely to fall further behind unless there was a change in strategy. Breuer told the Supervisory Board that the bank was at a turning point and there were four options about what kind of bank Deutsche Bank could become: 'Global' universal bank (like Chase or Citigroup), 'Traditional' universal bank (like Commerzbank, Unicredito or HypoVereinsbank), 'Focused' advisory bank like Dresdner Bank or an 'Integrated capital market and advisory bank' (like Merrill Lynch, Goldman Sachs, UBS, Credit Suisse or Morgan Stanley Dean Witter). Breuer's recommendation on behalf of the Management Board was to aim to be an integrated bank, which promised the highest valuation (price/book value ratio) and return on equity, but also posed the highest share volatility relative to the total market. This option would build on the successful divisions and a leading position in Europe but divest the bank of its mortgage banking (Eurohypo), some insurance (Nürnberger, Gerling) and financial services (Deutsche Financial Services). The data presented below demonstrate the large and growing importance of Ackermann's GCI Division, which generated over half of the bank's revenue and almost 60 per cent of its profit by 2000. But just as the future strategy crystallised, the bank was struck by the death of one of its key leaders.

Table 16: Revenues by division from 1998 to 2000 (January to May).

	€ Millions			Per cent of Total		
	1998	1999	Jan–May 2000	1998	1999	Jan–May 2000
GCI	4,761	9,596	6,536	36.5	48.1	55.8
Asset Management	953	1,519	797	7.3	7.6	6.8
Retail and Private Banking	4,303	4,807	2,371	32.9	24.1	20.3
Corporates and Real Estate	2,707	3,126	1,401	20.7	15.7	12.0
Global Technology and Services (profit centre)	337	897	602	2.6	4.5	5.1

Table 17: Profit from ordinary activities by division before tax.

	€ Millions			Per cent of Total		
	1998	1999	Jan–May 2000	1998	1999	Jan–May 2000
GCI	520	2,225	1,931	22.0	56.8	59.7
Asset Management	379	581	318	16.0	14.8	9.8
Retail and Private Banking	576	201	527	24.3	5.1	16.3
Corporates and Real Estate	803	927	418	33.9	23.7	12.9
Global Technology and Services (profit centre)	90	-16	39	3.8	-0.4	1.2

Source: Presentation on Group Strategy to Shareholder Representatives in the Supervisory Board – Backup slides, 24 July 2000, HADB, V27/x256.

On 22 December 2000, in heavy weather, the small plane carrying 47-year-old Edson Mitchell to his holiday home in Maine crashed, killing him and his pilot. The news was a devastating personal blow to senior managers at the bank and a shock for the bank's Global Markets business, which he had built up so successfully over nearly six years. The bank's share price stumbled, but quickly recovered as Ackermann and Breuer set about reassuring the bank's clients and investors. Mitchell's central role as a force of energy and imagination in the bank, expanding the Global Markets business so rapidly through a mixture of personal charisma, talent and ambition was critical to the reorientation of the bank in the second half of the 1990s. He created a huge and mainly loyal team of traders and market makers who focused intently on the revenues that would generate their annual compensation and bonuses. The bank's large balance sheet and opportunities for growth attracted a high calibre of ambitious and innovative traders,

Anshu Jain joined Deutsche Bank in 1995. He became head of the Global Markets division in 2001 following the death of Edson Mitchell. He became a member of the Management Board in 2009.

many of whom drifted away after his death. There were several contenders to replace Mitchell, but Ackermann chose Anshu Jain quite quickly. He had proved himself as Mitchell's lieutenant and had the leading expertise in fixed income business.

Despite Mitchell's death, the reorganisation pressed forward and in February 2001 the bank was restructured into two main divisions: Private Clients and Asset Management (PCAM) and the Corporate and Investment Bank (CIB). They were supported by a Group Corporate Center that took responsibility for Risk, Finance, Human Resources and IT, and by DB Services. This structure separated the control functions from the operational functions of the bank, which was to prove problematic, although CIB had its own Risk and Resources Committee led by Hugo Bänziger as Chief Credit Risk Officer; Richard Evans was Chief Market Risk Officer. The Corporate Investments (CI) section managed the bank's investments and equity holdings during the period of divestment (described below).

As head of Sales and Trading in CIB, Ackermann took over control of Global Markets and Global Equities as well as two new units in Global Debt Origination and Global Credit Products. Jain succeeded Mitchell as head of Global Markets, Kevin Parker led Global Equities, Tom Gahan led Global Credit Products and Grant Kvalheim led Global Debt Origination. A joint venture between Global Credit Products and Corporate Finance would manage real estate lending and trading assets, in order to build on the bank's position 'as a major lender in this sector, as well as one of the

Figure 27: Group management structure 2001.

Management Board					
Corporate Center Breuer (Spokesman), Börsig (Chief Financial Officer), Fischer (Chief Risk Officer/Operating Officer), von Heydebreck (Chief Human Resources), Lamberti (Chief Information Officer)					
Corporate and Investment Bank Ackermann (Chairman)			Private Clients and Asset Management Breuer (Chairman)		
Ackermann		v. Boehm-Bezing	Lamberti	v. Heydebreck	Philipp
Sales and Trading	Corporate Finance	Transaction Banking	Personal Banking	Private Banking	Asset Management
CIB Global Technology			PCAM Global Technology		
DB Services					
Corporate Investments Breuer (Chairman)					

largest players in the CMBS [Commercial Mortgage-Backed Securities] market, we are well positioned to be a dominant force in the Real Estate banking market'.[30] Clearly, building the bank's business in the securitisation of mortgages was an important part of this restructuring. Overall, the strategic objective for CIB was 'to reach, and sustain, the position of global no. 1 – with a dominant position in Europe – in corporate and institutional banking, as measured by financial performance, market share and client franchise'.[31] These were huge ambitions for a European bank.

3. Selling the Family Silver

As the bank was reoriented to align more with US banks in the bulge bracket, the balance sheet and mobilisation of capital were reassessed. There were three key drivers: regulatory capital requirements, return on equity target and external credit rating. First, prudential regulation requires banks to hold capital in low-risk and low-return assets in case their riskier ventures generate losses, but the low returns on regulatory capital means that financial institutions try to minimise this, for example by moving some business to subsidiaries or special purpose vehicles. Secondly, the return on equity target of 25 per cent could be made easier to achieve by reducing the bank's outstanding equity. Furthermore, the bank's external credit rating determined how much it cost to raise capital or borrow, so keeping the AAA rating from agencies like Moody's and Standard & Poor's was critical to the bank's leveraged business model. Together these elements created a motivation to increase capital and reduce equity outstanding. The compensation deals for staff that included shares were a further consideration in the need to have a buoyant share price. Buying back the bank's shares from the market would help with achieving the target return on equity of 25 per cent and could be financed through the sale of industrial holdings to avoid reducing the coverage of regulatory capital. These industrial shares, the legacy of the German style of universal banking, had been a main source of revenue for the bank during most of the period under review, creating hidden reserves because of the excess of market value over the book value of these assets as well as a steady flow of dividend revenue. But being a 'Hausbank' also brought its own burdens. Deutsche Bank was involved in liquidity injections and bailouts of several of the companies in its portfolio in the 1990s such as Metallgesellschaft (in 1994), Klöckner-Humboldt-Deutz (in 1995) and Philipp Holzmann (in 1999).[32] The insider control of companies by big banks was also challenged by the public, by the spread of US accounting practices and by the emphasis on shareholder returns as part of the consolidation of international business through mergers and acquisitions.[33] Deutsche Bank was certainly not alone in divesting the industrial shareholdings that it had accumulated over time, but the bank became a major focus of public attention because of its leading role in the German economy and the country's financial system.

As returns on the portfolio in the form of dividends fell in the early 1990s, selling off these assets in order to put the funds to more productive use was repeatedly discussed. Reviews in 1992 and 1994 resulted in reduction of some holdings, such as Daimler-Benz and Karstadt, to diversify the portfolio away from a focus on the automotive industry, insurance and retail and to aim at a participation of 10–15 per cent. In 1994, sales from the portfolio generated capital gains before tax amounting to DM 1.5 billion.[34] But capital increases of some firms such as Allianz, Munich Re and Daimler-Benz later in the year diluted the bank's holdings, and also reduced the return on the portfolio. Further sales in 1996 were aimed at industrial holdings with below average performance or 'of minor significance' to the bank.[35] The management was also sensitive to public debates in the mid-1990s about excessive power exercised by banks in Germany through the universal banking model of supervisory board representation and holdings of industrial shares.[36] For this reason, and in order to increase transparency and flexibility, placing the shareholdings in a special subsidiary or spinning them out of the main bank was attractive, but needed to be done in a tax efficient way.[37]

The shares in Daimler-Benz/Chrysler were among the last to be sold, partly because they were especially lucrative. In 1992 almost half of the bank's own dividend payment to shareholders could be covered by dividend income from these industrial investments, of which about half came from Daimler-Benz alone.[38] In 1998 Daimler-Benz merged with Chrysler, reducing the bank's stake in the company but generating an extraordinary dividend for Deutsche Bank of DM 3.2 billion in a year when total net income for the bank was DM 3.4 billion. The bank's participation in Daimler-Benz/Chrysler (and advisory fees during the merger) helped sustain revenues during these difficult years in international markets. Nevertheless, the way was prepared to reduce the portfolio to realise its market value.

The 1998 Annual Report signalled that the bank intended to manage the portfolio 'more actively and more flexibly'.[39] At the beginning of December 1998 Breuer announced that most of the industrial portfolio would be transferred to a separate legal entity, DB Investor, headed by Axel C. Pfeil and located in Eschborn.[40] Facing the same external pressures, Dresdner Bank and Munich Re followed similar procedures. Deutsche Bank's portfolio of directly held industrial shareholdings, amounting to a market value of DM 42 billion at the end of 1998, were distributed to fully owned subsidiaries, avoiding taxation on the transfer because the assets formed part of new partnerships. This was a landmark in the bank's development, making it possible to sell off the industrial holdings in a more tax efficient way. Deutsche Bank AG realised about one third of the profit from the difference between the book value and market value through this transfer, allowing increased dividend to shareholders from DM 1.80 per share to DM 2.20 in May 1999. At the end of 1999 the German government announced its intention to reduce capital gains tax on sales of corporate shareholdings in German companies from 50 per cent to zero, which would allow the realisation of even more of the profits from the bank's portfolio. In the end the law took six months to pass through the German parliament and became effective at the start of 2002, but Deutsche Bank began to accelerate its programme of divestment while deferring its tax obligations until the law was passed.

The intention to begin selling the bank's industrial shares was intimated clearly to the market, with the annual reports repeatedly stating the policy of significantly reducing the bank's shareholdings while maximising the revenue from selling them, but it met with public criticism for reducing the bank's stable assets.[41] During 1999 the bank sold a quarter of its holdings in Allianz, which contributed to a total revenue of €2.2 billion from securities for sale in that year. The next year, the bank sold 42 per cent of its remaining shares in Allianz, generating a further €2.3 billion. This marked a change in the relationship between these two titans of German business as they unwound their co-ownership just as the Dresdner merger deal failed. In 2001, sales of a quarter of the bank's stake in Munich Re generated €1.4 billion and continued the gradual separation of banking and insurance businesses in Germany. Table 18 shows that major industrial holdings were concentrated by value in three companies and that by 2003 Daimler-Chrysler shares were the only remaining large shareholding, with all of Munich Re sold off and only a remnant of Allianz shares still in the bank's ownership. By the time the reduction in tax burden became effective in January 2002, the bank had already sold off most of its major industrial shareholdings.

The last shares in Allianz were sold in 2008 and the Daimler stake was finally sold in 2009 after a steady reduction from 2004. As the industrial shareholdings were sold off, the bank embarked on a programme of share repurchases in 2002. The share buyback was carefully designed to beat the average market price while shares earmarked for retirement were purchased systematically. The purchases were synchronised with sales of industrial securities to fund the operations and kept the target Tier 1 regulatory capital constant at 8 per cent.

In the early 2000s, as the bank's strategy was being reshaped, the returns from the industrial portfolio were negatively affected by the weak performance in global equity markets due to the dot-com bubble bursting, the terrorist attacks in New York in September 2001 and SARS (severe acute respiratory syndrome) affecting global business. The bank's recorded income fell sharply from almost €7 billion in 2000 to €1.8 billion in 2001. Partly this reflected the fact that in 2001 the bank was listed in New York and moved to US accounting standards (US GAAP) which required reporting of tax liabilities differently. But the fall in income also reflected falling commission and trading income and the costs from restructuring. We have seen that the timing of the programme of sales was affected by changes in the German tax law that altered the

Table 18: Deutsche Bank Industrial Holdings in non-bank listed companies, 1995–2003.

Year (as of 31 December)		Allianz AG	Daimler-Benz/ DaimlerChrysler AG	Munich Re AG	Share of 3 companies in total market value (%)	TOTAL market value
1995	% of company capital	10	24.4	10		
	market value in billion DM	6.379	9.063	2.53	76.1	23.612
1996	% of company capital	10	22.6	10		
	market value in billion DM	6.363	12.227	3.052	79.9	27.073
1997	% of company capital	10	21.8	10		
	market value in billion DM	10.448	14.152	5.585	84.1	35.881
1998	% of company capital	9.3	12	10		
	market value in billion DM	13.891	19.732	7.114	89.2	45.668
1999	% of company capital	7	11.9	9.6		
	market value in billion euro	5.675	9.219	4.342	87.5	21.995
2000	% of company capital	4.2	12.1	9.7		
	market value (holdings over 5%) in billion euro	3.987	5.312	6.521	88.2	17.933
2001	% of company capital	4	12.1	7.2		
	market value (over €150 million) in billion euro	2.806	5.861	3.889	84.2	14.909
2002	% of company capital	3.2	11.8	0		
	market value (over €150 million) in billion euro	0.783	3.403	0	88.2	4.746
2003	% of company capital	2.5	11.8	0		
	market value (over €150 million) in billion euro	0.965	4.4	0	90.6	5.919

Source: Deutsche Bank, annual reports. Note: 1995–1998 DM billion; 1999–2003 euro billion. From 1995 to 2000 Total Market Value is of companies in which Deutsche Bank held at least a 5 per cent stake. From 2001 the Total Market Value is of companies in which Deutsche Bank's interest was at least €150 million.

incentives for holding on to the equity of these companies, but the underlying decision to divest was taken before this change was implemented and formed part of the reinvention of the bank into a global investment bank.

4. The Rise of the Global Investment Bank, 2001–2004

In the first few years after the restructuring, the Corporate and Investment Bank (CIB) Division drove ahead on the basis of the rapidly growing Eurobond business. As the leading European corporate and investment bank, Deutsche Bank dominated Euro-denominated fixed income business, which created important positive benefits for other areas of the bank's business such as foreign exchange trading, advising and IPOs. But the difficult trading conditions in the early 2000s required a continued focus on cutting costs, and in particular reducing staff numbers across the bank's divisions, both internationally and in Germany.

By November 2001, CIB was still third in the world (behind JP Morgan and Citigroup), but the gap between Deutsche Bank and the second-place Citigroup was growing and the diagnosis was that the bank's size was too small in the US.[42] The bank pursued a carefully monitored programme of reducing costs while maximising revenues, but these efforts were made more difficult because of high loan loss provisions in 2002 that increased the cost base for the bank.[43] This prompted Anshu Jain to suggest securitising the loan portfolio to reduce regulatory capital. He also recommended marking the loan book to market, assessing the portfolio's 'market value' through the cost of hedging.[44] Given the cost of funds, a significant part of the bank's loan portfolio could be considered value-destroying since returns were lower than the cost of funds. To deal with this situation, in early 2003 Jain and Bänziger proposed a new Loan Exposure Management Group within CIB to arrange hedging for all new loans with terms over 180 days for international, large and medium-sized German borrowers and for real estate sub-investment grade portfolios. The goal was to reduce regulatory capital and increase the reported return on equity of the bank's lending by buying credit default swaps (CDS) and other credit derivatives.[45]

The terrorist attack on the Twin Towers in New York City on 11 September 2001 marked another major blow to the bank. One employee was killed and the collapse of the towers damaged the Bankers Trust building on nearby Liberty Street beyond repair. Ackermann flew out immediately to New York to support the bank's employees and to relocate its operations. He was prominent in the spirit of recovery in New York, taking part in a gala at the Metropolitan Opera and singing 'New York, New York' on stage with New York City Mayor Rudolph Giuliani. But the bank lost some of its

The long-awaited listing of Deutsche Bank shares on the New York Stock Exchange on 3 October 2001, only three weeks after the attack on the World Trade Center.

lustre as a result of the delay in bringing the damaged building down while Deutsche Bank sued its insurers to minimise its losses. In 2004, after the case was settled, the bank transferred the remnants of the building to the Lower Manhattan Development Corporation, which led the costly dismantling undertaken to minimise the releasing of hazardous substances in the building's fabric. It was only fully demolished in 2011, finally removing a dark reminder of the attack.

In 2002 Ackermann also pushed through fundamental changes to the management of the bank. In order to streamline cost-cutting, ensure focus on the collective goals for return on equity and to bring the management closer to operations he proposed a new Group Executive Committee (GEC). The GEC of the 1990s had similarly included heads of division, but by 2002 the dual 'virtual holding' structure of the bank left Ackermann's GEC with a much narrower grouping that was vested with greater power. One motive for creating the GEC was that, under German law, members of the Management Board had to disclose their salaries and compensation. If the compensation to the main division heads was disclosed, there would be a public backlash as well as disquiet within the bank since their compensation was so high. This meant that Ackermann was reluctant to bring his lieutenants onto the Management Board. The GEC was a way to shift effective management of the bank from the figureheads on the Management Board to those with greater operational understanding of the bank's business.

The formal agreement by the Group Board was:

> The Board of Managing Directors [= Management Board] forms, together with the Global Heads of Group Divisions CIB and PCAM as well as CI Division and possibly other members selected by the Group Board, the 'Group Executive Committee'. The Group Executive Committee performs advisory, co-ordinating and decision-preparing functions for the Board of Managing Directors. The members of this Committee are appointed and dismissed by the Group Board.[46]

Figure 28: Management structure as of 31 January 2002.

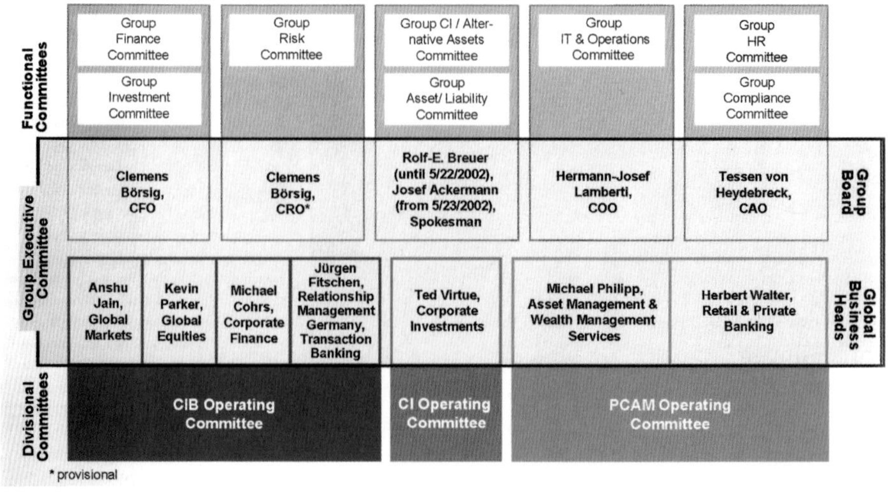

Source: *Forum*, March 2002, p. 18.

The members of the Group Executive Committee in autumn 2004, from the left: Kevin Parker, Michael Cohrs, Anshu Jain, Jürgen Fitschen, Clemens Börsig, Josef Ackermann, Hermann-Josef Lamberti, Tessen von Heydebreck, Pierre de Weck, Rainer Neske, Tom Hughes.

The GEC met monthly and was initially chaired by Breuer as Spokesman of the Management Board. The first GEC meeting was held in February 2002, where Breuer suggested, and the members agreed, that there should be no formal terms of reference for the new committee. From the 25 June 2002 meeting, the GEC began to meet in the morning before the Group Management Board, so it was able to report its recommendations to the Management Board.[47] This further increased the influence and power of the GEC vis-à-vis the Management Board since the change in timing meant that recommendations went from the GEC to the Board rather than from the Board to the GEC. Power in the bank had moved from the Management Board to the Group Executive Committee just as Ackermann took over as Spokesman on 23 May 2002. Over the next few years, Ackermann quickly advanced the bank's transformation to an integrated capital markets bank to rival the US conglomerates.

In addition to these challenges within the bank, Ackermann found himself in court over bonuses paid to senior executives in Mannesmann, for which he was a member of the supervisory board. Deutsche Bank owned a 5 per cent stake in Mannesmann, which was the target of a hostile takeover bid by Vodafone at the end of 1999. The deal was a landmark challenge to so-called 'Deutschland AG' whereby German industry operated in an environment that allowed long-term planning and stakeholder engagement without the need to fear hostile takeovers. Mannesmann's workers council strongly opposed the deal, as did the German Chancellor Gerhard Schröder, but in the end the bid was successful. Ackermann was among six senior executives charged in February 2003 for approving the bonuses paid to Mannesmann managers, which the prosecution alleged were bribes to get them to accept the Vodafone takeover. At the GEC meeting in February 2003 Ackermann 'expressed his complete lack of understanding of the state prosecutor's reported allegations'.[48] The case proved to be a public relations disaster for the bank and for Ackermann, who confirmed the German public's suspicion of him as an arrogant foreigner when he flashed a two-finger Victory sign at the start of the trial. The case ultimately was dismissed and no criminal activity was proven, but it revealed the lingering clash between the German antipathy to hostile takeover of German companies and the American-inspired bonus culture of international corporate business by 2000. The case also pushed Ackermann into the front line of the German public and press battle against the dominant Anglo-American style of business, and Deutsche Bank's transformation into a US-style investment bank.

At the start of the Mannesmann trial on 21 January 2004 Josef Ackermann showed the victory sign. This spontaneous gesture earned him a lot of criticism.

In August 2004 *The Economist* published a highly critical article about Deutsche Bank, arguing that it had essentially turned itself into a hedge fund.[49] Ackermann responded in a letter to the editor pointing out factual errors in the piece, but the perception that Deutsche Bank had left behind its traditional commercial and retail banking business in an effort to model itself on Goldman Sachs or other US banks was widely reported at the time. A key element was the shift to trading on the bank's own account rather than on behalf of customers, either through participating in hedge funds or operating proprietary trading desks within the bank (such as Greg Lippmann's desk described below). The change in the bank's profile was reflected in its balance sheet. Traditional loans and deposits fell from about 40 per cent of assets and 60 per cent of liabilities respectively in 2000 to 20 per cent and 40 per cent by 2003. This was partly due to the integration of the new US entities: Bankers Trust in 2000 and Zurich Scudder Investments in April 2002. But the change in the bank's balance sheet also reflected the new business model driven by increases in trading and sales activity that created new assets and liabilities in the form of capital market instruments and derivatives. One of the outcomes of the bank's new shape was that the ratio of net loans to deposits also fell, from 87 per cent in 1993 to 45 per cent in 2003, increasing the reported liquidity of the balance sheet and Tier 1 capital and also the bank's leverage (assets compared to shareholders' equity).[50]

In September 2004 the Group Executive Committee met offsite in Nice to review the bank's performance and structure. As a result of these deliberations, from 21 September, Jürgen Fitschen, who had previously been in charge of customer relationship management and transaction banking, was appointed head of regional management worldwide and chair of a specific Management Committee for Germany, which was designed to signal the bank's continued commitment to German corporate finance. But at the same time, CIB was streamlined into two main sections: Global Banking (led by Michael Cohrs) and Global Markets (led by Anshu Jain), so that the core parts of the investment bank were being run from London. In October 2004, Ulrich Cartellieri abruptly left the Supervisory Board as the investment bank took on greater prominence and the German business was downgraded.[51] The bank's press release noted that Cartellieri left 'due to differences of opinion on the bank's strategy' after 16 years on the Management Board followed by seven years on the Supervisory Board.[52] Over the previous year, the press had reported conflicts with Ackermann, stemming from the talks of merging with Citigroup in 2003–04 and the relative neglect of domestic branch business.[53] The bank that entered the final years before the global financial crisis of 2007 was therefore a very different institution from the one that had existed at the beginning of the millennium, with more emphasis on credit derivatives, more power in London and greater reliance on investment banking. These developments increased its vulnerability to the looming crisis in global markets.

During 2005 and 2006, the bank also embarked on a series of acquisitions and joint ventures in a 'bolt-on' strategy of growth.[54] By May 2006 there were 41 deals in various stages of development worth a total investment of about €15 billion including mortgage originators (Chapel, MortgageIT), retail banks (Berliner Bank, Banco Urquijo, Banca Popolare Italiana), insurance (Abbey Life) and other specialist financial services providers. These plans were mainly focused in Europe, but China also offered significant potential.

International Expansion: China

Deutsche Bank had more than a century of presence in China dating from its first branch in Shanghai, opened in 1872, albeit with long interruptions. As the People's Republic of China emerged from its decades of relative isolation in the 1980s and 1990s, the paths for banks to enter the market was carefully managed by the People's Bank of China to encourage investment in Chinese institutions and joint ventures. Accession to the World Trade Organization (WTO) in 2001 promised an acceleration in opening up the Chinese financial system to foreign participation. In 1981 Deutsche Bank opened a representative office in Beijing, followed by two more in Guangzhou in 1994 and in Shanghai in 1995, which were converted into branches in 1995 and 1999, respectively.[55] The Shanghai branch was authorised to undertake local currency renminbi (RMB) business in 2002. In January 2003 Deutsche Bank applied for a branch licence in Beijing and began to make plans for a securities business, including an application in March 2003 to replace the existing Beijing representative office with a 'Deutsche Bank AG (Securities) Beijing Representative Office'.[56] The search for a Chinese partner for a securities company joint venture was underway by the third quarter of 2002.[57] In 2002 the bank won the contract to be sole financial adviser to PetroChina's $15 billion West-East Pipeline Project, and financial adviser with JP Morgan for PetroChina's $5 billion acquisition of Husky Energy. In addition, the bank signed a contract to manage international payments transfers in dollars and euros for China Post through the European electronic payment system Eurogiro.[58] In January 2008, once regulations allowed, Deutsche Bank opened its subsidiary Deutsche Bank China but most of its business was directed through three joint ventures. This was a common strategy due to regulatory constraints on the share of local banks that could be owned by foreigners and because of the cultural barriers and complex regulatory structures that needed to be navigated in the rapidly changing Chinese financial sector.

Two major investments in 2005 marked Deutsche Bank's serious entry into the Chinese market. In March 2005, Deutsche Asset Management embarked on a joint venture with Harvest Fund Management (嘉实基金), beginning with 19.5 per cent and increasing this stake to 30 per cent ownership in 2008. Harvest Fund was

Advertising accompanied the founding of Deutsche Bank (China) Co., Ltd., referring to Deutsche Bank's first presence in China in 1872.

led by the young and dynamic CEO Henry Zhao. By the end of 2007, Harvest had RMB 252 billion under management, making it China's largest asset management joint venture and the third largest Chinese firm in the sector by assets. In the summer of 2005, Deutsche Bank agreed to embark on an investment of up to 14 per cent in Hua Xia Bank (华夏银行), a well-established joint stock commercial bank based in Beijing.[59] Hua Xia was founded in 1992 and made its IPO on the Shanghai Stock Exchange in September 2003, becoming a publicly traded company. Code-named 'Project Rooster', negotiations were underway by July 2005 and focused early on the potential to a separate joint venture for affluent customers.[60] Chinese regulations capped foreign bank ownership to below 10 per cent so Deutsche Bank's stake was initially 9.9 per cent. The purchase was agreed in principle in October 2005 and completed in May 2006. In 2007 the banks co-operated in issuing a credit card and there were hopes of selling other higher value-added products through the Hua Xia branch network, but it proved challenging to generate a significant positive return on the investment. In 2008 the bank proposed issuing new shares and Deutsche Bank was invited to increase its holdings to 12.3 per cent. This generated some discussion at the Supervisory Board, since on financial grounds alone there was no case for increasing the stake, but the Management Board believed it would demonstrate commitment to Hua Xia's expansion in China, and bring important reputational benefits for Deutsche Bank with the Chinese government.[61] In 2010 the stake in Hua Xia was increased again to 19.99 per cent (the maximum allowed) at a cost of €636 million. By this time the bank had 349 retail branches in 32 cities and was the thirteenth largest bank in China.[62] But in June 2010, the GEC agreed not to extend the bank's retail presence any further and in 2016 the stake in Hua Xia was sold.[63] Instead, the focus was on securities markets. In 2009 Deutsche Bank invested in 33 per cent of Zhong De Securities in a joint venture with Shanxi Securities Co. Ltd. In the meantime, however, the realignment of Deutsche Bank's exposure to the US market was underway.

International Expansion: Russia

Another area of international expansion that straddled the global financial crisis was the investment in Russia. As noted in 'Crisis and Fresh Opportunities', in the late 1990s the bank extended into a broad range of banking and financial services in Russia, partly through Deutsche Morgan Grenfell and partly through a subsidiary launched in April 1998. Although the rouble crisis hampered operations in Russia in the short term, the bank's presence grew and became profitable, generating a net income of €32.7 million in 1999 mainly due to fixed income trading and fee generation from the restructuring of Russian industry.[64] In 1998, Deutsche Bank led the group of 19 banks that negotiated over the Russian bond default, which further increased its profile during this volatile political period as Vladimir Putin rose to power. At the start of March 1999, the group of banks voted to depose Deutsche Bank from the head of the group after it agreed unilaterally to accept the government's restructuring offer of 10 per cent in cash and the rest in new bonds. Putin himself had close links with Germany, having worked for five years, from 1985 to 1990, in Dresden for the Soviet KGB intelligence service. From its outlets in Moscow, Deutsche Bank was also able to build leadership in Eurobond issuing and underwriting in the mid-2000s, and in 2003 Private Wealth Management services were introduced. By 2003, negotiations to acquire a 40 per cent stake in the brokerage house United Financial Group (code-named 'Sputnik'), were at the final due diligence stage.[65] UFG had been founded in 1994 by American and ex-Credit Suisse First Boston banker Charles Ryan and by Boris Fyodorov, a former finance minister under Gorbachev and Yeltsin. But the GEC was cautious, noting 'political ramifications of the Project, the likely need to increase the country limit for Russia, the interest of Global Markets to chart an independent course for its business in Russia, and whether there were any particular liabilities' for this participation in a Russian bank under local law.[66] The concerns were overcome and on 9 September 2003 the Management Board approved the acquisition of the brokerage and investment banking parts of UFG; the deal for a reported $70 million was completed in November.[67] Political links were particularly important in Russia, and Tessen von Heydebreck, for instance, met with Putin in the summer of 2004 and Ackermann developed a working relationship with him.[68] In February 2006 Deutsche Bank took over the remaining 60 per cent of UFG, including equities and corporate finance. A similar strategy was followed with UFG Asset Management. Just four days before the Lehman Brothers collapse in September 2008, the bank announced that it would take a 40 per cent stake in UFG Asset Management.[69] The rest was acquired three years later in 2011. Charles Ryan was kept on as CEO of Deutsche Bank Group in Russia before becoming chairman of UFG Asset Management in 2008. Igor Lijevsky then took over as CEO in Russia (until 2012). In June 2008 Putin was quoted as remarking to Ackermann that Deutsche Bank had done 'good work' in Russia in 2007 through $16 billion of IPOs and advising on mergers and acquisitions worth $22 billion, and that 'the fact that Deutsche Bank is a bridge between the Russian and German economies is of particular importance'.[70] Ackermann responded effusively saying that of the bank's 1,000 employees in Russia, 'mainly these are Russian geniuses'.

5. Anticipating the Downturn, 2005–2007

With the surge in the US housing market in 2004, innovations were beginning to take place in asset-backed securities (ABS) to provide greater liquidity. These securities had been traded for a long time based on a range of assets including student loans, credit cards and car loans. Investment banks provided credit default swaps (CDS) to 'insure' against losses, but there were no standardised CDS contracts and no secondary market where they traded; the CDS contracts tended to be drawn up on a bespoke basis by the main investment banks for their customers. Credit default swaps were developed in the 1990s within JP Morgan to allow its customers to lay off default or counterparty risk by entering a contract with a third party to take on that risk, for a fee. With increased demand to offer CDS on ABS including residential mortgage-backed securities (RMBS), the cost of devising bespoke contracts was rising and in early 2005 a group of traders met to devise a standard contract; the first meeting was held at Deutsche Bank's New York offices over a Chinese takeaway meal. Deutsche Bank's senior CDO trader, Greg Lippmann, and Hiroki (Rocky) Kurita, who oversaw subordinate and investment grade ABS trading, hosted traders and document lawyers from Goldman Sachs, JP Morgan Chase and Citibank.[71] By June 2005, a standardised credit default contract was agreed that allowed more trades to take place and therefore greater fee income for the banks. In his book on the crisis, the *Wall Street Journal*'s Gregory Zuckerman relates how shortly after the contract was created Angela Chang, a broker at Deutsche Bank, sold Michael Burry's Scion fund CDS protection for six tranches of RMBS with a $10 million face value of BBB subprime mortgages for 155 basis points above LIBOR ($155,000 p.a. each or $1 million for all six).[72] Chang was selling the CDS protection on behalf of a European pension fund with Deutsche Bank earning fees for the trade. This was Burry's first short of the US housing market. Mid-2005 was thus a crucial moment in the run-up to 2007–08; the game was on.

In mid-March 2005 Deutsche Bank's Risk Committee met to discuss the bank's risk profile and the outlook seemed rosy.[73] The bank was in the middle of a third share buyback programme of 45.5 million shares and had completed 82 per cent of the programme at an average price of €61.24. Provisions for credit losses were forecast to be 25 per cent below plan in the first quarter of 2005 and the risk profile was well diversified and of good quality. Basel II preparation was on track. PCAM hedge fund investments increased sharply from €89 million to €293 million in January 2005 but most hedging was around equity. As part of a periodic review, credit risk management (CRM) reviewed clients for potentially excessive leverage in the current low return environment but found no evidence of 'undue risk'. Credit exposure (marked to market) from option sellers was mainly in fund management (vis-à-vis AXA, Dexia, Natixis) and with liquidity providers (Merrill Lynch, Citibank, JP Morgan and UBS); all big names that seemed to pose very little risk. The bank was in a comfortable and liquid position with adequate capital to take advantage of new opportunities.[74]

But it was also clear at this time that there were operational risks in a fast-changing market. In 2000 and 2001 Deutsche Bank participated as an underwriter in two of WorldCom's bond offerings with a total volume of $17 billion. When WorldCom went bankrupt in 2002, investors sought damages from Deutsche Bank and another 16 underwriters based on an alleged breach of financial due diligence. In March 2005, Deutsche Bank agreed to a $325 million out-of-court settlement without any admission of wrongdoing, as did most of the other accused banks (including Citigroup $2.6 billion, Bank of America $0.5 billion). The net loss was only €50 million after insurance recoveries, so it did not make a serious dent in the balance sheet, but the episode did expose operational risks.[75] The extraordinarily rapid growth in credit derivatives also created problems for back office processing and compliance because of the scale of the business.[76] The International Swaps and Derivatives Association (ISDA) calculated that there were about $12.4 trillion worth of credit risk covered by credit derivative contracts by June 2005 compared with less than $3 trillion in 2003.[77] By this time, Deutsche Bank was the largest dealer in credit derivatives with a global market share of over 14 per cent, and almost a quarter of the bank's traded volumes were affected by unsigned confirmations due to lags in finalising paperwork.[78] Anshu Jain addressed this situation partly through a new document management programme and hiring back office staff in low-cost centres such as Bangalore in India.

Meanwhile, the May 2005 report on hedge funds noted that the number of firms in the portfolio had increased by 42 per cent to 489, and the number of funds in these firms by 63 per cent or by over 1,500.[79] The hedge fund portfolio was 'one of the most profitable industry portfolios of the bank'. Nevertheless, key risks included short-fall of staff expertise, weak infrastructure among smaller funds and sensitivity to severe market disruptions. In addition, it was recognised that 'highly complex transactions increase operational risk and can decrease system's liquidity'. However, stress testing was comforting since in 'a downside scenario combining several substantial adverse market movements' the portfolio quality would fall only one notch to iBB- and the resulting fall in market value could be covered by collateral calls.[80] The Group Credit Policy Committee (GCPC), which was the most important sub-committee of the Risk Committee, remarked on the operations problems, such as processing documentation, that might arise from the rapid increase in number of counterparties and transactions, and noted that Global Markets management was committed to improving process controls.[81] New counterparties were generally lower rated so the bank compensated with higher documentation standards and higher margining requirements. Given the increasing competition in established hedge fund products, market participants were branching out into less liquid assets including equity investments and real estate. By 2005 the bank also became more aware of market risk from the weaknesses in the US real estate market.

Karen Weaver was the bank's global head of Securitization Research and an expert in real estate markets, based in New York.[82] In April 2005 she travelled to California to visit mortgage sellers in an effort to help her assess the quality of MBS. She later described the moment when the chief underwriter of one of the largest subprime mortgage lenders admitted that they were considering these loans as merely bridging loans that would need to be repaid by taking out new mortgages. This meant that the lender was not concerned about the client's underlying ability to repay on the basis of their income,

the mortgages 'were just hot potatoes being passed on to the next lender and the next deal'.[83] Driven by fees and incentives to increase the volume of lending, mortgage lenders were signing up borrowers who did not have the financial basis to repay their loan unless the value of their home increased and they were able to remortgage. This left the entire business vulnerable to a decline, or even a standstill, in housing prices. At an investor meeting hosted by Deutsche Bank Securities in mid-May 2005, Weaver warned that the California market in particular was vulnerable because of low affordability rates of borrowers (i.e. high loan to value of the homes and low quality of borrowers' income).[84] But she did not expect a nationwide downturn in housing prices at this stage and, overall, affordability rates were still high so 'we don't agree that we are about to see a bubble burst in U.S. housing'.[85] An exception was California where prices were soaring, affordability was falling and

Karen Weaver was global head of Securitization Research at Deutsche Bank in New York and pointed out the vulnerability of the US real estate market in 2005.

there was a surge in interest-only mortgage lending. She recommended that clients try to go long on older vintages of MBS that might be of higher quality and to use synthetic instruments to short the more recent 2005 portfolios.[86] Deutsche Bank continued to build out its MBS group within the Global Markets Division with new hires in 2005, thus 'underscoring the firm's commitment to the industry'.[87] In September 2005 Weaver reported again to the bank's clients on the risks of a downturn in the US housing market. By this time, therefore, senior analysts at the bank were aware of the vulnerability of the RMBS market to a downturn in real estate prices and publicly warning of the risks. Weaver's colleague Eugene Xu also published this warning in early September 2005 after noticing that mortgage lending standards were deteriorating; he was confident that he was the first to draw attention to the potential disruption in the market.[88]

The first challenge to the models underpinning the CDO market came in May 2005 in the corporate sector. Standard & Poor's downgraded US automakers General Motors (GM) and Ford from BBB to BB, causing turmoil in the market in corporate CDOs and large losses among some hedge funds.[89] At Deutsche Bank, rumours of difficulties at hedge funds prompted a 'thorough analysis of our clients and [we] spoke directly with selected funds' which reassured the bank that there were 'no substantial problems with Deutsche Bank's hedge fund clients'.[90]

In the wake of this shudder in the markets, in June 2005 the Risk Committee of the Supervisory Board of Deutsche Bank considered synthetic collateralised debt obligations (CDOs) in detail, partly to explain to the Committee what these instruments were and partly to discuss the May 2005 market turmoil.[91] A synthetic CDO is a CDO referenced to an underlying portfolio of synthetic credit positions (i.e. credit default swaps and not actual loans). Standardised products were available related to various indices including iTRAXX Europe, CDX NA and Asian indices. Richard Evans, head of Group Market Risk, explained that the value of each tranche was driven by the risk of pool losses to which each tranche is exposed. The market prices of synthetic CDOs tended to move in a way broadly correlated with spreads reflecting their risk, but in May 2005 the tranche prices moved apart in the wake of Standard & Poor's downgrading of US automotive companies. The presentation to the Risk Committee emphasised that 'Deutsche Bank is a major market maker in synthetic CDO product trading indices and bespoke tranches across the seniority structure'.[92] In the subsequent discussion in the Risk Committee, Ackermann noted 'the need to compensate reduced customer flow business to a certain degree with proprietary trading', although this comment was not specifically aimed at CDO business.[93]

Meanwhile, other parts of the bank were lagging behind the trading and sales divisions. At the end of July 2005 Kevin Parker,[94] head of Asset Management, presented his strategy to recover the performance of asset management to the Supervisory Board.[95] Despite major restructuring, the division was due to report flat net income before tax in 2005 (c. €400 million) and this generated a fresh programme to cut costs and reduce operational complexity while at the same time increasing profits by shifting to higher margin products. At the beginning of July, the Management Board agreed to sell the loss-making asset management businesses in the UK and Philadelphia to Aberdeen Asset Management.[96] An important conclusion was that 'investment in high-margin business is required to sustain 2006 profitability'.[97] To increase revenues, the Japan and Asia-Pacific business was repositioned from traditional institutional to higher margin (and more risky) products such as so-called alternative investments, which included real estate, infrastructure, quantitative strategies, hedge funds and private equity fund of funds. A drastic decline of over 50 per cent in total headcount drove a planned reduction of 20 per cent in operating costs (ex-bonus). Scudder Investments was to be restructured into DWS by the end of 2005 to operate mutual funds and retail-structured products, and one of the key strategic goals was to build DWS into a top five global retail franchise. The other strategic goal was to build the #1 Alternative Investment Management business, which would be achieved through rebranding this business under RREEF Alternative Investment Managers from September 2005.[98] Traditional institutional investment (cash, equity, fixed income and insurance) would have its hub in Frankfurt. The Asset Management Division was thus poised to enter a higher risk strategy just as market risk accelerated.

At the end of June 2005, when the standardised CDS contract was being finalised, the Group Credit Policy Committee (GCPC) for the first time considered the Group's portfolio of securitisation-related exposures to assess their credit risk.[99] By this point the total credit limits amounted to €91.5 billion, although utilisation was only €14.6 billion. About 17 per cent of the underlying assets for these securities were residential mortgages which were considered 'highly diversified and adequately collateralized'. There were no loan loss provisions and no losses were expected even if interest rates rose and property values fell. The GCPC noted 'a key business risk' if Deutsche Bank's own ratings fell in an emergency and it was unable to borrow to cover liabilities, but noted that 'there has never been a significant drawdown of liquidity backstop facilities, not even in the aftermath of 9/11'. Finally, the GCPC proudly noted that 'in the last years DB has established itself as one of the top players in the USD1 trillion Term Securitisation market, with a 2004 total transaction volume of about USD50bn'. Key competitors were Credit Suisse First Boston (CSFB), Citigroup, Lehman Brothers, Morgan Stanley and Merrill Lynch. The GCPC approved the securitisation industry batch and the Management Board also formally noted it on 13 July 2005 and it passed through the Risk Committee on 8 September 2005. Even as new innovations in the market would increase the pace of securitisation, the bank was clearly taking on a prominent role in this market.

Mid-2005 was also the period in which the sale of Deutsche Bank's 37.7 per cent interest in Eurohypo was planned, which reduced the bank's exposure to the low margin real estate market in Germany. The sale was spread over two tranches over the fourth quarter of 2005 and first quarter of 2006. This promised to increase Basel Tier 1 capital ratio by 17 basis points, the German regulatory ratio (KWG) by 97 basis points and deliver economic capital relief of €985 million.[100] The bank also launched a further buyback of 25.6 million shares at an average price of €69.13, mainly in the first quarter of 2005. These initiatives reoriented the bank further away from the domestic retail market and reduced outstanding equity.

Deutsche Bank's global head of ABS and CDO Trading, Greg Lippmann, developed his famous shorting strategy at about the same time, based on quantitative research by Eugene (Youyu) Xu.[101] Xu held a PhD from the University of California, Los Angeles

(UCLA) and had been researching mortgage-backed securities since the mid-1990s, first at Credit Suisse and then from 2000 at Deutsche Bank. In order to assess the risk in the RMBS market he related historic default rates across different US metropolitan areas to changes in property prices and found that they were strongly negatively correlated: i.e. as house price inflation slowed, default rates increased. These data suggested that while a portfolio of RMBS might seem diversified by type of borrower and location, the 'risk in the asset class remains a macroeconomic risk […] ultimately driven by 3 things: home prices, interest rates (payment shocks and ability to refinance/move) and unemployment'.[102] The models used by ratings agencies for RMBS were based on the performance of the housing market only since the late 1990s (when the market had been booming) and so Xu believed that they underestimated the downside risks. At the time, house prices in many areas were rising at about 12 per cent p.a., which encouraged borrowers to take on larger debts in the expectation that persistently rising house prices would help pay off or refinance the loan. Looking closely at the underlying mortgages, Lippmann and Xu recognised that most were on fixed rates that would expire in about two years when the interest rate charged rose. At this point, properties would need to be remortgaged (if they had held their value) or the borrower would default. Further fragility in the system arose from high loan to value, interest-only payment deals, low credit scores among borrowers and poor (or no) documentation offered at the time of borrowing.

On 19 September 2005 Lippmann sent two presentations to Amin Arjomand (managing director in the Distressed Products Group at Deutsche Bank Securities Inc.) entitled 'The Bear Case for Home Equity Mezzanines' and 'Long Equity Short Portfolio Sep 2005' which set out 'the bear case for the product' and 'a way to do it with little to no negative carry'.[103] The CDOs could be shorted by buying protection on them – essentially paying out regular premiums against a future default; if the products did collapse, the protection would result in a massive payment to the bank. In an interview to the Financial Crisis Investigation Committee, Lippmann said he pitched the idea to his managers, Rajeev Misra (global head of Global Credit Trading) and Richard d'Albert (head of the Securitized Products Group) around this time. Although the likelihood that the scheme would pay off might be only 30 per cent, it would still be worth the gamble since the payments to buy the protection that shorted the CDOs were relatively cheap; nobody in the market expected them to default.[104] Moreover, Deutsche Bank's position overall was biased in favour of the optimistic view of the market, so it made sense for the bank to pay modest premiums to bet on a pessimistic view, even if it was unlikely to occur. According to Lippmann and Xu, the likelihood that the RMBS CDO market would collapse was high and rising, but selling the idea of shorting didn't require Deutsche Bank managers to share this view: it was just prudent from the bank's point of view to take some balance in their position if it wasn't too costly. This was also a lucrative fee-generating deal that could be offered to Deutsche Bank's customers.

One final piece of the puzzle that helped the short on the market was the introduction on 19 January 2006 of a tradable index of home equity asset-backed securities. Markit, a company based in London, gathered CDS data from 16 international banks including Deutsche Bank and compiled a set of indices each based on 20 RMBS. The index made it easier to see and monitor the increasing cost of insuring RMBS against default. This made the quality of the RMBS more transparent and, in particular, it became much clearer to the market that the new RMBS were of much lower quality than the older securities, i.e. the quality of the assets in the market was deteriorating. It also made it easier to short the RMBS market.

Lippmann later stated that, in early 2006, as CDO prices continued to rise, his boss had asked him to encourage other clients to buy short positions to create a market to allow Deutsche Bank to sell these positions later to suit their overall portfolio and expectations. The bank also wanted verification that Lippmann's strategy made sense, by seeing others willing to short the market.[105] This required Lippmann to try to sell the trade as a useful product to his clients, but he was unable initially to convince many that shorting the RMBS market was worth the relatively modest payments to buy this protection. After repeated challenges, his presentation grew significantly from the original 'book' in September 2005 to include other factors that might affect the likelihood of subprime mortgage holders to default. Hedge funds tended to be receptive to the deal, while insurance companies like AIG told Lippmann he was 'crazy'. Lippmann guessed he had sold protection to more than 50 but fewer than 100 customers, including early takers like John Paulson, Michael Burry, Elliott Associates and Baupost, and later Philip Falcone at Harbinger Capital. Most of his pitches were in the second half of 2006 and first quarter of 2007 and he estimated that he visited about 250 hedge funds over a two-year period.[106]

By February 2007 the sales pitch for Lippmann's trade had been enhanced to stress its essential characteristics and developments since 2005.[107] Data back to 1975 were used to show longer term trends in the key variables. From 2003 to 2005 spreads on Baa2 and Baa3 bonds had narrowed, despite the increased risk of default due to the deteriorating condition of loans, which now included more interest-only and other riskier mortgage products. Near the end of 2005, the spreads widened but then strong demand for RMBS from CDO managers tightened the spread again, making these securities appear less risky. But 'The demand from CDOs is a result of worldwide excess capital chasing yieldy products' and Lippmann warned that 'such demand may prove elusive in an adverse market environment'.[108] From May 2006 spreads began to widen again for the rest of that year and so in Lippmann's analysis: 'Already there have been a few 2005 and 2006 deals either downgraded or placed on downgrade watch. Previously, rating actions on structured products within two years of their issuance were virtually unheard of.'[109] Crucially, the model still did not require house prices to fall, just to grow more slowly or not at all. '[A]t 4% home price appreciation, we expect the net loss rate to be close to 10%, enough to wipe out most BBB-bonds. At 0%, net loss rates is [sic] expected to be in high teens, enough to wipe out almost all BBB bonds' in a typical subprime pool.[110]

It is difficult to calculate exactly how short Lippmann's desk eventually became because the trades were always marked to market, but he estimated that by February 2007 he was short $5–10 billion.[111] From this peak, he began to reduce the short trades under instruction from his bosses in Deutsche Bank. By this time he could sell on his short positions at a considerable profit as doubts about the reliability of the underlying assets had grown.

Ironically, just as Lippmann was building up the short position in the subprime market, another part of the bank turned to the origination of mortgages in the US under the guidance of Philip Weingord, head of Global Markets North America. The bank would thus be active in all stages of the production line or value chain for RMBS in the same way that its competitors were, such as Bear Stearns, Lehman Brothers, Merrill Lynch and Credit Suisse. In 2004, the bank experimented with a small Correspondent Lending Group in Boca Raton, Florida, which bought closed subprime mortgages (i.e. those that could not be repaid early), and with Berkshire Mortgage, which specialised in multi-family commercial mortgages. In September 2005 Weingord began to consider buying Chapel Funding, a subprime mortgage lender based in California, for about $3 million and the deal was announced in May 2006.[112] The next month the bank announced the acquisition of MortgageIT, based in New York, which was aimed more at prime borrowers. The Chapel acquisition was announced exactly a year after Karen Weaver's tour of the real estate market in California had convinced her that the market was in trouble. Between them the two companies had 2,200 employees.[113] Jain was keen that net revenue would accrue to Global Markets but not the costs; the companies would be expected to cover their own costs. The Chapel Funding deal was completed in September 2006 and MortgageIT in January 2007 (for $430 million, about $100 million more than planned in May 2006).[114] The CEO of MortgageIT, Doug Naidus, became head of Mortgage Origination for Deutsche Bank. In July 2006 Jain noted some 'near term challenges' over the acquisitions, including reputational issues from 'predatory lending' but noted in mitigation that MortgageIT prohibited such practices, there was mandatory 'training to spot predatory lending practices', it did not engage in subprime and there was an automated system to detect excess fee payments, although Jain recommended 'additional investment in compliance technology and personnel'.[115] By October 2007 Ackermann stressed the need for the new acquisition to break even.[116] In May 2012 the bank admitted that up to 2009 MortgageIT had submitted certifications that some of its mortgages were eligible for state insurance, which they were not, and paid $202.3 million to the Department of Justice. Ackermann later described MortgageIT as 'the biggest mistake of my time as CEO'.[117]

Meanwhile, at the end of 2006, the bank renewed its risk strategy for 2007. The underlying assumptions for the coming year were that global growth would slow 'somewhat', Germany's credit environment would remain stable and there would be no overall weakening of credit demand. Credit spreads would 'widen moderately' and commodity prices would remain volatile.[118] The plan included yielding about €1.9 billion in free capital to allow further growth, acquisitions or share buyback. If the free capital was used for share buybacks then the 2007 average active book equity of €29.8 billion would result in a return on equity of 25 per cent – Ackermann's holy grail. This was to be achieved by expanding Global Markets. The plan for 2007 anticipated a 23 per cent increase in total risk-weighted assets in Global Markets due to ambitious targets for equity and credit derivatives, warehousing from the securitisation business and a weaker US dollar. Risk-weighted assets from margin business had increased from €53 billion in December 2004 to €64 billion in December 2005. By September 2006 it was at €65 billion, but was expected to rise to €82 billion in 2007. There were ambitious plans for 2007 as the market peaked.

When CDO managers announced they were going to issue a CDO, they went to brokers to buy up the underlying collateral. A range of suppliers would offer RMBS at different prices and the CDO manager would pick which ones to put into the CDO based on the target risk profile. This left a warehousing risk for CDO issuers such as Deutsche Bank since the RMBS had to be held until all the collateral was acquired and then the tranches of the CDO had to be sold. The bank was therefore selling RMBS and CDOs to customers at the same time as shorting the market to managing its own risk exposure.

In August 2006, as Lippmann, just promoted to global head of ABS and CDO Trading in June, continued to report an active market in CDOs despite his pessimistic view of its future, Richard Axilrod of Moore Capital questioned Lippmann's strategy that linked CDOs to the housing market assets that underlay them, predicting that since house price inflation was already slowing, '[i]f this thing doesn't work by year end it isn't going to'.[119] Lippmann responded by email that 'in a normal market your logic would be inarguable, but the demand for this crap is virtually entirely technically driven, all cdos. And each person at the cdo table thinks someone else is the fool.' He described how 'bbb sold mostly ponzi-like to other cdos with limited distribution in europe and asia […] again hard to call that smart money'. He also recalled that 'In 05 for a time, we sold EVERY SINGLE one [AAA CDO] to AIG. They stepped out of the market in march of 06 after speaking with me and our research people (and I don't doubt other dealers). Since then it has been more hit and miss for us. Sometimes we sell to European banks but often (and for the last 3 deals) we are forced to put it into our commercial paper conduit. […] Why have we done this? It is not without reluctance and we are looking for ways to get out of this risk, but for now the view has been, we like the fees and the league table credit (and dammit we have a budget to make).'[120]

In addition to giving a sense of the communications at the time, this quotation reveals a lot about the way the market was working; the fee-generating CDO market fed on itself, by being both a source of demand and supply. It also points to the appetite of AIG, which was ultimately to require a massive bailout from the US government. Furthermore, by this time the market was beginning to become thin and CDOs were being taken in by Deutsche Bank's own conduit. In the email quoted above, Lippmann also explained the motivation behind the business as the drive to achieve volume for league tables, fees and targets. Deutsche Bank's CDO Primary Update Progress Report in October 2006 noted that the volume of CDO deals in the marketplace had 'ramped up' in 2006 with 50 deals expected to be closed by the year end.[121] Deutsche Bank ranked third behind Merrill Lynch and Citigroup as bookrunner for Global CDOs with about 7 per cent of the total amount issued. The full year forecast was for 12 deals each for CDOs of US collateralised loan obligations (CLO) and Mezzanine ABS, seven European CLOs and five Investment Grade Synthetic.

Insights into Anshu Jain's concerns are evident in his correspondence with customers. In October 2006 Derek Kaufman of JP Morgan wrote to Jain to let him know how much he appreciated a recent deal with Deutsche Bank that had allowed him to buy $350 million of mezzanine protection on a portfolio of BBB and BBB- subprime MBS.[122] Deutsche Bank had then sold the risk to other investors. The email subject line was 'Deutsche at its best'. Jain's reply reflected slight concern over the appetite to short the market, asking 'given we have just acquired a couple of RMBS originators, both prime and sub prime … how concerned should I be?'.[123] Kaufman was reassuring:

'unlike Greg [Lippmann], I am not in the camp that housing Armageddon is around the corner' and Kaufman's main motivation was to balance his other business 'without worrying too much about the tail risk of a housing collapse'.[124] But Lippmann's approach didn't require a housing collapse: in February 2007 he noted, 'we need 15–35% of the people to default to make 100% so we are not betting on a system meltdown but rather a squeeze on the weakest credits'.[125]

In February 2007 the subprime market faltered. New Century, a major subprime lender, announced that it would have to restate earnings for the first three quarters of 2006 and its shares fell 12 per cent in 10 days. NovaStar shares fell 50 per cent on news that their loan loss reserves were only just over 1 per cent of their $2.1 billion portfolio in the fourth quarter of 2006. At the start of the month, Lippmann was circulating a range of people in an email 'loop of negative news' but noted that 'there are very few abs people on this loop as i dont want to scare the buyers of abs/cdo managers […] please please do not forward these emails outside of your firm … i do not want to be blamed by the new issue people for destroying their business'.[126] At the end of the month, Greg Lippmann circulated a *Wall Street Journal* article on 'Subprime Game's Reckoning Day'.[127] For him, mixing mezzanine tranches of CDOs into other CDOs resembled a Ponzi scheme since 'every mezz cdo has 5–15% other mezz cdos'.[128] The pyramid of debt was beginning to topple.

The ABX index fell sharply in February 2007 but then recovered through the spring. By June 2007, the indices for most of the 2006 RMBS had returned to par, but the catastrophic collapse was just around the corner. Lippmann recalled several meetings with Anshu Jain at the start of 2007 where he was challenged to justify continuing his short position (then $4–5 billion) and was able to convince senior management that his strategy was useful to the bank, which at this point had long positions in RMBS of over $100 billion.[129] Meanwhile, Deutsche Bank reduced its inventory of subprime ABS from €5.4 billion at the end of 2006 to €600 million by June 2007.[130] This was the moment when the need to radically reduce the bank's exposure was decided.

The Deutsche Bank's derivatives offsite meeting with customers in Barcelona in July 2007 became notorious during the crash because of the evidence of excess at the end of the boom. The Rolling Stones were brought in to entertain the 600 attendees at considerable expense, a tradition at this annual meeting which had previously featured Kylie Minogue and Rod Stewart. *Huffington Post* reported that the band were paid $5.4 million for their 80-minute set and that Mick Jagger concluded with the jibe 'Thank you for having us. The best part is, it's coming out of your bonuses.'[131] But it was also at this meeting that Anshu Jain felt the mood of an impending downturn in the US housing market and decided to de-risk the bank's portfolio. David Folkerts-Landau later recalled how major hedge fund managers at a dinner in Barcelona predicted an oncoming crisis and Jain gathered his senior managers together late that night and instructed them to begin to run down their risk positions.[132] This was not a universally popular move, removing bankers from the party before it was over. Publicly, he remained confident, reassuring the conference in a speech, quoted in the press, that the subprime panic was overblown. 'The problem with the sub-prime sector is one of vintage,' he said. 'In certain market sectors, the underlying loans themselves have been shown to be of lesser quality than earlier loans. In the past, this deterioration in quality would have been obscured for a time by the market's relative opacity. In this case, the introduction of the ABX index provided transparency that enabled a more rapid correction.'[133] But Jain's early decision to reverse the exposure from the summer of 2007 saved Deutsche Bank from the worst excesses of its peers in the US, and limited the initial losses from the collapse of the RMBS business.

6. Conclusions

Chapter VI has described the dramatic changes in the structure and purpose of Deutsche Bank that fulfilled many of the aims of Herrhausen's initial foray into investment banking at the end of the 1980s. His goal had been to develop Anglo-American investment banking expertise and to operate on a global level, and grow to a size that allowed it to compete not only in Germany but in Europe and beyond. But achieving this vision proved extraordinarily difficult. The bank's split personality during these reforms reflected the lack of consensus among many in the bank and among the bank's stakeholders in Germany about the direction the management were taking. In Germany, the bank and its senior managers were subjected to strong criticism while internationally the strategy was viewed as aggressive, but also admired. And the results were stellar by many measures. Shareholder dividends tripled from €1.50 in 2003 to €4.50 in 2007. The magic 25 per cent pre-tax return on equity was finally almost achieved in 2005 and then exceeded in 2006 (33 per cent) and 2007 (29 per cent), bringing performance up to the level of its peers. At the same time the cost/income ratio fell from a peak of 82 per cent in 2003 to 70 per cent by 2006, still higher than the average of its peers at 64 per cent, but on the right trajectory.[134]

These achievements in the cost/income ratio were achieved despite a sharp increase in salaries and other compensations for some of Deutsche Bank's employees. The salaries and bonuses of the bank's traders and senior managers soared in the industry-wide competition for talent that could deliver revenue and profits. In the run-up to the global financial crisis, this strategy seemed to be working as the cost/income ratio fell. But the Management Board came under sustained criticism for large salaries from the 1990s onwards and Figure 29 shows that this attention was due to the increase in the real value of compensation that started well before the diversion to investment banking. In the 20 years from 1970 to 1990, the average value of compensation paid to Management Board members (not including share options or expenses) almost doubled, even when taking into account changes in the cost of living (as expressed in the German Consumer Price Index). From 1990, when the bank embarked on its investment operations in London, the pace of annual increases in compensation rose sharply. After 1999, with the Bankers Trust acquisition, there was a jump in average compensation, but during the securitisation boom (when traders were drawing huge salaries from the bank) the compensation to the Management Board stopped increasing. Nevertheless, the increase from the 1990s far outstripped the rise in the cost of living in Germany so that the nominal value reached €7 million per annum in 2003, equivalent to €8.4 million in 2015 dollars. In the wake of the global financial crisis both nominal

Figure 29: Average Management Board member compensation, 1970–2018 (in euro million).

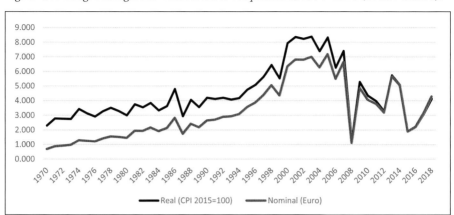

Source: Deutsche Bank, Annual reports 1970–2017. Total compensation includes bonuses, allowances and equity packages. Real values compared to German Consumer Price Index (CPI) in 2015.

and real compensation declined so that in 2018 the average purchasing power for a Management Board member was about the same as in the late 1980s.

Although the levels of compensation after 2012 were on average lower than during the boom period, they still remained high, especially considering that the bank was making losses overall. Moreover, the average also does not capture the distribution across individuals and is affected periodically by members not in office for the entire year. During the mid-2000s, for example, when the Management Board was small and the GEC included highly paid executives not included in the data presented in Figure 29, Ackermann's compensation as CEO accounted for about 40 per cent of the total. Despite the shortcomings in the data, the trends are a useful guide.

When assessing the rise of Global Markets, it is important to recall that the different parts of the bank (retail and wholesale; global, local and European) were interdependent. Deutsche Bank could not expect to retain its major German and European customers unless it was able to offer a wide spectrum of financial services that rivalled its US and Swiss competitors. On the other hand, the risky global wholesale trading and sales side of the bank relied on the AAA external credit rating delivered by the safe funding streams of commercial and retail banking. Moreover, in the mergers and acquisitions wave in financial services in the 1990s the bank needed to grow to protect itself from being taken over and to provide a balance sheet large enough to leverage profitably. After absorbing Bankers Trust and Scudder in 2002, the bank mainly grew organically, albeit with some acquisitions and some disposals in Europe and the Far East. Meanwhile, the trading and sales business during the securitisation boom was responsible for at least half of gross revenue, which promoted Ackermann and then Jain to leading positions in the strategic management of the bank. Moreover, the reliance on this income made it difficult to rein this business back even when it might appear risky. By 2005 71 per cent of Deutsche Bank's revenues were generated abroad, making it the most 'global' of any major bank, slightly ahead of UBS (70 per cent) and Credit Suisse (65 per cent) but well ahead of other European competitors like Société Générale and BNP Paribas, which each earned less than half of their revenues outside their home country.[135] Income before taxes in the flagship CIB division grew from €2.8 billion in 2004 to €6.1 billion in 2006 and, despite the collapse in the second half of 2007, it still managed to record income of €5.1 billion for the year. This very rapid expansion at times outpaced the

Since the 1990s, sales and trading of debt securities, equities, foreign exchange, precious metals and commodities have substantially contributed to the bank's earnings. Centres of this business are the worldwide trading rooms such as in Frankfurt (top, 1992, and bottom, 2001) …

infrastructure of internal controls and compliance, which left a legacy to be confronted in the aftermath of the crisis. Nevertheless, as the global financial crisis was about to break with the collapse of Lehman Brothers in September 2008, the bank had prepared itself for the end of the boom. How it dealt with the crisis and its aftermath is the subject of the next chapter.

… as well as in London (top) and New York, both 2010.

VII. Global Financial Crisis, 2008–2012

The global financial crisis is often dated from the dramatic collapse of Lehman Brothers on 15 September 2008, which abruptly choked off global liquidity and left many of the world's international banking conglomerates suddenly illiquid or even insolvent.[1] Certainly the Lehman Brothers debacle was among the most dramatic failures and it generated memorable images on TV of workers leaving their offices immediately with their personal belongings in boxes. But it was the last straw rather than the cause of the collapse; the crisis had been brewing for months before this event. Chapter VI has described the shudder in the markets in early 2007 that prompted Karen Weaver to reassess Deutsche Bank's exposure to the US subprime mortgage market. But there were problems closer to home. In July 2007 Deutsche Bank played a major role in the €3.5 billion bailout of German bank IKB, which had invested heavily in the subprime market. The German government and the German financial industry grouped together to support IKB in order to avoid a systemic crisis. Almost at the same time several Landesbanken also required bailouts, including West LB and Sachsen LB. The seemingly unadventurous and highly competitive German market was revealed to have embarked on the rollercoaster of global securitisation. The market recovered from this wobble, but the cracks were clearly showing. Looking back on the summer's events from early September 2007, the Deutsche Bank Risk Committee viewed the bailout of IKB as 'a watershed event' that caused the market to lose faith in the so-called 'conduits' that banks were using to channel their risky securities trading off of their balance sheets.[2] When these arm's length institutions came under pressure, their losses came back on to their parent bank's balance sheet, threatening their solvency.

On 2 August 2007, the Bundesbank was forced to issue a special press release after the IKB bailout stating that 'fears concerning a banking crisis in Germany are entirely without foundation [...] to compare the current economic situation with the 1931 banking crisis [...] is completely absurd'.[3] A week later, on 9 August, BNP Paribas suspended trading in three of its funds based on underlying subprime mortgage assets, claiming that it was unable to value these assets because the market for ABS had dried up. This made public the problems in the market as collateral lost its value and European banks went to the ECB for liquidity. This time the Bundesbank reassured the public, 'the pricing of risks is now returning to normal [...]. European and German economic data remain positive.'[4] Just over a month later a relatively minor British bank, Northern Rock, suffered a bank run and had to be bailed out by the Bank of England. Like other institutions, Northern Rock had offered mortgage loans using funds borrowed on the short-term interbank funding market and, when it was no longer able to sell these mortgages on to other financial institutions, or to continue to borrow itself, the bank became illiquid.[5] While sticking plasters were applied to these individual collapses, they were a symptom of a wider systemic problem that was soon evident in the core of the global financial system in Wall Street.

The fall in the US subprime mortgage market in the summer of 2007 took six months to claim the next large victim. On 16 March 2008 Bear Stearns, an 85-year-old Wall Street investment firm, was sold to JP Morgan Chase for a minimal $2.00 per share in a deal brokered by the US government.[6] At its peak in 2007, Bear Stearns' share price had been nearly $172, but it was rocked by the collapse of two of its mortgage-related hedge funds in the summer of 2007 and found that its access to interbank funds dried up as other banks suspected that it might not be able to repay. Nevertheless, the sale of this failed bank to JP Morgan Chase (with state backing) seemed to suggest that the market as a whole could survive even while some players might not. This episode also appeared to demonstrate the commitment of the US government and Federal Reserve to avoiding large bank failures in the US. On the same day as the sale of Bear Stearns was announced, the Fed announced its Primary Dealer Credit Facility, which provided cash to major investment banks against a broad range of collateral. On 17 March 2008 Deutsche Bank Securities Inc. borrowed a modest $500 million against $525 million in municipal bonds, but it did not use the facility again.[7]

A few months later, in July 2008, Ackermann was interviewed at the National Press Club, as chairman of the Institute of International Finance (IIF) when the Institute published its report on the banking industry.[8] He acknowledged that there were 'fundamental challenges in the global economy. But the financial crisis, in itself, as an impact on the financial sector, I'm a bit more confident that we are seeing the end pretty soon.' When asked to define 'pretty soon' he answered, 'Five years. (Laughs, laughter.) No, no, no. I always say three to six months.'[9] For Deutsche Bank, as for the global banking system as a whole, even five years was to prove an optimistic prediction.

1. Performance Through the Crisis

Partly due to the de-risking described in Chapter VI, Deutsche Bank initially demonstrated considerable resilience. By coincidence, the annual press conference in early February 2008 held to announce Deutsche Bank's 2007 results took place on Josef Ackermann's sixtieth birthday.[10] The Group Executive Committee (GEC) gathered just before the press conference to toast their leader with champagne and present him with their joint gift of flowers, a case of Bordeaux and a box of cigars.[11] The press conference that followed was upbeat, stressing that the bank was in a strong position having reduced its exposure to risky assets and built up its liquidity to 'prepare for additional potential headline risk'.[12] Through the second half of 2007 the bank had sold off long positions on asset-backed securities and commercial mortgage-backed securities through its subsidiary Winchester Capital, and wrote down the value of residential mortgage-backed securities.[13] Overall the bank was net short of US subprime securities by €1.4 billion by September 2007, which was unchanged at the end of the year.[14] But net default risk for US subprime was valued at €1.7 billion because of exposures to several companies specialising in packaging mortgages into securities, and to other borrowers, such as IKB and its special purpose vehicle Rhineland Funding. Meanwhile, the value of residential mortgage-backed securities that the bank was holding as it prepared CDOs for itself or others was rapidly reduced. While it held these assets, the bank was vulnerable to a collapse in their price. As noted above, at the start of 2007 this so-called 'warehouse' of securities amounted to €2.4 billion, but this was reduced rapidly to €8 million by November 2007.[15] The reduction in warehousing was achieved partly through completing and selling 15 CDOs with assets of $11.5 billion from December 2006 to December 2007, making Deutsche Bank the industry's fourth largest CDO issuer. One of the last was the $1.1 billion CDO known as Gemstone 7, which accumulated warehoused securities from October 2006 until it was closed in March 2007 with $400 million in securities left unsold. Commerzbank bought $16 million in Gemstone assets.[16] Deutsche Bank was heavily criticised by the US Senate Subcommittee investigation of the causes of the global financial crisis for marketing Gemstone 7 at a time when many in Deutsche Bank had already anticipated a decline in the value of the underlying securities.[17] By July 2008 the underlying assets for Gemstone 7 were almost worthless.

For the 2007 results press conference, GEC members were instructed to wear 'a dark suit with a lightly coloured shirt (not white!)' and a tie of contrasting colours and to remember that they were likely to be photographed throughout and so to 'show your best face at all times'.[18] It was clearly important to demonstrate unity among the bank's leadership and to avoid adverse press comment during a difficult time in the markets; appearances mattered. The speech drafted for Chancellor Merkel to present at Ackermann's birthday

Last meeting of the Management Board of Deutsche Bank in the premises of the old Deutsche Bank towers in Frankfurt on 17 September 2007. The building was then completely refurbished and reoccupied at the end of 2010. From the left: Anthony Di Iorio, Hugo Bänziger, Josef Ackermann and Hermann-Josef Lamberti.

party more than two months later recalled the press conference as offering news 'welcomed by the entire financial industry with relief'.[19] The apparent strength of Deutsche Bank despite shudders in global financial markets was reassuring. Of course some institutions had failed, but it still seemed that these banks could be treated as isolated victims of bad decisions in a declining market rather than a systemic problem.

On 7 February 2008, Ackermann was able to announce to his press audience that the bank had exceeded its 25 per cent return on equity target for the second year, increasing net income from €6.1 billion in 2006 to €6.5 billion in 2007, and that the Management Board was planning an increased dividend. The bank's strategy was 'we stay the course'.[20] The underlying data, however, were more challenging than the headline figures. The bank had already reported that Global Markets' trading losses in the third quarter of 2007 reached €1.561 billion although they showed a profit for the year as a whole during the boom of €423 million.[21] The 'safe' side of the bank had helped to balance these losses and kept the funding base to allow the bank to sustain its liquidity when trust in the interbank market was eroding. This allowed Deutsche Bank to write down its impaired assets when the US property market entered a sustained downturn.

A few months later, in April 2008, *Bloomberg* published its account of how much major investment banks had been forced to mark down their assets due to the subprime crisis.[22] The total for the 70 banks reviewed was $247.9 billion, of which Deutsche Bank accounted for $7.5 billion or 3 per cent. This was quite modest considering the bank's leading position in the market as a whole. Its competitors, including UBS ($38 billion), Citigroup ($35.3 billion) and Merrill Lynch ($31.7 billion), were much more deeply affected. The UBS portfolio was particularly weak with a focus on poorer quality securities backed by mortgages issued in 2006 and 2007, which were at the highest probability of default. In early 2008, therefore, Ackermann and the management team had some reason to be sanguine about the bank's prospects. At the end of June 2008, Ackermann evaluated the current situation, telling the Risk Committee of the Supervisory Board, 'whilst the financial markets were still very volatile, he was of the opinion that the worst should be over' although the bank's share price was still relatively low.[23] One particularly embarrassing episode was that the bank became the owner of the Cosmopolitan Casino in Las Vegas just as the banking system was coming under fire for gambling away its customers' deposits. After the developer Bruce Eichner defaulted on a $760 million loan in early 2008, the bank found it had little choice but to continue construction of the casino in order to sell the project as a going concern. Finishing the project required further investment of about $4 billion, making it the most expensive casino in Las Vegas, before it could be sold off to Blackstone in 2014 for $1.73 billion. In 2009 the bank had to write down the value of the casino twice for a total of €575 million because of the impact of the poor US economic outlook on hotel and casino revenues.[24]

Through the summer of 2008 the news from global financial markets did not improve and the dam was about to burst. The evening of Lehman's collapse, on Monday 15 September 2008, Ackermann took part in a teleconference of the board of directors of the Association of German Banks.[25] Lehman Brothers' German subsidiary had been suspended with €6 billion in protected deposits, and the directors of the Association were concerned about how the burden of covering these liabilities would be distributed.

Given that Deutsche Bank was the major contributor to the national deposit protection scheme, Ackermann remarked that

> even in the case of liquidity assistance from central banks, the ultimate default to be borne would be considerable. A fundamental discussion ('Grundsatzdiskussion') on the future of deposit protection was necessary. The remit of the German Deposit Protection could not be to bear defaults caused exogenously. At the present time, in which many banks are suffering from the financial market crisis and also have to bear consolidation burdens, banks cannot be subjected to such additional burdens.[26]

Three days later, on Thursday 18 September, Ackermann was scheduled to fly to Sochi to have dinner with President Putin as part of the effort to enhance the bank's presence in Russia.[27]

The specific exposure to Lehman Brothers had been reduced significantly from June 2007 so that, at the time it closed over a year later, Deutsche Bank owed Lehman on a net basis rather than the other way around. The drain of funds from Lehman was accelerated as press reports and market gossip suggested that Lehman would soon follow Bear Stearns.[28] In the second week of September, as Lehman's weaknesses were exposed, Deutsche Bank staff completed more than 80,000 trades with 14 counterparties to ensure that its deals could settle even if Lehman collapsed.[29] Deutsche Bank's credit exposure to Washington Mutual (the largest US bank failure when it collapsed on 25 September 2008) had also been reduced from September 2007 from a gross limit of over €300 million to only about €50 million by July 2008. The collapse of Icelandic banks caused some losses despite de-risking of direct exposure, such as cancelling €2 billion in liquidity facilities.[30] But the efforts to protect the bank from the collapse of counterparties and reduce its own direct exposure to subprime seemed to have worked.

Deutsche Bank was even able to recover some funds. Ackermann was proud to have refused state funds from Germany, but Deutsche Bank benefited indirectly from the $105 billion US government bailout of AIG because it was a creditor of this failed US insurance company, getting $11.8 billion in compensation for a combination of insurances it had bought from AIG and collateral it had offered.[31] Deutsche Bank stood to benefit when the Fed included American-based subsidiaries of foreign banks in the US Emergency Economic Stabilization Act, given Deutsche Bank's €462 billion in assets in US subsidiaries.[32] Deutsche Bank's New York branch borrowed $76.9 billion under the Federal Reserve's Term Auction Facility (TAF) from the end of January 2008 to April 2009. The TAF provided short-term loans to banks in the US against a range of different types of collateral when the interbank market was not working. Dresdner Bank borrowed $123.3 billion and Commerzbank $51.16 billion from the Federal Reserve in this way.[33]

Despite this relatively rosy picture, Deutsche Bank was severely affected when the largest financial crisis since the 1930s brought financial trading to a halt. Hugo Bänziger, the bank's chief risk officer,[34] flew home to Frankfurt from the EU meeting of economic and finance ministers in Nice on 12–13 September 2008 to deal with the calls on the bank. Borrowers were unable to roll over short-term credits and many did not have enough cash to meet their own obligations. As a result of Bänziger's policies in

2007–08 Deutsche Bank was liquid and able to meet the calls on its own liabilities over the first few days, but losses quickly began to accumulate at a rate of $400 million per day. In the period from 1 September to 15 October 2008, Global Markets alone posted a total loss of €1.907 billion, of which €1.3 billion was from credit proprietary trading business associated with the internal group of traders called Saba Principal Strategies, led by Boaz Weinstein.[35] Weinstein had a meteoric career at Deutsche Bank, arriving in the late 1990s and becoming managing director after only three years at the age of 27. By 2008 he was co-head of Global Credit Trading along with Colin Fan. One important outcome of the crisis was the Management Board's decision to shut down proprietary trading entirely, including hedge funds, so that by October 2008 equity proprietary trading was at 25 per cent of the levels of summer 2008.[36] Weinstein left the bank and reorganised his hedge fund, Saba Capital Management, outside the bank.

Greater market risk increased the value of the bank's risk-weighted assets (RWA) by $60 billion, requiring an additional $6 billion in capital to meet the bank's obligations under the Basel minimum capital requirements. Hugo Bänziger put together a task force to resolve this problem as quickly as possible in early October 2008, reassuring Ackermann that a solution could be found to keep the bank well within its regulatory capital requirements and not vulnerable to needing a government bailout from the state. Bänziger called all major counterparties such as UBS, Credit Suisse, JP Morgan, Bank of America, Goldman Sachs and Barclays and collateralised their trading balances using the extensive liquidity available from the ECB, the Fed and the Bank of England to reduce the value of risk-weighted assets. This was an important step in the bank's ability to avoid requiring bailout funding from the German state. He also converted $5 billion of contingent capital into Tier 1 capital.[37] In November 2008 Ackermann 'stressed the importance of the ongoing RWA reduction initiative' led by Bänziger and CFO Stefan Krause.[38]

Deutsche Bank's refusal to take state money was resented by the German government since it showed a lack of solidarity with the rest of the German banking system. The €500 billion package that the government agreed in October 2008 came with strings attached, including capping salaries and suspending bonuses. Ackermann was reported as having said he would be ashamed to take government money for Deutsche Bank, which the government feared would deter weaker banks from coming forward and thus undermine the efforts to stabilise the German system. In the end, the take-up of the support was slower than anticipated. The German government's bailout of its domestic institutions included €3–5 billion for Commerzbank/Dresdner Bank as well as about €50 billion to bail out five Landesbanken, and a further €24 billion for IKB and Hypo Real Estate, as discussed below.[39] In December, Ackermann reportedly proposed an alternative: that the government create a 'bad bank' to take the damaged assets off the banks' balance sheets, and there were efforts to use the government support to take over some of the bad assets on Postbank's balance sheet, but these ideas were ultimately abandoned.[40] There needed to be a quid pro quo for government support, but Deutsche Bank was not willing to cede any control or autonomy.

In a public 'road show' presentation in Zurich at the start of October 2008, and again at the meeting of the Risk Committee of the Supervisory Board in Berlin near the end of that month, Ackermann was able to claim that 'Deutsche Bank remains a relative winner through the crisis'.[41] This was reflected in a positive income before interest and taxes of €3.4 billion in the year from the third quarter of 2007 to the third quarter of 2008. Most competitors had much poorer outcomes, including losses at Credit Suisse (-€1.4 billion), UBS (-€18.8 billion), Citigroup (-€23 billion) and Merrill Lynch (-€25.4 billion), although JP Morgan Chase and Goldman Sachs both outperformed Deutsche Bank on this score. Through Bänziger's operations, the bank also built up a comfortable Tier 1 capital ratio of over 10 per cent, which reduced the need to recapitalise. Nevertheless, the share price was hit hard with a 55.4 per cent fall between 12 September (just before Lehman Brothers' collapse) and 27 October 2008. This was a larger fall than all its competitors except for Morgan Stanley. Shareholders had lost confidence.

Despite this brave outlook in the midst of the crisis, the final results for 2008 as a whole were a huge disappointment for Ackermann.[42] After they were announced in January 2009 Ackermann was under such strain that he fainted at an evening reception in Berlin.[43] Pre-tax losses for the year amounted to €5.7 billion. The value of financial assets fell by almost €10 billion, offset by gains in interest income on traditional lending. But the bank bounced back the following year with pre-tax profits of €5.2 billion and net income of €5.0 billion, posting a pre-tax return on equity of 15 per cent. The turn-around was particularly striking in Corporate and Investment Banking where 2008 pre-tax losses of €7.4 billion were turned into profit of €4.3 billion the following year. This recovery was reflected in a significant recovery in the share price. Meanwhile, the faltering of other European banks created opportunities for Deutsche Bank to make acquisitions such as Postbank, Sal. Oppenheim and ABN AMRO, as discussed below.

Economic summit at the Federal Chancellery in April 2009: Deutsche Bank's CEO Josef Ackermann served as one of the federal government's advisers.

Figure 30: Deutsche Bank total assets (bars, left-hand-side axis) and net income before tax (line, right-hand-side axis), 2005–2012 (in euro million).

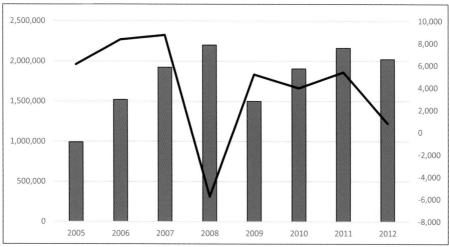

Source: Deutsche Bank, Annual Reports. Figures are for 31 December each year.

Figure 30 shows the rapid increase in the value of the bank's total assets reported in the years before the crisis so that, by 2008, total assets were valued at €2.2 trillion. The figure also shows the 'V'-shaped recovery after substantial losses in 2008, in both net income before tax and total assets.

The crisis pushed Deutsche Bank even more into the spotlight because of its senior role in the German system. As the public face of the bank, Ackermann came under considerable fire in the media over the collapse of German bank IKB, which had amassed over €20 billion of subprime and other asset-backed securities before requiring a bailout at the end of July 2007. It emerged that Ackermann contacted the German financial regulatory authority BaFin about IKB's deteriorating condition in July 2007 and the bank suspended its trading limit with IKB on 27 July. IKB's CEO, Stefan Ortseifen, claimed that Deutsche Bank contributed to the collapse both by selling large amounts of subprime products to IKB during the boom as well as cutting its line of credit just when IKB needed it when the crisis broke. Deutsche Bank refuted these suggestions on the basis that it had never advised IKB.[44] In the criminal court trial against Stefan Ortseifen in May 2010, Ackermann as a witness recalled repeatedly asking for more details from IKB about the value of the assets in its Rhineland subprime funding vehicle.[45] Deutsche Bank was not responsible for the bank's ultimate collapse; this was down to IKB and its conduits' commitment to the subprime real estate market. But the allegations of mis-selling after the profits built by Deutsche Bank during the boom dogged the final years of Ackermann's tenure at the bank. Moreover, being the largest German bank gave Deutsche Bank a high profile in general public complaints about bankers' greed and the role of financial institutions in the German economy and society. The next preoccupation in the German market was Hypo Real Estate.

2. Hypo Real Estate

One of the biggest casualties in the German market was Hypo Real Estate (HRE). Deutsche Bank was at the forefront of emergency negotiations with the German finance ministry, the Bundesbank and BaFin to shore up the bank in the largest bailout in German history. The bank was formed in 2003 as a spinoff of the German and international real estate business of HypoVereinsbank and was initially successful. In July 2007 HRE took over the Irish Depfa bank which doubled its balance sheet and extended its activities into public sector real estate and infrastructure. The bank's business model, however, left it highly vulnerable to the looming financial crisis; it was financing long term mortgages and infrastructure investments through short-term money market funding. When global money markets tightened in 2007 and property prices began to decline, the bank suffered from illiquidity and was then pushed to the brink of insolvency after the collapse of Lehman Brothers in September 2008 caused international money markets to freeze. Depfa was particularly heavily indebted to global money markets when the crisis struck. Deutsche Bank's own exposure gave it a strong interest in HRE's survival; at the time it had €48 million in net margin exposure, €285 million in senior unsecured bonds and €760 million in covered bonds (*Pfandbriefe*). But even more damaging was the liability of Deutsche Bank as the largest contributor to the German financial industry's deposit insurance – it would have had to cover 26 per cent of €17 billion.[46]

On 22 September 2008 the head of HRE's management board, Georg Funke, and Christopher Flowers (whose fund had bought 25 per cent of HRE in May 2008) called Ackermann to discuss an emergency line of credit, and over the next two days there was a series of working meetings between representatives of HRE and Deutsche Bank in Frankfurt.[47] On 23 September, Kurt F. Viermetz, the chairman of the supervisory board of Hypo Real Estate Group, appealed directly to the German Finance Minister Peer Steinbrück asking that 'you, together with the Deutsche Bundesbank, should work with the leading banks in the private banking industry to ensure that Hypo Real Estate Group obtains a back-stop line of €20 billion beyond the previous framework, which will secure the Group's funding at least until the very next year'.[48] Otherwise he warned of further crises in the German financial system. That afternoon, Ackermann, Bänziger and Deutsche Bank's head of Corporate Development (AfK), Axel Wieandt, met again with Flowers.[49] HRE hoped to arrange a €15 billion credit against collateral, but it was quickly apparent that credit from Deutsche Bank alone would not be sufficient.[50]

Two days later, on 25 September, Wieandt emailed Ackermann and Bänziger with the news that HRE had outstanding money market funding liabilities of €51 billion of which 82 per cent was due by the end of the year.[51] So far a short-term bridge of €15 billion was under discussion but this left €27 billion due by the end of the year. On the plus side, there were €46 billion of unencumbered assets, a commercial real estate portfolio of €26 billion and a public sector/infrastructure portfolio of €20 billion. But altogether Wieandt calculated that the actual collateral value of all these assets was no more than €16 billion. This was the ceiling on what could be provided in terms of credit from private sector banks. Additional government support was necessary either through a state guarantee or by the government buying up some of the bank's assets.

The debate between the banks, the government and the regulators was set to continue. On 25 September, Ackermann met with Chancellor Merkel for an hour at noon and then with Finance Minister Steinbrück in the afternoon to discuss the situation.[52] The first rescue package was agreed in a series of meetings at BaFin with HRE, representatives of the Bundesbank and the Auditing Association of German Banks (PdB) as well as telephone conferences with the Association of German Banks over the weekend of 26–28 September 2008.[53] On Friday, Funke claimed that HRE itself was still profitable and that the liquidity problem was limited to Depfa. The next morning the group met again and it was obvious that multilateral support from the banking system would be required. The meeting reconvened that afternoon with Ackermann and Bänziger from Deutsche Bank and Martin Blessing from Commerzbank. Bänziger argued that the situation could become worse than Lehman Brothers, yet it was clear that there would be no European Central Bank bailout for European institutions. Bundesbank president Axel Weber responded that he had discussed the situation with ECB chairman Jean-Claude Trichet. Euro area liquidity could only be given to solvent banks and so it was necessary first to ensure HRE's solvency. This would require a €35 billion line of credit. Ackermann and Blessing insisted that the private banking sector could not afford the full rescue and there would need to be some state participation.

By this time, the government had a troubled history of trying to rescue failing banks. Axel Weber noted that after suffering through the IKB bailout there was less political willingness on the part of the government to be involved in helping Hypo Real Estate. The first bailout of IKB in early August 2007 had been a joint effort of German commercial banks and the state-owned Kreditanstalt für Wiederaufbau (KfW). KfW was the major shareholder of IKB, but there was still public controversy over using state funds to bail out a bank that had engaged in investing in risky securities. A deal had been hastily agreed on 29 July 2007 after it emerged that IKB had a subprime exposure of about $19 billion, putting at risk an estimated €3.5 billion that needed to be covered.[54] KfW agreed to be responsible for 70 per cent if the main German banking associations covered the rest. Half of the 30 per cent allocated to the banking associations would be borne by the Deposit Protection Fund (*Einlagensicherungsfonds*, ESF) of the private sector banks. But this deal was in the end not enough and had to be followed by a second and then a third bailout. The German government had to go back with more funds to shore up IKB with another €1 billion in February 2008 before it was finally sold to Lonestar, a Texas investment fund, in August 2008. In total the restructuring support amounted to €9 billion and drew the critical attention of the European Commission.[55] In September 2008, memories of this debacle and the political backlash it had provoked were still fresh.

Nevertheless, Ackermann repeated in the afternoon meeting on 27 September 2008 that a solution was only possible with the help of the federal government.[56] The meeting then adjourned and reconvened at 9 p.m. to discuss various proposals, but both Blessing and Ackermann continued to insist that the state must contribute. Ackermann suggested that the Deposit Protection Fund could be used to guarantee €24 billion but Weber rejected this since if the ESF's available funds fell there could be a run on German banks. This left the group in a stalemate until the next morning when BaFin president Jochen Sanio admitted that the rescue could only be achieved with some political participation. Blessing and Ackermann then presented a draft scheme for German banks to contribute €15 billion and the ESF €20 billion. They also proposed a cap on the banks' guarantee for losses at €7 billion, but this was deemed unacceptable. State Secretary Jörg Asmussen was brought into the meeting and the haggling continued until a deal agreed with the Chancellor and the Finance Minister was put to the banks at 11.30 p.m.: €35 billion total to be shared 50 per cent by the state and 50 per cent by the banks, but putting a cap on the losses to be guaranteed by the banks was not acceptable. Blessing and Ackermann rejected this package and promptly withdrew from the negotiations. Within half an hour, however, Ackermann was back in the room having spoken to Finance Minister Steinbrück on the phone. He reassured the group that the banks wanted to negotiate and that Steinbrück would speak to Chancellor Merkel again. At 1 a.m. on Monday Asmussen came back with the government's final offer of 60 per cent to come from the finance industry, 40 per cent to be contributed by the state and a cap of €8.5 billion on initial losses by the banks, any losses beyond this to be covered by the state. Ackermann immediately called Chancellor Merkel to confirm this agreement. A mere five minutes later, at 1.10 a.m. on Monday 29 September, the Bundesbank and BaFin issued a joint press release just before the Australian stock markets opened. On Monday afternoon, Deutsche Bank's GEC expressed its support for the proposed solution.[57] These intense discussions demonstrate Ackermann's personal importance and close connections with the government, and Chancellor Merkel in particular, as well as the ability of the Deutsche Bank leadership (with support from Blessing of Commerzbank) to convince the state to be bailed in to the resolution of HRE.

On Wednesday 1 October 2008 there were further telephone calls between Ackermann, Weber, Bänziger and Flowers. At a meeting with the Bundesbank on 2–3 October the loss guarantees for €8.5 billion to be provided by the banks were distributed: €4.5 billion would come from the Deposit Protection Fund of the Association of German Banks, €1.6 billion from the savings banks and Landesbanken, €1.4 billion from the insurance industry, €600 million from the National Association of German Co-operative Banks (BVR) and DZ-Bank and €400 million from the Association of German Public Banks (VÖB, development banks). This distributed HRE's immediate losses throughout the German banking and insurance sectors. In addition, a syndicate of banks would provide €15 billion in credit, led by Deutsche Bank contributing €5 billion.[58] The total rescue package was €35 billion, but it didn't last long.

Deutsche Bank's investigations of the Depfa subsidiary in Dublin during the first week of October turned up fresh revelations that meant the bailout would need to be in excess of €35 billion. On the evening of Saturday 4 October the press announced that the first bailout deal had been abandoned.[59] Ackermann met with Bänziger and Axel Weber that afternoon and then there was another marathon meeting at BaFin lasting from 5 p.m. to 2 a.m. the next day. On Sunday, Ackermann, Weber and Bänziger met at Frankfurt airport and flew to Berlin to meet with Chancellor Merkel to finalise negotiations for a second bailout package. In Ackermann's calendar the meeting with Merkel was noted as lasting from 8 p.m. on Sunday until 2 a.m. the following day.

On Monday 6 October a teleconference took place among the board of directors of the Association of German Banks to conclude the final details of the rescue package. Deutsche Bank staff were especially thanked for their efforts in putting the deal together.[60] Ackermann updated his Management Board the next day in Frankfurt noting that if the rescue were not completed, the impact on German financial markets would be severe and that 'The most important goal was to regain confidence in the banking sector and financial markets overall.'[61]

The new deal totalled €50 billion. The Bundesbank provided a bridging loan until the end of October of €35 billion. This would be underwritten by €15 billion in a state-guaranteed note issued by HRE and a €20 billion note issued by the Bundesbank. A syndicate of financial institutions led by Deutsche Bank was to subscribe to the state-guaranteed HRE note with maturity at the end of March 2009. In addition, HRE would issue a further note (without a state guarantee) for €15 billion that would also be subscribed by financial institutions and would have priority claim on collateral. These notes were considered eligible collateral for ECB funding, thus allowing the participating banks to borrow from the ECB. The financial system continued to provide its guarantee for €8.5 billion in losses. In this way a breathing space of a few months was secured by €30 billion from the private sector and €20 billion directly from the Bundesbank. Deutsche Bank agreed to take €6 billion of each of HRE's notes, bringing its contribution to 40 per cent of the private sector – just less than a quarter of the total package. The risks turned on the quality of the €60 billion of collateral assets put up by HRE, which Deutsche Bank due diligence had valued at €22 billion if they were liquidated or perhaps €46 billion if the bank continued as a going concern.[62]

Thirteen institutions contributed. Deutsche Bank's share was €12 billion, far ahead of the next largest contributor, which was Commerzbank with €5 billion. Postbank, which Deutsche Bank had just agreed to buy, was also due to make a contribution of €2 billion and had an exposure to HRE of €1 billion in bonds.[63] Deutsche Bank AG's own exposure was €632 million.[64] The Management Board finally agreed the rescue package on 28 October 2008.

In addition to the financial support, Deutsche Bank provided managerial assets. The nasty surprise hidden in the Irish Depfa balance sheet discredited HRE's management board. On 13 October Axel Wieandt left Deutsche Bank to replace Georg Funke as CEO of Hypo Real Estate Holding AG, returning to Deutsche Bank in June 2010 for a year before moving on to Credit Suisse. Michael Endres, a retired member of Deutsche Bank's Management Board, became chairman of HRE's supervisory board.

In the end, Hypo Real Estate was unable to trade its way out of its immediate troubles and, once its notes were due to be redeemed at the beginning of April 2009, the German government made an offer of €1.39 per share to take over the bank entirely. The €290 million for this operation came from the Financial Market Stabilisation Fund set up in October 2008 to rescue the German banking system and was Europe's largest bailout. HRE was divided into a 'bad bank' and a 'good bank' to isolate its impaired assets in the autumn of 2010. The 'bad bank' took over a nominal value of about €210 billion, or about half the value of the entire 2008 balance sheet.[65] The entanglement with HRE demonstrated the importance of Deutsche Bank in the German state's reaction to the global financial crisis, the lack of clarity and consensus in the fevered atmosphere of a bailout and the ability of Ackermann to take the negotiations past a stalemate to gain his position. These characteristics were on display again in the bank's negotiations to take over assets of ABN AMRO.

3. 'Project Erasmus': ABN AMRO and Fortis

In October 2007 a consortium of Royal Bank of Scotland (RBS), Santander and Belgian bank Fortis had taken over ABN AMRO (ABN) for the enormous sum of €71 billion, the largest ever bank merger deal at the time.[66] As part of this deal the European Commission required Fortis to sell some of ABN AMRO's assets in the Netherlands to conform to anti-competition rules. Fortis began to negotiate a sale to Deutsche Bank of 15 commercial banking units, a commercial bank (Hollandsche Bank Unie NV) and 14 advisory branches of a leasing and factoring enterprise (IFN). The group had some one thousand employees and about 12 per cent of the Dutch market share including 32,000 commercial clients.[67] Michael Cohrs introduced the possibility of Deutsche Bank taking over ABN AMRO's commercial banking activities in the Netherlands in April 2008, five months before the collapse of Lehman Brothers. The project was code-named 'Erasmus'. Ackermann summarised the GEC discussion that the deal was feasible only if it was equity financed and the credit provisions 'conformed to Deutsche Bank's standards and synergies were improved'.[68] The GEC declined to recommend the proposal to the Management Board at this point but Cohrs continued negotiations and on 2 July 2008 Deutsche Bank made an offer of €709 million.[69] The bank remained concerned about the quality of the assets remaining on the balance sheet and requested a 'credit umbrella' to get compensation for unexpected losses after conclusion of the purchase. Although Fortis and ABN AMRO publicly agreed to the deal, with ABN AMRO providing credit risk coverage for about €10 billion of risk-weighted assets, it also required approval from the Dutch central bank DNB (De Nederlandsche Bank). In early September 2008 DNB deemed that the credit coverage terms offered by Deutsche Bank were inadequate since the risk that the actual assets in the bank's portfolio turned out to be worse than expected was entirely borne by ABN. Deutsche Bank sought to rescue the deal by making another offer that would require ABN to cover *unexpected* losses only up to nine months after the deal was concluded and then capping the liability afterwards. But in the first week of September 2008, DNB warned Deutsche Bank that they were unlikely to approve the proposal and the deal was never formally signed off before the collapse of Lehman Brothers threw international banking markets into turmoil.[70]

A few weeks later, at the start of October 2008, the Dutch authorities had to bail out and nationalise ABN AMRO at a cost to the Dutch government of €12.8 billion. In December 2008 as conditions continued to deteriorate, the Dutch government also took over the Dutch part of Fortis for a further €6.5 billion. This interrupted the negotiations, but the EU continued to insist that some of the commercial banking business needed to be separated out in order to meet their rules for the limits on market concentration. Deutsche Bank hoped to renew its offer, but the deadline expired at the end of October 2008 and ABN AMRO rejected the old terms. To overcome the impasse, Credit Suisse was mandated by the EU as a trustee to enforce a solution by 14 August 2009.

Almost a year after the first offer, Project Erasmus was still under negotiation. At the end of July 2009 a new scheme was proposed to Deutsche Bank's Group Investment Committee (GIC) which was responsible for analysing strategic investments. By this time, Deutsche Bank was ready to offer €638 million with the protection of a credit umbrella and €441 million without.[71] Importantly, the 2008 financial returns had not yet been audited so there could still be some nasty surprises. On the positive side, the deal would make Deutsche Bank the fourth largest commercial bank in the Netherlands with a market share of 14 per cent. From a Group perspective it would contribute to strengthening the 'stable' businesses of the bank, to re-weight the business portfolio and improve the Group's overall credit rating. Deutsche Bank's Global Transaction Banking (GTB) Division believed that the Dutch bank could be returned to profit by 2012 even without the credit umbrella and recommended the deal should be submitted. The GIC board, however, agreed instead to revert to the original July 2008 offer, which had a larger up-front cash total but greater protection against undisclosed and unexpected losses. There followed a series of exchanges over the terms of a deal between the Dutch Ministry of Finance, the ABN CEO, the European Commission and Credit Suisse, but the Dutch Ministry of Finance confirmed the collapse of negotiations on 17 September 2009. This was not the end of the story.

Having come to the brink of failure, the parties returned to the negotiating table and on 20 October 2009 Deutsche Bank announced that it had concluded an outline agreement on the basis of the July 2008 offer. The deal was finally signed off on 23 December 2009 and completed in April 2010 for the original price of €700 million in cash. The balance of responsibility for unexpected losses on the loan portfolio ended up with ABN taking on 75 per cent and Deutsche Bank 25 per cent. This was less than Deutsche Bank's original proposal for 100 per cent cover in July 2008 but better than the 50/50 risk-sharing proposed by ABN AMRO and the Dutch Ministry of Finance. The transaction to acquire the shares was finally concluded at the start of April 2010, making Deutsche Bank the fourth largest provider of commercial banking services in the Netherlands, although it was never able to challenge the market dominance of incumbents ING, Rabobank and the nationalised ABN AMRO in what remains a highly concentrated banking market.[72] During 2013 the Dutch operations were scaled down (including telling 78 per cent of its 23,000 customers to move to another bank) with a renewed focus on commercial banking services for corporate clients.[73]

By taking over parts of ABN AMRO's commercial banking activities in the Netherlands, Deutsche Bank's management sought to continue to rebalance the bank away from the risky investment banking business and to build up the commercial and retail side of the business, including wealth management. This was part of a strategy that also led to the bank taking over private wealth manager Sal. Oppenheim Group in a deal announced a week later, on 28 October 2009. The cost was €1 billion and was scheduled to be completed in the first quarter of 2010. Thus, the crisis created opportunities for Deutsche Bank to extend the 'safe' banking side of the business through new acquisitions.

4. Trouble at the Top: Ackermann's Extended Leadership

In the wake of the crisis, it was clear that changes needed to be made to allow the bank to weather the instability that was certain to follow. Layoffs among investment bankers were mirrored by investments in wealth management and commercial and retail banking (represented in the divisions for Global Transaction Banking, Asset and Wealth Management and Private & Business Clients) and there was a strong focus on sustaining the bank's liquidity and external credit rating. In January 2009, however, after the Postbank and ABN AMRO acquisitions, and in the wake of the massive losses reported in 2008, Ackermann made a decision to leave Deutsche Bank a year before his second term expired in 2010. According to Ackermann's biographer, the timing was partly sparked by the reorganisation of UBS, which created an opportunity for Ackermann to return to Switzerland and take on the role of chairman of the board of directors.[74] Although the timing of this opportunity was too tight for Ackermann, there were other possibilities in Switzerland and he still planned to leave at the next annual meeting in May 2009.

By this time personal conflict at the top of Deutsche Bank's leadership between Clemens Börsig as Chairman of the Supervisory Board and Ackermann as Chairman of the Management Board (CEO) was unsettling, and the issue of succession became a general preoccupation within and outside the bank. In 2002, after serving his two years as a 'lame duck' Spokesman of the Management Board, Rolf-E. Breuer had moved to become Chairman of the Supervisory Board. Almost immediately, however, he was implicated in a scandal involving allegations by businessman Leo Kirch against Deutsche Bank. Kirch claimed that Breuer had undermined his company's reputation in an interview with *Bloomberg* in February 2002 that contributed to the company's collapse. At the start of 2006 the Federal Court of Justice (*Bundesgerichtshof*, BGH) confirmed that Breuer had a case to answer and his position as head of the Supervisory Board became untenable. After years of legal wrangling, Deutsche Bank settled the case, paying Kirch's estate €928 million in 2014. Breuer's prolonged fall from grace had long-lasting effects on the leadership at the top of Deutsche Bank. In 2006, Breuer was replaced by the CFO, Clemens Börsig, who had a troubled relationship with Ackermann. This marked a departure from the usual pattern by which the Chair of the Supervisory Board was usually a former Spokesman of the Management Board, as had been the case for Kopper and Breuer and with one exception all their predecessors since Abs. In the run-up to the global financial crisis the Supervisory Board became a rather passive audience for the quarterly reports from the Management Board, which in turn relied on Ackermann's Group Executive Committee. The formal governance of the bank became more distant from the operations details at a crucial time of financial innovation and risk-taking.

In the weeks before the 2009 annual general meeting, Ackermann told a small circle of colleagues, including a four-member search committee chaired by Börsig, about his plans to leave.[75] A first step in the succession planning was that the Management Board was reinvigorated by adding key heads of division out of the Group Executive Committee. At its meeting of 17 March 2009, the Supervisory Board agreed to bring Cohrs, Jain, Fitschen and Neske onto the Management Board from the beginning of April 2009. The GEC membership was increased from 10 to 12. Meanwhile, Börsig was lined up to succeed Ackermann as CEO at the next Supervisory Board meeting, but his ambitions were thwarted. The succession was bungled at this critical moment when the bank was just emerging from the 2008 crisis. Stefan Baron, Deutsche Bank's head of Communications from 2007 to 2012, relates that the employee members of the Supervisory Board resisted the appointment of Börsig to CEO and also of Henning Kagermann (then CEO of SAP) as his own successor as Chair of the Supervisory Board.[76] Allegations also emerged that the bank's internal security had been set to investigate one of the bank's shareholders after Börsig had drawn attention to them.[77] This raised further resistance to Börsig in the Supervisory Board. In these circumstances, at short notice the Supervisory Board asked Ackermann to continue in post and this was confirmed at an extraordinary meeting of the Supervisory Board on 27 April 2009. Thus, at the same time as announcing that the bank had returned to profit, Ackermann agreed to continue for a further three years beyond his original term, until 2013, in order to end the confusion over the bank's future leadership. This proved to be a critical decision both for Ackermann and for the bank's fortunes. The conflict between Börsig and Ackermann continued, the bank's underlying strategy was left unrefreshed and Ackermann became increasingly drawn towards more external public activities beyond the day-to-day management of the bank itself. Among these was the European sovereign debt crisis described in the next section. Deutsche Bank would have been involved in any case because of its own exposure and its position as the leading German bank, but Ackermann's statesmanship as head of the Institute of International Finance raised the bank's profile and influence in the negotiations.

5. Greek Sovereign Debt Crisis

The financial crisis that erupted in the autumn of 2008 had profound effects on the fiscal positions of many countries, particularly Ireland and Greece, within the Eurozone. In Ireland, the problem was prompted by the state's decision to bail out Irish banks, which caused a huge fiscal deficit. The problems in Greece were more fundamental, arising from structural fiscal deficits. In mid-2009 the country was heading for a fiscal deficit of 10 per cent of GDP, but in October a new government was elected and the deficit was revealed as having been under-reported in official statistics and would reach 12.7 per cent for 2009. The debt burden (interest and repayments) threatened to exceed GDP and Greece was poised for a major sovereign debt crisis as repayments of €53 billion were due in 2010.[78] Of Greece's outstanding debt of €293 billion at the end of 2009, about €90 billion was held by European banks; €23 billion of that by German banks. The sovereign debt crisis threatened the fragile international banking system but it also became an issue focused on the opposing sides of Germany and Greece.[79]

As recounted by many observers of the crisis, the political obstacles to a bailout or a restructuring agreement were enormous, but this was especially true for Germany. The German election of September 2009 returned Angela Merkel as Chancellor and Wolfgang Schäuble replaced Peer Steinbrück as Finance Minister. Both Schäuble and Bundesbank president Axel Weber took a hard line on the need for Greece to pay back its debts by reinforcing fiscal discipline and austerity at home. At the same time, the

German media were adamant that private bank lenders should bear a fair share of the cost of reducing Greece's debt rather than having the burden land on European tax payers through government support.[80] Political and ideological pressures meant that Chancellor Merkel became a key antagonist for the Greek government, refusing a compromise until the last moment in April 2010 when Greece's first tranche of debt came due. A deal was struck with the Greek government, the ECB and the IMF in May 2010, including a €750 billion stabilisation package to forestall the immediate crisis, but it did not create a sustainable foundation for the longer term.

Josef Ackermann, as chairman of the Institute of International Finance (IIF) and CEO of Deutsche Bank, was perfectly placed to play a leading role in negotiating the restructuring of Greek debt. The IIF was founded to bring banks together to discuss and resolve issues associated with the 1982 developing country sovereign debt crisis and had evolved into an important forum for international banks on other issues. For instance, the IIF responded to regulatory changes designed at the Bank for International Settlements after the crisis and acted as the key liaison group for international banks with public sector institutions. Thomas Mayer, chief economist of Deutsche Bank and head of Deutsche Bank Research from January 2010 to May 2012, also contributed prominently to the sovereign debt debate, proposing a European Monetary Fund to help with Eurozone sovereign debt restructuring.[81] In February 2010 Ackermann reportedly travelled to Athens to meet with Greek Prime Minister George Papandreou to discuss a scheme to provide Greece with a package of €30 billion in 10-year bonds, but it did not in the end achieve German government support.[82] Ackermann's role heightened Deutsche Bank's profile in the negotiations, but there were also more fundamental reasons why the bank was central to restructuring Greece's debt.

Much of Deutsche Bank's exposure to Greek sovereign debt arose from the significant amount of Greek bonds bought by Postbank, which came onto Deutsche Bank's balance sheet in 2010. In mid-2011 UBS and the *Guardian* published research showing that Postbank's net exposure to Greek sovereign debt was €1.2 billion or 21 per cent of total equity compared with €400 million for Deutsche Bank.[83] Overall, Deutsche Bank was in a much less precarious position than Commerzbank, which held about €2.2 billion of Greek sovereign debt. Hypo Real Estate (HRE) had accumulated even larger amounts so that its exposure to Greece amounted to €8.8 billion.[84] After the HRE bailout, most of the losses on these assets would fall to the government and the German taxpayer, so Merkel's government had an incentive to resolve the Greek sovereign debt crisis with as little writing down as possible of the value of existing bonds.

Table 19 shows Deutsche Bank's exposure to sovereign debt of five Eurozone countries in difficulty in 2010, of which a total of €6.9 billion or 57 per cent came to the bank with Postbank. Within a year Deutsche Bank had reduced its net exposure dramatically, particularly by divesting its Italian bonds.

After the short breathing space afforded by the stabilisation package in May 2010, another pinch point was due to arrive at the start of July 2011 when another set of bonds would need to be rolled over or redeemed. Given the strong political need for private sector involvement in debt restructuring, European finance ministers approached the IIF to co-ordinate discussions with affected banks and other financial institutions. The

Table 19: Deutsche Bank's net sovereign debt exposure to selected European states, 2010–2012.

Net sovereign exposure in € million	2010	2011	2012
Portugal	(12)	(45)	153
Ireland	237	181	400
Italy	8,011	1,767	2,969
Greece	1,601	448	39
Spain	2,283	1,318	1,659
Total	12,120	3,669	5,220

Source: Deutsche Bank, Annual Reports 2010, 2011, 2012. Parentheses = short position.

IIF set up a Greece Task Force and on 27 June 2011 had its first meeting with the Eurogroup Working Group chaired by Vittorio Grilli, Director General of the Italian Treasury.[85] Time was clearly short to devise a plan in time for the 3 July deadline to conclude a deal with Greece and allow the IMF to release the next €12 billion of its funding. Euro area finance ministers hoped that the banks would agree to roll over their maturing bonds into new five-year bonds, but this would require them to take losses onto their profit and loss statement in their balance sheets. The banks hoped to avoid booking losses. The French came up with a complex solution including a special purpose vehicle and enhancing collateral on the debt to avoid impairment and losses.[86] The IIF had a less complicated plan to have a debt buyback supported by the EU and IMF, and a rollover with enhanced collateral. But such a tangled web of accounting would require time, which had run out.[87] In these final negotiations, Deutsche Bank's Charlotte Jones,[88] Hugo Bänziger and Stefan Krause were keenly involved.

On 29 June 2011 a working group of major German financial institutions met with representatives of the Bundesbank, BaFin and Ministry of Finance to draft a 'declaration on the German financial industry's contribution to solving the Greek situation' and Schäuble requested the heads of German financial institutions to sign it the following day.[89] The intention was to provide a signal of the intentions of private sector creditors that could reassure official creditors and the IMF enough to allow the release of the IMF funding a few days later. In the declaration the banks agreed to roll over, extend or reinvest the bonds maturing until the end of 2014 into new instruments, although the nature and structure of these instruments had yet to be resolved. The total face value of the package was €2 billion, which included Deutsche Bank's €65 million trading book and €736.7 million of Postbank's bonds. Deutsche Bank thus accounted for 40 per cent of the total.[90] Bänziger expected Schäuble also to ask that the relevant bonds include all those maturing by 2020, which increased the total to €4 billion, but for Deutsche Bank this included only a further €78 million held by DB Bauspar. Bänziger reassured his colleagues on the Management Board that the declaration was not binding, but, rather, represented an offer to engage in negotiations. It also avoided rolling over maturing bonds into new five-year off market rate bonds, which would require losses to be recorded on the banks' bottom line. In the end, €3.2 billion was the headline total that banks agreed somehow to roll over or extend. When this intention was announced, Ackermann reassured the public: 'We are convinced that Greece has to be helped further ... and are very confident we will find a solution that will give satisfactory answers to all participants.'[91]

In the end, the Greek government imposed a further round of austerity on its suffering population and on 21 July 2011 Merkel, Trichet and French President Nicolas Sarkozy hammered out a deal that released the IMF's funding and ECB bond purchases. Ackermann, as head of both the IIF and Deutsche Bank, arranged for private bank creditors to swap their maturing bonds for new 30-year bonds while at the same time reducing their value by 21 per cent. Of course, the 2011 deal was not the final solution to Greek sovereign debt and a series of subsequent agreements pushed the problem further into the future. In March 2012 the IIF agreed a deal for major banks (including Deutsche Bank and Commerzbank) to exchange their bonds again, reducing their value by 50 per cent as part of yet another EU support package. In the meantime, however, Deutsche Bank was able to reduce its exposure through write-downs and hedging without impairing the bank's profit and loss statement, so that by the end of 2012 it posted only €39 million of net exposure to Greek sovereign debt.

6. The End of the Ackermann Era

Even as Ackermann was enjoying his national and international statesmanship, there was increasing speculation about who would succeed him at the head of the bank. In mid-June 2010 Michael Cohrs abruptly announced that he wished to leave the bank as of September.[92] The GEC immediately agreed that Global Banking would be integrated with Anshu Jain's Global Markets within two weeks, greatly increasing his management portfolio and making Jain the sole head of the Corporate and Investment Bank. At the extraordinary GEC meeting where this was announced, 'Ackermann reiterated that this management change is no signal for his succession as CEO and Chairman of the GEC of DB; he reiterated that his contract expires in 2013'. He also characterised the merging of Global Banking and Global Markets as 'the logical finalization of the strategic steps taken in prior years and is the model used by most of DB's key competitors'.[93] But it was clear that there would be further changes at the top of the bank.

Having bungled the transition so seriously in 2009, the Supervisory Board met first in August 2010 to begin the process while Ackermann still had two and a half years left on his contract.[94] Ackermann himself came to favour Axel Weber, then head of the Bundesbank. He was a talented economist and had leadership experience, but little actual banking experience, which was an important weakness. When he left the Bundesbank in April 2011 he still seemed a legitimate possibility, but his candidacy faced a backlash in the press and within Deutsche Bank.[95] For a time Hugo Bänziger was also considered a possibility, having worked closely with Ackermann and contributed materially to the bank's survival in 2008. He prepared a strategy for how he would take the bank forward should he become CEO, including reducing the investment bank in anticipation of the new capital requirements of Basel III and building up the transaction bank.[96] But his proposals were not taken up. Anshu Jain tended to be more optimistic that the bank's previous business model could be restored with some cost-cutting. In mid-2010, for example, he reported that 'Global Markets gained best market share ever' and that Deutsche Bank 'was well positioned for returning markets'.[97] But without fluent German it was not clear that he could run Germany's premier financial institution. A compromise was finally reached to have Jain and Jürgen Fitschen as co-CEOs from 2012, although it was clear that Jain would be the driving force. Fitschen was the same age as Ackermann and did not have as strong a background in the complex global trading markets that characterised the bank's international base. On the other hand, he did have a strong background in international relationship management and transaction banking, as well as the key knowledge and connections with the German market. Jain was also a choice that reflected continuity since he was close to Ackermann and had taken over key responsibilities while Ackermann pursued his public international roles.

The choice of Ackermann's successor was highly contested in the spring and summer of 2011. The Supervisory Board eventually decided to repeat the succession style of Hermann J. Abs with two co-Spokesmen/CEOs. But the choice of a new Chair for the Supervisory Board also provoked controversy that attracted unwelcome publicity. Ackermann expressed his wish to be elected to succeed Börsig as Chair of the Supervisory Board, and the board approved this suggestion of the nomination committee in July 2011 to complete the succession package.[98] The outcome quickly attracted further criticism, particularly from external investors. The traditional path from Spokesman of the Management Board to the Chair of the Supervisory Board that Kopper and Breuer had followed was no longer acceptable. Partly, this was because Ackermann's role from 2006 was CEO, so that he was not the 'one among equals' that his predecessors had been when elected spokesman. This change was actually introduced by Breuer in March 2005 when he argued that the term spokesman 'no longer corresponded to reality and was internationally unusual'.[99] In November 2011 Ackermann was persuaded to retract his nomination and another solution quickly had to be found.

Paul Achleitner had been head of Goldman Sachs Germany before joining Allianz as chief financial officer (CFO) in January 2000, where he had presided over the sale of Allianz's industrial holdings and also the costly acquisition and later sale of Dresdner Bank. He was therefore very much a part of the dismantling of Germany's iconic industry-finance nexus. However, after more than a decade at Allianz he was ready for a change and he agreed to move to Deutsche Bank from May 2012.

Ackermann's departure after 10 years at the head of the bank predictably led to a change of guard. Hugo Bänziger left the bank and Jain reportedly hoped to appoint William Broeksmit to replace him as chief risk officer. Broeksmit had come with Jain from Merrill Lynch as part of Edson Mitchell's recruitment drive in 1996 and led the development of derivatives trading. But BaFin reportedly blocked Broeksmit's appointment on the grounds that he had insufficient leadership experience, and Stuart Lewis was appointed chief risk officer instead.[100] Broeksmit left the bank the following year. Hermann-Josef Lamberti also retired from the Management Board and was replaced as chief operating officer (COO) by Henry Ritchotte, another recruit from the mid-1990s, who had started in hedge fund management before heading Global Markets in Tokyo during the financial crisis. In 2008 he was appointed co-COO of Global Markets under Jain and then COO at CIB from 2010. Meanwhile, Achleitner reinvigorated the Supervisory Board with people with specialist business experience including John

Cryan, former CFO of UBS, as head of the Audit Committee. Finally, the GEC was expanded from 12 to 18 members.

At Ackermann's final AGM, interjections by shareholders disrupted proceedings; a call to remove Börsig from office led to claims by shareholder Ruth Kirch (widow of Leo Kirch who had sued Breuer) against Börsig that he had choked off discussion. Approval of the Supervisory Board's performance in 2011 passed by a relatively low 77 per cent and a legal case was brought against the bank for improper proceedings. Paul Achleitner's election (along with two other nominations to the Supervisory Board) passed, but had to be confirmed at an Extraordinary Meeting almost a year later, in April 2013. Fitschen and Jain had their work cut out to restore harmony between the bank and its stakeholders.

The prolonged debate over Ackermann's succession was a distraction for the bank during a period when it should have been establishing its post-crisis profile and reassessing its business model. Arguably, the ability to recover profitability in the short term had the perverse effect of relaxing the pressure to make fundamental changes beyond cost-cutting. But the legacies of the Ackermann era would soon push the bank into a fresh era of challenge and controversy.

VIII. Renewed Crisis, 2012–2020

When Josef Ackermann left Deutsche Bank it seemed that the bank was in reasonably good shape. The return to profit had been swift, Deutsche Bank had helped restore parts of the German financial system and new acquisitions on the retail and private clients side seemed poised to rebalance the bank's portfolio from the excesses of the 2000s. But serious underlying problems soon became obvious, including the fallout from unethical and illegal activity that the bank had been engaged in during the boom of the 2000s. Furthermore, efforts to reshape the bank did not achieve an effective rescaling of the investment banking business or fundamentally change the bank's business model and infrastructure quickly enough. This left Deutsche Bank vulnerable as profits slumped and the bank's reputation ebbed away. In the first years after the 2008 crisis competitors who had fared worse in the short term had taken the opportunity to reorganise and by 2013 were pulling ahead. The bank soon found itself in a downward spiral of trying to cut costs and staff while still trying to compete in global markets and keep customers. As the bank had learned in the 1990s, an investment bank's most important assets are not on its balance sheet but at its desks. The human resource was easy to attract but just as easy to lose in a liquid market for talent. Underpinning these two issues were problems with information technology systems that proved unfit for the bank's purpose, making it even more difficult to cut costs. The Ackermann era had ended with a record of profits and expansion, but failures in operational risk management, a lack of investment in IT infrastructure and inadequate compliance left the bank extremely vulnerable. The next decade, therefore, was one of ebbing market share, falling share price and rapid turnover at the top. The bank entered the most serious challenge in its 150-year history: how to arrest the decline and restore confidence and profitability.

1. Anshu Jain and Jürgen Fitschen, 2012–2015

The appointment of Anshu Jain as one of Josef Ackermann's successors was a strong signal of continuity. Jain was instrumental in building the investment bank through Global Markets and CIB, especially in the years after Edson Mitchell's death near the end of December 2000. He had unrivalled market experience and expertise as well as a dynamic global approach that reflected the bank's strategy and profile during the decade of Ackermann's reign. He famously built a cohort of bankers and traders within Deutsche Bank known as Anshu's Army because of their numbers and their commitment to his leadership. But the challenge facing Jain and Fitschen was the opposite of that which Ackermann had faced in 2002. Then, the task had been to build the bank's scope and reputation in global markets and make a success of the acquisition of Bankers

Trust while retaining its domestic market. The challenge in 2012 was to reshape the bank away from the global trading model that Jain had helped to build. Jürgen Fitschen (the same age as Ackermann and 15 years older than Jain) was a useful partner, with a deep understanding of the domestic banking market, having been head of regional management and chairman of the Management Committee Germany. He also had extensive experience in the bank's Asian offices. After a brief tenure on the Management Board from 2001 to 2002, he had been a GEC member since 2002 and a Management Board member once again since early 2009 (associated with CIB), but he was not the charismatic and powerful leader that Jain was; his was not the driving force for change.

Launching the new leadership, the bank reconfirmed that the Group Executive Committee (GEC) had 'no decision-making authority', but, rather, 'serves as a tool to co-ordinate our businesses and regions, discusses Group strategy and prepares recommendations for Management Board decisions'.[1] Jain and Fitschen explained that the GEC was being expanded to better reflect the bank's 'global footprint' and the bank leadership's focus would be on 'evolution not revolution'.[2] The expansion from 12 to 18 members meant that the GEC now reflected 'the balance of the business divisions, regions and infrastructure functions'.[3] Regional heads outside Europe reported to Fitschen, who also continued to be responsible for Germany, while Stephan Leithner was regional manager for Europe (excluding Germany and UK) as well as head of human resources, legal and compliance.

Jürgen Fitschen (left) and Anshu Jain became the two Co-Chief Executive Officers of Deutsche Bank in 2012. Jain left the Board in 2015, and Fitschen one year later.

At the end of May 2012 when Ackermann's term formally finished, Michael Boddenberg, the CDU Hessian Minister of Federal Affairs and Representative of the State of Hessen at the federal government, wrote to Jain to congratulate him on his promotion, but he also had some warnings to offer:

> For the people in Germany, Deutsche Bank has become synonymous with the banking industry itself and its Management Board Chairmen are always subject to raised levels of scrutiny. As a consequence, Deutsche Bank has a special responsibility for the public image of the financial sector. The international financial crisis has presented huge challenges for governments as well as financial institutions. It has necessitated extensive regulatory measures to stabilize the banking sector. However, just as important – if not more so – is the need to win back the public's trust in our financial system. Indeed, it is the investment banking division that you were hitherto responsible for that has been the target of much public criticism.[4]

After three months of consultation, in September 2012 Jain and Fitschen launched their Strategy 2015+ setting the targets that they hoped the bank would achieve over the next three years. Under Ackermann there had been a commitment to grow the so-called stable businesses (PBC, GTB) but this proved difficult to implement.[5] The new approach vowed to continue this process but also to emphasise the opportunities to renew investment banking and the competitiveness of this part of the bank. The strategy was framed around five 'Cs': capital, costs, competencies in core businesses, clients and culture. Rather than marking a radical departure from the bank's basic business model, the plan aimed at 'reinforcing [the bank's] commitment to the universal banking model, to its home market of Germany and to its global positioning'. The goal was to make Deutsche Bank the 'leading client-centric global universal bank'.[6] Jain's and Fitschen's understanding was that the global financial crisis had consolidated the market for global banking because of the many mergers and acquisitions, so that the top five were gaining market share.[7] This provided opportunities for Deutsche Bank in global investment banking rather than a reason to get out of this business. At the same time, it was vital to cut costs quickly in order to return the bank to profitability. In the years to come, the bank continued to rely on its investment banking revenue for its overall performance despite the rhetoric around balancing the bank's provision.

There were three top priorities within the 2015+ strategy: improving Tier 1 capital to over 10 per cent, reducing the ratio of costs to income to less than 65 per cent and raising post-tax return on equity from 8 per cent to over 12 per cent. Of these three priorities only the first was achieved. The immediate focus of Strategy 2015+ was on growth while cutting costs, both by reducing staff numbers and by investing about €4 billion in better IT systems. Geographically, the areas for expansion were in Germany, the Americas and the Asia Pacific region while the bank planned to contract elsewhere in Europe. This included investing in Postbank's retail operations but exiting from the non-customer bank. They also promised to invest in advisory centres and devolve more local decision-making to local offices, particularly to service the needs of the Mittelstand. In Corporate Banking & Securities, the core of the investment bank, a reduction of

900 front-office employees was announced, plus a further 600 infrastructure employees. Bonuses would be linked more closely to the performance of the bank's share price and less would be paid out in relation to business performance. An independent panel was set up to review compensation. At the time of the announcement, it seemed that considerable progress had already been made; variable compensation was reduced from 22 per cent to 11 per cent of net revenues between 2006 and 2011, but there was more to do in this area as bankers came under sustained attack from the public for their excesses, and jobs were going. In order to focus on cost-cutting and de-risking, which would contribute to all three targets of Strategy 2015+, from November 2012 a specialist Non-Core Operations Unit (NCOU) pulled together the loss-making activities and portfolios that were due to be run down, including the trading securitisation portfolio and other assets, as well as Postbank's structured credit portfolio. Essentially, the NCOU isolated the bank's 'bad' assets while they were sold off or restructured. These were ambitious plans that seemed to rely heavily on cost-cutting. By the end of 2014 the ratio of costs to income was still 86.7 per cent, a reduction from 92.5 per cent in 2012, but it demonstrated little progress towards the target of 65 per cent by 2015. The pre-tax return on equity was only 2.6 per cent in 2013 and 5 per cent in 2014. Meanwhile, the bank announced a net loss of €92 million in the third quarter of 2014 and Moody's downgraded the bank from A2 to A3, although it was able to report a small profit for the year as a whole.

The goal of increasing the bank's capital was more successful. An ambitious programme of share issues and other debt issues increased the bank's capital during 2013. On 18 February 2014, the US authorities passed legislation to increase the capital and liquidity required for foreign banking organisations in the US and Deutsche Bank was required to submit their plan for complying by the start of 2015. This increased the urgency, but looking for wealthy and liquid investors in the first years after the financial crisis was a difficult task. In 2008, the Qatari sovereign wealth fund had supported Barclays and allowed that bank to avoid going to the state for a bailout, although five years later this deal was under legal attack. The Qataris also supported Credit Suisse during the crisis.[8] In May 2014, as part of a €8 billion share capital increase, Jain was able to bring the Qatari al-Thani family's investment vehicles, Paramount Services Holdings Ltd. and Supreme Universal Holdings Ltd., into Deutsche Bank as a stable investor committed to taking a long-term view of the bank's prospects. By 2019 these two investment vehicles still held 6.1 per cent of the bank's outstanding shares. Despite these headline investments, the capital increase in 2014 actually increased the proportion of shares held in Germany from 50 to 57 per cent. Jain's strategy bore fruit; by 2014 shareholders' equity had increased by €14 billion over 2012, increasing the Tier 1 capital resources of the bank to 9.7 per cent by the end of 2013 and 11.7 per cent by 2014. Increasing shareholder equity also facilitated the process of de-leveraging the bank's balance sheet (leverage being total assets compared to shareholder equity). During the first two years of the co-CEO regime, the bank's net income before taxes grew dramatically from €800 million in 2012 to €3 billion in 2014, but the ratio of costs to income still remained high, at almost 87 per cent, well above the Strategy 2015+ target of about 65 per cent. Compensation and benefits paid to employees remained at about the same level as in the heyday of 2006 before the crisis.

The bank's Strategy 2015+ was revised and relaunched as Strategy 2020 at the annual general meeting (AGM) of May 2015. While performance had improved, especially in the restructured Deutsche Asset & Wealth Management, the shape of the bank was not changed dramatically, so revenues still depended heavily on the investment banking business. Corporate Banking & Securities accounted for about a quarter of net revenues and almost half of pre-tax profits in 2014 compared to 55 per cent in 2012. Investment in operational infrastructure, including spending on technology-related regulatory and control infrastructure, amounted to €5.8 billion in the three years to the end of 2014, after having lacked investment during the crucial years of expansion from the 1990s.[9] Strategy 2020 set a more modest target of creating 'a leading global bank based in Germany' rather than the previous strapline of 'the leading client-centric global universal bank'. This reflected a simpler and narrower focus for the bank's business. There were two key headline aims: shrinking the investment bank and selling off Postbank. The strategy was to prepare Postbank for an IPO in 2016 on the basis that the bank's 'ability to fully realise the value of our acquisition of Postbank eroded in the face of the changed regulatory environment and our revised strategy'.[10] Jain announced at the 2015 AGM that Christian Sewing would lead the restructuring of the retail business in the wake of this decision. The second part of the strategy was aimed at the balance sheet of the investment bank, which had attracted so much negative comment but generated so much of the bank's revenue. This part of the bank was to be reduced from over €900 billion in leverage exposure in the first quarter of 2015 to closer to €650 billion by 2018.

The strategy was too little too late for many investors. The litigation scandals described below also sapped Jain's ability to be an effective leader, particularly when the investment bank was being further downgraded by rating agencies. At the May 2015 AGM, the approval of the acts of management of the members of the Management Board for the 2014 financial year were all around 61 per cent for each member, including Fitschen and Jain, although the Supervisory Board received a 91.5 per cent approval rating.[11] In the face of this lack of confidence from investors, Jain reconsidered his position and went to see Achleitner who accepted Jain's resignation, effective in June.

During Jain and Fitschen's joint tenure, the bank continued to be criticised by supervisors. For example, in July 2013 the Financial Supervisory Service in South Korea found that the bank's Seoul branch '"systematically violated" laws governing Korea's capital markets'.[12] In July 2014, the *Wall Street Journal* leaked parts of a letter from the Federal Reserve Bank of New York (FRBNY) to Deutsche Bank executives dating from December 2013, which reportedly noted that financial reports by some of Deutsche Bank's US arms were 'of low quality, inaccurate and unreliable. The size and breadth of errors strongly suggest that the firm's entire U.S. regulatory reporting structure requires wide-ranging remedial action', as the shortcomings amounted to a 'systemic breakdown'.[13] A New York Fed senior vice-president was quoted as saying that 'since 2002, the FRBNY has highlighted significant weaknesses in the firm's regulatory reporting framework that has remained outstanding for a decade'.[14] In January 2015, *The Times* reported that the UK Financial Conduct Authority (FCA) had allegedly put Deutsche Bank under 'enhanced supervision' in autumn 2014, indicating concerns 'due to a serious failure of culture, governance or standards'.[15] This scrutiny from supervisors, and the regulatory changes developed at the Bank for International Settlements and the Financial Stability Board, exposed the bank's struggling IT and compliance infrastructure as well as requiring increased capital to be put aside against risky assets and litigation.

In the wake of the global financial crisis there was considerable public and political frustration that the burden fell on taxpayers and not on the bankers and traders who had become rich building a tower of unsustainable debt. Unlike the earlier isolated cases of Enron, WorldCom or the rogue trading scandals in Barings and at Société Générale in the 1990s and 2000s, few traders and executives were initially tried on criminal charges. For most bankers, if they kept their jobs, it seemed that life returned to 'normal' with perhaps slightly smaller bonuses. Nevertheless, investigations into fraud and other criminal activity by traders during the boom attracted the attention of the US Department of Justice and New York banking authorities as well as the ECB in Frankfurt and the FCA in the UK. From 2010, official investigations into the global financial crisis began to explore how much bankers knew about the fragility of the US housing market and in what ways they contributed to the ultimate crisis of the global financial system. Michael Lewis's journalistic account of Greg Lippmann's trades for Deutsche Bank was the main subject of his bestselling book *The Big Short: Inside the Doomsday Machine*, published in March 2010. The Hollywood film based on the book, starring Brad Pitt and Ryan Gosling, brought the story to an even wider audience in 2015. The distinctive Deutsche Bank logo featured in many scenes. In the US, the Financial Crisis Inquiry Commission interviewed hundreds of bankers and collected thousands of pages of emails and other evidence, even referencing *The Big Short* in its investigations. The Commission's investigation provided a road map for a series of legal cases against international banks and their employees.

2. Legal Woes I: LIBOR

There were two main areas of investigation: mis-selling residential mortgage-backed securities (RMBS) and rigging benchmark interest rates. We turn first to the LIBOR scandal.

Interbank Offered Rates (IBOR) are rates offered for short-term and medium-term balances from other banks. The most famous is the London (L)IBOR, but they are also quoted in Euro (EURIBOR) and Tokyo and other markets. These rates emerged in the late 1960s as part of the syndicated loan market and eventually evolved into a benchmark rate for many other financial products. From 1981, LIBOR was set by the Chicago Mercantile Exchange through a poll of reporting banks; from 1986 the process was taken over by the British Bankers' Association in London.[16] Every day each reporting bank on the panel submitted the interest rate that it believed it would have to pay if it borrowed from other banks. Because there were not that many transactions in the interbank market, the rate submitted was an estimate and therefore difficult to verify. A proportion of the highest and the lowest bids was excluded and a single rate was determined from the average of the others. The IBOR panels for each international currency had 12–16 banks; Deutsche Bank was one of six global banks that sat on all the panels setting IBOR for the US dollar, British pound, Swiss franc, the euro, Japanese yen and the Canadian dollar. The importance of this system is not only for the interbank market itself but because these IBOR rates were then used to price a wide range of financial products including interest rate swaps, forward rate agreements and currency swaps.[17] Changes in LIBOR, therefore, could affect a wide sweep of local and international financial transactions across a range of markets. In mid-2008 the Bank of England estimated that outstanding contracts in the over-the-counter derivatives market amounted to $700 trillion, of which 60 per cent, or $420 trillion, was explicitly linked to LIBOR.[18] In addition, LIBOR was used for 65–75 per cent of syndicated lending in the US and the UK, and about 30–40 per cent of smaller corporate loans in the UK. They also found that LIBOR could 'feed its way through to the rate charged by banks on fixed rate mortgages' in the UK.[19] When deals can run into the multiple billions, even a small difference in the rate applied can generate huge revenues for traders and banks. In its report on the investigation of the manipulation of LIBOR at Deutsche Bank the FCA deemed that some 'Derivatives Traders were motivated by profit and sought to benefit their (and thus Deutsche Bank's) derivative trading positions by attempting to influence the final benchmark rates. [...] In addition to written requests, Derivatives Traders often made oral requests. These included in person requests in London by Derivative Traders sitting in close proximity to the Submitters and requests made via the telephone.'[20] At Deutsche Bank, the individuals sat in the same area and this allowed discussion between the two parties to move the rate up or down, a practice which was captured in email correspondence or telephone recordings. In the case of Deutsche Bank's Tokyo office the person who set the rate and the derivatives trader using it were even the same person, so they could pitch it high or low depending on their position in the market.[21]

As noted above, setting IBOR in London (LIBOR) was managed by the British Bankers' Association (BBA), and Deutsche Bank was a member of the polling group. In April 2008 as markets became volatile and risks increased, the BBA became concerned about the setting of LIBOR.[22] It seemed as if some banks were persistently low and others high; rumours began to circulate about the way that submissions to the poll were managed. This included allegations in the financial press of manipulation. In October 2008, when the markets were still dealing with the fallout of the Lehman collapse, the Federal Reserve Bank of New York president Tim Geithner raised the issue with Bank of England Governor Mervyn King.[23] At this point it seemed that some in the polling group were submitting artificially low quotes in order to give a better image of their banks' reputation (i.e. that they were able to borrow on the interbank market at a lower rate). The British Bankers' Association conducted an internal review, but there were no fundamental reforms. Thus, the potential for manipulating LIBOR was an open secret by the autumn of 2008.

The rumours about LIBOR that circulated in 2008 were mainly about possible 'low balling' of the rate to enhance the banks' reputation but there was also speculation that the rate could be manipulated for profit. In May 2008 the BBA wrote to the polling banks, including Deutsche Bank, to warn them that there were indications that the LIBOR was too low to be realistic and asking the senior management to 'do what is necessary within your organization to effect appropriate rates to be set'.[24] Despite this warning, the New York State Department of Financial Services (NYDFS) found that 'Despite this awareness, it was not until 2011 that Deutsche Bank took steps to introduce IBOR-specific systems and controls'.[25] Allegations that senior managers at Deutsche Bank were aware of the risk that the bank's employees were manipulating the rate for several years before undertaking a review was one of the key failings identified by regulators. In the end the bank paid total fines of $2.5 billion (£1.66 billion), mainly to the US regulators who fined the bank $2.1 billion. In addition, 'ten of the individuals centrally involved in the misconduct were terminated as a result of the investigation' although four were subsequently 'reinstated pursuant to a German Labour Court determination'.[26] The total fines were distributed across the NYDFS ($600 million), Commodity Futures Trading Commission (CFTC, $800 million), US Department of Justice ($775 million) and the equivalent of $340 million to the UK Financial Conduct Authority.

The case against Deutsche Bank brought by the UK Financial Conduct Authority, as the home authority for LIBOR, finally settled with a fine of £226.8 million on 23 April 2015. By settling at an early stage of the FCA's investigation, the bank 'qualified for a 30% (stage 1) discount under the Authority's executive settlement procedures. Were it not for this discount, the Authority would have imposed a financial penalty of £324,000,000 on Deutsche Bank.'[27] But even with the reduction Deutsche Bank's fine was higher than the £160 million paid by UBS or £59.5 million by Barclays. The FCA found 'Serious misconduct by Deutsche Bank […]: first, through Deutsche Bank's attempted manipulation of IBOR rates and improper influence over IBOR submissions, second, through its systems and controls failings and, third, through serious deficiencies in the way Deutsche Bank dealt with the Authority in relation to IBOR matters. The direct involvement of Managers and Senior Managers in many aspects of Deutsche Bank's misconduct aggravates the seriousness of the breaches.'[28] The allegations dated back to 2006 when Jain was the head of Global Markets. On the first count, the FCA found that misconduct was spread through many sections of the Global Markets division and evidence was presented from Tokyo, London, New York and Frankfurt. The FCA's published judgement found at least 29 managers, derivative traders and money market traders who were implicated in the misconduct, mainly in London. One senior manager was cited as being 'aware of traders making request to submitters to manipulate Deutsche Bank's IBOR submissions' from as early as 2006 and 'sought personally on one occasion to improperly influence LIBOR submissions' by instructing a colleague to 'make sure our libors are on the low side for all ccy [currencies]'. On the second count, after the bank found evidence of trader manipulation, it established a LIBOR steering committee of senior compliance officers in June 2011, but the FCA found that 'it was not until February 2013 that systems and controls fully addressing the inherent conflict of interest […] were in place'.[29]

The third count against Deutsche Bank was the bank's 'failure to have any IBOR-specific systems and controls in place and, moreover, its failure to address this absence of any IBOR-specific systems and controls even after being put on notice of the risk of misconduct'.[30] Deutsche Bank had 'seriously defective systems and controls in place to support audit and investigation of Trader misconduct more generally' and specifically that 'Deutsche Bank's systems for identifying and recovering recordings of Trader telephone calls and mapping trading books to Traders were inadequate'.[31]

Back in Germany, after an initial investigation in 2013 revealed irregularities, BaFin ordered a special audit by Ernst & Young, which also reported in 2015. The BaFin letter from Frauke Menke, department president of BaFin, to the Deutsche Bank Management Board relating to the report (dated 23 May 2015) was later leaked to the *Wall Street Journal* in mid-July 2015.[32] Deutsche Bank disputed some of the interpretations in the letter. The letter noted that 'overall, the [Ernst & Young] report discloses major misconduct by various traders of Deutsche Bank, and by at least one member of the management of Deutsche Bank, London Branch, as well as in part major failures by members of the Management Board or the Group Executive Committee'. Although Ernst & Young found 'no indications' that current or former members of the Management Board knew about manipulations before 2011, BaFin's view of the report was that 'a business and organizational environment was created which was favourable to incorrect IBOR submissions or even made them possible in the first place'. The report focused on Global Finance and Foreign Exchange (GFFX), led by Alan Cloete, and specifically the Money Market Derivatives (MMD) desk in GFFX, where Christian Bittar was considered by Cloete to be at the time 'one of the top money market traders in the industry'.[33] One of the aspects was 'reorganization of the seating order in the trading division in London in the year 2005, which resulted in traders and submitters sitting together [...]. The reorganization of the GFFX sectors was initiated by Mr. Jain who was also decisively responsible for this' although it was implemented by Cloete.[34] Profits in the MMD desk increased 'substantially' from August 2007 to March/April 2010, prompting 'two internal investigations at the bank' conducted by Broeksmit and by the Business Integrity Review Group (BIRG). BaFin's letter deemed that these exercises 'were not completely independent, not comprehensive and did not go deep enough'. Broeksmit's investigation in January 2009 found that 'the profits of the MMD desk/of Mr. Bittar were real and had not been caused by false valuations or internal transactions'. The letter noted that the BIRG investigation 'was supposed to look for fraud in this situation [...] but BIRG found nothing'. Bittar was fired from Deutsche Bank in 2011 and convicted in a London court in March 2018 (after pleading guilty) of conspiring to rig the EURIBOR rate. He was ultimately sentenced to a prison term of five years. In terms of the culture of GFFX, the BaFin letter considered that 'The focus in the GFFX division was clearly on the business figures and not on compliance by the employees' and that 'Mr. Bittar's supervisors (Mr. Nicholls, Mr. Cloete and Mr. Jain) were aware of and tolerated the fact that Mr. Bittar regularly exceeded trading limits'.

The letter also reviewed the senior management. One of the interesting elements in the BaFin letter was a description of a phone call between Jain and Ackermann in June 2008 in which Ackermann expressed 'his anger about "cultural deficits" in Global Markets divisions which he said he would no longer tolerate because this unnecessarily endangered the reputation of the bank'.[35] Jain was head of Global Markets, within which GFFX was situated, and therefore, in the BaFin letter he was deemed 'responsible in these functions for the GFFX division'. Frauke Menke found that 'Due to the large number of charges involving Mr. Jain as well as due to the substantial importance of the issue involving "reference interest rates", I consider the failures with which Mr. Jain is charged to be serious. They display improper management and organization of

Table 20: Costs and reserve for litigation, 2012–2018 (in euro billion).

Year	Litigation Costs	Litigation Reserves	Mortgage Repurchase Demands	Mortgage Repurchase Reserves
2012	2.607	2.4	4.6	0.5
2013	3.036	2.3	4.6	0.5
2014	1.571	3.2	5.0	0.5
2015	5.0	5.5	4.8	0.5
2016	2.397	7.6	0.8	0.1
2017	0.213	2.0	n/a	n/a
2018	0.088	1.2	n/a	n/a

Source: Deutsche Bank, Quarterly Reports, Presentations. Year-end figures. Litigation reserves varied during the year; in September 2013 reserves amounted to €4.1 billion.

the business.' The leak of the BaFin letter through the *Wall Street Journal* in July 2015 (after Jain had stepped down) added to growing public criticism of the trading culture of Deutsche Bank.

In another important case during the Jain–Fitschen era, in December 2013 the bank settled with the US Federal Housing Finance Agency to pay $1.9 billion over a charge of mis-selling $14.2 billion worth of RMBS to Fannie Mae and Freddie Mac from 2005 to 2007. The bank did not acknowledge liability. The case had loomed over the balance sheet since September 2011, before Jain and Fitschen took control of the bank, and settling it removed some uncertainty. The immediate financial impact was minimised by the significant allocation of capital made for potential legal claims arising from the global financial crisis from 2011 onwards. In 2014 this had amounted to €3.2 billion and by 2015 the bank had €5.5 billion set aside for legal contingencies. Table 20 shows the resources expended and reserved for litigation and for outstanding demands for repaying mis-sold mortgage products.

On 7 June 2015, after the LIBOR settlement became public, the Supervisory Board met and accepted Jain's resignation as of the end of the month, while Fitschen stayed on until the next annual general meeting in May 2016. At the same time as Jain, several other members also stepped down from the Management Board, including Stefan Krause (CFO), Stephan Leithner (CEO Europe, responsible for HR, Legal and Compliance from June 2012) and Henry Ritchotte (chief operating officer, COO, from 2012).

3. John Cryan and Jürgen Fitschen, 2015–2017

When Jain stepped down, the Supervisory Board had to appoint a successor swiftly. At the time, the bank was under extreme pressure from its shareholders, rating agencies, customers and employees; the succession at the top was a vital component of rebuilding the bank's reputation. The chosen man, John Cryan, might be considered the antithesis of Anshu Jain. A member of the Supervisory Board since 2013, he had chaired the Audit Committee during the various supervisory authority reviews. In the 1990s he was at

S. G. Warburg in London when Michael Cohrs and Maurice Thompson were there, but rather than leave when UBS took over he stayed, rising to become CFO at UBS just as the global financial crisis struck in September 2008. He thus avoided the blame for the crisis and was instrumental in the post-crisis reforms, which gave him important experience for Deutsche Bank. Three years later, in 2011, Cryan left UBS to manage the Singapore sovereign wealth fund Temasek in London. He had a solid demeanour and a leadership style that was certainly very different from that of Jain and Ackermann, which had often attracted the ridicule and disgust of the German public who perceived it as brash and sometimes arrogant. Cryan's style was more consultative, canvassing views across relevant teams before making decisions, although this sometimes meant that decisions could be slow. Promoting Cryan was a signal that the bank would change its path from the one that had led to the scandals that plagued Ackermann's and Jain's time in the

John Cryan came from the Supervisory Board, which he had belonged to since 2013. From 2015 to 2018, he was Deutsche Bank's Chief Executive Officer.

2000s. Although Cryan had a good command of German, Fitschen's role was extended so that he had the support of an experienced co-CEO for the first year. This also ensured continuity after Jain's abrupt departure.

There is no doubt that Cryan inherited a crisis-ridden bank. On top of the IBOR scandals, the 2015 annual results announced at his first AGM were worse than during the global financial crisis, with the bank posting a pre-tax loss of almost €6.8 billion, due in no small part to litigation fines. As a result, the Management Board agreed not to take bonuses for 2015. But this crisis atmosphere also provided an opportunity to overhaul the bank and to make a break with the Ackermann/Jain era. The Group Executive Committee (GEC) originated by Ackermann and continued by Jain and Fitschen was quickly dismantled so as to bring power back to the Management Board and the Supervisory Board. Cuts in the investment banking business signalled in Strategy 2020 continued, while costs were also attacked aggressively elsewhere. The investment banking business was split from Corporate Banking & Securities into two separate entities again: Global Markets and Corporate and Investment Banking (CIB). Nevertheless, Cryan made it clear that he was not going to eliminate investment banking: 'in response to all the well-meaning demands for an exit from investment banking and above all from securities trading, let me say: we are committed, unreservedly, to this business. It represents an indispensable element of our strategy – the only way we have of providing our corporate clients with capital market expertise and global access.'[36] It was also crucial to sustain the bank's revenue, since it still contributed for almost half of the bank's income. The aim was to focus on a smaller range of customers and to reduce the footprint, for example, by withdrawing from the Russian capital markets business.

Among the new Management Board members taking up office in 2015 and 2016 were the first women since Ellen R. Schneider-Lenné, who had died prematurely 20 years earlier, in 1996; Sylvie Matherat took up a new role as chief regulatory officer (CRO), and Kim Hammonds soon replaced Ritchotte as COO. Jeffrey Urwin (CIB) was new to the bank, but Garth Ritchie (Global Markets) joined Christian Sewing (Private, Wealth & Commercial Clients) and Karl von Rohr (HR and Legal) as experienced veterans. Among those continuing on the Management Board were Stuart Lewis (CRO) and Marcus Schenck (CFO), an investment banker who had come from Goldman Sachs in 2014. In January 2016, Quintin Price from Blackrock had replaced Michele Faissola on the board, in charge of Asset Management, but Price resigned in June due to ill health and amid falling flows of funds into Deutsche Asset Management's mutual funds.[37] He was replaced by AXA France chairman and CEO Nicolas Moreau in October 2016. Together with Cryan, these 10 individuals made up the new Management Board and Germans were now a minority on the Management Board of the 'German bank'. Figure 31 shows how the bank's operations were reorganised.

Strategy 2020, announced only weeks before Jain's departure, was continued but revamped in October 2015 to be even more ambitious. This included a specific target to reduce total costs by €5 billion, or 18.5 per cent, by 2018, which should be achieved partly by IT efficiencies, but also by closing branches in Germany, cutting more jobs and further slimming down the investment bank. As with Jain's and Fitschen's Strategy 2015+, the inability to cut costs was to be the key weakness in Cryan's strategy. Given the stickiness of costs, the collapse in Global Markets income in the third quarter of 2015 and the minimal net income achieved through 2016, due partly to litigation costs, meant that the bank was unable to turn around its bottom line. The sale of the 20 per cent stake in Hua Xia Bank in November 2016 allowed the situation to appear better by €793 million, but the fall in equity markets in the third quarter of 2015 hit the bank strongly, damaged as it was by the fines announced by various national regulatory authorities, especially the United States Department of Justice's open settlement demand for $14 billion which leaked in mid-September 2016 (discussed below).

Figure 31: Core corporate divisions: Jain/Fitschen to Cryan/Fitschen.

Previous Division	Function	New Division
Corporate Banking & Securities (CB&S)	Sales and Trading	Global Markets
	Corporate Finance	Corporate and Investment Banking (CIB)
Global Transaction Banking (GTB)	Global Transaction Banking	
Private & Business Clients (PBC)	Private and Business Clients	Private, Wealth & Commercial Clients (PW&CC)
Deutsche Asset & Wealth Management (AWM)	Private Wealth Management	
	Asset Management	Deutsche Asset Management

Source: Deutsche Bank, Presentation, AGM 2016, 16 May 2016.

Certainly, the reputational challenges that Cryan and his team faced were enormous. At Cryan's first AGM in May 2016, the compensation system for members of the Management Board was narrowly rejected. Achleitner was forced to defend himself from critics who blamed him for not getting rid of Jain earlier. His defence was that getting the right strategy was more important than the leadership and that he was 'convinced that it's worth giving one's all for an institution like Deutsche Bank. And I am certain that, in giving my all, I can serve this institution. I am sticking to my duty and to my responsibilities.'[38] Only weeks before the AGM, the chairman of the Integrity Committee, Georg Thoma, left the Supervisory Board amid media reports of a dispute over his investigations into senior executives' involvement in the bank's regulatory scandals. The deputy Chairman of the Supervisory Board and chairman of the General Staff Council of Deutsche Bank, Alfred Herling, told the press: 'With his overzealousness and judicial self-fulfilment, Dr. Thoma is increasingly encountering criticism.'[39] Such public disagreement in the Supervisory Board was a further blow of confidence.

In 2015 the bank set aside €5.5 billion in litigation provisions and increased this to €7.6 billion in 2016. Clearly, settling these cases and either releasing or spending this capital was critical to the bank's reputation and viability. Here, Cryan relied heavily on Karl von Rohr who was head of legal matters on the Management Board. Von Rohr had joined the bank in 1997 working in human resources, rising to global chief operating officer for regional management in 2013 and was brought on to the Management Board in November 2015. The regulatory cases settled or dismissed in Cryan's first year included the following:[40]

- 'BaFin closed special audits including those on interbank offered rates (IBOR), Monte dei Paschi di Siena and precious metals with no further action against the Bank or its employees (Feb 2016)
- Commodity Futures Trading Commission dropped its investigations into alleged foreign-exchange manipulation (Oct 2016)
- Settlements of large matters with respect to RMBS: civil claims arising from DB's pre-financial crisis RMBS business in the US settled with Department of Justice (Dec 2016)
- Russia/ UK Equities Trading: regulatory enforcement investigations into DB's anti-money laundering control function settled with FCA [£163 million] and [NY]DFS [$425 million] (Jan 2017)
- Kaupthing CLNs: claims regarding DB-issued leveraged credit-linked notes referencing Kaupthing settled with plaintiffs (Oct 2016)
- IBOR: Agreements-in-principle to settle four class actions in the US (Dec 2016 and Jan 2017)
- Precious Metals: US civil litigations regarding the daily setting of gold and silver fixes settled with plaintiffs (Jan. 2016)
- High Frequency Trading/ Dark Pools: allegations whether marketing materials adequately disclosed certain features and/or technical problems related to the Bank's dark pool and order router settled with SEC, New York Attorney General and FINRA (Dec 2016)

- Schickedanz: agreement reached including claim on alleged wrongful advice in relation to the "Arcandor" bankruptcy (Dec 2016).'

During Cryan's first full year, these cases were a persistent drain on the energy of the bank as well as the balance sheet. By 2017 only €2 billion needed to be set aside for potential litigation claims and this fell to €1.2 billion in 2018.

Another way to shore up the balance sheet and release Tier 1 capital was by selling off individual businesses. US private client business Alex. Brown had come to Deutsche Bank with the acquisition of Bankers Trust in 1999 and was sold to Raymond James Financial Inc. in September 2016, although the two companies agreed a distribution arrangement to co-operate on equity new issue securities for a further seven years.[41] In the summer of 2007, while markets were wobbling, Deutsche Bank had bought Abbey Life from Lloyds TSB for £977 million. Nine years later, also in September 2016, it was sold for just £935 million to British holding company Phoenix Group. After lengthy negotiations with regulators over remitting the proceeds, Deutsche Bank was able to sell its stake in Hua Xia Bank in November 2016 to PICC Property and Casualty Company Ltd. and the credit card agreement between the two banks was ended. After considerable negotiation, the deal to sell the retail commercial and private banking business in Poland to Santander for €305 million was announced at the end of 2017. The transaction was finally closed almost a year later. These sales generated cash at a time when litigation fines were still hanging over the bank's future.

In early 2017 the Management Board reassessed Jain's Strategy 2020 and Cryan's October 2015 amendments. After two years of losses, clearly more needed to be done to bring the bank to a more stable foundation and on 5 March 2017 yet another relaunch heralded a further major restructuring. The bank was to be comprised of three corporate divisions instead of four, aiming at streamlining systems and reinforcing the presence in Germany. Global Markets, Corporate Finance and Transaction Banking were combined into a single entity, Corporate and Investment Banking, with the emphasis on corporate orientation rather than wholesale or institutional trading and sales. Postbank and the German retail business were combined to create Private & Commercial Banking. Deutsche Asset Management would form the third division. The plan was to partially spin it out through an IPO into a separate subsidiary after integrating Sal. Oppenheim's operations. Accompanying this new structure, a further €8 billion share issue would boost the bank's capitalisation. The aim was that the balance of the bank would move more towards the stable businesses, and the corporate centre would be pruned and costs cut further. The geographical footprint would shrink so that Private & Commercial Banking was more concentrated in Germany with a smaller physical presence; 187 branches were closed by the end of September 2017. The CIB would continue to operate in Europe, North America and Asia Pacific to meet the needs of customers, but it, too, would be focused primarily on Germany and Europe. The strategy made a clear commitment to 'maintain a strong, but more focused US footprint'.[42] To support the reforms, the Supervisory Board appointed Schenck (CFO) and Sewing (PW&CC) as co-deputy CEOs to support Cryan.

A key part of the renewed vision, with its focus on Germany, Europe and stable business, was to reverse Jain's decision to sell off Postbank. Instead, Postbank would be integrated into Deutsche Bank's retail operations, generating a target €900 million in synergy savings. By 2016, Postbank had been brought back to net profit after recording a loss of €2.6 billion in 2015, due in no small measure to job cuts, including about 550 FTE in 2016. In addition, revenues were increased through changes to Bauspar interest provisions in the last quarter of 2015 and the sale of some investment securities. On the other hand, charges for litigation and the drain from the 'bad bank' NCOU offset some of these gains. A new pricing model and extended advisory services helped to offset the decline in interest income that all retail operations faced in the global low interest rate environment. Christian Sewing and Frank Strauß as co-heads of the Private & Commercial Bank led this transformation. During 2017, integration plans were drawn up and negotiations with labour unions progressed. The two brands would persist, although there would be a single legal entity with one head office, management team and IT platform.[43] Sewing's retail empire was getting stronger while Cryan's legal struggles continued.

4. Legal Woes II: RMBS and Foreign Exchange

As noted above, after the global financial crisis there was a public backlash against large banks and this was particularly intense in Germany. While Deutsche Bank became embroiled in the legal cases that were co-ordinated among British, American and European banking regulators, the bank came under increasing scrutiny and criticism as part of the general investigations of the global financial crisis. The US Congressional investigations of the financial crisis exposed fresh evidence from many banks of the poisonous culture at trading desks (including the publication of internal email correspondence) which spurred the Obama administration's quest for public compensation from investment banks. In January 2012 President Obama announced a task force to investigate bank fraud, and a series of high-profile cases were pursued by the Department of Justice as well as by the New York banking regulator and the Office of the Comptroller of the Currency. Deutsche Bank was not the most deeply involved bank in most of these scandals and the fines levied against it were not among the highest. For example, only weeks after Obama's task force was announced, the Department of Justice agreed a $25 billion settlement with five US banks over mortgage foreclosures. But this was just the start.

By August 2017 total fines paid by financial institutions in relation to the credit crisis in the US amounted to over $150 billion.[44] Cryan had managed to settle a number of Deutsche Bank's cases by this time, so with less than $10 billion in fines they featured further down this disreputable league table than they might otherwise have, in fourth place. Bank of America accounted for more than a third of the total fines charged on the major banks, including $16.6 billion to settle the case of RMBS mis-selling in August 2014. This bank was particularly hard hit because it had acquired Countrywide and Merrill Lynch during the crisis and then was responsible for their misdeeds. Similarly, JP Morgan Chase paid the second largest amount of fines by 2017, partly on behalf of Bear Stearns and Washington Mutual, the two early collapses in the crisis, including $13 billion over its RMBS operations.

Figure 32 shows the annual total fines levied for non-compliance from 2009 to 2017. European banks paid about 36 per cent of the total, mainly to US regulators. Overall, the fines charged by European regulators amounted to only 6 per cent of the total. The US authorities, with their higher fine levels and overlapping supervisory and regulatory agencies accumulated the bulk of the fines, and American banks paid close to two-thirds of the total.

The RMBS mis-selling probe was one of the most prominent efforts by the US Department of Justice to bring banks to account. While the large American banks were dealt with relatively swiftly, Deutsche Bank was towards the back of the queue and the delay and uncertainty made things worse. In mid-September 2016, on the eighth anniversary of the Lehman Brothers collapse, the press published the confidential Department of Justice's opening settlement demand against Deutsche Bank of $14 billion.[45] The impact was seismic. The demand amounted to almost half the bank's total net revenues in 2015. The bank's share price fell to an all-time low as it was forced to admit that the rumours were indeed true. The bank's public response was that 'Deutsche Bank has no intent to settle these potential civil claims anywhere near the number cited. The negotiations are only just beginning. The bank expects that they will lead to an outcome similar to those of peer banks which have settled at materially lower amounts.'[46] But the publicity surrounding this enormous figure made these claims seem hollow; the number stuck in the minds of investors, ratings agencies and customers. The share price fell 7.6 per cent on the news and the credit default swap price (the cost

In many places around the world, such as here in London, people protested against the financial system in 2011.

Figure 32: Annual total fines paid by banks due to non-compliance, 2009–2017 (in US dollar billion).

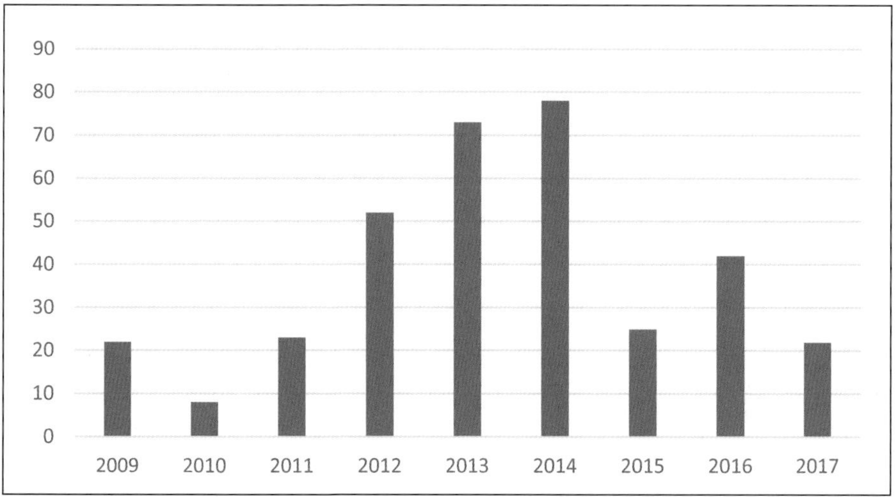

Source: Boston Consulting Group, 'Global Risk 2018: Future-Proofing the Bank Risk Agenda', February 2018.

of insuring the bank's debt against default) rose about 8 per cent.[47] These were existential threats at a time when the bank might need to raise capital and had only set aside €5.5 billion for fines. The negotiations then continued for two months, prolonging the uncertainty hovering over the bank's future.

In January 2017 the bank finally settled with the Department of Justice over mis-selling RMBS, agreeing to a fine of $3.1 billion and providing $4.1 billion worth of 'consumer relief to eligible consumers'.[48] At the beginning of February, Cryan made an official apology on behalf of the bank, stressing: 'It was generally the misconduct of a relatively small number of individuals pursuing their own short-term interests that jeopardised Deutsche Bank's most valuable asset: its reputation.'[49] As stated in the Deutsche Bank Mortgage Settlement, the relief for consumers included '(a) loan forgiveness or forbearance, or assistance with refinancing, to underwater homeowners and distressed borrowers; (b) loan originations meeting specified borrower and loan characteristics; (c) principal forgiveness where foreclosure is not pursued and liens are released; (d) affordable housing development financing through certain federal tax incentive programs'.[50] This was the largest fine for a single bank's activities, although others had paid more on behalf of institutions they had absorbed during the crisis.

Not all cases were related to the run-up to the global financial crisis. In September 2015, for example, Deutsche Bank was fined $2.5 million by the US Commodity Futures Trading Commission for failing to properly report its swaps transactions from January 2013 to July 2015.[51] Another major category of financial crime was charges of collusion in the setting of currency foreign exchange rates to increase profits for traders at the expense of their customers. Again, Deutsche Bank was fined $205 million over allegations that traders operated through chat rooms to manipulate foreign exchange rates.[52] In May 2015, five banks were fined (Citicorp [$925 million], JP Morgan Chase

& Co. [$550 million], Barclays PLC [$650 million], The Royal Bank of Scotland plc [$395 million] and UBS AG [$203 million]), for the activities of their traders (self-styled as 'The Cartel') who manipulated the $/€ exchange rate. At the same time Barclays settled related claims with the New York State Department of Financial Services (NYDFS), the Commodity Futures Trading Commission (CFTC) and the United Kingdom's Financial Conduct Authority (FCA) for an additional combined penalty of approximately $1.3 billion.[53] Deutsche Bank's alleged control and compliance failings were shared by many others in the industry.

Despite the success in settling the largest outstanding legal actions, the more fundamental changes in the bank seemed not to be delivering on the bottom line and the share price continued to fall. Cryan began his statement to shareholders in the Annual Report for 2017 with the defensive statement that 'our results were actually better than they may seem at first glance'.[54] The outcome for the year was especially adversely affected by the need to recalculate deferred tax benefits after cuts to the US corporate tax rate, and this tipped the bank into a third straight year of losses under Cryan's leadership. The falling share price made it more costly to raise capital, but new investors nevertheless came on board. From April 2017 the Chinese conglomerate group HNA acquired shares both directly and through subsidiaries and options with UBS to accumulate a stake of 9.9 per cent. However, they proved a less stable investor once the Chinese economy began to falter in 2018 and they reduced their investment. There were also reports that Cryan refused to meet with HNA's CEO Adam Tan as the share price stumbled in 2017.[55] By the start of June 2018 HNA's Cayman Islands subsidiary C-QUADRAT held 7.64 per cent of voting rights. Stephen A. Feinberg began to build up a holding through his private equity company Cerberus Capital Management of just over 3 per cent of shares from November 2017. Blackrock remained a major shareholder throughout.[56]

In the end, despite two major strategic revamps, the required changes were not happening fast enough for investors. In April 2018, the Supervisory Board announced that Cryan would step down. Paul Achleitner was also under fire at this point as the most senior person in the bank, who had presided over three CEOs and persistent losses, but he retained the confidence of his Supervisory Board colleagues through the succession to the next CEO. After Ackermann's 10-year stint at the top, the Management Board prepared to welcome its fourth CEO in six years. How had it come to this?

5. Performance, 2012–2018

To understand the context for the prolonged struggle in the bank's performance from 2012 to 2018, we can look first to the causes of the securitisation boom that led to the global financial crisis. The 'great moderation' of the 1990s and 2000s, characterised by low interest rates and moderate inflation, fired up the US real estate market. It also exposed the frailty of the short-term structure of most mortgages that relied on sustained or rising property values for refinancing. But it was the way that banks and other financial institutions used the mortgages that transformed these features into a global crisis. In February 2017 Cryan issued a public apology after settling major legal issues:

I would like to take this opportunity to express, also on behalf of the Management Board of Deutsche Bank, our deep regret for what happened. We would like to apologise sincerely. Serious errors were made – for example, with regard to our residential mortgage backed securities business in the US between 2005 and 2007, about which we recently reached a settlement with the Department of Justice. In this matter, conduct at that time did not meet our standards and was completely unacceptable. Unfortunately the same also applies in other instances. [...] It was generally the misconduct of a relatively small number of individuals pursuing their own short-term interests that jeopardised Deutsche Bank's most valuable asset: its reputation. Many more people felt the repercussions – not only clients and investors, but also all of our decent, honest colleagues who identify so strongly with Deutsche Bank.[57]

So where did the bank go wrong? Indulging in counterfactual scenarios is tempting but ultimately dangerous; which turning points to choose, what features to leave constant and which elements of the present or past should be changed? Some indications can be taken from comparison. Being smaller and less ambitious globally may not have saved Deutsche Bank from the worst effects of the crisis in global markets. Examples of those that suffered include Commerzbank, which had to accept a government bailout and partial state ownership. IKB and HRE were also drawn fatally into global markets despite remaining smaller and primarily domestic-focused. Even the German retail giant Postbank ended up exposed to both the securitisation and sovereign debt crises.

Where were the models that successfully avoided the worst excesses of the era? Banks in Canada and Australia did not avoid the backlash from the global financial crisis entirely, but they were not as highly leveraged as many European and American banks. In 2006 and 2007 the Canadian banking system's leverage ratio was below 2 per cent compared with 15 per cent in Germany and about 7 per cent in the USA.[58] This was not due to the wisdom and conservatism of their management boards, but, rather, to the strong frameworks and priorities in the prudential supervision systems.[59] While the healthy profits of Canadian banks were protected by anti-competitive regulation, they were also prevented from engaging in the securitisation boom to the same extent as American and European banks. Indeed, the structure of the Canadian banking system meant that it weathered the two major crises of the twentieth century (1930s and 2008) without the same repercussions as in the USA or Europe. This comparison suggests that national structures should bear some responsibility for the problems at the core of German universal banks. But Deutsche Bank was not merely a passive victim of the global financial crisis and its aftermath. The prolonged litigation over a range of violations across the European and American jurisdictions makes clear that internal compliance and governance structures were inadequate. This inability to mitigate operational risk before and after the crisis would have existed even without the generalised market risk in 2007–08.

This observation suggests a further source of frailty, which was also shared by the sector as a whole: the incentives built into employment contracts and the highly competitive nature of the labour market in financial firms. By 2007, a minority of senior bankers trading in the markets had any experience before 1987. This was a generation weaned on the excesses of the champagne lunches and bonuses of the 1980s and the ability to make easy profits in the 1990s (so long as emerging markets were avoided). From the 1980s, the City of London and Wall Street drew in legions of young, ambitious graduates who hoped and then expected to get rich through designing and selling financial products to an increasingly global market. Forty-year-old senior bankers in 2007 were part of a transactional rather than relational generation. They might be loyal to their immediate managers, as evidenced in the frequent movement of entire teams between banks, but they were also attached to their bonuses and enhanced compensation as a measure of their status – not as strongly to their customers or their employers. This made for a slippery labour market, where a bank's key assets – its traders and market makers – could disappear overnight to a competitor. Managers needed to reward these employees in order to retain them. We have seen that this aspect of human resources was critical from the beginning of Deutsche Bank's move to London capital markets when it bought Morgan Grenfell, and again when it embarked on the US market through, for example, Frank Quattrone's group. The expectations of the 'prima donnas' needed to be met with tangible evidence of how much they were valued through retention bonuses and guaranteed compensation contracts. By the 2000s, most participants knew no other labour market or motivation. Did this mark the end of the global Hausbank?

The distinctive nature of the German financial system was usually identified across three dimensions; the Hausbank, the universal bank and the identity of interests between business, finance and the state characterised by the shorthand 'Deutschland AG'. The Hausbank concept emphasises the relational nature of banking with long-term and exclusive relationships between customers and their chosen bank, but in practice it was a reality for only part of the bank's history. Companies might have a primary banking relationship, but they also increasingly built multiple relationships, particularly in the late twentieth century as financial needs became more complex. This is especially true for large firms.[60] We have seen that Herrhausen's and Kopper's global strategy in the 1980s was prompted by the need to protect the bank's domestic customer relations by providing the full range of capital market services that they demanded. Deutsche Bank did not abandon its Hausbank role, but its corporate customers moved on to more transactional relationships with their banks. Nor did Deutsche Bank abandon its universal banking identity, although this too shifted to a global platform. Throughout the 1990s and 2000s it consciously pursued the model of the leading global universal banks like UBS, Citigroup and JP Morgan. The protection of the universal bank character in Germany was the key area of dispute through the 1990s whereas there was little mention of Hausbank in the debate. Meanwhile, Deutschland AG was dismantled by the state as well as by the banks themselves. In the 1990s the largest state financial deals were the privatisations of public assets and we have seen that the German state was content to favour American firms over German banks for this business. Indeed, this was a key driver for Deutsche Bank to compete with the US universal banks. Deutsche Bank's reorientation in global markets and the reframing of its domestic market relations needs to be viewed in the context of changes initiated outside the bank rather than only by choices made by the bank's leaders themselves. There was no cosy traditional

German banking culture that Deutsche Bank could have relied on when the globalisation of financial markets accelerated at the end of the 1980s.

On the other hand, Germany's unusually competitive and expensive domestic retail market was an important handicap. The bank experimented with ways to overcome this by segmenting the market and moving to online services, and latterly considering consolidation through merger. The decade of low interest rates after 2008 further compressed the ability to generate profits from traditional lending. Nevertheless, the repeated restructuring of the bank demonstrated the management's struggle to find ways to have effective governance as well as managerial control over its increasingly complex operations. Here, no doubt, mistakes were made. Despite its contribution to restoring stability in the German and European financial systems at the time of the two crises of the 2000s, Deutsche Bank became a lightning rod for public criticism of global banking and its excesses.

Certainly, other choices could have ameliorated the situation, even without the benefit of hindsight. More investment in compliance and IT infrastructure, wiser international acquisitions, or a speedier adjustment of the bank's business model to the new global regulatory and market environment would have left Deutsche Bank in a stronger position. Indeed, in an interview in August 2018 Jürgen Fitschen expressed his view that taking government support during the financial crisis would have contributed to a faster change in the balance sheet structure of the bank and perhaps a faster recovery.[61]

As the 'German Bank', Deutsche Bank's rising and falling fortunes have always followed those of Germany, from its contribution to the first globalisation in the late nineteenth century, interwar instability, through the Nazi period and the rebuilding of the post-war economy, finally culminating in the reunification of Germany. In the 1990s and 2000s Deutsche Bank was the most visible part of Germany's engagement in financial globalisation as the leading European universal bank. For 20 years, from its first major move into the London market in 1989, this seemed to be a mark of success, but it left behind a legacy of weakness that the bank's management spent the 10 years after the global financial crisis struggling to repair.

The key challenge from 2012 was to ensure the bank's future viability and this required increasing capital, increasing revenue and cutting costs. These imperatives drove the bank's key performance indicators, which included Tier 1 capital and the cost/income ratio. How did the bank perform? At the end of 2018 the ratio of costs to income was almost exactly where it had been in 2012: 92.7 per cent, which compared unfavourably with the average for 2001–2005 of 80.6 per cent. But the intensive effort to cut costs deeply affected the bank's workforce. The number of posts (full-time equivalent) was reduced by over 9 per cent overall, including heavy cuts within Germany, where there was a 12 per cent loss in jobs, or over 5,600 (net), from the start of 2012 to the end of 2018. Over 540 branches closed in Germany alone and more than 900 worldwide. Increasing share capital and selling off risky businesses meant that the Tier 1 capital ratio achieved its target, but this was not reflected in the rating agencies' view of the bank, which was steadily downgraded, partly due to German legislation in 2016 that meant that long-term lenders would be less likely to get their money back if the bank collapsed. Deutsche Bank now had among the highest funding costs of European banks, which reversed its business model during the boom that relied on leveraging cheap funding.[62] Table 21 shows some key indicators for the bank during the period from 2012. Particularly striking is the decline in the share price (adjusted for capital

Table 21: Selected indicators, 2012–2018.

	2012	2013	2014	2015	2016	2017	2018
Branches	2,984	2,907	2,814	2,790	2,656	2,425	2,064
thereof in Germany	1,944	1,924	1,845	1,827	1,776	1,570	1,409
Employees (full-time equivalent)	98,219	98,254	98,138	101,104	99,744	97,535	91,737
thereof in Germany	46,308	46,377	45,392	45,757	44,600	42,526	41,669
Long-term rating							
Moody's Investors Service	A2	A2	A3	A3	Baa2	Baa2	Baa3
Standard & Poor's	A+	A	A	BBB+	BBB+	BBB-	BBB-
Share Price High €	33.41	32.89	34.05	29.83	19.72	17.82	16.46
Share Price Low €	18.82	25.04	20.22	18.46	8.83	13.11	6.68
Income (loss) before income taxes, € m.	814	1,456	3,116	(6,097)	(810)	1,228	1,330
Net income (loss), € m.	316	681	1,691	(6,772)	(1,356)	(735)	341

Note: share price from daily highs and lows.

Figure 33: Total assets of Deutsche Bank, 1997–2018 (in euro billion).

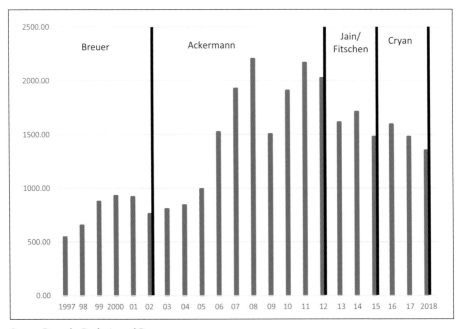

Source: Deutsche Bank, Annual Reports.

increases in 2014 and 2017). From its highest in 2012 to its lowest in 2018, the share price fell by 80 per cent.

Figure 33 shows the growth in the total assets of the bank under the four leadership teams from 1997 to 2018. The rapid expansion during Ackermann's reign reflected the increased leverage that was reversed in part under Jain, Cryan and Sewing. After 2012, structural changes, de-leveraging and sales of some units meant that the value of the bank's assets shrank back to the levels of before the financial crisis.

Figure 34 shows the phenomenal rise in the bank's share price under Ackermann, followed by the equally dramatic collapse in the financial crisis of 2007–08. The restructuring of the bank under Cryan failed to reverse the decline, which continued through the start of his successor's leadership. As discussed below, Christian Sewing stepped into the CEO role in early April 2018.

Figure 35 shows the return on average shareholders' equity, one of the consistent key performance indicators for the bank. From 2000 there was an increase in recorded profitability until the peak in 2006, but this was followed by a steady decline punctuated by losses in 2008, 2016 and 2017.

Figure 34: Adjusted closing daily share price of Deutsche Bank, January 1998–September 2019 (in euro).

Note: To reflect the capital increase in 2017, the historical share prices up to and including 20 March 2017 (last trading day cum rights) have been adjusted with retroactive effect by multiplication with the correcting factor of 0.8925 (R-Factor). To reflect the capital increase in 2014, the historical share prices until and including 5 June 2014 have been adjusted with retroactive effect by multiplication with the correcting factor of 0.9538 (R-Factor). To reflect the capital increase on 6 October 2010, historical share prices from before that day have been adjusted with retroactive effect by multiplication with the correcting factor of 0.912477 (R-Factor).

Figure 35: Adjusted return on average shareholders' equity (post-tax) of Deutsche Bank, 2000–2018 (in per cent).

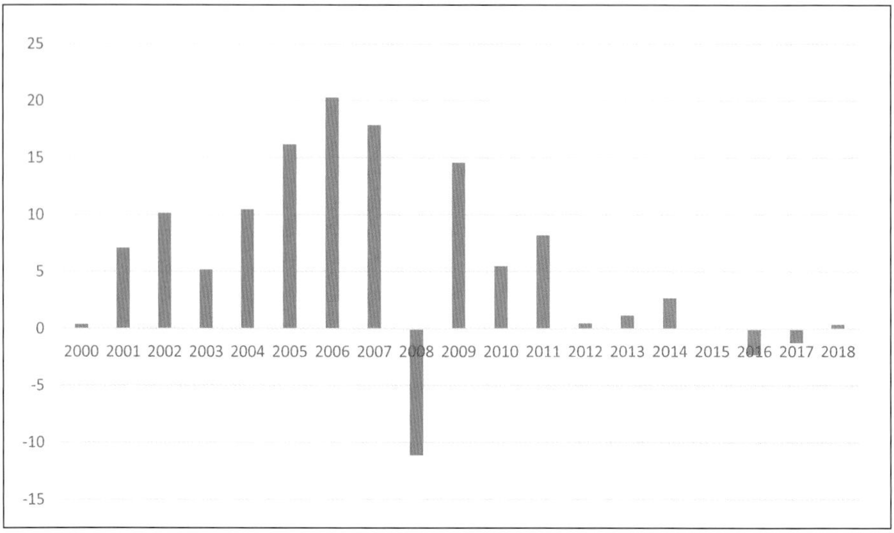

Source: Deutsche Bank, Annual Reports 2000–2018.

Overall, the bank's performance in the 10 years since the global financial crisis was clearly reflected in its returns and the share price. The unrelenting decline in the bank's share value reflected the lack of confidence in the management's ability to turn around the bank's fortunes despite the intensive efforts described in this chapter. Ultimately, it was not possible to cut costs fast enough as revenues shrank.

6. Christian Sewing, 2018–2020

Christian Sewing's appointment in April 2018 was initially met with some relief. He was a Deutsche banker in the old style, having started as a 19-year-old apprentice at a regional branch in Bielefeld before rising to the top management position. Except for two years, he spent his entire career at Deutsche Bank and had proved himself in the bold reshaping exercises while he was on the Management Board. In contrast, Sewing's co-deputy CEO, Marcus Schenck, left the bank after only four years. The choice of new CEO reflected the direction the bank was taking, away from investment banking and increasing the retail and commercial banking divisions. Thus, at the end of April 2018 Sewing announced a new target to generate 50 per cent of revenues from the Private & Commercial Bank and asset management and a further 15 per cent from Global Transaction Banking.[63] Corporate banking would become more focused on Europe where Sewing noted the bank was 'deeply rooted', while the bank's Global Equities business would be reviewed 'with expectation of reducing its platform'.[64] While Sewing may have had a homely profile, he also had a ruthless track record in reducing costs; he was instrumental in cutting thousands of retail jobs as head of Private, Wealth & Commercial Clients. Under Cryan, he sold the bank's businesses in Poland and

Portugal and the commercial banking business in China. On taking office, he immediately imposed austerity on the bank, cutting fruit bowls for staff and first-class rail travel. At the same time, the Management Board concluded the decision to shift the bank's New York offices away from their Wall Street home to Columbus Circle in midtown Manhattan by 2021.[65]

On 21 May 2018, soon after Sewing took office and three days before the annual general meeting, Deutsche Bank's chief economist, David Folkerts-Landau, gave a lengthy interview to the *Handelsblatt*, signalling the new departure for the bank, now under German leadership once again.[66] Achleitner, as Chairman of the Supervisory Board, faced a potential vote of no confidence at the annual general meeting because of the failure to turn around the bank's fortunes. Folkerts-Landau used the interview to give a ringing endorsement of Achleitner and Sewing. Given the timing and the nature of his intervention, it is worth assessing this key interview from a bank insider. After three non-German CEOs (Ackermann, Jain and Cryan) and one German joint CEO (Fitschen), Folkerts-Landau asserted:

> The difficult truth is, fundamental, strategic decisions made by the management and Supervisory Board from the mid-1990s through 2012 put the bank in this situation. These transformative decisions were based on a profound misjudgement of the cultural differences between Anglo-Saxon investment banking and the way in which the banking business was conducted in Germany.[67]

This language and references to cultural conflict hark back to the emotions expressed at the time of the takeover of Morgan Grenfell almost 30 years earlier. Then, too, the

60 Wall Street has been home to Deutsche Bank in New York since 2003. In May 2018, the bank decided to move its headquarters to Columbus Circle in Midtown Manhattan by 2021.

'Anglo-Saxon' style of banking was believed to be at the heart of the bank's inability to integrate the investment banking business effectively and challenged the bank's core values as a German universal bank. But this cultural debate also masked the fact that some leaders of the bank were not really committed to engaging in the global financial services sector. In the 1980s, Herrhausen and Kopper recognised that entering this business was not just the only way to grow the bank's international footprint, but also the only way to protect its domestic market from foreign competition. Germany's companies were becoming global, the state was divesting itself of key assets and the traditional German way of Hausbank, through exclusive and comprehensive bank/firm relationships, was eroding. Herrhausen and Kopper viewed the change in strategy not as a choice but as a necessity. Thirty years later this turning point for the bank appeared to Folkerts-Landau to be a critical mistake.

Nevertheless, Folkerts-Landau praised the efforts and experience of Edson Mitchell in delivering the Herrhausen/Kopper vision in the 1990s, even though it changed the balance of the bank perhaps more than anticipated: 'If you hire a plumber to build your house, don't be surprised if it ends up with too many bathrooms.' For him the 'truly fateful and transformational event' that pushed the bank in the wrong direction was the appointment of Ackermann as Spokesman of the Management Board in 2002, and Anshu Jain's promotion to head Global Markets to replace Mitchell. He laid the blame quite squarely on Ackermann and Jain, who presided over the bank's huge expansion in the 2000s. For Folkerts-Landau, putting aside the mistakes of the past by restoring the German characteristics of Deutsche Bank was the strong message in advance of Sewing's first AGM as CEO.

One of Sewing's challenges was the legacy of Cryan's effort to raise funds by spinning out part of the asset management business, which was rebranded to DWS in December 2017. The IPO of 22.5 per cent of DWS took place on 23 March 2018, with Karl von Rohr as the chair of the DWS Supervisory Board and Nicolas Moreau as its CEO. The goal had been to raise funds and reduce the core bank's regulatory capital while also increasing the operational independence (and compensation rules) for the asset management business. But the initial performance was disappointing; the share price lost almost a third of its value, reaching €22.4 by January 2019 compared to €33.04 at the company's launch. In 2018 there was a net outflow of funds of €22.3 billion.[68] Moreau moved out of the bank in October 2018 and was replaced by Asoka Wöhrmann, who had been in charge of the German private client business in the Private & Commercial Bank. He also had extensive career experience in DWS. This marked a move away from hiring leaders in asset management from outside the bank (and outside Germany). Despite this challenging start, DWS asset management became a cornerstone of Sewing's plans for the reorganisation of the bank (discussed below); the DWS share price recovered in the early months of 2019, the net outflows were reversed and assets under management recovered in the first half of the year.

The bank's IT woes also continued as costs increased and progress on streamlining systems was slower than planned. As COO, Kim Hammonds was able to streamline the bank's IT systems by, for example, reducing the number of payments systems from 40 to 8. In March 2018, she was quoted as remarking at an internal function that

Deutsche Bank was the 'most dysfunctional company' for which she had worked. It was announced that she would leave soon after Sewing's arrival in April 2018.[69] Frank Kuhnke replaced her but did not join the Management Board until 1 January 2019. At that point two thirds of the Management Board were German, compared to one third under Cryan.

And the legal challenges kept coming. At the end of November 2018, the police very publicly raided Deutsche Bank's head office seeking evidence related to allegations of money-laundering arising from a leak of documents on offshore banking from a law firm in Panama, a cache which became known as the 'Panama Papers'.[70] This marked a low point for the bank's public reputation both in Germany and internationally and reportedly prompted a more fundamental reassessment of the bank's strategy, which began to be developed in a programme code-named 'Cairo'.

Despite a very challenging year, the 2018 results finally showed a return to profit and the bank's management took their bonuses for the first time in three years. The bank was able to meet its targets in cutting the number of employees on a full-time equivalent basis by about 6,000 during the year, of which about half were from CIB.[71] In the Private & Commercial Bank, most of the reduction arose from the sale of the Poland retail business, so the impact was not felt so strongly by the bank's German workforce.

This positive turn laid the foundations for Project Cairo, but in January an approach from Commerzbank provided another option. In early 2019, rumours began to circulate about a possible merger between Deutsche Bank and Commerzbank. The speculation arose partly because a major shareholder, Cerberus, had significant stakes in both banks and partly because the German government was believed to favour a single, stronger, national champion as the landscape of European finance seemed about to change.[72] This was the second time that collaboration between Commerzbank and Deutsche Bank was contemplated. In August 2016 Cryan and his counterpart at Commerzbank, Martin Zielke, informally discussed potential collaboration or merger, but both banks chose instead to continue with their own restructuring plans and the talks were abandoned. The rationale for a merger at that point arose partly from the unusual structure of the German banking system. In 2016 Germany had 1,600 credit institutions, which was three times as many as any other euro-area country. The largest five banks had only 31 per cent of total assets, which was the lowest concentration in the Eurozone, where the average was 46 per cent.[73] The result of the UK referendum in June 2016 heralded the likely exit of the UK from the European Union and increased attention on Frankfurt as an alternative financial centre for Europe. Stronger German banking institutions could assist in attracting such business and increase the benefits for Germany. In their times, both Cryan and Sewing were critical of the structure of the German banking system, that it was too fragmented and there were too many banks, so consolidation in some form was an obvious option.[74] Two years after the first talks with Commerzbank were abandoned, potential consolidation loomed again. *Bloomberg Businessweek* reported that 'at a strategy conclave in Hamburg on Sept. 14–15 [2018], the supervisory board and top managers [of Deutsche Bank] examined potential combinations with partners in Germany and abroad and decided the time isn't right for such a deal'.[75] Other reports of this meeting suggested that the favoured partner for Deutsche Bank's management was UBS rather than Commerzbank.[76]

In January 2019, Zielke reportedly came back to Deutsche Bank's CEO to explore a merger once more.[77] According to some indicators, the fragmentation of German banking was even increasing: the share of total assets of the top five banks fell to 29 per cent in 2018. Informal talks began and, amid increasing speculation, on 17 March the Management Board publicly announced that it was reviewing its strategic options and that there were ongoing discussions with Commerzbank. Labour unions opposed the merger, which likely would require massive reductions in staff to achieve the necessary synergies.[78] The formal talks lasted six weeks but on 25 April 2019 they were abandoned. In the end, the potential synergies were not considered big enough to risk a merger. The opportunity also came at a time when Sewing and his team were developing their own fundamental reforms, and this option was deemed more advantageous for the bank than a risky merger.[79] The positive 2018 performance may have boosted confidence to pursue Project Cairo, although the share price remained low. After the talks ended, Sewing remarked, 'we simply have too many banks in Germany and Europe, so there is an urgent need for consolidation. And yes, it is right and important to have a large German bank. However, a merger of Deutsche Bank and Commerzbank simply did not fit the bill – that was a business decision of both companies.'[80] Deutsche Bank was big enough to compete on its own, but needed to be more profitable, which required more dramatic changes to improve the cost/income ratio and to realign the bank's business.

Christian Sewing has been a member of Deutsche Bank's Management Board since 2015. He became CEO in April 2018. In July 2019, he announced a new strategy – including the withdrawal from equities trading.

In early July 2019, as the bank approached its 150th anniversary, Sewing revealed his new strategy for the bank. In many ways it marked a deliberate re-emphasis of the bank's traditional role as a global Hausbank. By exiting equity sales and trading and focusing more on transaction banking and developing its corporate relationships, the Management Board hoped finally to turn the bank's fortunes around. The heart of German industry, the Mittelstand, which had been shifted from corporate to private banking in 2002, was to be returned to a revitalised corporate bank. The other core business units were asset management (DWS), private/retail banking and an investment bank without equities trading, but instead focused on fixed income securities, advisory services, real estate and foreign exchange. The bank aimed to remain global, following customers across the US, Asia and Europe, particularly marketing its services as a 'global Hausbank' for the German Mittelstand through its presence in 60 countries.[81] The headroom to allow these changes to be implemented would come from radically reducing staff numbers by up to 18,000, exiting from equities and releasing capital by de-leveraging and creating a Capital Release Unit to reduce risk-weighted assets. The global investment bank, which had occupied so much of the management's time and characterised the change in the culture of the bank in the 1990s, would continue, but with a narrower range of integrated services to serve corporate and financial clients.

In July 2019, Sewing reassured his staff that the new direction the Management Board had launched was in part a return to Deutsche Bank's 'DNA', observing:

> Almost 150 years ago, we were founded as a bank that serves German and European companies worldwide, that provides a global network and that paves the road to Europe for international companies and investors. This is exactly the role that the Corporate Bank which we are forming will play.[82]

As stated in the introduction, the story of the 150 years of Deutsche Bank told in this volume does not provide a road map or a blueprint for the bank's future. The global economy now differs in many ways from the first globalisation in the nineteenth century when the bank was launched. Nevertheless, inspiration can still be taken from a thorough understanding of the bank's origins and development, its sources of resilience and frailty over the course of the bank's extended history.

Notes

In the Age of the First Globalisation, 1870–1914

I. The Founding of Deutsche Bank and the Beginnings of the Business, 1870–1875

1   Brecht, *The Threepenny Opera*, p. 166.
2   See, for example, Stern, *Gold and Iron*.
3   On the so-called founders' boom of banks, see, first of all, Helfferich, *Siemens*, vol. 1, pp. 212f. Then Burhop, *Kreditbanken*.
4   In fact, there is no new research on this. The multitude of newly founded banks – Wehler speaks of 186 founded incorporated banks between 1869 and 1872 (see Wehler, *Gesellschaftsgeschichte*, vol. III, p. 101) – most likely were the sort of brokerage banks that actually exclusively engaged in stock market listings and stock transactions. From the older literature, see, first, the not very significant study by Kleine-Natorp, *Verfassung*. The dissertation by Wunderlich, *Entwicklung*, is more informative.
5   Tilly, *Verkehrs- und Nachrichtenwesen*, p. 588.
6   Wehler, *Gesellschaftsgeschichte*, vol. III, pp. 101f. The crisis not only contributed to 186 of the newly founded incorporated banks failing, but also had a severe impact on banks like Disconto-Gesellschaft, which had focused on the serious discounting of exchange rates for trade and industry.
7   Fischer, *Bergbau*, p. 538.
8   Bondi, *Außenhandel*, p. 145.
9   Cf. Tilly, *Verkehrs- und Nachrichtenwesen*, pp. 584f.
10   Findlay/O'Rourke, *Power and Plenty*, pp. 402–7.
11   In general on this see Osterhammel, *Transformation*.
12   Bondi, *Außenhandel*, p. 146.
13   Urbig, *Vorkriegsgründungen*, p. 24.
14   On Comptoir d'Escompte in this period, see Bonin, *Le Comptoir*; Torres, *Banquiers d'avenir*, pp. 10–23.
15   Wallich, *Aus meinem Leben*, pp. 52–104.
16   Cf. Cassis, *Capitals of Capital*, pp. 7–73.
17   Stern, *Gold and Iron*, passim.
18   On Bamberger, see Koehler, *Bamberger*, and Kopper, *Bamberger*.
19   Bamberger, *Erinnerungen*, p. 385.
20   Engelberg, *Bismarck*, p. 72.
21   Ibid., p. 79.
22   Gall, *Bismarck*, pp. 493f.
23   Otto, *Entstehung*, p. 92. On the background, see Schneider, *Imperial Germany's Gold Mark*. Cf. finally also Ziegler, *Entstehung*.
24   Bamberger, *Reichsgold*.
25   See Schneider, *Imperial Germany's Gold Mark*, p. 122.
26   Lumm, *Helfferich*; Williamson, *Helfferich*, pp. 20–22, gives insight into Helfferich's (pupil) relationship with Bamberger.
27   Helfferich, *Siemens*, vol. 1, p. 214.
28   On the composition of this committee, see Gall, *Deutsche Bank*, pp. 6f.; Seidenzahl, *100 Jahre*, pp. 9–21.

29   *Jahres-Bericht und Mitglieder-Verzeichniß der Deutschen Gesellschaft der Stadt New York am 16. Januar*, New York, 1860. Among the members of Deutsche Gesellschaft who were in the founding circle of Deutsche Bank were Heinrich Hardt, Eduard von der Heydt, Friedrich Kapp, Gustav Kutter, Wilhelm Loeschigk, Hermann Marcuse, Wilhelm Platenius, Hermann Rose and Otto Wesendonck.
30   Cf. Bippen, *Meier*; Duensing, *Meier*.
31   Concept Brief to die Herren Wendelstaedt, Cöln, Al. Heimendahl, Crefeld, G. Gebhard, Elberfeld, Ludwig Bamberger, Paris, Hermann Marcuse, Frankfurt a.M., Frege & Co., Leipzig, Leop. Schöller, Düren, undated, probably July 1869, HADB, K1/1000.
32   *Bataviaasch Handelsblad*, 14 November 1863 and 16 March 1867, HADB, SG8/48; Mackenzie, *Realms*, p. 119.
33   Denkschrift über Aufgaben und Ziele der neu zu errichtenden Deutschen. Confidentiell, Berlin, July 1869, HADB, K1/1000, printed in Pohl, *Documents*, in: *Studies* no. 21, pp. 729–37.
34   Delbrück, *Aufzeichnungen*, pp. 175–8.
35   On this see Gall, *Deutsche Bank*, pp. 10–11.
36   Quoted in Pohl, *Documents*, in: *Studies* no. 21, p. 730.
37   Siemens to Gwinner, 11 April 1899, HADB, S1245.
38   Luckemeyer was the brother of Mathilde Wesendonck (née Agnes Luckemeyer), the muse of composer Richard Wagner. She was married to Otto Wesendonck, who likewise was one of the initial subscribers of Deutsche Bank.
39   Pohl, *Selected Documents*, in: *Studies* no. 1–22, p. 772; *Hirth's Parlaments-Almanach*, vol. 8, Berlin, 1869, p. 188.
40   List of the Administrative Board members in HADB, SG5/1/1. On Pustau see Leutner/Mühlhahn, *Handlungsmuster*, p. 22.
41   'Herman Marcuse', *New York Times*, 20 April 1900. Seidenzahl, *100 Jahre*, p. 15, completely misjudges the significance of Marcuse's activity in the United States.
42   Wright/Smith, *Mutually Beneficial*, pp. 38f.
43   Statuten-Entwurf der Deutschen Bank Aktien-Gesellschaft, Berlin, 1870, § 2, HADB, SG30/302.
44   First financial advertisement of Deutsche Bank from 24–25 March 1870, printed in Pohl, *Documents*, in: *Studies* no. 1–22, p. 780.
45   Ibid.
46   HADB, P51, Bl. 5–10, printed in Pohl, *Documents*, in: *Studies* no. 1–22, pp. 738f.
47   Pohl, *Documents*, in: *Studies* no. 1–22, p. 738.
48   Ibid., p. 739.
49   Ibid.
50   Ibid., p. 769.
51   Ibid., p. 739.

52 Helfferich, *Siemens*, vol. 1, p. 216.

53 Ibid.

54 Cf. for the final draft of the statute of 25 February 1870 the 'Statut der Deutschen Bank Aktien-Gesellschaft genehmigt durch Allerhöchsten Erlass Sr. Majestät des Königs von Preussen vom 10.3.1870', Berlin 1870, §§ 15–37, HADB, SG30/302.

55 On the history of stock law, see Horn, *Unternehmensorganisation*.

56 Statut der Deutschen Bank, § 17, HADB, SG30/302.

57 Statut der Deutschen Bank, § 28, HADB, SG30/302.

58 Financial advertisement of Deutsche Bank from 24–25 March 1870, printed in Pohl, *Documents*, in: Studies no. 1–22, pp. 780–82.

59 Gall, *Deutsche Bank*, p. 7; Helfferich, *Siemens*, vol. 1, p. 218; also Pohl, *Documents*, in: Studies no. 1–22, p. 773.

60 List of the first subscribers of Deutsche Bank AG, dated 21 March 1870, reprinted in Pohl, *Documents*, in: Studies no. 1-22, pp. 776–9.

61 On this, see Deutelmoser, *Kilian Steiner*.

62 See, for example, the list of subscribers on the initial offering of Deutsche Bank shares, IV. Serie, 1881, in: HADB, S4210.

63 Bol, *Aktionärsstruktur*, p. 137. The previously cited list of subscribers, however, proves that even among the shareholders who allowed themselves to be represented and did not appear by name there were unlikely to be any individual, dominant investors.

64 Wallich, *Aus meinem Leben*, p. 116.

65 List of Administrative Board members of 1870 in Pohl, *Documents*, in: Studies no. 1–22, pp. 780–82. Composition of the Administrative Board in 1876 in Deutsche Bank, Annual Report 1876.

66 Wallich, *Aus meinem Leben*, p. 123.

67 'Berliner Börse vom 22. bis 28.1.1870', *Der Aktionär*, 30 January 1870, HADB, SG10/1.

68 'Berliner Börse vom 9. bis 15.12.1871', *Der Aktionär*, 17 December 1871, HADB, SG10/2.

69 Friedrich Dernburg, 'Doktor Georg Siemens. Ein Vierteljahrhundert Bankchef', *Berliner Tageblatt*, 7 April 1895.

70 Helfferich, *Siemens*, vol. 1, pp. 221f.

71 Georg Siemens to Carl Siemens, 26 January 1870, SAA, F137, here quoted in Helfferich, *Siemens*, vol. 1, p. 223.

72 Georg Siemens to Adelbert Delbrück, 22 March 1870, Abschrift, HADB, P51.

73 Kilian Steiner to Ludwig Bamberger, 14 February 1870, transcript of the letter in: HADB, SG18/8 .

74 On Wallich see Frost, *Hermann Wallich*; Helfferich, *Siemens*, vol. 1, pp. 224f.; Wallich, *Aus meinem Leben*, pp. 115–28. On the influence of Paris on Wallich, cf. Brötel, Die deutsche 'Kolonie', pp. 324ff. and 357ff.

75 Helfferich, *Siemens*, vol. 1, p. 225.

76 Georg Siemens to Rudolf Siemens, 13 April 1870, quoted in Helfferich, *Siemens*, vol. 1, p. 226; translation quoted in Gall, *Deutsche Bank*, p. 14.

77 Deutsche Bank, Annual Report 1870.

78 Wallich, *Aus meinem Leben*, p. 124. Siemens rejected Mölle's joining the Management Board, although at the time Platenius resigned he was still in the field in Le Mans. As Mölle was a lawyer, Siemens felt that his appointment directly threatened his own position in the bank, which is why he mentioned to his father that he himself was contemplating not returning to the bank; cf. Helfferich, *Siemens*, vol. 1, p. 228.

79 Quoted in Helfferich, *Siemens*, vol. 1, p. 228.

80 Wallich, *Aus meinem Leben*, pp. 123f.

81 Pohl, *Selected Documents*, in: Studies no. 1–22, pp. 785–91.

82 At least as long as it was not necessary to make immediate payments or pay within a very short time; when immediate payment became the norm, the volume of acceptance credits and, correspondingly, of bill discounting gradually declined; Riesser, *German Great Banks*, pp. 277, 297f.

83 Details in Rozumek, *Rembours* (*Rembourskredit*); Spalding, *Überseegeschäft*.

84 According to Max Steinthal, Wallich familiarised himself so thoroughly with 'the principles and the technical handling of overseas trade … that he often stated in later years that he did not understand how someone could have difficulties with this material; everything was, after all, so self–evident!' Memorial service on Friday 11 May 1928, in the Deutscher Saal of Deutsche Bank for the deceased Mr Consul Hermann Wallich, p. 8, HADB, SG1/83.

85 Exposé by Hermann Wallich for the Administrative Board, October 1877, HADB, S4499, printed in Pohl, *Documents*, in: Studies no. 1–22, p. 787.

86 Chapman, *Rise*, pp. 123–5.

87 Pohl/Raab-Rebentisch, *Deutsche Bank in Hamburg*, p. 16.

88 Seidenzahl, *100 Jahre*, p. 35.

89 Deutsche Bank, Annual Report 1871, p. 4.

90 Frost, *Hermann Wallich*, p. 58.

91 Dahlem, *Professionalisierung*, pp. 39f.

92 Pohl/Burk, *Deutsche Bank in London*, pp. 23f. and 35f.

93 For example, Mölle and Wallich writing to the branch in Bremen, 9 February 1872, with the news that a one sixteenth per cent reduction in commission had been implemented, HADB, F1/167.

94 Mölle and Wallich to Bremen branch, 23 October 1871, HADB, F1/167. In addition, Siemens to Bremen branch, 2 January 1872, HADB, F1/167, in which he praises the success of the business there, but, at the same time, also asks for understanding 'that we certainly do not have the intention of preventing you from expanding it [overseas business] by means of formal concerns. Otherwise, though, we ask [you] to consider that we, as long as binding agreements have not been reached about the extent to which we can make use of the credit of the German Bank, must reserve a portion of our credit with said [bank] for our branches in Yokohama and Shanghai.'

95 Seidenzahl, *100 Jahre*, p. 35.

96 Pohl/Burk, *Deutsche Bank in London*, pp. 26 and 33.

97 Wallich to Pietsch, 15 March 1873, HADB, F1/167.

98 Deutsche Bank, Annual Report 1873, p. 3.

99 Pohl/Burk, Deutsche Bank in London, p. 24.

100 Wallich and Koch to Bremen branch, 6 March 1873, HADB, F1/167.

101 Secretariat to London Agency, 25 November 1899, HADB, S4187, Bl. 297f.

102 Mölle and Wallich to Bremen branch, 31 October 1871, HADB, F1/167.

103 On Knoop see Dahlmann, *Ludwig Knoop*.

104 Wallich and Siemens to Bremen branch, 31 March 1876, HADB, F1/167.

105 Bremen branch to Berliner Vorstand, 16 June 1876, HADB, F1/166.

106 Wallich and Steinthal to Bremen branch, 17 June 1876, HADB, F1/167.

107 Helfferich, *Siemens*, vol. 1, p. 267.

108 Seidenzahl, *100 Jahre*, pp. 36f. For example, the bank also transferred the sum of 20.25 million marks to Spain in the early twentieth century for the acquisition of the Caroline Islands efficiently and without saying a word; Wallich, *Aus meinem Leben*, p. 125.

109 Wallich, *Aus meinem Leben*, p. 125.

110 Deutsche Bank, Annual Report 1873, p. 4.

111 Plumpe, *Deutsche Bank in Ostasien*, p. 36.

112 Seidenzahl, *100 Jahre*, pp. 37f.

113 Wallich to Bremen branch, 21 July 1876, HADB, F1/167.

114 Dahlem, *Professionalisierung*, p. 45.

115 Seidenzahl, *100 Jahre*, pp. 38f.

116 Deutsche Bank, Annual Report 1876, p. 5; Annual Report 1877, p. 3.

117 On Paul Lichtenstein see Skal, *History*, p. 211.

118 Bremen branch to Knoblauch & Lichtenstein, 19 May 1876, HADB, F1/166.

119 Siemens and Wallich to Knoblauch & Lichtenstein, 5 October 1877, HADB, A1343.

120 Deutsche Bank, Annual Report 1882, p. 3. See also Kobrak, *Banking on Global Markets*, pp. 26–8.

121 Deutsche Bank, Annual Report 1873, p. 6.

122 Dahlem, *Professionalisierung*, pp. 38f.

123 Fürstenberg, *Lebensgeschichte*, p. 208.

124 Riesser, *German Great Banks*, pp. 191f.

125 Ibid., p. 167.

126 Fuchs, *Gustav Schröter*, p. 12.

127 Helfferich, *Siemens*, vol. 1, p. 329.

128 Riesser, *German Great Banks*, p. 220.

129 Pohl, *Selected Documents*, in: Studies no. 1–22, pp. 785–91.

130 On this see Münch, *Adolph von Hansemann*, p. 261.

131 Helfferich, *Siemens*, vol. 1, p. 307. See also Heuß, *Georg von Siemens*, p. 311.

132 Riesser, *German Great Banks*, pp. 215–18.

133 Seidenzahl, *100 Jahre*, p. 43.

134 Helfferich, *Siemens*, vol. 1, p. 286.

135 Mölle and Wallich to Bremen branch, 4 March 1872, HADB, F1/167. The attempt to interest the Berlin public in the AG Weser, however, was not successful; see Wallich to Bremen branch, 9 March 1872, HADB, F1/167. Deutsche Bank itself subscribed to 50,000 shares but refused 'to acquire the remaining of the unsubscribed shares' because there was not sufficient interest; Mölle and Wallich to Bremen branch, 14 March 1872, HADB, F1/167.

136 Deutsche Bank, Annual Report 1875, p. 5.

137 On this event, see HADB, A134. A thorough account is in Helfferich, *Siemens*, vol. 2, pp. 14–21. Aktuell hierzu Bähr, *Werner von Siemens*, pp. 282–5.

138 Helfferich, Siemens, vol. 1, p. 330.

139 Deutsche Bank, Annual Report 1875, p. 5.

140 Speech by Max Steinthal at the memorial service on Friday 11 May 1928, in Deutscher Saal of Deutsche Bank for the deceased Herr Consul Hermann Wallich, p. 12, HADB, SG1/83.

141 Steinthal, *Gedenkfeier Wallich*, p. 14.

142 Numbers in Seidenzahl, *100 Jahre*, p. 40.

143 Wallich to Bremen branch, 25 June 1873, HADB, F1/167.

144 Seidenzahl, *100 Jahre*, p. 41.

145 Delbrück to Konsul Plenge, 21 April 1874, HADB, F1/167.

146 Bremen branch to Direktion in Berlin, 27 May 1875, HADB, F1/166.

147 Ibid.

148 Siemens to Bremen branch, 28 July 1875, HADB, F1/167.

149 Helfferich, *Siemens*, vol. 1, p. 292.

150 Seidenzahl, *100 Jahre*, pp. 41f., who relies on Hermann Wallich's memoirs.

151 Helfferich, *Siemens*, vol. 1, p. 292.

152 Siemens and Wallich to Bremen branch, 17 September 1875, HADB, F1/167.

153 Bremen branch to Direktion in Berlin, 18 September 1875, HADB, F1/166.

154 Bremen branch to Direktion in Berlin, 20 September 1875, HADB, F1/166.

155 Bremen branch to Direktion in Berlin, 21 September 1875, HADB, F1/166.

156 Wallich to Bremen branch, 22 September 1875, HADB, F1/167.

157 Bremen branch to Direktion in Berlin, 23 September 1875, HADB, F1/166.

158 Steinthal and Koch to Bremen branch, 24 September 1875, HADB, F1/167.

159 Bremen branch to Direktion in Berlin, 25 September 1875, HADB, F1/166.

160 Bremen branch to Hamburg branch, 2 October 1875, HADB, F1/166.

161 Report by the Management Board on previous use of its share capital, 26 October 1875, HADB, S4510. See Gall, *Deutsche Bank*, p. 29.

162 Seidenzahl, *100 Jahre*, p. 40.

163 Gall, *Deutsche Bank*, p. 22.

164 Helfferich, *Siemens*, vol. 1, pp. 288–300.

165 Georg Siemens to Elise Görz, 9 March 1872, quoted in Helfferich, *Siemens*, vol. 3, p. 269.

166 Georg Siemens to Elise Görz, 13 March 1872, quoted in Helfferich, *Siemens*, vol. 3, pp. 272f.

167 Georg Siemens to Marie Siemens, 6 March 1872, quoted in Helfferich, *Siemens*, vol. 3, p. 280.

168 Elise Siemens to Ehepaar Siemens, 4 November 1873, quoted in Helfferich, *Siemens*, vol. 3, p. 284.

169 Georg Siemens to Joseph Görz, 22 May 1874, quoted in Helfferich, *Siemens*, vol. 3, pp. 285f.

170 Gall, *Deutsche Bank*, p. 15.

171 Elise Siemens to to her parents, 9 February 1878, quoted in Helfferich, *Siemens*, vol. 3, p. 292.

172 Seidenzahl, *Pamphlet*.

173 Quoted in Heuß, *Georg von Siemens*, p. 315.

174 The draft of the letter is largely reproduced in Helfferich, *Siemens*, vol. 1, pp. 322–6.

175 Ibid., p. 325.

176 Karl Helfferich wrote Georg Siemens's biography at the behest of Siemens's widow. It was published in three volumes in the early 1920s. Helfferich undoubtedly knew Georg Siemens's character better than anyone, particularly since he had married one of Siemens's daughters and had unrestricted access to his entire estate. It is owing to the fact that Helfferich documented part of the correspondence in the third volume of the biography that a considerable number of original sources survived even though large parts of his estate were later lost.

177 Georg Siemens to Johann Georg Siemens, 14 July 1875, quoted in Helfferich, *Siemens*, vol. 3, p. 288.

178 Elise Siemens to her parents, 27 April 1880, quoted in Helfferich, *Siemens*, vol. 3, pp. 293f.

179 Fürstenberg, *Lebensgeschichte*, p. 202.

II. Consolidation in a Difficult Time: The Era of Wallich, 1876–1887

1 Rosenberg, *Große Depression*.
2 Spree, *Wachstumstrends*.
3 Cf. e.g. Wengenroth, *Unternehmensstrategien*; in general, see Aldenhoff-Hübinger, *Agrarpolitik*.
4 On tariff policies, see Findlay/O'Rourke, *Power and Plenty*, pp. 395–402. See also Cameron, *Concise Economic History*, pp. 278–82.
5 On Bismarck's swing towards protective tariffs, see Engelberg, *Bismarck*, pp. 297–319.
6 Georg Siemens on tariff reform, quoted in Helfferich, *Siemens*, vol. 3, p. 167.
7 Seidenzahl, *Pamphlet*.
8 Rosenberg, *Große Depression*; Grundsätzlich Baltzer, *Berliner Kapitalmarkt*.
9 Ziegler, *Eisenbahnen*, pp. 211–29.
10 Wallich and Koch to Bremen branch, 11 April 1876, HADB, F1/167.
11 Bremen branch to Müller & Krüger, New York, 2 May 1876, HADB, F1/167.
12 Wallich to Bremen branch, 5 May 1876, HADB, F1/167.
13 Siemens and Wallich to Bremen branch, 12 May 1876 (Minutes of the Meeting of the Committee of Five, 8 May 1876, intus), HADB, F1/167.
14 Bremen branch to Deutsche Bank Berlin, 16 June 1876, HADB, F1/166.
15 Wallich and Steinthal to Bremen branch, 17 June 1876, HADB, F1/167.
16 Bremen branch to Deutsche Bank Berlin, 12 July 1876, HADB, F1/166.
17 Bremen branch to Deutsche Bank Berlin, 25 July 1876, HADB, F1/166.
18 Ibid.; Hermann Wallich, who had been in Bremen right then for the semi-annual inspection, shared the view of the Bremen branch, by the way.
19 Steinthal and Koch to Bremen branch, 1 August 1876, HADB, F1/167.
20 Compilation in letter from Bremen branch to Direktion, 7 September 1876, HADB, F1/166.
21 The bank's tax burden, by the way, was not uniform, particularly since the legal situation in the young Reich was completely disparate and complicated because the federal states had the exclusive right to levy direct taxes where they were sovereign. Correspondingly, income and corporate taxes also varied, though primarily only in rudimentary form before Prussia made progress in legislation at the end of the century. But that did not lead to uniformity either, nor did it affect what is called corporate tax today; on the legal situation, see Ullmann, *Steuerstaat*, pp. 59ff. The taxation of corporations in the nineteenth century proceeded analogously to the nonuniform income tax of natural persons, so that it generally consisted of a state tax plus municipal charges. In addition, there were other federal taxes, for example, in Bremen an assets tax of one-eighth per cent, which the branch located there had to pay on the capital being utilised in Bremen. Berlin saw no possibility for Bremen to avoid taxation. Deutsche Bank Berlin to Bremen branch, 9 October 1876, HADB, F1/167.
22 Bremen branch to Direktion in Berlin, 25 July 1876, HADB, F1/166.
23 Cf. Correspondence between the branch in Bremen with Knoblauch & Lichtenstein in the first half-year of 1878, HADB, F1/166.
24 Wallich and Steinthal to Bremen branch, 22 November 1878, HADB, F1/167.
25 Transcript of the minutes of the directorate meeting on 6 December 1878, HADB, F1/167.
26 Ibid.
27 Bremen branch to Direktion, 20 March 1882, HADB, F1/166.
28 Delbrück and Kapp to Bremen branch, 22 March 1882, HADB, F1/167.
29 Deutsche Bank, Annual Report 1886, p. 3.
30 Riesser, *German Great Banks*, p. 272.
31 Koch and Krug to Bremen branch, 28 February 1880, HADB, F1/167; Bremen branch to Direktion, 1 March 1880, HADB, F1/166.
32 Helfferich, *Siemens*, vol. 2, pp. 35ff.
33 Fürstenberg, *Lebensgeschichte*, pp. 199–202.
34 Helfferich, *Siemens*, vol. 2, p. 34.
35 Bremen branch to Deutsche Bank Berlin, 7 May 1881 and frequently, HADB, F1/166.
36 Georg Siemens to Elise Siemens, 10 July 1882, quoted in Helfferich, *Siemens*, vol. 3, pp. 300f.
37 Georg Siemens to Elise Siemens, 16 September 1882, quoted in Helfferich, *Siemens*, vol. 3, p. 302.
38 Kobrak, *Banking on Global Markets*, pp. 26–8.
39 On Villard see Kobrak, *Banking on Global Markets*, p. 30f.
40 Georg Siemens to Elise Siemens, 2 September 1883, quoted in Helfferich, *Siemens*, vol. 3, pp. 307f.
41 Ibid., p. 308.
42 'I think that we in Berlin also need to address the American matters; after all, America is closer to us than Italy, despite the Gotthard,' he wrote to Kilian Steiner on 22 June 1883, quoted in Helfferich, *Siemens*, vol. 2, p. 232.
43 Kobrak, *Banking on Global Markets*, pp. 34f.
44 Ibid., pp. 36f.
45 Gall, *Deutsche Bank*, p. 57.
46 Wallich, *Aus meinem Leben*, p. 142.
47 Ibid., pp. 142–6.
48 Wallich and Steinthal to Bremen branch, 30 April 1879, HADB, F1/167. See also Helfferich, *Siemens*, vol. 2, p. 27.
49 Siemens to Bremen branch, 4 February 1883, HADB, F1/167, with a detailed description of the negotiations.
50 Siemens and Koch to Bremen branch, 19 February 1883, HADB, F1/167. There is a summary of the whole matter in Siemens to Bremen branch, 22 February 1883, HADB, F1/167.
51 Summary in Helfferich, *Siemens*, vol. 2, pp. 27–34.
52 A typical example is the application for a Bremen conversion bond of December 1880, which Deutsche Bank, together with the Disconto-Gesellschaft, the Seehandlung and the banks Warschauer and Mendelssohn, wished to acquire; Siemens and Wallich to Bremen branch, 9 December 1880; Bremen branch to Deutsche Bank Berlin, 9 December 1880 and further correspondence up to 14 December 1880, HADB, F1/166–167. The concrete form the bond then took was entirely unsatisfactory, however.
53 Seidenzahl, *100 Jahre*, p. 44.
54 Ibid., pp. 45–8.
55 Ibid., pp. 49f.
56 Ibid., p. 53f.
57 Deutsche Bank, Annual Report 1887, p. 3.
58 Helfferich, *Siemens*, vol. 2, p. 184.
59 Model, *Effektenbanken*, pp. 118 and 123.
60 Helfferich, *Siemens*, vol. 1, p. 335.

III. The Expansive Years: The Era of Siemens, 1887–1900

1 Deutsche Bank, Annual Report 1890, p. 3.
2 Ibid., 1895.
3 Ibid., pp. 3f. See Buchner, *Möglichkeiten*.
4 Buchner, *Spielregeln*. See also Fohlin, *Finance Capitalism*, ch. 4.
5 Riesser, *German Great Banks*, p. 205.
6 Deutsche Bank, Annual Report 1900, Balance Sheet of the Headquarters and Branches.
7 Weber, *Bankplatz*, p. 68.
8 Deutsche Bank, Annual Report 1900, pp. 9, 11.
9 Model, *Effektenbanken*, p. 128.
10 On this and the following, see Seidenzahl, *100 Jahre*, pp. 56–62.
11 On this, see Historische Gesellschaft der Deutschen Bank (ed.), *Deutsche Bank in Frankfurt am Main*, pp. 40–44.
12 Köster, *Standort Weiß-Blau*; Pohl/Raab-Rebentisch, *Deutsche Bank in Leipzig*.
13 Deutsche Bank, Annual Report 1897, p. 3.
14 Fürstenberg, *Lebensgeschichte*, p. 208.
15 For the fundamentals on this, see Schinckel, *Bankunternehmungen*.
16 On this and the following, see Pohl, *Deutsche Bank Buenos Aires*, pp. 16–45.
17 Helfferich, *Siemens*, vol. 2, pp. 166f.
18 For the fundamentals, see Meleghy, *Vermittlerrolle*, pp. 39–42, 58–62.
19 For details, see Müller-Jabusch, *Fünfzig Jahre*; Plumpe, *Deutsche Bank in Ostasien*, pp. 23–90.
20 Müller-Jabusch, *Fünfzig Jahre*, pp. 34–8. For a thorough account of the areas of conflict, see Merker, *Konfrontation*, pp. 53–60.
21 For a thorough account of this, see Hertner, *Deutsche Bank in Italien*. See also Hertner, *Starting from Scratch?*.
22 Helfferich, *Siemens*, vol. 2, pp. 206–13.
23 The falling-out turned out to be so severe that Siemens once again threatened to resign in order to force Jonas to do so; he accused Jonas of causing important railway projects in Italy to fail; ibid.
24 On the Italian syndicate, see Hertner, *Deutsche Bank in Italien*, pp. 35–77, here pp. 44–54. Helfferich, *Siemens*, vol. 2, pp. 217f.
25 Strasser, *Die deutschen Banken im Ausland*, p. 69.
26 Helfferich, *Siemens*, vol. 2, pp. 218–22.
27 For a thorough account of this, see ibid., pp. 169–78.
28 Bernhard von Bülow to Georg Siemens, 23 May 1899; Gwinner to M. W. Radulowitsch, 1 May 1900; Deutsche Bank Sekretariat to Emil Goldschmidt, Wien, 7 May 1900, HADB, OR1733.
29 On their structure, see Radu, *Auguren*.
30 Barth, *Hochfinanz*.
31 Reinhard, *Unterwerfung*, pp. 950–65.
32 This was all well known already by contemporaries; see Scharlach, *Unsere Banken*, Teil I.
33 Helfferich, *Siemens*, vol. 2, p. 279.
34 Faust, Ein 'deutsches Indien in Afrika'?, pp. 38–65.
35 For details, see Scharlach, *Unsere Banken*, Teil I, pp. 196–9.
36 Scharlach, *Unsere Banken*, Teil II.
37 Helfferich, *Siemens*, vol. 2, p. 287.
38 Ibid., p. 287f.; Fuchs, *Max Steinthal*, pp. 23ff.
39 Deutsche Bank, Annual Report 1895, p. 6.
40 Deutsche Bank to Gebr. Bethmann, 17 January 1893, IStG Frankfurt, Bethmann-Archiv, V222.
41 Fürstenberg, *Lebensgeschichte*, p. 340.
42 Deutsche Bank, Annual Report 1899, pp. 4f.; Koch,

Goldverkehr. Friedrich Koch was Rudolph Koch's son and thus had relatively unrestricted access to the relevant information in London.
43 Siemens to Otto Braunfels, quoted in Helfferich, *Siemens*, vol. 2, p. 289.
44 Deutsche Bank, Annual Report 1890, p. 4.
45 On this, see Pohl, *Deutsche Bank Buenos Aires*, pp. 28–45. Helfferich, *Siemens*, vol. 2, pp. 197–206.
46 Helfferich, *Siemens*, vol. 2, p. 205.
47 Kobrak, *Banking on Global Markets*, pp. 62–91.
48 Letter, printed in Helfferich, *Siemens*, vol. 3, p. 344.
49 On Adams see Kobrak, *Banking on Global Markets*, pp. 70f.
50 Ibid., p. 101.
51 Ibid., p. 100.
52 Ibid.
53 See, e.g. Pohl, *Stambul*.
54 This is how it was presented in Deutelmoser, *Kilian Steiner*, pp. 223–57.
55 Deutelmoser, *Kilian Steiner*, p. 230.
56 Ibid., p. 231f. The relationship between Georg Siemens and Alfred Kaulla was not easy because Siemens did not completely trust Kaulla.
57 Deutelmoser, *Kilian Steiner*, pp. 226f.
58 Foreign Office, signed by Bismarck, to Deutsche Bank, 2 September 1888, HADB, OR5.
59 Seidenzahl, *100 Jahre*, pp. 64–6. Pohl, *Stambul*, pp. 23ff.
60 Seidenzahl, *100 Jahre*, p. 81.
61 Georg Siemens to Bauer (Wiener Bankverein), 18 January 1899, HADB, OR1733.
62 Esteves, *Imperialism*.
63 See the section 'Deutschland in der Weltwirtschaft', in Tilly, *Zollverein*, pp. 104–30.
64 Bähr, *Werner von Siemens*, pp. 234–41.
65 Ibid., pp. 328–38.
66 For a comprehensive account of this, see Pinner, *Emil Rathenau*. In addition, there are numerous documents in Pohl, *Emil Rathenau*.
67 Bähr, *Werner von Siemens*, pp. 355f.
68 Ibid., p. 359.
69 Pinner, *Emil Rathenau*, pp. 97f.
70 Pohl, *Emil Rathenau*, pp. 39–41.
71 On this, see Bähr, *Werner von Siemens*, pp. 360f.
72 Pohl, *Emil Rathenau*, p. 59f.
73 Georg Siemens to Hermann Görz, 23 May 1894, quoted in Helfferich, *Siemens*, vol. 2, p. 123.
74 Bähr, *Werner von Siemens*, pp. 351–71.
75 Pinner, *Emil Rathenau*, pp. 146–56.
76 Pohl, *Emil Rathenau*, p. 59.
77 Cf. in Pinner, *Emil Rathenau*, pp. 186–222.
78 Seidenzahl, *100 Jahre*, pp. 136f.
79 Ibid., p. 137.
80 Pinner, *Emil Rathenau*, pp. 378f.
81 Helfferich, *Siemens*, vol. 2, p. 125. Pohl, *Emil Rathenau*, pp. 126f.
82 Pohl, *Emil Rathenau*, pp. 129–67, with lots of material and numerous photographs of AEG's expansion projects.
83 Helfferich, *Siemens*, vol. 2, p. 138.
84 Ibid.
85 Georg Siemens to Hermann Görz, 6 October 1900, quoted in Helfferich, *Siemens*, vol. 2, p. 139.
86 Ibid.
87 Jacob-Wendler, *Elektroindustrie*.
88 Helfferich, *Siemens*, vol. 2, p. 143.
89 Wessel, *Kontinuität*, pp. 53–70.

90 'During this time Papa was together with Dr Siemens, who now has a lot of trouble. At Deutsche Bank 1.1 million has been squandered by forgeries of brokers' certificates by an official. The directors replaced the sum.' Walther Rathenau to Mathilde Rathenau, 1 August 1891, in: Walther Rathenau, *Briefe*, pp. 363f.

91 For stock market transactions in securities, the broker had to confirm every concluded deal on the same day by means of a broker's certificate. See *Handwörterbuch des Kaufmanns. Lexikon für Handel und Industrie*, vol. 4, Hamburg, 1927, p. 926.

92 Data in Helfferich, *Siemens*, vol. 2, p. 184. Cf. Barth, *Banken und Kapitalexport*.

93 Deutsche Bank, Annual Reports, ongoing.

94 On the propaganda that boiled over not least into the so-called Agriculture-Industry-State Debate that took place as this time, see Regulski, *Handelsvertragspolitik*.

95 Karl Helfferich, Die Novelle zum deutschen Bankgesetz vom 7. Juni 1899, in: *Neue Freie Presse* 20 June–7 July 1899, reprinted in: Helfferich, *Studien*.

96 Ferguson, *The World's Banker*; Liedtke, *Rothschild*.

97 Müller-Jabusch, *Fünfzig Jahre*, pp. 34–8, who describes the structure of the 'Comprador Department' in detail and points out that it was entirely indispensable to all European banks in China but could also be associated with significant losses. Osterhammel, *China*, pp. 174, 185ff., confirms this finding but nevertheless indicates that towards the end of the nineteenth century this system had already passed its peak.

98 Gleeson-White, *Double Entry*, pp. 146–60.

99 Georg Siemens to Geheimrat Braunfels, 26 July 1899, quoted in Helfferich, *Siemens*, vol. 2, p. 289.

100 Fahrmeir/Lesczenski, *Finanzdienstleister*, pp. 21–44.

101 On the following, see, above all, Dahlem, *Professionalisierung*, pp. 95–103.

102 Gwinner to Julius Frey, 8 March 1909, HADB, S1929.

103 Dahlem, *Professionalisierung*, p. 99.

104 Ibid., pp. 101f.

IV. On the Path to Success: The Gwinner Era, 1901-1914

1 Deutsche Bank, Annual Report 1900, p. 4.

2 Holtfrerich, *Quantitative Wirtschaftsgeschichte*; now Böse, *Kartellpolitik*.

3 On the crisis of the mortgage banks, cf. Redenius, *Strukturwandel*, pp. 78f; Sattler, *Pfandbrief*, pp. 75–82.

4 Kritzler, *Preußische Hypotheken-Aktienbank*.

5 On the general success of these kinds of solutions in the area of public bonds, cf. Esteves, *The Bondholder*.

6 Deutsche Bank, Annual Report 1905.

7 Barth, *Hochfinanz*; Kirshner, *Appeasing Bankers*.

8 Georg von Siemens, Die nationale Bedeutung der Börse, in: *Die Nation*, 6 October 1900, pp. 6–8.

9 Dahlem, *Professionalisierung*, p. 56.

10 'Behrensstraße 9-13', *Plutus*, 12 February 1910, p. 130.

11 When he wanted to introduce typewriters in the bank's offices, Arthur von Gwinner recalls having encountered resistance, *Lebenserinnerungen*, p. 98.

12 Gwinner, *Lebenserinnerungen*, p. 100.

13 'Umschau', *Plutus*, 5 February 1910, pp. 104f.

14 'Behrensstraße 9-13', *Plutus*, 12 February 1910, pp. 130f.

15 Pinner, *Wirtschaftsführer*, p. 222. Pinner was evidently alluding to Arthur Gwinner's nervous breakdown, the fairly early retirements of Hermann Wallich and Max Steinthal from the Management Board, of Ludwig Roland-Lücke's repeated vacating of his offices.

16 Reinhard, *Unterwerfung*, especially ch. XVII.

17 For a general account, see Osterhammel, *Transformation*, p. 487.

18 Fischer, *Weltwirtschaft*, pp. 11–15.

19 Transactions by country (alphabetical): Summary of the contents of the files transferred from Berlin to Frankfurt am Main, HADB, ZA17/1187.

20 Cassis, *Financial Centres*, p. 301; van der Wee/Goossens, *Belgium*, p. 128.

21 On the involvement of German banks in Belgium before 1914, see Bitsch, *La Belgique*, pp. 141–4.

22 Carrein/Mestdagh, *Inventaris*, pp. 11–27.

23 Memo of 'Société Commerciale Belgo Allemande du Congo SA, Brüssel,' 5 January 1912, BArch, R 8119 F, 7455; 'Sekretariat – Katanga-Konzession,' BArch, R 8119 F, 8632. Cf. the list of syndicate business transactions in Brussels before 1914 in HADB, S3920. The German press expressly welcomed these kinds of engagements; see 'Deutsches Kapital am belgischen Kongo,' *Berliner Tageblatt* (Morgenausgabe, 3. Beiblatt), 6 January 1912.

24 Bitsch, *La Belgique*, p. 143.

25 Berlin office to Brussels branch, 13 February 1911, HADB, S3919.

26 Deutsche Bank (Foreign Department) to Brussels branch regarding Banque Centrale de Liège, 20 July 1912, GSA 2 – Depot Joseph Cuvelier, Deutsche Bank, 1726. Cf. the list of syndicate business transactions in Brussels before 1914 in HADB, S3920.

27 'Interessen in Belgien vor 1914', July 1940, p. 8, HADB, B271.

28 Dr O. Sarrazin (chairman of Allgemeiner Deutscher Sprachverein) to Gwinner, 17 February 1912, HADB, S3919.

29 Brussels branch to Berlin office, 15 April 1911, HADB, S3919.

30 Cf. correspondence in GSA 2 – Depot Joseph Cuvelier, Deutsche Bank, 3863, 3866 and 3884.

31 'Interessen in Belgien vor 1914', July 1940, p. 9, HADB, B271.

32 Max Schinckel to the management of Disconto-Gesellschaft, 29 October 1913, HADB, K1/783, Bl. 223–227.

33 Carrein/Mestdagh, *Inventaris*, pp. 26f. The London branch, for instance, attached a great deal of importance to maintaining relations with the important Swiss trading company of Gebrüder Volkart; London branch to Brussels branch, 10 February 1910, GSA 2 – Depot Joseph Cuvelier, Deutsche Bank, 10.

34 Deutsche Bank Berlin to Brussels branch, 17 March 1911, HADB, S3919.

35 Kautz to Gwinner, 13 December 1911, HADB, S3919.

36 Deutsche Bank, Annual Report 1911, p. 6.

37 Heinemann to Richarz, 16 July 1913, HADB, S3773.

38 Pohl, *Deutsche Bank Buenos Aires*, pp. 58f. For details on DUEG, see Hertner, *Globale Elektrifizierung*. On the capital investments, see Jacob-Wendler, *Elektroindustrie*, p. 72.

39 Loscertales, *Investitionen*, chs V and VI.

40 The following is according to Kobrak, *Banking on Global Markets*.

41 Pak, *Gentlemen Bankers*, p. 18. Within Morgan's syndicate, Deutsche Bank was ranked ninth before 1914, with $51 million in volume.

42 For details on this, see Kobrak, *Banking on Global Markets*, pp. 126–43.

43 File on the Guatemala Railway Company, HADB, A35–A40.
44 Gwinner's correspondence with James Speyer, New York, and with Edgar Speyer, London, HADB, A1353.
45 Gwinner to James Speyer, 29 May 1904, HADB, A1323.
46 Pak, *Gentlemen Bankers*, ch. 1.
47 Obituary of 1 April 1934, *New York Herald*, HADB, A465.
48 Jacob Schiff to Gwinner, 26 September 1904, HADB, A465.
49 Jacob Schiff to Gwinner, 9 January 1905, HADB, A465.
50 Gwinner to Edgar Speyer, 14 January 1905, HADB, A1323.
51 Edgar Speyer to Gwinner, 22 January 1905, HADB, A1323.
52 Memo by Mankiewitz, 30 November 1909, HADB, A465.
53 Memo by Gwinner for Blinzig, 23 December 1909, HADB, A465.
54 Memo by Gwinner for Mankiewitz, 29 January 1906, HADB, S4487.
55 Memo by Mankiewitz for Gwinner, 31 January 1906, HADB, S4487.
56 McNeese, *Robber Barons*.
57 Barth, *Hochfinanz*, pp. 120ff.
58 See on this Mejcher, *Die Bagdadbahn*.
59 Pohl, *Stambul*, pp. 51–5.
60 Ibid., pp. 56ff.; Barth, *Hochfinanz*, pp. 202ff.
61 These rights had already been conceded earlier on. Cf. Baumgart/Benneckenstein, *Interessen. Zur britischen Haltung*. For more details, see Mejcher, *Britische Erdölpolitik*. Lastly, see Earle, *Turkish Petroleum Company*.
62 Pohl, *Stambul*, p. 66.
63 Barth, *Hochfinanz*, pp. 204–8.
64 See on this Williamson, *Karl Helfferich*, pp. 76–80.
65 Pohl, *Stambul*, p. 77.
66 See on this Canis, *Weg*, pp. 283ff.
67 See the 21-page report of Helfferich to Gwinner, 13 May 1909, in which he developed a precise analysis of the domestic political situation in the Ottoman Empire, HADB, OR1742. Cf. also Gutsche, *Monopole*, pp. 160–64.
68 Gwinner to Adams, 8 December 1902, HADB, A45.
69 Deutsche Bank to the editors of *Osmanischer Lloyd*, 21 December 1908, HADB, S3910. Cf. also Historische Gesellschaft der Deutschen Bank, *100 Jahre Deutsche Bank in Istanbul*, pp. 12–31.
70 On this, see the manuscript, Aufzeichnungen des Geheimrat Dr Helfferich, Geschichte der Bagdadbahn bis zum Ausgleich mit Großbritannien 1912 (10 pages). In particular, however, see: Tätigkeit des Herrn Geheimrat Karl Helfferich in türkischen Sachen nach Rückkehr aus der Türkei (60 pages), especially p. 33: 'We are shaking our heads and wondering what happened with our good sense and understanding. Considering that our policy for years has been to simply accept all the unpleasant and dubious effects of the Moroccan question, as a primary way to maintain our position among the Islamite peoples whom we need as a counterweight to England, it's just incredible that our position is being abandoned in the blink of an eye without any reflection, merely to oblige the wishes and personal vanity of our Austrian ally', HADB, OR1741.
71 Deutsche Bank participated in the launching of Turkish Petroleum Company, yet it did not develop any large activity prior to the war. After the war, access to the (now Iraqi) oil sources was divided up by the victorious powers among themselves; Karlsch/Stokes, *Faktor Öl*, p. 74.
72 Pohl, *Stambul*, p. 80.
73 Hertner, *Balkan Railways*, pp. 148f.
74 Deutsche Bank, Annual Report 1913, p. 10.
75 Earle, *Turkish Petroleum Company*. See also Baumgart/Benneckenstein, *Interessen*.
76 Helfferich to Anatolian Railway Company, 4 August 1913, HADB, OR1599, with the request to find out whether the Ottoman government was prepared to sign a contract acceptable to the bank.
77 Helfferich to Hugo Stinnes, 3 October 1913, HADB, OR1599.
78 Anatolian Railway to Supervisory Board in Berlin, 28 February 1914, HADB, OR1599; communication that the Stinnes deal was known. In the enclosure was a confidential report of the Commercial Intelligence Branch of the Board of Trade, of 13 February 1914, with details of the business deal.
79 Helfferich, *Staatsschuld*.
80 Details can be found in: Europäische Kapitalinteressen in den Friedensverträgen, HADB, OR1273
81 Williamson, *Karl Helfferich*, pp. 111–21. See also the letter of Deutsche Bank to Foreign Office of 28 November 1912 with the plan that derived from Helfferich for splitting up Turkish claims again the Balkan states; HADB, OR1273.
82 Deutsche Bank, Annual Report 1913, p. 11.
83 Cf., for instance, Baumgart/Benneckenstein, *Mineralölwirtschaft*. See also Gutsche, *Monopole*.
84 Karlsch/Stokes, *Faktor Öl*, pp. 49–52. Moreover, see Förster, *Geschichte*, pp. 75ff.
85 Karlsch/Stokes, *Faktor Öl*, p. 69.
86 Ibid., p. 75.
87 Competition with Disconto-Gesellschaft was already depicted quite early on in Haase, *Erdöl-Interessen*.
88 On Georg Spies, cf. the introduction by Wolfgang Sartor in: Spies, *Erinnerungen*.
89 Spies to Gwinner, 1 July 1904, HADB, S1633.
90 Spies to Zeller, 24 July 1904, HADB, S1633.
91 Spies to Gwinner, 20 August 1904, HADB, S1633.
92 Gwinner's annotation on letter of Spies to Gwinner, 7 May 1905, HADB, S1633.
93 Spies to Heinemann, 28 April 1905, HADB, S1633.
94 Karlsch/Stokes, *Faktor Öl*, p. 74.
95 Owing to drastically reduced production volumes in Galicia, oil production in Romania became increasingly important for the group around Disconto-Gesellschaft, cf. Karlsch/Stokes, *Faktor Öl*, p. 75.
96 Cf. confidential correspondence with Georg Spies, vols I–III, HADB, S1633–S1636.
97 Spies to Gwinner, 28 July 1905, HADB, S1633.
98 Heinemann to Gwinner, 8 August 1905, HADB, S1633.
99 Gwinner (from St Blasien) to Heinemann, 11 August 1905, HADB, S1633.
100 Heinemann to Gwinner, 2 September 1905, HADB, S1633.
101 Karlsch/Stokes, *Faktor Öl*, pp. 76–8.
102 This was by no means in the interest of German policy, which favoured a stronger confrontation with Standard Oil. However, Deutsche Bank did not have a choice, as Gwinner explained in 'strict confidence' to Georg Spies

on 3 July 1909; HADB, S1677; report on conversation with Reichskanzler, Legationsrat Goebel, Referenten im AA. Here Gwinner reported that the bank was compelled to reach an agreement with the Americans, 'and that in the future, although we were able to save the distinctiveness of our Deutsche Verkaufs-Gesellschaft, we will only be entitled to provide 20% of German petroleum consumption, and the Americans will dictate the prices'. That was the case because '1) our Russian allies did everything possible to come to an understanding with the Americans and have not felt the slightest desire, especially in Germany, to lose out on money in deference to German-national or sentimental considerations; 2) we have actually recorded losses of 2–3 million marks annually in German sales alone'; 3) on account of riots in Russia, production and exports had fallen sharply there; 4) there was a lack of government support, for not even the state was buying the petroleum it needed from Steaua. Gwinner had pointed out 'that if the empire could decide to make petroleum imports a state privilege, let's say, create a petroleum monopoly, even in its most modest form, then we would again have some freedom to operate along with the Russians. If it came up, you could say something like this to the king as well as to Mr Sturdza.'

103 On the EPU, see Karlsch/Stokes, *Faktor Öl*, pp. 75–8.
104 Gwinner to Spies, 28 September 1906, HADB, S1634.
105 Ibid.
106 Spies to Gwinner, 3 October 1906, HADB, S1634: 'If I have been raising a hue and cry for years now, I have not done so because I enjoy nagging – which, if I judge correctly, is alien to my character – but rather did so out of duty. What happened to me in Berlin was similar to Anderson's [sic!] fairy tale, where a king in underpants believes he's dressed in velvet and gold – and it became my duty to provide a place to change clothes in our Berlin office. […] Far be it for me to be hostile or ambitious, elbowing my way to becoming a sort of petroleum general, as Dr Herz assumes that I am doing and which actually makes his whole attitude towards me clear. Yet I know well from our business that, when it comes to *his* essential interests, there is no consideration shown for others, including myself. […] EPU is his, the Steaua is mine – or vice versa if he would like. Since I was 21 years old, meaning now for 24 years, I have headed businesses on my own and am too independent of a character to ever subordinate myself to a younger gentleman. As soon as Dr Herz finds contentment in his own sphere of activity and stops dominating mine, he will find in me once more the good comrade I was.'
107 Gwinner to Spies, 28 September 1906, HADB, S1634.
108 Gwinner, who had hired Herz, ultimately distanced himself from him due to the latter's 'high-handedness'; Herz was dismissed by the bank in 1908, HADB, S1622.
109 Gwinner (from Frankfurt) to Spies, 12 April 1907, HADB, S1634.
110 Spies to Gwinner, 16 April 1907, HADB, S1634.
111 Gwinner to Spies, 6 February 1908, HADB, S1634.
112 Gwinner to Herz, 18 November 1907, HADB, S1677.
113 Gwinner to Herz, 10 March 1908, HADB, S1634.
114 Gwinner to Spies, 9 March 1908, HADB, S1634.
115 Heinemann's annotation to a newspaper article in 'Burza' of 13 September 1908, HADB, S1634.
116 Gwinner to Heinemann, 16 October 1908, HADB, S1634.

117 HADB, S1654.
118 Gwinner to Spies, 28 January 1909, HADB, S1635.
119 Deutsche Bank to Spies, 28 March 1909, HADB, S1654. Spies was guaranteed a bonus of £300 per month as a delegate of Deutsche Bank Group in EPU for the period from 1 March 1909 to 14 May 1910.
120 Spies to Gwinner, 4 February 1909, HADB, S1635.
121 Ibid.
122 Spies to Gwinner, 12 February 1909, HADB, S1635.
123 Spies to Gwinner, 7 May 1910, HADB, S1654. For Spies, additional collaboration with EPU would depend on changes within the organisation.
124 Heinemann and Gwinner to Spies, 10 August 1911, HADB, S1636.
125 Heinemann to Steinthal, 12 August 1911, HADB, S1636.
126 On the pros and cons, see Heinemann to Steinthal, 12 August 1911, HADB, S1636.
127 Steinthal to Spies, 29 July 1911, HADB, S1636.
128 Karlsch/Stokes, *Faktor Öl*, pp. 79–84.
129 A. E. Wassermann to Credit Suisse, 11 April 1912, HADB, S1677.
130 Gwinner, *Lebenserinnerungen*, p. 99.
131 Canis, *Weg*, pp. 117ff., 403ff.
132 Special issue of the journal *Export*, 25 August 1892: Über den Nutzen der Errichtung einer deutschen Bank im Sultanat Marokko, HADB, S814.
133 Gutsche, *Imperialismus*, pp. 125f.
134 See newspaper clipping collection on: Marokko 1902–1942, BArch, R 8119 F, 8633. See also files: Marokkanische Staatsbank 1907–1914, newspaper clippings, HADB, S2857.
135 Gwinner to Regierungsrat von Hake, 17 June 1902, BArch, R 8119 F, 8633.
136 Roland-Lücke to Deutsche Bank London Agency, 13 May 1903, HADB, S2857.
137 Ibid.
138 Deutsche Bank to Marokkanische Gesellschaft, 12 November 1903, HADB, S2857.
139 Roland-Lücke to Leipzig branch, 25 March 1905, BArch, R 8119 F, 8633.
140 Memo by Roland-Lücke, 12 May 1905, BArch, R 8119 F, 8633, Bl. 72–75. Roland-Lücke also described his impressions in a detailed letter to Arthur Gwinner, in particular explaining the presumed role of Disconto-Gesellschaft and the dubious nature of most of the project proposals, 3 August 1905, BArch, R 8119 F, 8633, Bl. 121–130.
141 Deutsche Bank Berlin to Hamburg branch, 27 April 1905, HADB, S670.
142 Riese to Deutsche Bank, 25 April 1905, HADB, S670.
143 Gwinner to Riese, 12 May 1905, HADB, S670.
144 Deutsche Bank to Hässner, 21 August 1905, HADB, S2857.
145 Warburg to Mankiewitz, 31 May 1905, BArch, R 8119 F, 8633.
146 Mankiewitz to Warburg, 6 June 1905, BArch, R 8119 F, 8633.
147 Beit to Roland-Lücke, 7 July 1905, BArch, R 8119 F, 8633
148 Roland-Lücke to Beit, 8 July 1905, BArch, R 8119 F, 8633.
149 Gwinner to Klönne, 30 July 1905, BArch, R 8119 F, 8633.
150 Heinemann to Riese, 9 August 1905, HADB, S670.
151 Gwinner to Riese, 24 February 1906, BArch, R 8119 F, 8633, Bl. 201–203.

152 Roland-Lücke to Berthold Jahn, Tangier, 7 September 1906, HADB, S2857; Roland-Lücke to Ph. Holzmann, 6 September 1906, HADB, S670.

153 Correspondence of Roland-Lücke with Berthold Jahn, Tangier, 6–7 September 1906, HADB, S670, S2857. On the government bond of Deutsche Bank to Hässner, 17 April 1907, HADB, S2857.

154 Memo on Morocco by Roland-Lücke, 12 May 1906, BArch, R 8119 F, 8633, Bl. 204f.

155 Ibid.

156 Memo by Roland-Lücke, 10 July 1906; conference minutes 11 July 1906; the syndicate's charter, 30 July 1906, in: HADB, S813.

157 On this, see the description in an open letter from Casablanca of August 1907. The author was a German businessman based there; Carl Ficke, BArch, R 8119 F, 8633, Bl. 272f.

158 Entry of 2 September 1911, BArch, R 8119 F, 8633, Bl. 307.

159 Hamburg branch to Deutsche Bank, 20 September 1911, reply of 7 October 1911, BArch, R 8119 F, 8633, Bl. 308-312.

160 Memo by Gwinner, 13 February 1913, BArch, R 8119 F, 8633, Bl. 333.

161 Gwinner, *Lebenserinnerungen*, pp. 90–96.

162 Helfferich, *Siemens*, vol. 2, pp. 133ff.

163 Münch, *Adolph von Hansemann*, pp. 372f. Siemens had always understood the bank's transactions in Austria as a personal matter but had at times behaved ineptly; cf. also Helfferich, *Siemens*, vol. 2, p. 178.

164 Gwinner, *Lebenserinnerungen*, p. 95.

165 Ibid.

166 Mankiewitz to Popper, 19 September 1908, HADB, S4162.

167 Memo for Kraetzig, 12 February 1909, HADB, S4162.

168 Gwinner to Mankiewitz, 19 December 1908, HADB, S2938.

169 Gwinner to Board, 10 December 1909, HADB, S2938.

170 Heinemann to Leth, Postsparkassenamt, 27 July 1914, HADB, S2938.

171 Memo by Mankiewitz, 8 August 1903, BArch, R 8119 F, 7530.

172 Frey to Gwinner, 30 November 1904, BArch, R 8119 F, 7530.

173 Frey to Gwinner, 18 March 1904, BArch, R 8119 F, 7530.

174 Gwinner to Frey, 22 April 1904, BArch, R 8119 F, 7530.

175 For instance, Frey to Gwinner, 28 December 1907, BArch, R 8119 F, 7530.

176 Thielemann to Deutsche Bank, 17 June 1903, BArch, R 8119 F, 7533.

177 Roland-Lücke to Thielemann, 23 June 1903, BArch, R 8119 F, 7533.

178 Details can be found in Bommarius, *Fürstentrust*. See also Rasch, *Unternehmer*, pp. 445ff.

179 Historische Skizze, in: *Berliner Börsen-Courier*, 16 April 1910, HADB, S217.

180 *Berliner Börsen-Courier* of 27 March 1909, HADB, S217.

181 *Frankfurter Zeitung*, 11 October 1910, HADB, S217.

182 Memo by Klönne on a conversation with Prince Hohenlohe, 17 September 1910, HADB, S217.

183 Ibid.

184 Constantinople branch to Klönne, 7 October 1910, HADB, S217.

185 Klönne to Constantinople branch, 11 October 1910, HADB, S217.

186 Deutsche Bank made efforts to hold on to Witscher following the collapse of Handelsvereinigung and the takeover of the branches of Palästina-Bank by Deutsche Orientbank in 1914: 'We cannot let him go to Diskonto-Gesellschaft [sic!]. I am always thinking that he could stay as correspondence head in Berlin, learning the ropes there and working part-time on the liquidation of Palästina-Bank. We could then see later on where we could send him'; Mankiewitz to Kiehl, Frankfurt am Main branch, 15 June 1916, HADB, S217.

187 Constantinople branch to Deutsche Bank, 28 January 1911, HADB, S217.

188 Bommarius, *Fürstentrust*, shows that the Passage store was a big flop. To generate 'artificial' sales, products were sold at their cost price, a circumstance that could not be maintained long-term.

189 Gwinner to James Speyer, 26 March 1913, HADB, A1353.

190 Gwinner to Mankiewitz, 19 December 1908, HADB, S2938.

191 Reulecke, *Geschichte*, pp. 203f.

192 Deutsche Bank, Annual Report 1913, p. 11.

193 Deutsche Bank, Annual Reports 1900 and 1913.

194 Seidenzahl, *100 Jahre*, pp. 194–200.

195 Ibid., p. 203. Cf. also HADB, SG1/47.

196 Compilation in: HADB, SG 1/36.

197 Ibid.

198 Hilferding, *Finance Capital*, section III.

199 Seidenzahl, *100 Jahre*, p. 201.

200 Wellhöner, *Großbanken*.

201 Quoted in Krenn, *Macht*, p. 20.

202 Seidenzahl, *100 Jahre*, pp. 202f.

203 Zilch, *Plan*.

204 Münch, *Adolph von Hansemann*, pp. 259f.

205 Weber, *Bankplatz*, p. 68.

206 Model, *Effektenbanken*, p. 128.

V. The Group: Organisational Structures, Personnel Development and Regional Form, 1870–1914

1 The most comprehensive study thus far of Deutsche Bank's organisational development is Dahlem, *Professionalisierung*, who has designed several 'virtual' organisational plans of the bank; these will be referred to separately.

2 On this, Helfferich, *Siemens*, vol. 1, pp. 319f.

3 Burhop, *Banken*.

4 Quoted in Helfferich, *Siemens*, vol. 1, p. 321.

5 Wehler (ed.), *Friedrich Kapp*.

6 Deutsche Bank, Annual Reports 1876–1913.

7 On the organisational structure of banking operations, cf. Buchwald, *Technik*, pp. 32f. An essential account is: Krause, *Archivalische Quellen*, esp. chart, p. 10.

8 Wichmann, *Lehrling*.

9 Diedrichs, *Verwendung*.

10 Fuchs, *Die Deutsche Bank in Berlin*, p. 6.

11 Deutsche Bank, Annual Reports 1877, 1892, 1900, 1903, 1913.

12 Fuchs, *Die Deutsche Bank in Berlin*, p. 2.

13 Deutsche Bank, Annual Report 1913, p. 9.

14 Deutsche Bank, Annual Reports 1894–1914.

15 Carl Michalowsky to Georg von Simson (Bank für Handel und Industrie), 10 August 1911, HADB, S4414.

16 Fuchs, *Die Deutsche Bank in Berlin*, p. 7.

17 Ibid., p. 10.
18 Fuchs, *Arthur von Gwinner*, pp. 6f.
19 Fuchs, *Die Deutsche Bank in Berlin*, p. 7.
20 Münch, *Adolph von Hansemann*, p. 77. It is indisputable that there was a certain similarity between the two banks. The only question is whether it is a matter of intentional imitation or whether the similarity developed on its own, from the way the business was run; cf. Disconto-Gesellschaft, *Die Disconto-Gesellschaft 1851–1901*, ch. VIII.
21 On this, see Pohl, *Gebäude*.
22 Weber, *Bankplatz*, p. 73.
23 Fuchs, *Die Deutsche Bank in Berlin*, p. 4.
24 Ibid., p. 5.
25 On the architectural form of the Berlin banking quarter in Friedrichstadt, cf. Gall, *Deutsche Bank*, pp. 125f.
26 Steckner, *Bildhauer*.
27 Gwinner and Michalowsky to *Berliner Tageblatt*, 1 February 1912, HADB, S4487.
28 Henning, *Innovationen*.
29 Gall, *Deutsche Bank*, pp. 114f.
30 Michalowsky to Georg Manasse, Stettin, 26 March 1909, HADB, S4414.
31 Michalowsky to Hofprediger D. Rogge, 17 December 1906, HADB, S4487.
32 Wallich, *Lehr- und Wanderjahre*, pp. 239–57.
33 Michalowsky to Kurt Ulfert, Grottkau in Schlesien, 7 July 1910, HADB, S4414.
34 See also Michalowsky to the Directorate of Rheinische Creditbank, 12 January 1909, HADB S4188: 'The fact that our agency has not been able to take all the recommendations into account that you make for young people interested in employment here can be explained: it accumulates these applications to such an extraordinary extent that it is by no means able, in light of such circumstances, to meet everyone's wishes.'
35 Otto Roese to Gwinner, 21 June 1910, HADB, S4188.
36 Michalowsky to Court Chaplain D. Rogge, 17 December 1906, HADB, S4487.
37 Ibid.
38 Stillich, *Schulbildung*.
39 Gall, *Deutsche Bank*, p. 114.
40 Henning, *Innovationen*, pp. 60f.
41 Roese to Deutscher Bankbeamten-Verein, 23 February 1911, HADB, S4414.
42 Personnel file of Paul Vernickel, HADB, P1/25.
43 Gwinner, *Lehrlingszeit*, p. 49.
44 Bremen branch to Deutsche Bank Berlin, 7 September 1876, HADB, F1/166.
45 Burhop, *Banken*, p. 8.
46 Michalowsky to Heinrich Ref, 4 January 1909, HADB, S4414.
47 Michalowsky to Court Chaplain D. Rogge, 17 December 1906, HADB, S4487.
48 Hohorst/Kocka/Ritter, *Sozialgeschichtliches Arbeitsbuch*, p. 107. On average, an industrial worker in 1913 earned 1,083 marks annually; skilled workers in large cities were paid much more.
49 The data are from the annual reports of Deutsche Bank for 1876, 1896, and 1913. See there also precise details on the bank's social benefits.
50 In general, research today emphasises that 'bank officials' were at the top of the income hierarchy among employees; however, there were significant differences within that group itself; on this, refer to Schulz, *Die Angestellten*, p. 22.

51 In 1891, under the name of Klub der Beamten der Deutschen Bank (Deutsche Bank Staff Club), a meeting place was created, at the suggestion and with the support of the bank, which offered employees – especially unmarried ones – an opportunity to have good, reasonably priced meals while at the same time reinforcing their sense of community and esprit de corps; see N. N., Deutsche Bank, in: *Unser Kaiserpaar*, p. 285.
52 Carl Michalowsky to Ernst Michalowsky, 5 August 1911, HADB, S4414.
53 Michalowsky to Weber, 8 October 1910, HADB, S4414.
54 Henning, *Innovationen*, p. 55.
55 Ibid., p. 62.
56 Deutsche Bank, Annual Report 1913, Gewinn- und Verlustkonto.
57 Fuchs, *Max Steinthal*, p. 9.
58 Steinthal retired from the Management Board in 1905, but that did little to change his work behaviour: 'Since his departure from the Management Board, Steinthal has shown up at Deutsche Bank with the same regularity he always had; as far as I know, he has hardly been able to reduce his working hours'; Fürstenberg, *Lebensgeschichte*, p. 211.
59 Gwinner to *Berliner Tageblatt*, 13 May 1912, HADB, S4487. This information was expressly 'confidential and not intended for publication'.
60 'I believe,' noted Carl Fürstenberg, 'that Wallich's importance for developing Deutsche Bank's international relations cannot be overestimated'; Fürstenberg, *Lebensgeschichte*, p. 210.
61 Georg Siemens to Elise Görz, 8 March 1872, quoted in Helfferich, *Siemens*, vol. 3, pp. 268f.
62 Williamson, *Karl Helfferich*, pp. 111ff. At least Carl Michalowsky did not like to see him leave: 'I view Helfferich's departure with great regret and will miss him not only as a capable and efficient colleague without equal, but also as a dear, close friend'; Michalowsky to Klönne, 26 January 1915, HADB, S4414.
63 Cf. the documentation in: HADB, SG1/64.
64 Memo on a conversation with Dr Weigelt, 30 July 1968, HADB, SG1/61.
65 Weitenweber [= Müller-Jabusch], Carl Klönne, p. 180. For a similar account: Fürstenberg, *Lebensgeschichte*, pp. 194f.
66 Weitenweber [= Müller-Jabusch], Carl Klönne, p. 180.
67 'Rauhe Sitten in alter Zeit', *Deutsche Sparkassenzeitung*, 16 June 1966, no. 46, p. 2.
68 On the backgrounds of banking elites in the Wilhelmine Empire, see Reitmayer, *Bankiers*, pp. 120–46.
69 *Neue Freie Presse*, no. 2006, 30 March 1870, p. 9.
70 Georg Siemens to Elise Görz, 8 March 1872, quoted in Helfferich, *Siemens*, vol. 3, pp. 268f.
71 Georg Siemens to Elise Görz, 9 March 1872, quoted in Helfferich, *Siemens*, vol. 3, p. 271.
72 Georg Siemens to Elise Görz, 12 March 1872, quoted in Helfferich, *Siemens*, vol. 3, p. 272.
73 Theodor Barth, Georg von Siemens, in: *Biographisches Jahrbuch und Deutscher Nekrolog*, vol. VI, from 1.1. to 31 December 1901, Berlin 1904, pp. 63–5, in: HADB, SG1/96/3.
74 Fuchs, *Max Steinthal*, p. 194.
75 See 'Neue Bankdirektoren', *Plutus*, 13 January 1912, p. 33: Steinthal had moved to the Supervisory Board

'in order to – as bank officials told it – be able to have dinner at home at least once a week'.

76 Pohl, *Koch*.

77 As a former employee in the secretariat recollected: 'Koch was more an organiser than a businessman and was not highly regarded by his colleagues'; communication of Schulze to Fitger, 8 March 1965, HADB, SG1/48. The judgement of Peter Brunswig, who had worked with Koch during his early years at the bank, was even more negative, although Brunswig very much appreciated his way of conducting himself later on: 'We young employees did not think very much of him; in contrast to the tireless and rather exaggerated hustle and bustle, he liked to take things more easily, living as a grand seigneur and hardly impressing us'; Peter Brunswig, Lebenserinnerungen: Die Deutsche Bank, typescript, p. 4, HADB, SG1/18.

78 Wallich, *Aus meinem Leben*, p. 136.

79 Arthur Gwinner thought that Siemens's lifestyle had destroyed him; otherwise, Siemens 'would have had the strength to be fit until the age of 80'; Gwinner, *Lebenserinnerungen*, p. 61.

80 Gwinner to James Speyer, 20 May 1905, HADB, A1353, with a detailed description of his state of health.

81 Helfferich, *Siemens*, vol. 3, p. 384.

82 Note by Schulze, formerly of the secretariat at Deutsche Bank Berlin, 4 June 1968, HADB, SG1/33/2.

83 Max Steinthal, *Arthur von Gwinner*, p. 3. Here Steinthal is referring to Elkan Heinemann, Emil Georg (von) Stauß and Alfred Blinzig.

84 Dr Kurt Weigelt, interview on 30 July 1968, HADB, SG1/33/2.

85 On Gwinner, see Wixforth, Arthur (von) Gwinner. On the 'treadmill': Pinner, *Wirtschaftsführer*, p. 222.

86 Max Steinthal to Elise Siemens, 11 August 1899, quoted in Helfferich, *Siemens*, vol. 3, p. 370.

87 Cf. the documentation in: HADB, SG1/69.

88 Note by Schulz, formerly of the secretariat at Deutsche Bank Berlin, 4 June 1968, HADB, SG1/69.

89 His brother Emil had refused to write a biography of Karl, as he would then also have had to describe his weaknesses. Karl was, according to the memory of his brother (interview of 27 February 1962) 'a purely rational man, who hardly had a sense of humour, although he was significant not only as a banker but also as a scientist'; interview in: HADB, SG1/37.

90 Heinemann owed his career to the retirement and/or death of Siemens. One employee from the old Berlin secretariat believed he could remember Siemens saying that Heinemann was not fit for the top management since he wasn't fit for the lowest level, either; cf. file memo by Fitger, 5 March 1965, HADB, SG1/36.

91 On Elkan Heinemann, cf. Seidenzahl, *Elkan Heinemann*.

92 Fuchs, *Gustav Schröter*.

93 'Preussische Peers', *Plutus*, 5 February 1910, pp. 104f., here p. 104.

94 Deutsche Bank Secretariat in Berlin to Hamburg branch, 14 May 1913, HADB, S4246.

95 Members of the Management Board and proprietors of Disconto-Gesellschaft, compilation in: HADB, SG18/8.

96 Memorial service on Friday, 11 May 1928, in Deutscher Saal of Deutsche Bank for the deceased Consul Hermann Wallich, p. 7, HADB, SG1/83.

97 *Verhandlungen des Reichstags*, vol. 169, Berlin 1900, 148. Sitzung, 14 February 1900, p. 4128.

98 Reitmayer, *Bankiers*, p. 207.

99 Ibid., p. 65.

100 Pinner, *Wirtschaftsführer*, p. 187.

101 An essential account on this is Urbig, *Vorkriegsgründungen*.

102 Helfferich, *Siemens*, vol. 1, pp. 252–61.

103 Hertner, *German Banks*.

104 Hertner, *Die Deutsche Bank in Italien*.

105 On Speyer, cf. the draft by Ludwig Roland-Lücke of 8 May 1905: Verhältnis zu den Firmen Speyer's, HADB, A1323.

106 Cf. the chart 'Der Konzern der Deutschen Bank' of 1908/09, reproduced in Lansburgh, *Beteiligungssystem*.

107 On this, see Scholtyseck/Bormann, *Bank- und Börsenplatz*, pp. 70–102.

108 For details, see Frost, *Macher*.

109 According to Peter Brunswig, who starting working in the secretariat of the Management Board in 1904, it was the bank's luck 'and gave it a big head start over the other big banks that it was able to implement its later expansion to a large extent not by establishing branches from Berlin, but by taking over locally established banks. In so doing, they gained these old businessmen as people of the new office, to which they could then – if need be – add a young bank official who had proven himself in Berlin'; Brunswig, Lebenserinnerungen: Die Deutsche Bank, typescript, p. 2, HADB, SG1/18.

110 Cf. for example, the draft by Ludwig Roland-Lücke of 8 May 1905: Verhältnis zu den Firmen Speyer's, HADB, A1323.

111 Koch to Gwinner, 14 April 1909, HADB, S4453.

112 Cf. correspondence of Deutsche Bank Headquarters in Berlin with the Bremen branch, 1871–1888, HADB, F1/166 and F1/167.

113 'Shortly before the outbreak of the First World War, the bank's branch in Frankfurt was prepared to grant the Kalle company an unsecured loan, which the headquarters prevented, to the annoyance of Frankfurt', cf. letter of the Frankfurt branch to secretariat, 30 June 1914, as well as the reply of 2 July 1914, HADB, S4253.

114 Siemens and Steinthal to Bremen branch, 5 October 1876, HADB, F1/167.

115 On this, see also Spalding, *Überseegeschäft*, p. 564.

116 Wallich, *Aus meinem Leben*, pp. 141–54.

117 Urbig, *Vorkriegsgründungen*, p. 26.

118 Fuchs, *Die Deutsche Bank in Berlin*, p. 7.

119 Max Steinthal, *Paul Mankiewitz*.

VI. From Troublemaker to Top Dog: Deutsche Bank in Politics and Society before the First World War

1 For a detailed account of this, see Münch, *Adolph von Hansemann*.

2 E.g. Stern, *Gold and Iron*. In general, see the sketch with anecdotes by Achterberg, *Berliner Hochfinanz*.

3 For the fundamentals, see Damm, *Selbstpräsentation*, pp. 82–104.

4 Helfferich, *Germany's Economic Progress and National Wealth*.

5 Gall, *Deutsche Bank*, pp. 89f.

6 Reitmayer, *Bankiers*, pp. 152f.

7 Jörg Lesczenski, 'Im Reich der Industrie', p. 189.

8 Hutten-Czapski, *Sechzig Jahre*, p. 385.

9 Speier, *Die Angestellten*, pp. 124–32.

10 Fuchsbauer, *Angestelltenversicherung*.

11 Mielke, *Hansa-Bund*, here p. 189. The constitutive executive committee under the leadership of Jakob Riesser comprised numerous important names of Berlin's high finance world.

12 Winkler (ed.), *Organisierter Kapitalismus*.

13 Riesser, *German Great Banks*.

14 Hentschel, *Wirtschaft*. See also Wellhöner, *Großbanken*.

15 Doerry, *Übergangsmenschen*, for example, obviously characterises this type too strongly.

16 Gwinner, *Lebenserinnerungen*, p. 107f.

17 For the fundamentals on this, see Plumpe, *Boden*.

18 Barth, *Hochfinanz*.

19 Kirshner, *Appeasing Bankers*.

20 A typical example of this is Hauser, *Les méthodes*.

21 On this, see Canis, *Weg*, pp. 403–56.

22 Dresdner Bank was the only major German bank that succeeded in establishing a sort of indirect agency in Paris prior to 1914 by acquiring a majority share of J. Allard & Co.; Strasser, *Die deutschen Banken im Ausland*, p. 65.

23 Hertner, *Die Deutsche Bank in Italien*, pp. 35–78. On the Triple Alliance, see Afflerbach, *Der Dreibund*.

24 Cf., e.g., already Strasser, *Die deutschen Banken im Ausland*, pp. 67–71; Toniolo, *One Hundred Years*.

25 See the articles by the colonial enthusiast Julius Scharlach, *Unsere Banken*, Teil I and II, who, in light of the banks' lack of interest, finally suggested that a colonial bank be founded, which obviously did not come to pass.

26 Gwinner and Wassermann to Foreign Office re: Bulgarian Financing Transactions, 22 September 1915, HADB, S2473. The management of the bank presented the preceding development of the Bulgarian bond as different from what it actually had been: it claimed that the bank did not invest in the bond in 1913–14 because the Bulgarian government had not been friendly towards Germany. Since that had changed in the meantime, the bank could reconsider its own position. Deutsche Bank certainly would have participated if the Bulgarian bond had come about in a way that would not burden the German market, but the international syndicate that would have been necessary for this had not emerged up to that point; Helfferich to Foreign Office, 23 April 1914; Helfferich to Salomonsohn, 13 May 1914; Helfferich to Foreign Office, 15 May 1914, HADB, S2473.

27 Reitmayer, *Bankiers*, p. 296.

28 Georg Siemens to Elise Siemens, 28 October 1900, quoted in Helfferich, *Siemens*, vol. 3, p. 376; translation quoted in Gall, *Deutsche Bank*, p. 98.

29 There is a somewhat overstated but nevertheless enlightening perspective on German-British relations in Straub, *Kaiser Wilhelm II*, pp. 269ff.

30 Roland-Lücke to all branches, 14 December 1901, HADB, S92.

31 Deutsche Bank to Speyer & Co., 26 January 1903, HADB, S92.

32 Minutes of the constitutive meeting of the representative committee for the preparation of the return visit of the English journalists, 24 April 1903, HADB, S92.

33 E.g. London branch to Deutsche Bank Berlin, 1 July 1908, HADB, S92: the *Morning Post* had allegedly criticised German expansion in Argentina and simultaneously spread anti-English sentiments among the German public.

34 Heinemann to Leth, Postsparkassenamt Wien, 27 July 1914, HADB, S2838.

35 On this, see now Herr, *Centralverband*, pp. 43ff.

36 Mielke, *Hansa-Bund*; Herr, *Centralverband*, pp. 230–34.

37 Dorrmann, *Eduard Arnhold*, p. 57.

38 Apt, *25 Jahre*, p. 7.

39 Baumgart, *Unsere Reichsbank*. On this cf. also Lumm, *Karl Helfferich*, pp. 30–35.

40 On this see Torp, *Weltwirtschaft*.

41 Torp, *Challenges of Globalization*.

42 Cheque transactions were conditionally freed from taxation only in 1908; see Spengler, *Enstehung*.

43 For a thorough account of this, see Offer, *The First World War*.

44 Gwinner, *Lebenserinnerungen*, pp. 101–4.

45 On the banking inquiry and its impacts, see Wandel, *Banken*, p. 83. Müller, *Entstehung*, pp. 82f.

46 Mankiewitz and Michalowsky to Commerzbank in Lübeck, 8 January 1913, HADB, S4400.

47 Zilch, *Plan*.

48 This is presented as early as in Mayer, *Adelsmacht*. See the contributions in: Kocka (ed.), *Bürgertum im 19. Jahrhundert*. On their self-understanding, see the recent work by Groppe, *Im deutschen Kaiserreich*.

49 Achterberg, *Berliner Hochfinanz*, pp. 43–7.

50 Ralf Lindemann, *Das weiße Schloss am Meer. Schloss Dwasieden in Sassnitz auf der Insel Rügen*, Sassnitz, 2003.

51 Heß, *Junker*. Arthur Gwinner complained that the 'cultivation of the agricultural part of Krumke [had] been a constant source of bother and loss'; Gwinner, *Lebenserinnerungen*, p. 109.

52 For average yearly salaries, cf. Hohorst/Kocka/Ritter, *Sozialgeschichtliches Arbeitsbuch*, pp. 107–10.

53 Ullmann, *Steuerstaat*, pp. 45f.

54 On this, see Martin, *Jahrbuch*. On this, see Gajek, *Sichtbarmachung*. See also the study by Augustine, *Patricians*.

55 *Die Nation*, 26 October 1901, HADB, NL 48/1.

56 A very instructive work on this is Oepen-Domschky, *Kölner Wirtschaftsbürger*.

57 Reichert, *Gelehrtes Leben*. See also the comparison of Hampe to the industrialist Carl Duisberg in Plumpe, *Boden*.

58 See the relevant remarks for characterising a major industrialist in Powell, *Dance*, p. 107. Cf. also Zunkel, *Verhältnis*. Bank managers who had the pertinent tendencies thus did not strive to get to the top of their banks at any cost; on this Föhl/Wolff, *Alfred Wolff*, esp. ch. IV.

59 Siemens to his wife, 13 March 1872, quoted in Helfferich, *Siemens*, vol. 3, pp. 272f.

60 Quoted in Wilhelmy-Dollinger, *Salons*, p. 256.

61 Ibid., pp. 290–95.

62 Ibid., p. 295.

63 Fürstenberg, *Lebensgeschichte*, pp. 504f.

64 A sort of 'psychogram' of Emil Rathenau can be found in Pinner, *Emil Rathenau*, pp. 350–408.

65 For example, Plumpe, *Carl Duisberg*.

66 Lesczenski, *August Thyssen*.

67 Auerbach, *Ernst Abbe*, pp. 427ff.

68 Oepen-Domschky, *Kölner Wirtschaftsbürger*.

69 Knoch, *Grandhotels*.

70 Budde, *Weg ins Bürgerleben*.

71 Gwinner, *Lebenserinnerungen*, p. 109.

72 In general on this, see Reitmayer, *Bankiers*.

73 Wallich, *Lehr- und Wanderjahre*.

74 Pak, *Gentlemen Bankers*.
75 Jüngst Volkov, *Walther Rathenau*, ch. 5.
76 Heinemann, who was not uncontroversial at the bank on account of his 'dithering', seems to have been particularly sensitive to anti-Jewish resentments and anti-Semitism; his departure from Deutsche Bank and his move abroad, in any case, took place very abruptly in 1923.
77 Barkai, *Oscar Wassermann*.
78 Ibid., p. 36.
79 In general on this, see Reitmayer, *Bankiers*, pp. 165ff.
80 Ibid., pp. 173–6. Concerning Elkan Heinemann, a former colleague recalled: 'At Deutsche Bank, namely, one paid attention to keeping the Jewish influence from dropping below a certain level.' It is unclear what this

recollection was about; it is difficult to utilise as historical evidence; Fitger, 5 March 1965, HADB, SG1/36.
81 Compilation of biographies by the Institut zur Erforschung historischer Führungsschichten, HADB, ZA17/22.
82 Reitmayer, *Bankiers*, p. 269.
83 Gall, *Deutsche Bank*, p. 124.
84 For a comprehensive account, see Tatzkow/Frost, *Max Steinthal*, pp. 10–41.
85 Dorrmann, *Eduard Arnhold*, pp. 125, 204.

Conclusion: Deutsche Bank, 1870–1914

1   Cf. Hook, *Entwicklung*.

Between State and Market, 1914–1989

Introduction

1   Barth, *Auswirkungen*.
2   *Frankfurter Zeitung*, 5 March 1914.
3   Kobrak/Hansen (eds), *European Business, Dictatorship, and Political Risk, 1920–1945*; Jones/Lubinski, *Managing Political Risk*.
4   Westerhuis/Kipping, *Managerialization*.

I. The End of the World Economy: War, Revolution and Inflation

1   'Der Juli 1914', *Die Bank*, 1914, p. 758.
2   'Krieg', *Plutus*, 1 August 1914, p. 594.
3   Gwinner and Helfferich to the management of the Anatolian Railway Company, 12 August 1914, HADB, OR1029.
4   Max Schinckel, 8 August 1914, HADB, K1/784, Sheet 152.
5   Clark, *Sleepwalkers*.
6   Cf. on this also Barth, *Auswirkungen*.
7   Münkler, *Der Große Krieg*, p. 19.
8   Urbig to Heinemann, 5 September 1914 with Karbe's report on the closure of the German branches in London on 5 August 1914, HADB, S4190.
9   Pohl/Burk, *Deutsche Bank in London*, p. 53.
10 Cf. Roberts, *Saving the City*; also Mendel, *Geldmarkt*.
11 In addition to Deutsche Bank, Dresdner Bank and Disconto-Gesellschaft had branches in London. Commerz- und Disconto-Bank had a share in the London and Hanseatic Bank Ltd.
12 Report by Ernst Morgenstern to the management of Deutsche Bank, 15 August 1914, p. 6, HADB, S4190. Cf. also Rudolf Frensel's position on asset transactions of the London branch after the start of the war, 9 February 1929, HADB, NL6/7.
13 Roberts, *Saving the City*, p. 144.
14 William Plender to FA. Harper, Battock & Goode, 28 September 1914, HADB, S4190.
15 'Enemy Banks', *The Times*, 5 January 1917, HADB, NL6/3; Russell to Norddeutsche Bank, 8 November 1916, HADB, K1/852.
16 Max von Rapp, *The London Branch*, 17 October 1918, pp. 6f., HADB, S4190.
17 Ibid., p. 7.
18 Ibid., p. 11.
19 Pohl/Burk, *Deutsche Bank in London*, pp. 55f.
20 Cf. Cassis, *Capitals of Capital*, pp. 134–67.
21 Kobrak, *Banking on Global Markets*.
22 Ibid., p. 208.
23 Schmidt to Blinzig, 23 December 1914, HADB, A1027.
24 Adams to Gwinner, 22 September 1914, p. 7, HADB, A457.
25 Schmidt to Blinzig, 10 May 1915, HADB, A464; cf. also reports in HADB, S4190.
26 Schmidt to Blinzig, 9 June 1915, HADB, A464.
27 See on this Kobrak, *Banking on Global Markets*, pp. 169–98.
28 Ibid., pp. 177f.
29 Ibid., pp. 180ff.
30 Wilkins, *History*, pp. 63–5.
31 BAT, Annual Report 1913, pp. 12f.
32 See on this: *50 Jahre Deutsche Ueberseeische Bank*; Pohl, *Deutsche Bank Buenos Aires*.
33 BAT, Report of 22 September 1914, HADB, S3773.
34 Schmidt to Heinemann, 6 September 1915, HADB, S3773.
35 King, *Hongkong Bank*, p. 620.
36 Müller-Jabusch, *Fünfzig Jahre*, p. 248.
37 Moazzin, *From Globalization to Liquidation*.
38 Müller-Jabusch, *Fünfzig Jahre*, p. 243.
39 Historical Association of Deutsche Bank (ed.), *A Century of Deutsche Bank in Turkey*.
40 Ibid., pp. 48f.; Feldman, *Deutsche Bank*, pp. 139–41.
41 Historical Association of Deutsche Bank (ed.), *A Century of Deutsche Bank in Turkey*, pp. 34f.
42 Note on the letter from Gwinner/Strauß to Riese, 23 March 1915, HADB, OR461.
43 Feldman, *Deutsche Bank*, pp. 142f.
44 Report by Winkler to the construction management office in Constantinople from 19 June 1916, HADB, OR1704. Cf. Kaiser, Baghdad Railway.
45 Barth, *Trade and Finance*.
46 Authorisation from the Senior President, Potsdam, to Deutsche Bank from 2 August 1914 to send encoded telegrams to neutral countries and various reports from Axhausen to Gwinner, August 1914, HADB, A461; Gross (Credit Suisse) to Heinemann, 29 April 1916, HADB, S3773. For more information on the Swiss banks during the war, see Mazbouri, *Aufstieg*, pp. 454–62.
47 *The Economist*, 18 December 1915, War Supplement, p. 9.
48 Euwe, *Amsterdam*, p. 157.
49 Zeidler, *Die deutsche Kriegsfinanzierung*, p. 423.

50 Frey, *Niederlande*, pp. 164–70.

51 Urbig to Norddeutsche Bank, 12 December 1918, HADB, K1/787; cf. also unpublished typescript from Bernd A. Wilken, H. Albert de Bary & Co. NV, Amsterdam (1919–1993), p. 8, HADB, K20/7.

52 Bleichröder to Deutsche Bank Brussels branch, 28 July 1914, GSA 2 – Joseph Cuvelier repository, Deutsche Bank, 3884.

53 Disconto-Gesellschaft, Annual Report 1914, p. 13.

54 Georg Solmssen to the management of Disconto-Gesellschaft, 2 December 1914, in: James/Müller (eds), *Georg Solmssen*, p. 91.

55 HADB, B271.

56 Deutsche Bank Brussels branch to management of the Reichsbank, 18 June 1915, GSA 2 – Joseph Cuvelier repository, Deutsche Bank, 3891. For more on the monetary importance of Belgium for the German Empire, see Zilch, *Okkupation und Währung*, pp. 97–241.

57 Cf. generally also Meißner, *Bruch oder Kontinuität?*.

58 Keynes, *Consequences*, p. 49. On the DÜEG see Hertner, *Globale Elektrifizierung*.

59 Seidenzahl, *100 Jahre*, p. 257.

60 Benfey, *Entwicklung*, p. 213.

61 Deutsche Bank tried, without success, to secure funds and assets during the war; Allenhoven to Kautz, 17 February 1916; Report from C. Christion, 12 April 1918, HADB, S529.

62 Feldman, *Deutsche Bank*, p. 181.

63 Ibid.

64 Cf. Feldman, *German Business Interests*; Hamlin, *Germany's Empire*, pp. 286–9.

65 On the change in ownership of Steaua Română and its further development, see Marguerat, *La Steava Romana, 1903–1939*.

66 Cf. Deutsche Bank, Annual Report 1914, p. 6.

67 Helfferich, *Entstehung*, p. 9.

68 Quoted in Feldman, *Deutsche Bank*, p. 134.

69 Cf. Deutsche Bank, Annual Report 1916, p. 8.

70 Wixforth, *Karl Helfferich*; Williamson, *Karl Helfferich*.

71 After being appointed state secretary he handed this role to Paul Mankiewitz.

72 Karl Helfferich, 'Deutschlands finanzielle Rüstung', *Norddeutsche Allgemeine Zeitung*, 16 August 1914, printed in: idem., *Reden und Aufsätze aus dem Kriege*, Berlin 1917, pp. 69–74, here p. 74.

73 Cf. Feldman, *Deutsche Bank*, p. 134.

74 Gwinner and Helfferich to the Management of the Anatolian Railway, 12 August 1914, HADB, OR1029.

75 Holtfrerich, *The German Inflation*.

76 Kiehling, *Funktionsverlust*.

77 Kobrak, *Banking on Global Markets*, p. 177.

78 Deutsche Bank, Annual Report 1914, p. 8.

79 Ibid., and Wixforth, *Instrumente*.

80 Roth, *Staat und Wirtschaft*; Rohlack, *Kriegsgesellschaften*; van de Kerkhof, *Von der Friedens-zur Kriegswirtschaft*.

81 Deutsche Bank, Annual Report 1918, p. 23.

82 'Deutsche Bank prospering', *St Louis Republic*, 21 May 1916 (and other newspaper reports in HADB, SG10/47).

83 Lampe, *Bankbetrieb*, p. 107.

84 Deutsche Bank, Annual Report 1917, p. 12.

85 Lampe, *Bankbetrieb*, p. 98.

86 Ritschl, *The Pity of Peace*, p. 63.

87 Feldman, *Deutsche Bank*, p. 135.

88 Hardach, *Mobilmachung*, p. 372

89 Münkler, *Der Große Krieg*, p. 590.

90 This is also the assessment in Feldman, *Deutsche Bank*, p. 135.

91 The bank already had communities of interest since 1898 with Hannoversche Bank and Oberrheinische Bank in Mannheim. To this were added communities of interest with Essener Credit-Anstalt (1903), Essener Bankverein, Siegener Bank für Handel und Gewerbe und Sächsische Bank in Dresden, Oldenburgische Spar- und Leihbank and the Privatbank zu Gotha (all in 1904), Württembergische Vereinsbank in Stuttgart (1906), Süddeutsche Bank and Rheinische Creditbank (1911).

92 Deutsche Bank, Annual Report 1914, p. 17.

93 Dahlem, *Professionalisierung*, p. 56.

94 Cf. Frost, *Macher*, pp. 22–33.

95 Seidenzahl, *100 Jahre*, pp. 114f.

96 Michalowsky to the colleagues of the Management Board, 16 November 1916, HADB, S4091.

97 Report by Michalowsky, 8 December 1916, quoted in Feldman, *Deutsche Bank*, p. 136.

98 Michalowsky to Zilske, 2 February 1917, HADB, S4080.

99 Cf. Feldman, *Deutsche Bank*, pp. 173ff.

100 Bol, *Aktionärsstruktur*, pp. 182-3; Historische Gesellschaft der Deutschen Bank (ed.), *Die Deutsche Bank in Hannover*.

101 Some examples include the acquisition of Lübecker Privatbank in 1927 or Hildesheimer Bank in 1928; Deutsche Bank, Annual Report 1927, p. 19.

102 Pohl, *Konzentration*, pp. 285ff.

103 Michalowsky to the colleagues of the Management Board, 16 November 1916; Report from Michalowsky about the supervisory board meeting of Schlesischer Bankverein on 15 March 1916, 24 March 1916, p. 2, HADB, S4091.

104 Deutsche Bank, Annual Report 1925, p. 21.

105 Hook, *Die wirtschaftliche Entwicklung*, p. 43 and Panel 3 (Appendix).

106 On the business policies of German companies in general during the First World War, see Plumpe, *Logik*.

107 Cf. Kobrak, *Banking on Global Markets*, pp. 180–82; see also Wixforth, *Kriegseinsatz und Kriegsfolgen*, p. 377.

108 Cf. Founding in HADB, S1837; Köster, *Standort weiß-blau*, p. 30; Hamlin, *Germany's Empire*, pp. 233–5.

109 Deutsche Bank to Prussian Minister for Public Works Paul von Breitenbach, 12 May 1915, HADB, S693. Cf. Bechtloff, *Die Mitropa AG*, pp. 64–113, esp. pp. 72, 94–6, and 112–13.

110 For contracts and correspondence pertaining to the Tetralin consortium see: HADB, S1725.

111 Cf. also Kreimeier, *The Ufa-Story*.

112 Cf. Feldman, *Deutsche Bank*, pp. 151–4.

113 Cf. Pohl, *Philipp Holzmann*.

114 Mankiewitz to Paul Klaproth, 30 January 1920, HADB, S3987. Cf. also Historical Association of Deutsche Bank (ed.), *Historical Review* No. 10 (2006), '150th anniversary of the birth of Arthur von Gwinner'; *Historical Review* No. 15 (2007), 'The life and work of Paul Mankiewitz'.

115 See on this in general Feldman, *The Great Disorder*.

116 Lampe, *Bankbetrieb*, p. 107. The real returns on shares had a strongly negative trend starting in 1918; cf. Ronge, *Die langfristige Rendite*, p. 183.

117 Deutsche Bank, Annual Report 1919, p. 13

118 Lampe, *Bankbetrieb*, p. 211, fn. 56; Holtfrerich, *The German Inflation*, pp. 287f.

119 Lampe, *Bankbetrieb*, p. 214.
120 Feldman, *Deutsche Bank*, pp. 178f.; Köster, *Standort weiß-blau*, p. 52.
121 Cf. Thamm, *Anspruch*, pp. 89ff.
122 Deutsche Bank, Annual Report 1918, p. 13.
123 Cf. Thamm, *Anspruch*, pp. 92ff.
124 Minutes recorded by Burath, 27 November 1918, BArch, R 8119 F, 8891.
125 Announcement by the company employees' council, 29 January 1919, BArch, R 8119 F, 8891.
126 Works Council Act of 4 February 1920, paragraph 73.
127 Feldman, *Deutsche Bank*, pp. 160–65.
128 Deutsche Bank, Annual Report 1918, p. 22.
129 Deutsche Bank, Annual Report 1922, p. 20.
130 Lampe, *Bankbetrieb*, pp. 159f.
131 Ibid., pp. 289f. and 293.
132 Deutsche Bank, Annual Report 1919, p. 13. Cf. on the German banks' business strategies during inflation Wixforth, Kollaps and Wixforth, *German Banks*.
133 Lampe, *Bankbetrieb*, p. 239.
134 Feldman, *Deutsche Bank*, pp. 192–4.
135 Lampe, *Bankbetrieb*, p. 331.
136 Cf. Geyer, *Verkehrte Welt*, pp. 220f.
137 Cf. Bormann/Scholtyseck/Wixforth, *Zentralinstitute*, pp. 166–74; Pohl, *Sparkassen*, pp. 92–8; Hardach, *Entstehung*.
138 Tilly, *German Banks and Foreign Investment*; Barth, *Mitteleuropakonzepte*.
139 Deutsche Bank, Annual Report 1917, p. 12.
140 Feldman, *Deutsche Bank*, pp. 159f.
141 The German banks had been pushing since late 1917 for compensation for their loans and credits in Russia (HADB, S3110).
142 Panwitz, *Das Haus des Kranichs*, pp. 233–6.
143 Note by Berne (undated), HADB, S53595.
144 Management of Disconto-Gesellschaft to Deutsche Bank, 21 March 1921, HADB, S3595.
145 Both banks were, inter alia, leaders in the consortium for Russian state loans and state-guaranteed railroad obligations, which also sought compensation after the Rapallo Treaty; Mendelssohn & Co. to Foreign Office, 19 December, 1924, HADB, S3139.
146 Pohl, *Geschäft und Politik*, pp. 57ff.
147 Cf. Dahlmann, *Otto Wolff*, pp. 42–50.
148 Fritz Seidenzahl, Das Russengeschäft, HADB, S3839; cf. also Lutz, *Siemens im Sowjetgeschäft*.
149 This rediscount was increased in autumn 1926 to 50 per cent; Pohl, *Geschäft und Politik*, p. 86.
150 The exporters covered the remaining 40 per cent with additional guarantees.
151 Financing exports to Russia (1931–1939), HADB, S3838; Consortium agreements of the banks of 1926, HADB, S3111; Industrie-Finanzierungs-AG Ost, Circular, 5 August 1926, HADB, S3840; cf. also the archives of the Reich Chancellery. Weimar Republic – Cabinet Marx III/IV, Volume 1, Documents, No. 26, Cabinet meeting on 16 June 1926, Agenda item 1. Credit for Russia, p. 58.
152 Seidenzahl, *Russengeschäft*, p. 13, HADB, S3839.
153 Wolfram Doellen, 'Um die deutschen Rußlandkredite. Deutsch-amerikanische Zusammenarbeit', *Berliner Börsen-Zeitung*, 8 October 1927, HADB, S3111.
154 Tilly, *German Banks and Foreign Investment*.
155 Cf. Wixforth, *Visier*.
156 This included, inter alia, in 1921 the Bank for the Electrification of Poland (Warsaw), in 1922 the founding of a large logging company to exploit the

Białowieża Forest and in 1925 the financing of a canal installation for the city of Łódź (HADB, S3313).
157 Benfey, *Entwicklung*, p. 118.
158 Stauß/Lehmann to the management of the branches, 19 February 1921, BArch, R 8119 F, 8979; Memo to Dr Kessler with regard to Bulgaria, 25 October 1930, HADB, S3914.
159 Note regarding the closure of the Constantinople branch, 26 April 1919, BArch, R 8119 F, 8960.
160 Deutsche Bank to the representatives of the Allied governments at Versailles, 13 May 1919, BArch, R 8119 F, 8960.
161 Note regarding business conditions at the Constantinople branch, 28 January 1927, BArch, R 8119 F, 8960.
162 Historical Association of Deutsche Bank (ed.), *A Century of Deutsche Bank in Turkey*, pp. 39–47.
163 Heinemann to the Deutsche Wirtschaftsverband für Mittel- und Südamerika, 24 March 1917, HADB, S196.
164 Cf. Pohl, *Deutsche Bank Buenos Aires*, pp. 66ff.
165 Deutsche Bank, Berlin headquarters, to the management of the Banco Alemán Transatlántico, 12 November 1926, BArch, R 8119 F, 8639.
166 Cf. *50 Jahre Deutsche Ueberseeische Bank*, pp. 42f.
167 In the spring the headquarters still had 745 employees; BAT, Annual Report 1924, p. 16.
168 BAT, Annual Reports 1924 and 1927.
169 Meeting with the Deutsch-Asiatische Bank on 2 July 1919, BArch, R 8119 F, 8386.
170 Still in November 1922, for example, 'the question of the bank's disputes with the debtors of the Chinese departments [of DAB] [were] still entirely unresolved', Deutsch-Asiatische Bank, supervisory board meeting minutes from 7 November 1922, p. 1, BArch, R 8119 F, 8386. On the negotiations with the Chinese, see also the minutes of the meeting of the business committee on 28 May 1924, BArch, R 8119 F, 8386.
171 Enclosure in the letter from Urbig to Kurt Weigelt, 24 October 1933, S. 3, BArch, R 8119 F, 8383.
172 Müller-Jabusch, *Franz Urbig*, pp. 179ff.
173 Memo from Franz Urbig, 27 August 1924, HADB, K7/5/II-1.
174 Urbig to the management board of the Deutsch-Asiatische Bank, 12 October 1926, HADB, K7/5/II-1.
175 DAB, Annual Reports 1915–1927, 1928, p. 6.
176 DAB, Annual Report 1930, p. 8.
177 DAB, Annual Report 1929, p. 9.
178 Plumpe, *Deutsche Bank in East Asia*, p. 76.
179 Kurt Meißner to Paul Bonn, with an essay entitled 'Concerning the upcoming closure of the Kobe office of the Deutsch-Asiastische Bank', 30 March 1931, BArch, R 8119 F, 8383, sheet 80. On Meißner, see Friese, *Meißner*.
180 Urbig to the management board of the Deutsch-Asiatische Bank, 12 October 1926, HADB, K7/5/II-1.
181 Memo from Franz Urbig for the supervisory board of the Deutsch-Asiatische Bank (DAB), 23 October 1933, p. 5, BArch, R 8119 F, 8383. On the various strategic options, see also a memo about a meeting of the supervisory board of DAB on 8 November 1933, BArch, R 8119 F, 8383.
182 Feldman, *Deutsche Bank*, pp. 190f.
183 Born, *Helfferich*.
184 Cf. Rupieper, *Cuno Government*, pp. 42ff.
185 Bergmann, *Weg*.
186 Ferguson, *Paper and Iron*.

187 Kobrak, *Banking on Global Markets*, p. 208.
188 Minutes of the branch directors meeting on 11 March 1926, HADB, SG8/5.
189 Kobrak, *Banking on Global Markets*, pp. 218–22.
190 Cf. also Schacht's letter to Wassermann, 13 September 1927, HADB, S4382.
191 Feldman, *Deutsche Bank*, p. 228.
192 Cf. Ritschl, *Deutschlands Krise und Konjunktur*.
193 Feldman, *Deutsche Bank*, p. 200.
194 Deutsche Bank, Annual Reports 1925 and 1928.
195 Deutsche Bank, Annual Report 1926, p. 20.
196 Deutsche Bank, Annual Report 1928, p. 24
197 Minutes of the branch directors meeting on 11 March 1926, p. 2, HADB, SG5/8.
198 Deutsche Bank, Annual Report 1928, p. 20.
199 The 'Law on Tax Mitigation and Easing of the Economic Situation' of 31 March 1926, made, above all, investments of up to 25 per cent advantageous from a taxation standpoint, because they were not treated as taxable business assets, in order to prevent double taxation ('intercorporate privilege'); Fiedler, *Fusionen und Übernahmen*, p. 225.
200 Deutsche Bank, Annual Report 1924, p. 28; Deutsche Bank, Annual Report 1928, p. 26.
201 This cannot be precisely determined from the published balance sheet figures; cf. Hook, *Entwicklung*, p. 66.
202 Cf. Feldman, *Hugo Stinnes*, pp. 936ff.
203 Feldman, *Deutsche Bank*, pp. 201f.
204 Cf. Feldman, *Automobilindustrie*; Pierer, Die Bayerischen Motoren Werke bis 1933.
205 Budraß, *Adler und Kranich*.
206 Wellhöner/Wixforth, *Unternehmensfinanzierung*.
207 Fohlin, *Finance Capitalism*, p. 122.
208 Deutsche Bank und Disconto-Gesellschaft, Aufsichtsrats-Mandate der Deutschen Bank und Disconto-Gesellschaft (self-published 1930), HADB, B361/1930.
209 RGBl, Part I, No. 63, 1931, Decree of the Reich President on Stock Corporation Law, Bank Supervision and Tax Amnesty, 21 September 1931, pp. 493–509 (Art. VIII, Para. 3 and 4, p. 500)
210 Deutsche Bank, Annual Report 1926, p. 17.
211 Krenn, *Macht*, pp. 213–26. In this regard, Deutsche Bank stood in contrast to most other banks, which had fewer connections in industry (ibid., p. 136).
212 Deutsche Bank, Annual Reports, various years.
213 Bol, *Aktionärsstruktur*, p. 105.
214 Ziegler, *Aufsichtsräte*; Marx/Krenn, *Kontinuität und Wandel*; Fiedler, *Eigentümer und Netzwerke*.
215 Sibylle Lehmann-Hasemeyer and Alexander Opitz have shown that the banks' links to politics through Management Board and Supervisory Board positions were especially strong in the interwar years. Cf. Lehmann-Hasemeyer/Opitz, *Value*.
216 Steinthal had been on the supervisory board since 1905 and had been the deputy chairman of the board for many years.
217 This corresponds to the general finding that in companies with diversified holdings the Supervisory Board often is in a weaker position; cf. Wiethölter, *Interessen und Organisation*, pp. 302f.
218 Cf. Gehlen, *Aktienrecht und Unternehmenskontrolle*.
219 Bol, *Corporate Governance*, p. 30.
220 Bol, *Aktionärsstruktur*.
221 Bol, *Corporate Governance*, pp. 92f.
222 Cf. Feldman, *Deutsche Bank*, pp. 245.

223 For contemporary criticism of the collegial system, cf. ibid., p. 213.
224 Seidenzahl, *100 Jahre*, p. 278.
225 Minutes of the branch directors' meeting on 11 March 1926, pp. 5f., HADB, SG8/5.
226 Ibid.
227 Deutsche Bank, Annual Report 1924, p. 23. On the following statement, see generally Weihe, *Personalpolitik*.
228 Deutsche Bank, Annual Report 1924, p. 23.
229 Letter to the editors of *Abendblatt*, 22 November 1927, HADB, B236/1.
230 The bank did, in fact, have to defend itself in March 1927 from the accusation of having chosen older – and more expensive – employees to let go and of not having considered social criteria; Report on 27 February 1928, HADB, B236/2.
231 Employees of Deutsche Bank, including all banks acquired until now, 19 January 1929, HADB, B236/2.
232 Report, 9 March 1927, HADB, B236/2.
233 Contract terms of contract employees 1925–1927, HADB, B236/1.
234 Minutes of the branch directors meeting on 11 March 1926, HADB, SG8/5.
235 Monthly income of contract employees in Berlin, 25 March 1929, HADB, B236/2.
236 See for example the exchange of letters between Georg Solmssen and Otto Urbig, 26 November/31 December 1931, HADB, P2/U51.
237 Report on employees (1929), HADB, B236/2.
238 Deutsche Bank, Annual Report 1926, p. 22.
239 Deutsche Bank, Annual Report 1924, p. 23; Lampe, *Bankbetrieb*, p. 271.
240 Lampe, *Bankbetrieb*, p. 290.
241 Deutsche Bank, Annual Report 1924, p. 24.
242 Dickhaus, *Innovationen*; Obst, *Bankbuchhaltung*, pp. 175–211.
243 Deutsche Bank, Annual Report 1927, p. 20
244 Memo by Georg Solmssen, 16 September 1926, HADB, NL3/79, quoted in James/Müller (eds), *Georg Solmssen*, pp. 235–8, here p. 236.
245 Ibid., pp. 235–8.
246 See also Thomes, *Die 'Fusion der Elefanten' 1929*.
247 Memo by Georg Solmssen, 16 September 1926, HADB, NL3/79, quoted in James/Müller (eds), *Georg Solmssen*, pp. 235–8.
248 Minutes of the branch directors meeting on 11 March 1926, HADB, SG8/5.
249 Seidenzahl, *100 Jahre*, pp. 295ff.
250 Cf. e.g. Rummel, *Rentabilitäts- und Organisationsfragen*.
251 Pohl, *Konzentration*, p. 353.
252 On the technical aspects of the merger, cf. ibid., pp. 354ff. By spring 1929 Osnabrücker Bank had already been taken over by Deutsche Bank.
253 Speech by Wassermann at the general meeting on 29 October 1929, in: Stenographic notes of the extraordinary general meeting of Deutsche Bank on 29 October 1929, HADB, B270.
254 Feldman, *Deutsche Bank*, pp. 254f.
255 Deutsche Bank, Annual Report 1929, p. 30; Pohl, *Konzentration*, p. 357.
256 Meeting with branch directors, 13 September 1929, HADB, SG5/8.
257 Cf. letter from the Management Board to the branch directors, 6 September 1929, HADB, SG5/8.
258 Minutes of the branch directors meeting, 2 September 1936, HADB, SG5/8.

259 Pohl, *Konzentration*, p. 356.
260 Deutsche Bank, Annual Report 1929, p. 30.

II. Age of Extremes: Crisis, Dictatorship and Expansion

1 Fehr to Carl Boschwitz, 29 October 1929, HADB, A1252.
2 'Reactions of the Wall Street slump', *The Economist*, 23 November 1929.
3 Deutsche Bank, Annual Report 1929, p. 34; cf. on the effects of the Wall Street Crash on the German financial system in general: Balderston, *The Origins and Course*, pp. 155–63.
4 Deutsche Bank, Annual Report 1930, p. 9.
5 Temin, Transmission; James, *The End of Globalization*.
6 Eggenkämper/Modert/Pretzlik, *Die Frankfurter Versicherungs-AG 1865–2004*.
7 Abraham, *Konzernkrach*, pp. 81ff.; Fiedler, *Netzwerke des Vertrauens*, pp. 96–105.
8 Cf. Gustav Stolper, Finanzskandale, in: *Der deutsche Volkswirt*, 6 (1931/32), pp. 179–81.
9 Geyer, *What Crisis?*.
10 Deutsche Bank und Disconto-Gesellschaft, Annual Report 1929, p. 26.
11 Deutsche Bank und Disconto-Gesellschaft, Annual Report 1931, p. 13.
12 Köster, *Standort weiß-blau*, p. 77; Bähr, *Wandlungen*, pp. 121–33.
13 Hook, *Entwicklung*, p. 74.
14 Schubert, *The Credit-Anstalt Crisis of 1931*.
15 For a critical view on this, esp. James, *The German Slump*; cf. also on international cross-holdings, Feinstein/Watson, *Private International Capital Flows*.
16 Bähr, *Bankenkrise*, pp. 25f.
17 For a detailed discussion of this, see ibid., pp. 31ff.
18 Kaminsky/Reinhart, *The Twin Crises*.
19 Ferguson/Temin, *Made in Germany*.
20 Schnabel, *The German Twin Crisis of 1931*, p. 827. In addition to Born, *Bankenkrise* see James, *Causes*; Gold, *Bankinsolvenzen*; Balderston, *German Banking*; Balderston, *The Origins and Course*.
21 Brüning, *Memoiren 1916–1934*, pp. 313f.
22 'Memo on Events in July in the Banking World', 1 October 1931, BArch, R431/647, Copy in HADB, NL3/63.
23 Hardach, *Weltmarktorientierung*, p. 151.
24 Feldman, *Deutsche Bank*, pp. 253f.
25 Kopper, *Marktwirtschaft*, p. 100
26 Born, *Bankenkrise*, p. 95; cf. on Nordwolle Wixforth, *Beziehungen*, p. 16.
27 Pohl, *Konzentration*, p. 365.
28 Deutsche Bundesbank, *Deutsches Geld- und Bankwesen*, p. 123.
29 Koeppel, *Öffentlichkeit und Aktienrecht*.
30 The emergency decree of 19 September 1931 prohibited the buyback of shares. This stipulation was also incorporated in the Reich Credit Law of 1934.
31 Untersuchung des Bankwesens 1933, Untersuchungsausschuß für das Bankwesen (ed.), *1933*, Teil II: S*tatistiken*, Berlin 1933, p. 266; Terberger/Wettberg, *'Aktienrückkauf'*, p. 15.
32 Schnabel, *German Twin Crisis*, p. 850.
33 The bank was able to increase the number of accounts to 837,000 by 1930, 137,000 of which were savings accounts (Deutsche Bank und Disconto-Gesellschaft, Annual Report 1930, p. 13); for a comparative

assessment of the banks' deposits, Schnabel, *German Twin Crisis*, p. 854.
34 Karl Nordhoff, 'Über die Liquiditätsfrage', in: *Untersuchung des Bankwesens 1933*, Part I, vol. 1, Berlin 1933, pp. 477–91, here p. 491; cf. also Balderston, *The Origins and Course*, p. 171.
35 Schnabel, *Role of Liquidity*.
36 Holtfrerich, *Amerikanischer Kapitalexport*, p. 501.
37 Committee for the Assessment of Production and Sales in the German Economy (Ausschuss zur Untersuchung der Erzeugungs- und Absatzbedingungen der Deutschen Wirtschaft), *The Reichsbank*, p. 86.
38 Schnabel, *German Twin Crisis*, p. 834.
39 Irmler, *Bankenkrise*, p. 286; Accominotti/Eichengreen, *The Mother of All Sudden Stops*; Accominotti, *International Banking*.
40 Feldman, *Deutsche Bank*, p. 248.
41 Ibid., p. 262.
42 Deutsche Bank und Disconto-Gesellschaft, Annual Report 1932, p. 13 and 1933, p. 11
43 Cf. Deutsche Bank und Disconto-Gesellschaft, Annual Reports 1931–1935.
44 Feldman, *Deutsche Bank*, pp. 240–42; Feldman, *Jakob Goldschmidt*; Boris Gehlen, *'Avantgarde'*.
45 Cf. e.g. Solmssen to Schlitter, 20 January 1930, quoted in James/Müller (eds), *Georg Solmssen*, pp. 276f., here p. 276.
46 For a comprehensive analysis, see Born, *Bankenkrise*, pp. 64ff.
47 Barkai, *Oscar Wassermann*, p. 49; cf. for a more detailed account of the chronology Priester, *Geheimnis*.
48 Solmssen and Frank to Brüning, 1 August 1931, quoted in James/Müller (eds), *Georg Solmssen*, pp. 311–313.
49 Born, *Bankenkrise*, p. 87.
50 In 1930 72 per cent of Deutsche Bank und Disconto-Gesellschaft's nostro accounts consisted of foreign currency receivables; Hook, *Entwicklung*, pp. 58f.
51 Cf. the assessment in Bähr, *Bankenkrise*, pp. 58–61.
52 Deutsche Bank und Disconto-Gesellschaft, Annual Report 1931, p. 14; Seidenzahl, *100 Jahre*, p. 337; Bähr, *Bankenkrise*, pp. 101f.
53 Deutsche Bank und Disconto-Gesellschaft, Annual Report 1931, p. 14.
54 Bähr, *Bankenkrise*, p. 114.
55 Ministerial meeting on 20 June 1931, Records of the Reich Chancellery, Brüning Cabinet I/II, Doc. No. 339, p. 1228; Feldman, *Deutsche Bank*, pp. 270f.
56 Cf. on the international debt negotiations, Bennett, *Germany*.
57 Seidenzahl, *100 Jahre*, p. 347.
58 Addresses by Wilhelm Keppler and Gottfried Feder at the meeting of the Investigation Committee on 6 September 1933, in: *Untersuchung des Bankwesens 1933*, Part I, vol. 1, pp. 12–19, here pp. 13f. and 18.
59 Address by Schacht at the meeting of the Investigation Committee 6 September 1933, in: *Untersuchung des Bankwesens 1933*, Part I, vol. 1, pp. 9–12, here pp. 11 and 10, respectively.
60 Cf. on the bank hearings, Seidenzahl, *100 Jahre*, pp. 348–55 and Kopper, *Marktwirtschaft*, pp. 86–112.
61 Hans Rummel, The Profitability of the Banks, their Expenses and Calculations – Attempts to Increase Profits, Reduce Expenses and Increase Earnings, in: *Untersuchung des Bankwesens 1933*, Part I, vol. 1, p p. 421–74.
62 On the development of the KWG, see Müller, *Entstehung*.

63 Kopper, *Marktwirtschaft*, p. 125.
64 Balderston, *German Banking*, p. 588.
65 'Reich Credit Law' of 5 December 1934, in: RGBl, I, 1934, p. 1204, paragraph 4; Cf. Bähr, *Modernes Bankrecht*, p. 209.
66 On Ernst cf. Gloe, *Planung*, pp. 70f.
67 Mertens, *Aktiengesetz*; Bähr, *Modernes Bankrecht*, pp. 212f.
68 James, *The Nazi Dictatorship and the Deutsche Bank*, pp. 24f.
69 Ibid., p. 4.
70 Solmssen to Adolf von Batocki-Friebe, 29 October 1930, quoted in James/Müller (eds), *Georg Solmssen*, pp. 295f, here p. 295.
71 Müller, *50 Jahre*; Volkswirtschaftliche Abteilung to Abteilung für Bücherei- und Archivwesen beim Magistrat für Stadt Berlin, 14 September 1945, BArch, R 8119 F, 10914.
72 Numerous reports in BArch, R 8119 F, 10913, 10914, 10915, 23980, 23981.
73 Feldman, *Deutsche Bank*, p. 250.
74 Solmssen to Adolf von Batocki-Friebe, 29 October 1930, quoted in James/Müller (eds), *Georg Solmssen*, p. 295.
75 Kopper, *Marktwirtschaft*, p. 44.
76 Ibid., pp. 75f.
77 Fischer, *Hjalmar Schacht*; Kopper, *Hjalmar Schacht*.
78 Kopper, *Marktwirtschaft*, p. 109; James, *Verbandspolitik*, pp. 80–100.
79 Barkai, *Oscar Wassermann*, p. 92; Kopper, *Bankiers unterm Hakenkreuz*, pp. 207–20; Balderston, *German Banking*, p. 600.
80 Kopper, *Marktwirtschaft*, p. 134.
81 Feldman, *Deutsche Bank*, pp. 249f.
82 Barkai, *Oscar Wassermann*, p. 96.
83 Urbig to Ernst Enno Russell, 18 January 1934, HADB, P1/14; translated in James, *The Nazi Dictatorship and the Deutsche Bank*, pp. 43f.
84 Barkai, *Oscar Wassermann*, p. 101.
85 Solmssen to Urbig, 9 April 1933, quoted in James/Müller (eds), *Georg Solmssen*, pp. 356ff., here p. 357. Quote translated in James, *The Nazi Dictatorship and the Deutsche Bank*, p. 45.
86 Quoted in Sommerfeldt, *Ich war dabei*, p. 41. Translated in James, *The Nazi Dictatorship and the Deutsche Bank*, p. 46.
87 Seidenzahl, *100 Jahre*, p. 360.
88 Cf. e.g. James, *The Deutsche Bank and the Nazi Economic War Against the Jews*, p. 44.
89 Cf. on this Frei, *Wirtschaft*.
90 Ziegler, 'A Regulated Market Economy', pp. 142f.
91 James, *The Nazi Dictatorship and the Deutsche Bank*, pp. 92–107.
92 Attack against Mosler due to Jewish heritage, June 1939, HADB, B203, Envelope 144.
93 Ritter von Halt and Karl Kimmich had even studied law after their apprenticeships in banking and obtained doctorates; Ruppmann, *Generationsforschung*, p. 23.
94 James, *The Nazi Dictatorship and the Deutsche Bank*, pp. 53–5; Weihe, *Personalpolitik*, pp. 100–143.
95 James, *The Deutsche Bank and the Nazi Economic War Against the Jews*, p. 28.
96 James, *The Nazi Dictatorship and the Deutsche Bank*, pp. 48–50. James considers this number to be too high, but does not provide reasoning for this interpretation.
97 On Karl Ritter von Halt see Kopper, *Bankiers unterm Hakenkreuz*, pp. 151–62.
98 James, *The Nazi Dictatorship and the Deutsche Bank*, p. 58f.
99 Cf. for example the correspondence between the DAF, Ritter von Halt and the Hildesheim and Goslar branches due to the dual functions of an employee (1939), HADB, P2a/K10; correspondence between Halt and Höß, the district leader of the NSDAP in Prague, with regard to the promotion of Erich Rudolph, Troppau (1939–1940), HADB, P2a/R32.
100 Cf. correspondence with regard to the termination without notice of an SA member in December 1938, HADB, P2a/W27.
101 James, *The Nazi Dictatorship and the Deutsche Bank*, p. 110.
102 Kopper, *Marktwirtschaft*, p. 353.
103 James, *The Deutsche Bank and the Nazi Economic War Against the Jews*, p. 31.
104 The NSDAP in Munich sought in May 1933, for example, to replace the branch director there with Rudolf Weydenhammer, a party member; Memo by Ernst A. von Lewinski, 16 May 1933, HADB, P2a/W2.
105 Cf. on Miethe HADB, P2/M426; see also Stiftung Topographie des Terrors (ed.), *Volksgerichtshof*, pp. 121ff. and 222.
106 Frost, *Rösler*.
107 Schmidt, Notes on the Economic Upswing in Early May 1933, BArch, R 8119 F, 23980.
108 Ibid., p. 2.
109 Ibid., p. 1.
110 Schmidt, Wirtschaftspolitik des italienischen Faschismus, 13 April 1933, BArch, R 8119 F, 23980.
111 Ibid., p. 6; p. 1; pp. 3f.
112 Schieder, *Das italienische Experiment*; Schieder, *Fatal Attraction*.
113 Salaries of directors, authorised representatives and senior officials 1933–43, HADB, B382; Payments to upper-level officials, 1 September 1933, HADB, B389.
114 Bähr, *Modernes Bankrecht*, p. 210.
115 Banken, *Hitlers Steuerstaat*, pp. 404–27.
116 Weihe, *Personalpolitik*, pp. 144–54.
117 Kopper, *Marktwirtschaft*, p. 148.
118 Gesetz über Aktiengesellschaften und Kommanditgesellschaften, 30 January 1937, RGBl., I, 1937, pp. 107ff. Cf. also Mertens, *Aktiengesetz*.
119 Hook, *Entwicklung*, table 5.
120 Minutes of the directors meeting on 6 October 1936, HADB, SG5/8.
121 Cf. also James, *The Nazi Dictatorship and the Deutsche Bank*, p. 25ff.
122 Minutes of the directors meeting on 6 October 1936, p. 7, HADB, SG5/8.
123 Deutsche Bank und Disconto-Gesellschaft, Annual Report 1936, p. 5.
124 Cf. Lorentz, *Commerzbank*.
125 Pohl, *Konzentration*, p. 407.
126 Report on the semi-annual meeting of 30 June 1938 in Berlin on 30 August 1938, p. 3, HADB, SG5/8.
127 Ibid.
128 James, *The Deutsche Bank and the Nazi Economic War Against the Jews*, pp. 64f.
129 Ziegler, *Die Dresdner Bank und die Juden*, pp. 182–202.
130 James, *The Deutsche Bank and the Nazi Economic War Against the Jews*, p. 206.
131 Report on the semi-annual meeting of 30 June 1938 in Berlin on 30 August 1938, p. 3, HADB, SG5/8.
132 Deutsche Bank, Annual Report 1937, p. 18 and 1940, p. 16.
133 Köhler, *Das Ende*; Panwitz, *Das Haus des Kranichs*, pp. 272–8.

134 Cf. Gall, *Abs*, pp. 58–65.

135 James, *The Deutsche Bank and the Nazi Economic War Against the Jews*, pp. 77–82.

136 Bajohr, *'Aryanisation' in Hamburg*; Bajohr, *'Arisierung' als gesellschaftlicher Prozeß*.

137 Wixforth, *Die Banken in den abhängigen und besetzten Gebieten Europas 1938–1945*, pp. 200–204.

138 Köhler, *Die 'Arisierung' der Privatbanken*; Köhler, *Business as usual?*.

139 Ziegler, *Die Dresdner Bank und die Juden*, pp. 436–48.

140 Lorentz, *Commerzbank*, p. 250.

141 Herbst, *Banker in einem prekären Geschäft*, p. 130ff.

142 Ritschl, *Deutschlands Krise und Konjunktur*, p. 109.

143 Born, *Bankenkrise*, pp. 148f.

144 Minutes of the branch directors meeting, 2 September 1931, pp. 8–11, HADB, SG5/8.

145 Kobrak, *Banking on Global Markets*, p. 246.

146 By summer, only $3 million worth of bonds was left. The buyback continued in the following years. Abs referred in summer 1938 to the need to buy back remaining dollar obligations in order to 'further consolidate our creditworthiness internationally'; Kobrak, *Banking on Global Markets*, p. 239; Memo on the directors meeting of 17 September 1935; Report on the semi-annual meeting of 30 June 1938 in Berlin on 30 August 1938, p. 2, HADB, SG5/8.

147 Kobrak, *Banking on Global Markets*, pp. 245–7.

148 See also Schlieper's pessimistic remarks, memo on the directors meeting of 17 September 1935, pp. 9–10, HADB, SG5/8.

149 Cf. Hermann Willink (Hamburg branch) to the Economic Group Private Banks (1936) with a statement of imports and exports, HADB, F2/1111.

150 Pohl, *Deutsche Bank Buenos Aires*, pp. 77ff.

151 Report of the Management Board of BAT, Berlin, 30 September 1939, BArch, R 8119 F, 8644.

152 Report of Management Board member Walther Greamer in the shareholder meeting of BAT, 9 May 1940, BArch, R 8119 F, 8644.

153 Report of the Management Board of the BAT, Berlin, 22 September 1936, BArch, R 8119 F, 8645.

154 According to Anton Walter's memories of his time at BAT's branch in Spain between 1935 and 1942, HADB, NL12/3.

155 Abs to Councillor of State Helmuth Wohltat, 28 April 1939, BArch, R 8119 F, 8635.

156 Cf. the situational reports of the DAB from China in August 1937 in HADB, K7/19/I-4.

157 Cf. the (unsigned) memo of 17 July 1935 on the letter from the Leadership of the NSDAP Auslands-Organisation to Reichsbank Director Hasse of 5 July 1935, HADB, K7/26/II-1. Quote, ibid., p. 1. According to its own reports, the DAB had, depending on the branch, an average of a good third of the German China trade at the beginning of the 1930s, cf. ibid., pp. 1f.

158 DAB, Minutes of the meeting of the supervisory board, 27 June 1939, HADB, K7/11/I-1. On the situation of the international banks, especially HSBC and Chartered Bank, see Siu, *British Banks*.

159 Müller-Jabusch, *50 Jahre*, pp. 305ff.

160 Memo by Franz Urbig, 15 January 1935, HADB, K7/26/II-1; see also the memo by Franz Urbig on a conversation with Private Secretary Dr Voss (Foreign Office), 4 April 1935, HADB, K7/26/II-1.

161 Urbig to August Reiss (Deutsch-Asiatische Bank, Shanghai), 3 February 1936, HADB, K7/26/II-2.

162 DAB, Minutes of the meetings of the supervisory board of 3 March 1941 and 1 June 1942, HADB, K7/11/I-1. Above all, the strong position of the semi-public Yokohama Specie Bank led to the DAB's withdrawal from Kobe in 1932, according to Urbig in March 1941.

163 Müller, *Eine deutsche Bank für Japan*.

164 Hook, *Entwicklung*, table 2.

165 Bulletin to the sub-branches, 8 June 1934, HADB, F55/3192.

166 Schlieper, *Banken und Aussenhandel*, p. 20.

167 Deutsche Bank, Annual Report 1938, p. 8; cf. the report, prepared for the economic department, 'New German Banking Work in Europe' as well as the writings of Schmidt to the Elberfeld branch, 31 December 1941, BArch, R 8119 F, 10913.

168 Minutes of the directors meeting of 6 October 1936, p. 13, HADB, SG5/8.

169 Schlieper, *Banken und Aussenhandel*, p. 15.

170 Ibid.

171 Economic Group Private Banks to Reich Group Banks, 18 March 1937, HADB, F2/1111.

172 Schlieper, *Banken und Aussenhandel*, p. 14.

173 Memo about the trip of Dr Moehle to Russia, 18 March 1934, HADB, S3111.

174 Pollem's report on the Russia Business for Dr Schlitter, 24 June 1935; Report on Russian Prewar and Postwar Debt (1932), HADB, S3111.

175 Report to Hans Leibkutsch, Financing Exports to Russia 1926–1941, 2 January 1974, HADB, S3838.

176 Volkmann, *Sowjetunion*, p. 307.

177 Directors meeting of 6 October 1936, p. 11, HADB, SG5/8.

178 Pollems, Report on Business in Russia over the Past Years, October 1937, HADB, S3111.

179 Seidenzahl, *Das Russengeschäft*, p. 13, HADB, S3839.

180 Pollems to Rummel, 16 October 1937, HADB, S3111.

181 Pollems to Seidenzahl, 18 March 1969, HADB, S3838.

182 Pollems to Schlieper, 13 May 1936, HADB, S3111.

183 Memo by Abs, 4 July 1942, BArch, R 8119 F, 24154.

184 James, *The Deutsche Bank and the Nazi Economic War Against the Jews*, pp. 172f.

185 Overy/Otto/Houwink ten Cate (eds), *Die 'Neuordnung' Europas*; Buchheim/Boldorf (eds), *Europäische Volkswirtschaften*.

186 Cf. also Tooze, *The Wages of Destruction*.

187 See balance sheets and summaries of the individual balance sheet items 1933–1944, HADB, B305-B319

188 Earnings from ongoing investments, HADB, B314

189 Gall, *Abs*, pp. 89ff.

190 Wixforth, *Expansion*.

191 Cf. Schlieper's statements in the directors meeting of 6 October 1936, p. 11, HADB, SG5/8.

192 Abs represented the bank abroad starting in 1937, but did not officially join the bank until 1 January 1938; Minutes of the directors meeting on 9 September 1937, HADB, SG5/8.

193 Personnel file of Pollems, HADB, P1/36

194 Nachrichten-Abteilung, Documents of Johannes Kiehl, BArch, R 8119 F, 10917.

195 James, *The Nazi Dictatorship and the Deutsche Bank*, p. 161f.

196 Dickhaus, *Kredite für den Holocaust?*.

197 Memo 2 April 1943, HADB, F119/848.

198 Personnel record of Pohle, HADB, P2a/P9. Cf. James, *Banks and Business Politics in Nazi Germany*, pp. 52–6.

199 On Weigelt, see Linne, *Afrika als 'wirtschaftlicher Ergänzungsraum'*.

200 Personnel record of Weigelt, HADB, P2/W135.
201 Cf. correspondence in BArch, R 8119 F, 7465.
202 Kurzmeyer was briefly even considered as a candidate for leading Mendelssohn; Köhler, *Die 'Arisierung' der Privatbanken*, p. 251; on Kurzmeyer's biography see Steinberg, *Gold Transactions*, pp. 59–66.
203 For a detailed analysis see Feldman, *Austrian Banks*, pp. 117ff.
204 Report on the relationship between DB und CABV, 5 July 1938, HADB, B56.
205 James, *The Nazi Dictatorship and the Deutsche Bank*, pp. 119f.
206 Draft of a friendship agreement, 26 March 1938, HADB, B56.
207 Report of 5 July 1938 on the relationship between DB und CABV, HADB, B56; Note by Ulrich on 17 February 1941 and analysis of 19 February 1941 with regard to the planned role of the CABV in south-eastern Europe, BArch, R 8119 F, 24158.
208 Feldman, *Austrian Banks*, pp. 395ff.
209 Memo by Mosler, 12 May 1938, HADB, B51; Feldman, *Austrian Banks*, pp. 40–1
210 Note on the transfer of the majority share in CABV from VIAG to Deutsche Bank, 2 March 1942, HADB, B56.
211 Report by Abs, 2 March 1942, HADB, B56.
212 Joham to Abs, 27 October 1941, HADB, B74.
213 Negotiations of January/February 1941, HADB, B59.
214 James, *The Nazi Dictatorship and the Deutsche Bank*, p. 175.
215 Memo, 'Die Südostausdehnung der Creditanstalt', 30 July 1942, HADB, B54.
216 Cf. Proceedings in the records of the General Secretariat with regard to the Regional Bank of Bosnia and Hercegovina, HADB, B85.
217 Memo by Kurzmeyer, 20 September 1940 and letter from CABV to the RWM with regard to the distribution of share capital in the Jugoslawischer Bankverein, 6 July 1939, HADB, B69; Abs to Rösler, 13 February 1940 and Abs to Pohle, 26 October 1940, HADB, B176.
218 Report on discussions with the Greek banks on 17 and 18 June 1941, BArch, R 8119 F, 24158; Co-operation Agreement, 17 June 1941, HADB, B78.
219 Pollems, Minutes of the Founding of a 'Aktiengesellschaft Braunkohle von Griechenland' (Joint-Stock Company Lignate from Greece), 3 October 1941, HADB, B78.
220 Minutes of the 3rd Meeting of the Foreign Trade Committee of the Board of the German Reichsbank, 19 December 1939, p. 3, BArch, R 8119 F, 349, Sheet 119.
221 Cf., for example, Osterwind to Abs with regard to the agent in Bucharest at the Athénée Palace Hotel, 6 May 1941, BArch, R 8119 F, 24154.
222 Statements by Abs, Minutes of the Southeast Conference in Vienna, 15 to 17 July 1942, p. 19, BArch, R 8119 F, 11726.
223 Hasslacher to Abs, 7 July 1939, HADB, B69.
224 Memo by Fischböck, 6 July 1939, HADB, B69.
225 Abs to Hasslacher, 11 July 1939, HADB, B69.
226 James, *The Deutsche Bank and the Nazi Economic War Against the Jews*, pp. 169–71.
227 Kiehl, Note with regard to Loan and Banking Transactions in the Future Polish State, 1 November 1939, BArch, R 8119 F, 24222.
228 Anonymous, Proposal on the matter of a possible shares in the Polish banking system, 7 September 1939, p. 1, BArch, R 8119 F, 24222.
229 Report of 6 September 1939, BArch, R 8119 F, 24222.
230 Cf. Loose, *Kredite für NS-Verbrechen*, pp. 98ff.
231 Deutsche Bank had maintained its presence in Upper Silesia (Katowice branch) after the Geneva Convention of May 1922 ran out, whereas Dresdner Bank had decided in 1938 to withdraw; cf. Wixforth, *Expansion*, pp. 433f.
232 Kiehl to Gdynia (Katowice), 13 October 1939, BArch, R 8119 F, 24222.
233 Feldman, *Austrian Banks*, pp. 189–223; cf. Wixforth, *Wiedererwerbung*.
234 Kiehl, Note with regard to bank branches in Russian territories, 2 August 1941, BArch, R 8119 F, 24222.
235 Circular letter from Kiehl and Rummel to the branches entitled 'Representation in the Ostland Territory', 4 November 1941, HADB, F88/1609.
236 Gall, *Abs*, pp. 110f.
237 Schmidt, Report on the Branches in Upper Silesia, 28 September 1939, BArch, R 8119 F, 10913.
238 This had already been considered and discussed in November 1938, cf. Note by Kiehl, 25 November 1938, BArch, R 8119 F, 24222.
239 Abs, Note with regard to Creditanstalt-Bankverein Krakau-Lemberg, 18 August 1943, HADB, B137.
240 Feldman, *Austrian Banks*, pp. 191–6.
241 Kiehl to Theusner, 19 September 1939, BArch, R 8119 F, 24222.
242 James, *The Nazi Dictatorship and the Deutsche Bank*, p. 167.
243 Kiehl to Theusner, 1 August 1941, BArch, R 8119 F, 24222.
244 Dr Schlotterer, Reich Economics Ministry, to the German banks, 20 September 1940, p. 1. Cf. also Schlotterer's explanatory letter of 2 October 1940, BArch, R 8119 F, 7465.
245 Report by E. W. Schmidt, 16 August 1940, BArch, R 8119 F, 10913.
246 Memo by Pollems for Kimmich and Abs, 30 September 1940, BArch, R 8119 F, 7465.
247 Statements by Feske, Minutes of the Southeast Conference in Vienna, 15 to 17 July 1942, p. 18, BArch, R 8119 F, 11726.
248 The de Bary bank was a subsidiary of Disconto-Gesellschaft until 1929 and was combined with the Amsterdam branch of Deutsche Bank at the time of the merger, but run under Dutch law.
249 Kimmich, Note for Abs, 13 August 1940 and 17 October 1940, HADB, B128.
250 Kimmich to Schacht, 13 November 1940, HADB, B128.
251 Pollems, Support points for German banks in Brussels, 3 March 1941; Becker (Bank Commissar of Brussels) to Abs, 17 March 1941, HADB, B128.
252 Cf. on the competition with the other banks the branch's report on 8 October 1941, HADB, B128.
253 Wald to Kimmich, 2 August 1940; Authorisation of the Head of the Civil Administration on 20 December 1940 for the acquisition of the shares of the Bank Générale of the Société Générale de Belgique, HADB, B101.
254 Franz Stiller (Brussels) to Abs, 29 August 1941, HADB, B154.
255 Memo Abs, 16 September 1941, HADB, B154.
256 Gall, *Abs*, pp. 79ff.
257 Memo Ulrich, 21 September 1943, HADB, B154.
258 Gall, *Abs*, pp. 88–93.
259 Naasner, *SS-Wirtschaft und SS-Verwaltung*.

260 Banken, *Edelmetallmangel und Großraubwirtschaft*.
261 Steinberg, *Gold Transactions*, pp. 39–58.
262 Ibid., p. 16; Deutsche Bank was thus slightly less involved in the gold transactions than Dresdner Bank; cf. on this Bähr, *Goldhandel der Dresdner Bank*.
263 Steinberg, *Gold Transactions*, p. 67.
264 Fest, *Hermann J. Abs*, p. 31.
265 Deutsche Bank, Annual Reports 1942 to 1944. See Bähr, *Modernes Bankrecht*, pp. 217–21.
266 Hook, *Entwicklung*, table 5.
267 Directors meeting on 25 March 1941 in Berlin concerning the full year results as of 31 December 1940, p. 5, HADB, SG5/8.
268 Memo, Besprechung der südwestdeutschen Filialen in Heidelberg, 9 May 1944, p. 2, HADB, SG5/8.
269 Bericht über die Halbjahressitzung in Berlin am 30 August 1938, p. 2, HADB, SG5/8.
270 Hook, *Entwicklung*, p. 45.
271 James, *The Nazi Dictatorship and the Deutsche Bank*, pp. 192–9.
272 Cf. Bähr, *'Bankenrationalisierung' und Großbankenfrage*; Bähr, *Modernes Bankrecht*.
273 Kopper, *Marktwirtschaft*, pp. 351–3.
274 Gall, *Abs*, pp. 114f.
275 Ibid., p. 115.
276 Deutsche Bank, Annual Report 1943, p. 2.
277 Directors meeting on 5 November 1942 in Berlin, p. 7, HADB, SG 5/8.
278 Sonderrundschreiben der Zentrale für die Direktoren der Hauptniederlassungen, S31/43, 17 November 1943, HADB, F63/250.
279 Personalbestand 1939–1944, HADB, B237.
280 Heimerzheim, *Karl Ritter von Halt*, pp. 126–8.
281 The material costs of the bombing were already estimated at RM 14 million in May 1944, cf. 'Aktennotiz über die Besprechung der südwestdeutschen Filialen in Heidelberg', 9 May 1944, p. 2, HADB, SG5/8.
282 One side effect was that the bank's personnel costs and cost of materials fell by RM 19 million between 1939 and 1944; pension commitments also declined during the war; cf. memo, 'Besprechung der südwestdeutschen Filialen in Heidelberg', 9 May 1944, p. 2, HADB, SG5/8.
283 James, *The Nazi Dictatorship and the Deutsche Bank*, p. 219.
284 Ibid., pp. 206–9.
285 Spoerer, *Zwangsarbeit*; Herbert, *Hitler's Foreign Workers*.
286 Schmidt, Aktennotiz zum Arbeitseinsatz, 9 August 1944, BArch, R 8119 F, 23981.
287 Müller, *Die Bank, ihre Akten und der Kalte Krieg*, p. 395.
288 Kopper, *Bankiers*, pp. 221–47, here pp. 222f.
289 Holtfrerich, *Deutsche Bank*, pp. 357ff.
290 Perhaps for this reason there was greater continuity at banks than in industry; cf. Joly, *Kontinuität*; Fiedler/Lorentz, *Kontinuitäten*, p. 67; Ruppmann, *Generationsforschung*, p. 42.
291 Seidenzahl, *100 Jahre*, pp. 375ff.
292 Quoted in Holtfrerich, *Deutsche Bank*, p. 397.
293 Ibid., p. 397ff.
294 Steinberg, *Gold Transactions*, pp. 65f.
295 Holtfrerich, *Deutsche Bank*, pp. 401–2 and 497. Deutsche Bank received a total of DM 416 million as compensation for defaulted debts of the Third Reich; Seidenzahl, *100 Jahre*, p. 385.
296 Scholtyseck, *Wiedervereinigung*.
297 In the British zone: Rheinisch-Westfälische Bank in Düsseldorf, Norddeutsche Bank in Hamburg and Nordwestbank in Hanover. In the French zone: Rheinische Kreditbank in Ludwigshafen, Oberrheinische Bank in Freiburg and Württembergische Vereinsbank in Reutlingen. The American military government established Bayerische Creditbank in Munich, Hessische Bank in Frankfurt and Südwestbank in Mannheim and Stuttgart.
298 Cf. Horstmann, *Alliierten*.
299 Plassmann to Oesterlink, 20 December 1949, HADB, NL39/3.
300 Ahrens, *Exempelkandidat*, p. 656.
301 This argument was advanced by the economist Ernst W. Schmidt in 1949: Memorandum, 'Die Dezentralisierung der Großbanken für die Sitzung des Bundestagsausschusses "Geld und Kredit"', 7 November 1949, HADB, ZA47/8 and V1/2027.
302 Memorandum, 'Filialgroßbanken', four pages, undated, HADB, V1/2027 and ZA47/64.
303 Hermann J. Abs, Carl Goetz and Paul Marx, 'Vorschlag betreffend die zukünftige Struktur der deutschen Aktienbanken', 31 May 1950, HADB, V1/2026 and ZA47/64.
304 Erhard Ulbricht, Die Deutsche Bank Ende 1937 und ihre Nachfolgebanken Ende 1953, 17 December 1956, HADB, V1/5169.
305 Seidenzahl, *100 Jahre*, pp. 385f.
306 Erhard Ulbricht, Die Deutsche Bank Ende 1937 und ihre Nachfolgebanken Ende 1953, 17 December 1956, HADB, V1/5169.
307 After the reunification of Deutsche Bank in 1957, Karl Ritter von Halt continued to serve the bank for several years, chairing its advisory council in Bavaria; Deutsche Bank, Annual Report 1958, p. 37.
308 Deutsche Bank, Annual Report 1957, p. 17; cf. Hannah, *Transformation*, pp. 199f.
309 Priemel, *Betrayal*; Wiesen, *West German Industry*.
310 Ahrens, *Exempelkandidat*; Ahrens, *Unternehmer*. See also Simpson, *War Crimes*.
311 Brünger, *Geschichte und Gewinn*, esp. pp. 145–7, 163–39, 214–16.
312 Mausbach, *Morgenthau*; Buchheim, *Wiedereingliederung*.
313 JCS 1067, Art. 47.
314 Holtfrerich, *Deutsche Bank*, p. 441.
315 The meeting was to discuss Adenauer's earlier financial claims against Deutsche Bank; Gall, *Abs*, pp. 124–6.
316 Ibid., pp. 137–9.
317 Schwarz, *Adenauer*, pp. 702f.; Conze et al., *Das Amt und die Vergangenheit*, pp. 443f.
318 Gall, *Abs*, p. 145.
319 Ibid., pp. 142–63.
320 Harries, *Financing the Future*, p. 36.
321 See Kobrak, *Banking on Global Markets*, p. 264f.
322 Personalakte Gdynia, HADB, P1/39.
323 Grünbaum, *Reconstruction*, p. 44; Pohl, *Wiederaufbau*.
324 Paul Krebs, HADB, SG18/12b.
325 Harries, *Financing the Future*, pp. 46–8.
326 Niederschrift über die Bankenbesprechung vom 14. November 1951 in der Rheinisch-Westfälischen Bank in Köln betreffend die Finanzierung mittel- und langfristiger Exportgeschäfte, 17 November 1951, p. 3, HADB, V1/2140.
327 Ibid. The consortium banks could declare their funds in the new institution as 'liabilities to banks'.
328 Rheinisch-Westfälische Bank, Einladungsschreiben betr.

Finanzierung mittel- und langfristiger Exportgeschäfte, 6 November 1951, p. 3, HADB, V1/2140.

329 Grünbacher, *Reconstruction*, pp. 234–57.

330 Kopper, *Bankiers*, p. 257; Holtfrerich, *Deutsche Bank*, p. 377.

331 Gall, *Abs*, pp. 193 and 229f.

332 Kopper, *Bankiers*, p. 254.

333 Gall, *Abs*, pp. 167ff.

334 See Rombeck-Jaschinski, *Schuldenabkommen*; Fisch, *Reparationen*; Buchheim, *Schuldenabkommen*.

335 Gall, *Abs*, p. 165.

336 Abs, *Entscheidungen*, p. 123.

337 Gall, *Abs*, pp. 171f.

338 Goschler, *Wiedergutmachung*, pp. 257ff.; Wolffsohn, *Globalentschädigung*; Wolffsohn, *Wiedergutmachungsabkommen*.

339 Gall, *Abs*, pp. 176f. The agreement with Israel was highly contentious for German politicians and only ratified in the Bundestag with the help of the SPD. Cf. Wolffsohn, *Globalentschädigung*; Wolffsohn, *Wiedergutmachungsabkommen*.

340 Guinnane, 'Financial Vergangenheitsbewältigung'.

341 Abs, *Entscheidungen*, pp. 175–9.

342 See Abs's comments in: Niederschrift über die Besprechung betreffend die Auslandsabteilung und Aussenhandelsfragen am 9. Mai 1952 im Hause der Hessischen Bank, Frankfurt-Main, 12 May 1952, pp. 1–2, HADB, V1/2006.

343 Abs, *Entscheidungen*, pp. 143–54. For a detailed financial analysis of the agreement, see Galofré-Vilà et al., *The Economic Consequences*.

344 Fisch, *Reparationen*, pp. 117–29.

345 Tooze, *Reassessing*, p. 56. On the financial burden of debt repayment and reparations, see Deutsche Bundesbank, *Deutsches Geld- und Bankwesen*, pp. 342–4.

346 Abs, *Entscheidungen*, pp. 197–202.

347 Gall, *Abs*, p. 197.

348 Galofré-Vilà et al., *The Economic Consequences*.

349 Kopper, *Bankiers*, p. 253.

350 Abs, *Entscheidungen*, p. 55.

351 Kobrak, *Banking on Global Markets*, pp. 266ff.

352 Abs, *Aktuelle internationale Finanzierungsfragen*, p. 395.

353 Guinnane, 'Financial Vergangenheitsbewältigung'.

354 Gall, *Abs*, p. 192.

355 The German Foreign Exchange Act of 1938 remained in force until September 1949 and was replaced by the Allied foreign exchange rules; Wolf, *Währungsreform*, p. 73; on the continuity, see Gross, *Gold*.

356 Eichengreen, *Globalizing Capital*, pp. 106–9.

357 Wolf, *Währungsreform*, p. 109.

358 Bericht 'Zentrale/Auslandsabteilung' (o. D.), p. 2, HADB, V1/2014.

359 Protokoll über die Außenhandelssitzung der Schwesterbanken, 14–15 September 1953, p. 28f., HADB, V1/2007.

360 Bericht v. Osterwind in der Besprechung über die Auslandsabteilung und Außenhandelsfragen, 9 May 1952, p. 4, HADB, V1/2006.

361 Holtfrerich, *Deutsche Bank*, p. 518.

362 Ibid., p. 501.

363 Protokoll der Außenhandelssitzung der Schwesterbanken, 14–15 September 1953, HADB, V1/2007.

364 Osterwind, Bericht über das Auslandsgeschäft in der Außenhandels-Fachherrensitzung, 19 March 1954, p. 6, HADB, V1/2006.

365 Given the large number of existing accounts, it was decided on 13 April 1954 to 'exercise great restraint when opening new nostro accounts as saturation point appeared to have been reached'; Comments by Regling, Aussprache unter den Schwesterbanken, 12 February 1957, p. 9, HADB, V1/2011.

366 Protokoll über die Außenhandels-Fachherrensitzung am 19 March 1954, p. 1, HADB, V1/2006.

367 Bericht 'Zentrale/Auslandabteilung' (o. D.), p. 3, HADB, V1/2014.

368 Protokoll über die Außenhandels-Fachherrensitzung am 12 November 1953, HADB, V1/2006.

369 Ressorteinteilungen des Vorstandes, 2 January 1954, HADB, ZA16/x40.

370 Bericht 'Zentrale/Auslandsabteilung' (o. D.), pp. 1–2, HADB, V1/2014.

371 See, for example, the extent of the foreign trips planned for 1956, Protokoll der Aussprache der Schwesterbanken über Fragen des Auslandsgeschäftes am 12 December 1955, pp. 4f. HADB, V1/2009.

372 Aussprache über Fragen des Auslandsgeschäfts, 14 January 1953, pp. 1f., HADB, V1/2007.

373 Ibid., pp. 6f., 11.

374 Regling, Dezentrale Bearbeitung des Auslandsgeschäftes nach Fusion, 4 April 1957, p. 1, HADB, ZA1/146; Ulrich's words at the meeting of the head offices and foreign departments had a similar thrust, 4 February 1958, p. 1, HADB, V1/2012.

375 Pirkham to Abs/Osterwind, Neuorganisation des Auslandsgeschäftes der drei Zentralen der Deutschen Bank, 13 June 1957; Osterwind, Gedanken zur Organisation des Auslandsgeschäfts, Frühjahr 1957; Pirkham to Abs/Osterwind, Zentrale Erfassung des Engagements ausländischer Banken, 15 April 1957, HADB, ZA1/146.

376 Memo, Organisation der drei Zentralen, 1 June 1959; Geschäftsordnung für den Vorstand, July 1957, HADB, V2/146.

377 Bericht 'Das Auslandsgeschäft' (o. D.), HADB, V5/25-1

378 Ulrich, Note about meeting between Abs, Klasen, Osterwind and Ulrich on 30 June 1958 concerning foreign business, 2 July 1958, p. 3, HADB, V2/144.

379 Besprechung über die Auslandsabteilung und Außenhandelsfragen, 9 May 1952, p. 3; Protokoll der Sitzung der Auslands-Fachherren am 19 March 1954, HADB, V1/2006.

380 Aussprache unter den Schwesterbanken über Fragen des Auslandsgeschäftes, 13 October 1955, p. 7, HADB, V1/2009.

381 Kopper/Pohl/Rebentisch, *Stationen*, p. 110.

382 BAT, Annual Report 1943–1958, pp. 13f.

383 Report by Regling, Außenhandelssitzung der Schwesterbanken, 14–15 September 1953, pp. 30f., HADB, V1/2007.

384 Ausführungen Osterwinds auf der Zusammenkunft der Außenhandelsfachherren des Bereiches der Zentrale Frankfurt, 28 March 1960, p. 3, HADB, ZA1/152.

385 Ausführungen Abs auf der Besprechung über die Auslandsabteilung und Außenhandelsfragen am 9 May 1952, p. 2, HADB, V1/2006.

386 Gall, *Abs*, p. 260ff.

387 Ibid., p. 265.

388 Feldman, *Austrian Banks*, pp. 390–1.

389 Protokoll der Außenhandelssitzung, 6 October 1954, pp. 10f., HADB, V1/2009; Sattler, *Vermögensfragen*, pp. 213f.

390 Historische Gesellschaft der Deutschen Bank e.V. (Hg.), *100 Jahre Deutsche Bank in Istanbul*, pp. 61, 66.

391 Gall, *Abs*, pp. 271f.

392 Kleinschmidt, Außenwirtschaftsbeziehungen; Kleinschmidt/Atilgan (eds), *Wirtschaftsbeziehungen*.

393 Ulrich, Note about meeting between Abs, Klasen, Osterwind and Ulrich on 30 June 1958 concerning foreign business, 2 July 1958, HADB, V2/144.

394 Protokoll der Außenhandelssitzung der Schwesterbanken, 14–15 September 1953, p. 15, HADB, V1/2007.

395 See speech by Goldenberg on the occasion of the meeting of the foreign trade experts, 13 April 1956 and Memo by Goldenberg, 20 April 1956, HADB, V1/2006.

396 On the economic effects of European integration, see Ambrosius, *Integration*.

397 Arbeitstagung der Auslandabteilungen, 16 January 1959, HADB, V1/2013.

398 Protokoll der Außenhandelssitzung, 6 October 1954, p. 12, HADB, V1/2009.

399 Ulrich, Note about meeting between Abs, Klasen, Osterwind and Ulrich on 30 June 1958 concerning foreign business, 2 July 1958, HADB, V2/144.

400 Pollems to Abs, 5 August 1955; Note by Bindert, 23 November 1959; Abs to Schaefer, 8 December 1959, HADB, V1/4034.

401 Pohl, *Geschäft*, pp. 111ff.; see also Spaulding, *Reconquering*.

402 Lahr to Wolf von Amerongen, 26 August 1963; Wolf von Amerongen to Abs, 4 September 1963, HADB, V1/4034.

403 Bauert-Keetman, *Unternehmens-Chronik*, pp. 197ff.

404 Ibid., pp. 230ff.; Plumpe, *Deutsche Bank in East Asia*, p. 78.

405 DAB, supervisory board minutes, 24 November 1950, HADB, K7/31/I-1; Report 'Deutsch-Asiatische Bank' (o. D.), HADB, V1/653.

406 Abs in the foreign trade meeting on 14–15 September 1953, p. 13, HADB, V1/2007.

407 Bernardini, *Pragmatism*, p. 90.

408 Bericht der Deutsch-Asiatischen Bank, Mai 1953, p. 5f., HADB, V1/654; on the Ostausschuss, see Rudolph, *Wirtschaftsdiplomatie*.

409 Norddeutsche Bank to Abs, 6 January 1955, HADB, V1/653; Bernardini, *Pragmatism*. pp. 100–106.

410 Memo, 9 June 1954, HADB, V10/207.

411 Bauert-Keetman, *Unternehmens-Chronik*, pp. 230ff.

412 Ibid.

413 Witting's report to Klasen on meetings in Hong Kong, 29 October 1957, HADB, V10/208.

414 Aussprache unter den Schwesterbanken über Fragen des Auslandsgeschäftes, 6 October 1954, p. 11, HADB, V1/2009.

415 Report by Wittings to Klasen about his trip to Japan, 31 October 1957, HADB, V10/208.

416 Kobrak, *Banking on Global Markets*, pp. 262–5.

417 See, for example, Brunner (Arnhold and S. Bleichroeder, New York) to Klasen betr. Kooperation mit der DAB, 25 May 1954, HADB, V10/207.

418 Ulrich, Note about meeting between Abs, Klasen, Osterwind and Ulrich on 30 June 1958 concerning foreign business, 2 July 1958, p. 2, HADB, V2/144.

419 Ibid.

420 Personnel file of Wolff, HADB, K8/119.

421 Two other Deutsche Bank representatives also joined the supervisory board in 1959: Ulrich and Osterwind; Ulrich, Note about meeting between Abs, Klasen, Osterwind and Ulrich on 30 June 1958 concerning foreign business, 2 July 1958, p. 2, HADB, V2/144.

422 BAT, Annual Report 1961, p. 13.

423 Pohl, *Deutsche Bank Buenos Aires*, pp. 92–108.

424 BAT's shareholding in 1953 was 10 per cent and increased to 22 per cent by 1966; Abs to Management Board of Deutsche Bank, 28 November 1967, HADB, V25/x438.

425 Ulrich to Osterwind, 13 November 1962, HADB, V10/47. However, Deutsche Bank offered the Spanish banks favourable borrowing facilities. In 1959, these already amounted to DM 20 million; Arbeitstagung der Auslandsabteilungen, 16 January 1959, HADB, V1/2013.

426 BAT, Annual Report 1943–1958, p. 14.

427 Ibid., pp. 12f.

428 BAT, Annual Report 1960, p. 11.

429 BAT, Annual Report 1961, pp. 11f.

430 BAT, Annual Report 1959, p. 12 and 1960, p. 11. Deutsche Bank's share in West Germany's Latin American business had already reached 17.4 per cent by 1959, see Thierbach to Ulrich, 24 June 1966, HADB, V10/47.

431 The project's total costs of DM 35 million would probably have overstretched BAT. Ulrich, Note about meeting between Abs, Klasen, Osterwind and Ulrich on 30 June 1958 concerning foreign business, 2 July 1958, p. 2, HADB, V2/144.

432 BAT, Annual Report 1963, p. 10.

433 Gall, *Abs*, pp. 301ff.

434 Investitionen der DB in ihren Beteiligungen im Ausland, undated, HADB, V5/22.

435 Gall, *Abs*, pp. 294f.

436 Arbeitstagung der Auslandsabteilungen, 16 January 1959, p. 3, HADB, V1/2013.

437 Abs, *Schutz*, p. 78.

438 Deutsche Bank, Annual Report 1959, p. 20.

439 Gall, *Abs*, pp. 314f.

440 In 1966, for example, the bank issued a DM 100 million warrant bond on behalf of the South African Highveld Steel and Vanadium Corporation; Büschgen, *Deutsche Bank*, p. 677.

441 Gall, *Abs*, pp. 280ff.

442 Memo, 'Einiges über das Auslandsgeschäft der Deutschen Bank', 29 October 1963, p. 1, HADB, V5/22.

443 Report, 'Das Auslandsgeschäft' (o.D.), HADB, V5/25-1.

444 Osterwind at the meeting of the foreign trade experts, 28 March 1960, p. 2, HADB, ZA1/152.

445 Bericht 'Das Auslandsgeschäft' (o.D.), p. 7, HADB, V5/25-1.

III. Deutschland AG: Rhenish Capitalism and the World Market

1 Full Management Board meetings took place twice a month until the late 1960s, then weekly, usually on a Tuesday.

2 Deutsche Bank, Annual Report 1967, p. 28.

3 Supervisory Board minutes, 26 January 1971, p. 5, HADB, V1/575.

4 Büger/Lamberti, *Lessons*, p. 35.

5 Weiss, Interview, 29 October 2013, HADB, ZA17.

6 Platthaus, *Herrhausen*, p. 96.

7   McKinsey had previously made overtures to Deutsche Bank in the mid-1960s. Unlike with Dresdner Bank, however, these did not lead to long-term co-operation; cf. correspondence between Ulrich and John G. McDonald (Managing Director at McKinsey), February 1965, HADB, ZA47/644. In 1980, McKinsey analysed the bank's overheads to identify possible cost savings at head office; Maßfeller to Management Board secretaries, 26 February 1980, HADB, V1/643. On the role of management consulting firms in the bank reforms since the 1960s, cf. Kipping/Westerhuis, *Managerialization*.

8   Büschgen, *Deutsche Bank*, pp. 550f.

9   Ferslev, Interview, 1 April 2014, HADB, ZA17.

10 Barkhausen, Notiz über Besprechung der Personaldezernenten, 8 May 1974, HADB, V12/x432.

11 Ibid.

12 Die Auslandsfilialen der Deutschen Bank, Proposal for the meeting of the Management Board on 16 October 1979, 12 October 1979, HADB, V25/x682.

13 Thierbach to Management Board, 29 June 1976, HADB, V25/x668.

14 Zentrale Planungsabteilung, Stand des internationalen Geschäftes der DB-Gruppe in 1978, 15 August 1979, HADB, V25/x668.

15 Central Foreign Department, 31 December 1969, HADB, V1/2864.

16 Hollenberg to Thierbach, 23 July 1973, HADB, V5/110.

17 Aussprache über das Auslandsgeschäft, 1 December 1972, HADB, V5/110.

18 Cartellieri, Überlegungen zu unserem Auslandsgeschäft, 17 May 1972, HADB, V5/110.

19 Das Auslandsgeschäft im Jahre 1970, HADB, V5/16.

20 Mertin to Ulrich, 27 November 1969, HADB, V10/94.

21 Ulrich to Thierbach, 27 November 1969, HADB, V10/94.

22 Hollenberg to Thierbach, 28 December 1971, HADB, V5/110.

23 Blessing/Behrendt to Thierbach, 19 June 1973, HADB, V5/110.

24 Arbeitskreis Ausland, Das internationale Geschäft der Deutschen Bank, June 1976, p. 11, HADB, V25/x668.

25 Thierbach/Kopper, Organisatorische Umstrukturierung im internationalen Geschäft (March 1977), HADB, V25/x668.

26 Geschäftsverteilungsplan, 'Zentrale/Internationale Abteilung' (March 1977), HADB, V5/110.

27 Mohr, Bilanzberichterstattung Auslandsfilialen, 25 July 1978, HADB, V30/351.

28 Aussprache über das Auslandsgeschäft, 14 November 1979, p. 8, HADB, V30/351.

29 Bericht über die Untersuchung der Zentrale Auslandsabteilung (1971), HADB, V5/25; Hollenberg, Planung und Organisation der ZAA und des Auslandsgeschäftes der DB in den 70iger Jahren, 5 June 1974, HADB, V5/110.

30 Aussprache über das Auslandsgeschäft, 1 December 1972, HADB, V5/110.

31 Ibid., 7 December 1969, HADB, ZA1/199. From 1957 to 1971, Osterwind was the Management Board member with primary responsibility for international business.

32 Wagner to Thierbach, 2 March 1979; Hollenberg/Rehbaum, Entwicklung im internationalen Geschäft, 25 January 1979, HADB, V5/25-1.

33 Ibid. and Kunder to Thierbach, 6 December 1973; 'Mitarbeiter im Ausland' (as of January 1979), HADB, V5/25-1.

34 Das internationale Geschäft der Deutschen Bank, June 1976, pp. 18–20, HADB, V25/x668.

35 Ibid., p. 20.

36 Weiterbildung Bereich Ausland, report 1977, HADB, V5/25.

37 Circular letter to the personnel managers of the main branches, 30 November 1976; Dorner/Osenberg, circular dated 29 June 1977, HADB, V5/25.

38 Guth, Anmerkungen zur Konzernentwicklung, 28 March 1985, p. 11, HADB, ZA18/x698.

39 Deutsche Bank, Annual Report 1988, p. 41.

40 Breuer, Interview, 21 June 2013, HADB, ZA17.

41 Weiss, Interview, 29 October 2013, HADB, ZA17.

42 Michael Endres received the support of Robet Ehret, Hans Feith and Stuttgart director Nikolaus Kunkel as well as Wilfried Guth and F. Wilhelm Christians; Endres, Interview, 12 September 2013, HADB, ZA17.

43 Cf. Weiss, Interview, 29 October 2013, HADB, ZA17: 'My friends advised me (and it was good advice) that if you want to get anywhere at Deutsche Bank, you must at least have worked in the lending business and be able to point to it on your CV; after all, the lending business is the sine qua non of banking.'

44 Weiss, Interview, 29 October 2013, HADB, ZA17. Promotions throughout the entire bank were announced on two set dates a year.

45 Kopper, Interview, 6 March 2013, HADB, ZA17.

46 Osenberg, Interview, 1 April 2014, HADB, ZA17. On HR policy in general, see Büschgen, *Deutsche Bank*, pp. 553ff.

47 Endres, Interview, 12 September 2013, HADB, ZA17.

48 Platthaus, *Herrhausen*, p. 115.

49 Sattler, *Ernst Matthiensen und Alfred Herrhausen*, p. 308.

50 Weiss, Interview, 29 October 2013, HADB, ZA17.

51 Osenberg, Interview, 1 April 2014, HADB, ZA17.

52 Breuer, Interview, 21 June 2013, HADB, ZA17.

53 Platthaus, *Herrhausen*, pp. 160 and 239; there was evidently considerable disagreement between Christians and Herrhausen; cf. Kopper, Interview, 6 March 2013, HADB, ZA17.

54 Platthaus, *Herrhausen*, p. 90.

55 Cf. Bosetzky, *Mikropolitik*.

56 Breuer, Interview, 21 June 2013; Weiss, Interview, 29 October 2013, HADB, ZA17.

57 Krupp, Interview, 2 July 2013, HADB, ZA17.

58 Osenberg, Interview, 1 April 2014, HADB, ZA17.

59 Kopper, Interview, 6 March 2013, HADB, ZA17.

60 Büschgen, *Deutsche Bank*, p. 566.

61 Organisationsplan, 1 September 1972; Geschäftsverteilungsplan, April 1977, HADB, SG8/14.

62 Dividend payments in per cent lasted until 1976.

63 Büschgen, *Deutsche Bank*, pp. 571–81.

64 Chandler, *Strategy and Structure*.

65 Ahrens, *Identitätsmanagement*; Ramm, *Organisationsstrukturen*, p. 6.

66 Ferslev, *Recollections*, p. 33.

67 Albrecht/Endres/Hess/Schaub to Guth and Christians, 13 February 1985, HADB, ZA25/x27. According to the recollections of Endres, Guth and Christians were soon to leave the bank anyway and had little interest in the project, while Herrhausen took the view that this work should instead be given to one of the bank's departments; Endres, Interview, 12 September 2013, HADB, ZA17.

68 Cf. Kapitel III.3.

69 Herrhausen to Management Board, 9 December 1985, HABD, ZA47/625.

70 Strategische Konzernentwicklung, 1 October 1986, HADB, ZA18/x698.
71 Ferslev, Aurora – Ortsbestimmung, 9 August 1985, HADB, ZA18/58.
72 Herrhausen, *Koordinierung und Steuerung des Konzerns, in: db-aktuell 112 (1986)*, pp. 13–15, here p. 14.
73 Büschgen, *Deutsche Bank*, p. 535.
74 Endres, Interview, 12 September 2013, HADB, ZA17.
75 Breuer, Interview, 21 June 2013; cf. also Krupp, Interview, 2 July 2013, HADB, ZA17.
76 Interview, Frowein, 24 July 2014, HADB, ZA17.
77 Rede Koppers vor leitenden Angestellten der Bank, 19 December 1989, p. 1, HADB, V40/x207.
78 Pfaff in the Supervisory Board meeting on 3 July 1990, p. 23, HADB, V17/x94; cf. also Strukturprojekt, annex for the Management Board meeting on 27 March 1990, V40/x173; Weiss, Vorschläge zur Organisation und Kostensenkung, 19 January 1984, HADB, ZA18/58.
79 Deutsche Bank, Annual Report 1988, p. 40.
80 Strategische Planung, Notiz von Schultze-Kimmle, 1 October 1986, p. 13, HADB, ZA18/x698.
81 Feldman, *Deutsche Bank*, p. 267.
82 See chapter II.4. and Hook, *Entwicklung*, p. 45.
83 Holtfrerich, *Deutsche Bank*, p. 508.
84 On the following, see Gonser, *Kapitalismus*; Büschgen, *Deutsche Bank*, p. 699.
85 Erhard Ulbricht, Die Deutsche Bank Ende 1937 und ihre Nachfolgebanken Ende 1953, 17 December 1956, HADB, V1/5169.
86 Frost, *Wünsche*, pp. 47f.
87 Cf. Jansen to Ulrich u. Klasen betr. Kleinkundengeschäft der First National City Bank, 17 August 1955, HADB, SG8/16.
88 Besprechung wegen Kreditorenwerbung, 19 April 1956, HADB, SG8/16.
89 Logemann, *Americanization*.
90 Competition from American banks was much discussed at management level; cf. Thierbach, Konkurrenz von Filialen US-Amerikanischer Banken in Deutschland, 25 April 1957, HADB, V5/21; Thierbach to Ulrich, 10 December 1964, HADB, V10/47; Management Board minutes, 11–12 February 1965 and 31 March/1 April 1965, HADB, V10/73; see Sattler, *Investmentsparen*, pp. 47f.
91 Ambrosius, *Wachstum*, p. 157.
92 Supervisory Board minutes, 9 January 1970, p. 6, HADB, V1/573.
93 Büschgen, *Deutsche Bank*, p. 710.
94 Logemann, *Different Paths*, pp. 529ff.
95 Frost, *Wünsche*, p. 79.
96 Deutsche Bank, Annual Report 1969, pp. 31 and 40.
97 Frost, *Wünsche*, pp. 81ff.
98 Supervisory Board minutes, 26 January 1971, p. 7, HADB, V1/575.
99 Frost, *Wünsche*, pp. 70f.
100 Marktanteil Inlandsgeschäft 1970–1980, Anhang A III-7, HADB, ZA4/x877; cf. also Supervisory Board minutes, 11 July 1978, p. 7, HADB, V1/574.
101 Besprechung wegen Kreditorenwerbung, 19 April 1956, HADB, SG8/16.
102 See also Bähr, *Errichtung*.
103 Frost, *Wünsche*, p. 75.
104 Besprechung wegen Kreditorenwerbung, 19 April 1956, p. 3, HADB, SG8/16.
105 Deutsche Bundesbank, Deutsches Geld- und Bankwesen, pp. 306-8; Sattler, Investmentsparen, pp. 64f.

106 Cf. ibid., pp. 58f.
107 Müller, *DWS*, p. 77.
108 Notiz Sekretariat Düsseldorf betr. EWG-Broschüre 'Der Aufbau eines Europäischen Kapitalmarktes' vom November 1966, 12 October 1967, p. 5, HADB, ZA43/17.
109 Müller, *DWS*, pp. 102–8.
110 Deutsche Bank, Annual Report 1967, p. 20.
111 Müller, *DWS*, pp. 109–13.
112 Dietrich, *Vermögenspolitik*.
113 Linder, *Volksaktienbewegung*, p. 107; Edelmann, *Privatisierung*, p. 71.
114 Büschgen, *Deutsche Bank*, p. 719.
115 Müller, *DWS*, p. 259.
116 Ambrosius, *Wachstum*, p. 158; Pohl/Jachmich, *Verschärfung*, pp. 207f.
117 Ibid., p. 216.
118 Tatsachen und Zahlen zur vorgesehenen Änderung der Besteuerung von Kreditinstituten, 4 October 1967, HADB, ZA40/88.
119 Abs to Federal Minister of Finance Franz J. Strauß, 18 May 1967; Note, Besprechung im Bundesaufsichtsamt für das Kreditwesen am 3. Februar 1967, 13 February 1967, HADB, V1/3769.
120 Janberg to Vierhub (Dresdner Bank), 13 February 1967, HADB, V1/3769.
121 Bundesverband des Privaten Bankgewerbes, Steuerprivilegien im Kreditgewerbe, Rundschreiben 28 July 1967, HADB, ZA40/88; cf. also Deutsche Bank, Annual Report 1967, p. 19.
122 Supervisory Board minutes, 21 October 1970, p. 3, and 26 January 1971, p. 4, HADB, V1/573.
123 Supervisory Board minutes, 27 March 1974, p. 3, HADB, V1/573.
124 Zentrale Planungs-Abteilung, Die Bank im Markt (1978), HADB, ZA4/x877.
125 Christians in the Supervisory Board meeting on 25 January 1977, p. 3, HADB, V1/574.
126 Zentrale Planungsabteilung, Die Bank im Markt (1978), p. 1, HADB, ZA4/x877.
127 Supervisory Board minutes, 21 October 1970, p. 3, and 26 January 1971, p. 5, HADB, V1/573.
128 Deutsche Bank, Annual Report 1979, p. 33.
129 Zentrale Planungsabteilung, Die Bank im Markt (1978), Anhang II-1, HADB, ZA4/x877.
130 On the decline in the commercial banking business, see Kleffel's remarks in the Supervisory Board meeting on 27 October 1976, p. 13, HADB, V1/574.
131 Zentrale Planungsabteilung, Die Bank im Markt (1978), appendix II-1, HADB, ZA4/x877; see also the remarks by Christians in the Supervisory Board meeting on 30 January 1984, p. 6, HADB, V1/576.
132 Marktanteil Inlandsgeschäft 1970-1980, HADB, ZA4/x877; comments by van Hoovens at the Supervisory Board meeting on 5 July 1982, pp. 7ff., HADB, V1/576.
133 Ibid.
134 Frost, *Wünsche*, pp. 202–5.
135 Supervisory Board minutes, 21 October 1981, p. 10, HADB, V1/575.
136 Van Hooven in the Supervisory Board meeting on 5 July 1982, p. 8, HADB, V1/576.
137 Supervisory Board minutes, 21 October 1981, p. 11, HADB, V1/575.
138 Supervisory Board minutes, 8 April 1975, HADB, V1/574.
139 Comments by Zapp in the Supervisory Board meeting on 30 January 1984, p. 11, HADB, V1/576.

140 Van Hooven in the Supervisory Board meeting on 5 July 1982, pp. 10f., HADB, V1/576.
141 Lamberti/Büger, *Lessons*, pp. 35–7.
142 Deutsche Bank, Annual Report 1987, p. 37.
143 Ibid., p. 38.
144 Discussion in the Supervisory Board meeting on 22 October 1979, p. 10, HADB, V1/575.
145 Weiss, *Probleme*. See comments by Weiss in the Supervisory Board meeting on 21 October 1981, p. 12, HADB, V1/575.
146 Supervisory Board minutes, 21 October 1981, p. 10, HADB, V1/575.
147 Supervisory Board minutes, 5 July 1982, p. 3, HADB, V1/576.
148 Deutsche Bank, Annual Report 1987, pp. 41 and 56.
149 Büschgen, *Deutsche Bank*, p. 727.
150 Deutsche Bank, Annual Report 1988, p. 35.
151 Supervisory Board minutes, 14 December 1988, p. 5, HADB, V1/620.
152 Büschgen, *Deutsche Bank*, pp. 728–31; Supervisory Board minutes, 21 October 1992, HADB, V17/x94.
153 Supervisory Board minutes, 27 January 1987, p. 9, HADB, V1/620.
154 Weiss, Unsere Geschäftspolitik in Italien, Spanien und Portugal, 24 January 1989, p. 10, HADB, V32/x331.
155 Van Hooven to Christians, Herrhausen and Kopper, 6 October 1986, HADB, ZA47/540.
156 However, the branch opened in Paris in 1977 explicitly did not handle retail banking business; see remarks by Frowein, Aussprache über das Auslandsgeschäft am 6 October 1977, HADB, V5/111.
157 Aufnahme des Privatkundengeschäftes durch die DB Lux, Proposal for the Mangement Board meeting on 8 July 1986, dated June 1986, HADB, ZA47/551; see Kopper, *Reiche Deutsche*.
158 Quote by Ronaldo Schmitz in the Supervisory Board meeting on 29 October 1997, p. 5, HADB, V40/x110; Weiss/Schmitz to Supervisory Board, 29 September 1997, HADB, V50/434; Annex to the letter from Weiss to Emilio Botín (Santander), 6 December 1996, HADB, V32/x161.
159 Weiss, Unsere Geschäftspolitik in Italien, Spanien und Portugal, 24 January 1989, Anlage Spanien, HADB, V32/x331.
160 Blessing, Vertretung der Deutschen Bank in Mailand, 4 April 1974, HADB, ZA47/574; Blessing/Minners, Errichtung einer Niederlassung in Italien, 8 September 1978, HADB, ZA1/97-1; Proposal for Thierbach, Errichtung einer Niederlassung in Italien, 14 November 1978, HADB, ZA47/540.
161 Van Hooven to Christians, Herrhausen and Kopper, 6 October 1986, HADB, ZA47/540.
162 Weiss, Unsere Geschäftspolitik in Italien, Spanien und Portugal, 24 January 1989, Anlage Italien, HADB, V32/x331.
163 Aktennotiz Deutsche Bank – Italien, 3 October 1984; Memo 'Banca Cattolica del Veneto' for Kopper for the Management Board meeting on 6 November 1984; Kopper to the President of the Banca d'Italia Ciampi, 15 November 1984, HADB, V40/x77.
164 Ferslev and Vontz to Kopper, 27 October 1986, HADB, ZA47/540.
165 Vontz and Ferslev, Proposal for the Supervisory Board, 20 November 1986, HADB, ZA47/540.
166 'Vergleich der Banca d'America e d'Italia (BAI) mit unseren Filialbezirken', Bericht der Zentrale/Rechnung und Planung to Management Board, 16 December 1986, HADB, ZA18/318.
167 Vontz and Ferslev, Proposal for the Supervisory Board, 20 November 1986, HADB, ZA47/540.
168 Erwerb der Banca Popolare di Lecco SpA (BPL) durch die Banca d'America e d'Italia (BAI) zum Preis von bis zu DM 800 Mio, Vorlage der Abteilung für Konzernentwicklung, 8 October 1993, p. 1, HADB, V17/x94.
169 Kopper/Weiss to Supervisory Board, 29 May 1995, HADB, V32/x366.
170 Vontz and Ferslev, Proposal for the Supervisory Board, 20 November 1986, p. 5, HADB, ZA47/540; Christians in the Supervisory Board meeting on 1 December 1986, p. 4, HADB, V1/620.
171 Deutsche Bank SAE Working-Meeting Commercial Banking – Strategic Plan 1996–1998, 27 November 1995, HADB, V32/x171; Retail Banking – 'The Experiences of Deutsche Bank Spain', 30 January 1997, HADB, V32/x161.
172 Von Boehm-Bezing/von Heydebreck to Supervisory Board, Erwerb des Crédit Lyonnais Belgium, 17 November 1998, HADB, V40/x111; quote in annex, p. 2.
173 Deutsche Bank Polska SA (DB Polska), Proposal for the Management Board meeting on 9 July 1996, 4 July 1996, HADB, V24/x301.
174 Frost, *Wünsche*, pp. 140–53.
175 Kopper, *Strategische Ausrichtung*.
176 Kabinettsausschuß für Wirtschaft, Band 1. 1951–1953.
177 Abs continued to serve on the Supervisory board after 1967.
178 See Christians, *Wege*.
179 Platthaus, *Herrhausen*, pp. 133–50 and passim.
180 On the differences between Erhard and Abs see Gall, *Abs*, pp. 240ff; Hentschel, *Erhard*.
181 Berghahn, *Americanisation*, pp. 152–79; Hüttenberger, *Wirtschaftsordnung*, p. 302.
182 Gall, *Abs*, p. 331.
183 Stock Corporation Act, 6 September 1965, BGBl. I, p. 1089.
184 Abs to Management Board with list of mandates, 24 September 1968, HADB, V10/94; see Gall, *Abs*, pp. 330–50.
185 Gall, *Abs*, pp. 399–406; Brünger, *Geschichte und Gewinn*.
186 Ibid., pp. 209–14, 355–360; Feldman, *Deutsche Bank*, Introduction, pp. xviii–xx.
187 Gall, *Abs*, pp. 408–39.
188 Zapp, Proposal for the Management Board meeting, 1 October 1979, p. 1, HADB, V35/x548 (underlining in the original).
189 Platthaus, *Herrhausen*, p. 138. See also Rother, *Kunstförderung*.
190 Kunst in der Bank. Das Kunstkonzept der Deutschen Bank, 21 November 1986, HADB, V35/x548.
191 Van Hooven, *Meistbegünstigt*, p. 64.
192 Stenographic minutes on the press conference on the 1973 financial statements, 2 April 1974, pp. 20f., HADB, ZA3/x169.
193 *Bild*, 17 April 1974.
194 Sattler, *Wissenschaftsförderung*, pp. 603f.
195 Platthaus, *Herrhausen*, p. 140.
196 Ibid., pp. 139–42.
197 This was also coming increasingly from abroad: see 'The Power of the German banks', *The Economist*, 14 November 1970.

198 Guth, *Verantwortung der Banken*; see also Sattler, *Stabilisierung*.
199 Interview with Franz H. Ulrich, *Capital*, 1 June 1970.
200 Interview with Herrhausen, *Der Spiegel*, 18 June 1979, pp. 81–5, here p. 81.
201 Exchange of letters between Ulrich and Ministerial Director Wilhelm Hankel (Federal Ministry of Economics), January 1970, HADB, ZA47/625.
202 Mertin, *Ausgliederung industrieller Beteiligungen aus der Bank*, 16 April 1970, HADB, ZA18/58.
203 Grawert-May, *Börsenkapitalisierung der drei Großbanken und ihrer Beteiligungen*, 5 September 1975, HADB, V1/600. Including the temporarily held Flick shares in Daimler-Benz, the market value of the industrial shareholdings was as high as DM 6 billion.
204 *Mitgeteilte Aktienbestände und GmbH-Anteile* (as of 31 January 1965), HADB, ZA47/625.
205 *Bericht to Ulrich*, 29 March 1974, HADB, V6/100.
206 See *Bestandsentwicklung der inländischen Schachtelbeteiligungen ab 1948* (Stand 1 March 1983), HADB, V6/100.
207 *Industrie-Schachtelbeteiligungen per 31 December 1969*, HADB, ZA18/58.
208 Ahrens/Bähr, *Ponto*, pp. 131ff.
209 Mertin, *Ausgliederung industrieller Beteiligungen aus der Bank*, 16 April 1970, HADB, ZA18/58.
210 Siara (Zentrale Steuer-Abteilung), *Memo dated 9 February 1973*, HADB, ZA18/59.
211 Mertin, *Ausgliederung industrieller Beteiligungen aus der Bank*, 16 April 1970, HADB, ZA18/58.
212 Ulrich to Abs and die Vorstände, 4 March 1970, HADB, ZA47/625; see Supervisory Board minutes, 30 January 1973, pp. 10–11, HADB, V1/573.
213 'Schmidt gegen Banken', *Wirtschaftswoche*, 29 June 1973. However, this was not regarded as promising from a constitutional perspective; see Werner to Ulrich, 29 June 1973, HADB, V6/100.
214 Ulrich, *Industrieller Aktienbesitz der Geschäftsbanken*, 10 July 1973, HADB, V6/100. See also Presse-Information, 11 March 1974, HADB, ZA47/625.
215 Pöhl to Ulrich, 19 March 1974, and annex, 19 March 1974, HADB, ZA47/625.
216 See Sattler, *Stabilisierung*.
217 Ahrens/Bähr, *Ponto*, p. 201.
218 Report 'Monopolkommission', 26 July 1976, HADB, V6/100; Reply by Dr Christians to Graf Lambsdorff, 17 April 1979, HADB, ZA47/625.
219 Bundesministerium der Finanzen (ed.), *Bericht der Studienkommission*.
220 Hahn, *Energiekrise*, pp. 255f.
221 'Panic over', *The Economist*, 26 May 1979.
222 Ahrens/Bähr, *Ponto*, pp. 186–9. The Quandt family had previously offered the shares to Deutsche Bank, which declined them. The supervisory board mandates were held by Dresdner Bank rather than being transferred to the Kuwaiti investors.
223 Ulrich, *Notiz über Gespräch mit Schmidt am 13 January 1975*, HADB, ZA47/601; Hiß, *Aufzeichnungen des Gesprächs mit Schmidt u. Friderichs am 15 January 1975*, HADB, V25/3.
224 Cabinet minutes of the German Federal Government, 94th meeting on 15 January 1975 (online); see; Feldenkirchen, 'Vom Guten das Beste', pp. 345f. The share package was sold through a specially established holding company.
225 See numerous documents in HADB, ZA47/601 and

226 Ulrich in the Supervisory Board meeting on 28 January 1975, p. 14, HADB, V1/574.
226 Qtd. in Ahrens/Bähr, *Ponto*, p. 190.
227 'KWG-Novelle: Sieg für die Banken', *Wirtschaftswoche*, 30 October 1981; Ehrlicher, *Wende*, p. 320.
228 Christians in the Supervisory Board meeting on 5 July 1983, p. 4, HADB, V1/576.
229 Ferslev, *Recollections*, p. 22.
230 Proposal by Wieland and Bilstein for the Management Board meeting, 22 November 1985, and annex 'Übernahme- und Platzierungskonzept der Friedrich Flick Industrieverwaltung KGaA', HADB, V29/107.
231 AfK, *Durchführung des Übernahme- und Platzierungskonzepts*, 6 March 1986, p. 6, HADB, V29/106; Comments by Christians in the Supervisory Board meeting on 22 January 1986, pp. 7f., HADB, V1/620.
232 AfK, *Durchführung des Übernahme- und Platzierungskonzepts*, 6 March 1986, p. 12, HADB, V29/106. The operating result increased by 35.1 per cent compared to the figure for 1985. Without the Flick deal, the increase would have been just 7 per cent.
233 Offer by Friedrich Flick KG to Deutsche Bank, 3 December 1985; Christians and Herrhausen to Flick, 17 December 1985, HADB, V29/107.
234 Wieland/Bilstein to Blessing, 22 November 1985, HADB, V29/107; Ferslev, *Recollections*, p. 25.
235 Büschgen, *Deutsche Bank*, pp. 688f.; Altenburg, *Gedanken*, pp. 98–101.
236 Herrhausen to Management Board, 10 December 1985, HADB, ZA47/625.
237 From 31 December 1987, the Accounting Directives Act (*Bilanzrichtliniengesetz*) required banks to report shareholdings of 20 per cent or more in detail; Wieland/Christoffers, *Unser industrieller Anteilsbesitz*, 28 April 1987, HADB, ZA47/625.
238 Weber to Christians, 14 April 1986, HADB, ZA47/625.
239 Monopolkommission, *Ordnungspolitische Leitlinien*.
240 Wieland/Ferslev, *Unser industrieller Anteilsbesitz*, 20 October 1986, HADB, ZA47/625.
241 Ferslev, *Recollections*, pp. 26–7; Wieland/Christoffers, *Unser industrieller Anteilsbesitz*, 28 April 1987, HADB, ZA47/625.
242 Deutsche Bank, Annual Report 1959, p. 20.
243 Ambrosius, *Wachstum*, p. 154.
244 Gall, *Abs*, p. 287.
245 Deutsche Bank, Annual Report 1959, p. 20.
246 Deutsche Bank, Annual Report 1964, p. 27.
247 Büschgen, *Deutsche Bank*, pp. 675–7.
248 Deutsche Bank, Annual Report 1964, p. 27.
249 See 'Issue of Foreign Loans in the Federal Republic of Germany', in: Monthly Report of the Deutsche Bundesbank, April 1968, pp. 3–9, here p. 7.
250 Schenk, *Origins*.
251 Management Board minutes, 6–7 September 1965, p. 3, HADB, V10/73
252 Abs, *Finanzierungsfragen*, p. 393.
253 Abs, *Bemerkungen zum Eurodollarmarkt*, 19–20 November 1965, p. 2, HADB, V1/3657.
254 Otmar Emminger to Central Bank Council, 12 January 1968, HADB, V1/2907.
255 Emminger to Central Bank Council, 12 January 1968 (table 1), HADB, V1/2907.
256 Ulrich, *The Eurodollar Market*.
257 R. Steinig, *London – ein Come-back als internationaler Kapitalmarkt*, 15 January 1964, HADB, ZA43/17.

258 Deutsche Bank, Annual Report 1963, p. 21.

259 Abs, *Rolle der Geschäftsbanken*, p. 118.

260 Management Board minutes, 4–5 October and 6 December 1960, HADB, V10/71.

261 Memorandum über die Zusammenarbeit DB-BSGB-AB, 8 April 1963, ZA47/599.

262 Deutsche Bank, Annual Report 1963, pp. 22f.

263 Management Board minutes, 4–5 October and 6 December 1960, HADB, V10/71; Abs, Memo on Europäisches Emissionssyndikat, 4 January 1968, HADB, ZA43/17.

264 Circular to directors, 20 January 1964, HADB, ZA47/599.

265 'Internationaler "Informationsring"?', *Der Volkswirt*, 13 December 1963, copy in HADB, ZA47/599.

266 Economics Department, Amerikanische Bankenaktivitäten in der Bundesrepublik, 21 June 1968, HADB, V5/21.

267 Thierbach to Ulrich, 10 December 1964, HADB, V10/47.

268 Deutsche Bank, Annual Report 1967, p. 27.

269 Report by Klasen in the Management Board meeting on 4–5 September 1967, HADB, V10/74; Deutsche Bank, Annual Report 1968, p. 32; Büschgen, *Deutsche Bank*, pp. 753f.

270 Storck, *Euromarkt*, pp. 62f.

271 Straumann, *Finanzplatz*.

272 Abs in the Management Board meeting on 6–7 December 1965, p. 14, HADB, V10/73; Supervisory Board minutes, 21 October 1970, p. 3, HADB, V1/575.

273 Ulrich to Osterwind, 4 February 1970, HADB, V25/x289.

274 Guth in the Management Board meeting on 25 November 1969, HADB, V10/75. The banks had a gentlemen's agreement with the Bundesbank that they would not overburden the capital market and that they would notify the central bank in advance of bond issuance plans so as to enable co-ordination.

275 Osterwind, Aussprache über das Auslandsgeschäft, 17 December 1969, p. 2, HADB, ZA1/199.

276 Memo, 'Zusammenarbeit mit der Compagnie Financière de la Deutsche Bank AG', 20 August 1970, HADB, ZA47/551.

277 Thierbach/Fried, Überschlägige Schätzung der Kosten und Einnahmen einer DB-Filiale in Luxemburg, 13 February 1970, HADB, ZA47/551.

278 Proposal for the Management Board meeting on 28 April 1970; Management Board minutes, 6 July 1970, HADB, ZA47/551.

279 Circular to the main branches, 4 December 1970; Report by Storck, 21 April 1971, HADB, ZA47/551.

280 Memo, 'Zusammenarbeit mit der Compagnie Financière de la Deutsche Bank AG', 20 August 1970 HADB, ZA47/551.

281 Management Board minutes, 25 August 1970, HADB, ZA47/551; Report by Storck in the meeting with the directors of the main branches on 1 October 1979, HADB, ZA1/82; Büschgen, *Deutsche Bank*, p. 667.

282 Supervisory Board minutes, 25 October 1978, p. 2, HADB, V1/574.

283 Büschgen, *Deutsche Bank*, pp. 677f.

284 Abs, Bemerkungen zum Eurodollarmarkt, 19–20 November 1965, p. 3, HADB, V1/3657.

285 See 'Issue of Foreign Loans in the Federal Republic of Germany', in: Monthly Report of the Deutsche Bundesbank, April 1968, pp. 3–9, here pp. 5–7;

286 Osterwind at the meeting of the Credit Committee of the Supervisory Board on 2 December 1969, p. 3, HADB, V10/75.

287 Supervisory Board minutes, 30 January 1973, p. 3, HADB, V1/573; Supervisory Board minutes, 27 January 1976, p. 10, HADB, V1/574.

288 Guth in Management Board meeting on 25 November 1969, p. 2, HADB, V10/75.

289 Büschgen, *Deutsche Bank*, p. 682.

290 Guth in the Supervisory Board meeting on 21 October 1981, pp. 8–9, HADB, V1/575.

291 Stand des internationalen Geschäfts in der DB-Gruppe in 1978, 15 August 1979, HADB, V25/x668.

292 Guth, Internationales Geschäft, 16 December 1980, HADB, V25/x668.

293 Ehret at the meeting of the Supervisory Board on 27 October 1976, p. 11, HADB, V1/574; Storck's report in the meeting with the directors of the main branches on 1 October 1979, HADB, ZA1/82.

294 Büschgen, *Deutsche Bank*, p. 668. Deutsche Bank sought to increase oversight of business risks at DB Lux; Storck to ZIA, 23 August 1984, and appendix 'Grundsätze der Zusammenarbeit mit der Deutschen Bank AG', HADB, ZA1/82.

295 For the following see Kobrak, *Banking on Global Markets*, pp. 311–17.

296 For more details on the complex tax- and business-related issues concerning EAB and Deutsche Bank's investment in it, see Thierbach to Leibkutsch, 20 January 1970, and report dated 20 February 1970, HADB, V10/204.

297 Cf. foundation agreement of the EABs, 19 April 1968, HADB, ZA47/643.

298 Deutsche Bank, Annual Report 1968, p. 32; Circular by Klasen/Ulrich to directors, 2 January 1969, HADB, V10/204.

299 Bank of New York asked in 1969 to join EBIC, but the idea was not pursued; Cf. correspondence between Thierbach, Ulrich and Burgard, July 1969, HADB, V10/96.

300 The two EAB banks were combined in a US holding company in 1977: European American Bankcorp.

301 Thierbach to Klasen, 20 December 1968, HADB, V10/200.

302 Jürgens/Seipp to Guth, 30 November 1971; Report 'Deutsche Bank und Schweizerische Bankgesellschaft gemeinsam im Effekten- und Emissionsgeschäft in den USA', undated, HADB, V25/74.

303 Christians at the Supervisory Board meeting on 26 January 1972, p. 10, HADB, V1/575.

304 Seipp to Management Board, UBS-DB Corporation, Bericht über das Geschäftsjahr 1972, 29 March 1973, HADB, V25/74.

305 Bericht über das Board Meeting der UBS-DB am 17 October 1972, HADB, V25/74.

306 Anderson (Merrill Lynch) to Christians, 15 August 1974; Christians to Anderson, 30 August 1974, HADB, V12/x355.

307 UBS-DB Corporation, Bericht über das Geschäftsjahr 1972, HADB, V25/74.

308 UBS-DB Corporation – Geschäftspolitische Analyse, January 1977, HADB, V25/74.

309 Hausser, Zusammenfassender Bericht 'Recommendations regarding foreign access to the US securities markets, 22 August 1973, HADB, V25/74; 'Auslandsbanken sollen nicht an die US-Börsen', *Handelsblatt*, 28 August 1973.

309 Christians, Report to the Management Board of Deutsche Bank, 31 August 1977; Grasnick/Koenig, UBS-DB Corporation, Note for the Management Board, 16 March 1978, HADB, V25/74.

310 Büschgen, *Deutsche Bank*, pp. 758f.

311 Report on trip by Blessing, 2 May 1984, HADB, ZA25/x123.

312 Büschgen, *Deutsche Bank*, p. 756.

313 Corporate bonds also gained importance, but only gradually; Thierbach to Ulrich, 30 May 1968, HADB, V10/96.

314 Buhr (Tokyo) to Krebs, 18 June 1970, HADB, V25/x743.

315 Bericht 'Wertpapiergeschäft Tokyo – Geschäftsmöglichkeiten', 3 September 1973, HADB, ZA1/283.

316 Eröffnung der DUB-Filiale Tokyo, 21 June 1971, HADB, V25/x743.

317 DAB, Annual Report 1970, p. 22.

318 Blomeyer to Klasen, 5 December 1969 mit Anlage 'Gedanken zur Lage unserer Bank', HADB, V10/211.

319 Memorandum zur Lage der DAB, 30 July 1962, HADB, V10/209.

320 Bericht über Verhandlungen mit Ponto, 20 July 1971; Aktenvermerk 'Flurbereinigung', 29 December 1971, HADB, K7/7/III-1.

321 Aktenvermerk 'Sitz der EAB', 23 December 1971, HADB, K7/7/III-1.

322 Van der Bey, Kurzbericht über Aufenthalt in Tokyo, 8 March 1971, HADB, ZA1/356.

323 Bericht 'Überlegungen zu einer Erweiterung unserer Investment- bzw'. Merchant-Banking Interessen auf Asien, 9 November 1973; Seipp to Guth, 16 November 1973, HADB, ZA1/283.

324 Bergmann/v. Benckendorff, Bericht über Besuch in Hongkong, 16 November 1972, HADB, ZA1/356.

325 Bericht Gaewert-May to Thierbach, Merchant Banking in Südost-Asien, 11 November 1974, HADB, ZA1/283.

326 Breuer/von der Bey, Merchant Banking in Süd-Ost-Asien, 17 December 1973, HADB, ZA1/283.

327 Ibid.

328 Auslandsumsätze und Engagements der Deutschen Bank 1960–1971, 7 October 1971, HADB, V5/22.

329 Konferenz zur Erörterung einer vorgeschlagenen neuen Form der Zusammenarbeit auf dem Anleihesektor in Europa, 13 February 1967, HADB, ZA43/17; report by Abs in the Management Board meeting on 6–7 March 1967, HADB, V10/74.

330 Thierbach to Guth, 21 December 1971, HADB, ZA18/217.

331 Management Board minutes, 25 August 1970, ZA47/551.

332 Report by Guth on EAC meeting, 15 March 1977, HADB, ZA47/594.

333 Supervisory Board minutes, 27 October 1976, p. 9, HADB, V1/574.

334 ZIA, Rechenschaftsbericht 1980, 16 April 1981, p. 9, HADB, V25/x682.

335 Guth in the Supervisory Board meeting on 27 October 1976, pp. 9–10, HADB, V1/574.

336 Guth in the Supervisory Board meeting on 25 October 1978, p. 5, HADB, V1/574.

337 Guth, Anmerkungen zur Konzernentwicklung, 28 March 1985, p. 6, HADB, ZA18/x698.

338 Büschgen, *Deutsche Bank*, pp. 758f.

339 Guth, Internationales Geschäft, 16 December 1980, HADB, V25/x668.

340 Deutsche Bank, Annual Report 1968, pp. 29f.

341 Economics Department, Deutsch-Sowjetischer Handel, 3 December 1971, HADB, V5/22.

342 Cf. Christians to Abs, 12 May 1975, HADB, V1/4034. Christians referred to a book recently published by Manfred Pohl on the financing of the 'Russian business' between the two world wars, which he believed offered useful pointers for the new negotiations.

343 Pohl, *Geschäft und Politik*, p. 150.

344 On the preparations, see the comments by Christians in the Management Board meeting on 14 July 1969; Report on Christians' trip, 16 December 1969, HADB, ZA1/418; see Christians, *Wege*, pp. 29ff.

345 Konsortialvereinbarung sowie Vertrag zwischen der Deutschen Bank und der Bank für Außenhandel der UdSSR, 1 February 1970, HADB, ZA1/419.

346 Report by Christians, 6 July 1972, HADB, V1/4034.

347 Herbst betr. Deutsch-sowjetische Wirtschaftsbeziehungen, 26 January 1970, AAPD, 1970, vol. 1, doc. 23, pp. 86–8.

348 Taubner, Bericht 'Röhrenkredite von 1970–1982', Juli 1985, p. 6, HADB, ZA47/567.

349 Taubner, Proposal for the Management Board meeting on 5 August 1969, p. 2, HADB, V10/93.

350 Management Board minutes, 14 July 1969 and 24 November 1969, HADB, ZA1/418.

351 Finanzkredit an die Bank für Außenhandel (o.D.), HADB, ZA1/418.

352 Ulrich in the Management Board meeting on 25 November 1969, HADB, V10/75.

353 Taubner, Bericht 'Röhrenkredite von 1970–1982', July 1985, p. 6, HADB, ZA47/567.

354 Ibid.

355 Cf. Rede Ulrichs bei der Eröffnung der Repräsentanz, 22 March 1973, HADB, ZA1/155.

356 Linss, Aussichten der künftige Entwicklung unseres Ostgeschäftes (undated, probably 1971), HADB, ZA1/1179; Bindert, Memo, Vertretung in Moskau, 5 August 1971, HADB, ZA47/564.

357 Christians and Ulrich to the head of the Soviet Foreign Trade Bank Ivanov, 13 July 1972, HADB, ZA1/151; cf. also on the preliminary soundings Dinkelmann to Ulrich, 15 January 1973, HADB, ZA1/155.

358 Zentrale Auslandsabteilung, Eröffnung einer Vertretung in Moskau, 25 August 1972, HADB, ZA1/151; Aktennotiz, 22 March 1973, HADB, ZA1/155.

359 The representative of the Bank for Foreign Trade of the USSR asked Ulrich during the opening of the representative office in Moscow to put together a 'group of customers who would come into consideration for joint business opportunities'; Aktennotiz, 22 March 1973, HADB, ZA1/155.Cf. also Rede Ulrichs bei der Eröffnung der Repräsentanz, 22 March 1973, HADB, ZA1/155.

360 Ibid.

361 Linss, Unser Anteil am Ostgeschäft, 3 April 1973, HADB, ZA1/155.

362 Memorandum 'Finanzierung von Comecon-Staaten', 5 January 1973, HADB, ZA1/1178.

363 Blessing/Linss, Gewährung eines Eurokredits an die Außenhandelsbank der UdSSR, 26 February 1973, HADB, ZA1/1178.

364 Economics Department, Finanzprobleme im Osthandel, 22 September 1980, p. 5, HADB, ZA1/1183.

365 Taubner to Christians, 13 August 1976, HADB, ZA47/564.

366 Lebahn and Hofmann-Werther (Moscow), Neue Modelle der Exportfinanzierung, 11 October 1979, HADB ZA47/565.

367 Taubner, Bericht 'Röhrenkredite von 1970–1982', Juli 1985, pp. 7–14, HADB, ZA47/567.

368 Lebahn, Das Sowjetuniongeschäft der Deutschen Bank in den 80er Jahren, 28 July 1981, HADB, ZA47/565.

369 Pohl, *Geschäft und Politik*, p. 173; Lebahn to Christians, 26 June 1982, HADB, ZA1/1178.

370 Lebahn to Christians, 24 November 1983, HADB, ZA47/566.

371 Thierbach to Bank Handlowy, Warsaw, 9 July 1969, HADB, ZA/1178; Unsere künftige Einstellung zum DDR-Geschäft, 21 June 1972, HADB, ZA/1179.

372 Economics Department, Ost-Westhandel und Westverschuldung der Staatshandelsländer, 15 June 1976, HADB, ZA1/120 (data in appendix I, p. 3).

373 Burghardt to Thierbach, 8 October 1973, HADB, ZA1/1179.

374 Burghardt to Linss, 26 November 1973, HADB, ZA1/1179.

375 Aufzeichnungen von Seitz betr. Internationale Verschuldungskrise, 13 August 1982, AAPD, 1982, vol. 2, doc. 225, pp. 1189–94; cf. also Cline, *International Debt Reexamined*, pp. 26–9, 80.

376 Schmidt, Finanzierungsformen im Ostgeschäft, 23 September 1980, p. 3, ZA1/1183.

377 Steves (Ost-Ausschuß) betr. Lage in Polen, 31 December 1981, HADB, ZA1/1178; see also Bartel, *Fugitive Leverage*.

378 Economics Department, Zur Kreditwürdigkeit der europäischen RGW-Länder, May 1981, HADB, ZA1/120.

379 Ibid.

380 Martiny, Finanzprobleme im Osthandel, 5 September 1980, p. 2, HADB, ZA1/1183.

381 Schmidt, Finanzierungsformen im Ostgeschäft, 23 September 1980, p. 3, HADB, ZA1/1183.

382 Guth in the Supervisory Board meeting on 9 July 1981, p. 4, HADB, V1/575; Marx and Krumnow, Gentlemen's Agreement über die Konsolidierung, 6 February 1984, HADB, ZA1/82.

383 Cf. Devlin, *Debt and Crisis*.

384 Cf. Kopper, *Recycling*.

385 Cf. Altamura, *European Banks*.

386 Aufzeichnungen von Seitz betr. Internationale Verschuldungskrise, AAPD, 1982, vol. 2, doc. 225, pp. 1189–94.

387 Bericht Blessing, 28 February 1972; Krebs and Storf, Auslandsverschuldung Brasiliens, 12 November 1973, HADB, V1/560.

388 Guth to Herrhausen, Thierbach and Kopper, 25 May 1977, HADB, ZA16/x149.

389 Ibid.

390 Blessing and Trouvain to Herrhausen, 12 August 1977, HADB, V30/351.

391 Rischbieter, *Risiken*, pp. 480–83.

392 Hollenberg (ZIA) to Herrhausen, Thierbach and Kopper, 21 August 1978, HADB, V30/351.

393 Meissner (ZIA/Rechnungswesen) to Mertin, 26 July 1978, HADB, V30/351.

394 Bericht der Volkswirtschaftlichen Abteilung, 23 September 1977; Länderlimite im internationalen Geschäft – Grundsätze und Regeln, 19 August 1977, HADB, ZA16/x149.

395 Arendt (Zentrale Außenhandelsfinanzierung) to Herrhausen, 28 June 1977, HADB, V30/351.

396 Cf. Sattler, *Geschäft mit den Staatsschulden*, pp. 436–40.

397 Economics Department, Lateinamerika, 8 January 1980, HADB, V29/5; Blessing to Management Board, 2 June 1977; Economics Department, Tendenzen der außenwirtschaftlichen Entwicklung bis 1982, September 1977, HADB, ZA16/x149.

398 Economics Department, Beurteilung von Länderrisiken, Dezember 1981, p. 5, HADB, V29/5.

399 Guth in the Supervisory Board meeting on 19 October 1982, p. 9, HADB, V1/576.

400 Economics Department and ZIA to Kopper and Herrhausen, Bewertung von Länderrisiken und Kernobligo-Richtlinien, 26 January 1982 and Anlagen, HADB, V29/5.

401 Economics Department, Länder nach Gefährdungsgruppen (April 1987), HADB, V29/6.

402 Trouvain to Guth, 27 July 1982, HADB, V29/5.

403 Economics Department, Kreditbedarf 1984/90 der Länder, für die wir Risikovorsorge getroffen haben – eine Modellrechnung, August 1984, HADB, V30/860.

404 Cf. z.B. Economics Department, Entwicklungsländer: Alternative Entwicklungen der Zahlungsbilanz bis 1982, HADB, ZA1/82; Auswirkungen fallender Ölpreise auf hochverschuldete Länder, 13 February 1986; Zur aktuellen Zinsdiskussion, 23 July 1987, HADB, V29/6.

405 Büschgen, *Deutsche Bank*, pp. 549–53.

406 Cf. Economics Department, Entwicklungsländer: Alternative Entwicklungen der Zahlungsbilanz bis 1982, p. 13, HADB, ZA1/82.

407 Report by Christians in the Supervisory Board meeting on 31 March 1981, p. 2, HADB, V1/575.

408 Ulrich in the Supervisory Board meeting on 21 October 1981, p. 4, HADB, V1/575.

409 Report by Guth in the Supervisory Board meeting on 25 January 1982, p. 4; cf. also Guth, 30 March 1982, p. 6, HADB, V1/576.

410 Storf, Internationale Schuldenkrise, 15 September 1986, p. 6, HADB, V29/6; Blessing, Kreditbedarf der Länder, für die wir Risikovorsorge getroffen haben, 1984–1990, HADB, V30/860.

411 Loan loss provisions were tax deductible.

412 Blessing, Kreditbedarf der Länder, für die wir Risikovorsorge getroffen haben, 1984–1990, HADB, V30/860. See also Boughton, *Silent Revolution*; Copelovitch, *International Monetary Fund*.

413 Speech manuscript by Guth for the Supervisory Board meeting on 25 October 1983, p. 3, HADB, V1/576.

414 Blessing, Kreditbedarf der Länder, für die wir Risikovorsorge getroffen haben, 1984–1990, HADB, V30/860.

415 Ibid.

416 Note on 'Internationales Risk Management', 28 April 1983, p. 15, HADB, V29/860.

417 Ibid., p. 2.

418 Report by Guth in the Supervisory Board meeting on 19 October 1982, p. 8, HADB, V1/576; Notiz über 'Internationales Risk Management', 28 April 1983, HADB, V30/860.

419 Supervisory Board minutes, 3 July 1984, S, 10f., HADB, V1/576.

420 Speech manuscript by Guth for the Supervisory Board meeting on 25 October 1983, p. 7, HADB, V1/576.

421 Cartellieri to Management Board, 11 August 1986 and Economics Department, Beteiligung an 'organisierten' Krediten für Entwicklungsländer, 5 August 1986, HADB, V29/6.

422 Speech manuscript by Guth for the Supervisory Board meeting on 25 October 1983, p. 7, HADB, V1/576.

423 Economics Department/ZIA, Internationale Schuldenkrise, 15 September 1986, HADB, V29/6; on the role of international organisations, see Woods, *The Globalizers*.

424 Economics Department, Kreditbedarf 1984/90 der Länder, für die wir Risikovorsorge getroffen haben – eine Modellrechnung, August 1984, HADB, V30/860.

425 Herrhausen, *The Time Is Ripe*.

426 Platthaus, *Herrhausen*, pp. 176–213.

427 Herrhausen, *The Time Is Ripe*.

428 Notiz für Zapp betr. Mexiko, 23 August 1989, HADB, ZA1/x2853.

429 In 1989, the bank had a coverage ratio of 77 per cent of unsecured exposures in the countries hit by balance of payments difficulties; Burgard in the Supervisory Board meeting on 4 July 1989, p. 10, HADB, V1/620.

430 Berghoff/Rischbieter, *Debt and Credit*, pp. 496ff. See also Darity/Horn, *Loan Pushers*, pp. 74f.

431 Deutsche Bank, Annual Report 1989, p. 24.

432 Cf. Cabinet minutes of the German Federal Government, 47th meeting on 25 July 1984, item 4 (online). See list of the syndicate dated 16 July 1984, HADB, V40/x51.

433 Bericht über Empfang Christians durch Gorbatschow, 18 April 1985, AAPD, 1985, vol. 1, doc. 94, pp. 495–501.

434 Herrhausen, 'Deutsche Bank moves on into the Future', address given at the Executives Meeting, 30 March 1988, HADB, V30/321.

435 Cf. Gaertner/Albrecht/Schaub, Ausbau des Investment Banking im Konzern Deutsche Bank, 14 June 1984, HADB, ZA18/57.

436 Guth, Anmerkungen zur Konzernentwicklung, 28 March 1985, p. 3, HADB, ZA18/x698.

437 Ehrlicher, *Wende*, pp. 331f.

438 Herrhausen at the Supervisory Board meeting on 5 July 1988, p. 5, HADB, V1/620.

439 Herrhausen, Vortrag vor den Leitern der DB-Auslandsniederlassungen und -töchter, 17 October 1987, p. 1, HADB, V30/321.

440 AfK, Anforderungen an die Bank auf dem Weg in die 90er Jahre, 28 August 1987, HADB, ZA18/59.

441 Herrhausen, Vortrag vor den Leitern der DB-Auslandsniederlassungen und -töchter, 17 October 1987, p. 10, HADB, V30/321.

442 Die Bank im Markt 1984, p. 3, HADB, ZA4/x877.

443 Herrhausen, 'Deutsche Bank moves on into the Future', address given at the Executives Meeting, 30 March 1988, p. 14, HADB, V30/321.

444 Cf. Gaertner/Albrecht/Schaub, Ausbau des Investment Banking im Konzern Deutsche Bank, 14 June 1984, p. 11, HADB, ZA18/57.

445 AfK, Anforderungen an die Bank auf dem Weg in die 90er Jahre, 28 August 1987, pp. 11f., HADB, ZA18/59.

446 Ausbau des Investment Banking im Konzern Deutsche Bank, 14 June 1984, p. 4, HADB, ZA18/57.

447 Sitzung mit den Hauptfilialdirektoren, 2 July 1984, HADB, ZA18/57.

448 Internationales Geschäft – Konzernentwicklung und -koordination, 19 April 1988, HADB, ZA18/2.

449 Ibid.

450 Ibid.

451 Ibid.

452 Herrhausen at the Supervisory Board meeting on 4 July 1989, p. 5, HADB, V1/620.

453 Internationales Geschäft – Konzernentwicklung und -koordination, 19 April 1988, HADB, ZA18/2.

454 Herrhausen, 'Deutsche Bank moves on into the Future', address given at the Executives Meeting, 30 March 1988, p. 15, HADB, V30/321.

455 Guth, Anmerkungen zur Konzernentwicklung, 28 March 1985, pp. 17f., HADB, ZA18/x698.

456 Herrhausen, 'Deutsche Bank moves on into the Future', address given at the Executives Meeting, 30 March 1988, p. 15, HADB, V30/321.

457 Cf. Gaertner/Albrecht/Schaub, Ausbau des Investment Banking im Konzern Deutsche Bank, 14 June 1984, p. VIII, HADB, ZA18/57.

458 Von Brentano to Kopper, 26 June 1989, HADB, V30/1382.

459 Herrhausen at the Supervisory Board meeting on 5 July 1988, p. 3, HADB, V1/620.

460 Ibid., p. 6.

461 Albrecht/Schaub to Shareholdings Department, 16 December 1983, HADB, ZA18/57.

462 Miesel/von Brentano, Das internationale Investment Banking der DB, 12 June 1984, HADB, ZA18/57.

463 Supervisory Board minutes, 22 October 1984, pp. 9–10, HADB, V1/576.

464 Altenburg, *Gedanken*, pp. 96f.

465 Platthaus, *Herrhausen*, pp. 226ff.

466 'Investment Banking – Standort und Strategie', Memo by Kopper, 30 October 1989, HADB, V33/127/1.

467 Sattler, *Ernst Matthiesen und Alfred Herrhausen*, p. 316. The comprehensive biography by Friederike Sattler *Herrhausen: Banker, Querdenker, Global Player* was not available upon completion of the manuscript.

Globalisation and Crisis, 1989–2020

I. The Acquisition of Morgan Grenfell

1 Burk, *A Brief History*, pp. 128–9.

2 Büschgen, *Deutsche Bank*, p. 771.

3 'Deutsche Bank in British Deal', *New York Times*, 7 November 1984.

4 Burk, *A Brief History*, pp. 128–9.

5 Letter from Sir Peter Carey (Morgan Grenfell Group) to Herrhausen, 3 February 1987, HADB, V27/x46.

6 Ibid.

7 Memo by Heintzeler and Ferslev, 23 January 1987, p. 6, HADB, V33/127/1.

8 Ibid.

9 Ibid.

10 Ibid., p. 10.

11 Management Board minutes, 26 January 1987, HADB, ZA18/55.

12 Letter from John A Craven (Phoenix Securities) to Breuer, 9 February 1987, HADB, ZA18/55.

13 'Eagle/Bulldog', 20 February 1987, HADB, V33/127/2. This paper was viewed by Schneider-Lenné again on 4 September 1988. The report is not signed.

14 Ibid., p. 3.

15 Memo by CBBB [unknown], 20 July 1988, HADB, V33/127/2.

16 'Eagle/Bulldog', 20 February 1987, pp. 4–5, HADB, V33/127/2.
17 Ibid., p. 6.
18 Ibid., pp. 6–7.
19 Ibid., pp. 8–9.
20 Memo by ten Brink, 22 January 1987, HADB, V33/127/1.
21 Details in this paragraph from Deutsche Bank Living History Project interview with Sir John Craven, 22 November 2013, HADB, ZA17. See also CV 'John A. Craven', 13 November 1989, HADB, V33/127/2.
22 Letter from Breuer to Craven, 27 April 1987, HADB, V27/x46. The letter is addressed to Craven as CEO of Phoenix Securities.
23 Ibid.
24 Details in this paragraph from Deutsche Bank Living History Project interview with Sir John Craven, 22 November 2013, HADB, ZA17.
25 Dobson relates the same account of relations with IndoSuez – that they agreed not to engage in a hostile takeover. Deutsche Bank Living History Project interview with Michael Dobson, 14 January 2014, HADB, ZA17.
26 Ibid.
27 Memorandum from Morgan Grenfell, 6 November 1987, HADB, V27/x46.
28 Ibid.
29 'German Solution', *The Economist*, 14 November 1987.
30 Memo by Ferslev and Heintzeler for Herrhausen, Breuer and Kopper, 29 June 1988, HADB, V33/127/2.
31 Memo by Heintzeler for Breuer, Herrhausen, Kopper, Schneider-Lenné and Ferslev, 2 September 1988, HADB, V33/127/2.
32 'Bulldog', Memo by Low for Schneider-Lenné, 12 September 1988, HADB, V33/127/1. Schneider-Lenné forwarded it to Breuer, Kopper and Heintzeler.
33 Deutsche Bank Living History Project interview with Lord Aldington (Charles Low), 24 September 2014, HADB, ZA17.
34 Burk, *A Brief History*, p. 131.
35 'Bulldog', Memo by Low for Schneider-Lenné, 12 September 1988, HADB, V33/127/1. Schneider-Lenné forwarded it to Breuer, Kopper and Heintzeler.
36 'Morgan Grenfell', Memo by Heintzeler for Breuer, Herrhausen, Kopper, Schneider-Lenné and Ferslev, 30 September 1988, HADB, V33/127/2. For the following ibid.
37 Big Bang in 1986 allowed entry of foreign firms and banks into the securities market at the same time as demand declined, decreasing margins and profits. Six smaller firms had closed between 1986 and 1988, cf. 'Morgan Grenfell Cuts Market Operations', *New York Times*, 7 December 1988.
38 'Operation Magic', J. O. Hambro Magan & Co., 18 July 1989, HADB, V33/127/2.
39 Büschgen, *Deutsche Bank*, p. 771.
40 'Morgan Grenfell Plc', Memo by Ferslev and Thelen for Kopper and Schneider-Lenné, 28 February 1989, HADB, V33/127/1.
41 'Magic', Memo by Kopper for the Management Board meeting on 18 April 1989, dated 13 April 1989, HADB, V33/127/1.
42 'Project Magic', J. O. Hambro Magan & Co., 18 July 1989, HADB, V33/127/2. On 4 July 1989, DB Investments was incorporated in London as wholly owned subsidiary of Deutsche Bank. It was this

subsidiary that formally took over Morgan Grenfell, suggesting that planning was certainly firming up by this time. The company received a certificate to commence business on 28 November 1989.
43 'Project Magic', J. O. Hambro Magan & Co., 18 July 1989, HADB, V33/127/2.
44 Memo by Ferslev and Thelen for Kopper, 21 July 1989, HADB, V33/127/2.
45 'Magic Fund Management, Additional Information', J. O. Hambro Magan & Co., 4 August 1989, HADB, V33/127/2.
46 Memo by Low for Thelen, copied to Schneider-Lenné, 17 August 1989, HADB, V33/127/1.
47 'Magic', Memo from Ferslev and Thelen, copied to Kopper, 22 August 1989, HADB, V33/127/2.
48 'Magic-Sitzung am 2. September 1989', 22 August 1989, HADB, V33/127/2.
49 Deutsche Bank Living History Project interview with Sir John Craven, 22 November 2013, HADB, ZA17.
50 'Magic', Memo by Ferslev and Thelen to Kopper and Schneider-Lenné for the Management Board meeting on 3 October 1989, dated 25 September 1989, HADB, V33/127/1.
51 Deutsche Bank Living History Project interview with Sir John Craven, 22 November 2013, HADB, ZA17.
52 Ibid.
53 'Magic – Zusammenfassendes Argumentarium', Memo by Fischer and Berlin, 2 November 1989, HADB, V33/127/1.
54 Memo by Ferslev and Thelen for Herrhausen, 12 October 1989, HADB, V33/127/1.
55 'Magic', Memo by Ferslev and Thelen to Kopper and Schneider-Lenné for the Management Board meeting on 3 October 1989, dated 25 September 1989, p. 2, HADB, V33/127/1.
56 'Investment Banking – Standort und Strategie', Memo by Kopper, 30 October 1989, HADB, V33/127/1. For the following quotes see ibid. (Underlining in the original).
57 Letter to Kopper from G. M. Magan, 1 November 1989, HADB, ZA18/54.
58 Extract of minutes of a meeting of the Board of Managing Directors, Munich, 26 November 1989, HADB, V33/127/2.
59 Supervisory Board minutes (extraordinary meeting), 26 November 1989, HADB, V1/620. Krumnow explained the balance sheet, goodwill calculation and overall price.
60 Ibid., p. 4.
61 Ibid.
62 Deutsche Bank Living History Project interview with Sir John Craven, 22 November 2013, HADB, ZA17.
63 Ibid.
64 Ibid.
65 Ibid.
66 'Talking Points for Alfred Herrhausen, Speaker of the Board of Managing Directors of Deutsche Bank, at an analysts meeting in London on Monday, November 27, 1989 and at a subsequent press conference', 25 November 1989, HADB, V33/127/2.
67 'Notes for Speech of Dr. H. at Morgan Grenfell to Morgan Grenfell's Staff', 25 November 1989, HADB, V33/127/2.
68 Extract of Minutes of a Meeting of the Board of Managing Directors, Munich, 26 November 1989, p. 2, HADB, V33/127/2.
69 Memorandum of Understanding, November 1989, p. 2, HADB, V33/127/2.

70 Quoted in memo from Craven to Jess and Steinmetz, 28 October 1992, HADB, V17/x37.
71 For the following paragraph and all quotes see Memorandum of Understanding, November 1989, HADB, V33/127/2.
72 Craven to Kopper, 15 June 1992, HADB, V17/x8.
73 Deutsche Bank Living History Project interview with Michael Dobson, 14 January 2014, HADB, ZA17.
74 Private and Confidential Minutes of Directors' Meeting, 21 March 1991, HADB, V17/x18.
75 Memo from Craven to all staff, 28 October 1994, HADB, V17/x38.
76 Deutsche Bank Living History Project interview with Sir John Craven, 22 November 2013, HADB, ZA17.
77 Letter from Schneider-Lenné to Sir Adrian Cadbury, 16 December 1992, Cadbury Archive, Cambridge University, CAD-02510. Cadbury was particularly interested in Schneider-Lenné's proposal that the number of supervisory board memberships allowed for any individual should be limited.
78 Schneider-Lenné, *Germany Case.*
79 Schneider-Lenné, *Governance of Good Business,* p. 76
80 Ibid., p. 77.
81 Schneider-Lenné, *The Role.*
82 Ibid., p. 302.

II. Building the Investment Bank, 1991–1998

1 Brandon Mitchener, 'Germany names Goldman to aid Telekom sale', *New York Times,* 26 November 1994.
2 Interview with Anshu Jain, 'The Transformation of Deutsche Bank' project, House of Finance, Frankfurt, 22 February 2006.
3 From 1984 to 1994 there was a 'Steering Committee Investment Banking' including Bain and Co. and chaired by Breuer in 1994. It was disbanded when the new investment bank was agreed in 1994 and had its last meeting in Sydney in early November 1994. See HADB, ZA18/60.
4 Christian Caryl, 'Fear and Loathing in Deutsche Bank', *Spectator,* 30 July 1994.
5 David Shirreff, 'In the line of fire', *Euromoney,* March 1994.
6 Mello/Parsons, *Maturity Structure;* Culp/Miller, *Metallgesellschaft.*
7 David Waller, 'Schneider affair errors leave dent in Deutsche Bank's reputation', *Financial Times,* 29 April 1994.
8 Memorandum by Legal Department Deutsche Bank AG, 23 December 1994, HADB, V17/x5.
9 'Wir reden hier eigentlich von Peanuts', 25 April 1994. Joachim Preuss, '"Peanuts" im Brunnen', *Der Spiegel,* 2 May 1994.
10 'Fugitive German Developer Arrested in South Florida', *New York Times,* 19 May 1995.
11 'Banker denies knowledge of Schneider's problems', *Wall Street Journal,* 25 September 1997.
12 'Schneider judge slams Deutsche risk control system', *Reuters,* 24 September 1997.
13 'Schneider given six years for fraud', *Financial Times,* 24 December 1997.
14 Memo by Ferslev to Kopper, 9 June 1992, HADB, ZA18/77.
15 Craven to Kopper, 16 June 1992, HADB, V17/x8.
16 Ibid.
17 Memo from Craven to Kopper, 13 October 1992, HADB, V17/x98.

18 Management Board minutes (in camera meeting), 24 November 1992, Frankfurt, HADB, V40/x177.
19 Ibid.
20 Investment Banking Review, 10 March 1994. Report of Investment Banking Committee set up by Breuer, HADB, V17/x38.
21 Investment Banking Review, Part I, 10 March 1994, HADB, V17/x38. The members were Jonathan Asquith (Morgan Grenfell), Thomas R. Fischer (Deutsche Bank AG OTC Derivatives), Steven Mobbs (Deutsche Bank AG London branch), Hung Tran (Co-Managing Director Deutsche Bank Research GmbH, formerly VP at Merrill Lynch and Salomon Bros in NY), Alexander von Ungern-Sternberg (Deutsche Bank AG Treasury co-ordinator). Underlining in the original.
22 Investment Banking Review, Part I, 10 March 1994, HADB, V17/x38.
23 Ibid.
24 'The Minority View: Division of Deutsche Bank Group – not a separate legal entity – managed out of head office', H. Tran, appended to Investment Banking Review, Part I, 10 March 1994, HADB, V17/x38.
25 Internal Morgan Grenfell memo by Craven of discussion with Breuer, Schmitz and Krumnow, 21 March 1994, HADB, V17/x38.
26 'Equity securities', Memo by Craven to Morgan Grenfell staff, 21 March 1994, HADB, V17/x38.
27 Memo for Breuer by Craven, 7 June 1994. This was also discussed at a meeting setting out responsibilities for Morgan Grenfell and Deutsche Bank in Asia attended by Breuer, Cartellieri, Craven, Dobson, von Maltzan, Murray, von Ungern-Sternberg on 14 June 1994, HADB, V17/x38.
28 Dennis Stevenson CBE to Craven and Dobson, 10 June 1994, HADB, V17/x38. Stevenson was knighted in 1999 and became Baron Stevenson of Coddenham. He was later CEO of HBOS from 2001 to 2009 and was heavily criticised by the Parliamentary Commission on Banking Standards over the 2008 collapse of HBOS.
29 'Investment Banking Review – Part II', 9 June 1994, HADB, V17/x38.
30 Ibid.
31 Ibid.
32 Memo from Jonathan Asquith to Investment Banking Review Committee, 9 June 1994, HADB, V17/x38. Asquith had missed the final Committee meeting because he was travelling back from Argentina. Asquith had been with Morgan Grenfell since 1979; he left the bank in 1997.
33 Ibid.
34 Ibid.
35 Ferslev to Kopper and Schmitz, 23 June 1994, HADB, ZA18/60. The paper itself is dated 22 June.
36 Jörg Eigendorf, 'Reif für die Top-Liga?', *Die Welt,* 31 July 2003.
37 J. A. Craven, 'The positioning of Morgan Grenfell in the Deutsche Bank Group', 17 June 1994, HADB, V17/x38. A week earlier in a memo to 'Colleagues' Craven asserted that 80 per cent of the investment in Morgan Grenfell was goodwill relating to 'a relatively small number of human assets who go in and out of the door every day. They are highly marketable highly self confident and prima donnaish […] and they have a clear idea of the sort of organisation they want to work for.' Memo by Craven, 10 June 1994, HADB, V17/x38.

38 Craven, 'The positioning of Morgan Grenfell in the Deutsche Bank Group', 17 June 1994, HADB, V17/x38.

39 Craven, Draft, Investment Banking in the DB Group, Appendix A, 29 June 1994, HADB, V17/x38.

40 Craven, Draft, Investment Banking in the DB Group, 29 June, HADB, V17/x38.

41 Manuscript note by Breuer to Craven, stamped 4 July 1994, HADB, V17/x38.

42 Memo from Craven to Breuer, Cartellieri, Schmitz and Schneider-Lenné, 13 July 1994, HADB, V17/x38.

43 Memo by Dobson, 22 August 1994, HADB, V17/x38.

44 Ibid.

45 Letter from Richmond-Watson to John Craven, 25 July 1994, HADB, V17/x38.

46 Investment Banking Initiative, minutes of meeting on 23 August 1994 by Droste; Memo by Craven to Cartellieri, Breuer, Schmitz, Schneider-Lenné, 25 August 1994, HADB, V17/x38. Droste was appointed head of European Industry Groups of Deutsche Bank's Global Investment Banking unit in 1999.

47 Craven to Cartellieri, Breuer, Schmitz, 25 August 1994, HADB, V17/x38.

48 Craven to Kopper, 26 August 1994, HADB, V17/x38.

49 Craven to Breuer, Schneider-Lenné, 1 September 1994, HADB, V17/x38.

50 Craven to Cartellieri, Breuer, Schmitz, Schneider-Lenné, 9 September 1994, HADB, V17/x38.

51 Note by Craven of meeting on 13 September 1994 with Cartellieri, Breuer, Schmitz, Schneider-Lenné and Droste, 15 September 1994, HADB, V17/x38.

52 Deutsche Bank, press release, 28 October 1994, HADB, V17/x38.

53 Memo by von Heydebreck to the Management Board, 26 October 1994, HADB, V40/x182.

54 Deutsche Bank, press release, 28 October 1994, HADB, V17/x38.

55 Ibid.; Memo by von Heydebreck to the Management Board, 26 October 1994, HADB, V40/x182.

56 Memo from Dobson to heads of working groups, 20 December 1994. The working groups were set up on 12 December 1994, HADB, V17/x39.

57 'Warburg's woes' (Lex column), *Financial Times*, 11–12 February 1995.

58 'Investment Bank London, Ein Zwischenbericht', speech manuscript of Schmitz, 31 January 1995, HADB, V37/x347; 'Top-Down Study for the Investment Bank', Memorandum by Craven, 3 February 1995, HADB, V24/x287.

59 Interview with Anshu Jain, 'The Transformation of Deutsche Bank' project, House of Finance, Frankfurt, 22 February 2006.

60 Memo signed by Schneider-Lenné, von Boehm-Bezing, Endres, Krumnow, Weiss and von Heydebreck, 3 March 1995, HADB, V37/x347 (in German) and HADB, V17/x39 (in English translation).

61 Ferslev to Craven, 7 February 1995, HADB, V17/x39.

62 Ibid.

63 Personal memo from von Boehm-Bezing to all members of the Management Board, 7 February 1995, HADB, V17/x39.

64 Ibid.

65 Telefax from Schmitz to Craven, 8 February 1995, HADB, V17/x39.

66 Memo from Craven to von Boehm-Bezing, Endres, Krumnow, Krupp, Weiss and von Heydebreck, copied to Breuer, Cartellieri, Kopper, Schmitz, Schneider-Lenné and Ferslev, 10 February 1995, HADB, V17/x39.

67 'Defining the Investment Banking Group', 3 February 1995, HADB, V24/x287.

68 Ibid.

69 Ibid.; underlined in the original.

70 A. von Ungern-Sternberg led the Treasury Products Working Party. Memo from J. C. Newman and J. M. Yallop to MG Group Board, 2 March 1995, HADB, V17/x39. The Working Party's report of 20 January 1995 is in HADB, ZA18/60. Members were von Ungern-Sternberg, B. Cuthbert, F. Dannemann, M. deSa, J. C. Newman, H. Schlawin, J. M. Yallop.

71 'Defining the Investment Banking Group', 3 February 1995, HADB, V24/x287. See also Paper sent from Mark Yallop to Craven, 31 January 1995. Enclosing Appendix to the 'Defining the Investment Bank' paper for the Management Board, HADB, V17/x39.

72 'Defining the Investment Banking Group', 3 February 1995, HADB, V24/x287.

73 Fax from Craven to Schmitz and Breuer, 16 February 1995. Enclosing amended paper 'Defining the Investment Banking Group', HADB, V17/x39.

74 Ibid.

75 Ibid.

76 Ibid.

77 Craven to Schneider-Lenné and Kopper, 20 February 1995, HADB, V17/x39.

78 Fax from Craven to Schmitz, 20 February 1995. Schmitz's name on the draft 20 February version is crossed out, HADB, V17/x39.

79 Draft memo by Craven, 24 February 1995, HADB, V17/x39.

80 'Defining the Investment Banking Group', revised version, 2 March 1995, HADB, V17/x39.

81 Signatories included Schneider-Lenné, Krumnow, von Heydebreck, Endres, Weiss, von Boehm-Bezing. Memo to all members of the Management Board for discussion at the Board meeting on 7 March 1995. Dated 3 March 1995, HADB, V37/x347. The memo was translated for Craven to be discussed at the Management Board on 7 March 1995, HADB, V17/x39.

82 'Investment Banking Division', note from Kopper to Management Board, 2 June 1995, HADB, V17/x8.

83 Note from Craven to Management Board members, 8 June 1995, HADB, V40/x69. Emphasis in the original.

84 Weiss to Management Board, 23 June 1995, HADB, V37/x346. This was in response to the position papers prepared by Dobson and others for the Management Board meeting on 25 June 1995.

85 Slides by Dobson from the Management Board meeting, attached to a memo to Schmitz 3 July 1995, HADB, V37/x346. Management Board minutes (in camera meeting), 25 June 1995, HADB, V40/x183.

86 'Investment Bank Possible Future Structure', Memo for Management Board on 25 June 1995, dated 19 June 1995, HADB, V17/x39.

87 Management Board minutes (in camera meeting), 25 June 1995, HADB, V40/x183.

88 'Brand name for investment banking', Position paper by Dobson to Management Board, HADB, ZA18/60.

89 Dobson to Schmitz 29 June 1995, HADB, V37/x346.

90 Craven to the Management Board members, 4 July 1995, HADB, V37/x346.

91 James Bethell, 'Kleinwort agrees £1bn Dresdner offer', *Independent*, 27 June 1995.

92 Richard W. Stevenson, 'Dresdner Bank bids $1.5 billion for Kleinwort', *New York Times*, 16 June 1995.

93 Erik Ipsen, 'Morgan Stanley and Warburg call off banking mega-merger', *New York Times*, 16 December 1994. A very similar sort of obstacle would later arise in the Dresdner–Deutsche Bank merger attempt.

94 'S. G. Warburg ärgert sich über die Deutsche Bank', *Frankfurter Allgemeine Zeitung*, 15 May 1995. Piers von Simson, Warburgs' M&A head, criticised Deutsche Bank's 'shocking and unacceptable behaviour' poaching its senior staff (ibid.)

95 'Warburg loses key men to Grenfell', *Financial Times*, 8 February 1995. See also the Lex column, ibid.

96 'Deutsche Bank announces appointment of Edson Mitchell as Head of Global Markets', Deutsche Bank, press release, 19 April 1995; John Wilcock, '$10m Deutsche raid on Merrill', *Independent*, 20 April 1995.

97 Craven to Schmitz, 9 March 1995, HADB, V17/x84.

98 Deutsche Bank Living History Project interview with Michael Dobson, 14 January 2014, HADB, ZA17.

99 Landon Thomas Jr, 'The High Price of Deutsche's Fall', *New York Times,* 1 January 2017. Philipp himself was promoted to the Management Board along with Mitchell on 1 June 2000.

100 Investment Banking Board minutes, 15 May 1995, HADB, V37/x153.

101 Investment Banking Board minutes, 18 July 1995, HADB, V37/x153.

102 Deutsche Bank Living History Project interview with Lord Aldington (Charles Low), 24 September 2014, HADB, ZA17. See also interview with Edson Mitchell, 'Edson Mitchell's Game Plan', *Euromoney*, September 1996.

103 Schmitz to Dobson, 11 May 1995, HADB, V37/x153.

104 Investment Banking Board minutes, 26 September 1995, Frankfurt, HADB, V37/x153.

105 Memo from Dobson to All Executives, Deutsche Morgan Grenfell, January 1996, HADB, V37/x126.

106 Regions included Germany, Europe, North America, Asia/Pacific.

107 Deutsche Bank Living History Project interview with Sir John Craven, 22 November 2013, HADB, ZA17.

108 'New Management Structure', *Forum Flash*, 9 July 1996, HADB V27/x91.

109 Andrew Garfield, 'Peter Young charged with Morgan Grenfell fraud', *Independent*, 19 October 1998. Roberts, *The City*, pp. 299–300.

110 Securities included Alulux Mining, Sandvest Petroleum, Opcon AB and Sendit B. Young was subsequently deemed unfit to face trial.

111 Augar, *Chasing Alpha*, p. 22–3.

112 Deutsche Bank Living History Project interview with Lord Aldington (Charles Low), 24 September 2014, HADB, ZA17.

113 Draft memo by Craven sent to Schmitz, Breuer and Dobson, 7 January 1997, HADB, V37/x158.

114 Schmitz to Craven, copied to Breuer and Dobson, 14 January 1997, HADB, V37/x158.

115 Draft memo by Craven sent to Schmitz, Breuer and Dobson, 7 January 1997, HADB, V37/x158.

116 Investment Banking Board minutes, 25 March 1996, HADB, V37/x153.

117 Investment Banking Board minutes, 29 July 1997, HADB, V37/x153.

118 Investment Banking Board minutes, 20 November 1996, HADB, V37/x153

119 Investment Banking Board minutes, 21 April 1997, HADB, V37/x153.

120 Investment Banking Board minutes, 4 November 1997, HADB, V37/x153.

121 Ibid.

122 Group Executive Committee minutes, 17–18 February 1997, HADB, V40/x194.

123 Investment Banking Board minutes, 4 February 1997, HADB, V37/x153.

124 Ibid.

125 Group Executive Committee minutes, 17–18 February 1997, HADB, V40/x194.

126 Ibid.

127 'Our Strategy', Paper presented by Thompson to the Board in September 1997, HADB, V37/x160.

128 Memo from McClelland and Thompson to Dobson, 29 November 1997; Memo from Thompson and McClelland to Schmitz, Ackermann and Dobson, 23 December 1997, HADB, V37/x160. McClelland was co-head of the IBD with Thompson at the time.

129 'The Creation of a "Corporate Bank"', Presentation prepared by Bilstein, Fitschen, McClelland, Mitchell and Philipp, 12 December 1997, HADB, V37/x501.

130 Ibid.

131 *Forum*, February 1998.

132 'Restructuring: At the Crossroads', *Forum*, April 1998, p. 10.

133 Ibid.

134 Baron, *Late Remorse*, p. XX.

135 Deutsche Bank, press release, 20 May 1998, HADB, V37/x266.

136 Ibid.

III. The Bankers Trust Acquisition, 1999

1 Deutsche Bank Living History Project interview with Ronaldo Schmitz, 24 September 2013.

2 Quoted in John Schmid, 'Deutsche Bank on the Prowl in U.S.', *International Herald Tribune*, 19 February 1997.

3 DBNA Strategic Plan Summary, Draft, 28 March 1994, HADB, V17/x24.

4 Ibid.

5 Investment Banking Board minutes, 17 October 1995, HADB, V37/x153.

6 Ibid.

7 Investment Banking Board minutes, 20 November 1995, HADB, V37/x153.

8 'Project Cardinal', Memo by Schmitt (AfK), Asquith (DMG CFO) and McClelland (DMG North America) to Schmitz for the Management Board meeting on 2 April 1996, 29 March 1996, HADB, V24/x299.

9 'Project Cardinal', Memo for Schmitz for the Management Board meeting on 19 March 1996, 18 March 1996, HADB, V24/x298.

10 Investment Banking Board minutes, 26 January 1996, HADB, V37/x153.

11 Investment Banking Board minutes, 27 February 1996, HADB, V37/x153.

12 'Project Cardinal', Memo by Schmitt (AfK), Asquith (DMG CFO) and McClelland (DMG North America) to Schmitz for the Management Board meeting on 2 April 1996, 29 March 1996, HADB, V24/x299.

13 Investment Banking Board minutes, 9 December 1997, HADB, V37/x153.

14 Investment Banking Board minutes, 26 July 1996, HADB, V37/x153.

15 Investment Banking Board minutes, 22 October 1996, HADB, V37/x153.

16 'Deutsche Bank North America', presentation by Carter McClelland to the Management Board, 16 December 1996, HADB, V40/x194.

17 Investment Banking Board minutes, 25 February 1997, HADB, V37/x153.

18 'The battle of the bulge bracket', *The Economist*, 26 November 1998.

19 Quoted in Peter Lee, 'Deutsche dumps its investment bankers', *Euromoney*, July 1998.

20 John Schmid, 'High-Tech Team Quits Deutsche Bank', *New York Times*, 15 July 1998.

21 Impermissable activities included merchant banking, commodities, insurance and real estate. Eligible securities included municipal bonds, US government bonds, private placement of commercial paper and real estate bonds.

22 Memo by Kohler and Otto (Legal) for Dobson, Schmitz, Asquith, McClelland, Mitchell, 23 January 1997, HADB, V37/x142c.

23 Memorandum from May 1996, sent by Barry Allardice to Schmitz and McClelland on 19 February 1997, HADB, V37/x142c.

24 Investment Banking Division, Strategy Plan, Deutsche Morgan Grenfell, Investment Banking Board, 21 April 1997, HADB, V37/x501.

25 Reported in John Schmid, 'Deutsche Bank on the Prowl in U.S.', *International Herald Tribune*, 19 February 1997.

26 Memo from Carter McClelland to Schmitz, including presentation on Project Penguin, 24 March 1997, HADB, V37/x142c.

27 Ibid.

28 Ibid.

29 Memo by von Heydebreck to Breuer and Schmitz, 11 April 1997, HADB, V37/x142c.

30 Memo by von Heydebreck to Schmitz, 16 April 1997, HADB, V37/x142c.

31 Letter from Newman to Schmitz, 11 April 1997, HADB, V37/x142c.

32 Memo from Allardice to Schmitz, copied to McClelland, 28 April 1997, HADB, V37/x142c.

33 'Penguin', Memo dictated by Schmitz, 16 May 1997, HADB, V37/x142c.

34 Memo by Schmitz to Breuer, 27 May 1997, HADB, V37/x142c.

35 Ibid.

36 Ibid.

37 'Deutsche Bank / Deutsche Morgan Grenfell in Mittel- und Osteuropa', Memo by Bilstein and Vontz for Management Board meeting on 3 December 1996, dated 14 November 1996, HADB, V24/x303; Memo for Management Board meeting on 21 October 1997, dated 16 October 1997, HADB, ZA1/x3959; Memo, 'Deutsche Bank Ltd. Moscow – request of increase of regulatory capital', 21 April 1999, HADB, ZA2/x981.

38 'Deutsche Bank versucht neuen Anlauf im Investmentbanking', *Frankfurter Allgemeine Zeitung*, 16 July 1998; 'Deutsche Bank on US expansion trail', *Financial Times*, 13 July 1998.

39 Project Liberty, Short Profile, for Discussion, 14 July 1998, HADB, V37/x266. Kobrak, in his history of Deutsche Bank in the US suggests the idea came from Edson Mitchell to Breuer. Kobrak, *Banking on Global Markets*, p. 334.

40 Saul Hansell, 'Bankers Trust Settles Suit with P. & G.', *New York Times*, 20 May 1996.

41 Ibid.

42 The example was included in a case: Michael Moffett and Barbara Petitt, Procter and Gamble versus Bankers Trust: Caveat Emptor, Thunderbird School of Global Management, 2005.

43 Wolfensohn had been owned by James Wolfensohn who left the firm to become the president of the World Bank in 1995.

44 Bankers Trust, Memo for Analysts' Meeting, 7 April 1997, HADB, K50/5/100.

45 Lehman Bros, Short Profile, for Discussion, 1 September 1998, HADB, V37/x501.

46 Memo from Lauk and Wieandt to Schmitz and Ackermann, 1 September 1998, HADB, V37/x501.

47 This view was also conveyed to Ackermann on 20 August 1998 by Wieandt and Caspar von Blomberg (SKPL), 'Strategic Options IBD', HADB, V50/366.

48 Memo from Lauk and Wieandt to Schmitz and Ackermann, 1 September 1998, HADB, V37/x501.

49 Project Liberty, Short Profile for Discussion, 14 July 1998, HADB, V37/x266. Alex. Brown and Sons Co. had been founded in New York in 1800 and purchased its first seat on the NYSE in 1933. In 1992 it led IPOs for AOL and Starbucks. In 2016 Raymond James bought the US private client services unit of Deutsche Asset & Wealth Management and operated it under the Alex. Brown brand.

50 JP Morgan, Company Update, 7 December 1998, HADB, V50/583.

51 Date of contact from 'Erwerb von Bankers Trust New York Corporation', Memo for Supervisory Board, 23 November 1998, HADB, V40/x111; 'Project Circle', Discussion Materials, 15 November 1998, HADB, V27/x92.

52 'Project Circle', Discussion Materials, 15 November 1998, p. 4, HADB, V27/x92.

53 'Project Circle', Presentation to the Steering Committee, 22 November 1998, HADB, V27/x92.

54 Kopper to members of the Supervisory Board, 24 November 1998, HADB, V37/x654. Kopper had become Chairman of the Supervisory Board in May 1997.

55 Supervisory Board minutes (extraordinary meeting), 29 November 1998, HADB, V37/x654.

56 'Erwerb von Bankers Trust New York Corporation', memo for Supervisory Board, 23 November 1998, HADB, V40/x111.

57 Kobrak, *Banking on Global Markets*, p. 340.

58 'Agreement and Plan of Merger by and among Deutsche Bank AG, circle Acquisition Corporation and Bankers Trust Corporation, dated as of November 29, 1998', memo by Hans-Dirk Krekeler for Ackermann, Breuer, Krumnow and Schmitz, 27 November 1998, HADB, V50/583. A US Holding Company (Circle Acquisition Corporation) was set up and owned 70 per cent ($6.3 billion equity) by DB AG Frankfurt and 30 per cent ($2.7 billion debt) by DB AG New York Branch. This company then paid $9 billion to BT shareholders. Presentation by Detlef Bindert, Deutsche Bank Group Treasurer to ISC Meeting, 29 April 1999, HADB, V50/583.

59 Annual General Meeting on 18 March 1999, Extract of speech of Dr Rolf-E. Breuer, HADB, V37/x654.

60 James, 'The Deutsche Bank and the Dictatorship 1933–1945'. In 2001 James completed a book length treatment of this era, *The Deutsche Bank and the Nazi Economic War Against the Jews*.

61 JP Morgan, Company Update, 7 December 1998, HADB, V50/583.

62 Ibid.

63 John Paulson to Rolf Breuer, 9 February 1999, HADB, V27/x20.

64 Integration Steering Committee minutes, 12 May 1999, HADB, V37/x654.

65 Benjamin Weiser, 'Bankers Trust admits diverting unclaimed money', *New York Times,* 12 March 1999.

66 JP Morgan, Company Update, 7 December 1998, HADB, V50/583.

67 Operating Committee of the America's Weekly Update, 22 January 1999, HADB, V50/364. Positions were booked to non-US entities.

68 Implementation Review Committee minutes, 24 August 1999, HADB, V37/x657.

69 Status of Retention Programme, 11 June 1999, HADB, V37/x657.

70 Implementation Review Committee minutes, 24 August 1999, HADB, V37/x657.

71 By 30 June 1999 31 per cent of the target staff had been laid off (2,626) using up 48 per cent of the restructuring provision (total DM1.241 billion). Integration Office Team/IRC minutes, 28 July 1999, HADB, V37/x657.

72 Email notice to members of the committees, 6 December 1999, HADB, V37/x657.

73 Fasttrack executive: newsletter for Senior Management for internal distribution only, July 1999, HADB, V37/x657.

74 Presentation to Integration Steering Committee meeting on 15 April 1999, HADB, V37/x657.

75 Fasttrack executive: newsletter for Senior Management for internal distribution only, July 1999, HADB, V37/x657.

76 Ibid.

77 Ibid.

78 'German companies adopt fund for slave laborers under Nazis', *New York Times*, 17 February 1999.

79 Spiliotis, *Verantwortung*; Niethammer, *Forced Labor*.

80 Management Board minutes, 17 December 1997, HADB, V40/x188. 'Biggest German bank admits and regrets dealing in Nazi gold', *New York Times*, 1 August 1998. One outcome from the Commission was Steinberg, *Gold Transactions*.

81 'Deutsche Bank linked to Auschwitz funding', *New York Times*, 5 February 1999.

82 Letter from Breuer to Alan G. Hevesi, 3 May 1999, HADB, V27/x20.

83 Letter from Hevesi to Alan Greenspan (Chair of Federal Reserve), William J. McDonough (Federal Reserve Bank of New York), Elizabeth McCaul (New York Superintendent of Banks), 5 May 1999, HADB, V27/x20.

84 Jesse Angelo, 'Goodbye, Newman: German Bank gives BT Chief das boot', *New York Post*, 30 June 1999.

85 Memo for members of the Management Board, 21 May 1999, HADB, V37/x654.

86 Ackermann speech at his final AGM on 31 May 2012, p. 10 (https://agm.db.com/en/docs/HV2012_Rede_ Ackermann_en.pdf; last accessed 8 March 2019).

87 Kobrak, *Banking on Global Markets*, p. 349.

IV. The Failed Merger with Dresdner Bank, 1999–2000

1 For a review of contemporary literature see, Berger/ Demsetz/Strahan, *The Consolidation*; Bliss/Rosen, *CEO Compensation*.

2 'Die blauen Herren des Geldes lassen sich Zeit', *Süddeutsche Zeitung*, 13 November 2000.

3 Ibid.

4 Allianz also owned 4.9 per cent of Deutsche Bank.

5 'Deutsche and Dresdner set to merge in search for growth', *Financial Times*, 8 March 2000; Eggenkämper/ Modert/Pretzlik, *Allianz*, p. 356.

6 'Neupositionierung des Privatkundengeschäfts in Deutschland – Grundkonzept, Feasibility, Schritte zur Umsetzung', Memo by von Heydebreck to Breuer, 28 March 1998, HADB, V27/x96.

7 Ibid., p. 4.

8 Koetter, *Evaluating*; see also Koetter, *Assessment*.

9 'Daphne & Chloe: Gemeinsame Vorlage', presentation dated 16 August 1999, HADB, V34/77.

10 Memo from Wieandt to von Heydebreck and Pauluhn, 18 August 1999, HADB, V34/77.

11 'Zusammenführung der Retailgeschäfte der Deutschen Bank (Deutsche Bank 24, Projektname ‚Daphne') und der Dresdner Bank (‚Chloé')', Memo by Wieandt and Pauluhn for Breuer and von Heydebreck, 20 August 1999, HADB, V34/77.

12 'Walter: "Wir wollen beide nicht fusionieren"', *Frankfurter Allgemeine Zeitung*, 28 September 1999.

13 'Deutsche Bank bedauert Scheitern der Gespräche mit Dresdner Bank', *Frankfurter Allgemeine Zeitung*, 6 October 1999.

14 Interview with Paul Achleitner, December 2018.

15 'Chronologie der Gespräche zwischen Deutsche Bank, Dresdner Bank und Allianz – November 1999 bis April 2000', 14 April 2000, HADB, V27/x2.

16 Eurohypo and Deutsche Hyp were the mortgage banks of Deutsche Bank and Dresdner Bank, respectively.

17 'Chronologie der Gespräche zwischen Deutsche Bank, Dresdner Bank und Allianz – November 1999 bis April 2000', 14 April 2000, p. 3, HADB, V27/x2.

18 Ibid., p. 4.

19 Supervisory Board minutes (extraordinary meeting), 8 March 2000, HADB, V40/x112.

20 Ibid.

21 'Chronologie der Gespräche zwischen Deutsche Bank, Dresdner Bank und Allianz – November 1999 bis April 2000', 14 April 2000, p. 6, HADB, V27/x2.

22 Ibid.

23 David Schirreff, 'No! To the Blender', *Euromoney*, 1 April 2000.

24 'Gemeinsame Erklärung der Vorstände der Deutsche Bank AG und Dresdner Bank AG gegenüber den Arbeitnehmervertretungen beider Gesellschaften', signed by Breuer and Walter, 13 March 2000, HADB, V40/x112.

25 'Außerordentliche Sitzung des Aufsichtsrats Deutsche Bank AG, Frankfurt, den 8. März 2000 – Verschmelzung mit der Dresdner Bank zur Deutsche Bank NEU', HADB, V37/x502.

26 Supervisory Board minutes (extraordinary meeting), 8 March 2000, HADB, V40/x112.

27 Deutsche Bank New would keep a minority stake of 10 per cent in Deutsche Bank 24 New and name its CEO and supervisory board head, while Allianz would name the chief financial officer and the deputy supervisory board head. Membership of the executive board and shareholder representation on the supervisory board of Deutsche Bank 24 New would be divided equally between Deutsche Bank New and Allianz.

28 Supervisory Board minutes (extraordinary meeting), 8 March 2000, p. 6, HADB, V40/x112.

29 'Chronologie der Gespräche zwischen Deutsche Bank, Dresdner Bank und Allianz – November 1999 bis April 2000', 14 April 2000, p. 7, HADB, V27/x2.

30 'Dresdner arm faces closure', Financial Times, 9 March 2000.

31 Quoted in David Schirreff, 'No! To the Blender', Euromoney, 1 April 2000.

32 'Deutsche and Dresdner set to merge in search for growth', Financial Times, 8 March 2000.

33 Memo by Wolfram Schmitt to Breuer and Labak, 14 March 2000, HADB, V27/x3.

34 Ibid.

35 'Deutsche Bank to Shut Bulk of Dresdner Kleinwort Unit', Bloomberg, 5 April 2000.

36 General Public Monitor: March 2000, Group Brand and Market Research, 4 April 2000, HADB, V27/x2.

37 Supervisory Board minutes (extraordinary meeting), 14 March 2000, HADB, V40/x112.

38 Ibid.

39 Letter from Dresdner Bank management board to Deutsche Bank Management Board, 29 March 2000, HADB, V38/x3.

40 Memo from Wieandt and Fremerey (Integration Office) to Schmitz, 16 March 2000, HADB, V27/x3.

41 Ibid.

42 Memo from Wieandt and Fremerey to Breuer, Ackermann and Schmitz enclosing revised discussion paper on Dresdner Kleinwort Benson, 17 March 2000, HADB, V27x/3.

43 Minutes of the meeting of the Integration committee at Dresdner Bank, minutes by Klaus Rosenfeld of Dresdner Bank, 17 March 2000, HADB, V27/x4.

44 'Deutsche admits DKB is for sale', Financial Times, 17 March 2000. See also Nicholas Bannister, 'Deutsche may break up the Kleinwort "jewel"', Guardian, 17 March 2000. 'Chronologie der Gespräche zwischen Deutsche Bank, Dresdner Bank und Allianz – November 1999 bis April 2000', 14 April 2000, p. 7, HADB, V27/x2.

45 Project Downtown, Discussion Materials on Investment Banking, 14 March 2000, HADB, V27/x7.

46 Memo, DKB – Discussion with Morgan Stanley Dean Witter (MSDW), 19 March 2000, HADB, V27/x7.

47 DKB – Evaluation of Options by Morgan Stanley Dean Witter, Memo by Wieandt and Fremerey for Breuer, Ackermann and Schmitz, 21 March 2000, HADB, V27/x3.

48 'Chronologie der Gespräche zwischen Deutsche Bank, Dresdner Bank und Allianz – November 1999 bis April 2000', 14 April 2000, p. 7, HADB, V27/x2.

49 Letter from Dresdner Bank management board to Deutsche Bank Management Board, 29 March 2000, HADB, V38/x3.

50 Ibid.

51 Ibid.

52 Ibid.

53 Ibid.

54 'Deutsche chief criticised over Dresdner deal', Financial Times, 3 April 2000.

55 Wieandt to Breuer, 'Optionen Dresdner Kleinwort Benson (DKB)', 3 April 2000, HADB, V27/x7.

56 'Deutsche Bank to Shut Bulk of Dresdner Kleinwort Unit', Bloomberg, 5 April 2000. See also the detailed reports in 'Dresdner, Deutsche Bank Clash', Wall Street Journal Europe, 5 April 2000; 'German bank merger in

57 Philip Eade, 'People: T. J. Lim', Euromoney, 1 December 2000.

58 Supervisory Board minutes, 5 April 2000, HADB, V40/x112.

59 'Chronologie der Gespräche zwischen Deutsche Bank, Dresdner Bank und Allianz - November 1999 bis April 2000', 14 April 2000, p. 8, HADB, V27/x2; Ad-hoc Release Dresdner Bank AG, 5 April 2000, 3.18 p.m.

60 Reuters, 8 April 2000.

61 Letter to Members of Staff, 11 April 2000, HADB, V27/x79.

62 Supervisory Board minutes (extraordinary meeting), 20 April 2000, HADB, V40/x112. Bloomberg reported that Renner and Mönig-Raane had called the meeting on 13 April 2000. Letter from Mönig-Raane to Kopper, 12 April 2000, HADB, V40/x112.

63 'Renner – Arbeitgeber-Unterstützung für Breuer nicht einhellig', Reuters, 8 April 2000. Also quoted in Süddeutsche Zeitung, 8 April 2000. Clippings in HADB, V40/x112.

64 Group Brand and Market Research, De-Merger: Impact on Target Groups (April 2000), 27 April 2000, HADB, V27/x2.

65 'Deutliche Image-Belastungen, aber kein Worst Case Szenario', Memo by Habig and Hörter for Breuer and members of the Management Board, 27 April 2000, HADB, V27/x2.

66 Eggenkämper/Modert/Pretzlik, Allianz, p. 356.

67 Chris Isidore, 'Stock deal valued by firms at $33b joins two of banking's biggest names', CNN Money, 13 September 2000. In this article Deutsche Bank was reported as considering buying JP Morgan.

68 Ibid.

69 'Kleinwort Benson chairman quits over strategy', Independent, 1 March 1997.

V. The Retail Bank: Cinderella or Fairy Godmother?

1 Brunner et al., System.

2 Up to 4,000 GDR-mark per head for citizens below 60 years and up to 6,000 GDR-mark for citizens above 59. For higher amounts the exchange rate was 2:1.

3 See Osenberg, East. Axel Osenberg was a member of the management board of Deutsche Bank-Kreditbank in Berlin.

4 'The Battle Plans of Hilmar Kopper', Euromoney, January 1994.

5 The Deutsche Bank Berlin, located in West Berlin since 1949, was also rolled into Deutsche Bank in April 1991.

6 Die Zeit, 17 August 1990.

7 Büschgen, Deutsche Bank, pp. 734–5.

8 See Osenberg, East.

9 Frost, Wünsche, pp. 96–7.

10 Supervisory Board minutes, 22 July 1997, HADB, V40/x110.

11 Report by Georg Krupp to the Supervisory Board, 22 July 1997, HADB, V40/x110; Management Board minutes, 12 May 1992, HADB, V40/x178.

12 Deutsche Bank, Annual Report 1999.

13 Supervisory Board minutes, 3 July 1990, p. 21, HADB, V17/x94.

14 Büschgen, Deutsche Bank, p. 702. By 1993 there were one million in the higher income retail group, who generated 15 per cent of the division's profits.

15 Supervisory Board minutes, 3 July 1990, p. 22, HADB, V17/x94.
16 Frost, *Wünsche*, pp. 101, 213–14.
17 Büschgen, *Deutsche Bank*, pp. 642–4.
18 Management Board minutes (in camera meeting), 25 November 1991, HADB, V40/x176.
19 Ibid.
20 Ibid.
21 Management Board minutes, 14 January 1992, HADB, V40/x178.
22 Management Board minutes, 17 March 1992, HADB, V40/x178. 'Stand und Umsetzung des Projekts zur Wiederherstellung der Profitabilität im Kreditgeschäft des GB Privatkunden', Memo by Pauluhn and Becker for Management Board meeting on 10 May 1994, HADB, V24/x278.
23 Management Board minutes, 29 August 1994, HADB, V40/x181.
24 'Neue Struktur der Bank im Inland', *Forum Flash*, 12 November 1996.
25 Memo by Gerard, Pauluhn, Juncker and Guterman for the Management Board, 12 November 1996, HADB, V27/x91.
26 Management Board minutes, 15 November 1994, HADB, V40/x182.
27 DeYoung, *Performance*.
28 Management Board minutes, 4 July 1994, HADB, V40/x181.
29 'Projekt "Alternative Vertriebswege" im Unternehmensbereich Privat- und Geschäftskunden', Memo by Steinig and Pauluhn, 7 October 1996, HADB, V34/22.
30 'Aufbau einer Direktbank', Memo by Sefranek/Pauluhn for Management Board meeting on 30 January 1995, HADB, V24/x286.
31 Ibid.
32 Management Board minutes, 5 September 1995, HADB, V40/x184.
33 'Business Plan für die BANK 24 – 1995 bis 2000', Presentation dated 22 August 1995, HADB, V26/x54.
34 Management Board minutes, 2 May 1995, HADB, V40/x183.
35 'Direktbank: Geschäftsleitung und Standort', Memo by Steinig and Pauluhn for Management Board meeting on 21 February 1995, HADB, V24/x287.
36 'Projekt "Alternative Vertriebswege" im Unternehmensbereich Privat- und Geschäftskunden', Memo by Steinig and Pauluhn, 7 October 1996, HADB, V34/22.
37 Ibid.
38 Management Board minutes, 12 November 1996, HADB, V40/x186.
39 Management Board minutes, 3 December 1996, HADB, V40/x186.
40 Supervisory Board minutes, 28 January 1997, V40/x110.
41 Memo by von Heydebreck to Breuer, 28 March 1998, HADB, V27/x96.
42 Supervisory Board of Bank 24 AG minutes, 4 November 1998, HADB, V34/26.
43 Ibid.
44 'Neuausrichtung UB Privat- und Geschäftskunden', status report for the Supervisory Board meeting, 27 January 1999, HADB, V40/x111.
45 Frost, *Wünsche*, pp. 107–19.
46 Supervisory Board minutes, 23 October 2000, HADB, V40/x112.
47 Frost, *Wünsche*, p. 113.
48 'Deutsche Bank begins retail overhaul', *Financial Times*, 13 September 2002.
49 In May 2018, Deutsche Bank Privat- und Geschäftskunden AG was merged with Postbank, becoming DB Privat- und Firmenkundenbank AG.
50 Rainer Neske, Deutsche Bank Private & Business Clients, presentation for Supervisory Board, 2 February 2005, p. 7, HADB, V51/x389.
51 Ferslev, *Corporate Strategy at Deutsche Bank 1985–1997*, pp. 33–4.
52 Ibid., p. 34.
53 'Ich war elektrisiert' (Interview with Edmund Stoiber), *Capital*, issue no. 9, 1997.
54 Supervisory Board minutes, 9 July 1996, HADB, V18/x28a; Management Board minutes, 15 September 1997, HADB, V40/x188.
55 'Built in Bavaria', *The Economist*, 24 July 1997.
56 'Strategic Scan', AfK Presentation 15 May 2006, HADB, V50/x66.
57 Ibid.
58 Supervisory Board of Deutsche Bank Privat- und Geschäftskunden AG minutes, 14 July 2006, HADB, V34/29.
59 Supervisory Board of Deutsche Bank Privat- und Geschäftskunden AG minutes, 13 October 2006, HADB, V34/29.
60 Deutsche Bank's purchase of Norisbank did not include staff, systems platforms and the main product 'easy credit'. The refreshed Norisbank started operating in September 2007. See Frost, *Wünsche*, pp. 127–9.
61 Helmut Kohl to Kopper, 28 September 1995, HADB, V38/x6.
62 Kopper to Kohl, 23 October 1995, HADB, V38/x6.
63 Ibid.
64 Ibid.
65 BIS Triennial Survey of Foreign Exchange, April 1998 (https://www.bis.org/publ/r_fx98statanx.pdf).
66 EMU Preparations in Deutsche Morgan Grenfell, February 1998, HADB, V37/x304.
67 Comment to Dr Brun's EMU Monitoring First Report to Management Board, 23 December 1997, HADB, V37/x304.
68 Schmitz to Cohrs and Friedrich Schmitz, 17 February 1998, HADB, V37/x304.
69 Ibid.
70 Ackermann and Schmitz to the GCI Board, 20 March 1998, HADB, V37/x304.
71 Memo from DMG EMU Project Team to GCI Board, 2 April 1998, HADB, V37/x304.
72 Deutsche Bank, Annual Report 1999.
73 'The Battle Plans of Hilmar Kopper', *Euromoney*, January 1994.
74 Ibid., p. 29.
75 Ibid., pp. 29–30.
76 Ibid., p. 30.
77 Memo by Wintels and Pradelli (AfK) for von Boehm-Bezing, Breuer and von Heydebreck, 15 July 1999, HADB, V27/x215.
78 Thelen (AfK) to Breuer, 2 July 1999, HADB, V27/x215.
79 Memo by Wintels and Pradelli (AfK) for von Boehm-Bezing, Breuer and von Heydebreck, 15 July 1999, HADB, V27/x215.
80 Deutsche Bank, Annual Report 2001.
81 Memo Kors Korsmeier (AfK), 17 January 2002, HADB, F199/53.

82 Presentation by Rainer Neske, head of PBC, at the Goldman Sachs Annual European Financials Conference, Berlin, 12 June 2008 (https://www.db.com/ir/en/download/Neske_GS_Conf_Berlin_12_June_2008_final.pdf).

83 Patrick Jenkins, 'Josef Ackermann hits a crossroads', *Financial Times*, 13 July 2004.

84 Norisbank data from Deutsche Bank media release, 4 August 2006. Berliner Bank data from Deutsche Bank Media Release, 2 January 2007 and Deutsche Bank Annual Review 2007, p. 39. Data for Postbank from its Annual Report 2007.

85 'Deutsche Post hints at sale of bank stake', *Financial Times*, 8 November 2007.

86 'Commerzbank CEO flags interest in buying Postbank', *Reuters*, 23 November 2007.

87 Daniel Schäfer and Marcus Theurer, 'Sandkastenspiele', *Frankfurter Allgemeine Zeitung*, 28 March 2008.

88 'Deutsche Bank avoids losses that peers couldn't escape', *International Herald Tribune*, 8 February 2008

89 James Wilson, 'Postbank sale talks "moving quickly"', *Financial Times*, 25 June 2008.

90 Deutsche Bank Ad Hoc announcement dated 12 September 2008.

91 Deutsche Bank Ad Hoc announcement dated 14 January 2009.

92 Email from Ackermann and Neske to all permanent staff, *Deutsche Bank Group Internal Communications*, 26 November 2010.

VI. The Road to 2007

1 November 2007 Securitisation Industry Batch, dated for the Risk Committee meeting on 6 December 2007, HADB, V50/x97.

2 United States Senate Permanent Subcommittee on Investigations, *Wall Street and the Financial Crisis: Anatomy of a Financial Collapse,* 2011 (= PSI Report), p. 335.

3 November 2007 Securitisation Industry Batch, dated for the Risk Committee meeting on 6 December 2007, HADB, V50/x97.

4 The proposal from the end of April was approved without any adjustment by the Management Board on 2 May 1994, HADB, V40/x181.

5 Memo by v. Maltzan (Trading & Sales), Bilstein (Corporate Finance) and Rolls (DBNA) to Schmitz and Breuer for the Management Board meeting on 26 April 1994, 22 April 1994, HADB, V24/x278.

6 Hill later wrote a book about his role in financial innovation, see Hill, *Finance Monsters*.

7 Memo by v. Maltzan (Trading & Sales), Bilstein (Corporate Finance) and Rolls (DBNA) to Schmitz and Breuer for the Management Board meeting on 26 April 1994, 22 April 1994, HADB, V24/x278.

8 Ibid.

9 Ibid.

10 Timmermann to Krumnow, 2 May 1994, HADB, V24/x278.

11 Memo for Management Board meeting on 5 May 1998, 'DMG/Mortgage-backed Securities (MBS) and DBNA: Newport Funding Corp., Delaware (NFC)', 24 April 1998, HADB, V50/353.

12 Ibid.

13 'Newport Funding Corp.', Memo for Management Board, 14 April 1998, HADB, V50/353.

14 Memo from Allardice, Hamilton and Hendel to Krumnow, 1 May 1998, HADB, V50/364.

15 Letter by Detlef Bindert (Group Treasurer) to John Keleghan (Controller DMG New York), 19 May 1998, HADB, V50/364.

16 Schmitz to Ackermann, Allardice, Mitchell, Philipp, 19 June 1998, HADB, V50/364.

17 John J. Gentile, Assistant Regional Director Broker-Dealer inspection Program (SEC) to Robert Lynch, Managing Director (DB Securities Inc.), 31 July 1998, HADB, V50/364.

18 Memo by Bänziger to Ackermann and Schmitz, 12 August 1998, HADB, V50/364. Haircuts are the reduction in the value of an asset compared to its face value, often due to the risk that the borrower will be unable to repay the full amount.

19 Operating Committee of the Americas Weekly Update, 29 January 1999, HADB, V50/364.

20 Deutsche Morgan Grenfell, Global Markets Research, 'Mortgage-Backed Security Research Real Estate Collateral Risk', 3 May 1998, HADB, V50/364.

21 Memo from Nathan Muller and Michelle Cenis to Krekeler, 24 April 1998, HADB, V50/364. GACC was a subsidiary of Deutsche Bank specialising in MBS.

22 Krekeler to Schmitz, Allardice, Gary Hendel, Fritz Link, 28 April 1998, HADB, V50/364. Allardice had replaced McClelland as CEO for the Americas in March 1998.

23 Memo from Schmitz to Mitchell, 5 May 1998. Presentation 'Discussion of MBS Business' is dated 1 May 1998, HADB, V50/353.

24 Memo from Mitchell to Schmitz, 8 May 1998, HADB, V50/364.

25 These MBS were risk weighted at 0 per cent compared to the on-balance sheet Securities Inventory (50 per cent), Secured Lending (100 per cent) and Whole Loans (100 per cent). Memo from Mitchell to Schmitz, 8 May 1998, HADB, V50/364.

26 Bänziger to Ackermann, 14 October 1998, HADB, V50/364.

27 Kopper to the Supervisory Board of Deutsche Bank AG, 21 September 2000, HADB, V22/x1.

28 Mitchell joined the Management Board in June 2000. Presentation on Group Strategy to Shareholder Representatives in the Supervisory Board, 24 July 2000, HADB, V27/x256.

29 Net income before tax and goodwill amortisation, after restructuring charges and capital charge on the basis of allocated book equity.

30 Internal Memo to CIB staff from Ackermann and von Boehm-Bezing, 21 February 2001, p. 2, HADB, ZA17/1177.

31 Ibid., p. 1.

32 Janssen, *Banking Strategies*, p. 107.

33 See, e.g. Kellermann, *Disentangling Deutschland AG*.

34 Memo by AfK, signed by Ferslev and Schäffner, 29 August 1994, HADB, V24/x282.

35 'Verkauf ausgewählter Industriebeteiligungen', Memo for Management Board by Schäffner and Schneider, 16 January 1996, HADB, V24/x296.

36 'Möglichkeiten zur Ausgliederung bzw. Abspaltung des Beteiligungsbesitzes', Memo by Ferslev and Schäffner for Management Board meeting 14–15 October 1996, 10 October 1996, HADB, V24/x303.

37 Memo by Pfeil and Schäffner, 5 November 1998, HADB, V38/x3.

38 Memo by Ferslev and Bilstein for Management Board members, 21 December 1992, HADB, ZA18/284.

39 Deutsche Bank, Annual Report 1998, p. 43.

40 Letter by Breuer to Members of the Group Executive Committee, 9 December 1998, HADB, V27/x373.

41 Jörg Eigendorf, 'Reif für die Top-Liga?', *Die Welt*, 31 July 2003.

42 'CIB Business Challenges and PCAM Connectivity', Presentation by Fitschen for G40 Conference on 16–17 November 2001, HADB, V50/442.

43 Minutes of the meeting of the GEC Off-site in Rome, 26 October 2002, HADB V50/x126.

44 Ibid.

45 'CIB Loan Exposure Management: organisation, governance and financial impact', presentation by Jain and Bänziger to GEC, 18 February 2003, HADB, V50/x261.

46 GEC minutes, 19 February 2002, HADB, V50/x126. Initial members of the GEC were Börsig, Fitschen, von Heydebreck, Ackermann, Parker, Cohrs, Lamberti, Walter, Virtue, Philipp, Jain.

47 GEC minutes, 28 May 2002, HADB, V50/x126.

48 GEC minutes, 18 February 2003, HADB, V50/x126.

49 'A giant hedge fund', *The Economist*, 26 August 2004.

50 Janssen, *Banking Strategies*, p. 109.

51 Robert von Heusinger, 'Goodbye, Deutsche Bank', *Die Zeit*, 30 September 2004.

52 Deutsche Bank, press release, 28 October 2004.

53 Edward Taylor, 'Deutsche Bank to lose a key board member', *Wall Street Journal*, 23 September 2004. 'Has Deutsche Bank lost its way?', *Business Week*, 22 November 2004. 'Nationale Verschwörung', *Der Spiegel*, 10 May 2004.

54 Corporate Development (AfK), 'Strategic Scan', 15 May 2006, HADB, V50/x66.

55 Deutsche Bank had already considered converting its Shanghai and Beijing representative offices into branches in November 1995, see memo by Simon Murray and Jürgen Fitschen for Cartellieri, 21 November 1995, HADB, V24/x294.

56 Letter to Shang Fulin (China Securities Regulatory Commission) from Ackermann and Fitschen, 4 March 2003, HADB, V50/x257.

57 Email from Ken Borda to CIB Executive Committee, 11 September 2002, HADB, V50/x257.

58 Ibid.

59 Memo by Frank Strauß, Philipp von Girsewald and Till Staffeldt for Group Board, 13 October 2005, HADB, V50/x231.

60 Memo by Till Staffeldt (Deutsche Bank AG Singapore) to Axel Wieandt, 26 July 2005, HADB, V50/x231.

61 Supervisory Board minutes, 6 February 2008, HADB, V51/x727.

62 Deutsche Bank, press release, 6 May 2010. Data from end 2009.

63 GEC minutes, 21 June 2010, HADB, V50/x694.

64 Email from Hubert Pandza to Ackermann, 31 January 2000, HADB, V50/342.

65 GEC minutes, 17 June 2003, HADB, V50/x126.

66 GEC minutes, 22 July 2003, HADB, V50/x126.

67 GEC minutes, 25 September 2003, HADB, V50/x126.

68 GEC minutes, 20 July 2004, HADB, V50/x126; 'Putin lockt Ackermann', *Der Spiegel*, 30 June 2008; Markus Balser and Martin Hesse, 'Putin und seine Freunde', *Süddeutsche Zeitung*, 27 November 2010.

69 Deutsche Bank, press release, 'Deutsche Bank and UFG Asset Management enter into strategic partnership', 11 September 2008.

70 Deutsche Bank, Press release, 23 June 2008 (https://www.db.com/russia/en/content/1087.htm).

71 FCIC Interview with Greg Lippmann, 20 May 2010. This meeting took place in February 2005 according to Zuckerman, *Trade*. Lippmann joined Deutsche Bank from Credit Suisse First Boston in 2000 and was part of the Securitised Products Group from March 2000. In 2002–03 he took over CDO trading in Deutsche Bank Securities Inc. (DBSI) and became head of ABS trading for North America and global head of CDO trading in June 2004. In June 2006 he was promoted to global head of ABS trading and CDO trading.

72 Zuckerman, *Trade*.

73 The Risk Committee was a committee of the Supervisory Board and met every two months to discuss the bank's exposure.

74 Deutsche Bank Risk Profile, presentation for Risk Committee, 18 March 2005, HADB, V50/x135.

75 Ibid., p. 48.

76 Memo by Jain to Ackermann, 'Derivatives Documentation', 13 October 2005, HADB, V50/x267.

77 Ibid.

78 Ibid.

79 Industry Batch, Hedge Funds, 6 May 2005, HADB, V50/x135.

80 Hedge Funds Industry Batch April 2005, GCPC comments, Memo by Bänziger, 17 May 2005, HADB, V50/x135.

81 Ibid.

82 Karen Weaver joined Deutsche Bank in 2000 as head of Deutsche Bank's Securitisation Research division, from CSFB and was based in New York. She left Deutsche Bank in 2010.

83 Weaver, *Subprime*. See also interview with Weaver quoted in NBC New, 'The Hansen Files: "If you had a pulse, we gave you a loan"' (last updated 22 March 2009). http://www.nbcnews.com/id/29827248/print/1/displaymode/1098/ (accessed 11 October 2019).

84 Karen Sibayan, 'DBSI debates California exposure', *Asset Securitization Report*, 23 May 2005, pp. 10–11.

85 Ibid., p. 11.

86 Ibid.

87 Deutsche Bank, media Release, New York, 11 May 2005. https://www.db.com/newsroom_news/archive/medien/deutsche-bank-continues-mbs-build-out-with-two-key-hires-en-11957.htm (accessed 11 October 2019).

88 FCIC Interview with Eugene Xu, 20 May 2010. Jacqueline Simmons and Elena Logutenkova, 'Deutsche Bank avoids subprime loan fallout', *International Herald Tribune*, 30 July 2007.

89 Scheicher, *CDO Market Pricing*, p. 14.

90 Hedge Funds Industry Batch April 2005, GCPC comments, Memo by Bänziger, 17 May 2005, HADB, V50/x135.

91 Deutsche Bank Risk Profile, presentation for Risk Committee, 10 June 2005, HADB, V50/x135.

92 Ibid.

93 Risk Committee minutes, 10 June 2005, HADB, V50/x135.

94 Parker joined the bank in 1997 from Morgan Stanley where he was head of Asian derivatives and global head of equity derivatives. He joined the GEC in 2002 as head of Global Equities and became head of Asset Management in autumn 2004. He left the bank in 2012.

95 Deutsche Asset Management, Supervisory Board Presentation by Kevin Parker, 28 July 2005, HADB, V50/x139.

96 BNP Paribas and Schroders also competed to take over the £46.3 billion in assets under management. Cost was £220 million up front and up to £45 million a year later depending on how much of the funds under management were retained. Sale included Morgan Grenfell European Growth Trust, which had been managed by Peter Young until the 1996 scandal.

97 Deutsche Asset Management, Supervisory Board Presentation by Kevin Parker, 28 July 2005, p. 29, HADB, V50/x139.

98 Deutsche Bank acquired Chicago-based real estate investment manager RREEF in 2002 for $490 million.

99 'Securitisation Industry Batch – June 2005', Memo by Bänziger, 28 July 2005, HADB, V50/x139.

100 Deutsche Bank Risk Profile, presentation for Risk Committee, 2 December 2005, p. 12b, HADB, V50/x139.

101 On Eugene Xu, see Jonathan R. Laing, 'Coming Home to Roost', *Wall Street Journal*, 13 February 2006; Jacqueline Simmons and Elena Logutenkova, 'Deutsche Bank avoids subprime loan fallout', *International Herald Tribune*, 30 July 2007.

102 'Shorting Home Equity Mezzanine Tranches', September 2005. Flip Book. PSI Report, p. 343, Footnote 1301; PSI Report and Appendix, Vol. 5, Part II, p. 126, Footnote Exhibits p. 0878.

103 Email from Lippmann to Amin Arjomand (DBSI), 19 September 2005, PSI Report and Appendix, Vol. 5, Part II, p. 123, Footnote Exhibits p. 0875.

104 FCIC Interview with Greg Lippmann, 20 May 2010.

105 Ibid.

106 Ibid.

107 'Shorting Home Equity Mezzanine Tranches', February 2007. Flip Book. PSI Report, p. 345, Footnote 1314; PSI Report and Appendix, Vol. 5, Part II, pp. 173–245, Footnote Exhibits pp. 0925-0997.

108 Ibid., p. 175, Footnote Exhibits p. 0927.

109 Ibid., p. 176, Footnote Exhibits p. 0928.

110 Ibid., p. 195, Footnote Exhibits p. 0947.

111 FCIC Interview with Greg Lippmann, 20 May 2010.

112 'Strategic Scan', presentation by AfK, 15 May 2006, HADB, V50/x66.

113 'Project Maiden – Supplementary Overview of Governance Structure', Memo by Jain to Group Board, 11 July 2006, HADB, V51/x729.

114 'Strategic Scan', presentation by AfK, 15 May 2006, HADB, V50/x66.

115 'Project Maiden – Supplementary Overview of Governance Structure', Memo by Jain to Group Board, 11 July 2006, HADB, V51/x729.

116 GEC minutes, 22 October 2007, HADB, V50/x108.

117 Quoted in 'Deutsche Bank Settles Lawsuit with the US', *Spiegel Online*, 11 May 2012 (http://www.spiegel.de/international/business/deutsche-bank-reaches-settlement-with-us-justice-department-a-832642.html).

118 Group Risk Strategy and Capital Planning, 2007, presentation for Risk Committee, 1 December 2006. Approved by the Management Board on 21 November 2006, HADB, V50/x38.

119 Email from Axilrod to Lippmann, 26 August 2006, PSI Report and Appendix, Vol. 5, Part II, pp. 161–2, Footnote Exhibits p. 0913-0914.

120 Email from Lippmann to Axilrod, 26 August 2006, PSI Report and Appendix, Vol. 5, Part II, p. 161, Footnote Exhibits p. 0913.

121 CDO Primary Update Progress Report, presentation October 2006, PSI Report and Appendix, Vol. 5, Part II, p. 257, Footnote Exhibits p. 1009.

122 Email from Derek Kaufman (JP Morgan) to Anshu Jain, 25 October 2006, PSI Report and Appendix, Vol. 5, Part IV, p. 1781, Footnote Exhibits p. 5852. Kaufman was head of Global Fixed Income in JP Morgan Chase's Proprietary Positioning Group. He left JP Morgan in April 2008 for Citadel Investment Group.

123 Email from Jain to Kaufman, 25 October 2006, PSI Report and Appendix, Vol. 5, Part IV, p. 1781, Footnote Exhibits p. 5852.

124 Email from Kaufman to Jain, 25 October 2006. Jain forwarded this correspondence to Michele Faissola, Philip Weingord, Rajeev Misra and Pablo Calderini. Misra forwarded on to Lippmann, d'Albert and Boaz Weinstein. PSI Report and Appendix, Vol. 5, Part IV, p. 1780, Footnote Exhibits p. 5851.

125 Email from Lippmann to Warren Dowd (DBNA San Francisco), 13 February 2007, PSI Report and Appendix, Vol. 5, Part IV, p. 1800, Footnote Exhibits p. 5871.

126 Email from Lippmann to Wyck Brown (Braddock Financial), 1 February 2007, PSI Report and Appendix, Vol. 5, Part II, p. 169, Footnote Exhibits p. 0921.

127 Email from Lippmann, 27 February 2007, PSI Report, p. 349, Footnote 1340; PSI Report and Appendix, Vol. 5, Part II, p. 270, Footnote Exhibits p. 1022.

128 Email from Lippmann to Kent Baum (DBNA San Francisco), 4 December 2006. PSI Report and Appendix, Vol. 5, Part II, p. 267, Footnote Exhibits p. 1019.

129 PSI Report, p. 344–5.

130 Briefing for Ackermann for Luncheon for Henry Paulson, Secretary of the Treasury, 14 June 2007, HADB, V50/x381. In mid-June 2007, Ackermann was invited to a small luncheon for US Treasury Secretary Paulson with various Fed and Treasury officials, and the heads of Morgan Stanley, JP Morgan Chase and Merrill Lynch to discuss the market.

131 *Huffington Post*, 17 July 2007 (https://www.huffingtonpost.com/2007/07/17/rolling-stones-play-priva_n_56513.html). *Der Spiegel* put the cost at €4 million, cf. 'Deutsche Bank bestellte Rolling Stones für Privatkonzert', *Spiegel Online*, 13 July 2007 (http://www.spiegel.de/wirtschaft/analysten-veranstaltung-deutsche-bank-bestellte-rolling-stones-fuer-privatkonzert-a-494279.html).

132 'Schicksalhafte Fehler der Führungsspitze' (Interview with David Folkerts-Landau), *Handelsblatt*, 22 May 2018.

133 Quoted in Gillian Tett and Joanna Chung, 'Leverage is to blame, says markets veteran', *Financial Times*, 12 July 2007.

134 Peers include BNP Paribas, Citigroup, Credit Suisse, Goldman Sachs, JP Morgan Chase, Lehman Bros, Merrill Lynch, Morgan Stanley, UBS (2007 excluding Merrill Lynch, Citi and UBS).

135 Dr Josef Ackermann's CEO Decade, Draft, 14 April 2012.

VII. Global Financial Crisis, 2008–2012

1 Ball, *The Fed*.

2 Deutsche Bank Risk Profile, presentation for Risk Committee, 4 September 2007, HADB, V50/x133.

3   Bundesbank, press release, 2 August 2007.
4   Bundesbank, press release, 14 August 2007.
5   Northern Rock was taken over by the British government in February 2008.
6   There are many books on the collapse of Bear Stearns including Cohan, *House of Cards*.
7   Federal Reserve Board (https://www.federalreserve.gov/regreform/reform-pdcf.htm).
8   July 2008 Ackermann National Press Club, Chairman of IIF Final report on banking industry (CSPAN video) (https://www.c-span.org/video/?206454-1/state-banking-industry).
9   Ibid.
10 His birthday party with 30 invited guests was famously held on 22 April at the Federal Chancellery hosted by Angela Merkel.
11 Email from Kiersten Winhart, 16 January 2008, HADB, V51/x727.
12 'Hot Topics 4Q2007' prepared to supplement the fourth quarter results but not for public disclosure, 7 February 2008, HADB, V51/x727.
13 Ibid.
14 November 2007 Securitisation Industry Batch, dated for the Risk Committee meeting on 6 December 2007, HADB, V50/x97.
15 Ibid.
16 PSI Report, p. 372.
17 Ibid., p. 375.
18 Briefing Notes for GEC Members, Annual Press Conference, Frankfurt, 7 February 2008, HADB, V51/x727.
19 https://netzpolitik.org/wp-upload/ackermann-abendessen.pdf (last access 18 February 2019).
20 Ackermann's presentation for Analyst Meeting, 2007 Full Year Review, 7 February 2008, p. 9 (https://www.db.com/ir/en/download/Ackermann_FY2007_Analysts_Final.pdf; last access 8 March 2019).
21 'Hot Topics 4Q2007' prepared to supplement the fourth quarter results but not for public disclosure, 7 February 2008, HADB, V51/x727.
22 'Subprime banking losses reach USD290 billion', *DB Intranet*, 23 April 2008. $290.2 billion includes $42.3 billion of increased provision for bad credit.
23 Risk Committee minutes, 25 June 2008, HADB, V50/x38.
24 The bank also owned 25 per cent of Station Casinos, operating 19 Nevada casinos until 2016.
25 Josef Ackermann Kalender, HADB, V50/x572.
26 Teleconference minutes of the board of directors of the Association of German Banks on 15 September 2008, HADB, V50/x272.
27 Josef Ackermann Kalender, HADB, V50/x572.
28 Ball, *The Fed*.
29 Deutsche Bank Risk Profile, presentation for Risk Committee, 29 October 2008, p. 24, HADB, V51/x727.
30 Ibid., pp. 26–27.
31 'Deutsche Bank erhält 12 Milliarden Dollar von AIG', *Frankfurter Allgemeine Zeitung*, 17 March 2009. AIG, Press Release, 'AIG discloses counterparties to CDS, GIA and Securities Lending Transactions', 15 March 2009.
32 Deutsche Bank Risk Profile, presentation for Risk Committee, 29 October 2008, p. 91, HADB, V51/x727.
33 Federal Reserve Board (https://www.federalreserve.gov/regreform/reform-taf.htm).
34 Bänziger had joined the Management Board in May 2006 after Clemens Börsig had become Chairman of the Supervisory Board.
35 Josef Ackermann 'Current Risk Environment and Perspectives', presentation to the Risk Committee of the Supervisory Board, 29 October 2008, HADB, V51/x727.
36 Ibid., p. 5.
37 Interview with Hugo Bänziger, 14 December 2018.
38 GEC minutes, 24 November 2008, HADB, V50/x108.
39 Estimates by Martin Hellwig, 'Germany and the Financial Crisis 2007–2017', mimeo, (https://www.riksbank.se/globalassets/media/konferenser/2018/germany-and-financial-crises-2007-2017.pdf).
40 'The bottomless pit', *Spiegel Online*, 23 December 2008 (https://www.spiegel.de/international/business/germany-s-faltering-bank-bailout-program-the-bottomless-pit-a-598207.html).
41 Josef Ackermann 'Current Risk Environment and Perspectives', presentation to the Risk Committee of the Supervisory Board, 29 October 2008, p. 7, HADB, V51/x727. Road Show presentation, Zurich, 2 October 2008 (https://www.db.com/ir/de/download/CEO_Roadshow_Zurich_October_2008.pdf).
42 Baron, *Late Remorse*, pp. 168–9.
43 Ibid.
44 Legal and Reputational Risk Report by Hugo Bänziger, October 2008, p. 22, HADB, V51/x727.
45 'Deutsche Bank CEO rejects blame for IKB collapse', *Reuters*, 12 May 2010.
46 Deutsche Bank Risk Profile, presentation for Risk Committee, 29 October 2008, p. 28, HADB, V51/x727.
47 HRE-Rettung – Ablauf der Ereignisse, 24 July 2009, HADB, V50/x572. Time line is from this document, prepared in advance of the Bundestag hearings on HRE. Ackermann recalled receiving a midnight phone call that HRE needed to be rescued. Interview with Josef Ackermann, 16 November 2018.
48 Viermetz to Steinbrück, 23 September 2008, HADB, V50/x572.
49 Josef Ackermann Kalender, HADB, V50/x572.
50 Note by BaFin, Summary of Discussions at BaFin headquarters 26–28 September 2008, HADB, V50/x572.
51 Email from Axel Wieandt to Ackermann and Bänziger, 25 September 2008, HADB, V50/x572.
52 Josef Ackermann Kalender, HADB, V50/x572.
53 Note by BaFin, Summary of Discussions at BaFin headquarters 26–28 September 2008, HADB, V50/x572.
54 Note, re: IKB Deutsche Industriebank AG, teleconference of the board of directors of the Association of German Banks on 30 July 2007, HADB, V50/x54. Documents for the board of directors meeting of the Association of German Banks on 12 November 2007, HADB, V50/x48.
55 'State aid: Commission approves restructuring of German bank IKB', European Commission, press release, IP/08/1557, 21 October 2008.
56 Note by BaFin, Summary of Discussions at BaFin headquarters 26–28 September 2008, HADB, V50/x572.
57 GEC minutes, 29 September 2008, HADB, V50/x108.
58 Letter from Deutsche Bundesbank, 3 October 2008, HADB, V50/x572.

59 Jonathan Gould, 'Hypo Real fights for life after rescue collapses', *Reuters*, 4 October 2008, 10:05 p.m. (https://www.reuters.com/article/businesspro-us-hyporealestate-idUSTRE4932O520081004).

60 Teleconference of the board of directors of the Association of German Banks on 6 October 2008, 7 October 2008, HADB, V50/x572.

61 Excerpt of the Minutes of the meeting of the Management Board, 7 October 2008, HADB, V50/x572.

62 Update to Board Memo 6 Oct 2008, 28 October 2008, HADB, V50/x572.

63 Ibid.

64 Ibid.

65 Buder et al., *The Rescue*.

66 For a narrative account of ABN AMRO up to this point see Smit, *The Perfect Prey*.

67 Project Erasmus, presentation for Group Investment Committee, 29 July 2009, HADB, V50/x621. The GIC was chaired by the CFO, Stefan Krause.

68 GEC minutes, 21 April 2008, HADB, V50/x108.

69 'Project Erasmus', presentation for Group Investment Committee, 29 July 2009, HADB, V50/x621.

70 Memo for the Management Board, 'Project Erasmus: update', 5 September 2008, HADB, V50/x555.

71 Ibid.

72 De Nederlandsche Bank, Perspective on the Structure of the Dutch Banking Sector: efficiency and stability through competition and diversity (2015).

73 Deutsche Bank Press Release 29 November 2013, KOPIE Persbericht: Afronding strategische heroriëntatie Deutsche Bank in Nederland (https://deutschebank.nl/nl/content/over_ons_nieuws_en_publicaties_nieuws_3239.html).

74 Baron, *Late Remorse*, pp. 171–2.

75 Ibid., p. 176.

76 Ibid., p. 176–7.

77 'Probe Shows Deutsche Bank Spied on Board Members and Shareholder', *Spiegel Online*, 6 July 2009. (http://www.spiegel.de/international/business/snooping-scandal-probe-shows-deutsche-bank-spied-on-board-members-and-shareholder-a-634561.html). Two Deutsche Bank employees were charged and went to court.

78 Tooze, *Crashed*, pp. 324–5.

79 Ibid., p. 327.

80 Ibid., p. 330.

81 *The Economist*, 18 February 2010. See also, Mayer, *Europe's Unfinished Currency*.

82 'Josef Ackermann: The Secret 2010 Financial Support Plan for Greece and Why it was Sunk', *To Vima*, 9 October 2014 (https://www.tovima.gr/2014/10/09/international/josef-ackermann-the-secret-2010-financial-support-plan-for-greece-and-why-it-was-sunk/). Also in Tooze, *Crashed*, p. 328.

83 'Greece debt crisis: how exposed is your bank?', *Guardian* (Datablog), 17 June 2011 (https://www.theguardian.com/news/datablog/2011/jun/17/greece-debt-crisis-bank-exposed#data).

84 'German Banks can Stomach Greek Debt', *Financial Times*, 29 September 2011.

85 Email from Charles Dallara (IIF) to Josef Ackermann, 27 June 2011, HADB, V50/x564. The Eurogroup is an informal body of Eurozone finance ministers.

86 Fédération bancaire française to Ministère de l'Économie, des Finances et de l'Industrie, 24 June 2011, HADB, V50/x564.

87 IIF, 'Proposed Ideas from Private Sector Holders of Greek Sovereign Debt: a global perspective', 26 June 2011, HADB, V50/x564.

88 At the time, Charlotte Jones was CFO Group Reporting and later served as deputy CFO of Deutsche Bank Group until 2013.

89 Email from Arne Wittig to Ackermann, Bänziger, Fitschen, Jain, Krause, Lamberti, Neske, 30 June 2011, HADB, V50/x564.

90 Including the trading book, the inclusion of which was not clear at the time. Briefing by Bänziger attached to email from Arne Wittig to Ackermann, Bänziger, Fitschen, Jain, Krause, Lamberti, Neske, 30 June 2011, HADB, V50/x564.

91 'German banks Agree to Billions in Greek Debt Relief', *Spiegel Online*, 30 June 2011 (https://www.spiegel.de/international/germany/deal-in-sight-german-banks-agree-to-billions-in-greek-debt-relief-a-771656.html).

92 GEC minutes (extraordinary meeting), 14 June 2010, HADB, V50/x694.

93 Ibid.

94 Baron, *Late Remorse*, p. 208–9.

95 'Prospect fades of D Bank role for Weber', *Financial Times*, 14 February 2011.

96 Interview with Hugo Bänziger, December 2018.

97 GEC minutes, 19 July 2010, HADB, V50/x694.

98 Baron, *Late Remorse*, pp. 221–3.

99 Chairman's committee minutes, 17 March 2005, HADB, V50/x135.

100 Edward Taylor, 'German regulator vetoes key Deutsche Bank exec', *Reuters*, 16 March 2012; Martin Hesse, 'Jains Wunschkandidat fällt durch', *Spiegel Online*, 15 March 2012 (https://www.spiegel.de/wirtschaft/unternehmen/bafin-blockiert-jain-vertrauten-broeksmit-als-deutsche-bank-vorstand-a-821653.html).

VIII. Renewed Crisis, 2012–2020

1 Deutsche Bank, Financial Report 2012, p. 5.

2 'Jürgen Fitschen and Anshu Jain host Day One town hall', *DB Intranet*, 1 June 2012.

3 Ibid.

4 Letter from Michael Boddenberg to Jain, 30 May 2012, HADB, V39/3. English translation in Jain's files.

5 See, for example, Ackermann's Investor Road Show Presentation, Boston and New York, 11–12 March 2008 (https://www.db.com/ir/en/download/Roadshow_US_East_Coast__11-12_March_2008_Ackermann.V2.pdf).

6 Deutsche Bank, Annual Report 2012, p. 7.

7 Fitschen and Jain, Investor Day presentation, 11 September 2012 (https://www.db.com/ir/en/download/Co-CEO_Investor_Day_Final.pdf).

8 Augar, *The Bank That Lived a Little*, pp. 217–21.

9 Presentation at AGM May 2015 (https://agm.db.com/en/docs/HV2015_Praesentation_en.pdf).

10 Deutsche Bank, AGM 2015, Key Topics (Convenience Translation). (https://agm.db.com/en/docs/HV2015_Schwerpunktthemen_en.pdf).

11 https://agm.db.com/en/docs/HV2015_Abstimmungsergebnisse_en.pdf. Votes were based on about 30 per cent of total capital. In April 2016 Fitschen was acquitted in a court case related to his testimony in the Kirch Group case.

12 Kanga Kong, 'Deutsche Bank Warned', *Wall Street Journal*, 5 July 2013.

13 David Enrich, Jenny Strasburg and Eyk Henning,

'U.S. Rebuked Deutsche Bank on Controls', *Wall Street Journal*, 23 July 2014.

14 Ibid.

15 Harry Wilson and James Hurley, 'Deutsche Bank under investigation by regulator', *The Times*, 30 January 2015 (https://www.thetimes.co.uk/article/deutsche-bank-under-investigation-by-regulator-svs6b3g8rbb); FCA, *Tackling Serious Failings in Firms*, June 2014, p. 9 (https://www.fca.org.uk/publication/corporate/tackling-serious-failings-in-firms.pdf).

16 Lopes, *Libor and Euribor*.

17 J. Gyntelberg and P. Wooldridge, 'Interbank Fixings during the Recent Turmoil', *BIS Quarterly Review*, March 2008.

18 'Supplementary Memorandum from the Bank of England' to the House of Commons, Treasury Select Committee, November 2008 (https://publications.parliament.uk/pa/cm200708/cmselect/cmtreasy/1210/1210we05.htm).

19 Ibid.

20 FCA, Final Notice, 23 April 2015, p. 12 (https://www.fca.org.uk/publication/final-notices/deutsche-bank-ag-2015.pdf).

21 Ibid.

22 BBA board meeting cited in FCA at which a senior manager was present where manipulation was discussed, FCA, Final Notice Deutsche Bank, 23 April 2015.

23 Augar, *The Bank That Lived a Little*, pp. 222–3.

24 NYDFS, Consent Order in the Matter of Deutsche Bank AG and Deutsche Bank AG, New York Branch, 23 April 2015 (https://www.dfs.ny.gov/docs/about/ea/ea150423.pdf).

25 Ibid., p. 16.

26 Ibid., p. 17.

27 FCA, Final Notice, Deutsche Bank, 23 April 2015, p. 1.

28 Ibid., p. 2.

29 Ibid., p. 22–4.

30 Ibid., p. 3.

31 Ibid.

32 David Enrich, Jenny Strasburg and Eyk Henning, 'Germany Blasts Deutsche Bank Executives Over Culture', *Wall Street Journal*, 16 July 2015. The draft convenience translation of the BaFin letter is available here (accessed 7 October 2019): http://graphics.wsj.com/documents/doc-cloud-embedder/?sidebar=0#2167237-deutsche. Deutsche Bank's comments published on the site: 'Deutsche Bank strongly disputes BaFin's criticisms, while saying in a statement that it expresses "deep regret for the wrongdoing that occurred" and saying that the bank has improved its internal procedures. The bank said that "the report includes statements that are taken out of context. It would be unwarranted to infer conclusions about the conduct of the bank or any individuals at this stage, especially because their detailed responses are submitted privately out of respect for the regulatory process." https://www.wsj.com/articles/germany-blasts-deutsche-bank-executives-over-broken-culture-1437068759.

33 Barney Thompson, 'Euribor messages amounted to market manipulation, court told', *Financial Times*, 3 May 2018.

34 Draft convenience translation of the BaFin letter 2015.

35 Ibid.

36 Cryan speech at 2016 AGM, 19 May 2016, p. 16 (https://agm.db.com/en/docs/HV2016_Rede-Cryan-Fitschen_en.pdf).

37 Madison Marriage, 'Morale flags for staff at Deutsche Asset Management', *Financial Times*, 17 October 2016.

38 Achleitner speech at 2016 AGM, 19 May 2016 (https://agm.db.com/en/docs/HV2016_Rede-Achleitner_en.pdf).

39 Quoted in Georg Meck, 'Ziemlich böse Freunde', *Frankfurter Allgemeine Sonntagszeitung*, 24 April 2016. 'Georg F. Thoma to leave the Supervisory Board of Deutsche Bank', Deutsche Bank, Media Release, 28 April 2016.

40 Deutsche Bank Fourth Quarter 2016 results, Presentation, 2 February 2017 (https://www.db.com/ir/en/download/Deutsche_Bank_4Q2016_results.pdf).

41 Raymond James, Press Release, 6 September 2016.

42 Deutsche Bank, Interim Report, 30 September 2017, p. 18.

43 Deutsche Bank, Interim Report, 30 September 2017.

44 Kara Scannell and Claire Manibog, 'US haul from credit crisis bank fines hits $150 bn', *Financial Times*, 6 August 2017. The total worldwide was estimated to be $321 billion from 2009 to 2016.

45 Arno Schueetze, 'Deutsche Bank to fight $14 billion demand from US authorities', *Reuters*, 16 September 2016 (https://www.reuters.com/article/us-deutsche-bank-mortgages-idUSKCN11L2VQ).

46 Ad hoc press release, 'Deutsche Bank confirms negotiations with DoJ regarding RMBS', 15 September 2016.

47 Schueetze, 'Deutsche Bank', 16 September 2016.

48 https://www.db.com/newsroom_news/settlement-statement-with-translations.pdf.

49 Letter from Cryan, 'Management Board apologises for former misconduct', 3 February 2017 (https://www.db.com/newsroom_news/2017/ghp/statement-from-john-cryan-on-misconduct-and-legacy-issues-en-11471.htm).

50 https://www.db.com/newsroom_news/settlement-statement-with-translations.pdf. The deal was probably concluded at the end of 2016.

51 https://www.cftc.gov/PressRoom/PressReleases/pr7255-15.

52 Consent Order, New York State Department of Financial Services, 20 June 2018 (https://www.dfs.ny.gov/about/ea/ea180620.pdf).

53 Department of Justice, Press Release, 10 May 2015 (https://www.justice.gov/opa/pr/five-major-banks-agree-parent-level-guilty-pleas).

54 Deutsche Bank, Annual Report 2017.

55 'At Last, Deutsche Bank's John Cryan and Big Shareholder HNA Meet', *Wall Street Journal*, 14 November 2017.

56 In 2018 Douglas L. Braunstein, CEO of Hudson Executive Capital LP, also became a major shareholder with 3.14 per cent of shares.

57 Letter from Cryan, 'Management Board apologises for former misconduct', 3 February 2017 (https://www.db.com/newsroom_news/2017/ghp/statement-from-john-cryan-on-misconduct-and-legacy-issues-en-11471.htm).

58 OECD Data (https://data.oecd.org/corporate/banking-sector-leverage.htm). Leverage is measured by the ratio between the financial assets of the banking sector and their equity (shares and other equity). Assets include currency and deposits, debt securities and loans, as recorded on the asset side of the financial balance sheets. Excludes insurance corporations and pension funds.

59 Calomiris and Haber, *Fragile by Design*.

60 Deeg, *Industry and Finance*.

61 'Fitschen: Staatshilfe hätte der Deutschen Bank geholfen', *Frankfurter Allgemeine Zeitung*, 28 August 2018.

62 'Deutsche Bank's funding woes deepen', *Financial Times*, 10 February 2019. Moody's Investor Service, 'Change in Insolvency Legislation Drives German and Italian Bank Rating Actions', 26 January 2016. https://www.db.com/ir/en/download/Moody_s_on_German_Italian_Banks_26_Jan_2016.pdf. This brings German legislation in line with European new rules that prioritised depositors when a bank collapses and seeks to reduce the burden on the taxpayer.

63 https://www.db.com/newsroom_news/2018/deutsche-bank-announces-actions-to-reshape-its-corporate-and-investment-bank-and-additional-cost-cutting-measure-en-11567.htm

64 Ibid.

65 The decision was announced in early May 2018.

66 'Schicksalhafte Fehler der Führungsspitze', *Handelsblatt*, 22 May 2018; Daniel Schäfer and Michael Brächer, 'Blame game: Deutsche Bank chief economist lashes out at former CEO Ackermann', *Handelsblatt*, 23 May 2018 (https://www.handelsblatt.com/today/finance/blame-game-deutsche-bank-chief-economist-lashes-out-at-former-ceo-ackermann/23582210.html).

67 Ibid.

68 DWS Quarterly Statement Q4, 1 February 2019. One-third of the outflow was the loss of a large low-margin insurance mandate.

69 Georg Meck, '"Die unfähigste Firma überhaupt"', *Frankfurter Allgemeine Sonntagszeitung*, 25 March 2018; Michael Maisch and Daniel Schäfer, 'Top exec calls Deutsche Bank "dysfunctional"', *Handelsblatt*, 26 March 2018. Patrick Jenkins and Laura Noonan, 'How Deutsche Bank's high-stakes gamble went wrong', *Financial Times*, 9 November 2017.

70 The papers of the legal firm Mossack Fonseca were initially leaked to *Süddeutsche Zeitung* from 2015. https://www.icij.org/investigations/panama-papers/

71 Presentation for Fourth Quarter 2018 and full-year results. (https://www.db.com/ir/en/download/Deutsche_Bank_Q4_2018_results.pdf).

72 'Scholz offen für Großbanken-Fusion', *Frankfurter Allgemeine Zeitung*, 12 January 2019; Stephen Morris, David Crow and Olaf Storbeck, 'Deutsche and Commerzbank: Why Berlin is backing a merger', *Financial Times*, 4 March 2019.

73 European Central Bank, Report on Financial Structures, 2017.

74 Cryan quoted in James Shotter, 'Deutsche Bank and Commerzbank held tie-up talks', *Financial Times*, 31 August 2016. Sewing in 'Eins und eins ergibt nicht zwei' (interview with Sewing), *Frankfurter Allgemeine Sonntagszeitung*, 28 April 2019.

75 Steven Arons, 'A New CEO Plans Deep Cuts to Save Deutsche Bank', *Bloomberg Businessweek*, 20 September 2018 (https://www.bloomberg.com/news/articles/2018-09-20/a-new-ceo-plans-big-cuts-to-mend-deutsche-bank).

76 Nicholas Comfort, Birgit Jennen and Steven Arons, 'Deutsche Bank watchdogs prefer merger with European firm, not Commerzbank', *Bloomberg*, 16 January 2019 (https://www.bloomberg.com/news/articles/2019-01-16/deutsche-bank-watchdogs-said-to-favor-europe-deal-to-commerzbank).

77 Olaf Storbeck, Stephen Morris and Laura Noonan, 'How Deutsche Bank woes led to radical action', *Financial Times*, 22 July 2019.

78 'Deutsche Bank faces resistance to Commerzbank merger plan', *Bloomberg News*, 12 March 2019.

79 'Eins und eins ergibt nicht zwei' (Interview with Sewing), *Frankfurter Allgemeine Sonntagszeitung*, 28 April 2019.

80 Ibid.

81 https://www.deutsche-bank.de/fk/de/im-fokus/globale-hausbank.htm?#pi_15954.

82 Message from CEO Christian Sewing to the Staff, 7 July 2019. https://www.db.com/newsroom_news/2019/deutsche-bank-s-transformation-a-message-from-ceo-christian-sewing-to-the-staff-en-11540.htm (accessed 11 October 2019).

Glossary

AAPD	Akten zur Auswärtigen Politik der Bundesrepublik Deutschland	CFTC	Commodity Futures Trading Commission
		CLO	collateralised loan obligation(s)
ABS	asset-backed securities	CMBS	commercial mortgage-backed securities
ABX	index for asset-backed securities	CMOs	collateralised mortgage obligation(s)
ADP	Automatic Data Processing, Inc.	COMECON	Council for Mutual Economic Assistance
AEG	Allgemeine Elektricitäts-Gesellschaft	COO	chief operating officer
AfK	Group Strategy (= Abteilung für Konzernentwicklung)	CORE	Corporates and Real Estate
		CPI	Consumer Price Index
AIG	American International Group, Inc.	CRM	credit risk management
AG	Aktiengesellschaft	CRO	chief risk officer
AGM	annual general meeting	CSFB	Credit Suisse First Boston
AKA	Ausfuhrkredit-Aktiengesellschaft		
APC	Alien Property Custodian	DAB	Deutsch-Asiatische Bank
Arbed	Aciéries Réunies de Burbach-Eich-Dudelange	DAF	German Labour Front (= Deutsche Arbeitsfront)
BaFin	German Federal Financial Supervisory Authority (= Bundesanstalt für Finanzdienstleistungsaufsicht)	Danat-Bank	Darmstädter und Nationalbank
		DAPG	Deutsch-Amerikanische Petroleum-Gesellschaft
BAI	Banca d'America e d'Italia	DASA	Deutsche Aerospace Aktiengesellschaft
BArch	Federal Archives of Germany	DB	Deutsche Bank
BASF	Badische Anilin- & Soda-Fabrik AG	DB24	Deutsche Bank 24
BAT	Banco Alemán Transatlántico	DB Lux	Deutsche Bank Luxembourg S.A.
BBA	British Bankers' Association	DBNA	Deutsche Bank North America
BCT	Banco Comercial Transatlántico	DBSC	Deutsche Bank Securities Corporation
BDI	Federation of German Industries (= Bundesverband der Deutschen Industrie)	DBSI	Deutsche Bank Securities, Inc.
		DEAG	Deutsche Erdöl AG
BdL	Bank deutscher Länder	DEMAG	Deutsche Maschinenbau-Aktiengesellschaft
BEC	Banque Européenne de Crédit à Moyen Terme	DFS	Deutsche Financial Services
BGH	Federal Court of Justice (= Bundesgerichtshof)	DIT	Deutscher Investment Trust
BHF-Bank	Berliner Handels- und Frankfurter Bank	DIHT	Association of German Chambers of Industry and Commerce (= Deutscher Industrie- und Handelstag)
BIRG	Business Integrity Review Group		
BIS	Bank for International Settlements		
BMW	Bayerische Motorenwerke	DKB	Dresdner Kleinwort Benson
BPL	Banca Popolare di Lecco	DLJ	Donaldson, Lufkin & Jenrette
BT	Bankers Trust	DLR	Deutsche Luft-Reederei
BUB	Böhmische Union-Bank	DM	Deutschmark
Bufa	Bild- und Filmamt	DMG	Deutsche Morgan Grenfell
BVR	National Association of German Co-operative Banks (= Bundesverband der Deutschen Volksbanken und Raiffeisenbanken)	DNB	De Nederlandsche Bank
		DNVP	German National People's Party (= Deutschnationale Volkspartei)
BZW	Barclays de Zoete Wedd	DOR	Deutsche Ozean-Reederei
		DPAG	Deutsche Petroleum-Aktiengesellschaft
CABV	Creditanstalt-Bankverein	DUB	Deutsche Ueberseeische Bank
CDO	collateralised debt obligation(s)	DUEG	Deutsch-Ueberseeische Elektricitäts-Gesellschaft
CDU	Christian Democratic Union of Germany (= Christlich Demokratische Union)	DVP	German People's Party (= Deutsche Volkspartei)
CDS	credit default swaps		
CEO	chief executive officer	DWS	Deutsche Gesellschaft für Wertpapiersparen
CFDB	Compagnie Financière de la Deutsche Bank AG		
CFO	chief financial officer	EAB	European American Bank(s)
CHADE	Compañia Hispano-Americana de Electricidad	EBIC	European Banks' International Company
CI	Corporate Investments	ECB	European Central Bank
CIB	Corporate and Institutional Banking (until 1998); Corporate and Investment Bank(ing) (from 2001)	ECM	equity capital markets
		ECSC	European Coal and Steel Community
		EEC	European Economic Community

EMU	European Monetary Union
ENEL	Ente Nazionale per l'Energia Elettrica
EOS	Erdölsyndikat
EPU	Europäische Petroleum-Union
ESF	Deposit Protection Fund (= Einlagensicherungsfonds)
EU	European Union
Euras	European Asian Bank
EURIBOR	Euro Interbank Offered Rate
FAVAG	Frankfurter Allgemeine Versicherungs-AG
FCA	Financial Conduct Authority
FCIC	Financial Crisis Inquiry Commission
Fed	Federal Reserve Bank/System
Finag	Deutsches Finanzierungsinstitut AG
F & F	Finanza & Futuro
FINRA	Financial Industry Regulatory Authority
FRBNY	Federal Reserve Bank of New York
FTE	full-time equivalent
FTSE100	Financial Times Stock Exchange 100 Index
FX	foreign exchange
GAAP	Generally Accepted Accounting Principles
GACC	German American Capital Corporation
GARIOA	Government Aid and Relief in Occupied Areas
GCI	Global Corporates and Institutions
GCPC	Group Credit Policy Committee
GDP	gross domestic product
GDR	German Democratic Republic
GEC	Group Executive Committee
GEFA	Gesellschaft für Absatzfinanzierung mbH
GFFX	Global Finance and Foreign Exchange
GIC	Group Investment Committee
GM	General Motors
GSA	National Archives of Belgium
GTB	Global Transaction Banking
GTS	Global Technology & Services
HADB	Historical Archives of Deutsche Bank
HAPAG	Hamburg-Amerikanische Packetfahrt-Action-Gesellschaft
HBV	Gewerkschaft Handel, Banken und Versicherungen
HR	Human Resources
HRE	Hypo Real Estate
HSBC	Hongkong & Shanghai Banking Corporation
IB	Investment Bank(ing)
IBD	Investment Banking Division
IBM	International Business Machines
IBMC	Investment Banking Management Committee
IBOR	Interbank Offered Rate(s)
ICI	Imperial Chemical Industries
IFAGO	Industriefinanzierungs-Aktiengesellschaft Ost
IIF	Institute of International Finance
IKB	Industriekreditbank
IMF	International Monetary Fund
IOS	Investors Overseas Services
IPO	initial public offering(s)
IRC	Integration Review Committee
ISC	Integration Steering Committee
ISDA	International Swaps and Derivatives Association
IStG	Institut für Stadtgeschichte
IT	information technology
JCS	Joint Chiefs of Staff

KfW	Kreditanstalt für Wiederaufbau
KGaA	partnership limited by shares (= Kommanditgesellschaft auf Aktien)
KGB	Committee for State Security (of the Soviet Union)
KWG	German Banking Act (= Kreditwesengesetz)
k.u.k.	Imperial and Royal (= kaiserlich und königlich)
LIBOR	London Interbank Offered Rate
LLC	Limited Liability Company
M&A	mergers & acquisitions
MBB	Messerschmitt-Bölkow-Blohm
MBIA	Municipal Bond Insurance Association
MBS	mortgage-backed securities
MG	Morgan Grenfell
MGAM	Morgan Grenfell Asset Management
Mitropa	Mitteleuropäische Schlafwagen- und Speisewagen-Aktiengesellschaft
MM	Money Market(s)
MMD	Money Market Derivatives
MNC	multinational corporation
MSDW	Morgan Stanley Dean Witter
NATO	North Atlantic Treaty Organization
NCOU	Non-Core Operations Unit
NSBO	National Socialist Factory Cell Organisation (= Nationalsozialistische Betriebszellenorganisation)
NSDAP	National Socialist German Workers' Party (= Nationalsozialistische Deutsche Arbeiterpartei)
NYDFS	New York State Department of Financial Services
NYSE	New York Stock Exchange
o.D.	undated
OEG	Ostafrikanische Eisenbahngesellschaft
OM	Organisation and Management
OMGUS	Office of Military Government, United States
OTC	over-the-counter
PBC	Private & Business Clients
PC	personal computer
PCAM	Private Clients and Asset Management
PdB	Auditing Association of German Banks (= Prüfungsverband deutscher Banken)
PPAG	Petroleum Producte Aktiengesellschaft
PSI	United States Senate Homeland Security Permanent Subcommittee on Investigations
PW&CC	Private, Wealth & Commercial Clients
PWM	Private Wealth Management
RBS	Royal Bank of Scotland
repo	repurchase operation/agreement
RM	Reichsmark
RMB	Renminbi/Chinese Yuan
RMBS	residential mortgage-backed securities
RWA	risk-weighted assets
SA	Sturmabteilung
SAA	Siemens Archives
SARS	Severe Acute Respiratory Syndrome
SEC	United States Securities and Exchange Commission
SF	Structured Finance
S&P	Standard & Poor's
SKPL	Corporate Strategy (= Strategische Konzernplanung)

SMEs	small and medium-sized enterprises
SPD	Social Democratic Party of Germany (= Sozialdemokratische Partei Deutschlands)
SPV	special purpose vehicle
SS	Schutzstaffel
TAF	Term Auction Facility
UCI	Unicredito Italiano
UCLA	University of California, Los Angeles
Ufa	Universum-Film Aktiengesellschaft
UFG	United Financial Group
UK	United Kingdom
US	United States
USD	United States dollar
US GAAP	United States Generally Accepted Accounting Principles
USSR	Union of Soviet Socialist Republics

VEW	Vereinigte Elektrizitätswerke Westfalen AG
VIAG	Vereinigte Industrie-Unternehmungen Aktiengesellschaft
VÖB	Association of German Public Banks (= Bundesverband Öffentlicher Banken Deutschlands)
VW	Volkswagen
West LB	Westdeutsche Landesbank
WTO	World Trade Organization
ZAA	Central Foreign Department (= Zentrale Auslandsabteilung)
ZIA	Central International Department (= Zentrale Internationale Abteilung)

Primary Sources and Archives

United States Senate Permanent Subcommittee on Investigations Committee on Homeland Security and Governmental Affairs: Wall Street and the Financial Crisis: Anatomy of a Financial Collapse. Majority and Minority Staff Report, 13 April 2011 (= PSI Report)

https://www.hsgac.senate.gov//imo/media/doc/Financial_Crisis/FinancialCrisisReport.pdf

Wall Street and the Financial Crisis: Anatomy of a Financial Collapse. Report and Appendix before the Permanent Subcommittee on Investigations Committee on Homeland Security and Governmental Affairs United States Senate. One Hundred Twelfth Congress. First Session, Volume 5 of 5, Parts II–IV, April 13, 2011 (= PSI Report and Appendix, Vol. 5, Part II–IV).

https://www.govinfo.gov/content/pkg/CHRG-112shrg66050/pdf/CHRG-112shrg66050.pdf (Vol. 5, Part II)
https://www.govinfo.gov/content/pkg/CHRG-112shrg66051/pdf/CHRG-112shrg66051.pdf (Vol. 5, Part III)
https://www.govinfo.gov/content/pkg/CHRG-112shrg66052/pdf/CHRG-112shrg66052.pdf (Vol. 5, Part IV)

Financial Crisis Inquiry Commission (FCIC) Staff Audiotape of Interview with Greg Lippmann, Deutsche Bank, 20 May 2010

http://fcic.law.stanford.edu/interviews/view/15 (part 1)
http://fcic.law.stanford.edu/interviews/view/16 (part 2)
http://fcic.law.stanford.edu/interviews/view/17 (part 3)

Financial Crisis Inquiry Commission (FCIC) Staff Audiotape of Interview with Eugene Xu, Deutsche Bank, 20 May 2010

http://fcic.law.stanford.edu/interviews/view/125 (part 1)
http://fcic.law.stanford.edu/interviews/view/126 (part 2)

BArch – German Federal Archives, Berlin-Lichterfelde
Cadbury Archive, Cambridge University
GSA – National Archives of Belgium, Depot Joseph Cuvelier, Deutsche Bank, Brussels
HADB – Historical Archives of Deutsche Bank, Frankfurt am Main
IStG – Institut für Stadtgeschichte (Bethmann Archives), Frankfurt am Main
SAA – Siemens Archives, Berlin

Bibliography

Abraham, Erich W.: *Konzernkrach. Hintergründe, Entwicklungen und Folgen der deutschen Konzernkrisen*, Berlin 1933

Abs, Hermann J.: Fragen des deutschen Vermögens im Ausland, in: idem, *Zeitfragen der Geld- und Wirtschaftspolitik. Aus Vorträgen und Aufsätzen*, Frankfurt am Main 1959, pp. 56–72

Abs, Hermann J.: Der Schutz privater Investitionen im Ausland, in: idem, *Zeitfragen der Geld- und Wirtschaftspolitik. Aus Vorträgen und Aufsätzen*, Frankfurt am Main 1959, pp. 72–9

Abs, Hermann J., Die Rolle der Geschäftsbanken in der Finanz- und Kreditpolitik eines integrierten Europas (Rede vor dem Europäischen Forum in Alpbach, 30.8.1957), in: idem, *Zeitfragen der Geld- und Wirtschaftspolitik. Aus Vorträgen und Aufsätzen*, Frankfurt am Main 1959, pp. 116–26

Accominotti, Olivier/Eichengreen, Barry: The Mother of all Sudden Stops: Capital Flows and Reversals in Europe, 1919–1932, in: *Economic History Review* 69 (2016), no. 2, pp. 469–92

Accominotti, Olivier: International Banking and Transmission of the 1931 Financial Crisis, in: *Economic History Review* 72 (2019), no. 1, pp. 260–85

Achterberg, Erich: *Berliner Hochfinanz. Kaiser, Fürsten, Millionäre um 1900*, Frankfurt am Main 1965

Afflerbach, Holger: *Der Dreibund. Europäische Großmacht- und Allianzpolitik vor dem Ersten Weltkrieg*, Wien 2002

Ahrens, Ralf: Der Exempelkandidat. Die Dresdner Bank und der Nürnberger Prozess gegen Karl Rasche, in: *Vierteljahrshefte für Zeitgeschichte* 52 (2004), no. 4, pp. 637–70

Ahrens, Ralf: Unternehmer vor Gericht. Die Nürnberger Nachfolgeprozesse zwischen Strafverfolgung und symbolischem Tribunal, in: Jürgen Lillteicher (ed.), *Profiteure des NS-Systems? Deutsche Unternehmen und das Dritte Reich*, Berlin 2006, pp. 128–53

Aldenhoff-Hübinger, Rita: *Agrarpolitik und Protektionismus. Deutschland und Frankreich im Vergleich 1879–1914*, Göttingen 2002

Altamura, Edoardo C.: *European Banks and the Rise of International Finance: The Post-Bretton Woods Era*, London/New York 2016

Ambrosius, Gerold: Europäische Integration und wirtschaftliche Entwicklung der Bundesrepublik Deutschland in den fünfziger Jahren, in: Helmut Berding (ed.), *Wirtschaftliche und politische Integration in Europa im 19. und 20. Jahrhundert*, Göttingen 1984, pp. 271–94

Ambrosius, Gerold: Intensives Wachstum (1958–1965). Das Kreditwesen der Bundesrepublik Deutschland, in: Hans Pohl (ed.), *Geschichte der deutschen Kreditwirtschaft seit 1945*, Frankfurt am Main 1998, pp. 149–202

Apt, Max: *25 Jahre im Dienste der Berliner Kaufmannschaft*, Berlin 1927

Auerbach, Felix: *Ernst Abbe. Sein Leben, sein Wirken, seine Persönlichkeit nach den Quellen und aus eigener Erfahrung geschildert*, Leipzig 1918

Augar, Philip: *Chasing Alpha: How Reckless Growth and Unchecked Ambition Ruined the City's Golden Decade*, London 2009

Augar, Philip: *The Bank That Lived a Little. Barclays in the Age of the Very Free Market*, London 2018

Augustine, Dolores L.: *Patricians and Parvenus. Wealth and High Society in Wilhelmine Germany*, Oxford/Providence, RI 1994

Ausschuß zur Untersuchung der Erzeugungs- und Absatzbedingungen der deutschen Wirtschaft: *Die Reichsbank. Verhandlungen und Berichte des Unterausschusses für Geld-, Kredit- und Finanzwesen (V. Unterausschuß)*, Berlin 1929

Bajohr, Frank: *'Aryanisation' in Hamburg. The Economic Exclusion of Jews and the Confiscation of their Property in Nazi Germany*, New York/Oxford 2002

Bajohr, Frank: 'Arisierung' als gesellschaftlicher Prozeß. Verhalten, Strategien und Handlungsspielräume jüdischer Eigentümer und 'arischer' Erwerber, in: Irmtrud Wojak/Peter Hayes (eds), *Arisierung im Nationalsozialismus. Volksgemeinschaft, Raub und Gedächtnis*, Frankfurt am Main 2000, pp. 15–30

Bähr, Johannes: *Der Goldhandel der Dresdner Bank im Zweiten Weltkrieg*, Leipzig 1999

Bähr, Johannes: Bankenrationalisierung' und Großbankenfrage: Der Konflikt um die Ordnung des deutschen Kreditgewerbes während des Zweiten Weltkrieges, in: Harald Wixforth (ed.), *Finanzinstitutionen in Mitteleuropa während des Nationalsozialismus* (= Geld und Kapital, Bd. 4, 2000), Stuttgart 2001, pp. 71–94

Bähr, Johannes: Modernes Bankrecht und dirigistische Kapitallenkung. Die Ebenen der Steuerung im Finanzsektor des 'Dritten Reichs', in: Dieter Gosewinkel (ed.), *Wirtschaftskontrolle und Recht in der nationalsozialistischen Diktatur*, Frankfurt am Main 2005, pp. 199–223

Bähr, Johannes: *Werner von Siemens 1816–1892. A Biography*, Munich 2018

Bähr, Johannes: Wandlungen im Zeitalter der Extreme (1918–1945), in: Johannes Bähr/Paul Erker/Maximiliane Rieder, *180 Jahre Krauss Maffei. Die Geschichte einer Weltmarke*, München 2018, pp. 101–74

Balderston, Theo: German Banking between the Wars. The Crisis of the Credit Banks, in: *Business History Review* 65 (1991), no. 3, pp. 554–605

Balderston, Theo: *The Origins and Course of the German Economic Crisis, November 1923 to May 1932*, Berlin 1993

Ball, Lawrence M.: *The Fed and Lehman Brothers: Setting the Record Straight on a Financial Disaster*, Cambridge 2018

Baltzer, Markus: *Der Berliner Kapitalmarkt nach der Reichsgründung 1871. Gründerzeit, internationale Finanzmarktintegration und der Einfluss der Makroökonomie*, Berlin 2007

Bamberger, Ludwig: *Reichsgold. Studien über Währung und Wechsel*, Leipzig 1876

Bamberger, Ludwig: *Erinnerungen.* Ed. by Paul Nathan, Berlin 1899

Banken, Ralf: *Edelmetallmangel und Großraubwirtschaft. Die Entwicklung des deutschen Edelmetallsektors im 'Dritten Reich' 1933–1945*, Berlin 2009

Banken, Ralf: *Hitlers Steuerstaat. Die Steuerpolitik im Dritten Reich* (= Das Reichsfinanzministerium im Dritten Reich, Bd. 2), Berlin 2018

Barkai, Avraham: *Oscar Wassermann und die Deutsche Bank. Bankier in schwieriger Zeit*, München 2005

Baron, Stefan: *Late Remorse. Joe Ackermann, Deutsche Bank and the Financial Crisis. An Inside Report*, Berlin 2014

Bartel, Fritz: Fugitive Leverage: Commercial Banks, Sovereign Debt, and Cold War Crisis in Poland, 1980-1982, in: *Enterprise and Society* 18 (2017), no. 1, pp. 72–107

Barth, Boris: *Die deutsche Hochfinanz und die Imperialismen. Banken und Außenpolitik vor 1914*, Stuttgart 1995

Barth, Boris: Banken und Kapitalexport vor 1914. Anmerkungen zum Forschungsstand der politischen Ökonomie, in: Manfred Köhler/Keith Ulrich (eds.), *Banken, Konjunktur und Politik. Beiträge zur Geschichte deutscher Banken im 19. und 20. Jahrhundert*, Essen 1995, pp. 42–54

Barth, Boris: Mitteleuropakonzepte und die deutsche Exportwirtschaft in der Weimarer Republik, in: Boris Barth *et al.* (eds.), *Konkurrenzpartnerschaft. Die deutsche und die tschechoslowakische Wirtschaft in der Zwischenkriegszeit*, Essen 1999, pp. 112–31

Barth, Boris: Trade and Finance in the Great War. German Banks and Neutral Scandinavia 1914-1918, in: Philip L. Cottrell/Even Lange/Ulf Olsson (eds.), *Centres and Peripheries in Banking. The International Development of Financial Markets*, Ashgate 2007, pp. 3–12

Barth, Boris: Die Auswirkungen des Kriegsausbruchs auf eine globalisierte Weltwirtschaft, in: Jürgen Angelow/Johannes Großmann (eds), *Wandel, Umbruch, Absturz. Perspektiven auf das Jahr 1914*, Stuttgart 2014, pp. 43–56

Bauert-Keetman, Ingrid: Unternehmens-Chronik. Deutsch-Asiatische Bank, European Asian Bank, Deutsche Bank (Asia) 1889–1987, MS, Hamburg/Wuppertal 1988

Baumgart, Inge/Benneckenstein, Horst: Die Interessen der Deutschen Bank am mesopotamischen Erdöl, in: *Jahrbuch für Wirtschaftsgeschichte* 29 (1988), no. 1, pp. 49–65

Baumgart, Inge/Benneckenstein, Horst: Die Deutsche Bank in der europäischen Mineralölwirtschaft vor 1914, in: *Jahrbuch für Wirtschaftsgeschichte* 30 (1989), no. 4, pp. 45–60

Baumgart, Willy: *Unsere Reichsbank. Ihre Geschichte und Verfassung*, Berlin 1915

Bechtloff, Gudrun: *Die Mitropa AG. Ein privatrechtliches Unternehmen des Schlafwagen- und Speisewagenverkehrs im Spannungsfeld wirtschaftlicher Interessen und staatlicher Einflüsse und Abhängigkeiten von 1916–1990*, Frankfurt am Main 2000

Benfey, Fritz: *Die neuere Entwicklung des deutschen Auslandsbankwesens 1914–1925 (unter Berücksichtigung der ausländischen Bankstützpunkte in Deutschland)*, Berlin 1925

Bennett, Edward W.: *Germany and the Diplomacy of the Financial Crisis, 1931*, Cambridge, Mass. 1962

Berger, Allen N./Demsetz, Rebecca S./Strahan, Philip E.: The Consolidation of the Financial Services Industry: Causes, Consequences, and Implications for the Future, in: *Journal of Banking and Finance* 23 (1999), no. 2–4, pp. 135–94

Berghahn, Volker: *The Americanisation of West German Industry, 1945–1973*, Leamington Spa/New York 1986

Bergmann, Carl: *Der Weg der Reparation: Von Versailles über den Dawesplan zum Ziel*, Frankfurt am Main 1926

Bernardini, Giovanni: Principled Pragmatism: The Eastern Committee of German Economy and West German–Chinese relations during the early Cold War, 1949–1958, in: *Modern Asian Studies* 51 (2017), no. 1, pp. 78–106

Bippen, Wilhelm von: 'Meier, Hermann Henrich', in: *Allgemeine Deutsche Biographie* 52 (1906), pp. 291–4

Bitsch, Marie-Thérèse: *La Belgique entre la France et l'Allemagne 1905–1914*, Paris 1994

Bliss, Richard T./Rosen, Richard J.: CEO Compensation and Bank Mergers, in: *Journal of Financial Economics* 61 (2001), no. 1, pp. 107–38

Böse, Christian: *Kartellpolitik im Kaiserreich. Das Kohlensyndikat und die Absatzorganisation im Ruhrbergbau 1893–1919*, Berlin 2018

Bol, Angela: Die Aktionärsstruktur der Deutschen Bank, 1870–1929, in: *Jahrbuch für Wirtschaftsgeschichte/ Economic History Yearbook* 59 (2018), no. 1, pp. 135–56

Bol, Angela: Corporate Governance: Normen, Legitimation und Praktiken in deutschen Unternehmen, 1870–1930, Diss., Wien 2018

Bommarius, Christian: *Der Fürstentrust. Kaiser, Adel, Spekulanten*, Berlin 2017

Bondi, Gerhard: *Deutschlands Außenhandel 1815–1870*, Berlin 1958

Bonin, Hubert: Le Comptoir national d'escompte de Paris, une banque impériale (1848–1940), in: *Revue française d'histoire d'outre-mer* 78 (1991), no. 293, pp. 477–97

Bormann, Patrick/Scholtyseck, Joachim/Wixforth, Harald: Die kreditgenossenschaftlichen Zentralinstitute vom Beginn des Ersten Weltkriegs bis zur bedingungslosen Kapitulation des NS-Staats (1914-1945), in: Timothy Guinnane *et al.*, *Die Geschichte der DZ Bank. Das genossenschaftliche Zentralbankwesen vom 19. Jahrhundert bis heute*, München 2013, pp. 145–294

Born, Karl Erich: 'Karl Helfferich', in: *Neue Deutsche Biographie* 8 (1969), pp. 470–72

Bosetzky, Horst: *Mikropolitik. Netzwerke und Karrieren*, Wiesbaden 2019

Boughton, James M.: *Silent Revolution: The International Monetary Fund, 1979–1989*, Washington DC 2001

Brecht, Bertolt: *Collected Plays: Two*, London 2015

Brötel, Dieter: Die deutsche 'Kolonie' in Paris: Imperiale Aktivitäten jüdisch-deutscher Bankiers 1860-1880, in: Markus A. Denzel (ed.), *Deutsche Eliten in Übersee (16. bis frühes 20. Jahrhundert). Büdinger Forschungen zur Sozialgeschichte 2004 und 2005*, St Katharinen 2006, pp. 319–60

Brünger, Sebastian: *Geschichte und Gewinn. Der Umgang deutscher Konzerne mit ihrer NS-Vergangenheit*, Göttingen 2017

Brüning, Heinrich: *Memoiren 1916–1934*, Stuttgart 1970

Brunner, Allan D. *et al.*: *Germany's Three-Pillar Banking System: Cross-Country Perspectives in Europe.* Occasional Paper 233, International Monetary Fund, Washington DC 2004

Buchheim, Christoph: Das Londoner Schuldenabkommen, in: Ludolf Herbst (ed.), *Westdeutschland 1945–1955. Unterwerfung, Kontrolle, Integration*, München 1986, pp. 219–29

Buchheim, Christoph: *Die Wiedereingliederung Westdeutschlands in die Weltwirtschaft 1945–1958*, München 1990

Buchheim, Christoph/Boldorf, Marcel (eds), *Europäische Volkswirtschaften unter deutscher Hegemonie 1938–1945*, München 2012

Buchner, Michael: Möglichkeiten und Grenzen staatlicher Finanzmarktregulierung. Die Reaktionen der Berliner Fondsbörse auf die Einschränkung des Terminhandels in Wertpapieren durch das Börsengesetz von 1896, in: *Archiv für Sozialgeschichte* 56 (2016), pp. 189–217

Buchner, Michael: *Die Spielregeln der Börse. Institutionen, Kultur und die Grundlagen des Wertpapierhandels in Berlin und London, ca. 1860–1914*, Tübingen 2019

Buchwald, Bruno: *Die Technik des Bankbetriebs. Ein Hand- und Lehrbuch des praktischen Bank- und Börsenwesens*. 7. verb. Aufl., Berlin 1912

Budde, Gunilla: *Auf dem Weg ins Bürgerleben. Kindheit und Erziehung in deutschen und englischen Bürgerfamilien 1840–1914*, Göttingen 1994

Buder, Matthäus et al.: The rescue and restructuring of Hypo Real Estate', in: *EU Competition Policy Newsletter* 3 (2011), pp. 41–4

Budraß, Lutz: *Adler und Kranich. Die Lufthansa und ihre Geschichte 1926–1955*, München 2016

Bundesministerium der Finanzen (ed.): *Bericht der Studienkommission 'Grundsatzfragen der Kreditwirtschaft'*, Bonn 1979

Burhop, Carsten: *Die Kreditbanken in der Gründerzeit*, Stuttgart 2004

Burhop, Carsten: Banken, Aufsichtsräte und Corporate Governance im Deutschen Reich (1871–1913), in: *Bankhistorisches Archiv* 32 (2006), no. 1, pp. 1–25

Burk, Kathleen: A Brief History of Morgan Grenfell 1838–1998. Life, Death and Rebirth, in: Manfred Pohl/Kathleen Burk, *Deutsche Bank in London 1873–1998*, Munich/Zurich 1998, pp. 105–40

Büschgen, Hans E.: Deutsche Bank from 1957 to the Present. The Emergence of an International Financial Conglomerate, in: Lothar Gall et al., *The Deutsche Bank 1870–1995*, London 1995, pp. 523–796

Calomiris, Charles W./Haber, Stephen S.: *Fragile by Design: The Political Origins of Banking Crises and Scarce Credit*, Princeton 2014

Cameron, Rondo: *A Concise Economic History of the World: From Paleolithic Times to the Present*, Oxford 1989

Canis, Konrad: *Der Weg in den Abgrund. Deutsche Außenpolitik 1902–1914*, Paderborn 2011

Carrein, Kristof/Mestdagh, Jurgen/Vancoppenolle, Chantal (eds): *Inventaris van het archief van Deutsche Bank. Succursale de Bruxelles (1904–1933)*, Bruxelles 2005

Cassis, Youssef: *Capitals of Capital. The Rise and Fall of international Financial Centres 1780–2009*. 2nd edition, Cambridge 2010

Cassis, Youssef: Financial Centres, in: Youssef Cassis/Richard S. Grossman/Catherine R. Schenk (eds), *The Oxford Handbook of Banking and Financial History*, Oxford 2016, pp. 293–317

Chapman, Stanley: *The Rise of Merchant Banking*, London 1984

Christians, F. Wilhelm: *Wege nach Rußland. Bankier im Spannungsfeld zwischen Ost und West*. 2., erw. u. aktual. Aufl., Hamburg: Hoffmann und Campe, 1990 (zuerst 1989)

Clark, Christopher: *The Sleepwalkers. How Europe Went to War in 1914*, London/New York 2012

Cline, William R.: *International Debt Reexamined*, Washington DC 1995

Cohan, William D.: *House of Cards: A Tale of Hubris and Wretched Excess on Wall Street*, London/New York 2009

Conze, Eckart et al.: *Das Amt und die Vergangenheit. Deutsche Diplomaten im Dritten Reich und der Bundesrepublik*, 2. Aufl., Berlin 2010

Copelovitch, Mark S.: *The International Monetary Fund in the Global Economy. Banks, Bonds, and Bailouts*, Cambridge/New York 2010

Culp, Christopher L./Miller, Merton H.: Metallgesellschaft and the economics of synthetic storage, in: *Journal of Applied Corporate Finance* 7 (1995), no. 4, pp. 62–76

Dahlem, Markus: *Die Professionalisierung des Bankbetriebs. Studien zur institutionellen Struktur deutscher Banken im Kaiserreich 1871–1914*, Essen 2009

Dahlmann, Dittmar: Ludwig Knoop: ein Unternehmerleben, in: idem/Carmen Scheide (eds), '… das einzige Land in Europa, das eine große Zukunft vor sich hat.' *Deutsche Unternehmen und Unternehmer im Russischen Reich im 19. und frühen 20. Jahrhundert*, Essen 1998, pp. 361–78

Dahlmann, Dittmar: Das Unternehmen Otto Wolff: vom Alteisenhandel zum Weltkonzern (1904–1929), in: Peter Danylow/Ulrich S. Soénius (eds), *Otto Wolff. Ein Unternehmen zwischen Wirtschaft und Politik*, Berlin 2005, pp. 13–97

Damm, Veit: *Selbstpräsentation und Imagebildung. Jubiläumsinszenierungen deutscher Banken und Versicherungen im 19. und frühen 20. Jahrhundert*, Leipzig 2007

Darity, William A./Horn, Bobbie L.: *The Loan Pushers. The Role of Commercial Banks in the International Debt Crisis*. Cambridge, Mass. 1988

Deeg, Richard: Industry and Finance in Germany since Unification, in: *German Politics & Society* 28 (2010), no. 2, pp. 116–29

Delbrück, Adelbert: *Aufzeichnungen unseres Vaters Adelbert Delbrück. Für die Enkel und Urenkel gedruckt*, Leipzig 1922

Deutelmoser, Otto K.: *Kilian Steiner und die Württembergische Vereinsbank*, Ostfildern 2003

Deutsche Bundesbank: *Deutsches Geld- und Bankwesen in Zahlen 1876–1975*, Frankfurt am Main 1976

Devlin, Robert: *Debt and Crisis in Latin America: The Supply Side of the Story*, Princeton 1993

DeYoung, Robert: The financial performance of pure play Internet banks, in: *Economic Perspectives* 25 (2001), no. 1, pp. 60–78

Dickhaus, Monika: Innovationen im deutschen Bankwesen 1918–1931, in: *Scripta Mercaturae* 25 (1991), no. 1/2, pp. 73–124

Dickhaus, Monika: Kredite für den Holocaust? Die Deutsche Bank und J.A. Topf & Söhne, Erfurt 1933-1945, in: Dieter Ziegler (ed.), *Banken und 'Arisierungen' in Mitteleuropa während des Nationalsozialismus* (= Jahrbuch für mitteleuropäische Banken- und Sparkassengeschichte 2001), Stuttgart 2002, pp. 211–34

Diedrichs, Johann: *Die Verwendung maschineller Hilfsmittel im Bankbetrieb*, Berlin 1923

Dietrich, Yorck: Vermögenspolitik, in: *Geschichte der Sozialpolitik in Deutschland seit 1945, Bd. 4: 1957–1966. Bundesrepublik Deutschland. Sozialpolitik im Zeichen des erreichten Wohlstandes*, Baden-Baden 2007, pp. 795–17

Disconto-Gesellschaft, *Die Disconto-Gesellschaft 1851–1901, Denkschrift zum 50jährigen Jubiläum*, Berlin 1901

Doerry, Martin: *Übergangsmenschen. Die Mentalität der Wilhelminer und die Krise des Kaiserreichs*. 2 Bde., Weinheim 1986

Dorrmann, Michael: *Eduard Arnhold (1849–1925). Eine biographische Studie zu Unternehmer- und Mäzenatentum im Deutschen Kaiserreich*, Berlin 2002

Duensing, Monika: 'Meier, Hermann Henrich', in: *Neue Deutsche Biographie* 16 (1990), pp. 642f.

Earle, Edward M.: The Turkish Petroleum Company – A Study in Oleaginous Diplomacy, in: *Political Science Quarterly* 39 (1924), no. 2, pp. 265–79

Edelmann, Heidrun: Privatisierung als Sozialpolitik. 'Volksaktien' und Volkswagenwerk, in: *Jahrbuch für Wirtschaftsgeschichte/Economic History Yearbook* 40 (1999), no. 1, pp. 55–72

Eggenkämper, Barbara /Modert, Gert/Pretzlik, Stefan: Die Frankfurter Versicherungs-AG 1865-2004, München 2004

Eggenkämper, Barbara/Modert, Gerd/Pretzlik, Stefan: *Allianz. The Company History 1890–2015*, Munich 2015

Ehrlicher, Werner: Von der 'wirtschaftlichen Wende' zur Wiedervereinigung, in: Hans Pohl (ed.), *Geschichte der deutschen Kreditwirtschaft seit 1945*, Frankfurt am Main 1998, pp. 299–354

Eichengreen, Barry: *Globalizing Capital. A History of the International Monetary System*. 2nd edition, Princeton

Engelberg, Ernst: *Bismarck. Das Reich in der Mitte Europas*, Berlin 1990

Esteves, Rui Pedro: Between Imperialism and Capitalism. European Capital Exports Before 1914, *Working Papers 8022, Economic History Society*, 2008 (http://www.ehs.org.uk/dotAsset/4fe8d90b-39f9-4ed2-9fe5-16c700cef2d9.pdf)

Esteves, Rui Pedro: The Bondholder, the sovereign, and the banker: sovereign debt and bondholders' protection before 1914, in: *European Review of Economic History* 17 (2013), no. 4, pp. 389–407

Euwe, Jeroen: Amsterdam als Finanzzentrum für Deutschland, 1914–1931, in: Hein A. M. Klemann/Friso Wielenga (eds.), *Deutschland und die Niederlande: Wirtschaftsbeziehungen im 19. und 20. Jahrhundert*, Münster 2009, pp. 153–72

50 Jahre Deutsche Ueberseeische Bank, Berlin 1936

Fahrmeir, Andreas/Lesczenski, Jörg: Vom Finanzdienstleister zum 'Arzt der Wirtschaft'. Gründung, Wandel und Ausbau der DTG, 1890 bis 1933, in: Dieter Ziegler/Jörg Lesczenski/Johannes Bähr (eds), *Vertrauensbildung als Auftrag. Von der Deutsch-Amerikanischen Treuhand-Gesellschaft zur KPMG AG*, München/Berlin 2015, pp. 21–63

Faust, Julian F.: Ein 'deutsches Indien in Afrika'? Investitionen in koloniale Eisenbahnen in Indien und Ostafrika vor dem Ersten Weltkrieg, MS, MA, Göttingen 2014

Feinstein, Charles H./Watson, Katherine: Private International Capital Flows in Europe in the Inter-War Period, in: Charles H. Feinstein (ed.), *Banking, Currency, and Finance in Europe Between the Wars*, Oxford 1995, pp. 94–130

Feldenkirchen, Wilfried: 'Vom Guten das Beste'. Von Daimler und Benz zur DaimlerChrysler AG. Band 1: Die ersten 100 Jahre 1883–1993, München 2003

Feldman, Gerald D.: The Great Disorder. Politics, Economics, and Society in the German Inflation, 1914–1924, Oxford 1993

Feldman, Gerald D.: The Deutsche Bank from World War to World Economic Crisis, in: Lothar Gall *et al.*, *The Deutsche Bank 1870-1995*, London 1995, pp. 129–276

Feldman, Gerald D.: German Business Interests and Rumanian Oil in the First World War, in: Roland Schönfeld (ed.), *Germany and Southeastern Europe – Aspects of Relations in the Twentieth Century* (= Deutschland und Südosteuropa – Aspekte der Beziehungen im Zwanzigsten Jahrhundert), München 1997, pp. 23–36

Feldman, Gerald D.: *Hugo Stinnes. Biographie eines Industriellen 1870–1924*, München 1998

Feldman, Gerald D: Die Deutsche Bank und die Automobilindustrie, in: *Zeitschrift für Unternehmensgeschichte* 44 (1999), no. 1, pp. 3–14

Feldman, Gerald D.: *Austrian Banks in the Period of National Socialism*, Cambridge 2015

Ferguson, Niall: *Paper and Iron. Hamburg Business and German Politics in the Era of Inflation, 1897–1927*, Cambridge 1995

Ferguson, Niall: *The World's Banker: The History of the House of Rothschild*, London 1998

Ferguson, Thomas/Temin, Peter: Made in Germany: the German Currency Crisis of July 1931, in: *Research in Economic History* 21 (2003), pp. 1–53

Ferslev, Hans-Peter: Recollections of the Group Strategy department, in: Historical Association of Deutsche Bank (ed.), *Corporate Strategy at Deutsche Bank 1985–1997*, Frankfurt am Main 2017, pp. 17–77

Fest, Joachim: Hermann J. Abs im Gespräch mit Joachim Fest, in: Karl B. Schnelting (ed.), *Zeugen des Jahrhunderts. Porträts aus Wirtschaft und Gesellschaft*, Frankfurt am Main 1981, pp. 11–56

Fiedler, Martin: Netzwerke des Vertrauens: Zwei Fallbeispiele aus der deutschen Wirtschaftselite, in: Dieter Ziegler (ed.), *Großbürger und Unternehmer. Die deutsche Wirtschaftselite im 20. Jahrhundert*, Göttingen 2000, pp. 93–115

Fiedler, Martin: Fusionen und Übernahmen in der deutschen Industrie 1898–1938, in: *Jahrbuch für Wirtschaftsgeschichte/Economic History Yearbook* 43 (2002), no. 2, pp. 209–39

Fiedler, Martin/Lorentz, Bernhard: Kontinuitäten in den Netzwerkbeziehungen der deutschen Wirtschaftselite zwischen Weltwirtschaftskrise und 1950, in: Volker Berghahn/Stefan Unger/Dieter Ziegler (eds), *Die deutsche Wirtschaftselite im 20. Jahrhundert. Kontinuität und Mentalität*, Essen 2003, pp. 51–74

Fiedler, Martin: Eigentümer und Netzwerke: Zum Verhältnis von Personal- und Kapitalverflechtung in deutschen Großunternehmen, 1927 und 1938, in: Hartmut Berghoff / Jörg Sydow (eds), *Unternehmerische Netzwerke. Eine historische Organisationsform mit Zukunft?*, Stuttgart 2007, pp. 97–117

Findlay, Ronald/O'Rourke, Kevin H.: *Power and Plenty. Trade, War, and the World Economy in the Second Millennium*, Princeton 2007

Fisch, Jörg: *Reparationen nach dem Zweiten Weltkrieg*, München 1992

Fischer, Albert: *Hjalmar Schacht und Deutschlands 'Judenfrage'. Der 'Wirtschaftsdiktator' und die Vertreibung der Juden aus der deutschen Wirtschaft*, Köln/Weimar/Wien 1995

Fischer, Wolfram: Bergbau, Industrie und Handwerk 1850-1914, in: Hermann Aubin/Wolfgang Zorn (eds),

Handbuch der deutschen Wirtschafts- und Sozialgeschichte. Bd. 2, Stuttgart 1976, pp. 527–62

Fischer, Wolfram: *Die Weltwirtschaft im 20. Jahrhundert,* Göttingen 1979

Föhl, Thomas/Wolff, Stephan: *Alfred Wolff und Henry van de Velde. Sammelleidenschaft und Stil,* Berlin/München 2018

Förster, Fren: *Geschichte der Deutschen BP 1904–1979,* Hamburg 1979

Fohlin, Caroline: *Finance Capitalism and Germany's Rise to Industrial Power,* Cambridge 2007

Frei, Norbert: Die Wirtschaft des 'Dritten Reiches'. Überlegungen zu einem Perspektivenwechsel, in: ders./Tim Schanetzky (eds), *Unternehmen im Nationalsozialismus. Zur Historisierung einer Forschungskonjunktur,* Göttingen 2010, pp. 9–24

Frey, Marc: *Der Erste Weltkrieg und die Niederlande. Ein neutrales Land im politischen und wirtschaftlichen Kalkül der Kriegsgegner,* Berlin 1998

Friese, Eberhard: 'Meißner, Kurt', in: *Neue Deutsche Biographie* 16 (1990), pp. 701f.

Frost, Reinhard: 'Rösler, Oswald', in: *Neue Deutsche Biographie* 21 (2003), pp. 743f.

Frost, Reinhard: *Wünsche werden Wirklichkeit. Die Deutsche Bank und ihr Privatkundengeschäft,* München 2009

Frost, Reinhard: *Wo Macher Zukunft gestalten. 100 Jahre Deutsche Bank an Rhein und Ruhr,* Köln 2014

Frost, Reinhard: *Hermann Wallich. A Banker in Paris, Shanghai and Berlin,* Berlin 2017

Fuchs, Max: *Die Deutsche Bank in Berlin. Den Herren Mitgliedern der Schiffbautechnischen Gesellschaft aus Anlass ihres Besuches am 20. November 1909 gewidmet von der Deutschen Bank Berlin,* Berlin 1910

Fuchs, Max: *Max Steinthal zu seinem achtzigsten Geburtstag am 24. Dezember 1930,* Berlin 1930

Fuchs, Max: *Arthur von Gwinner. Eine Widmung zu seinem fünfundsiebzigsten Geburtstag,* Berlin 1931

Fuchs, Max: Gustav Schröter †. Ein Gedenkblatt, in: Monatshefte für die Beamten der Deutschen Bank und Disconto-Gesellschaft, Jan./Feb. 1932, pp. 10–15

Fuchsbauer, Erich: *Die Angestelltenversicherung im deutschen Bank-Gewerbe,* Nürnberg 1929

Fürstenberg, Carl: *Die Lebensgeschichte eines deutschen Bankiers 1870–1914.* Ed. Hans Fürstenberg, Berlin 1931

Gajek, Eva Maria: Sichtbarmachung von Reichtum. Das Jahrbuch des Vermögens und Einkommens der Millionäre in Preußen, in: *Archiv für Sozialgeschichte* 54 (2014), pp. 79–108

Gall, Lothar: *Bismarck. The White Revolutionary.* Vol. 2: *1871–1898,* London 1986

Gall, Lothar: The Deutsche Bank from its Founding to the Great War 1870–1914, in: Lothar Gall et al., *The Deutsche Bank 1870–1995,* London 1995, pp. 1–127

Gall, Lothar: *Der Bankier Hermann Josef Abs,* München 2004

Galofré-Vilà, Gregori et al.: The Economic Consequences of the 1953 London Debt Agreement, in: *European Review of Economic History* 23 (2019), no. 1, pp. 1–29

Gehlen, Boris: 'Avantgarde', 'Establishment' und sozialer Komment in der Hochfinanz der Weimarer Zeit zwischen Inklusion und Exklusion, in: *Bankhistorisches Archiv* 36 (2010), pp. 61–81

Gehlen, Boris: Aktienrecht und Unternehmenskontrolle. Normative Vorgaben und unternehmerische Praxis in der Hochphase der Deutschland AG, in: Ralf Ahrens/Boris Gehlen/Alfred Reckendrees (eds), *Die 'Deutschland AG'. Historische Annäherung an den bundesdeutschen Kapitalismus,* Essen 2013, pp. 165–93

Geyer, Martin H.: *Verkehrte Welt. Revolution, Inflation und Moderne. München 1914–1924,* Göttingen 1998

Geyer, Martin H.: What Crisis? Speculation, Corruption, and the State of Emergency during the Great Depression, in: *Bulletin of the German Historical Institute* (Washington DC) 55 (2014), pp. 9–35

Gleeson-White, Jane: *Double Entry. How the Merchants of Venice Created Modern Finance,* London 2013

Gold, Ernst Adolf: Die Bankinsolvenzen seit der Stabilisierung und ihre Ursachen, in: *Zeitschrift für handelswissenschaftliche Forschung* 25 (1931), pp. 450–71

Goschler, Constantin: *Wiedergutmachung. Westdeutschland und die Verfolgten des Nationalsozialismus 1945–1954,* München 1992

Groppe, Carola: *Im deutschen Kaiserreich. Eine Bildungsgeschichte des Bürgertums 1871–1918,* Köln/Wien/Weimar 2018

Gross, Stephen G.: Gold, Debt and the Quest for Monetary Order: The Nazi Campaign to Integrate Europe in 1940, in: *Contemporary European History* 26 (2017), no. 2, pp. 287–309

Grünbacher, Armin: *Reconstruction and Cold War in Germany. The Kreditanstalt für Wiederaufbau (1948–1961),* Aldershot 2004

Guth, Wilfried: Verantwortung der Banken – heute, in: ders., *Weltwirtschaft und Währung. Aufsätze und Vorträge 1967–1989,* Mainz 1989, pp. 373–98

Gutsche, Willibald: Monopole, *Staat und Expansion vor 1914. Zum Funktionsmechanismus zwischen Industriemonopolen, Großbanken und Staatsorganen in der Außenpolitik des Deutschen Reiches 1897 bis Sommer 1914,* Berlin 1986

Gwinner, Arthur von: Meine Lehrlingszeit, in: *Monatshefte für die Beamten der Deutschen Bank 1927,* no. 12, pp. 49–51

Haase, Friedrich: *Die Erdöl-Interessen der Deutschen Bank und der Direction der Disconto-Gesellschaft in Rumänien,* Berlin 1922

Hamlin, David: *Germany's Empire in the East. Germans and Romania in an Era of Globalization and Total War,* Cambridge 2017

Hannah, Leslie: The Twentieth Century Transformation of Banking and its Effect on Management Training for Bankers, in: Edward Green/Kostas Kostis (eds), *The Human Factor in Banking History. Entrepreneurship, Organization, Management and Personnel,* Athens 2008, pp. 189–207

Hardach, Gerd: *Weltmarktorientierung und relative Stagnation: Währungspolitik in Deutschland 1924–1931,* Berlin 1976

Hardach, Gerd: Die Entstehung des Drei-Säulen-Modells in der deutschen Kreditwirtschaft 1871-1934, in: Institut für bankhistorische Forschung (ed.), *Geschichte und Perspektiven des Drei-Säulen-Modells der deutschen Kreditwirtschaft* (= Bankhistorisches Archiv, Beiheft 46), Stuttgart 2007, pp. 13–39

Hardach, Gerd: Die finanzielle Mobilmachung in Deutschland 1914–1918, in: *Jahrbuch für Wirtschaftsgeschichte/Economic History Yearbook* 56 (2015), no. 2, pp. 359–87

Harries, Heinrich: *Financing the future: KfW, The German Bank with a Public Mission,* Frankfurt am Main 1998

Hauser, Henri: *Les méthodes allemandes d'expansion économique,* Paris 1915

Heimerzheim, Peter: *Karl Ritter von Halt – Leben zwischen Sport und Politik,* Sankt Augustin 1999

Helfferich, Karl: Die türkische Staatsschuld und die Balkan-Staaten, in: *Bank-Archiv* 12 (1913), Nr. 11, pp. 167–75

Helfferich, Karl: *Deutschlands Volkswohlstand von 1888 bis 1913*, Berlin 1913

Helfferich, Karl: Die Entstehung des Weltkrieges im Lichte der Veröffentlichungen der Dreimächteverbände, in: ders., *Reden und Aufsätze aus dem Kriege, Berlin 1917*, pp. 9–66

Helfferich, Karl: *Georg von Siemens. Ein Lebensbild aus Deutschlands großer Zeit*. 3 Bde., Berlin 1921–1923

Helfferich, Karl: *Studien über Bank- und Geldwesen*, Paderborn 2013 (Nachdruck der Ausgabe von 1900)

Henning, Friedrich-Wilhelm: Innovationen und Wandel der Beschäftigtenstruktur im Kreditgewerbe von der Mitte des 19. Jahrhunderts bis 1948, in: Hans Pohl (ed.), *Innovationen und Wandel der Beschäftigtenstruktur im Kreditgewerbe* (= Bankhistorisches Archiv, Beiheft 12), Frankfurt am Main 1988, pp. 47–66

Hentschel, Volker: *Wirtschaft und Wirtschaftspolitik im wilhelminischen Deutschland. Organisierter Kapitalismus und Interventionsstaat?*, Stuttgart 1978

Hentschel, Volker: *Ludwig Erhard. Ein Politikerleben*, München 1996

Herbert, Ulrich: *Hitler's Foreign Workers. Enforced Foreign Labor in Germany under the Third Reich*, Cambridge 1997

Herbst, Ludolf: Banker in einem prekären Geschäft: Die Beteiligung der Commerzbank an der Vernichtung jüdischer Gewerbeunternehmen im Altreich (1933–1940), in: ders./Thomas Weihe (eds), *Die Commerzbank und die Juden 1933–1945*, München 2004, pp. 74–137

Herr, Laura: '… dem Bankiersstande die frühere Ansehen zurückzugewinnen.' Der Centralverband des Deutschen Bank- und Bankiersgewerbes 1901 bis 1933, Diss. phil., Heidelberg 2018

Herrhausen, Alfred: The Time Is Ripe, in: *IDS Bulletin* 21 (1990), no. 2, pp. 52-54

Hertner, Peter: The Deutsche Bank in Italy and on the Italian Capital Market up to the Outbreak of the First World War, in: *Studies on Economic and Monetary Problems and on Banking History* No. 1–22, Mainz 1988, pp. 685–726

Hertner, Peter: German Banks abroad before 1914, in: Geoffrey Jones (ed.), *Banks as Multinationals*, London 1990, pp. 99–119

Hertner, Peter: The Balkan Railways, international capital and banking from the end of the nineteenth century until the outbreak of the First World War, in: Gerald D. Feldman/Peter Hertner (eds), *Finance and Modernization. A Transnational and Transcontinental Perspective for the Nineteenth and Twentieth Centuries*, Abingdon/London 2008, pp. 125–53

Hertner, Peter: Globale Elektrifizierung zu Beginn des 20. Jahrhunderts. Das Beispiel der Deutsch-Ueberseeischen Elektricitäts-Gesellschaft in Buenos Aires, 1989 bis 1920, in: Hartmut Berghoff/Jürgen Kocka/Dieter Ziegler (eds), *Wirtschaft im Zeitalter der Extreme. Beiträge zur Unternehmensgeschichte Österreichs und Deutschlands. Im Gedenken an Gerald D. Feldman*, München 2010, pp. 47–80

Hertner, Peter: Starting from scratch? The beginnings of Banca Commerciale Italiana 1893–1894, in: Carmen Hofmann/Martin L. Müller (eds), *History of Financial Institutions. Essays on the History of European Finance, 1800–1950*, London 2016, pp. 13–37

Heß, Klaus: *Junker und bürgerliche Großgrundbesitzer im Kaiserreich: landwirtschaftlicher Großbetrieb, Großgrundbesitz und Familienfideikommiß in Preußen (1867/71–1914)*, Stuttgart 1990

Heuß, Theodor: Georg von Siemens, in: Theodor Heuß, *Deutsche Gestalten. Studien zum 19. Jahrhundert*, Tübingen 1951

Hilferding, Rudolf: *Finance Capital. A Study of the Latest Phase of Capitalist Development*. Ed. Tom Bottomore, London 1981 (first published in German 1910)

Hill, Howard B.: *Finance Monsters: How Massive Unregulated Betting by a Small Group of Financiers Propelled the Mortgage Market Collapse into a Global Financial Crisis*, CreateSpace Independent Publishing Platform 2014

Historische Gesellschaft der Deutschen Bank (ed.): *Die Deutsche Bank in Frankfurt am Main*, München/Zürich 2005

Historische Gesellschaft der Deutschen Bank (ed.): *100 Jahre Deutsche Bank in Istanbul*, Frankfurt am Main 2009

Historische Gesellschaft der Deutschen Bank (ed.): Vor hundert Jahren: Die Deutsche Bank kommt nach Belgien, in: *Bank und Geschichte – Historische Rundschau*, Nr. 21, 2010

Hohorst, Gerd/Kocka, Jürgen/Ritter, Gerhard A.: *Sozialgeschichtliches Arbeitsbuch*. Bd. 2: *Materialien zur Statistik des Kaiserreichs 1870–1914*. 2., durchges. Aufl., München 1978

Holtfrerich, Carl-Ludwig: *Quantitative Wirtschaftsgeschichte des Ruhrkohlenbergbaus im 19. Jahrhundert*, Dortmund 1973

Holtfrerich, Carl-Ludwig: Amerikanischer Kapitalexport und Wiederaufbau der deutschen Wirtschaft 1919–23 im Vergleich zu 1924–29, in: *Vierteljahrschrift für Sozial- und Wirtschaftsgeschichte* 64 (1977), no. 4, pp. 497–529

Holtfrerich, Carl-Ludwig: *The German Inflation 1914–1923. Causes and Effects in International Perspective*, Berlin/New York 1986 (translated by Theo Balderston)

Holtfrerich, Carl-Ludwig: The Deutsche Bank 1945–1957: War, Military Rule and Reconstruction, in: Lothar Gall et al., *Die Deutsche Bank 1870–1995*, London 1995 pp. 357–521

Hook, Walter: *Die wirtschaftliche Entwicklung der ehemaligen Deutschen Bank im Spiegel ihrer Bilanzen*. 2. Aufl., Heidelberg 1956

Hooven, Eckart van: *Meistbegünstigt: Bericht eines Zeitzeugen des Jahrgangs 1925*, Frankfurt am Main 2002

Horn, Norbert: Aktienrechtliche Unternehmensorganisation in der Hochindustrialisierung (1860–1920). Deutschland, England, Frankreich und die USA im Vergleich, in: Norbert Horn/Jürgen Kocka (eds), *Recht und Entwicklung der Großunternehmen im 19. und frühen 20. Jahrhundert*, Göttingen 1979, pp. 123–89

Horstmann, Theo: *Die Alliierten und die deutschen Großbanken. Bankenpolitik nach dem Zweiten Weltkrieg in Westdeutschland*, Bonn 1991

Hüttenberger, Peter: Wirtschaftsordnung und Interessenpolitik in der Kartellgesetzgebung der Bundesrepublik 1949–1957, in: *Vierteljahrshefte für Zeitgeschichte* 24 (1976), no. 3, pp. 287–307

Hutten-Czapski, Bogdan von: *Sechzig Jahre Politik und Gesellschaft*. Band 1, Berlin 1936

Irmler, Heinrich: Bankenkrise und Vollbeschäftigungspolitik (1931–1936), in: Deutsche Bundesbank (ed.), *Währung und Wirtschaft in Deutschland 1876–1975*, Frankfurt am Main 1976, pp. 283–330

Jacob-Wendler, Gerhart: *Deutsche Elektroindustrie in Lateinamerika: Siemens und AEG (1890–1914)*, Stuttgart 1982

James, Harold: The Causes of the German Banking Crisis of 1931, in: *Economic History Review* 37 (1984), no. 1, pp. 68–87

James, Harold: *The German Slump: Politics and Economics, 1924–1936*, Oxford 1986

James, Harold: The Deutsche Bank and the Dictatorship 1933–1945, in: in: Lothar Gall *et al.*, *The Deutsche Bank 1870–1995*, London 1995, pp. 277–356

James, Harold: *Verbandspolitik im Nationalsozialismus. Von der Interessenvertretung zur Wirtschaftsgruppe: Der Centralverband des Deutschen Bank- und Bankiergewerbes 1932–1945*, München 2001

James, Harold: *The End of Globalization. Lessons from the Great Depression*, Cambridge 2001

James, Harold: *The Deutsche Bank and the Nazi Economic War against the Jews. The Expropriation of Jewish-Owned Property*, Cambridge 2001

James, Harold: *The Nazi Dictatorship and the Deutsche Bank*, Cambridge 2004

James, Harold: Banks and Business Politics in Nazi Germany, in: Francis R. Nicosia/Jonathan Huener (eds), *Business and Industry in Nazi Germany*, New York/Oxford 2004, pp. 43–65

James, Harold /Müller, Martin L. (eds), *Georg Solmssen – ein deutscher Bankier. Briefe aus einem halben Jahrhundert 1900–1956*, München 2012

Janssen, Sven: *British and German Banking Strategies*, Basingstoke/New York 2009

Joly, Hervé: Kontinuität und Diskontinuität der industriellen Elite nach 1945, in: Dieter Ziegler (ed.), *Großbürger und Unternehmer. Die deutsche Wirtschaftselite im 20. Jahrhundert*, Göttingen 2000, pp. 54–72

Jones, Geoffrey/Lubinski, Christina: Managing Political Risk in Global Business: Beiersdorf 1914–1990, in: *Enterprise & Society* 13 (2012), no. 1, pp. 85–119

Der Kabinettsausschuß für Wirtschaft, Vorgeschichte und Einrichtung, in: *Kabinettsausschuß für Wirtschaft. Band 1. 1951–1953, herausgegeben für das Bundesarchiv von Friedrich P. Kahlenberg bearbeitet von Ulrich Enders*, München 1999

Kaiser, Hilmar: The Baghdad Railway and the Armenian Genocide, 1915–1916. A Case Study in German Resistance and Complicity, in: Richard G. Hovannisian (ed.), *Remembrance and Denial. The Case of the Armenian Genocide*, Detroit 1999, pp. 67–112

Kaminsky, Graciella L./Reinhart, Carmen M.: The Twin Crises: The Causes of Banking and Balance-of-Payment Problems, in: *American Economic Review* 89 (1999), no. 3, pp. 473–500

Karlsch, Rainer/Stokes, Raymond G.: *Faktor Öl. Die Mineralölwirtschaft in Deutschland 1859–1974*, München 2003

Kellermann, Christian: Disentangling Deutschland AG, in: Stefan Beck/Frank Klobes/Christoph Scherrer (eds), *Surviving Globalization? Perspectives for the German Economic Model*, Springer 2005, pp. 111–32

Kerkhof, Stefanie van de: *Von der Friedens- zur Kriegswirtschaft. Unternehmensstrategien der deutschen Eisen- und Stahlindustrie vom Kaiserreich bis zum Ende des Ersten Weltkrieges*, Bochum 2006

Keynes, John Maynard: *Die wirtschaftlichen Folgen des Friedensvertrages*, München/Leipzig 1921

Keynes, John Maynard: *The Economic Consequences of the Peace. The Collected Writings of John Maynard Keynes*, vol. 2, London 1971 [first published 1919]

Kiehling, Harmut: Der Funktionsverlust der deutschen Finanzmärkte in Weltkrieg und Inflation 1914–1923, in: *Jahrbuch für Wirtschaftsgeschichte* 39 (1998), no. 1, pp. 11–58

King, Frank H. H.: *The Hongkong Bank in the Period of Imperialism and War, 1895–1918*, Cambridge 1988

Kirshner, Jonathan: *Appeasing Bankers. Financial Caution on the Road to War*, Princeton 2007

Kleine-Natorp, Heinrich: *Verfassung und Geschichte der Maklerbanken*, München/Leipzig 1913

Kleinschmidt, Christian: Strategische Außenwirtschaftsbeziehungen. Die Bundesrepublik, die Türkei und der Kalte Krieg 1945–1970, in: *Jahrbuch für Wirtschaftsgeschichte/Economic History Yearbook* 53 (2012). H. 1, pp. 43–67

Kleinschmidt, Christian/Atilgan, Inanc (eds): *Deutsch-türkische Wirtschaftsbeziehungen. Eine Bestandsaufnahme*, Klagenfurt 2013

Kobrak, Christopher/Hansen, Per H. (eds): *European Business, Dictatorship, and Political Risk, 1920–1945*, New York 2004

Kobrak, Christopher: *Banking on Global Markets. Deutsche Bank and the United States, 1870 to the Present*, Cambridge 2008

Koch, Friedrich: *Der Londoner Goldverkehr*, Stuttgart 1905

Kocka, Jürgen (ed.): *Bürgertum im 19. Jahrhundert*. Bd. II: *Wirtschaftsbürger und Bildungsbürger*, Göttingen 1995

Koehler, Benedikt: *Ludwig Bamberger. Revolutionär und Bankier*, Stuttgart 1999

Köhler, Ingo: *Die 'Arisierung' der Privatbanken im Dritten Reich. Verdrängung, Ausschaltung und die Frage der Wiedergutmachung* (= Schriftenreihe zur Zeitschrift für Unternehmensgeschichte 14). 2. Aufl., München 2008

Köhler, Ingo: Business as usual? Aryanization in practice, 1933–1938, in: Hartmut Berghoff/ Jürgen Kocka/ Dieter Ziegler (eds), *Business in the Age of Extremes. Essays in Modern German and Austrian Economic History*, Cambridge 2013, pp. 172–88

Köhler, Ingo: Das Ende des Bankhauses Mendelssohn 1938. Aderlass des Bankwesens durch 'Arisierungen', in: Dieter Lindenlaub/Carsten Burhop/Joachim Scholtyseck (eds), *Schlüsselereignisse der deutschen Bankengeschichte*, Stuttgart 2013, pp. 270–82

Koeppel, Wilhelm: Öffentlichkeit und Aktienrecht zur Kurspflege, in: *Bank-Archiv. Zeitschrift für Bank- und Börsenwesen* 31 (1931), pp. 74–6

Köster, Roman: *Standort Weiß-Blau. 125 Jahre Deutsche Bank in Bayern*, München 2017

Koetter, Michael: Evaluating the German bank merger wave, ECB Discussion Paper, Series 2: Banking and Financial Studies, 12/2005

Koetter, Michael: An Assessment of Bank Merger Success in Germany, in: *German Economic Review* 9 (2008), no. 2, pp. 232–64

Knoch, Habbo: *Grandhotels. Luxusräume und Gesellschaftswandel in New York, London und Berlin um 1900*, Göttingen 2016

Kopper, Christopher/Pohl, Manfred/Raab-Rebentisch, Angelika: *Stationen*, Frankfurt am Main 1995

Kopper, Christopher: *Hjalmar Schacht. Aufstieg und Fall von Hitlers mächtigstem Bankier*, München 2006

Kopper, Christopher: The Recycling of Petrodollars, in: *Revue d'Économie Financière* (2009), special issue, pp. 37–46

Kopper, Christopher: *Ludwig Bamberger. Vom Revolutionär zum Vater der Goldmark*, Berlin 2015

Kopper, Christopher: Reiche Deutsche und transnationale Vermögensanlage. Die Rolle der Banken in der Professionalisierung der Anlageberatung und die

Internationalisierung der Vermögensanlage seit den 1970er Jahren, in: Eva Maria Gajek/Anne Kurr/Lu Seegers (eds), *Reichtum in Deutschland. Akteure, Räume und Lebenswelten im 20. Jahrhundert*, Göttingen 2019, pp. 182–97

Kopper, Hilmar: Strategische Ausrichtung einer Universalbank auf einen gemeinsamen EG-Finanzmarkt, in: *Österreichisches Bank-Archiv* 38 (1990), no. 2, pp. 67–72

Krause, Detlef: Archivalische Quellen zu den Organisationsstrukturen der Banken, GUG-Arbeitspapier 1/1998

Kreimeier, Klaus: *The Ufa Story: A History of Germany's Greatest Film Company 1918–1945*, New York 1996

Krenn, Karolin: *Alle Macht den Banken? Zur Struktur personaler Netzwerke deutscher Unternehmen am Beginn des 20. Jahrhunderts*, Wiesbaden 2012

Krenn, Karoline/Marx, Christian: Kontinuität und Wandel in der deutschen Unternehmensverflechtung. Vom Kaiserreich bis zum Nationalsozialismus, 1914–1938, in: *Geschichte und Gesellschaft* 38 (2012), no. 4, pp. 658–701

Kritzler, Ernst: Preußische Hypotheken-Aktienbank, Deutsche Grundschuldbank, Pommersche Hypotheken-Aktienbank: Krise und Sanierung, in: *Die Störungen im deutschen Wirtschaftsleben während der Jahre 1900ff*, Leipzig 1903 (Schriften des Vereins für Socialpolitik), Bd. 6, pp. 1–82

Lamberti, Hermann-Josef/Büger, Matthias: Lessons Learned: 50 Years of Information Technology in the Banking Industry – The Example of Deutsche Bank AG, in: *Business & Information Systems Engineering* 1 (2009), no. 1, pp. 26–36

Lampe, Winfried: *Der Bankbetrieb in Krieg und Inflation. Deutsche Großbanken in den Jahren 1914 bis 1923*, Stuttgart 2012

Lansburgh, Alfred: Das Beteiligungssystem im deutschen Bankwesen, in: *Die Bank* (1910), Bd. 1, pp. 497–508

Lesczenski, Jörg: *August Thyssen 1842–1926: Lebenswelt eines Wirtschaftsbürgers*, Essen 2008

Lesczenski, Jörg: 'Im Reich der Industrie lebt ein Mann …, der ein Unikum ist.' August Thyssen (1842–1926), in: Werner Plumpe (ed.), *Unternehmer – Fakten und Fiktionen. Historisch-biografische Studien*, München 2014, pp. 169–95

Lehmann-Hasemeyer, Sibylle/Opitz, Alexander: The value of active politicians on supervisory boards: evidence from the Berlin stock exchange and the parliament in interwar Germany, in: *Scandinavian Economic History Review* 67 (2019), no. 1, pp. 71–89

Leutner, Mechthild/Mühlhahn, Klaus: Interkulturelle Handlungsmuster. Deutsche Wirtschaft und Mission in China in der Spätphase des Imperialismus, in: dies. (eds), *Deutsch-chinesische Beziehungen im 19. Jahrhundert. Mission und Wirtschaft in interkultureller Perspektive*, Münster 2001, pp. 9–42

Lewis, Michael: *The Big Short: Inside the Doomsday Machine*, New York 2010

Liedtke, Rainer: *N. M. Rothschild & Sons: Kommunikationswege im europäischen Bankenwesen im 19. Jahrhundert*, Köln/Weimar/Wien 2006

Lindemann, Ralf: *Das weiße Schloss am Meer. Schloss Dwasieden in Sassnitz auf der Insel Rügen*, Sassnitz 2003

Lindner, Axel: *Die Volksaktienbewegung in Deutschland. Ihre Motive und Zielsetzungen, ihre Projekte und Erfahrungen*, Winterthur 1964

Linne, Karsten: Afrika als 'wirtschaftlicher Ergänzungsraum'. Kurt Weigelt und die kolonialwirtschaftlichen Planungen im 'Dritten Reich', in: *Jahrbuch für Wirtschaftsgeschichte/ Economic History Yearbook* 47 (2006), no. 2, pp. 141–62

Loose, Ingo: *Kredite für NS-Verbrechen. Die deutschen Kreditinstitute in Polen und die Ausraubung der polnischen und jüdischen Bevölkerung 1939–1945*, München 2007

Lopes, Daniel Seabra: Libor and Euribor: from normal banking practice to manipulation to the potential for reform, in: Ismail Ertürk/Danela Gabor (eds.), *The Routledge Companion to Banking Regulation and Reform*, Abingdon/New York 2017, pp. 225–49

Lorentz, Bernhard: Die Commerzbank und die 'Arisierung' im Altreich. Ein Vergleich der Netzwerkstrukturen und Handlungsspielräume von Großbanken in der NS-Zeit, in: *Vierteljahrshefte für Zeitgeschichte* 50 (2002), no. 2, pp. 237–68

Loscertales, Javier: *Deutsche Investitionen in Spanien 1870–1920*, Stuttgart 2002

Lumm, Karl von: *Karl Helfferich als Währungspolitiker und Gelehrter. Erinnerungen von Karl von Lumm*, Leipzig 1926

Lutz, Martin: *Siemens im Sowjetgeschäft. Eine Institutionengeschichte der deutsch-sowjetischen Beziehungen 1917–1933*, Stuttgart 2011

Mackenzie, Compton: *Realms of Silver. One Hundred Years of Banking in the East*, London 1954

Marguerat, Philippe: La Steava Romana, 1903–1939. Une grande entreprise industrielle entre la Deutsche Bank et la Banque de Paris et des Pays-Bas, in: Olivier Feiertag/Isabelle Lespinet-Moret (eds), *L'économie faite homme. Hommage à Alain Plessis*, Genf 2011, pp. 265–73

Martin, Rudolf: *Jahrbuch des Vermögens und Einkommens der Millionäre in Preußen*, Berlin 1912

Mausbach, Wilfried: *Zwischen Morgenthau und Marshall. Das wirtschaftspolitische Deutschlandkonzept der USA 1944–1947*, Düsseldorf 1996

Mayer, Arno J.: *Adelsmacht und Bürgertum. Die Krise der europäischen Gesellschaft 1848–1914*, München 1984

Mayer, Thomas: *Europe's Unfinished Currency; the political economy of the Euro*, London/New York 2012

Mazbouri, Malik: Der Aufstieg des Finanzplatzes im Ersten Weltkrieg. Das Beispiel des Schweizerischen Bankvereins, in: Roman Rossfeld/Tobias Straumann (eds), *Der vergessene Wirtschaftskrieg. Schweizer Unternehmen im Ersten Weltkrieg*, Zürich 2008, pp. 439–64

McNeese, Tim: *The Robber Barons and the Sherman Antitrust Act: Reshaping American Business*, New York 2009

Meißner, Jochen: Bruch oder Kontinuität? Die Bedeutung des Ersten Weltkrieges für die deutschen Auslandsinvestitionen in Lateinamerika, in: Boris Barth/Jochen Meißner (eds), *Grenzenlose Märkte? Die deutsch-lateinamerikanischen Wirtschaftsbeziehungen vom Zeitalter des Imperialismus bis zur Weltwirtschaftskrise*, Münster 1995, pp. 185–203

Mejcher, Helmut: Die Britische Erdölpolitik im Nahen Osten, 1914–1956, in: ders., *Zeithorizonte im Nahen Osten. Studien und Miszellen zur Geschichte im 20. Jahrhundert*, Berlin 2012, pp. 1–23

Mejcher, Helmut: Die Bagdadbahn als Instrument deutschen wirtschaftlichen Einflusses im Osmanischen Reich, in: ders., *Zeithorizonte im Nahen Osten. Studien und Miszellen zur Geschichte im 20. Jahrhundert*, Berlin 2012, pp. 35–67

Meleghy, Gyulya: Die Vermittlerrolle der Banken bei deutschen Investitionen in Nord- und Mittelamerika bis zum Ersten Weltkrieg, Diss., Köln 1983

Mello, Antonio S./Parsons, John E.: Maturity Structure of a Hedge Matters: lessons from the Metallgesellschaft Debacle, in: *Journal of Applied Corporate Finance* 8 (1995), no. 1, pp. 106–20

Mendel, Joseph: Geldmarkt, Finanzen, Börse und Warenmärkte im Weltkriege. Eine international-vergleichende Übersicht, in: *Weltwirtschaftliches Archiv* 5 (1915), pp. 145–84

Merker, Peter: Zwischen Konfrontation und Kooperation: Das deutsch-chinesische Handelsverhältnis in Hankou. Interessenlagen, Interaktionen, Konfliktfelder, Interventionsmuster, in: Mechthild Leutner/Klaus Mühlhahn (eds), *Deutsch-Chinesische Beziehungen im 19. Jahrhundert. Mission und Wirtschaft in interkultureller Perspektive*, Münster 2001, pp. 43–85

Mertens, Bernd: Das Aktiengesetz von 1937 – unpolitischer Schlussstein oder ideologischer Neuanfang?, in: *Zeitschrift für Neuere Rechtsgeschichte* 29 (2007), pp. 88–117

Mielke, Siegfried: *Der Hansa-Bund für Gewerbe, Handel und Industrie 1909–1914. Der gescheiterte Versuch einer antifeudalen Sammlungspolitik*, Göttingen 1976

Moazzin, Ghassan: From Globalization to Liquidation: The Deutsch-Asiatische Bank and the First World War in China, in: *Cross-Currents: East Asian History and Culture Review* 4 (2015), no. 2, pp. 601–29

Model, Paul: *Die großen Berliner Effektenbanken. Aus dem Nachlasse des Verfassers herausgegeben und vervollständigt von Dr. jur. Ernst Loeb*, Jena 1896

Monopolkommission: Ordnungspolitische Leitlinien für ein funktionsfähiges Finanzsystem, *Sondergutachten* 26, Baden-Baden 1988

Müller, Christoph: *Die Entstehung des Reichsgesetzes über das Kreditwesen vom 5. Dezember 1934*, Berlin 2003

Müller, Martin L.: *DWS. Eine Erfolgsgeschichte*, München 2006

Müller, Martin L.: Die Bank, ihre Akten und der Kalte Krieg. Die Überlieferung der Berliner Zentrale der Deutschen Bank, in: Hartmut Berghoff/Jürgen Kocka/Dieter Ziegler (eds), *Wirtschaft im Zeitalter der Extreme* (= Schriftenreihe zur Zeitschrift für Unternehmensgeschichte, Bd. 20), München 2010, pp. 394–409

Müller, Martin L.: 50 Jahre Historisches Institut der Deutschen Bank, in: *Archiv und Wirtschaft* 44 (2011), no. 4, pp. 160–70

Müller, Martin L.: Eine deutsche Bank für Japan. Die Deutsche Bank für Ostasien im Zweiten Weltkrieg – ein Beitrag zum Verhältnis zwischen Politik und Finanzwirtschaft im Nationalsozialismus (ungedr. MS)

Müller-Jabusch, Maximilian: *Fünfzig Jahre Deutsch-Asiatische Bank, 1890–1939*, Berlin 1940

Müller-Jabusch, Maximilian: *Franz Urbig. Überarb. u. ergänz. Neudruck der Erstauflage von 1939*, Berlin 1954

Münch, Hermann: *Adolph von Hansemann*, München/Berlin 1932

Münkler, Herfried: *Der Große Krieg. Die Welt 1914–1918*, Berlin 2014

Naasner, Walter: *SS-Wirtschaft und SS-Verwaltung. 'Das SS-Wirtschafts-Verwaltungshauptamt und die unter seiner Dienstaufsicht stehenden wirtschaftlichen Unternehmungen' und weitere Dokumente*, Düsseldorf 1998

Neebe, Reinhard: *Weichenstellung für die Globalisierung. Deutsche Weltmarktpolitik, Europa und Amerika in der Ära Ludwig Erhard*, Köln/Weimar/Wien 2004

Niethammer, Lutz: From Forced Labor in Nazi Germany to the Foundation 'Remembrance, Responsibility and Future', in: Michael Jansen/Günter Saathoff (eds), *'A Mutual Responsibility and a Moral Obligation'. The Final Report on Germany's Compensation Programs for Forced Labor and other Personal Injuries*, Basingstoke 2009, pp. 15–85

N. N., Deutsche Bank, in: *Unser Kaiserpaar. Gedenkblätter zum 27. Februar 1906*, Berlin 1906, pp. 281–6

Obst, Georg: *Bankbuchhaltung. Buchhaltung, Statistik und Kalkulation im Bankbetriebe*, Stuttgart 1925

Oepen-Domschky, Gabriele: *Kölner Wirtschaftsbürger im Deutschen Kaiserreich. Eugen Langen, Ludwig Stollwerck, Arnold von Guilleaume und Simon Alfred von Oppenheim*, Köln 2003

Offer, Avner: *The First World War: An Agrarian Interpretation*, Oxford 1989

O'Malley, Chris: *Bonds Without Borders: A History of the Eurobond Market*, Chichester 2014

Osenberg, Axel: Deutsche Bank moves East, in: Andreas R. Prindl (ed.), *Banking and Finance in Eastern Europe*, New York/London 1992, pp. 80–85

Osterhammel, Jürgen: *China und die Weltgesellschaft. Vom 18. Jahrhundert bis in unsere Zeit*, München 1989

Osterhammel, Jürgen: *The Transformation of the World. A Global History of the Nineteenth Century*, Princeton 2014 (translated by Patrick Camiller)

Otto, Frank: *Die Entstehung eines nationalen Geldes: Integrationsprozesse der deutschen Währung im 19. Jahrhundert*, Berlin 2002

Overy, Richard/Otto, Gerhard/Houwink ten Cate, Johannes (eds): *Die 'Neuordnung' Europas. NS-Wirtschaftspolitik in den besetzten Gebieten*, Berlin 1997

Pak, Susie J.: *Gentlemen Bankers. The World of J. P. Morgan*, Cambridge, Mass. 2013

Panwitz, Sebastian: *Das Haus des Kranichs. Die Privatbankiers von Mendelssohn & Co. (1795–1938)*, Berlin 2018

Pierer, Christian: *Die Bayerischen Motoren Werke bis 1933. Eine Unternehmensgründung in Krieg, Inflation und Weltwirtschaftskrise*, München 2011

Pinner, Felix: *Emil Rathenau und das technische Zeitalter*, Leipzig 1918

Pinner, Felix: *Deutsche Wirtschaftsführer*. 15., erw. Auflage, Charlottenburg 1925

Platthaus, Andreas: *Alfred Herrhausen. Eine deutsche Karriere*, Berlin 2006

Plumpe, Werner: Deutsche Bank in East Asia 1872–1988, in: Historical Association of Deutsche Bank (ed.), *Deutsche Bank in East Asia*, Munich/Zurich 2004, pp. 23–89

Plumpe, Werner: *Deutsche Bank in China*, Munich/Zurich 2008

Plumpe, Werner: Die Logik des modernen Krieges und die Unternehmen: Überlegungen zum Ersten Weltkrieg, in: *Jahrbuch für Wirtschaftsgeschichte/Economic History Yearbook* 56 (2015), no. 2, pp. 325–58

Plumpe, Werner: *Carl Duisberg 1861–1935. Anatomie eines Industriellen*, München 2016

Plumpe, Werner: Den Boden verloren! Die multiple Krise des Bürgertums im Zeitalter des Ersten Weltkriegs, in: Manfred Hettling/Richard Pohle (eds), *Bürgertum. Bilanzen, Perspektiven, Begriffe*, Göttingen 2019, pp. 205–35

Pohl, Hans/Jachmich, Gabriele: Verschärfung des Wettbewerbs (1966–1973), in: Hans Pohl (ed.),

Geschichte der deutschen Kreditwirtschaft seit 1945, Frankfurt am Main 1998, pp. 203–48

Pohl, Hans: Die Sparkassen vom Ausgang des 19. Jahrhunderts bis zum Ende des Zweiten Weltkriegs, in: ders./Bernd Rudolph/Günther Schulz, *Wirtschafts- und Sozialgeschichte der deutschen Sparkassen im 20. Jahrhundert*, Stuttgart 2005, pp. 21–248

Pohl, Manfred: Wiederaufbau, Kunst und Technik der Finanzierung 1947–1953 – Die ersten Jahre der Kreditanstalt für Wiederaufbau, Frankfurt am Main 1973

Pohl, Manfred: Art. 'Koch, Rudolph von', in: *Neue Deutsche Biographie* 12 (1980), p. 277

Pohl, Manfred: *Konzentration im deutschen Bankwesen (1848–1980)*, Frankfurt am Main 1982

Pohl, Manfred: Die Gebäude der Deutschen Bank. Ein Rückblick, in: Bernhard Leitner *et al.* (eds), *Taunusanlage 12*, Frankfurt am Main 1985, pp. 97–131

Pohl, Manfred: Documents on the History of the Deutsche Bank, in: *Studies on Economic and Monetary Problems and on Banking History* no. 1–22, Mainz 1988, pp. 727–39

Pohl, Manfred: Selected Documents on the History of the Deutsche Bank, in: *Studies on Economic and Monetary Problems and on Banking History* no. 1–22, Mainz 1988 pp. 769–91

Pohl, Manfred: *Deutsche Bank Buenos Aires 1887–1987*, Mainz 1987

Pohl, Manfred: *Emil Rathenau und die AEG*, Mainz 1988

Pohl, Manfred: *Geschäft und Politik. Deutsch-russisch/ sowjetische Wirtschaftsbeziehungen 1850–1988*, Frankfurt am Main 1988

Pohl, Manfred/Raab-Rebentisch, Angelika: *Die Deutsche Bank in Hamburg 1872–1997*, München 1997

Pohl, Manfred/Burk, Kathleen: *Deutsche Bank in London 1873–1998*, Munich 1998

Pohl, Manfred: *Von Stambul nach Bagdad. Die Geschichte einer berühmten Bahn*, München 1999

Pohl, Manfred: *Philipp Holzmann. Geschichte eines Bauunternehmens 1849–1999*, München 1999

Pohl, Manfred/Raab-Rebentisch, Angelika: *Die Deutsche Bank in Leipzig 1901–2001*, München/Zürich 2001

Powell, Anthony: *A Dance to the Music of Time*. Vol. 6: *The Kindly Ones*, London 1962

Priemel, Kim Christian: *The Betrayal: The Nuremberg Trials and German Divergence*. Oxford 2016

Priester, Hans E.: *Das Geheimnis des 13. Juli: ein Tatsachenbericht von der Bankenkrise*, Berlin 1932

Radu, Robert: *Auguren des Geldes. Eine Kulturgeschichte des Finanzjournalismus in Deutschland 1850–1914*, Göttingen 2017

Rasch, Manfred: *Der Unternehmer Guido Henckel von Donnersmarck. Eine Skizze*, Essen 2016

Rathenau, Walther: *Briefe*, Teilband I: *1871–1913*, ed. by Alexander Jaser/Clemens Picht/ Ernst Schulin (Bd. V 1 der Walther-Rathenau-Gesamtausgabe), Düsseldorf 2006

Redenius, Oliver: *Strukturwandel und Konzentrationsprozesse im deutschen Hypothekenbankwesen*, Wiesbaden 2009

Reichert, Folker: *Gelehrtes Leben. Karl Hampe, das Mittelalter und die Geschichte der Deutschen*, Göttingen 2009

Reinhard, Wolfgang: *Die Unterwerfung der Welt. Globalgeschichte der europäischen Expansion 1415–2015*, München 2016

Reitmayer, Morten: *Bankiers im Kaiserreich. Sozialprofil und Habitus der deutschen Hochfinanz*, Göttingen 1999

Regulski, Christoph: *Die Handelsvertragspolitik im Kaiserreich. Regierungshandeln, Verbandspolitik und publizistische Debatte seit den 1890er Jahren*, Marburg 2001

Reulecke, Jürgen: *Geschichte der Urbanisierung in Deutschland*, Frankfurt am Main 1985

Riesser, Jakob: *The German Great Banks and Their Concentration in Connection with the Economic Development of Germany*, Washington DC 1911

Rischbieter, Julia Laura: Risiken und Nebenwirkungen. Internationale Finanzstrategien in der Verschuldungskrise der 1980er Jahre, in: *Geschichte und Gesellschaft* 41 (2015), no. 3, pp. 465–93

Ritschl, Albrecht: *Deutschlands Krise und Konjunktur: Binnenkonjunktur, Auslandsverschuldung und Reparationsproblem zwischen Dawes-Plan und Transfersperre 1924–1934*, Berlin 2002

Ritschl, Albrecht: The Pity of Peace. The German Economy at War, 1914–1918 and Beyond, in: Stephen Broadberry/Mark Harrison (eds), *The Economics of World War I*, Cambridge 2005, pp. 41–76

Roberts, Richard: *The City: A Guide to London's Global Financial Centre*, London 2008

Roberts, Richard: *Saving the City. The Great Financial Crisis of 1914*, Oxford 2013

Rohlack, Momme: *Kriegsgesellschaften (1914–1918). Arten, Rechtsformen und Funktionen in der Kriegswirtschaft des Ersten Weltkrieges*, Frankfurt am Main 2001

Rombeck-Jaschinski, Ursula: *Das Londoner Schuldenabkommen. Die Regelung der deutschen Auslandsschulden nach dem Zweiten Weltkrieg*, München 2005

Ronge, Ulrich: *Die langfristige Rendite deutscher Standardaktien: Konstruktion eines historischen Aktienindex ab Ultimo 1870 bis Ultimo 1959*, Frankfurt am Main 2002

Rosenberg, Hans: *Große Depression und Bismarckzeit. Wirtschaftsablauf, Gesellschaft und Politik in Mitteleuropa*, Berlin 1967

Roth, Regina: *Staat und Wirtschaft im Ersten Weltkrieg. Kriegsgesellschaften als kriegswirtschaftliche Steuerungsinstrumente*, Berlin 1997

Rozumek, Paul: Rembours (Rembourskredit), in: *Handwörterbuch des Kaufmanns. Lexikon für Handel und Industrie*, Hamburg/Berlin 1927, Bd. 4, pp. 635–8

Rudolph, Karsten: *Wirtschaftsdiplomatie im Kalten Krieg. Die Ostpolitik der westdeutschen Großindustrie 1945–1991*, Frankfurt am Main 2004

Rummel, Hans: *Rentabilitäts- und Organisationsfragen im Kreditgewerbe*, Berlin 1935

Rupieper, Hermann J.: *The Cuno Government and Reparations 1922–1923. Politics and Economics*, The Hague/Boston/ London 1978

Ruppmann, Reiner: Generationsforschung in der Unternehmensgeschichte. Das Beispiel des Vorstandes der Deutschen Bank 1919–1957?, in: *Akkumulation* 20 (2004), pp. 19–39

Sattler, Friederike: Offene Vermögensfragen? Die Dresdner Bank und ihr beschlagnahmtes Auslandsvermögen in den Niederlanden nach 1945, in: Ralf Ahrens (ed.), *Umbrüche und Kontinuitäten in der mitteleuropäischen Kreditwirtschaft nach dem Zweiten Weltkrieg* (= Geld und Kapital, Bd. 9, 2005/6), Stuttgart 2008, pp. 197–219

Sattler, Friederike: 'Investmentsparen' – ein früher Durchbruch der Geschäftsbanken zu breiteren Privatkundenkreisen?, in: Ralf Ahrens/Harald Wixforth (eds), *Strukturwandel und Internationalisierung im Bankwesen seit den 1950er Jahren* (= Geld und Kapital Bd. 10, 2007/2008), Stuttgart 2010, pp. 35–70

Sattler, Friederike: Bewusste Stabilisierung der Deutschland AG? Alfred Herrhausen und der Diskurs über die 'Macht der Banken', in: Ralf Ahrens/Boris Gehlen/Alfred Reckendrees (eds), *Die 'Deutschland AG'. Historische Annäherungen an den bundesdeutschen Kapitalismus*, Essen 2013, pp. 221–46

Sattler, Friederike: Ernst Matthiensen und Alfred Herrhausen. Zwei Wege an die Spitze bundesdeutscher Großbanken, in: Werner Plumpe (ed.), *Unternehmer – Fakten und Fiktionen. Historisch-biografische Studien*, München 2014, pp. 295–327

Sattler, Friederike: Das Geschäft mit den Staatsschulden. Banken, Finanzmärkte und die Securitization of Debt nach der Ölpreiskrise 1973/1974, in: *Geschichte und Gesellschaft* 41 (2015), no. 3, pp. 418–46

Sattler, Friederike: Wissenschaftsförderung aus dem Geist der Gesellschaftspolitik. Alfred Herrhausen und der Stifterverband für die deutsche Wissenschaft, in: *Vierteljahrshefte für Zeitgeschichte* 64 (2016), no. 4, pp. 597–636

Sattler, Friederike: *Der Pfandbrief 1769–2019. Von der preußischen Finanzinnovation zur Covered Bond Benchmark*, Stuttgart 2019

Sattler, Friederike: *Herrhausen: Banker, Querdenker, Global Player. Ein deutsches Leben*, München 2019

Scharlach, Julius: Unsere Banken und die Kolonien, Teil I, in: *Bank-Archiv* 5 (1906), Nr. 17, pp. 195–200

Scharlach, Julius: Unsere Banken und die Kolonien, Teil II, in: *Bank-Archiv* 5 (1906), Nr. 18, pp. 209–12

Scheicher, Martin: How has CDO Market Pricing changed during the Turmoil? Evidence from CDS Index Tranches, ECB Working Paper Series, no. 910, June 2008

Schenk, Catherine R.: The Origins of the Eurodollar Market in London: 1955–1963, in: *Explorations in Economic History* 35 (1998), no. 2, pp. 221–38

Schenk, Catherine R.: Summer in the City: Banking Failures of 1974 and the Development of International Banking Supervision, in: *English Historical Review* 129 (2014), no. 540, pp. 1129–56

Schieder, Wolfgang: Das italienische Experiment. Der Faschismus als Vorbild in der Krise der Weimarer Republik, in: *Historische Zeitschrift* 262 (1996), no. 1, pp. 73–125

Schieder, Wolfgang: Fatal Attraction: The German Right and Italian Fascism, in: Hans Mommsen (ed.), *The Third Reich Between Vision and Reality. New Perspectives on German History 1918–1945*, Oxford/New York 2001, pp. 39–58

Schinckel, Max: Unsere überseeischen Bankunternehmungen, in: *Bank-Archiv* 5 (1906), Nr. 23, pp. 265–69

Schlieper, Gustaf: *Banken und Aussenhandel. Vortrag im Deutschen Institut für Bankwissenschaften und Bankwesen am 3. März 1936*, Berlin 1936

Schnabel, Isabel: The German Twin Crisis of 1931, in: *Journal of Economic History* 64 (2004), no. 3, pp. 822–71

Schnabel, Isabel: The Role of Liquidity and Implicit Guarantees in the German Twin Crisis of 1931, in: *Journal of International Money and Finance* 28 (2009), no. 1, pp. 1–25

Schneider, Sabine: Imperial Germany's gold Mark and the creation of an international currency, 1871–1914, in: *The Economic History Society: Annual Conference, Keele University, 6–8 April 2018, Programme including New Researchers', Papers & Abstracts of the other Academic Papers*, pp. 121–25

Schneider-Lenné, Ellen R.: The Germany Case, in: *Annals of Public and Cooperative Economics* 64 (1993), no. 1, pp. 63–70

Schneider-Lenné, Ellen: The Governance of Good Business, in: *Business Strategy Review* 4 (1993), no. 1, pp. 75–85

Schneider-Lenné, Ellen R.: The Role of German Capital Markets and the Universal Banks, Supervisory Boards, and Interlocking Directorships, in: Nicholas Dimsdale/Martha Prevezer (eds), *Capital Markets and Corporate Governance*, Oxford 1994, pp. 284–305

Scholtyseck, Joachim: Die Wiedervereinigung der deutschen Großbanken und das Ende der Nachkriegszeit im Epochenjahr 1957, in: *Bankhistorisches Archiv* 32 (2006), no. 2, pp. 137–45

Scholtyseck, Joachim/Bormann, Patrick: *Der Bank- und Börsenplatz Essen. Von den Anfängen bis zur Gegenwart*, München 2018

Schubert, Aurel: *The Credit-Anstalt Crisis of 1931*, Cambridge 1991

Schubert, Michèle: Zum Wirken Paul Fridolin Kehrs für ein deutsches historisches Zentralinstitut oder: Der lange Weg zum Kaiser-Wilhelm-Institut für Deutsche Geschichte, in: *Die Kaiser-Wilhelm-/Max-Planck-Gesellschaft und ihre Institute. Studien zu ihrer Geschichte*, Berlin 1996, pp. 423–44

Schulz, Günther: *Die Angestellten seit dem 19. Jahrhundert*, München 2000

Schwarz, Hans-Peter: *Adenauer. Der Aufstieg. 1876–1952*. 3. Aufl., Stuttgart 1991

Seidenzahl, Fritz: *100 Jahre Deutsche Bank 1870–1970*, Frankfurt am Main 1970

Seidenzahl, Fritz: Elkan Heinemann, in: *Studies on Economic and Monetary Problems and on Banking History* no. 1-22, Mainz 1988, pp. 47–51

Seidenzahl, Fritz: A Forgotten Pamphlet by Georg Siemens, in: *Studies on Economic and Monetary Problems and on Banking History* no. 1-22, Mainz 1988, pp. 187–92

Simpson, Christopher: *War Crimes of the Deutsche Bank and the Dresdner Bank: The Omgus Report*, New York 2002

Siu, Man-han: British Banks and the Chinese Indigenous Economy: The Business of the Shanghai Branch of the Chartered Bank of India, Australia and China (1913–37), in: Hubert Bonin/Nuno Valério/Kazuhiko Yago (eds), *Asian Imperial Banking History*, London 2015, pp. 93–119

Skal, Georg von: *History of German Immigration in the United States and Successful German-Americans and Their Descendants*, New York 1908

Smit, Jeroen: *The Perfect Prey: The Fall of ABN AMRO, or What Went Wrong in the Banking Industry*, Amsterdam 2009

Sommerfeldt, Martin H.: *Ich war dabei. Die Verschwörung der Dämonen*, Darmstadt 1949

Spalding, William F.: Überseegeschäft, in: *Handwörterbuch des Bankwesens*, Berlin 1933, pp. 564–7

Spaulding, Robert M.: 'Reconquering Our Old Position'. West German Osthandel Strategies of the 1950s, in: Volker R. Berghahn (ed.), *Quest for Economic Empire. European Strategies of German Big Business in the Twentieth Century*, Providence, RI/Oxford 1996, pp. 123–43

Speier, Hans: *Die Angestellten vor dem Nationalsozialismus. Ein Beitrag zum Verständnis der deutschen Sozialstruktur 1918–1933*, Göttingen 1977

Spengler, Mark: *Die Entstehung des Scheckgesetzes vom 11. März 1908*, Frankfurt am Main 2008

Spies, Georg: *Erinnerungen eines Auslandsdeutschen. Nach der Originalausgabe von 1926 und dem nachgelassenen*

Originalmanuskript bearbeitet und neu herausgegeben von Wolfgang Sartor, St Petersburg 2002

Spiliotis, Susanne-Sophia: *Verantwortung und Rechtsfrieden. Die Stiftungsinitiative der deutschen Wirtschaft*, Frankfurt am Main 2003

Spoerer, Mark: *Zwangsarbeit unter dem Hakenkreuz. Ausländische Zivilarbeiter, Kriegsgefangene und Häftlinge im Deutschen Reich und im besetzten Europa 1939–1945*, Stuttgart/München 2001

Spree, Reinhard: *Wachstumstrends und Konjunkturzyklen in der deutschen Wirtschaft von 1820 bis 1913. Quantitativer Rahmen für eine Konjunkturgeschichte des 19. Jahrhunderts*, Göttingen 1978

Sorkin, Adam Ross: *Too Big to Fail: The Inside Story of How Wall Street and Washington Fought to Save the Financial System – and Themselves*, New York 2009

Steckner, Cornelius: *Der Bildhauer Adolf Brütt. Schleswig-Holstein, Berlin*, Weimar: Autobiographie und Werkverzeichnis, Heide 1989

Steinberg, Jonathan: *The Deutsche Bank and Its Gold Transactions During the Second World War*, Munich 1999

Steinthal, Max: Paul Mankiewicz. Rede, gehalten bei der Trauerfeier in der Deutschen Bank am 25. Juni 1924, in: *Bank-Archiv* 23 (1924), Nr. 19, pp. 251–3

Steinthal, Max: Arthur von Gwinner †, in: *Monatshefte für die Beamten der Deutschen Bank und Disconto-Gesellschaft*, 1932, Januar–Februar-Heft, pp. 1–9

Stern, Fritz: *Gold and Iron. Bismarck, Bleichröder, and the Building of the German Empire*, New York 1977

Stiftung Topographie des Terrors (ed.), *Der Volksgerichtshof 1934–1945. Terror durch Recht*, Berlin 2018

Stillich, Oskar: Die Schulbildung der Bankbeamten, in: *Zeitschrift für die gesamte Staatswissenschaft* 72 (1916), no. 1, pp. 103–13

Storck, Ekkehard: *Euromarkt. Finanz-Drehscheibe der Welt*, Stuttgart 1995

Strasser, Karl: *Die deutschen Banken im Ausland. Entwicklungsgeschichte und wirtschaftliche Bedeutung*. 2., durch ein Vorwort ergänzte Aufl., München 1925

Straub, Eberhard: *Kaiser Wilhelm II. in der Politik seiner Zeit. Die Erfindung des Reiches aus dem Geist der Moderne*, Berlin 2008

Straumann, Tobias: Finanzplatz und Pfadabhängigkeit: Die Bundesrepublik, die Schweiz und die Vertreibung der Euromärkte (1955–1980), in: Christoph Merki (ed.), *Europas Finanzzentren. Geschichte und Bedeutung im 20. Jahrhundert*, Frankfurt am Main 2005, pp. 245-268

Tatzkow, Monika / Frost, Reinhard: Max Steinthal – Bankier, Kunstsammler, Berliner, in: Max Steinthal: *Ein Bankier und seine Bilder*, Berlin 2004, pp. 10–41

Temin, Peter: Transmission of the Great Depression, in: *Journal of Economic Perspectives* 7 (1993), no. 2, pp. 87–102

Terberger, Eva/Wettberg, Stefanie: Der Aktienrückkauf und die Bankenkrise von 1931, AWI-Discussion Paper No. 418, Universität Heidelberg, 2005

Thamm, Imke: *Der Anspruch auf das Glück des Tüchtigen. Beruf, Organisation und Selbstverständnis der Bankangestellten in der Weimarer Republik*, Stuttgart 2006

Thomes, Paul: Die 'Fusion der Elefanten' 1929. Zur Konzentration von Kapital und Macht in der Weimarer Republik am Beispiel der Disconto-Gesellschaft und der Deutschen Bank, in: Dieter Lindenlaub/Carsten Burhop/Joachim Scholtyseck (eds), *Schlüsselereignisse der deutschen Bankengeschichte*, Stuttgart 2013, pp. 244–56

Tilly, Richard: Verkehrs- und Nachrichtenwesen, Handel, Geld-, Kredit-, Versicherungswesen 1850–1914, in: Hermann Aubin/Wolfgang Zorn (eds), *Handbuch der deutschen Wirtschafts- und Sozialgeschichte*. Bd. 2, Stuttgart 1976, pp. 563–96

Tilly, Richard H.: *Vom Zollverein zum Industriestaat. Die wirtschaftlich-soziale Entwicklung Deutschlands 1834 bis 1914*, München 1990

Tilly, Richard: German Banks and Foreign Investment in Central and Eastern Europe before 1939, in: David F. Good (ed.), *Economic Transformations in East and Central Europe. Legacies from the Past and Policies for the Future*, London/New York 1994, pp. 201–29

Toniolo, Gianni: *One Hundred Years, 1894–1994. A Short History of the Banca Commerciale Italiana*, Mailand 1994

Tooze, Adam: *The Wages of Destruction. The Making and Breaking of the Nazi Economy*, London 2006

Tooze, Adam: Reassessing the Moral Economy of Post-war Reconstruction: The Terms of the West German Settlement in 1952, in: *Past & Present* 210 (2011), suppl. 6, pp. 47–70

Tooze, Adam: *Crashed. How a Decade of Financial Crises Changed the World*, London/New York 2018

Torp, Cornelius: Weltwirtschaft vor dem Weltkrieg. Die erste Welle ökonomischer Globalisierung vor 1914, in: *Historische Zeitschrift* 279 (2004), no. 3, pp. 561–609

Torp, Cornelius: *The Challenges of Globalization. Economy and Politics in Germany, 1860–1914*, New York/Oxford 2014

Torres, Félix: *Banquiers d'avenir. Des Comptoirs d'Escompte à la Naissance de BNP Paribas*, Paris 2000

Ullmann, Hans-Peter: *Der deutsche Steuerstaat. Geschichte der öffentlichen Finanzen vom 18. Jahrhundert bis heute*, München 2005

Ulrich, Franz Heinz: The Eurodollar Market: A view from the Federal Republic of Germany, in: Herbert V. Prochnow, *The Eurodollar*, Chicago 1970, pp. 175–87

Urbig, Franz: Die Vorkriegsgründungen deutscher Banken und Bankfilialen im Ausland, in: *Der deutsche Volkswirt*, Beiheft zu Nr. 22, 28.2.1936, pp. 24–7

Volkmann, Hans-Erich: Die Sowjetunion im ökonomischen Kalkül des Dritten Reiches 1933–1941, in: ders., Ökonomie und Expansion. Grundzüge der NS-Wirtschaftspolitik, München 2002, pp. 303–22

Volkov, Shulamit: *Walther Rathenau. Weimar's Fallen Statesman*, New Haven, Conn. 2012

Wallich, Hermann: Aus meinem Leben, in: *Zwei Generationen im deutschen Bankwesen 1833–1914*, Frankfurt am Main 1978, pp. 29–155

Wallich, Paul: *Lehr- und Wanderjahre*, in: Zwei Generationen im deutschen Bankwesen 1833–1914, Frankfurt am Main 1978, pp. 159–362

Wandel, Eckhard: *Banken und Versicherungen im 19. und 20. Jahrhundert*, München 1998

Weaver, Karen: The Subprime Mortgage Crisis: Boom, Bust, and Blame, in: *Journal of Structured Finance* 23 (2017), no. 2, pp. 96–8

Weber, Hanns: *Bankplatz Berlin*, Wiesbaden 1957

Wee, Herman van der/Goossens, Martine: Belgium, in: Rondo Cameron/V. I. Bovykin (eds), *International Banking 1870–1914*, Oxford 1991, pp. 113–29

Wehler, Hans-Ulrich (ed.), *Friedrich Kapp: Vom radikalen Frühsozialisten des Vormärz zum liberalen Parteipolitiker des Bismarckreiches. Briefe 1843–1884*, Frankfurt am Main 1969

Wehler, Hans-Ulrich: *Deutsche Gesellschaftsgeschichte* Bd. III. *Von der 'Deutschen Doppelrevolution' bis zum Beginn des Ersten Weltkrieges 1849–1914*, München 1995

Weihe, Thomas: *Die Personalpolitik der Filialgroßbanken 1919–1945. Interventionen, Anpassung, Ausweichbewegungen*, Stuttgart 2006

Weiss, Ulrich: Probleme und Grenzen der Technik, in: *Zeitschrift für das gesamte Kreditwesen* Nr. 2, 15.1.1981

Weitenweber, Andreas [= Müller-Jabusch, Maximilian], Carl Klönne, in: *Die Bank. Wochenhefte für Finanz-, Kredit- und Versicherungswesen* 36 (1943), no. 10, pp. 178–84

Wellhöner, Volker: *Großbanken und Großindustrie im Kaiserreich*, Göttingen 1989

Wellhöner, Volker/Wixforth, Harald: Unternehmensfinanzierung durch Banken – ein Hebel zur Etablierung der Bankenherrschaft? Ein Beitrag zum Verhältnis von Banken und Schwerindustrie im Kaiserreich und der Weimarer Republik, in: Dietmar Petzina (ed.), *Zur Geschichte der Unternehmensfinanzierung*, Berlin 1990, pp. 11–33

Wengenroth, Ulrich: *Unternehmensstrategien und technischer Fortschritt. Die deutsche und die britische Eisen- und Stahlindustrie 1865–1895*, Göttingen 1986

Wessel, Horst A.: *Kontinuität im Wandel. 100 Jahre Mannesmann 1890–1990*, Düsseldorf 1990

Westerhuis, Gerarda/Kipping, Matthias: The Managerialization of Banking: From Blueprint to Reality, in: *Management and Organizational History* 9 (2014), no. 4, pp. 374–93

Wichmann, Karl: Unser ältester Lehrling erzählt … Eine Lehrzeit in der Deutschen Bank, 1872–1875, in: *Monatshefte für die Beamten der Deutschen Bank*, 1928, Märzheft, pp. 37–9

Wiesen, Jonathan: *West German Industry and the Challenge of the Nazi Past, 1945–1955*, Chapel Hill/London 2001

Wiethölter, Rudolf: *Interessen und Organisation der Aktiengesellschaft im amerikanischen und deutschen Recht*, Karlsruhe 1961

Wilhelmy, Petra: *Der Berliner Salon im 19. Jahrhundert (1780–1914)*, Berlin 1989

Wilhelmy-Dollinger, Petra: *Die Berliner Salons. Mit kulturhistorischen Spaziergängen*, Berlin 2000

Williamson, John G.: *Karl Helfferich 1872–1924. Economist, Financier, Politician*, Princeton 1971

Wilkins, Mira: *The History of Foreign Investment in the United States, 1914–1945*, Cambridge, Mass. 2004

Winkler, Heinrich August (ed.): *Organisierter Kapitalismus. Voraussetzungen und Anfänge*, Göttingen 1974

Wixforth, Harald: Die Banken und der Kollaps der Mark. Zur Lage des Bankwesens während der Inflation von 1918 bis 1923, in: Manfred Köhler/Keith Ulrich (eds), *Banken, Konjunktur und Politik. Beiträge zur Geschichte deutscher Banken im 19. und 20. Jahrhundert*, Essen 1995, pp. 55–73

Wixforth, Harald: 'Die Wiedererwerbung der Filialen ist als Repatriierung anzusprechen' – Die Expansionsbestrebungen der Österreichischen Creditanstalt-Wiener Bankverein in das Sudetenland 1938/39, in: *Bankhistorisches Archiv* 27 (2001), no. 1, pp. 62–77

Wixforth, Harald: German Banks and their Business Strategies in the Weimar Republic: New Findings and Preliminary Results, in: Makoto Kasuya (ed.), *Coping with Crisis. International Financial Institutions in the Interwar Period*, Oxford 2003, pp. 133–52

Wixforth, Harald: *Die Expansion der Dresdner Bank in Europa* (= Die Dresdner Bank im Dritten Reich, Bd. 3), München 2006

Wixforth, Harald: Arthur (von) Gwinner [1856-1931], in: Hans Pohl (ed.), *Deutsche Bankiers im 20. Jahrhundert*, Stuttgart 2008, pp. 165–80

Wixforth, Harald: Karl Helfferich [1872–1924], in: Hans Pohl (ed.), *Deutsche Bankiers des 20. Jahrhunderts*, Stuttgart 2008, pp. 195–209

Wixforth, Harald: Die Banken in den abhängigen und besetzten Gebieten Europas 1938–1945: Instrumente der deutschen Hegemonie?, in: Christoph Buchheim/Marcel Boldorf (eds), *Europäische Volkswirtschaften unter deutscher Hegemonie 1938–1945*, München 2012, pp. 185–207

Wixforth, Harald: Banken im Visier der Diplomatie. Die Auseinandersetzung über die Präsenz deutscher Banken im polnischen Teil Oberschlesiens in der Zwischenkriegszeit, in: Lutz Budraß/Barbara Kalinowska-Wójcik/Andrzej Michalczyk (eds), *Industrialisierung und Nationalisierung. Fallstudien zur Geschichte des oberschlesischen Industriereviers im 19. und 20. Jahrhundert*, Essen 2013, pp. 191–221

Wixforth, Harald: Instrumente der Kriegswirtschaft oder der wirtschaftlichen Selbsthilfe – Die Kriegskreditbanken 1914–1918, in: *Jahrbuch für Wirtschaftsgeschichte/Economic History Yearbook* 56 (2015), no. 2, pp. 389–419

Wixforth, Harald: Die Beziehungen der Norddeutschen Wollkämmerei und Kammgarnspinnerei zu den Banken, in: IBF Paper Series 04-17, 2017

Wixforth, Harald: Kriegseinsatz und Kriegsfolgen – der Norddeutsche Lloyd im Ersten Weltkrieg und in der Nachkriegsinflation, in: Vierteljahrschrift für Sozial- und Wirtschaftsgeschichte 105 (2018), no. 3, pp. 365–90

Wolf, Herbert: Von der Währungsreform bis zum Großbankengesetz (1948–1952), in: *Geschichte der deutschen Kreditwirtschaft seit 1945*, Frankfurt am Main 1998, pp. 59–110

Wolffsohn, Michael: Das Deutsch-Israelische Wiedergutmachungsabkommen von 1952 im internationalen Zusammenhang, in: Vierteljahrshefte für Zeitgeschichte 36 (1988), no. 4, pp. 691–732

Wolffsohn, Michael: Globalentschädigung für Israel und die Juden? Adenauer und die Opposition in der Bundesregierung, in: Ludolf Herbst/Constantin Goschler (eds), *Wiedergutmachung in der Bundesrepublik Deutschland*, München 1989, pp. 161–90

Woods, Ngaire: *The Globalizers: the IMF, the World Bank and their Borrowers*, Ithaca, NY 2006

Wright, Robert E./Smith, George David: *Mutually Beneficial. The Guardian and Life Insurance in America*, New York/London 2004

Wunderlich, Lothar: Die Entwicklung der deutschen Maklerbanken, Diss., Würzburg 1923

Zeidler, Manfred: Die deutsche Kriegsfinanzierung 1914 bis 1918 und ihre Folgen, in: Wolfgang Michalka (ed.), *Der Erste Weltkrieg. Wirkung – Wahrnehmung – Analyse*, München 1994, pp. 415–55

Ziegler, Dieter: *Eisenbahnen und Staat im Zeitalter der Industrialisierung: Die Eisenbahnpolitik der deutschen Staaten im Vergleich*, Stuttgart 1996

Ziegler, Dieter: Die Aufsichtsräte der deutschen Aktiengesellschaften in den zwanziger Jahren. Eine empirische Untersuchung zum Problem der 'Bankenmacht', in: Zeitschrift für Unternehmensgeschichte 43 (1998), no. 2, pp. 194–215

Ziegler, Dieter: *Die Dresdner Bank und die deutschen Juden* (= Die Dresdner Bank im Dritten Reich, Bd. 2), München 2006

Ziegler, Dieter: 'A Regulated Market Economy': New Perspectives on the Nature of the Economic Order of the Third Reich, 1933–1939, in: Hartmut Berghoff/Jürgen Kocka/Dieter Ziegler (eds), *Business in the Age of Extremes. Essays in Modern German and Austrian Economic History*, Cambridge 2013, pp. 139–52

Ziegler, Dieter: Die Entstehung der Reichsbank 1875. Die erste deutsche Einheitswährung und der Goldstandard, in: Dieter Lindenlaub/Carsten Burhop/Joachim Scholtyseck (eds), *Schlüsselereignisse der deutschen Bankengeschichte*, Stuttgart 2013, pp. 166–77

Zilch, Reinhold: Der Plan einer Zwangsregulierung im deutschen Bankwesen vor dem ersten Weltkrieg und seine Ursachen, in: B. A. Aisin/Willibald Gutsche (eds), *Forschungsergebnisse zur Geschichte des deutschen Imperialismus vor 1917*, Ost-Berlin 1980, pp. 229–56

Zilch, Reinhold: *Okkupation und Währung im Ersten Weltkrieg. Die deutsche Besatzungspolitik in Belgien und Russisch-Polen 1914–1918*, Goldbach 1994

Zuckerman, Gregory: *The Greatest Trade Ever: How John Paulson Bet Against the Markets and Made $20 Billion*, London/New York 2010

Zunkel, Friedrich: Das Verhältnis des Unternehmertums zum Bildungsbürgertum zwischen Vormärz und Erstem Weltkrieg, in: M. Rainer Lepsius (ed.), *Bildungsbürgertum im 19. Jahrhundert, Teil 3: Lebensführung und ständische Vergesellschaftung*, Stuttgart 1992, pp. 82–101

Picture Credits

Index